A Dictionary of
Ancient History

A Dictionary of
Ancient History

edited by

Graham Speake

BLACKWELL
Reference

Copyright © Basil Blackwell Ltd. 1994
First published 1994

First published in USA 1994

Blackwell Publishers
108 Cowley Road
Oxford OX4 1JF
UK

238 Main Street
Cambridge, Massachusetts 02142
USA

British Library Cataloguing in Publication Data

A CIP catalogue record for this book is available from the British
Library.

Library of Congress Cataloging-in-Publication Data

Dictionary of ancient history / edited by Graham Speake.
    768p. 229 × 152mm
    Includes bibliographical references.
    ISBN 0–631–18069–9
    1. Civilization, Classical—Dictionaries. 2. History, Ancient—
Dictionaries. 3. Rome—History—Dictionaries. 4. Greece—
History—Dictionaries. 5. Classical dictionaries. I. Speake,
Graham, 1946– .
DE5.D53 1994
930′.03—dc20   93–1437
                                                         CIP

Typeset in 10 on 12 pt Sabon
by Graphicraft Typesetters Ltd., Hong Kong
Printed in Great Britain by BPCC Wheatons Ltd.

This book is printed on acid-free paper

Contents

List of contributors   vii

Preface   ix

Dictionary entries A–Z   1

Bibliography   685

Appendixes
  Genealogies   736
  Maps   744

To Jennifer

Contributors

Richard J. Brickstock (RJB) teaches archaeology and ancient history at the University of Durham and is Curator of the university's Museum of Archaeology. His primary research interest is the coinage of the Roman Empire.

Roger Brock (RB) is a Lecturer in Classics at the University of Leeds, with a particular interest in Greek history and historiography.

George Cawkwell (GLC) is an Emeritus Fellow of University College, Oxford, where he has tutored in ancient history since 1949. His special interest is Greek history of the pre-Hellenistic period.

Tim Cornell (TC) is Senior Lecturer in History at University College London. Sometime Assistant Director of the British School at Rome, he works on the history of ancient Italy and the Roman Republic.

Hugh Elton (HE) is Visiting Assistant Professor in the Department of History at Rice University, Texas. His particular interest is the history of the late Roman Empire.

James Longrigg (JL) is Senior Lecturer in Classics at the University of Newcastle upon Tyne. His primary research interests are in ancient philosophy and science, and he is author of a recent study of Greek rational medicine.

David Preest (DP) taught classics at the Royal Grammar School, Newcastle upon Tyne, and at Highgate School. He now works in the Education Centre at St Alban's Abbey.

Louis P. Rawlings (LPR) is currently conducting research for a Ph.D. in history at University College London. His interests centre on the warfare and society of Greeks, Romans, and Celts.

Ellen Rice (EER) is Senior Research Fellow in Ancient History and Archaeology at Wolfson College, Oxford. She is a specialist in Hellenistic history and the author of a recent study of Ptolemy Philadelphus.

Harry Sidebottom (HS) teaches at the universities of Oxford and London. He is the author of several studies in Greek culture and Roman power, and is writing a book on violence and warfare in the Roman Empire.

Graham Speake (GS) is Publications Director at the Oxford Centre for Islamic Studies and a Senior Member of Christ Church. His research interests focus on ancient Greek literature and its transmission.

Preface

———◆———

This book is intended as a layman's guide to the history of the ancient Greco-Roman world. The word 'history' is interpreted loosely and is more easily understood in the sense of what is today fashionably described as 'total history'. Thus, in addition to entries on the personalities and events that have shaped the course of military and political history, the reader will find entries on ancient literature, philosophy, art, religion, and society. The aim is therefore to provide an accessible information resource to the ancient world as a whole.

For practical purposes, however, the limits of the book have had to be strictly prescribed. Chronological coverage extends from 776 BC, the year in which the first Olympic Games were held, to the fall of the Roman Empire in the west in AD 476. There are occasional nods in the direction of both the Bronze Age and the Byzantine Empire to round off a particular story, but these periods are not formally covered. The geographical span is the world of the Greeks and Romans and those peoples who impinged directly on it such as Persia and Carthage. Nevertheless, we are looking at the better part of three continents across a time-span in excess of 1,250 years, which working back from today would take us almost to the death of Bede in AD 735.

The only aspect of the ancient world that we are conscious of excluding is mythology. We are absolved from this by the existence of another volume in the series, Pierre Grimal's *Concise Dictionary of Classical Mythology*, edited by Stephen Kershaw (1990). The publisher helpfully distinguishes the two books by describing that one as being concerned with the 'pretend' people of antiquity while ours is concerned with the 'real' people. We have, however, been permitted to include a few 'pretend' people in this volume: it would, for example, be absurd to try to tell the story of Greek medicine without reference to Asclepius or of the Delphic oracle without Apollo; we have also included some of the heroes of early Roman legend such as Lars Porsenna and Coriolanus.

In addition to providing a concise definition of whatever the reader chooses to look up, the dictionary aims to be diverting in the best possible sense. A system of cross-references (set in small capital letters) is designed to beckon the reader to other entries which contain related information. Similarly, most entries are equipped with suggestions for further reading, of which full details are given in the Bibliography. These suggestions range from the general to the strictly academic, but the vast majority are in English and are to be found in most libraries.

Compiling this book has been rather like re-running the course for Part One of the Classical Tripos at Cambridge which the editor ran for the first time a quarter of a century ago. (It has also dominated an equivalent period of his life.) It has been a privilege to work with a team of contributors every bit as congenial, inspiring, and energetic as fellow undergraduates. Roger Brock provided entries on archaic Greek history; George Cawkwell on classical Greek history; Ellen Rice on Hellenistic history; Tim Cornell, Hugh Elton, David Preest, Louis Rawlings, and Harry Sidebottom wrote on the Roman Republic; Richard Brickstock on the Roman Empire; and James Longrigg on philosophy and natural science; all other entries were written by the editor. Tutorial guidance, for which this is a poor but none the less sincere acknowledgement, was provided by George Cawkwell, Tim Cornell, Anne Gosling, Martin Millett, and Nigel Wilson. Administrative assistance was given by Blackwells who have all along been the most accommodating and supportive of publishers. Moral fibre and constructive criticism were supplied in generous measure by my wife Jennifer. My profound thanks are due to them all.

My greatest debt, however, is reserved for Dr W. W. Cruickshank, my Latin master at St Paul's, who taught me more about the ancient world and about scholarly standards than anyone else has ever done. If I may adapt the words of my Cambridge teacher Roger Dawe, Dr Cruickshank has become a legendary figure. The legends are all true.

GS
Christ Church, Oxford
30 January 1993

A

Academy the philosophical school founded by PLATO (*c*.385 BC). It derived its name from its situation in the olive grove sacred to the hero Academus on the outskirts of Athens. The school was organized upon a corporate basis, and Plato's primary aim was to subject potential statesmen to an educational process designed to produce the philosophical insight necessary for government. The curriculum was probably similar to that described in the *Republic* and included mathematics, political theory, and dialectic. Plato himself taught there for almost 50 years and was succeeded by SPEUSIPPUS and XENOCRATES. This first Old Academy was succeeded by the second or Middle Academy under ARCESILAUS OF PITANE and Polemon which embraced the doctrines of scepticism (*see* SCEPTICS) and engaged in controversy with the STOICS. A reconciliation, however, was effected by Antiochus of Ascalon (*c*.78 BC), who reverted to the teachings of the Old Academy. In the 5th century AD the school became the centre of NEOPLATONISM, particularly under the headship of PROCLUS, and was finally dissolved by Justinian.

See also CARNEADES; EDUCATION.

JL

Field (1930).

Acarnania region in north-west Greece to the west of AETOLIA from which it is divided by the river Acheloüs. The coast was colonized by CORINTH in the 7th century BC. In the 5th century an Acarnanian Confederacy invited Athens to intervene against the Corinthians and later against the Spartans. Submitting to AGESILAUS in 390, the Acarnanians were ruled by Sparta until they joined the Second Athenian Confederacy in 375. The Acarnanian Confederacy was refounded *c.*230 and survived until 30 BC when the people were drafted into NICOPOLIS.

See also LEUCAS.   GS

Larsen (1968).

Accius   (170–*c.*85 BC), Latin writer. Lucius Accius was the last real tragedian and the first great grammarian at Rome (*see* SCHOLARSHIP, LATIN; TRAGEDY, ROMAN). Born at Pisaurum in Umbria, he was a friend of PACUVIUS and later of CICERO. He wrote prolifically in verse and prose but was most admired as a tragedian. The titles of 46 plays are known, most of them based on Euripidean originals, but some (*Brutus*, *Decius*) are concerned with themes from Roman history.   GS

Beare (1964).

Achaea   region in central Greece comprising south-east Thessaly and the north coast of the Peloponnese. In the archaic period the Achaeans sent colonists to CROTON and other cities in south Italy. By the 5th century BC they had formed an ACHAEAN LEAGUE, but this did not play an active part in Greek politics until the 3rd century. After 146 BC the area was incorporated into the Roman province of MACEDONIA. Under the Empire Achaea formed a separate province which included all of central Greece, the Peloponnese, and the Cyclades and was administered from Corinth.   GS

Larsen (1968).

Achaean League   confederation of Greek states. The Achaean League had been an active federal body in the Peloponnese in the 5th century BC, but fell into obscurity and was reconstituted in 280 BC as a confederacy of Achaean, and later also non-Achaean, cities. League affairs were directed by two annually elected generals (after 255 by only one), federal magistrates, a council, and an assembly. There were regular, as well as specially summoned, meetings to decide important issues. The confederation is praised by POLYBIUS. Its most powerful generals in the 3rd century were ARATUS, LYDIADAS, and PHILOPOEMEN, whose basic hostility towards Sparta led them to adopt shifting pro- and anti-Macedonian policies.   EER

CAH VII.1; Green (1990); Gruen (1984); Larsen (1968).

Achaemenids   Persian dynasty. All the kings of PERSIA came from this family, allegedly descended from an eponymous Achaemenes, perhaps four generations before CYRUS.

See also ARTAXERXES I–III; CAMBYSES; DARIUS I–III; XERXES.   RB

Achaeus (fl. c.246–213 BC), Seleucid general. Achaeus was a Seleucid prince who supported SELEUCUS II CALLINICUS in the civil war against ANTIOCHUS HIERAX in 226 BC. Appointed governor of Asia across the Taurus Mountains by ANTIOCHUS III THE GREAT, he regained much of Seleucid Asia Minor from ATTALUS I SOTER of Pergamum. Achaeus declared independence in 220 BC, maintaining himself in a 'kingdom' in PHRYGIA. At Sardes his mercenaries betrayed him to Antiochus, who murdered him savagely and recovered Asia Minor by 213 BC.   EER

CAH VII.1; Green (1990); Hansen (1971).

Achilles Painter (fl. mid-5th century BC), Greek vase painter. This painter is named after a red-figure amphora in the Vatican illustrating the hero Achilles and the slave girl Briseis. He is credited with painting more than 200 vases – nearly 100 white-ground *lekythoi*, some 90 in red figure, and a small number of black-figure Panathenaic prize amphorae.
    See also PAINTING, GREEK.   GS

Arias and Hirmer (1962); Kurtz (1975).

Achilles Tatius (2nd century AD), Alexandrian novelist. Achilles was the author of *Leucippe and Cleitophon*, a rhetorical prose romance (*see* NOVEL, GREEK) in eight books concerning the amorous adventures of its eponymous heroes. Set in the contemporary world of the eastern Mediterranean, it was written for an erudite Alexandrian élite. But it was widely read (and copied) in medieval Byzantium and despite its racy subject-matter was much admired.   GS

Bartsch (1989); Reardon (1989).

Acragas later Agrigentum, city in Sicily founded c.582 BC from GELA. It gained early prominence under the tyrant PHALARIS, and in 480 BC it helped GELON defeat the Carthaginians at HIMERA. A well-preserved series of Doric temples bears witness to the city's prosperity at this time. Sacked by Carthage in 406, it recovered under TIMOLEON, only to suffer again during the PUNIC WARS. It was repopulated by the Romans and became an important trading station.   GS

Finley (1979).

Acropolis literally an 'upper city'. An acropolis was a fortified hill such as formed the nucleus of many Greek city-states. Its original purpose was to serve as a stronghold and place of refuge in time of war. Later, in the classical and Hellenistic periods, it was often used as a religious sanctuary and provided with handsome buildings. The best-known example is the acropolis of ATHENS.

See also FORTIFICATIONS, GREEK.   GS

Hopper (1971).

Acta   a loose title covering the enactments of a Roman emperor or emperors. Developed from the Republican system whereby MAGISTRATES swore to respect the pre-existing laws of Rome, under the Empire emperors and magistrates took a simliar oath to observe the *Acta* of previous rulers. The *Acta* encompassed the CONSTITUTIONES *principis* and, with the increasingly autocratic nature of the Principate in the second half of the 1st century AD, came to apply, in addition, to the enactments of the living emperor. The *Acta* of a bad or unpopular ruler could, however, be excluded from the oath, so that no oath was taken to observe the *Acta* of Tiberius, Gaius (Caligula), Galba, Otho, Vitellius, Domitian, or Caracalla. However, although some of the *Acta* of these rulers were specifically rescinded (*rescissio actorum*), the better laws were sometimes allowed to survive, and were presumably included in the oath of observance.   RJB

Cracknell (1964); Nicholas (1962).

Acta Diurna   an official Roman gazette, instituted by CAESAR in 59 BC as a daily record of public business in the city. During the early Empire its circulation extended to the provinces and the armies. In addition to official events it listed day-to-day happenings (often of a trivial nature) including births and deaths of prominent people, and perhaps also the results of sporting events such as chariot races. It was a mine of information for historians like TACITUS.   TC

Acta Senatus   proceedings of the Roman Senate. The *Acta Senatus* (or *Commentarii Senatus*) were the enactments of the SENATE under the Roman Empire. Preserved as an official record of the Senate's proceedings, they were available for consultation by senators, and were the responsibility of an individual senator appointed, from the reign of Tiberius onwards, by the emperor. These records do not survive, but appear to have provided material for historians such as TACITUS or his sources.   RJB

Cracknell (1964); Nicholas (1962).

Actium   battle in 31 BC. Off Actium, a promontory on the west coast of Greece, Octavian's 400 ships defeated the 500 ships of ANTONY and CLEOPATRA on 2 September 31 BC, and Octavian (AUGUSTUS) became master of the Roman world. It is uncertain whether Antony, weakened by desertions, was trying to break through the blockade of Actium or to fight a decisive action. In the end Antony and Cleopatra fled to Egypt with 60 ships, but his remaining forces surrendered to Octavian.

See also NICOPOLIS.   DP

Carter (1970).

Acts of the Pagan Martyrs Alexandrian document. The Acts of the Pagan Martyrs, the *Acta Alexandrinorum,* are a series of papyri surviving in only very fragmentary form. They document the anti-Roman movement in Alexandria in the first two centuries AD, and are so named because of the readiness of nationalistic leaders to face martyrdom. They record imperial hearings, some perhaps wholly or partly fictional, consisting of verbal exchanges between the emperor, attended by his CONSILIUM PRINCIPIS, and named nationalists.   RJB

Millar (1977); Musurillo (1954); Scullard (1982).

Adlectio means of admission to the Roman Senate. *Adlectio,* or adlection, was a power by which Roman emperors, including Augustus and Claudius, bestowed membership of the senatorial order, and thus exercised control over the membership of the SENATE. It was also a device, used extensively from the Flavian period onwards, to accelerate the careers of existing senators, e.g. an ex-QUAESTOR adlected *inter praetorios* (to the rank of ex-PRAETOR) was allowed to miss out the praetorship and proceed directly to the consulship. From the time of Macrinus (AD 217–18), and commonly in the 4th century AD, it was even possible to be adlected *inter consulares* (to the rank of ex-CONSUL).

See also CURSUS HONORUM.   RJB

Millar (1977); Salmon (1968).

Adoptio the legal process of adoption at Rome. Adoption was a means of acquiring PATRIA POTESTAS and was restricted to men until the time of DIOCLETIAN. The adopted person became legally indistinguishable from the natural children of the adoptive father, enjoying the same rights of succession as well as the name and social rank of the father, while at the same time losing all such rights in his or her previous family. An alternative system for adopting a person who had *patria potestas* in his own right was known as *adrogatio.* This effectively involved the suppression of one family by another and required the approval of the Comitia Centuriata (later the lictors). For *adrogatio* the adopting party had to be childless and over the age of 60. Caesar's

adoption of Octavian (AUGUSTUS) was legalized by a posthumous grant
of *adrogatio*.   GS

Adrogatio   *see* ADOPTIO.

Adultery   In Greek law adultery was regarded as a declaration of war
against a man's property. DRACO's code permitted a man to kill another caught in the act with his wife, mother, sister, or daughter.
SOLON decreed that an offended husband must repudiate his wife but
that he could take the law into his own hands when dealing with the
adulterer. The latter could also be prosecuted by other interested parties
and could attempt to buy himself out of the situation. Some marriage
contracts preserved in papyri detail fines for adultery.

  In Roman Republican law it was only a wife's adultery that was
recognized and retribution was left to the offended husband or family.
Adultery by the husband was never in itself a crime. Under Augustus
the *Lex Iulia de adulteriis coercendis* (18 BC) established procedures
and penalties for adultery in criminal law. Such cases were tried by a
special court before a praetor. Both guilty parties were generally punished by banishment and some confiscation of property. Stiffer penalties were introduced by the Christian emperors.

  See also MARRIAGE; WOMEN.   GS

CAH X; Gardner (1986); Parker (1983).

Advocatus   Roman advocate. Those involved in a civil trial could
entrust the presentation of their case to an advocate. In the late Republic, under the influence of Greek rhetoric, some members of the
Roman élite made a speciality of being advocates, the most famous
being CICERO. Advocates were debarred from taking fees (although
they became legal by the end of the 2nd century AD). Instead, the
advocate formed links of obligation and friendship (*amicitia*) with other
members of the élite.

  Advocates were not legal experts, and are thus to be distinguished
from jurists (until the late Empire). Advocates were more concerned
with the art of persuasion than the science of law.

  See also EDUCATION; JURISPRUDENCE; LAW, ROMAN.   HS

Jolowicz and Nicholas (1972); Schulz (1946).

Aediles   Roman magistrates. The original two aediles were officials of
the PLEBS subordinate to the tribunes (TRIBUNUS PLEBIS). From 367 BC
two more aediles were elected from the PATRICIANS. After plebeians were
allowed to be senior ('curule') MAGISTRATES, the link with the tribunate
was forgotten and the aediles acted together as a 'college', although
the 'curule' aediles had to be patricians in alternate years. The aediles

functioned in three main areas: care of the city, including supervision of markets and some police duties; care of the ANNONA; and the giving of certain games. Although the aedileship, which ranked above the quaestorship and below the praetorship, was inessential for the CURSUS HONORUM, the giving of games made this annual magistracy attractive to ambitious politicians. Augustus transferred the games to the PRAETORS and the care of the *annona* to the *praefectus annonae*.   HS

Jolowicz and Nicholas (1972).

Aedui   Gallic people. The Aedui lived in central Gaul between the rivers Loire and Saône. They were generally pro-Roman. In 60 BC their chieftain Divitiacus visited Rome to seek protection from ARIOVISTUS. In 58 Divitiacus supported CAESAR against the HELVETII, although his brother, Dumnorix, opposed him. The Aedui provided auxiliaries for Caesar's Gallic campaign, but after Dumnorix became chief and was killed by Roman troops in 54 they became disillusioned and joined VERCINGETORIX.   LPR

Chadwick (1970).

Aegae   modern Vergina, capital of ancient MACEDONIA until the reign of ARCHELAUS. The remains of a royal palace and burial ground have been excavated. Aegae remained the burial place of Macedonian kings even after the transfer of the capital to Pella. One of the tombs, unrobbed and containing spectacular grave goods, has been identified as that of PHILIP II.   GS

Andronikos (1974); Hammond and Griffith (1979).

Aegina   Greek island. Aegina was a major naval and commercial power in archaic Greece, a rival of Athens and Corinth. Trade made Aegina wealthy: she struck the earliest Greek COINAGE; she was an original participant at NAUCRATIS; and Sostratus, the richest of all Greek traders, was Aeginetan. Aegina was founded from Epidaurus, but broke away and initially had closer ties with Argos; by the early 5th century BC, however, she was probably a member of the PELOPONNESIAN LEAGUE. From the early 7th century she pursued a chronic feud with Athens, even siding with Persia before Marathon, although she made a vital contribution to the Greek cause at SALAMIS. Hostilities resumed in the PENTECONTAETIA: Aegina was defeated and became a tributary ally of Athens. In 431 the Athenians expelled the Aeginetans and occupied the island themselves; the Aeginetans were restored by Lysander in 405, but the island was of little importance thereafter.   RB

Amit (1973); Figuera (1981, 1991).

Aegospotami   inlet on the east coast of the Thracian CHERSONESE, where the Athenian fleet beached (despite the advice of the exiled ALCIBIADES) and was decisively defeated (405 BC) in the final engagement of the PELOPONNESIAN WAR. Accounts of the battle differ, but probably the Spartan LYSANDER, whose fleet was stationed on the opposite shore, deceived the Athenians into abandoning thoughts of battle that day and dispersing for provisions. Lysander took the whole fleet save for the nine ships that escaped with CONON.   GLC

Kagan (1987).

Aelian   (c.AD 170–c.235), Roman sophist. Claudius Aelianus gave up a teaching career to devote himself to writing (in Greek). His 17 books of *Animal Stories* and 14 books of *Stories from History*, praised by contemporaries for their simple elegance, read more like juvenile collections of inconsequential anecdotes. His 20 *Rustic Letters* are entertaining but none the less contrived. Fragments of lost philosophical works display Stoic sympathies.   GS

Bowersock (1969).

Aemilia, Via   Roman road. The Via Aemilia, a later extension of the Via FLAMINIA, ran 176 miles north-west from ARIMINUM (Rimini) on the Adriatic to Placentia (Piacenza) on the river Po. It was built by M. Aemilius Lepidus, consul of 187 BC, using the army with which he had just defeated the Ligures. As many of the main towns of CISALPINE GAUL lay on its route, it helped to romanize the district, which is still known as Emilia today.

See also ROADS, ROMAN.   DP

Chevallier (1976); Potter (1987); Wiseman (1987).

Aemilianus   *see* TREBONIANUS GALLUS; VALERIAN.

Aeneas Tacticus   (fl. mid-4th century BC), Greek military writer. Typical of the ever-increasing professionalism of the age, Aeneas (sometimes identified with a general of the ARCADIAN LEAGUE) wrote a number of books, of which only that concerning the defence of cities has survived. Some devices recommended are of comic ingenuity, but the principal military interest of the work is the demonstration that cities were then assaulted, not starved into submission as in the 5th century.   GLC

Whitehead (1990).

Aeolis   see ARCHITECTURE, GREEK; DIALECTS, GREEK.

Aeolis that part of north-west Asia Minor, including the island of LESBOS, that was originally occupied by Greeks from Thessaly and Boeotia (*see* DIALECTS, GREEK). The territory extended from the Hellespont in the north to Smyrna in the south. Settlement was largely coastal, but colonies were also planted along river valleys and as far away as Magnesia on the Maeander. An Aeolian League was founded, perhaps for religious purposes: it offered little or no resistance to invaders.

GS

Bean (1979a).

Aequi Italian people. The Aequi occupied the upper Anio valley and the hills to the east of PRAENESTE. They were enemies of Rome during the early 5th century BC, and together with the VOLSCI they frequently invaded LATIUM. In time their raids ceased, and they were defeated by CAMILLUS in 388 BC. In 304 the Romans occupied their territory and massacred the population. Little is known of their language and culture: there are no documents and little archaeological evidence apart from a few hillforts.

TC

CAH VII.2; Salmon (1982).

Aerarium Roman treasury. The *aerarium Saturni* in the temple of Saturn near the CAPITOL was the main treasury of Rome. It was also the main repository for official documents (*see* SENATUS CONSULTUM). The *aerarium* was run by the QUAESTORS, under the supervision of the SENATE. Caesar placed two AEDILES in charge. Augustus entrusted the *aerarium* first to two *praefecti* (28 BC), then to a pair of PRAETORS (23 BC). Claudius returned it to the quaestors, before Nero again placed two *praefecti* in charge. Under the Empire some state revenues were diverted from the *aerarium* to the *fiscus* (*see* FINANCE, ROMAN).

In AD 6 Augustus founded the *aerarium militare* to pay donatives to discharged soldiers. It was run by three ex-praetors and financed by the revenues from the inheritance and sales taxes (*see* VECTIGAL).

See also TRIBUNUS AERARIUS; TRIBUTUM.

HS

Aerarius Roman citizen class. The *aerarii* were a class of Roman citizens who had been condemned by the CENSORS to be tax-payers and nothing more. They paid TRIBUTUM at a higher rate than other citizens and were relegated from their voting century to a supernumerary one with no voting influence. The censors could also remove an *aerarius* from his TRIBUS and place him in a less favoured one.

See also COMITIA; VOTING.

HS

Nicolet (1980).

Aeschines (c.398/7–c.322 BC), Athenian orator. Of humble origins, Aeschines had a chequered career as soldier, actor, and minor government official until 348 BC (or perhaps 347/6) when he was appointed ambassador to Arcadia. Supported by EUBULUS, he went to Megalopolis determined to oppose the expansionist policies of PHILIP II of Macedon and to establish a common peace; but he returned with a change of heart, perhaps swayed by the indifference of the Greek states. In 346 he accompanied DEMOSTHENES on the embassy of Philocrates which negotiated a treaty with Philip. Accused of treason by both Demosthenes and Timarchus, Aeschines counter-attacked with a successful prosecution *Against Timarchus* and in 343 cleared his name with another speech *On the Embassy*. He represented Athens at a meeting of the DELPHIC AMPHICTYONY in 339 and after the defeat at CHAERONEA in 338. His last speech (*Against Ctesiphon*), attacking the proposal (first made in 336) to confer a crown on Demosthenes, was not heard until 330, when Demosthenes (*On the Crown*) successfully defended himself. Aeschines went into exile and taught rhetoric at Rhodes until his death.

Aeschines is more important for his role in history (his speech to the Delphic Amphictyony provoked a war) than for his skill in oratory, at which he was markedly inferior to Demosthenes. Only three speeches survive, but he was by all accounts an impressive performer.   GS

Hammond and Griffith (1979); Hornblower (1983); Kennedy (1963).

Aeschylus (525/4–456 BC), Greek tragedian. Aeschylus fought for Greece at Marathon in 490 and probably also at Salamis in 480. He was prolific (he is said to have written 90 plays) and popular (he won 13 victories in the dramatic competitions at Athens). He made at least two visits to the court of HIERON I in Sicily, on the second of which he died at Gela.

Seven plays survive, one of which (*Prometheus*) is probably spurious. The earliest (*The Persians*), produced in 472, treats the Persian defeat at Salamis and is the only surviving TRAGEDY to be based on a historical event. As drama it is somewhat amorphous; as history it is restrained and impartial. In the *Oresteia* (*Agamemnon*, *Choephori*, *Eumenides*), the only intact Greek trilogy, the action moves from Argos via Delphi to the court of the Areopagus in Athens which purveys the justice of Zeus. *Suppliants* and *Seven against Thebes* also raise moral and political issues of contemporary relevance.   GS

Griffith (1977); Lloyd-Jones (1971); Macleod (1982); Meier (1993); Podlecki (1966).

Aesop (6th century BC), writer of Greek fables. By tradition Aesop was a Thracian slave who worked on Samos and was then freed. But his *oeuvre* is an omnium gatherum of early fables by many hands, first brought together in the late 4th century BC by DEMETRIUS OF PHALERUM. The earliest editions to survive, the so-called Augustana and another by Babrius, date from about AD 100.

See also FABLE, GREEK.   GS

Perry (1952).

Aetius (d. AD 454), Roman general. Flavius Aetius, son of Gaudentius, a high-ranking officer under Theodosius I, became effective ruler of the western empire under VALENTINIAN III, despite the opposition of PLACIDIA. With help from the HUNS, he held Gaul against further advances by the Visigoths and Burgundians, but later (451) needed the help of THEODORIC's Visigoths against an invasion by ATTILA the Hun. Aetius was killed by Valentinian, who was convinced (by PETRONIUS MAXIMUS) of Aetius' treason.   RJB

Bury (1958); Grant (1979).

Aetna volcano and city in Sicily. Eruptions of the volcano (height 10,705 feet), attributed to the movements of a subterranean giant, were recorded in 475, 396, and 122 BC. The city, formerly known as CATANA, was founded by HIERON I after he deported its original inhabitants to LEONTINI and replaced them with Dorian mercenaries. These were in turn expelled in 461 BC when the city regained its old name.
                                                                              GS

Finley (1979).

Aetolia region in north-west Greece to the east of ACARNANIA and north of the Corinthian Gulf. A country of rugged mountains and remote unfortified villages, it remained a tribal state into the 4th century BC. It was, however, sufficiently united to repel the invasion of DEMOSTHENES in 426 BC and by the end of the 4th century had developed into an efficient federal state or SYMPOLITEIA (*see* AETOLIAN LEAGUE).   GS

Larsen (1968).

Aetolian League Greek confederation. The Aetolian League was established as a federal state by the 4th century BC, replacing the earlier tribal organization of the Aetolian people. It had an assembly of male citizens, a representative council, a standing executive committee, and annually elected officials. Thermon was its religious centre. During the 3rd century the League controlled the DELPHIC AMPHICTYONY. Naturally hostile towards Macedonia, the League was initially allied with Rome, but shifting relations and involvement with ANTIOCHUS III THE GREAT guaranteed Roman hostility. The Aetolians were reduced to subject allies in 189 BC, and the League declined in importance.

See also NAUPACTUS. EER

CAH VII.1; Green (1990); Larsen (1968).

Africa Roman province. Africa became a Roman province after the destruction of CARTHAGE in the Third PUNIC WAR (149–146 BC). The new province was governed by a praetor from UTICA, 30 miles north-west of Carthage. The province (roughly equivalent to modern Tunisia) was extended by Caesar, who added the Numidian kingdom of JUBA I, to the west (46 BC), and Augustus reorganized Africa as a senatorial province, under a proconsul based at Carthage. The proconsul commanded Legion III Augusta, but Gaius (AD 37) handed the legion to an imperial legate, and c.200 NUMIDIA became a separate province under the legate. None the less, the proconsulate of Africa remained one of the highest senatorial appointments.

Augustus began a thorough process of romanization, and the fertile soils of the coastal strip, in combination with an extremely extensive irrigation system, combined to make Africa the granary of Rome. Under Augustus the province extended east to the border with CYRENAICA, although under Tiberius an insurrection led by Tacfarinas (AD 17) was not defeated until 24, after which the frontiers were gradually pushed southwards, reaching their furthest extent under Septimius Severus and Caracalla. Claudius I extended Roman territory west to the Atlantic, establishing the two provinces of MAURETANIA Tingitana and Mauretania Caesariensis (AD 44). Elaborate building campaigns (e.g. at LEPTIS MAGNA) belong particularly to the reigns of African emperors, who included Titus and Domitian (Vespasian's wife was African), Clodius Albinus, the Severi, and Macrinus. Africa remained prosperous almost throughout, until it fell to the VANDALS, who took Carthage in AD 439.

See also AUGUSTINE; CYPRIAN; LIBYA; TERTULLIAN. RJB

Millar (1981).

Africanus (c.AD 160–240), Greek Christian writer. Sextus Julius Africanus was born in Jerusalem and visited Rome c.220 on an embassy to ELAGABALUS. He wrote five books of *Chronographies*, a world history which was the model for EUSEBIUS' *Chronicle*, and a 24-book encyclopaedia (*Kestoi*, 'Amulets') of miscellaneous information. Fragments of both works survive, as do his letters to ORIGEN and one Aristides. GS

Thee (1984).

Afterlife Ancient religion subscribed almost universally to belief in some sort of life after death. BURIAL PRACTICES continued largely unchanged throughout classical antiquity, but the manner in which the deceased survived them was endlessly debated.

In HOMER's world cremation and/or burial of the body enabled the soul to enter Hades, the subterranean abode of the dead to which all mortals must go. Heroes (*see* HERO CULT) were spared this cheerless fate and were transported to Elysium, the Isles of the Blest, for a life of endless pleasure. According to HESIOD certain categories of mortals had once been favoured with some such agreeable existence; and one of the HOMERIC HYMNS (7th century BC) states that initiates of the secret ELEUSINIAN MYSTERIES can look forward to happiness after death, while those who 'do wrong and fail to honour Persephone' are condemned to eternal punishment.

The philosophers, notably DIOGENES OF SINOPE ('the Cynic') and PLATO, later questioned the initiate's automatic entitlement to immortality. This led to greater emphasis on good behaviour as an additional (but not alternative) criterion for selection. Plato was deeply influenced by theories of reincarnation and the divine origin of the soul, which had become current in the 6th century BC with the introduction of ORPHISM and which he expounded in the *Phaedo*. While Platonic ideas on immortality were easily adapted to subsequent speculation on the nature of the soul, ARISTOTLE's belief in the afterlife as a purely intellectual experience made little impact on later popular thinking.

See also LUCRETIUS; PYTHAGORAS.   GS

Easterling and Muir (1985).

Agatharchides (2nd century BC), of Cnidus, Alexandrian geographer and historian. Agatharchides was a prolific writer and prominent figure at the court of Ptolemy VI. His historical works (*Events in Asia* and *Events in Europe*) are lost but enough of his geography (*On the Red Sea*) is quoted by DIODORUS SICULUS and Photius to make possible an assessment of his achievement as the most significant Alexandrian writer of the 2nd century BC.   GS

Fraser (1972).

Agathocles (361–289 BC), tyrant of Syracuse. Agathocles, son of a Syracusan immigrant brought in by TIMOLEON, was a successful mercenary but initially unsuccessful revolutionary. Finally overthrowing the oligarchs bloodily in 317 BC, he ruled Syracuse as tyrant supported by the lower classes. When his designs on eastern Sicily were thwarted by Carthage, Agathocles invaded Africa and seriously threatened Carthage with the military help of OPHELLAS of Cyrene. After various vicissitudes, he abandoned his army and escaped to Syracuse (307) where he continued to rule cruelly and ambitiously. He took the title 'king' in 304, but claimed to have restored Syracusan freedom. The historian TIMAEUS excoriates him.

See also CALLIAS OF SYRACUSE; MAMERTINES; SICILY.   EER

CAH VII.1; Finley (1979); Green (1990).

Agathon (c.447–c.401 BC), Greek tragedian. The plays of Agathon are lost; but we know from fragments that he invented plots that were not mythological. His appearance in Plato's *Symposium* (as the guest of honour) suggests that he was successful; and he was sufficiently well known to be ridiculed (for his effeminacy) by Aristophanes in *Thesmophoriazusae*. Like EURIPIDES, he left Athens c.407 for the Macedonian court of Archelaus where he died.   GS

Lévêque (1955).

Ager Campanus   see CAMPANIA.

Ager publicus   Roman public land. *Ager publicus* was land owned by the Roman people and administered by the state. Its origins are obscure, but common land undoubtedly existed very early. It was continually supplemented by conquest, as the Romans seized a substantial proportion of the territories of defeated Italian communities. Some of this land was distributed to Roman citizens in allotments, as in the case of VEII; in more distant or hostile regions conquered land became the territory of newly founded colonies (*see* COLONIZATION, ROMAN). But a substantial residue was left in public ownership. In theory this *ager publicus* could be rented by Roman citizens for cultivation or grazing, but in practice much of it was occupied by wealthy land-owners who annexed it to their estates. It thus became a major issue for the PLEBS, who agitated for its redistribution and for limits on the amount that any individual could occupy. A limit of 500 *iugera* (about 300 acres) was imposed by the Licinio-Sextian laws (367 BC), and subsequent laws restricted the numbers of animals that could be grazed. But these limits were frequently ignored, especially after the Second PUNIC WAR, when many rebel communities were punished with further loss of territory, and at a time when large slave-run estates were growing. This formed the background to the reforms of Tiberius GRACCHUS, who sought to enforce the old limits and to redistribute the remaining *ager publicus*.

See also STOLO.   TC

CAH VIII.

Agesilaus (*c*.444–360 BC), king of Sparta, 401–360. Despite lameness, Agesilaus succeeded AGIS II through the influence of LYSANDER and led an expedition against Persia (396), quickly dispensing with Lysander. Only moderately successful against the satraps of Asia Minor, he was called home (394), encountering the Boeotians at Coronea with honours even. After the failure of ANTALCIDAS to secure peace with Persia, he re-emerged and conducted various land campaigns, Teleutias his step-brother operating by sea. When Athens resumed open imperialism, Antalcidas led Sparta into the King's Peace (387/6) which Agesilaus exploited to Sparta's advantage against MANTINEA, Phlius, and especially THEBES where he was blamed for Phoebidas seizing the Cadmea (382). He campaigned against Thebes after its liberation. At the renewal of the King's Peace (371) he confronted EPAMINONDAS and excluded Thebes. After LEUCTRA he spent his time bitterly opposing Persia for recognizing independent MESSENIA.   GLC

Cartledge (1987).

Agis II king of Sparta, *c*.427–401 BC. Agis won the first battle of MANTINEA (418) which restored Spartan prestige. In command at Decelea, he ravaged Attica severely in the last years of the PELOPONNESIAN WAR, dying shortly after punishing ELIS for insubordination.   GLC

Kagan (1987).

Agis III king of Sparta, 338–330 BC. Agis led Peloponnesian opposition to Macedonian rule and died in battle against ANTIPATER near Megalopolis.   GLC

Agis IV (*c*.262–241 BC), king of Sparta. Agis proposed dealing with a severe economic crisis at the time of his accession in 244 BC by cancelling debts and redistributing land. To achieve these idealistic goals, he deposed his co-king Leonidas II and the civic magistrates who opposed him. After absence in 242 helping ARATUS OF SICYON against the Aetolians, Agis returned home to find his support eroded, himself betrayed by his uncle Agesilaus, and Leonidas back in power. His opponents executed him in 241.   EER

CAH VIII; Cartledge and Spawforth (1989); Forrest (1980); Green (1990); Jones (1967).

Agon   *see* GAMES, GREEK.

Agora   the market-place and civic centre of a Greek POLIS, the equivalent of the Roman FORUM. Generally bordered by stoas and other public buildings, the agora provided a large open space in which any form of business – commercial, social, political, judicial, religious, intellectual – could be transacted. The agora at ATHENS evolved naturally to serve the needs of the day. The Hellenistic agora (e.g. at PRIENE) was purpose-built to an established design.   GS

Thompson and Wycherley (1972).

Agoracritus (late 5th century BC), Greek sculptor. A native of Paros and a pupil of PHEIDIAS, Agoracritus probably worked mostly in Attica. He is credited with statues in both marble and bronze, but his best-known work was the marble statue of Nemesis at Rhamnus. Fragments of the original, including a colossal female head, have facilitated identification with a number of Roman copies.

See also SCULPTURE, GREEK.   GS

Robertson (1975).

Agricola (AD 40–93), Roman politician. Gnaeus Julius Agricola is the most famous Roman governor of BRITAIN thanks to a detailed biography, almost amounting to panegyric, by his son-in-law TACITUS. His distinguished career, spanning more than 25 years, included three appointments in Britain: his first post was as a military tribune in Britain (58–61); he commanded Legion XX (70–73/4) under Cerialis; and, after holding the consulship in Rome (77/8), he became governor of Britain (78–84). As governor he was almost constantly on campaign – Tacitus admits Agricola was over-fond of military glory – defeating the Ordovices (78) and the BRIGANTES, reaching the Tyne–Solway (79), and occupying the Scottish lowlands (80). After building roads and forts (81), he continued the advance into Scotland (*see* CALEDONIA) (82/3), establishing a legionary fortress at Inchtuthil, and defeated the Caledonians at Mons Graupius (84, site unknown). Recalled by Domitian, who rightly considered his plans over-ambitious, he spent the rest of his life in retirement in Rome.   RJB

Hanson (1987); Mattingly and Handford (1970); Scullard (1979); Todd (1981).

Agriculture Life was hard for the Greek farmer according to HESIOD. The soil was poor (except in the few fertile plains) and the climate difficult. Estates were small and land needed to be left fallow for at least a year after a season's cultivation. Corn and vegetables showed a poor return when compared with olives, grapes, and animal husbandry. In the classical period the growth of towns created a demand for more food which could only be met by a more scientific rotation of crops and use of manure that facilitated continuous cultivation of the soil and by an expansion and specialization of the labour force (*see* SLAVERY, GREEK). Farming was big business in Ptolemaic Egypt.

Agriculture was infinitely more professional in Roman Italy. Technology kept pace with demands for improved irrigation, specialist implements, and labour-saving machinery. Tools for lopping and pruning were introduced; sickles were improved; and an ox-powered machine for reaping with a battery of sharp knives (*vallus*) was invented. Estates grew to enormous proportions and cheap labour was provided by prisoners of war. A change came about under the Empire with a return to smaller estates in the hands of tenants who paid a share of their produce (DECUMA) as rent. But improvements in techniques continued to be made, advice was freely available from the literati (*see* CATO; COLUMELLA; HYGINUS; VARRO; VIRGIL), and the adoption of scientific methods quickly spread throughout the provinces.

See also ARBORICULTURE; BEE-KEEPING; ENGINEERING; HORSES; INDUSTRY; LATIFUNDIA; VITICULTURE.   GS

Hanson (1983); Rostovtzeff (1941, 1957); Westermann (1955); White (1967, 1970, 1975).

Agri Decumates   Roman territory in Germany. The *Agri Decumates* comprised the triangle of land north of the Upper Rhine and the Upper Danube, mostly occupied by the Black Forest. VESPASIAN (AD 69–79) conquered the area, and DOMITIAN (81–96) established the first bases of the LIMES, providing a northern frontier. The new territory became part of the province of Upper Germany, but became increasingly untenable with the barbarian incursions of the 3rd century AD, and was abandoned by Gallienus *c.259/60*.

See also ALAMANNI; GERMANIA.   RJB

Millar (1981).

Agrippa   (*c.63–12* BC), Roman soldier. Marcus Vipsanius Agrippa was the exact contemporary of Octavian (AUGUSTUS), and his staunchest supporter. Octavian's victory at ACTIUM (31 BC) was largely due to Agrippa, and Agrippa was Octavian's colleague as consul in 28 and 27. In 21 he married Augustus' only daughter, JULIA MAJOR, and their eldest children were rapidly marked out for the succession. To marry Julia, Agrippa divorced his second wife, Marcella, niece of Augustus: his first, Attica, bore him Vipsania Agrippina, future wife of TIBERIUS. Agrippa, granted *imperium* in 23, served in the east (23–22) and in Gaul and Spain (20–19), and acted as Augustus' deputy in Rome in the intervening period (21). In 18 Agrippa was granted proconsular *imperium maius* for five years, and *tribunicia potestas*, powers (renewed in 13) similar to those of Augustus himself. He returned to the east, and in 13 went to Pannonia, but died on his return to Italy.

RJB

Salmon (1968); Scullard (1982); Syme (1939); Wright (1937).

Agrippa I (AD 10–44), king of Judaea, 41–4. Agrippa (the Herod Agrippa of Acts 12) was the son of Aristobulus, one of the sons of HEROD THE GREAT. Herod's kingdom had been split between three other sons, HEROD ANTIPAS, Philip, and Archelaus: by virtue of his friendship with GAIUS and CLAUDIUS I, Agrippa succeeded to the portions of his uncles Philip (Ituraea) and Herod (Galilee, 39), and became king of Judaea (originally Archelaus' territory, but a province since AD 6).

RJB

Bowersock (1983); Salmon (1968); Scullard (1982).

Agrippa II *see* BERENICE.

Agrippa Postumus (12 BC–AD 14), son of M. Agrippa. Agrippa Postumus was the third son of Marcus AGRIPPA and JULIA MAJOR, daughter of AUGUSTUS. Born after Agrippa's death in 12 BC, he was adopted in AD 4 by Augustus, but his depraved behaviour led Augustus to disinherit and exile him (AD 7). DIO CASSIUS' allegation that Augustus secretly visited Agrippa in exile is probably false. Agrippa was killed immediately after Augustus' death, perhaps on the latter's orders, although TACITUS blames TIBERIUS.

RJB

Scullard (1982); Wells (1984).

Agrippina the Elder (*c.*14 BC–AD 33), wife of GERMANICUS. Vipsania Agrippina, daughter of Marcus AGRIPPA and JULIA MAJOR, Augustus' daughter, married Germanicus and bore him nine children. Proud and imperious, and popular with the army after accompanying Germanicus on campaign, she came into conflict with Tiberius after her husband's death (AD 19), finally committing suicide after the deaths in prison of her eldest sons, Nero and Drusus Caesar. Her surviving children were GAIUS (Caligula), AGRIPPINA THE YOUNGER, DRUSILLA, and Julia Livilla.

RJB

Scullard (1982); Wells (1984).

Agrippina the Younger (AD 15–59), eldest daughter of GERMANICUS and AGRIPPA THE ELDER. Julia Agrippina conspired with her lover Aemilius Lepidus against her brother GAIUS (Caligula), and later became the mistress of PALLAS. Her third husband was her uncle CLAUDIUS I (48): she persuaded him to adopt NERO (50, her son by her first husband, Gnaeus Domitius Ahenobarbus), and became virtual ruler at Rome. She almost certainly poisoned Claudius, but was driven from court (55) by Nero and assassinated. RJB

Salmon (1968); Scullard (1982); Wells (1984).

Ahenobarbus *see* DOMITIUS AHENOBARBUS.

Alamanni German people. The Alamanni, whose origins are obscure, first appear fighting alongside the CHATTI in Raetia against Caracalla (AD 213). Their attacks on Roman territory finally forced the abandonment of the AGRI DECUMATES (c.260), and they occupied the area to the south. Their raiding continued through the 4th century, despite a defeat by JULIAN at Argentorate (Strasbourg, 357), and in the 5th century they settled within the empire, in Alsace and northern Switzerland. RJB

Thompson (1965); Todd (1975).

Alani Asiatic people. The Alani, originally one of the nomadic SARMATIAN peoples, had, by the 1st century BC, occupied the plains between the Don and the Volga. They failed to break through into the Roman or Parthian empires until, in the 4th century AD, pressure from the migrating HUNS forced them westwards: they joined the Germanic invasions of Gaul (406) and Spain (409), and (after defeat by the VISIGOTHS) were absorbed by the VANDALS. RJB

Todd (1972, 1975).

Alaric (c.AD 360–410), king of the Visigoths, c.395–410. Alaric fought in the army of GOTHS that helped THEODOSIUS I against Eugenius (394), then led a revolt which threatened Constantinople, ravaged Thessaly, and occupied Greece. Alaric withdrew to Epirus (397), and ARCADIUS granted him the title Master of Soldiers in Illyricum. He invaded Italy (401), but was twice defeated by STILICHO (402; 403). Stilicho's death prompted a further invasion: Alaric besieged Rome three times (408–10), the second time attempting to install a usurper (Attalus), and eventually sacked it (24 August 410): he left after three days with much booty and many captives (including PLACIDIA) and died while preparing to invade Africa. RJB

Bury (1958); Matthews (1990); Todd (1972).

Alba Longa city in Italy. According to tradition, Alba Longa was founded by Iulus, the son of Aeneas, and was ruled by his descendants as the chief city of Latium. Alba Longa was conquered and destroyed by TULLUS HOSTILIUS, who moved its population to Rome. Despite modern doubts about Alba Longa's existence, in classical times the Romans and Latins celebrated an annual festival near the supposed site of the ancient city.   LPR

CAH VII.2.

Albinus *see* CLODIUS ALBINUS.

Albion *see* BRITAIN.

Alcaeus (born *c*.620 BC), Greek lyric poet. Alcaeus was actively involved in the turbulent politics of his native Lesbos, first as an ally, later a critic, of the tyrant PITTACUS. Exiled more than once, he was finally pardoned *c*.580 and returned home, but nothing is known of his later life. His lyrics, which survive in numerous fragments, are, like those of his contemporary SAPPHO, passionate, personal, and vivacious. Many relate to political events of the time; others are more conventional hymns to gods, drinking songs, and love poems. Both the form and the content of his verses provided models for the *Odes* of HORACE.
                                                                                       GS

Andrewes (1956); Kirkwood (1974); Page (1955).

Alcamenes (late 5th century BC), Greek sculptor. Probably an Athenian, Alcamenes was both a pupil and a rival of PHEIDIAS. Apart from a bronze athlete and a chryselephantine Dionysus, all his recorded works were marble statues of gods. The group of Procne and Itys in the Athenian Acropolis Museum may be his work; the figures from the west pediment of the temple of Zeus at Olympia, attributed to Alcamenes by Pausanias, are almost certainly not.

See also SCULPTURE, GREEK.   GS

Capuis (1968); Robertson (1975).

Alcibiades (*c*.450–404 BC), Athenian leader. Alcibiades, a pupil of SOCRATES, had outstanding political and military gifts but was greatly suspect for his extravagant tastes and conduct. He masterminded the coalition that nearly defeated Sparta at MANTINEA (418), and was responsible for the reduction of MELOS (416) and the Sicilian expedition (415). He was suspected of mutilating the HERMAE and profaning the ELEUSINIAN MYSTERIES, but was obliged to continue as general. Before effecting anything in Sicily, he was recalled for trial. Anticipating the worst, he made his way to Sparta where allegedly he urged Spartan support for Syracuse and fortification of Decelea. In 412 he went out to Ionia and forwarded revolts of Athens's subjects. In fear of Spartan disfavour, he fled to TISSAPHERNES, satrap in Sardes, seeking to soften Persian hostility to Athens. Joining the Athenians at Samos, he continued efforts to win over Tissaphernes and stopped the Athenian fleet sailing home to put down the oligarchic revolution. Recalled in 411, he did not return to Athens before defeating Sparta at CYZICUS and capturing Byzantium (410) and being assured of a changed mood in Athens. Sent out again to Ionia (407), he was absent when his fleet was defeated off NOTIUM. Alcibiades deemed it expedient to retire to his property in Thrace, where he tried to warn the Athenian generals of the dangers of their position at AEGOSPOTAMI. Fearing Sparta, he sought refuge with PHARNABAZUS but was murdered (404). It was disastrous for Athens not to have made better use of his very great abilities.   GLC

Ellis (1989); Kagan (1987).

Alcmaeon (fl. early 5th century BC), Greek physician. Alcmaeon of Croton is the only Greek medical author before HIPPOCRATES whose theories have survived in any form. While only fragments of his book survive, they clearly reveal the same rational outlook characteristic of the Ionian natural philosophers. Furthermore, just as ANAXIMANDER had viewed the cosmos in terms of a balance between equal opposed forces, so Alcmaeon regarded health as due to the equilibrium (*isonomia*) of the powers composing the body, whereas the supremacy (*monarchia*) of any one of them caused disease. This theory of health subsequently attained a wide currency. Although influenced by Ionian philosophy Alcmaeon rejected the dogmatic, *a priori* approach of these philosophers and adopted a much more empirical attitude. In the course of his investigations he discovered passages (*poroi*) linking eye to brain and inferred that all the senses were linked to the brain and that the brain was the seat of thought and feeling. He thus became one of the earliest protagonists in the long debate as to whether the heart or brain was the seat of intelligence.

See also ANATOMY.   JL

Guthrie, vol. 1 (1962); Kirk, Raven, and Schofield (1983); Longrigg (1993).

Alcmaeonids Athenian noble family. The Alcmaeonids were one of the leading families of archaic Athens. The first notable figure, Megacles, executed the supporters of CYLON, leading to the family's exile under a curse, a recurrent theme in attacks on them. His son Alcmaeon commanded the Athenian forces in the First SACRED WAR, and founded the family fortune through friendship with Alyattes of Lydia. His son Megacles married the daughter of CLEISTHENES OF SICYON, their son being the legislator CLEISTHENES, and was prominent in the dynastic struggles surrounding PEISISTRATUS. The family's claim to have been in exile throughout the tyranny was inaccurate, since Cleisthenes was archon in 525/4 BC; but they played a leading role in its overthrow, exploiting their association with Delphi. However, they were suspected of collusion with the Persians at MARATHON, hence the subsequent ostracism of Megacles and XANTHIPPUS. Thereafter the family is only represented in politics by descendants by marriage, notably PERICLES and ALCIBIADES.

RB

Davies (1971) no. 9688.

Alcman   (7th century BC), of Sparta, Greek lyric poet. Alcman is the earliest choral poet of whose work substantial fragments survive. His six books of graceful lyrics included ritual hymns, marriage songs, love poems, nature poems, and myths. Literary remains support the evidence of archaeology that 7th-century SPARTA was a flourishing cultural centre.

GS

Page (1951).

Aleuadae   leading family of Larisa. They accepted Persian influence in THESSALY and assisted XERXES' invasion in 480 BC. In the 4th century they similarly treated with MACEDONIA.

GLC

Westlake (1935).

Alexander I   king of Epirus, 342–330 BC. Installed as ruler of the Molossian kingdom by PHILIP II of Macedon (342), he united EPIRUS. Summoned by TARENTUM, he conquered much of southern Italy, but after a defeat he was murdered.

GLC

Hammond (1967).

Alexander I   king of Macedon, c.494–452 BC. Alexander I 'the Philhellene' perforce joined XERXES in his invasion of Greece (480) and was used as envoy by MARDONIUS. On his own initiative he visited the Greeks by night before PLATAEA and was allowed to compete in the OLYMPIC GAMES.

GLC

Hammond and Griffith (1979).

Alexander II   king of Macedon, 369–368 BC. In his short reign Alexander intervened in THESSALY and is believed by some to have made military reforms attributed by most to his younger brother, PHILIP II.

GLC

Hammond and Griffith (1979).

Alexander III the Great (356–323 BC), king of Macedon. Alexander was the son of PHILIP II and his Epirote queen OLYMPIAS. Tradition maintains that he was tutored by ARISTOTLE. As heir apparent, he fought campaigns on his father's behalf (*see* map on page 748) but after a quarrel was sent into exile with some of his friends (337 BC). He returned after Philip's murder in 336, in which he was probably not involved, and was acclaimed king although he was careful to eliminate possible rivals. His control over Greece was voted by the League of CORINTH; his savage destruction of Thebes clearly indicated his intentions. Alexander undertook the invasion of Asia which had been initiated by Philip. From 334 to 330 he conquered the Persian empire and its Great King DARIUS III. Three major battles occurred: at the GRANICUS RIVER (334), ISSUS (333), and GAUGAMELA (331). After Issus, Alexander liberated Egypt from the Persians and founded ALEXANDRIA. Although he was *de facto* king of Persia, Alexander continued to campaign for several more years. The murders of PHILOTAS, PARMENION, and CLEITUS THE BLACK suggest that his character was deteriorating (*see* CURTIUS).

After a long sojourn in BACTRIA, where he married the captive ROXANE, and in Central Asia, he reached INDIA in 327 BC and conquered native kings like PORUS, not without stiff opposition. His army mutinied at the Hyphasis (Beas) River (the easternmost tributary of the Indus), and refused to proceed further to the Ganges. Alexander thereupon built a fleet (commanded by NEARCHUS and ONESICRITUS) to sail down the Indus and up the Persian Gulf. He and his troops were nearly wiped out crossing the Gedrosian desert. The returning expedition reached Babylon, where Alexander fell ill and died on 10 June 323 BC, probably of fever brought on by excess, although poison was alleged. A brilliant general who was admired and emulated in antiquity as in modern times, Alexander was none the less a cruel and autocratic ruler whose conviction of his own invincibility led to megalomaniac intentions and pretensions to divinity. Although he founded many cities, these were for strategic reasons rather than for the spread of Hellenism. His expedition had a disastrous effect upon the population and economy of Macedon. EER

Bosworth (1988a); Hammond (1989); Hammond and Walbank (1988); Lane Fox (1973).

Alexander IV (323–*c*.311 BC), king of Macedon. Alexander was the posthumous son of ALEXANDER THE GREAT and ROXANE, declared at birth joint king with his half-uncle PHILIP III ARRHIDAEUS. A useful pawn in the power struggles of the DIADOCHI, Alexander fell under the control first of ANTIPATER in 320, then OLYMPIAS in 319, and finally CASSANDER in 316.

He was killed by Cassander after 311, and is perhaps the occupant of Tomb III at Vergina (ancient AEGAE) in Macedonia.   EER

Andronikos (1974); CAH VII.1; Hammond and Walbank (1988).

Alexander V   king of Macedon, 295–294 BC. Alexander was the youngest son of CASSANDER who fought his brother Antipater for the Macedonian throne after the death of their elder brother. To further his claims he rashly sought help from PYRRHUS of Epirus and DEMETRIUS I POLIORCETES, who each had designs upon the same throne. Pyrrhus installed Alexander as king, but Demetrius had him murdered and was himself acclaimed king by the Macedonian army in 294.   EER

Errington (1990); Hammond and Walbank (1988).

Alexander, Severus   *see* SEVERUS ALEXANDER.

Alexander of Corinth   (*c*.290–*c*.245 BC), Greek general. Alexander inherited the Macedonian military command of the strategic areas Corinth and Euboea from his father the younger Craterus, who was son of the general CRATERUS and a half-brother of ANTIGONUS II GONATAS. Alexander declared himself independent *c*.253–*c*.249, making an alliance with the ACHAEAN LEAGUE and consolidating his position. Macedonia was forced to acquiesce in his usurpation, but Alexander's death left his widow as ruler in Corinth, which was soon recovered by Antigonus.   EER

CAH VII.1; Hammond and Walbank (1988).

Alexander of Pherae   tyrant, 369–359 BC. Succeeding his uncle JASON as TAGUS and tyrant, Alexander aroused opposition especially from Larisa which was aided by ALEXANDER II of Macedon. He was defeated by PELOPIDAS of Thebes at Cynoscephalae (364). First ally, then foe, of Athens, he won a minor naval victory at Peparethus (361) before being murdered by relatives.   GLC

Westlake (1935).

Alexander Balas   (fl. 161–145 BC), Seleucid king. Alexander, the pretended son of ANTIOCHUS IV EPIPHANES, was backed as king by the Pergamene ATTALUS II PHILADELPHUS who resented the support of the legitimate king DEMETRIUS I SOTER for a false claimant to the Cappadocian throne of ARIARATHES V. Secure after Demetrius' death in 150, Alexander was recognized (for their own ends) by Rome, Pergamum, Cappadocia, and Egypt. An incompetent ruler and pawn of Ptolemy

VI, Alexander died fighting the true successor DEMETRIUS II NICATOR and the turncoat Ptolemy.

See also PTOLEMY VI–XV.   EER

CAH VII.1; Green (1990); Gruen (1984).

Alexander Polyhistor (*c*.100–*c*.40 BC), Greek historian. Alexander 'the very learned' was a Greek from Miletus who became a prisoner of war at Rome. Later freed and taking the name Lucius Cornelius Alexander, he was a pedagogue and taught HYGINUS. He died in a fire. Influenced by CRATES OF MALLUS, he wrote prolifically on philosophy, literature, and history. He recorded Jewish apologetic writing and Greco-Jewish poetry, thereby helping to transmit Jewish historical tradition to the western world.   EER

Davies and Finkelstein (1989); Schürer (1973–87); Stern (1974–84).

Alexandria city in Egypt. Alexandria was founded by ALEXANDER THE GREAT in 331 BC when he liberated Egypt from the Persian empire. It was the first of his eponymous city foundations. Tradition maintains that Alexander took a personal interest in its design, selecting sites for temples and the agora. His appointed governor CLEOMENES OF NAUCRATIS oversaw the city's completion. After Alexander's death, PTOLEMY (later I) became satrap and later king of Egypt, and chose Alexandria as his Greek capital. Situated in the western Delta near the Canopic mouth of the Nile and possessing excellent natural harbours, Alexandria soon became a rich commercial centre for trade in the eastern Mediterranean. The city grew rapidly during the 3rd century and was lavishly adorned by PTOLEMY I, II, and III. The MUSEUM and LIBRARY made Alexandria a great centre of learning throughout the Hellenistic age and attracted scholars and writers (among them APOLLONIUS RHODIUS, CALLIMACHUS, ERATOSTHENES, and THEOCRITUS; *see also* JEWISH LITERATURE; MEDICINE; NEOPLATONISM; SCHOLARSHIP, GREEK). There were extensive palaces, a temple of SARAPIS, the PHAROS (a lighthouse ranked among the seven wonders of the world), and the opulent tomb of Alexander which was the focus of the Ptolemaic ruler cult. The large Jewish community which occupied a separate quarter had special privileges of self-government. Roman and Byzantine Alexandria remained an important city until the Arab conquest.   EER

Davies and Finkelstein (1989); Fraser (1972); Jones (1983); Stillwell (1976).

Alexandrian poetry, Greek By the end of the 4th century BC the power struggles that were the inevitable consequence of Alexander the Great's extension of the Greek world began to subside and made way for a cultural flowering that bears comparison with that of 5th-century BC Athens. The new city of Alexandria provided the focus for much of the literary activity of this HELLENISTIC age. Poets wrote for a large cosmopolitan readership that was well educated and highly sophisticated, and they employed great originality in adapting most of the traditional forms to its taste. Much of their work (including all tragedy) is lost, but the revival of epic is well represented by APOLLONIUS RHODIUS, mime by HERODAS, pastoral poetry by THEOCRITUS, elegy and epigram by CALLIMACHUS and MELEAGER, and didactic poetry by ARATUS. These writers provided much of the inspiration for subsequent generations of Roman poets.   GS

Fraser (1972); Hutchinson (1988); Pfeiffer (1968); Tarn and Griffith (1952); Webster (1964).

Alexandrian poetry, Latin Throughout the classical period Latin writers were directly influenced by and profoundly respectful of their Greek predecessors. The Alexandrian poetry of the Hellenistic age began to make its mark on Rome in the 2nd century BC with the epigrams of Catulus and the *Erotopaegnia* of Laevius. But it was in the mid-1st century BC that a group of poets, dubbed *neoterici* ('the moderns') by Cicero (*Att.* 7.2.1), abandoned the established literary traditions of Latin epic and tragedy and substituted both the form and the content of Alexandrian Greek models. Foremost among this group, and its sole surviving representative, was CATULLUS whose choice of metres, cult of erudition, and passionately personal style of writing are characteristic of the new fashion. Its influence remained strong in the early works of VIRGIL, the APPENDIX VIRGILIANA, and the elegies of PROPERTIUS and OVID.   GS

Ross (1969).

Alexis (*c*.372–*c*.270 BC), Greek comic poet. Alexis came from Thurii in south Italy but spent most of his long life in Athens. He is said to have written 245 plays, spanning the transition from Middle COMEDY to New Comedy. Surviving fragments indicate that his plots treated mythical as well as contemporary subjects. He exerted considerable influence on Roman playwrights such as PLAUTUS.   GS

Webster (1970).

Algebra *see* DIOPHANTUS.

Alimenta Roman system of poor relief. Originating as an act of private charity and first employed in the 1st century AD, the practice was later institutionalized and administered by state or local officials. It required a benefactor to invest capital in mortgage on land from which the interest could be distributed among poor children in Italian towns. Such endowments were made by both private individuals (e.g. PLINY THE YOUNGER) and emperors (NERVA; TRAJAN). Pliny suggests that it was done primarily to increase the birth rate among the poor and to improve the supply of recruits to the legions.   GS

Hands (1968); Rostovtzeff (1957).

Allectus *see* CARAUSIUS.

Allies *see* SOCII.

Allobroges Gallic people. The Allobroges lived in the region of modern Savoy between the rivers Rhône and Isère and Lake Geneva. They were defeated by Gnaeus DOMITIUS AHENOBARBUS in 121 BC and became part of the Roman province of Gallia Narbonensis. In 63 BC their ambassadors provided vital evidence against CATILINE. However, exasperated by debts owed to PUBLICANI and mistreatment by the Roman governor, they revolted, but were crushed in 61.   LPR

Chadwick (1970).

Alphabet, Greek After the Mycenaean period, during which a script known as Linear B was used, the Greeks seem to have lost the art of writing. When they regained it, sometime in the 8th century BC, they developed a new alphabet for it, derived from the Phoenician but with the important innovation of representing vowels. At first there were several local variants, but Ionic eventually prevailed and was officially adopted by Athens in 403 BC. Later in antiquity a cursive script was developed for use in letters and accounts, though books continued to be written in uncial (capital) letters until the 9th century AD.
See also NUMBERS.   GS

Jeffery (1990); Powell (1991); Reynolds and Wilson (1991).

Alphabet, Latin The original Latin alphabet consisted of 20 letters: A B C D E F H I K L M N O P Q R S T V X; G Y Z were added later in antiquity and J U W in the Middle Ages. Some scholars argue that the Romans received their alphabet directly from the Greeks via their colony at Cumae in Campania; others that the ETRUSCANS acted as intermediaries in providing a common origin for OSCAN and Umbrian scripts as well as Latin. The earliest Latin inscription is found on a fragment of pottery from Gabii in Latium of *c*.800 BC (*see* EPIGRAPHY, LATIN). The alphabet is an enduring element of Rome's legacy to the modern world.

See also LATIN LANGUAGE.   GS

Allen (1978); Palmer (1954).

Amasis   (6th century BC), Greek potter. Amasis, whose name is Egyptian, worked in Athens at the same time as EXECIAS. Nine vases survive with his signature as potter. They are all painted by the same artist, who is therefore known as the Amasis Painter; potter and painter may be the same man. The Amasis Painter is credited with over 100 black-figure vases.
    See also PAINTING, GREEK; POTTERY, GREEK.   GS

Boardman (1974); Karouzou (1956).

Ambarvalia   Roman festival. The Ambarvalia was a ceremony held annually in May in which a procession of priests traced a boundary around the city at a radius of around 5 Roman miles (about 4 miles). The chief ritual was the sacrifice of a pig, an ox, and a sheep. The aim was evidently to purify the borders of the Roman state. The festival must therefore date from a time (probably before 600 BC) when Rome controlled only a very restricted territory.   TC

Scullard (1981).

Ambitus   literally 'going round'. *Ambitus* was canvassing for public office and a regular feature of Roman electioneering. Advice to a candidate on how to canvass support is offered in the *Commentariolum Petitionis*, a pamphlet sometimes attributed to Quintus CICERO. However, *ambitus* came to be equated with illicit electoral practices, especially bribery. Attempts to regulate canvassing and to prevent corruption go back at least to the 4th century BC and in the late Republic many laws *de ambitu* ('concerning canvassing') were passed, but to little practical effect.   DP

Lintott (1990); Taylor (1949).

Ambracia   modern Arta, city in north-west Greece. Originally a colony of CORINTH, Ambracia was subdued by a combination of Acarnanians and Athenians in 426 BC. Subdued again by PHILIP II of Macedon, it passed in 294 to PYRRHUS who made it the capital of EPIRUS and provided it with fine buildings. Besieged by the Romans in 189, it then became a free city.   GS

Hammond (1967).

Ambrose, St   (*c*.AD 339–97), bishop of Milan. Born at Trier and educated in Rome, Ambrose was appointed (*c*.370) governor of Aemilia with his headquarters at Milan. Though not yet baptized, he was chosen as bishop in 374 by popular demand. As the champion of orthodox CHRISTIANITY against ARIANISM, paganism, and Judaism and a brilliant preacher, he exercised influence over successive emperors and was partly responsible for the conversion of St AUGUSTINE. His letters, panegyrics, and sermons are an important source on the early Church. PAULINUS wrote his *Life*.   GS

Brown (1967); Matthews (1990).

Ammianus Marcellinus (*c*.AD 330–95), Roman historian. Ammianus Marcellinus was a native of Antioch, became a staff officer of the general Ursicinus, in the east (354), and then in Gaul, first on a mission to kill the usurper Silvanus (355) and thereafter under JULIAN's command. He followed Ursicinus back east (357), took part in the resistance to a Persian invasion (359), and joined Julian's invasion of Persia (363). In 371 he was in Antioch, once more a civilian, and later moved to Rome, where, probably in the late 380s, he wrote a *History*, in Latin, continuing the histories of TACITUS from 96 down to his own day. The first 13 of his 31 books are lost: the remainder cover the years 354–78, for which they are a primary source. Much space is devoted to Julian, a fellow pagan whom he greatly admired. Using many sources, showing good judgement, and generally impartial, he was the last great Roman historian.

See also HISTORIOGRAPHY, ROMAN.   RJB

Hamilton and Wallace-Hadrill (1986); Matthews (1989).

Ammon Egyptian god. Originally peculiar to Egyptian THEBES, Ammon (or Amun) achieved national status under the Egyptian empire and was introduced to the Greek world through the colony at CYRENE. His oracle at Siwa rivalled those at Delphi and Dodona (*see* ORACLES) and was visited by CIMON, LYSANDER, and ALEXANDER THE GREAT. In Greece he was identified with ZEUS.   GS

Parke (1967b).

Amphictyonic League *see* DELPHIC AMPHICTYONY.

Amphipolis city in northern Greece in a strategic position on the east bank of the river Strymon. First colonized by Athens in 437/6 BC after earlier failed attempts, Amphipolis fell to BRASIDAS in 424 without resistance. Despite restoration to Athens under the Peace of NICIAS (421), it retained its independence until occupied by PHILIP II of Macedon in

357. Ceded to Rome after PYDNA, it became the capital of Roman MACEDONIA. GS

Hammond and Griffith (1979).

Amphitheatre   an elliptical arena surrounded by raised seating for the staging of spectator sports in the Roman world. The earliest examples were temporary structures built of wood, but by about 80 BC the first permanent amphitheatre had been erected, at POMPEII. Its arena was sunk below ground level and the seating rested on earth banks supported by stone retaining walls with external staircases. This model was soon followed in the provinces at Syracuse, Merida, Cirencester, and Caerleon. But it was not long before architects introduced a free-standing structure with masonry vaulting to provide spectators with easy access and means of circulation. Those at Verona, Pola, Nîmes (NEMAUSUS), Arles (ARELATE), and El Djem, characteristic gestures of imperial munificence, are among the most impressive of all surviving Roman monuments. This style allowed for the construction of underground chambers beneath the arena to accommodate men, animals, and props for the performances. Such chambers exist in fairly simple form at Pozzuoli (PUTEOLI), El Djem, and Sarmizegetusa; but the most elaborate example, and also the most famous of all amphitheatres, is the COLOSSEUM at Rome. Even here, however, the seating was in wood until the great fire of AD 217.

See also GAMES, ROMAN. GS

Ward-Perkins (1977).

Amphora   *see* POTTERY, GREEK.

Ampliatio   Roman legal institution for adjournment. During the Republic criminal trials could be adjourned if the jury felt that a decision could not be reached on the evidence as presented. The case then had to be reiterated and the evidence elucidated more thoroughly. In theory an infinite number of such repetitions was possible, but in the late 2nd century BC abuses gave rise to laws restricting *ampliatio* to one or two in any one trial. TC

Amynander   (fl. 209–c.189 BC), king of Athamania, the region between MACEDONIA and AETOLIA. Initially among those attempting to dissuade PHILIP V from the First MACEDONIAN WAR, he later joined Philip and attended the peace negotiations at Phoenice in 205. Amynander joined Rome in the Second, helping FLAMININUS against Philip at CYNOSCEPHALAE in 197. In 192–1 he joined ANTIOCHUS III THE GREAT and

Aetolia against Rome and Philip, who unseated him. Despite his shifting allegiances, Rome pardoned and restored him in 189.   EER

Gruen (1984); Hammond (1967); Hammond and Walbank (1988); Walbank (1940).

Amyntas   king of Macedon, 393–370 BC. Amyntas consolidated the kingdom against the Illyrians, joined the Spartans against OLYNTHUS in 382, and shared in the renewal of the King's Peace in 371. He was the father of PHILIP II.   GLC

Hammond and Griffith (1979).

Anacreon   (c.575–c.490 BC), Greek lyric poet. Anacreon was born at Teos in Asia Minor, but after the Persian occupation of Ionia c.540 he joined the new colony at Abdera in Thrace. He was much in demand as a poet, song writer, and entertainer and was summoned first to the court of POLYCRATES on Samos c.532 and later to Athens by HIPPARCHUS, son of Peisistratus, c.522. His songs, characterized by witty imagery expressed in simple forms, remained popular throughout the 5th century and continued to be imitated into the Byzantine period.   GS

Bowra (1961); Kirkwood (1974).

Anatomy   In the *Iliad* wounds are described with an anatomical accuracy that has led to the claim that this knowledge was derived from the dissecting table. But, as the treatises in the Hippocratic Corpus clearly reveal, knowledge of internal organs remained, even in the 5th and 4th centuries BC, at a very primitive level. There is no strong evidence at this time to suggest that anatomical knowledge was based upon systematic dissection of animals or man. Religious scruples prohibited human dissection in ancient Greece. Although Chalcidius describes ALCMAEON as the 'first to dare to approach the excision of the eye', it is extremely doubtful that this evidence indicates dissection pursued as part of a systematic, investigative process. DIOCLES is said to have been the first to write a textbook on anatomy (unquestionably animal anatomy). This work may have influenced ARISTOTLE's anatomical investigations.

It was not until the 3rd century BC at Alexandria, under the protection and provision of the first Ptolemies, that medical researchers first began, on a regular basis, to dissect and even vivisect humans. Freed from the inhibitions and religious prejudices in vogue in mainland Greece, HEROPHILUS and ERASISTRATUS attained levels of sophistication in anatomy largely unsurpassed until the Renaissance. Despite their impressive achievements, the schools they founded dissipated their energies in sectarian strife and none of their followers made any really significant contribution. Nor did the practice of human dissection continue as a permanent legacy. By the 2nd century AD it was already a thing of the past, as the writings of Rufus and SORANUS reveal. Even GALEN rarely had the opportunity to practise human dissection. His dissections were based primarily upon a large variety of animals, especially the Barbary ape. After Galen original anatomical investigation virtually ceased and later medical writers confined themselves to summarizing and commenting upon the views of their predecessors.

See also MEDICINE.   JL

Longrigg; Temkin and Temkin (1967).

Anaxagoras (*c*.500–428 BC), Greek natural philosopher. Anaxagoras of Clazomenae came to Athens at the age of 20. He became the teacher and friend of PERICLES. Like EMPEDOCLES, Anaxagoras sought a pluralist solution to circumvent PARMENIDES' arguments. He denied that there was an original unity and postulated a plurality of eternal, qualitatively different substances that filled the whole of space. He accepted the negation of coming-into-being and passing-away, but replaced the former with the aggregation of indestructible elements and the latter with their segregation. He introduced a motive force (mind: *nous*) to account for motion. Anaxagoras seems to have considered that Empedocles had not fully satisfied the demands of ELEATIC logic since he allowed secondary substances to come into being as various combinations of his four elements. Anaxagoras, therefore, denied the existence of elements simpler than and prior to common natural substances, maintaining that every natural substance must itself be elementary, since it cannot arise from what is not itself. Furthermore, to avoid being confuted by ZENO OF ELEA, he held that matter was infinitely divisible; that, however far any piece of matter might be divided, it always contained portions of every other substance in the same ratio; and that its predominant ingredients were responsible for its most distinctive features. This theory was not influential, doubtless as much because of its subtlety and sophistication as because of its lack of economy.   JL

DSB I (1970); Guthrie, vol. 2 (1965); Kirk, Raven, and Schofield (1983).

Anaxandridas II king of Sparta, *c*.560–520 BC. Anaxandridas, together with the ephor CHILON, presided over a shift in Spartan policy from conquest to diplomacy. By using mythological propaganda which represented Sparta as heir to the whole Peloponnese and by assisting the overthrow of tyrannies, Sparta built up a league of dependent allies. Anaxandridas was the father of DORIEUS and LEONIDAS and, by his second wife, of CLEOMENES I.   RB

Cartledge (1979); Forrest (1980).

Anaxilas tyrant of Rhegium, *c*.494–476 BC. Anaxilas attempted to maintain the position of Rhegium against the threat of HIPPOCRATES and GELON. He organized the seizure of Zancle by Samian exiles in 473, later taking control himself and resettling the city, and supported the appeal of his father-in-law Terillus for Carthaginian aid against THERON. But Gelon's victory at HIMERA did not lead to reprisals, and HIERON I later married Anaxilas' daughter.   RB

Burn (1984); Dunbabin (1948).

Anaximander (*c*.610–540 BC), Greek natural philosopher. Traditionally regarded as THALES' pupil and successor, Anaximander of Miletus held that his first principle (the *Apeiron*) was infinite and indeterminate. He invested it with certain of the attributes of the Olympian gods, describing it as 'divine' and 'ageless and deathless', and believed that it enfolded and steered the innumerable worlds, which were themselves the (successive?) products of a number of pairs of opposites which separated off from the *Apeiron* to 'pay justice and retribution to one another for their injustice according to the assessment of Time'. He thus conceived of the world as a cosmos, subject to the rule of law that imposed a balance upon the warring opposites. His ASTRONOMY is highly rational, and his theory that the heavenly bodies wheel round the earth in great circles marks the first expression of the great contribution of the Greeks to astronomy, namely the formulation of geometrical systems to represent the motions of the heavnly bodies. He held similar rational beliefs (though not evolutionary as some believe) regarding the origin of human and animal life. He is credited with introducing the gnomon into Greece (*see* TIME, MEASUREMENT OF) and with being the first 'to draw the inhabited world on a tablet' (*see* MAPS).

See also PHYSICS; ZOOLOGY.   JL

Kahn (1960); Kirk, Raven, and Schofield (1983).

Anaximenes of Lampsacus (*c*.380–320 BC), Greek historian. Anaximenes wrote histories of Greece, PHILIP II of Macedon, and ALEXANDER THE GREAT whom he is said to have tutored. The eleventh speech of the Demosthenic corpus, answering Philip's letter declaring war in 340 BC, is from Anaximenes, as is perhaps that letter itself. Other writings included a treatise on rhetoric addressed to Alexander.   GLC

Anaximenes of Miletus (fl. *c.*546 BC), Greek natural philosopher. Traditionally regarded as the third of the Milesian philosophers (after THALES and ANAXIMANDER), Anaximenes wrote a book on natural philosophy, less poetical in style, however, than that of Anaximander. His first principle, air (*aēr*), was able to change into different forms (and so create the world and everything in it) by a process of condensation and rarefaction. When rarefied, air became fire; when condensed, wind, cloud, water, earth, and stone. Like the *Apeiron*, air seems to have been regarded as all-encompassing and divine, as possessing a directive capacity and an ability to initiate change within itself. Compared with Anaximander's, Anaximenes' astronomy is retrograde. He believed that the earth was flat and floated on air, and that the heavenly bodies were fiery leaves.

See also DIOGENES OF APOLLONIA; PHYSICS. JL

Guthrie, vol. 1 (1962); Kirk, Raven, and Schofield (1983).

Andocides (*c.* 440–*c.*390 BC), Athenian orator. Andocides was one of the ten 'canonical' ATTIC ORATORS and an eloquent supporter of democratic principles. In 415 he admitted involvement in the sacrilegious mutilation of the HERMAE and went into exile. In 411 and again in 408 he attempted unsuccessfully to return, despite a speech *On his Return*, delivered in the Ecclesia. He was readmitted in 403 and three years later was again charged with impiety. His defence, *On the Mysteries*, succeeded, unlike a later discourse, *On the Peace*, recommending a treaty with Sparta in 392, for which he was again exiled. GS

Hornblower (1983); Kennedy (1958, 1963).

Andocides Painter (fl. late 6th century BC). Andocides was the name of an Athenian potter whose signature is found on nine vases. Four of them were painted by the so-called Andocides Painter, to whom 12 vases in all are assigned, all of them red-figure. Possibly a pupil of EXECIAS, he is credited with the invention of the red-figure technique.

See also PAINTING, GREEK. GS

Arias and Hirmer (1962); Boardman (1974).

Andriscus (fl. *c.*153–148 BC), Macedonian pretender. Andriscus, an adventurer from the Troad, claimed to be the son of PERSEUS and heir to the Macedonian throne. Handed over to Rome by the Seleucid DEMETRIUS I SOTER (who needed Roman help), Andriscus escaped and with Thracian help won control over Macedonia by 149 BC. Rome awoke to the danger and sent METELLUS MACEDONICUS, who defeated

Andriscus with the help of ATTALUS II's navy. He was captured, marched in Metellus' triumph, and was executed.   EER

CAH VIII; Green (1990); Gruen (1984).

Androtion   (*c*.410–340 BC), Athenian politician and historian. Son of Andron who shared in the FOUR HUNDRED, Androtion had an active career, including an embassy to MAUSOLUS and prosecution for official conduct. Exiled after 346, he lived in Megara, writing a history of Athens, from which the Aristotelian *Constitution of Athens* probably derives.   GLC

Jacoby (1954).

Annales   Roman records. *Annales* were historical records which registered events year by year. The best-known example was the chronicle kept by the PONTIFEX Maximus and known as the *Annales Maximi*. This chronicle apparently recorded a wide range of events both sacred and secular under the heading of the current magistrates, and was maintained down to the time of P. Mucius Scaevola, who was Pontifex Maximus in the time of the Gracchi. The records went back certainly before 400 BC and perhaps to the start of the Republic. The *Annales Maximi* were both a model and a major source of information for Roman historians. '*Annales*' later became a general term for history, and was adopted by ENNIUS as the title for his historical epic, but more strictly a work entitled 'annals' indicated a historical account with a year-by-year arrangement.

See also ARCHIVES, ROMAN; HISTORIOGRAPHY, ROMAN.   TC

Frier (1979); Momigliano (1990).

Annona   Roman corn supply. Under the Republic corn imported to Rome came mainly from SICILY and SARDINIA. The Senate exercised a general supervision, and MAGISTRATES could act to relieve famine and prevent speculation. Gaius GRACCHUS introduced a state-subsidized distribution of cheap corn to Roman citizens. The distributions were opposed by the OPTIMATES and abolished by SULLA, but were soon restored, and in 58 BC CLODIUS made the distribution free. Caesar reduced the numbers eligible and placed the distribution under two new AEDILES. Augustus, after some experimentation, gave control to a *praefectus annonae*, a high EQUESTRIAN official. Under the Empire most imported corn came from AFRICA and EGYPT.   HS

Garnsey, Hopkins, and Whittaker (1983); Garnsey and Saller (1987); Rickman (1980).

Antalcidas (4th century BC), Spartan leader. Antalcidas was probably the political opponent of AGESILAUS and was regularly used in negotiations with Persia from 392 to 367 BC. He represented Sparta at the Sardes peace conference in 392, negotiated the King's Peace of 387/6 and, by visiting Susa in 372/1, brought about a renewal of the King's Peace in 371. Failing in 367 to stop Persia favouring Thebes, he committed suicide. GLC

Cartledge (1987).

Antenor (6th century BC), Greek sculptor. Antenor worked in Athens where he produced the bronze group of the tyrannicides HARMODIUS AND ARISTOGEITON, stolen by the Persians in 480 BC. His signature appears on the base belonging to one of the Caryatids of the ERECHTHEUM. Stylistic similarities suggest that he may also have worked on the figures for the east pediment of the temple of Apollo at Delphi which was rebuilt c.520 BC at the expense of the ALCMAEONIDS. GS

Boardman (1978).

Anthemius (d. AD 472), western Roman emperor, 467–72. Anthemius, grandson of Arcadius' Praetorian Prefect Anthemius, married MARCIAN's daughter Euphemia. In 467 the eastern emperor LEO chose Anthemius as his western counterpart, hoping to unite the two empires against the VANDALS. Anthemius' reign was largely occupied with trying, unsuccessfully, to resist the depredations of the Visigoths under EURIC, and, latterly, in conflict with RICIMER who, in April 472, declared OLYBRIUS emperor. Rome was besieged and Anthemius captured and beheaded (July). RJB

Bury (1958); Grant (1985).

Anthesteria Greek religious festival. The Anthesteria, which was held over three days in the month of Anthesterion (near the end of February), was the oldest of the festivals of DIONYSUS. On the first day new wine was opened and offered to the god; on the second, a public holiday, there was a drinking contest and at night a symbolic marriage of the wife of the ARCHON basileus to the god; on the third the dead were commemorated and evil spirits expelled.

See also FESTIVALS, GREEK. GS

Burkert (1985); Pickard-Cambridge (1968).

Anthology, Greek The *Greek Anthology* is a vast collection of more than 6,000 EPIGRAMS from every period of Greek literature on every conceivable topic. The earliest anthology, the so-called *Garland* of MELEAGER, made in the 1st century BC, contained the work of about 50

poets. It is lost, but together with several later compilations it formed the basis of the surviving Byzantine anthology that was made in the 10th century. This so-called Palatine Anthology (from the Palatine Library in Heidelberg), supplemented by the later edition of Planudes, contains poems by 320 writers, including a surprising number of jewels.   GS

Cameron (1993).

Anthology, Latin The *Latin Anthology* is a collection of about 380 Latin poems, made in the Vandal kingdom of Africa in the early 6th century AD. Much of it is by African poets of poor quality; but it does transmit the *Pervigilium Veneris*, a poem of 93 lines of uncertain date and unknown authorship written to celebrate the spring festival of Venus Genetrix, and some poems by the younger SENECA.   GS

Antigonus I Monophthalmus (*c*.382–301 BC), Macedonian dynast. Antigonus 'the one-eyed' was a commander in ALEXANDER THE GREAT's army and appointed satrap of PHRYGIA in 333 BC. During the struggles of the DIADOCHI over Alexander's kingdom, Antigonus was appointed supreme commander in Asia in 321. His military successes and increasing power led to a coalition against him, although the short-lived peace of 311 confirmed his position in Asia. Persistently attacking his rivals and intervening in Greece (through his son DEMETRIUS I POLIORCETES), Antigonus declared himself 'king' in 306. He was defeated and killed at the battle of IPSUS in 301 by a coalition of CASSANDER, LYSIMACHUS, PTOLEMY I, and SELEUCUS I NICATOR.   EER

Billows (1990); CAH VII.1; Green (1990); Hammond and Walbank (1988).

Antigonus II Gonatas (*c*.320–239 BC), king of Macedon. Antigonus (the meaning of Gonatas is unknown) was the son of DEMETRIUS I POLIORCETES and was his deputy in mainland Greece. He contended the Macedonian throne after the deaths of LYSIMACHUS and PTOLEMY CERAUNUS, finally attaining it *c*.277 BC despite later opposition by PYRRHUS. Antigonus and his Spartan ally AREUS I defeated Pyrrhus and CLEONYMUS in the Peloponnese in 272. Athens and Sparta unsuccessfully rose against him in the War of CHREMONIDES. He perhaps aided the Seleucids against the Ptolemies in the Second and Third Syrian Wars. Throughout the mid-3rd century Antigonus sought to contain the growing power of the anti-Macedonian ACHAEAN LEAGUE. A pupil of the philosopher ZENO OF CITIUM, he invited the poet ARATUS and the historian HIERONYMUS to his sophisticated court.
See also ALEXANDER OF CORINTH.   EER

CAH VII.1; Errington (1990); Green (1990); Hammond and Walbank (1988); Tarn (1913).

Antigonus III Doson (*c.*263–221 BC), king of Macedon. Antigonus (the meaning of Doson is unknown) became regent for, and stepfather of, the boy king PHILIP V in 229 BC, but was declared king himself *c.*227/6. He restored Macedonia's position in Greece by defeating the Aetolians and Thessalians in 228, and launched an expedition to Caria in 227. ARATUS OF SICYON invoked his help for the ACHAEAN LEAGUE against the aggressions of CLEOMENES III of Sparta, and in 224 Antigonus invaded the Peloponnese and founded the Hellenic League of allies under Macedonian hegemony. They defeated Cleomenes at Sellasia in 222. Returning to Macedonia to face the Illyrians, Antigonus suffered a burst blood vessel and died in 221 after ensuring Philip V's accession.

EER

CAH VII.1; Errington (1990); Green (1990); Hammond and Walbank (1988).

Antigonus of Carystus (3rd century BC), Greek sculptor and writer. A native of Euboea, Antigonus was based at Athens but worked also at PERGAMUM where he contributed to ATTALUS I SOTER's Gallic victory monument. Of his writings, only a collection of anecdotes survives. His (lost) personal memoirs, *Lives of Philosophers*, used by DIOGENES LAERTIUS, were highly regarded and popular. He also wrote on art history and lexicography. GS

Wilamowitz-Moellendorff (1881).

Antimachus (late 5th century BC), Greek poet and scholar. A native of Colophon, Antimachus wrote epic and elegiac poetry that is now lost but was much admired by Plato and imitated by Apollonius Rhodius. More importantly, he produced the first known 'edition' of the works of Homer, anticipating the scholar poets of Alexandria by a century or more.

See also SCHOLARSHIP, GREEK. GS

Pfeiffer (1968).

Antioch city in Phrygia. First colonized by Seleucid settlers from Magnesia on the Maeander, Antioch was given its independence by the Romans after their defeat of ANTIOCHUS III THE GREAT (191 BC). Incorporated in the Roman province of GALATIA in 25 BC, it received the status of a Roman colony and the name Caesarea Antiochia. Under Diocletian it became part of Pisidia. GS

Gruen (1984).

Antioch city in Syria. Antiocheia on the Orontes (now Antakya in Turkey) was founded by SELEUCUS I NICATOR in 300 BC as his Anatolian capital. It lay on the east bank of the Orontes river at the edge of a fertile plain. Its harbour at the river's mouth was Seleuceia in Pieria, and a road also ran to the seaport Laodicea. Its population was composed of Athenian and Macedonian colonists, and there was a large Jewish community. Its location and natural resources ensured commercial success. Annexed by POMPEY in 64 BC, Antioch was capital of the Roman province of SYRIA. It became an important Christian city and intellectual community.

See also SELEUCEIA ON TIGRIS.   EER

Downey (1961, 1963); Grainger (1990a); Green (1990); Liebeschuetz (1972).

Antiochus I (fl. 69–31 BC), king of Commagene. Antiochus was a grandson (through his mother) of the Seleucid ANTIOCHUS VIII GRYPUS. As an ally of Rome, he was rewarded by POMPEY in 64 BC with extra territory, and sent him troops in the CIVIL WAR. After helping Rome's enemy PARTHIA, he was besieged by VENTIDIUS and later by Mark ANTONY. By 31 his brother had replaced him as king. He built himself a remarkable funerary sanctuary at Nimrud Dagh in the Anti-Taurus Mountains.

See also COMMAGENE.   EER

Akurgal (1978); Goell (1952); Smith (1988); Sullivan (1990); Yarshater (1983).

Antiochus I Soter   (324–261 BC), Seleucid king. Antiochus was the son of SELEUCUS I NICATOR, and governed the eastern territories before acceding to the throne in 281 BC. He was a prolific city-founder, but his reign was troubled by wars. He fought Egypt in 279, won his title Soter ('Saviour') in a victory *c*.275/4 over the Gauls of GALATIA, and lost the First Syrian War (274–271) to PTOLEMY II. Much of Seleucid Asia Minor was lost through the revolt of EUMENES I in 262.

See also COLONIZATION, HELLENISTIC.   EER

CAH VII.1; Grainger (1990a, b); Green (1990).

Antiochus II Theos   (*c*.287–246 BC), Seleucid king. Antiochus 'the god' was the younger son of ANTIOCHUS I SOTER and succeeded him in 261 BC. He fought the Second Syrian War against PTOLEMY II (260–*c*.253), and in alliance with Macedonia recovered much of Seleucid Asia Minor. He repudiated his queen LAODICE I and heirs in favour of the Ptolemaic BERENICE SYRA in 253/2. He died in mysterious circumstances in 246, and was perhaps buried in the Mausoleum at Belevi near Ephesus. The succession was contested bloodily.   EER

CAH VII.1; Green (1990).

Antiochus III the Great   (*c*.242–187 BC), Seleucid king. Antiochus, younger son of SELEUCUS II CALLINICUS, succeeded in 223 BC. He invaded Egypt in the Fourth Syrian War (219), but was defeated by PTOLEMY IV at RAPHIA (217). A civil war against Antiochus' cousin and general ACHAEUS, who declared himself independent, was finally settled in 213 with the help of the Pergamene ATTALUS I SOTER. Antiochus undertook a great expedition to the east (212–206), in which he gained Armenia and regained Parthia. An unsuccessful siege of BACTRIA forced recognition of EUTHYDEMUS' independence. He reached India and returned via Arabia. Antiochus attracted Rome's attention when, in collusion with PHILIP V, he attacked Egypt (the Fifth Syrian War, 202–195), and invaded Thrace (196). He invaded Greece at the Aetolians' request, but was defeated by the Romans at THERMOPYLAE in 191. An unsuccessful naval campaign against Rome, RHODES, and Pergamum was followed by a decisive land defeat at MAGNESIA (190). The peace treaty of Apamea (188) imposed the harshest terms. Antiochus lost most of Asia Minor and was murdered the next year.   EER

CAH VII.1, VIII; Green (1990); Gruen (1984).

Antiochus IV Epiphanes   (*c*.215–*c*.164 BC), Seleucid king. Antiochus 'the [god] made manifest', third son of ANTIOCHUS III THE GREAT, was taken to Rome as a hostage after MAGNESIA but became king in 175. He paid lip service to Roman demands but quietly consolidated his foreign alliances. During the Sixth Syrian War (170–168) he invaded Egypt three times and interfered until ordered away by Rome. His policy of hellenization in Judaea caused a serious Jewish revolt under JUDAS MACCABAEUS in 167. Jewish hostility and extreme personal eccentricity explain Antiochus' unfavourable reputation.

See also PTOLEMY VI–XV.   EER

CAH VII.1, VIII; Davies and Finkelstein (1989); Green (1990); Gruen (1984); Morkholm (1966).

Antiochus VII Sidetes   (*c*.159–129 BC), Seleucid king. Antiochus 'of Side' was a son of DEMETRIUS I SOTER who claimed the throne after his elder brother DEMETRIUS II was taken captive in Parthia in 139 BC. He defeated the pretender DIODOTUS TRYPHON in 138, and temporarily reestablished Seleucid political control over the Jewish Hasmonaean state. His expansionist ambitions led in 129 to his death in battle against the Parthians, who released his brother to oppose him, and saw the end of Seleucid claims in the east.

See also JEWS.   EER

CAH VIII; Green (1990).

Antiochus VIII Grypus Seleucid king, 125–96 BC. Antiochus 'the hook-nose' finally attained the throne after defeating his father DEMETRIUS II's usurper (helped now by Ptolemy VIII who had originally raised the usurper). He struggled for power with his half-brother ANTIOCHUS IX after murdering their dominating mother (daughter of Ptolemy VI). The brothers had each other's wives murdered (both daughters of Ptolemy VIII and CLEOPATRA III). Antiochus VIII established supremacy by 108 BC but was assassinated by a minister in 96. His five sons bitterly contested the succession. EER

Green (1990); Sullivan (1990).

Antiochus IX Cyzicenus Seleucid king, 113–95 BC. Antiochus 'of Cyzicus' was the son of ANTIOCHUS VII SIDETES, and through his mother the half-brother of ANTIOCHUS VIII GRYPUS against whom he revolted in 114/13 BC. The dynastic quarrel led to the murder of both their wives (who were sisters). Antiochus IX's power was limited to coastal areas by 108, but he claimed the throne again after Antiochus VIII's assassination in 96. He was murdered in 95 by one of his five nephews, who contested the succession with his own son. EER

Green (1990); Sullivan (1990).

Antiochus Hierax (c.263–226 BC), Seleucid ruler of Asia Minor. Antiochus 'the hawk' was the second son of ANTIOCHUS II THEOS and LAODICE I, ruling jointly with his brother SELEUCUS II CALLINICUS at the end of the Third Syrian War (c.242–241 BC). Their subsequent civil war led to the partition of the empire before 236, with Antiochus in control of Asia Minor and supported by PONTUS, CAPPADOCIA, BITHYNIA, and GALATIA. The Pergamene ATTALUS I SOTER defeated Antiochus and his Gallic mercenaries by c.228 and won much Seleucid territory. Antiochus fled and was murdered in Thrace.
See also ARIARATHES III. EER

CAH VII.1; Green (1990); Hansen (1971).

Antipater (397–319 BC), Macedonian general and regent. Antipater served first under PHILIP II, and then was ALEXANDER THE GREAT's viceroy in Macedonia and general in Europe during the king's eastern expedition (334–323 BC). Although distrusted by OLYMPIAS, he performed loyally and supplied reinforcements to Alexander. He suppressed the revolt of AGIS III in 331, and (after Alexander's death) defeated the rebellious Greeks in the Lamian War (323–322), installing an unpopular oligarchy in Athens. In 321 he joined the other DIADOCHI against PERDICCAS, and was appointed regent for the two kings ALEXANDER

IV and PHILIP III ARRHIDAEUS whom he took back to Macedonia. His death intensified the struggles over the succession and empire.   EER

CAH VII.1; Errington (1990); Green (1990); Hammond and Griffith (1979); Hammond and Walbank (1988).

Antipater of Idumaea (fl. c.70–43 BC), Arab governor. Antipater governed Idumaea in southern Judaea and supported HYRCANUS II in his contested bid for the high priesthood of the Jews, arguing his case before POMPEY. In 55 BC he aided GABINIUS in the restoration of Ptolemy XII, but in the Alexandrian War of 47 he led Jewish troops in support of Julius CAESAR against Ptolemy XIII. Caesar appointed him governor of Judaea, but he was murdered in 43 and succeeded by his son HEROD THE GREAT.
    See also PTOLEMY VI–XV.   EER

Davies and Finkelstein (1989); Grainger (1991); Schürer (1973–87); Sullivan (1990).

Antiphon (c.480–411 BC), Athenian orator. Earliest of the so-called ATTIC ORATORS, Antiphon was a professional speech writer and teacher of rhetoric at Athens. He supported the oligarchic coup of the FOUR HUNDRED in 411, but when the regime fell he was tried for treason. Thucydides (8.68) comments that 'his speech in his own defence seems to have been the best one ever made up to my time', but it did not save his life.
    Of his surviving works, the *Tetralogies* are a set of rhetorical exercises or models for the prosecution and defence in invented homicide cases. We also have three speeches written for real murder trials (*Against a Stepmother*, *On the Choreutes*, and *On the Murder of Herodes*) and fragments of a manual *On the Art of Public Speaking*. In the history of letters Antiphon occupies an important place as the creator (with THUCYDIDES) of literary Attic prose.   GS

Due (1980); Kagan (1987); Kennedy (1963).

Antisthenes (c.445–360 BC), Greek philosopher. Antisthenes was the founder of what subsequently became known as the CYNIC school of philosophy. A pupil and friend of SOCRATES, he established his school at Cynosarges outside the walls of Athens where he taught that virtue was the sole basis of happiness and was attained through freedom from wants and desires. Since he held that virtue was based upon knowledge, he believed that it was teachable and sought to do so by investigating the meaning of words. He believed that whoever gained a knowledge of virtue could not act other than virtuously and that, once attained, this knowledge could never be lost.

See also DIOGENES OF SINOPE. JL

Dudley (1937).

Antistius Labeo *see* LABEO.

Antium city in Italy. Antium, modern Anzio, is on the coast, some 30 miles south of Rome. Inhabited from the beginning of the Iron Age, Antium was an important settlement in the 6th century BC and a member of the LATIN LEAGUE. Around 500 BC it was occupied by the VOLSCI, and it was their principal centre until defeated by Rome in the LATIN WAR (341–338 BC). Its fleet was destroyed (*see* ROSTRA) and a Roman garrison was established there (*see* COLONIZATION, ROMAN), the existing inhabitants becoming Roman citizens. A generation later it was notorious as a centre of PIRACY, and the Romans received complaints on this score from ALEXANDER THE GREAT and DEMETRIUS I POLIORCETES. In classical times it was a fashionable resort, and the birthplace of CALIGULA and NERO. TC

Stillwell (1976).

Antonia (36 BC–AD 37), daughter of the triumvir, Mark ANTONY. Antonia was the younger of two daughters named Antonia born to Mark Antony and OCTAVIA, sister of Octavian (AUGUSTUS). Married to DRUSUS, step-son of Augustus, she bore him three children who achieved prominence: GERMANICUS; CLAUDIUS; and Livia Julia (Livilla), who married first Gaius CAESAR and then DRUSUS, son of Tiberius, and became mistress of SEJANUS. Antonia herself precipitated the downfall of Sejanus with a letter to Tiberius questioning his loyalty. RJB

Kokkinos (1992); Scullard (1982); Wells (1984).

Antonine Wall *see* WALL OF ANTONINUS.

Antoninus Pius (AD 86–161), Roman emperor, 138–61. Titus Aurelius Fulvius Boionius Arrius Antoninus (Antoninus Pius), a competent and moderately distinguished senator, was adopted by HADRIAN on 25 February 138, granted all the imperial powers, and obliged to adopt two sons of his own, his nephew (the future emperor Marcus AURELIUS) and Lucius VERUS. Antoninus succeeded Hadrian without incident (July 138), and it was probably his insistence on Hadrian's deification that earned him the name Pius. He made no dramatic changes in the administration, and the reign was largely peaceful: the only serious military activity was in Britain, where the governor Q. Lollius Urbicus (139–45) advanced the frontier from the WALL OF HADRIAN to the

Forth–Clyde line, where the WALL OF ANTONINUS was constructed, only to be abandoned after Pius' death. In Germany the frontier was also advanced, and the LIMES strengthened. Pius' rule was firm, but lenient in the enforcement of the law. Communications with the provinces were improved, and public buildings were maintained. There was less building activity in Rome than under Hadrian, but a temple of Antoninus and his wife (the elder Faustina), and a temple of the Deified Hadrian, belong to the reign. Pius was hard-working, and financially able, bequeathing a full treasury to Marcus Aurelius (March 161).   RJB

Grant (1985); Wells (1984).

Antonius, Lucius (fl. 50–40 BC), brother of Mark ANTONY. Lucius Antonius, after serving under Mark Antony during the Mutina campaign, led an army himself as consul in 41 BC, championing the dispossessed land-owners against Octavian and the veterans, and claiming to be acting on his brother's behalf. He was forced to surrender at Perugia early in 40, and died soon after while on a mission in Spain for Octavian.   DP

Carter (1970); Syme (1939).

Antonius, Marcus (fl. 102–87 BC), Roman orator, grandfather of Mark ANTONY. Marcus Antonius, as praetor in 102 BC, fought against the Cilician pirates. He triumphed on his return in 100, and was elected consul for 99. As censor in 97 he may have been responsible for admitting Italians to the citizenship, an act rescinded two years later by L. CRASSUS. He and Crassus were also rivals in oratory, Antonius preferring a simple style which could include exhibitionist gestures like bearing the breast of his client Aquilius. He was murdered by the Marians in 87.   DP

Badian (1964); Gruen (1968).

Antony, Mark (c.82–30 BC), triumvir. Marcus Antonius, a natural soldier and capable politician, rose to power as an adherent of Caesar. He served under him in Gaul (52–51 BC), represented his interests at Rome as tribune (49), and commanded the left wing at PHARSALUS. During much of 49–47 he looked after Italy in Caesar's absence. After Caesar's assassination in 44 he skilfully used his position as remaining consul to inherit Caesar's party, while being conciliatory towards the conspirators. The arrival of Octavian (see AUGUSTUS), Caesar's heir, upset his calculations, and Antony found himself fighting Octavian and the Republicans in April 43. But by the end of 43 Octavian, LEPIDUS, and Antony had formed the Second TRIUMVIRATE.

Antony gained the military credit when he and Octavian defeated Brutus and Cassius at PHILIPPI in 42, but misused his strong position when, with Lepidus fading, he took the east for himself, and allotted the west to Octavian. The eastern provinces were richer and easier to govern, but Octavian in Italy was well placed to win the propaganda war. Distance increased their natural antipathy, and the Triumvirate had to be patched up at Brundisium in 40, when Antony married Octavian's sister, OCTAVIA, and at Tarentum in 37. After 37 they never met, and Antony became increasingly identified with the Hellenic east, where he had built up an economic and strategic base by forming a close personal alliance with CLEOPATRA VII, queen of Egypt. Although he lost 22,000 men in an unsuccessful invasion of Parthia (36), he reorganized the eastern provinces astutely, and conquered Armenia in 34. But when he celebrated a triumph for Armenia in Alexandria, and in the Donations of Alexandria assigned Roman provinces to Cleopatra and her children, he alienated sufficient Italian opinion for Octavian to be able to declare a national war against Cleopatra. Defeated at ACTIUM, Antony died by suicide at Alexandria.

Antony received a bad press in the ancient tradition, written by the winners, but Octavian never underestimated his quality as a general or as a man.   DP

Carter (1970); Huzar (1978); Syme (1939).

Anytus   (fl. c.400 BC), Athenian politician. Anytus is said to have been the first man to bribe an Athenian jury. As leader of the restored democracy, he shared in the prosecution of SOCRATES (399 BC).   GLC

Apaturia   Greek family festival. The Apaturia, which was held over three days in the month of Pyanopsion (late October), was an Ionian festival at which new members were enrolled in the PHRATRY and thereby given access to civic rights. A father introduced his son at the age of three, and again as a young adult; a husband introduced his newly married wife. An equivalent festival for Dorian Greeks was known as the Apellai (*see* APELLA).

See also MARRIAGE, GREEK.   GS

Burkert (1985).

Apella   Spartan assembly. The name Apella is often given by modern scholars to the Spartan assembly, because it met at the Apellai, festivals of Apollo, although it has been argued that its official title was 'Ecclesia'. Its status was defined by the *Rhetra* ('Enactment') attributed to Lycurgus, which established the frequency, location, and procedure for meetings. It was presided over initially by the GEROUSIA, and later by the EPHORS. It was open to all citizens, probably from the age of 20, and was the supreme decision-making body for matters of policy; but it was limited to accepting or rejecting proposals formulated by the Gerousia, and decision was by acclamation, not voting (like its elections to the Gerousia and, probably, ephorate). Its only attested judicial function was settling disputed royal successions.   RB

Andrewes (1966); De Ste Croix (1972); Forrest (1980); MacDowell (1986).

Apelles   (4th century BC), Greek painter. A native of Colophon, Apelles studied at Ephesus and Sicyon before moving to Pella where he became artist in residence at the court of PHILIP II and ALEXANDER THE GREAT, both of whom he painted. He also travelled to Egypt, but most of his work was done in the eastern Aegean. Of his 30-odd recorded paintings, more than half are portraits, the most famous being an Aphrodite Anadyomene at Cos. All are lost, but some found their way to Italy where they no doubt inspired much of the art of POMPEII. Later writers rated him the greatest of the painters of the Hellenistic period.
   See also PAINTING, GREEK.   GS

Robertson (1975).

Apennine culture   the material culture of peninsular Italy during the Middle and Later Bronze Age (*c*.1500–1000 BC). It is marked by a distinctive type of incised pottery, which is widely distributed throughout peninsular Italy, with particular concentrations in central upland areas (hence the name). The evidence suggests that transhumant pastoralism was of major economic importance, but excavations at sites such as Luni sul Mignone in south Etruria have shown that sedentary agriculture was also practised.   TC

Potter (1979); Ridgway and Ridgway (1979); Trump (1966).

Aphrodisias   city in Caria. The site of a shrine dedicated to the goddess Ishtar/Astarte/Aphrodite, Aphrodisias played little part in history until the MITHRIDATIC WARS in which it supported Rome. Rewarded by SULLA, favoured by Julius CAESAR, and enriched by successive emperors, it became a free city and an important cultural and intellectual centre. Though the seat of a bishop, it long remained a centre of paganism. Recent excavations have revealed impressive remains.   GS

Erim (1986).

Aphrodite   Greek goddess. Her oriental origins and identification with the Semitic goddess Astarte indicate that Aphrodite was a good deal older than Greek cult traditions imply. Apart from her principal role as goddess of love, beauty, and fertility, she was at times associated with marriage, vegetation, war, animals, and the sea. She was worshipped throughout the Greek world from Cyprus to Sicily with particular cult centres in Paphos, Delos, Sparta, Cythera, and Eryx. In literature she was celebrated by SAPPHO and AESCHYLUS; in sculpture famously by AGORACRITUS, ALCAMENES, PHEIDIAS, and PRAXITELES; in painting by APELLES. She was identified by the Romans with Venus, the mother of Aeneas.   GS

Friedrich (1979); Grimal (1986).

Apicius   the name given to several gourmets at Rome, notably Marcus Gavius Apicius in the 1st century AD. But the cookery book *De Re Coquinaria,* a compilation of earlier and later recipes, ascribed in manuscripts to Caelius Apicius, was written later, probably in the 4th century, and presents a challenge to cooks and critics alike.   GS

Edwards (1988).

Apollo   Greek god. The cult of Apollo is associated with Dorian, Cretan, and Hittite traditions. He has been described as 'the most Greek of the gods' and in art he represents the ideal of adult male beauty. His particular responsibilities included MUSIC, prophecy (*see* DIVINATION; ORACLES), archery, MEDICINE (later shared with his son ASCLEPIUS), and the care of flocks. He was worshipped throughout the Greek world, but especially on DELOS (where he was born) and at DELPHI, the seat of his oracle, where the PYTHIAN GAMES were held in his honour. Introduced early to Italy, he was popular with the ETRUSCANS and was endowed with similar attributes by the Romans.

See also BASSAE; DIDYMA.   GS

Grimal (1986); Guthrie (1950).

Apollodorus   (*c.*180–*c.*110 BC), of Athens, Greek scholar. A pupil of ARISTARCHUS at Alexandria, Apollodorus fled to Pergamum *c.*146, and possibly returned later to his native Athens. His works (now lost) included a verse chronicle, based on ERATOSTHENES but introducing various innovations in chronology, of the years from the fall of Troy to 144 BC; monographs on Homeric geography and religion; and studies of Epicharmus and Sophron. But the handbook of mythology attributed to him is a later compilation.   GS

Pfeiffer (1968).

Apollodorus of Athens   (late 5th century BC), Greek painter. Apollodorus was a leading painter of his day. But all his works are lost and very few are even recorded, so there is nothing with which to corroborate the judgement of ancient writers. HESYCHIUS called him the 'shadow painter . . . he mimicked form through shading and colour'. PLINY THE ELDER said 'he opened the gates of art which ZEUXIS entered' and was the first to represent people with 'the appearance of reality'.

See also PAINTING, GREEK. GS

Robertson (1975).

Apollodorus of Damascus (1st century AD), architect and town planner. Apollodorus was a Greek from Syria who served with TRAJAN on his Dacian campaigns as a military engineer and built a wooden bridge across the Danube. Returning to Rome as the emperor's architect, he designed Trajan's Column (the frieze on which commemorates the Dacian triumph), Trajan's Forum (see FORUM ROMANUM), and a number of adjacent buildings. Under Hadrian he was banished and eventually executed. His work on *Engines of War* survives.

See also ARCHITECTURE, ROMAN. GS

Rossi (1971).

Apollonis of Cyzicus (fl. *c*.223–*c*.183 BC), queen of Pergamum. Apollonis was the wife of ATTALUS I SOTER and the mother of four sons, including kings EUMENES II SOTER and ATTALUS II PHILADELPHUS. These two sons erected a temple in her honour at Cyzicus. Book 3 of the Greek ANTHOLOGY contains 19 epigrams describing the relief sculptures on this temple, all of them mythological scenes illustrating filial piety and devotion. After their deaths Apollonis and her husband were worshipped in the divine ruler cult at Pergamum. EER

Allen (1983); Hansen (1971).

Apollonius of Perge (fl. *c*.200 BC), Greek mathematician and astronomer. Little is known about Apollonius. Of the dozen or so works attributed to him only two have survived: the *Cutting-off of a Ratio* (two books in Arabic translation) and the *Conics* (of which four books survive in the original Greek, three in Arabic translation, and the eighth is lost). His chief claim to fame in modern times rests upon the latter work, which represents the culmination of the study of conics over two centuries. His terminology and innovative methodology became canonical and not only superseded the work of his predecessors, but also influenced Descartes, Fermat, and Newton. In astronomy it seems likely that it was Apollonius who first established the equivalence of eccentric and epicyclic models of planetary motion. His work in this respect was subsequently adopted and elaborated by HIPPARCHUS and PTOLEMY.

See also MATHEMATICS.   JL

DSB I (1970); Heath (1921).

Apollonius of Tyana (b. *c*.4 BC), Neopythagorean philosopher and mystic. Apollonius was born at Tyana in Cappadocia around the beginning of the Christian era. He led the life of an ascetic wandering teacher and attained such fame for his thaumaturgical powers that he was equated by anti-Christian writers with Christ. His biography by Philostratus survives.

See also NEOPYTHAGOREANISM.   JL

Apollonius Dyscolus (2nd century AD), of Alexandria, Greek grammarian. Named Dyscolus ('hard to please') for his crabby and pedantic manner, Apollonius wrote voluminously on the parts of speech. His four books of *Syntax* survive, as do individual treatises on the *Adverb*, *Conjunction*, and *Pronoun*. His own writing is careless, but he exerted considerable influence on subsequent generations and, together with his son HERODIAN, is regarded as the greatest of the original Greek grammarians.   GS

Blank (1982).

Apollonius Rhodius (3rd century BC), Greek epic poet and scholar. Despite his sobriquet, apparently earned from his migration to Rhodes, Apollonius was a native of Alexandria. Little is known for certain about his life except that he was chief librarian to Ptolemy II, after ZENODOTUS and before ERATOSTHENES. He followed literary tradition in composing an epic poem, *Argonautica*, in four books on a mythological subject, Jason's quest for the golden fleece; but he followed his contemporary CALLIMACHUS in filling his work with obscure allusions and antiquarian curiosities. Reports of a feud between the two poets are based on unreliable evidence.   GS

Hutchinson (1988); Pfeiffer (1968); Webster (1964).

Appellatio in Roman law, an appeal to a higher magistrate to adjust the judgement of a lower magistrate in a civil case. The appeal involved a fresh trial in which new evidence could be considered. Further appeals could be made, right up to the emperor. The right to appeal did not exist before the end of the Republic.   HE

Nicholas (1962).

Appendix Virgiliana a collection of minor Latin poems traditionally ascribed to the young VIRGIL. Though the attribution is disproved for most of the poems, they represent an interesting sample of second-rate verse of the 1st century AD. The collection includes: *Catalepton*, 15 poems in various metres; *Ciris*, an epyllion telling the story of Scylla; *Copa*, an elegiac invitation to drink; *Culex*, an epic pastiche on the death of a gnat; *Dirae*, a farmer's lament; *Lydia*, a lover's lament; *Moretum*, a description of country life; *Priapea*, three Priapic poems; and two elegies for MAECENAS. Even ancient authorities doubted the authenticity of *Aetna*, a didactic poem on vulcanology.   GS

Appia, Via   Roman road. The Via Appia ran in a straight line south-east from Rome to CAPUA, before turning to cross Italy and finish at BRUNDISIUM (Brindisi), the main port for Greece. It was begun in 312 BC by the censor Appius CLAUDIUS CAECUS and finished by 244 BC. As the oldest and the longest (234 miles) trunk road in Italy, and the main route south from Rome, it was not surprisingly known as 'the queen of roads'.

See also ROADS, ROMAN.   DP

Chevallier (1976); Potter (1987); Wiseman (1987).

Appian (1st–2nd centuries AD), Greek historian of Rome. Appian (Appianus) was born in Alexandria, probably in the reign of Domitian. He held an administrative post in Alexandria and experienced the Jewish revolt (AD 115–17), before moving to Rome, where he was probably an equestrian advocate of the imperial treasury. Appian gained the post of PROCURATOR from the emperor Antoninus Pius.

Appian wrote a *History of Rome's Wars* from earliest times to the reign of Trajan. The work, in 24 books (nine survive complete and seven in fragments), successively dealt with the peoples Rome conquered. This allowed Appian to give the viewpoint of the conquered and include information a Roman historian would not. Books 13–17 deal with Rome's CIVIL WARS. Despite some misunderstanding of Republican conditions, Appian's work shows awareness of economic and social as well as political factors and provides our only continuous narrative from the Gracchi to ACTIUM.   HS

Gabba (1956).

Apuleius   (b. *c.*AD 125), Latin novelist. Apuleius was born at Madaurus in Africa and studied at Carthage, Athens, and Rome. His marriage to a wealthy widow provoked scandal and he was accused of procuring her by magic. His defence against the charge (*Apologia*) was brilliantly successful, enhancing his reputation as a poet, philosopher, rhetorician, and (subsequently) priest. His *Metamorphoses* (or *Golden Ass*), based on a Greek model, is the only Latin novel to survive intact.

See also NOVEL, LATIN.   GS

Hägg (1983); Martin (1987); Tatum (1979); Walsh (1970); Winkler (1985).

Apulia   region of south-east Italy, lying between ancient Calabria (the 'heel') and Samnium. It was a fertile farming region, especially in the coastal plains and the northern parts, while the southern hills and western reaches were famous for wool. Its inhabitants included Peucetii and Daunii and spoke OSCAN. Initially strongly influenced by the Greek colonies of MAGNA GRAECIA, the region became subject to Rome during the later 4th century BC. During the war against PYRRHUS it remained loyal, though some discontent emerged during the Second PUNIC WAR and SOCIAL WAR, leading to severe Roman punishment.   HE

Potter (1987).

Aqueduct   Rome's first aqueduct was built in 312 BC by Appius CLAUDIUS CAECUS. Known as the Aqua Appia and financed by the spoils of war, it brought a supply of water from springs to the east of the city through a 10-mile tunnel to a population already greater than 150,000. It was insufficient and within 40 years work had begun on another, the Anio Vetus, from a source 40 miles away in the Apennines. Two more aqueducts were built in the 2nd century BC, one of them using a high-level construction for the first time, and a further three in the 1st century BC. By the end of the 1st century AD, when FRONTINUS was appointed *curator aquarum* and began writing his two-volume study of the Roman water supply, the city had nine aqueducts. He had plans drawn of the whole system, he regularized the work of maintenance (heaviest in the overhead sections, much less in the tunnels), and he acted against abuses of the system (such as illicit tapping of the supply and corrupt practices among the distributors). It is estimated that the total supply to the city at the time amounted to about 130 million gallons per day. Costs of building and upkeep were high, and most small towns settled for underground systems. But spectacular examples survive of the elevated supplies to Carthage, Segovia, and Nîmes (NEMAUSUS).   GS

Ashby (1935); Hodge (1992).

Aquileia   city in northern Italy at the head of the Adriatic. Founded by the Romans as a Latin colony in 181 BC largely for military purposes (*see* COLONIZATION, ROMAN), Aquileia commanded important routes over the Julian Alps. It grew into a prosperous commercial centre, exploiting nearby goldfields and trading in amber. With a population approaching 100,000 it became one of Italy's largest cities until destroyed by the Goths in AD 403 and again by ATTILA in 452.   GS

Stillwell (1976).

Aquincum   modern Budapest, city on the river Danube. Founded as a Roman legionary camp in the time of Tiberius, Aquincum became the capital of PANNONIA in AD 106, a *municipium* in 124, and a *colonia* in 194. Like CARNUNTUM it was overrun by the Huns in the early 5th century. Most of the military installations are hidden under the modern city but parts of the civilian town are visible.   GS

Stillwell (1976).

Arabia   The Arabian peninsula was inhabited by the NABATAEANS in the north and Arab peoples in the south. The desert interior was crossed by important caravan routes. Arabia produced and exported incense, and re-exported spices and luxuries from India. ALEXANDER THE GREAT planned a circumnavigation. During Hellenistic times the Ptolemies explored the Red Sea area, and the Seleucids established colonies in the Persian Gulf. In the 1st century AD Roman control of Egypt and the direct sea route to India (bypassing the southern Arabian kingdoms) decreased the importance of the caravan routes. Nabataean Arabia became a Roman province in AD 106. The provincial capital was Bostra.
                                                                      EER

Bowersock (1983); Potts (1990); Sullivan (1990).

Ara Pacis   literally the 'altar of peace'. The Ara Pacis, set up by the Senate in the Campus Martius in 9 BC, commemorates and illustrates an event that took place in Rome on 4 July 13 BC. Both the event – a procession of officials and members of the imperial family – and the monument celebrated AUGUSTUS' safe return from Gaul and Spain and the peace that he had imposed on the empire. It was reconstructed in 1937.   GS

Moretti (1948); Strong (1976).

Aratus   (*c*.315–*c*.240 BC), Greek poet. Aratus was born in Cilicia but educated at Ephesus and Athens. Invited to Pella *c*.277, he joined the court circle of ANTIGONUS II GONATAS, for whom he wrote hymns and the surviving didactic poem *Phaenomena* which treats astronomy and meteorology. This achieved instant success and received close attention from commentators. Later he visited the Syrian court of Antiochus and edited the works of Homer.   GS

Hutchinson (1988); Webster (1964).

Aratus of Sicyon   (271–213 BC), head of the ACHAEAN LEAGUE. Aratus freed Sicyon from tyranny in 251 BC and united it with the anti-Macedonian Achaean League, receiving Ptolemaic financial help. Aratus became the League's general in alternate years after 245 (though not unopposed). After joining many Peloponnesian cities to the League,

Aratus faced aggression from CLEOMENES III of Sparta and turned towards Macedon. ANTIGONUS III DOSON successfully intervened at Aratus' request (225), and later sent to him the future PHILIP V. Aratus joined Philip in the Social War against Aetolia (220–217), but later felt betrayed when Philip invaded the Peloponnese and destroyed Messene (214). Aratus died claiming Philip poisoned him. His *Memoirs* were used by POLYBIUS and in PLUTARCH's *Life of Aratus*.

See also DEMETRIUS OF PHAROS; LYDIADAS. EER

CAH VII.1; Green (1990); Walbank (1933).

Arbitration *see* JUDICIAL PROCEDURE.

Arbogastes *see* THEODOSIUS I.

Arboriculture Trees were central to the ancient economy. First in importance came the olive, of which 27 varieties were known. A whole technology developed for the extraction of its oil. TIMBER was required for the building of houses and ships, for wagons and carts, for weapons and war machines, for furniture and sculpture, for tools and fuel. For these purposes the following trees were available: fir, pine, beech, oak, sycamore, cedar (after the conquests of Alexander), and some larch, plane, acacia, and willow. Forests were extensive to the north of the Mediterranean and continued to be exploited throughout the period, though Attica may have become deforested at an early stage. To the south, supplies were more meagre, but along the banks of the Nile planting and cutting were organized on scientific lines. Orchards of fruit and nut trees flourished everywhere yielding the following crops: apple, pear, cherry, plum, peach, lemon, pomegranate, fig, date, carob, pistachio, walnut, and almond. Their methods of cultivation are described in literature (especially THEOPHRASTUS) and papyri.

See also BOTANY; FOOD AND DRINK. GS

Meiggs (1982).

Arcadia region in southern Greece. Landlocked and mountainous, Arcadia was a land of villages where an archaic dialect and many local myths and customs survived (*see* DIALECTS, GREEK). It played little part in Greek politics, coming early under the influence of Sparta. MERCENARIES were its most famous export. In the 4th century BC an ARCADIAN LEAGUE was formed to counter Sparta's newly weakened position.

See also MEGALOPOLIS. GS

Arcadian *see* DIALECTS, GREEK.

Arcadian League   a confederacy of Greek states founded in the aftermath of LEUCTRA when Spartan control of the Peloponnese was relaxed. The moving spirit was Lycomedes of Mantinea, the guardian angel EPAMINONDAS. Owing to XENOPHON's reticence the league's evolution is obscure, but its heyday was the 360s after which it was debilitated by the abiding rivalry of Tegea and Mantinea. MEGALOPOLIS was founded as its capital, where the council (with its steering committee of 50 *demiurgi*) and the assembly of 'Ten Thousand' met, and the 'general' commanded the standing army. The league probably owed more to imitation of the BOEOTIAN CONFEDERACY than of democracies.

GLC

Larsen (1968).

Arcadius   (AD 377/8–408), eastern Roman emperor, 395–408. Flavius Arcadius, elder son of THEODOSIUS I and Flacilla, was created Augustus in 383, was regent in Constantinople during Theodosius' campaign against Eugenius, and became eastern emperor on Theodosius' death (395). Weak and unintelligent, he was dominated by his Praetorian Prefect RUFINUS (395), then by the Lord Chamberlain Eutropius (396–9), who arranged Arcadius' marriage (395) to Eudoxia, daughter of Bauto (consul in 385). Arcadius approved the rebellion of GILDO, without offering practical support, but generally took little interest in events. After the death of Eudoxia (mother of THEODOSIUS II and PULCHERIA) in 404, Arcadius was dominated by Anthemius, Praetorian Prefect.

RJB

Bury (1958); Grant (1985); Liebeschuetz (1990).

Arcesilaus I–IV   kings of Cyrene. The kings of Cyrene were alternately called Battus and Arcesilaus. Of Arcesilaus I (*c*.590–575 BC?), son of the founder, little is known; Battus II enlarged Cyrene with new colonists; but Arcesilaus II (*c*.560) quarrelled with his brothers, who left to found Barce, was defeated in battle, and was assassinated in a palace intrigue. After unrest under Battus III, the king's powers were limited, but Arcesilaus III (*c*.525), under whom Cyrene submitted to Persia, attempted to recover them; he was exiled, tried to return by force, and was murdered. His grandson, Arcesilaus IV (patron of PINDAR), was deposed by a democratic revolution *c*.440.

RB

Chamoux (1953); Mitchell (1966).

Arcesilaus of Pitane   (*c*.316–242 BC), Greek philosopher. Arcesilaus, founder of the Second or Middle ACADEMY, initially studied philosophy at Athens under THEOPHRASTUS. He was subsequently persuaded by

Crantor to join the Academy, of which he later became head. Arcesilaus adopted the Socratic practice of arguing for and against any given point of view without reaching any conclusions, which led to a suspension of judgement. This sceptical attitude, which underlies his polemic against the Stoic theory of truth, was further developed by CARNEADES. In ethics Arcesilaus maintained as his main moral principle that one should follow 'what is reasonable' (*to eulogon*).

See also SCEPTICS.   JL

Long (1974).

Archaic period   The 'archaic' period in Greek culture extends from the end of the GEOMETRIC PERIOD to the advent of the CLASSICAL PERIOD, roughly 700 to 480 BC. The growth of overseas trade and COLONIZATION resulted in the adoption of oriental styles and exotic materials, especially precious metals and ivory. After the mid-7th century BC Greek sculptors and architects found new inspiration in Egypt, and Greek art entered a monumental phase. In the 6th century columnar ARCHITECTURE became established and the Doric, Ionic, and Aeolic orders were distinguished. SCULPTURE of the human figure became more relaxed and more realistic, characterized by the so-called archaic smile. Vase PAINTING blossomed with the adoption of the black-figure technique, while potters experimented with new shapes and glazes. Striking innovations also occurred in the minor arts, notably, GEMS, scarab SEALS, metalwork, and coins. By the end of the period nearly every Greek POLIS had issued its own silver COINAGE.   GS

Charbonneaux, Martin, and Villard (1971); Hurwit (1985); Jeffery (1976); Johnston (1976); Murray (1993).

Archelaus   king of Macedon, 413–399 BC. Archelaus contributed more to the development of Macedon than his eight predecessors: he built roads and fortifications, made military reforms, and moved the capital from AEGAE to Pella. PLATO denounced his violent and abominable methods and SOCRATES refused to visit him; but EURIPIDES wrote the *Bacchae* there.   GLC

Hammond and Griffith (1979).

Archelaus   (1st century BC), Greek general of Mithridates VI. Archelaus was perhaps from Sinope or Amisus in PONTUS. During the First MITHRIDATIC WAR (88–85 BC), he led the troops of MITHRIDATES VI EUPATOR through BITHYNIA and central Greece, but was defeated on the mainland by SULLA in 87 and instructed by Mithridates to negotiate a peace. In 83, shortly before the Second Mithridatic War, he deserted to Rome to escape accusations of treason, and fought with LUCULLUS during the Third Mithridatic War in 74.   EER

Green (1990); Sherwin-White (1984); Sullivan (1990).

Archidamus II king of Sparta, *c*.469–427 BC. Archidamus acted strenuously against the Messenian revolt (465) and led invasions of Attica in 431, 430, and 428. In 429 he commenced the siege of PLATAEA. The first decade of the PELOPONNESIAN WAR (431–421) was early called the 'Archidamian War'. THUCYDIDES depicts him in 432 anticipating a long-lasting war, urging caution and alliance with Persia. He was father of AGIS II and AGESILAUS.   GLC

De Ste Croix (1972).

Archidamus III king of Sparta, 360–338 BC. The son of AGESILAUS, Archidamus spent his reign vainly trying to undo the consequences of LEUCTRA, campaigning in Arcadia to counter Theban influence. At the head of 100 men he made a spirited riposte in defence of Sparta against EPAMINONDAS (362). ISOCRATES' *Archidamus* professes to express his opposition to the peace of 366/5. In 342, despairing of his cause in Greece, he went to Italy where he was killed.   GLC

Archilochus (7th century BC), of Paros, Greek poet. Archilochus was the illegitimate son of the noble Telesicles and a slave girl. He left Paros in poverty and disgrace for THASOS and became a mercenary, eventually dying in battle against the Naxians. He was the first major literate poet and was ranked with Homer by the ancients. He adapted the traditions of oral epic and song to new forms, composing satirical iambics and sensuous elegiacs that aroused controversy at the time but guaranteed him an outstanding posthumous reputation. The surviving fragments have been substantially augmented by recently discovered papyri.   GS

Fränkel (1975); West (1974).

Archimedes (*c*.287–212 BC), Greek mathematician, astronomer, and inventor. Born at Syracuse, Archimedes, the greatest mathematician of antiquity, invented war machines to defend the city against the Romans under MARCELLUS. He was killed at the fall of the city. Other inventions by him included a screw for raising water, an endless screw, a compound pulley (used for launching ships), and two *sphaerae* (a planetarium and a star-globe which were taken to Rome). He also discovered a means to determine the proportions of gold and silver in a crown made for HIERON II (Archimedes' Principle). He developed the method of exhaustion and applied it to the calculation of areas and volumes (including the area enclosed within a segment of a parabola), the area bounded by certain spirals, and the surface area and volume of a sphere. He also calculated an improved value for π and designed his own tomb incorporating a sphere inside a cylinder to commemorate his discovery that the sphere occupies two-thirds of the space. His extant works include *On the Sphere and the Cylinder*; *On the Measurement of the Circle*; *On Conoids and Spheroids*; *On Spirals*; *On the Equilibrium of Planes* (where the theory of the lever is propounded); *On the Quadrature of the Parabola*; *The Sand Reckoner* (which is our best evidence for the heliocentric system of ARISTARCHUS OF SAMOS); *On the Method of Mechanical Theorems*; and *On Floating Bodies*. Two geometrical works, *A Book of Lemmas* and *On the Heptagon in a Circle*, have survived in Arabic sources. Virtually all his work on astronomy has been lost except for a method of calculating the sun's diameter described in *The Sand Reckoner*. After the rediscovery of his works in the Renaissance, Archimedes exercised a profound influence upon the subsequent development of MATHEMATICS and mathematical physics.

See also ENGINEERING.   JL

DSB I (1970).

Architecture, Greek Building in stone is the most tangible legacy of the Greeks. Suitable materials – limestone, marble, and conglomerate – were widely available from the 6th century BC. Earlier, and humbler, structures in brick and wood have not survived.

Temples: A Greek temple was built to house the image of a god. Worship and sacrifice took place at an altar inside the precinct (*temenos*) but outside the building. By the end of the 7th century BC the plan of the temple had been established: a central hall (*cella*), approached through a porch (*pronaos*), with a second porch often at the rear (*opisthodomos*), surrounded by a colonnade (*peristylion*), all standing on a stepped platform. At first it was only the platform that was built of stone: the temple of Hera at OLYMPIA still had wooden columns and beams and mud-brick walls when erected *c*.600 BC. But a few years later the temple of Artemis at CORCYRA was built entirely of stone and was the first to have its pediments filled with sculpture. Temples were generally aligned east–west and the cult statue was placed at the western end of the *cella*. Apart from minor regional variations (e.g. a preference for the Ionic over the Doric order in the eastern Aegean) and stylistic refinements (e.g. a gradual tendency to emaciate and taper the columns and a substantial increase in the amount of sculptural decoration), this plan remained unchanged for three centuries.

The Doric and Ionic (and the latter's prototype, Aeolic) orders were distinguished in the 6th century BC, the Corinthian not until the later 5th century. The Doric column rises from the top (third) step of the platform (stylobate) with no base and has 20 shallow flutes. Its height, including the capital, is generally five and a half times its base diameter. The capital consists of a simple moulding (*echinus*) topped by a rectangular slab (*abacus*). The architrave, of plain blocks, spans the columns. The frieze consists of triglyphs with vertical grooves, alternating with metopes, square slabs set back from the line of the triglyphs, which could be painted or sculptured or both. Above the frieze are the cornice (*geison*) and the gutter (*sima*).

The Ionic and Corinthian orders differ from the Doric principally in the shape of their columns. The Ionic is lighter in its proportions and has more complex mouldings. It rises from a moulded base and has 24 deeper flutes, separated by flat strips. The capital has a carved moulding surmounted by a pair of volutes. The architrave is divided into three projecting bands. Above this is a row of small projecting blocks (dentils) and/or a continuous sculptured frieze. The Aeolic column, probably an early form of Ionic, has a spreading, double-spiral capital.

The first Corinthian column is found in the temple of Apollo at BASSAE (*c*.430 BC). Like the Ionic, it rises from a base and has volutes on its capital, but these grow out of one or more bands of acanthus leaves. Its advantage over its Ionic relative is that all four of its faces are the same. This order finds its most monumental form in the temple of Olympian Zeus at ATHENS (2nd century BC). It was later adopted as the standard for Roman imperial architecture. Very rarely columns were replaced by sculptured figures (Caryatids if female, Atlantes if male). The most famous example of this is the porch of the Caryatids on the ERECHTHEUM at Athens.

SCULPTURE was regularly applied to the metopes, frieze, and pediments and would be painted, as would the triglyphs and cornice. But the columns and the outside walls of the *cella* were left white, as were the capitals unless covered with stucco. The overall effect of a temple was therefore extremely colourful and required the close collaboration of architect, sculptor, and painter.

Other Religious Buildings: Altars were occasionally of monumental proportions, even as early as the archaic period. But the most famous example is that of Zeus and Athena at PERGAMUM which dates from the 2nd century BC. It took the form of a raised Ionic portico, decorated in high relief.

Religious sanctuaries generally occupied dramatic locations and were sometimes approached by way of a monumental gateway (PROPYLAEA). The finest example is the entrance to the acropolis at Athens which included a combination of Doric and Ionic orders.

Some sanctuaries (DELPHI, EPIDAURUS, OLYMPIA) include circular buildings (*tholoi*) which take the form of a chamber surrounded by concentric colonnades. It is presumed, but not certain, that their function was religious. More certain is the function of the treasuries that have been found at Delphi and Olympia. As well as being depositories, they provided their donors with an opportunity for conspicuous artistic display.

Tombs were rarely monumental before the 4th century BC. But the Nereid monument at Xanthus represents an innovation in adapting the form of an Ionic temple to a tomb. The MAUSOLEUM at Halicarnassus was the model for many later monuments. Macedonian rulers were buried in monumental tombs that were buried under mounds of earth (*see* AEGAE).

Buildings for Entertainment: The THEATRE is one of the most evocative and enduring forms of Greek architecture. Impressive examples survive throughout the Greek world, many of them continuing to present festivals of ancient drama. Smaller than the theatre, and often associated with it, was the ODEUM (or concert hall), which was used for musical competition and possibly also for theatrical rehearsal.

Special buildings were also associated with the GAMES. Athletic events were generally presented in the STADIUM, a running track that was one stade (600 Greek feet, *c*.200 yards) in length. Like the theatre, it often made use of a natural slope to support the surrounding banks of seats. Establishments for exercise and training included the GYMNASIUM, where athletes could practise running and throwing, and the palaestra, a smaller structure for boxing, wrestling, and jumping. Equestrian events took place in the hippodrome (*see* CIRCUS) of which surviving remains are few.

Urban Buildings and Planning: The civic centre of a Greek city was the AGORA (or market-place). Here were facilities for commerce, often protected by a STOA (or portico); for assembly, in a bouleuterion (council chamber) or prytaneion (committee room); and for the distribution of water at fountain houses. Private HOUSES lined the adjacent streets and were usually simple in design. Many cities were planned so that their streets followed an orderly grid pattern. According to Aristotle, this system was invented by HIPPODAMUS of Miletus, but remains suggest that it had been in existence since archaic times.

See also HERMOGENES; ICTINUS; TOWN PLANNING.   GS

Berve and Gruben (1963); Coulton (1977); Lawrence (1984); Tomlinson (1989); Wycherley (1967).

Architecture, Roman Roman architecture represents a combination of two inherited traditions, namely Etruscan and Greek, overlaid by a number of independent innovations. Etruscan elements included an emphasis on grand façades, especially on temples where the colonnade was often only at the front, and an increased width in proportion to length. The most obvious Greek contribution was that of the three orders: Doric, Ionic, and Corinthian, to which the Romans added a fourth, composite. Structural developments centred on the introduction of the arch and its progeny, the vault and the dome, facilitated by the discovery of an effective concrete and more general use of brick and veneer. The distinctively Roman characteristics may be summarized as an increasing emphasis on secular and utilitarian forms, such as the AMPHITHEATRE, THEATRE, CIRCUS, AQUEDUCT, and BATHS; the greater significance of interior space, notably in the progression from the Greek temple, which merely provided congregations with a background, to the BASILICA, which actually accommodated them; and the requirements of grandeur and sheer scale to symbolize the Roman achievement, which are well represented, for example, in the TRIUMPHAL ARCH.

Temples: The earliest Roman temples followed the Etruscan model: a flight of steps at one end led to a portico on a raised platform behind which was the *cella*. The addition of columns, either free-standing or engaged, along the sides and sometimes at the end was due to Greek influence. Internally from the 1st century BC a domed apse was often placed on the back wall of the *cella*. The finest surviving example of such a temple is the Maison Carrée at Nîmes (NEMAUSUS) (*c.*16 BC).

Circular temples were popular from an early date, their form deriving from the Greek *tholos*. The so-called temple of Vesta in the Forum Boarium dates from the late 2nd century BC and is the oldest marble temple in Rome to survive. The culmination of this form is seen in the PANTHEON, built under Hadrian, where unparalleled attention is devoted to the proportions and decoration of the interior.

It is in the eastern provinces, where Rome found difficulty in making any impact on a thoroughly hellenized culture, that the monumental scale of temple architecture is best observed. The temple of Bel at PALMYRA and the precinct of Jupiter at Baalbek, where columns stand to a height of 65 feet, have more to do with imperial propaganda than with religion.

Urban Architecture and Planning: The civic centre of every Roman town was the FORUM. More symmetrical than the Greek AGORA, it served the same purpose in providing facilities for commerce, assembly, and the dispensing of justice. The principal innovation in this context was the replacement of the Greek STOA with the BASILICA or public hall which served a variety of purposes.

Roman town planners adopted the rectangular grid pattern of their Greek predecessors (*see* TOWN PLANNING), but the main axes were given greater emphasis by the addition of two broad streets running at 90 degrees to each other. These streets were known as the *cardo*, which ran north–south, and the *decumanus*, which ran east–west. The forum was located at their intersection.

Roman HOUSES were similar in plan to Greek houses – a number of connecting rooms grouped around a central courtyard (*atrium*) – but perhaps a higher proportion of them rose to a second storey. As city populations increased, however, and as land became more expensive, Roman architects devised a more efficient use of space with the apartment block or tenement (*insula*) which often had as many as five storeys and generally occupied one block of the grid. But because they ran such a high risk of fire and collapse their height was limited by Augustus to 70 feet and by Trajan to 60 feet.

The development of the arch had important consequences for the supply of water to city centres (*see* AQUEDUCT) and for the spanning of rivers. The earliest stone bridge across the Tiber (*pons Aemilius*) dates from the 2nd century BC, but most bridges outside Rome date from the imperial period. The most impressive surviving example was built across the Tagus gorge at Alcantara in AD 106. Bridges had clear military applications too as exemplified by Trajan's bridge over the Danube which was designed by APOLLODORUS OF DAMASCUS: this bridge had a wooden superstructure spanning stone piers and was more than 1,200 yards long.

Country Houses and Palaces: The country house (or *villa rustica*) played an important part in the romanization of the provinces, and most surviving examples date from the imperial period. Such villas, particularly common in the north-west provinces, functioned as self-sufficient estates and often covered a considerable acreage. Looking rather like an enclosed village, a typical establishment consisted of a main residence of some distinction in its own enclosure, with another, larger enclosure adjacent to it lined with cottages and barns.

The urban villa (or *villa urbana*) had quite a different purpose, though it too functioned as a working farm. Generally located near a city, it provided its wealthy owner with a rural seat where he could escape the pressures of city life and enjoy the pleasures of the countryside. CICERO had such a property at Tusculum, and HORACE took particular pleasure in his Sabine farm which he received as a result of imperial patronage.

The idea of the urban villa was taken up by the emperors and developed to extremes of extravagance and luxury that were more suited to palaces than villas. The first such residence, the DOMUS AUREA, was built by NERO to form a royal park within the city of Rome. HADRIAN preferred a rural location for his sumptuous villa at Tivoli. Here the architect blended buildings and landscape in a sophisticated series of pavilions and pools, temples and baths, courtyards and libraries, which owes much to the emperor's own tastes and travels.

The 4th-century villa at Piazza Armerina in Sicily, famous for its well-preserved MOSAICS, is perhaps the last representative of the imperial hunting lodge. DIOCLETIAN built a vast fortified palace for his retirement at Split in Dalmatia. The severe symmetry of its plan is a reflection of the military rigour with which he reorganized the empire.

See also GARDENS; VITRUVIUS.   GS

Boëthius (1978); MacDonald (1982, 1986); McKay (1975); Nash (1968); Percival (1976); Ward-Perkins (1977).

Archives, Greek   The earliest archives were the records kept by religious centres such as DELPHI. In most classical cities public documents were inscribed on stone and set up in public, in scattered locations, apart from law codes such as those of GORTYN and of SOLON (inscribed on wood) at Athens. Athens only acquired an organized public record office, the Metroön, at the end of the 5th century BC. Certain Hellenistic cities attached important inscribed documents to archival walls, but full-scale bureaucratic documentation was confined to Ptolemaic Egypt, encouraged by the ready availability of papyrus.   RB

Posner (1972); Sherwin-White (1985); Thomas (1989).

Archives, Roman   The Roman Republic kept large numbers of records, both at Rome and elsewhere, though they were not systematically organized until the late 4th century BC. Though many of the records themselves are lost, the subject-matter is often recorded. In Rome, details were kept of citizenship, *senatus consulta*, taxes, land allocations, magistracies, festivals, triumphs. Outside Rome, records were kept of tax returns and censuses, and during the Empire, of imperial rescripts and land-holdings. Military units kept their own extensive records. Much historical information was recorded in the ANNALES *Maximi*, an annual chronicle kept by the Pontifex Maximus until *c*.120 BC.

See also COMMENTARII; FASTI; TABULARIUM.   HE

Frier (1979); Posner (1972).

Archon   Athenian state official. In the classical period Athens had nine archons: the Archon Basileus ('King'), the Archon Eponymos, who gave his name to the administrative year (from 683 BC), the Polemarch, and six Thesmothetai. The first three originated earlier: the Basileus was supposed to have replaced an actual king and inherited many traditional religious functions; the later Eponymos administered more recent cults, including the City DIONYSIA. The Polemarch had traditionally been the commander-in-chief, but by the Persian Wars his duties had been taken over by the office of STRATEGOS; he remained responsible for certain military and religious ceremonies. The principal duties of all archons were judicial, presiding in the courts: the Basileus was particularly concerned with homicide, the Eponymos with widows, orphans, and property, and the Polemarch with non-citizens. Traditionally, the Thesmothetai were a more recent creation, to regulate legal matters: they administered the courts and oversaw most public cases. From 487/6 BC archons were chosen by lot from a shortlist produced by the tribes; each served once, for one year only; eligibility was at first socially limited (*see* SOLON), but effectively unrestricted from the mid-5th century.

See also AREOPAGUS.   RB

Develin (1989); Rhodes (1981).

Arelate   modern Arles, city in southern Gaul. Built on the site of a Greek settlement, Arelate was linked to the sea by a canal in 104 BC and subsequently became a prosperous port. CAESAR used it as a naval station in 49 BC, and in 46 it received a colony of veterans. Enlarged under AUGUSTUS and Christianized under CONSTANTINE I, Arelate was occasionally used as a residence by 4th-century emperors and in the 5th century succeeded AUGUSTA TREVERORUM as imperial capital in the west. It was destroyed by Visigoths c.480.   GS

Matthews (1990); Stillwell (1976).

Areopagus   Athenian council. The Council of the Areopagus (named after its usual meeting place, the Hill of Ares) was the traditional council of elders at Athens, composed of ex-ARCHONS with membership for life. Originally, as the only permanent body, it possessed extensive powers, notably 'guardianship of the laws', and wide judicial functions which probably included the scrutiny of magistrates entering and leaving office, hearing cases of EISANGELIA for treason (after Solon), and perhaps oversight of public behaviour; but its power and influence were gradually limited by the development of the BOULE. However, the change to selection of archons by lot probably did not greatly alter its character, and it retained considerable prestige. Through the reforms of EPHIALTES the Areopagus was reduced to a court, mainly for cases of intentional homicide; but in the 4th century BC its powers were again gradually increased, to include oversight of magistrates' adherence to the laws, a supervisory role in some state affairs, and important judicial functions, particularly through the procedure of *apophasis* for treasonable political conduct, which it might initiate itself; the most celebrated instance is the HARPALUS affair. Given its character, it was prominent in the idealized picture of the 'ancestral constitution' constructed by conservatives, and outlived the democracy long into the Roman era.

RB

Hansen (1991); Rhodes (1981); Wallace (1989).

Ares Greek god. Ares was traditionally of Thracian origin. As the god of war he was never popular, even on Olympus, and his cult was of little significance outside THEBES. He sometimes received sacrifices from warring armies, and ALCAMENES made a statue of him. By the Romans he was identified with MARS and accorded greater honour.

GS

Grimal (1986); Guthrie (1950).

Areus I (c.312–265 BC), king of Sparta. Areus was the first Spartan king to adopt the trappings of Hellenistic monarchy, and issue silver coinage. His anti-Macedonian Peloponnesian alliance unsuccessfully attacked Aetolia in 280 BC, and, after intervening in Crete, he returned to defend Sparta in 272 against attack by CLEONYMUS and PYRRHUS of Epirus. In the War of CHREMONIDES his Peloponnesian alliance failed to force the Isthmus and relieve Athens, and he was killed at Corinth in 265/4.

EER

CAH VII.1; Cartledge and Spawforth (1989); Forrest (1980); Jones (1967).

Argei effigies used in Roman festivals. The *argei* were straw puppets which were carried in procession around the city on 16–17 March and on 14 May. At the end of the May ceremony they were thrown into the Tiber from the Sublician Bridge, a ritual interpreted by both ancient and modern scholars as a substitute for human sacrifice. The central area where the processions took place may represent the extent of the city at a very early stage of its development.

TC

Palmer (1970); Scullard (1981).

Arginusae three islands east of Mytilene, where Athens heavily defeated the Spartan fleet under Callicratidas in 406 BC. The generals, intent on pursuing the Spartans, instructed two trierarchs, THERAMENES and THRASYBULUS, to gather up the survivors from damaged and sunken ships; a storm prevented this. In the subsequent unjustly conducted trial the generals blamed the trierarchs who blamed the generals, and despite SOCRATES' protest against the procedure the generals were condemned to death.

See also PELOPONNESIAN WAR.

GLC

Kagan (1987).

Argos city in southern Greece. In the 9th–7th centuries BC Argos dominated the Peloponnese, and under PHEIDON (c.665 BC) it was the strongest power in Greece. Eclipsed first by CORINTH and then by SPARTA, Argos was neutral towards Persia but seized every opportunity to oppose Sparta, making alliances with Athens in 461 and 420, with Corinth in 395, with THEBES in 362, with PHILIP II of Macedon in 338, and finally with the ACHAEAN LEAGUE. In 195 it was liberated from Spartan control by FLAMININUS.

See also NEMEAN GAMES.   GS

Tomlinson (1972).

Arianism Christian heresy. The Arian heresy, which denied the consubstantial nature of the Trinity, was named after its founder Arius (*c*.AD 260–336) who began to propagate it in Alexandria *c*.320. Arius was excommunicated by his bishop at a synod *c*.321 but the doctrine continued to find favour with the masses. At the Council of NICAEA, called by the emperor CONSTANTINE I in 325, Arianism was condemned by ATHANASIUS. Arius himself was exiled, but recalled in 335 (a year before his death) through the good offices of EUSEBIUS. The heresy outlived him and was espoused by Constantine's successor, CONSTANTIUS II. Not until the Council of Constantinople (381) was it finally driven from the empire, and in Spain and North Africa it survived into the 5th century.

See also AMBROSE; BASIL THE GREAT; GREGORY OF NAZIANZUS; GREGORY OF NYSSA.   GS

Chadwick (1986b); Kelly (1977).

Ariarathes III (fl. 255–220 BC), king of Cappadocia. Ariarathes proclaimed himself independent of Seleucid authority *c*.255–250 BC, and was the first ruler of Cappadocia to issue coinage using the royal title. His marriage to a daughter of ANTIOCHUS II THEOS increased his territory but gave the Seleucids an ally in a strategic area. He supported ANTIOCHUS HIERAX in his fraternal war against SELEUCUS II CALLINICUS (both were his brothers-in-law).   EER

CAH VII.1; Magie (1975).

Ariarathes IV (220–163 BC), king of Cappadocia. Ariarathes succeeded his father ARIARATHES III as independent ruler, strengthening his alliance with the Seleucids by marrying a daughter of ANTIOCHUS III THE GREAT. Punished with Antiochus after the Roman victory at MAGNESIA in 190 BC, he switched his allegiance to PERGAMUM. He married his daughter to EUMENES II SOTER and remained a faithful ally of Pergamum and Rome, fighting on their side against PHARNACES I of Pontus.

See also PONTUS.   EER

CAH VIII; Gruen (1984); Hansen (1971); Magie (1975).

Ariarathes V   (fl. 163–130 BC), king of Cappadocia. Ariarathes, who had studied philosophy in Athens with CARNEADES, succeeded his father Ariarathes IV despite claims from a supposed elder brother Orophernes. When Rome advised him against marrying the Seleucid DEMETRIUS I's sister (the widow of PERSEUS of Macedon), Demetrius helped Orophernes dethrone Ariarathes in 160 BC. Rome divided Cappadocia between them, but Ariarathes recovered the kingdom c.157 with the help of his Pergamene brother-in-law ATTALUS II PHILADELPHUS. He aided Attalus against PRUSIAS II of Bithynia in 155, and died helping Rome against the Pergamene pretender ARISTONICUS in 130.
  See also ALEXANDER BALAS.   EER

CAH VIII; Gruen (1984); Hansen (1971); Magie (1975).

Aricia   city in Italy. Aricia, modern Ariccia, was a prominent city in early Latium, being a meeting place for the LATIN LEAGUE. It allied with ARISTODEMUS to defeat Arruns, the son of PORSENNA, c.504 BC. In c.496, after being defeated at Lake REGILLUS, Aricia became an important ally of Rome. After its defeat in the LATIN WAR (341–338), it was awarded Roman citizenship. Despite being sacked by MARIUS in 87 BC, it remained prosperous well into the Principate.   LPR

CAH VII.2.

Ariminum   modern Rimini, an Umbrian town which became a Latin colony in 268 BC. It was an important harbour on the Adriatic, and as terminus of the Via FLAMINIA and Via AEMILIA it controlled communications between Rome and upper Italy. It was the first city to be captured by Caesar after his fateful crossing of the Rubicon in 49 BC. An arch of Augustus and a marble bridge of Tiberius survive in the modern town, together with a circuit of Roman walls.   DP

Salmon (1969); Stillwell (1976).

Ariovistus   (1st century BC), German king. Ariovistus led the German confederation of tribes known as the Suebi into Gaul on the invitation of the ARVERNI and Sequani to fight the AEDUI. But he seized the opportunity to win hegemony in Gaul by defeating a united Gallic force in 61 BC. He was recognized as 'Friend of the Roman people' in 59, but a year later he was attacked and defeated by CAESAR.   LPR

Chadwick (1970).

Aristagoras   (fl. c.500 BC), ruler of Miletus. Aristagoras was left as regent by his cousin HISTIAEUS. About 500 BC he promoted an abortive expedition, with Persian support, against Naxos; fear of the consequences led him to raise the IONIAN REVOLT. In the early stages he obtained support from Athens and Eretria (though not from Sparta), but after later reverses he withdrew to Myrcinus, where he was killed by the Thracians.   RB

Aristarchus of Samos (fl. *c.*310–230 BC), Greek mathematician and astronomer. Aristarchus was a pupil of STRATON. His only surviving treatise, *On the Sizes and Distances of the Sun and Moon*, marks the first attempt to determine astronomical distances and dimensions by mathematical deductions from a set of (six) hypotheses. This treatise has a geocentric basis. Aristarchus' chief claim to fame, however, was for being the first to put forward a heliocentric hypothesis. Hellenistic astronomers, unable to accept Aristarchus' bold assertion that the orbit of the earth was but a point compared with the vast distance of the stars, rejected this hypothesis primarily on the ground that some parallactic displacement of the stars should be apparent. Copernicus, however, in putting forward his own belief in heliocentricity, first recorded – then subsequently suppressed – the precedent of Aristarchus.

See also ASTRONOMY.   JL

DSB I (1970); Heath (1913).

Aristarchus of Samothrace (*c.*216–*c.*144 BC), Greek scholar. Aristarchus lived most of his life in Alexandria where he became chief librarian in succession to Apollonius Eidographus. In the persecution of scholars by Ptolemy VIII (145 BC) he escaped to Cyprus, where he died. He was a pioneering critic of classical texts, producing as many as 200 commentaries on the poets and Herodotus. Large excerpts of his work on Homer survive.

See also SCHOLARSHIP, GREEK.   GS

Pfeiffer (1968).

Aristeas (7th century BC), of Proconnesus, Greek travel writer. Aristeas is a shadowy figure, of whom our knowledge derives mostly from Herodotus (4.13–16). It seems that he was a devotee of Apollo, and at a time when Greeks were colonizing the Black Sea shore he joined an expedition to explore the lands of the Hyperboreans, favourites of Apollo. The fabulous story of his travels deep into Scythia was told in his (lost) poem *Arimaspea*.   GS

Bolton (1962).

Aristides (*c.*525–467 BC), Athenian politician. Aristides was probably archon in 489/8 BC, and possibly strategos at MARATHON the previous year. Political conflict with THEMISTOCLES, perhaps over the shipbuilding programme, caused his ostracism in 482; but he was recalled in the crisis of Xerxes' invasion, and commanded with distinction at SALAMIS and PLATAEA. He collaborated with Themistocles on the rebuilding of Athens's walls and in 478, while commanding the Athenian contingent at Byzantium campaigning against Persia, presided over the creation of the DELIAN LEAGUE, including the initial assessment of tribute.   RB

Davies (1971) no. 1695; Meiggs (1972); Sansone (1989).

Aristides, Aelius   (AD 117–c.180), Greek writer and orator. Born at Hadrianutherae in Mysia, Aristides studied in Athens and Pergamum and travelled widely (to Egypt, Cyzicus, and Rome) before settling in Smyrna. A hypochondriac, he sojourned long in the Asclepieum at Pergamum where many (including Marcus AURELIUS) came to hear him declaim. A large corpus of his writings (hymns, panegyrics, diaries, speeches) survives.   GS

Bowersock (1969).

Aristobulus of Alexandria   (2nd century BC), Jewish writer. Aristobulus, known as 'the Peripatetic', wrote a commentary on the Pentateuch which he dedicated to Ptolemy VI Philometor. Excerpts preserved in Eusebius anticipate the allegorical interpretation of scripture, later developed by PHILO. His suggestion that Plato and Pythagoras, as well as some of the poets, owed their beliefs to Mosaic Law is the earliest evidence of a link between Jewish and Greek philosophy.   GS

Fraser (1972).

Aristobulus of Cassandreia   (?c.380–?c.290 BC), historian of ALEXANDER THE GREAT. Aristobulus accompanied Alexander's expedition, perhaps as an engineer or technician since he supervised the restoration of CYRUS' tomb at Pasargadae in Persia. Allegedly long afterwards he wrote a history of Alexander's campaign, basically apologetic although sober and much admired in antiquity. Aristobulus was used as one of two main sources for ARRIAN's history of Alexander, and also as a source for geographical information about India by STRABO.   EER

Bosworth (1980, 1988a, b); Pearson (1960).

Aristocracy   see OLIGARCHY.

Aristodemus   (6th century BC), tyrant of Cumae. According to DIONYSIUS OF HALICARNASSUS, who probably used a source independent of Roman tradition, Aristodemus 'the Effeminate' defeated an Etruscan army outside Cumae by killing its general (*c.*524 BC). In 504 he defeated the army of PORSENNA at Aricia and then made himself tyrant. After the battle of Lake REGILLUS (*c.*496) he harboured TARQUINIUS SUPERBUS. Although popular with the poor because of his land reforms, he was ousted *c.*492. LPR

CAH VII.2; Frederiksen (1984).

Aristogeiton *see* HARMODIUS AND ARISTOGEITON.

Aristomenes (fl. *c.*660 BC), Messenian soldier. Aristomenes was a folk hero of the Messenian resistance to SPARTA as recounted by Pausanias (4.6–24). The tradition of this struggle was much embellished after the refoundation of Messene in 369 BC, and must be treated sceptically, but he is usually associated, following Pausanias, with the Second Messenian War, *c.*660 BC. Some scholars have argued, however, that RHIANUS, on whom Pausanias drew, linked Aristomenes with a Messenian revolt *c.*490 BC.

See also MESSENIA. RB

Cartledge (1979); Huxley (1962); Pearson (1962); Wade-Gery (1966).

Aristonicus (d. 128 BC), Pergamene pretender. Aristonicus, perhaps an Attalid, led a revolt after the death of ATTALUS III PHILOMETER and his bequest of Pergamum to Rome. Whether his motives were anti-Roman, self-serving, or socially progressive, the revolt appealed to disfranchised classes throughout Asia Minor to whom he promised social and economic freedom in his ideal state Heliopolis (City of the Sun). Aristonicus faced a large Roman army joined by frightened native rulers. He was eventually defeated and captured in 130 BC, and Pergamum passed into Roman control.

See also ARIARATHES V; NICOMEDES I–IV. EER

CAH VIII; Green (1990); Gruen (1984); Hansen (1971); Sherwin-White (1984).

Aristophanes (*c.*445–*c.*385 BC), of Athens, Greek comic poet. Aristophanes was the most celebrated writer of Greek COMEDY and the only representative of Old comedy whose works survive intact. Of about 40 plays he is known to have written, 11 are preserved. His first play was staged in 427, four years after the outbreak of the Second Peloponnesian War and two years after the death of Pericles. His last was produced in 388.

As a professional playwright Aristophanes' prime concern was to make his audience laugh and so to win prizes in the dramatic competitions. In this he was eminently successful, winning four first prizes and three seconds. In appealing to the conservative prejudices of his audience, he struck at soft targets without malice: contemporary politicians (especially CLEON), philosophers (notably SOCRATES), other dramatists (AESCHYLUS, EURIPIDES, and CRATINUS), the military, the bureaucracy, the judiciary, the gods, homosexuals, musicians, and scientists. Bawdy slapstick overrides more serious concerns such as the war and abuse of power. Aristophanes' influence on contemporary politics was as slight as it was immense on the development of comedy. His supreme value to historians is in providing a satirical commentary on post-Periclean Athenian society.   GS

Cartledge (1990); De Ste Croix (1972); Dover (1972).

Aristophanes of Byzantium   (*c*.257–*c*.180 BC), Greek scholar. A pupil of CALLIMACHUS and ZENODOTUS, Aristophanes succeeded ERATOSTHENES as chief librarian at Alexandria *c*.195 BC. 'He was the perfect scholar', writes Pfeiffer, describing as 'epoch-making' his contributions to the study of texts (epic, lyric, and dramatic), language (grammar, punctuation, and accentuation), literary criticism (summaries of the plays), colometry, lexicography, and antiquities.

   See also SCHOLARSHIP, GREEK.   GS

Pfeiffer (1968).

Aristophon   (4th century BC), Athenian politician. Though exempt from taxation for his part against the THIRTY TYRANTS, Aristophon was in the course of his 100 years prosecuted 75 times under the *graphai paranomon* (procedure for dealing with unconstitutional proposals) but never successfully. He was general in 363/2; he attacked TIMOTHEUS in the courts for his conduct of the SOCIAL WAR (357–355); and he opposed the Peace of PHILOCRATES (346). He died before 330.   GLC

Aristotle   (384–322 BC), Greek philosopher. Aristotle was born at Stagira in Chalcidice. He entered the ACADEMY in his 18th year and remained there for 20 years until PLATO's death in 347 BC. He then went to Assos in the Troad to join a community of Platonists and there married Pythias, the adopted daughter of the tyrant HERMIAS. After three years at Assos he went to Mytilene on Lesbos, where he collaborated with THEOPHRASTUS and carried out many of his zoological investigations. In 343/2 he was invited by Philip II to Pella as tutor to ALEXANDER THE GREAT. He returned to Athens in 335 and began teaching at the Lyceum (*see* PERIPATETIC SCHOOL). He remained at Athens until shortly after the death of Alexander, when there was an outburst of anti-Macedonian feeling. A charge of impiety was brought against him and lest the Athenians should 'sin twice against philosophy' he retired to Chalcis, where he died in 322.

Aristotle's works cover every branch of philosophy and science known in his day. His comprehensive system exercised a powerful influence in late antiquity and, transmitted largely through the work of Arab scholars, dominated European intellectual life from the 13th century to the Renaissance. A vast number of works are attributed to him. His earlier, popular, published works are now lost, as are his selections of materials for scientific treatises. A collection of philosophical and scientific treatises, however, has survived which provides valuable evidence of Aristotle as a teacher and researcher. These works which had not been prepared for publication seem to be in the form of memoranda for his own use. While Plato is the main influence upon Aristotle, certain important aspects of the former's philosophy, like the separate existence of the forms, are rejected by him. Aristotle's work was long regarded as a closed system of doctrines all held simultaneously by him, but the work of Jaeger, especially, has shown that there is more development in his doctrines than had previously been recognized. Jaeger's thesis too, that Aristotle originally endorsed and then progressively freed himself from Plato's influence, has been widely accepted. Recent research, however, suggests that some of the works where Aristotle opposes Plato can plausibly be assigned to his period at the Academy and that some later works, conversely, seem to reveal increased sympathy with Plato's aims.

See also AFTERLIFE; ANATOMY; BOTANY; DEMOCRACY; DOXOGRAPHERS; EDUCATION; METEOROLOGY; MONARCHY; RHETORIC, GREEK; ZOOLOGY.   JL
Ackrill (1981); DSB I (1970); Jaeger (1948); Lloyd (1968).

Aristoxenus   (4th century BC), Greek philosopher and musical theorist. After an early musical training, Aristoxenus of Tarentum came to Athens where he studied with the Pythagorean Xenophilus and later with ARISTOTLE, who passed him over in favour of THEOPHRASTUS in his choice of successor to the headship of the Lyceum. Aristoxenus' theory of harmonics was influential for several centuries despite being criticized by PTOLEMY for excessive empiricism and lack of a sound mathematical basis. Aristoxenus also believed in the moral and educational value of MUSIC. According to CICERO (*Tusc.* 1. 19) he regarded the soul as a harmony (*intentio, harmonia*) of the body, a view which he seems to have taken from the Pythagoreans. Although a prolific author, only a portion of the second book of his *Elements of Rhythm* and parts of three books of his *Principles and Elements of Harmonics* have survived.   JL
DSB I (1970).

Armenia   Armenia lies to the north and east of the Euphrates, east of Cappadocia, south-east of the Black Sea, and west of Media. It was a satrapy of the Persian empire, and after ALEXANDER THE GREAT became part of the Seleucid empire. After the defeat of the Seleucid ANTIOCHUS III THE GREAT at MAGNESIA in 190 BC, the Armenians declared independence. Armenia Maior (the region east of the Euphrates) was united under King Artaxias. TIGRANES I greatly expanded Armenia's boundaries and founded a new capital, TIGRANOCERTA. His alliance with MITHRIDATES VI of Pontus in 69 involved Armenia in war with Rome. Tigranes surrendered, ceded his new territories, and remained a Roman vassal. During the Roman Empire Rome and Parthia struggled continually to control Armenia (Armenia Minor west of the Euphrates remained a separate kingdom under different rulers). It was temporarily annexed by TRAJAN, divided between Byzantium and the SASSANIANS in AD 387, and conquered by the Arabs c.AD 653.   EER

Burney and Lang (1971); CAH VII.1, VIII; Der Nersessian (1969); Jones (1983); Sherwin-White (1984); Sullivan (1990).

Arminius (*c.*18 BC–AD 21), chief of the CHERUSCI. Arminius owes his fame largely to the rashness of VARUS. He became a Roman citizen, serving in the *auxilia* and gaining equestrian rank. Rebelling against Rome, he ambushed Varus' three legions in the Teutoburg Forest, and destroyed them (AD 9). GERMANICUS' campaigns failed to inflict a decisive defeat on Arminius (14–16), but war with the MARCOMANNI (under MAROBODUUS) turned Arminius' attention away from Rome, and in 21 he was assassinated.   RJB

Salmon (1968); Scullard (1982).

Arms and armour, Greek   Although the advent of the HOPLITE brought a basic uniformity of equipment, variation in detail remained, even within an army, since hoplites normally provided their own equipment. The round bronze shield (*hoplon*), supported by a band round the left forearm and gripped by a handle at the rim, was a constant, as were the greaves; but corslets might be formed of two large bronze plates or be a composite of bronze scales on leather, fastened by shoulder-flaps; and helmets varied in the form and presence or absence of crest, cheek-pieces, and nose-guard. The principal offensive weapon was the thrusting spear, supplemented in close combat by a short sword.

In the Macedonian PHALANX, the *sarissa*, a pike some 17 feet long, was the main weapon; defensive armour was reduced to a helmet and greaves, with a small shield slung around the neck, since the *sarissa* required both hands. The élite corps, the hypaspists, used the same equipment but were capable of superior mobility and tactical flexibility.

Conversely, cavalry (*see* HIPPEIS) became more heavily armed: whereas previously they had normally worn only leather armour, and used javelins or lances, in the 4th century BC they acquired metal corslets and helmets and heavier swords and spears, though horse-armour remained rare.

Light troops tended to be mercenaries, particularly PELTASTS whose equipment, the curved light shield (*pelta*) and javelin, was less expensive than hoplite armour, as well as archers (whose bows were apparently less powerful than the oriental type) and slingers. Missile troops, effective both in skirmishing and sieges, were supplemented by the evolution in the 4th century BC of artillery capable of firing arrows and stones over long distances.

See also ARMY, GREEK.   RB

Snodgrass (1967).

Arms and armour, Roman   The earliest known Roman ARMY was based on heavy infantry. The richest class was equipped as Greek-style HOPLITES, with a thrusting spear (*hasta*), round shield, helmet, corslet, and greaves. The next three classes were also armed with the *hasta*, but carried a large oval shield (*scutum*), and were progressively less heavily armoured. They were supported by spear-armed cavalry and light infantry armed with javelins or slings. By the time of the PUNIC WARS the first two lines of the legions were armed with a heavy javelin (*pilum*). The third line retained the *hasta*. They had all adopted the *scutum* and a Spanish, primarily thrusting, sword (*gladius*). The richer legionaries wore mail armour (*lorica hamata*), the rest a breastplate (*pectorale*), and a greave was worn on the left leg only. The legions also contained spear-armed cavalry and infantry armed with light javelins.

By the time of CAESAR the *pilum* and mail armour were standard in the legions, and greaves had been abandoned. This equipment remained essentially unchanged under the Principate. The *scutum* became shorter, more curved, and sometimes rectangular. In the mid-1st century AD plate armour (*lorica segmata*) began to replace mail. Another type of body armour was scale armour (*lorica sequamata*). Auxiliary units were similar, but inferior, in equipment, except that they used a lighter javelin (*lancea*). Auxiliary cavalry had a longer sword (*spatha*) and lighter shield. Some auxiliary units had specialist weapons such as bows, but usually Roman armies relied on non-regular contingents for such troops.

In the 3rd century AD legionary equipment became lighter as cavalry equipment became heavier. Legionaries wore leather body armour, and carried a light spear (*spiculum*) and the *spatha*. Heavy cavalry units (*cataphracti*), riding armoured horses and armed with a lance (*contos*), became the main striking force. Uniformity was probably never high within units as equipment tended to be used until worn out.

See also STANDARDS; WARFARE, ROMAN.   HS

Barker (1981); Bishop and Coulston (1993); Robinson (1975).

Army, Greek   In the early archaic period the armies of Greek states consisted principally of aristocratic champions and their companions, since ARMS AND ARMOUR were costly and not widely distributed. In the late 8th and early 7th centuries BC warfare was revolutionized by the advent of HOPLITE armour. This, by extending the opportunity to fight effectively and by requiring new tactics whereby soldiers operated as a coherent unit, established the hoplite phalanx as the polis army: those who could afford it equipped themselves, and the army was normally formed by the calling up of specified age-classes of citizen hoplites. Hoplite warfare opened the possibility of proper training, exploited early by Sparta and, much later, by specialist units in other states (e.g. the Theban SACRED BAND), and established the pattern of classical WARFARE, in which cavalry, being relatively scarce, played a limited part (*see* HIPPEIS), while light troops, though effective in suitable terrain, tended to be regarded as inferior and were often mercenaries, particularly specialists such as slingers and archers. Generals tended to be magistrates rather than career soldiers (*see* STRATEGOS), training (except at Sparta) was sketchy, and scope for manoeuvre was limited, so the level of tactical sophistication was low, although the Thebans gradually developed the ploy of concentrating force in one wing. Commissariat provision was also rudimentary: much warfare was local, and elsewhere troops generally lived off the land or supplied themselves.

In the course of the 4th century BC the Greek army evolved. The value of light troops was increasingly appreciated, and PELTASTS were regularly deployed, particularly as MERCENARIES, which many Greek rulers and states, including Athens, employed as a supplement or alternative to citizen troops. The greatest changes were made by PHILIP II of Macedon, who developed a professional and diverse army: the infantry was divided into the relatively inflexible PHALANX, the more mobile hypaspists, and the light troops, while expansion of his cavalry arm turned it into a genuine striking force. As the career of ALEXANDER THE GREAT showed, the variety of the Macedonian army offered a solution to any problem, allowing greater tactical flexibility and hence genuine battle plans. Philip also maintained a corps of engineers who, assisted by the development of artillery, enabled him to storm cities, rather than merely reduce them by starvation (*see* SIEGECRAFT, GREEK). The Macedonian army was also much larger than its predecessors: whereas large Greek states could field a maximum of 10,000–15,000 men, Alexander's army was three or four times that size. Hellenistic armies remained diverse, professional forces, capable of moving with impressive rapidity over long distances; contact with India also introduced ELEPHANTS to the battlefield, a powerful if unreliable resource.

RB

Adcock (1957); Greenhalgh (1973); Hammond and Griffith (1979); Lazenby (1985); Pritchett (1965–91); Snodgrass (1967).

Army, Roman The earliest Roman army we can reconstruct in any detail consisted of a citizen levy serving without pay and providing its own equipment. Citizens were organized into seven groups by property qualifications, an arrangement traditionally credited to SERVIUS TULLIUS. The richest provided the cavalry (*see* EQUESTRIAN ORDER). The next five groups provided infantry with progressively diminishing amounts of equipment. The poorest group (the PROLETARII) was not considered eligible to serve in the army (*see* COMITIA). The demands of lengthy campaigns led to the introduction of pay, traditionally in 406 BC.

By the time of the PUNIC WARS the army had changed. POLYBIUS gives a detailed description. Commanded by MAGISTRATES or ex-magistrates, the army was organized into legions, which consisted of three lines of heavy infantry, the *hastati*, *principes*, and *triarii*, each made up of ten units called maniples, which in turn were composed of two centuries (each *centuria*, commanded by a *centurio*, numbered 60 *hastati* or *principes* or 30 *triarii*). These were supported by cavalry and light infantry. A minimum property requirement for service remained. On campaign, Rome's troops were accompanied by an at least equal number of troops drawn from her Italian allies (*see* SOCII). Polybius also gives a detailed description of Roman marching camps. These orderly and defended camps were of considerable importance in the conduct of Roman WARFARE.

MARIUS is traditionally seen as reorganizing the army. The property qualification for service was removed, and the legions' internal organization altered to 10 cohorts, each of six centuries. The enfranchisement of all Italy south of the river Po after the SOCIAL WAR led to the abolition of the distinction between the legions and their Italian allies. Henceforth the main distinction lay between the legions and the auxiliary units recruited outside Italy.

The growth of the Roman empire under the Republic led to increasing professionalization of the Roman army. Lengthy campaigns abroad separated the troops from their Italian roots, and necessitated the appointment of generals for longer tenures of command. A vicious circle was created whereby the troops came to expect their commander, to whom they swore their military oath (SACRAMENTUM), to win them bonuses, especially land, on their discharge; the commander looked to his troops to support him in politics.

AUGUSTUS established a standing army, fixing the terms of military service (see STIPENDIUM). The army was composed of permanent units: legions recruited from citizens, and auxiliaries (AUXILIA) recruited from non-citizens. He also instituted new units at Rome, the PRAETORIAN GUARD, the Urban Cohorts, and the para-military fire brigade (VIGILES), as well as establishing a standing NAVY.

As the Principate progressed, the stationing of troops near to the new linear frontiers, and the tendency for army camps to become permanent bases, removed much of the strategic flexibility of the empire's forces. The political and economic crisis of the 3rd century (see ROME, HISTORY) led to changes in the composition of the Roman army. More reliance was placed on cavalry, more barbarians were enlisted, and a split appeared between the troops on the frontier and those with the emperors. The changes culminated in the reforms of CONSTANTINE I, who established mobile field armies and static frontier troops.

See also ARMS AND ARMOUR, ROMAN; LEGATI; PRAEFECTUS; STANDARDS.

HS

Brunt (1971a); Gabba (1976); Jones (1964); Keppie (1984); Webster (1985).

Arrian (?c.AD 90–?c.160), Greek historian. Lucius Flavius Arrianus came from BITHYNIA and studied under the Stoic EPICTETUS. He had an active career in the Roman civil service under HADRIAN, and subsequently became an Athenian citizen and civic official. Arrian published Epictetus' *Discourses* and wrote works on geography, hunting, tactics and military expeditions, and local history. He is justly famous for his *Anabasis*, the most important history of ALEXANDER THE GREAT's campaign. Arrian discerningly combined his main sources, PTOLEMY I SOTER and ARISTOBULUS, with other 'tales'. The resulting coherent, convincing, and sober picture of Alexander – although flattering – contrasts with the romantic, sensational view found in DIODORUS SICULUS and CURTIUS. His literary style is clear if not elegant, and often depends on rhetorical devices. Arrian also wrote the *Indica*, an account of Alexander's Indian expedition based on NEARCHUS OF CRETE, and a history of the years after Alexander's death. This fragmentary work provides crucial evidence for the early years of the DIADOCHI.

EER

Bosworth (1980, 1988a, b); Stadter (1980).

Arsacids (c.250 BC–c.AD 230), Parthian dynasty. The Arsacids were a dynasty of independent kings founded by Arsaces, a barbarian who invaded and conquered the Seleucid satrapy of Parthyene after the

revolt of its satrap, and that of DIODOTUS I of Bactria, from ANTIOCHUS
II THEOS. An alliance was later concluded between PARTHIA and Bactria
for mutual security. The kingdom, centred on modern Iran, included
territories from Mesopotamia to India. Nearly 40 Arsacid kings ruled,
each taking the name Arsaces as a royal title. They adapted Persian
customs and Persian religion, claiming descent from the ACHAEMENIDS.
After several wars with Rome the Arsacids were finally dislodged by
SASSANIANS c.AD 227.   EER

Debevoise (1938); Eddy (1961); Frye (1984); Sullivan (1990); Yarshater (1983).

Arsinoë I (c.300–c.270 BC), queen of Egypt. Arsinoë was the daughter of King LYSIMACHUS of Thrace, whose alliance with Egypt was
cemented by her marriage in c.289–c.285 BC to Prince Ptolemy, later
PTOLEMY II PHILADELPHUS. Her three children included the heir PTOLEMY
III and BERENICE SYRA. She was accused of treason and repudiated
probably between 281 and c.279, perhaps at the instigation of her
successor ARSINOË II. She was banished to Coptus in Upper Egypt and
died there in obscurity.   EER

Macurdy (1932).

Arsinoë II Philadelphus (c.316–270 BC), queen of Egypt. 'Brother-
loving' Arsinoë was the daughter of PTOLEMY I and BERENICE I. Married
first to LYSIMACHUS, she was widowed in 281 BC. Trying to win the
Macedonian throne for her sons, she married its claimant, her half-
brother PTOLEMY CERAUNUS, who killed two sons and was killed himself
in 279. Returning to Egypt c.276 she married her full brother PTOLEMY
II. She exercised great influence on public affairs, culture, and court
life, and was deified while alive.   EER

CAH VII.1; Fraser (1972); Green (1990); Macurdy (1932).

Arsinoë III Philopator (c.235–204 BC), queen of Egypt. 'Father-
loving' Arsinoë was the daughter of PTOLEMY III and BERENICE II EUERGE-
TIS, a cultivated woman of great charm according to ERATOSTHENES. She
married her full brother PTOLEMY IV in 217 BC, although she reputedly
found his excesses repugnant. She was banished from court at an
uncertain date by her husband's unscrupulous ministers, and murdered in obscure circumstances, probably shortly after Ptolemy's death
in 204, to prevent her acting as regent for their young son PTOLEMY V.
                                                                       EER

Fraser (1972); Macurdy (1932).

Art *see* ARCHITECTURE; GEMS; JEWELLERY; MOSAIC; PAINTING; POTTERY;
SCULPTURE.

Artabazus (5th century BC), Persian general. Artabazus commanded the Parthians and Chorasmians in the army of XERXES. He was chosen to command the force that in late 480 escorted Xerxes back to Persian-controlled territory. He returned to joint command of the army at PLATAEA where, despite HERODOTUS' account of his rapid departure before the battle, he seems to have acquitted himself well. In the 470s he was satrap of Dascylium, but was probably not the Artabazus who faced CIMON in 450. GLC

Dandamaev (1989).

Artabazus (4th century BC), Persian satrap. A member of the family which held Dascylium as almost a hereditary fiefdom, Artabazus loyally fought against Datames in the Satraps' Revolt (360s BC), but revolted from ARTAXERXES III in the 350s, securing help from CHARES and later from Pammenes of Thebes. He fled to PHILIP II of Macedon (c.351), returning in 345 by the good offices of his brother-in-law Mentor. Loyal to DARIUS III, he deserted Bessus and went over to ALEXANDER THE GREAT in 330. GLC

Artaphernes (fl. c.515–495 BC), Persian noble. Artaphernes, a half-brother of DARIUS I, was appointed satrap of Sardes by him c.512 BC. He defended Sardes against Greek attack early in the IONIAN REVOLT, and was one of the leaders of the Persian counter-offensive. Although responsible for the execution of HISTIAEUS, he imposed a moderate settlement on Ionia: tribute was more methodically assessed, but not increased, and an arbitration mechanism for disputes between cities was established. His son, also Artaphernes, commanded Persian troops at MARATHON and in Xerxes' invasion. RB

Artaxerxes I Macrocheir king of Persia, 464–424 BC. Artaxerxes 'the long-armed' inherited an empire vulnerable to Athenian naval attack, with major expeditions in 460 and 450, and to internal revolt in Egypt (460–454) and elsewhere. He therefore made a deal with Athens, the so-called Peace of CALLIAS, delimiting spheres of influence. Wooed by Sparta in the opening years of the PELOPONNESIAN WAR, he seemed to be about to accept alliance when he died. GLC

Dandamaev (1989); Gershevitch (1985).

Artaxerxes II Mnemon king of Persia, 404–359 BC. Artaxerxes 'the mindful' was the son of DARIUS II and the elder brother of CYRUS THE YOUNGER who in 401 revolted and was defeated at CUNAXA. The main events of his reign were the signing of the King's Peace (387/6; *see* ANTALCIDAS) which brought an end to Greek efforts to liberate the

Asiatic Greeks, two unsuccessful attempts in the 380s and 370s to subdue Egypt, the conclusion of the war against EVAGORAS of Cyprus, and the partial suppression of the Satraps' Revolt (*see* MAUSOLUS) – all in all hardly illustrious but perhaps not Artaxerxes' fault.   GLC

Dandamaev (1989).

Artaxerxes III Ochus king of Persia, 359–338 BC. Son of ARTAXERXES II, Artaxerxes III (the meaning of Ochus is unknown) began by completing the suppression of the Satraps' Revolt (*see* MAUSOLUS), requiring the western satraps to disband their mercenary armies, and reasserting Persian influence on Greek politics. Some disorders continued (*see* ARTABAZUS), but the Egyptian Revolt was finally extinguished (343). He prepared to face invasion by PHILIP II of Macedon but died.   GLC

Dandamaev (1989).

Artemidorus (*c*.150–*c*.100 BC), of Ephesus, Greek geographer. Artemidorus is known to us only from the work of STRABO, for whom he was a major source. He travelled widely, visiting Rome, Spain, and the Atlantic seaboard as well as Egypt, Ethiopia, and the Red Sea. He made good use of his predecessors AGATHARCHIDES and ERATOSTHENES to produce his own geography of the world (in 11 books) which was much admired in antiquity.   GS

Artemis Greek goddess. The cult of Artemis, which was universal in ancient Greece, is of uncertain origin but had early associations with Crete and Asia Minor. As the goddess of hunting and mistress of the animals (Potnia Theron, as she is called in HOMER) she is very old indeed, perhaps Palaeolithic. Though a virgin goddess, her other responsibilities were fertility and childbirth. Cult centres included Brauron, Sparta, Perge, and EPHESUS (where her temple was one of the wonders of the ancient world). In art she is often winged and dressed for hunting; but at Ephesus her maternal role manifested itself in numerous breasts. The Romans identified her with DIANA.   GS

Grimal (1986); Guthrie (1950).

Artemisia I (fl. *c*.480 BC), Carian queen. Artemisia inherited the throne of Halicarnassus on the death of her husband. As a Persian vassal, she commanded a small contingent from Halicarnassus and its subject islands at SALAMIS, attracting the admiration of Xerxes, according to Herodotus, who reports several good stories about his fellow Halicarnassian (7.99, 8.68f., 87f.).   RB

Hornblower (1982).

Artemisium the northern point of Euboea where the first naval battle of the PERSIAN WARS (480 BC) occurred. HERODOTUS recounts various preliminary Greek successes, but these are dubious. In the principal encounter the Greeks were 'roughly handled'. They withdrew to SALAMIS having heard that THERMOPYLAE had fallen; but since they later refused to face the Persian fleet on the open sea, they had probably been defeated.   GLC

Burn (1984).

Arval Brothers Roman college of priests. The Arval Brothers were the earliest college of PRIESTS at Rome, but had to be revived by Augustus. Their 12 members, coopted for life, in imperial times included the emperor. Their main festival was held in May for the agriculture goddess Dea Diva, to whom their sacred grove at the fifth milestone on the Via Campana was dedicated. Besides prayers for the fields (*arvum*, a ploughed field, gave them their name) they also offered sacrifice for the safety of the emperor.   DP

Scullard (1981); Syme (1980).

Arverni Gallic people. The Arverni lived in south central Gaul in the Auvergne mountains. Under their leader, Bituitis, they were defeated by Gnaeus DOMITIUS AHENOBARBUS in 122 BC. Struggling for hegemony of Gaul with the AEDUI, they invited ARIOVISTUS across the Rhine. An Arvernian noble, VERCINGETORIX, led the revolt against CAESAR in 52 BC in which the Arverni took a leading role. Caesar's only defeat occurred in their territory, at Gergovia.   LPR

Chadwick (1970).

Asclepiades (4th–3rd century BC), of Samos, Greek poet. Asclepiades, who wrote under the name of Sicelides, worked mostly in Alexandria where he was a major figure in the development of the EPIGRAM as a vehicle for personal expression. Highly esteemed by Theocritus (7.40), he exercised profound influence over Callimachus. About 40 of his (mostly erotic) poems survive in the ANTHOLOGY.   GS

Cameron (1993); Fraser (1972); Webster (1964).

Asclepius Greek god. Asclepius, son of APOLLO, was the god of MEDICINE. Though most likely of Thessalian origin, his cult was centred at EPIDAURUS, whence other shrines were established, notably those at ATHENS, COS, PERGAMUM, and Rome. INCUBATION was a central feature of the ritual for those seeking a cure (cf. Aristophanes, *Plutus* 653ff.), though exercise, bathing, and changes in diet were also prescribed

The god's sanctuaries functioned like spas with facilities provided for an extended stay. In art he is mature, kindly, and usually bearded; his usual attribute is the snake, symbol of rejuvenation.   GS

Grimal (1986); Guthrie (1950).

Asellio (mid-2nd century–89 BC), Roman historian. Sempronius Asellio's history, which does not survive, broke new ground by rejecting the traditional annalistic form (*see* ANNALES) and concentrating on contemporary events in the manner of POLYBIUS, whom he had met as a young man while serving in Spain under SCIPIO AEMILIANUS. He is perhaps identical with the A. Sempronius Asellio who, as praetor in 89 BC, was murdered by money-lenders in the Forum for giving judgement in favour of debtors.   TC

Badian (1966b).

Ashoka (269–232 BC), Mauryan king. Ashoka was the grandson of SANDRACOTTUS who as king united central and north INDIA. An active missionary of Buddhism, Ashoka maintained contacts with the west. PTOLEMY II sent an envoy to him, and a famous rock-cut inscription from Kandahar (*c.*256 BC) records embassies sent to Ptolemy, an Alexander (identity uncertain), ANTIGONUS II GONATAS, ANTIOCHUS II THEOS, and MAGAS of Cyrene. His death marked the beginning of the end of the Mauryan empire.   EER

Narain (1957); Sedlar (1980); Smith (1981); Thapar (1966, 1973); Woodcock (1966).

Asia as a Roman province. The province comprised the western part of Asia Minor, consisting of the Ionian coast, the islands, LYDIA, and the Troad, bounded by BITHYNIA to the north, GALATIA to the east, and LYCIA to the south. The region was rich in cities, of which the most prominent were EPHESUS and PERGAMUM. Rivalry between these and other cities was common, being shown in widespread building programmes. The wealth for this competition was provided by the harbours of the Ionian coast, linking the interior of Asia Minor with the Mediterranean and facilitating export of cloth and grain.

This region came under Roman control following the death of King ATTALUS III PHILOMETOR of Pergamum in 133 BC, who bequeathed it to Rome in his will. A senatorial commission under Scipio Nasica was sent to organize the province, but its work was upset by the revolt of ARISTONICUS and the province had to be secured by force before Aquilius could complete the settlement in 129. Some cities (including Pergamum) remained completely free, while others seem to have enjoyed local self-government.

Once the province had been created, it was exploited by Roman governors and entrepreneurs, particularly the PUBLICANI, resulting in strong resentment and large debts. This led in 88–84 to its participation in the MITHRIDATIC WARS, when MITHRIDATES VI occupied the area, cancelled debts, and organized the murder of some 80,000 Italian residents. After Mithrides was driven out, SULLA plundered part of the province, removed most city privileges, and made Asia responsible for paying for the war and five years' back taxation, a sum of 20,000 talents. Unable to pay, the provincials were forced to borrow from money-lenders. It was not until 70 BC that LUCULLUS was able to solve these problems, clearing the province of debt in four years. Made a senatorial province by AUGUSTUS, Asia was very prosperous under the Empire, but was split into seven provinces by DIOCLETIAN.   HE

Magie (1975); Sherwin-White (1977, 1984).

Aspasia (fl. 450–430 BC), mistress and latterly wife of PERICLES. Aspasia was much celebrated in a world where WOMEN did not attain celebrity. In Plato's *Menexenus* SOCRATES is depicted repeating a sample funeral oration he had heard her utter; she was well enough known to be spoken of on the comic stage, and was credited with urging Pericles to suppress the revolt of Samos (441) and to pass the MEGARA Decree (433/2). She was also said to have been tried for impiety. All this is very doubtful but testifies to her exceptional qualities and influence.

GLC

Assembly *see* APELLA; COMITIA; ECCLESIA.

Astronomy NAVIGATION, AGRICULTURE, and TIME-keeping stimulated interest in the heavenly bodies among peoples of antiquity. The Egyptians and Babylonians, especially, made astronomical investigations and noted various astronomical cycles for calendaric purposes. The Greeks, too, used the rising and setting of certain stars as calendaric markers and others as navigational aids. The Presocratic philosophers imported rational attitudes into astronomy and thereby paved the way for its development as a science. During this period several important ideas were put forward, notably the sphericity of the earth, the view that the moon derives its light from the sun, and the correct explanation of solar and lunar eclipses.

The great contribution of the Greeks to astronomy was their formulation of geometrical systems to represent the apparent motions of the heavenly bodies. The origin of this idea might be traced back to ANAXIMANDER, who, by developing the assumption that the world is orderly, gave the heavenly bodies a proportionate arrangement based upon circular orbits. However, the Pythagoreans contributed most to the development of scientific astronomy in this way and brought about its close and fruitful marriage with MATHEMATICS. Important developments of this idea took place in the ACADEMY when EUDOXUS OF CNIDUS answered the problem raised by PLATO of how the apparently irregular motions of the planets might be derived from combinations of uniform, regular, circular motions by putting forward separate systems of homocentric spheres. This work was subsequently improved and elaborated upon by CALLIPPUS; later difficulties led to this system being supplanted by others that included eccentrics and epicycles. The most influential of these was that of PTOLEMY who, incorporating HIPPARCHUS' solar and lunar theory, formulated a system which was almost universally accepted as the foundation of astronomical science for about 1,400 years. ARISTARCHUS' heliocentric system, put forward in answer to this same problem, was formulated too early since Hellenistic astronomers were not ready to accept his assumption that the stars are so vastly distant and the earth's orbit so slight in comparison that the parallactic displacement of the stars was so small as to be unnoticeable.

See also APOLLONIUS OF PERGE; ARCHIMEDES; CALLIPPUS; HERACLIDES PONTICUS; METON; PYTHAGORAS.   JL

Dicks (1970); Heath (1913).

Atellana Fabula   Atellan farce was a form of native Italian burlesque, named after the town of Atella in Campania but known at Rome by the 3rd century BC. In the 1st century BC it acquired a literary form in the hands of Pomponius and Novius. The subject-matter was drawn from the provincial Italian demi-monde but the technique owed much to Greek New COMEDY. An Atellan farce was sometimes performed after a tragedy, in the manner of a Greek SATYR PLAY.

See also MIME, LATIN.   GS

Beare (1964).

Athanasius, St   (AD 295–373), archbishop of Alexandria. A native of Alexandria, Athanasius was the champion of orthodox Christianity against the heresy of ARIANISM. He was appointed archbishop of Alexandria in 328 but was five times unseated and exiled. A friend of Sts PACHOMIUS and Antony, he promoted monasticism both in Egypt and in the west and worked to heal schism in the Church. His surviving writings include a treatise *On Incarnation* but not the eponymous creed which was written in Latin, probably by St AMBROSE.

See also NEW TESTAMENT.   GS

Cross (1974); Kazhdan (1991).

Athaulf (d. AD 415), leader of the Visigoths, 410–15. Athaulf, or Ataulf, an Ostrogoth, succeeded his brother-in-law ALARIC as king of the Visigoths. In 412 he crossed from Italy into Gaul, and suppressed Jovinus, in revolt against HONORIUS. As Honorius failed to provide the Gallic province demanded by the Goths, Athaulf refused to return Honorius' half-sister PLACIDIA, and himself married her (414). Athaulf reinstated the usurper Attalus, but was forced into Spain by CONSTANTIUS (III), where he was murdered. RJB

Bury (1958); Matthews (1990), Todd (1972).

Athena Greek goddess. Athena is most closely, but by no means exclusively, identified with Athens whose patron she was. She had Minoan and Mycenaean connections and was associated with cities and citadels throughout Greece. Her particular responsibilities range from war (in which capacity she protects her city as she once protected Achilles at Troy) to arts and crafts. Her chief sanctuary is the PARTHENON where the climax of the PANATHENAEA was annually celebrated. In art she is armed, an ice maiden, often with an owl, especially on coins. The Romans identified her with MINERVA. GS

Grimal (1986); Guthrie (1950); Herrington (1955).

Athenaeus (2nd–3rd century AD), Greek writer. Born at Naucratis in Egypt, Athenaeus probably spent at least some time in Rome, given the Roman setting for his surviving work, *Deipnosophistae*. This is the record of conversation at a SYMPOSIUM which in the course of several days ranges over matters of law and medicine, art and literature, philosophy and science. Its principal value is in its extensive quotation of otherwise lost earlier writers. GS

Athens, history *To 490 BC*: Athens was continuously occupied through the Dark Ages (hence Athenian claims to be autochthonous), and became a prosperous and advanced city with overseas contacts in the geometric period. In the mid-8th century BC a period of introspection and relative isolation began: the multiplication of graves and wells in Attica suggests an increasing population, forming new settlements in the extensive territory of Attica – Athens established no colonies at this stage. At some point she made the transition from kings to magistrates (the list of eponymous ARCHONS goes back to 683), though power rested with the aristocratic EUPATRIDAE, particularly in the AREOPAGUS. During the 7th century BC Athens became subject to the same tensions which had earlier affected the Peloponnese: about 632 Cylon made an abortive attempt to become tyrant; the coup failed for want of popular support, but its suppression also allowed aristocratic rivals to have the ALCMAEONIDS expelled for sacrilege.

The legislation of DRACO was probably an attempted concession to anti-Eupatrid pressure, but must have been insufficient, since in 594 SOLON was appointed archon and arbitrator to resolve Athens's social problems. His economic measures brought some immediate relief, while the creation of a council to serve the assembly and the opening of legal process to the people, including the institution of the HELIAEA, took the first steps to the genuine enfranchisement of the whole community; but his attempts to alter the basis of office-holding from birth to wealth had only limited success: aristocratic in-fighting continued, and was only finally suppressed by the firm establishment of PEISISTRATUS as tyrant in 546.

The 'Golden Age' of Peisistratid rule saw the development of Athens as the political, cultural, and religious centre of Attica, and a further increase in Athenian power. Already in the late 7th century Athens had colonized the Troad, perhaps in part to control the important Black Sea corn route, and her position on the Hellespont was now renewed and strengthened. She had also wrested control of Salamis from her neighbour MEGARA, and had according to tradition long been involved in a regional power struggle with AEGINA. Athenian troops had also fought in the First SACRED WAR.

The fall of the tyranny was followed by a fresh aristocratic struggle, quickly resolved by the reforms of CLEISTHENES, which bound Attica together as a political unity and gave Athens the essentials of democracy. Commitment to the new order was cemented by abortive Spartan interventions, and by Athenian victories over Boeotian and Chalcidian invaders in 506. Athenian self-confidence can be seen in her bold intervention in the IONIAN REVOLT, and in the series of reforms which developed the implications of democracy, including the election of archons by lot and the implementation of OSTRACISM.   RB

Forrest (1966); Jeffery (1976); Rhodes (1981).

490–318 BC: By victory at MARATHON (490) and by her vigorous part in the defeat of XERXES' army (480–479) Athens won the prestige to assume leadership on sea against Persia (*see* CIMON; DELIAN LEAGUE). In the PENTECONTAETIA she developed a maritime empire (*see* PERICLES; THEMISTOCLES), and since this depended on those who rowed the ships, the remains of the aristocratic state had to give way to democracy (*see* EPHIALTES for his curtailment of the powers of the AREOPAGUS). Under the leadership of Pericles Athens became the cultural centre of Greece and policy was wisely conducted.

After the outbreak of the PELOPONNESIAN WAR (431) and Pericles' death (429), the democracy under populist leaders became 'radical', and with the failure of the Sicilian expedition (415–413), which caused enormous losses of men and ships, complete military disaster threatened. The oligarchic revolution of 411 (*see* FOUR HUNDRED; THERAMENES) ensued but was short-lived. Despite the successes of ALCIBIADES, LYSANDER with Persian support proved too strong. At AEGOSPOTAMI (405) Athens lost her navy and therewith her empire, and was starved into submission. Another oligarchic revolution followed (404) (*see* CRITIAS; THIRTY TYRANTS). When THRASYBULUS returned with a band of exiles, Sparta hesitated to crush him, and democracy was re-established. Despite the judicial murder of SOCRATES (399), it endured unchallenged until the end of the LAMIAN WAR (323–322).

Down to the SOCIAL WAR (357–355) policy was principally concerned with the recovery of empire, but while Sparta and Persia held power, Athens had to proceed cautiously, and from 378 to LEUCTRA (371) the Second Athenian Confederacy practised its laudable professions. Thereafter ambition was more naked and the revolt of the allies (357) brought a change of policy (*see* EUBULUS). From 355 Athens was obsessed with the menace of PHILIP II of Macedon. He deceived her into making the Peace of PHILOCRATES (346) and finally totally defeated the Greeks at CHAERONEA (338), Athens suffering especially (*see* AESCHINES; DEMOSTHENES). During the Lamian War Athens briefly recovered full liberty, but ANTIPATER put a stop to that by installing a Macedonian garrison and instituting an oligarchy.

See also ARISTOPHON; CALLISTRATUS; CLEON; CLEOPHON; CONON; DEMADES; LYCURGUS; NICIAS; PHOCION; TIMOTHEUS.   GLC

Hammond (1959); Hignett (1952); Jordan (1972); Kagan (1987); Meiggs (1972); Ostwald (1986); Pickard-Cambridge (1914); Strauss (1986).

318–31 BC: Still the symbolic heart of Greece, Athens fell prey to the rivalries of the DIADOCHI who struggled to control her. For some 60 years after ALEXANDER THE GREAT's death, Athens was threatened by Macedonian domination. CASSANDER, and then DEMETRIUS I POLIORCETES, subdued her, although there was constant internal unrest and frequent revolt (a major revolt against Demetrius occurred in 287 BC). The War of CHREMONIDES (*c.*266–261) ended in the defeat of Athens by ANTIGONUS II GONATAS, and meant the loss of her independence until 228. In the 2nd century a neutral Athens was spared the consequences of the wars which established Roman rule in Greece, but her support for MITHRIDATES VI of Pontus led to her capitulation when besieged by SULLA (87–86).

Throughout the Hellenistic period Athens faded in political importance and no longer held centre stage in Greek affairs. Although still a centre of culture (for example, the comic poet MENANDER and the philosophers EPICURUS and ZENO OF CITIUM lived and worked in Athens in the 3rd century), Athens could hardly compete in wealth and glamour with the new capitals of the Seleucid and Ptolemaic kings

(ALEXANDRIA in Egypt was arguably more influential and productive in cultural terms too). None the less, throughout the Roman Empire it was an almost obligatory part of an upper-class Roman man's EDUCATION to study philosophy, rhetoric, literature, and history in Athens.

See also CALLIAS OF SPHETTUS; DEMETRIUS OF PHALERUM; DEMOCHARES; LACHARES; LEOSTHENES; OLYMPIODORUS; PHAEDRUS OF SPHETTUS; STRATOCLES.

EER

CAH VII.1, VIII; Ferguson (1911); Green (1990); Mossé (1973).

Athens, topography (See map on page 758.) The ACROPOLIS always provided the focus for Athenian architecture, not least under PEISISTRATUS and his sons, but all buildings were destroyed by the Persians in 480 BC. The present buildings – the PARTHENON, the ERECHTHEUM, the PROPYLAEA, and the temple of Athena Nike – date from the second half of the 5th century and owe their inspiration to PERICLES. Later accretions were few (a circular temple of Rome and Augustus was built east of the Parthenon soon after 27 BC) and pagan worship continued on the acropolis until the 5th century AD.

The steep southern slope of the acropolis lent itself naturally to the construction of theatres. Oldest was the THEATRE of Dionysus (c.500 BC but rebuilt in the 4th century). Best preserved is the ODEUM of Herodes Atticus (c.AD 160). Between them ran the Stoa of Eumenes (2nd century BC) above which was the sanctuary of Asclepius (418 BC).

North of the acropolis was the AGORA, the civic centre of ancient Athens. This large rectangular area, bordered by stoas and temples, among them the so-called THESEUM, contained a variety of buildings including the Bouleuterion (meeting place of the BOULE), the HELIAEA (lawcourts), the Prytaneion (see PRYTANIS), and the mint (see COINAGE, GREEK). It was diagonally bisected by the processional Panathenaic Way and the area in the middle was reserved for the musical and dramatic contests of the PANATHENAEA. Various buildings of the Roman period such as the market and library of Hadrian lay to the east.

West of the acropolis the Hill of Ares (or AREOPAGUS) provided the meeting place for the council of elders, and beyond it, the Pnyx, that of the ECCLESIA or citizens' assembly. The city was encircled by walls built in the 480s BC by THEMISTOCLES. The principal gateway was the Dipylon in the north-west, beyond which lay the Ceramicus or main cemetery. To the south-west the Long Walls (see WALLS, LONG) were built in the 450s to connect Athens with PIRAEUS.

GS

Hopper (1971); Stillwell (1976); Thompson and Wycherley (1972); Travlos (1971); Wycherley (1978).

Athletics see GAMES, GREEK.

Athos, Mount   rocky headland at the south-eastern tip of CHALCIDICE. In 492 BC the invading Persian fleet was smashed on the rocks by a storm. Ten years later XERXES dug a canal through the neck of the peninsula to provide a passage for his fleet. The mountain, sacred to Zeus in antiquity, rises out of the sea to a height of 6,670 feet. ALEXANDER THE GREAT rejected a scheme that it should be fashioned in his own image.   GS

Atomists   The atomic theory was originated by LEUCIPPUS and further developed by DEMOCRITUS in an attempt to circumvent the arguments of the ELEATICS. The theory was subsequently adopted and adapted by EPICURUS to serve as the basis for his ethical theory. Agreeing with the Eleatics that generation and destruction are, in the literal sense, impossible, Leucippus sought to explain coming-into-being and passing-away by the aggregation and segregation of a plurality of corporeal particles, each of which shared certain features of the Eleatic One-Being, in that it was homogeneous, uncreated, and indestructible. He refused to accept, however, the Eleatic denial of empty space and baldly declared that his atomic particles moved eternally at random throughout an infinite void. Collisions between these particles set up vortices which caused like atoms to tend towards like, ultimately bringing about the formation of innumerable worlds scattered throughout the void.

See also MEDICINE; PHYSICS.   JL

Bailey (1928); Kirk, Raven, and Schofield (1983).

Atossa   (fl. *c.*520–490 BC), queen of Persia. Atossa was the daughter of CYRUS and wife successively of CAMBYSES, the usurping Magus, and DARIUS I, an indication of her importance, as is her securing the succession for XERXES, the eldest of her four sons.   RB

Attalus   *see* ALARIC; ATHAULF.

Attalus I Soter   (269–197 BC), king of Pergamum. Attalus succeeded his adoptive father EUMENES I (241 BC), and took the titles 'king' and 'Soter' ('saviour') after his victory over marauding Galatians before 230. His defeat of ANTIOCHUS HIERAX *c.*228 won Pergamum most of Seleucid Asia Minor, although much was later lost to ACHAEUS. Alarmed by the ambitions of the Macedonian PHILIP V, Attalus joined Rome and the AETOLIAN LEAGUE in the First MACEDONIAN WAR (215–205), and defended Pergamum against Philip's ally PRUSIAS I of Bithynia. Attalus and RHODES defeated Philip at the battle off Chios in 201. During the

Second Macedonian War (200–197) he waged naval warfare in the Aegean as a Roman ally.

See also APOLLONIS OF CYZICUS; EUMENES II. EER

Allen (1983); CAH VII.1, VIII; Green (1990); Gruen (1984); Hansen (1971); McShane (1964).

Attalus II Philadelphus (220–138 BC), king of Pergamum. 'Brother-loving' Attalus, a pupil of CARNEADES, succeeded his brother EUMENES II SOTER in 159 BC, having previously served him and Rome loyally. Rome helped him win two wars against the Bithynian PRUSIAS II. He supported ALEXANDER BALAS for the Seleucid throne when DEMETRIUS I SOTER threatened the disputed Cappadocian throne of Attalus' relative ARIARATHES V. He helped Rome defeat the Macedonian pretender ANDRISCUS in 148, and MUMMIUS to destroy Corinth in 146. He dedicated a (now reconstructed) STOA in the Athenian Agora. EER

Allen (1983); CAH VIII; Green (1990); Gruen (1984); Hansen (1971); McShane (1964).

Attalus III Philometor (*c.*170–133 BC), king of Pergamum. 'Mother-loving' Attalus was the son of EUMENES II SOTER and successor in 138 BC to his uncle ATTALUS II PHILADELPHUS. A colourful personality, Attalus is attested both as a popular benefactor and as an evil tyrant who dabbled in poisons and torture. In his will he bequeathed Pergamum to Rome for obscure reasons which perhaps included a recognition of Rome's power and an attempt to avert social unrest. The Pergamene dynasty ended with his death despite the revolution incited by ARISTONICUS. EER

Allen (1983); CAH VIII; Gruen (1984); Hansen (1971); McShane (1964).

Atthis a type of antiquarian chronicle, concerned with the history of Attica, which became fashionable at Athens in the 4th and 3rd centuries BC. Chief among the Atthidographers was PHILOCHORUS. Only fragments of their work survive, but they were clearly much preoccupied with local cults and festivals, and their influence on the subsequent development of Alexandrian scholarship has been demonstrated.

See also HELLANICUS; HISTORIOGRAPHY, GREEK. GS

Jacoby (1949).

Attic *see* DIALECTS, GREEK.

Attica region of central Greece to the south-east of Boeotia. Cut off from the rest of Greece by mountains and otherwise encircled by sea,

Attica constituted a natural unit that became a political unit (*see* SYNOECISM) by the end of the GEOMETRIC PERIOD (though by tradition the unification was achieved by Theseus). Once densely forested, its hillsides were mostly bare by the CLASSICAL PERIOD, but its plains were fertile and arable. It was also rich in natural resources: there was good clay for POTTERY, fine-grained MARBLE for building, and LEAD and SILVER were mined at LAURIUM. Its capital was ATHENS, located in the centre of the largest plain but with easy access to excellent harbours at PIRAEUS and Phalerum and with good overland communications with the rest of the region.   GS

Traill (1975).

Atticism   a rhetorical movement that gained momentum in the mid-1st century BC as a reaction to Asianic bombast. Proclaiming a return to classical stylistic models, exemplified by the 10 ATTIC ORATORS, it aimed to replace the pretentiousness and banality of Hellenistic Greek with a purer, plainer language. Atticism in its turn became exaggerated, but it did play an important role in maintaining the cosmopolitan nature of the Greek world through the medium of a universal educated language. The works of Atticist writers of the 2nd century AD such as LUCIAN set literary standards that endured until the Renaissance.   GS

Reynolds and Wilson (1991); Wilson (1983).

Attic Orators   Ten Attic orators were canonized, probably by the Alexandrians: AESCHINES, ANDOCIDES, ANTIPHON, DEMOSTHENES, DINARCHUS, HYPERIDES, ISAEUS, ISOCRATES, LYCURGUS, LYSIAS.   GS

Atticus   (110–32 BC), Roman literary patron and publisher. Titus Pomponius Atticus is best known as the close friend and correspondent of CICERO. In 85 BC he left Rome for Athens (whence his *cognomen*) where he lived until the mid-60s and cemented his life-long friendship with Cicero, whose mentor and publisher he became. Though not politically active himself, he wielded considerable influence by befriending the leading men of his day.
See also BOOKS, LATIN.   GS

Shackleton Bailey (1965–70).

Attila   (*c*.AD 404–53), king of the HUNS, 434–53. Attila and his brother Bleda inherited an empire that included modern Austria, Hungary, Romania, and southern Russia, which they ruled jointly until 444, when Bleda was put to death by Attila. Attila made an advantageous settlement with THEODOSIUS II, and concentrated on extending his power eastwards until 441, when he attacked the eastern Roman empire, inflicting a humiliating defeat on Theodosius (443): the annual Roman tribute of 700 pounds of gold was trebled. A further invasion (447), a Hun army this time threatening Constantinople, enabled Attila to dictate still harsher terms (448). The Roman tribute was discontinued by MARCIAN (450), but Attila turned his attention towards the western empire, encouraged by an appeal from VALENTINIAN III's sister Honoria. An invasion of Gaul (451) was frustrated by AETIUS and THEODORIC, while his invasion of Italy (452) destroyed Aquileia but failed to reach Rome (*see* LEO I THE GREAT). After Attila's death, his empire fell apart.   RJB

Bury (1958); Thompson (1975).

Aufidius Bassus   (d. after AD 54), Roman historian. Aufidius Bassus, who lived into the reign of NERO, wrote a *History* of some authority which is now lost, but was available to and used by TACITUS. Bassus' *History* began *c.*44 BC and continued to at least AD 31, perhaps as late as AD 50, and was continued by PLINY THE ELDER (*a fine Aufidii Bassus*). An earlier work, on the Germanic Wars (*Bellum Germanicum*), covered the years *c.*AD 4–16.   RJB

Scullard (1982); Syme (1958).

Augures   Roman priests. The augurs formed a college, at first (under the kings) consisting of three life-long patrician members. In 300 BC the college was enlarged (to nine), and plebeians were admitted, by the law of Q. OGULNIUS. Sulla increased their number to 15, Caesar to 16. Their function was to ascertain from signs such as the flight of birds whether the gods approved or disapproved of proposed actions, and to advise the Senate and magistrates accordingly.
    See also AUSPICIUM; PRIESTS, ROMAN.   TC

Beard and North (1990); Linderski (1986).

Augusta Treverorum   modern Trier, city in north-east Gaul. Once the capital of the TREVERI, the city owes its name to the presence of AUGUSTUS during his visit to Gaul in 15–13 BC. It soon became prosperous as the seat of the procurator of Belgica and the two Germanies, and from the late 3rd century was the imperial capital in the west until that role was transferred to ARELATE in the early 5th century. From 259 to 273 it was the centre of a breakaway Gallic empire established by POSTUMUS. Some splendid buildings survive, including the imperial basilica and baths and the Porta Nigra.   GS

Matthews (1990); Stillwell (1976); Wightman (1970).

Augustales   Roman local officials. The Augustales were municipal priestly officials concerned with the cult of the emperor, in whose honour they put on games and other entertainments. They were established under AUGUSTUS in the cities of Italy, in each of which they formed a college of six members. The priesthood proved especially attractive to wealthy freedmen, who were barred from holding magistracies but found in the service of the imperial cult a means of fulfilling their social aspirations and expressing their loyalty to the established order.

See also RULER CULT, ROMAN.   TC

Taylor (1931).

Augustan age   The Principate of AUGUSTUS (27 BC–AD 14) marks a high point in the literature of Rome. After nearly a century of political turmoil, civil war, and revolution the *Pax Augusta* paved the way for a cultural flowering comparable with that of Periclean Athens. With the sting taken out of politics the orators were silenced, and prose writing as a whole was reduced to a trickle with the important exception of the historian LIVY. The Augustan solution was cause for celebration above all by poets. This duty was discharged by HORACE and VIRGIL, Augustan poets *par excellence*, who rejoiced in calling themselves *vates* (prophets). Less politically engaged but equally important as representatives of Augustan values are the love poets TIBULLUS, PROPERTIUS, and OVID. The combination of tradition and originality that was the key to the success of the Augustan revolution is mirrored in the output of the Augustan poets. With them Latin poetry came of age.   GS

Lyne (1980); Syme (1939); Williams (1968).

Augustine, St   (AD 354–430), Latin Christian writer. Aurelius Augustinus was born at Thagaste in Numidia, the son of a pagan father and Christian mother (Monica). As a teacher of rhetoric he moved from Carthage to Rome in AD 382 and on to Milan in 384 where he was converted to Christianity and patronized by Bishop AMBROSE. Returning to Africa, he was ordained priest in 391 and in 395 became bishop of Hippo. His writings, notably the *Confessions* and *City of God*, profoundly influenced the development of Christian thought.   GS

Brown (1967); Chadwick (1986a).

Augustulus   *see* ROMULUS AUGUSTULUS.

Augustus Roman imperial title. Augustus was the quasi-religious name (chosen in preference to the more kingly 'Romulus') conferred on Octavian by the Senate on 16 January 27 BC after his 'restoration of the Republic'. AUGUSTUS clearly intended his successor Tiberius to assume the title 'Augustus', and all subsequent emperors except Vitellius did so. Augustus' widow LIVIA was designated 'Augusta' in his will, and from Domitian's reign onwards that title was normally conferred on the emperor's wife.

See also CAESAR; DIOCLETIAN.   RJB

Grant (1985).

Augustus (63 BC–AD 14), first Roman emperor, 31 BC–AD 14. Augustus was born Gaius Octavius on 23 September 63 BC, the only son of Gaius Octavius (a first-generation senator from Velitrae, south-east of Rome) and Atia, niece of Julius CAESAR. He was introduced to public life by Caesar, and posthumously adopted in Caesar's will (44), taking the name Gaius Julius Caesar Octavianus; contemporaries generally called him Caesar (modern writers use Octavian).

The Senate supported him against Mark ANTONY. On CICERO's initiative, Octavian was appointed senator and propraetor, and he became consul in 43, aged 19. The Second TRIUMVIRATE (23 November 43) gave Octavian control of Italy, while Antony held the east. Octavian strengthened his position by marriage to Scribonia, a relative of Sextus POMPEIUS. Scribonia bore him his only child, JULIA MAJOR, but he subsequently divorced her, and instead married LIVIA. AGRIPPA's victory over Antony at ACTIUM (31 BC), followed by Antony's suicide after Octavian's invasion of EGYPT (30 BC), left Octavian as master of the Roman world.

Octavian took care to emphasize the traditional Republican precedents for his powers: he held the consulship continuously from 31 to 23, but in 27 he resigned all extraordinary powers and 'transferred the state to the free disposal of the Senate and people'. He was granted a province consisting of Spain, Gaul, and Syria (which contained the majority of the military forces), and the title 'Augustus' (held by all emperors except VITELLIUS). He retained Egypt as his own estate by right of conquest, and as PRINCEPS was also able to dominate the remaining provinces through his pre-eminent prestige (*auctoritas*). In 23 BC Augustus was seriously ill, after which he ceased to rely on continuous consulships, and instead his power of IMPERIUM was declared *maius*, and he was granted tribunician power (*tribunicia potestas*). A settlement in 19 BC further enlarged his constitutional powers.

Augustus gradually reduced the number of legions from 60 to 28, reorganized the fleet, and created a permanent imperial bodyguard (the PRAETORIAN GUARD) and a POLICE force for Rome (the Urban Cohorts).

He established an advisory body, the CONSILIUM PRINCIPIS, revised the membership of the SENATE, and gradually overhauled the entire administrative and financial structure of the state. Augustus' search for a successor was frequently frustrated: his nephew MARCELLUS (husband of Julia) died in 23 BC. Augustus next adopted the infant sons of Julia and Agrippa, Gaius and Lucius CAESAR (17 BC), and finally, having survived both Caesars, turned to his stepson TIBERIUS.

There was considerable military expansion in the earlier parts of the reign: Agrippa campaigned in the east, and completed the conquest of Spain; Tiberius and his brother DRUSUS annexed Raetia and Noricum, and advanced the frontier to the Danube (16–15 BC). However, this expansionist policy was halted by the Pannonian/Illyrian revolt (AD 6–9), and the loss of VARUS' three legions in Germany (AD 9). Augustus was an immensely able administrator, who brought peace and stability to the Roman empire. His many building works include the ARA PACIS, and his surviving literary work, the *Res Gestae* (or MONUMENTUM ANCYRANUM), records his achievements as he wished them to be remembered.

See also ARMY, ROMAN; COINAGE, ROMAN; CYRENE, EDICTS OF; FINANCE, ROMAN; NAVY, ROMAN.   RJB

Grant (1985); Jones (1970); Millar (1977); Salmon (1968); Scullard (1982); Syme (1939); Wells (1984).

Aulus Gellius   *see* GELLIUS.

Aurelian (*c.*AD 214–75), Roman emperor, 270–5. Lucius Domitius Aurelianus, an Illyrian soldier born near Sirmium, was proclaimed emperor in succession to CLAUDIUS II by the Illyrian legions. Easily disposing of Claudius' brother QUINTILLUS, he eventually succeeded in reuniting the Roman empire under a single ruler. Having defeated a Germanic invasion of Italy in two major battles, Aurelian began work on a defensive wall around Rome (271). In late 271 he moved east against the Palmyrene empire of ZENOBIA and Vaballathus. Egypt was reconquered by the future emperor PROBUS (271), while Aurelian first defeated the GOTHS in Moesia before retaking, in succession, Antioch, Emessa, and Palmyra (272). A second invasion of the east was necessitated by rebellions in Palmyra and Egypt, before Aurelian was able to proceed against the Gallic empire of TETRICUS: the latter surrendered to Aurelian during a hard-fought battle near Châlons (273). Aurelian celebrated the reunification of the empire with a triumph at Rome (274) Zenobia and Tetricus marching as captives in the procession. Thereafter he was able to institute a series of reforms, including a major overhaul of the much-degraded currency, but his reorganization of the frontier defences (which included the abandonment of DACIA) was incomplete when he was assassinated.

See also WALL OF AURELIAN. RJB

Grant (1985); Parker (1958).

Aurelius (AD 121–80), Roman emperor, 161–80. Marcus Annius Verus (Marcus Aelius Aurelius Verus after adoption; known as Marcus Aurelius as emperor) was adopted, at Hadrian's instigation, by his uncle ANTONINUS PIUS in AD 138, along with Lucius VERUS, 10 years his junior. The Antonine dynasty was further established by Aurelius' marriage to the younger Faustina (145), daughter of Pius. Aurelius succeeded Pius without incident (July 161), and took Verus (died 169) as his colleague. Verus lacked Aurelius' ability and dedication to duty, and, although their powers were almost equal, Aurelius clearly remained pre-eminent.

Aurelius' reign was one of almost constant warfare, first in the east against a Parthian invasion. Aurelius appointed Verus commander-in-chief, but Verus' inadequacy was outweighed by the competence of the subordinate commanders (also appointed by Aurelius), and in 166 the emperors celebrated a double triumph. However, the empire was hit by plague brought back from the east, and thereafter Aurelius was occupied with the Marcomannic Wars. The weakening of the northern frontier to supply the army of the east allowed a massive incursion by Germanic tribes from across the Danube. Aurelius brought the situation under control in 168, but in 170 both Italy (as far as Aquileia) and Greece were invaded. From 172 Aurelius gained the upper hand, making an advantageous peace with the MARCOMANNI, but in 175 he was diverted by the unsuccessful rebellion of AVIDIUS CASSIUS, governor of Syria, before returning to the Danube in 178. The war was going well when he died in March 180, to be succeeded by his son COMMODUS (appointed joint emperor in 177), the first emperor since Vespasian to have a son to succeed him.

In general, Aurelius' administration was conservative and lacking in innovation. His *Meditations*, which survive, record the maxims, passing thoughts, and philosophizings of a noble, but rather austere, character.

See also FRONTO; STOICS. RJB

Birley (1987); Staniforth (1964); Wells (1984).

Aurelius Antoninus (Caracalla) (AD 188–217), Roman emperor, 211–17. (Lucius) Septimius Bassianus, elder son of Septimius SEVERUS and JULIA DOMNA, was created Caesar by Severus in 196. He took the name Marcus Aurelius Antoninus, but later became known by the nickname

Caracalla, derived from the type of long, flowing cloak that he favoured. Promoted to Augustus in 198, he accompanied his father on campaign in Britain (208–11), sharing with him the front-line command. On Severus' death in February 211 he became joint emperor with his brother GETA, whom he hated, immediately abandoning the newly won territory in Britain and returning to Rome. Early in 212 he arranged Geta's murder, and ruled alone for a further five years until assassinated by his Praetorian Prefect, MACRINUS, when on campaign in Syria (April 217). Caracalla spent most of his sole reign abroad, first in Germany, where a victory was won against the ALAMANNI but other tribes had to be bribed to withdraw (213). In 214 he moved east, suffering a defeat at the hands of the Armenians (215), before declaring war on Parthia (216). During the reign the increasingly blurred distinction between citizens and non-citizens was removed by the *Constitutio Antoniniana* (212), which granted Roman CITIZENSHIP to virtually all free inhabitants of the empire.   RJB

Birley (1988); Grant (1979); Parker (1958); Wells (1984).

Aurelius Victor   (d. after AD 389), Roman historian. Sextus Aurelius Victor, an African and a pagan, was appointed governor of Lower Pannonia by JULIAN with the rank of consular, and honoured with a bronze statue (361). In 389 he was city prefect at Rome. Described by AMMIANUS MARCELLINUS as a model of respectability, he probably provided Ammianus with material, and himself wrote a history of Rome from Augustus to Julian (360) in the form of brief imperial biographies.   RJB

Hamilton and Wallace-Hadrill (1986); Pichlmayr (1911).

Aureolus   (d. AD 268), Roman general. Marcus Aelius Aureolus, a cavalry general under GALLIENUS, helped the latter crush the usurper Ingenuus at Mursa (258–9), and also dealt with MACRIANUS and his father (261). Left in charge of Italy while Gallienus campaigned against the GOTHS, Aureolus revolted (268), but was driven back into Milan. Gallienus was murdered during the ensuing siege, but Aureolus was obliged to surrender to the new emperor CLAUDIUS II and was put to death.   RJB

Grant (1985); Parker (1958).

Ausonius   (*c*.AD 310–95), Latin poet. Decimus Magnus Ausonius was born at Bordeaux and educated there and in Toulouse. After 30 years as a teacher of rhetoric at Bordeaux, he was summoned to the imperial court at Trier to teach GRATIAN, son of the emperor Valentinian. With Gratian's accession in AD 375 he entered public life, becoming praetorian prefect of Gaul and later consul. After Gratian's murder in 383 he retired to Bordeaux. His poetry was voluminous and earned admiration at court and in literary circles at Rome. Much of it survives, perhaps the best being the *Mosella*, a description of the river in 483 hexameters. Other works include epigrams, eulogies (*see* PANEGYRIC), and letters to PAULINUS of Nola.   GS

Binns (1974); Matthews (1990).

Auspicium in Roman divination, a sign sent by the gods to indicate approval or disapproval of a proposed human action. Such signs were thought to be present in the behaviour of animals (especially, but not exclusively, the flight of birds) and in other natural phenomena. The 'public auspices' of the Roman state were taken by senior magistrates in consultation with the AUGURES, and any major public event, such as an election or a military campaign, was said to take place 'under the auspices' of the magistrate who conducted it.   TC

Dumézil (1970); Linderski (1986).

Auxilia Roman auxiliaries. *Auxilia* were non-citizen troops recruited from outside Italy: units included both infantry and cavalry, and specialists such as archers and slingers. Under the Empire these war bands, led by their own tribal leaders, were gradually transformed: infantry were organized into *cohortes*, cavalry into *alae*, normally 500 or 1,000 strong, commanded by equestrian prefects, and there were also some mixed units (*cohortes equitatae*). Many units were stationed close to home, but after the revolt of CIVILIS (AD 69) were more frequently posted abroad. Local recruiting continued, so that many units changed markedly in character. Auxiliaries, normally discharged after 25 years' service, were then granted CITIZENSHIP, a privilege which up to AD 140 included their descendants, so that their citizen offspring could enter the legions. On Trajan's Column auxiliaries are fighting in much the same manner as the legionaries, and the distinction between them was largely lost after Caracalla's (*see* AURELIUS ANTONINUS) general extension of citizenship.
  See also ARMY, ROMAN.   RJB

Connolly (1981).

Aventine part of Rome. One of the hills of Rome, the Aventine lay to the south of the city centre, overlooking the TIBER to the north-west and the Forum Boarium to the north. To its north-east it was separated from the PALATINE by the Murcia valley, eventual site of the Circus Maximus. It was enclosed within the WALL OF SERVIUS but excluded from the POMERIUM.

The hill itself had strong Latin connections and was the site of a Latin temple to DIANA as early as the 6th century BC, and later temples to Juno, Jupiter, and Mercury. Under AUGUSTUS it formed *regio* xiii of Rome, while an eastern outcrop formed *regio* xii and was known as 'little Aventine'.

See also ROME, TOPOGRAPHY.   HE

Platner and Ashby (1929); Richardson (1992); Robinson (1992).

Avidius Cassius (d. AD 175), Roman general. Avidius Cassius, son of Heliodorus (a Syrian orator), was VERUS' chief commander during the Parthian War, remained in Syria as governor, and was made commander-in-chief of the east by Marcus AURELIUS. In 175 Cassius rebelled, encouraged, according to DIO, by the empress FAUSTINA. Cassius posed a serious threat, holding Syria and Egypt (chief source of Rome's grain), but was murdered after three months, before Aurelius could move against him.   RJB

Millar (1981); Parker (1958).

Avitus (d. AD 456), western Roman emperor, 455–6. Marcus Maecilius Flavius Eparchius Avitus, AETIUS' Prefect of Gaul, made peace with THEODORIC (436), and gained Theodoric's aid against ATTILA (451). After the deaths of VALENTINIAN III and PETRONIUS MAXIMUS (455), and the VANDAL invasion of Rome, Avitus was declared emperor in Gaul (July 455). Despite military successes, Avitus was unpopular in Rome, and rebellion led by RICIMER and MAJORIAN led to his deposition (October 456), shortly before his death.   RJB

Bury (1958); Grant (1985).

B

Babylon city in Mesopotamia. Babylon had been the capital of southern Mesopotamia since the reign of Hammurabi (1792–1750 BC). It was rebuilt by Nebuchadnezzar II (604–562 BC) whose embellishments included the wondrous Hanging Gardens. It fell to the Persians in 539 and was the Great King's winter residence. It was described by HERODOTUS who visited c.450. ALEXANDER THE GREAT took it in 331 and died there in 323. It lost its primacy when SELEUCUS I NICATOR moved his capital to SELEUCEIA ON TIGRIS.   GS

Roaf (1990).

Bacchanalia rites in honour of Bacchus (DIONYSUS), performed by women in secret and at night. Greek in origin, the worship arrived in Rome from south Italy. Although long accepted by the Romans, in 186 BC, after men had been admitted to the rites and allegations of immorality and crime had prompted fears for public safety, Bacchic worship was suppressed throughout Rome and Italy by a still extant decree of the Senate.   DP

North (1979).

Bacchiads see CORINTH.

Bacchus see BACCHANALIA; DIONYSUS.

Bacchylides (c.510–c.450 BC), Greek lyric poet. A native of Ceos, Bacchylides was invited with his uncle SIMONIDES to Syracuse by HIERON I in the 470s, and was later exiled from Ceos to the Peloponnese. A papyrus discovered in 1896 preserves 20 poems almost complete, a mixture of victory odes (similar but inferior to those of his contemporary and rival PINDAR) and dithyrambs on mythological subjects. His hymns, songs, and love poems are lost.   GS

Bowra (1964); Calder and Stern (1970).

Bactria satrapy of the Persian empire. Bactria included the territory of northern Afghanistan and Central Asia. It was a satrapy under the ACHAEMENIDS, was conquered with difficulty by ALEXANDER THE GREAT, and was Seleucid until the revolt of DIODOTUS I, who declared independence. ANTIOCHUS III THE GREAT was forced to confirm EUTHYDEMUS as legitimate king, and the kingdom of the Bactrian Indo-Greeks grew large and powerful. Its chief city was Bactra, and an important Greek city was found at Aï Khanum.

See also DEMETRIUS I OF BACTRIA; MENANDER; ROXANE.   EER

CAH VIII; Eddy (1961); Frye (1984); Holt (1988); Narain (1957); Tarn (1984); Woodcock (1966); Yarshater (1983).

Baetica region in southern SPAIN. When the province of Further Spain was divided in two by AUGUSTUS in 27 BC, Baetica, the more civilized southern half, was assigned to the Senate, while the emperor retained control of LUSITANIA. The principal administrative centres were Gades, Hispalis, Astigi, and Corduba. Latin rights (see IUS LATII) were enjoyed by many towns, and the Guadalquivir valley developed a wealthy economy and a cultured society.   GS

Keay (1988).

Balbinus (c.AD 170–238), Roman emperor, 238. Decius Caelius Calvinus Balbinus, an experienced senator of distinguished family, was declared co-emperor with PUPIENUS by the Senate after the death of GORDIAN I (238). Balbinus was civil head while Pupienus commanded the army. The opposition of the army and common people necessitated the elevation of GORDIAN III, grandson of Gordian I, as Caesar: this was insufficient, however, to save Balbinus and Pupienus, who were murdered by the Praetorian Guard.   RJB

Grant (1985); Parker (1958).

Balbus (fl. 70–40 BC), agent of Caesar. Lucius Cornelius Balbus, a native of Gades (Cadiz), was brought to Rome in 60 BC by Julius CAESAR, whom he served as secretary and agent. He tried to attach CICERO to the First TRIUMVIRATE in 60, and in the 50s 'there can have been few intrigues conducted . . . without the . . . mediation of Balbus' (Syme). In 56 he was successfully defended by Cicero when his enemies contested the citizenship given him by POMPEY in 72. After Caesar's death he transferred his services as agent to Octavian, and in 40 he became Rome's first foreign-born consul. On his death he left the citizens as much money as had Julius Caesar. DP

Syme (1939).

Ballista *see* SIEGECRAFT, ROMAN.

Banking Banking in early Greece was a monopoly of the temples: individuals could both deposit and borrow money on interest from priests. But in the 5th century BC much of the business was taken over by money-changers (*trapezitae*) who set up 'tables' in public places and operated a system based not on COINAGE but on letters of credit. A third system of banking was adopted by certain cities, notably Cos and Miletus, whose financial transactions were so complicated that they needed professional fund managers. These specialists worked with the mints and the administration to create city banks which in some places had a banking monopoly.

All three systems continued to operate in the Hellenistic world, but Ptolemaic Egypt developed a unique system of its own. A central state bank was opened in Alexandria which had branches all over the country. It was like a Greek city bank but on a much larger scale. It had custody of both public and private funds and was responsible for the collection and distribution of state revenues. It remained in operation during the period of Roman rule.

In the Republican period banking at Rome was controlled by small firms run by *equites* and merchants rather than professional bankers. Bills of exchange obviated the transfer of actual cash and facilitated payments both to and from the provinces. This system spread throughout the empire, but the business of lending was gradually lost to the owners of large estates. After the collapse of the COINAGE in the 3rd century AD banking became a government monopoly.

See also FINANCE. GS

Rostovtzeff (1941, 1957).

Barbarians For the Greeks 'barbarians' were all those who did not speak Greek (but said 'barbar . . .'). After the Persian Wars the word was used especially of the Medes and Persians, and it also acquired the connotation of 'brutal, uncultivated'. The Romans too applied the word to foreigners in general and to Persians in particular. After the Augustan age they used it of any hostile people, especially the German tribes. GS

Bar-Kochba (d. AD 135), Jewish leader. Simon Ben Koziba or Bar-Kochba ('Son of the Star') led a Jewish revolt (AD 132–5) precipitated by HADRIAN's decision to build a colony, Aelia Capitolina, on the site of JERUSALEM, destroyed by Titus in AD 70. Bar-Kochba succeeded in taking Jerusalem, but the city fell to Sextus Julius Severus (134) and was again destroyed. The rebellion brought disaster upon the JEWS, and irrevocable separation between Judaism and Christianity.   RJB

Perowne (1960); Salmon (1968); Wells (1984).

Basilica Replacing the STOA in the Greek AGORA, the basilica, an aisled hall, became an essential adjunct of the Roman FORUM. As a public building, often with an apse at one end or at both, it served a variety of purposes. The earliest known example was built at Rome in 184 BC and took the form of a long covered hall with a timber roof supported on columns. It provided facilities for commerce, assembly, and legal proceedings. The word was later extended to cover any large hall in a commercial, domestic, military, or religious context. The basilica was the architectural forebear of the earliest churches at Rome when CHRISTIANITY first showed its face.   GS

Coulton (1976); Ward-Perkins (1977).

Basil the Great, St (c.AD 330–79), bishop of Caesarea in Cappadocia. Basil was the brother of St GREGORY OF NYSSA and friend of St GREGORY OF NAZIANZUS. All three were Cappadocians by birth and their influence combined to defeat the heresy of ARIANISM at the Council of Constantinople in 381. Basil became a hermit in 358 and devised the monastic rule which is still observed in the Eastern Orthodox Church. In 370 he succeeded EUSEBIUS as bishop of Caesarea where he died. Sermons, letters, and tracts survive, including an essay on the value of pagan literature.   GS

Cross (1974); Kazhdan (1991).

Bassae In terms of its location, decoration, and state of preservation, the temple of Apollo at Bassae is one of the finest surviving examples of a Greek temple. Designed by ICTINUS, the architect of the PARTHENON, it has a Doric peristyle but a *cella* lined with engaged Ionic columns and a single free-standing Corinthian column (perhaps the earliest example) in the centre. The frieze (now in the British Museum) ran continuously around the inside of the *cella*.   GS

Lawrence (1984); Stillwell (1976).

Bastarnae Germanic people. The Bastarnae suddenly appeared north of the Danube c.200 BC, threatening the Greek cities of the Black Sea coast. PLAUTIUS SILVANUS AELIANUS made peace with the Bastarnae (AD 60s), and by Domitian's day they seem to have been confined to an area well north of the Danube. PROBUS (276–82) settled 100,000 Bastarnae within the Roman empire, in Thrace (but had difficulty in controlling them), and DIOCLETIAN settled others in Pannonia.   RJB

Mommsen (1968); Salmon (1968); Todd (1975).

Batavi   Germanic people. The Batavi, settled on the Rhine delta, were incorporated into the Roman empire c.12 BC. They paid no taxes, but provided soldiers: in AD 68 the Batavian cohorts (imperial bodyguard) contributed to NERO's downfall. In 69 the Batavians, led by CIVILIS, revolted, and although at first claiming to support VESPASIAN, sought their independence. They were joined by most of the German peoples, but were finally quelled by Petilius Cerialis (70).   RJB

Millar (1981); Thompson (1965).

Baths   The bath complex was one of the most characteristic features of Roman architecture and society. The earliest known example was built at POMPEII in the early 1st century BC and none existed in Rome until about 20 BC. But in the imperial period the fashion spread rapidly throughout the provinces until no community was without at least one, and most private residences had their own domestic facilities. There was considerable variation in size and layout, but the essential elements of the baths were a hot room (*caldarium*), a warm room (*tepidarium*), and a cold room (*frigidarium*). Common additions were a room for changing (*apodyterium*), an area for exercise (*palaestra*), and a swimming pool (*natatio*). Further attachments might include GARDENS, meeting rooms, libraries, and lecture theatres. Structurally, the development of the baths was made possible by the availability of concrete and the vaulted arch. Architecturally, the plan, exemplified by the baths of Trajan, Caracalla, and Diocletian in Rome, was generally symmetrical, externally austere, but internally ornate. Culturally, the baths provided a leisure centre that was widely enjoyed by all classes of society. Their endowment offered the wealthy conspicuous opportunities for public munificence. In the eastern provinces they usurped the role of the Hellenistic GYMNASIUM.   GS

Ward-Perkins (1977).

Bee-keeping   Bees were valued by the ancients both for their honey, which had the importance of sugar today, and for their wax. Bee-keeping was therefore an important ingredient of the ancient economy: it was widely practised throughout the Mediterranean region and carefully studied by scholars. It was regulated by law at Athens and subjected to special taxes in several cities. Areas famed for honey production included Attica, Thasos, Cos, Rhodes, Lycia, Caria, Cyprus, Syria, Sicily, and southern Spain. ARISTOTLE studied bees scientifically. Other writers on the subject included COLUMELLA, HYGINUS, NICANDER, the elder PLINY, VARRO, and VIRGIL.

See also FOOD AND DRINK.   GS

Rostovtzeff (1941, 1957).

Belgae Gallic confederation. The Belgae were a warlike confederation of tribes who lived between the rivers Rhine and Loire. Some Belgic tribes, such as the Atrebates, had territory in southern Britain. The Belgae opposed CAESAR in 57 BC but were outmanoeuvred and defeated piecemeal, although the Roman victory was incomplete. In 56 the Morini and Menapii aided the VENETI, in 54 the Eburones ambushed and destroyed one of Caesar's legions, and in 52 the Belgae joined VERCINGETORIX. After Vercingetorix's defeat Commius, chief of the Atrebates, fled to Britain, where he strengthened his territory in Sussex and Hampshire with survivors of the Gaulish Atrebates.

See also GERMANI.   LPR

Chadwick (1970).

Bellum Africum a Roman historical work that covers CAESAR's campaign in Africa of 47–46 BC. The author, who is unlikely to be the same as the author of either the BELLUM ALEXANDRINUM or the BELLUM HISPANIENSE, appears to have been an eye-witness, but is unaware of the reasons for strategic or tactical decisions, which suggests that he was a junior officer. Despite attempted fine writing, the text is somewhat monotonous.

See also THAPSUS.   HS

Bellum Alexandrinum a Roman historical work which continued CAESAR's commentaries on the CIVIL WAR from where they stopped in Alexandria to the battle of ZELA. The author is unknown, but since antiquity he has often been considered to have been Hirtius, one of Caesar's officers and consul in 43 BC, who added an eighth book to Caesar's commentaries on the GALLIC WARS.

See also BELLUM AFRICUM; BELLUM HISPANIENSE.   HS

Bellum Hispaniense a Roman historical work dealing with CAESAR's Spanish campaign which culminated at MUNDA. The author, seemingly an eye-witness, appears barely literate, although he attempts to lift his prose, and is thus extremely unlikely to be the same as the author of either the BELLUM AFRICUM or the BELLUM ALEXANDRINUM.   HS

Berenice (b. AD 28), daughter of AGRIPPA I. Berenice, eldest daughter of Agrippa I of Judaea, married her uncle Herod, king of Chalcis, and bore him two sons. She then became queen to her brother, Agrippa II, before marrying King Polemon of Cilicia, whom she deserted to return to Agrippa. Berenice opposed the Roman massacre of the Jews (AD 65), but supported Rome during the first Jewish revolt. She became TITUS' mistress, but was eventually repudiated to satisfy Roman prejudices.

RJB

Bowersock (1983).

Berenice I (c.340–c.275 BC), queen of Egypt. Berenice, a Macedonian widow, was the second wife (and perhaps a relative) of PTOLEMY I, supplanting as queen her relation Eurydice whom she had accompanied to Egypt. Their son PTOLEMY II inherited the throne, eventually ruling jointly with their daughter ARSINOË II. Berenice's previous children include MAGAS of Cyrene and a wife of PYRRHUS of Epirus. Berenice was posthumously deified, and worshipped with her husband.   EER

CAH VII.1; Fraser (1972); Macurdy (1932).

Berenice II Euergetis (c.273–221 BC), queen of Egypt. Berenice, 'the benefactor', the daughter of MAGAS of Cyrene, was betrothed to the future PTOLEMY III whom she married (after various vicissitudes) upon his accession in 246 BC. A constellation was named the 'Lock of Berenice' in honour of the hair she dedicated to ensure Ptolemy's safe return from a war in support of BERENICE SYRA. After Ptolemy III's death she ruled jointly with her son PTOLEMY IV, but was murdered probably with his connivance.   EER

CAH VII.1; Fraser (1972); Macurdy (1932).

Berenice Syra (c.280–c.246 BC), Seleucid queen. Berenice 'the Syrian' was the daughter of PTOLEMY II and ARSINOË I. In a political alliance she was married to the Seleucid ANTIOCHUS II THEOS, who renounced his queen, LAODICE I, and established Berenice at Antioch. When Antiochus died, Berenice's brother PTOLEMY III invaded Syria to support the claims of her son to the Seleucid throne, but Laodice murdered mother and child before help arrived. In revenge, Ptolemy III waged the Third Syrian War against Laodice's son SELEUCUS II CALLINICUS.   EER

CAH VII.1; Green (1990); Macurdy (1932).

Berlin Painter (fl. 500–480 BC), Greek vase painter. The Berlin Painter is named after a tall amphora in Berlin that illustrates Hermes and two satyrs. Nearly 300 vases have been ascribed to him, though none is signed. His preference was for large pots, and he painted both black-figure and red-figure Panathenaic amphorae as well as many other shapes. His favourite subjects were gods, heroes, and athletes.

GS

Arias and Hirmer (1962); Kurtz (1983).

Bibulus (fl. 65–48 BC), Roman politician. Marcus Calpurnius Bibulus, the husband of CATO's daughter Porcia, tried as consul in 59 BC to veto the agrarian laws of his colleague Caesar. On being forcibly prevented, he withdrew to his house where he tried to make Caesar's subsequent laws invalid by watching for omens. In 52 he proposed Pompey's election as sole consul, and in 51 he governed Syria. He worried himself to death, trying to prevent Caesar's fleet crossing to Epirus in the winter of 49–48.

DP

Gruen (1974); Taylor (1949).

Biography, Greek As a discrete literary form, biography was a late developer in the ancient world. Character sketches had appeared in prose since Herodotus, and there are passages in Thucydides that are quite close to the genre. Isocrates and Xenophon developed the art of the prose encomium, and the PERIPATETICS, writing in the wake of Aristotle, produced biography of a sort, devoid of any critical awareness and based on scandal, legend, and polemic. In the 3rd century BC Antigonus of Carystus wrote about his contemporaries with a new sense of realism, and the Alexandrians added biographical data to their researches. But it was not until PLUTARCH, writing in the early 2nd century AD, that the art of biography (which he distinguished from history) really flowered, bringing together psychological and dramatic interests to produce a text that is informative, readable, and edifying.

See also DIOGENES LAERTIUS; HISTORIOGRAPHY, GREEK.

GS

Momigliano (1971); Russell (1973).

Biography, Latin The writing of biography at Rome was as much indebted to native traditions of composing obituaries and eulogies in praise of famous men as it was to Greek models. The biographical element is often central to CICERO's speeches, as is the autobiographical to the memoirs of such Republican figures as C. Gracchus and Sulla and, later, members of the imperial family such as Augustus, Tiberius, Hadrian, and Severus. Encomiastic biography developed from nostalgic opposition to the early Principate (exemplified by studies of the younger Cato by Brutus and Cicero) to TACITUS' life of his father-in-law Agricola. NEPOS was perhaps the first at Rome to imitate the Hellenistic Greek biographers and produce *Lives* that were uncritical but full of antiquarian interest. Similar interests inspired SUETONIUS who had access to imperial files and correspondence and wrote of his subjects as private individuals. He was imitated by the author(s) of the HISTORIA AUGUSTA.

See also HISTORIOGRAPHY, ROMAN; JEROME. GS

Dorey (1967); Geiger (1985); Momigliano (1971).

Bion (2nd–1st century BC), of Smyrna, Greek poet. Bion spent most of his life in Sicily and followed THEOCRITUS and MOSCHUS in the tradition of pastoral poetry. Seventeen short poems (most of them erotic, not all of them complete) are preserved by Stobaeus. The 98-line *Lament for Adonis*, a passionate song written to be recited, may also be ascribed to him. GS

Webster (1964).

Bion of Borysthenes (*c.*325–*c.*255 BC), Greek philosopher. Born into slavery, Bion was later set free and inherited his master's fortune. He went to Athens and studied at the Academy under XENOCRATES and at the Lyceum under THEOPHRASTUS. He was, however, more strongly influenced by CRATES OF THEBES, the Cynic, and by the atheist and hedonist Theodorus. He adopted the CYNICS' caustic humour, shamelessness, and criticism of convention. Happiness, he believed, was attained by adapting to circumstances. He travelled from place to place lecturing for a fee. JL

Kindstrand (1976).

Birthdays In classical Greece the birth of a child was an occasion for family and friends to make visits and offer gifts to the child, but the subsequent anniversary of the event seems not to have been celebrated. In the Hellenistic world rulers marked the anniversary of their birthday with a feast, though this may have been more directly related to the award of divine or heroic honours. Only in Roman times did the practice of celebrating birthdays by giving presents become universal through all strata of society. Not only individuals, but cities and institutions were honoured on their anniversary, which was an occasion for paying respect to their guardian spirit or *genius*. The 1,000th birthday of Rome was celebrated by the emperor PHILIP I on 21 April AD 248.

See also GAMES, ROMAN. GS

Bithynia   territory in Asia Minor. Bithynia lies on the south-west shore of the Black Sea in northern Asia Minor. Held only tenuously by the ACHAEMENIDS and ALEXANDER THE GREAT, Bithynia became independent when the Thracian Zipoetes proclaimed himself king in 297/6 BC. By a combination of expansion and diplomacy the kings maintained themselves against the Seleucids, PONTUS, PERGAMUM, and GALATIA. They founded many cities. NICOMEDES IV bequeathed his kingdom to Rome in 75/4, and in 64 POMPEY created the Roman province of Bithynia and Pontus (PLINY THE YOUNGER was governor under TRAJAN during a period of severe financial mismanagement). It became an imperial province under Marcus AURELIUS.   EER

CAH VII.1, VIII; Eddy (1961); Gruen (1984); Jones (1983); Magie (1975); Sherwin-White (1984); Sullivan (1990).

Biton   see CLEOBIS AND BITON.

Black-figure   see PAINTING, GREEK.

Boadicea   see BOUDICCA.

Boeotia   region in central Greece between Attica and Phocis with sea coasts on both the Gulf of Corinth and the Straits of Euboea. Its hinterland offered rich farming land, divided into two plains by Lake Copais, the western dominated by Orchomenos and the eastern by THEBES. The people spoke an Aeolic dialect and were regarded as slow by other Greeks. Similarities in coinage suggest that some progress towards Boeotian unity was made in the 6th century BC but it was not until 447 that the BOEOTIAN CONFEDERACY was formed. Boeotians took no part in Greek expansion overseas but made significant contributions to music and poetry.
See also TERRACOTTA.   GS

Buck (1979); Larsen (1968).

Boeotian   see DIALECTS, GREEK.

Boeotian Confederacy   After defeating Athens at Coronea (447 BC) THEBES established a federal constitution for BOEOTIA, described by the OXYRHYNCHUS HISTORIAN under the year 395 BC. Of the 11 'divisions', each providing one Boeotarch, 60 councillors for the federal council, and 1,000 hoplites and 100 cavalry for the army, Thebes predominated with four. Citizenship was based on property. Each division had four councils, each in turn serving as probouleutic to the whole. There was one central council (*pace* Thucydides 5.38). The confederacy, dissolved in 386 under the King's Peace, was refounded after 378 with the seemingly more democratic constitution of a federal general assembly, but it increasingly served Theban interests. It continued into the Roman period. GLC

Larsen (1968).

Boii Gallic people. The Boii settled around Bononia (Bologna) in the late 5th century BC. Together with the Insubres they invaded Italy but were defeated at Telamon in 225 BC by the Romans. In 218 they supported HANNIBAL, and fought on until 192. Another branch of the Boii lived in Bohemia, but were driven out by BUREBISTAS in 50 BC, when they joined the HELVETII. After Caesar's victory they were allowed to settle in Aeduan territory. LPR

Chilver (1941).

Bononia city in Italy. Bononia, modern Bologna, occupies a vital strategic site at the foot of the Apennines and controls the route from peninsular Italy to the Po valley. Possibly the oldest city in Europe, it was a flourishing VILLANOVAN settlement, dating from before 1000 BC. Around 500 BC it was taken over by the ETRUSCANS, who called it Felsina. By 350 BC, however, the Etruscans had been driven out by invading Gauls, and the city became the capital of the BOII. When the Romans conquered the region in the 190s, they founded the Latin colony of Bononia (191 BC), which was to become one of the most prosperous cities in the empire, and has flourished ever since. TC

Scullard (1967); Stillwell (1976).

Books, Greek In the 5th century BC there was a bookstall in the Athenian market and a copy of Anaxagoras cost one drachma. Before that, PEISISTRATUS is said to have ordered the writing down of the works of Homer in the mid-6th century; but there was probably no large-scale copying or circulation of texts until EDUCATION created a demand for the poets and philosophers. In the Hellenistic period books were much more freely available and private individuals were able to form their own LIBRARIES.

The first books were in fact rolls, made from strips of the papyrus plant that grew (almost exclusively) in the Nile delta. The text was written in vertical columns, which the reader gradually unwound from one roll and wound up on the other. Given that there was no word division and some texts were more than 20 feet long, reading was a cumbersome business. The Egyptian monopoly created problems and an interruption of the supply of papyrus necessitated the development of an alternative: at Pergamum animal skins were treated to make parchment (or vellum). This, together with the introduction of the codex (or bound book of leaves as we know it) after the 2nd century AD, revolutionized publishing and reading.

See also SCHOLARSHIP, GREEK.   GS

Lewis (1974); Reynolds and Wilson (1991); Roberts and Skeat (1983); Wilson (1983).

Books, Latin Books were in general circulation at Rome by the 1st century BC when we hear of booksellers such as the Sosii and publishers such as ATTICUS. Large private LIBRARIES were already in existence, but the first public library was founded in 39 BC by C. Asinius POLLIO; two more were founded by Augustus, and throughout the empire libraries became a feature of private and imperial opulence. The copying of texts and the mechanics of book production were done by slaves whose carelessness vexed Cicero. Authors enjoyed no copyright protection or royalty terms so the role of a literary patron such as MAECENAS was all the more important. In the early Empire books became fashionable items for collectors but were also in demand for educational purposes. The establishment of a core curriculum for schools ensured a demand for, and therefore the survival of, a canon of standard texts. Nevertheless circulation remained relatively limited and a writer's fame spread through public recitations much more than by the sale of texts.   GS

Quinn (1979); Reynolds and Wilson (1991).

Botany Plants provide a major part of human food, drink, medicine, and materials in everyday use. Thus some knowledge of them goes back to prehistoric times. Popular interest, frequently shrouded in superstition, is evidenced in the earliest Greek literature. Rational study of plants, however, begins with the Presocratic philosophers. EMPEDOCLES speculated about the sex and growth of trees, and Menestor based his botanical theory upon the dualism of hot and cold. Although some 300 herbal drugs are mentioned in the Hippocratic Corpus, little information is provided about the plants themselves. *Nature of the Child*, however, does discuss in detail germination of seeds and growth of plants and provides an early attempt at a vegetable physiology.

Botany began to emerge as a separate science in the second half of the 4th century BC when it engaged the interest of the ACADEMY. More interest is displayed in the Lyceum. ARISTOTLE regarded plants as being of a lower order than animals, possessing only the three lowest faculties of soul, nutrition and growth, and reproduction. Although there are numerous botanical passages in his work, there are no detailed studies to match those in his zoological works. His philosophical outlook, however, underlies THEOPHRASTUS' two botanical works, *History of Plants* and *Causes of Plants*, which represent antiquity's highest achievement in botany. Later writers derived much of their botanical knowledge from Theophrastus.

The herbals of DIOCLES, Crateuas, and DIOSCORIDES are also important for the history of botany. Crateuas incorporated coloured illustrations of plants along with descriptions of their medical use. Dioscorides used this work as a source for his influential *Materia Medica*. After Dioscorides, although GALEN emphasized the medical importance of botanical knowledge, there were no significant advances in botany in classical antiquity.

See also FOOD AND DRINK; MEDICINE.   JL

Sarton (1970).

Boudicca (d. AD 61), queen of the Iceni, British people. Boudicca, widow of King Prasutagus, led the Iceni in revolt against Rome, for on Prasutagus' death (AD 60/1), officials acted to absorb his kingdom, scourged Boudicca, and raped her daughters. Boudicca was joined by the Trinovantes, and they overwhelmed Colchester and sacked London and VERULAMIUM. The governor SUETONIUS PAULINUS, however, returned from Wales, and Boudicca's forces were routed somewhere in the Midlands. Boudicca appears to have escaped, but poisoned herself.

RJB

Salway (1981); Scullard (1979); Webster (1978).

Boule Athenian council. The Boule was the most important administrative body at Athens. SOLON instituted a tribal council of 400 members, but the Council under the democracy was the work of CLEISTHENES. Its 500 members were chosen by lot, 50 per tribe, from the DEMES by a system of quotas proportional to population; none served more than twice, and not in consecutive years. Each tribal contingent served for one-tenth of the conciliar year as the executive committee (*see* PRYTANIS) which summoned meetings and prepared business; the Boule was required to meet daily, except for holidays, normally in the Bouleuterion, the state council building.

The Boule's most important function was to prepare business for the assembly (ECCLESIA): no question could be discussed there without prior consideration by the Boule. In some cases the Council presented a detailed proposal, which might be modified, but in others it simply raised a matter and invited proposals and debate from the floor.

It also performed a range of administrative functions, including oversight of public buildings and sanctuaries, the navy and dockyards, and the cavalry, and in these limited capacities it might issue decrees of its own. Most significantly, it oversaw foreign policy, because of the frequency of its meetings and its greater confidentiality, and the state finances. Much of this administrative work was actually discharged by committees answering to the Boule. Its judicial powers included over-sight and scrutiny of magistrates and officials; but it could normally impose only limited penalties, and cases were often referred to the courts.

RB

Hansen (1991); Rhodes (1972).

Boxing *see* GAMES, GREEK.

Brasidas (*c*.472–422 BC), Spartan leader. Brasidas was devoted to utterly defeating Athens and liberating her subject cities. As ephor in 431/30 he probably urged rejection of Athenian peace offers and is constantly associated with efforts to break the strategic deadlock. In 424 he took an army, largely of helots (*see* SERFS), to Thrace and liberated a number of cities including AMPHIPOLIS, where he defeated CLEON. Both men died in the battle.

GLC

Kagan (1975).

Brennus (4th century BC), Gallic chief. According to LIVY, Brennus led a Celtic warband, the SENONES, into peninsular Italy in 390 BC. He routed a Roman army at the river Allia and captured Rome, although the CAPITOL was saved by MANLIUS. He demanded 1,000 pounds of gold to withdraw and, when the Romans objected to the weights, he threw his sword into the scales saying '*vae victis*' ('woe to the vanquished').

LPR

CAH VII.2; Cottrell (1960).

Brennus (3rd century BC), Gallic chieftain. Brennus led a Galatian invasion into Greece in 279 BC, overrunning Macedonia after killing PTOLEMY CERAUNUS. Stopped at THERMOPYLAE by a Greek coalition, Brennus drew away the Aetolians by sending a secondary force to attack Aetolia, turned the pass, and attacked DELPHI during a ferocious snowstorm. When Brennus was wounded, the Gauls retreated north and were harassed by the Thessalians. He killed himself in despair, and the Greek victory passed into legend.

EER

Hammond and Walbank (1988); Hubert (1987); Rankin (1987).

Bridges *see* ARCHITECTURE, ROMAN.

Brigantes British people. The Brigantes, a federation of upland peoples, occupied most of northern England, and were, according to TACITUS, the largest tribe in Britain. In the early years of Roman occupation the client kingdom of Brigantia, under Queen Cartimandua, provided a northern buffer for the province, but in the AD 70s it was conquered by Cerialis and AGRICOLA. By the early 2nd century AD the Brigantian capital was Aldborough (Isurium Brigantum).   RJB

Hartley (1988); Salway (1981); Scullard (1979).

Britain as a Roman province. Britain was first invaded by the Romans under Julius CAESAR (55, 54 BC). He defeated Cassivellaunus and con-quered south-east Britain, but then withdrew. In AD 43 CLAUDIUS I invaded, and south-east Britain was organized as a Roman province. Aulus PLAUTIUS (43–7) extended occupation to the Severn and the Wash, and OSTORIUS SCAPULA (47–52) defeated CARATACUS. The revolt of BOUDICCA (601) was put down by SUETONIUS PAULINUS. Under Petilius Cerialis (71–4), FRONTINUS (74–8), and AGRICOLA (78–84), the advance was con-tinued. However, under TRAJAN the Tyne–Solway line became the effective northern frontier, soon marked by the WALL OF HADRIAN (al-though under Antoninus Pius the frontier was briefly advanced to the WALL OF ANTONINUS on the Forth–Clyde line).

Under Virius Lupus (197–202) Britain was divided into two prov-inces (reducing the power of the governor, who had hitherto com-manded three legions), and further subdivided into four by Diocletian. In the later 3rd century a series of Shore Forts was constructed to guard against increasing Saxon piracy. In the 4th century JULIAN sent Lupicinus to contain barbarian unrest (360), and a major raid in 367 required rebuilding by Count Theodosius (369). Roman occupation formally ended in 410, when Honorius told the Britons to arrange their own defence against Saxon invasion, and an appeal to AETIUS (446) was unavailing.

Britain was prosperous for long periods: the economy was princi-pally agricultural, but the Romans exploited mineral wealth, particu-larly LEAD. British exports included hunting dogs, and bears for the Roman arena; the *birrus Britannicus,* a hooded cloak of goats' hair; and the *tapete Britannicum,* a woollen blanket.

See also CARAUSIUS; CLODIUS ALBINUS; CONSTANS; CONSTANTIUS I; EBURACUM; GALLIC EMPIRE; LONDINIUM; MAGNENTIUS; Magnus MAXIMUS; Septimius SEVERUS.   RJB

Salway (1981); Scullard (1979); Wacher (1980).

Britannia *see* BRITAIN.

Bronze The age of bronze had bowed to that of IRON before the start of our period, but the alloy remained in use throughout antiquity for various utilitarian purposes such as domestic utensils, furniture, LAMPS and handles as well as for SCULPTURE, ARMS AND ARMOUR, and COINAGE. COPPER was found not only in CYPRUS but also in Euboea in Greece, in Bruttium, Elba, and Etruria in Italy, and in Spain. TIN was imported from further afield: from Spain, Brittany, and Cornwall. For monumental sculpture, casting by the lost-wax process was the most commonly employed method. Heads and limbs were cast separately and adjusted to fit the body. Ornament was hammered in repoussé and the plates joined together with rivets. Earlier examples were chiselled, wrought, and welded. Bronzes were often gilded or silvered to make them shine, and lacquered for protection. The metal retained its value and was easily melted down, so few statues have survived intact. GS

Charbonneaux (1958); Healy (1978).

Bructeri Germanic people. The Bructeri were settled around the Ems and the upper Lippe (near modern Munster). They submitted to TIBERIUS (AD 5–6) and their territory was laid waste by GERMANICUS (14–15), but they remained free. Bordering on Roman territory, the Bructeri were rapidly involved in the revolt of CIVILIS (69–70), but the suppression of the revolt, and feuds with neighbouring tribes, broke the power of the Bructeri, who troubled the Romans little thereafter. RJB

Millar (1981); Mommsen (1968); Thompson (1965).

Brundisium city in Italy. Brundisium, modern Brindisi, a city of the MESSAPII, lay on the east coast of Italy in Calabria. It was heavily hellenized, but little is known of its history before 244 BC when a Roman colony was established there. Blessed with a good harbour, it formed the eastern end of the Via APPIA and the usual departure point for crossings to Greece and Epirus. HE

Potter (1987).

Bruttii Italian people. The Bruttii inhabited south-west peninsular Italy (modern Calabria, the 'toe'), a region famed for ships' TIMBER. The SABELLI conquered them c.390 BC and introduced the OSCAN language, but the Bruttii rebelled successfully in 356. Having conquered several Greek colonies in the region, they became partly hellenized, leading to their support of PYRRHUS against Rome in the 270s. But after Pyrrhus' defeat Roman punishment involved the loss of some territory. This process was repeated at the end of the 3rd century after the Bruttii supported HANNIBAL in the PUNIC WARS, resulting in a virtual loss of independence.   HE

Potter (1987).

Brutus, Lucius Junius   (6th century BC), founder of the Roman Republic. L. Junius Brutus organized the coup which overthrew his cousin TARQUINIUS SUPERBUS and established the Roman Republic. As one of two newly elected CONSULS in 509 BC he made the people swear never to tolerate a king, and when his sons formed a plot to reinstate Tarquin, he was obliged to execute them. Shortly afterwards he died in battle against the Etruscans. The legend of Lucius Brutus strongly influenced the outlook and behaviour of his descendant, M. Junius BRUTUS, the murderer of Caesar.   TC

Broughton (1951); Ogilvie (1976).

Brutus, Marcus Junius   (85–42 BC), tyrannicide. Marcus Junius Brutus' one known lapse from moral integrity was his extortion of 48 per cent interest on a loan to Cyprian Salamis in 53 BC. Although POMPEY had killed his father in 77 and his mother Servilia had been Caesar's lover, Brutus joined Pompey in the CIVIL WAR, convinced of the justice of the Republican cause. Caesar pardoned him after PHARSALUS, and he became a humane governor of CISALPINE GAUL in 46. Although *praetor urbanus* in 44, he was persuaded by CASSIUS LONGINUS to follow the example of his reputed ancestor, Lucius Junius BRUTUS, and free Rome from tyranny. He thus became moral leader of the conspiracy that killed Caesar. Forced out of Italy by popular resentment, Brutus and Cassius built up a powerful presence in the east against the Second TRIUMVIRATE, but were defeated at PHILIPPI in 42 BC by the triumviral army under ANTONY, whom the upright Brutus had refused to kill along with Caesar. Brutus and his wife Porcia, CATO's daughter, both committed suicide.   DP

Clarke (1981); Syme (1939).

Brutus Albinus   (d. 43 BC), Roman politician. Decimus Junius Brutus Albinus as a young man commanded victorious fleets for Caesar. But in 44 BC, although Caesar had appointed him governor of CISALPINE GAUL and consul-designate for 42, he joined the conspiracy against him. He was besieged by ANTONY at Mutina in Cisalpine Gaul, and even after the siege had been lifted in April 43, he was forced by the disloyalty of his troops to flee to Macedonia and was killed *en route*.   DP

Syme (1939).

Brygos Painter   (fl. 500–480 BC), Greek vase painter. Brygos was the name of an Athenian potter whose signature is found on 13 cups. Five of these were decorated by the so-called Brygos Painter whose work has been identified on more than 200 vases, most of them cups. His subjects included dynamic representation of revelry and battle, as well as more traditional mythological scenes.   GS

Arias and Hirmer (1962); Boardman (1975).

Bureaucracy, Roman   Under the Republic the SENATE controlled the administration, appointing MAGISTRATES and provincial governors. Most officials were unsalaried, and control of provinces was often haphazard, depending on governors, who often amassed fortunes by plundering their provinces, and on the PUBLICANI, the often corrupt representatives of private corporations.

Under the Empire professional governors, assisted by a professional staff, were more carefully supervised, and financial control was exercised by independent PROCURATORS. A regular civil service was gradually established; the career structures of senators and equestrians were gradually regularized (*see* EQUESTRIAN ORDER); the POSTAL SERVICE (*cursus publicus*) was improved; the FINANCES were reformed and measures taken against the farming of TAXATION. Under CLAUDIUS I (AD 41–54) there was a rapid expansion of the civil service and of a centralized bureaucracy, and in particular of the secretariat, in which the most powerful posts were held by freedmen. HADRIAN (117–38) replaced the freedmen with equestrians, establishing for equestrians the steady career structure already enjoyed by senators. Henceforth civil servants were public servants rather than personal agents of the emperor. Septimius SEVERUS (193–211) reduced the potential power of provincial governors, subdividing provinces and therefore the armies within them. Increasing use was made of equestrian rather than senatorial legionary commanders and governors, particularly by GALLIENUS, beginning a separation of civil and military administration which DIOCLETIAN's reforms almost completed. Diocletian subdivided the provinces still further, and CONSTANTINE I completed the transformation, so that the PRAETORIAN PREFECTS, instead of acting as the emperors' deputies, became the civil administrators of particular portions of the empire.

See also NOTITIA DIGNITATUM.   RJB

Parker (1958); Salmon (1968); Wells (1984).

Burebistas   (1st century BC), Dacian king. Burebistas created a large empire in the mid-1st century BC at the expense of the Celts, Thracians, and Greek cities on the shore of the Black Sea. In the CIVIL WAR, POMPEY negotiated with him. In 44 BC Caesar was preparing to march against

Dacia, but Burebistas was assassinated, and his empire fragmented, before the expedition was sent. Burebistas was advised by a philosopher-wizard called Decaeneus.

See also DECEBALUS.   HS

Burgundians   see GERMANI.

Burial practices, Greek   Both cremation and inhumation were practised by the Greeks throughout antiquity. In Homer the dead were always cremated, perhaps because this was thought to enable the soul to escape the body more rapidly. But regardless of whether it had been burned or not, what mattered most was that the body should receive proper burial rites. This need be no more than the symbolic scattering of a handful of dust. But failure to do this was a serious offence incurring the anger of the deceased, the wrath of the Erinyes (Furies), and pollution of the land. This applied even to enemies of the state. The only exceptions were traitors, suicides, and executed criminals. After burial a period of mourning was observed. Appropriate tribute would be paid to the virtues of the deceased which in the case of those killed in war might take the form of a laudatory funeral oration. Finally a memorial might be commissioned, either monumental or literary. Demonstrations of grief were often lavish, and regular attempts were made at Athens to curb excessive expenditure.

See also AFTERLIFE.   GS

Garland (1985); Kurtz and Boardman (1971); Parker (1983).

Burial practices, Roman   Roman practices were derived partly from Greek and partly from Etruscan models. The choice between cremation and inhumation often depended on economic or practical considerations, but there was a gradual tendency to prefer cremation. The Roman understanding of burial required that no bones should be visible above ground and this encouraged the use of subterranean vaults. Well-to-do families purchased and enclosed a plot outside the city to serve as a burial ground. The site was marked by an architectural monument beneath which the ashes of the dead were buried inside an urn. Communal vaults (or *columbaria*) were available for the urns of poorer people. Despite numerous local variations, a number of types of monumental tomb may be distinguished: large circular mausolea, perhaps inspired by that of AUGUSTUS, rectangular house tombs, altar tombs, tower tombs, and so on (*see also* CATACOMBS; SARCOPHAGI). Roman funerals were often the occasion for great ceremonial display. In the late Empire the traditional funeral oration developed into a new literary genre known as the PANEGYRIC.   GS

Toynbee (1971).

Byzantium   city on the European shore of the Bosphorus, south of the Golden Horn. The original Greek colony was founded in the mid-7th century BC by Megarians, perhaps assisted by Greeks from other cities. After a period under Persian control (512–478 BC) it was an (occasionally rebellious) ally of Athens and stoutly resisted the besieging forces of PHILIP II of Macedon in 340–339. Having suffered repeated attacks from its neighbours in the 3rd century, it supported Rome in the eastern wars, in return for which it was rewarded with Roman protection and privileges. These privileges were lost when it supported PESCENNIUS NIGER against Septimius SEVERUS and was besieged (AD 193–5). Rebuilt by Septimius, the city quickly regained its prosperity. Its strategic location, controlling the entrance to the Black Sea, recommended it to CONSTANTINE I who chose it as the site for his New Rome. After its dedication in 330 it became known as CONSTANTINOPLE.

GS

Stillwell (1976).

C

Caecilius Statius   (d. 168 BC), Latin comic poet. Caecilius Statius was brought to Rome as a prisoner of war from northern Italy *c*.222 BC and subsequently freed. He associated with ENNIUS and was regarded as the best comic writer of his day. He wrote for the masses, and his plays were still performed in Cicero's day. His debt to MENANDER is demonstrated by GELLIUS who quotes several passages alongside their Greek originals.

See *also* COMEDY, ROMAN.   GS

Beare (1964); Wright (1974).

Caecina Alienus   (d. AD 79), Roman soldier. Aulus Caecina Alienus supported the unsuccessful rebellion of VINDEX in AD 68, and in the following year, with Fabius VALENS, supported VITELLIUS against OTHO in his successful bid for the throne, defeating Otho's forces near Cremona. He then deserted to the cause of VESPASIAN (also 69), but in 79 was involved in a plot against Vespasian with EPRIUS MARCELLUS, which was rapidly suppressed by TITUS, and Caecina himself was executed.   RJB

Grant (1979); Salmon (1968); Wellesley (1975).

Caecina Severus   (d. after AD 21), Roman soldier. Aulus Caecina Severus, a military commander of great experience, served under both Augustus and Tiberius. As legate of Moesia, he helped TIBERIUS quell a major revolt in Pannonia and Dalmatia (AD 6–9), and he was GERMANICUS' second-in-command during the campaigns on the Rhine frontier (14–16) following Varus' disaster (9). Harassed by the Cherusci under ARMINIUS, he successfully extricated his forces (15), and was voted an honorary triumph in that year.   RJB

Grant (1971c); Salmon (1968); Scullard (1982).

Caelius (82–48 BC), Roman orator and politician. Marcus Caelius Rufus was a witty but wayward luminary who moved in fashionable circles in the 50s BC. When he broke off his affair with CLODIA in 56, she sought her revenge in the courts where he was successfully defended by his friend CICERO. Tribune in 52, aedile in 50, praetor in 48, he joined MILO in a rebellion which ended with their deaths.   GS

Wiseman (1985).

Caelius Mons   part of Rome. The Caelian was one of the hills of Rome, lying to the south of the ESQUILINE and east of the PALATINE. According to legend its name was derived from Caeles VIBENNA, an Etruscan adventurer who settled there in the 6th century BC. It was enclosed within the WALL OF SERVIUS. During the Republic it was densely populated, but after a fire in AD 27 it became an aristocratic suburb and little remains of earlier structures. Notable buildings included Agrippina's temple to CLAUDIUS, the villa of Elagabalus, and the baths of Helena. Under AUGUSTUS it formed *regio* ii of Rome.   HE

Platner and Ashby (1929); Richardson (1992); Robinson (1992).

Caepio (fl. 110–105 BC), Roman politician. Quintus Servilius Caepio was praetor in 109 BC. In 107 he triumphed over the Lusitani in Spain, and was consul in 106. After this he was sent to Gaul where he defeated the Tectosages and captured Tolosa. He then failed to support Mallius against the CIMBRI, leading to the Roman defeat at Arausio. Once he returned to Rome he was prosecuted by NORBANUS in 103 and exiled to Smyrna.   HE

Gruen (1968).

Caere   city in Italy. Caere, modern Cerveteri, was a wealthy Etruscan city which reached the peak of its prosperity in the 6th century BC. In 535 BC, in alliance with CARTHAGE, Caere defeated the Phocaean Greeks in a naval battle off Corsica. By 390 BC it had become a close friend of Rome, giving shelter to the Vestal Virgins during the attack by BRENNUS. The cemetery outside the city at Banditaccia was laid out like a town, the tombs representing houses. Excavations there have revealed much information about Etruscan culture and everyday life.   LPR

CAH VII.2; Ogilvie (1976).

Caesar   Roman imperial title. Caesar was the family NAME of Gaius Julius CAESAR and thus also of Octavian (AUGUSTUS), his adoptive son. Each subsequent emperor (the AUGUSTUS) assumed the name 'Caesar' as part of his titulature, and emperors frequently granted that title to their sons (adoptive or otherwise): the appellation came to designate the heir(s) to the throne. The tetrarchic system of DIOCLETIAN comprised two emperors (Augusti) and their juniors, the Caesars.   RJB

Grant (1985).

Caesar, Gaius (20 BC–AD 4), son of AGRIPPA. Gaius Caesar, eldest son of Marcus Agrippa by his third wife, AUGUSTUS' daughter JULIA MAJOR, was adopted by Augustus, together with his brother Lucius (17 BC–AD 2), and clearly intended as Augustus' successor. Formally introduced to public life by Augustus (5 BC), Gaius married OCTAVIA's granddaughter LIVILLA, and received a special grant of proconsular *imperium* in the eastern provinces (1 BC), and the consulship (AD 1), but died in AD 4.   RJB

Grant (1979); Salmon (1968); Wells (1984).

Caesar, Julius (100–44 BC), Roman dictator. Gaius Julius Caesar's political career down to 60 BC was typical of a successful and talented noble of patrician lineage; like many of his class he leant towards the *popularis* cause (*see* POPULARES). Unlike POMPEY, Caesar held the regular offices of quaestor (68), aedile (65), and practor (62), his one unusual achievement being his election as Pontifex Maximus in 63. He stressed his connection with earlier *populares* in his funeral speech for his aunt Julia, the widow of MARIUS, and in his opposition in 63 to CICERO and RABIRIUS, both involved in putting Roman citizens to death without trial.

After his return in 60 from a successful military governorship in Spain, he began increasingly to occupy the centre of the political stage. Waiving his claim to a triumph in order to stand for the consulship of 59, he brilliantly exploited the current bafflement of Pompey and CRASSUS to create the First TRIUMVIRATE. In 59 he overcame conservative opposition and passed laws to benefit the poor and the provinces, and won for himself a five-year command in Gaul and Illyricum. Although he was absent from Rome for the next 10 years, the immense wealth from his conquests, his presence south of the Alps most winters, and the publication of his slanted campaign records (the *Commentarii*) enabled him to retain his influence on Roman politics. In 56 he was able to renew the Triumvirate, thus keeping the threatening Lucius DOMITIUS AHENOBARBUS out of the consulship, and to extend his Gallic command for five more years. His brilliant conquest of Gaul (*see* GALLIC WARS), in essentials complete by 56, was delayed until 51 by a series of revolts, culminating in that of VERCINGETORIX. In 49 his loyal, experienced army was willing to follow him across the Rubicon into Civil War, when the OPTIMATES, rightly seeing Caesar as a major threat to their power, refused to allow him to stand for the consulship *in absentia* and sought ways of prosecuting him.

Caesar's victory over Pompey at PHARSALUS was followed by campaigns in Egypt, Pontus, Africa, and Spain (48–45) which made him master of the Roman world. His successive consulships, his progressively longer grants of dictatorial powers, and his acceptance of extravagant honours, sometimes implying royal or divine status, made it clear that he intended to retain his absolute predominance. But he used it to pass as many constructive reforms as possible. A flood of shrewd, sane measures, such as his compromise solution of the debt problem and his policy of colonies abroad, improved life for many Romans, Italians, and provincials, while his reform of the calendar (*see* TIME, MEASUREMENT OF), with minor adjustments, survives to this day. He did not solve the central constitutional problem. The 60 members of the plot to kill him could declare that he intended to make himself king. Even if this allegation was untrue, Caesar had obviously ended the Republic. Caesar made the decisions now, not the other *nobiles*; nor did he care about cloaking their impotence with the trappings of power. The nobility found this unacceptable, and killed him on the Ides of March (the 15th) 44 BC.   DP

Grant (1974); Syme (1939); Yavetz (1983).

Caesarion   (47–30 BC), son of Cleopatra. Caesarion, officially titled Ptolemy XV Caesar, was the son of CLEOPATRA VII and, allegedly (although this is still disputed), Julius CAESAR. Both mother and son went to him in Rome. When Caesar was murdered in 44 BC, Cleopatra returned to Egypt, killed her husband, and declared Caesarion joint ruler. He was sent away for safety during the war of Octavian (AUGUSTUS) against Cleopatra and Mark ANTONY, but, after Cleopatra's suicide, he was killed on Octavian's orders.   EER

Green (1990); Sullivan (1990); Volkmann (1958).

Caledonia   region of north Britain, specifically the Highlands of Scotland beyond the Firth of Forth. The Caledonians were defeated by AGRICOLA at Mons Graupius in AD 84 and a legionary fortress was built at Inchtuthill on the Tay, but their territory was never incorporated into the empire. During the 2nd century the WALLS OF HADRIAN and ANTONINUS were built to consolidate the frontier. But Septimius SEVERUS' invasion of Scotland in 209 encountered serious opposition and the Roman garrison withdrew to the line of Hadrian's Wall.   GS

Hanson (1987); Salway (1981).

Calendars *see* TIME, MEASUREMENT OF.

Caligula *see* GAIUS.

Callias (5th century BC), Athenian politician. Of immense wealth and considerable political influence, Callias, son of Hipponicus, was related by marriage to CIMON. He went on an embassy to ARTAXERXES I in the 460s and negotiated the so-called Peace of Callias with Persia in 450/49 and the Thirty Years' Peace with Sparta in 446.   GLC

Callias (4th century BC), Athenian politician. Like his grandfather CALLIAS, Callias was virtually a professional diplomat. He thrice successfully negotiated peace with Sparta, the third time being in 372/1. He clashed in the courts with ANDOCIDES and seems to have squandered a great deal of the family wealth. His house at Piraeus was a meeting place for SOPHISTS.   GLC

Callias of Sphettus (fl. *c*.295–*c*.265 BC), Ptolemaic commander. Callias, of the Attic deme Sphettus, was exiled from Athens in the 290s BC and joined the Ptolemies. After Athens revolted from DEMETRIUS I POLIORCETES in 287, Callias returned and, using Ptolemaic mercenaries, helped his brother PHAEDRUS OF SPHETTUS in gathering the harvest before the retaliatory Macedonian siege. He represented Athens in the peace negotiations and, although remaining in Ptolemaic service, continued to work on behalf of Athens, which voted him full civic honours.   EER

Green (1990); Osborne (1979); Shear (1978).

Callias of Syracuse (fl. *c*.325–*c*.285 BC), Greek historian. Callias probably lived at the court of AGATHOCLES of Syracuse, and wrote a history of his reign in 22 books. Since it was the only favourable picture of this unpopular tyrant, DIODORUS SICULUS (perhaps following TIMAEUS) accused Callias of accepting royal bribes. The scant remains of the history permit no independent assessment of its contents, but it was used by CALLIMACHUS and DIONYSIUS OF HALICARNASSUS.   EER

Tillyard (1908).

Callicrates of Leontium (fl. *c*.181–149/8 BC), Achaean politician. Callicrates openly endorsed a pro-Roman policy for the ACHAEAN LEAGUE after PHILOPOEMEN's death, and opposed the pro-Achaean views of Lycortas (father of POLYBIUS). As general of the Achaean League (180–179 BC), Callicrates' actions in the Peloponnese accorded with Rome's wishes. When the pro-Achaean party went as hostages to Rome after PYDNA (168), Callicrates' policies were continued until his death.

Callicrates correctly foresaw Rome's inevitable domination, but was excoriated in Polybius' history.   EER

Errington (1969); Green (1990); Gruen (1984).

Callimachus (3rd century BC), Greek poet and scholar. Born in Cyrene, Callimachus became a leading figure in the literary élite of Ptolemaic Alexandria, employed in the LIBRARY and author of its catalogue but never librarian. Apart from the monumental catalogue (in 120 books), his prose works included a collection of wonders of the world, a chronology of dramatists, and numerous monographs on games, winds, foreign customs, local nomenclature, nymphs, birds, rivers, etc. Surviving poetry includes the (fragmentary) *Aetia* (four books of subtle aetiological studies), *Hecale* (a narrative poem on Theseus), six erudite *Hymns*, and 63 witty epigrams preserved in the ANTHOLOGY.   GS

Fraser (1972); Hutchinson (1988); Pfeiffer (1968); Webster (1964).

Callippus (fl. *c*.330 BC), Greek astronomer. Callippus of Cyzicus worked with ARISTOTLE 'to correct and complete the discoveries of EUDOXUS [OF CNIDUS]'. To the latter's theory of concentric spheres, designed to account for the motions of the sun, moon, and planets, he added two spheres in each case for the sun and moon and one for each of the planets. He proposed a year length of 365¼ days and introduced, as an improvement on METON'S nine-year cycle, the 76-year cycle named after him.
See also ASTRONOMY.   JL

Dicks (1970); Heath (1913).

Callisthenes (*c*.?380–327 BC), Greek historian. Callisthenes of Olynthus was a relative of ARISTOTLE and an established writer who accompanied ALEXANDER THE GREAT'S expedition as official historian. He objected to Alexander's introduction of the Persian custom of *proskynesis* (obeisance), and was implicated in the Pages' Conspiracy for which he was arrested. He died in captivity or was executed. His unfinished history, intentionally favourable to Alexander, may have influenced later histories of the early years of the campaign.
See also HISTORIOGRAPHY, GREEK.   EER

Bosworth (1980, 1988a, b); Hammond (1989); Lane Fox (1973); Pearson (1960).

Callistratus (fl. 392–361 BC), Athenian statesman, financier, and orator. Callistratus began his political career by prosecuting the ambassadors who had been willing to accept a peace between Sparta and

Persia in 392. He was prominent in the foundation of the Second Athenian Confederacy (378) which was a reaction against Sparta. By 372/1, when he shared in the renegotiation of the King's Peace (*see* CALLIAS), he had become opposed to THEBES, and he proposed the dispatch of an Athenian army to help Sparta in 370/69. In 366, when his pro-Spartan policy had gone awry, he was prosecuted. His influence rose again in 362 but he had to go into exile. He unwisely returned and was put to death. GLC

Calpurnius Siculus (mid-1st century AD), Latin poet. Titus Calpurnius Siculus is the author of seven eclogues in the tradition of THEOCRITUS and VIRGIL. Nothing is known of his life but internal evidence supports a Neronian date and his name may indicate a Sicilian origin. His verses were imitated by NEMESIANUS. GS

Cambyses king of Persia, 530–522 BC. Cambyses was the son of CYRUS; in 526–5 BC he invaded and conquered Egypt. Herodotus' unfavourable assessment of Cambyses and his achievement is exaggerated, being derived from Egyptian priests whose privileges Cambyses had curtailed. But resistance kept Cambyses in Egypt almost until his death, and his behaviour may have provoked the revolt in Persia in that year, the details of which remain mysterious. RB

CAH IV; Cook (1983).

Camillus (fl. 401–367 BC), Roman general. Marcus Furius Camillus was a celebrated general of the early Republic who became semi-legendary. His early successes (*c*.396 BC) included the capture of VEII and Falerii from the ETRUSCANS. After the sack of Rome by the Gauls in 390 he was responsible for much of the recovery and led successful campaigns against the AEQUI and VOLSCI. He organized the suppression of MANLIUS and may have instigated a reform of the ARMY. HE

CAH VII.2.

Camp *see* ARMY, ROMAN.

Campania region of Italy. Campania lay on the west coast of Italy, south of LATIUM and north of LUCANIA. The region contained a number of good harbours, including PUTEOLI, and was very fertile, largely thanks to the volcanic soil in the Ager Campanus, the plain to the north and east of Naples, which is dominated by the still-active volcano VESUVIUS.

From *c*.750 BC Campania was colonized by Greeks, who established settlements at CUMAE, Dicaearchia (PUTEOLI), and Naples, and by Etruscans, who founded CAPUA, Nola, POMPEII, and HERCULANEUM. By 400

BC the region had been overrun by OSCAN-speaking SABELLI from the interior (although Naples retained its Greek character until late antiquity) and in the later 4th century BC it was conquered by Rome. Campania was fully romanized in the 1st century BC, when colonies of veteran soldiers were settled there, and it became renowned for the luxury seaside villas owned by wealthy Roman magnates.

See also WINE.   HE

D'Arms (1970); Frederiksen (1984).

Campus Martius part of Rome. The Campus Martius lay outside the city walls to the north-west in a bend of the river Tiber. Originally a pasture belonging to the Tarquins, after their expulsion it was taken over by the state. As Roman citizens in arms were not allowed inside the city walls, the Campus Martius was used for army musters and exercises, and for meetings of the militarily based COMITIA *centuriata*. It was also the recreation ground for the Romans. Its name came from an altar to Mars built there. Gradually buildings took over its south end: in 221 BC Gaius FLAMINIUS built the Circus Flaminius and next to it in 52 BC Pompey constructed Rome's first permanent theatre.   DP

Platner and Ashby (1929); Richardson (1992); Robinson (1992).

Canals Canals for drainage and irrigation were commonplace, not only in Egypt and Mesopotamia where life depended on them, but throughout the ancient world. In Greece the plain of Boeotia and in Italy the valley of the Po, as well as Latium and Etruria, were kept drained by canals. Navigable canals were rarer, but they too existed in Egypt and Mesopotamia. PTOLEMY II PHILADELPHUS cut a canal from the Nile to the Bitter Lakes, thus linking the Mediterranean with the Red Sea. Xerxes cut through the isthmus of ATHOS to ensure the safety of his fleet. And numerous attempts were made on the Isthmus of CORINTH, but none of them was successful.   GS

Cannae battle in 216 BC. At Cannae, in Apulia, the Carthaginian general HANNIBAL and 40,000 men encircled and virtually annihilated the two consular armies of Terentius VARRO and Aemilius PAULLUS, numbering 80,000. It was the worst defeat ever suffered by the Romans. A number of Rome's allies, including CAPUA, joined Hannibal after the battle, but not in sufficient numbers to inhibit Rome's capacity to resist.   LPR

Lazenby (1978).

Capito (d. AD 22), Roman jurist. Gaius Ateius Capito was of undistinguished family but became consul in AD 5 and *curator aquarum*

(AD 13–22). As a jurist he specialized in sacral and constitutional law; but his writings were overshadowed by LABEO and were soon regarded as obsolete. According to POMPONIUS, their rivalry was the origin of the opposing schools of jurists named after SABINUS and Proculus.   GS

Capitol part of Rome. The Capitol was one of the hills of ROME, and of all of them the best fitted for natural defence. From early times it was both the religious centre of the city and the citadel. It consisted of two summits, the *Capitolium* and the *Arx*. The former was the site of the great temple of JUPITER Best and Greatest, which was traditionally attributed to TARQUINIUS SUPERBUS (the date has been confirmed by archaeology). The archaic temple survived until 83 BC, when it was burnt down; its successor was destroyed in the CIVIL WAR of AD 69. The *Arx* was dedicated to JUNO, whose sacred geese woke the garrison and saved the citadel from an attack by the Gauls in 390 BC (*see* BRENNUS). In 344 BC a temple to Juno Moneta was built there.   TC

Nash (1968); Platner and Ashby (1929); Richardson (1992); Robinson (1992).

Cappadocia territory in Asia Minor. Cappadocia is a mountainous region lying west of COMMAGENE, north of CILICIA, east of GALATIA, and south of PONTUS. The ACHAEMENIDS ruled it through Iranian satraps, one of whom refused to submit to ALEXANDER THE GREAT and was killed by PERDICCAS (322 BC). Lying between Syria and western Asia Minor, Cappadocia was strategically important to the Seleucids. ARIARATHES III declared independence *c*.255, although the houses continued to be allies and to intermarry. After ANTIOCHUS III'S defeat at MAGNESIA, ARIARATHES IV adopted a pro-Roman policy. Annexed in AD 17, it formed a Roman province with Galatia (AD 72–113) after which TRAJAN formed the province of Cappadocia and Pontus.

See also ARIARATHES V.   EER

CAH VIII; Eddy (1961); Gruen (1984); Jones (1983); Magie (1975); Sherwin-White (1984); Sullivan (1990).

Capua city in Italy. Capua lay on the Volturnus river in CAMPANIA, at the heart of the Campanian plain. The city was founded by ETRUSCANS probably in the 7th century BC, but in 423 BC it was taken over by OSCAN-speaking SABELLI. In 338 it was defeated by Rome and received Roman citizenship. Capua remained a large, prosperous city, and the Oscan language continued to be used. Capua sided with HANNIBAL in 216, but in 211 was recaptured by the Romans, who stripped it of much territory. Nevertheless, Capua continued to prosper.   HE

Frederiksen (1984).

Caracalla see AURELIUS ANTONINUS.

Caratacus (fl. mid-1st century AD), British chief. Caratacus inherited half of the kingdom of the Catuvellauni from his father Cunobelinus (c.AD 40–3). In attacking the Dobunni and Atrebates, he provided a pretext for CLAUDIUS I's invasion of Britain (43), as the Atrebatic leader, Verica, appealed to Rome. Defeated in the south-east, Caratacus organized further resistance in Wales, until defeated by OSTORIUS SCAPULA. The Brigantian queen, Cartimandua, surrendered him to the Romans (51), who granted him honourable retirement in Rome.
See also PLAUTIUS.   RJB

Salway (1981); Scullard (1979).

Carausius (d. AD 293), Roman usurper in Britain, AD 287–93. Marcus Aurelius Mausaeus Carausius was a Manapian (from the Low Countries) of low birth. MAXIMIAN made him commander of the Channel fleet, based at Boulogne, but later, suspecting him of corruption, ordered his execution. Carausius escaped to Britain, setting up an independent kingdom that included part of Gaul, and ruled until 293 when CONSTANTIUS I retook Boulogne, and Carausius himself was assassinated and succeeded by his treasurer Allectus (293–6).   RJB

Grant (1985); Salway (1981); Scullard (1979).

Carbo (fl. 92–82 BC), Roman politician. Gnaeus Papirius Carbo was tribune in 92 BC, fought in the SOCIAL WAR, and supported CINNA's attack on Rome in 87. He became consul in 85 and remained sole consul after Cinna's death in 84, following a moderate policy. In 82 he was consul with MARIUS' son and fought unsuccessfully against SULLA and his lieutenants. Carbo then fled to Africa where he was executed by POMPEY.   HE

Badian (1964).

Caria region in south-west Asia Minor including the Greek cities of CNIDUS and HALICARNASSUS. Parts of the coast were hellenized as a result of early COLONIZATION but the interior remained Carian, a land of villages with a common sanctuary at Mylasa. Having suffered under Lydian and Persian rule, the Carians joined the IONIAN REVOLT and subsequently the DELIAN LEAGUE. A deliberate programme of hellenization begun under MAUSOLUS enabled Caria to be assimilated easily into the Hellenistic world.   GS

Bean (1980).

Carinus (*c*.AD 249–85), Roman emperor, AD 283–5. Marcus Aurelius Carinus, elder son of CARUS, was created Caesar (282), and elevated to Augustus shortly before Carus invaded Persia (283), leaving him as regent. Joint emperor with his brother NUMERIAN after Carus' death (late 283), he put down the rebel M. Aurelius Julianus in Illyricum (284), and came close to defeating his rival DIOCLETIAN in the Margus valley (285), but was murdered by a tribune whose wife he had seduced.

RJB

Grant (1985); Parker (1958).

Carnea Greek religious festival. The Carnea, the most important festival of the Dorians, was celebrated annually in the month Karneios (late summer) in honour of APOLLO. Its origin is uncertain, but at Sparta it glorified the military way of life with sacrificial banquets and running races. A major musical contest was also included. Wars were halted for the duration of the festival which accounted for the Spartans' late arrival at MARATHON and the inadequacy of their force at THERMOPYLAE.

See also FESTIVALS, GREEK.

GS

Burkert (1985).

Carneades (*c*.214–129 BC), Greek philosopher. Carneades of Cyrene was the founder of the New or Third ACADEMY which superseded the Middle Academy of ARCESILAUS. He studied in the Academy originally under Hegesinus and eventually succeeded him as its head sometime before 155 BC, when he was sent by the Athenians on an embassy to Rome. Just as Arcesilaus had attacked the early STOICS, so Carneades combatted the theories of CHRYSIPPUS. Although he did not publish his views, they were recorded by his pupils, notably Clitomachus. Carneades agreed with Arcesilaus that no proposition can certainly be established as true or false and judgement must, therefore, be reserved. Conclusions of varying degrees of probability could be drawn, however, and these supplied a guide to conduct.

JL

Long (1974).

Carnuntum Roman city on the Danube. Founded as a legionary base under Tiberius, it became a *municipium* under Hadrian and a *colonia* under SEVERUS who was proclaimed emperor there in AD 193. It was regularly visited by emperors including Marcus AURELIUS who wrote the second book of his *Meditations* there. It was equipped with fine public buildings which proved too much of a temptation to the neighbouring barbarians who destroyed it *c*.AD 400.

GS

Mócsy (1974).

Carrhae battle in 53 BC. Eager to win a military reputation, CRASSUS DIVES led seven legions into Mesopotamia to attack the Parthians. At Carrhae (modern Harran) he was tricked into a parley with the Surenas and was killed. Leaderless, the legions were harassed by Parthian horse archers, until many men were killed or captured along with the legionary standards. The disgrace was keenly felt by the Romans, and the return of the standards in 20 BC was paraded as one of AUGUSTUS' great achievements.   LPR

Sherwin-White (1984).

Carthage Carthage lay on a small peninsula projecting into the Gulf of Tunis. It had a fortified acropolis (Byrsa) and was surrounded by a large walled circuit. On the southern part of the peninsula lay Carthage's superb harbour (Cothon) with inner (naval) and outer (commercial) sections. The agora lay between harbour and acropolis. The city was founded, according to tradition, in 814 BC as a Tyrian colony, though there is no archaeological evidence for occupation before c.750. As a PHOENICIAN colony, Carthage worshipped gods such as Baal-Hammon, Tanit, and Melkart, cults which are said to have involved human sacrifice.

Carthage's success was the result of its powerful maritime trading position. Its site gave it easy access to both eastern and western basins of the Mediterranean while at the same time acting as a conduit for trade with Africa. It dominated western Mediterranean trade by force (building a large and aggressive fleet in the process), exploiting under-developed Spanish and African tribes. By the 4th century BC it was also developing the agricultural potential of the region. Carthaginian colonies were set up along the African coast and the Berbers were brutally brought under control.

This aggressive trade policy inevitably brought conflict, particularly as Carthage expanded into Spain and SICILY, though it avoided involvement in Italy by allying with first the Etruscans, then the Romans. In 535 BC a Greek fleet was defeated off Corsica, allowing Carthage to consolidate its position in Spain, Sardinia, and western Sicily. Hostilities continued with the Sicilian Greeks throughout the 5th and 4th centuries, but Carthage was never able to gain lasting control of more than half the island, and in 307 the Syracusans even landed a force in Africa. In 280 Carthage provided a fleet to aid Rome in the war against PYRRHUS.

Hostilities with Rome eventually came about as a result of conflicting interests in Sicily, leading to Carthaginian defeats in all three PUNIC WARS (264–241, 218–201, 149–146 BC) and the deliberate destruction of Carthage. Despite the destruction, the site was quickly reoccupied by the Romans. Although Gaius GRACCHUS' attempt to found a colony (Junonia) there failed (122), Julius Caesar and Augustus were more successful.

In the last years of the Republic and under the Empire Carthage's prosperity quickly recovered, a result partly of the new colonies, and partly of the vast market for corn provided by the growing city of Rome. Its advantageous geographical position also enabled Carthage to promote the export of products from North African farms (olive oil) and workshops (pottery). As one of the larger cities in the Mediterranean, Carthage had a strong educational record. It later became an important Christian centre, propounding orthodoxy against the DONATISTS, and acting as home for AUGUSTINE, CYPRIAN, and TERTULLIAN. In AD 439 Carthage was captured by the VANDALS, though trade continued and the recapture of the region by Belisarius in 534 probably caused more disruption to economic life. HE

Charles-Picard and Charles-Picard (1961); Warmington (1969a).

Cartography   *see* MAPS.

Carus   (*c*.AD 229–83), Roman emperor, AD 282–3. Marcus Aurelius Carus, Praetorian Prefect under PROBUS, was proclaimed emperor by the army in Raetia (282). After Probus' murder Carus announced his elevation (without requesting the Senate's approval), and named his sons CARINUS and NUMERIAN first Caesar and then Augustus. Leaving Carinus as regent, Carus defeated the QUADI and SARMATIANS on the Danube and then invaded Persia, capturing the capital Ctesiphon, before his death, probably due to an army conspiracy. RJB

Grant (1985); Parker (1958).

Carvilius   (fl. 235 BC), freedman of Spurius Carvilius Maximus. According to PLUTARCH, Carvilius was the first to open an elementary school at Rome. Informal teaching academies had no doubt long been in existence but Carvilius may have been the first to set up as a professional. He is also credited by Plutarch with being the first to distinguish the letters C and G.

See also ALPHABET, LATIN; EDUCATION. GS

Marrou (1956).

Caryatid   *see* ARCHITECTURE, GREEK.

Cassander   (*c*.358–297 BC), king of Macedon. Cassander, son of ANTIPATER, joined ALEXANDER THE GREAT in Babylon in 324 BC.

Threatened when POLYPERCHON was appointed successor to Antipater in Europe (319), Cassander subdued several Greek cities including Athens. Polyperchon invoked OLYMPIAS, but in 316 Cassander arranged her murder. He allied himself with the other DIADOCHI against ANTIGONUS I MONOPHTHALMUS, and murdered ALEXANDER IV and ROXANE c.309 to increase his power in Macedonia. He proclaimed himself king after 305. He joined in the defeat of Antigonus at IPSUS in 301, after which his rule in Macedonia was secure. He founded the city of THESSALONICA, naming it after his wife, a daughter of PHILIP II.   EER

CAH VII.1; Errington (1990); Green (1990); Hammond and Walbank (1988).

Cassiterides   literally the 'tin islands'. The term was applied loosely to all the tin-bearing regions of north-west Europe, and by Strabo specifically to the Scilly Isles (where there is no tin). The TIN route was first exploited by the Carthaginians who were possessive about it. According to Diodorus, the metal was exported from Ictis (St Michael's Mount) to Corbilo (?St Nazaire) on the Loire and thence overland to the mouth of the Rhône. Cornish tin became less important after the 1st century AD when deposits in SPAIN were discovered.   GS

Cassius, Avidius   see AVIDIUS CASSIUS.

Cassius, Dio   see DIO CASSIUS.

Cassius Longinus   (d. 42 BC), tyrannicide. Gaius Cassius Longinus, as quaestor to CRASSUS in 53 BC, escaped from CARRHAE and successfully governed Syria till 51. He commanded a Pompeian fleet in the CIVIL WAR, but was pardoned by CAESAR and became praetor for 44. However, in his bitterness at Caesar's domination, he promoted the conspiracy to kill him. Forced out of Rome after the murder, he and BRUTUS gained control of the provinces and the armies of the east. In the autumn of 42 their 19 legions held the Via Egnatia at PHILIPPI against the forces of the Second TRIUMVIRATE. In the first battle Cassius, thinking wrongly that Brutus had done as badly as himself, committed suicide.   DP

Rawson (1991); Syme (1939).

Cassius Vecellinus   (fl. 502–485 BC), Roman statesman. Although probably not a patrician, Spurius Cassius was consul three times (502, 493, and 486 BC). In 493 he concluded a treaty of alliance with the LATIN LEAGUE, and another in 486 with the HERNICI. But his proposal to distribute AGER PUBLICUS to the PLEBS (486) gave rise to the suspicion that he was aiming at kingship, and he was tried and condemned to death.

See also SOCII.   TC

Broughton (1951); Ogilvie (1965).

Catacombs early Christian cemeteries. Catacombs consisted of rows of underground galleries containing tiers of rock-cut tomb chambers, hollowed out to receive as many as four corpses each. The most famous and most extensive are at Rome where they stretch for more than 350 miles. They bear clear similarity to *columbaria* (*see* BURIAL PRACTICES, ROMAN) but are more closely related to Jewish family tombs. Outside Rome, catacombs have been found in Albano, Alexandria, Hadrumetum, Malta, Naples, and Syracuse. The extent of the Roman catacombs bears witness to the size of the Christian community there. Paintings on the walls and ceilings demonstrate the beginnings of Christian art. In the 4th century the catacombs ceased to be used for burial but the tombs of martyrs became places of pilgrimage.

See also CHRISTIANITY; PAINTING, ROMAN.   GS

Hertling and Kirschbaum (1960).

Catana Greek colony in Sicily. Founded from Sicilian NAXOS *c.*729 BC, the city enjoyed independence until the 5th century BC when it fell under Syracusan control. Under HIERON I its name was changed to AETNA, but in 461 BC it was renamed Catana. Occupied by DIONYSIUS I in 403, it remained under Syracusan influence until taken by Rome in 263. Under Roman rule it flourished and acquired fine buildings, most of which have succumbed to volcanic activity.   GS

Dunbabin (1948); Stillwell (1976).

Catiline (*c.*108–62 BC), Roman conspirator. Lucius Sergius Catilina, member of an obscure patrician family and legate of SULLA, was propraetor of Africa in 67–66 BC, but an extended prosecution stopped him from standing for the consulship until 64. When the COMITIA voted for CICERO and Gaius Antonius instead, Catiline championed the discontented elements in Italy, basically debtors, dispossessed peasants, and the poor, but including a dozen senators and some municipal aristocrats. When even this support failed to win him the consulship for 62, he organized a widespread if ramshackle rebellion. Frightened out of Rome by Cicero, he joined his forces in Etruria, but was defeated and killed by Antonius in January 62. Doubtless frustrated political ambition caused Catiline's conspiracy, but, had he succeeded, the poor might not have complained about that.

See also SALLUST.   DP

Fuhrmann (1992); Gruen (1974); Habicht (1990).

Cato (234–148 BC), Roman statesman. Marcus Porcius Cato the Censor was born in TUSCULUM of a well-to-do EQUESTRIAN family, and was brought up on a family estate in the Sabine hills. A NOVUS HOMO, he rose to prominence thanks to the patronage of L. Valerius Flaccus, a patrician neighbour who recognized his early promise. After serving with distinction in southern Italy and Sardinia in the Second PUNIC WAR (he fought at METAURUS), Cato passed rapidly through the CURSUS HONORUM, holding the plebeian aedileship in 199 BC and the praetorship in 198. He was consul in 195 and CENSOR in 184, each time with Valerius Flaccus as his colleague. As consul in 195, Cato campaigned in Hither Spain and won a decisive battle at Emporiae (modern Ampurias).

Throughout his political career Cato adopted a conservative stance and voiced his opposition to the rapid cultural changes then taking place. He attacked the corruption and dishonesty of the NOBILES, whom he viewed as irresponsible and decadent, and devoted much of his later career to uncovering political scandals and prosecuting those who fell short of his own austere standards. He instigated the trials of the SCIPIOS and was largely responsible for their downfall. His unceasing campaign against the growth of luxury expressed itself in support for sumptuary legislation (i.e. laws restricting personal consumption), and culminated in his famous censorship (184).

Cato was noted for his hostility to the Greeks and their culture. His target, however, was not Hellenism as such but rather the pretentious and indiscriminate adulation of everything Greek that had become fashionable at Rome. Cato saw this as a decadent fad, and attacked it from a position of strength, because he had a deeper understanding of Greek culture than most of his opponents. This is evident from his own literary activity. Cato was the father of Latin prose. His published speeches revealed a mastery of Greek rhetorical technique and knowledge of the Attic orators; his treatises on medicine, the art of war, and agriculture (the latter still survives) recall the encyclopaedic work of XENOPHON; finally, his history of Rome and Italy (entitled *Origines*) took its didactic purpose from Xenophon, its facts from TIMAEUS, and its method from POLYBIUS (*see also* HISTORIOGRAPHY, ROMAN).

Cato remained active to the end of his long life. In his last years he became obsessed with the threat of the old enemy, Carthage, and Rome entered the Third PUNIC WAR largely at his insistence.   TC

Astin (1978); Scullard (1973); Toynbee (1965).

Cato Uticensis (95–46 BC), Roman politician. Marcus Porcius Cato Uticensis passionately tried to maintain the dying Republic. Emulous of his great-grandfather, CATO the Censor, he was wedded to tradition

and rectitude. In 63 BC he persuaded the Senate to execute the followers of CATILINE. His opposition to unconstitutional demands precipitated the First TRIUMVIRATE and eventually the dictatorship he was
fighting against. Sent away from Rome by his enemies in 58 to annex
Cyprus, on his return he supported his brother-in-law DOMITIUS
AHENOBARBUS' campaign against the First Triumvirate, and was praetor
in 54. He saw the necessity for POMPEY to be sole consul in 52, and
inspired the intransigence towards CAESAR which caused the CIVIL WAR.
In 46 he killed himself at Utica in Africa on hearing of Caesar's victory
at THAPSUS.   DP

Scullard (1982); Syme (1939); Taylor (1949).

Catullus (c.84–54 BC), Latin poet. Gaius Valerius Catullus was born
at Verona of a prosperous family. Coming to Rome c.62 BC, he moved
in fashionable literary circles and began a stormy affair with Lesbia
(probably CLODIA) which dominated his life and poetry. The poems,
which survived in a single (now lost) manuscript, are arranged in three
groups, possibly by the poet himself: 1–60 are short poems including
lyrics, love poems, occasional pieces, and political satire; 61–68 are
longer poems mostly in hexameters and elegiacs; 69–116 are EPIGRAMS.
Profoundly influenced by Hellenistic models, the poems are none the
less original, passionate, and strikingly sincere.
    See also ALEXANDRIAN POETRY, LATIN.   GS

Lyne (1980); Quinn (1972); Ross (1969); Wiseman (1985).

Catulus, Quintus Lutatius (c.152–87 BC), Roman politician. Quintus
Lutatius Catulus was a conservative senator noted for his cultural
interests and literary patronage. CICERO introduced him as a character
in the *De Oratore*, and his funeral oration on his mother was the first
to be delivered on a Roman woman. He was three times defeated for
the consulship until helped to success by MARIUS in 102 BC. He and
Marius then defeated the CIMBRI in 101 and held a joint triumph, with
Catulus building a portico on the Palatine out of the spoils. But Catulus
became resentful of Marius' greater reputation, and led the opposition
to him. When Marius and CINNA captured Rome in 87, they arraigned
him and he committed suicide.   DP

Badian (1964); Gruen (1968).

Catulus, Quintus Lutatius (d. 61 BC), Roman politician. Quintus
Lutatius Catulus rose to prominence as a supporter of SULLA and was
consul in 78 BC. As proconsul in 77 he successfully led the government's forces against the revolt of his former colleague LEPIDUS. A

leading conservative figure in the Senate during the 70s and 60s, he opposed the grant of extraordinary powers to POMPEY in 67 and 66, and as censor in 65 blocked the move of his colleague CRASSUS to give citizenship to the Transpadani. In 63 he was beaten in the election for Pontifex Maximus by Julius CAESAR.   DP

Gruen (1974).

Caudine Forks   battle in 321 BC. At a narrow defile near Capua called the Caudine Forks a Roman army, led by the consuls Veturius Calvinus and Spurius Postumius, was trapped by the Samnites. After negotiating a truce and surrender, the Romans were forced to walk under a 'yoke' of spears with great disgrace. The peace was not ratified in Rome and so the Second SAMNITE WAR continued.   LPR

Salmon (1967).

Celsus   (fl. *c*.AD 178), Greek anti-Christian philosopher. Celsus was the author of *The True Account*, the first comprehensive philosophical polemic against Christianity, written *c*.AD 178. ORIGEN quotes about three-quarters of this work in his own treatise, *Contra Celsum*, some 70 years later. Celsus writes from a Greek and Platonic point of view, but certain objections to Christianity are put into the mouths of Alexandrian Jews. His criticisms were subsequently taken over by the NEOPLATONISTS in their polemics against Christianity.   JL

Chadwick (1986b); de Lange (1976).

Celsus, Aulus Cornelius   (fl. 1st century AD), Roman encyclopaedist. Aulus Cornelius Celsus wrote an encyclopaedia during the reign of Tiberius which dealt with agriculture, medicine, military arts, rhetoric, philosophy, and jurisprudence. Apart from a few fragments of other sections, only eight books on MEDICINE survive. Well organized and written in excellent Latin, the *De Medicina* subsequently became a model for Renaissance writers. The work is important for the evidence it provides of Hellenistic medical doctrines and for the brief, but judicious, summary of the history of medicine up to the author's own day. Such is the level of medical knowledge revealed here that some have claimed that Celsus must himself have been a doctor. A vigorous controversy has arisen around this issue. Others, however, maintain that Celsus was a literary author (rather than a mere translator) who selected his material with sound judgement and critical appraisal from a variety of sources.   JL

Phillips (1973); Scarborough (1969).

Celsus, Publius Juventus   (fl. *c*.AD 100), Roman jurist. Publius Juventus Celsus had a distinguished public career, serving as praetor (AD 106 or 107), governor of Thrace, twice as consul, and proconsul of Asia. He succeeded Pegasus as head of the Proculian school of jurists. Extracts survive from his *Digesta*, which was based on earlier writings now lost.   GS

Celtiberians   Spanish people. The Celtiberians were a warlike Gallic tribe of central Spain (Aragon). They served as mercenaries for both sides in the PUNIC WARS. In 195 BC Marcus Porcius CATO invaded Celtiberia, and in 178 BC Tiberius Sempronius GRACCHUS negotiated a treaty which gave Rome nominal control. However, the Celtiberians revolted a number of times (154–151 and 144 BC), until in 134 they were besieged in NUMANTIA by SCIPIO AEMILIANUS. Reduced to cannibalism, they surrendered in 133.   LPR

Knapp (1977).

Celts   a barbarian people whose heartland was originally in central Europe. By 500 BC the Celts had spread out from France, Germany, Bohemia, Austria, and Switzerland into parts of Spain, Britain, Ireland, the Low Countries, and northern Italy (*see* CISALPINE GAUL). In the 4th and 3rd centuries they moved further south and east into central Italy, the Balkans, and Asia Minor (*see* GALATIA). Most of them were subsequently absorbed into the Roman empire or wiped out by other barbarian movements, but on the north-west fringes of Europe their culture survived in Brittany, Ireland, Wales, and Scotland. They were distinguished by their language, their beliefs, and their art, but they never formed a political entity. In antiquity they were famous for their skill in warfare: in 390 BC under BRENNUS they sacked Rome, and in 279 BC under another BRENNUS they attacked Delphi. But Julius CAESAR greatly exaggerated the influence of their religious leaders, the Druids, in his work *On the Gallic War*.
See also GAULS.   GS

Hubert (1987); Momigliano (1975a); Powell (1960); Rankin (1987).

Censor   Roman magistrate. The censorship was created in the mid-5th century BC to take over from the CONSULS the holding of the CENSUS. There were always two censors. They were at first elected every four years, but from 209 BC every five years, and held office for 18 months, or, if it came sooner, until they had finished the census and held a ceremony of purification (*lustrum*). The censorship was an inherently important office which came to stand at the head of the CURSUS HONORUM and was usually held by ex-consuls.

The censors, as well as holding the census, which allowed them, if in agreement, to enact various punishments against Roman citizens (*see* AERARIUS), leased out important state contracts (*see* PUBLICANI), and held a general supervision of public morals. The latter was of great political importance, as it meant that the censors could remove men from the SENATE. From the time of Sulla to the end of the Republic the intense competition amongst the élite made the appointment of censors extremely irregular. Under the Principate the emperor took over the role of the censors. This process culminated in DOMITIAN becoming censor for life.

See also MAGISTRATES, ROMAN; ROADS, ROMAN.   HS

Jolowicz and Nicholas (1972); Nicolet (1980); Soulahti (1963).

Census   Roman register. The census was thought by the Romans to have been instituted by SERVIUS TULLIUS to register Roman citizens for military and financial purposes. Originally the responsibility of the kings, under the Republic it was first held by the CONSULs then, from *c.*443 BC, by the CENSORs.

The census, which was held in the CAMPUS MARTIUS every four years until 209 BC and every five years after then, required by law adult male Roman citizens to register their names, ages, and property, and give details of women and children in their family. The citizens were then divided into tribes (*see* TRIBUS) and five property classes which were further divided into *seniores* and *iuniores* (*see* COMITIA). The EQUESTRIAN centuries were registered separately in the FORUM. The census combined legal equality for Roman citizens with political and social inequality, as the richer classes had more political power and, originally at least, more military responsibilities.

In the late Republic the census was taken irregularly in Italy, and ceased to be taken during the 1st century AD when the establishment of a professional ARMY, the end of popular VOTING, and Italy's exemption from direct TAXATION had removed its necessity. Under the Republic censuses were occasionally taken in the provinces. These became more regularized under the Empire.

See also AERARIUS; POPULATION.   HS

Nicolet (1980).

Centumviri   Roman jury. The *centumviri* (= '100 men') were a panel from which juries were drawn to form special civil courts dealing with INHERITANCE cases. During the Republic the panel actually numbered 105 (most but not necessarily all of them senators), three from each of the 35 TRIBUS. Under the Empire it increased to at least 180. It is not known what caused a given case to be brought before the centumviral courts, or whether they had any wider jurisdiction than cases involving succession. The cases were of great legal importance, and engaged the talents of orators such as L. CRASSUS and PLINY THE YOUNGER. TC

Brunt (1988); Kelly (1975).

Centuria, Centurio *see* ARMY, ROMAN.

Centuriation Roman land measurement system. Centuriation was a Roman technique for dividing large areas of land into sections. It was particularly used in COLONIAE. The area was divided into squares (*centuriae*) of 200 *iugera* by a gridded network of roads running north–south and east–west. In practice this theoretical framework was often adjusted to local conditions with variations in both area and size of the subdivisions, but traces of it often survive in modern field and road networks in Italy.

See also GROMATICI. HE

Cercidas (*c*.290–*c*.220 BC), of Megalopolis, Greek writer. In public life Cercidas was prominent as a diplomat (he led an embassy to ANTIGONUS III DOSON), an army commander (at the battle of Sellasia), and a lawgiver. He also gained a reputation as a Cynic philosopher and lyric poet. Surviving fragments of his *Meliambi* express moralizing and satirical sentiments. GS

Webster (1964).

Ceres Roman goddess. Ceres was an ancient Italian corn goddess. Her early history is obscure, but she was worshipped in Rome from very early times. In 493 BC a temple of Ceres was dedicated and became an important cult centre for the PLEBS. By this date her worship had elements derived directly from that of the Greek goddess DEMETER who had major cult centres in Sicily and at Cumae and with whom she is normally identified. Her festival, the Cerialia, was celebrated at Rome on 19 April. HE

Ogilvie (1969); Scullard (1981).

Chabrias (*c*.420–356 BC), Athenian general. Chabrias was so frequently employed as general from 390 until his death in 356 during the SOCIAL WAR that he was really a professional soldier. When not engaged by Athens he sought service in Egypt. In the 370s he played a large part in the defence and extension of the Second Athenian Confederacy. From 369 to 366 he was the general used by CALLISTRATUS in his pro-Spartan policy and the two were prosecuted on succeeding days in 366, trials which much impressed the youthful DEMOSTHENES. He was celebrated for a hoplite tactic he used in 378 in defence of Boeotia.   GLC

Parke (1933).

Chaeronea   city in western Boeotia, where PHILIP II of Macedon decisively defeated the Greeks in 338 BC. The Macedonian army comprised 30,000 foot and 2,000 horse, the Greek perhaps similar. Philip executed a controlled withdrawal; the Greek line opened up; and Alexander and the cavalry delivered the knock-out blow. Casualties were appalling: the whole Theban SACRED BAND was destroyed; Athens lost 3,000 killed or captured; others probably fared equally badly.   GLC

Cawkwell (1978).

Chalcidian League   In 432 BC, when POTIDAEA revolted from Athens, the cities of CHALCIDICE formed a confederacy centred on OLYNTHUS. Despite an attempt to dissolve it in the Peace of Nicias (421), it survived until the King's Peace (387/6). When it endeavoured covertly to resurrect itself, Sparta took Olynthus (379). Reborn in the 370s, it opposed Athenian attempts to regain AMPHIPOLIS and allied with PHILIP II of Macedon. He captured Olynthus in 348 and dissolved the league.
                                                                          GLC

Larsen (1968); West (1918).

Chalcidice   promontory in MACEDONIA culminating in the peninsulas of Kassandra, Sithonia, and ATHOS. The name derives from the large number of colonies planted there by CHALCIS in Euboea in the 8th century BC. After the Persian Wars Chalcidice was subject to Athens until the formation of the CHALCIDIAN LEAGUE in 432 BC. After the dissolution of the league in 348 the region was overrun by PHILIP II.   GS

Chalcis   chief city in EUBOEA. Chalcis lies on the west coast of Euboea at the narrowest point of the Euripus channel. Throughout antiquity it was a flourishing commercial centre, known for its pottery and metalwork. It played a prominent part in the COLONIZATION of Magna Graecia and the north Aegean (*see* CHALCIDICE). Subject to Athens for most of the 5th and 4th centuries, the city was garrisoned by PHILIP II in 338. For siding with the ACHAEAN LEAGUE it was partly destroyed by the Romans in 146 BC.   GS

Chares   (*c.*395–324 BC), Athenian general. Chares held office very frequently between 367 and 324. His harsh treatment of Athens's allies (notably CORCYRA) contributed to the outbreak of the SOCIAL WAR (357–355) and moved ISOCRATES to attack him (though not by name) in *On the Peace*. To raise pay for his mercenary army, he served under ARTABAZUS, a rebel satrap, winning a great victory, 'sister to Marathon', and causing ARTAXERXES III to threaten intervention if Athens did not withdraw him and end the Social War. Active in the north Aegean against the Thracian king Cersobleptes, and regaining Sestos, he was unsuccessful against PHILIP II of Macedon. In 335 Alexander demanded his surrender but he survived to resist Macedon until his death.   GLC

Chares of Lindus   (fl. *c*.300 BC), Greek sculptor. Chares was a pupil of LYSIPPUS and worked as a sculptor in Antioch and Rhodes. His most famous creation was the colossal bronze statue of Helios, known as the Colossus of Rhodes, which was erected as a thank offering for the delivery of the city from the siege of DEMETRIUS I POLIORCETES in 304 BC. It stood more than 100 feet high but was snapped off at the knees by an earthquake in 220 BC.   GS

Charidemus   (*c*.395–333 BC), Euboean mercenary captain. In service with the Thracian king Cersobleptes, Charidemus secured for Athens restoration of the Chersonese and was granted Athenian citizenship. As general, he was active against PHILIP II in defence of Olynthus, incurring bitter hatred from the Macedonians, and in 335 Alexander required Athens to exile him. He fled to DARIUS II and was executed for insolence.   GLC

Chariot racing   *see* GAMES, ROMAN.

Chariton   (1st century BC–1st century AD), Greek novelist. Probably born in Aphrodisias, Chariton is the author of *Chaereas and Callirhoe*, the earliest surviving Greek novel. A tale of love and adventure, set in 5th-century Syracuse, it presents romance within a historical framework.
See also NOVEL, GREEK.   GS

Perry (1967); Reardon (1989); Winkler and Williams (1982).

Charon of Lampsacus   (5th century BC), Greek historian. Only a few fragments remain of his varied writings, and opinions have differed over his precise date. His work was compared with that of HERODOTUS and he dealt with the flight of THEMISTOCLES, so the loss is considerable.
See also HISTORIOGRAPHY, GREEK.   GLC

Pearson (1939).

Charops   (d. *c.*159 BC), Epirote leader. Charops was educated at Rome and continued his family's pro-Roman affiliation. The Roman victory over the Macedonian PERSEUS in 168 BC made Rome dominant in northern Greece. Charops used Roman influence for personal political advantage, perhaps even encouraging the general PAULLUS to ravage Epirus in order to be rid of his political opponents there. He remained powerful in Epirus until his death, although he eventually lost Roman support. POLYBIUS denounced him virulently.   EER

Gruen (1984); Hammond (1967).

Chatti   German people. The Chatti occupied the Fualda, Lahn, and Eder region. Overrun by DRUSUS in 10/9 BC, they joined the revolt of AD 9, and were attacked by GERMANICUS (15), who burnt their capital, Mattium. They were in frequent conflict with the CHERUSCI, and fought the Hermunduri (58) for the possession of salt-beds. They took part in the revolt of CIVILIS (69–70), and were attacked by DOMITIAN (83, 89), but are infrequently mentioned thereafter.   RJB

Thompson (1965); Todd (1975).

Chauci   German people. The Chauci, a tribe of soldiers and fisher-men settled between the lower Ems and the Elbe, were subjugated by the elder DRUSUS (12–11 BC), but Roman domination does not appear to have continued beyond AD 17. Described by TACITUS as 'the noblest people of Germany', they raided the coast of Roman Gaul during the 1st century AD, and joined in the Batavian revolt (69–70), but are little heard of thereafter.
See also CHERUSCI.   RJB

Thompson (1965); Todd (1975).

Chersonese, Taurian   modern Crimea. Colonists from MILETUS in the 7th century BC were the first to found Greek cities in the Crimea, attracted no doubt by the natural defences of the peninsula as well as its fertile plains and FISHING grounds. The chief city was Panticapaeum where the SPARTOCIDS ruled from 438 to 110 BC. They brought great prosperity to the region by exporting grain to Greece.   GS

Rostovtzeff (1941).

Chersonese, Thracian   Gallipoli peninsula. Ionian Greeks planted colonies on the Thracian Chersonese in the 8th and 7th centuries BC, notably at Cardia and SESTOS. The peninsula had strategic importance in that it commanded the Dardanelles; it also produced a valuable surplus of grain. Acquired for Athens by the PHILAIDS in the mid-6th century, it remained largely under Athenian control until ceded to PHILIP II in 338 BC.

See also THRACE.   GS

Cherusci   German people. The Cherusci, settled in the Upper Weser valley, were the leading tribe in central Germany in the time of Augustus and Tiberius. Subjugated by the elder DRUSUS in 12–11 BC, they revolted (with the CHAUCI) in AD 2, and again under ARMINIUS (9), who led them against GERMANICUS (14–16), and against the Alamanni under MAROBODUUS, as well as in civil war. The tribe is seldom mentioned after Arminius' death (21).   RJB

Mommsen (1968); Thompson (1965); Todd (1975).

Children   *see* ADOPTIO; INHERITANCE; MARRIAGE.

Chilon   (fl. *c*.556 BC), Spartan ephor. Chilon was EPHOR in 556 BC, the first to make the office politically influential, and is reputed to have collaborated with King ANAXANDRIDAS in major changes in Spartan policy; Anaxandridas' second wife probably came from Chilon's family. Chilon's reputation for practical wisdom caused him to be considered one of the SEVEN SAGES, and later Spartans worshipped him as a hero.   RB

Cartledge (1979).

Chios   island in the eastern Aegean. Traditionally colonized by IONIANS and a member of the Ionian Confederacy, Chios enjoyed political stability and cultural prosperity in the archaic and classical periods. A thriving commercial centre, famous for its WINE and figs, it had its own silver COINAGE by 600 BC. After the Persian Wars Chios was a member of the DELIAN LEAGUE and subsequently of the Second Athenian Confederacy, becoming independent in 354 BC. Its prosperity continued into the Roman period but attracted the attentions of MITHRIDATES VI who plundered it. Regaining its independence in 86 BC, it remained a free city until the reign of VESPASIAN.   GS

Boardman and Vaphopoulou-Richardson (1986).

Choregus   patron of the chorus at the dramatic festivals at Athens. The LITURGY system required wealthy citizens to undertake the *choregia* which involved the assembling, paying, and equipping of a chorus (but not the actors) at the various festivals. For dithyramb the system was in place by 509 BC and the choregus was chosen by the 10 tribes. For TRAGEDY and COMEDY at the DIONYSIA he was appointed by the Archon

Eponymos and at the LENAEA by the Archon Basileus. Other *choregoi* supported the performance of dithyramb at the PANATHENAEA and THARGELIA. A tripod was awarded to the winning choregus for dithyramb, but not to victors for comedy and tragedy: their names were recorded on stone inscriptions.

See also DIDASCALIA.   GS

Pickard-Cambridge (1968).

Chorus   *see* CHOREGUS; COMEDY, GREEK; TRAGEDY, GREEK.

Chremonides   (fl. 270–240 BC), Athenian politician. Chremonides studied philosophy with ZENO OF CITIUM and was active in Athens's struggles against ANTIGONUS II GONATAS. He proposed the decree which joined Athens to an anti-Macedonian alliance under the Spartan AREUS I (the resulting war *c.*266–261 BC is therefore called the 'War of Chremonides'). Athens, although aided by PTOLEMY II, was forced to surrender. Chremonides fled to Egypt and was admiral in a Ptolemaic fleet defeated by the allies of ANTIOCHUS II THEOS in the Second Syrian War.

See also ATHENS, HISTORY.   EER

CAH VII.1; Ferguson (1911); Mossé (1973).

Christianity   The first Christians were mostly devout JEWS and as such the early Church was accorded the same degree of tolerance by Rome as was enjoyed by Judaism. But Judaea was a turbulent province and relations between Jews, Christians, and Romans deteriorated rapidly. When the great fire broke out at Rome in AD 64, NERO blamed the Christians and subjected them to persecution. Christians were persecuted again under DOMITIAN in the 90s, especially in Asia where there was further trouble during PLINY THE YOUNGER's governorship of Bithynia (112). A period of calm ensued during which Christianity spread and, despite pogroms under Marcus AURELIUS (48 Christians were martyred at Lyon in 177), by 200 it was distinguished from Judaism and established as a major religion in its own right. The 3rd century was marked by widespread persecution and increasing hostility, but as the empire began to crumble so the faith gathered strength and the blood of martyrs became the seed of the Church. The Church also gained intellectual credibility, thanks largely to the work of ORIGEN.

Order was restored to the empire by DIOCLETIAN and it was he who launched in 303 the last and most terrible onslaught on the Christians. Under the influence of GALERIUS buildings were razed, books burned, recalcitrant believers (after 304) slain in countless (and no doubt exaggerated) numbers. The persecution lasted 10 years and ended in failure. The Church emerged stronger than ever: its refugees became the first monks; its final triumph was symbolized by the conversion of the emperor CONSTANTINE I in 312. By the Edict of Milan (313) he brought an end to the persecution and at the Council of NICAEA (325) at which he presided Christianity in effect became the religion of the empire. Despite its shortlived restoration under JULIAN (360–3), paganism was in terminal decline. The victory of the Church was sealed by THEODOSIUS I.

See also ARIANISM; CATACOMBS; DONATISTS; GNOSTICISM; NESTORIANISM; NEW TESTAMENT; PELAGIANISM.   GS

Chadwick (1986b); Lane Fox (1986).

Chrysippus (*c*.280–207 BC), Stoic philosopher. Chrysippus came to Athens *c*.260 BC from Soli in Cilicia. He attended at first the lectures of ARCESILAUS, then head of the ACADEMY, but was later converted to Stoicism by Cleanthes, whom he succeeded as head of the Stoa in 232 BC. He spent the rest of his life elaborating the doctrines of ZENO OF CITIUM and Cleanthes into a unified system and defending it against the attacks of the Academy.

See also CARNEADES; STOICS.   JL

Long (1974).

Chrysostom, St John (*c*.AD 347–407), bishop of Constantinople. A native of Antioch, John was trained in law under LIBANIUS but pursued a monastic calling (*c*.373–81). Returning to Antioch, he was ordained and became a celebrated preacher (whence his nickname 'golden mouth'). Summoned to Constantinople as bishop (398), he fell foul of the empress Eudoxia, was deposed (403), banished (404), and died in exile. Numerous sermons and letters survive.   GS

Chadwick (1986b); Kazhdan (1991); Liebeschuetz (1990).

Cicero, Marcus Tullius (106–43 BC), Roman orator. Marcus Tullius Cicero was born an equestrian and was thus a NOVUS HOMO in Roman politics. He first established his reputation as an advocate in political trials, most notably with his defence of ROSCIUS GALLUS in 80 BC and his prosecution of VERRES in 70. In the latter trial Cicero defeated HORTENSIUS HORTALUS, whom he then replaced as the leading orator at Rome. Posing as a moderate among the POPULARES, Cicero supported POMPEY in the 60s, speaking in favour of the *lex Manilia* of 66 which gave Pompey the command against MITHRIDATES VI. Having been quaestor in 75 and praetor in 66, Cicero played on fears of CATILINE to win election in 64 to be consul in 63.

After the election of 64 Cicero allied himself to the OPTIMATES, although posing as a *popularis* to stop an agrarian reform bill proposed by Rullus. In his consulship of 63 Cicero's attacks drove Catiline into an open rebellion, which was easily crushed. The temporary union of the propertied against Catiline inspired Cicero to dream of creating a 'Union of the Orders' (*Concordia Ordinum*), a chimera he followed for the rest of his life.

The First TRIUMVIRATE of 59 curtailed Cicero's influence. In 58 CLODIUS, attacking the dubious legality of Cicero's execution of the Catilinarian conspirators, secured Cicero's exile. Returned in 57 at the instigation of Pompey, Cicero accepted the invidious position of defending in court his personal enemies (GABINIUS, Vatinius) at the behest of the triumvirs. In 51–50 Cicero was forced to serve as governor of the province of Cilicia, a post he regarded as a second exile.

Cicero returned to Rome in 49 to the CIVIL WAR. After some indecision, he joined the Republican side, but made no positive contribution to its cause. In the aftermath of the battle of PHARSALUS Cicero accepted a pardon from CAESAR. Cicero, however, welcomed the assassination of Caesar in 44. He now called for the death of Mark ANTONY in the *Philippic* orations and attempted to manipulate Octavian (AUGUSTUS) in the Optimate cause. With the formation of the Second TRIUMVIRATE in 43, Cicero's name appeared on the PROSCRIPTION lists, and he was killed making an ineffectual attempt to escape by sea.

Cicero was a prolific author in various genres. Although most is now lost, he took his poetry seriously, composing, among other works, the epics *On his Consulship* and *On his own Times*. The majority of his correspondence was not written for publication. Collected as letters *To Atticus*, *To his Friends*, *To his Brother Quintus* CICERO, and correspondence with BRUTUS, it gives a vivid insight into the political and social life of his times (*see* EPISTOLOGRAPHY, LATIN). As Cicero's 58 surviving speeches, from the *Pro Quinctio* in 81 to the 14th *Philippic* in 43, were composed for differing audiences and ends, they vary widely in content and tone. Cicero's philosophical works (famous among which are *On the Republic* and *On the Laws*) synthesized Greek philosophy and made it available to a Latin audience. Cicero also wrote on RHETORIC, which he saw as closely related to philosophy.

HS

Dorey (1965); Douglas (1968); Fuhrmann (1992); Habicht (1990); Rawson (1975); Stockton (1971).

Cicero, Quintus Tullius (d. 43 BC), brother of CICERO the orator. Quintus Tullius Cicero, younger brother of Marcus but without his genius, was an able soldier and administrator. After his praetorship he governed Asia from 61 to 59 BC, and served as a legate first to Caesar in Gaul and Britain from 54 to 51 and then to his brother in Cilicia. In the CIVIL WAR he joined Pompey, but was pardoned after PHARSALUS. He perished in the proscriptions of 43. He may have written the pamphlet *Commentariolum Petitionis* ('Electioneering Advice') for Marcus. DP

Rawson (1975); Wiseman (1987).

Cilicia   territory in Asia Minor. Cilicia, the eastern part of Turkey's south coast, consists of remote, mountainous Cilicia Tracheia (west) and fertile Cilicia Pedias (east). Persian control was ended by ALEXANDER THE GREAT, and Cilicia was disputed in Hellenistic times by the Ptolemies and Seleucids. Cilicia Tracheia became notorious for pirates, leading to a special Roman provincial command for the general area *c*.102. POMPEY suppressed them only in 67 BC, joining Pedias and its interior to the province. The province of Cilicia was later broken up and fell under the successive control of GALATIA, CAPPADOCIA, and COMMAGENE. Vespasian in AD 72 recreated the province of Cilicia from Tracheia and Pedias. EER

Bean (1979); CAH VII.1; Eddy (1961); Jones (1983); Magie (1975); Ormerod (1924); Sherwin-White (1984); Sullivan (1990).

Cimbri   German people. The Cimbri and TEUTONES entered Noricum in 113 BC and defeated a Roman army. In 109 they requested land in Transalpine Gaul to settle, but the Senate refused. This was followed by a disastrous attack by Junius Silanus. At Arausio (Orange) in 105 they defeated CAEPIO, but then advanced into Spain, giving MARIUS time to train a new army. CATULUS delayed the Cimbri in 102 BC while Marius destroyed the Teutones, and in 101 Marius slaughtered the Cimbri at Vercellae. LPR

Chadwick (1970).

Cimmerians   Asiatic tribe. Driven from their homeland in south Russia by the SCYTHIANS, the Cimmerians invaded Asia Minor in great numbers in the late 8th century BC, destroying the Phrygian kingdom and attacking Lydia and Ionia: Magnesia and Sardes were sacked and Ephesus attacked; GYGES died fighting them; but they established no empire and, weakened by plague, were finally driven from Anatolia by Alyattes, father of Croesus. RB

Burn (1960); CAH III.2.

Cimon   (*c*.510–450 BC), Athenian aristocrat. Son of MILTIADES, Cimon was frequently general in the 470s and 460s and passionate in conducting war against Persia. In 476 he took Byzantium from PAUSANIAS and Eion from the Persians, and in 469 at the battle of EURYMEDON he smashed a Persian land and sea force heading for Ionia. Despite suppressing the revolts of Naxos (470?) and Thasos (465), he acquired a reputation for leniency to members of the DELIAN LEAGUE. When Sparta, faced with a helots' (see SERFS) revolt, appealed for help, he called on the Athenians 'not to see Greece lame nor Athens deprived of her yoke-fellow', a notable call for shared hegemony against Persia. After the reforms of EPHIALTES he was ostracized but recalled in 451 to make the Five Years' Truce with Sparta. He set sail for Cyprus on a final campaign against the Persians and died. He supported the values of the landed aristocracy (as his sons' names show: Lacedaemonius, Eleius, Thessalus).

GLC

Meiggs (1972).

Cincinnatus   (5th century BC), Roman hero. L. Quinctius Cincinnatus was a historical figure celebrated in later legend as a model of ancient virtue and simplicity. During an emergency in 458 BC, when a Roman army was trapped by the AEQUI at Algidus, he was summoned while ploughing and appointed DICTATOR. In the space of 15 days Cincinnatus raised an army, defeated the enemy, triumphed, laid down his office, and returned to the plough.   TC

Broughton (1951); CAH VII.2.

Cinna   (d. 84 BC), Roman politician. Lucius Cornelius Cinna as consul in 87 BC attacked SULLA's actions of 88. Driven out of Rome and illegally deposed, he returned by force with the cooperation of MARIUS and SERTORIUS. He attempted to curb Marius' massacres, and after Marius' death his government seems to have aimed at conciliation. In 84, with war against Sulla inevitable, he was killed in a mutiny.   HS

Badian (1964); Bennett (1923).

Circus   an arena for chariot racing, the Roman equivalent of the Greek hippodrome (see ARCHITECTURE, GREEK). Shaped like an elongated horseshoe, it had raised seating all round, and at the open end stables for up to 12 teams of horses. The oldest circus at Rome is the Circus Maximus which lies between the Aventine and Palatine hills and dates from the earliest times. It was reconstructed by Julius CAESAR with three tiers of seating, the upper two being wooden, and again by TRAJAN who embellished it with marble both inside and out. The track was 600 yards long and 150 yards wide, so a single lap was about 1,500 yards; there were seven laps to a race. A central reservation (*spina*) divided the length of the course, decorated with shrines and statues, and with turning posts at each end. The sport attracted a mass following and supporters divided themselves into factions that were identified by their colours: Reds, Whites, Greens, and Blues. In addition to the Circus Maximus, which could seat about 200,000 people, three other circuses were built at Rome and numerous other examples are known throughout the empire.

See also GAMES, ROMAN.   GS

Cameron (1976); Humphrey (1986).

Cirta   modern Constantine, city in Numidia. Capital of the kingdom ruled by SYPHAX and MASSINISSA, Cirta was sacked by JUGURTHA in 112 BC. Given by Caesar to his friend Sittius after THAPSUS (46 BC), it was subsequently incorporated in the province of Africa. During the Empire it enjoyed great prosperity as a source of grain, copper, and marble. Under CONSTANTINE I it was renamed Constantina and became the capital of NUMIDIA.   GS

Cisalpine Gaul   Roman province. Cisalpine Gaul was the region of north Italy bounded on the north and west by the Alps and on the south by the Apennines and river Rubicon. From early times it was occupied by CELTS, whose frequent invasions of peninsular Italy were resisted by the Romans. The Roman conquest began in the later 3rd century BC with the capture of MEDIOLANUM (Milan) in 222 and the subsequent foundation of colonies such as Cremona, Bononia, Mutina, and Parma. The conquest was finally consolidated at the end of the 2nd century. The area north of the Po received Roman citizenship in 49. In 42 BC it was formally incorporated into Italy by the Second TRIUMVIRATE. An area of rich agricultural land and numerous cities, Cisalpine Gaul became the most prosperous region of the Roman empire.   HE

Chilver (1941); Potter (1987).

Citizenship, Greek   Citizenship meant membership of a POLIS, participation in its political and religious activities, and acceptance of its laws; it was also linked to the right to own land. Normally it was inherited through the father, though at Athens after 451/450 BC both parents had to be citizens. In oligarchies full political citizenship might be further restricted by qualifications of wealth or family, giving rise to inferior citizen statuses. In the 6th and 5th centuries BC citizenship was jealously guarded: acceptance was by formal procedure, citizen lists were regularly scrutinized, and citizenship was rarely granted to outsiders, although the Athenians made block grants in exceptional circumstances to the Plataeans (428/7), the Samians (405), and the 'liberators' (401/400). But in the 4th century the tendency to grant honorary citizenship for political reasons increased, and in the Hellenistic period it was a normal way of rewarding and attracting benefactors.   RB

Ehrenberg (1969); Manville (1990); Osborne (1981–3).

Citizenship, Roman   Roman citizenship entailed a complex of rights and privileges, including the vote (*suffragium*), the right to make legally binding contracts (*commercium*), and the capacity to contract a legal MARRIAGE (*conubium*). It also implied a corresponding set of obligations, principally taxation and military service. Citizenship was flexible, however, and did not automatically mean the same for all citizens. It was possible to hold partial citizenship, e.g. 'citizenship without vote' (*see* MUNICIPIUM), and for non-citizens to possess some of its privileges. LATINI, for example, had the rights of *commercium*, *conubium*, and a limited right to vote. The extent of a citizen's privileges also depended on wealth and status (*see* CENSUS; PROLETARII).

Citizenship could be obtained in different ways, most obviously by inheritance (from a citizen father who had formed a legal marriage); but Roman citizenship was never confined exclusively to citizens by birth, and from the earliest times Rome had opened its door to outsiders. Latini could become Romans simply by taking up residence at Rome, and slaves automatically became citizens when formally manumitted. Citizenship could also be granted to outsiders (individuals or groups) as a reward for services rendered, and under the Empire became automatic for men who completed their service in the AUXILIA. Conquered peoples in Italy were sometimes given full or partial citizenship (*see* e.g. CAMPANIA; LATIN WAR; TUSCULUM), and after the SOCIAL WAR all of Italy was incorporated. Under the Principate the emperors gave citizenship to favoured individuals, cities, and sometimes whole provinces, a process that culminated in AD 212 in Caracalla (*see* AURELIUS ANTONINUS) giving citizenship to all free inhabitants of the empire.
                                                                              TC

Nicolet (1980); Sherwin-White (1973).

City-state   *see* POLIS.

Civilis (d. *c.*AD 70), Batavian commander. Gaius Julius Civilis, a Batavian of royal descent, commanded an auxiliary infantry unit in the Roman army. Imprisoned on suspicion of rebellion (68), he was acquitted by GALBA. Incited by VESPASIAN's supporters, he rebelled against VITELLIUS (69), and then turned the rebellion into a nationalistic uprising.

He was rapidly joined by Germanic tribes from both sides of the Rhine, but was eventually forced to surrender by Petilius Cerialis (70) and probably executed.   RJB

Drinkwater (1983); Wellesley (1975).

Civil wars, Roman   After the ARMY reforms of MARIUS, a vicious circle became established whereby the troops looked to their commander for rewards and the commander looked to his troops for support. When deprived by SULPICIUS Rufus and Marius of his command against MITHRIDATES VI, SULLA in 88 BC was the first Roman general to march on Rome. In 87, with Sulla in the east, CINNA and Marius seized Rome. Returning in 83, Sulla defeated NORBANUS and CARBO to retake Rome.

The civil wars that ended the Republic began in 49 BC when CAESAR drove POMPEY from Italy. The battles of PHARSALUS, THAPSUS, and MUNDA secured Caesar's dominance. After the assassination of Caesar the civil wars began again, Octavian (AUGUSTUS) first fighting ANTONY, before joining with him to defeat Caesar's enemies at PHILIPPI. Augustus successively removed by force his rivals, Sextus POMPEIUS, LEPIDUS, and Antony (at ACTIUM), to establish the Principate.

Under the Julio-Claudians the 'secret' that the monarchy rested on military force was kept until the 'year of the four emperors' (AD 69), when GALBA, OTHO, and VITELLIUS fought for the throne before VESPASIAN established the Flavian dynasty. Although there were rebellions (AVIDIUS CASSIUS), major civil wars did not reappear until after the death of PERTINAX in 193. DIDIUS JULIANUS then seized power, and Septimius SEVERUS went into revolt. The provincial armies were by now ready to follow their commanders against each other or Rome. Didius Julianus soon died, and Severus defeated two rivals, CLODIUS ALBINUS and PESCENNIUS NIGER, to establish the Severan dynasty. Civil war was avoided under the dynasty with one exception, the defeat of the short-lived interloper MACRINUS, until the murder of SEVERUS Alexander in 235. The 3rd century then saw endemic civil war until DIOCLETIAN temporarily restored order. The late Empire continued to suffer from periodic outbreaks of civil war.

See also ARMS AND ARMOUR, ROMAN; WARFARE, ROMAN.   HS

Birley (1988); Brunt (1971a, 1988); Wellesley (1975).

Classical period   The 'classical' period of Greek culture extends from the end of the PERSIAN WARS to the death of ALEXANDER THE GREAT, roughly 480 to 323 BC. It represents the maturity of the flowering that began in the ARCHAIC PERIOD. The geographical focus was the city of Athens where an enlightened regime and a period of relative peace and prosperity created an intellectual climate that was uniquely receptive to new ideas and new areas of creativity. Pioneering activity extended to almost every field of cultural endeavour.

In literature the telling of stories, which had first blossomed in the EPIC POETRY of earlier centuries, evolved in new directions: the dramatists responded to the need for public entertainment with their masterpieces of TRAGEDY and COMEDY, and a new prose tradition of HISTORIOGRAPHY emerged. Just as innovative were the developments in LYRIC POETRY, in RHETORIC, and in philosophical writing. Philosophical inquiry, notably in ethics and metaphysics, was transformed by the teaching of men such as SOCRATES, PLATO, and ARISTOTLE. The latter also made significant contributions to the study of natural and political science, and the scientific practice of MEDICINE was initiated. Finally, the visual arts reached maturity. ARCHITECTURE with its newly defined columnar orders (Doric, Ionic, and now also Corinthian) made a monumental but gracious impact on the landscape. SCULPTURE and PAINTING achieved excellence by means of the techniques of harmony and perspective. POTTERY and the mostly anonymous painters of pots explored new shapes and achieved a new and sublime realism which has a timeless appeal.

GS

Charbonneaux, Martin, and Villard (1973); Ling (1989).

Claudian (*c.*AD 370–404), Latin poet. Claudius Claudianus was born in Alexandria and moved to Rome *c.*394 where he became court poet to the emperor HONORIUS and his regent STILICHO. Moving to the imperial capital at Milan, he obtained senatorial rank and was employed by Stilicho as a professional laureate and propagandist. He introduced the Greek tradition of poetic PANEGYRIC to the western empire; other surviving works include occasional poetry and historical and mythological epics.

GS

Binns (1974); Cameron (1970).

Claudius I (10 BC–AD 54), Roman emperor, AD 41–54. Tiberius Claudius Nero Germanicus was the youngest son of DRUSUS (son of LIVIA) and the younger ANTONIA. His childhood was unhappy: treated as a fool by Antonia and Livia, he was largely excluded from public life because of physical disabilities, devoting much of his time to antiquarian studies. In January 41 he was proclaimed emperor by the Praetorian Guard after the murder of his nephew GAIUS (Caligula): he was of the Claudian family, but had inherited Julian blood through his mother, and so was an acceptable candidate. He is portrayed as an ineffectual glutton, ruled by his freedmen and wives, but he was at first more vigorous. Anxious to acquire military prestige, he began the conquest of BRITAIN (43), although entrusting the campaign to Aulus PLAUTIUS (he himself spent only 16 days in Britain). For the sake of efficiency, the administration was increasingly centralized, freedmen achieving great power (at the expense of senatorial magistrates): the most important were NARCISSUS, secretary-general (*ab epistulis*); PALLAS, financial secretary (*a rationibus*); Callistus, legal secretary (*a libellis*); and Polybius, librarian and privy seal (*a studiis*). Claudius acted to safeguard Rome's grain supply, building a new harbour at OSTIA, and reorganized the imperial and state FINANCES. Various senatorial conspiracies against Claudius included that of the consul Gaius Silius (48), who went through a marriage ceremony with Claudius' third wife, MESSALINA (by whom Claudius had two children, Britannicus and Octavia). Both conspirators were put to death, and Claudius, advised by his friend L. VITELLIUS and by Pallas, married for a fourth time, to his niece, the younger AGRIPPINA. He adopted her son (NERO) and married him to Octavia, marking him out for the succession ahead of Britannicus. Agrippina achieved extraordinary power in Claudius' final years, and almost certainly murdered him (with poisoned mushrooms) to ensure her son's succession.   RJB

Grant (1985); Levick (1990); Scullard (1982); Wells (1984).

Claudius II (*c*.AD 214–70), Roman emperor, AD 268–70. Marcus Aurelius Claudius 'Gothicus', proclaimed emperor after GALLIENUS' assassination, was one of a series of Illyrian soldier-emperors who effected a revival of Roman military fortunes. Claudius put down the usurper AUREOLUS, and, with AURELIAN as his cavalry general, defeated an invasion of Italy by the ALAMANNI. His greatest success was against the GOTHS (hence the title 'Gothicus') in the Balkans, whose forces he broke up after inflicting heavy defeats at Doberus and Naissus. However, pre-occupied with these barbarian invasions, Claudius was unable to reclaim either the Gallic provinces or Palmyra for Rome, dying of plague at Sirmium (early 270).   RJB

Grant (1985); Parker (1958).

Claudius, Appius (5th century BC), Roman lawgiver. Appius Claudius was the only one of the DECEMVIRI to hold office for two years running (451–450 BC), and was the leader of the tyrannical regime established by the second decemvirate. He was also responsible for its downfall, when he attempted to seduce Verginia, a young plebeian girl who was killed by her own father in order to save her from Appius' lust. This tragedy provoked the popular uprising which overthrew the decemvirs.
                                                                    TC

Broughton (1951); Wiseman (1979).

Claudius Caecus   (fl. 312–279 BC), Roman statesman. Appius Claudius Caecus rose to prominence as CENSOR in 312 BC. Apart from the construction of two great public works, the Via APPIA and Rome's first AQUEDUCT (the Aqua Appia), Appius' censorship was marked by extreme political radicalism. He reorganized the tribes so as to increase the voting power of the lower classes in the COMITIA. He also admitted sons of freedmen into the Senate. He aroused furious opposition, among others from his own colleague, who resigned, leaving Appius to continue as sole censor. He was consul in 307 and 296 (when he fought successfully against the Etruscans), and praetor in 295. At the end of his life (279) he successfully persuaded the Senate to reject a peace offer from PYRRHUS.   TC

Broughton (1951); CAH VII.2.

Claudius Pompeianus   (d. after AD 193), Roman soldier and administrator. Tiberius Claudius Pompeianus, governor of Lower Pannonia during the Germanic invasions of 166–7, was promoted by Marcus AURELIUS after the death of VERUS (169): he married Verus' widow, Marcus' daughter Lucilla, and acted as regent in Rome during Marcus' absence (169–76). Passed over for the succession in favour of COMMODUS, and discarded by him, Pompeianus retained sufficient standing for DIDIUS JULIANUS to appeal to him (unavailingly) when deposed by Septimius SEVERUS (193).
See also PERTINAX.   RJB

Parker (1958).

Claudius Pulcher   (d. 48 BC), Roman politician. Appius Claudius Pulcher, elder brother of CLODIUS and CLODIA and a leading figure in the senatorial establishment, was consul in 54 BC, and then governed Cilicia from 53 to 51. CICERO, who succeeded him as governor, tried to remedy his abuses there. Appius then became censor in 50 and used the office as a partisan tool against CAESAR's supporters. He helped to win POMPEY to the Republican cause, but died in 48 as Republican governor of Achaea. He was an expert on religious matters and wrote a book on augury, which he dedicated to Cicero.   DP

Gruen (1974); Rawson (1991).

Claudius Quadrigarius   (1st century BC), Roman annalist. Quintus Claudius Quadrigarius wrote a history of Rome which survives in only a few fragments. It covered events from the Gallic sack of Rome (390 BC) to Sulla (70s BC) in at least 23 books. Quadrigarius was a contemporary of the annalists VALERIUS ANTIAS and MACER and, later, a major source for LIVY.

See also HISTORIOGRAPHY, ROMAN.   HE

Badian (1966b).

Clearchus (450–401 BC), Spartan soldier. After the Peloponnesian war, in which he served mostly in the Hellespontine area, Clearchus was in 403 appointed governor at Byzantium where he behaved tyrannically. When recalled, he refused to obey and was condemned to death. An army was sent against him, so he fled to CYRUS THE YOUNGER who made him commander of the Greeks in his army. In the battle of CUNAXA (401) he disobeyed Cyrus' order to advance obliquely and Cyrus was killed. On the return march Clearchus was arrested by TISSAPHERNES and executed.   GLC

Parke (1933).

Cleisthenes of Athens (fl. *c*.525–505 BC), Athenian statesman. Cleisthenes was the son of the ALCMAEONID Megacles and grandson of CLEISTHENES OF SICYON. He was archon under the Peisistratids in 525/4 BC; after the overthrow of the tyranny, he headed a faction opposed to that of ISAGORAS. Although he was initially defeated, his proposals for political reform attracted a popular support which overrode the Spartan-supported backlash and reversed his brief exile. His interlocking reforms created a new geographically based structure of DEMES, TRITTYES, and tribes which elected a new BOULE. The old tribal structure, dominated by aristocratic clans, was not abolished, but largely superseded: Cleisthenes' system removed control of citizenship from the PHRATRY and cut across old loyalties, creating alternative power bases, while the invention of OSTRACISM offered a peaceful resolution of factional strife. All this was probably reinforced by appeals to an ideology of equality, and Cleisthenes was later regarded as one of the architects of Athenian DEMOCRACY.   RB

CAH IV; Forrest (1966); Kearns (1985); Murray (1993).

Cleisthenes of Sicyon tyrant of Sicyon, *c*.600–570 BC. Cleisthenes was a descendant of Orthagoras, first tyrant of SICYON, but seems to have seized power from his brothers. His policies were uniformly hostile to Argos, including a tribal reform which apparently also had anti-Dorian overtones. A quarrel with the Delphic oracle led to his participation in the First SACRED WAR, and he established a marriage connection with the ALCMAEONIDS.   RB

Andrewes (1956); Griffin (1982).

Cleitarchus (*c*.350–?280 BC), Greek historian. Cleitarchus may have accompanied ALEXANDER THE GREAT's expedition, and perhaps lived in Alexandria, but details of his life are lacking. At an unknown date and using unknown sources, he wrote a history of Alexander in at least 12 books. His lost history is generally considered the main influence on the so-called 'Vulgate' tradition about Alexander: a highly coloured, sensational picture seen in the later histories of DIODORUS SICULUS, CURTIUS, and TROGUS.

See also ARRIAN. EER

Bosworth (1988a, b); Pearson (1960).

Cleitus the Black (*c*.380–328/7 BC), Macedonian general. Cleitus was a distinguished cavalry commander under ALEXANDER THE GREAT. He saved Alexander's life at the battle of the GRANICUS RIVER in 334 BC, but was killed by him in 328 during a drunken quarrel in which he mocked Alexander for adopting oriental customs and neglecting the Macedonians. The episode was later invoked as evidence for the sharp decline in Alexander's moral character. EER

Bosworth (1988a); Hammond (1989); Lane Fox (1973).

Cleitus the White (d. 318 BC), Macedonian general. Cleitus was an officer of ALEXANDER THE GREAT. During the LAMIAN WAR he was an admiral of the Macedonian fleet which defeated Athens at Amorgos and finally closed the Dardanelles to the allied Greeks in 322 BC. ANTIPATER rewarded him with the satrapy of LYDIA in 321. Expelled by ANTIGONUS I MONOPHTHALMUS in 319, Cleitus joined POLYPERCHON. He failed to prevent Antigonus from crossing the Bosporus, was defeated by NICANOR OF STAGIRA, and killed in Thrace. EER

Billows (1990); Hammond and Walbank (1988).

Clement of Alexandria, St (*c*.AD 150–215), Greek Christian writer. Titus Flavius Clemens, probably Athenian by birth, was educated in Alexandria. He became head of the Catechetical School (an establishment for the instruction of converts) there in 190 but in the persecution of 202 he fled to Cappadocia where he died. He was succeeded by ORIGEN. His learning was wide and catholic, fusing elements of pagan and Christian thought. His surviving works include the *Protrepticus* urging the superiority of Christianity, and the *Paidagogus* on Christian morality. GS

Chadwick (1966); Lilla (1971).

Cleobis and Biton traditionally two of the happiest men. According to HERODOTUS (1.31), Solon on a visit to CROESUS refused to name his wealthy host the happiest of men because he was still living. Instead he chose first an Athenian called Tellus and secondly Cleobis and Biton, two young Argive brothers who had harnessed themselves to their mother's cart and drawn it six miles to the Heraeum. They were rewarded with death while they slept in the temple. Their statues have been found at Delphi.   GS

Cleomenes I   king of Sparta, c.520–489 BC. Cleomenes, son of ANAXANDRIDAS, was the most powerful archaic Spartan king, but his reputation has always been mixed. His defeat of Argos at SEPEIA eliminated Sparta's rival for a generation; he helped Athens overthrow the Peisistratid tyranny; and his intervention in AEGINA stiffened resistance to Persia, although he refused several calls for Spartan aid overseas. But his overbearing actions in support of ISAGORAS alienated Athens and weakened Sparta's standing *vis-à-vis* her allies, and his machinations within Sparta, notably against DEMARATUS, culminated in treasonable plotting in exile, imprisonment, and death.

See also PELOPONNESIAN LEAGUE.   RB

Cartledge (1979); Forrest (1980); Huxley (1962).

Cleomenes III   (c.260–219 BC), king of Sparta. Cleomenes was the son of Leonidas II (deposed by AGIS IV), and inherited and implemented Agis' ideas of social and economic reform. His extension of Spartan power in the Peloponnese alarmed ARATUS OF SICYON, who invited the Macedonian ANTIGONUS III DOSON to help the ACHAEAN LEAGUE against Cleomenes. Defeated at the battle of Sellasia in 222 BC, he fled to his ally Egypt, was arrested, and killed himself escaping from prison after the accession of PTOLEMY IV.   EER

CAH VII.1; Cartledge and Spawforth (1989); Forrest (1980); Green (1990); Jones (1967).

Cleomenes of Naucratis   (fl. 332–322 BC), governor of Egypt. Cleomenes was appointed by ALEXANDER THE GREAT in 332–331 BC as governor of eastern Egypt (under the supervision of two Macedonian military commanders), and oversaw the completion of ALEXANDRIA. He declared himself satrap, but was eventually forgiven and confirmed as such despite exploiting Egypt's wealth for his personal benefit. After Alexander's death he was appointed assistant to the new satrap PTOLEMY (later I) but was soon executed by him.   EER

Bosworth (1988a); CAH VII.1.

Cleon   (fl. 430–422 BC), Athenian statesman. Cleon dominated Athenian politics after PERICLES. He advocated severity in maintaining loyalty in the empire, proposing the execution of all adult males of Mytilene (427) and Scione (423); and, refusing to compromise with Sparta, he counselled the rejection of peace (425). Inheriting from NICIAS the conduct of a force to help DEMOSTHENES capture the Spartans on Sphacteria (see PYLOS), he won great credit for that success and conceived military ambitions. When sent as general to counter BRASIDAS and recover Amphipolis (422), he proved incompetent and was killed. Both THUCYDIDES and ARISTOPHANES were hostile towards him and compared him unfavourably with Pericles.   GLC

Kagan (1975).

Cleonymus (fl. 305–270 BC), Spartan pretender. Cleonymus was guardian to his nephew AREUS I (acceded 309–308 BC) but never renounced his own claim to the Spartan throne. He led a mercenary force to Tarentum in 303, and temporarily seized Corcyra. His anti-Macedonian alliance with PYRRHUS of Epirus raised his hopes for the throne, eased Pyrrhus' intervention in the Peloponnese, and posed problems for Macedon. Cleonymus and Pyrrhus attacked Sparta in 272 but were defeated by Areus and ANTIGONUS II GONATAS.   EER

Cartledge and Spawforth (1989); Forrest (1980); Jones (1967).

Cleopatra II (c.185–116/115 BC), queen of Egypt. Cleopatra, the daughter of PTOLEMY V EPIPHANES, married her brother Ptolemy VI and was co-regent with him and their mutual brother Ptolemy VIII during the Sixth Syrian War against ANTIOCHUS IV EPIPHANES (170–168 BC). A widow in 145, Cleopatra married Ptolemy VIII. He murdered her son, also married her daughter (his niece) CLEOPATRA III, and later killed his son by Cleopatra II. In the struggle for power Cleopatra promised the throne to her Seleucid son-in-law DEMETRIUS II NICATOR, but her husband helped to kill him. A public reconciliation was somehow declared in 124, and until her death in 116/115 Cleopatra ruled jointly with Ptolemy VIII and Cleopatra III.
       See also PTOLEMY VI–XV.   EER

Green (1990); Macurdy (1932).

Cleopatra III (fl. 142–101 BC), queen of Egypt. Cleopatra was the daughter of Ptolemy VI and his sister CLEOPATRA II. In 142 BC she married, and was made co-regent with, her uncle Ptolemy VIII (also married to her own mother) who played daughter against mother. After various struggles, the three ruled jointly from 124 until Ptolemy VIII's death in 116. In the contested succession she supported her second son who may none the less have caused her death in 101.

See also PTOLEMY VI–XV.   EER

Green (1990); Macurdy (1932); Sullivan (1990).

Cleopatra VII (69–30 BC), queen of Egypt. Cleopatra, the last Ptolemaic queen, was the daughter of Ptolemy XII and from 51 BC uneasy co-ruler with her younger brother and husband Ptolemy XIII. She was supported against her brother's faction by Julius CAESAR, who fought her side in the Alexandrian War in which Ptolemy XIII was killed in 47. She married her other brother Ptolemy XIV, relying on Caesar's legions. After the birth of her (and allegedly Caesar's) son CAESARION, she moved to Rome but returned after Caesar's murder in 44. Ptolemy XIV died, supposedly through poison, and Cleopatra declared Caesarion joint ruler. After summoning her to Tarsus, Mark ANTONY spent the winter of 41 in Alexandria, and their permanent alliance in 37 led to Cleopatra's involvement in Antony's civil war against Octavian (later AUGUSTUS). Rome declared war on her in 32, and she and Antony were defeated at ACTIUM. Cleopatra avoided capture and humiliation by succumbing to the fatal bite of an asp.
    See also BELLUM ALEXANDRINUM.   EER

Green (1990); Macurdy (1932); Sullivan (1990); Volkmann (1958).

Cleophon (fl. 430–405 BC), Athenian politician. As 'leader of the people' from 410 to 404 BC, Cleophon opposed peace with Sparta after CYZICUS (410), possibly after ARGINUSAE (406), certainly after AEGOSPOTAMI (405), and introduced the *diobelia*, a form of dole. XENOPHON showed his contempt by naming him only once. THUCYDIDES must have had him in mind when making his remarks about the successors of PERICLES (2.65). The comic poet PLATO used his name as a title, a sign of his importance.   GLC

Kagan (1987).

Cleophrades Painter (fl. *c*.500–480 BC), Greek vase painter. Cleophrades was the name of an Athenian potter, whose signature is found on the fragments of a cup. The cup's painter, generally known as the Cleophrades Painter, has been credited with more than 100 vases and is regarded as one of the greatest artists of the late archaic period.   GS

Arias and Hirmer (1962); Boardman (1975).

Cleruchy a type of overseas settlement practised by classical Athens, in which land was taken from an existing state and distributed in allotments (*kleroi*) to poor Athenians, who retained their original citizenship. Cleruchies generally had a security function, and many were punitive, following revolt or conquest; but in some cases the original inhabitants were compensated by reduced tribute. Although they were an unpopular feature of the 5th-century BC empire and explicitly forbidden in the charter of the Second Athenian Confederacy, Athens established several new cleruchies when given the opportunity in the following century.　　　　　　　　　　　　　　　　　　　　　　　　RB

Brunt (1966); Figuera (1991); Graham (1964); Hornblower and Greenstock (1986); Meiggs (1972).

Clientela　form of Roman patronage. *Clientela* is a Latin term used to describe the relationship of clients and patrons. Clients received food or financial support, legal assistance, and other benefits. In return, they gave deference and support to their PATRONUS in political and personal affairs. They were also obliged to greet him each morning, to receive handouts, and to accompany him on his way to the Forum. This relationship had no legal status and rested on purely moral ties, but it was accepted that clients and patrons could not testify against each other.　　　　　　　　　　　　　　　　　　　　　　　　　　　　　HE

Brunt (1988); Saller (1982); Wallace-Hadrill (1989).

Cloaca Maxima　Roman sewer. The Cloaca Maxima was the main sewer of Rome, draining via the FORUM into the TIBER. Originally a natural water course, it was canalized and, after 200 BC, covered over. Work on it was traditionally ascribed to TARQUINIUS SUPERBUS, but most of the surviving remains were constructed by Vipsanius AGRIPPA. It was said to be a favoured place to deposit unsatisfactory emperors.　　HS

Nash (1968); Richardson (1992).

Clocks　*see* TIME, MEASUREMENT OF.

Clodia　(*c*.95–45 BC), Roman courtesan. Clodia, sister of CLODIUS and Appius CLAUDIUS PULCHER and wife of Q. Metellus Celer (consul 60 BC), came from the heart of the Roman ruling class. She was allegedly dominated by her desire for sexual gratification and political influence. CATULLUS was rejected by her, and puzzled over their relationship in his Lesbia poems. In 56, when she had accused her ex-lover CAELIUS of attempted murder, CICERO in his defence accused Clodia of incest with Clodius and the killing of her husband.　　　　　　　　　　　　　　　DP

Balsdon (1962); Gruen (1974); Wiseman (1985).

Clodius　(*c*.92–52 BC), Roman politician. Publius Clodius' adventurous career began when he caused a mutiny in LUCULLUS' army in 68 BC, and continued with his trial in 61 for attending in female attire the festival of the Bona Dea from which men were excluded. In 59 he became a plebeian by adoption so that he could hold the tribunate for 58. As tribune he successfully campaigned against CICERO, who was exiled, and passed a series of radical measures to limit the power of the *nobiles* and to benefit the poor. These included legalizing *collegia* (GUILDS) and a free corn distribution (ANNONA) for the inhabitants of the city. His gangs which resulted from the revived *collegia* clashed with the gangs of MILO until Clodius was killed in a fight in January 52.

DP

Gruen (1968, 1974); Lintott (1968); Scullard (1982).

Clodius Albinus (d. AD 197), Roman general. Decimus Clodius Septimius Albinus, distinguished general under Marcus AURELIUS and COMMODUS, and governor of Britain from *c*.191, rivalled Septimius SEVERUS and PESCENNIUS NIGER for the imperial throne in 193. He was initially bought off by Severus with the title of Caesar and a false promise of succession to the empire. Proclaimed Augustus by his troops, Albinus crossed into Gaul (196), but was defeated by Severus near Lyon and committed suicide.

RJB

Grant (1985); Parker (1958); Scullard (1979).

Clubs   *see* GUILDS.

Cnidus   Greek city in south-west Asia Minor. Originally settled by colonists from Sparta, Cnidus made good use of its strategic location and two harbours. It founded colonies of its own in Sicily and the Lipari islands and formed commercial links with Naucratis. After the Persian Wars it joined the DELIAN LEAGUE, but in 413 BC it switched allegiance to Sparta. In the 4th century a medical school was founded and the city produced a number of scientists. Decline set in in the 2nd century but it was a free city under the Roman Empire.

GS

Bean (1980).

Codex   *see* BOOKS, GREEK; LAW, ROMAN.

Coelius Antipater   (late 2nd century BC), Roman historian. Lucius Coelius Antipater was a jurist and rhetorician and the teacher of Lucius CRASSUS. He wrote a history of the Second PUNIC WAR in seven books, using both Roman and Carthaginian sources, which survives only in fragments. The idea of writing a historical monograph was a novelty

at Rome and derived from Hellenistic models. Coelius was later used
as a source by LIVY.   HE

Badian (1966b).

Cohort   *see* ARMY, ROMAN.

Coinage, Greek   The Greeks imitated coinage from its inventors in
Lydia, where coins of electrum (a gold–silver alloy) were being minted
in the second half of the 7th century BC; Aegina minted the earliest
coinage outside Anatolia, quickly followed by Corinth and Athens
(*c.*570–550), and the practice spread rapidly through the Greek world.
Early Greek coins were almost always SILVER, struck by hand between
two dies, or a die and a punch. Initially they had only an obverse
design, the reverse bearing a geometrical mark from the punch; but
reverse designs are found by the late 6th century; and some south
Italian coins bear the same design in relief and intaglio on obverse and
reverse.

Early coins are mainly of large denomination and value, and hence
impractical for retail trade. Since they also apparently circulated locally in most cases, and always carry a civic badge and/or name, it is
thought that they were originally intended for state purposes, such as
taxation or payment to mercenaries, and were meant to be retained
locally. Coins which do circulate widely come from areas like Athens
with abundant silver (*see* LAURIUM), and were probably viewed first as
bullion of guaranteed origin and quality. In due course small denominations naturally emerged, as minute silver coins: BRONZE small change
only became common in the 4th century, when GOLD coins also became more frequent. Inter-state trade was complicated by the variety
of weight standards for the drachma current in different cities; this in
turn had to be fitted in with the eastern system of staters and minae
(*see* WEIGHTS).

The study of coins offers a wealth of information. First, their date
must be established: this can be determined by type and design, style,
fabric, and from the context of their finding, particularly in coin hoards;
multiple examples offer scope for increasing precision. Coins themselves require care as dating indicators, because of the tendency of
valuable coins to remain in circulation. In some cases coins can be
assigned to a mint and even identified with particular dies, and hence
types can be placed in sequence; the origin and purity of their metal
content can also be analysed.

Hence, coins are valuable evidence for the economic life and history
of individual cities, and through their circulation they can help to
illustrate patterns of TRADE; coin designs, too, often allude to sources

of wealth. They can also be informative for political history, particularly in areas poorly covered by our literary sources: some eastern Hellenistic kings are only known from their coinage. Thus, the formation of inter-state groupings may be indicated by shared types with common features, while independence may be asserted by divergent or overstruck coinage; likewise, types may reflect the propaganda of individual rulers (or claimants to power) or states, and imitation may reflect the influence of another state, or an attempt to lay claim to the qualities of a predecessor (Alexander, above all).   RB

Head (1911); Jenkins (1990); Kraay (1976)

Coinage, Roman Early Rome had no coinage. Instead money took the form of uncoined bronze measured by weight, with fixed quantities of metal being officially designated as monetary units. The basic unit was the *as*, a pound (327.45 grammes) of bronze. This rudimentary system perhaps goes back to the 6th century BC.

The earliest Roman bronze coins, dating from the 280s BC, were *asses*: that is, bronze coins weighing a pound. Shortly before that (*c*.310 BC) Roman silver coins had been issued, but were minted in Campania, probably at Naples; another 'Romano-Campanian' silver issue was produced during the war against PYRRHUS. Only in 269 BC were silver coins minted at Rome; further issues followed at irregular intervals down to the Second Punic War.

These early coins carried a variety of different designs (coin types): the head of a deity (Hercules, Apollo, Mars, etc.) usually appeared on the obverse, and a conventional design (horses, lions, dolphins, etc.) on the reverse. Some obviously symbolic types include the helmeted head of Roma, a female personification of the state, and the infants Romulus and Remus with the wolf. They also bore the legend 'ROMANO' or, later, 'ROMA'.

During the 3rd century economic difficulties caused the bronze denominations to be devalued. The *as* was reduced, first to the 'semilibral' ($\frac{1}{2}$ lb) standard, then in 211 BC to the 'sextantal' ($\frac{1}{6}$ lb) standard. The latter change coincided with the introduction of a new currency system, based on the *denarius* ('tenner'), a silver coin worth 10 (sextantal) *asses*, with its fractions the *quinarius* (5 *asses*) and the *sestertius* ($2\frac{1}{2}$ *asses*). With certain adjustments (such as the revaluation of the *denarius* to 16 *asses*, and the reduction of the *as* to a token coin), this system lasted to the end of the Principate.

The Roman mint was on the CAPITOL in the temple of Juno Moneta (hence the word 'money'), and was supervised by junior magistrates called *tresviri monetales* ('moneyers'). During the 2nd century the name of the chief moneyer came to be engraved on the coins, and from *c.*150 BC displaced the legend 'ROMA'. Early *denarii* bore the head of Roma on the obverse and the Dioscuri on the reverse, but in the Gracchan age the reverse types began to show scenes chosen by the moneyers, usually historical episodes involving their ancestors. In the 1st century the types became more political, and began to serve the interests of the rival dynasts; this culminated in 44 BC with coins bearing the portrait of the dictator CAESAR.

This precedent was followed by the emperors, whose portraits appeared on almost all issues from Rome, and from LUGDUNUM, where a second imperial mint was opened by AUGUSTUS. The reverse types of imperial coins stressed the achievements of the emperor and his family, and were an important vehicle of official propaganda.

The *denarius* remained the basic unit of the Roman currency system until the 3rd century AD. Under Augustus and his successors a fixed relationship of 1 : 50 was established between gold and silver, with the gold *aureus* (2.75 ounces) being the equivalent of 25 silver *denarii* (1.375 ounces each). But under Nero the weight of the *aureus* and the silver content of the *denarius* were both reduced, a precedent followed by many later emperors. Under Marcus Aurelius the silver content of the *denarius* was 75 per cent, and under Septimius Severus 50 per cent. During the 3rd-century crisis the whole system collapsed, with the government issuing worthless money and the population of the empire reverting to transactions in kind. A new coinage was established under Diocletian and Constantine, based on the gold *solidus* at 72 to the pound, which lasted into the Middle Ages.   TC

Burnett (1987); Carson (1990); Crawford (1985); Kent (1978); Sutherland (1974).

Collegia   *see* GUILDS.

Colonia   *see* COLONIZATION, ROMAN.

Colonia Agrippinensis   modern Cologne, city on the Rhine. The city was first founded in 38 BC by AGRIPPA, and two legions were stationed nearby by AUGUSTUS. The legions were later transferred, but the fleet remained (*see* NAVY, ROMAN) and in AD 50 Claudius founded a colony in the name of his wife AGRIPPINA. It was the capital of Germania Inferior. An important centre of INDUSTRY, the city was well fortified and did not fall to the FRANKS until 463.   GS

Stillwell (1976).

Colonization, Greek   (*See* map on page 744.) A colony was a new community, usually sent out from a single existing polis, though joint foundations are attested. It was independent from the start, while retaining sentimental and religious ties with its mother city; CORINTH was an exception in treating her colonies as dependencies. According to foundation traditions, would-be colonizers usually consulted the Delphic oracle. The settlers usually numbered a few hundred able-bodied men, led by an *oecist* (founder). On arrival, he marked out the city, dividing the land into plots for housing within the walls and allotments outside; each settler received an equal assignment. After his death, the *oecist* was worshipped as a hero. Although an alien intrusion, colonies usually established a *modus vivendi* with the indigenous population, which tended to be less politically and culturally advanced, and many settlers must have married native women.

Renewed Greek exploration overseas after the Dark Ages had been characterized by mixed settlements of Greeks and non-Greeks. The high era of Greek colonization proper began about the middle of the 8th century BC, and extended to the early 6th century. During this period Greek cities were planted in the western Mediterranean as far afield as MASSILIA and CYRENE, though most densely in southern Italy and Sicily (the area known as MAGNA GRAECIA), around the Black Sea, and in CHALCIDICE; the principal colonizers were the Euboean cities of CHALCIS and ERETRIA, Corinth, MEGARA, and Achaea in the Peloponnese, MILETUS, and various Aegean islands.

The principal motive was a desire for land, created by rising population and/or precipitated by agricultural crisis, and exemplified by traditions of settlers driven out or forbidden to return and by the choice of rich land for many colonial sites. Conversely, regions with larger territories colonized late, like Attica, or not at all, like Boeotia. Shortage of land might also generate political motives: the foundation traditions of TARENTUM and Cyrene both refer to political strife, while colonization by PHOCAEA was a response to Persian expansion.

The other major motive was TRADE. Most of the Black Sea colonies were established by Miletus for commercial reasons in otherwise unappealing areas. The establishment of such settlements was often less formal, and a distinction is frequently drawn between *emporia* (trading posts) and colonies proper, though the clusters of cities around the Hellespont and the Straits of Messina provide numerous examples of regular colonies motivated by trade. Even in predominantly agricultural colonies, trade was often a consideration: SYRACUSE and Tarentum possess magnificent harbours, and many colonies had access to marketable commodities.

During the 6th century the rate of colonization slowed, and the failure of DORIEUS about 510 BC suggests that unclaimed land was becoming scarce. Classical colonies tended to be instruments of policy, designed for influence, territorial control, or the protection of trade

routes, like THURII and AMPHIPOLIS, and populations were more frequently mixed. Even in the 4th century the colonizing instinct was not
dead, and we possess several foundation decrees for new settlements.
See also CLERUCHY.   RB

Boardman (1980); Dunbabin (1948); Forrest (1957); Graham (1964); Murray
(1980).

Colonization, Hellenistic ALEXANDER THE GREAT founded many cities,
most named Alexandria after him (the practice of naming cities after
living mortals is previously unknown in Greece). Some were meant to
be Greek cities proper, like ALEXANDRIA in Egypt; others were fortified
military settlements with a mixed population of veterans and indigenous peoples; others were temporary military outposts. These cities
were founded for strategic or commercial purposes, not to spread
Greek civilization throughout Asia.

The city foundations of the Hellenistic kings did increase the
hellenization of the Greek east. The Seleucids, especially ANTIOCHUS I
SOTER, founded many new cities, both urban centres (like ANTIOCH in
Syria and SELEUCEIA ON TIGRIS) as well as colonies on important frontiers. Immigration from Macedonia and Greece was encouraged (cities
were often named for places back home: Beroea in Syria nostalgically
recalls Macedonian Beroea). There was little integration with native
populations. Also, old cities were often refounded with new dynastic
names (many cities were given the names Antiocheia, Seleuceia, etc.),
and several existing settlements could be synoecized into a new city.

The Ptolemies established colonies throughout EGYPT for military
purposes. Soldiers were given a share of land (a *kleros*, after which they
are known as cleruchs, *see* CLERUCHY) in return for military service;
both grant and obligation were hereditary. The cleruchs did not form
cities in the Greek political sense.   EER

Bagnall (1976); Cohen (1978); Grainger (1990a).

Colonization, Roman As Rome conquered Italy, large amounts of
land were annexed and colonized by the Romans. From the earliest
times colonies were founded on the borders of LATIUM. After 338 BC
colonies were founded further afield. The colonists, who included allies (SOCII) as well as Romans, gave up their existing citizenship and
became citizens of the colony, which had the same status as existing
Latin communities. They were therefore known as 'Latin colonies'.

Rome's reluctance to keep a NAVY led to the establishment of small
strong-points on the coast. These were too small to form autonomous
communities and the settlers kept their Roman CITIZENSHIP. These minor
settlements were thus known as 'colonies of Roman citizens'.

As it became increasingly difficult to persuade colonists to give up their Roman citizenship, Latin colonies ceased to be founded (Aquileia in 181 BC being the last) and instead large colonies of Roman citizens began to be set up (the first two being Parma and Mutina in 183). In 177 colonization ceased, presumably because after the conquest of the Po valley there was no strategic need, and land in Italy was not available for settlement. The end of colonization contributed to the problem faced by the Gracchi. Gaius GRACCHUS revived the practice of colonization, which in the late Republic was used by revolutionary politicians to reward their supporters. The purpose of colonization had moved from strategic to social and economic interests: discharging veterans and resettling the poor.

Gaius Gracchus attempted to found the first overseas colony at Carthage. Overseas colonies were controversial and remained infrequent until CAESAR and AUGUSTUS solved the demographic problem which underlay the unrest of the late Republic by massive colonization abroad.

After HADRIAN, colonization came to a halt, and the title *colonia* became a much-sought-after mark of status for existing cities.

See also MUNICIPIUM. HS

Brunt (1971a); CAH VII.2; VIII; Keppie (1983); Salmon (1969); Sherwin-White (1973).

Colosseum More properly known as the Amphitheatrum Flavium, the Colosseum was so named in the Middle Ages for its proximity to a colossal statue of Nero. The finest surviving example of a Roman AMPHITHEATRE, it was begun by VESPASIAN, completed by his sons TITUS and DOMITIAN, and officially opened in AD 80. The area it covers is an ellipse measuring 205 by 170 yards. It could seat an audience of about 70,000. GS

Nash (1968).

Colossus of Rhodes *see* CHARES OF LINDUS.

Columella (mid-1st century AD), Latin writer. Lucius Junius Columella was a native of Cadiz where he was born of a land-owning family. After military service he moved to Italy where he farmed estates and composed treatises on AGRICULTURE. His *De Re Rustica* (12 books, of which Book 10, on GARDENS, is in verse) survives intact and is based largely on his own experience. One book of a shorter manual on ARBORICULTURE, *De Arboribus*, also survives. GS

White (1970).

Comedy, Greek   Comedy was first formally adopted as part of the City DIONYSIA at Athens in 486 BC, though its informal origins were much older. It was not peculiar to Athens (both Sicily and Megara claimed it as their invention), but Athens provided the necessary social and political conditions that enabled it to blossom. There were two distinct phases.

Old Comedy was already in its final stages when ARISTOPHANES began writing in the 420s. The plot was invariably a fantasy and the chorus a gaggle of fantastic creatures (clouds, wasps, frogs, etc.). All actors were men and masked. Costume and language alike were grotesque and indecent. Contemporary public figures, intellectuals, and the gods were ridiculed with uninhibited zest but with little real malice. The playwright and the audience were in league against the establishment of the day. Aristophanes' last plays were written in the 4th century after the fall of Athens and represent a transitional stage, sometimes called Middle Comedy, in which the satire was aimed less at politicians and more at society.

New Comedy, whose chief surviving representative is MENANDER, continued the trend away from fantasy and politics towards the realities of everyday life. Actors were still masked but wore ordinary clothes. The chorus was now irrelevant to the plot which usually turned on a recognition scene. The tone was less boisterous, more serious, more versatile, more subtle, but still very funny – a Hellenistic comedy of manners which found a home in the adaptations of PLAUTUS and TERENCE.

See also ALEXIS; CRATINUS; DIPHILUS; EPICHARMUS; EUBULUS; EUPOLIS; HERMIPPUS; MACHON; PHERECRATES; PHILEMON; PLATO.   GS

Dover (1972); Hunter (1985); Pickard-Cambridge (1962); Sandbach (1977).

Comedy, Roman   The origins of Roman comedy are obscure. Certainly it included some native elements (*see* ATELLANA FABULA; MIME, LATIN; SATIRE), but probably fewer than chauvinistic scholars liked to think. Essentially it was Greek comedy made Roman. The Greek models, traditionally first introduced in translation by LIVIUS ANDRONICUS, were the exponents of Attic New Comedy, notably PHILEMON, DIPHILUS, and MENANDER. Greek elements that were retained included metre, costume, and character types. But whereas Greek audiences were fairly prosperous and middle-class, the Roman poets, particularly PLAUTUS and CAECILIUS STATIUS, were writing for the masses. They therefore substituted a blend of farce and comic opera for social and political comment; they exchanged the mannered moralizing of the chorus for the coarse and extravagant language of a much less sophisticated demimonde; they provided escapist entertainment in a fantastic setting with no regard for dramatic consistency and subtlety of interpretation. For

Plautus the scene is simply here, the time now; the play is the thing and the object is to make the audience laugh. TERENCE wrote for a more aristocratic audience and a more mature Rome, but he operated within the same literary parameters as his predecessors. Roman literary and theatrical tastes, however, soon diverged: while the lions roared in the theatre, the poets' caravan moved on.   GS

Beare (1964); Duckworth (1952); Hunter (1985); Sandbach (1977); Segal (1987).

Comitia   Roman assemblies. *Comitia* were assemblies of the Roman people summoned in groups (*see* ARMY, ROMAN; CURIAE; TRIBUS) by a MAGISTRATE. These assemblies were the *Comitia curiata, centuriata*, and *tributa*.

The *Comitia curiata*, presided over by a CONSUL, PRAETOR, or (for religious purposes) PONTIFEX Maximus, was the oldest. But by historical times the people no longer attended, each of the 30 *curiae* was represented by a LICTOR, and its functions were curtailed to the confirmation of the election of magistrates and certain wills and adoptions.

The *Comitia centuriata*, which met outside the POMERIUM (usually in the CAMPUS MARTIUS), presided over by a consul or praetor, was open to all citizens. Its organization into 193 centuries based on wealth gave the élite, if unified, a dominance in VOTING. After 218 BC it was no longer the chief legislative assembly, an exception being declarations of war and peace, but it retained the election of consuls and praetors, and the trial of certain capital crimes (*see* IUDICIA POPULI).

The *Comitia tributa* (confusingly the similar CONCILIA *plebis* were often called *Comitia tributa*), which met in the Campus Martius for elections and in the FORUM for legislation or trials, presided over by a consul, praetor, or, sometimes, a 'curule' AEDILE, was open to all citizens divided into the 35 tribes. It legislated on anything except what was restricted to the *Comitia centuriata*, judged minor trials, and elected 'curule' aediles, QUAESTORS, and lower magistrates.

Roman assemblies only voted on measures put to them by magistrates. They had no power to initiate or amend. Popular participation was probably higher in the *Contiones*, assemblies for discussion summoned by a magistrate in which the people were not divided into groups. Under the Principate the assemblies steadily lost all their functions.

See also LAW, ROMAN.   HS

Nicolet (1980); Taylor (1966).

Comitium   place of assembly in Rome. The Comitium existed from an early date as a consecrated area in the heart of the city where assemblies (COMITIA) took place. It was a circular stepped area in front of the CURIA in the north-east corner of the FORUM. Different places were employed for assemblies depending on which assembly (*see* CONCILIA) was meeting and for what purpose.   HS

Nash (1968); Nicolet (1980); Richardson (1992).

Commagene region of northern Syria. Commagene became independent of the Seleucid empire in 163 BC when its governor revolted and established a line of Greco-Iranian kings claiming descent from DARIUS I and ALEXANDER THE GREAT. ANTIOCHUS I helped POMPEY in 64 BC and was rewarded with extra territory. Sympathy with PARTHIA led to Roman hostility, and the Commagene kings were successively deposed and reinstated by Rome for a century. In AD 72 Vespasian annexed the kingdom to the province of Syria.   EER

Goell (1952); Jones (1983); Magie (1975); Sullivan (1990); Yarshater (1983).

Commentarii Roman records or memoranda which were originally private in nature, but acquired a public function. Initially they were used in business or legal contexts, but soon also by priestly colleges, magistracies, and provincial governors. Later the term referred to the emperor's records of campaigns and letters and legal decisions. It could also refer to literary works, derived from diaries or notes, such as CAESAR's *Commentarii*.

See also ARCHIVES, ROMAN.   HE

Commerce *see* BANKING; COINAGE; TRADE.

Commodus (AD 161–92), Roman emperor, AD 180–92. Lucius Aelius Aurelius Commodus, only surviving son of Marcus AURELIUS and FAUSTINA, was created Augustus in AD 177. Sole ruler from 180 to 192, he preferred the dissolute life in Rome, abandoning Aurelius' Danubian war, against the advice of CLAUDIUS POMPEIANUS. His contempt for the Senate, and his determination to rule through favourites, precipitated a series of plots, the first led by his sister Lucilla (182), who was subsequently executed. A prolonged reign of terror included the banishment and execution of his wife Crispina (183). Commodus finally fell victim to a palace plot (192), and his memory was condemned by Senate and people alike.   RJB

Grant (1985); Parker (1958); Wells (1984).

Communications *see* NAVIGATION; ROADS; TRAVEL.

Concilia   Roman assemblies. *Concilia* was a term for all Roman assemblies (*see* COMITIA), but usually referred to the specific *Concilium plebis* (sometimes called the *Comitia tributa*). This was only open to plebeians, PATRICIANS being excluded. The PLEBS, divided into the 35 tribes (TRIBUS), met for elections in the CAMPUS MARTIUS and for legislation and trials in the FORUM, presided over by a TRIBUNUS PLEBIS or AEDILE of the *plebs*. After 287 BC, when PLEBISCITA acquired the force of law, the *Concilium plebis* became the main legislative assembly. It also elected tribunes and aediles of the *plebs*, and, especially before the institution of the public courts (QUAESTIO), acted as a court. Provincial councils were also called *Concilia*.   HS

Nicolet (1980); Taylor (1966).

Confarreatio   *see* MARRIAGE, ROMAN.

Conon   (*c*.450–389 BC), Athenian general. After AEGOSPOTAMI (405) Conon escaped with eight ships to EVAGORAS in Cyprus where he awaited a chance to restore Athens's fortunes. Serving under PHARNABAZUS, he destroyed Sparta's control of the sea at Cnidus (394), returning in glory to Athens in 393 to assist in rebuilding the walls of PIRAEUS and re-establish Athenian power under cover of friendship with Persia. After Sparta complained, he was recalled to Sardes. TIMOTHEUS was his son.   GLC

Consecratio   Roman consecration. The formal process of consecrating a building, or the land on which it stood, was carried out by an official appointed for the purpose by the COMITIA or, later, by the emperor. It involved a religious ceremony in the presence of the PONTIFICES, usually consisting of prayers recited by the dedicator while holding one of the doorposts. The prayers, which announced that the building was being presented to a god, were dictated by a pontiff, who held the other doorpost. Elements of this ritual are still retained in Christian consecration ceremonies.   TC

Consilium Principis   Roman privy council. The *Consilium Principis*, initially an unofficial advisory body formed by AUGUSTUS to help him with legal decisions, was formalized by HADRIAN (AD 117–38) to improve the standard of justice. Its members, regularly appointed and salaried, included some of the most famous jurists of the day, NERATIUS PRISCUS, Salvius JULIANUS, and Juventus CELSUS. From the time of Septimius SEVERUS (193–211), the praetorian prefect (*see* PRAEFECTUS PRAETORIO) presided over the *Consilium* in the emperor's absence, and the prefect was frequently a lawyer (e.g. PAULUS, ULPIAN). The *Consilium* was further reorganized under Severus Alexander to include 70 members (20 equestrians, 50 senators), and was superseded by the CONSISTORIUM.

RJB

Crook (1955); Millar (1977); Parker (1958); Salmon (1968).

Consistorium Roman imperial council. The *Sacrum Consistorium*, the Roman imperial council, was established early in the reign of CONSTANTINE I, extending the powers of the existing imperial council (the CONSILIUM) to include some powers previously exercised by the praetorian prefects (*see* PRAEFECTUS PRAETORIO). The *Consistorium* was a standing committee for the transaction of administrative and judicial business. It consisted of permanent members, appointed by the emperor: all bore the title *comes*, but were graded in three ranks. Its chief officials were the *quaestor sacri Palatii*, responsible for the issue of edicts and rescripts, and the MAGISTER OFFICIORUM, and, below them, two chancellors, controlling the FISCUS and the RES PRIVATA. RJB

Millar (1977); Parker (1958).

Consolatio ad Liviam When Augustus' stepson DRUSUS died in 9 BC, there was deep public mourning. The *Consolatio* is an elegy in 474 lines addressed to Drusus' mother LIVIA, incorrectly attributed to Ovid. It may be no more than an artificial exercise in the established genre of lament or *epicedium*. GS

Constans (AD 320–50), Roman emperor, AD 337–50. Flavius Julius Constans, youngest son of CONSTANTINE I and Fausta, was created Caesar on 25 December 333. After Constantine's death (337) he inherited Italy, Africa, and Illyricum, and in spring 340 he defeated and killed his elder brother CONSTANTINE II, adding Britain, Spain, and Gaul to his kingdom. Constans campaigned against the SARMATIANS, defeated the FRANKS (341–2), and visited BRITAIN (winter 342/3). He was defeated and killed by MAGNENTIUS. RJB

Grant (1985); Salway (1981).

Constantia *see* LICINIUS.

Constantina *see* GALLUS; MAGNENTIUS.

Constantine I the Great (*c.*AD 273–337), Roman emperor, AD 307–37. Flavius Valerius Constantinus, born at Naissus in Dacia, was the son of CONSTANTIUS I and his concubine (perhaps wife) HELENA. He served at DIOCLETIAN'S court after Constantius' elevation (Caesar, 293), and then on the staff of GALERIUS. In 306 he was allowed to join Constantius in Britain, and was hailed as Augustus by the troops after Constantius' death at York (306). Galerius refused to confirm him, and Constantine accepted the lesser title of Caesar: Constantine's reign is normally dated from 307 when he married Fausta, daughter of MAXIMIAN (31 March 307), and was recognized as Augustus by Maximian.

A conference attended by Diocletian, Maximian, and Galerius (Carnuntum, 308) again formally demoted Constantine, but he refused to acquiesce. He consolidated his control of Britain and Gaul, and successfully checked Germanic incursions on the Rhine frontier. His principal rival was Maximian's son, MAXENTIUS: in 312 Constantine invaded Italy, and Maxentius was defeated and killed at the MILVIAN BRIDGE (312). Constantine's victory is commemorated by the Arch of Constantine in Rome. Now unchallenged ruler of the west, Constantine was recognized as senior Augustus by the Senate. Uneasy peace between Constantine and LICINIUS was broken by an indecisive war (316): Constantine eventually defeated and deposed Licinius (324), and thereafter Constantine ruled as sole Augustus.

Constantine, an immensely able soldier and administrator, completed the major reorganizations begun by Diocletian. The PRAETORIAN GUARD was replaced by a bodyguard of Germanic cavalry, and the four praetorian prefects (see PRAEFECTUS PRAETORIO) became powerful financial and judicial administrators. Many Germanic tribesmen served in the new mobile field army, a central force with a large cavalry element: commanded by two MAGISTRI MILITUM, it was designed to move rapidly in support of static frontier forces, which were also strengthened and reorganized. The COINAGE was again reformed, with the successful introduction of a lighter gold coin, the *solidus* (struck at 72 to the pound). Taxes were increased (often levied in kind), and the BUREAUCRACY was further enlarged: the imperial council, the CONSILIUM, was replaced by the CONSISTORIUM.

Constantine established a new capital, CONSTANTINOPLE, at Byzantium (Istanbul), begun in 324 and dedicated on 11 May 330. Adorned with splendid buildings, it had its own SENATE, which soon matched that of Rome in status. Under Constantine, the empire became Christian. Galerius had already issued an edict of toleration (311): Constantine ascribed his victory at the Milvian Bridge to the Christian God, and, with Licinius, issued a further edict of toleration (to Christians and pagans alike), the Edict of Milan (313). Although himself baptized only on his death-bed, he actively encouraged the Christianization of the empire, the building of churches, and the advancement of Christian officials (see also ARIANISM; CHRISTIANITY; EUSEBIUS; NICAEA, COUNCIL OF).

Constantine executed his wife Fausta and his eldest son Crispus (son of Minervina; created Caesar, 317) in 326, on suspicion of treason, and is suspected of ordering the massacre of his relatives that followed his death in May 337 (among them his nephews Delmatius, created Caesar in 335, and Hannibalian, Rex in Cappodocia and Pontus from 335), that cleared the way for the succession of his sons by Fausta: CONSTANTINE II, CONSTANTIUS II, and CONSTANS.   RJB

Barnes (1982); Grant (1985); Holland Smith (1971); MacMullen (1969); Parker (1958).

Constantine II (c.AD 316–40), Roman emperor, AD 337–40. Flavius Claudius Constantinus, eldest son of CONSTANTINE I and Fausta, was created Caesar on 1 March 317. After Constantine's death the empire was split between Constantine II, CONSTANTIUS II, and CONSTANS. Already established for some years in Gaul, Constantine became senior Augustus in the west, ruling Gaul, Britain, and Spain. Unable to dominate Constans as he wished, Constantine invaded Italy in spring 340, but was defeated at Aquileia, and killed.   RJB

Grant (1985); Jones (1964).

Constantine III   *see* BRITAIN; CONSTANTIUS III.

Constantinople   modern Istanbul. Dedicated by CONSTANTINE I in AD 330 on the site of ancient BYZANTIUM, Constantinople was from the start a Christian city. Originally designated New Rome, it remained the capital of the eastern Roman empire, and of its successor the Byzantine empire, until the Ottoman conquest in 1453. New land walls protected an area that was five times the size of its predecessor and no expense was spared in building and adorning the new city. Construction was not completed until the reign of CONSTANTIUS II who also established a constitutional structure based on the Roman model with a senate, quaestors, tribunes, and praetors. Like Rome, the city was divided into 14 administrative regions (*see* REGIO), each governed by a *curator*, and one of the consuls was normally based there. Monuments surviving (in part) from the 4th century include the Hippodrome and the aqueduct of Valens. In the 5th century the city again doubled in size when the present walls were built by THEODOSIUS II in 443. Walls were also built around the sea front, making a circuit of about 12 miles. A university was founded in 425 with 10 chairs of Greek grammar and 10 of Latin, five for Greek rhetoric and three for Latin, two for law, and one for philosophy. The patriarch of Constantinople emerged victorious from the Christological controversies arising from the heresy of ARIANISM and was accorded equal honours with the bishop of Rome. Remains survive of some 5th-century churches and palaces but the greatest monuments date from the time of Justinian.

GS

Hearsey (1963); Maclagan (1968); Wilson (1983).

Constantius I Chlorus   (AD 250–306), Roman emperor, AD 305–6. Flavius Julius Constantius (Flavius Valerius as Caesar), an Illyrian and successful general, married MAXIMIAN's step-daughter Theodora and became Maximian's deputy and Caesar in the west (293). He retook Boulogne from CARAUSIUS (293), reconquered BRITAIN, defeating ALLECTUS (296), and then defeated the ALAMANNI at Langres (298). After Maximian's abdication, Constantius became western Augustus (March 305). An invasion of Britain by the Picts allowed Constantius to request the return of CONSTANTINE (his eldest son, by the concubine Helena), held as a potential hostage by Galerius: after a victory over the Picts, Constantius died at York (25 July 306), to be succeeded by Constantine.

RJB

Grant (1985); Parker (1958).

Constantius II   (AD 317–61), Roman emperor, AD 337–61. Flavius Julius Constantius, second son of CONSTANTINE I and Fausta, was created Caesar on 8 November 324, and after Constantine's death inherited Thrace and the east (September 337). Constantius fought a series of wars against SHAPUR of Persia, then moved against MAGNENTIUS, usurper in the west. He defeated Magnentius at Mursa (351), taking Italy (352) and finally Gaul (353). Thereafter he ruled the whole empire, using his cousins as deputies, first GALLUS, Caesar in the east (351–4), and then JULIAN, Caesar in the west (355–60). Conflict with Julian, following the latter's rebellion, was only averted by Constantius' death (November 361).

See also ARIANISM.

RJB

Grant (1985); Kent (1981).

Constantius III   (d. AD 421), Roman emperor, February–September AD 421. Flavius Constantius, an Illyrian, succeeded STILICHO as effective ruler of the western empire under HONORIUS. He suppressed the usurper Constantine III in Gaul (411), and also Heraclian (413) in Italy. He negotiated successfully with the Goths, for the return of PLACIDIA, whom he married (417), and for their aid against other Germanic tribes in Spain, rewarding them with federate territory in south-west Gaul. In February 421 Honorius named him co-emperor.

RJB

Bury (1958); Grant (1985); Matthews (1990).

Constantius Gallus *see* GALLUS.

Constitutiones Roman imperial enactments. *Constitutiones* were the means by which the Roman emperor introduced new laws, a development from the Republican practice whereby the possessor of IMPERIUM could issue his own summary of the principles of the LAW. The emperor became virtually the sole source of new legislation: early emperors preferred to pass most of their legislation through the Senate, as *Senatus consulta*; but from the reign of HADRIAN (117–38) onwards it became more usual for the emperor to issue personal pronouncements, in the form of *edicta* (edicts, fiats), *decreta* (judicial decisions), or *rescripta* (written replies on legal points), which together made up his *constitutiones*.   RJB

Cracknell (1964); Salmon (1968).

Consul Roman magistrate. The consulate was the supreme magistracy of the Roman Republic. The Romans dated their Republic from 509 BC when two annually elected MAGISTRATES took over the powers of the king (REX). The consuls, who were known as PRAETORS until the 4th century BC, were elected by the COMITIA *centuriata* and gave their names to the year. While limited by annual tenure and the existence of a colleague, the consular power (IMPERIUM) was a general authority both civic and military, subject to some specific limitations (*see* PROVOCATIO) in Rome (*domi*) but unlimited abroad (*militiae*). The consuls normally commanded Rome's armies in the field until the time of SULLA, after which provincial commands were usually held by ex-consuls or ex-praetors while the consuls remained in Italy.

Under the Principate the emperor appointed the consuls. The two who took up office on 1 January gave their names to the year and were called *ordinarii*. Unlike under the the Republic, when consuls served all year, the *ordinarii* were replaced later in the year by a varying number of pairs of other consuls known as *suffecti*. The consulate remained an important post, consuls presiding in the SENATE and at some elections, having some jurisdiction, and giving games, and ex-consuls going on to govern the major provinces of the empire.

See also CENSOR; DICTATOR; INTERREX; PROCONSUL.   HS

Jolowicz and Nicholas (1972); Millar (1977).

Contract A contract in Roman LAW (*ius civile*) was a free agreement resulting in obligations, normally between two parties. Various types of contract were distinguished by the jurist GAIUS (2nd century AD), and reaffirmed in the 6th century by Justinian: (1) *re*, which involved the handing over of an object; a loan of e.g. money, to be repaid in kind by a certain date (*mutuum*); a loan of an object for use, to be returned by a specified date *(commodatum)*; a loan of property, without any right of use, to be returned upon demand (*depositum*); a pledge (*fiducia*) requiring SECURITY; (2) *verbis*, a formal declaration (STIPULATIO), such as MARRIAGE; (3) *literis*, a written entry, recorded in the account books of a creditor; (4) *consensu*, an agreement made by simple consent, e.g. an agreement of sale or hire. Most contracts imposed obligations on both parties, though some, such as *mutuum*, left only one party under obligation. RJB

Cracknell (1964); Nicholas (1962).

Cookery *see* APICIUS; FOOD AND DRINK.

Copper Copper is one of the principal ingredients of BRONZE and there was a constant demand for it, not only for COINAGE, but also to provide the materials for weapons, statuary, furniture, tools, surgical instruments, and other everyday articles. Plentiful supplies were available. The Greeks found copper in CYPRUS, TARTESSUS, and Euboea and later in Thessaly, Palestine, Egypt, and Mesopotamia. The Romans exploited deposits also in Spain, Etruria, Elba, Noricum, Numidia, Raetia, and Dalmatia. But Cyprus remained the most important single source throughout the period. The mines were worked by slaves. GS

Healy (1978).

Corbulo (d. AD 66/7), Roman general. Gnaeus Domitius Corbulo, a leading general under Claudius and Nero, won victories against the FRISII (47) and the CHAUCI, and campaigned against the Parthians (58–60), temporarily installing a Roman nominee, Tigranes IV, in Armenia. He became governor of Syria and, finally, as commander of all Rome's eastern armies, negotiated a peace with Parthia which lasted for half a century (63). However, Corbulo was forced to commit suicide by Nero, who feared disloyalty.
See also VOLOGESES I. RJB

Grant (1979); Scullard (1982).

Corcyra modern Corfu, island off north-west Greece. Corcyra was colonized and so named by Corinthians *c.*734 BC. It joined CORINTH in the foundation of DYRRHACHIUM but was disaffected by the behaviour of PERIANDER. For much of the 5th and 4th centuries it was allied with Athens against Corinth, and in 373 it withstood a prolonged siege by the Spartan fleet. After a brief occupation by AGATHOCLES of Syracuse it was absorbed by EPIRUS until 229 when it came under Roman protection. The Romans used it principally as a naval station and it was here that Octavian assembled his fleet before the battle of ACTIUM.

GS

Hammond (1967).

Corinna (3rd century BC?), Greek lyric poet. Some date the works of Corinna (of which two long fragments survive) as early as the 6th century BC. Others follow the Suda tradition in linking her with Pindar in the 5th century. The dialect is Boeotian, but the spelling and metre argue for an Alexandrian date as does the obscure mythological content.

GS

Kirkwood (1974).

Corinth Corinth was one of the most important and prosperous Greek cities, owing to the commercial advantages of her position on the Isthmus. Her prosperity developed under the oligarchy of the Bacchiad clan, especially through her COLONIZATION which included SYRACUSE and CORCYRA. During this period Corinthian POTTERY became the finest in Greece. About 650 BC the Bacchiads were supplanted by the tyranny of CYPSELUS and PERIANDER who, while continuing their policies, also developed the urban centre. The tyranny was replaced c.584 by an oligarchy aligned with Sparta. In the late 6th century, however, Corinth favoured Athens and opposed Spartan attempts to intervene there; but as Athenian power increased, a conflict of interests led to tension: there were intermittent hostilities from 460, and Corinth did much to precipitate the PELOPONNESIAN WAR, in which she suffered from her proximity to Athens. Disaffected with Sparta after 404, Corinth joined an anti-Spartan coalition in an indecisive war (394–386) during which she briefly formed a political union with ARGOS; thereafter, she was loyal to Sparta until after Sparta's collapse at LEUCTRA. She opposed Philip II at CHAERONEA, but after defeat became the centre of the League of Corinth (*see* CORINTH, LEAGUE OF), her loyalty guaranteed by a garrison on the Acrocorinth, which ensured Macedonian control for most of the Hellenistic period. After the Roman liberation (196 BC), Corinth became the centre of the ACHAEAN LEAGUE, and was consequently destroyed by MUMMIUS ACHAICUS in 146 after the Achaean War. Refounded in 44 BC, she became the capital of the province of Achaea.

RB

Gruen (1984); Salmon (1984).

Corinth, League of modern name for the league comprising all the Greek states except Sparta, founded by PHILIP II of Macedon after CHAERONEA (338 BC). Philip's purposes were to ensure peace within

Greece and support for his attack on Persia. A council of cities' representatives met at Corinth or, in times of peace, at the national festivals. There were military but no financial obligations. Philip or his deputy was the 'leader' (*hegemon*) and, although freedom and autonomy were guaranteed, there were forces stationed in Corinth, Thebes, Chalcis, and Ambracia under Macedonian commanders, apt instruments of domination.   GLC

Cawkwell (1978); Hammond and Griffith (1979).

Corinthian order   *see* ARCHITECTURE, GREEK.

Coriolanus   Roman hero. According to an ancient legend, Gnaeus Marcius Coriolanus took his name from the town of Corioli, which he is said to have captured. Later he was accused of tyranny and left Rome, taking refuge among the VOLSCI. In 491 BC he led a Volscian army against Rome, but was turned back by appeals from his wife and mother. The Volsci then put him to death. PLUTARCH's account of his life survives.   HE

Cornelia   (2nd century BC), mother of the Gracchi. Cornelia was the daughter of SCIPIO AFRICANUS, Hannibal's conqueror, and the wife of Tiberius Sempronius GRACCHUS, soldier and administrator. After her husband's death she engaged the rhetorician Diophanes and the Stoic Blossius as tutors to her sons Tiberius and Gaius GRACCHUS. Plutarch says she influenced Gaius to drop controversial measures, and claims that she may have been the force behind Tiberius' laws in 133 BC, vexed that the Romans still called her Scipio's daughter rather than mother of the Gracchi.   DP

Dixon (1988).

Cornelius Nepos   *see* NEPOS, CORNELIUS.

Cornelius Palma   *see* PALMA FRONTONIANUS.

Corn supply   *see* ANNONA.

Corsica   island in the western Mediterranean. A settlement at Alalia on the east coast was founded by Greek colonists from Phocaea *c.*565 BC, but *c.*535 it was attacked and resettled by Etruscans with Carthaginian help. The island remained under Etruscan and then Carthaginian influence until the First PUNIC WAR, after which Rome amalgamated it into a single province with SARDINIA. Under the Empire it became a separate senatorial province and was a place of exile, e.g. for SENECA THE YOUNGER.   GS

Cos island in the eastern Aegean. First colonized by Carians, and later by Dorians from Epidaurus, Cos was a member of the Delian League after the Persian Wars and supported Athens in the Peloponnesian War. In the SOCIAL WAR, however, the island revolted from Athens and came under the influence of MAUSOLUS until absorbed by ALEXANDER THE GREAT in 334. Under the Romans it was declared a free city. It was the home of the physician HIPPOCRATES and an important centre of the cult of ASCLEPIUS.

See also MEDICINE; SILK; WINE.   GS

Sherwin-White (1978); Stillwell (1976).

Crassus, Lucius Licinius (140–91 BC), Roman statesman. Lucius Licinius Crassus was a noble politician who started his career as a *popularis* (*see* POPULARES) but later became a strong supporter of the Senate. As consul in 95 with SCAEVOLA he deprived illegally enfranchised Italians of their citizenship; but at the end of his life he supported the efforts of DRUSUS to extend citizenship to all Italians. His pupil CICERO admired him as Rome's greatest orator to date and made him the principal speaker in his dialogue *De Oratore*.   DP

Badian (1964); Gruen (1968); Rawson (1991).

Crassus, Marcus Licinius (fl. 30–27 BC), Roman soldier and administrator. Marcus Licinius Crassus, grandson of the triumvir, held the consulship of 30 BC with Octavian (AUGUSTUS) in spite of having previously sided with Sextus POMPEIUS and with ANTONY. As proconsul of Macedonia from 28 to 27, he successfully pacified Thrace, but Octavian's wish to monopolize military glory meant that he was denied the SPOLIA OPIMA for killing a king of the Bastarnae. This incident may have helped persuade Octavian to regularize his constitutional position in 27 BC.   DP

Carter (1970); Syme (1939).

Crassus Dives (*c*.112–53 BC), triumvir. Marcus Licinius Crassus, an aristocratic politician who fled to Spain after CINNA's takeover of Rome in 87 BC, joined SULLA in 83 and commanded the victorious right wing in the battle of the Colline Gate (82). He enriched himself in the proscriptions, and used his fortune and forensic skills to build up political support. He showed excellent generalship in his defeat of SPARTACUS (72–71), but was annoyed by POMPEY claiming a share in the credit for killing some fugitives. As consuls in 70 he and Pompey swept away many of Sulla's constitutional reforms. From 67 to 60 Crassus tried to counter Pompey's growing prestige by extending his own influence. He sponsored schemes to annex Egypt and to redistribute AGER PUBLICUS. He was an early supporter of CATILINE, but took no part in his conspiracy. On Pompey's return he at first joined OPTIMATE opposition to him, but by 60 had allied with Pompey and CAESAR in the First TRIUMVIRATE, after meeting optimate opposition himself. During Caesar's absence in Gaul discord between Pompey and Crassus grew, but Caesar reconciled them at Luca and arranged for Crassus to have Syria after their second joint consulship in 55. Crassus' passion for military distinction led him to convert his governorship of Syria into a war against Parthia, and he was killed at CARRHAE in 53.   DP

Adcock (1966); Marshall (1976); Ward (1977).

Craterus (c.?370–321 BC), Macedonian general. Craterus was an infantry commander of ALEXANDER THE GREAT at the GRANICUS RIVER, ISSUS, and GAUGAMELA. When the army divided, he frequently held separate commands. In 324 BC Alexander ordered him to lead veterans back to Macedonia and replace ANTIPATER as regent. After Alexander's death in 323, Craterus was responsible for PHILIP III ARRHIDAEUS, and helped Antipater in the Lamian War. He joined the coalition against PERDICCAS, but was killed by EUMENES OF CARDIA in 321.   EER

Bosworth (1988a); CAH VII.1; Green (1990); Hammond and Walbank (1988).

Crates of Mallus (fl. 2nd century BC), librarian. Crates was the first head of the library at PERGAMUM (under EUMENES II SOTER). He wrote upon Greek literature with a philosophical (largely Stoic) and antiquarian bias. He adopted an allegorical mode of exposition favoured by the STOICS but disliked by the Alexandrians. His chief work was a comprehensive commentary on Homer. During a visit to Rome (probably in 168 BC) he greatly stimulated by his lectures Roman interest in SCHOLARSHIP.
   See also LIBRARIES.   JL

Pfeiffer (1968).

Crates of Thebes (c.365–285 BC), Greek philosopher. Crates attended the lectures of the Megarian Bryson, but was subsequently converted to Cynicism by DIOGENES OF SINOPE. He thereupon renounced his great wealth and led a wandering life, preaching voluntary poverty and independence. DIOGENES LAËRTIUS also records (6.98) that he wrote tragedies of an elevated and philosophical nature.

See also CYNICS. JL

Dudley (1937).

Cratinus (*c*.484–*c*.419 BC), of Athens, Greek comic poet. Cratinus was the oldest and the most successful (he won nine first prizes) of the representatives of Old COMEDY most admired by Horace ('*Eupolis atque Cratinus Aristophanesque poetae*'). He wrote mythological burlesques and political satires (usually attacking PERICLES), but only fragments survive. ARISTOPHANES ridiculed him in *Knights* as a drunkard, to which he responded with the prize-winning *Bottle*. GS

Pickard-Cambridge (1962).

Cresilas (fl. *c*.450–420 BC), Greek sculptor. Cresilas was a Cretan from Cydonia but worked mostly in Athens. His signature has been found on three statue bases at Athens, one at Delphi, and one in the Argolid. Surviving Roman copies of his work include the statue of a wounded Amazon, which was entered for a competition at Ephesus against PHEIDIAS, POLYCLEITUS, Phradmon, and Cydon, and the portrait bust of Pericles. GS

Robertson (1975).

Crete island in the eastern Mediterranean. Cretan history is overshadowed by its Bronze Age prehistory, but much can be learned of Cretan society in the 5th century BC from the GORTYN LAW CODE. Until the Roman conquest in 67 BC it remained a land of small city-states, often at war with one another and notorious for PIRACY. Under Roman rule the island was incorporated into the province of CYRENAICA. GS

Willetts (1965).

Crispus *see* CONSTANTINE I.

Critias (*c*.460–403 BC), Athenian aristocrat, leader of the THIRTY TYRANTS. In 411 BC Critias seems to have sided with THERAMENES and proposed the recall of ALCIBIADES. He soon retired to Thessaly and engaged in an obscure revolutionary movement. By 404 he was the embittered, out-and-out oligarch, idealizer of Sparta, who by extreme violence sought to extirpate democracy for ever. Clashing with Theramenes, he had him executed. He was himself killed in battle against THRASYBULUS. GLC

Ostwald (1986).

Croesus   king of Lydia, 560–546 BC. Croesus, son of Alyattes, completed the Lydian subjugation of the Greek cities on the Ionian mainland. Alarmed by the Persian overthrow of his brother-in-law, Astyages king of Media, Croesus launched a pre-emptive invasion, but was defeated and conquered by CYRUS I. Proverbially wealthy, he courted Greek opinion by generous hospitality and lavish gifts and dedications, especially at DELPHI, and reaped a posthumous reputation for piety, demonstrated by the tradition of his miraculous deliverance from a burning pyre.

See also EPHESUS.   RB

Boardman (1980); CAH III.2.

Croton   city in Calabria on the toe of Italy. Founded by Achaean colonists in 710 BC, Croton flourished in the archaic period and founded a colony of its own at Caulonia. PYTHAGORAS made it his home c.530 BC, revised the constitution, and founded a religious brotherhood which governed the city and survived (after removal to Tarentum) until the late 4th century. In 510 Croton defeated and destroyed its rival SYBARIS and emerged supreme among the Achaean cities of south Italy. But decline set in in the 5th century and the city's fortunes were eclipsed by the Second PUNIC WAR.   GS

Dunbabin (1948)

Crypteia   Spartan secret police. According to Plutarch, young Spartans armed with daggers were 'from time to time' sent out into the countryside (presumably of Messenia) to live off the land and murder any helots (*see* SERFS) they encountered at night. Aristotle attributed the institution to LYCURGUS. Parallels elsewhere suggest it may have been an initiatory 'walk-about'; but helots were treated harshly and the Crypteia was no doubt part of the oppression.   GLC

Michell (1964).

Cumae   city in Italy. Traditionally Cumae was the first Greek city in Italy, founded near Naples by CHALCIS c.750 BC. The city was powerful and prosperous in the 6th and 5th centuries BC. In 474 BC Cumae and SYRACUSE defeated the Etruscans, ending their domination of Campania. In 420 Cumae was conquered by the Oscan-speaking SABELLI. In 338 BC it received 'citizenship without vote' (*see* MUNICIPIUM) from Rome, remaining loyal throughout the Republic.

See also ARISTODEMUS.   LPR

CAH VII.2; Frederiksen (1984).

Cunaxa   north of Babylon, site of a battle (401 BC) at which CYRUS THE YOUNGER, with the Ten Thousand, fought ARTAXERXES II and died. Accounts of the battle are confused by the absurd numbers attributed to Artaxerxes' army. Cyrus' main weapon was the Greek HOPLITES on the right wing under CLEARCHUS. But he disobeyed Cyrus' last-minute order to advance obliquely and they missed Artaxerxes in the middle of his slightly longer front. The hero of the day for Artaxerxes was TISSAPHERNES.   GLC

Cawkwell (1972b).

Curia   Roman Senate House. The Curia, in which the SENATE usually met, was situated in the FORUM to the north of the COMITIUM. The PLEBS used it as a pyre for CLODIUS. Caesar began a new Curia (Iulia), which was dedicated by Augustus, on a slightly different site. The building, dominated inside by a statue of victory, needed restoration by Domitian and Diocletian after fires, and is still standing today.   HS

Nash (1968); Robinson (1992), Zanker (1988).

Curiae   divisions of the Roman people. The early Roman community was divided into 30 units called *curiae*. These were subdivisions of the TRIBUS, 10 to each tribe. Almost everything about them is obscure. It is probable, but not certain, that all free Romans, not just patricians, were enrolled in the *curiae,* and that membership was determined by birth. Under the kings the political and military organization of the state depended on the *curiae*, but under the Republic they had only residual functions, for instance in religious festivals such as the FORNACALIA. They also formed the constituent units of Rome's earliest assembly, the COMITIA *curiata*, which in historical times conferred *imperium* on the chief magistrates (a 'rubber-stamp' function) and witnessed adoptions and wills (though this archaic method of making a will had became obsolete by the 1st century BC). The IGUVIUM TABLES indicate the existence of something similar to *curiae* among the Umbrians.   TC

Momigliano (1963b); Palmer (1970).

Cursus honorum   political ladder at Rome. The *Cursus honorum* was the ascending order of magistracies held by Roman politicians which was regulated by a series of laws passed in the course of the Republic. The basic pattern in the late Republic, which was confirmed by SULLA in 81 BC, was preliminary military service followed by the offices of QUAESTOR, PRAETOR, CONSUL, and CENSOR, which could only be held in that sequence. If the non-obligatory offices of AEDILE or TRIBUNUS PLEBIS were held, these came between quaestorship and praetorship. The minimum ages for quaestors, praetors, and consuls were 30, 39, and 42 respectively: to gain a magistracy 'in one's own year', as Cicero did the consulship for 63, meant at the earliest possible age. The same office could only be held again after a 10-year gap. This *Cursus honorum* continued under the Empire, although Augustus reduced the minimum age for the quaestorship to 25 and for the praetorship to 30. Imperial patronage could also waive the rules for specially favoured candidates.

See also ADLECTIO.   DP

Astin (1958); CAH VIII.

Cursus publicus   *see* POSTAL SERVICE.

Curtius   (?1st century AD), historian of ALEXANDER THE GREAT. Quintus Curtius Rufus wrote a Latin history of Alexander in 10 books, of which the last eight remain. His identification with other namesakes is uncertain, his date is widely disputed, and his reasons for writing are unknown. His rhetorical picture of Alexander differs from ARRIAN, and shares many features with the so-called Vulgate tradition seen in DIODORUS SICULUS. His view that Alexander's character deteriorated dramatically derives from Peripatetic tradition.   EER

Atkinson (1980); Bosworth (1988b); Heckel (1984).

Cybele   ancient goddess. Cybele was an Anatolian mother goddess known to the Greeks as Meter Oreia (Mother of the Mountains) or simply Meter. As a goddess of fertility she was early associated with DEMETER but had no mythology of her own. Her cult was introduced to Rome in 204 BC, a temple was built on the Palatine, and a spring festival (Megalesia) held annually in her honour. It subsequently spread throughout the empire.   GS

Burkert (1985).

Cyclades   group of islands in the southern Aegean forming a circle (*kuklos*) around DELOS. After the Persian Wars they were naturally incorporated in the Delian League and they remained largely under Athenian influence until the SOCIAL WAR (357–355) when they revolted. Subjected alternately to Macedon and Egypt, and finally to Rome, they suffered much from Cretan PIRACY, inter-state rivalries, and the MITHRIDATIC WARS.

See also MELOS; NAXOS; PAROS.   GS

Cyclic poets The *Iliad* and the *Odyssey* were not the only examples of heroic poetry known to the ancients. Summaries by Proclus (2nd century AD) describe a number of poems belonging to the Trojan Cycle which were already lost: *Cypria, Aethiopis, Sack of Troy, Little Iliad, Homecomings*, and *Telegony*. Other parts of the Epic Cycle were supplied by poems of which we know even less: *Epigoni, Titanomachia, Oedipodea*, and *Thebais*.   GS

Davies (1989); Huxley (1969); Murray (1934).

Cylon *see* ATHENS, HISTORY to 490 BC.

Cynics The Cynics were followers of DIOGENES OF SINOPE, who had been given the nickname of *kuōn* (dog) because of his rejection of conventions, his adoption of poverty, and his practice of shamelessness. But since ANTISTHENES influenced Diogenes, many consider him to be the true founder of the sect. Diogenes' most faithful disciple was CRATES OF THEBES. After flourishing in the 3rd century BC, Cynicism gradually declined in the 2nd and 1st centuries. It revived, however, during the 1st century AD at which time several Cynics were banished for their opposition to the emperors.   JL

Dudley (1937).

Cynoscephalae battle in 197 BC. At Cynoscephalae in Thessaly, Titus Quinctius FLAMININUS ended the Second MACEDONIAN WAR by defeating PHILIP V. Although Philip held the higher ground, part of his phalanx had not formed up when it was attacked. When the Macedonians raised their pikes in a gesture of surrender, the Romans did not understand and massacred them.   LPR

Walbank (1940).

Cyprian, St (*c*.AD 200–58), bishop of Carthage. Thascius Caecilius Cyprianus was born at Carthage where he taught rhetoric before being converted to Christianity *c*.246 and elected bishop in 248. For 10 years he suffered intermittent persecution and exile, and finally martyrdom. A collection of letters and treatises survives concerned with contemporary theological issues, notably the terms for reconciling apostates.   GS

Lane Fox (1986).

Cyprus island in the eastern Mediterranean. Cyprus had been primarily Greek-speaking since the Bronze Age and its archaic Achaean DIALECT and syllabic script survived into the classical period. It was a land of petty kingdoms but its resources of COPPER made it a prize possession. There had been a Phoenician colony at Citium since the 9th century, and in the archaic period the island was controlled briefly by Assyria and later by Egypt. Apart from a spell of independence under EVAGORAS of SALAMIS, Cyprus was under Persian control almost continually from 525 to 333 BC when it was liberated by ALEXANDER THE GREAT. The island was then ruled by the Ptolemies until Rome took it in 58 BC and incorporated it in the province of CILICIA.   GS

Casson (1937); Stylianou (1989); Tatton-Brown (1987).

Cypselus   tyrant of Corinth, *c*.655–625 BC. Cypselus, encouraged by the Delphic oracle, seized power in CORINTH by overthrowing the exclusive aristocracy of the Bacchiads. He furthered Corinthian expansion by extensive colonization on the Adriatic coast, rewarded Delphi with rich dedications, strengthened the walls of Corinth, and is said to have been sufficiently popular to need no bodyguard. He was succeeded by his son PERIANDER.   RB

Andrewes (1956); Salmon (1984).

Cyrenaica   Roman province. Cyrenaica, centred on Cyrene, was part of the North African coastal strip, sandwiched between the provinces of Africa and Egypt. Bequeathed to Rome by Ptolemy Apion (96 BC), it was organized formally as a province (74 BC), and CRETE was added to its territory (67 BC). It remained a senatorial province under the Empire, although the emperor's ability to interfere is apparent from the Edicts of CYRENE. Originally a prosperous province, exporting grain, its prosperity decreased in the 2nd century, a series of Jewish revolts during Trajan's reign leading to widespread devastation. It was later incorporated into the province of EGYPT.   RJB

Millar (1981); Scullard (1982).

Cyrene   city in Libya. Founded by colonists from Thera under Battus *c*.630 BC, Cyrene flourished on the strength of its trade in corn, oil, wool, and silphium, and in the 6th century founded colonies of its own. Apart from a spell of Persian control (*c*.525–475), Battus and his successors (*see* ARCESILAUS I–IV) ruled like kings until *c*.440 when a democratic constitution was imposed. After submitting to ALEXANDER THE GREAT, Cyrene and its neighbouring cities were under Ptolemaic control until 96 BC (but *see* MAGAS) when they were bequeathed to Rome. In 74 BC the province of CYRENAICA was formed.   GS

Boardman (1980); Chamoux (1953); Stillwell (1976).

Cyrene, Edicts of   The Edicts of Cyrene, preserved on an inscription, are four edicts of AUGUSTUS (7/6 BC), and one senatorial edict (4 BC). The Augustan edicts relate to tensions between Romans and Greeks: two concern jury composition, one a case of MAIESTAS, and one the performance of LITURGIES. They demonstrate Augustus' use of his power of IMPERIUM *maius* to impose direct rule in a province (CYRENAICA) nominally controlled by a senatorial governor.   RJB

Scullard (1982); Wells (1984).

Cyrus   king of Persia, 560/59–530 BC. Cyrus, son of Cambyses and the Median Mandane, was the founder of the Persian empire. In 550 the Persians under Cyrus overthrew their Median overlords. Next he defeated CROESUS and took control of LYDIA and its Greek tributaries (probably 546). The conquest of BABYLON followed in 539, ending the Jewish captivity. Either before or after this there were campaigns in the east, and he died fighting the Massagetae, east of the Aral Sea. His later years also saw the construction of a new capital and palace complex at Pasargadae, where his tomb survives.   RB

CAH IV; Cook (1983); Stronach (1978).

Cyrus the Younger   (423–401 BC), Persian commander. The younger son of DARIUS II, Cyrus rebelled against his brother ARTAXERXES II. Born after Darius' accession, Cyrus cannot have been more than 15 when sent down in 408 to Sardes to command the western satrapies and collaborate with Sparta. On close terms with LYSANDER, he ensured Spartan victory. Then gathering an army, half Greek MERCENARIES, he made his famous 'march up country' (*Anabasis*) and died at CUNAXA (401). XENOPHON lived to tell his tale.   GLC

Dandamaev (1989).

Cyzicus   city on the south shore of the Sea of Marmora. By tradition Cyzicus was founded twice by Miletus, once in 756 BC and again in 675: the latter date is the more probable. Its strategic location on an important trade route guaranteed its prosperity, as is attested by its celebrated electrum coinage. It was a member of the Delian League and was the scene of ALCIBIADES' defeat of the Spartan fleet in 410. It remained prosperous into the Hellenistic period and under Roman rule was a free city until AD 25.

See also APOLLONIS OF CYZICUS.   GS

Hasluck (1910).

D

Dacia Roman province. Dacia was an extensive province, established in AD 106, bounded to the south by the Danube (to the south of which lay MOESIA), and consisting largely of the plateau of Transylvania. The threat from the Dacian tribes, united under DECEBALUS, prompted an inconclusive campaign under DOMITIAN (86–9), followed by further campaigns under TRAJAN (101–2; 105–6) which finally resulted in the death of Decebalus and the fall of his capital Sarmizegetusa. The Roman victory is commemorated on Trajan's Column in Rome. The new province was bounded by the Aluta to the east, and to the west by the river Theiss, falling short of the Carpathians in the north. It was extensively settled and gold, silver, and iron mines were exploited by the Romans. Dacia was later subdivided into three districts (Dacia Inferior (118); Dacia Superior (118); Porolissensis (124)), but abandoned c.270 when repeated Gothic invasions made it impractical to hold.   RJB

Millar (1981); Wilkes (1983).

Dalmatia Roman province. Dalmatia was the province north of Macedonia, on the east coast of the Adriatic. The Dalmatians, a people of the Illyrian group, were compelled to acknowledge Roman supremacy as early as 156/5 BC, but were not subdued until conquered by Octavian (AUGUSTUS) (35–33 BC). Dalmatia became part of the senatorial province of ILLYRICUM (27 BC), but rose in revolt in 16 BC, 11/10 BC, and again in the great Illyrian–Pannonian revolt of AD 6–9, which was finally put down by TIBERIUS. A revolt by Camillus Scribonianus, the governor of Dalmatia (42), also failed.

The name Dalmatia probably became current under the Flavians: before that, after the creation of the separate province of PANNONIA,

Dalmatia was probably known as Illyricum Superior, or Upper Illyricum. Diocletian's reorganization split the province between two *dioceses*: Dalmatia (in the north, capital Salonae) belonged to Pannonia, and Praevalitana or Praevalis (in the south, capital Scodra) to MOESIA.   RJB

Millar (1981); Wilkes (1969).

Damocles   (fl. mid-4th century BC), Syracusan nobleman. Damocles was an obsequious courtier of DIONYSIUS II, tyrant of Syracuse. When he expressed envy of the tyrant's happiness, Dionysius invited him to a sumptuous feast, but suspended a sword by a horse-hair over his head. The experience cured Damocles of his envy of the tyrant.   GS

Damophon   (2nd century BC), Greek sculptor. A native of Messene, Damophon seems to have worked only in the Peloponnese. He restored the statue of Zeus by PHEIDIAS at OLYMPIA which had been damaged by earthquake. He produced a colossal group for the temple of Despoina at Lycosura, parts of which survive. And he made statues of gods and goddesses for other temples in Achaea and Messenia, including a head of Apollo recently found at Messene.   GS

Robertson (1975).

Danube   (Latin Danuvius), river in central Europe. The Greeks knew its lower course as far as the Iron Gates and named it the Ister ('the greatest of all rivers that we know', according to Herodotus). But they were ignorant of its source. The upper course became known to the Romans when they pushed north from Italy in the 2nd century BC but was not identified with the Ister until Octavian's Illyrian campaign of 35 BC. With the exception of DACIA, the length of the river formed the northern frontier of the Roman empire from its source near that of the RHINE to its debouch into the Black Sea. The other Danubian provinces were RAETIA, NORICUM, PANNONIA, DALMATIA, MOESIA, and THRACE.
See also LIMES.   GS

Alföldy (1974); Mócsy (1974); Wilkes (1969).

Darius I   king of Persia, 522–486 BC. Darius, probably a cousin of CAMBYSES, took power after overthrowing, with six Persian nobles, the usurper Gaumata (or, some believe, Cambyses' brother Bardiya) and suppressing widespread revolt in the Persian empire. Having campaigned in India and, unsuccessfully, in Scythia, he reorganized the empire into its developed system of satrapies and tribute. He also built elaborate palace complexes at Susa and PERSEPOLIS. Despite minor advances in the west, it was the IONIAN REVOLT, and a desire for revenge, which drew his attention to Greece; but his first expedition failed at MARATHON, and he died before the second, which was inherited by his successor, XERXES. RB

Burn (1984); CAH IV; Cook (1983).

Darius II king of Persia, 423–404 BC. The son of ARTAXERXES I and father of CYRUS THE YOUNGER, Darius acceded through palace intrigue and his reign was marked by internal troubles. In the west he was very successful. When Athens gave help to the rebel satrap of Caria, Amorges, Darius broke off the alliance he had renewed with Athens, allied with Sparta (412), and, ably served by TISSAPHERNES, maintained Sparta. Cyrus came down to Sardes (408), resolved to finish the war and to contest the succession. GLC

Dandamaev (1989).

Darius III king of Persia, 336–330 BC. Darius was installed after the eunuch Bagoas had murdered the son of ARTAXERXES III. He confronted the Macedonian invasion, but was twice defeated: at ISSUS (333), after which he proposed a peace making the Euphrates the frontier, and at GAUGAMELA (331), which signalled the end of the ACHAEMENIDS. Darius fled and was murdered by Bessus, satrap of Bactria. He was buried at Persepolis. GLC

Dandamaev (1989).

Datis (fl. *c*.490 BC), Median soldier. Datis may have held command in the later stages of the IONIAN REVOLT. After the failure of MARDONIUS' expedition in 492 BC, he led an amphibious expedition against Eretria and Athens, which was checked at MARATHON. His treatment of Delos suggests an able diplomat who knew Greece, and the participation of HIPPIAS hints at political aims at variance with Mardonius' plans for conquest. RB

Burn (1984).

Dead Sea Scrolls a collection of Hebrew and Aramaic manuscripts discovered in 1947 in the caves at Qumran at the north-west end of the Dead Sea. The scrolls have been scientifically dated to the 1st century BC and 1st AD and were produced by an ascetic Jewish community sometimes identified with the Essenes. Nearly all the books of the canonical Old Testament (SEPTUAGINT) are represented, at least in part, alongside many apocryphal writings and works not previously known (including hymns, commentaries, and rulebooks). They provide unique contemporary evidence for Jewish life and thought at the time of the birth of CHRISTIANITY. GS

Vermes (1987); Vermes and Vermes (1977).

Decarchy   Decarchies were boards of 10, set up by LYSANDER after the PELOPONNESIAN WAR (404) to administer liberated cities of the Athenian empire. When Lysander was temporarily discredited in 403, they were dissolved by a board of EPHORS which ordered the establishment of 'ancestral constitutions'. Lysander hoped to restore them in Asia in 396, but AGESILAUS denied him this opportunity. Both men discredited Sparta, preferring personal and violent methods of control.   GLC

Cartledge (1987).

Decebalus   (d. AD 106), king of the Dacians. Decebalus led the Dacian attempts to retain their independence from Rome. In AD 85 he invaded MOESIA, and although eventually defeated by DOMITIAN (89), was confirmed as king of DACIA. The growing threat posed by the Dacian army, into which Decebalus introduced Roman discipline, led to TRAJAN's campaigns against him. After the first (101–2) Decebalus was reduced to client status (acknowledging Rome's supremacy); after the second (105–6) he committed suicide.   RJB

Millar (1981); Salmon (1968).

Decemviri   Roman lawgivers. In 451 BC the Roman constitution was suspended, and instead of consuls a board of 10 men ('decemvirs') was appointed, all of them PATRICIANS. One of their tasks was to codify the laws, and in the first year they duly produced 10 tables. In 450 a second decemvirate took office, this time including plebeians, and produced two further tables. They then began to behave tyrannically, and tried to perpetuate their rule, but were overthrown by a popular uprising, which restored the earlier constitution (*see* VALERIUS POTITUS). Much is uncertain in the story, parts of which are pure romance (*see* Appius CLAUDIUS), but the TWELVE TABLES are historical.   TC

CAH VII.2.

Decentius   *see* MAGNENTIUS.

Decius   (*c.*AD 200–51), Roman emperor, AD 249–51. Gaius Messius Quintus Decius, a Pannonian, was governor of Lower Moesia (234–8) and later city prefect. Sent by PHILIP I to restore order in the Danubian armies, Decius was created emperor by the soldiers, against his will. A battle was fought near Verona, and Philip and his son were killed. Decius took the additional name 'Trajanus' and, aiming to restore traditional Roman discipline and values, set the soldiers to work building roads and instituted a persecution of the Christians. However, further

Gothic invasions recalled Decius to the Danubian frontier, and both he and his elder son Herennius were killed at Abrittus. RJB

Grant (1985); Parker (1958).

Decuma Roman tax. The *decuma* ('tithe') was a tax on agricultural land amounting to 10 per cent of the annual produce. In theory Roman citizens occupying AGER PUBLICUS were liable to the *decuma*, though in practice it was often not collected. The TAXATION of certain provinces (ASIA; SICILY) also took the form of a *decuma*. It was handled by PUBLICANI, who paid an agreed sum to the treasury and bore the risks of collecting a variable tax. TC

Badian (1972a).

Decuriones Roman local councillors. *Decuriones* were recruited from ex-magistrates in Latin and Roman colonies and MUNICIPIA and held office for life. Though there were age, status, and wealth requirements, these were often disregarded, particularly among more powerful families. The *decuriones* controlled all aspects of local affairs, together forming the town council. Thus they sent petitions to emperors and governors, dealt with local administration, and voted for local honours, including statues. They also collected taxes and were personally responsible for shortfalls, a liability that led to frequent attempts to avoid the office in the late Empire. HE

Dediticii Roman subjects. *Dediticii* were persons or communities who made a complete surrender of rights and property to Rome, usually to avoid annihilation. They had no political rights. Theirs was usually a temporary status and they could be assigned various rights by Rome. *Dediticii* were usually well treated.

See also PEREGRINI. HE

Sherwin-White (1973).

Delian League modern name for the Greek alliance organized by Athens to carry on the war against Persia after the PERSIAN WARS. In 478 BC the Greeks, disgusted by the conduct of PAUSANIAS commanding the operations of the 'Hellenic League', persuaded Athens to form a new organization. Each member state swore 'to think the same people friends and enemies as the Athenians', thus putting Athens as leader (*hegemon*) at the centre. A synod met on Delos, but Athens was not a member and so not beholden to majority opinion. Executive officers were appointed by Athens; the commanders of league forces were Athenian generals responsible to Athens alone. At first the allies jointly contributed as many ships as Athens. When the balance of power turned in Athens's favour, and since she could not be coerced by majority opinion, degeneration was inevitable. There was no precise moment when league became empire. ARISTIDES and CIMON were leading spirits; THEMISTOCLES and PERICLES sought empire.   GLC

Hornblower (1983); Meiggs (1972).

Delmatius   *see* CONSTANTINE I.

Delos   island in the CYCLADES. Traditionally the birthplace of Apollo and Artemis, it was an important centre of the cult of APOLLO and the venue of a great annual Ionian festival. In an attempt to assert Athenian leadership over the IONIANS, PEISISTRATUS purified the sanctuary in 543 BC by removing the surrounding tombs. After the PERSIAN WARS it was the natural choice for placing the treasury of the DELIAN LEAGUE, founded in 478, until the latter was removed to Athens in 454. In 426 Delos was purified again and the Athenians decreed that thereafter no one was to die or give birth on the island. It remained mostly under Athenian control until 314 when it gained its independence, and as the centre of an island confederacy achieved great prosperity. It remained an important commercial centre and slave market into the Roman period when it became a free port; but decline set in after it was sacked in 88 BC during the First MITHRIDATIC WAR and it was devastated by pirates in 69. Extensive remains survive of the Hellenistic town including some fine private HOUSES, temples, a theatre, colonnades, and agoras. Delos is the subject of a hymn by CALLIMACHUS.
See also TRADE.   GS

Stillwell (1976).

Delphi   *The Sanctuary:* Delphi is dramatically situated on the southern slopes of Mount Parnassus in Phocis overlooking the Gulf of Corinth about 2,000 feet below. The place was known to Homer as Pytho, after the resident dragon (Python) that was slain by APOLLO. The sanctuary was dedicated to Pythian Apollo in whose honour the PYTHIAN GAMES were celebrated. By the end of the 8th century BC it was enclosed by a wall, and in the 7th century the first temple of Apollo was built. This temple was destroyed by fire in 548 and replaced by a larger one, built with the help of the ALCMAEONIDS. This was in turn destroyed by earthquake in 373 and the present temple was erected on the site of its predecessors. Marked by an *omphalos* (navel), it was regarded as the centre of the world. The temple survived intact into the Roman period and was restored by DOMITIAN.

Delphi was a shrine of supranational significance and its political independence was vital to its reputation. Local inhabitants provided staff for the oracle, but after the First SACRED WAR (c.595–586) the sanctuary was administered by a confederacy known as the DELPHIC AMPHICTYONY. XERXES attacked Delphi in 480, but the Persian defeat was marked by the setting up of many statues, trophies, and treasuries. Later in the century Delphi became involved in rivalry between Greek states and a Second Sacred War was fought (c.449). Further bickering in the 4th century provoked a Third Sacred War (c.356–346) which was only resolved by the intervention of PHILIP II of Macedon. In 279 the Gauls under BRENNUS attacked but were repulsed, but in 189 Delphi fell to the Romans. SULLA plundered the sanctuary in 86 BC and NERO removed 500 statues. Other emperors such as Hadrian and the Antonines restored its outward appearance which was admired by PAUSANIAS; but the reputation of the oracle had been permanently impaired and, despite an attempt to revive it under JULIAN, it was finally closed by THEODOSIUS I in AD 390.

The Oracle: By the 8th century BC Delphi had emerged as the most important oracular shrine in mainland Greece. Its purpose, stated in the *Homeric Hymn to Apollo*, was to enable Apollo to provide the Greeks with 'unfailing advice through prophetic utterances in the rich temple'. The procedure for consultation was complex and reports of it are clothed in mystery, though PLUTARCH, who was a priest at Delphi in the 1st century AD, is a valuable source for that period. Only men were admitted. A goat was sacrificed. If the omens were favourable the inquirer paid a fee and entered the temple. The question was delivered to the Pythia (priestess) either orally or in writing, who then prophesied. Her response, induced by some form of ecstatic trance, was recorded by her attendant prophets, usually in verse, and was often ambiguous and sometimes unwelcome but almost invariably true. Questions might cover a wide range of political, religious, or personal issues, though after the 4th century BC, when political decisions were generally taken autocratically, the oracle's influence declined and inquiries were largely confined to private concerns.

See also DIVINATION; ORACLES. GS

Fontenrose (1978); Morgan (1990); Parke (1967a); Parke and Wormell (1956).

Delphic Amphictyony Greek confederacy. The Delphic Amphictyony, or union of 'dwellers around', consisted of 12 tribes organized originally around the shrine of Demeter at Anthela and, later, the temple of Apollo at DELPHI. It was administered mainly by its representative council (*Synhedrion*). Its principal concern was the upkeep of the temple and cult of Apollo, but it also regulated the behaviour of members towards each other and the cult centre, and could impose religious and financial sanctions or, in extreme cases, levy a SACRED WAR against offenders;

hence membership was liable to be manipulated, and the Amphictyony was sometimes exploited for political ends.　RB

Cawkwell (1981); Ehrenberg (1969); Parke and Wormell (1956).

Demades (c.380–319 BC), Athenian politician. Demades was prominent in the two decades after CHAERONEA (338 BC) and was often thought to have been a traitor. Captured in the battle and released by PHILIP II, he negotiated the Peace of Demades in which Athens fared well. After the sack of THEBES (335) he persuaded Alexander not to insist on the surrender of hostile politicians. He made peace with ANTIPATER after the battle of Crannon (322) and was sent in 319 to persuade him to remove the garrison from Piraeus. All this, coupled with his proposal (324) that Alexander should be added to the Twelve Gods, earned him the abuse of the war politicans, perhaps unjustly. He was a celebrated orator.　GLC

Hammond and Walbank (1988).

Demaratus king of Sparta, c.515–491 BC. Demaratus maintained a steady opposition to CLEOMENES I, causing Cleomenes to engineer his deposition as allegedly illegimate about 491, and he subsequently fled to Persia. He accompanied XERXES' invasion as adviser and, perhaps, potential satrap of the Peloponnese, and is prominent in the narrative of HERODOTUS, for whom he was clearly an important source.　RB

Cartledge (1979).

Deme unit of Athenian POPULATION. The deme was the basic Athenian community and administrative unit, a village or city ward. Many already existed in the archaic period; but under the reforms of CLEISTHENES 139 demes became the lowest tier of the political structure, divided into 10 tribes by distribution in TRITTYES. Political identity thus became based on locality: citizenship depended on deme membership, which was hereditary, each deme maintaining a list of its own members and registering new citizens at adulthood; and membership of the BOULE was distributed among the demes by a system of quotas proportional to population, since demes varied in size from hamlets to substantial towns. Politically, demes reflected the national system: each had magistrates, the most important being the demarch, and an assembly in which it managed its own affairs. Demes also had their own financial and religious organization.　RB

Osborne (1985, 1990); Whitehead (1986).

Demeter Greek goddess. Demeter was the goddess of corn and the fruits of the earth. Through her daughter Persephone, wife of Hades, she was closely connected with the underworld: 'the Two Goddesses' were central to the cult of the ELEUSINIAN MYSTERIES. Demeter was also honoured throughout Greece at the festival of the THESMOPHORIA. In literature she is celebrated in a *Homeric Hymn to Demeter*. In art she carries an ear of corn, a torch, or a sceptre and is often shown with Persephone and the Eleusinian hero Triptolemus. The Romans identified her with CERES. GS

Burkert (1985); Guthrie (1950).

Demetrius (1st century AD?), Greek prose writer. The author and date of the extant treatise *On Style* are unknown, but it may have been the work of Demetrius of Tarsus who was a friend of Plutarch. As a textbook on the theory of literary styles it is of considerable interest and displays Peripatetic sympathies. GS

Russell (1981).

Demetrius I Poliorcetes (336–283 BC), king of Macedon. Demetrius was the son of ANTIGONUS I MONOPHTHALMUS and fought with him in the struggles among the DIADOCHI. He helped defeat EUMENES OF CARDIA in 317–316 BC. He lost to PTOLEMY I at Gaza in 312 but defeated the Ptolemaic fleet off Cypriot Salamis in 306, after which Antigonus and Demetrius, first among the Successors, styled themselves 'kings'. When RHODES refused to help Antigonus, Demetrius besieged the island for one year, unsuccessfully (305/4 BC). This episode gave him the nickname 'Poliorcetes' ('besieger'). The death of Antigonus at IPSUS (301) meant Demetrius' exclusion from Asia, but he opposed CASSANDER in Greece and entered Athens in 294. After engineering the murder of Cassander's son ALEXANDER V, Demetrius was proclaimed king of Macedon (294). His son ANTIGONUS II GONATAS consolidated their control in Greece, but Demetrius lost Macedon in 288 to LYSIMACHUS and PYRRHUS. Returning to recover Asia, he was captured by SELEUCUS I NICATOR and died in captivity in 283. EER

CAH VII.1; Errington (1990); Green (1990); Hammond and Walbank (1988).

Demetrius II (c.276–229 BC), king of Macedon. Demetrius was the son of ANTIGONUS II GONATAS. During the War of CHREMONIDES, Demetrius defeated an attack on Macedon by Alexander of Molossia (son of PYRRHUS of Epirus) and dethroned him in 264 BC. Upon accession to the Macedonian throne in 239, Demetrius married Alexander's daughter, thus allying the two kingdoms and involving him in the 'Demetrian War', in which Macedon and Epirus fought the AETOLIAN and ACHAEAN LEAGUES over territorial expansion in western Greece. Although he had some successes, Demetrius was called north to fight a barbarian invasion. His death there in 229 left his young son PHILIP V to rule a weakened Macedonia.   EER

CAH VII.1; Errington (1990); Green (1990); Hammond and Walbank (1988).

Demetrius I Soter   (187–150 BC), Seleucid king. Demetrius 'the saviour' was the heir to the Seleucid kingdom, although it passed first to his uncle ANTIOCHUS IV EPIPHANES and then infant cousin. Demetrius escaped from Rome where he was held hostage and won the throne in 162 BC. He supported a pretender against the Cappadocian ARIARATHES V (who had refused to marry his sister), and was in turn threatened by the pretender ALEXANDER BALAS whom Ariarathes' ally ATTALUS II PHILADELPHUS raised against him. Demetrius died in battle against Balas in 150.
   See also JUDAS MACCABAEUS.   EER

CAH VIII; Green (1990); Gruen (1984); Sherwin-White (1984).

Demetrius II Nicator   (c.161–125 BC), Seleucid king. Demetrius 'the conqueror', helped by Ptolemy VI (whose daughter he married), finally attained the throne in 145 BC after the defeat of his father's usurper, ALEXANDER BALAS. In 144 he was forced to share the kingdom with another pretender, DIODOTUS TRYPHON. Released from a decade of capture by the Parthians, he overcame the claims of his brother ANTIOCHUS VII SIDETES to the throne, but lost it to a third pretender raised up against him by PTOLEMY VIII.
   See also CLEOPATRA II.   EER

CAH VIII; Green (1990); Gruen (1984).

Demetrius I of Bactria   (c.200–c.170 BC), king of Bactria. Demetrius succeeded his father EUTHYDEMUS, and, although details of his reign are lacking, followed a plan of expansion into eastern Seleucid satrapies which had been reconquered by ANTIOCHUS III THE GREAT. He annexed Arachosia and Drangiana to his kingdom, but Bactrian expansion into India, and the issue of bilingual coinage, probably did not happen until the reign of a later namesake. This obscure period of various Euthydemid kings came to an end when the throne was usurped by a Eucratides. After his murder the Bactrian empire passed largely into Parthian control.   EER

CAH VIII; Frye (1984); Narain (1957); Tarn (1984); Woodcock (1966).

Demetrius of Phalerum   (c.350–c.280 BC), Athenian politician. Demetrius was a pro-Macedonian statesman and Peripatetic philosopher whom CASSANDER installed as ruler of oligarchic Athens in 318/17

BC. He enacted legislation and sumptuary laws in accordance with his philosophical principles (he is often considered a 'philosopher–king'), and ruled until expelled by DEMETRIUS I POLIORCETES in 308/7. He fled to Alexandria and advised PTOLEMY I. His prolific writings include philosophical and rhetorical works, political speeches, moral treatises, and works of popular interest. EER

CAH VII.1; Ferguson (1911); Green (1990); Mossé (1973).

Demetrius of Pharos (fl. 229–214 BC), Illyrian dynast. Demetrius ruled his petty state as a reward for betraying Corcyra to Rome in 229 BC. He fought with ANTIGONUS III DOSON against CLEOMENES III at Sellasia in 222. Contravening his treaty with Rome, Demetrius with SCERDILAIDAS ravaged the Aegean islands, and, when Rome expelled him from Pharos in 219, he fled to PHILIP V. He encouraged Philip's disastrous anti-Roman policies, and died in 214 during an ill-advised Macedonian expedition against Messene in the Peloponnese. EER

CAH VIII; Gruen (1984); Hammond (1967); Hammond and Walbank (1988); Walbank (1940).

Demiurgi literally public workers, those who lived by trade or commerce in a Greek state. At Athens they were a citizen class (after the EUPATRIDAE and Georgi) comprising all who did not work on the land, and in 580 BC they supplied two of the 10 archons. Elsewhere they performed different functions, e.g. in the ACHAEAN and ARCADIAN LEAGUES they formed a council. GS

Demochares (c.360–275 BC), Athenian orator and statesman. Demochares was the nephew of DEMOSTHENES, and a confirmed democrat opposed to Macedonian intervention in Athens. He fought against CASSANDER and his partisan DEMETRIUS OF PHALERUM, and went into exile c.303 BC returning only after Athens successfully revolted from DEMETRIUS I POLIORCETES in 287. He and OLYMPIODORUS recovered Eleusis from ANTIGONUS II GONATAS. He obtained financial aid for Athens from Macedon's enemies, and public vindication for Demosthenes. He wrote orations and a history. EER

Ferguson (1911); Green (1990); Mossé (1973).

Democracy The essential tenets of democratic ideology were equality and freedom: equal access to and participation in the judicial and administrative machinery, and freedom from both domination by others and interference in or regulation of one's private life. Political equality meant that the citizen ASSEMBLY was the supreme deliberative body; all magistrates and any council would have inferior power and be accountable to the people as delegates, not representatives in the modern sense. Since all citizens were equal, and equally capable, this frequently meant the use of sortition and rotation, allowing all to exercise power in turn and no one to become indispensable, though positions requiring particular skills, such as financial and military offices, were often exceptions.

Although theoretically universal, Greek democracies were restricted by modern standards: at best, all adult males were enfranchised. Since the majority prevailed in the assembly, democracy could be seen as government of the many (rather than the few) in the interest of the poor, the majority of citizens. Equally, a constitution which enfranchised many, but not all, free men might be termed a democracy in some quarters; the term embraced a variety of possibilities, as Aristotle's discussions in the *Politics* make clear, and Athenian democracy, the best–attested form, may not be representative, given Athens's population, power, and wealth.

Philosophers, especially Plato, tended to criticize democracy from an upper-class standpoint, disliking the licence allowed to individuals, disparaging the judgement of the masses (Aristotle excepted), and regarding democratic equality as spurious and unrepresentative of unequal talents and resources.

See also MONARCHY; OLIGARCHY; TYRANNY.   RB

Finley (1985); Hansen (1991); Ostwald (1969); Raaflaub (1989); Sinclair (1967).

Democritus (b. *c*.460 BC), Greek philosopher. Democritus was born at Abdera in Thrace. He is said to have travelled widely in Egypt and Asia and to have visited Athens. His only certain teacher was LEUCIPPUS. The date of his death is unknown, but he is said to have lived to a great age. He was popularly known as the 'Laughing Philosopher', moved to laughter by the follies of mankind, as HERACLITUS is said to have been moved to tears. He was an encyclopaedic writer and his works resemble those of Aristotle in their impressively comprehensive range. Only fragments, however, have survived. Over 60 titles are attributed to him, arranged in tetralogies. These are divided into five main sections – ethical, physical, mathematical, musical, and technical – together with a few unclassified works.

Democritus adopted and further elaborated the atomic theory which Leucippus had put forward to circumvent ELEATIC logic and rehabilitate the reality of the physical world. They both held that everything came into being through the chance collision of solid, indivisible, homogeneous particles, which moved eternally in infinite numbers through an infinite void. The atomic theory of matter, with its mechanical view of causation, however, was largely rejected in antiquity in favour of teleology and a continuum theory.

See also ATOMISTS; EPICURUS; PHYSICS; ZOOLOGY. JL

Bailey (1928); Kirk, Raven, and Schofield (1983).

Demophanes and Ecdelus (3rd century BC), liberators of Megalopolis. Demophanes and Ecdelus were exiled from Megalopolis and became followers of the philosopher ARCESILAUS in Athens. They achieved a legendary reputation as liberators. They freed Megalopolis from the tyrant Aristodemus, and helped ARATUS OF SICYON in 251 BC to liberate Sicyon from its tyrant. At an uncertain date they were called to Cyrene to reorganize the constitution, and were teachers of PHILOPOEMEN. EER

CAH VII.1; Errington (1969); Walbank (1933).

Demosthenes (c.460–413 BC), Athenian general. After a chastening experience in AETOLIA (426 BC), Demosthenes heavily defeated a Peloponnesian army in Amphilochia. In 425, temporarily a private citizen, he perceived the real weakness of Sparta to be Messenian nationalism and used a force going to Sicily to fortify PYLOS. When Sparta occupied Sphacteria, he blockaded and, with the help of a force brought by his collaborator CLEON, captured the Spartans. For demographic reasons this was the biggest disaster Sparta sustained in the war. Other large designs – the attacks on Megara and Boeotia – miscarried. Sent with reinforcements to Sicily (413), he promptly decided on withdrawal. Blocked by NICIAS, he was captured and executed. GLC

Kagan (1975).

Demosthenes (384–322 BC), Athenian orator. Demosthenes was born into a property-owning middle-class Athenian family, but his father died when he was seven and his guardians embezzled his inheritance. This motivated him to study oratory, perhaps under ISAEUS, and his earliest surviving speeches, *Against Aphobus* and *Against Onetor* (364–361), represent his attempt to recover his fortune. The outcome is uncertain, but his future career was set and he became a professional speech writer.

Demosthenes' entry into politics is marked by a speech he wrote for Diodorus, *Against Androtion* (355), delivered shortly after the end of the SOCIAL WAR (357–355). He seems initially to have supported the policies of EUBULUS in advocating the maintenance of peace and modest economic expansion. His first speech to the Assembly, *On the Symmories* (354), argued for enlarging the class of taxpayers contributing to the upkeep of the fleet. His growing interest in foreign affairs is evinced by subsequent speeches on behalf of the Megalopolitans

(352, against Sparta), against the honouring of CHARIDEMUS (352, for his hand in the return of the Chersonese), and *On the Liberty of the Rhodians* (351/50). PHILIP II's aggression against Thrace after 352 represented a threat to Athens and provided the focus for all of Demosthenes' future activity.

In his *First Philippic* (351) Demosthenes urged more vigorous action on behalf of Amphipolis but he failed to persuade. In 349 OLYNTHUS was attacked and Demosthenes responded with his three *Olynthiacs* demanding immediate support. Three expeditions were voted, but the city was betrayed and fell to Philip in 348. Two years later Demosthenes joined the embassy to Pella that negotiated the peace of PHILOCRATES. He had hoped to prevent Philip's entry into central Greece, but he and Athens were deceived. Athenian resistance now seemed pointless, and in his speech *On the Peace* Demosthenes argued for the preservation of the treaty. Meanwhile ISOCRATES called on Philip to assume hegemony of all Greece.

In his *Second Philippic* Demosthenes returned to the attack, denouncing Philip, seeking allies, and criticizing AESCHINES. His quarrel with the latter he brought to a head in 343 with a speech *On the False Embassy*, suggesting that Aeschines was responsible for Philip's intervention in Phocis. After 342, as Philip's designs on Greece became transparent, so Demosthenes' invective against him (*On the Chersonese* and *Philippics 3–4*) grew in proportion. Demosthenes gladly accepted Philip's declaration of war in 340, and Athens was decisively defeated at CHAERONEA in 338. Still Demosthenes remained in office and in 336 he was offered a crown in return for his services to Athens. Aeschines questioned the legality of this; Demosthenes defended himself brilliantly with his speech *On the Crown*, forcing his opponent into exile.

Demosthenes continued to enjoy high office under Macedonian rule until 324 when he was convicted on a charge of corruption (*see* HARPALUS) and went into exile. Later recalled to Athens, he was condemned to death after the Macedonian victory at Crannon (*see* LAMIAN WAR). In 322 he fled and died by his own hand on the island of Calauria. He holds supreme place among the orators for his single-minded passion, his integrity, and his clarity of expression.   GS

Cawkwell (1978); Ellis and Milns (1970); Hammond and Griffith (1979); Kennedy (1963); Luce (1982); Pearson (1976); Sealey (1993).

Dentatus   (d. *c*.270 BC), Roman hero. Manius Curius Dentatus was a successful soldier, defeating the SAMNITES and SABINES in 290 BC and PYRRHUS in 275. He was also responsible for draining Lake Velinus and building Rome's second aqueduct. Dentatus was consul in 290, 275, and 274 and celebrated triumphs in 290 and 275. According to legend he lived sparely and was incorruptible.   HE

Devotio Roman general's prayer. To avoid disaster in battle, a Roman general could 'devote' himself and the enemy army to the gods. He then charged into their ranks. If he died, the vow had been fulfilled; if not, then an image of the general had to be buried to propitiate the gods. The first known *devotio* was performed in 340 BC by the consul Decius Mus, the second by his son at Sentinum in 295.   LPR

Scullard (1981).

Diadochi successors of ALEXANDER THE GREAT, 323–301 BC. Diadochi ('Successors') is the customary name applied to the officers of Alexander the Great who were rivals in the struggle for personal power and division of the empire after Alexander's death. After the early deaths of ANTIPATER, CRATERUS, EUMENES OF CARDIA, and PERDICCAS, the Diadochi consisted of ANTIGONUS I MONOPHTHALMUS, CASSANDER, LYSIMACHUS, PTOLEMY I, and SELEUCUS I NICATOR. The 'Age of the Diadochi' conventionally extends from Alexander's death to the battle of IPSUS in 301 BC.   EER

CAH VII.1; Green (1990).

Dialects, Greek Inscriptions suggest that each city-state had and used its own dialect, but within this plethora a pattern of five major groups emerges. (*See* map on page 746.) Ionian Greeks settled in a broad band across the Aegean from Attica and Euboea through the Cyclades to the south-west seaboard of Asia Minor. To the north of them Aeolic Greeks occupied the lands from Boeotia and Thessaly to Lesbos and the north-west of Asia Minor. The Arcadians continued to speak an archaic Greek which is similar to that of Cyprus and Pamphylia and is sometimes called Achaean. These three groups can be classed together as East Greek. West Greek is represented by two further groups. North-west Greeks occupied Elis, Aetolia, and central Greece and infiltrated the Aeolic lands of Boeotia and Thessaly. The Dorians occupied the rest, that is Magna Graecia, Corfu, Ambracia, the south and east Peloponnese, Crete, the Dodecanese, and the southern shore of western Asia Minor.

Dialects seem to have developed rapidly and independently of one another: it is no longer thought possible to link them with particular migrations, though the spread of Doric no doubt gives an indication of the penetration achieved by the so-called Dorian invasion. Different genres of literature developed their own preferred dialects which did not necessarily correspond with that of the writer's home city. Attic, originally a branch of Ionic, eventually conquered the entire Greek-speaking world and evolved into *koine*, the lingua franca of the Hellenistic period.

See also GREEK LANGUAGE.   GS

Buck (1955); Palmer (1980).

Diana Roman goddess. Diana was an old Italian goddess, originally a 'wood spirit' who gradually became also a goddess of women. Her chief cult centre was at Aricia near Rome. As the Latin League had its headquarters there, the founding by Servius Tullius of Diana's first temple in Rome on the AVENTINE was possibly an attempt to transfer these headquarters to Rome. The votive offerings found at Aricia show Diana as a goddess of childbirth and women as well as a goddess of the chase and wild animals, like the Greek ARTEMIS, with whom Diana was identified as early as the 6th century BC. In Italy her cult was especially associated with slaves, and her festival day, 13 August, was a holiday for slaves.   DP

Ogilvie (1969); Scullard (1981).

Diaspora *see* JEWS.

Dicaearchus (fl. 326–296 BC), Greek philosopher. Dicaearchus of Messene was a pupil of ARISTOTLE. Only fragments of his works survive. They provide evidence of a wide range of political, biographical, literary, philosophical, and geographical works which influenced many later authors including ERATOSTHENES, CICERO, JOSEPHUS, and PLUTARCH.
    See also MAPS.   JL

DSB IV (1971).

Dicastery Athenian court or jury. Originally the people sat as a court, but the increase of legal business required a system of organized courts which was probably introduced by EPHIALTES. Every year 6,000 citizens volunteered for jury service. PERICLES initiated payment for service, but it was only a subsistence wage. Juries were large – 500, 700, on occasion all 6,000 – so bribery was not practicable (but *see* ANYTUS). Without a judge to guide them, jurors voted as they saw fit. Naturally, Athenian justice was political, which is why ARISTOPHANES ridiculed and the THIRTY TYRANTS abolished the Ephialtic system.
    See also JUDICIAL PROCEDURE, GREEK; LAW, ATHENIAN.   GLC

MacDowell (1978).

Dictator Roman magistrate. The dictatorship was an extraordinary magistracy designed to operate for no more than six months at a time of crisis. Unlike any other magistrate, the dictator had no colleague and was not elected by the people. Instead he was nominated by a CONSUL, although his powers had to be confirmed in the COMITIA *curiata*. The other MAGISTRATES remained in office, but were subordinate to the dictator who was not subject to veto (INTERCESSIO) or right of appeal (PROVOCATIO). The dictator appointed his own deputy, the *magister* *equitum*. Possibly in 300 BC the dictatorship became subject to *provocatio*, and in 217 BC FABIUS MAXIMUS VERRUCOSUS was elected dictator by the people.

The dictatorship in its original form did not survive into the late Republic. SULLA and CAESAR held the dictatorship, but theirs were very different from earlier dictatorships, being imposed by military force and held for longer than six months.   HS

Jolowicz and Nicholas (1972).

Didascalia   Originally meaning simply the production of a play, the word was later used to refer to the official record of the plays performed at the DIONYSIA together with the names of the CHOREGUS and the poet, actors, and musicians associated with each performance. These were inscribed in stone and sizeable fragments survive. Aristotle composed a (lost) book of *Didascaliae* on which the Alexandrians drew when writing their synopses and lives of the poets.   GS

Pickard-Cambridge (1968).

Didius   (d. 89 BC), Roman politician. Titus Didius was a prominent politician of OPTIMATE leanings. As *tribunus plebis* in 103 BC, Didius vainly attempted to prevent NORBANUS' prosecution of CAEPIO. As consul in 98 he helped pass the *lex Caecilia Didia,* which gave the SENATE greater control over legislation. His military career won him two TRIUMPHS, for victories in Macedonia (100 or 99) and Spain (93), but he was killed fighting in the SOCIAL WAR.   HS

Gruen (1968).

Didius Julianus   (AD 133–93), Roman emperor, AD 193. Marcus Didius Julianus, a rich but undistinguished senator, bought the imperial throne in AD 193 after the murder of PERTINAX, by outbidding the city prefect, Flavius Sulpicianus, offering the Praetorian Guard 25,000 *sestertii* per man. However, he failed to pay the promised amount, and commanded little support elsewhere. With the approach of Septimius SEVERUS, the Senate deposed Julianus, after just 66 days, and condemned him to death.   RJB

Grant (1985); Wells (1984).

Didyma   in Ionia, site of a temple and oracle of Apollo near MILETUS. The oracle was very ancient (inscriptions date from 600 BC) and of international standing. The first temple was sacked by DARIUS I in 494 BC and the oracle fell silent until the arrival of ALEXANDER THE GREAT, whose victory at GAUGAMELA it foretold. Work began *c.*300 on a new and enlarged temple (nearly 360 feet long) and continued for almost 500 years. The oracle flourished until the 3rd century AD. The Great Didymeia, festivals of athletics, music, oratory, and drama, were celebrated every fourth year from c.200 BC.

See also ORACLES.   GS

Bean (1979a); Parke (1967a).

Didymus (1st century BC), Alexandrian scholar. Didymus was an amazingly prolific writer, reputedly the author of 3,500 or 4,000 books, for which he acquired the nickname *chalcenterus* ('brazen guts'). Scarcely an original scholar, he is important for sifting and preserving the work of his predecessors, notably ARISTARCHUS OF SAMOTHRACE on Homer. He also wrote widely on dramatic texts and lyric poetry, contributing much of value to the SCHOLIA.   GS

Fraser (1972); Pfeiffer (1968).

Dies fasti   *see* FASTI; TIME, MEASUREMENT OF.

Dinarchus   (c.360–c.290 BC), Athenian orator. Dinarchus was born a Corinthian but lived in Athens where, as a metic, he was debarred from speaking in public. He composed speeches for others, of which three survive, all concerned with the HARPALUS affair of 324, one of them *Against Demosthenes*. Described by Hermogenes as 'gingerbread Demosthenes', he was the last, and least, of the so-called ATTIC ORATORS.   GS

Kennedy (1963).

Dio Cassius (c.AD 163–c.235), Roman historian. Cassius Dio Cocceianus was born in Bithynia but came to Rome as a young man and entered the Senate, rising to the consulate under Septimius Severus. His *Roman History* was largely written during his withdrawal from public life during the reign of Caracalla, after which he was, successively, proconsul of Africa, governor of Dalmatia and then Pannonia, and finally consul again (229). Of the 80 books of Dio's *History*, covering Roman history down to AD 229, books 36–60 (68 BC to AD 46) survive largely intact, while Xiphilinus (11th century) and Zonaras (12th century) summarize much of the rest.   RJB

Grant (1979); Millar (1964); Scott-Kilvert and Carter (1987).

Dio Chrysostom (c.AD 40–112), Greek orator and philosopher. Dio of Prusa in Bithynia was given the sobriquet 'golden-mouthed' because of his eloquence. After embarking upon an oratorical career at Rome, he subsequently became influenced by STOIC philosophy. His opposition to DOMITIAN resulted in banishment both from Rome and from his native province. After spending many years as a wandering teacher of philosophy, he was later reinstated and held in high regard by NERVA and TRAJAN. Eighty speeches, not all of them genuine, are attributed to him on political, philosophical, mythological, and literary subjects. Some of them are epideictic, whereas others deal with real situations. Stoic influences are clearly apparent. His main literary models were PLATO and XENOPHON. His style is refined and largely free from rhetorical exaggeration.   JL

Diocles (fl. late 4th century BC), Greek physician. Diocles of Carystus was a contemporary of Aristotle and the first physician to write in Attic. The Athenians called him a 'younger Hippocrates' and Pliny describes him as 'next after Hippocrates in time and fame'. Only fragments of his works remain, dealing with animal ANATOMY, physiology, aetiology, symptomatology, prognostics, dietetics, and BOTANY. These fragments reveal the influence of Aristotle as well as that of the Hippocratic writings and of 'Sicilian' MEDICINE. GALEN tells us that Diocles was the first to write a book on anatomy (i.e. on animal anatomy) and it may well have been Diocles' influence which led to the introduction of systematic animal dissection within the Lyceum. In physiology Diocles seems to have integrated his 'Sicilian' legacy with the Hippocratic tradition to form a comprehensive and integrated synthesis when he brought the four-element theory into conformity with the humoral theory (*see* ELEMENTS). He seems also to have exercised an important influence upon the development of the theory of *pneuma*. Diocles was the first to write a herbal on the medical use of plants, which THEOPHRASTUS seems to have used extensively. He is also credited with the invention of a type of head bandage and a spoon-like device for the extraction of arrows.   JL

Jaeger (1940); Longrigg (1993).

Diocletian (*c.*AD 240–313), Roman emperor, AD 284–305. Diocles, an Illyrian of low birth who had risen through the ranks to the consulship, was chosen by the army of the east to replace NUMERIAN, and after the assassination of CARINUS (spring 285) became sole ruler of the empire. Gaius Aurelius Valerius Diocletianus, as he was known after his accession, undertook a massive reorganization of the administration of the empire. He established a tetrarchic system of government, appointing MAXIMIAN as Augustus in the west (286), GALERIUS (293) as his own deputy (Caesar) in the east, and CONSTANTIUS I CHLORUS as Maximian's Caesar (293). There was no formal partition of the empire, but each ruler held a particular area of responsibility. Diocletian, based at

Nicomedia (Izmit), remained the senior figure. Diocletian envisaged the retirement of the Augusti after 20 years and the automatic succession of the Caesars: he forced Maximian's retirement at the same time as his own (1 May 305), but the system broke down following the death of Constantius (306).

Diocletian's other reforms included a major reorganization of the army, which was much increased in size: each ruler commanded a mobile field force, largely made up of cavalry, designed to provide swift support for other units, strung out along the frontiers. The civil administration was improved by the subdivision of each province into two, each governor (no longer a military commander, and thus less able to rebel) responsible to the governor-general of one of 13 dioceses: these governors were responsible to one of four praetorian prefects (one for each emperor, see PRAEFECTUS PRAETORIO). Less successful were Diocletian's attempts to re-establish a stable currency (c.294), and to beat inflation with an *Edict of Maximum Prices* (301) for all goods, transport, and wages. Included as part of the general emphasis on old-style values and discipline was a revival of paganism, accompanied by a persecution of the Christians.

See also CHRISTIANITY.   RJB

Grant (1985); Parker (1958); Williams (1985).

Diodorus Siculus   (1st century BC), Greek historian. A native of Agyrium in Sicily, Diodorus wrote a history of the world (or *Library*) in 40 books from earliest times to AUGUSTUS. Some passages reflect autopsy, but essentially he epitomized, his value varying with his sources. Books 1–5 and 11–20 are complete, the rest fragmentary. It is generally thought that 11–15 draw on EPHORUS, 18–20 on HIERONYMUS, save for Sicilian matter. His method was to insert passages of epitomized narrative quite fitfully into a framework of dates derived from a chronographic source (which is generally reliable). His inaccuracies, confusions, and doublets astound, but without him knowledge of Greek history would be gravely diminished.   GLC

Sacks (1990).

Diodotus I   (fl. *c.*256–*c.*248 BC), king of Bactria-Sogdiana. Diodotus was the Seleucid satrap of BACTRIA, rebelling and declaring independence at an indeterminate date during the reign of ANTIOCHUS II THEOS, after which he issued coinage in his own name. Arsaces I of PARTHIA feared his growing power. Although the chronology is uncertain, he was succeeded by his son Diodotus II (in whose reign an alliance with Parthia was concluded), who was himself replaced by EUTHYDEMUS.   EER

CAH VIII; Frye (1984); Narain (1957); Tarn (1984); Woodcock (1966).

Diodotus Tryphon (fl. 142–137 BC), Seleucid king. Diodotus challenged the throne of DEMETRIUS II by supporting as king the son of the pretender ALEXANDER BALAS. He killed the boy, and ruled independently over Seleucid territory in Judaea, where Jewish disturbances had made Demetrius unpopular. His intervention in internal conflicts there led to the creation of the independent Hasmonaean state in 143/2 BC. He was defeated by Demetrius' brother ANTIOCHUS VII SIDETES, who also claimed the throne, and killed himself in 137.

See also JEWS.   EER

CAH VIII; Green (1990); Gruen (1984).

Diogenes of Apollonia (fl. *c*.440 BC), Greek philosopher. Diogenes, whose views are parodied in ARISTOPHANES' *Clouds* (423 BC), revived the monistic theory of ANAXIMENES that air is the first principle in a post-Parmenidean age. He believed that air was divine, endowed with intelligence, all-controlling, and capable of transformation through rarefaction and condensation. He wrote a number of treatises, including a work *On Nature*, which reveals strong eclectic tendencies. The influences of EMPEDOCLES, ANAXAGORAS, and LEUCIPPUS are clearly apparent. Diogenes may also have been a physician and the author of a medical treatise. He based his theory of health and his physiological theories generally upon his unifying hypothesis and exercised through them an important influence upon the history of MEDICINE, particularly in pneumatic theory.   JL

Guthrie, vol. 2 (1965); Kirk, Raven, and Schofield (1983); Longrigg (1993).

Diogenes of Sinope (*c*.400–325 BC), Greek philosopher. Diogenes was the principal representative of the CYNIC sect. He appears to have come to Athens after 362 BC where he lived in extreme poverty. There he came under the influence of ANTISTHENES. He advocated and practised an ascetic life-style, based upon self-sufficiency and a rigorous training of the body to have as few needs as possible. He believed that happiness was attained by satisfying only natural needs in the easiest practical way. Conventions contrary to these principles he considered to be unnatural and were ignored. For this reason he was called *kyōn* (dog) from which the name Cynic is derived. He expounded his principles with a caustic wit, and is said to have written dialogues and tragedies. Aspects of his philosophy were later adopted by the STOICS.

See also CRATES OF THEBES.   JL

Dudley (1937).

Diogenes Laërtius (*c*.AD 200–50), Greek biographical doxographer. Diogenes of Laërte in Cilicia was the author of *The Lives and Opinions*

of Eminent Philosophers (from Thales to Epicurus) in 10 books. The work, which is highly anecdotal and not always accurate, is a compilation of earlier biographers and epitomizers of philosophical doctrines. The opinions of each thinker are set out in two distinct biographical presentations: one a summary account, based largely upon a less reliable source, and the other a more detailed exposition, drawn from a more dependable epitome. Thus his reliability varies from passage to passage.

See also DOXOGRAPHERS.   JL

Dion (*c.*408–354 BC), Syracusan politician. Dion was the brother-in-law of DIONYSIUS I and an associate of PLATO, with whose aid he attempted to make DIONYSIUS II a philosopher-king. The tyrant's resistance and opposition from PHILISTUS led to Dion's exile about 366. He returned in 357 and expelled Dionysius, but failed to win control of the city until 354; growing increasingly autocratic, he was assassinated shortly thereafter.   RB

Berve (1956); Lintott (1982).

Dionysia Athenian festivals in honour of DIONYSUS. The Rural Dionysia was celebrated annually in the demes of Attica in the month of Poseideon (December). The centrepiece of this merry festival was a phallic procession of which a description is provided by ARISTOPHANES (*Ach.* 241–79). Dramatic competition was often included and there is evidence for TRAGEDY, COMEDY, and dithyramb (*see* LYRIC POETRY, GREEK) in many demes. Remains of theatres survive at Rhamnous and Thoricus.

The City (or Great) Dionysia, in honour of Dionysus Eleuthereus, was a very popular festival at the end of March when Greeks from all over the Hellenic world converged on Athens. A public holiday was declared and the assembly prorogued. The god's statue was carried in procession from the Academy to his temple on the south slope of the acropolis where bulls were sacrificed. After further sacrifice and a parade of imperial tribute in the adjacent theatre, four days of dramatic competition followed (reduced to three during the Peloponnesian War) at which tragedies, comedies, and SATYR PLAYS were performed. Inscriptions allow us to trace the history of the festival from *c.*501 to 328 BC; and there is evidence for the continuation of the dithyrambic competition until *c.*AD 200. As at the LENAEA each poet presented only one play. Poets were selected by the Eponymos ARCHON, to whom they 'applied for a chorus'. Five judges assessed the plays and the victor received a crown of ivy.

See also CHOREGUS; FESTIVALS, GREEK.   GS

Easterling and Muir (1985); Pickard-Cambridge (1968).

Dionysius I tyrant of Syracuse, 405–367 BC. Dionysius came to power as a result of Carthaginian attacks on the Greek cities of Sicily. Initial failure and a disadvantageous peace provoked a popular uprising which Dionysius crushed, cementing his position as tyrant with assistance from his ally Sparta. After securing his position in eastern Sicily, fortifying Syracuse, and making thorough preparations, Dionysius attacked the Carthaginians, capturing Motya, thwarted a counter-attack on Syracuse by HIMILCO, and made a more favourable peace (397–392). He next intervened in southern Italy, extending his influence over much of MAGNA GRAECIA; he also established a diplomatic and colonial foothold in the Adriatic and was active against the Etruscans (390–384). Renewed fighting with Carthage (383–375) ended, after a heavy defeat at Cronium, in peace on less favourable terms, not altered by a final war (368), which was unresolved at his death. He was succeeded by his son, DIONYSIUS II.   RB

Caven (1990); Sanders (1987).

Dionysius II tyrant of Syracuse, 367–344 BC. Dionysius succeeded his father DIONYSIUS I and reigned for 10 years, initially under the influence of DION and PLATO, and later of PHILISTUS. Driven out in 357 by Dion, whom he had exiled, Dionysius took refuge in Locri. After Dion's fall, he returned to Syracuse (347/6), but was driven out by TIMOLEON (344) and died in exile in Corinth.   RB

Berve (1967); Lintott (1982).

Dionysius of Halicarnassus (later 1st century BC), Greek historian of Rome. Dionysius of Halicarnassus, the Greek rhetorician and historian, arrived in Rome in 30 BC and remained for many years. Here he taught RHETORIC and wrote numerous works of literary criticism, most notably on THUCYDIDES and the Greek orators. Dionysius' self-styled memorial was his *Roman Archaeology* (often called *Antiquities*) in 20 books, the first 11 of which survive plus fragments of the rest. This work traced the rise of Rome from its beginnings to the First PUNIC WAR, where POLYBIUS' work began. His principal thesis was that Rome was a Greek city with civilized institutions and a respectable pedigree. The work used a wide range of Greek and Latin sources, including antiquarians, and although not a success as a work of literature, it is a mine of information for historians and forms a valuable supplement to LIVY.   HS

Gabba (1991).

Dionysius Periegetes (1st–2nd century AD), Greek geographer. A native of Alexandria, Dionysius wrote a *Description of the Earth* in 1187

hexameters, based largely on ERATOSTHENES. This survives in so many manuscripts, as well as in Latin versions by Avienus and Priscian, that it must have been adopted as a school text in Byzantium. His poem on birds is known to us from a prose paraphrase.   GS

Dionysius Thrax   (*c.*170–*c.*90 BC), Alexandrian scholar. 'Thrax' because his father's name was thought to be of Thracian origin, Dionysius was an Alexandrian and a pupil of ARISTARCHUS OF SAMOTHRACE. Later he moved to Rhodes where he taught grammar and literature. He devoted himself primarily to the interpretation of Homer, but he is best known for his *Greek Grammar* which was enormously influential, attracted much comment, and remained in use as a textbook until the Renaissance.   GS

Pfeiffer (1968).

Dionysus   ancient god. Dionysus had early connections with Thrace and Asia Minor (his other name, Bacchus, is Lydian). The name Dionysus appears in Mycenaean contexts but he is of little importance in Homer. A fragment of a *Homeric Hymn to Dionysus* survives, and he is central to the development of LYRIC POETRY and TRAGEDY. As the god of wine he was honoured at a number of merrymaking festivals, notably the ANTHESTERIA, LENAEA, and the Rural and City DIONYSIA. All these centred on Attica but his cult was widespread in northern Greece. His attributes were the mask and the thyrsus (sacred wand), the vine and the cantharus (drinking horn). His adherents devoted themselves to orgiastic mysteries which the Roman Senate took steps to suppress (*see* BACCHANALIA).   GS

Burkert (1985); Guthrie (1950).

Diophantus   (fl. 2nd–3rd century AD), Greek mathematician. The greatest achievement of Greek MATHEMATICS was in geometry. 'Algebra', as we now call it, was relatively neglected and it is only in the work of Diophantus of Alexandria that we have any systematic treatment of this branch of mathematics among the Greeks (who never in fact achieved a fruitful union between algebra and geometry). Diophantus, whose work is in a tradition which goes back ultimately to Babylonian mathematics, was the first Greek to make any approximation to an algebraical notation. Few of his works survive: six of the original 13 books of his logistical work, the *Arithmetica*; a treatise on polygonal numbers; and some propositions in the theory of numbers which survive from a lost work, the *Porismata*, quoted in the *Arithmetica*.   JL

DSB IV (1971).

Dioscorides (fl. AD 50–70), Greek physician and botanist. Pedanius Dioscorides of Anazarbus served as a physician in the Roman army and wrote during the reign of Nero a *Materia Medica* in five books which provided a systematic and rational account of some 600 plants and their medical properties as well as 35 animal products and 90 minerals. This work, which superseded all earlier botanical treatises, was translated into Latin by at least the 6th century and into Arabic by the 9th. Its influence upon Islamic, medieval, and Renaissance BOTANY and therapy was considerable. Dioscorides played an important role in determining modern plant nomenclature and many of the medicines described by him appear in modern pharmacopeias. JL

DSB IV (1971).

Diphilus (4th–3rd century BC), Greek comic poet. Born at Sinope, Diphilus lived mostly at Athens but died at Smyrna. An older contemporary of MENANDER, he was a prolific and successful writer of New COMEDY, said to be the author of 100 plays (60 titles are known) and winner of three first prizes. Like PHILEMON, he was much quarried by PLAUTUS and TERENCE, but only fragments of his Greek survive. GS

Webster (1970).

Dithyramb *see* LYRIC POETRY, GREEK.

Divination The interpretation of signs as a means of predicting future events is an aspect of folk religion that occurred throughout antiquity. Signs were dispensed by all the gods, but above all by ZEUS. Their interpretation was an art bestowed by APOLLO upon the mortal seer (*mantis* in Greek, *vates* in Latin). Divination was a family profession and the seer received his gift of inspiration from his forebears. CICERO in his treatise *On Divination* divided the phenomena requiring interpretation into natural and artificial.

Naturally occurring phenomena included dreams and visions, particularly those experienced during INCUBATION (e.g. at a shrine of ASCLEPIUS) or through necromancy (calling up spirits of the dead). Artificial phenomena ranged from observing the flight of birds; a sneeze, a stumble, or a chance encounter; inspecting the entrails, particularly the liver, of sacrificial animals which was especially important before an army joined battle; to the use of inanimate objects such as drawing lots, throwing dice, and the random reading of books (bibliomancy, e.g. *sortes Homericae, sortes Virgilianae*). Celestial phenomena, such as thunder and lightning, comets, meteorites, and eclipses, and monstrous births, either human or animal, portended change or disaster and were recorded by priests (*see also* AUSPICIUM; HARUSPICES).

As with ORACLES, complete trust was placed by the ancients in the art of the seer whose interpretation of signs frequently influenced the pattern of events. Like today's professional footballers, good seers changed sides for high prices. Some philosophers, notably the Epicureans, expressed scepticism; and in the 4th century AD the emperor THEODOSIUS I formally brought pagan divination to an end; but in most Greek villages to this day the *mantis* is alive and well.

See also METEOROLOGY.   GS

Dodds (1951); Halliday (1913); Lawson (1910).

Divorce   *see* MARRIAGE.

Dodona   in Epirus, the site of a sanctuary and oracle of Zeus. Dodona claimed to be the oldest of the ORACLES in Greece. According to Homer the god himself spoke through the medium of a sacred oak tree, and the place was inhabited by prophets known as Selli. When Herodotus visited it in the 5th century BC, the oracle was administered by three priestesses. Questions to the oracle were inscribed on tablets of lead, many of which survive. Most were from private individuals, but a few came from cities seeking an alternative to DELPHI. A fine theatre was built in the time of PYRRHUS; but the sanctuary was sacked by the Romans in 167 BC and the oracle fell silent.   GS

Parke (1967b).

Dolabella   (*c*.80–43 BC),   Roman commander. Publius Cornelius Dolabella, an unscrupulous aristocrat, married CICERO's daughter, Tullia, against her father's wishes in 50 BC. He fought for CAESAR in the CIVIL WAR, but as tribune in 47 clashed with ANTONY over debt. After Caesar's murder Antony allowed him to assume the vacant consulship (44), and he went out to govern Syria. The Senate outlawed him for killing TREBONIUS, the Republican governor of Asia, and after being defeated by CASSIUS LONGINUS he committed suicide.   DP

Syme (1939).

Dominium   ownership in Roman law. Rights of ownership were generally similar to rights over people, deriving from rights over family. Thus cows and children were both owned in the same way by family heads (*see* PATRIA POTESTAS). This ownership was proved by the SACRAMENTUM. Items could also become legally owned after a period of a year (movable) or two years (non-movable), if bought in good faith from a non-owner and not previously stolen.   HE

Nicholas (1962).

Domitian (AD 51–96), Roman emperor, AD 81–96. Titus Flavius Domitianus, second son of Vespasian and Flavia Domitilla, was thrown into sudden prominence by the elevation of his father (AD 69), narrowly escaping death during the storming of the Capitol by VITELLIUS' supporters. The Senate appointed him praetor with consular powers, although the real power lay with MUCIANUS pending Vespasian's arrival in Rome. Domitian was honoured, along with his brother TITUS, with the titles *princeps iuventutis* and Caesar, but neither Vespasian nor Titus allowed him any real power. He succeeded Titus (September 81), in spite of the latter's failure to grant him the powers of *imperium proconsulare* and *tribunicia potestas* in advance. From the start the Senate resented Domitian, who owed his position entirely to his father, having no record of distinguished service. Domitian's reign was openly autocratic, and characterized by contempt for the Senate. He took the censorship in perpetuity, and allowed equestrians access to posts previously reserved for senators. Domitian encouraged informers (*delatores*), and many senators were executed or exiled. There were several senatorial conspiracies, including that of L. Antonius Saturninus, governor of Upper Germany. Domitian's memory was damned after his death, and TACITUS and the younger PLINY (no doubt not discouraged by TRAJAN) are uniformly hostile. However, Domitian proved himself an able administrator and commander: he restored the state finances, was firm in the maintenance of law and order, and continued the building programme of his predecessors. He won the devotion of the armies with a successful campaign against the CHATTI beyond the Rhine (83), and AGRICOLA continued the Roman advance in Britain; but the incursions of the Dacians on the Danube front under DECEBALUS, against whom several campaigns were necessary between 85 and 92, made it impractical to hold the Scottish Lowlands. Domitian was assassinated by a palace conspiracy that included his wife Domitia.

RJB

Grant (1985); Jones (1979); Salmon (1968); Wells (1984).

Domitius Ahenobarbus, Gnaeus (d. *c*.104 BC), Roman soldier and administrator. Gnaeus Domitius Ahenobarbus ('bronze beard') belonged to one of the noble families that dominated the Senate in the last century of the Republic. From 122 to 120 BC he was largely responsible for the conquest and organization of the southern strip of Gaul as the province of Transalpine or Narbonese Gaul. His conquest of the ALLOBROGES there was achieved with the aid of elephants. A milestone records his construction of the Via Domitia to the Pyrenees and Spain. He was the ancestor of NERO.

DP

Rivet (1988).

Domitius Ahenobarbus, Gnaeus   (d. 31 BC), Roman soldier and administrator. Gnaeus Domitius Ahenobarbus, 'the best of all his family' according to Syme, began as a Republican. Gaining an unsolicited pardon from CAESAR after Corfinium in 49 BC, he later commanded a Republican fleet against the Second TRIUMVIRATE. In 40 POLLIO won him for ANTONY. He served as governor of Bithynia and officer in Antony's Parthian campaign of 36. Just before ACTIUM he deserted to Octavian, objecting to Cleopatra's presence in Antony's camp, and died soon after.   DP

Carter (1970); Syme (1939).

Domitius Ahenobarbus, Lucius   (d. 48 BC), Roman noble. Lucius Domitius Ahenobarbus, a wealthy land-owner and 'consul-designate from his cradle' in Cicero's phrase, helped lead the *nobiles* against the First TRIUMVIRATE. He had little success in this, either as praetor in 58 BC or in his threat to recall CAESAR from Gaul, the scene of his grandfather's triumphs, if he were elected consul for 55: his election was postponed until 54. His march northwards in 49, unsupported by POMPEY, resulted in capitulation at Corfinium, though, pardoned by Caesar, he lived to fall at PHARSALUS.   DP

Syme (1939).

Domitius Ahenobarbus, Lucius   (d. AD 25), Roman general. Lucius Domitius Ahenobarbus, from a distinguished Roman family, was arrogant, rude, and extravagant, but also a successful general. Consul in 16 BC, he held commands on the Danubian frontier during Tiberius' years of retirement on Rhodes (6 BC onwards). He was allied to AUGUSTUS' family through his marriage to ANTONIA, elder daughter of Mark ANTONY and Octavia; his son married the younger AGRIPPINA; and his grandson and namesake became the emperor NERO.   RJB

Salmon (1968); Scullard (1982); Wells (1984).

Domus Aurea   The Domus Aurea (Golden House) was built by NERO to replace an earlier palace, the Domus Transitoria, that was destroyed in the great fire of Rome in AD 64. Its park covered an area of about 125 acres between the Palatine, Caelian, and Esquiline hills. The architecture, which made great play of vaults, domes, and arches, represented a monumental version of the aristocrat's villa familiar from the wall paintings of POMPEII. Some remains of it survive, built into the substructure of the baths of Trajan.

See also GARDENS; PAINTING, ROMAN.   GS

Boëthius (1960).

Donatists   members of a schismatic church in North Africa named after Donatus who was chosen bishop of Carthage in place of the elected Bishop Caecilian (AD 311). Caecilian's consecrator had allegedly surrendered scriptures in the persecution of DIOCLETIAN and, despite attempts by the Roman state and church to intervene, the schism prospered. It survived condemnation by AUGUSTINE (*c*.398) and by a council of 500 bishops in 411 and may have lasted until the Arab conquest.   GS

Frend (1985).

Donatus   (mid-4th century AD), Latin grammarian. Aelius Donatus lived in Rome where he was the revered teacher of JEROME. His *Ars Grammatica* in two parts (*Ars Minor* for beginners and *Ars Maior* for advanced students) became the standard textbook for Latin grammar in the Middle Ages. His commentary on TERENCE also survives, but not his commentary on Virgil, though extracts from it are preserved by SERVIUS.   GS

Holtz (1981); Kaster (1988).

Dorians   one of the principal Greek racial groups. The Dorians appear to have entered Greece from the north during the Dark Ages, occupying most of the Peloponnese and spreading through the southern Aegean islands, particularly CRETE, to the coast of south-western Asia Minor. They shared a distinct DIALECT of Greek and the worship of Apollo, and the three Doric *phylai* (*see* PHYLE) are found in many Dorian states. Dorians felt a common racial identity in the classical period, contrasting their own austerity and physical superiority with the effeminate weakness of the IONIANS.   RB

Alty (1982); Craik (1980); Will (1956).

Doric   *see* DIALECTS, GREEK.

Doric order   *see* ARCHITECTURE, GREEK.

Dorieus   (fl. *c*.515 BC), Spartan colonist. Dorieus, son of ANAXANDRIDAS, left Sparta to found a colony in Libya *c*.514 BC, resenting the succession of his half-brother CLEOMENES I. Driven out by the Carthaginians and Libyans, he returned home briefly before leading a second colony to Sicily. *En route* he supported CROTON against SYBARIS, but he was killed in Sicily (*c*.510) and the colony failed.   RB

Burn (1984); Dunbabin (1948).

Douris (fl. 500–470 BC), Greek potter and vase painter. In the course of a long career Douris signed two vases as potter and 39 as painter, and he has been credited with the painting of some 300 vases in all, most of them cups. In his early years he was influenced by ONESIMOS, but his style continued to develop and several distinct periods in his work can be identified.   GS

Arias and Hirmer (1962); Boardman (1975).

Doxographers   writers on the doctrines of the philosophers. THEO-PHRASTUS seems to have been the first to write a special work upon the opinions of his predecessors when he collected the doctrines of the Presocratic philosophers and Plato in the 16 books of his *Physikon Doxai*, arranging them according to topics. (Aristotle, however, probably initiated this genre of literature by discussing the theories of his predecessors in the introductory chapters of his various works, see especially *Metaphysics* A.) Theophrastus' work became the standard authority for what is known as the doxographical tradition. It is the source for subsequent collections of opinions which took different forms: some were arranged according to subjects (following Theophrastus), some were bibliographical (*see* DIOGENES LAËRTIUS), and some arranged various philosophers into master/pupil relationships or 'successions' (e.g. Sotion).   JL

Kirk, Raven, and Schofield (1983).

Draco   (fl. *c*.621/20 BC), Athenian lawgiver. Draco was the author of the first Athenian law code, published in 621/20 BC. Publication of laws in writing represented a concession by the aristocracy, probably in response to the failed *coup d'état* of CYLON; but Draco's code became notorious for the severity of its penalties, allegedly prescribing death for most offences (hence our 'draconian'). Draco's legislation was superseded by that of SOLON, except for the law of homicide, which remained the basis of classical Athenian practice, and little other reliable information concerning it survives. The 'Draconian Constitution' in Aristotle's *Athenian Constitution* is an interpolated conservative fiction.   RB

Gagarin (1981, 1986); Rhodes (1981); Stroud (1968).

Drama   *see* COMEDY; TRAGEDY.

Dreams   *see* DIVINATION.

Dress, Greek   Our knowledge of Greek dress derives principally from vase painting and sculpture. Greek men commonly wore a loose-fitting tunic (*chiton*), made of linen or wool, over which they wrapped a cloak (*himation*). A young man's tunic would reach to his knees, an older man's to his ankles. Labourers wore either a single garment (*exomis*), fastened over the left shoulder only, or a loin cloth (*zoma*). Athletes wore nothing. A shorter cloak or cape (*chlamys*) was worn for hunting or riding. Men usually went bareheaded, but a broad-brimmed hat (*petasos*) might be worn by huntsmen and travellers and a skull cap (*pilos*) by labourers. All classes commonly went barefoot, but sandals, shoes, or boots were sometimes worn outdoors. In the archaic period women generally wore a draped, sleeveless tunic (*peplos*), folded and drawn in at the waist by a girdle, and over it a cloak or shawl (*kredemnon* or *pharos*). In the classical period women's dress was more restrained than before and much more like men's, that is a long *chiton* worn under a *himation*, but with a brighter range of colours and patterns. JEWELLERY, especially pins and brooches, was worn by both sexes in all periods. Most men wore beards.   GS

Symons (1987a).

Dress, Roman   Roman men wore a tunic (*tunica*), like the Greek *chiton* but shorter, and over it a TOGA. The latter may have been inherited from the Etruscans, but it became the standard uniform of the Roman citizen. More than one tunic might be worn in cold weather. Stripes on the tunic distinguished senators and *equites*. An outer cloak (*lacerna*) was worn by travellers. A ceremonial cloak (*trabea*) was worn at outdoor events by the equestrian order, the consul, the augurs, and some priests. Headgear might take the form of a hood (*cucullus*) or, on journeys and at the Saturnalia, a skull cap (*pilleus*). Leather shoes (*calcei*) were worn in the city and boots (*perones*) in the country; soldiers wore heavy marching boots (*caligae*). Roman women wore a shirt-like under-tunic (*tunica inferior*), sometimes with a leather band (*strophium*) below the breasts. Over it unmarried women wore a *tunica exterior* which reached the ground. Married women wore a much fuller garment (*stola*) which had to be gathered up into folds under the breast by means of a girdle. Over this they draped an outdoor shawl (*palla*). Coiffure was simple at first but became very elaborate during the Empire. JEWELLERY, especially rings and brooches, was worn by both men and women. Most men were clean shaven.   GS

Symons (1987b).

Drusilla (AD 17–38), daughter of GERMANICUS. Julia Drusilla, second daughter of Germanicus and AGRIPPINA THE ELDER, is chiefly remembered as the favourite sister of the emperor GAIUS (Caligula), with whom she is said to have committed incest. He named Drusilla as his heir, and, after her death in AD 38, he ordered her deification. Her widower, Aemilius Lepidus, conspired against Gaius, implicating both of Drusilla's sisters (the younger AGRIPPINA and Julia Livilla) in the plot.   RJB

Salmon (1968); Scullard (1982).

Drusus, Marcus Livius   (d. 109 BC), Roman politician. Marcus Livius Drusus was tribune in 122 BC and cooperated with FANNIUS in opposing Gaius GRACCHUS. By promoting popular measures such as the founding of colonies and exempting Latins from corporal punishment he undermined Gracchus' position as reformer. As consul in 112, and subsequently as proconsul, he fought the barbarian Scordisci in the Balkans, celebrating a triumph in 110. He became censor in 109, but died in office.   HE

Stockton (1979).

Drusus, Marcus Livius   (d. 91 BC), Roman tribune. Marcus Livius Drusus was the son of DRUSUS, brother-in-law of CAEPIO, and a supporter of Lucius CRASSUS. In 91 BC he became tribune, and attempted to defuse current crises, drawing support from both the Senate and the people. He proposed a reform of the courts, probably by enrolling 300 EQUESTRIANS in the Senate and drawing juries from this larger body, land distributions, and the extension of Roman citizenship to all Italians. This made him unpopular with wealthy land-owners, including senators (led by the consul of 91, Philippus), the people (who did not wish to share their privileges), and even some Italians (who would lose land in exchange for citizenship). His known links with Italian leaders such as Poppaedius Silo led to (groundless) fears concerning his loyalty. Already under severe pressure, Drusus' position was further weakened by Crassus' death. His legislative programme collapsed, and at the end of the year he was assassinated, hastening the onset of the SOCIAL WAR.   HE

Gabba (1976); Gruen (1968).

Drusus, Nero Claudius   (38–9 BC), Roman soldier. Nero Claudius Drusus, step-son of AUGUSTUS, was the son of LIVIA by her first husband, Tiberius Claudius Nero. Drusus was not considered a possible successor of Augustus on account of his Claudian ancestry, and was opposed to the Principate, favouring the restoration of the Roman Republic. However, he proved himself able, and both he and his elder brother TIBERIUS served Augustus loyally. Drusus was quaestor in 16 BC, although under age for the post, and served with distinction with Tiberius on the Rhine frontier, defeating the Raetians and the Vindelicians. In 13 BC he was appointed governor of the Three Gauls (Aquitania,

Lugdunensis, and Belgica), and conducted several brilliant military campaigns in the north against the Germanic tribes, advancing as far as the river Elbe, before being killed in a fall from his horse. He had three children, GERMANICUS, LIVILLA, and CLAUDIUS I, through his wife, the younger ANTONIA.   RJB

Salmon (1968); Scullard (1982).

Drusus, Julius Caesar (13 BC–AD 23), son of TIBERIUS. Julius Caesar Drusus was the son of Tiberius by Vipsania Agrippina, and therefore not a blood relative of Augustus. Because of this, Drusus' advancement was subordinated to that of GERMANICUS, Tiberius' nephew. Competent, though allegedly cruel, Drusus suppressed a mutiny in Illyricum (14), and became heir apparent to Tiberius after Germanicus' death (19). He died in 23, perhaps poisoned by his wife Livilla (Livia Julia, Germanicus' sister), mistress of SEJANUS.   RJB

Scullard (1982); Wells (1984).

Ducetius (fl. c.460–440 BC), Sicel leader. Ducetius emerged c.460 BC as leader of a confederation of the Sicels, the indigenous Sicilian population. Though initially allied with democratic SYRACUSE against the remnants of its tyranny, which had been hostile to the Sicels, he turned to founding Sicel cities and attacking Greek ones. Heavily defeated by Syracuse c.450, Ducetius surrendered and was sent into exile in Corinth. Though he soon returned to found another city before his death, the Sicel movement collapsed.   RB

CAH V; Freeman (1891); Rizzo (1970).

Dura Europus city in Mesopotamia. Dura Europus was founded as a military colony by SELEUCUS I NICATOR c.300 BC. The lofty site, on the middle Euphrates in modern Syria, commands the river crossing and the Mesopotamian plain. In 114 BC Dura was conquered by PARTHIA, and the Greek city became gradually orientalized. In AD 165 this prosperous city was conquered by the Roman emperor Lucius VERUS and became an important military outpost. It was besieged and destroyed c.AD 257 by the Sassanian king SHAPUR I. Archaeological excavation has revealed a citadel, governor's palace, Greek and oriental temples, a Christian church, a synagogue with well-preserved paintings, and important related artefacts and documents.   EER

Hopkins (1979); Perkins (1973); Weitzmann and Kessler (1990).

Duris (c.340–c.260 BC), tyrant of Samos and historian. Duris was a pupil of THEOPHRASTUS and became tyrant of Samos. Few details of his life are known, but he was a prolific writer. He wrote histories of Greece, Macedonia, and Samos, a life of AGATHOCLES of Syracuse, and various anecdotal works. He produced so-called 'tragic history', characterized by a sensational, emotional style, and was criticized in antiquity, although his life of Agathocles was used by PLUTARCH.

See also HISTORIOGRAPHY, GREEK.   EER

Kebric (1977).

Dyrrhachium   modern Durazzo (Durrës), city on the eastern shore of the Adriatic. Jointly founded *c.*625 BC by Corinth and Corcyra as the colony Epidamnus, it was a major port for trade with ILLYRICUM. Under PYRRHUS it became part of Epirus, but was besieged by Illyrians in 229 and then occupied by the Romans who used it as a base for operations in Greece and the Balkans.

See also EGNATIA, VIA.   GS

E

Eburacum modern York, legionary fortress in Roman Britain. Founded as a camp for the Ninth Legion in AD 71, a more permanent fort was built by AGRICOLA and strengthened under TRAJAN in 108. In 122 the Sixth Legion replaced the Ninth, and when BRITAIN was divided into two provinces Eburacum became the capital of Lower Britain. Both Septimius SEVERUS and CONSTANTIUS I died there and CONSTANTINE I was proclaimed emperor there. It was a bishopric by 314.　　GS

Salway (1981).

Ecclesia Greek citizens' assembly. In theory, the Ecclesia, the citizen body meeting in assembly, was the dominant political organ; in practice, in many states its power was limited by restrictive qualifications for CITIZENSHIP, by its procedural machinery, and by the diversion of powers to magistrates, councils, and courts (*see* OLIGARCHY), and only in a DEMOCRACY such as Athens was its authority supreme.

At Athens the Ecclesia was open to all male citizens over 20. It met on the Pnyx, which accommodated about 6,000 in the 5th century BC and perhaps 8,000 in the 4th (in either case a minority of citizens). In the 5th century there was probably only one fixed meeting a month, which might be supplemented *ad hoc*; but after about 400 (when attendance was also paid) there were four per month. The BOULE provided presidents and prepared business, but any citizen was entitled to speak and to make or amend a proposal; voting was by show of hands. Decrees of the assembly tended to concern policy rather than administration, but they covered all areas of government, especially foreign policy. In the 4th century the freedom of the assembly in practice was restricted by the existence of a published law code and of

NOMOTHETAE, although these were theoretically subject to the people; furthermore, unlike judicial verdicts, its decisions might be reviewed and reversed. The assembly itself functioned as a court in cases of EISANGELIA (until about 355 BC) and elected magistrates, notably STRATEGOI.   RB

See also APELLA.

Hansen (1983, 1987, 1989, 1991); Starr (1990).

Ecdelus   *see* DEMOPHANES AND ECDELUS.

Eclecticism   the selective amalgamation of elements from different systems of thought. Eclecticism began first in the 2nd century BC and coincided with a general decline in the quality of Greek thought. The four major schools of philosophy, the Peripatetic, the Stoic, the Epicurean, and the Platonic (converted to Scepticism by ARCESILAUS), were all permanently established at Athens. Their traditional opposition eventually gave way to recognition of similarities between them and the distinctive doctrines of each school were allowed to fade into the background. Thus, for example, the doctrines of the ACADEMY, the PERIPATETICS, and the STOICS were regarded as essentially indistinguishable; elements of Platonism and Aristotelianism were incorporated into Stoicism; and the NEOPLATONISTS selected elements from Platonism, Aristotelianism, and elsewhere to form a comprehensive new system.
                                                                          JL

Zeller (1883).

Economics   *see* BANKING; COINAGE; INDUSTRY; TRADE.

Edictum   Roman edict. Edicts, the primary means by which a Roman emperor legislated, could be on almost any subject and, together with *decreta* and *rescripta*, made up the imperial CONSTITUTIONES. Republican and early imperial urban magistrates could issue an *edictum perpetuum* for their period of office, both interpreting and altering the laws: Hadrian abolished this privilege by codifying the *edicta*, which became permanent and binding, and alterations were thereafter made by imperial edict.
    See also LAW, ROMAN.   RJB

Cracknell (1964); Salmon (1968).

Education   Education in antiquity was based largely on the study of RHETORIC with the aim of producing effective public speakers, but there were considerable local variations.

At SPARTA, despite a flourishing archaic culture, education in the classical period was geared solely to the production of an efficient military élite. Both boys and girls were removed from parental care at the age of seven and lodged in state-run barracks where the emphasis was on sport and physical education, though not to the exclusion of reading, writing, and MUSIC.

At ATHENS more liberal conditions prevailed. Elementary schooling was not compulsory: it was private and fee-paying, but not expensive. From the age of six most pupils, girls as well as boys, attended three schools: one for gymnastics (*paidotribes*), one for music and poetry (*kitharistes*), and one for the three Rs (*grammatistes*). Most teachers were slaves, though the head was usually a freedman. After elementary school the sons of wealthier parents might continue their education to the age of 18 at a senior school offering professional training in LAW or MEDICINE or rhetoric or by attending courses given by the SOPHISTS. Best known were Plato's ACADEMY, Aristotle's Lyceum (*see* PERIPATETIC SCHOOL), and ISOCRATES' school of rhetoric.

In the Hellenistic world the pattern set in classical Athens was formalized into a structure that continued into the Middle Ages. Education remained private but there was a gradual trend towards state ownership with the establishment of the GYMNASIUM and public LIBRARIES. Schooling was now concentrated in one building, and pupils were divided into age groups: up to 14 (*paides*), 14–18 (*epheboi*), 18 plus (*neoi*). Elementary schooling was little changed, but secondary education offered a broader syllabus now, and at the tertiary level high standards were set, especially at Alexandria, Athens, Pergamum, and Rhodes. Teachers were respected but still not highly paid except at the top.

At Rome a boy was traditionally educated by his father from the age of 7 to 16 when he was apprenticed to an advocate (ADVOCATUS) and subsequently sent on military service. But there were schools from the 3rd century BC (*see* CARVILIUS) and the Hellenistic model of primary and secondary schooling for girls as well as boys was gradually introduced, though with much less emphasis on physical education. At the tertiary level the study of Greek rhetoric, established at Rome in the 2nd century BC, was supplemented in the next century by that of Latin, and the greatest distinction was to be 'learned in both tongues'. For rhetoric the best school was at Athens, and Greek teachers were always in demand at Rome; but for law Rome's supremacy went unchallenged. The growth of educational opportunity necessitated a degree of state control and state support, and the emperors took a personal interest by endowing chairs and municipal schools (*see* CONSTANTINOPLE).

Methods that were developed in Greece were systematized at Rome, and the seven liberal arts, identified by MARTIANUS CAPELLA but based on

Plato's *quadrivium* (arithmetic, astronomy, geometry, and music) and Isocrates' *trivium* (grammar, rhetoric, and dialectic), constituted the curriculum for medieval education.

See also EPHEBI; IUVENES; QUINTILIAN.   GS

Bonner (1977); Clarke (1971); Marrou (1956).

Egeria   (4th century AD), Christian pilgrim. Egeria was a wealthy nun from the western Mediterranean who made a pilgrimage to the Holy Land and Egypt in 381–4. The account of her *Travels*, which survives in part, is the earliest known record of Christian pilgrimage and provides valuable evidence of the contemporary topography and liturgy of the Holy Land.   GS

Hunt (1982); Wilkinson (1981).

Egnatia, Via   Roman road. Following the line of existing trade routes, the Via Egnatia was built by the Romans *c*.130 BC from the Adriatic to BYZANTIUM. From two starting points, at Apollonia and DYRRHACHIUM, it crossed the mountains into Macedonia and passed through Heraclea, Pella, and THESSALONICA before following the coast to the Bosphorus. As the Balkan extension of the Via APPIA, it was the principal route from Rome to the east.

See also ROADS, ROMAN.   GS

Egypt   *Before 331 BC*: Greeks were present in Egypt from at least the 7th century BC as traders and, more significantly, mercenaries, employed in their thousands by the pharaohs of the XXVIth Dynasty. Under Amasis Greek trade was regulated by being concentrated at NAUCRATIS. Greek states and tyrants had diplomatic links with Egypt, but these were broken by the Persian conquest under CAMBYSES. Thereafter, rebellious Egypt offered opportunities for Greek intervention against Persia: Athenian successes in the mid-5th century were short-lived, but a further revolt *c*.405–343, in which Greek mercenaries were employed by both sides, was suppressed only just before the arrival of Alexander.   RB

Austin (1970); Boardman (1980); CAH III.3; Cook (1983).

Ptolemaic kingdom: Egypt was liberated from the Persians by ALEXANDER THE GREAT in 332/1 BC. He founded the city of ALEXANDRIA in the Nile Delta. Alexander appointed CLEOMENES OF NAUCRATIS governor, but after 323 the DIADOCHI appointed PTOLEMY (later I) as satrap. Ptolemy and his descendants established themselves as hereditary monarchs and ruled Egypt until the death of CLEOPATRA VII in 31 BC. The 3rd century saw strong government by able kings (although Nubia revolted at the end of the century), enviable prosperity (through a tightly regulated economy), and military successes. Egypt formed a naval protectorate in the Aegean and won several wars against Syria. The 2nd and 1st centuries were troubled by brutal dynastic quarrels and the meddlings of Syria and Rome.

Papyrus documents provide evidence for all aspects of life in Greek and Roman Egypt outside Alexandria. Greek culture seems to have been a thin veneer spread over the native population. The flourishing culture of the Greek cities apart, life remained largely unchanged for the Egyptian peasant. There was little cultural amalgamation of language or religion. Similarly, the Greeks remained Greek and were not egyptianized except in religious iconography.

See also ARSINOË I–III; BERENICE I, II; CLEOPATRA II, III, VII; ISIS; PTOLEMY I–XV.   EER

Bagnall (1976); Bowman (1986); Eddy (1961); Fraser (1972); Green (1990); Lewis (1986); Pomeroy (1990); Sullivan (1990); Thompson (1988).

Roman province: Egypt, kingdom of the Ptolemies, passed into the hands of Octavian (AUGUSTUS) in 30 BC, after the defeat of Mark ANTONY and CLEOPATRA VII. It became the personal province of the Roman emperor, administered by an equestrian prefect based in Alexandria. Augustus preserved the existing administrative system with only minor modifications, but extracted the maximum in revenue. A new flat-rate poll-tax was introduced (the *laographia*), paid in full by the bulk of the population. Roman citizens were exempt, as were the citizens of the three Greek-style cities in Egypt (Alexandria, Naucratis, and Ptolemais), and some of the priests of each temple. Three main districts, the Nile Delta, the 'Seven Nomes and Arsinoe' (Middle Egypt), and the Thebaid (Upper Egypt), were administered by *epistrategoi*, and the subdivisions (nomes) by *strategoi* ('generals', though lacking any military function, since there was a Roman army of occupation). The principal towns of each nome were known as *metropoleis*: at least some of the inhabitants (*metropolitai*) paid the poll-tax at a reduced rate. This taxation proved a heavy burden on the province, which decreased in prosperity as the revenues were spent elsewhere. In the 4th century, however, there was something of a revival, and throughout the period, Egypt was a major supplier of corn to Rome. In contrast to other provinces, there was little in the way of romanization: Alexandria remained a centre of Greek culture and learning, while the languages and customs of the interior changed as little under the Romans as they had in the Hellenistic period.   RJB

Bowman (1986); Lewis (1983); Lindsay (1963); Millar (1981).

Eisangelia Athenian impeachment. *Eisangelia* ('denunciation') might be used by any citizen to initiate a prosecution for certain offences: the most important forms of *eisangelia* were to the ECCLESIA, for treason or corruption, or to the Council (BOULE), for misconduct in office by any official. Until about 355 BC, when referral became automatic, the Ecclesia might hear cases itself, or refer them to a court; the Council heard its cases initially, but referred them to a court if a penalty beyond its competence was required. Prosecutions seem to have been frequent, and the ease of procedure and elasticity of charges opened them to abuse.   RB

Hansen (1975, 1991); MacDowell (1978); Rhodes (1981).

Eisphora Greek property tax. The term *eisphora* ('contribution') is attested for a tax on land or property in various Greek states. At Athens it appears in the later 5th century BC as an extraordinary levy. In 378/7 it was reorganized: all rateable property was valued, and those liable to *eisphora* were divided into groups (*see* SYMMORIA), the sum raised by each levy being a stipulated percentage of the total, and individual, assessment. Subsequently, efficiency was increased by exacting the sum from the 300 richest citizens, who were reimbursed by the symmories; finally, the levy was fixed at 10 talents annually.
    See also FINANCE, GREEK.   RB

Brun (1983); De Ste Croix (1953); Thomsen (1964).

Elagabalus (AD 204–22), Roman emperor, AD 218–22. Varius Avitus Bassianus, son of Julia Soaemias, became emperor through the machinations of his grandmother Julia Maesa, sister of JULIA DOMNA. Maesa, banished from court by MACRINUS, returned to her native Emesa, where Bassianus became chief priest of Elah-Gabal, the sun god. Maesa claimed that Bassianus was the bastard son of Caracalla, and had him proclaimed emperor under the names Marcus Aurelius Antoninus. Much of Macrinus' army deserted to Antoninus, and the latter's reign was reckoned from the date of a decisive battle near Antioch (8 June 218). The religious title Elagabalus (Heliogabalus to ancient authors) took precedence over the emperor's other titles, and the reign was characterized by religious excess, cruelty, and immorality. Eventually Maesa took steps to replace him: Elagabalus was persuaded to adopt his cousin SEVERUS ALEXANDER as his heir (221), and in the following year Elagabalus and his mother were murdered by the praetorians (March 222), leaving Alexander as emperor.   RJB

Grant (1985); Parker (1958); Wells (1984).

Eleatic 'school'   (6th and 5th centuries BC). Although PLATO (*Sophist* 242D) traces back the 'Eleatic tribe' of philosophers to Xenophanes, and ARISTOTLE seems to have taken this remark seriously, there is no close intellectual connection between Xenophanes and the Eleatic philosopher PARMENIDES. It is also unlikely that there was a school in the accepted sense. Parmenides, following his remorseless deductive logic, denied all motion and change and concluded that what exists must be single, indivisible, and changeless. These startling conclusions were defended by ZENO OF ELEA, who revealed paradoxes in generally accepted ideas of plurality, divisibility, and change. Finally, MELISSUS put forward a modified version of Parmenides' conclusions levelled against later pluralists (EMPEDOCLES, ANAXAGORAS), who sought to circumvent Eleatic argument.

   See also ATOMISTS; DEMOCRITUS; PHYSICS.   JL

Guthrie, vol. 2 (1965); Raven (1948).

Elements   A survey of pre-philosophical Greek poetry reveals that belief in the four great cosmic masses – earth, air, fire, and water – as primary components of the universe was not of immemorial antiquity. Both Homer and Hesiod, however, recognized a simple division of the world into four separate regions and the precedent of this poetic tetrad must have contributed towards the widespread acceptance of the later four-element theory. While the Milesian philosophers (THALES, ANAXIMANDER, ANAXIMENES) isolated these four cosmic masses and gave them important roles in their PHYSICS, these are only part of a larger inventory of generated and corruptible natural forms. EMPEDOCLES' unique contribution was to focus exclusively upon earth, air, fire, and water as basic elements. By giving these four forms permanence and immutability, as well as equality of status, he replaced the wider Milesian series and established these four as the canonical tetrad. Unlike ATOMISM, its great rival in antiquity and later, Empedocles' theory was capable of being supported by appeals to empirical phenomena and was subsequently adopted – and adapted – by the ACADEMY, the PERIPATETICS, and the STOICS, each in their different ways, and exercised a dominant influence in natural science for almost two millennia.

   See also DIOCLES.   JL

Longrigg (1975, 1976).

Elephants   The Greeks possessed ivory (*see* SEALS) long before they ever saw an elephant. They first encountered elephants in war in 326 BC when ALEXANDER THE GREAT defeated PORUS at the Hydaspes. Alexander did not himself use them in battle but his successors did. These were Indian elephants such as PYRRHUS took on his expedition to Italy in

280. The elephants used by the Carthaginians and the Ptolemies were the smaller African Forest subspecies which they found in the Atlas Mountains and Ethiopia respectively. The Carthaginians employed them to great effect against REGULUS in 255, but the Romans had learnt how to deal with them before ZAMA (202). At Rome they appeared more often in GAMES and processions than in battle, though some were used at PYDNA.   GS

Scullard (1974).

Eleusinian mysteries   the most famous and most revered of the Greek mystery cults. The sanctuary at Eleusis in Attica was sacred to DEMETER and the cult is first attested in the *Homeric Hymn to Demeter*. Secrets of the cult were revealed only to initiates and our knowledge of the rituals is sketchy. Initiation was available to all who spoke Greek and were free from blood-guilt (women and slaves included); it was believed to ensure happiness in the AFTERLIFE. A major festival took place in the autumn month of Boedromion: a public procession followed the Sacred Way from Athens to Eleusis accompanied by dancing, chanting, and mumming. At Eleusis the initiates crowded into the Telesterion, a darkened hall, where various rituals were recited, mysteries revealed, and rites performed. Similar practices were enacted in other parts of Greece, and another mystery cult was established by the followers of Orpheus (*see* ORPHISM), but Eleusis retained its prominence until the cult was proscribed by THEODOSIUS I, and the sanctuary was sacked by the Goths *c*.AD 400.   GS

Burkert (1987); Easterling and Muir (1985); Mylonas (1961).

Elis   region in southern Greece. The state of Elis, in the north-west Peloponnese, achieved early distinction because its territory embraced OLYMPIA and its people presided at the OLYMPIC GAMES. Otherwise famous for horse-breeding, they played little part in politics until 420 BC when their ally Sparta supported a rival city. They promptly allied with Argos and then Athens, in return for which they were ravaged by AGIS II in 399 and deprived of territory. Elis joined the ACHAEAN LEAGUE in 191.   GS

Stillwell (1976).

Empedocles   (*c*.492–432 BC), Greek philosopher. Empedocles, who is described by LUCRETIUS as 'scarce born of mortal stock', combined the roles of philosopher, statesman, poet, orator, and healer. He later became a favourite subject for apocryphal stories. A native of Acragas, he was the author of two hexameter poems of considerable poetic merit: a physical poem *On Nature* and a religious work, entitled

Katharmoi (*Purifications*). Since the former seems to leave no room for an immortal soul and the latter expounds a belief in transmigration, controversy has arisen regarding this alleged inconsistency. Parallels between the two works, however, point to the unity and consistency of Empedocles' thought. The physical poem is the first pluralist answer to PARMENIDES. While accepting many of the latter's arguments, he postulated four 'roots' or ELEMENTS – earth, air, fire, and water. These four eternally distinct substances fill the whole of space, and by their combination and separation under the contrary influences of two motor causes, Love and Strife, bring about the generation and dissolution of 'mortal things'. Coming-into-being and passing-away are thus only relative and simply the compounding (in different ratios) and dissolution of particles of the four eternal and unchanging elements. Empedocles postulated a cosmic cycle, in which Love (which brings together unlike particles of the elements) and Strife (which joins like to like) predominate in turn. Adopted and adapted by the ACADEMY, the PERIPATETICS, and the STOICS, Empedocles' four-element theory dominated natural science for nearly two millennia and his corpuscular theory of matter influenced considerably the ATOMISTS too.

See also BOTANY; MEDICINE; PHYSICS; ZOOLOGY.   JL

Guthrie, vol. 2 (1965); Kirk, Raven, and Schofield (1983).

Endoios (fl. *c.*530–500 BC), Greek sculptor. Endoios was an Athenian whose work is represented by a number of surviving fragments. His marble statue of the seated Athena from the acropolis was seen by PAUSANIAS. The relief of a seated potter, also from the acropolis, bears his signature. On stylistic grounds he is credited with the head of a youth in Copenhagen, the ball-player base in Athens, and some of the sculpture of the Siphnian treasury at DELPHI.   GS

Boardman (1978).

Engineering The essential processes of AGRICULTURE, METALworking, POTTERY, and WEAVING had all been discovered during the Neolithic and Bronze Ages. Most of the fundamental devices for the redeployment of animal energy – lever, pulley, inclined plane, and windlass – were inherited by the Greeks and Romans from earlier civilizations. Despite some impressive achievements in civil engineering, such as the tunnel of Eupalinus built at SAMOS *c.*530 BC to carry water through an intervening mountain, and the more diverse legacy of ROADS, BRIDGES, AQUEDUCTS, THEATRES, and AMPHITHEATRES constructed to high standards by the Romans, technological progress in classical antiquity remained comparatively backward and relatively few advances were made in technical knowledge.

Inventions were limited to the gear, screw, rotary mill, water mill, screw press, dioptra, torsion catapult, water clock, water organ, concrete, glass blowing, hollow bronze casting, and some mechanical toys operated by wind, water, or steam. No great store was apparently set by material progress, and the potential use of applied mechanics to achieve such progress went largely unrecognized.

The main source of power was animal energy; but its exploitation was limited by a failure to devise an efficient harness. Neither wind, nor water, nor steam was effectively utilized as a power source. Although the water wheel was invented in the 1st century BC, it does not appear to have been used to any considerable extent until the 3rd century AD. This slow diffusion has been accounted for by the absence of fast-flowing streams in Greece and Italy. But since this problem could have been overcome by powering the wheels from aqueducts, the main reason should be sought elsewhere. The windmill was not used by the Greeks and Romans as a power source (although HERON describes a machine in which wind power seems to have been used to operate an organ).

One area where mechanical ideas were applied and developed, however, was WARFARE. THUCYDIDES (4. 100) describes the use of a primitive flame thrower by the Boeotians at Delium. But it was during the Hellenistic period especially that mechanical devices began to be exploited for purposes of SIEGECRAFT. PLUTARCH (*Life of Marcellus* 14–17) describes how the engines of ARCHIMEDES, which included catapults of various types, kept the Romans at bay during the siege of SYRACUSE in 212 BC. The earliest type of catapult, which was something like a cross-bow (*gastrophetes*), does not seem to have been used until the 4th century BC. Later, more effective weapons were developed, particularly those incorporating the torsion principle to exploit the power of skeins of twisted hair or sinew. Archimedes is held to have devised a monster capable of firing a stone weighing almost 175 lb a distance of 200 yards.

One invention of Archimedes which had a civil rather than a military application was the water-lifting device still known as the Archimedean screw. This was used in irrigation and the draining of mines and possibly even for pumping out the bilges of ships. Other ingenious devices invented during the Hellenistic age were intended purely for amusement rather than to harness the forces of nature for practical purposes. Heron describes in his *Pneumatics* the inventions of Ctesibius which included a water clock, a water organ, and a double pump for raising water which was used in fire engines. Heron also describes other devices for pouring wine (the *clepsydra*), for pouring libations, and for the automatic opening of temple doors. Among these inventions is a ball rotated by steam.

The failure of the Greeks to develop their technology and employ devices like the steam-powered ball for practical ends has frequently been attributed to the existence of SLAVERY within their society. But even if it had occurred to them to employ this device for practical purposes, the problems, particularly in metallurgy, which they would have had to overcome to make an efficient steam engine were formidable. A comparison with Egypt, where slavery manifestly did not inhibit developments in mechanics, suggests that this explanation is untenable. A psychological explanation seems more plausible: the Greeks judged the value of labour by the social status of the people who performed it. They were therefore contemptuous of manual work. In their eyes the value of science was reduced when it became a means to an end.

JL

Finley (1965); Hodges (1977); Landels (1978); White (1984).

Ennius (239–169 BC), Roman poet. Quintus Ennius was the greatest of the early Latin poets. Like many figures of early Latin literature he was an outsider whose native language was not Latin, but probably Messapic, the language of Rudiae, his home town in the heel of Italy. Ennius was also fluent in Greek and OSCAN. He served with the Roman army in Sardinia during the Hannibalic War, and was brought to Rome in 204 BC by CATO the Censor, a lifelong friend. He was also a client of M. FULVIUS NOBILIOR, whom he accompanied on a campaign in 189. He became a Roman citizen in 184.

Ennius' literary works included tragedies, comedies, and satires, but his greatest claim to fame was the *Annals*, an epic poem of over 20,000 lines, of which no more than about 600 survive in fragmentary quotations. It covered all of Roman history from the beginnings to his own time, and celebrated the heroic achievements of the Roman people and its leaders, from Romulus to Fabius Maximus and Scipio Africanus. Ennius worked on it until his death in 169 BC. The *Annals* became a national epic, and occupied a central place in Roman education until displaced by VIRGIL's *Aeneid*.

TC

Kenney and Clausen (1982); Skutsch (1985).

Epaminondas (d. 362 BC), Theban statesman and general. With PELOPIDAS, Epaminondas was the architect of Theban hegemony. At the peace conference at Sparta (372/1), after a famous confrontation with AGESILAUS, he insisted on recognition of the restored BOEOTIAN CONFEDERACY and Thebes was excluded from the peace. Twenty days later at LEUCTRA he destroyed Spartan military power and reputation. In 370/69 he went to assist the Arcadians, invaded Laconia, liberated Messene, and patronized the foundation of Megalopolis. Thereafter

Sparta was more of a nuisance than a menace. He planned naval expansion (364). In 362 he went to victory and death at MANTINEA.

GLC

Buckler (1980); Cawkwell (1972a).

Ephebi literally 'youths', but at Athens after 335 BC members of a military academy. After the defeat at CHAERONEA a system of compulsory military service was introduced for male citizens between the ages of 18 and 20. The first year was spent in barracks receiving instruction, the second patrolling the state frontiers. It was the (belated) Athenian response to the Spartan system of EDUCATION. It ceased to be compulsory after 305 and was reduced to one year by 282. By the end of the 2nd century the academy had lost most of its military appurtenances but it survived as an educational establishment until the 3rd century AD.

GS

Marrou (1956).

Ephemerides alleged Royal Journals of ALEXANDER THE GREAT. The *Ephemerides* were used by ARRIAN and PLUTARCH as evidence for the last days of Alexander the Great. Athenaeus attests that EUMENES OF CARDIA compiled Alexander's journals, and others are variously associated with them. Although Alexander must have had official journals, they are probably not the *Ephemerides*, since these only cover Alexander's drinking bouts and final illness. This material is seriously contaminated, and probably forged for purposes of political propaganda.

EER

Bosworth (1988a, b); Pearson (1960).

Ephesus city in Asia Minor. Ephesus was founded by Ionian colonists at a strategic site half-way down the coast of Asia. In the 6th century BC it was occupied by CROESUS who contributed to the building of the temple of ARTEMIS and moved the city further inland. Successively under Lydian, Persian, and Athenian control, the city remained prosperous and, though back under Persian rule in the 4th century, was able to undertake the rebuilding of the temple (after a fire in 356) on a scale that merited its inclusion among the seven wonders of the world. Under LYSIMACHUS *c.*290 the city was moved to another site with a better harbour and rebuilt on a magnificent scale. It was the capital of the Roman province of ASIA. Impressive remains survive.

GS

Bean (1979a).

Ephialtes (d. 461 BC), Athenian statesman and opponent of CIMON. In 462/1 Ephialtes carried the reform of the AREOPAGUS whereby it retained jurisdiction in murder cases but lost its role as guardian of the laws. Little is known about this reform but it was clearly of the greatest importance in the development of democracy. Ephialtes was murdered shortly afterwards.   GLC

Ostwald (1986); Wallace (1989).

Ephor   Spartan official. The five ephors were the principal Spartan magistrates. They were elected from and by the whole citizen body, probably by acclamation, like the members of the GEROUSIA, and served for a year, once only. They presided over the assembly (at least in the 5th century BC) and had wide judicial and executive powers. In particular, they served as a check on the kings, with whom they exchanged monthly oaths, the ephors pledging their support, the kings promising to uphold the constitution. The date of their establishment is uncertain: Herodotus attributes it to LYCURGUS, others to King Theopompus (c.700 BC?), while the ancient list of ephors began in 754 BC. Although not mentioned in the Lycurgan *Rhetra*, ephors are found in Sparta's colony THERA, and their early low profile may be due to relative unimportance: CHILON was traditionally the first noteworthy ephor.   RB

Andrewes (1966); De Ste Croix (1972); Forrest (1980); MacDowell (1986).

Ephorus   (4th century BC), Greek historian. Ephorus of Cyme was a contemporary of THEOPOMPUS and likewise a pupil of ISOCRATES. He wrote a universal history in 30 books going down to the siege of Perinthus (340 BC), the last book, covering the Third SACRED WAR, being the work of his son Demophilus. DIODORUS SICULUS used him for the Greek parts of his books 11–15. Although Ephorus took substantial passages from other authors word for word, he was a true historian, not a mere epitomist like Diodorus. It is highly fortunate that we can balance his account against that of XENOPHON.

See also HISTORIOGRAPHY, GREEK.   GLC

Barber (1935).

Epic poetry, Greek   Epic poetry, that is extended verse narrative celebrating the heroic exploits of mythical or historical characters, often flourishes in illiterate societies. By the time of HOMER (8th century BC), when Greek literature was first written down, it had already existed for a very long time. Apart from Homer, we have only fragments of other early epics (*see* CYCLIC POETS): they filled in the gaps, and would fill in more, had more survived; but they never challenged the supremacy that Homer won and maintained throughout antiquity. For all practical purposes early Greek epic means Homer.

The origins of epic are obscure but probably lay in hymns to the gods that were sung at religious festivals such as the early Delphic contests recalled by Pausanias (10.7). The legendary Orpheus and Musaeus are mentioned as poets in this context as well as Homer and HESIOD. Bards were travelling folk who sang to the accompaniment of a lyre, just as the blind Demodocus sings of the Trojan War in the *Odyssey* (8.72). The form was the hexameter verse. Each performance was a symphony in jazz, a finely crafted medley of stock repertoire and improvisation. People with such gifts were rare and held an honoured place in society.

Oral epic died with the introduction of writing but the genre continued, despite the greater popularity of LYRIC POETRY. Some poets told the same old stories, others used epic as a vehicle for new ideas about religion, others found new subject-matter in more recent history (e.g. Choerilus on the Persian Wars). None was very successful and none has survived. Epic enjoyed revivals in the 3rd century BC at Alexandria, as represented by the *Argonautica* of APOLLONIUS RHODIUS written for a sophisticated readership, and in the 4th–5th centuries AD with the heroic poems of QUINTUS and NONNUS.

See also ANTIMACHUS; OPPIAN; RHIANUS; XENOPHANES.   GS

Kirk (1976); Lord (1960); Murray (1934).

Epic poetry, Latin   Like Latin comedy, Latin epic was a Greek form made Roman; unlike comedy, it endured. LIVIUS ANDRONICUS in the 3rd century BC must be credited with the first translation into Latin of Homer's *Odyssey*. But NAEVIUS was the first Latin writer to produce an original epic poem with his *Bellum Punicum*. ENNIUS too followed Hellenistic practice in presenting historical record as epic poetry; his adoption of the Greek hexameter was fundamental to the development of the Latin genre. The narrative verse form remained in use down to the Augustan age, though only scattered fragments survive.

The *Aeneid* of VIRGIL is the coping stone of the Latin epic achievement. Selective borrowing from his predecessors, Greek as well as Latin, complemented by the poet's own imagination and originality, results in the most satisfying example of epic poetry in any literature. Augustus provided the *casus scribendi*: Virgil rose to it magnificently.

Epic after Virgil continued to flourish. Mythological subjects were generally favoured until LUCAN, writing in the time of Nero, chose a theme from recent history for his *De Bello Civili*. The artificial rhetorical style, which is used so effectively by him, pervades less happily the works of most subsequent writers of the genre. VALERIUS FLACCUS reverts to traditional subject-matter with his version of the Jason voyage, as does STATIUS in his *Thebais* and *Achilleis*. SILIUS ITALICUS, however, is in the tradition of Lucan (whose rhetoric he eschews) with his *Punica*

on the Second Punic War. The last classical poet to attempt mythological epic is CLAUDIAN in the 4th century with his polished *De Raptu
Proserpinae*. Of all the Greek literary genres adapted by the Romans
for their own purposes epic was perhaps the most successful and
exercised the widest influence on later European literatures.   GS

Bowra (1945); Burck (1979); Cairns (1989); Camps (1969); Hutchinson (1993);
Williams (1968).

Epicharmus   (6th–5th century BC), Greek comic poet. Epicharmus was
one of the earliest comic poets. He wrote at Syracuse during the reigns
of Gelon and Hieron I (485–467) and possibly for many years before
then. Aristotle said that his plays contributed to the development of
COMEDY but sadly none survives. Titles (37 are known) and fragments
suggest considerable versatility and a fondness for mythological burlesque.   GS

Pickard-Cambridge (1962).

Epictetus   (*c*.AD 55–135), Stoic philosopher. Epictetus of Hierapolis
in Phrygia was a slave in the household of Epaphroditus, a freedman
of Nero, who allowed him to attend the lectures of the Stoic Musonius
Rufus. Expelled from Rome in AD 90 with other philosophers by
DOMITIAN, he settled in Epirus and taught there. Although he himself
wrote nothing, much of his teaching was recorded by ARRIAN and
preserved in two treatises, the *Discourses of Epictetus* in four books
and the shorter and more popular work, the *Encheiridion*. The philosophy of Epictetus was intensely practical. He believed that the only
way to achieve happiness was through absolute trust in divine
providence and indifference to external circumstances.
   See also STOICS.   JL

Long (1974).

Epictetus of Athens   (fl. 520–500 BC), Greek potter and vase painter.
Epictetus signed a number of vases as both potter and painter. He is
regarded as one of the greatest archaic cup painters, and about 100
vases have been attributed to him. With the ANDOCIDES PAINTER he comes
at the start of red-figure, and some of his early cups are 'bilingual'
(red-figured outside and black-figured inside).   GS

Arias and Hirmer (1962); Boardman (1975).

Epicurus   (341–270 BC), Greek philosopher. The founder of the Epicurean school of philosophy was born in Samos of Athenian parents.
He learned about the atomic theory from Nausiphanes. After teaching

for some time at Mytilene and Lampsacus, he settled in Athens in 307/6 BC where he bought a house with a garden and established there his school of philosophy (consequently known as the 'Garden'). He wrote a large number of treatises, most of which are lost. Apart from a few mutilated papyri, fragmentary quotations, three letters, and two collections of maxims, our knowledge of Epicurus' system largely depends upon the *De Rerum Natura* of LUCRETIUS.

Epicurus' philosophy had a practical purpose: to achieve a life free from anxiety. To attain this ideal of *ataraxia* and to free mankind from its fears of the gods' intervention, of death, and of punishment after death, Epicurus adopted the atomic theory of LEUCIPPUS and DEMOCRITUS. He held that the soul, too, was a complex of atomic particles, which disintegrated upon death and, by explaining the physical world in terms of purely natural causes, he sought to dispel all fear of supernatural intervention. To escape the rigid determinism of Democritean atomism, where everything is subject to the strict law of mechanical necessity, Epicurus held that the atoms move naturally downwards because of their weight, unless they are in collision with other atoms. To account for these collisions he postulated that some atoms spontaneously, at random, and without any external cause deviate slightly from the perpendicular and by this deviation (*parenklisis, clinamen*) he sought to preserve free will and ensure that human actions are not predetermined from birth.

See also ATOMISTS; PHYSICS.

JL

Bailey (1928).

Epidamnus *see* DYRRHACHIUM.

Epidaurus city in the Argolid, site of the principal sanctuary of ASCLEPIUS. The cult seems not to have been established before the 4th century BC when Epidaurus became identified with the god's birthplace and he superseded his father APOLLO as resident deity. The site is extensive but most of the buildings, including the great temple of Asclepius, are ruinous, having been sacked by SULLA in 86 BC. Most noteworthy are the Abaton or Enkoimeterion where pilgrims slept hopeful of a cure (*see* INCUBATION), the tholos or rotunda, a small circular building with an outer peristyle of 26 Doric columns, and the THEATRE, the best preserved in Greece. All date from the 4th century.

GS

Stillwell (1976); Tomlinson (1983).

Epigrams, Greek The word 'epigram' was originally used of any verse inscription such as might be found on a tombstone or piece of pottery. In the classical period it acquired a literary form, usually as an elegiac couplet or two. Still largely funerary, epigrams were written by poets from SIMONIDES to ARISTOTLE. In the Alexandrian period the epigram moved finally from an epigraphic context to a purely literary one and became a major vehicle for poetic expression. CALLIMACHUS was a master of the genre. Some 6,000 epigrams on a wide range of subjects are preserved in the Greek ANTHOLOGY.

See also ASCLEPIADES; LEONIDAS OF TARENTUM; MELEAGER; PHILETAS. GS

Cameron (1993); Lausberg (1982); Webster (1964).

Epigrams, Latin The earliest Latin epigrams were funerary inscriptions. As a literary genre, they first took the form of epitaphs on poets such as Ennius, Pacuvius, Naevius, and Plautus. The erotic epigram, based on Greek models, first appeared in the 2nd century BC according to Gellius, but it was CATULLUS in the 1st century who really perfected and popularized this form. Most writers thereafter tried their hand at composing epigrams, though few have survived. The most successful and prolific exponent of the genre was MARTIAL, whose epigrams, preserved in 12 books, enjoyed a wide readership and provide good evidence for social history. GS

Epigraphy, Greek Epigraphy is the study of inscriptions, writings on stone, pottery, and metal (excluding coins); their study requires particular techniques, and they are an essential historical source.

Methods: Relatively few inscriptions survive intact, as most stones have been damaged over time or reused for building. Fragments of inscriptions may be recognized through similarities in stone, lettering, or content, and can be pieced together by direct fit, features in the stone such as cracks or colouring, or through textual considerations (*see below*). The surviving letters, which are often badly worn, are read directly, or from photographs or impressions in paper or latex ('squeezes'), which can reveal features not immediately apparent on inspection. It may then be possible to supplement a fragmentary text, especially if the length of the line is known, and hence the approximate number of missing letters; this is easiest in those inscriptions, mainly Attic, that use the grid system known as *stoichedon*. Line length can also be inferred from the use of formulaic expressions.

Inscriptions which do not contain a dating formula and cannot be dated from internal references to known events or individuals can often be approximately dated through features of expression or (more usually) through the style of lettering and the forms of individual letters, since many archaic Greek states had local forms of the ALPHABET which gradually altered, and even the later standard alphabet continued to develop in the Hellenistic and Roman periods.

Content: Inscriptions may be divided into public and private documents. Among public decrees, the most basic are concerned with laws, either law codes like that of GORTYN, or the homicide law of DRACO at Athens, reinscribed in the late 5th century BC, or individual enactments for the future. Foreign policy is a fertile area: the development of the Athenian empire must be mainly reconstructed from the evidence of documents such as treaties, decrees of the assembly, and the 'Athenian Tribute Lists', the detailed annual records of the fraction of contributions dedicated to Athena. Financial records (catalogues, inventories, and accounts) are especially valuable because they concern matters often poorly covered by literary narratives and illuminate the internal workings of a state as well as its policies. Public documents often obliquely illuminate legal and constitutional machinery. The fragments of pottery used in OSTRACISM likewise throw light on politics and politicians in 5th-century Athens, and epigraphy is essential for prosopography, the study of individual public figures and their interactions. The habit in cities of the Hellenistic period of preserving relevant decrees in ARCHIVES helps to reconstruct their history and that of the Hellenistic kingdoms, and inscriptions are equally illuminating for the activities of the Roman Republic and Empire in the Greek-speaking world.

Private documents, which include contracts and other legal documents, manumissions, gravestones, dedications, wills, graffiti, and curse tablets, provide evidence on aspects of economic, social, and private life, including trade and commerce, craft, wealth and status, slavery, literacy, and religious organization and belief; they are also often valuable for prosopography as illustrations of careers and family relationships.   RB

Jeffery (1990); Meiggs and Lewis (1988); Tod (1948); Woodhead (1981).

Epigraphy, Latin   The Romans were no less addicted than the Greeks to the habit of inscribing texts on durable surfaces for the purpose of permanent record. Roman inscriptions survive from all periods of Roman history and all parts of the Roman world (a recent estimate puts the total at over 300,000, itself perhaps only a 5 per cent sample of what once existed).

Latin inscriptions are found mostly in the western (Latin-speaking) half of the empire. In the Greek east the majority of inscriptions were naturally in Greek, and this continued to be so throughout the history of the empire and into the Byzantine period (*see* EPIGRAPHY, GREEK).

The history of Latin epigraphy begins early, indeed before Rome itself. A text on a fragment of pottery recently unearthed at Gabii in Latium dates from c.800 BC, and is the earliest known alphabetic text in any language. However, only a tiny handful of Latin inscriptions survives from before 600 BC, and not more than about 70 from before 400. The figures then increase substantially, especially for the last century of the Republic; but the overwhelming majority of Latin inscriptions (probably over 95 per cent) date from the imperial period, most of them from the 2nd and early 3rd centuries AD.

Although some important historical inscriptions date from the Republic (for example the senatorial decree regulating the BACCHANALIA (186 BC), and the law of Gaius GRACCHUS on RES REPETUNDAE (122), both on bronze tablets), it is in imperial history that the evidence of inscriptions has made the most decisive contribution. Apart from major historical texts, among which the *Res Gestae* of AUGUSTUS holds pride of place, the importance of inscriptions is that they illuminate aspects of Roman life not dealt with in literary sources: they cover a wider social spectrum, and document the life of the provinces as well as Rome and Italy.

The majority of inscriptions were put up to honour or commemorate individuals (less frequently groups, although units of the Roman army are an exception) and vary in type from the simplest gravestones to the most elaborate monumental texts. Although formal and sometimes pompous, they nevertheless give a sense of vitality and immediacy as tangible records of the lives of real people. A major concern is to register personal achievement in a wide variety of fields. Inscriptions record the careers of senators, equestrian administrators, soldiers of all ranks, local councillors, priests, craftsmen, traders, or simply slaves who had been freed and become successful in later life. Such texts, when analysed in bulk, provide invaluable evidence for social history, for the reconstruction of administrative hierarchies, the organization of the army, and the existence and nature of all manner of public and private associations.

While inscriptions are undoubtedly free from the aristocratic bias of the literary sources, they nevertheless do not represent all of society. Carving inscriptions was a professional craft, and to put one up, however modest, cost a certain amount of money. It follows that only the better-off are represented in the evidence. Large classes of people, including the mass of the rural peasantry, the urban proletariat, and slaves (other than those who were freed and made good) are almost entirely absent. TC

Gordon (1983); Humphrey (1991); Keppie (1991); Millar (1983); Susini (1973).

Epirus territory in north-western Greece. Epirus comprised much of modern Albania and the area of western Greece north of the Ambracian Gulf. It was separated from the rest of Greece by the Pindus mountain range. Epirus was inhabited by tribes, the most prominent being the Molossi who formed a Molossian state under King Neoptolemus (*c.*370–368 BC). ALEXANDER I OF EPIRUS (brother-in-law of PHILIP II of Macedon) unified Epirus under the Molossian kingship. King PYRRHUS (319–272), who reigned after suppressing serious dynastic trouble, built a capital at Ambracia and enlarged and beautified the ancient sanctuary of the Oracle of Zeus at DODONA. The Molossian monarchy fell in 232 and an Epirote Confederacy was created. Epirus became embroiled in the MACEDONIAN WARS between Macedonia and Rome. The Molossian state alone supported PERSEUS and was savagely sacked by Rome in 167. In honour of his victory at ACTIUM in Epirus in 31 BC, Octavian founded the Roman colony of NICOPOLIS there.   EER

Hammond (1967); Hammond and Griffith (1979); Hammond and Walbank (1988).

Epistolography, Greek   Several categories of letters surviving from antiquity may be distinguished. A large number of private letters are preserved in papyri, providing important evidence of the state of the Greek language and of the prevailing economic and social conditions in Egypt. Some official correspondence between governments survives, notably that of the Hellenistic kings. Letters were used as a vehicle for the expression of new ideas in religion, philosophy, and science, e.g. those of ARCHIMEDES, EPICURUS, ERATOSTHENES, and PAUL. In the 2nd century AD an epistolary genre of historical fiction, intended to entertain readers, was developed by Alciphron, AELIAN, and Philostratus. Later, in the 4th century, a group of literary epistolographers emerged who wrote letters designed for publication: BASIL THE GREAT, GREGORY OF NAZIANZUS, John CHRYSOSTOM, JULIAN, LIBANIUS, and SYNESIUS. Finally there are groups of letters attributed to various public figures such as DEMOSTHENES, ISOCRATES, and PLATO. While a few of these have some claim to authenticity and contain material of considerable interest, the majority are best regarded as spurious. By the 1st century BC there existed a large corpus of letters attributed to Alexander the Great which, like those of PHALARIS, contribute more to fantasy than to history.   GS

Exler (1923).

Epistolography, Latin   The art of writing personal letters, for which the need grew with the expansion of the empire, was one of Rome's principal literary accomplishments. By far the most important witness to the genre is provided by the correspondence of CICERO which includes nearly 800 letters written by him between the years 68 and 43 BC and more than 100 written to him by others. He wrote either in his own hand, with pen and ink on papyrus, or by dictation to his secretary TIRO who generally kept a copy. These copies, together with those to ATTICUS and his brother Quintus CICERO, form the nucleus of the surviving corpus. They provide a unique insight into the personality of the writer and the background to the politics of the day.

The verse epistles of HORACE and OVID are more important as poems than letters; and the younger SENECA's *Epistolae Morales* belong in the tradition of Epicurus' philosophical letters. Vital information about the social and political history of Rome under Trajan is preserved by the correspondence of the younger PLINY (10 books). The letters of FRONTO to Marcus Aurelius are inconsequential but of some literary interest. Prominent letter writers of the later Empire include AMBROSE, AUGUSTINE, AUSONIUS, JEROME, PAULINUS, SIDONIUS APOLLINARIS, and SYMMACHUS.   GS

See also POSTAL SERVICE.

Shackleton Bailey (1965–70).

Eprius Marcellus   (d. AD 79), Roman orator. Titus Clodius Eprius Marcellus, one of the foremost orators of his age, successfully defended himself against a Lycian claim for damages (AD 57), and was involved in a number of other trials during the reign of Nero. He was appointed governor of Asia by VESPASIAN, but, in an episode recorded by DIO CASSIUS, he was implicated in a plot with CAECINA ALIENUS against Vespasian (79), and forced to commit suicide.   RJB

Grant (1971c); Scullard (1982).

Epulones   Roman college of priests. The most junior of the four main colleges of Roman PRIESTS, the Epulones were created in 196 BC by the tribune Licinius Lucullus. Initially three in number, they were increased to seven, and later, under Caesar, to 10. Their duties were to organize public banquets that occurred as part of festivals, especially that of Jupiter.   HE

Scullard (1981).

Equestrian order   Roman class. The equestrians were an élite group below the SENATE. In the constitution attributed to SERVIUS TULLIUS the first 18 centuries in the COMITIA *centuriata* were reserved for equestrians: Roman cavalry who were supplied with a horse by the state. By *c.*400 BC these were augmented by those who supplied their own horse. The latter, while not enrolled by the CENSORS in the equestrian centuries, possessed some of the status marks of equestrians. In the 3rd century BC the equestrians lost their military function but retained their social eminence.

Probably in 129 BC senators, but not their sons, were debarred from the equestrian centuries. By now equestrian status, in its wider sense, was available to citizens of free birth with a property qualification of 400,000 sesterces. While the majority of equestrians were land-owners, and thus had a general community of interest with the Senate, some engaged in public contracting (PUBLICANI), from which senators were excluded. The possibility of tension existed between the Senate and the *publicani* as they exploited the provinces in different ways. This tension was played out in the struggle for control of the courts (QUAESTIO) from the tribunate of Gaius GRACCHUS to 70 BC, when the juries were divided between senators, equestrians, and men from the TRIBUNUS AERARIUS class.

AUGUSTUS revived the rituals around the public horse and established four panels of equestrian jurors, to which GAIUS added a fifth. Qualifications for equestrian status in its wider sense remained free-born citizenship and property of 400,000 sesterces. The proliferation of equestrian posts (PRAEFECTUS; PROCURATOR) led to the establishment of an equestrian career structure comparable to the senatorial CURSUS HONORUM. In the late 3rd century AD equestrians replaced senators in almost all posts, and by the end of the 4th century the equestrian order had ceased to be a distinct class in Roman society.   HS

Badian (1972a); Brunt (1988); Jones (1964); Millar (1977, 1981).

Erasistratus (fl. *c*.260 BC), Greek physician. After studying MEDICINE first at Athens then at Cos, Erasistratus emigrated to Alexandria (see ANATOMY) where he advanced the anatomical researches of HEROPHILUS, notably into the brain, heart, and nervous and vascular systems. In physiology he combined pneumatic theory with STRATON's physics to explain such processes as respiration and digestion. His careful dissections, together with those of Herophilus, provided a basis and stimulus for the anatomical and physiological investigations of GALEN more than four centuries later.   JL

DSB IV (1971); Longrigg (1993).

Eratosthenes (*c*.275–*c*.195 BC), Alexandrian scholar. Eratosthenes was born in Cyrene and educated there and in Athens before being summoned to Alexandria by Ptolemy III. There he became chief librarian in succession to APOLLONIUS RHODIUS and tutor to the royal family. His scholarly output was prodigious and wide-ranging. Literary studies included a voluminous work *On Old Comedy* and a grammar. But his books on chronology and GEOGRAPHY display a truly scientific bent: he established a complete system of dating based on the Olympic lists and he calculated the circumference of the earth with unprecedented mathematical precision.

See also MAPS.   GS

Fraser (1972); Pfeiffer (1968); Webster (1964).

Erechtheum an Ionic temple standing on sloping ground to the north of the PARTHENON on the acropolis at Athens. It served a variety of cult functions. Built of marble between 421 and 405 BC, it is unusual in having porches projecting asymmetrically from two sides. The central block is a plain rectangle divided into four compartments with a portico at the east end and a wall with engaged columns at the west. The north porch, which stands on lower ground, comprises a lofty Ionic colonnade. The south porch, known as the porch of the Caryatids, is much smaller and has a flat roof supported by draped female figures in place of columns. A frieze decorated with sculptures ran right round the building.   GS

Hopper (1971); Lawrence (1984).

Eretria city in Euboea. Eretria was a leading power in archaic EUBOEA, extensively involved in trade and colonization. Rivalry with CHALCIS eventually precipitated the LELANTINE WAR which cannot have harmed Eretria seriously since she remained prosperous; but her support for Miletus in the IONIAN REVOLT brought Persian retaliation, and in 490 the city was sacked and depopulated. Eretria was re-established, but was dominated by Athens, Macedon, and Rome in turn.   RB

Boardman (1980); Jeffery (1976).

Eretria Painter (fl. *c*.430–420 BC), Greek vase painter. The Eretria Painter is named after a decorated distaff (*epinetron*), found near Eretria but now in Athens, which depicts Alcestis and her friends. His delicate miniaturist style was well suited to small shapes. Some 150 vases are attributed to him.

   See also PAINTING, GREEK.   GS

Arias and Hirmer (1962); Lezzi-Hafter (1988).

'Ergamenes' (3rd century BC), king of Meroë in Sudan. 'Ergamenes' is the hellenized name of a native king who Diodorus says was contemporary with PTOLEMY II, had Greek education, studied philosophy, and curtailed the power of the Meroitic priesthood. 'Ergamenes' has been identified with various 3rd-century kings, some of whom had definite contacts with the Ptolemies, but it is not known if Diodorus' 'Ergamenes' really existed, or if he is a conflation of various Meroitic kings known to the Greeks.   EER

Adams (1977); Emery (1965); Shinnie (1967).

Erinna (late 4th century BC), Greek lyric poet. Erinna lived on Telos near Rhodes and wrote in a local Doric dialect. Her poem *The Distaff*

(of which 50 lines survive in a papyrus) is a lament of sweet sorrow for her friend Baucis. Three epigrams (two for Baucis) are preserved in the Greek ANTHOLOGY. She died aged 19. GS

Eros Greek god. Eros, god of sexual passion, enjoyed a variety of genealogies in early myth, not all of them divine, but he was most commonly thought to be the son of Hermes and Aphrodite. In art he is boyish and pretty, the object of both male and female desire, but in literature he is bitter-sweet and tricksome. Superficially innocent, he had the power to inflame hearts with his torch or wound them with his arrows. His cult was universal; as a god of fertility he was also worshipped in Thespiae and Athens. The Romans identified him with Cupid. GS

Grimal (1986); Guthrie (1950).

Eryx mountain and city in western SICILY. Founded by Elymians from SEGESTA, Eryx remained under Carthaginian control until 241 BC when most of Sicily fell to the Romans. The modern town of San Giuliano stands on the site of the sanctuary of Astarte (later Aphrodite). RB

Esquiline part of Rome. The Esquiline was one of the hills of Rome, lying south of the QUIRINAL, north of the CAELIUS MONS and the COLOSSEUM, and overlooking the Subura and the FORUM ROMANUM to the west. Two of its spurs, Cispius and Oppius (later forming the Augustan *regio* iii), were cut by the Subura and were later the site of Nero's DOMUS AUREA and the baths of TRAJAN. Beyond the Servian Wall lay the Esquiline plateau (Augustus' *regio* v) containing several large gardens. This was the city's main burial ground during the Republic. HE

Platner and Ashby (1929); Richardson (1992); Robinson (1992).

Ethiopia According to HOMER, the land of the Ethiopians was divided in two, one part being in the east and the other in the west, though both were at the world's end. This no doubt accounts for the fact that Ethiopians and Indians were commonly confused. But from the time of HERODOTUS Ethiopia was identified with the lands south of EGYPT. The area had been known to the Greeks since the 7th century BC and CAMBYSES II planned an expedition to capture it. The Ptolemies explored the coast as far as the Horn of Africa and opened up trade routes to connect the Red Sea port of Adulis with Aksum and Meroë.
See also ELEPHANTS. GS

Snowden (1970).

Etruscans   people of ancient Italy. The Etruscans inhabited an area of western central Italy bounded by the Tiber and the Arno. The problem of who they were and where they came from is tied up with the puzzle of their language, which is not Indo-European and has no structural or morphological similarity to any other known language. Its presence in a region of Italy that was neither backward nor remote is extremely mysterious. The most likely explanation is that it was brought from elsewhere, a theory that derives some support from an ancient legend that the Etruscans had migrated to Italy from the Near East. But any such migration, if historical, must have occurred in prehistoric times (certainly before 1000 BC), since archaeologists are convinced that Etruscan civilization was formed in Italy and developed from the preceding Iron Age VILLANOVAN CULTURE.

Etruscan civilization reached its cultural zenith in the archaic period (8th to 5th centuries BC), when powerful city-states emerged. These are conventionally divided into a southern group, including VEII, CAERE, TARQUINII, and Vulci; a northern group, comprising Volaterrae, Populonia, Vetulonia, and Rusellae; and an inland group, including Arretium, Cortona, Perusia, Clusium, and Volsinii. Our knowledge of these centres is based on archaeological evidence, particularly finds from their rich cemeteries, information in Greek and Roman historians, and Etruscan inscriptions, of which around 13,000 (mostly brief epitaphs) are now recorded. Although the language is not properly understood, the texts are written in the Greek alphabet, and the basic meaning of most of them can now be made out.

In the 6th century the Etruscans colonized other parts of Italy, and Etruscan settlements were established in the Po valley and in Campania. But the Etruscans never attempted to unify Italy; their city-states were fiercely independent, and there was intense rivalry, and sometimes armed conflict, between them. The political organization and social structure of the cities are not well understood, but there is evidence that in at least some of them, as at Rome, monarchical regimes were replaced by republics in the 6th and 5th centuries, and that wealth and power were concentrated in the hands of powerful aristocratic clans comparable to the Roman PATRICIANS. In many ways early Rome was very like its Etruscan neighbours, and had close (though not always friendly) links with them; but the theory that Rome was subjected to Etruscan rule in the 6th century is not supported by historical evidence.

In the 5th and 4th centuries Etruria was hit by economic recession and social crisis, and gradually fell victim to the growing power of Rome. The defeat and capture of Veii in 396 was the first stage in the Roman conquest of Etruria, which was finally completed when Volsinii was destroyed in 264. Even so, the remaining Etruscan cities preserved much of their ancient culture and unique social organization well into the Roman period; their language continued to be spoken at least until the 1st century BC, when it finally gave way to the universal spread of LATIN.   TC

Bonfante (1986, 1990); Bonfante and Bonfante (1983); CAH IV; Grant (1980); Pallottino (1975); Scullard (1967).

Euboea   island in the western Aegean. Of the seven city-states that originally divided Euboea between them, CHALCIS and ERETRIA emerged as the most powerful. Both cities played a prominent part in the COLONIZATION of Magna Graecia, the Aegean, and the eastern Mediterranean. In the 8th century BC they fought the LELANTINE WAR for control of Euboea's most fertile plain. For most of the 5th century the island was subject to Athens, but after LEUCTRA it passed to THEBES. Restored to Athens in 358, it was absorbed by Macedonia after CHAERONEA and fell to the Romans in 194. Its later history was undistinguished but the MARBLE of Carystus remained in demand at Rome.   GS

Boardman (1980).

Eubulides   (fl. *c*.140–120 BC), Greek sculptor. Eubulides of Athens came from a family of sculptors. His grandfather is credited with the seated statue of the philosopher Chrysippus of which a Roman copy survives. Eubulides the Younger worked with his father Eucheir on a large group of Apollo, Athena, Zeus, Mnemosyne, and the Muses, parts of which have come to light near the Ceramicus in Athens. Their neoclassical solemnity harks back to 5th-century styles.

   See also SCULPTURE, GREEK.   GS

Smith (1991); Webster (1964).

Eubulus   (*c*.405–335 BC), Athenian statesman. By 355 BC Athens was nearly bankrupt. Eubulus carried a law whereby surplus monies were concentrated in the Theoric Fund (*see* FINANCE, GREEK; THEORIKA) which he as Theoric Commissioner controlled and which could not be used for military purposes. By this means and with measures of the sort described in XENOPHON's *Revenues*, he restored prosperity. His policy, which DEMOSTHENES opposed, was to avoid unnecessary military involvement and concentrate on keeping PHILIP II out of Greece.   GLC

Cawkwell (1963).

Eubulus   (4th century BC), Greek comic poet. Eubulus wrote over 100 plays in the transitional genre known as Middle COMEDY. Titles of 58 are known and suggest a fondness for mythological burlesque and parody of the tragedians (especially Euripides). One fragment (74) describes the venal character of the Agora at Athens where everything from figs to lawsuits, porridge to witnesses, is for sale. Adaptations survive in the fragments of NAEVIUS.   GS

Hunter (1983a).

Euclid (fl. *c.295* BC), Greek mathematician. Euclid taught MATHEMATICS at Alexandria during the reign of PTOLEMY I. His main claim to fame rests upon his textbook, the *Elements* (*Stoicheia*) in 13 books (Books 14 and 15 are not by Euclid), which built upon and superseded the works of his predecessors. The work remained authoritative until the end of the 19th century. Books 1–6 of the *Elements* deal with plane geometry, 7–9 with the theory of numbers, 10 with irrationals, and 11–13 with stereometry. Other works of Euclid on geometry with the exception of the *Data* are now lost and known to us only from PAPPUS. However, several other works have survived, notably the *Phaenomena*, an astronomical textbook, and the *Optics*, an elementary treatise on perspective. The *Catoptrica*, however, a book on mirrors, is not by Euclid but is a later compilation.   JL

DSB IV (1971); Heath (1921).

Eudemus (4th century BC), Greek philosopher. Eudemus of Rhodes was a pupil of ARISTOTLE and, as part of the systematization carried out within the Lyceum, he composed histories of mathematics, astronomy, and theology. He also, following Aristotle's precedent, wrote a work on physics of which numerous fragments are preserved by Simplicius.

JL

DSB IV (1971).

Eudocia (d. AD 460), eastern Roman empress (Augusta, AD 423–50). Athenais, daughter of Leontius, a pagan Greek philosopher, married THEODOSIUS II (421), becoming a Christian and taking the name Aelia Eudocia. Their daughter, Licinia Eudoxia (b. 422), married VALENTINIAN III (437), after which Eudocia undertook a pilgrimage to Jerusalem, returning in 439. The eunuch Chrysaphius succeeded in convincing Theodosius that Eudocia had been unfaithful (*c.443*): she withdrew to Jerusalem, becoming involved in opposition to the religious orthodoxy established by the Council of Chalcedon.   RJB

Bury (1958); Grant (1985); Holum (1983).

Eudoxus of Cnidus (*c.400–347* BC), Greek mathematician, astronomer, and geographer. Eudoxus studied geometry with Archytas of

Tarentum. He also studied medicine under PHILISTION and philosophy under PLATO. After some time in Egypt studying ASTRONOMY with the priests at Heliopolis, where he published his calendaric treatise the *Eight-year Cycle*, he lectured in Cyzicus and the Propontis before returning to teach at Athens. In geometry he invented the general theory of proportion applicable to incommensurable as well as commensurable magnitudes (see Euclid Book 5). He also developed the so-called method of exhaustion, and was able to prove that the cone and pyramid are one-third respectively of the cylinder and prism with the same base and height. In astronomy he constructed an ingenious and influential geometric system based upon homocentric spheres to account for the apparent movements of the heavenly bodies. (CALLIPPUS later introduced some improvements and ARISTOTLE seems to have conceived of it as a purely mechanical system.) His description of the constellations and their risings and settings (the *Enoptron* or *Phaenomena*) was also highly influential. The *Gēs periodos* (*Description of the Earth*) in several books was a work of mathematical and descriptive geography.

JL

DSB IV (1971); Heath (1921).

Eudoxus of Cyzicus (2nd century BC), Greek explorer. Having travelled to Alexandria, Eudoxus was sent by PTOLEMY VIII Euergetes with an Indian sailor to discover the route to INDIA. He returned with a cargo of perfumes (which was confiscated) and was sent out again. This time he was blown off course down the East African coast where he saw wreckage of a ship from Spain. This convinced him that Africa could be circumnavigated, but two attempts ended in failure.

See also NAVIGATION.

GS

Thiel (1966).

Eugenius *see* THEODOSIUS I.

Euhemerus (fl. *c.*300 BC), Greek novelist. Euhemerus of Messene was the author of a philosophical novel, the *Sacred Scripture* (*Hiera Anagraphe*), which was influential in the Hellenistic world. In it he expressed the belief that the gods of mythology were originally great kings in their day, deified by their grateful subjects. He pretended to have found documentary evidence of this on an imaginary island, Panchaea, in the Indian Ocean. It is uncertain whether Euhemerus' aim was to rationalize atheistic beliefs, to support the traditional mythological beliefs expressed in Greek poetry, which did not clearly differentiate between gods and great men, or to provide justification

for Hellenistic ruler cults. A fragmentary version is preserved by
DIODORUS SICULUS.   JL

Fraser (1972).

Eumenes I king of Pergamum, 263–241 BC. Eumenes succeeded his
adoptive father PHILETAERUS as ruler of Pergamum in 263 BC. He declared independence from the Seleucid ANTIOCHUS I SOTER (although he
never took the title 'king'), and defeated him in 262, probably with
PTOLEMY II's assistance. Pergamene territory was thereby greatly extended, though partially recovered later by ANTIOCHUS II THEOS. Eumenes
bribed the Galatians not to plunder Pergamum, and began the great
building programme there. He was a patron of the philosopher
ARCESILAUS.   EER

Allen (1983); CAH VII.1; Green (1990); Hansen (1971); McShane (1964).

Eumenes II Soter king of Pergamum, 197–159 BC. Eumenes 'the
saviour' succeeded ATTALUS I SOTER in 197 BC and continued a pro-Roman
policy. He helped FLAMININUS in 195 against NABIS of Sparta, and in 192
against the invasion of Greece by ANTIOCHUS III THE GREAT, who unsuccessfully besieged Pergamum in 190. His distinguished participation
at MAGNESIA led Rome to grant Pergamum vast territories and later
support Eumenes against the envious Bithynian PRUSIAS I and PHARNACES
I of Pontus. Eumenes' complaint to Rome against PERSEUS hastened the
Third MACEDONIAN WAR, although Rome (probably wrongly) subsequently suspected Eumenes' loyalty. He decisively defeated the Galatian
threat to Pergamum, and beautified Pergamum through extensive
building (including the famous Great Altar).
    See also APOLLONIS OF CYZICUS; ARIARATHES IV; ATTALUS II PHILADELPHUS.
                                                                    EER

Allen (1983); CAH VIII; Green (1990); Gruen (1984); Hansen (1971); McShane
(1964); Sherwin-White (1984).

Eumenes of Cardia (*c*.362–316 BC), chief secretary to PHILIP II of
Macedon and ALEXANDER THE GREAT. Eumenes was the most senior Greek
at the Macedonian court, and held military as well as administrative
duties. Alexander the Great put him in charge of the Euphrates fleet,
and, after 324 BC, the cavalry. After Alexander's death he was appointed satrap of CAPPADOCIA. He supported Alexander's legitimate heirs
against the quarrelling generals, fighting alongside the kings' guardian
PERDICCAS until his death in 321. Eumenes next supported the new
regent POLYPERCHON against the generals, but was pursued and finally
defeated by ANTIGONUS I MONOPHTHALMUS at Gabiene in 316. His army

surrendered him and he was executed. The historian HIERONYMUS OF CARDIA served on his staff.   EER

Bosworth (1988a, b); CAH VII.1; Green (1990); Westlake (1969).

Eunapius (*c*.AD 345–*c*.420), Greek historian. Eunapius, a pagan SOPHIST and NEOPLATONIST, was born in Sardes, studied under Chrysanthius, and then under Prohaeresius in Athens, before returning to Sardes, where he taught RHETORIC. He composed a history, anti-Christian in outlook, designed to continue that of Dexippus, from 270 to 404. This history is now largely lost, but was an important source for ZOSIMUS and probably for AMMIANUS MARCELLINUS. A further work, *Lives of the Sophists*, survives.   RJB

Blockley (1983); Bury (1958); Wright (1922).

Eupatridae Athenian nobility. The Eupatridae ('well-born') were the original aristocracy of Attica, allegedly created and assigned their privileges by Theseus, but in practice, simply the leading families. In early Athens they monopolized the holding of office, particularly the archonships (and hence the Council of the AREOPAGUS); they probably controlled access to citizenship through the PHRATRIES, and dominated economic and religious life; but their position was undermined by SOLON, who created new classes based on wealth, not birth, as the basis of office-holding. Thereafter, despite resistance to the reforms, their position slowly declined, though they retained prestige, particularly through the priesthoods of old-established cults.   RB

Davies (1971); Rhodes (1981); Wade-Gery (1958).

Euphorion (3rd century BC), Greek lyric poet. Born at Chalcis on Euboea, Euphorion studied at Athens before being appointed chief librarian at Antioch where he remained. He wrote learned poetry (of which fragments survive) in difficult language on obscure mythological themes, plagiarizing his predecessors CALLIMACHUS and APOLLONIUS RHODIUS. But it has a charm that was admired by CATULLUS and the young VIRGIL.   GS

Van Groningen (1977); Webster (1964).

Euphranor (fl. *c*.370–330 BC), Greek painter and sculptor. Euphranor, of uncertain origin, worked mostly in Athens where he was highly regarded as both painter and sculptor. His paintings are lost but included a cavalry scene before the battle of MANTINEA (364 BC), Theseus with Democracy and Demos, and the Twelve Gods, all for the stoa of Zeus in the Athenian Agora. His only surviving sculpture is the headless

Apollo Patroös from the Agora. He also wrote treatises on colour and proportion.   GS

Palagia (1980).

Euphrates the longer and more westerly of the rivers of Mesopotamia. Though bridged at Zeugma and BABYLON, the Euphrates formed the frontier between the empires of Rome and PARTHIA. It also divided CAPPADOCIA from ARMENIA and SYRIA from MESOPOTAMIA. After the loss in AD 66 of Armenia, which had been a Roman protectorate since the time of POMPEY, the Romans built a line of forts along the upper course of the river.   GS

Euphron tyrant of Sicyon, 368–366/5 BC. Brought to power by a popular coup, Euphron went to Thebes to justify himself and was murdered by disgruntled compatriots. Having striven to keep Sicyon free from both Sparta and Thebes, he was honoured posthumously as 'founder' by the people.   GLC

Buckler (1980).

Euphronius (fl. c.515–480 BC), Greek potter and vase painter. Euphronius of Athens signed six surviving vases as painter and 10 as potter. The latter, all later than the former, were painted by other artists. With his contemporary and rival Euthymides he extended the conventions of red-figure vase-painting into dynamic representation of dancers and athletes in action.   GS

Arias and Hirmer (1962); Wegner (1979).

Eupolis (446–412 BC), Greek comic poet. One of the most respected and successful exponents of Old COMEDY (he won seven first prizes), Eupolis was the contemporary and rival of ARISTOPHANES. Numerous fragments survive from 19 of his plays, demonstrating that his subject-matter was similar to that of his rival; but unlike Aristophanes, whose plays generally supported the peace party, Eupolis argued for war. He died at sea.   GS

Euric (d. AD 484), king of the Visigoths, AD 466–84. Euric, probably the ablest Visigothic king, gained the throne by murdering his brother Theodoric II. Nominally a subordinate of the Roman emperor, but in fact an independent monarch, he brought most of Spain and Gaul under his control, becoming the most powerful Germanic king. NEPOS surrendered Auvergne and recognized Euric's possession of Gaul west of the Rhône and south of the Loire (475), and a later treaty added southern Provence.   RJB

Bury (1958); James (1980).

Euripides (*c*.485–406 BC), Greek tragedian. Euripides was the youngest of the three great Athenian tragedians. Unlike SOPHOCLES, he seems to have played no part in public life and, if we are to believe ARISTOPHANES, he was an intellectual recluse. He competed 22 times at the DIONYSIA, starting in 455, but won only four first prizes. In about 408 he moved to the court of Archelaus in Macedonia where he died.

Titles of some 80 plays are known, of which 19 survive intact. Of these, one (*Rhesus*) is probably spurious and another (*Cyclops*) is not a TRAGEDY but a SATYR PLAY. Ten of the 19 represent a selection which evolved in late antiquity for use in schools: *Alcestis, Andromeda, Bacchae, Hecuba, Hippolytus, Medea, Orestes, Phoenissae, Rhesus, Troades*. The remaining nine (*Cyclops, Electra, Helen, Heracleidae, Heracles, Ion, Iphigeneia in Aulis, Iphigeneia in Tauris, Supplices*) survive by chance from an unselected alphabetical Alexandrian edition. The extant plays range in date from 438 (*Alcestis*) to 405 (*Bacchae* and *Iphigeneia in Aulis*, both posthumous). After his death Euripides was the most revered of the tragedians and his plays were regularly revived. Labelled 'the most tragic of poets' by Aristotle, he was much ridiculed by Aristophanes and EUPOLIS.   GS

Conacher (1968); Whitman (1974); Zuntz (1955).

Eurymedon   river in southern Asia Minor. Near its mouth in 469 BC CIMON heavily defeated in one day a large west-bound Persian force on land and sea, destroying 200 ships.   GLC

Eusebius (*c*.AD 260–340), Greek church historian. Born and educated in Palestine, Eusebius escaped the persecution of Diocletian and became bishop of Caesarea *c*.314. Initially a supporter of Arius, he later joined the majority in condemning ARIANISM and signed the Nicene Creed. Befriended by CONSTANTINE I, he wrote a panegyric, the *Life of Constantine*, after the emperor's death in 337. His *Chronicle* is lost, but a Latin version of it by St JEROME survives. His most important work is the *Ecclesiastical History*, the principal source for knowledge of the early Church from its beginnings to the writer's own time (324) and the model for subsequent histories. It was translated into Latin (and extended to 395) by Rufinus of Aquileia and into Syriac in the 5th century.

See also OLYMPIC GAMES.   GS

Barnes (1982); R. M. Grant (1980).

Euthydemus (*c*.250–*c*.200/190 BC), king of Bactria-Sogdiana. Euthydemus took the throne of BACTRIA from Diodotus II, in mysterious circumstances and at an unknown date. He consolidated his kingdom into a strong state which also included Aria and Margiana. ANTIOCHUS III THE GREAT besieged him during his eastern expedition in 208 BC, could not subdue him, and reached a compromise two years later in which Euthydemus was recognized as legitimate king. He issued distinctive gold and silver coinage, and was succeeded by his son DEMETRIUS I OF BACTRIA. EER

CAH VIII; Frye (1984); Narain (1957); Tarn (1984); Woodcock (1966).

Eutropius (d. after AD 364), Roman historian. Eutropius served in JULIAN's Persian campaign (363) and was appointed *magister memoriae* under Valens. He produced a brief and generally impartial Survey (*Breviarium*) of Roman history up to the death of Jovian (364). Books 1–6 cover the Republic, books 7–10 the Empire, using LIVY, SUETONIUS, and other sources now lost. The latter portions are written from personal knowledge bearing interesting comparison with Julian and AMMIANUS MARCELLINUS. RJB

Grant (1979); Momigliano (1963a); Ruehl (1887).

Evagoras (*c*.435–374/3 BC), king of Cypriot Salamis. In 411 BC Evagoras seized the kingdom of SALAMIS from its pro-Phoenician ruler and for nearly four decades ruled sufficiently well for ISOCRATES to name him as an ideal monarch. He received CONON after AEGOSPOTAMI, provided a base for his fleet in the 390s, and allied with Athens. He openly revolted from Persia (*c*.390) and took 10 years to reduce, gaining an honourable peace which left him in power until his assassination. GLC

Stylianou (1989).

Execias (fl. *c*.550–530 BC), Greek vase painter and potter. Execias of Athens is regarded as the best of the black-figure vase painters. He began as a potter and in that capacity he signed 11 extant vases. Two of these – a neck amphora of Heracles and the lion in Berlin and an amphora with Achilles and Ajax playing draughts in the Vatican – he signed also as painter. And he has been recognized as the painter of more than 20 other vases as well as a number of terracotta plaques. Unlike other black-figure artists, he rises above convention to portray both the personality and the psychology of his figures.

See also PAINTING, GREEK. GS

Arias and Hirmer (1962); Boardman (1974).

Exsilium   the voluntary self-banishment from Roman territory of a person threatened with condemnation in a criminal trial. Originally an informal practice tolerated by the magistrates, it was institutionalized in the late Republic when it became a substitute for the death penalty, and condemned criminals were allowed time to escape. They were then stripped of their citizenship and forbidden to return by a solemn decree which refused them the basic necessities of life (*aquae et ignis indictio* – 'denial of water and fire'). In a non-technical sense *exsilium* was the general Latin term for any kind of exile, including RELEGATIO.

TC

F

Fabius Maximus Rullianus (fl. 325–295 BC), Roman general. Quintus Fabius Maximus Rullianus was one of Rome's greatest leaders in the age of the SAMNITE WARS. He was consul five times and dictator twice. In 310 BC he led a victorious expedition through central Etruria and into Umbria. His greatest achievement was his victory at the battle of Sentinum in 295, in which he defeated the Samnites with their Etruscan, Umbrian, and Gallic allies. This was the decisive moment in the Roman conquest of peninsular Italy. HE

CAH VII.2; Harris (1971).

Fabius Maximus Verrucosus, Cunctator (d. 203 BC), Roman dictator. Quintus Fabius Maximus Verrucosus triumphed over the LIGURES soon after his first consulship in 233 BC. He was consul again in 228, 215, 214, and 209 and dictator in 221 and 217. He was Rome's leading strategist in the first stage of the Second PUNIC WAR. After the Roman defeat at Lake TRASIMENE (217) he was elected dictator again and carried out an unpopular policy of avoiding pitched battles with HANNIBAL, to wear down his strength, whence his nickname 'Cunctator', the Delayer. Following the disastrous Roman defeat at CANNAE (216) this policy had to be continued for the next decade. Fabius was particularly opposed to SCIPIO AFRICANUS' plans to invade Africa in 205. Fabius succeeded in maintaining Roman morale during the war partly as a result of his keen religious observances. PLUTARCH's life survives. HE

Lazenby (1978); Scullard (1973).

Fabius Pictor (3rd century BC), Roman historian. Quintus Fabius Pictor came from an ancient patrician family and was himself a member of the Senate. He lived through the Second PUNIC WAR, which probably inspired him to write his history of Rome, the first ever by a Roman. Fabius wrote in Greek, probably because he wanted to break away from the native tradition of dry-as-dust ANNALES and to show his debt to Greek historiography. He no doubt hoped for Greek readers too. Only a few fragments of his work survive, not enough to give a clear idea of its character. He was used by POLYBIUS, LIVY, and DIONYSIUS OF HALICARNASSUS.

See also HISTORIOGRAPHY, ROMAN.   TC

Momigliano (1990).

Fable, Greek   The Greek fable, a moralizing tale set in the animal kingdom, forms part of the ageless tradition of folk mythology which occasionally rises to the surface in ancient literature. The earliest example is the story of the hawk and the nightingale in HESIOD; ARCHILOCHUS writes of the fox and the ape, and SEMONIDES of the dungbeetle who punished the arrogant eagle. Its purpose is always to demonstrate with discretion the path of truth and justice. After the 5th century BC the corpus of Greek fable was for ever associated with the name of its compiler, AESOP.   GS

Perry (1952).

Fable, Latin   The Latin fable, like its Greek predecessor usually an animal story with a simple moral, descends chiefly from the tradition associated with AESOP. Fables were transmitted by Ennius, Lucilius, and Horace; but the first collection in Latin was made by PHAEDRUS in the 1st century AD. In addition to material credited to Aesop, Phaedrus contributes more of his own verse compositions. More fables were written in prose in the 3rd century by Titianus, and a verse collection was made in the 4th century by Avianus.   GS

Fabricius Luscinus   (3rd century BC), Roman hero. Gaius Fabricius Luscinus was a leading commander in the campaigns against PYRRHUS and his Italian allies, and consul in 282 and 278 BC. He is said to have rejected both bribes from Pyrrhus and the overtures of traitors offering to poison Pyrrhus (*see also* DENTATUS). Although much of the reality of his career is uncertain, his name survived as a byword for old-fashioned Roman virtue: poor but incorruptible.   HS

Salmon (1967).

Falisci   Italian people. The Falisci occupied a region north of Veii and west of the Tiber, their main cities being Capena and Falerii. They were dominated politically by the ETRUSCANS of Veii, though their language was close to Latin. After defeats while resisting Roman expansion, Falerii was destroyed in 241 BC and was resettled by the Romans on a new site nearby. HE

Potter (1979, 1987).

Fannius (late 2nd century BC), Roman annalist. Gaius Fannius fought at Carthage (146 BC) and in Spain (141), and served as tribune (c.142), praetor (c.126), and consul (122). Originally a friend and associate of Gaius GRACCHUS, who helped him achieve the consulship of 122, Fannius later changed sides and opposed Gracchus' Italian legislation. His history, of which only fragments survive, dealt with contemporary events, probably covering the earlier history of Rome only in outline.

HE

Badian (1966b); Stockton (1979).

Fasces Roman symbol of office. *Fasces* were bundles of sticks, usually elm or birch, tied together by red thongs and with an axe bound into them. They symbolized the power of a magistrate to inflict corporal and capital punishment. They were originally introduced from Etruria under the kings. They were carried by the LICTORS who accompanied kings, praetors, consuls, dictators, emperors, and imperial legates. Within the city boundary only dictators carried axes in their *fasces*; others had them removed. HE

Fasti lists of Roman magistrates. Initially *fasti* were calendars showing the days on which public business and legal transactions were permitted. Lists of these *dies fasti* were published from as early as 304 BC. *Fasti* also included lists of consuls, triumphs, and priests, and versions of such lists going back to the beginning of the Republic are preserved in our sources. Their authenticity for the early 5th century BC is sometimes questioned, but most scholars accept that the surviving versions of the *fasti* provide a sound chronological framework for the history of the early Republic. HE

CAH VII.2.

Fausta *see* CONSTANTINE I.

Faustina the Elder *see* ANTONINUS PIUS.

Faustina the Younger (c.AD 125/130–75), wife of Marcus AURELIUS. Annia Galeria Faustina was the second daughter of ANTONINUS PIUS and Faustina the Elder. Intended by Hadrian to marry Lucius VERUS, she was betrothed instead to Marcus Aurelius (139), and married him in 145.

She bore him 13 children, including COMMODUS. Dio Cassius alleges that Faustina encouraged the revolt of AVIDIUS CASSIUS, fearing the loss of her own influence, should Marcus die before Commodus was old enough to become emperor.   RJB

Birley (1987); Parker (1958).

Favorinus (*c.*AD 80–*c.*150), sophist. Favorinus, a congenital eunuch from Arles, was one of the leading intellectuals of his day. After an education at Marseille, Greek remained his preferred language for both speaking and writing, though little of the latter survives. His teacher was DIO CHRYSOSTOM; his friends included PLUTARCH, and his pupils HERODES ATTICUS, FRONTO, and GELLIUS. At Rome he was a favourite of the emperor Hadrian.   GS

Bowersock (1969).

Felix (d. after AD 60), Roman procurator. Marcus Antonius Felix, brother of PALLAS, was a freedman of ANTONIA, the mother of CLAUDIUS I. Married to Drusilla, daughter of AGRIPPA I, he was made procurator of Judaea by Claudius (AD 52–60), and had to deal with increasing social unrest, and rioting between Greeks and Jews in Caesarea. St PAUL was tried by Felix, who considered him too dangerous to release, and Felix's successor, Festus, sent him to Rome.   RJB

Scullard (1982).

Festivals, Greek Festivals were the most important and the most conspicuous aspect of Greek public RELIGION. They were extremely numerous (more than 120 a year at Athens alone) and, while certain elements (such as processions, SACRIFICE, and feasting) might be common to most, the possibilities for local variation were endless. The majority were originally related to the cycle of the farmer's year and many followed soon after the harvest when there was more leisure. Festivals performed the double function of doing honour to the gods and providing entertainment for the people.

Of major international significance were the four great panhellenic festivals: the ISTHMIAN GAMES, NEMEAN GAMES, OLYMPIC GAMES, and PYTHIAN GAMES. These attracted visitors, both as spectators and as competitors in the GAMES, from all over the Greek world. Their value was threefold: they promoted the panhellenic idea which no single POLIS could do; they ensured a place for athletics and MUSIC in Greek EDUCATION; they provided patronage for poets (*see* PINDAR), painters (*see* EUPHRONIUS), and sculptors (*see* POLYCLEITUS) who were commissioned to celebrate victories.

Of local festivals the Athenian are the best documented: the PANATHENAEA in honour of Athena; the ANTHESTERIA, DIONYSIA, and LENAEA in honour of Dionysus; the THARGELIA for Apollo and the THESMOPHORIA for Demeter. The CARNEA was particularly associated with Sparta and the THEOXENIA with Delphi, the Heraea (in honour of HERA) with Argos and the Delia (for Apollo and Artemis) with DELOS. Despite the persistent veneer of piety, it was the secular aspect of Greek festivals that came to dominate their celebration. Some were entirely political in inspiration, such as the Eleutheria (or festival of Liberty) which after 479 BC into Roman times was celebrated every five years at PLATAEA in memory of that great victory.

See also APATURIA; THEOROI; TIME, MEASUREMENT OF. GS

Easterling and Muir (1985); Parke (1977); Pickard-Cambridge (1968).

Festivals, Roman Roman religious practice amounted to the regular, usually annual, repetition of well-defined rituals in honour of the gods. These festivals (*feriae*) were carefully ordered in the official state calendar (*see* TIME, MEASUREMENT OF), which was supervised by the PONTIFICES. Our knowledge of the pre-Julian calendar is based partly on literary accounts, especially the *Fasti* of OVID, and partly on an inscribed calendar from ANTIUM (the *Fasti Antiates Maiores*). This lists all the days of the year, indicating the religious status of each (i.e. whether it was a working day or a holiday), and adds the names of major public festivals on the appropriate days. Apart from around 40 fixed festivals (*feriae stativae*) there were a number of movable feasts (*feriae conceptivae*), such as the AMBARVALIA, which did not appear in the calendar but were held on days determined each year by the pontiffs.

The festivals themselves were of great antiquity, and it is generally agreed that the ones listed in the pre-Julian calendar go back at least to the 6th century BC. They reflect the needs of a simple agrarian community: to ensure the fertility of the soil and the health of the flocks, to promote childbirth, to placate the spirits of the dead, to avert disease and pestilence. A primitive warrior society is also implied in ceremonies such as the *Tubilustrium* ('purification of the trumpets') on 23 March and 23 May, and the *Armilustrium* ('purification of weapons') on 19 October. The rites performed at the various festivals were many and various; they were carried out on the city's behalf by the priests and magistrates. At some festivals the people took part as spectators; at others private ceremonies were carried out in each household by the head of the family.

See also ARGEI; FORNACALIA; LUPERCALIA; PARENTALIA; PARILIA; RELIGION, ROMAN; ROSALIA; SATURNALIA. TC

CAH VII.2; Michels (1967); Scullard (1981); Warde Fowler (1899).

Fetiales Roman priests. The Fetials (*fetiales*) were a 20-strong college of PRIESTS who were responsible for the ritual aspects of war. The Fetial procedure for declaration of war included a demand for the return of stolen property and compensation (*res repetundae*). If the demand was not met, the Fetials declared war by throwing a spear into enemy territory. The procedure legalistically and symbolically emphasized the rightness of the Roman cause. Hence the notion of the 'just war', that the Romans only fought in retaliation to external aggression. The Fetials gave advice to the Senate on the correct procedures and formulae for treaties. Their appointed leader, the *pater patratus*, was responsible for pronouncing the oaths and, perhaps in the early Republic, for conducting diplomacy during foreign crises.

LPR

Harris (1979).

Finance, Greek In the archaic period Greek states employed a primitive financial system. In Sparta, for example, although iron spits provided currency of a sort, payments to the state and to individuals were probably made in kind. Similarly, Athens did not introduce COINAGE before the time of the Peisistratids and, though large-scale overseas TRADE would have involved some exchange of precious metals, most internal dealings must have been in kind.

Athens, which provided the model for most other states, continued in a comparatively simple way through the 5th century BC. Various funds were established for specific items of expenditure (defence, embassies, sport, religion, etc.); these were serviced by specific taxes and administered by magistrates; any surplus at the end of the year was used for whatever purpose the people chose. There was no budget. Wars were financed by direct capital levies (EISPHORAI), though in the 420s the practice of borrowing temple treasures had begun. (Such depredations were to become a scandal in the 4th century at Olympia and Delphi.) Taxes were collected by private tax collectors, a system familiar from the Roman imitation.

The acquisition of empire greatly increased the amount of money available to the Athenian state. It was looked after by the 'Treasurers of the Greeks' (*Hellenotamiai*). After 454, when the treasury was moved from Delos to Athens, PERICLES drew on it for his building programme. In addition to tribute, there were a number of imperial taxes. The loss of it all in the PELOPONNESIAN WAR made Athenians nostalgic for imperial prosperity.

By the end of the Greek SOCIAL WAR (357–355) Athens was nearly bankrupt. Alternatives to imperial expansion had to be found. Hence the rise of politicians who were primarily financiers, notably EUBULUS and LYCURGUS, who would repair Athens's fortunes by the exploitation of peace and commerce.

In the Hellenistic period more complex financial systems were evolved, especially in Ptolemaic EGYPT.

See also BANKING; TAXATION, GREEK; THEORIKA; TREASURY.   GLC

Ehrenberg (1969); Heichelheim (1964); Michell (1957); Rhodes (1972).

Finance, Roman Under the Republic the Roman finances were managed by the Senate, and in particular by the CENSORS, who controlled the composition of the census classes, the sale or lease of public land, and the disposition of contracts, including the farming-out of provincial tax collection to equestrian syndicates. Financial administration was undertaken by QUAESTORS, and fines were levied by the AEDILES. Funds were held in a state treasury, the AERARIUM SATURNI, while a separate reserve fund was held in the *Aerarium sanctius*.

Under the Empire the emperor took over many of the functions of the censors, and sometimes held the office (Domitian held it for life). The state treasury was maintained, and quaestors continued to act in Rome and in the few provinces under senatorial control. However, the *Aerarium* (combined by Claudius into a single treasury) declined in importance relative to a new imperial treasury, the *Fiscus*, established for the revenues of the imperial provinces, whose affairs were administered by the emperor's financial agents (PROCURATORS), who rapidly became public officials. In addition, Augustus established a private treasury, the PATRIMONIUM CAESARIS, that received the revenues from crown property, including Egypt, as well as bequests and confiscated property; and also the *Aerarium militare*, to provide pensions for retired soldiers. Under Claudius the *procurator patrimonii* reported to PALLAS, who held the position of *a rationibus*, principal secretary in charge of imperial finances. Under the *procurator patrimonii* were the imperial procurators of all the provinces, including the senatorial ones. In addition, Claudius himself appointed the officials who administered the *Aerarium*, and by the end of the 2nd century AD the distinction between *Fiscus* and *Aerarium* had all but disappeared. Confusion between what had become the two principal treasuries, the *Fiscus* and the *Patrimonium*, caused Septimius SEVERUS to establish a new private treasury, the RES PRIVATA, which rapidly eclipsed the Patrimonium.

See also BANKING; BUREAUCRACY, ROMAN; CONSISTORIUM; TAXATION, ROMAN.   RJB

Grant (1979); Salmon (1968); Wells (1984).

Fire A number of methods of kindling fire were known in antiquity. Sticks could be rubbed together (or better, a fire-drill of laurel rotated in a fire-stick of ivy) until enough heat was generated by the friction. Tinder could be lit from a spark struck off a flint and another stone, or from the rays of the sun when concentrated by means of a piece of glass or crystal or a mirror. But since all these methods were more or less tedious and unreliable, the commonest practice was to retain a permanent fire in the hearth from which LAMPS etc. could readily be lit.

See also ELEMENTS.   GS

Fiscus *see* FINANCE, ROMAN.

Fishing Fish – salted, pickled, dried, or fresh – formed an important part of the staple diet of all sections of society (*see* FOOD AND DRINK). Fishing was practised locally in rivers, lakes, and coastal waters, but the Greeks also imported dried fish in large quantities from the rich fisheries of the Black Sea, the Sea of Marmora, and the rivers of the north including the Danube, the Dniester, and the Don. There are many references to fish and fishing in ancient literature and art. ARISTOTLE and his successors studied the science of ichthyology. OPPIAN's *Halieutica* provides detailed descriptions of various methods of catching fish. The Romans continued to import from the Black Sea, but it is possible that in some parts of the empire fishing in sea, river, and lake was a state-run monopoly. The production of fish sauce (*garum*), a favourite delicacy of Roman tables, was an important industry at POMPEII. GS

Rostovtzeff (1941).

Flaccus, Quintus Horatius *see* HORACE.

Flaccus, Verrius (1st century BC), Latin lexicographer. Verrius Flaccus was a freedman appointed by Augustus to teach his grandsons Gaius and Lucius CAESAR. A polymath like VARRO, he wrote on Etruscan antiquities and set up the calendar at Praeneste of which fragments survive. His most important work was the first Latin lexicon, *De Significatu Verborum*, of which an inferior abridgement is preserved by Pompeius Festus.   GS

Flamen Roman priest. A *flamen* was a priest appointed to serve the cult of a particular god. The best known is the priest of JUPITER, the Flamen Dialis, who was surrounded by mysterious taboos. He was forbidden to ride a horse, to set eyes on an army, to touch raw meat, she-goats, ivy, or beans, to have his hair cut by a slave, and so on. He and his wife, the *flaminica*, had to be patricians, free from bodily defects, and constantly dressed in special clothes. They were hardly allowed to leave the house, still less the city. Needless to say, it was a job that ruled out a political career. There were two other major *flamines* – of MARS and of QUIRINUS – about whom little is recorded; and virtually nothing is known of the minor *flamines*, at least 12 in number, who served lesser gods, some of them very obscure (e.g. Pales, Furria, Falacer, Pomona). Although the *flamines* were members of the pontifical college, they do not seem ever to have acted collectively.

See also PRIESTS, ROMAN.   TC

Beard and North (1990).

Flaminia, Via   Roman road. The Via Flaminia ran northwards from Rome to Fanum Fortunae on the Adriatic coast. Here it turned northwest and followed the coastline to its end in ARIMINUM (Rimini). It was 209 miles long, and was built by Gaius FLAMINIUS, censor of 220 BC. Its later repairers included AUGUSTUS who proclaimed in his *Res Gestae* 'I restored the Via Flaminia from Rome as far as Rimini.' Augustus' arch, marking the road's end at Rimini, can still be seen there.

See also ROADS, ROMAN.   DP

Chevallier (1976); Potter (1987); Wiseman (1987).

Flamininus   (*c*.228–174 BC), Roman politician. Titus Quinctius Flamininus was a leading figure in Rome's conquest of the Greek east. He was elected consul for 198 BC, when only 30, to command in the Second MACEDONIAN WAR. He defeated PHILIP V at CYNOSCEPHALAE (197), for which he won a triumph. He announced the freedom of Greece at the Isthmian Games of 196 and, after forcing NABIS of Sparta to give up Argos (195), evacuated Roman forces from Greece in 194. In 193 he scored a diplomatic success against the ambassadors of ANTIOCHUS III THE GREAT, and in 193/2 suppressed Nabis. After his censorship of 189 his influence declined, although in 183 he demanded the surrender of HANNIBAL from PRUSIAS I of Bithynia.

Flamininus was appreciative of Greek culture and an advocate of Greek local autonomy, but this 'philhellenic' policy should not disguise the fact that the nominally independent Greek states were intended to become client states of Rome.   HS

Badian (1970b); Gruen (1984); Scullard (1973).

Flaminius   (d. 217 BC), Roman politician. Gaius Flaminius, a NOVUS HOMO, was a radical reformer and a forerunner of the GRACCHI. As TRIBUNUS PLEBIS in 232 BC Flaminius distributed AGER PUBLICUS (the *ager Gallicus*) to poor citizens. When consul in 223 BC he won a triumph over the INSUBRES. In 220 BC as censor he built the Via FLAMINIA and the Circus Flaminius. Elected consul for 217 BC, he died when he led his army into the ambush prepared by HANNIBAL at Lake TRASIMENE. He was vilified by hostile, aristocratic-influenced sources as the man who started the 'demoralization of the people'. HS

Lazenby (1978); Scullard (1973); Taylor (1962).

Florianus (d. AD 276), Roman emperor, AD 276. Marcus Annius Florianus, praetorian prefect of TACITUS, seized the throne after the death of Tacitus at Tyana, but, although widely recognized (except in Egypt and Syria), reigned for only two to three months. His rival PROBUS, proclaimed less than a month after Florianus, evaded a pitched battle with the numerically superior forces of his enemy near Tarsus, and eventually, in autumn 276, Florianus was murdered by his own increasingly demoralized men. RJB

Grant (1985); Parker (1958).

Florus (1st–2nd century AD?), Roman historian. Florus, the author of an *Epitome* of Roman history, is often identified with Publius Annius Florus, the author of a dialogue 'Is Virgil an Orator or Poet?' The author of this said he came from Africa, visited Rome under DOMITIAN, and retired to Spain. He in turn is identified with the Florus who is said to have exchanged verses with HADRIAN.

The *Epitome* is a brief account (in two books) of Roman history arranged by wars from earliest days to AUGUSTUS. It draws chiefly on LIVY, but also shows awareness of, among others, CAESAR and SALLUST. The work is inaccurate, obscure, and rhetorical. HS

den Boer (1972); Kenney and Clausen (1982).

Food and drink The ancient diet was based on corn, fish, oil, and wine. Corn (wheat or barley) came in the form of bread or broth and might be accompanied by cheese or honey. Fish might be fresh or salted and many species were known. Olive oil was used in the preparation of many dishes and was the main source of fat. WINE was strong and sweet and usually mixed with water. Beer was a drink associated with BARBARIANS. Eggs and nuts were widely eaten. Butchered meat was a luxury, often available only after a SACRIFICE at a festival, but the Romans ate game and poultry and a little pork. Among vegetables, the commonest were beans, beet, garlic, marrows, onions, and radishes; among fruits, grapes and figs, but apples, pears, dates, and mulberries were also eaten, and later apricots, cherries, and peaches. Strongly flavoured sauces were favoured and a wide range of spices was imported from the Orient. Salt was in demand as a preservative as well as a flavouring and in many regions had to be imported. Throughout much of antiquity most people's diet was simple and, by modern standards, frugal. Under the later Empire extravagant luxury characterized the tables of the rich, and lavish banquets are described by JUVENAL and PETRONIUS. A collection of recipes, *On the Art of Cooking*, survives and is ascribed to APICIUS.

See also AGRICULTURE; ANNONA; ARBORICULTURE; BEE-KEEPING; FISHING; HUNTING; SYMPOSIUM; TRADE. GS

Miller (1969); Spiller (1991).

Fornacalia Roman festival. The Fornacalia ('festival of ovens') was a movable feast celebrated in February by the CURIAE. It involved a simple meal at the meeting house of each *curia*, with special cakes that had been baked (probably) in its communal oven. An assembly of all the *curiae* was then held on 17 February, the day of the Quirinalia, which was known as the 'Feast of Fools', because citizens who had forgotten which *curia* they belonged to were able to take part. TC

Scullard (1981).

Fortifications, Greek Although the Greeks always appreciated the defensive potential of an ACROPOLIS site, fortifications proper only developed in the 6th century BC. Town walls of stone masonry or brick were constructed in the classical period. These simple fortifications sufficed since sophisticated SIEGECRAFT was unknown; towns were captured by blockade. The developments of siege techniques in the 4th century (artillery in the form of catapults, and mobile towers on which it was mounted) necessitated stronger defensive measures. Walls had to be thicker and reinforced. As artillery came to be used by defenders, towers within the line of a wall gave more and better angles for effective shot. Taller walls and towers were needed to neutralize the machines designed to overlook them. Defensive ditches and curtain walls were introduced to impede the approach of the siege machines. Postern gates and sally-ports enabled defenders to emerge for skirmishes with the enemy. The many examples of extensive, well-preserved city walls attest to the importance placed upon effective defence even by small communities.

See also HARBOURS. EER

Connolly (1981); Lawrence (1979, 1984); Winter (1971).

Fortifications, Roman Roman fortifications initially followed the Etruscan pattern, where groups of hill-top villages were united into formidable towns: earlier palisades and ditches were replaced, around the 7th century BC, by massive terrace walls fronted by steep ramps and backed by earthen mounds. In 378 BC the Romans began the WALL OF SERVIUS: it was stone-built of rectangular blocks and included a massive terrace wall across the weakly defended eastern side of Rome.

From the mid-2nd century BC Roman fortifications declined, mirroring the lack of sophisticated siege warfare. Under the early Empire defences usually consisted of a wall or rampart, with a ditch in front. The only significant advance was the portcullis, a late Republican invention.

In the 2nd century AD Roman fortifications reflect more defensive thinking: the frontier fortifications of the WALL OF HADRIAN and the Germanic LIMES are massive in scale, but show no advance in thinking over the 5th century BC, consisting of forts or camps linked by wall or palisade. Late Roman fortifications, from the time of Diocletian onwards, were geared to prolonged defence, whereas during the early Empire the army normally intended to meet the enemy in the field. New forts were sited on raised ground, and the narrow V-shaped ditch of the early Empire gave way to a wide flat-bottomed ditch, set well away from the walls to create a killing zone. Walls were massive, with projecting towers to allow enfilading fire, and often included platforms for artillery: the two-armed bolt-firing torsion catapult (the *ballista*), or the single-armed stone-firing *onager*, or scorpion.   RJB

Connolly (1981); Hackett (1989).

Fortuna   Roman goddess. Fortuna was an ancient Italian deity who appears in various manifestations in Roman cult: Fors Fortuna, Fortuna Virilis, Fortuna Muliebris, Fortuna Virgo, Fortuna Primigenia, and so on. She is associated in legend with SERVIUS TULLIUS, whom she favoured and visited at night as a lover. Two temples to Fortuna are attributed to Servius, one of them in the Forum Boarium at the foot of the CAPITOL, where recent excavations have unearthed the foundations of an archaic temple dating to the 6th century BC. Shrines of Fortuna existed at other Italian towns, most notably PRAENESTE.   TC

Platner and Ashby (1929); Thomsen (1980).

Forum   Roman city centre. The forum, the equivalent of the Greek AGORA, lay at the heart of a Roman town or city. It was usually square or rectangular, surrounded on three sides by porticoes, with a BASILICA on the fourth side. The basilica was the local administrative centre. The surrounding portico could contain shops or trade stands, offices or shrines. The centre of the forum was also used as a market-place, being rented out to traders' stalls.   HE

Forum Romanum   and other *fora* in Rome. The Forum Romanum, the major FORUM of Rome, lay at the centre of the city, east of the CAPITOLINE and north of the PALATINE hills, overlooked by the ESQUILINE. It was a sprawling complex which was continuously redeveloped throughout Roman history: SULLA severely remodelled it, but many prominent Republican politicians and most emperors made some contribution. The area was first used as a meeting place after being drained in the 7th century BC, and some of its earliest public buildings, including the temple of VESTA and the Regia, date from before 600 BC. The first BASILICA was built in 184 BC and Augustus built a TRIUMPHAL ARCH there in 30 BC. Many of the original buildings were remodelled or rebuilt, but new construction continued as late as the 5th century AD. In addition to its judicial and religious functions, and its role as the political centre of the city, the Forum Romanum continued to operate as a market-place.

Rome contained numerous other *fora*, mostly situated in the flat areas in the centre, between the Velabrum and the Subura. The Forum of AUGUSTUS was dedicated to Mars Ultor in 2 BC. The Forum Pacis was dedicated by VESPASIAN in AD 75 to house the spoils of his victory in Jerusalem. The Forum Transitorium, dedicated by NERVA in AD 97, linked these two *fora* with the Forum Romanum, turning the whole area into a monumental park.

The Forum of TRAJAN, designed by APOLLODORUS OF DAMASCUS, was dedicated in AD 113 with the spoils of the Dacian War. It lay to the north-east of the Capitoline hill, partially cut out of the QUIRINAL. It is the most similar of Roman *fora* to those built in the provinces, square in plan with a large basilica on the north side. Behind the basilica libraries created a courtyard containing Trajan's Column.

See also ROME, TOPOGRAPHY.   HE

Grant (1970b); Platner and Ashby (1929); Richardson (1992); Robinson (1992).

Four-element theory *see* ELEMENTS.

Four Hundred revolutionary junta that overthrew the democracy at Athens in 411 BC and held power for four months. The Sicilian disaster (*see* PELOPONNESIAN WAR) and Spartan success in fomenting revolts within the empire made it seem that under the direction of a democracy Athens could not survive. Having prepared the ground with a reign of terror, the conspirators (chiefly ANTIPHON, PEISANDER, and THERAMENES) seized power, dissolving the democratic council of 500, establishing an oligarchic one of 400, and ruling without appointing the promised sovereign assembly of 5,000. But Theramenes insisted on its appointment, and the extreme oligarchs, who preferred peace with Sparta at any price, were ousted. The Five Thousand, membership of which was based on a property qualification, ruled Athens well until victory at CYZICUS (410) made the restoration of full democracy inevitable.

                                                                               GLC

Hignett (1952); Ostwald (1986).

Franks German peoples. The Franks, a 3rd-century AD coalition of Germanic tribes, made frequent incursions across the middle and lower Rhine into Roman Gaul and Spain (c.253–76). JULIAN defeated a major invasion (355), but the Salian Franks were allowed to settle within Gaul, and Frankish generals (e.g. Arbogastes) served in the Roman army. Around 425 the Franks began to expand again, and, after the death of AETIUS (454), gradually extended their power throughout Gaul.

RJB

James (1988).

Fratres Arvales *see* ARVAL BROTHERS.

Freedmen *see* SLAVERY.

Frisii German people. The Frisii, a seafaring people occupying Frisia, a North Sea coastal district, were subjugated by the elder DRUSUS in 12 BC. They revolted against Rome because of oppressive taxation (AD 28), and remained troublesome until defeated by CORBULO (47). They joined the Batavian revolt led by CIVILIS (69–70), but after their defeat they stayed loyal to Rome: they remained in their old settlements, and Frisian units fought in the Roman army.

RJB

Thompson (1965); Todd (1975).

Frontinus (c.AD 34–104), Roman politician and engineer. Sextus Julius Frontinus had a distinguished public career, becoming praetor in AD 70 and consul in 74 (and again in 98 and 100). As governor of BRITAIN (74–8) he subdued the Silures and founded the legionary camp at Exeter. When appointed *curator aquarum* by Nerva in 96, he began a two-volume study of the Roman water supply which survives. Other surviving works are the four books of military *Strategemata* and fragments of a manual on land surveying. His study of Greek and Roman warfare, *De Re Militari*, is lost but was used by Vegetius.

See also AQUEDUCT.

GS

Collingwood and Myres (1937); Hodge (1992).

Fronto (c.AD 100–170), Roman orator. Marcus Cornelius Fronto was born at Cirta in Africa but moved to Rome where he pursued a public career, becoming suffect consul in AD 143. A distinguished orator and teacher of rhetoric, he was appointed tutor to the future emperors Marcus AURELIUS and Lucius VERUS. Only fragments of his speeches survive, but his correspondence with Aurelius and others is partially preserved in a 5th-century palimpsest. The letters are of no historical interest and are mostly concerned with matters of language, literature, and rhetoric. GS

Brock (1911).

Fulvia (d. 40 BC), wife of CLODIUS, Curio, and ANTONY. Fulvia married successively husbands from important political families. As Antony's wife she may not have been as cruel as to pierce the tongue of CICERO's amputated head with a hair pin, as the stories say, but she certainly played a tough, prominent part in the war against Octavian (AUGUSTUS). After failure in this she escaped to Greece where she soon died. Claudia, her daughter by Clodius, became Octavian's first wife in 41 BC. DP

Balsdon (1962); Syme (1939).

Fulvius Flaccus (d. 121 BC), Roman politician. Marcus Fulvius Flaccus was a supporter of Tiberius GRACCHUS, to whose land commission he was appointed in 130 BC. Italian opposition to the commission led Flaccus to propose giving the allies (SOCII) Roman CITIZENSHIP. The Senate prevented him from carrying this out when consul in 125 by sending him to a war in Gaul. Returning to triumph in 123, he became TRIBUNUS PLEBIS in 122 and supported Gaius GRACCHUS, whose fate at the hands of OPIMIUS he shared.

See also AGER PUBLICUS; OPTIMATES; POPULARES; SCIPIO AEMILIANUS. HS

Stockton (1979).

Fulvius Nobilior (2nd century BC), Roman politician. Marcus Fulvius Nobilior, having been aedile in 196 BC and praetor in Spain in 193, was elected consul for 189. He defeated the AETOLIAN LEAGUE, capturing Ambracia, for which he obtained a triumph in 187. As censor in 179 he reformed the COMITIA *centuriata*. His appreciation of Greek culture (ENNIUS accompanied him to Aetolia) was expressed in a distinctively Roman fashion by looting Ambracia's art treasures. HS

Scullard (1973); Toynbee (1965).

Fuscus (d. AD 86), Roman soldier. Cornelius Fuscus, procurator of Pannonia in AD 69, supported VESPASIAN's bid for the empire. Promoted by the Flavians, Fuscus became praetorian prefect under Domitian, and commanded operations against an invasion of Moesia, led by DECEBALUS of DACIA (85). Domitian and Fuscus restored order in Moesia, and in 86 Fuscus crossed the Danube, intending to invade Dacia. However, he was pursued back over the river and killed, and his army annihilated. RJB

Salmon (1968).

G

Gabinius (d. 47 BC), Roman politician. Aulus Gabinius, as tribune in 67 BC, proposed the law giving POMPEY an unlimited command against the pirates. He served in the east under Pompey from 66 to 63, and became consul in 58. He was an energetic governor of Syria from 57 to 54: he tried to protect the provincials from the PUBLICANI, but was himself condemned for extortion on his return to Rome. Recalled to public life by CAESAR, he died as his legate in Illyricum in 47.   DP

Seager (1979); Syme (1939).

Gaiseric *see* VANDALS.

Gaius (AD 12–41), Roman emperor, AD 37–41. Gaius Julius Caesar Germanicus, youngest son of GERMANICUS, succeeded TIBERIUS as emperor. As an infant, he was paraded before the Rhine legions by his parents, his miniature uniform gaining him the nickname Caligula, 'Bootikins'. Caligula was initially popular (although not with the Senate): some sound measures were accompanied by extravagant shows. His cruelty and irresponsibility rapidly became apparent, and a serious illness (37) probably affected his sanity. Thereafter he ignored or humiliated the Senate, and proclaimed himself a divinity. He reportedly committed incest with his sisters (DRUSILLA, AGRIPPINA, and Julia Livilla), and made Drusilla his heir: her death (38) removed a moderating influence on his behaviour. His attempt to establish absolute monarchy provoked resentment among the old Claudian nobility, and among the Jews (*see* PHILO). In September 39 Caligula departed for the Rhine, putting down a plot led by Aemilius Lepidus, widower of Drusilla, and Lentulus Gaetulicus, in which Agrippina and Livilla were implicated. A planned expedition against Britain (spring 40) was never begun: instead, the troops were ordered to gather sea-shells (*musculi*). Caligula destroyed his remaining popularity by a series of taxes designed to fill the treasury, and finally, having alienated even the PRAETORIAN GUARD, was assassinated on 24 January 41. RJB

Barrett (1989); Grant (1985); Salmon (1968); Wells (1984).

Gaius (2nd century AD), Roman jurist. Gaius seems to have lived at Rome, but he held no public office and little is known of his life. Only in the 5th century was he recognized as one of the foremost Roman lawyers. His most important book, the *Institutes,* is a textbook of JURISPRUDENCE and is the only major work on classical law to survive in its original form. It was greatly admired by Justinian who made it the basis of his own *Institutes.* He also wrote studies of the Provincial Edict, the Urban Praetor's Edict, and the TWELVE TABLES, parts of which are preserved in later compilations.

See also CONTRACT; LAW, ROMAN. GS

Honoré (1962).

Gaius Caesar *see* CAESAR, GAIUS.

Galatia territory in central Asia Minor. Galatia was an area of PHRYGIA and CAPPADOCIA occupied by 'Gauls', tribal European CELTS who invaded Asia in 278 BC (*see* NICOMEDES I). Their marauding habits were not restrained by uneasy alliances with various Hellenistic powers. ATTALUS I SOTER and EUMENES II SOTER of Pergamum inflicted serious defeats in the 3rd and early 2nd centuries, but the Gauls continued to cause trouble. After MAGNESIA they became Roman allies. Galatia and adjoining territory became a Roman province in 25 BC. It later included parts of PONTUS and PAPHLAGONIA, and in AD 72 VESPASIAN joined to it Cappadocia and ARMENIA Minor. It was reduced in size under TRAJAN and again under DIOCLETIAN. EER

Allen (1983); Gruen (1984); Hubert (1987); Jones (1983); Magie (1975); Rankin (1987); Sullivan (1990).

Galba (3 BC–AD 69), Roman emperor, AD 68–9. Servius Sulpicius Galba, a stern disciplinarian from an ancient aristocratic family, replaced Gaetulicus as commander on the Upper Rhine (after Gaetulicus' rebellion against GAIUS), was appointed governor of Africa under Claudius, and was, for eight years, governor of Hispania Tarraconensis under NERO. He was persuaded by VINDEX to rebel against Nero, and received the support of OTHO, the future emperor, and of CAECINA ALIENUS. Vindex's rebellion was destroyed by RUFUS, who refused the throne for himself; and Galba, supported by the praetorian prefect Nymphidius

Sabinus, was recognized as emperor by the Senate (June 68); and Nero committed suicide. Galba now rapidly alienated most of his supporters: he replaced the popular Rufus, and also Sabinus; and, when the Germanic legions proclaimed VITELLIUS as emperor, he lost Otho's support by adopting as his heir L. Calpurnius Piso Frugi Licinianus. Otho promptly rebelled, and was proclaimed by the praetorians, who lynched Galba (January 69). RJB

Grant (1985); Wellesley (1975); Wells (1984).

Galba Maximus (fl. 211–193 BC), Roman commander. Publius Sulpicius Galba Maximus as consul for 211 BC defended Rome from HANNIBAL. He conducted the First MACEDONIAN WAR against PHILIP V with little success (210–206). Having been dictator in 203, as consul in 200 he commanded in the Second Macedonian War. He served as a legate (*see* LEGATI) of FLAMININUS in 197, on the senatorial commission to Greece in 196, and on an embassy to ANTIOCHUS III THE GREAT in 193. HS

Gruen (1984); Lazenby (1978); Scullard (1973).

Galen (c.AD 129–204), Greek physician. Galen of Pergamum is the most outstanding figure in medical science of the Greco-Roman period. After an excellent education in grammar, rhetoric, logic, and philosophy, he turned to MEDICINE at the age of 16, studying first at Pergamum, then at Smyrna and Alexandria. After a spell at Pergamum, where he was appointed doctor to the gladiators (AD 157), he left for Rome in 162. After a further period at Pergamum (166–9), he returned to Rome, where he became physician to the emperors, Marcus Aurelius, Commodus, and Severus.

Galen's literary output was prodigious. More than 430 titles have been listed and over 350 are authentic. Galen was committed to the integration of philosophy and medicine. In philosophy he was especially influenced by PLATO and ARISTOTLE and in medicine by the writings of HIPPOCRATES (or what he conceived to be such) and by the anatomical and physiological works of HEROPHILUS and ERASISTRATUS. The resulting tightly integrated and comprehensive system, offering a complete medical philosophy, came to represent the very embodiment of Greek and Roman medical knowledge and it dominated medicine until the Middle Ages and beyond.

See also ANATOMY; BOTANY. JL

Bowersock (1969); DSB V (1972).

Galerius (c.AD 250–311), Roman emperor, AD 305–11. Gaius Galerius Valerius Maximianus, a man of low birth from Serdica, became DIOCLETIAN's deputy (Caesar, 1 March 293). Based at THESSALONICA, he held particular responsibility for the Danubian frontier. He commanded the eastern armies against the Persian king, Narses (297), suffering a defeat at Carrhae that left Mesopotamia in Persian control, but followed up with a great victory in Armenia (298). The abdication of Diocletian (305) left Galerius as eastern Augustus, with his nephew MAXIMINUS DAIA as his Caesar. Technically the senior Augustus after CONSTANTIUS I's death (306), he struggled to maintain the tetrarchic system established by Diocletian, now threatened by the rival claims of CONSTANTINE I, MAXENTIUS, and MAXIMIAN. He intervened unsuccessfully in Italy (307) against the usurper Maxentius, and convened a conference at Carnuntum, chaired by Diocletian, which resulted in the appointment of LICINIUS as Augustus (308). Galerius issued an edict of religious toleration, shortly before his death (311).   RJB

Grant (1985); Parker (1958).

Galla Placidia   *see* PLACIDIA.

Gallia   *see* GAUL.

Gallic empire   *see* POSTUMUS; TETRICUS; VICTORINUS.

Gallic Wars   Between 58 and 51 BC CAESAR embarked upon the conquest and pacification of GAUL. His *De Bello Gallico* describes the course of his campaigns. Using the migration of the HELVETII as an excuse to intervene beyond his proconsular province, he drove out the Germans under ARIOVISTUS and broke up the confederation of BELGAE. In 56 he attacked the VENETI, while Publius Crassus (son of CRASSUS DIVES) conducted a brilliant campaign in Aquitania. So successful was Caesar that he attempted two invasions of BRITAIN, in 55 and 54. By skilfully exploiting the internal rivalries of the Gallic tribes, Caesar conquered them piecemeal. Celtic resentment was always apparent, however, and there were several revolts, the most serious being that of VERCINGETORIX. Caesar's subjection of Gaul combined clemency and severe brutality, and a number of tribes were virtually annihilated.   LPR

Cunliffe (1988); Hubert (1987).

Gallienus   (*c.*AD 218–68), Roman emperor, AD 253–68. Publius Licinius Valerianus Egnatius Gallienus, son of VALERIAN, created Augustus as his father's colleague (253), was sent to the Rhine frontier to prevent barbarian incursions (254), and then left in charge of the west when Valerian departed (256/7) to challenge SHAPUR I. Gallienus made no attempt to rescue his father, captured in 260, being preoccupied with frequent barbarian incursions and a succession of usurpers. He tolerated the existence of a break-away Gallic empire under POSTUMUS (259), and left the defence of the eastern provinces to ODAENATHUS of Palmyra, whom he appointed Roman commander in the east. Nevertheless, Gallienus' organizational changes laid the foundations for future military revival, by greatly increasing the role of cavalry, and through the appointment of equestrian commanders, allowing soldiers of ability to rise through the ranks to senior commands. However, his Hellenic sympathies resulted in his murder by a group of Illyrian generals, and replacement by CLAUDIUS II.

See also AUREOLUS; MACRIANUS; QUIETUS; THIRTY TYRANTS.   RJB

Connolly (1981); de Blois (1976); Grant (1985); Parker (1958).

Gallus (*c*.69–26 BC), Latin poet. Gaius Cornelius Gallus was born at Forum Iulii in southern Gaul but educated at Rome where he became a close friend of VIRGIL. In 30 BC he was appointed prefect of Egypt but power went to his head and he was driven to suicide. He wrote four books of love elegies which were greatly admired by his contemporaries but only a few lines survive.   GS

Ross (1975).

Gallus (AD 325–54), Caesar, AD 351–4. Flavius Claudius Constantius Gallus was the son of Julius Constantius and Galla, and thus a grandson of CONSTANTIUS I 'CHLORUSY'. Because of his youth, he was spared in the massacre of CONSTANTINE I's descendants (337) and lived in exile until recalled by CONSTANTIUS II. Gallus was appointed Caesar in the east (March 351) and married Constantius' sister Constantina, but proved so violent and irresponsible that he was recalled and executed.
          RJB

Grant (1985); Kent (1981).

Gallus, Trebonianus *see* TREBONIANUS GALLUS.

Games, Greek The public games (*agones*) of ancient Greece may have had their origins in the funeral games that were celebrated in honour of local heroes. But by the 8th century BC, when the OLYMPIC GAMES were founded, they had lost any funereal context and assumed a religious character as part of a major international festival. The aim was to do honour to the god or gods by means of the pursuit of human excellence in an intensely competitive situation. The participants were wealthy aristocrats who often devoted years of their lives to training on a paramilitary scale. Their approach was entirely professional and their efforts were the focus not just of personal ambition but of blatant political rivalry between states. Victors were fêted as national heroes, commemorated by artists and poets, and often rewarded with substantial financial or political prizes. The games also had economic significance in bringing together large groups of people who had to be housed, fed, and entertained for the duration of the festival, and they performed an important cultural service as patrons of the arts.

The events at most games were similar and were divided between MUSIC and athletics (except at Olympia where there seems never to have been a musical component). Musical events included singing (to the accompaniment of flute or lyre) and instrumental performance. Athletics involved running races, long jump, throwing the discus and javelin, wrestling, the pentathlon (all five), and boxing. Equestrian events were staged in the HIPPODROME. Athletes performed naked. There were separate events for men and boys. Women were not admitted either as participants or as spectators.

See also FESTIVALS, GREEK; GYMNASIUM; ISTHMIAN GAMES; NEMEAN GAMES; PINDAR; PYTHIAN GAMES; STADIUM. GS

Easterling and Muir (1985); Finley and Pleket (1976); Harris (1964); Poliakoff (1987).

Games, Roman The Roman public games (*ludi*), like their Greek predecessors, owed their origin and purpose to religious festivals and may represent a memory of Etruscan and Campanian funeral games. Unlike their four-yearly Greek models, they were mostly annual displays not of athletics but of military prowess and the chase. The earliest took the form of chariot races in honour of Mars. The *Ludi Romani* (or *Magni*) were held every September in honour of Jupiter and were controlled by magistrates. They began with a procession to the temple on the Capitol and continued with chariot races (*Circenses*) in the CIRCUS Maximus. From 240 BC they also included *ludi scaenici*, a celebration of music and literature which featured the production of drama such as the translations of Greek tragedy by LIVIUS ANDRONICUS. *Ludi scaenici* were later incorporated in a large number of games, but MIME and PANTOMIME gradually replaced TRAGEDY and COMEDY as the favoured genres.

Other major celebrations included the *Ludi Apollinares*, held in July from 208 BC in honour of Apollo under the direction of the *praetor urbanus* and consisting of *ludi scaenici* and games in the Circus. Similar events were staged at the *Ludi Megalenses,* held in April from 191 BC in honour of Cybele, the *Ludi Cereales,* also in April for Ceres, and the *Ludi Florales,* in April–May from 173 BC, a flower festival in honour of the goddess Flora. The HUNTING of wild animals was introduced into the games in the 2nd century BC and GLADIATORS had become popular by the end of the Republic. Under AUGUSTUS several new games were inaugurated: the *Martiales*, in May in honour of Mars; the *Augustales*, in October for the emperor; and the *Natalicii*, for the emperor's BIRTHDAY.

Ludi Saeculares (secular games) were staged at Rome every *saeculum* or (roughly) every 100 years. Perhaps first held in the first consulship of VALERIUS CORVUS (348 BC), these games were celebrated again in 249 and 146 BC but not (though planned) in the 40s. HORACE wrote his *Carmen Saeculare* for the games held by Augustus in 17 BC. Three nights and three days of sacrifices and *ludi scaenici* were followed by seven days of sports in the Circus. Subsequent celebrations occurred in AD 47 (for the 800th anniversary of the foundation of the city) and 248 (for the millennium), also in 88 and 204.

The OLYMPIC GAMES continued to be celebrated every four years without a break until they were finally suppressed in AD 393 by THEODOSIUS I. Meanwhile imitations of them, including athletic and musical competitions, were inaugurated by both NERO and DOMITIAN with the *Agon Neronianus* (60) and *Agon Capitolinus* (86) respectively.

See also GAMES, GREEK; NAUMACHIA; NICOPOLIS.　　　　　　　　　GS

Auguet (1972); Cameron (1976); Poliakoff (1987); Scullard (1981).

Gardens　The pleasure garden, as we know it, was a luxury in the ancient world. For most ordinary people gardening meant the cultivation of fruit and vegetables. Landscape gardening was not unknown in public places such as the Athenian Agora, and the sacred enclosure (*temenos*) of a temple was often cultivated. Royal parks existed in Persia and were imitated in the Hellenistic world and at Rome, e.g. in the DOMUS AUREA. But it was only in the late Roman country house or villa (*see* ARCHITECTURE, ROMAN) that the concept of a formal ornamental garden was developed with paths and peristyles, fountains and porticoes, as described by PLINY THE ELDER and as illustrated on the walls of houses at POMPEII.

See also BOTANY; COLUMELLA; EPICURUS.　　　　　　　　　　　　GS

Cunliffe (1971).

Gaugamela　battle in 331 BC. Gaugamela, near Arbela in Babylonia, was the site of ALEXANDER THE GREAT's third and final set battle against the massed army of the Persian king DARIUS III. The Persians were outmanoeuvred and defeated. Darius escaped to become a fugitive in Hyrcania. After this battle Alexander was hailed by his troops 'king of Asia', and the Persian empire was in effect conquered.　　　　EER

Bosworth (1988a); Hammond (1989); Lane Fox (1973); Marsden (1964).

Gaul Roman province. Gaul, from the 1st century BC to the 5th century AD, encompassed modern France, Belgium, and Luxembourg, as well as much of Switzerland, western Germany, and the Netherlands. Gallia, or Gaul, was initially divided, to Roman eyes, between CISALPINE GAUL (Gaul this side of the Alps) and TRANSALPINE GAUL (Gaul over the Alps). Cisalpine Gaul was settled and romanized, and effectively became part of Roman ITALY. Southern France, also extensively settled and romanized, became the province (*provincia*, hence Provence) of Gallia Narbonensis (121 BC). The rest of Gaul – the 'Three Gauls' of Aquitania, Lugdunensis, and Belgica – was conquered by Julius CAESAR between 58 and 51 BC (*see* GALLIC WARS).

The *pax Romana* brought great prosperity to Gaul, which figures prominently in the historical record, but provided surprisingly few prominent Roman equestrians or senators. Its pottery industries were particularly successful, mass-produced SAMIAN WARE being widely exported to Britain and even competing in the Italian market. Gaul's proximity to the frontier zone of the Rhine, in particular, assured its place in the events of the Empire, recorded by TACITUS, DIO CASSIUS, AMMIANUS MARCELLINUS, and others. The distinctive culture of Gaul, and its geography and history are described by several Greek and Roman authors, among them STRABO, DIODORUS SICULUS, and the elder PLINY.

Barbarian incursions in the 3rd century AD affected the prosperity of the province, although the effects were to some extent ameliorated by the establishment of the independent Gallic empire by POSTUMUS and his successors (258–73). Gaul gradually slipped from Roman control in the 5th century: successive barbarian invasions by, among others, the VANDALS and the GOTHS were partly countered by the extension of federate status to barbarian settlers, who then gradually established independent kingdoms: the VISIGOTHS inherited south-west Gaul, while the BURGUNDIANS controlled the south-east, and the FRANKS took over the north.

RJB

Drinkwater (1983); King (1990); Millar (1981).

Gauls generic term for continental Celtic peoples living in modern France, Belgium, Switzerland, northern Italy, and Austria. We have to rely on Greek and Roman accounts of their society and history since the CELTS had a primarily oral tradition which has not survived. Celtic society was based around kinship, with families forming clans, and clans forming tribes. A chieftain's power and status depended on the number of personal followers he possessed. The tribes were capable of making alliances with each other and with non-Gauls. Many Gauls served as mercenaries throughout the Mediterranean. From archaeology and the sources it is known that the Gauls had highly advanced metallurgical skills. A history of the Gauls is a history of their gradual conquest and integration into the Roman empire.   LPR

Chadwick (1970); Cunliffe (1988); Hubert (1987).

Gela   city on the south coast of SICILY. Founded by colonists from Crete and Rhodes in 688 BC, Gela flourished early and itself founded ACRAGAS. Under the tyrant HIPPOCRATES it reached the height of its power, only to lose it to Syracuse under his successor GELON. It remained a cultural centre for most of the 5th century, visited by AESCHYLUS who died there in 456. But in 405 it was destroyed by the Carthaginians and never fully recovered.   GS

Dunbabin (1948).

Gellius   (late 2nd century BC), Roman annalist. Gnaeus Gellius wrote an annalistic history (which now survives only in fragments) covering events from the foundation of Rome to at least 146 BC. His work was more detailed than that of earlier writers and comprised at least 97 books. He was later used as a source by DIONYSIUS OF HALICARNASSUS.
    See also HISTORIOGRAPHY, ROMAN.   HE

Badian (1966b); Rawson (1991).

Gellius   (c.AD 130–80), Latin writer. Aulus Gellius studied in Rome, where he mixed with leading intellectuals such as FAVORINUS and FRONTO, and in Athens, where he knew HERODES ATTICUS. On his return to Rome he practised law for a while, but little else is known of his life. His *Noctes Atticae* (19 of its 20 books survive) is a philological commonplace book, compiled in old age from notes written earlier. It is a reference work of archaizing erudition and a valuable source of anecdote and quotation from earlier writers.   GS

Holford-Strevens (1988); Kaster (1988).

Gelon   tyrant of Syracuse, 485–478 BC. Gelon served as cavalry commander to HIPPOCRATES, succeeding to the tyranny of Gela by supplanting his sons. In 485 he gained control of Syracuse by supporting the exiled land-owning aristocracy, made the city his capital, and vastly enlarged it, transplanting the population of Camarina and the aristocracy from Megara Hyblaea, together with many citizens of Gela, now ruled by HIERON I. At the height of his power, the Greeks appealed to him for aid against Persia; but Gelon committed himself to neither side, though he won a great victory over the simultaneous Carthaginian expedition at HIMERA in support of his ally THERON.   RB

Burn (1984); CAH IV; Dunbabin (1948).

Gems Engraved stones served a variety of purposes in antiquity: they were worn as ornaments; they were used as personal SEALS in place of signatures; and they were credited with certain magical and medicinal properties. The art was stimulated in the 7th century BC by the introduction of hard stones from the east – notably carnelian, chalcedony, and jasper – and the rediscovery of the cutting wheel which had not been in use in Greece since the Bronze Age. In the 6th century the scarab (beetle) form was introduced from Egypt and achieved popularity throughout the Mediterranean world. In Greece local styles soon emerged and artists of the 5th and 4th centuries, particularly Dexamenos who signed a number of works, attained an unparalleled mastery of the medium. Hellenistic engravers broadened the range of materials with agate, amethyst, beryl, garnet, rock crystal, sard, and sardonyx, and produced fine work in portraiture. They experimented also with new forms and made the first relief cameos, usually with sardonyx, the best of which were to come from imperial Rome. Engraved gems retained their popularity at Rome, their artists commonly reproducing the (since lost) works of their Greek predecessors (including miniature versions of full-size works of art).   GS

Boardman (1970); Richter (1968, 1971).

Genos Greek family or clan. The *genos* (Latin GENS) was the foundation of Greek society. Its members claimed descent from a single ancestor whose worship it was their duty to perform. Land was owned not by individuals but by the *genos*. Political power at Athens until the time of SOLON was largely in the hands of the aristocratic *gene* such as the EUPATRIDAE and some priesthoods were reserved for certain families (*see* PRIESTS, GREEK). One or more *gene* formed a brotherhood (PHRATRY) which in turn made up the tribe (PHYLE), a system that provided the political organization in most Greek states.   GS

Bourriot (1976); Manville (1990).

Gens Roman clan. According to a simple ancient definition, a *gens* comprised all those who had the same NAME (*nomen*: Julius, Cornelius, Sempronius, etc.). The first name (*praenomen*: Gaius, Marcus, Titus, etc.) identified the individual, and the third name (*cognomen*: Caesar, Cicero, Scipio, etc.), if any, specified a particular branch within the *gens*. In theory a *gens* traced its descent back to a single ancestor. Thus the Julii were descended from Iulus (the son of Aeneas), the Caecilii from Caeculus, and the Marcii from Marcus. A parallel is often drawn with Scottish clans such as MacDonald or MacGregor. But in most cases the supposed blood relationship between members of a *gens* was hardly demonstrable, and the *gens* as such was a very shadowy entity in historical times. Some *gentes* were distinguished by their own cults, unusual burial practices, and the use of particular forenames (the Sulpicii used the rare name Servius, the Claudii Appius; on the other hand Marcus was shunned by the Manlii). The TWELVE TABLES stated that if a man died intestate and without direct agnates, his property should be shared among the *gentiles,* but this does not mean that land was once held in communal ownership by the *gens.* This is one of many modern theories that attribute great importance to the *gens* in early times, but the evidence is woefully thin.

See also GENOS. TC

Brunt (1982).

Geography   The Greeks were the first geographers and, considering the limitations of their instruments, their achievements were remarkable. The Ionian philosophers were the first to attempt to relate the earth to the heavens. ARISTOTLE demonstrated the sphericity of the earth, earlier proposed by the Pythagoreans, and also introduced the division of the globe into zones. This, together with ERATOSTHENES' measurement of the earth's circumference and HIPPARCHUS' system of plotting by means of latitude and longitude, greatly enhanced the accuracy of MAPS. The work of PTOLEMY in the 2nd century AD was largely a synthesis of that of his predecessors but represents a summation of ancient knowledge that remained standard until modern times. Some geographical description is contained in the works of HECATAEUS OF MILETUS and HERODOTUS. Alexander's exploits revealed new horizons as is reflected in the writings of the Alexander historians, of AGATHARCHIDES, and of DIODORUS SICULUS. General treatises on the subject were produced by ARTEMIDORUS and STRABO, a school text by Pomponius MELA, and a verse description by DIONYSIUS PERIEGETES. Books 3–6 of the elder PLINY's *Natural History,* though devoted to geography, contain nothing of scientific value.

See also EUDOXUS OF CNIDUS; METEOROLOGY. GS

Aujac (1975); Bunbury (1883), Pédech (1976); Romm (1992); Warmington (1934).

Geometric period   The 'geometric' period of Greek culture extends from the end of the Dark Ages to the start of the ARCHAIC PERIOD, roughly 900–700 BC. It is named after a geometric style of vase PAINTING which first emerged in Athens *c.*900 BC. It was a creative period whose achievements included the invention of the Greek ALPHABET, the composition of the poems of HOMER, the rediscovery of figurative art, the rise of the POLIS or Greek city-state, the beginnings of COLONIZATION in the western Mediterranean, and the emergence of the great panhellenic sanctuaries at OLYMPIA and DELPHI.   GS

Coldstream (1968, 1977).

Geometry   *see* MATHEMATICS.

Germani   a series of tribes, originating in southern Scandinavia and the north German coast, who gradually migrated south-west from *c.*1000 BC, and in greater numbers from the 3rd century BC. The BELGAE, settled in northern and eastern Gaul, subdued by Caesar in 57 BC, are ambiguously referred to as 'Germani'. In common with German tribes, they were an agricultural people, preferring woodland sites for their towns. They worshipped Woden (= Mercury), Dorar/Thor (Hercules), and Ziu/Tiu (Mars) in sacred groves. Other German peoples included the SUEBI, arriving north of the Rhine and Main in the 1st century BC, and other groups from further east also migrated south-west: the BASTARNAE reached the Thracian border *c.*200 BC, pressured from behind by successive waves of Scandinavian tribes – the VANDALS from Jutland, the BURGUNDIANS from Bornholm, the Langobardi from Gotland, the Rugii from southern Norway, and the GOTHS from southern Sweden. *See also* ALAMANNI.   RJB

Thompson (1965); Todd (1972, 1975).

Germania   According to TACITUS, Germania was the land east of the Rhine and north of the Danube. He described its climate as severe and its scenery as grim, consisting mostly of rough forests and foul swamps. Its people he found idle, warlike, and boorish and he particularly criticized their addiction to gambling and beer, but he was aware that they posed a threat to the security of the empire. AUGUSTUS' attempts to annex the region were abandoned after the loss of VARUS' three legions in AD 9, but the Black Forest area was occupied by Vespasian (*see* AGRI DECUMATES), and under Domitian the two provinces of Germania Inferior (north) and Germania Superior (south) were established. But the raids of the local tribes were a constant problem (*see* ALAMANNI) and resulted in the loss of the Agri Decumates *c.*AD 260. The prosperity of the two Germanies was restored by their incorporation into the GALLIC EMPIRE in the late 3rd century.   GS

Thompson (1965).

Germanicus   (15 BC–AD 19), adopted son of TIBERIUS. Germanicus Julius Caesar was the adoptive name of Nero Claudius Germanicus, elder son of the elder DRUSUS and the younger ANTONIA. He was popular, but also vain and headstrong. He owed his rapid advancement to AUGUSTUS'

search for a Julian successor: Germanicus qualified through his mother; and his wife, the elder AGRIPPINA, was grand-daughter of Augustus. Tiberius was obliged to adopt his nephew Germanicus (AD 4), and to grant him seniority over his own son, the younger DRUSUS. Twice consul (12 and 18, the second time as the colleague and designated successor of Tiberius), Germanicus was granted proconsular *imperium* (14), commanding the armies of the Rhine. He quelled a mutiny after Tiberius' accession, and, after several inconclusive campaigns against ARMINIUS in Germany, celebrated a triumph in Rome (17), and was sent east to install a Roman nominee in Armenia. He died in October 19, accusing Gnaeus Calpurnius PISO of poisoning him.   RJB

Salmon (1968); Scullard (1982); Seager (1972b).

Gerousia   Spartan council. The Gerousia ('Council of Elders') consisted of 30 members including the two kings. Candidates had to be aged over 60 and were restricted, at least *de facto,* to certain aristocratic families; election was for life, according to the estimate by hidden judges of the volume of applause for each candidate. The Gerousia prepared business for and presented motions to the APELLA, with a right of subsequent veto; it had a wide judicial competence, and was regularly consulted by the EPHORS. The combination of its powers and prestige gave the Spartan constitution its oligarchic tendency.   RB

Andrewes (1966); De Ste Croix (1972); Forrest (1980); MacDowell (1986).

Geta (AD 189–212), Roman emperor, AD 211–12. Publius (originally Lucius) Septimius Geta, younger son of Septimius SEVERUS and JULIA DOMNA, was created Caesar in 198, and Augustus in 209. He accompanied his father and brother (CARACALLA) on campaign in Britain (208–11), taking charge of the supply lines. Geta and Caracalla inherited the empire jointly (February 211), but Caracalla arranged Geta's murder (February 212), and forbade his memory, ordering the erasure of his name from all inscriptions.   RJB

Grant (1985); Parker (1958); Wells (1984).

Gildo (d. AD 398), Moorish chieftain. Gildo, a Moor, aided the Romans during the rebellion of his brother Firmus in Africa (*c.*373). He was appointed Count of Africa, but revolted after THEODOSIUS I's death (395), proposing to transfer Africa from the western empire to the eastern. He prevented the corn ships from leaving for Italy (397): in reply, STILICHO sent an army under Gildo's brother Mascezel (398). Gildo's army offered no resistance, and he was executed.   RJB

Bury (1958); Hamilton and Wallace-Hadrill (1986).

Gladiators professional entertainers who fought each other to the death (*see* GAMES, ROMAN). Originating in the funeral games of the Etruscans, the first pairs appeared at Rome in 264 BC. Mostly prisoners of war or slaves (a few were volunteers), in the late Republic large numbers of gladiators were privately owned and shows were often paid for by men courting popularity. After Domitian only emperors could give shows at Rome. Three types of gladiator were distinguished: the Samnite, with an oblong shield, short sword, and visored helmet; the Thracian, more lightly armed with a round shield and scimitar; and the scantily clad *retiarius*, with a net, a dagger, and a trident.

GS

Grant (1971a); Wiedemann (1992).

Glass Until the discovery of glass-blowing technology, the production of glass was slow and laborious. The technique of modelling by hand spread from Egypt via Crete, and by the 7th century BC there were centres in Rhodes, Etruria, and the Veneto which specialized in the production of small, multi-coloured glass containers for perfume and ointment. Moulded glass was also used to make seal stones and in architectural decoration and in sculpture (e.g. in the chryselephantine statue of Zeus at OLYMPIA). Introduction of the blowpipe in the mid-1st century BC revolutionized the industry. Glass could now be produced quickly and cheaply, and with its versatility in size and shape it rivalled, and to a large extent superseded, more traditional materials such as POTTERY and metalwork. Within a generation factories had sprung up throughout the Mediterranean world. Blown glass was used for the manufacture of everyday household items and also for windows. Meanwhile glass decoration rapidly developed into one of the most spectacular art forms of the Roman empire.

See also INDUSTRY.

GS

Harden (1987); Henig (1983).

Glycerius (d. AD 474 or later), Roman emperor, AD 473–4. Glycerius, Count of the Domestics, was declared emperor in March 473 at the instigation of Gundobad, who had succeeded his uncle RICIMER as effective ruler of Italy. Glycerius is known to have successfully negotiated the diversion of an Ostrogothic invasion away from Italy towards Gaul. The eastern emperor LEO appointed a rival imperial candidate, Julius NEPOS, who, in June 474, deposed Glycerius. The latter was then ordained bishop of Salona.

RJB

Bury (1958); Grant (1985).

Gnosticism   a system of belief that broke with the Christian Church in the 2nd century AD. Derived from the Greek word *gnosis* ('knowledge'), Gnosticism embraced the Platonic dualism of spirit and matter (and so rejected the physical world as being incompatible with the divine) and the premiss that revelation of the divine was granted only to an élite. Knowledge of Gnostic beliefs, formerly confined to the writings of Christian polemicists such as IRENAEUS and TERTULLIAN, was greatly enhanced by the discovery in 1945 of Coptic texts in Upper Egypt dating from the 4th century. By the 3rd century Gnosticism ceased to pose a threat, though it survived long enough to influence the development of MANICHAEISM.   GS

Filoramo (1990); Martin (1987); Pagels (1979); Rudolph (1983).

Gold   Gold was used for COINAGE, JEWELLERY, and bullion. Limited sources were mined in Greece – in Siphnos, THASOS, Macedonia (PANGAEUS), and Thrace – and some may have been acquired through trade with Colchis and the SCYTHIANS. But gold remained a rarity in Greece until the conquests of Alexander opened up supplies in Persia, India, and Egypt. The Etruscans had access to large quantities of the metal and may have imported Greek expertise to work it. At Rome it was in short supply until the expansion of the empire revealed rich reserves in Spain, Gaul, Dalmatia, Dacia, and Egypt. After several centuries of lavish consumption, supplies began to dwindle again, and from the end of the 3rd century AD ownership was confined to the wealthiest members of imperial society, though gold coinage remained in wide circulation.   GS

Healy (1978); Strong (1966).

Gordian I   (*c.*AD 159–238), Roman emperor, AD 238. Marcus Antonius Gordianus, well born, wealthy, and experienced, and proconsul of Africa under MAXIMINUS THRAX, was declared emperor by a group of disaffected landowners in 238. Gordian's elevation was welcomed by the Senate in Rome, despite his advanced age, and he and his son (GORDIAN II) were recognized as joint emperors. However, Capelianus, governor of Numidia, remained loyal to Maximinus, and moved against Gordian in Carthage, who committed suicide after his son's death in battle, having reigned for 22 days.   RJB

Grant (1985); Parker (1958).

Gordian II   (*c.*AD 192–238), Roman emperor, AD 238. Marcus Antonius Gordianus, son and namesake of GORDIAN I, was recognized by the Senate as joint emperor, with his father, as an acceptable alternative to MAXIMINUS THRAX. However, with no regular troops at his disposal, he was defeated and killed outside Carthage by Capelianus, Maximinus' governor of Numidia. RJB

Grant (1985); Parker (1958).

Gordian III (AD 225–44), Roman emperor, AD 238–44. Marcus Antonius Gordianus, grandson of GORDIAN I through his daughter Maecia Faustina, was proclaimed Caesar (238) to calm opposition to the rule of BALBINUS and PUPIENUS. Created Augustus by the praetorians who murdered Balbinus and Pupienus, Gordian was dominated by his mother and then by his praetorian prefect Timesitheus (241–3). A major campaign against the invading Persians was begun in 242, with considerable success, but Timesitheus died in the winter of 243–4, and his replacement, PHILIP I, encouraged the troops to murder Gordian at Zaitha (February 244). RJB

Grant (1985); Parker (1958).

Gorgias (c.483–375 BC), Greek sophist. Gorgias of Leontini was primarily a teacher of RHETORIC (see Plato, *Gorgias* 449a, who treats him with respect). He came to Athens in 427 BC at the head of an embassy from LEONTINI and greatly impressed the Athenians with his oratory. His *Encomium of Helen*, *Defence of Palamedes*, and the fragment of his *Epitaphios* (Funeral Oration) clearly reveal his antithetical style with its balancing clauses and rhythms. His influence upon Attic prose writing is apparent in Antiphon, Thucydides, and Isocrates.

See also SOPHISTS. JL

Guthrie, vol. 3 (1969); Kennedy (1963).

Gortyn law code The law code of Gortyn in Crete, a codification of existing laws rather than an original code, was inscribed in columns on a circular architectural wall in the first half of the 5th century BC. Some 600 lines survive, concerned mainly with property and the family: topics covered include disputed ownership of slaves, rape and adultery, marriage and children, debts, and INHERITANCE law. The administration of justice is almost entirely in the hands of judges, though procedure is specified, while rights and sanctions vary according to a sharply defined hierarchy of social status; the code is thus also a valuable source for contemporary Cretan society. RB

CAH III.3; Meiggs and Lewis (1988) no. 41; Willets (1967).

Goths from southern Sweden. The Goths migrated gradually southwards: from AD 238 they raided Rome's Danubian provinces, Greece, and Asia Minor, and most of DACIA was abandoned to the Visigoths (*c.*270). The Ostrogoths established themselves between the Dnieper and the Don, until overrun by the HUNS (370), who also drove the Visigoths to invade MOESIA: VALENS was killed (378), but THEODOSIUS I defeated them, and then allowed them to settle. Under ALARIC the Visigoths invaded Italy, and sacked Rome (410). They moved into Gaul, founded the kingdom of Toulouse (419), and expanded into Spain. The Ostrogoths eventually invaded Italy, establishing a kingdom under Theodoric (493).

RJB

Heather (1991); James (1980); Thompson (1965); Todd (1972); Wolfram (1988).

Government   *see* DEMOCRACY; MONARCHY; OLIGARCHY; TYRANNY; *see also* BOULE; ECCLESIA; SENATE.

Gracchus, Tiberius   (d. *c.*154 BC), Roman statesman. Tiberius Sempronius Gracchus was best remembered as the husband of CORNELIA and the father of Tiberius and Gaius GRACCHUS. In 190 BC he was an envoy of SCIPIO ASIAGENUS to the east. One of the aediles in 182, he went on to be praetor, winning a triumph in Spain. Consul in 177, he crushed a revolt in Sardinia, gaining a second triumph. While censor in 169 he clashed with the PUBLICANI and earned a reputation for severity. He was consul a second time in 163 and died before 150.

HS

Bernstein (1978); Earl (1963).

Gracchus, Tiberius   (163–133 BC), Roman reformer, Tiberius Sempronius Gracchus, the son of Tiberius GRACCHUS (the consul of 177 BC) and CORNELIA, as TRIBUNUS PLEBIS in 133 BC embarked on radical measures to solve Rome's demographic problems. Continuous warfare had dislocated from their land many Italian peasants, from whom the legions were recruited. Gracchus proposed that all illegally held AGER PUBLICUS above 500 *iugera* (about 300 acres) should be reclaimed and redistributed to the poor. He took this bill straight to the people (*see* CONCILIA). This ignoring of the Senate (whose members as large landowners had a vested interest) was legal but against custom. Another tribune, M. Octavius, repeatedly vetoed the bill, until Gracchus had the people depose Octavius and elect a replacement, whereupon the bill was passed. A land commission was appointed, initially comprising Gracchus, his father-in-law Appius Claudius Pulcher, and his younger brother Gaius GRACCHUS.

When ATTALUS III PHILOMETOR of Pergamum died naming the Roman people as his heir, Gracchus had the people vote the new revenues to his land commission. This was in contradiction of the custom that the Senate dealt with foreign affairs. Senatorial opposition came to a head when Gracchus stood to be re-elected to the tribunate for 132. A mob of senators caught Gracchus by surprise, and the tribune and many of his followers were killed.

See also OPTIMATES; POPULARES HS

Badian (1972b); Bernstein (1978); Earl (1963); Stockton (1979).

Gracchus, Gaius (154–121 BC), Roman reformer. Gaius Sempronius Gracchus, the younger brother of Tiberius GRACCHUS (the tribune of 133 BC), undertook a series of radical reforms in 123 and 122 BC. He was made a member of his brother's land commission in 133, and continued its work until his death in 121. Elected TRIBUNUS PLEBIS for 123, he secured re-election for 122. After moves to avenge his brother, he proposed a package of reforms which far exceeded those of his brother. Most important of these were the founding of colonies to resettle the poor (*see* COLONIZATION, ROMAN), the provision of state-subsidized grain for citizens in Rome (*see* ANNONA), and the reorganization of the extortion court (*see* RES REPETUNDAE), replacing senatorial judges with men from the EQUESTRIAN ORDER.

In 122 a rival tribune, M. Livius DRUSUS, undermined Gracchus' popular support by proposing further colonies. As a result a proposal to enfranchise the Italians was defeated, and Gracchus failed to win re-election as tribune for 121. When his measures came under attack in 121, Gracchus turned to violence, and the Senate passed the first SENATUS CONSULTUM ultimatum calling on the consuls to save the state. The consul OPIMIUS had Gracchus killed, together with his ally FULVIUS FLACCUS and many of his supporters.

See also OPTIMATES; POPULARES. HS

Sherwin-White (1982); Stockton (1979).

Granicus river battle in 334 BC. The Granicus river, near the Hellespont in the Troad, was the site of ALEXANDER THE GREAT's first battle against the Persians. After crossing the Dardanelles from Thrace into Asia, Alexander encountered an advance Persian force. Although the enemy was drawn up in a favourable position on the far river bank, Alexander defeated it despite having to cross the river with his troops and attack.

EER

Bosworth (1988a); Hammond (1989); Lane Fox (1973).

Gratian (AD 359–83), Roman emperor, AD 367–83. Flavius Gratianus, elder son of VALENTINIAN I, was created Augustus (August 367) and married CONSTANTIUS II's daughter, Constantia (374). He succeeded

Valentinian as emperor in the west (Britain, Spain, and Gaul, November 375) and, in addition, dominated the portion of his younger brother, VALENTINIAN II (Italy, Illyricum, and Africa). An ardent Christian, Gratian incurred much resentment through his suppression of pagan institutions. He was overthrown and killed by Magnus MAXIMUS (383).

See also THEODOSIUS I.   RJB

Grant (1985); Matthews (1990); Salway (1981).

Greece, geography   The Greek landscape is noted for its variety. High, barren mountains (some perhaps more heavily forested in antiquity than they are today) are separated by narrow, fertile plains. The sea makes jagged, deep inroads into a long continental coastline and encircles innumerable islands. Rivers, raging torrents in winter but often dry in summer, cut passages through the highlands and irrigate the lowlands. Not one of them is navigable. The climate is equally varied: winter can be harsh in the mountains, but summer is long and hot, especially in the south. All these factors have influenced the development of human society.

The mountains present barriers to communications and encourage the growth of discrete communities, sometimes grouped into small confederacies, more often fiercely proud of their own independence: hence the emergence of the Greek city-state or POLIS. But only a fifth of the land is cultivable so an expanding population needed either to import food or to seek fresh pastures overseas: hence the principal motive for TRADE and COLONIZATION. Nowhere in Greece is more than about 60 miles from the sea; harbours are plentiful and safe; conditions for sailing, especially in summer, are generally favourable but occasionally treacherous: hence the Greek love (and fear) of the sea. The climate is also conducive to an outdoor life-style. Most business, both public and domestic, social and religious, cultural and commercial, is most naturally transacted in the open air, the consequences of which are most conspicuously manifested in ARCHITECTURE and TOWN PLANNING.

See also entries for separate states and regions.   GS

Cary (1949); Levi (1980).

Greece, history   *To 490 BC:* By the 8th century BC Greece had largely emerged from the Dark Ages which followed the destruction of Mycenaean civilization. New, substantial communities were replacing the scattered defensive post-Mycenaean settlements, and the forms of the POLIS were beginning to appear. Much of the Greek renaissance was due to the firm re-establishment of contacts with the Near East: eastern influences strongly shaped Greek culture, especially through the reintroduction of a written language. The new exploration of the

Mediterranean was led by Euboeans who developed trade routes to Syria in the east and Etruria in the west, but trade rivalries culminated in the LELANTINE WAR. Exploration was followed by the first wave of COLONIZATION, which placed Greek settlements all around the Mediterranean and the Black Sea. States with large territories were able to defer or avoid colonization, while SPARTA met her need for land by annexing MESSENIA.

The 7th century BC saw radical social change. The evolution of HOPLITE warfare extended responsibility for defence of the polis to a wider group than the ruling aristocrats and created an interdependent army. Trade likewise extended the spread of prosperity, leading to increased demand for land to own and increased competition in the display of wealth; this in turn, combined with the perennial uncertainties of subsistence agriculture, meant greater pressure on the poor. The resultant social tensions, and dissatisfaction with existing aristocratic regimes, led both to the publication of written law codes (*see* DRACO, LYCURGUS, ZALEUCUS) and to the emergence of TYRANNY in many states. These changes came earliest to the Peloponnese; the political and social development of ATHENS was more leisurely, while north of the Isthmus of Corinth, the various peoples remained inward-looking and dominated by aristocracies; only BOEOTIA (increasingly dominated by THEBES), THESSALY, and the oracle of DELPHI impinged significantly on affairs outside the region.

Sparta's internal reforms enabled her to escape tyranny. Her initial attempts at expansion were thwarted by Argos under PHEIDON, Messenian insurrection, and Arcadian resistance; but in the 6th century the policies of CHILON and ANAXANDRIDAS brought her control of the Peloponnese and dominance in Greece.

Meanwhile, political developments in the Near East came to affect the Greek world. The Greek cities of Asia Minor had come under the benign control of Lydia, now an ally of Media. CYRUS' conquest of Media and Lydia left these cities subject to Persia, which subsequently extended her control to the island states. Sparta, despite diplomatic ties with Lydia and eastern Greek cities, declined to intervene; but Athens, her energies released by the transition from tyranny to democracy, supported the IONIAN REVOLT, as did Eretria. The inevitable Persian retaliation was, despite the sack of Eretria, temporarily thwarted at MARATHON. Although Sparta played no military part in the events of 490, she had finally taken a clear stand against Persia and, despite the growing maritime power and influence of Athens, Sparta was the natural leader of the Greek coalition in 480.

See also SICILY. RB

Burn (1960, 1984); Bury and Meiggs (1975); Jeffery (1976); Murray (1993).

490–318 BC: The PERSIAN WARS (490–479 BC) were the watershed of Greek history. The defeat of XERXES assured Greece the freedom necessary for the flowering of intellect and culture in the CLASSICAL PERIOD, and the unity it required had to be maintained to keep the Persians at bay. SPARTA lacked the will to lead: ATHENS readily assumed first place. The DELIAN LEAGUE was formed and was gradually transformed into an Athenian empire. Sparta reacted in fear, and the first Peloponnesian War (459–446) ensued. When the Spartans concluded the Thirty Years' Peace, which forced Athens to give up her conquests on the mainland of Greece and carried a vague clause about autonomy, they believed the menace was ended. In truth in 446 Athens was poised for the great increase in power which occurred under PERICLES' leadership. Freed from war against Persia by the Peace of CALLIAS (449), but still keeping her hold over the cities of the empire, Athens crushed the revolt of Samos (440), founded AMPHIPOLIS (437), a city of the greatest strategic and economic importance, brought the Aegean ever more firmly under the control of her NAVY, and maintained a huge surplus of imperial funds as a war reserve. But above all she took over what Sparta had held, viz. the spiritual hegemony of Greece, as THUCYDIDES' Funeral Oration makes clear. Sparta feared even for her power in the Peloponnese. The PELOPONNESIAN WAR was the cataclysmic result. It sharpened the conflict, both economic and ideological, between rich and poor; it ended the Athenian empire; it brought Persia back into Greek affairs; and it left Sparta in bloody control of the Greek world.

The price of Spartan victory had been recognition of the Persian right to rule the Asiatic Greeks. In the 390s Sparta sought to liberate them, while suppressing liberty in Greece. With Athenian support Persia destroyed Spartan naval power at Cnidus (394), and THEBES and Athens opposed Spartan land power in the Corinthian War (395–387); but resurgent Athenian imperialism reunited Sparta and Persia in the King's Peace (387/6) (*see* ANTALCIDAS). This sealed the fate of the Asiatic Greeks for 50 years, broke up the BOEOTIAN CONFEDERACY, and checked Athenian imperialism. Spartan excesses, especially the occupation of the Theban Cadmea (382), moved Thebes to revolt and Athens to found the Second Athenian Confederacy. At LEUCTRA (371) Sparta was heavily defeated, and under the influence of EPAMINONDAS Messenia was liberated (369). Spartan power was thereby irreparably diminished while Thebes took over in much of the Peloponnese as well as in central Greece and Thessaly.

Despite another crushing Spartan defeat at MANTINEA (362), Theban power was debilitated by the Third SACRED WAR (357–346) and Athenian imperialism halted in the Greek SOCIAL WAR (357–355). Since the Satraps' Revolt (*c*.366–359) (*see* MAUSOLUS) had neutralized Persian influence in Greece, the way was open for PHILIP II of Macedon. He

terminated Athenian ambitions in the north, took Thessaly under his control, and, settling the Sacred War (346), had Greece at the mercy of his superb Macedonian ARMY. Bent on eastward expansion, he was obliged by the policy of the Athenian war party (*see* DEMOSTHENES) to return to Greece. The disastrous battle of CHAERONEA (338) ended Greek liberty. Philip established the League of CORINTH to secure his domination and support his attack on Persia. His assassination (336) merely delayed the stupefying expansion of Macedonian power which rendered Greece ever more unimportant. ALEXANDER THE GREAT's death (323) seemed to give Greece a chance, but the uprising of the LAMIAN WAR (323–322) resulted in a Macedonian garrison and an oligarchic constitution for Athens (*see* ANTIPATER). Greece was entirely at the mercy of Macedon.
GLC

Hammond (1959); Hornblower (1983); Sealey (1976).

318–31 BC: The focus of Greek history after ALEXANDER THE GREAT shifted away from the mainland and Aegean islands to the Asian empires founded by the DIADOCHI and their successors. Greece, especially ATHENS, continued to suffer from the threat, or indeed the reality, of Macedonian domination. Athens had lost her independence by the middle of the 3rd century BC, while experiencing severe unrest caused by the power struggles between pro-Macedonian oligarchs and anti-Macedonian democrats. The ACHAEAN LEAGUE intrigued with Macedon to get help in its perennial conflict with Sparta. SPARTA experienced dynastic struggles and attempts at extreme social and economic reforms. During these difficult decades various Hellenistic kings intervened for their own purposes and to block their rivals' designs, invariably proclaiming the 'freedom of the Greeks' and even the refoundation of the League of CORINTH. By the 2nd century BC the enemy was Rome. Roman wars against the Macedonian PHILIP V drew to her attention Philip's Greek allies, with disastrous consequences for them. Philip was finally subdued by FLAMININUS at CYNOSCEPHALAE in 197, and his son PERSEUS by Aemilius PAULLUS at PYDNA in 168. Macedonia thereupon became a Roman province. Roman attempts at limiting the power of the ACHAEAN LEAGUE culminated in the sack of CORINTH by MUMMIUS in 146, and Achaea was joined to the province of Macedonia.
EER

CAH VII.1, VIII; Ferguson (1911); Green (1990); Gruen (1984); Mossé (1973).

31 BC–AD 476: Greece was initially administered by Rome as a single province, MACEDONIA. In 27 BC the Peloponnese and southern and central Greece were organized as the senatorial province of ACHAEA (capital Corinth), although between AD 15 and 44 the provinces were temporarily reunited. In *c.*140 Epirus became a separate province, and

Thessaly was transferred from Achaea to Macedonia. From the time of Diocletian, Macedonia and Achaea fell into the diocese of MOESIA, part of the eastern half of the empire.

Greece enjoyed a privileged status because of Roman reverence for Greek culture, and Achaea in particular benefited from the favour of individual emperors: NERO toured Greece, and proclaimed its liberation (27 November AD 67), a move that extended the immunity from taxation (IMMUNITAS) already enjoyed by free cities such as Athens and Sparta to the whole of Achaea. The privilege was rapidly withdrawn by VESPASIAN. A Panachaean League, established by Augustus, was led by a 'Helladarch' and administered the imperial cult. HADRIAN created a wider Panhellenic League (Panhellenion) to which all the towns of Achaea sent representatives. Under Hadrian, who made Athens his headquarters between September 124 and April 125, an extensive programme of public works and building was carried out. A number of Greek cities flourished under the Empire, as did a number of wealthy land-owners. However, Greece was not immune from barbarian raids: in 170 Germanic tribes invaded Greece, reaching almost as far as Athens, and plundered Eleusis. From AD 238 onwards the GOTHS, in particular, made frequent incursions, and constituted a permanent threat. RJB

Grant (1979); Millar (1981); Mommsen (1968).

Greek language The origins of the Greek language lie beyond the chronological confines of this dictionary. Throughout antiquity language provided the Greek people with their principal unifying bond. The essential criterion for eligibility in the OLYMPIC GAMES was to be Greek-speaking: anyone who was not was a barbarian. The Greek world was defined by the spread of the Greek language, and by the 5th century BC there were few stretches of the Mediterranean and Black Sea coasts that were not included. Language also contributed to the sovereignty of each city-state (POLIS) since each developed and used its own dialect. These DIALECTS were mutually intelligible, but when treaties were drawn up between states using more than one dialect, copies were made in the language of each.

The political and commercial supremacy of Athens in the 5th century BC led to the widespread adoption of the Attic dialect throughout the Aegean area; the more enduring cultural and educational prestige of Athens extended it further afield and gave it a lasting primacy. With the rise of Macedon the nature of Hellenism changed: political and linguistic unity went hand in hand; as the city-states lost their sovereignty, so their dialects gradually died out. A new common dialect or *koine* took their place which, after the conquests of Alexander, became the common educated language for the entire Hellenistic world.

It was adopted as the language of Christianity and the language of the Byzantine empire. It is the language of the Greek world to this day and has exercised a major influence over all modern European languages.

GS

Allen (1987); Browning (1983); Buck (1955); Palmer (1980).

Gregory of Nazianzus, St (c.AD 329–90), bishop of Constantinople. Gregory was the son of a bishop of Nazianzus and the contemporary and friend of St BASIL THE GREAT. Like Basil, he became a monk, and later a priest. Summoned to Constantinople in 379, he assisted THEODOSIUS I in the suppression of ARIANISM and gained a reputation as a preacher. Appointed bishop of Constantinople in 380, he presided at the council of 381, but resigned the same year and returned home to write.

GS

Ruether (1969).

Gregory of Nyssa, St (c.AD 335–95), bishop of Nyssa. A younger brother of St BASIL THE GREAT, Gregory followed his brother into monastic life and was made bishop of Nyssa in 371. A famous preacher and an astute theologian, he assisted in the suppression of ARIANISM and after his brother's death (379) produced major works of exegesis, doctrine, and ascetics, many of which survive.

GS

Kazhdan (1991).

Gromatici Roman surveyors. The Roman system of CENTURIATION relied on an effective means of measuring areas of land and taking bearings on a square grid. The work was carried out by professional surveyors (*gromatici*) using a surveying instrument (*groma*) which enabled them to mark out lines at right angles from a central point. In addition to centuriation they were used to plan colonies, divide AGER PUBLICUS, measure estates, and assess land tax. Textbooks on the subject were written by FRONTINUS, HYGINUS, and others, extracts of which are preserved in the 6th-century *Corpus Agrimensorum Romanorum*.

GS

Dilke (1962).

Guilds In the Greek world guilds primarily served a religious function, though there was generally a social element too and political clubs existed in 5th-century BC Athens. Actors and musicians at the Dionysiac festivals formed their own societies, as did merchants, and others who followed the same craft, TRADE, or INDUSTRY. At Rome too all associations had a religious basis and the *collegia* were no exception. They were first and foremost the four colleges to which Roman PRIESTS belonged. Other *collegia* were more secular in their purpose, but each had a patron deity and meetings generally followed a ritual pattern. Tradesmen and craftsmen often formed their own guilds, primarily for social rather than economic reasons and to guarantee a decent burial for their dead. There were also *collegia* of military veterans and of young men (IUVENES) who practised sports together. Traditionally the first were founded by NUMA POMPILIUS and their centre of operations was on the Aventine. There seems to have been complete freedom of association until the 1st century BC when some became involved in political activities and had to be suppressed. A *lex Julia* of AUGUSTUS required that every guild should have senatorial or imperial sanction which was not generally unreasonably withheld.

GS

Gyges king of Lydia, *c*.675–650 BC. Gyges, the first of the Mermnad dynasty which ended with CROESUS, came to power by deposing the Heraclid Candaules, possibly aided by mercenaries. Initially allied with Assyria, he expanded Lydian power, attacking Greek cities in Ionia, but; he made lavish dedications at Delphi, supported Psammetichus I in Egypt against Assyria and died fighting the CIMMERIANS.   RB

Burn (1960).

Gylippus (late 5th century BC), Spartan general. Gylippus was sent in 415 BC to organize the defence of SYRACUSE. His energy and resolve succeeded in saving the city but he was unable to prevent the execution of NICIAS and DEMOSTHENES. After 413 he is not heard of until he was detected acquiring silver, forbidden in Sparta, and was probably executed.   GLC

Kagan (1987).

Gymnasium public sports ground open to all citizens. The principal element was a large open space for a running track, sometimes lined with one or more stoas. Usually associated with it was a *palaestra* or wrestling school. Other buildings might include BATHS, changing rooms, and various exercise rooms. At Athens gymnasia were supervised by a board of 10 superintendents. Elsewhere an honorary magistrate (gymnasiarch) hired professional trainers.

See also EDUCATION; GAMES, GREEK.   GS

H

—◆◆—

Hadrian (AD 76–138), Roman emperor, AD 117–38. Publius Aelius Hadrianus, from a family settled in Baetica (Spain), was TRAJAN's nearest male relative and ward. He served in Spain (90), Pannonia (95), Moesia (96), Germany (97); with Trajan in Dacia and the east; as governor of Lower Pannonia; and as governor of Syria (117). In 100 he married Trajan's nearest female relative, Vibia SABINA. Trajan's widow PLOTINA alleged that Trajan, on his death-bed, had adopted Hadrian, and the army acclaimed Hadrian as emperor. He abandoned Trajan's territorial gains from Parthia (while retaining ARABIA), and elsewhere introduced a fixed-frontier policy. This policy probably precipitated an alleged plot by four ex-consuls: before Hadrian reached Rome (July 118), the senators (including PALMA FRONTONIANUS) had been executed by the Senate, but Hadrian gained a lasting reputation for cruelty.

Hadrian travelled extensively, supervising the setting up of frontier defences, in particular the WALL OF HADRIAN in Britain, and the German and Raetian LIMES. Hadrian's largely peaceful reign was marred by a Jewish revolt (132–5), precipitated by his decision to rebuild JERUSUALEM as a colony. His peace policy, and financial reforms to ensure efficient collection of taxes, allowed an innovative and extensive building programme, particularly in Greece (which he visited in 124/5, 128, and 131). It included substantial rebuilding in Ostia and, in Rome, an enormous temple honouring Trajan and Plotina, a temple of Neptune (the Hadrianeum), a mausoleum (Castel Sant' Angelo), and the PANTHEON. His administrative reforms included codification of the LAW, and regularizing of the BUREAUCRACY. Increasingly ill from 135, and childless, Hadrian perhaps planned to adopt his nearest male relative, Cn. Pedanius Fuscus Salinator, grandson of SERVIANUS, but suddenly

executed both men, presumably suspecting a plot. He adopted Aelius
Verus (136), but Verus died (1 January 138), and Hadrian then adopted
a relative of Plotina, ANTONINUS PIUS, and obliged Antoninus to adopt
Marcus AURELIUS and Lucius VERUS.   RJB

Birley (1977); Grant (1985); Perowne (1960); Salmon (1968); Wells (1984).

Hadrian's Wall   *see* WALL OF HADRIAN.

Halicarnassus   modern Bodrum, Greek city in CARIA, home of
HERODOTUS. Traditionally founded *c.*900 BC from Troezen, by the 5th
century it was entirely Ionian with a strong Carian element. Its queen,
ARTEMISIA I, supported the Persians in 480 but it later became an Athenian naval base. In the 4th century MAUSOLUS made it the capital of his
satrapy and rebuilt the city on a grand scale (*see* MAUSOLEUM). But it
resisted ALEXANDER THE GREAT and was sacked.   GS

Bean (1980).

Hamilcar Barca   (d. 229 BC), Carthaginian general. Hamilcar Barca
had, as a young man, led a Carthaginian force in Sicily during the First
PUNIC WAR. In 241 BC he negotiated terms for peace with the Romans.
When Carthage's mercenaries revolted, Hamilcar conducted the
'Truceless War' (240–237). From 237 to his death in 229 he embarked upon the conquest of southern Spain. It appears that he was
attempting to build for Carthage an empire to counter that of Rome
in Italy. He took with him his three sons, HANNIBAL, HASDRUBAL, and
Mago, and reputedly made them swear never to be a friend of Rome.
                                                                    LPR

Warmington (1969a).

Hannibal   (*c.*246–182 BC), Carthaginian general. Hannibal Barca spent
his youth with his father, HAMILCAR BARCA, on campaign in Spain. In
222 BC, before his 25th birthday, he became commander-in-chief of
all Carthage's armies. After three years' success in Spain, he besieged
SAGUNTUM, precipitating the Second PUNIC WAR. He marched into Italy
with 40,000 men and 37 ELEPHANTS, crossing the Alps in winter in an
effort to forestall a Roman invasion of Africa. It appears his strategy
was to defeat Rome's armies and detach her allies, thus forcing her to
come to terms. However, despite Carthaginian victories at TICINUS,
TREBBIA, Lake TRASIMENE, and CANNAE, and the defection of some of
Rome's allies, notably CAPUA, the Romans would not capitulate.
Hannibal had to replace most of his losses with Gauls, a fact which
the Romans exploited by harping on the Italian fear of Celtic invasion.

Being dogged by the policy of FABIUS MAXIMUS VERRUCOSUS and constantly suffering manpower shortages, Hannibal's control was confined to southern Italy. After 16 years of maintaining himself unbeaten on Italian soil, with a mercenary army bound together purely by his leadership and charisma, he was recalled to fight SCIPIO AFRICANUS at ZAMA in 202. After his defeat and the end of the war, he devoted his attention to reforming the government of Carthage. In 196 he was elected suffete but made himself unpopular with the aristocracy. He fled into exile in 195, joining the Seleucid king ANTIOCHUS III THE GREAT. After the battle of MAGNESIA (190) he went to Bithynia where, in 182, to avoid Roman capture, he took poison. LPR

Lazenby (1978); Warmington (1969a).

Hannibalian *see* CONSTANTINE I.

Harbours The improvement of natural harbours and the subsequent creation of artificial ones were stimulated by the growth of trade that resulted from Greek COLONIZATION of the Mediterranean. Their fortification was initiated for purposes of defence by the tyrants of the late 6th century BC. By the 5th century the needs of commerce and defence could only be met by enclosing at least one harbour within the city walls. Towers, the forbears of LIGHTHOUSES, were built at the ends of moles so that the channel between them could be closed by chains. The complex of buildings generally included storehouses, ship sheds, and a market. The most elaborate example in the Greek world was at PIRAEUS. Hellenistic ports such as ALEXANDRIA relied much less on natural advantages. Commercial and military harbours were distinguished where nature allowed (e.g. Rhodes, Thasos), and only in imperial Roman times did architects gain complete mastery over nature. Successive emperors greatly improved the facilities at OSTIA. GS

Garland (1987); Meiggs (1960).

Harmodius and Aristogeiton Athenian tyrannicides. Harmodius and Aristogeiton, members of the aristocratic Gephyraei clan, assassinated Hipparchus (*see* HIPPIAS) in 514 BC; the sources stress various personal motives, while also suggesting a wider conspiracy against the tyranny. Harmodius was killed immediately; Aristogeiton died under torture. Although the tyranny survived for another four years, they were celebrated in song as liberators, and honoured by the later democracy with statues (*see* ANTENOR) and cult, and hereditary privileges for their descendants. RB

Fornara (1968, 1970); Taylor (1981).

Harpalus (c.355–323 BC), paymaster to ALEXANDER THE GREAT. Harpalus accompanied Alexander the Great's expedition as paymaster. Despite Harpalus' flight back to Greece in 333 BC, Alexander assigned him to the empire's treasury at Babylon in 331. He remained there during the Indian campaign, living so outrageously and extravagantly that at Alexander's return in 324 he fled (with troops and money) to seek refuge at Athens. He probably bribed Athenian politicians, including DEMOSTHENES, but escaped to Crete and was murdered.   EER

Badian (1961); Bosworth (1988a); Mossé (1973).

Harpocration, Valerius (2nd century AD), Alexandrian lexicographer. Harpocration was the author of a lost *Collection of Florid Expressions* and the extant *Lexicon of the Ten Orators*. This work is intended to aid the reader rather than the orator, but it does contain valuable evidence of the organization of the Athenian judiciary as well as extracts from the whole of Greek literature. His notes on architecture, religion, and society are also useful.   GS

Haruspices Etruscan priests who specialized in DIVINATION. They were regularly summoned from Etruria by the Romans to interpret omens and portents. They formed a highly respected priesthood in Etruria and also became important at Rome. Their main function was to predict the outcome of an action by examining the vital organs of sacrificial animals. They also gave advice on prodigies such as deformed births or phenomena like thunderbolts or earthquakes.   DP

Dumézil (1970); MacBain (1982).

Hasdrubal (d. 222 BC), Carthaginian general. Hasdrubal was appointed leader of the Carthaginian forces in Spain after the death of his father-in-law HAMILCAR BARCA in 229 BC. He was a skilful diplomat, and was recognized as overlord by many Spanish tribes. He founded New Carthage (Cartagena). In 226 the Romans obtained an undertaking from Hasdrubal that he would not cross the river Ebro in arms. In 222 he was assassinated by a disaffected Celtiberian.   LPR

Warmington (1969a).

Hasdrubal Barca (d. 207 BC), Carthaginian general. Hasdrubal Barca spent his childhood with his father, HAMILCAR BARCA, and brother, HANNIBAL, on campaign in Spain. In 219 BC he was left in command of Spain when Hannibal crossed the Pyrenees. In 215 he was defeated by Gnaeus and Publius Cornelius SCIPIO at Dertosa (Tortosa), which caused reinforcements intended for Hannibal to be diverted to Spain. Hasdrubal commanded one of the three Carthaginian armies which, in 211, defeated and killed the Scipios. In 208 he began a march to Italy to reinforce Hannibal. However, he was defeated by the consuls SALINATOR and Nero at the river METAURUS in 207 and his head was thrown into Hannibal's camp. LPR

Lazenby (1978).

Hecataeus of Abdera (4th–3rd century BC), Greek historian. Hecataeus received a philosophical training under the Sceptic PYRRHON of Elis but moved to Alexandria in the time of Ptolemy I. He wrote critical and grammatical works but is best known for his book *On the Egyptians*, substantial passages of which are preserved by DIODORUS SICULUS. He was concerned to promote Egypt as the source of Greek culture. GS

Fraser (1972).

Hecataeus of Miletus (6th–5th century BC), Greek geographer. Hecataeus was a member of the assembly at Miletus and argued in vain against the IONIAN REVOLT planned by Aristagoras in 498 BC. A pupil of the philosopher ANAXIMANDER, he travelled widely in the Mediterranean and Black Sea regions and wrote a description of his journeys. This *Periegesis* he illustrated with a MAP of the world on which HERODOTUS (4.36) poured scorn.

See also HISTORIOGRAPHY, GREEK. GS

Pearson (1939).

Hegesippus (mid-4th century BC), Athenian politician. Hegesippus, with DEMOSTHENES and others, sought to renew war with PHILIP II of Macedon after the Peace of PHILOCRATES (346 BC). In 344 he opposed further dealing with Philip who abruptly rebuffed him when sent on an embassy for the restoration of AMPHIPOLIS. In 342 he delivered a speech virtually recommending a breach with Philip. GLC

Cawkwell (1978); Hammond and Griffith (1979).

Helena, St (c.AD 255–330), mother of the emperor CONSTANTINE I. Of humble origins, Helena became the mistress and perhaps wife of CONSTANTIUS I to whom she bore Constantine c.273. Rejected by Constantius after his marriage to Theodora, step-daughter of MAXIMIAN, she returned to court only after her son's accession in 306. She and her daughter-in-law Fausta exerted considerable influence and both received the title Augusta c.325. An enthusiastic Christian, Helena visited the Holy Land in 326 where she founded churches in Jerusalem and Bethlehem and allegedly discovered the True Cross. She died in Rome where a mausoleum was built for her.　　　　　　　　　　　GS

Hunt (1982); Kazhdan (1991).

Heliaea　Athenian court of appeal. The Heliaea was instituted by SOLON as a court representing the people to which litigants might appeal against the verdict of an archon. Its form is controversial, but it was perhaps initially a judicial assembly, divided into jury courts (*see* DICASTERY) as appeals increased in frequency and eventually became the norm (*see* LAW, ATHENIAN). In the classical period the Heliaea was the largest court building, presided over by the Thesmothetai; but the term could be used for any court, or the courts in general (and likewise *heliastes* for juror).　　　　　　　　　　　　　　　RB

Hansen (1989); MacDowell (1978).

Heliodorus　(3rd or 4th century AD), Greek novelist. Heliodorus of Emesa in Syria was the author of the prose romance *Aethiopica*, the longest and, according to many, the best of the surviving Greek novels (*see* NOVEL, GREEK). Plot and narrative technique are well developed, though the work is shot through with religious piety. Some sources say Heliodorus became a Christian bishop: this is unlikely but the story may have helped the text to survive.　　　　　　　　　　　GS

Bartsch (1989); Hägg (1971, 1983); Reardon (1989); Sandy (1982); Winkler and Williams (1982).

Heliogabalus　*see* ELAGABALUS.

Hellanicus　(5th century BC), of Mytilene, Greek antiquarian. Hellanicus was a prolific writer whose work survives only in fragments. Subjects he covered included the manners and customs, history and mythology, of the cities, peoples, and regions of Greece and elsewhere. His ATTHIS was the first in a line of Athenian local histories, based on lists of kings and archons. His poor chronology drew the criticism of Thucydides (1.97).

See also HISTORIOGRAPHY, GREEK.　　　　　　　　　　　GS

Jacoby (1949); Pearson (1939).

Hellenistic period　The 'Hellenistic' period of Greek culture extends from the death of ALEXANDER THE GREAT to the end of the Ptolemaic dynasty when Roman domination of the Mediterranean world was complete, that is from 323 to 31 BC. Greece itself was no longer the heart of cultural activity and new centres of influence emerged in the newly extended Greek (or rather Hellenistic, i.e. Greek-speaking) world – at PERGAMUM in Asia, at ANTIOCH in Syria, and at ALEXANDRIA in Egypt.

For architects and town planners there was suddenly enormous scope to respond to the pride of the new rulers with the creation of cities resplendent with impressive public buildings and magnificent palaces that would in turn operate as centres of royal patronage for artists from all over the Greek world. SCULPTURE, both in relief and in the round, survives in sufficient quantity for us to observe the development of a new dramatic, almost melodramatic, realism of emotion and expression. Later in the period a new classicism drove sculptors back to the copying of earlier works. Small-scale works in clay and bronze exhibit the same trends as major sculpture. Vase PAINTING declined as an art after the end of the 4th century but wall painting and MOSAIC developed new techniques, for evidence of which we depend more on Roman copies than on surviving originals.

In the academic world innovative trends in SCHOLARSHIP informed the poetry of the Alexandrians. Philosophical inquiry followed new directions with EPICURUS and the STOICS, and notable advances were made in the fields of ASTRONOMY, MATHEMATICS, and GEOGRAPHY.   GS

Fraser (1972); Pfeiffer (1968); Pollitt (1986); Walbank (1981); Webster (1964).

Hellenotamiai   *see* FINANCE, GREEK.

Helots   *see* SERFS.

Helvetii   Gallic people. The Helvetii occupied Switzerland but, under pressure from Germanic tribes, they undertook a mass migration. In 58 BC, numbering 390,000, they headed west into the lands of the Sequani and AEDUI. This movement gave CAESAR the pretext to enter Gaul, as it posed a potential threat to the province of Transalpine Gaul. At Langres Caesar massacred 300,000 men, women, and children and forced the survivors to return home.   LPR

Chadwick (1970).

Helvidius Priscus   (d. *c.*AD 75), Roman fanatic. Helvidius Priscus was a Stoic philosopher of Republican leanings. He was banished by NERO in AD 66 during a purge of the STOICS, and was openly obstructive and discourteous to VESPASIAN. His publication of a provocative pamphlet entitled *In Praise of Cato* led to his banishment and condemnation, although Vespasian belatedly tried to cancel the order of execution. Herennius Senecio, the eulogist of Priscus, was himself executed by Domitian (*c.*93).   RJB

Salmon (1968).

Hephaestion (*c*.356–324 BC), Macedonian general. Hephaestion was a boyhood friend of ALEXANDER THE GREAT who accompanied the expedition as a senior military officer. He was appointed joint commander of the Companion Cavalry in 330 BC, and chiliarch (vizier) in 324. Although he was not universally popular with the Macedonians, his sudden death from fever caused Alexander excessive grief. An extravagant tomb was erected for him in Babylon, and he was given heroic honours.   EER

Bosworth (1988a); Hammond (1989); Lane Fox (1973).

Hephaestion of Alexandria (2nd century AD), Greek scholar. Hephaestion was the author of a treatise on metre in 48 books of which an abridgement survives. His work contributes to an understanding of the colometry of ARISTOPHANES and also preserves quotations from otherwise lost poets. He may have been the tutor of the emperor VERUS.   GS

Hephaestus Greek god. Hephaestus was the god of fire and of the smith's craft. But his cult was of Asian origin and seems first to have been associated with volcanic fire. In mythology he was lame, deformed, and an outcast among the Olympians. He was also an inventor and was for ever labouring to produce some new magic device. Thrown from Olympus by his mother HERA, he ensnared her in chains which only he could unpick. His recall was a favourite subject in vase painting. Only at Athens was he accorded his own temple, the so-called THESEUM. The Romans identified him with Vulcan.   GS

Grimal (1986); Guthrie (1950).

Hera Greek goddess. The cult of Hera, queen of the gods, daughter of Kronos and Rhea, was of great antiquity. Her marriage to ZEUS was commemorated at festivals throughout Greece when her statue was adorned as a bride and carried in procession. Her particular concern was to protect women, especially wives and mothers. She was worshipped at some of the most ancient temples in Greece, notably at Argos, Samos, and OLYMPIA. In art she is often depicted as a queen with sceptre and diadem. The Romans commonly identified her with JUNO.   GS

Grimal (1986); Guthrie (1950).

Heraclides Ponticus (4th century BC), Greek philosopher and astronomer. Born into an aristocratic family at Heraclea on the Black Sea, Heraclides joined the ACADEMY as a pupil of SPEUSIPPUS. After being narrowly defeated by XENOCRATES for the headship after Speusippus' death in 338 BC, he returned to Heraclea. Only fragments of his writings – mainly dialogues – have survived, but they reveal wide interests in ethics, politics, history, literature, physics, and astronomy. In physics he put forward a corpuscular theory to account for change, and in astronomy he is credited with belief in the axial rotation of the earth. The claim, however, that he maintained that Mercury and Venus revolved round the sun, while the sun itself moved around the earth, and that he was thus a precursor of Tycho Brahe, is spurious.   JL

DSB XV supp. 1 (1978).

Heraclitus (fl. *c.*500 BC), Greek philosopher. Although Heraclitus of Ephesus is traditionally held to have written a book, surviving fragments do not give the impression of extracts from a continuous written work but rather of a series of carefully formulated opinions or *gnomai* written in a deliberately terse, riddling, oracular style which aimed 'neither to say nor to conceal but to indicate the truth'. For this reason he was called 'the obscure one' (*skoteinos*). Heraclitus rejected the view of his predecessors that there is a single permanent imperishable entity behind the changes apparent in the phenomenal world and held that all things are in a state of balanced measured change. Following ANAXIMANDER, he conceived the world to be a ceaseless conflict of opposites regulated by an unchanging law designated as the *Logos*, which he considered to be coextensive with his primary cosmic constituent, fire. The world consisted broadly of three cosmic masses – earth, sea, and fire – which simultaneously changed into one another in such a way that their relative proportions (*Logos*) always remained the same. Fire, which was closely related to the *Logos*, was held to be the archetypal form of matter and possessed a directive capacity. Thus the world order was described by him as an 'ever-living fire being extinguished in measures and quenched in measures' (fr. 90). The soul, too, was made of fire and took part in the cycle of natural change. The dry soul was regarded as the wisest and best, and waking and sleeping and death were linked with the degree of fieriness in the soul. Human behaviour, too, was governed by the same *Logos*. Understanding of the *Logos*, of the underlying constitution of things, was necessary if our souls were not to become moistened and rendered ineffective by private folly.   JL

Kirk, Raven, and Schofield (1983).

Herbals *see* BOTANY.

Herculaneum   modern Ercolano, city on the bay of Naples to the west of VESUVIUS. An Etruscan foundation like its neighbour POMPEII, Herculaneum was occupied by Oscans and Samnites before coming under Roman control in the late 4th century BC. On the rebel side in the SOCIAL WAR, it became a *municipium* in 89 BC. Together with Pompeii it was destroyed in the eruption of Vesuvius in AD 79. Buried by tufa to a depth of 50 feet, buildings were badly damaged, furnishings much less so. The town was small but wealthy and built on a square grid plan. Grand public buildings and luxurious private villas have come to light. Remains of houses, shops, and apartment blocks provide detailed evidence of everyday life. One rural villa, the property of L. Calpurnius PISO CAESONINUS, has yielded a collection of sculpture and a library of papyrus rolls containing the works of the philosopher PHILODEMUS.   GS

Stillwell (1976).

Hermae   stone shafts or pillars surmounted by a bearded head, originally of the god Hermes, and with a phallus below. They were set up inside cities at street corners and between cities as milestones. Just before the departure of the Sicilian expedition in 415 BC (*see* PELOPONNE-SIAN WAR) the Hermae in Athens were mutilated, allegedly by ALCIBIADES, an act of sacrilege that caused confusion throughout the city.   GS

Hermes   Greek god. Originally a roadside demon, Hermes from earliest times haunted stone cairns and pillars (HERMAE). Thus he became the god of travellers, of merchants, and of shepherds. He was also associated with oratory; and having invented the lyre, he naturally became a patron of literature in general. Unusually he was connected with not only the upper world but also the lower where he guided souls with a magic wand. As messenger of the gods he was often depicted in art wearing sandals and a safari hat. His later representation, e.g. by PRAXITELES, as the ideal of male beauty demonstrates his transition to the god of athletic youth. He was identified by the Romans with MERCURIUS.   GS

Grimal (1986); Guthrie (1950).

Hermes Trismegistus   *see* HERMETICA.

Hermesianax   (3rd century BC), of Colophon, Greek lyric poet. Hermesianax was a pupil of PHILETAS and the author of *Leontion*, an elegiac poem in three books addressed to his mistress. One fragment, preserved by ATHENAEUS, comprises a bizarre catalogue of the love affairs of poets and philosophers from Orpheus to Philetas. Other fragments are less banal, but none displays any personal emotion.   GS

Webster (1964).

Hermetica   a collection of philosophical and religious texts in Greek, Latin, and Coptic attributed to the Egyptian god Thoth, later known as Hermes Trismegistus (both Hermes and Thoth were messengers of the gods). Dating from the 1st to the 3rd century AD, they demonstrate the extent to which Greco-Egyptian religion represented a fusion of the writings of Gnostics, Manichees, Platonists, Pythagoreans, Orphics, Isiacs, Mithraists, Magi, Chaldaeans, Jews, and Christians.   GS

Fowden (1986).

Hermias   (d. 341 BC), tyrant of Atarneus. THEOPOMPUS abused Hermias as a barbarian slave become tyrant by murdering his master; but he was accepted as Greek at the Olympic Games and for CALLISTHENES he was the philosopher-hero. A disciple of PLATO, he assembled at his court philosophers, notably ARISTOTLE, and played the philosopher-king. Private dealings assured PHILIP II of Macedon a bridgehead into Asia but led to Hermias' torture and death.   GLC

Cawkwell (1978); Hammond and Griffith (1979); Wormell (1935).

Hermippus   (5th century BC), Greek comic poet. Hermippus was the author of some 40 comedies, which he wrote between 435 and 415 BC, and was one of the rivals of ARISTOPHANES. Surviving fragments indicate a fondness for mythological burlesque as well as the usual political satire on figures such as CLEON, HYPERBOLUS, and ASPASIA. He also wrote some lyrics.   GS

Hermocrates   (fl. c.427–407 BC), Syracusan statesman. Hermocrates played a leading role in Syracusan resistance to Athenian intervention in Sicily. After the Athenian defeat, he commanded a Syracusan squadron against Athens in the Aegean, but was deposed and exiled in his absence by his enemies. In 408/7 he returned to Sicily and attempted to obtain his recall to Syracuse but died trying to seize the city by force.   RB

Freeman (1891–4); Westlake (1969).

Hermogenes   (2nd century BC), Greek architect. Hermogenes was an Ionian, perhaps from Priene, who had a strong preference for the Ionic as against the Doric order for temple architecture. He designed the temple of Dionysus on Teos and that of Artemis Leucophryene at

Magnesia. These buildings, and Hermogenes' writings about them, exercised considerable influence over Roman architecture of the Augustan period in general and VITRUVIUS' principles in particular.   GS

Lawrence (1984).

Hermogenes of Tarsus (c.AD 160–c.225), Greek rhetorician. In his youth Hermogenes achieved some distinction as an orator and was admired by Marcus AURELIUS. Later he turned to the theory of RHETORIC. Surviving works include two volumes on the *Doctrine of Style*, based on classical models (especially DEMOSTHENES), and a restatement of Hermagoras' rhetorical theories in the treatise *On Issues*. His works were standard textbooks in Byzantium.   GS

Hernici Italian people. The Hernici were an Italic people, possibly related to the SABINES, who occupied the strategically important valley of the Trerus (Sacco) in central Italy, between the AEQUI and the VOLSCI. Their main centres were Anagnia, Verulae, Ferentinum, and Aletrium, and they were organized in a federation. The Romans made a treaty with them in 486 BC similar to that with the LATIN LEAGUE. Anagnia revolted from Rome in 306 but was rapidly defeated, and incorporated with 'citizenship without vote' (*see* MUNICIPIUM).   TC

CAH VII.2.

Hero cult The hero in Greek religion occupied a status somewhere between that of gods and men. Heroes may be defined as the subjects of epic, especially Homeric, poetry – above all, those who died in the battles for Troy and Thebes. Their number, however, was not finite and additions continued to be made into the historical period (e.g. SOPHOCLES). Their cult was normally localized (often to an individual grave), related to the evolution of the POLIS, and an important element of group identity. With the exception of Heracles, no hero ever became a god. The cult, like that of the dead from which it is to be distinguished by its concern with a living presence, required sacrifice, libations, and offerings of food. The hero was then the guest of honour at an annual feast, a scene frequently depicted in art. Heroes were regarded as much less remote than gods and could be called upon for aid, as the Athenians called on Ajax and Telamon before the battle of SALAMIS. Their bones (e.g. those of Theseus removed to Athens c.470 BC) were believed to possess magical properties and there are parallels with the Christian cult of the saints.

See also AFTERLIFE; COLONIZATION, GREEK; RELIGION, GREEK.   GS

Burkert (1985); Farnell (1921).

Herod Agrippa   *see* AGRIPPA I.

Herod Antipas   (d. after AD 39), son of HEROD THE GREAT. Herod Antipas ('that fox') was granted Galilee and Peraea, part of his father Herod the Great's kingdom, which he ruled as tetrarch for 43 years (4 BC–AD 39). Deposed in favour of his nephew, AGRIPPA I, by GAIUS (Caligula), he died in exile in Spain. Antipas imprisoned John the Baptist after his emergence from the desert (*c.*27): the intrigues of his wife Herodias and step-daughter Salome later resulted in John's execution.   RJB

Bowersock (1983); Scullard (1982); Williamson (1981).

Herod the Great   (*c.*73–4 BC), king of Judaea 37–4 BC. Herod the Great was the vizier of HYRCANUS II of Judaea, who was overthrown by the Parthians (39 BC). Herod escaped to Rome, where the Senate proclaimed him king of Judaea, and he was installed by two legions sent by Mark ANTONY (37). Ituraea and other districts were added to Herod's kingdom by Augustus (23 and 20 BC). Herod ruled, by force, as a Hellenistic monarch, incurring the hatred of both the orthodox JEWS and the nationalists. According to JOSEPHUS, he took 10 wives: on his death, his kingdom was divided between three of his sons, HEROD ANTIPAS, Philip, and Archelaus.   RJB

Bowersock (1983); Scullard (1982).

Herodas   (3rd century BC), Greek mime poet. Herodas is the only surviving representative of Greek MIME. He seems to have moulded the content of SOPHRON to the form of HIPPONAX in order to produce his own miniature verse dramas. Eight of them survive almost intact in a papyrus of the 2nd century AD together with fragments of a ninth. Presumably intended for solo recital, they open an intriguing window on to everyday life of the period.   GS

Webster (1964).

Herodes Atticus   (*c.*AD 101–77), Greek sophist. Lucius Vibullius Hipparchus Tiberius Claudius Atticus Herodes was a wealthy Athenian who is best remembered as a patron of architecture, responsible for buildings all over Greece and Asia Minor. He also achieved distinction as a man of letters which brought him the friendship of powerful men such as the emperors HADRIAN, ANTONINUS PIUS, Marcus AURELIUS, and Lucius VERUS. He became consul in 143. His life was written by Philostratus.   GS

Ameling (1983); Bowersock (1969).

Herodian (c.AD 180–250), Greek grammarian. Taught at Alexandria by his father APOLLONIUS DYSCOLUS, Herodian moved to Rome where he produced a voluminous work of *General Prosody* which he dedicated to Marcus Aurelius. Extracts preserved by later writers reveal that it was concerned primarily with accentuation. Surviving works include a study of anomalous words and the *Philhetaerus*, a small Atticist lexicon.

GS

Herodotus (traditionally 484–c.425 BC), Greek historian. Herodotus was born in Halicarnassus, a city with both Greek and Carian elements, on the border between Greece and the Persian empire. According to tradition, he spent part of his early life in exile on Samos, and was involved in a rising against the Halicarnassian tyrant Lygdamis. He travelled widely, both in Greece and to 'barbarian' lands, including the Black Sea, Egypt, Phoenicia, and Babylon. He is said to have spent time in Athens, and to have joined the Athenian colony sent to THURII, where he died.

Herodotus' *Histories* ('Researches') are concerned with the conflict between Greece and Persia and its antecedents, which he traces back to the subjugation of the Greek cities of Ionia by CROESUS, and his misconceived attack on Persia; thereafter, the development and expansion of the Persian empire, until it comes into conflict with mainland Greece, forms the narrative frame. His preface also expresses a desire to preserve the memory of human achievement of all sorts, and the *Histories* are filled with tales of spectacular or unusual acts and artefacts. In particular, Persian imperial expansion allows him to include a wealth of geographic and ethnographic material which demonstrates both the diversity and the unity of mankind.

Apart from first-hand observation, Herodotus' information is largely derived from oral sources: eye-witnesses, the family traditions of Greek and oriental aristocrats, temple traditions, and the popular stories current in various cities. Beyond the range of oral tradition lies myth, hence the choice of Croesus, the earliest reliably attested aggressor, as a starting-point. Traditions are sifted, collated, and recounted, including variants and contradictions, but not uncritically: Herodotus feels bound to record, but encourages a critical attitude in his audience by a sceptical authorial stance. The work is meticulously structured: use of a flashback technique ('ring-composition') for excursuses maintains the forward flow of the principal narrative, and careful cross-referencing and marking of transitions prevent the audience from losing its place. Herodotus is prominent as first-person narrator: the vivid recreation of events, complete with direct speech, owes much to Homer, and sets a precedent for later Greek historians.

As his preface indicates, Herodotus' twin aims are commemoration and explanation. Different types of explanation complement one another; at one level, the narrative structure is explanatory: once responsibility has been traced back to Croesus, each event motivates the next, driven by human desires and emotions. But Herodotus also deploys a range of abstract concepts: fate, the instability of human prosperity, which attracts divine envy, leading to perpetual fluctuation in human fortunes and, more generally, a principle of reciprocity. These have a moral aspect, but Herodotus is more interested in causation than guilt or sin, and his god(s) are largely impersonal rather than traditionally Homeric. Likewise, he is famously even-handed in his treatment of Greeks and barbarians; he prefers Greek political freedom to oriental despotism, but eschews stereotypes, and recognizes admirable human achievements wherever they occur.

See also HISTORIOGRAPHY, GREEK.   RB

Dewald and Marincola (1987); Gould (1989); Lateiner (1989).

Heron   (fl. AD 62), Greek mathematician and inventor. A large number of works have survived under Heron of Alexandria's name, not all of them genuine, although some of the latter may have been based upon treatises actually written by him. These works fall broadly into two main categories, mathematical and technical. His mathematical works were directed primarily at solving practical problems, if necessary by approximation. Drawing upon Babylonian sources, he was able to solve quadratic equations arithmetically and determine the formula for the area of a triangle. His technical works, too, seem to have had utility as well as amusement as their primary aim, although theoretical discussion is not absent. These works present detailed descriptions of such various devices as siphons, a self-regulating lamp, an automatic theatre, a water organ, and a variety of mechanical toys, including a ball rotated by steam, the so-called 'steam-engine'.

See also ENGINEERING.   JL

DSB VI (1972); Landels (1978).

Herophilus   (fl. *c*.270 BC), Greek physician. After studying at Cos under PRAXAGORAS, Herophilus of Chalcedon moved to Alexandria where, under the first Ptolemies, the dissection (even vivisection) of human bodies was not invested with the inhibitions in vogue in mainland Greece. Working in this environment Herophilus discovered the nervous system and made impressive advances in anatomical knowledge of the brain, eye, liver, vascular, and reproductive systems. Together with ERASISTRATUS, he laid the foundations for the scientific study of ANATOMY.

JL

Longrigg (1993); von Staden (1989).

Hesiod (*c.*700 BC), Greek epic poet. Hesiod himself tells us (*Works* 63–40) that his father came from Cyme in Asia Minor and settled in Ascra, a village in Boeotia. Like Homer's, therefore, Hesiod's poems have an Ionian origin, though they are heavily influenced by their immediate Boeotian context: he worked as a shepherd on Mt Helicon where he received his calling to write poetry. His precise chronology is elusive: the story of his meeting and competing with Homer is probably a sophist's invention. Though commonly linked in antiquity, the two poets are poles apart in all but date.

Hesiod's principal surviving works are the *Theogony*, 1022 lines on the origins of the gods, and the *Works and Days*, 828 lines of friendly advice for the working man. The *Catalogue of Women*, a continuation of the *Theogony*, and the *Shield*, a narrative poem about Heracles, are almost certainly spurious.

See also EPIC, GREEK.   GS

Fränkel (1975); Janko (1982); Lamberton (1988).

Hesychius (5th century AD), of Alexandria, Greek lexicographer. Hesychius set out to produce a comprehensive alphabetical dictionary of all Greek words, based on the specialist lexica of earlier scholars. It survives, in abridged form (usually not stating the sources of the rare words), in a single manuscript of the 15th century which was used as printer's copy by its first editor Marcus Musurus in 1514.

                                                                                        GS

Wilson (1983).

Hibernia modern Ireland. In the 6th century BC the Greeks described Ireland as five days' voyage from Brittany. In the 3rd century ERATOSTHENES positioned it correctly on his map, but STRABO placed it north of Britain. PTOLEMY had some knowledge of the coastal perimeter, and Solinus (3rd century AD) recorded the absence of snakes. The CELTS found abundant copper and some gold. In the 5th century AD the Irish were evangelized by St PATRICK.   GS

Hierodouloi temple slaves or servants of the god. In different contexts the term might include sacred prostitutes, devotees of the god, or even manumitted slaves (whose freedom was guaranteed by the god).

See also SLAVERY, GREEK.   GS

Hieromnemones Greek religious officials. Their responsibilities might include management of finance, of estates, of archives, of the eponymous magistracies, and representation of their state at the DELPHIC

AMPHICTYONY. Their time in office varied from place to place but they generally formed a college of 24 members.   GS

Hieron I tyrant of Syracuse, 478–467 BC. Hieron ruled Gela for his brother GELON and subsequently succeeded him in the tyranny of Syracuse; his rule is said to have been less popular, and less secure, than Gelon's. He continued the policy of transplanting populations, transferring the inhabitants of Naxos and Catana to Leontini, and founding a new city, AETNA, in the territory of Catana. Interventions in southern Italy culminated in victory over the Etruscans, allies of Carthage, in 474. He promoted himself in Greece by competing in the games, by dedications at Olympia and Delphi, and by his patronage of poets, notably PINDAR.   RB

Andrewes (1956); Berve (1967); CAH V.

Hieron II (c.306–215 BC), king of Syracuse. Hieron first appears as a lieutenant of PYRRHUS in Sicily, then as an independent commander of the Syracusan army who seized power in Syracuse. He won a great victory over the MAMERTINES c.269 BC and was elected king, fabricating descent from the tyrants GELON and HIERON I. Wise alliances with Rome enabled Syracuse to remain at peace during the PUNIC WARS, and the city reached its peak during his reign. Hieron beautified Syracuse with grand building projects. He was a friend of ARCHIMEDES, and THEOCRITUS wrote an encomium about him. His fiscal system, the *lex Hieronica*, was adapted by the Roman provincial government.   EER

Finley (1979); Green (1990).

Hieronymus of Cardia (c.364–260 BC), soldier, administrator, and historian. Hieronymus fought alongside EUMENES OF CARDIA during the struggles among the DIADOCHI after ALEXANDER THE GREAT's death. After Eumenes' death in 316 BC, Hieronymus was rescued by ANTIGONUS I MONOPHTHALMUS whose family he served loyally. He was present at the battle of IPSUS in 301, was appointed governor of Boeotia by DEMETRIUS I POLIORCETES in 293, and spent the rest of his life at ANTIGONUS II GONATAS' court. He wrote an important history of the period 323–272 BC which was used by ARRIAN, DIODORUS SICULUS, and PLUTARCH, among others.
                                                                                    EER

Bosworth (1988a); Hammond and Walbank (1988); Hornblower (1981).

Hieronymus, Eusebius *see* JEROME, ST.

Hierosolyma *see* JERUSALEM.

Himera   battle in 480 BC. Terillus tyrant of Himera, expelled by THERON, appealed for assistance to Hamilcar, sufete of Carthage, who invaded with a force allegedly 300,000 strong, confronting 55,000 Sicilians. The battle, reputedly on the same day as SALAMIS, was a crushing victory for the Greeks under GELON, who none the less gave Carthage peace on moderate terms. Later generations suspected collusion between XERXES and Carthage to prevent Gelon from assisting mainland Greece.   RB

Burn (1984); CAH IV.

Himilco   (fl. 406–395 BC), Carthaginian general. Himilco's first successes as Carthaginian commander in Sicily were the capture of Acragas (406), Gela and Camarina (405). He successfully opposed the assaults of DIONYSIUS I on Phoenician Sicily, despite the destruction of Motya (398), but the Carthaginian counter-attack on Syracuse was disastrous: they were ravaged by plague and defeated, and Himilco and the Carthaginians were allowed to escape only at the price of their allies.
                                                                                          RB

Caven (1990); Freeman (1891–4).

Hippalus   (fl. c.100 BC?), Greek merchant. Hippalus was the first to exploit the value of the monsoon winds which enabled merchant seamen to cross the Indian Ocean. He sailed from Yemen to the mouth of the Indus and is credited with discovering the direct route to INDIA. The south-west monsoon, an African cape, and a sea were named after him.

See also NAVIGATION.   GS

Hipparchus of Athens   *see* HIPPIAS.

Hipparchus   (c.190–126 BC), Greek mathematician, astronomer, and geographer. Born at Nicaea in Bithynia, Hipparchus spent most of his life at Rhodes. His only extant work is his relatively early treatise in three books, *Commentary on the* Phaenomena *of Eudoxus and Aratus*, which criticizes the descriptions and placings of constellations and stars by them and provides a list of simultaneous risings and settings. Most of the rest of our knowledge of his ASTRONOMY is derived from PTOLEMY's *Almagest*. Hipparchus was the first to construct a theory of the motions of the sun and moon firmly based upon observational data and coupled with Babylonian eclipse records. He discovered the precession of the equinoxes, investigated the problem of the parallax, and devised the first practical method for determining the size and distance of the sun and moon. In MATHEMATICS he seems to have been the first to make systematic use of trigonometry; and his geographical work, *Against the Geography of Eratosthenes*, in at least three books, criticized ERATOSTHENES, showing that the distances and relationships given by him were inconsistent with each other and with other geographical data.   JL

DSB XV supp. 1 (1978).

Hippeis   Greek cavalry. Originally, HORSES were simply transport for infantrymen, and the Spartan Hippeis remained HOPLITES who rode to battle. Most states possessed insufficient land to support many horses, and the largest cavalry forces hardly exceeded a thousand; hence cavalry played a limited role in Greek warfare, scouting, harassing raiders and foragers, and pursuing or covering retreats. Furthermore, Greek horses were small, and lack of stirrups limited the effectiveness of shock charges. Only PHILIP II, by encouraging horse-breeding and gaining control of the cavalry of Thessaly, was able to develop his cavalry as a striking arm.

The Hippeis were also the second of SOLON's property classes (*see* PENTACOSIOMEDIMNI, ZEUGITAE, THETES), with a qualification of 300 measures of produce. Although Aristotle notes a link between cavalry power and oligarchy, a direct correlation between the Solonian class and the cavalry is debatable for archaic Athens and lacking in the classical period.   RB

Anderson (1961); Bugh (1988); Greenhalgh (1973).

Hippias   tyrant of Athens, 527–510 BC. Hippias succeeded his father PEISISTRATUS in 527, probably in partnership with his brother Hipparchus. They continued Peisistratus' moderate policies, but faced increasing aristocratic resistance; after the assassination of Hipparchus by HARMODIUS AND ARISTOGEITON, the regime became more oppressive. Spartan intervention against it was eventually successful, and the family withdrew to the Troad, and thence to Persia. Hippias accompanied the expedition to MARATHON in hopes of restoration; his fate thereafter is unknown.   RB

Berve (1967); CAH IV.

Hippias of Elis   (5th century BC), Greek sophist. Hippias was a well-known polymath who travelled all over Greece offering his services as a diplomat, teacher, and orator. His interests extended to astronomy, grammar, history, music, and poetry; and he made a significant contribution to mathematics with his discovery of the quadratrix, a regular curve that is not a circle. He figures in a number of Platonic dialogues.

See also HISTORIOGRAPHY, GREEK.   GS

Guthrie, vol. 3 (1969).

Hippocrates tyrant of Gela, 498–491 BC. Hippocrates took over the tyranny of GELA on the murder of his brother Cleander, who had overthrown the preceding oligarchy. He extended the power of Gela widely in eastern Sicily, gaining control of Zancle, Naxos, and Leontini; he defeated the Syracusans in battle, but failed to take the city, though he received as ransom for his prisoners the city of Camarina, which he 'refounded'. He died campaigning against the Sicels at Hybla, and was succeeded by his sons, who were soon supplanted by GELON.

See also ANAXILAS.   RB

Burn (1984); CAH IV; Dunbabin (1948).

Hippocrates (*c.*460–380 BC), Greek physician. Although Hippocrates is widely acclaimed as the 'Father of Medicine', relatively little is known about him. It may be accepted that he came from COS and was a contemporary of SOCRATES; that he was an Asclepiad, a member of a GUILD of physicians, which claimed descent from ASCLEPIUS, the god of healing; that he became the most famous physician and teacher of MEDICINE of his time and taught for a fee. Insufficient evidence, either of his methodology or of his doctrines, has survived to enable any one of the more than 60 treatises comprising the Hippocratic Corpus to be positively identified as having been written by him. It would, however, be paradoxical if, when so many works are ascribed to him, no genuine work of his has survived. Attempts to identify such a work are continually, but unsuccessfully, made.   JL

Lloyd (1978); Smith (1979).

Hippodamus (5th century BC), Greek town planner. Hippodamus was born in Miletus which, like many Ionian cities, had been destroyed by the Persians. The rebuilding of these cities provided opportunities for systematic planning. The plan adopted was the rectangular gridiron, which was not new, though Aristotle attributes its introduction to Hippodamus. His chief contribution seems to have been the adaptation of the plan to include the principal elements of the Greek city. He is credited with having designed the layout of PIRAEUS, of THURII (in 443 BC), and of RHODES (in 408 BC). Other cities that follow the 'Hippodamian' plan include MILETUS, PRIENE, and OLYNTHUS.

See also TOWN PLANNING.   GS

Ward-Perkins (1974).

Hippodrome *see* CIRCUS.

Hipponax (6th century BC), Greek lyric poet. Little is known about Hipponax except that he was a native of Ephesus and was exiled to Clazomenae where he lived in poverty. His verse, of which only fragments survive, is noted for outspoken realism and uninhibited satire, opening a window on to the harsh world of the 6th century. He is recalled by later poets as the inventor of the choliambic, the so-called limping iambic metre.

See also MIME, GREEK.   GS

West (1974).

Histiaeus (fl. *c.*515–493 BC), tyrant of Miletus. Histiaeus, Persian-sponsored tyrant of Miletus, won favour with DARIUS I by his loyalty during the abortive Scythian expedition; his reward, land at Myrcinus in Thrace, was revoked due to Persian mistrust by a summons to court, but Darius treated him as an honoured counsellor. Though he may not have masterminded the IONIAN REVOLT, his participation was inevitable, given the hostility of ARTAPHERNES and the involvement of ARISTAGORAS; but he failed to re-establish his authority and after some freebooting in the Hellespont and northern Aegean was eventually captured in Mysia and killed by his Persian enemies.   RB

Burn (1984); CAH IV.

Historia Augusta The *Historia Augusta*, or Augustan History, is a series of lives of emperors and usurpers from AD 117 to 284 (Hadrian to Carinus and Numerian). It was ostensibly produced by six biographers, Aelius Spartianus, Julius Capitolinus, Aelius Lampridius, Vulcatius Gallicanus, Trebellius Pollio, and Flavius Vobiscus, writing in the late 3rd and early 4th centuries AD. However, because of chronological inconsistencies apparent between the work of various 'authors', Hermann Dessau suggested that the Augustan History was the work of a single author, writing towards the end of the 4th century. This theory provides a reasonable explanation for the similarities with both EUTROPIUS (Life of Marcus) and AURELIUS VICTOR (Life of Severus). The History may originally have included Lives of Nerva and Trajan (96–117), taking up where SUETONIUS left off, but if so they are now lost, as are the Lives for 244–60. The work is of variable quality: the Lives of emperors from Hadrian to Caracalla contain material of value, much of it confirmed by epigraphic evidence; but material on junior figures and usurpers is either repetition from major Lives, or pure fiction. The Life of Elagabalus descends abruptly into fiction mid-way through, and the remainder of the 3rd-century *Lives* are of little value. RJB

Birley (1976); Dessau (1889); Syme (1968, 1971).

Historiography, Greek The beginnings of Greek historical writing, in the two generations before Herodotus, fall into three areas: genealogy, geography, and local history. The genealogical works of HECATEUS OF MILETUS and others aimed to organize the jumble of local mythologies into a single coherent system. Hecateus likewise pioneered geographical and ethnographic writing with his *Circuit of the World*. Local history begins with CHARON's history of Lampsacus and XANTHUS' treatment of Lydia, and we know of a number of other local historians who predate Thucydides. These authors were apparently parochial, concentrating on foundations, origins, and early history, and devoting little attention to recent history, apart from references to the Persian Wars. A further development, contemporary with Herodotus, was the development of chronography: the chronological works of HELLANICUS and HIPPIAS OF ELIS, among others, made possible the accurate relative dating of events, particularly in different parts of Greece.

The innovations of Herodotus and Thucydides did not replace these types of history. Local history continued to flourish: in particular, the ATTHIS of Hellanicus is the first of a series spanning the 4th century BC, while Sicily produced her own historians, notably PHILISTUS and TIMAEUS. Equally, the tradition of accounts of regions or peoples, especially outside the Greek world, continued, and the conquests of Alexander inspired a series of works with a geographical and ethnographic orientation which reflect the influence of Herodotus.

HERODOTUS reflects the preoccupations of his predecessors, but goes further, focusing on a great and universal event in the recent past and weaving together diverse parochial traditions into a coherent narrative. His decision to recreate the past in vivid narrative, including speeches, set a powerful precedent. THUCYDIDES' concentration on the military and political sphere was equally influential, and his scrupulous methodology set a new standard, rarely matched in practice. His concept of the utility of history, however, attracted fewer followers; rather, in the 4th century history came to be regarded as a repertory of moral and practical examples or lessons, a view already evident in XENOPHON's *Hellenica* (and quasi-historical works such as the *Hiero* and *Cyropaedeia*). Such histories consequently tended to become more episodic.

Conversely, EPHORUS attempted a universal history of Greece and its neighbours down to his own time. THEOPOMPUS' *Philippica* (a work also famous for its moral invectives) was the earliest example of a further sub-genre, biographical history, in which a dominant individual stands at the centre of the narrative, and of which the historians of Alexander, from CALLISTHENES onwards, are the most obvious exponents. In the early Hellenistic period DURIS and PHYLARCHUS amplified the desire for vivid narrative into a pursuit of emotional impact. POLYBIUS, last of the great Greek historians, reacted against this with the polemic characteristic of Greek historians discussing their predecessors: deliberately unsensational, his universal 'pragmatic' (military and political) history, charting the rise of Rome, combines analysis with a didactic purpose, and represents a return to the highest intellectual and methodological standards.

See also ANDROTION; BIOGRAPHY, GREEK; CALLIAS OF SYRACUSE; CLEITARCHUS; HIERONYMUS OF CARDIA; MEGASTHENES; ONESICRITUS; PHANODEMUS; PHILOCHORUS.   RB

Brown (1949); Fornara (1983); Jacoby (1923–58); Murray (1972); Pearson (1939, 1960).

Historiography, Roman   History was a Greek invention, and when the Romans began to write about their own past they were consciously adopting a Greek literary form (see HISTORIOGRAPHY, GREEK). The first Roman historian, FABIUS PICTOR, actually wrote in Greek. His example was followed by others, including POSTUMIUS ALBINUS. CATO attacked Albinus as a poseur, and himself showed that it was possible to write in Latin. His *Origines*, though unusual in method and scope, marked the beginning of Latin historiography. It was followed by a spate of Roman histories in Latin, most of them called ANNALES, by such writers as PISO FRUGI and GELLIUS. They were the forerunners of the late Republican annalists, Licinius MACER, CLAUDIUS QUADRIGARIUS, VALERIUS ANTIAS, and ultimately LIVY, whose work marks the apogee of this type of historiography, and is the only example to survive (albeit only in parts).

Most annalists covered the whole history of the city from its origins, and adopted a year-by-year arrangement in the manner of the *Annales Maximi*, which must have been one of their main sources; but they were also able to draw upon private family records and a substantial oral tradition.

In the Gracchan age some historians rejected annals as mere repetition of received facts, and turned instead to contemporary political history in the manner of THUCYDIDES and POLYBIUS. Early exponents include Sempronius ASELLIO and perhaps FANNIUS, though little is known of their works. A more substantial figure is SISENNA, himself a direct forerunner of SALLUST, whose *Histories* do not survive, but whose brilliant monographs on JUGURTHA and CATILINE are among the earliest extant works of Latin historiography.

Others wrote their memoirs, and refought old battles with the pen. They include Aemilius SCAURUS, RUTILIUS RUFUS, SULLA, and above all CAESAR, whose masterly *Commentarii* still survive. Another influential figure was Asinius POLLIO, who wrote a continuation of Sallust's *Histories* after retiring from the political stage.

Under the Principate everything changed. After Livy no major Latin historian attempted to rewrite the history of Republican Rome. This was not because Livy's work deterred all competitors, but because the issues were dead. The Julio-Claudian age offered the historian new possibilities – and new dangers. In AD 25 Cremutius Cordus paid with his life for expressing Republican sentiments in his history. The alternative to subversion was flattery, an example of which survives in the work of VELLEIUS PATERCULUS, whose adulation of Tiberius and SEJANUS adds an embarrassing touch to an otherwise pedestrian work. Other early imperial histories, by e.g. Cluvius Rufus, AUFIDIUS BASSUS, and PLINY THE ELDER, are all but completely lost, which makes it hard for us properly to assess the achievement of TACITUS.

Tacitus' masterly analysis of tyranny and its corrupting effects is set within an annalistic framework, but the personality of the emperor is always in the foreground. As Tacitus acknowledged, the nature of the regime inevitably pushed the historian towards BIOGRAPHY. Biography became the principal form of imperial history, and it reached its zenith in the incomparable *Lives of the Caesars* by SUETONIUS. Suetonius had many imitators, but none survives, with the exception of the mendacious and still puzzling HISTORIA AUGUSTA.

No later historian produced anything to rival Tacitus until AMMIANUS MARCELLINUS at the end of the 4th century; he was the last major historian of Rome. Otherwise historiography had by then degenerated into the production of epitomes for semi-literate people who could not cope with Livy and Tacitus, or Christian history, which made up in piety for what it lacked in political analysis.   TC

Dorey (1966); Grant (1970a); Laistner (1947); Momigliano (1990).

Homer (8th century BC), Greek epic poet. Homer, the poet of the *Iliad* and the *Odyssey*, almost certainly belongs to the end of the Dark Ages when Greek literature first began to be written down. The prevalence of Ionic in the language of the poems suggests that he came from Ionia, perhaps Chios (as maintained by Semonides) or Smyrna (by Pindar). There may be some truth in the tradition that he was blind, like the bards in the *Odyssey*. Little else about him is known, but the balance of scholarly opinion now supports the view that one man was responsible for both poems, and that the *Iliad* is the earlier of the two.

The metre, language, and structure of the poems are similar; and there are similarities of technique (extended similes, stock formulas, repeated passages, etc.) and of characterization. There are also undoubted differences in theme, pace, and subject-matter (but the *Iliad* is a poem of war while the *Odyssey* is a tale of adventure) and inconsistencies within the poems (though these are now mostly attributed to the oral origin and transmission of the poems).

The essential truth is that the *Iliad* and the *Odyssey* are not works of historiography, to be studied by readers as factual accounts of actual events, but the earliest and greatest examples of high-flown EPIC POETRY, intended to be recited for the entertainment of an audience. As such they were revered throughout antiquity and have exerted the most profound influence on all subsequent literature.   GS

Edwards (1987); Finley (1977); Griffin (1980); Kirk (1965, 1976); Parry (1971).

Homeric Hymns   The corpus of 'Homeric Hymns' contains four long poems (addressed to Aphrodite, Apollo, Demeter, and Hermes) which date from the post-Homeric period (650–400 BC) and 29 shorter poems which are probably later. As small-scale epics they are more akin to HESIOD than HOMER, but attribution of the *Hymn to Apollo* to Homer dates from Thucydides (3.104). The longer *Hymns* belong to the literary, rather than the devotional, tradition of Greek hymnography in which myth predominates.   GS

Clay (1989); Janko (1982).

Homosexuality   In Greek myth the gods practised homosexuality with no more inhibition than heterosexuality. The poets sang of the loves of men and boys from early archaic times. Artists frequently depicted older men making sexual advances towards younger men. Bisexuality was regarded as perfectly natural in the wealthier class of classical society and was not something either to hide or to flaunt. Relations between men and women were seen as primarily a means of procreation whereas those between men and men were often much more passionate. The latter could also be a means to political advancement and they were idealized by PLATO. Male prostitution, however, incurred the loss of citizenship at Athens and homosexuals were favourite targets for abuse by ARISTOPHANES. At Rome homosexuality was not uncommon and male prostitution was officially condoned. But in the 2nd century AD there was a change of attitude and a revulsion away from the blatant practices of earlier periods. Homosexuality was later condemned by the Church.   GS

Dover (1978).

Honestiores Roman upper class. The *honestiores* were the upper class in a two-tier social grouping created by HADRIAN (AD 117–38) that largely replaced the old distinction between Roman citizen and non-citizen. The *honestiores*, who included senators, equestrians, land-owners, soldiers, civil servants, and local town councillors, enjoyed superior legal rights to the lower class (the *humiliores* or *plebei*), and were punished less heavily by the courts. The distinction may have been designed to compensate town councillors and the like for the burdens of office placed upon them. It was a distinction that became enshrined in law, which still existed in the time of Justinian (527–65).   RJB

Grant (1979); Millar (1981).

Honorius (AD 384–423), western Roman emperor, AD 395–423. Flavius Honorius, younger son of THEODOSIUS I and Flacilla, was created Augustus in 393, and, after his father's death, became western emperor (395). He was dominated first by STILICHO (d. 408), and then by CONSTANTIUS III (d. 421). In 402, menaced by ALARIC, he moved the court to RAVENNA. He played little personal part in a reign which saw many usurpers (e.g. Constantine III in BRITAIN) and the sack of Rome (410).   RJB

Bury (1958); Grant (1985); Matthews (1990).

Hoplites Greek infantry. Hoplite armour and tactics appeared in the early 7th century BC; thereafter, hoplites were the standard heavy infantry of classical Greece. Equipped, usually at their own expense, with defensive armour, large round shield, thrusting spear, and sword, they fought in formation. The hoplite PHALANX required level open terrain to fight on; the initial collision and a phase of hand-to-hand fighting were followed by concerted pushing until one side gave way, but pursuit was limited by the weight of their armour.

See also ARMS AND ARMOUR, GREEK; ARMY, GREEK; WARFARE, GREEK.   RB

Hanson (1989, 1991); Pritchett, part IV (1985).

Horace (65–8 BC), Latin poet. Quintus Horatius Flaccus was born the son of a freedman at Venusia in Apulia. Educated at Rome under Orbilius and at Athens, he joined the army in 44 BC and served under Brutus as military tribune until PHILIPPI, when he says he deserted. Returning to Rome, he was pardoned and appointed archivist to the quaestors; but an early introduction to MAECENAS, performed by VIRGIL in 38 BC, enabled him to concentrate on writing. Under the patronage of Augustus he joined a literary élite and acquired his beloved Sabine farm. He never married and was buried alongside Maecenas. His biography by SUETONIUS survives.

Of his works the *Satires* (2 books) were written between 37 and 30 BC in the form of 'conversations' (*Sermones*). The *Epodes* (17 poems), also written in the 30s, imitate ARCHILOCHUS but also betray Hellenistic origins. The *Odes* (books 1–3 published in 23 BC, book 4 in 13) are lyrics on diverse themes which display complete mastery of form and economy of language. The *Carmen Saeculare* (17 BC) is a choral ode in praise of Augustus. The *Epistles* (20–17 BC) are versified dialogues on literary and philosophical subjects. The *Ars Poetica*, also an epistle in form, is an essay in literary criticism of uncertain date.

See also EPISTOLOGRAPHY, LATIN; LYRIC POETRY, LATIN; SATIRE.   GS

Brink (1971); Fraenkel (1957); Lyne (1980); Rudd (1966, 1986); Williams (1968).

Horse racing   *see* GAMES, GREEK.

Horses   Horses were bred on the plains of Thessaly and Macedonia, but the Greek horse seems to have been a puny beast unsuited to heavy labour on either the farm or the road. For the same reason horses were not much used in warfare (*see* HIPPEIS) where the absence of stirrups made riding precarious at the best of times. Furthermore they were expensive to feed and maintain, so their possession was restricted to the wealthy and their use to travel and sport. Equestrian events were popular at the GAMES from early times, and chariot racing became the Romans' favourite entertainment for which they imported large numbers of horses from Asia, Africa, and Spain. Above all, horses were used for HUNTING. XENOPHON wrote a treatise *On Horsemanship* which gives expert advice on how to choose, ride, exercise, jump, and armour a horse.   GS

Hyland (1990).

Hortensius Hortalus   (114–50 BC), Roman orator. Quintus Hortensius Hortalus, with his new, florid, 'Asianic' style of oratory, held the primacy at the Roman bar until defeated by CICERO in the case of VERRES in 70 BC. He continued to be an important orator, and he was a leader of the OPTIMATES, notably as consul in 69 and as a vehement opponent of POMPEY's extraordinary commands in 67 and 66. But towards the end of his life he put fishponds before politics and lived an indolent life of luxury in his parks and villas.   DP

Kennedy (1972); Rawson (1985); Syme (1939).

Horticulture   *see* GARDENS.

Houses, Greek   The first Greek houses were simple structures. Walls were built of sun-dried brick on a stone plinth and often coated with lime; roofs were of timber with terracotta tiles, or sometimes stepped or thatched. The commonest plan was a number of rooms arranged around a courtyard which was entered from the street through a porch. Apart from the door and a few windows, the street façade was plain; architectural decoration, if any, was restricted to the interior. Some houses rose to a second storey where the bedrooms and women's quarters were located, while the men's dining room (*andron*), kitchen, and storerooms remained on the ground floor. Water was available from wells and underground cisterns as well as from public fountains. There was effectively no sanitation before the Hellenistic period. Furniture was simple and austere.

Excavations at OLYNTHUS and in the Athenian Agora have revealed the foundations of houses of this type dating from the 5th and 4th centuries. In the Hellenistic period houses became more elaborate and more luxurious, though the same basic plan was retained, e.g. at PRIENE, DELOS, and Pella. Here the residences of wealthy merchants and courtiers were embellished with elegant GARDENS, wall PAINTINGS, and floor MOSAICS.

GS

Lawrence (1984).

Houses, Roman   There was more variety in the domestic architecture of the Roman world than of the Greek. The basic feature of the Italian town house (*domus*), which may be Etruscan in origin, was a central chamber (*atrium*) with a hole in the roof to admit light and rain (which was collected in a tank) and to emit smoke from the hearth. This functioned as the principal reception room, to which flanking rooms were added on both sides and at one end.

By the 1st century BC the majority of the urban population lived in apartment blocks (*insulae*) which rose to several storeys with the ground floor often occupied by shops and workshops. Owned by wealthy speculators and rented out to the masses, these flimsy structures were jerry-built and notoriously prone to overcrowding, fire, and collapse. Remains of more spacious and presumably less squalid blocks have been found at OSTIA.

In the provinces the influence of the Hellenistic peristyle is more pronounced, and the houses of the wealthy were decorated with sculpture, marbles, frescoes, and MOSAICS. Country houses assumed palatial proportions and played a major role in the spread of the Roman way of life throughout the empire.

See also ARCHITECTURE, ROMAN.   GS

McKay (1975); Ward-Perkins (1977).

Huns   Asiatic people. The Huns were a nomadic tribe first heard of
*c.*AD 370, when their formidable cavalry destroyed the OSTROGOTHS'
kingdom in the Ukraine, and drove the VISIGOTHS into the Roman empire
(376). Their continued advance precipitated the VANDAL invasion of Gaul
(406). ATTILA's empire (434–53) stretched from the Baltic to the Danube,
but his two sons were overwhelmingly defeated by their German subjects
(455), and the Huns were never again a great power.   RJB

Grant (1979); Maenchen-Helfen (1973); Thompson (1975).

Hunting   Hunting in the ancient world had the dual purpose of protecting the flocks from wild beasts and providing meat as a supplement to the diet. The animals most commonly hunted included hares,
usually on foot with dogs and nets; deer, with snares and nets; wild
boar, with hounds, hunters, and spears; and various birds, often with
hawks and falcons. The idea of hunting as sport came late, but the
Roman addiction to wild beast shows (*see* GAMES, ROMAN) meant that
huge numbers of animals had to be taken alive and shipped to Rome.
Many rural villas were built as hunting lodges, and the sport is nowhere better depicted than in the brilliant mosaics (4th century AD) at
Piazza Armerina in Sicily. Treatises on hunting survive by XENOPHON,
ARRIAN, OPPIAN, and NEMESIANUS.

See also HORSES.   GS

Hull (1964).

Hyginus   (*c.*64 BC–AD 17), scholar and librarian. Gaius Julius Hyginus
was a Spaniard and a freedman whom AUGUSTUS put in charge of his
newly founded library on the Palatine. A pupil of ALEXANDER POLYHISTOR
and a friend of OVID, he was inspired by VARRO to write textbooks on
agriculture, bee-keeping, and geography as well as a commentary on
VIRGIL, biographies of famous men, and various works on religion and
history.   GS

Hyperbolus   (d. 411 BC), Athenian politician. In 422 BC Hyperbolus
succeeded CLEON as 'leader of the people', holding power until his
ostracism (*c.*416) in which NICIAS and ALCIBIADES, both likely candidates
themselves, connived. He was murdered in Samos during the oligarchic revolution of 411.   GLC

Hyperides   (390–322 BC), Athenian orator. Hyperides studied under
PLATO and ISOCRATES before becoming a professional speech writer.

As a politician he was consistently anti-Macedonian, supporting DEMOSTHENES in the 340s but prosecuting him in 324. After the defeat at CHAERONEA in 338 he urged extreme measures to safeguard the city, including the manumission of slaves to supplement the army. He was largely responsible for the LAMIAN WAR against Macedon in 323–322: part of his funeral oration over the Athenian dead survives, as do fragments of four other speeches and one intact. He was executed in 322 on the orders of ANTIPATER.

See also LEOSTHENES.   GS

Hornblower (1983); Kennedy (1963).

Hyrcanus II (fl. 76–31/30 BC), Jewish high priest. Hyrcanus, grandson of John HYRCANUS, was expelled by his brother from the high priesthood. He was supported by ANTIPATER OF IDUMAEA, and POMPEY reinstalled him as high priest and ethnarch in 63 BC, although in 57 GABINIUS removed his temporal powers. Under Antipater's control, Hyrcanus helped Julius CAESAR in the Alexandrian War (47), and was reappointed ethnarch. In 40 the invading Parthians installed Hyrcanus' nephew in Jerusalem, and took Hyrcanus to Babylonia.

See also HEROD THE GREAT; JEWS.   EER

Davies and Finkelstein (1989); Schürer (1973–87); Sherwin-White (1984); Sullivan (1990).

Hyrcanus, John (134–104 BC), ruler of Judaea. John Hyrcanus was hereditary high priest of the JEWS in the independent Hasmonaean state established in Seleucid Palestine in 142 BC. He expanded the territory under Hasmonaean control, annexing Samaria and Idumaea. The policy of expansion and forcible conversion to Judaism was continued under the priesthoods of John's sons (Aristobulus the elder and Alexander Jannaeus), but continuing secularization led to popular discontent, quarrels with the Pharisees, and revolts.

See also HYRCANUS II; JUDAS MACCABAEUS.   EER

Davies and Finkelstein (1989); Eddy (1961); Schürer (1973–87); Sullivan (1990).

Hysiae *see* SPARTA.

I

Iamblichus (*c*.AD 250–325), Greek Neoplatonist philosopher. Iamblichus was born at Chalcis in Coele Syria. He later studied under PORPHYRY and founded his own school in Syria. His extant works comprise an encyclopaedia of Pythagoreanism, containing *The Life of Pythagoras*, the *Protrepticus*, and three mathematical treatises (the authorship of one of these is disputed), and the *De Mysteriis*, a work attributed to him on the authority of a lost work of PROCLUS which attempts to reconcile magical practices with Platonic philosophy. These works, though superficial, are valuable as source books and for the evidence they provide of the superstitions of the age.

See also NEOPLATONISM.

JL

DSB VII (1973).

Iazyges *see* SARMATIANS.

Iberia *see* SPAIN.

Ibycus (6th century BC), Greek lyric poet. Ibycus was a south Italian from Rhegium and presumably of distinguished family in view of the story that he could have become tyrant. From STESICHORUS he inherited the elaborate choral tradition of mythological narrative. But after his removal to the court of Polycrates on Samos he turned to lighter erotic themes, for which he was later remembered. A few fragments survive in both styles.

GS

Bowra (1961).

Ictinus (5th century BC), Greek architect. Ictinus, whose name is most likely a nickname (meaning 'kite'), was probably not an Athenian by birth. He is said to have been the architect of the Telesterion at Eleusis and of the temple of Apollo at BASSAE. But he is best known as the chief architect of the PARTHENON (448–438 BC), of which he wrote an account (now lost). All operations on the acropolis were directed by the sculptor PHEIDIAS, and, according to Plutarch, Ictinus was assisted by another architect, Callicrates.   GS

Ignatius, St   (c.AD 35–107), bishop of Antioch. Nothing is known of Ignatius' life until his journey from Antioch to martyrdom in Rome. En route he visited St POLYCARP at Smyrna and wrote letters of encouragement to the churches of Asia Minor and Rome. His martyrdom (traditionally in the Colosseum) is attested by Polycarp and ORIGEN. The authenticity of the letters was long disputed but is now generally accepted.   GS

Cross (1974).

Iguvium Tables   a set of seven inscribed bronze tablets discovered during the Renaissance at Iguvium (modern Gubbio) in Umbria. Written in the ancient Umbrian language, and therefore extremely difficult to interpret, they date from the 2nd and 1st centuries BC and record the activities of the *Fratres Atiedii*, a priestly college comparable to the Roman ARVAL BROTHERS. The Tables indicate that the people of Iguvium were divided into 10 groups similar to the Roman CURIAE.   TC

Momigliano (1963b); Poultney (1959).

Illyricum   Roman province. Illyricum was initially a vaguely defined area, comprising the territory of the Illyrian tribes east of the Adriatic, extending up to the Danube. It encompassed what became the provinces of PANNONIA and DALMATIA and the north-west of MACEDONIA. The first and second Illyrian Wars (229–228 BC; 219 BC) were fought by Rome against Scodra, in the south, but it was not until after the defeat of Genthius (167 BC) that Rome established any real control. In 148/7 BC Apollonia and Dyrrhachium became part of the province of Macedonia, but Illyricum was not fully subdued until Octavian (AUGUSTUS) conquered the Iapudes, the Pannonians, and the Dalmatians (35–33 BC). Illyricum was placed under senatorial control (27 BC), but passed to imperial control when the full conquest of the Pannonians extended the province to the Danube (13–11 BC). A major Illyrian–Pannonian revolt (AD 6–9) was finally subdued by TIBERIUS, after which Pannonia became a separate province. The remaining province, Illyricum Superior, became known as Dalmatia, probably under the Flavians. The name Illyricum continued, denoting a customs area embracing six provinces – Raetia, Noricum, Pannonia, Dalmatia, Moesia, and Dacia.

Diocletian's reforms created two dioceses – Moesia and Pannonia – that corresponded to east and west Illyricum (*I. orientale* and *I. occidentale*). RJB

Lengyel and Radan (1980); Millar (1981); Wilkes (1992).

Immunitas *Immunitas* granted immunity from certain taxes. It was a device used only rarely under the Roman Empire, and was usually confined to an individual town rather than a whole province. Used by AUGUSTUS as a reward for deserving communities, it did not necessarily give immunity from all TAXATION, but exempted the recipients from, for example, the TRIBUTUM *capitis*. CLAUDIUS I granted lengthy exemptions from taxation to towns hit by natural disasters, and NERO extended the immunity enjoyed by cities like Athens and Sparta to the whole province of Achaea. Even the notoriously parsimonius VESPASIAN occasionally granted immunity to a deserving community. RJB

Salmon (1968).

Imperator Roman commander; emperor. *Imperator* (the Greek equivalent was *autokrator*) was, under the Republic, a title borne by a military commander (a holder of IMPERIUM) who had been hailed *imperator* by his troops. It was a *cognomen* (i.e. it was added after his NAME) which the holder retained until after a triumph or until his command lapsed. Under the Empire only the emperor could be so saluted, because the generals who actually earned salutations served under the emperor's superior *imperium* (*imperium proconsulare maius*): the salutation, therefore, technically belonged to the emperor and was listed after his name (e.g. I mp. XI). In addition, *imperator* was used in another, distinct way: as an imperial title, a *praenomen* (i.e. it preceded the emperor's name) that ultimately developed into the title emperor. Soon the purple robe, symbol of an *imperator*, was reserved for the emperor alone. Octavian (AUGUSTUS) was called *imperator* from early in his career, but his immediate successors did not adopt the *praenomen* officially. However, OTHO (AD 69) did so, and from Vespasian's reign onwards (69–79) it became part of the imperial titulature, displacing PRINCEPS as the popular designation of the emperor. Thus, for example, Trajan's titles in 117 began 'Imp. Caesar' and ended 'Imp. XIII'. RJB

Millar (1981); Salmon (1968).

Imperium supreme command of Rome. *Imperium* signified supreme command: the holder had the right to command in war, to administer the law, and to inflict punishment (including the death penalty, subject to appeal, originally to the people, later to the emperor). PRAETORS and

CONSULS held IMPERIUM, as did ex-magistrates holding special appointments, such as the governorship of a province held *pro praetore* or *pro consule* (implying that the post-holder was technically the substitute of a praetor or consul). Normally the *imperium* of propraetors and proconsuls was restricted to a particular province (PROVINCIA), which initially indicated a particular sphere of influence, but came to denote a geographical area, e.g. the province of Asia, outside which the *imperium* lapsed. In the late Republic, and in the imperial period, one proconsul could be appointed to outrank the others, his *imperium* being designated greater (*maius*). Under the Empire it was the emperors who possessed *imperium proconsulare maius*, although it was occasionally granted to a second individual, to create a unified command for a particular campaign (e.g. Germanicus in the east in AD 17), or to designate the emperor's chosen successor (e.g. Agrippa in 18 BC, Tiberius in AD 13). Certain provinces were assigned to the emperor, who governed through deputies (normally ex-praetors or ex-consuls) holding the title *legatus Augustus pro praetore*, and wielding *imperium* in his name. The emperor could also interfere in provinces under senatorial control, such as Africa and Asia, by virtue of his greater *imperium* (this is demonstrated by the Edicts of CYRENE), and a special dispensation allowed him to wield his *imperium* from within Rome itself (where the power normally lapsed). A victorious general, holder of *imperium*, could be hailed by the troops as IMPERATOR, although in the imperial period the salutation passed to the emperor, as the possessor of *imperium maius*.   RJB

Millar (1981); Wells (1984).

Incubation   the practice of sleeping inside a sacred enclosure. The purpose of incubation (*enkoimesis* in Greek) was to induce a dream or vision in which the deity would reveal a cure for the suppliant's ailment or distress or the location of lost property. Most commonly associated with the cult of ASCLEPIUS, the practice is attested at EPIDAURUS, PERGAMUM, COS, Smyrna, and Rome. Votive offerings bear witness to the success of the procedure, which was introduced into Christianity after the collapse of paganism and is still followed in parts of Greece today, e.g. Tenos.

See also DIVINATION; MEDICINE.   GS

Hamilton (1906); Lawson (1910).

India   Rumours about the marvels and exotica of India had filtered to the west, but there was no accurate geographical knowledge until ALEXANDER THE GREAT. He penetrated modern Pakistan as far as the Hyphasis (Beas) river, the easternmost tributary of the Indus, and knew stories of the land beyond. His admiral NEARCHUS OF CRETE sailed down the Indus and up the Persian Gulf in 326–324 BC, and wrote an account of his journey. SELEUCUS I NICATOR ceded several eastern satrapies to the Mauryan king SANDRACOTTUS in 302, and sent his envoy MEGASTHENES to his court. Megasthenes travelled widely and wrote an influential eye-witness account. Sandracottus' grandson ASHOKA (269–232) sent embassies to several Hellenistic rulers. The Greco-Bactrian kings extended their rule into India in the 2nd century. The greatest of these 'Indo-Greek' kings was the Buddhist MENANDER (fl. 155–130). By the 1st century BC the Romans, eager to expand their luxury TRADE, established regular contact with India via an open-sea route which utilized the monsoon cycles.

See also DEMETRIUS I OF BACTRIA; EUDOXUS OF CYZICUS; HIPPALUS; NAVIGATION.   EER

CAH VIII; Narain (1957); Sedlar (1980); Smith (1981); Tarn (1984); Thapar (1966); Wheeler (1968); Woodcock (1966).

Industry   In Greece the heaviest and most highly organized industries were the mines and quarries (*see* COPPER; GOLD; LEAD; MARBLE; SILVER). Most were state-controlled and worked by slave labour. At LAURIUM in Attica, about which we are best informed, there were perhaps 20,000 slaves working during the Peloponnesian War, of whom 1,000 belonged to NICIAS. In Ptolemaic Egypt the gold mines were worked by prisoners of war and criminals under the direction of the king.

Manufacture was carried out by small-scale cottage industries. Small groups of craftsmen worked together in workshops (*ergasteria*) dedicated to a particular trade, e.g. potters, smiths, leather workers, etc. The practitioners of each trade often formed themselves into GUILDS. The 120 slaves employed by Cephalus to make shields for Athens during the Peloponnesian War were exceptional. Athenian potters, probably the best-studied group, may have numbered 500 in the 5th century BC but they usually worked in groups of five or six. Skills were highly developed, especially among craftsmen in POTTERY, metal, bone, wood, and leather.

Essential trades were practised in every state, but certain cities acquired a reputation for particular industries: Athens for painted pottery, Chalcis and Corinth for metalwork, Megara for cloaks, Miletus for textiles and furniture. Humbler crafts were often illustrated on vases: carpentry, shoemaking, smithing, and woodcarving. Domestic crafts such as spinning, WEAVING, and baking were done, mostly by WOMEN, at home.

In the Hellenistic world there was larger-scale production of some commodities: large jars at Cnidus and Rhodes; parchment at Pergamum;

papyrus and textiles in Egypt. The availability of labour did not encourage the development of labour-saving techniques and most trades continued as before except that there was more state intervention: brewers needed a licence; oil workers were state employees and mills had to be registered. Only in the building industry and military engineering did increases in demand result in improved technology.

In Republican Rome workshops and guilds multiplied. Increased specialization of craftsmen was sometimes counteracted by their incorporation into larger enterprises that combined the resources of industry, commerce, and agriculture. Under the Empire industry was decentralized. In the east, Asia Minor was renowned for carpets and clothing; Syria and Egypt for GLASS and linen; and the eastern provinces in general for leather goods and jewellery. No major industry remained in Greece. In the west, Italian industry was not protected and had to make way for the pottery of Gaul and Germany, glass from the Rhineland, cloaks from Gaul and Britain, lamps from Africa. The growing tendency towards mass production resulted in cheaper and more standardized goods at the expense of technical and artistic skills. Independent workshops were largely superseded by estate workshops, and throughout the empire many factories and guilds were regulated by the state. But small-scale industry was still not wiped out and many local shops continued to compete successfully with the large conglomerates. The urban prosperity of the empire depended far more on agricultural than industrial production.

See also AGRICULTURE; BANKING; ENGINEERING; TRADE.   GS

Hopper (1979); Rostovtzeff (1941, 1957)

Inheritance in Greek law   Partible inheritance appears universal in Greece, but regulations are also concerned with the preservation of the family (*oikos*). At Athens an estate was normally divided between surviving sons, grandsons, or great-grandsons; failing that, the property might pass through a female descendant (*epikleros*), who would marry her closest willing paternal relative, to her son as heir. A childless man might adopt a son as heir in his lifetime or by a will; intestate succession was governed by a fixed order of precedence, with males receiving preference. At Sparta women could own and inherit property; and, at least in the 4th century BC, Spartans could give or bequeath property as they wished; but the state may have tried to prevent the division of land allotments through adoption and legal restrictions. At Gortyn (*see* GORTYN LAW CODE) sons and daughters inherited on fixed terms, sons receiving double shares; heiresses inherited, but normally had to marry a kinsman.   RB

Harrison (1968); Lane Fox (1985); MacDowell (1986); Willets (1967).

Inheritance in Roman law   The Roman law of natural or intestate succession was that the property of a deceased person passed automatically to *sui heredes* – that is, persons (both male and female) in his PATRIA POTESTAS who became *sui iuris* on his death. In the absence of *sui heredes* it went to the nearest agnates (i.e. brothers and sisters), and then, if none such existed, to the GENS. This was the basic pattern of intestate succession according to the IUS CIVILE, but as early as the TWELVE TABLES the individual's right to make a will was recognized, a major step in the development of the idea of individual ownership of property.

All Romans of any substance made wills, and were terrified of intestacy. The basic ingredient of a will was the naming of one or more heirs (*sui heredes* had to be so named or specifically disinherited in the will), who were to take over all the assets and liabilities of the deceased and to give effect to legacies and other dispositions. The habit of naming friends in one's will became very common at Rome, as did that of legacy-hunting. Augustus' law prohibiting unmarried or childless men from giving and receiving legacies was a drastic restriction of these practices. Wills could be contested, and major disputes were heard before the CENTUMVIRI.   TC

Crook (1967); Watson (1971).

Insubres   Gallic people. The Insubres arrived in CISALPINE GAUL in the early 5th century BC, settling around MEDIOLANUM (Milan). In 225 BC the Insubres and BOII were defeated at Telamon by Rome. The Romans then invaded their territory, and in 222 defeated them at Clastidium before advancing to Mediolanum. In 218 Roman colonies were established at Placentia (Piacenza) and Cremona, but shortly afterwards the Insubres joined HANNIBAL. After his defeat they faced the wrath of Rome and finally submitted in 196.   LPR

Chilver (1941).

Intercessio   right of veto. In Roman constitutional practice, when a MAGISTRATE disagreed with his colleague the negative view always prevailed. Equal (or superior) magistrates therefore had the right to 'intercede' in favour of the *status quo*. DICTATORS, who had supreme power and were without colleagues, were consequently free from *intercessio*. The right of *intercessio* belonging to the TRIBUNUS PLEBIS was different in that it arose from the sacrosanctity of their persons, which allowed them to intercede physically against the oppression of magistrates, and in the course of time to put a stop to elections, legislation, senatorial decrees, and the acts of any magistrate (except for dictators). This 'tribunician veto' became an important negative force in Roman politics, and was frequently used as a weapon in the struggles of the late Republic. It was drastically curtailed by SULLA, but restored by POMPEY in 70 BC.   TC

Brunt (1971b).

Interest rates *see* BANKING.

Interrex According to tradition, when a king of Rome died, the patrician senators took turns to hold the office of *interrex* ('between-king'), each serving for five days, until a new king was chosen. The institution continued under the Republic, and was implemented in the event of an *interregnum* – that is, if both consuls died or if a year ended with no new consuls elected. The office was always confined to PATRICIANS.   TC

Ion (5th century BC), of Chios, Greek tragedian and lyric poet. Ion was a friend of AESCHYLUS and SOPHOCLES and a successful tragic poet of the 5th-century Athenian stage. He was included in the Alexandrian canon of tragedians. He also wrote elegies, epigrams, hymns, and satyr plays, and a number of prose works including one on the foundation of Chios and a book of memoirs. But very little of Ion survives. GS

Ionian Revolt (499–494 BC), a revolt against Persian rule. The Ionian Revolt began with the overthrow of Persian-sponsored tyrants in the Greek cities, inspired by ARISTAGORAS of Miletus. An initial campaign saw the sack of Sardes, with support from Athens and Eretria, though not Sparta, and insurrection spread to Caria and Cyprus. The Persian counter-offensive probably began in 497: Cyprus was reduced after a year, Caria was gradually pacified, and Greek resistance was effectively terminated in 494 by the battle of Lade, where the large Greek fleet was undermined by desertion and defeated, and the ensuing siege of Miletus. Although Aristagoras and HISTIAEUS probably had personal reasons for revolt, the principal Greek motives were opposition to tyranny and rejection of Persian rule; economic disruption due to the Persian conquest may have been an additional factor in places. The settlement imposed by ARTAPHERNES was moderate, but Darius' desire for revenge on Athens and Eretria was to lead to MARATHON and Xerxes' invasion of Greece.   RB

Burn (1984); CAH IV; Tozzi (1978).

Ionians one of the principal Greek racial groups, characterized by speaking a distinct DIALECT of Greek and by celebrating the APATURIA (*see also* DELOS). They claimed descent from the Athenian hero Ion;

Athens was traditionally regarded as the origin (*metropolis*) of the Ionian migration; and the four Ionian tribes (*see* PHYLE) are found in some Ionic states. The Ionian area covered Attica, Euboea, the Cyclades, and the central part of coastal western Asia Minor, which is often loosely termed 'Ionia' (hence the oriental use of 'Ionians' for Greeks in general), and cities colonized from the area. In archaic times 12 leading cities of Ionia formed the Ionian League, centred on the Panionion at Mycale near Miletus, which survived in some form into the 4th century BC. A sense of ethnic identity persisted in the classical period: Ionians saw themselves as intelligent and imaginative, in contrast to the stolidity of DORIANS.   RB

Alty (1982); Emlyn-Jones (1980); Huxley (1966); Will (1956).

Ionic *see* DIALECTS, GREEK.

Ionic order *see* ARCHITECTURE, GREEK.

Iphicrates (*c*.415–353 BC), Athenian general. Iphicrates was a typical professional soldier, commanding Athenian or mercenary armies for more than 35 years. Discovering the value of the light-armed, in 390 BC he brilliantly destroyed with his PELTASTS a division of Spartan HOPLITES. After the King's Peace (386) he served the Thracian king, then the Persian, returning to Athens in 373 for various campaigns, notably the attempt to regain AMPHIPOLIS (368–365). For his conduct in the Greek SOCIAL WAR (357–355) he was prosecuted unsuccessfully by ARISTOPHON and CHARES.   GLC

Best (1969); Parke (1933).

Ipsus battle in 301 BC. Ipsus in Phrygia was the site of a major battle among the DIADOCHI who struggled for power after ALEXANDER THE GREAT's death. Attempting to curb the growing power of ANTIGONUS I MONOPHTHALMUS and his son DEMETRIUS I POLIORCETES, a coalition of CASSANDER, LYSIMACHUS, SELEUCUS I NICATOR, and PTOLEMY I defeated and killed Antigonus at Ipsus. His death ended any possibility of reviving Alexander's empire under one ruler. The victors divided Antigonus' Asian empire.   EER

Bar-Kochva (1976); Billows (1990); Grainger (1990b).

Ireland *see* HIBERNIA.

Irenaeus, St (*c*.AD 130–200), bishop of Lyon. Probably a native of Smyrna, Irenaeus studied under St POLYCARP and later at Rome. He spent most of his life in Gaul, becoming bishop of Lyon c.178. A passionate defender of traditional Christianity, especially against GNOSTICISM, Irenaeus is regarded as the first great Catholic theologian and a link between east and west. His most important work is the treatise *Against All Heresies* of which Latin, Syriac, and Armenian versions survive in addition to the original (incompletely preserved) Greek. GS

Chadwick (1986b).

Iron Iron began to replace BRONZE as the metal most commonly used for making weapons and tools soon after the fall of Mycenae. It exists in small deposits on the Greek mainland but was mined in only a few places (e.g. Laconia) and most was imported. In the 8th century BC Pithecoussae on the island of Ischia was colonized for the sake of the iron from Elba. In the classical period the main source of supply was the land of the Chalybes in north-western Asia Minor and perhaps southern Russia, but manufacture of iron goods was centred on Attica. By the Hellenistic period deposits of iron were also mined in Cyprus, Palestine, and the Caucasus. The Romans exploited supplies in Spain, Gaul, Britain, Noricum, Nubia, and later Dacia and Dalmatia. Iron spits were used as currency at an early date, and swords of tempered steel were made in Greece before the 5th century BC. Wrought iron was used for making statues, but cast iron was not generally available because furnaces could not maintain sufficiently high temperatures. GS

Healy (1978); White (1984).

Isaeus (4th century BC), Athenian orator. By tradition Isaeus was born at Chalcis on Euboea c.420 BC, moved to Athens as a pupil of ISOCRATES, and later taught DEMOSTHENES. As a metic he wrote speeches for others to deliver. Eleven survive intact, all concerned with INHERITANCE, and a fragment of a twelfth on civil rights. They range in date from c.390 to c.350. His style was described by Dionysius of Halicarnassus as similar to that of LYSIAS; but while Lysias and Isocrates create an impression of simple honesty, Isaeus and Demosthenes provoke suspicion with their elaborate artifice. GS

Kennedy (1963).

Isagoras (fl. c.508 BC), Athenian politician. Isagoras was leader of the faction opposed to CLEISTHENES after the fall of the tyranny. At first successful, he became archon in 508/7 BC, but the popularity of Cleisthenes' reform proposals drove him to call in CLEOMENES I of Sparta.

Although Cleisthenes and his supporters were initially exiled, popular reaction led to Isagoras and the Spartans being besieged on the Acropolis and expelled from Attica.   RB

Isis Egyptian goddess. Isis was the wife of Osiris and the mother of Horus. The cult of the Egyptian gods was introduced into Greece during the 4th century BC by expatriate Egyptians. It spread rapidly and became thoroughly hellenized in its iconography, its language, and all external features. Worship of Isis was universal throughout the Greco-Roman world and became an established part of state religion. She was also at the centre of a mystery cult whose obscure rites were celebrated at Rome, Pompeii, and elsewhere and whose popularity is attested by APULEIUS. In addition to statues and monuments, her symbols are found on jewellery, tombs, and reliefs throughout the empire.
See also SARAPIS.   GS

Burkert (1987); Solmsen (1979); Witt (1971).

Ismenias (fl. *c*.410–382 BC), Theban statesman. As THEBES increasingly asserted her independence from Sparta, Ismenias and Androcleidas clashed with the pro-Spartan Leontiades. Ismenias, being rich, helped THRASYBULUS to return to Athens (403), and in 395 promoted the outbreak of the Corinthian War. In 382 Leontiades induced the Spartan Phoebidas to seize the Cadmea and arrest Ismenias as a warmonger. He was tried, by a court consisting of Spartans and allies, for collaborating with Persia and so forcing AGESILAUS to return from Asia, and was executed.   GLC

Cloché (1952).

Isocrates (436–338 BC), Athenian orator. Isocrates was born into a wealthy Athenian family and studied under Prodicus, GORGIAS, and THERAMENES. In the 390s he worked as a speech writer and opened a school of RHETORIC on Chios. Isocrates did not participate personally in affairs of state, and his speeches (21 survive) are more illustrative of, than they were influential upon, the political issues of the day.

His *Panegyricus* (380) argued for the unity of Greece under the joint leadership of Athens and Sparta, a principle that was incorporated into the peace made by TIMOTHEUS in 375. He then wrote to leading rulers in turn (AGESILAUS, DIONYSIUS I, ALEXANDER OF PHERAE, perhaps ARCHIDAMUS III), imploring them to lead a Greek crusade against Persia. In 355 after the SOCIAL WAR he argued (in *On the Peace*) for a common peace throughout Greece and (in the *Areopagiticus*) for the restoration of powers to the Areopagus. In the *Philippus* (346) he returned to the theme of a panhellenic crusade, calling on PHILIP II to lead it and expel the Persians from Asia Minor. In the *Panathenaicus* (339) he compared the achievements of Athens and Sparta, to the glory of the former. Disappointed by events, he starved himself to death in 338.

GS

Kennedy (1963); Luce (1982).

Issus battle in 333 BC. Issus, near Alexandretta in northern Syria, was the site of ALEXANDER THE GREAT's second major battle against the Persian army. After the GRANICUS RIVER, Alexander conquered western and southern Asia Minor and, proceeding towards Phoenicia and Egypt, met the main Persian force at Issus. The Persian cavalry, deployed in an unfavourable position, was defeated. The Macedonian infantry also triumphed over the Persians. Alexander refused to accept peace terms and continued towards Phoenicia.   EER

Bosworth (1988a); Hammond (1989); Lane Fox (1973).

Isthmian Games festival held at Corinth every second year in honour of POSEIDON. Various legends ascribed its foundation to Sisyphus, king of Corinth, and to Theseus, king of Athens. The latter tradition may have enhanced its popularity among the Athenians. It included athletic and equestrian events as well as competitions for music and poetry. It was at the Isthmian Games of 196 BC that Quinctius FLAMININUS proclaimed the freedom of Greece.

See also FESTIVALS, GREEK; GAMES, GREEK.   GS

Harris (1964).

Istri Illyrian people. The Istri inhabited the mountainous Istrian peninsula between Monte Maggiore and the river Arsia, famous for piracy. Having opposed the establishment of the Latin colony at AQUILEIA in 181 BC, they were conquered by the Romans in 178–177. However, this conquest was incomplete and they surrendered again to the Romans in 129. During the Civil War they supported Pompey against Caesar. After Augustus' reforms they became a part of Italy.   HE

Potter (1987); Stipcevic (1977); Wilkes (1992).

Italy, geography The dominant geographical feature of the Italian peninsula is the great chain of the Apennine mountains, which stretch for more than 600 miles from the Ligurian Alps in the far north-west to the extreme southern tip of Bruttium (the 'toe'). This vast mountain range, which rises in places to over 10,000 feet, is not easily traversed in summer, and often completely impassable in winter. The poor natural communications between different parts of Italy help to explain the marked cultural diversity of its regions, which has been such a distinctive feature of Italian history from the earliest times to the present day.

Along the edges of the Apennines lies a series of coastal plains, particularly on the western side, which is favoured by easier natural communications along the river valleys, and exceptionally fertile volcanic soil. The most important of these areas, Etruria, LATIUM, and CAMPANIA, form the cockpit of Italian history in antiquity; from the Iron Age onwards this Tyrrhenian lowland zone surpassed all other regions of peninsular Italy in economic prosperity, social development, and political power. The Adriatic side has fewer natural advantages: a narrow and inhospitable coastal strip in the north and centre, and an arid and infertile plateau in the south.

Peninsular Italy enjoys a typical 'Mediterranean' climate, with mild wet winters and hot dry summers, suitable for the cultivation of vines and olives. It is to be distinguished from 'continental Italy', the vast fertile plain of the Po valley. Although this region has a more extreme climate, and is naturally marshy and subject to flooding, under the Romans it was reclaimed by large-scale drainage works and became what it still is today – one of the most productive and affluent parts of Europe.   TC

Cary (1949); Cornell and Matthews (1982); Delano-Smith (1979); Walker (1967).

Italy, history *To 31 BC*: The history of Italy properly begins with the Roman conquest; before that there were only the separate histories of the different groups that inhabited the country. The regional diversity of Italy, which has always been one of its characteristic features, becomes evident in the archaeological record at the start of the Iron Age (*c.*1000 BC), when distinct local cultures emerge, and in the linguistic evidence, which shows that at least 40 different languages were spoken in Italy before Roman times.

There were three main cultural groupings in Italy on the eve of the Roman conquest (*c.*350 BC). The first comprises the urbanized communities of the coastal plains around the Tyrrhenian and Ionian coasts. City life in Italy began with the Greeks, who in the 8th and 7th centuries BC had founded colonies (*see* COLONIZATION, GREEK) around the southern shores from TARENTUM to CUMAE, an area later known as MAGNA GRAECIA. This movement had profound cultural effects on the native peoples of Italy and led ultimately to the formation of city-states on the Greek pattern among the LATINI (including Rome) and ETRUSCANS, and eventually also in Umbria and Apulia.

The second major grouping includes the OSCAN-speaking peoples of the central and southern Apennines and the central Adriatic region.

These peoples, who include the SAMNITES, Lucani (*see* LUCANIA), BRUTTII, Vestini, and Frentani, migrated southwards and eastwards in the 5th century in a general movement of expansion, and their warlike excursions menaced the cities of the coastal plains. By 400 BC many of the Greek cities on the Tyrrhenian coast had succumbed, and the Latins were hard pressed by the SABINES, AEQUI, and VOLSCI. But during the 4th century the roles were reversed, as the city dwellers, united and organized by Rome, overran the peoples of the Apennines in the SAMNITE WARS.

The third important element was the CELTS of northern Italy, who had invaded the Po valley during the 5th century, and in the 4th made occasional raids across the Apennines into peninsular Italy. It was during one of these that BRENNUS' war band captured Rome (390 BC). Rome subsequently organized the defence of Italy against the feared invaders, and her effective leadership had much to do with the later loyalty of the SOCII.

The Roman conquest, which was complete by 264 BC, united the diverse peoples of the peninsula in a system of military alliances. This system was tested by HANNIBAL's invasion, but emerged victorious and was further strengthened by the overseas wars of conquest in the 2nd century. But it was not until the SOCIAL WAR that true political union was achieved, and only in the later 1st century that local customs died out and Latin displaced the old languages. This transformation was caused partly by war and devastation in Italy itself, especially in the period from 91 to 71 BC, and partly by the mass resettlement of veteran soldiers in colonies in all parts of Italy by Sulla, Caesar, and Octavian. POMPEII only became a Roman town after it received a Sullan colony; before that it had been largely Oscan-speaking.

We can only properly begin to speak of Roman Italy in the reign of AUGUSTUS, when it was governed as a unified country and divided into 11 administrative districts. These were: I Latium and Campania; II Apulia; III Lucania and Bruttium; IV Samnium; V Picenum; VI Umbria; VII Etruria; VIII Aemilia; IX Liguria; X Venetia; XI Transpadana. (*See* map on page 756.)   TC

Pallottino (1991); Potter (1987); Salmon (1982).

31 BC–AD 476: During the Roman Empire Italy gradually lost its preeminent position, and eventually was treated much as the other provinces. Under the early Empire Italy was exempt from direct taxation and largely free from direct rule from Rome, but in the 2nd/3rd centuries AD Roman officials were appointed to cities, districts, and finally to all of Italy, and Diocletian removed Italy's tax exemptions.

Initially, the Roman legions were largely of Italian origin, as Roman CITIZENSHIP was universal in Italy but limited elsewhere: the spread of citizenship in the 1st/2nd centuries allowed legions to be made up to strength elsewhere. Likewise the percentage of offices held by Italian *equites* declined rapidly, but Italians retained a strong presence in the Senate (about half in the 3rd century).

Italy also declined in economic terms relative to the provinces: Gallic POTTERY replaced the Italian red-glazed 'Arretine Ware' in the 1st century, and Spanish wine eclipsed Italian. However, this may have been only a relative decline, as the prosperity of other provinces increased. Italy was largely peaceful: the only serious fighting was in the year of the four emperors (AD 69), in *c.*168, and in 238, before the barbarian raids and the civil wars of the mid-3rd century, which affected only the north of the country. In 271, following an invasion by the Iuthungi, Aurelian began a new defensive wall around Rome (WALL OF AURELIAN). The VISIGOTHS invaded in 401–3, ALARIC sacked Rome in 410, and the VANDALS did likewise in 455 (although by that time RAVENNA had replaced Rome as the capital of the western empire, 404). In 476 the last Roman emperor, ROMULUS AUGUSTULUS, was succeeded by the first barbarian king of Italy, ODOACER.

No new cities were founded after the reign of Augustus, but this is largely because Italy was already fully 'romanized'. Urban prosperity generally increased up to the 3rd century, and then faltered, in line with other provinces. Our knowledge of Italy is greatly augmented by the eruption of Vesuvius (AD 79), which preserved POMPEII and HERCULANEUM largely intact. In addition, large parts of OSTIA survive as they were rebuilt in the 2nd century AD. Ostia was one of a number of towns to benefit from its proximity to Rome: the first harbour was built by Claudius I and Nero (AD 42–62), and an inner one by Trajan.

Under Trajan (98–117) the ALIMENTA was introduced to provide for the children of the poor in Italian towns: the scheme was widespread and lasted into the 3rd century. Imperial control over Italy was extended in the 2nd century by the appointment of *curatores* (overseers), normally senators or equestrians, to control public finances. Such *curatores* continued to function in the 3rd and 4th centuries. Similarly, judicial officials (*iuridici*, judges, normally senators) were imposed in Italy by Marcus Aurelius (161–80) following Hadrian's appointment of four ex-consulars for the same purpose. In the 260s/270s the *iuridici* were replaced by a *corrector*. Everyday life seems to have been little disrupted by barbarian invasions, and central Italy remained peaceful: Italy became in effect a provincial backwater, dominated by Rome.

RJB

Millar (1981); Potter (1987).

Ituraeans Arab people. The Ituraeans' territory centred on Chalcis and Heliopolis. Mark ANTONY defeated and killed their tetrarch Lysanias

(35 BC), passing his lands to CLEOPATRA VII of Egypt. Octavian restored Ituraean semi-independence under Zenodorus (30 BC), but later (24) the kingdom was split up, much of it passing to HEROD THE GREAT. Herod's dominions passed to his son Philip (4 BC–AD 34); AGRIPPA I (37–44); and AGRIPPA II (53–c.93). Chalcis passed to Herod, brother of Agrippa I (AD 41–8), and Agrippa II (50–3), after which the region was fully absorbed into the Roman empire. The Ituraeans remained a primitive people, contributing archers to the Roman AUXILIA.   RJB

Bowersock (1983).

Iudex   Roman judge. The judge for a case was chosen by the participants, the plaintiff putting forward a name drawn from a panel of senators (though later including EQUESTRIANS), the defendant having the right to refuse an individual. Membership of the panel could only be avoided on grounds of being a minor or physically handicapped. Once chosen, judges were compelled to serve, though they could claim exemption on grounds of age, family size, or profession (doctor, philosopher, or orator). The precise nature of the case had already been decided by a magistrate, allowing it to take any form desired. The function of the *iudex* was to pronounce a verdict on it, possibly with the assistance of advisers. He was not bound by precedent, though this does seem to have influenced decisions.

See also JUDICIAL PROCEDURE, ROMAN.   HE

Nicholas (1962).

Iudicia populi   Roman popular appeal courts. During the early Republic these courts conducted trials in front of the people who were drawn up in military units outside the POMERIUM, the legal boundary of the city. They were the only courts permitted to condemn Roman citizens to death, which meant that all capital trials were eventually subject to their jurisdiction. These courts were used only for political offences, not for criminal cases.

See also COMITIA.   HE

Gruen (1968); Jones (1972); Nicholas (1962).

Ius civile   literally the 'law of the citizens', and as such to be differentiated from the IUS GENTIUM. But the term was also used by jurists to define the law deriving from statutes in contrast to that introduced by the magistrates, particularly the Praetor's edict (*see* EDICTUM).   TC

Jolowicz and Nicholas (1972).

Ius gentium   rather vague and confusing term in Roman law, used in the sources (and in modern handbooks) in a variety of different contexts.

Occasionally it means something like 'international law', and describes the legal relations between Rome and other states. Sometimes it refers to the 'law of nations' in a philosophical sense – that is, the concept of a universal or natural law implanted in the people of all nations by human reason. Thirdly, and most commonly, it is used, in contrast to the IUS CIVILE, to describe the law governing relations between Roman citizens and foreigners, and particularly matters dealt with by the PRAETOR Peregrinus.   TC

Jolowicz and Nicholas (1972).

Ius Italicum   The *ius Italicum* (Italian Right) was granted to a colony, or settlement of Roman citizens, in Roman territory outside Italy, which thus acquired the same status as Italy, enjoying immunity from TRIBUTUM *soli*. Most colonies of the late Republic and the early Empire up to the time of Hadrian were settlements of retired legionaries, who were already Roman citizens, so the *ius Italicum* was granted automatically. However, the title of *colonia* could also be granted to an existing city, and in these cases the grant of *ius Italicum* did not necessarily follow, but might be granted later as an additional privilege.
    See also COLONIZATION, ROMAN.   RJB

Millar (1981); Salmon (1968).

Ius Latii   The *ius Latii* (Latin Right) implied a status mid-way between that of Roman citizen and non-citizen, initially separating the inhabitants of Rome from those of the rest of Italy. In the early imperial period, when all Latin citizens were also Roman citizens, but before citizenship was extended throughout the empire (by Caracalla, in AD 212), the grant of Latin status was made to many provincial cities, whose local magistrates thus became Roman citizens. The right was normally granted as a preliminary step to granting the city the status of a MUNICIPIUM, which extended citizenship to all its inhabitants.   RJB

Scullard (1982).

Ius primae relationis   The *ius primae relationis* was the right to bring forward the first item of business at meetings of the Senate, a power traditionally held by the consuls. It was a significant right that AUGUSTUS lacked after giving up the consulship in 23 BC: as the holder of *tribunicia potestas*, he had the power to convene the Senate, but did not hold the *ius primae relationis*. Accordingly, in 22 BC it was arranged that it be granted to Augustus by special decree of the people (*lex de imperio*), on the initiative of the Senate, and subsequent emperors also obtained and exercised this right. RJB

Salmon (1968); Scullard (1982).

Iusiurandum the Latin term for an oath, sworn by one or both parties in a dispute in order to show their good faith. In judicial trials the plaintiff could invite the defendant to swear to the validity of his claim; if he refused he lost the case. But the defendant had the right to ask the plaintiff to swear in his turn, on the same conditions. The procedure was a way of producing an instant result, either in favour of the party who took the oath, or against the one who refused. TC

Iuvenes The *iuvenes* or *iuventus* were clubs of free-born young Roman men between the ages of 14 and 17 who met to practise sports together in preparation for their military service (*see* GUILDS). The institution had Republican origins but was strongly promoted by AUGUSTUS in the *municipia* as well as at Rome to invigorate the youth of Italy and encourage loyalty to the new social order. His grandsons, Gaius and Lucius, were honoured with the title 'Princeps Iuventutis'. Nero founded games known as the *Juvenalia* in AD 59 at which the sons of the nobility were encouraged to compete. In the 2nd century the institution of the clubs spread throughout the western provinces.

See also EDUCATION. GS

J

Janiculum part of Rome. The Janiculum was a long ridge, running north–south, lying on the right bank of the Tiber and overlooking the city of Rome. The name is apparently derived from JANUS. The ridge was the first line of defence against enemies coming from Etruria, but lay too far from the city to be enclosed in the WALL OF SERVIUS or WALL OF AURELIAN. The Janiculum also included the area closer to the Tiber, behind the ridge, that formed Augustus' *regio* xiv. This was mostly industrial and fell within Aurelian's Wall.   HE

Platner and Ashby (1929); Richardson (1992); Robinson (1992).

Janus Roman god. Janus, whose symbol was a head facing both ways, was originally a god of house doorways who became a god of city gates as well. Since to go through a door or city gate involved a new start, Janus also became god of beginnings. January, the first month of the reformed calendar (*see* TIME, MEASUREMENT OF), was named after him. He came first in a list of gods in a prayer, even before JUPITER. His blessing was sought for the beginning of each day and at births. The doors of his temple in the Forum were open in time of war. Peace (a rare event in Roman history) was symbolized by the 'closing of Janus'.   DP

Scullard (1981).

Jason tyrant of Pherae, *c*.380–370 BC. By force and threat of force, Jason united THESSALY and with the support of Polydamas of Pharsalus was appointed TAGUS. With the help of the Molossian king Alcetas, he commanded 8,000 cavalry and 20,000 infantry. He professed ambitions to unite Greece and attack Persia, a Panhellenist 'to judge by words, not deeds'. After LEUCTRA (371) the Thebans summoned him as ally to assist in the utter destruction of the Spartan army. He arrived and dissuaded them from risking what they had gained. In 370 he planned to go to Delphi (with a huge procession of victims) at the head of his army and preside over the festival. But he was assassinated and his real intentions remain unclear.   GLC

Westlake (1935).

Javolenus Priscus   (b. before AD 60, d. after 120), Roman jurist. Gaius Octavius Tidius Tossianus Javolenus Priscus was a legionary commander before becoming a *iuridicus* (governor's legal deputy) of Britain, suffect consul (AD 86), governor of Germania Superior and Syria, and proconsul of Africa. As a lawyer he headed the Sabinian school. His *Epistulae* (14 books) are lost but excerpts in Justinian justify his high reputation.

See also JURISPRUDENCE.   GS

Jerome, St   (AD 331–420), Latin Christian writer. Eusebius Hieronymus (Jerome) was born in Dalmatia but moved to Rome where he studied under Aelius DONATUS and was baptized. He travelled much, in the west (to Trier) and the east (to Syria where he learned Hebrew; Antioch were he learned Greek and was ordained; and Constantinople where he met GREGORY OF NAZIANZUS). Back in Rome (382–5) Pope Damasus persuaded him to revise the Latin Gospels. He then returned to the east, founded a monastery in Bethlehem, and devoted himself to scholarship. His most important works, written in fine Ciceronian prose, are the *Famous Men*, a biographical dictionary of 135 Christian writers, an expanded translation of EUSEBIUS' *Chronicle*, his revision of the Latin Bible (*see* VULGATE), and his correspondence.   GS

Kelly (1975)

Jerusalem   city in Judaea in Palestine. Jerusalem was the capital city of the JEWS and the site of the Temple. Palestine was included in ALEXANDER THE GREAT's empire, ruled by the Ptolemies in the 3rd century BC, and passed into Seleucid control in the 2nd century. ANTIOCHUS IV EPIPHANES tried to hellenize Judaea, and rededicated the Temple to Zeus in 167. The revolt of JUDAS MACCABAEUS ensued, leading to the rule of the Hasmonaean high priests in Jerusalem after 152. POMPEY intervened in their internal disputes, and in 63 BC captured Jerusalem. From 37 BC HEROD THE GREAT ruled as king, instituted a massive building programme, and lavishly rebuilt the Temple. After his death Jerusalem became part of the Roman province of Judaea. As the centre of the revolt of AD 66–70, the city and Temple were destroyed by TITUS. After

the revolt of BAR-KOCHBA in AD 132–5, HADRIAN rebuilt Jerusalem as a
Roman colony for non-Jews. CONSTANTINE I later erected several
Christian monuments.

See also HYRCANUS II; HYRCANUS, JOHN.   EER

Bickerman (1988); Davies and Finkelstein (1989); Finegan (1969); Grainger
(1991); Schürer (1973–87); Stillwell (1976).

Jewellery Most surviving Greek jewellery comes from funereal contexts and takes the form of bracelets, buttons, diadems, earrings,
necklaces, pins, rings, etc. GOLD has survived better than any other
metal, though SILVER was also used, as were less precious materials
such as BRONZE, IRON, and LEAD. Many techniques, such as filigree,
granulation, inlay, chasing, and repoussé, were no doubt acquired
from contact with Egypt and Mesopotamia. Our knowledge of ancient
jewellery is supplemented by references in literature and in inscriptions,
particularly temple inventories which list offerings of valuables to the
gods. Styles of decoration followed a similar progression to those of
the other arts, moving from simple and stylized forms to more complex
and realistic designs.

Hellenistic patterns informed the jewellery of the Roman world where
simplicity characterized cultivated taste into the early Empire. Standards of craftsmanship deteriorated but colourful effects were achieved
by the use of different stones. Writers such as PETRONIUS and the elder
PLINY inveighed against the moral depravity symbolized by the precious
metals, GEMS, and unguents then in vogue among the provincial and
freedman classes. In the later Empire men as well as women took to
wearing heavily jewelled belts, buckles, and brooches of considerable
splendour.

See also DRESS.   GS

Higgins (1980); Jacobsthal (1956).

Jewish literature in Greek. The Jews of the Diaspora more easily fell
under the influence of Hellenism than those in Palestine. In particular
the community in ALEXANDRIA, which became numerous after the mid-
2nd century BC, made a notable contribution to literary circles. Most
of it centred on the Septuagint, the Greek translation of the Bible that
was made then for the benefit of Jews who knew no Hebrew.
Apocryphal scriptures and semi-canonical books of prophecy were
composed; so also were biographical studies of such characters as
Abraham, Jacob, and Moses. Secular historical writing is represented
by the work of Demetrius, ALEXANDER POLYHISTOR, JOSEPHUS, and Justus;
prophetic literature by the *Sibylline Oracles*. PHILO was a philosopher
in the Greek tradition. Ezekiel wrote a tragedy on the *Exodus* of which

269 lines survive, and Theodotus wrote an epic *On the Jews* of which we have 47 lines.

See also ARISTOBULUS OF ALEXANDRIA. GS

Fraser (1972).

Jews In biblical times Palestine was the homeland of the Jews, and JERUSALEM in Judaea was their capital and site of the Temple. When the Persians invaded in 587 BC, destroying the first Temple built by Solomon, Nebuchadnezzar took the Jews into captivity in Babylonia. This is considered the beginning of the Diaspora (Dispersion) of the Jews. CYRUS allowed their return in 538. Those who returned to Palestine constructed the second Temple. Their political fortunes followed those of the Persian empire until it was destroyed by ALEXANDER THE GREAT. Thereafter the Jews of Palestine were ruled successively by the Ptolemies and Seleucids. The revolt of JUDAS MACCABAEUS in 167 BC led to the eventual establishment of the independent Hasmonaean state in Jerusalem, which lasted for some 80 years. Territorial expansion into neighbouring parts of Palestine proceeded rapidly. POMPEY the Great intervened in 63 BC, after which Rome appointed docile clients to powerful positions. The Roman province of Judaea was created in AD 6. There were serious revolts in Jerusalem in AD 66–70, AD 132–5, and in the reigns of ANTONINUS PIUS and Septimius SEVERUS.

After the Diaspora many Jews remained in Babylonia where there were flourishing communities. In the Hellenistic age many Jews emigrated from Babylonia and Palestine; ANTIOCH, ALEXANDRIA, CYRENAICA, and ROME all had large Jewish populations. Although many Jews spoke Greek and were to some extent hellenized, the Jews maintained their religious and ethnic identity and exclusivity. Jewish religious freedom was protected by law in the Roman empire, but Jewish unpopularity led to violent riots in Egypt, Syria, and Cyrenaica in the first centuries AD.

See also ANTIOCHUS IV EPIPHANES; ANTIPATER OF IDUMAEA; BAR-KOCHBA; DEAD SEA SCROLLS; DURA EUROPUS; HEROD ANTIPAS; HEROD THE GREAT; HYRCANUS II; HYRCANUS, JOHN; JOSEPHUS; PHILO OF JUDAEA. EER

Avi-Yonah (1984); Bickerman (1988); Davies and Finkelstein (1989); Eddy (1961); Goodman (1987); Grainger (1991); Green (1990); Schürer (1973–87); Sullivan (1990).

John the usurper see VALENTINIAN III.

John Chrysoston, St see CHRYSOSTOM, ST JOHN.

Josephus (b. *c*.AD 37), Jewish historian. Josephus, son of Matthias, was educated at a rabbinic school in Jerusalem. At the age of 26 he visited Rome, securing the release of some fellow priests through the good offices of Nero's wife, Poppaea. He returned to Jerusalem (AD 66), becoming one of the moderate leaders of the Jewish revolt, as commander of Galilee. Captured by the Romans (67), he was pardoned by VESPASIAN, and, after the sack of Jerusalem (70), accompanied TITUS to Rome, taking the name Flavius Josephus in honour of his patron Flavius Vespasian. Four Latin works written by Josephus in Rome survive, the most important being the *Jewish War* (*Bellum Judaiicum*, 66–70), and the *Jewish Antiquities*, a history of the Jews from Adam up to AD 66. Josephus' date of death is unknown, though his later works, a *Vita* (Life) and *Concerning the Antiquity of the Jews* and *in Apionen* ('against Apion') were written after 93.   RJB

Rajak (1983); Williamson (1981).

Jovian (*c*.AD 331–64), Roman emperor, AD 363–4. Flavius Jovianus, son of Varronianus, a Danubian, served as a senior staff-officer on JULIAN's Persian campaign. After Julian's death (June 363) he was chosen emperor, a compromise candidate, and was obliged to conclude an unpopular peace, surrendering DIOCLETIAN's territorial gains in order to extricate the Roman army. An ardent Christian, he immediately reversed the religious policies of Julian. He died at Dadastana while on his way to Constantinople (February 364).   RJB

Grant (1985).

Juba I (d. 46 BC), king of Numidia. Juba I, the son of Hiempsal II and king of NUMIDIA, was said as a young man to have been offended by Julius CAESAR and thus joined POMPEY in the CIVIL WAR. He aided CATO UTICENSIS and METELLUS SCIPIO, by whom he was supposedly promised the Roman province of AFRICA. Juba escaped from the defeat at THAPSUS in 46 BC but subsequently committed suicide.
See also JUBA II.   HS

Braund (1984).

Juba II (d. *c*.AD 23), king of Mauretania. Juba II, the son of JUBA I, was as a child paraded in the triumph of Julius CAESAR in 46 BC. Educated in Italy, he became a friend of AUGUSTUS and was given the African client kingdom of MAURETANIA, and, briefly, that of NUMIDIA. Of a scholarly disposition, he wrote prolifically in Greek and encouraged the spread of Greek and Roman culture in his kingdom.   HS

Braund (1984).

Judaea *see* JEWS.

Judas Maccabaeus   (fl. 166–160 BC), Jewish revolutionary leader. Judas Maccabaeus, a Jewish priest from the house of Hashmon, led a popular revolt in JERUSALEM after the Seleucid ANTIOCHUS IV EPIPHANES responded to various Jewish disturbances in 167 BC by rededicating the Temple to Zeus and garrisoning a new citadel. Judas reconsecrated the Temple in 164, but rivalries among the Greek generals in charge of suppressing the revolt led to a temporary truce. Judas accepted neither concessions nor the hellenized high priest, and continued the revolt as a political struggle. His death in 160 left the hellenizers in power, but the revolt led ultimately to the establishment of the independent Hasmonaean state.

See also JEWS.   EER

Bickerman (1988); CAH VIII; Davies and Finkelstein (1989); Eddy (1961); Green (1990); Schürer (1973–87).

Judicial procedure, Greek   The earliest judicial procedure was arbitration, the voluntary settlement of disputes by a judge or judges chosen from the elders or nobles; this precedes the emergence of written law in the 7th century BC (*see* DRACO; ZALEUCUS), which imposed controls on judges by regulating procedures and penalties. In some states the administration of justice was in the hands of magistrates or the council, and the assembly sometimes retained limited judicial powers; but even in oligarchies jury courts appear to have been the norm, though their composition varied widely. Although states had some capacity to initiate prosecutions, to imprison, and to exact penalties, including death, where their interests were concerned, the detection and prosecution of most offences devolved on individuals, who would prepare the case (including evidence) and present it in court; the Greeks had no professional lawyers or policemen, and litigants relied on friends, patrons, or orators for assistance.

The conduct of cases involving citizens of different states was often regulated by agreed conventions (*symbola* or *symbolai*), particularly those cases involving commerce and contracts, although in the 5th century Athens ordered the reference of many cases from allied courts to Athens for political reasons. Arbitration, which remained important in private disputes, was the only effective means of resolving interstate disputes peacefully, though it was hard to enforce; conversely, military sanctions might be invoked by supra-national bodies such as the DELPHIC AMPHICTYONY and the League of CORINTH.

See also LAW, ATHENIAN.   RB

Adcock and Mosley (1975); Bonner and Smith (1930–8); Cohen (1973); Gagarin (1986); Jones (1956); MacDowell (1986).

Judicial procedure, Roman The characteristic feature of Roman judicial procedure was that it was completed in two stages, the first before a magistrate (*in iure*), when the nature of the case was established, the second before a judge (*apud iudicem*), a private citizen appointed by the magistrate, who heard the case and gave judgement (*see* IUDEX). The earliest form was the so-called *legis actio* procedure, which required the parties to recite certain prescribed oral formulae stating the nature of their claims; any departure from the correct form of words could lose the whole case.

In the classical period this archaic and rigid type of action was replaced by the so-called formulary procedure, introduced probably in the 2nd century BC. It involved the use of written formulae drawn up by the praetor at the initial hearing, usually based on models set out in the edict (*see* EDICTUM). The system was flexible because formulae could be adapted to suit particular cases. This became the standard form of civil procedure.

During the Principate a different procedure was introduced, which did away with the two stages, and placed the whole administration of justice in the hands of state officials. This *cognitio extra ordinem*, as it was called, eventually replaced the formulary system; from now on all disputes were heard and decided in one go by officials appointed by the emperor or provincial governor.

These procedures were used in civil litigation, which included many cases that would nowadays be called criminal (e.g. theft, damage to property, assault, etc.). Special criminal procedures existed in Rome, but only for cases where the interests of the state were directly involved, e.g. theft or embezzlement of public property, treason, or abuses by state officials. For the development of these special procedures *see* QUAESTIO.

TC

Jolowicz and Nicholas (1972); Kelly (1975).

Jugurtha (d. 104 BC), Numidian leader. Jugurtha, an illegitimate grandson of MASSINISSA, served under SCIPIO AEMILIANUS at Numantia in 133 BC, and through his recommendation was adopted by King Micipsa of Numidia, who had two sons of his own. Within six years of the king's death in 118 Jugurtha had eliminated both sons and taken control of Numidia. SALLUST alleges that lavish bribery of influential friends at Rome allowed him a free hand in his schemes, but when he murdered some Italian residents at Cirta in 112 the Senate was forced to act. The Roman army sent against him in 111 at first achieved little, but eventually gained the upper hand under METELLUS NUMIDICUS and MARIUS who finished the war in 105. Jugurtha was captured and executed at Rome in 104. The war against Jugurtha was more important for the political upheavals it caused at Rome than for any change in

Rome's position in Africa, as Numidia was left in the hands of native rulers.   DP

Carney (1970); Paul (1984); Scullard (1982); Syme (1964).

Julia Domna (d. AD 217), wife of Septimius SEVERUS. Julia Domna, daughter of Julius Bassianus, a Syrian, and sister of Julia Maesa, was the second wife of Septimius Severus and the mother of CARACALLA and GETA. Domna was an able woman, who surrounded herself with a personal court of learned men, such as AELIAN, DIOGENES LAERTIUS, GALEN, OPPIAN, PAPINIAN, PAULUS, and ULPIAN, and was largely responsible for the great increase in eastern, particularly eastern religious, influences in the empire.   RJB

Birley (1988); Grant (1979); Parker (1958).

Julia Maesa   see ELAGABALUS; SEVERUS ALEXANDER.

Julia Major (39 BC–AD 14), daughter of AUGUSTUS. Julia, Augustus' only child, became a pawn in a series of dynastic alliances. Her first husband, Augustus' nephew, MARCELLUS, died in 23 BC. Within two years she married Marcus AGRIPPA, and subsequently bore him five children: Gaius CAESAR; Lucius Caesar; Julia; AGRIPPINA (the elder); and AGRIPPA POSTUMUS. After Agrippa's death, she married Augustus' step-son TIBERIUS (11 BC), but was exiled when her immoral behaviour finally came to Augustus' notice (2 BC).   RJB

Scullard (1982); Wells (1984).

Julia Mammaea   see SEVERUS ALEXANDER.

Julia Soaemias   see ELAGABALUS.

Julian (AD 332–63), Roman emperor, AD 360–3. Flavius Claudius Julianus, grandson of CONSTANTIUS I and Theodora through their son Julius Constantius, was appointed Caesar by his cousin CONSTANTIUS II (November 355). Julian had survived the massacre of Constantine's relatives (337), living in seclusion until the elevation of his half-brother GALLUS (351). He received a Christian education through the influence of his relative Bishop Eusebius of Nicomedia, but was more deeply influenced by pagan philosophers. As Caesar, Julian proved an unexpected success, winning a series of victories against the ALAMANNI and restoring the security of the Rhine frontier. When Constantius demanded the transfer of a large proportion of Julian's army to the east, the troops refused to go, instead proclaiming Julian Augustus (February

360). Conflict between Julian and Constantius seemed inevitible, but Constantius was delayed by SHAPUR II's incursions, and died in November 361, leaving Julian as sole emperor. Julian now publicly rejected CHRISTIANITY (hence his title 'the Apostate'), reinstituting pagan cults and introducing a pagan organization to rival that of the Christians. He proclaimed toleration, but actively discouraged Christianity, for example by forbidding Christians to teach in schools. Julian implemented an extensive programme of reforms, easing the tax burden by reducing the size, and increasing the efficiency, of the imperial bureaucracy. In March 363, eager to bring the inherited Persian war to a successful conclusion, Julian moved east, but was fatally wounded (perhaps murdered) during a skirmish (June 363), and succeeded by Jovian. Julian's reign is extensively documented, both in his own writings and those of AMMIANUS MARCELLINUS. RJB

Bowersock (1978); Browning (1975); Grant (1985); Lieu (1986).

Julianus *see* DIDIUS JULIANUS.

Julianus, Salvius (*c*.AD 100–169), Roman jurist. Publius Salvius Julianus was born near Hadrumetum in Africa and was a pupil of JAVOLENUS PRISCUS. His revision of the praetorian edict (*see* EDICTUM), which Hadrian invited him to undertake, gained him a high reputation and led to a distinguished public career. His offices included the quaestorship, praetorship, consulship (in 148), and the governorship of several provinces. As a lawyer he became the last recorded head of the Sabinian school and composed a *Digest* in 90 books, a highly original and influential work of which numerous excerpts appear in Justinian and later classical jurists.

See also JURISPRUDENCE; LAW, ROMAN. GS

Julius Africanus *see* AFRICANUS.

Julius Caesar *see* CAESAR.

Julius Nepos *see* NEPOS.

Juno Roman goddess. Juno was an old, very important Italian goddess. She was early identified with HERA through the similarity in their functions, and so was sister and wife of JUPITER. She was the protectress of women, especially when they married or gave birth, and her most famous festival, the Matronalia, was celebrated by matrons and virgins on 1 March. But she was also a great goddess of the state, and as Juno Regina she made up the Capitoline triad with Jupiter and MINERVA, while Virgil depicts her political power throughout the *Aeneid*.

DP

Ogilvie (1969); Scullard (1981).

Jupiter the chief Roman god. Jupiter, like the Greek ZEUS, was essentially a weather god, his name perhaps meaning 'father of the sky'. The Etruscan kings introduced the cult of 'the best and greatest Jupiter', in which he was associated with JUNO and MINERVA in a temple on the Capitoline hill. The *Ludi Romani* (*see* GAMES, ROMAN) in September, Rome's greatest festival with its solemn banquet, were in his honour. As sky god he was especially worshipped by farmers, but as a wielder of thunderbolts, and so able to punish, he was associated with oaths, treaties, and the laws of hospitality. White, symbol of the light of the day, was his colour, and his bird the eagle.

DP

Ogilvie (1969); Scullard (1981).

Jurisprudence Until the 3rd century BC the legal profession at Rome was tied exclusively to the priesthood. Though the monopoly was broken *c.*300 BC, the law retained its aristocratic associations and until the last years of the Republic jurists, such as SCAEVOLA, were always holders of high office and members of senatorial families. To them jurisprudence was a natural extension of the art of government. Under the early Empire jurists such as JAVOLENUS PRISCUS and JULIANUS were drawn from a wider circle but were still primarily public figures. From the time of Hadrian lawyers such as PAPINIAN, PAULUS, and ULPIAN exercised their influence rather as members of the imperial council (*see* CONSILIUM PRINCIPIS) and of one of the two legal schools, the Sabinian and the Proculian (*see* SABINUS). The universalization of the law required that its practice should become a science.

The role of the jurist was central to the Roman legal system. He drafted documents, advised on the conduct of law, and gave authoritative opinions (*responsa*) on questions of law laid before him. He exercised influence through the advice that he gave to magistrates (especially on the praetor's edict, *see* EDICTUM) and to judges, through his teaching, and through his writing; advocacy, however, was left to the ADVOCATUS. Almost nothing survives of the Republican literature and for knowledge of later writing we depend on extracts in Justinian's *Digesta*. It included commentaries, especially on the praetor's edict and on earlier jurists; collections of *responsa* and discussions of cases; monographs and textbooks, most notably the *Institutes* of GAIUS. The form was essentially an original Roman creation. Its influence on medieval and modern law has been fundamental.

See also CAPITO; CELSUS; GAIUS; LABEO; LAW, ROMAN; MAECIANUS; NERATIUS PRISCUS; POMPONIUS. GS

Frier (1985); Jolowicz and Nicholas (1972).

Justinian *see* LAW, ROMAN.

Juvenal (*c.*AD 55–128), Latin satirist. Decimus Junius Juvenalis moved from his native Aquinum to Rome where he lived in poor circumstances. He became a friend of MARTIAL, who addressed three epigrams to him; but, unlike other satirists, Juvenal writes little about himself and details of his life are sketchy. No other contemporary writer mentions him and his work did not become popular until the 4th century, when it was imitated by AUSONIUS. Fifteen satires (and fragments of a sixteenth) survive and present a powerful portrait of decadent Roman society at the close of the 1st century AD. Published between 110 and 128, the poems focus on the reign of DOMITIAN (81–96), when Juvenal may have suffered banishment, and seem motivated by a sense of personal failure and injustice. But brilliant use of rhetoric, allusion, and parody obscures the truth that Juvenal's Rome is a perennial one.

See also SATIRE. GS

Coffey (1989); Highet (1954); Hutchinson (1993); Rudd (1986).

K and L

Koine *see* DIALECTS, GREEK.

Labeo (*c*.48 BC–AD 11), Roman jurist. Marcus Antistius Labeo was a plebeian by birth but a pupil of CICERO. He rose to be praetor and refused the consulship offered him by Augustus. As a lawyer he was learned and innovative. As a writer he was prolific and is said to have written 400 books. But these are known only from quotations in other jurists and from excerpts in the *Digest*.   GS

Labienus (*c*.100–45 bc), Roman soldier. Titus Labienus, as tribune in 63 BC, cooperated with CAESAR in the prosecution of Gaius Rabirius, and from 58 to 51 was Caesar's senior officer in Gaul, taking command in his absence and successfully conducting independent operations. Although Caesar perhaps promised him a consulship for 48, Labienus deserted to POMPEY in 49, either because Pompey for him represented legitimate government or because as a native of Picenum he had always had close links with Pompey. He died at MUNDA. DP

Syme (1939).

Lachares (fl. *c*.301–295 bc), Athenian politician. Lachares supported CASSANDER in Athens after DEMETRIUS I POLIORCETES was defeated at IPSUS in 301 bc. Deploying mercenaries to defeat his opponents, he became virtual tyrant *c*.300. After Cassander's death in 297, hostility to Lachares grew in face of Demetrius' renewed threat to Athens. He forced his enemies to withdraw to Piraeus, remaining in control of Athens himself. Demetrius and Lachares' opponents successfully besieged Athens in 294, after which Lachares escaped to Boeotia.   EER

Ferguson (1911); Green (1990); Mossé (1973).

Laconia   region in south-east Greece to the east of MESSENIA and south of ARCADIA and the Argolid. The central plain of SPARTA is bounded by Mt Parnon to the east and Mt Taygetus to the west. It was settled by DORIANS in the 10th century bc and was entirely under Spartan control by the 8th. The rest of Laconia was the territory of nominally independent PERIOIKOI but in practice was ruled by Sparta. After the assassination of NABIS (192 bc) Laconia with Sparta was forced to become part of the ACHAEAN LEAGUE.   GS

Cartledge (1979).

Lactantius   (c.AD 240–320), Latin Christian writer. Lucius Caecilius Firmianus Lactantius was born a pagan in Africa whence he was summoned by DIOCLETIAN to Nicomedia to teach rhetoric. By 303 he had converted to Christianity when he lost his job in the persecution which inspired his Christian writings. His *Divine Institutes* is a wide-ranging work of Christian apologetic. Other works, written in good Ciceronian Latin, include a treatise *On the Wrath of God* and a pamphlet *On the Deaths of the Persecutors*.   GS

Ogilvie (1978); Wlosok (1960).

Lade   *see* IONIAN REVOLT.

Laelianus   *see* POSTUMUS.

Laelius   (2nd century BC), Roman politician. Gaius Laelius, 'the Wise', was a close friend of SCIPIO AEMILIANUS, under whom he served at the siege of CARTHAGE in 146 BC. Probably as consul in 140, he put forward, but then dropped, a proposal for agrarian reform. In 132 he aided the persecution of the supporters of the agrarian reformer Tiberius GRACCHUS.

Cicero judged Laelius the pre-eminent orator of his generation and made him a character in his dialogues.

See also TERENCE.   HS

Astin (1967); Rawson (1973).

Lamachus   (d. 415 BC), Athenian general. Lamachus was prominent enough in the 420s BC to be caricatured by ARISTOPHANES in the *Acharnians* (425) as a fire-eater. He went with ALCIBIADES and NICIAS on the Sicilian expedition (415) and advocated a strategy of prompt attack. He was killed in a skirmish.   GLC

Kagan (1987).

Lambaesis   modern Lambèse, fortified Roman camp in Numidia. First recorded in AD 81, it was the headquarters of the Third Augustan

Legion from the 2nd century AD. When NUMIDIA became a province in AD 192, Lambaesis was made its capital. Hadrian visited it in AD 128 and parts of his address to the troops survive on stone inscriptions. It was built to guard against invaders from the Sahara. GS

Stillwell (1976).

Lamian War (323–322 BC). After the death of ALEXANDER THE GREAT (323) Athens, allied with Aetolia and Thessaly and reinforced by 8,000 of Alexander's discharged mercenaries, rebelled against Macedonia. Having taken Thermopylae, the Athenian general LEOSTHENES besieged the Macedonian ANTIPATER in the strategically important city of Lamia. But the siege was raised in the spring of 322, the Macedonians gained the upper hand at Crannon in Thessaly, and the rebel alliance disintegrated. Athens was finished as a military power and suffered the indignity of a Macedonian garrison at Piraeus. As for the impassioned orators, HYPERIDES was put to death and DEMOSTHENES committed suicide.

See also CLEITUS THE WHITE. GS

Lamps Lighting was provided by simple oil lamps. They took the form of a circular fuel chamber with a spout to hold a wick and sometimes a handle. They were most commonly made of TERRACOTTA, pottery, or bronze. In classical Greece they were undecorated, but from the 3rd century BC moulded reliefs were added. In the 1st century AD Italian makers began producing volute lamps with dished tops, and variations on these were copied throughout the empire. The finest lamps, sometimes depicting celebrated works of sculpture, were produced in Athens and Corinth in the first half of the 3rd century AD.

See also FIRE. GS

Henig (1983).

Laodice I (fl. 261–c.241 BC), Seleucid queen. Laodice, probably a Seleucid princess, married ANTIOCHUS II THEOS but was repudiated c.253 BC when Antiochus cemented a Ptolemaic alliance by marrying BERENICE SYRA. Laodice established a rival court at Antioch and was perhaps involved in Antiochus' mysterious death in 246. She fiercely supported her son SELEUCUS II CALLINICUS as king, organizing his uprising and murdering Berenice and her infant son. The resulting war with Berenice's brother PTOLEMY III is known as the Third Syrian, or 'Laodicean', War (246–241). EER

CAH VII.1; Green (1990); Macurdy (1932).

Lares Roman household gods. Lares perhaps originally represented deified ancestors of the family. They were frequently associated with the PENATES, the gods of the hearth, as household spirits. Lares were also gods of the crossroads, both rural and urban, and thus became gods of travellers. Augustus restored the cult as the Lares Augusti, identifying himself with domestic harmony and security. HE

Ogilvie (1969).

Latial culture the Iron Age civilization of LATIUM Vetus. A local variant of VILLANOVAN, it is sometimes referred to in older works as 'Southern Villanovan'. The evidence comes exclusively from cemeteries. Analysis of grave goods has enabled scholars to trace the development of early Latin settlements, from small unsophisticated villages (c.1000–800 BC) to larger settlements, with increased wealth, craft specialization, foreign trade, and social differentiation (800–650), and finally to urbanized states (650–600). TC

CAH VII.2; Scullard (1980); Sestieri (1992).

Latifundia large estates. In the last two centuries of the Roman Republic the expansion of the empire caused the impoverishment of large numbers of Italian peasant farmers as they were separated from their lands by lengthy military service. The wars of expansion, however, enriched the élite and produced an influx of slaves into Italy. The result of these processes was the formation of *latifundia*, large estates owned by the élite and worked by slaves. *Latifundia* became the distinctive form of Italian AGRICULTURE but never completely ousted peasant farmers. With the cessation of expansion under the Principate, *latifundia* are commonly considered to have declined. HS

Cunliffe (1988); Hopkins (1978).

Latin language Latin was originally the language of LATIUM. It was a member of the Italic group of languages that crossed the Alps some time before the 8th century BC. As a branch of the Indo-European family it was related to GREEK, which already existed in southern Italy, and Celtic, which was spoken by the CELTS in the north, but not to its geographically near neighbour ETRUSCAN. All three languages contributed to the development of Latin which, as the language of Rome, became the lingua franca not only of Italy but of the empire. Indeed the language itself was one of the principal vehicles of romanization.

Colloquial Latin, the everyday language of educated people, is represented in the literature by such works as the plays of PLAUTUS and TERENCE and the letters of CICERO. Vulgar Latin, the language of uneducated Italians and provincials, is known from inscriptions, graffiti, and texts such as the *Satyricon* of PETRONIUS. Literary Latin may be divided into three periods: archaic Latin (before 100 BC) makes a crude and unpolished start with little attempt to break away from colloquial speech; classical Latin (roughly 100 BC–AD 14) is marked by increasing Greek influence and represents a golden age in both poetry and prose; silver Latin (after AD 14) is notable for its use of RHETORIC and the introduction of archaizing tendencies. From its adoption by the early Christian communities of the Roman world Christian Latin evolved into the language of the Middle Ages and of the western Church. GS

Allen (1978); Palmer (1954).

Latin League a modern phrase, with no precise equivalent in Latin or Greek, used here to refer to the federation of Latin states that fought against Rome at Lake REGILLUS and subsequently concluded the treaty of Sp. CASSIUS VECELLINUS. It is to be distinguished from the community of Latin peoples (including Rome) who met to take part in religious ceremonies, e.g. on the Alban Mount (*see* LATINI). As a result of the treaty of Sp. Cassius, Rome and the Latin League formed a military partnership, agreeing to help one another against external attack (at a time when the AEQUI and VOLSCI were becoming a menace) and to share the profits of victory. It also guaranteed the mutual rights of *conubium* and *commercium* between Rome and the Latins (*see* CITIZENSHIP, RO-MAN). The league was dissolved in 338 BC after the LATIN WAR. TC

CAH VII.2.

Latin War (341–338 BC). During the 4th century BC Roman territorial ambitions (signalled by e.g. the annexation of TUSCULUM in 381) began to be seen as a threat by the LATINI and their southern neighbours, the VOLSCI, Aurunci, Sidicini, and Campani, and in 341 they finally took up arms. The main engagement of the ensuing Latin War was at Veseris in 340 (scene of the DEVOTIO of P. Decius Mus) in which the Romans under T. Manlius TORQUATUS were victorious. The war ended with a settlement in 338, by which some Latin and Volscian cities were incorporated with full Roman citizenship (e.g. ARICIA and ANTIUM); the other Latins remained allies and continued to share mutual privileges with Rome (*conubium* and *commercium*, *see* CITIZENSHIP, ROMAN), but were forbidden to have any dealings with each other. From this time, Latin status meant that the city in question had a distinctive relationship with Rome, rather than being part of a wider community. By the same settlement the Campanians were incorporated with the limited form of citizenship known as 'citizenship without vote' (*see* MUNICIPIUM). TC

CAH VII.2; Sherwin-White (1973).

Latini people of Latium. The inhabitants of LATIUM Vetus formed a unified ethnic group. They shared a common name (the *nomen*

Latinum), a common sentiment, and a common language; they worshipped the same gods and had similar political and social institutions. This shared sense of kinship was expressed in a common myth of origin: they traced their descent back to Latinus (the father-in-law of Aeneas) who after his death was transformed into Jupiter Latiaris and worshipped on the Alban Mount. The annual festival in his honour (the *Feriae Latinae*) was attended by all the Latin peoples, including the Romans. In historical times the Romans and Latins had mutual rights of *conubium* and *commercium* (*see* CITIZENSHIP, ROMAN), which had been confirmed by the treaty of Spurius CASSIUS VECELLINUS (493 BC). After the LATIN WAR the Romans assumed the right to confer Latin status on whomsoever they chose, and from then on 'Latin' ceased to be an ethno-linguistic term and became a purely juridical category.   TC

Alföldi (1965); CAH VII.2.

Latium   region of Italy. Latium was a region whose borders only partly coincide with those of modern Lazio. Ancient sources make a useful distinction between Old Latium (Latium Vetus), the land of the ancient LATINI, bounded to the north-west by the rivers Tiber and Anio and to the east and south by a line running from PRAENESTE to ANTIUM, and Greater Latium (Latium Adiectum), which included the territory of the HERNICI, VOLSCI, and Aurunci, and extended south-eastwards as far as the borders of CAMPANIA. Under Augustus, Latium (Adiectum) was combined with Campania to form the first of the 11 regions of Italy (*see* ITALY, HISTORY). Physically it consists of a coastal plain (the name is connected etymologically with *latus*, 'broad') with mountainous spurs extending towards the sea from the Apennines. The defensible hilltop sites provided by these hilly outcrops were occupied by the earliest human settlements. Latium Vetus is dominated by the volcanic Alban Mount, which rises to over 3,000 feet, and was the site of the cult of JUPITER Latiaris, the patron god of the Latins.   TC

Laurium   district in southern Attica famous for its LEAD and SILVER mines. Exploitation may have begun very early but there is little evidence before the time of PEISISTRATUS when the demands of the COINAGE made the silver industry both economically and politically significant, and the profits financed the building of the Athenian NAVY. The mines were deep (some as much as 400 feet down) and reached by vertical shafts fitted with wooden ladders. They were owned by the state and worked by slaves in conditions of acute discomfort and considerable danger. They were closed when the Spartans captured Deceleia in 413 BC, and though they were reopened *c*.355 BC they never fully recovered and by the time of STRABO underground operations had ceased.

See also SLAVERY, GREEK.   GS

Healy (1978); White (1984).

Law, Athenian   The earliest Athenian law code was DRACO's, soon superseded by that of SOLON; the 'laws of Solon' was a conventional expression for Athenian law, although there was naturally much later legislation, and Athens did not have a coherent published law code until the reinscription of the laws was undertaken in the late 5th century BC. Initially, judicial administration was in the hands of magistrates, but Solon's institution of the HELIAEA and appeal to the people initiated a process which culminated in a system of jury courts (*see* DICASTERY), presided over by ARCHONS or magistrates, different officials having different competencies. Juries usually numbered several hundred, drawn from an annually constituted roster of 6,000, and from the time of Pericles were paid for their service. They were seen as representative of the people, though exceptionally (e.g. for EISANGELIA) the ECCLESIA itself functioned as a court, while the AREOPAGUS and other homicide courts operated separately.

Although public prosecutors were occasionally appointed, most cases were undertaken by private individuals. In private cases this was the victim (or, for homicide, a kinsman); but public cases might be brought by any citizen; these included certain offences against individuals which were felt to affect the whole community, or where the victim was seen as powerless. This volunteer system encouraged communal responsibility for justice; but it was open to abuse, and vexatious prosecutors (*sycophants*) were a perennial problem. Moreover, this system, and the possibility of indicting a speaker in the assembly for an illegal or 'unsuitable' proposal, encouraged the use of the courts for political ends. There were no legal experts: archon and jurors were amateurs, and litigants prepared and presented their own cases, sometimes with help from orators, since the crucial objective was to sway the jury.

See also EDUCATION; JUDICIAL PROCEDURE, GREEK; NOMOTHETAI; RHETORIC, GREEK.   RB

Cartledge, Millett, and Todd (1990); Harrison (1968–71); MacDowell (1963, 1978).

Law, Roman   Under the monarchy (753–510 BC), sovereign power was vested in the king (REX) by the COMITIA *curiata*, an assembly of the 30 *curiae* into which the three patrician tribes were divided. The king, who held office for life and was also chief priest (PONTIFEX Maximus), appointed an advisory body (the SENATE) made up exclusively of PATRICIANS, who enjoyed superior rights to the PLEBS, the latter being excluded from high office. The population was redivided into centuries by Servius Tullius (578–535 BC), the *Comitia curiata* being replaced by the *Comitia centuriata*.

Under the Republic (510–27 BC), the king's powers passed to two CONSULS elected by the *Comitia centuriata*. QUAESTORS were appointed to assist them and the powers of the Senate increased so that it became the state's permanent executive. From 494 BC the CONCILIUM *plebis*, the plebeian assembly, appointed two tribunes (*see* TRIBUNUS PLEBIS) to safeguard their interests. A new patrician and plebeian assembly, the *Comitia tributa*, first met in 489 BC, and by the 3rd century BC it had become the most important legislative body. The *plebs* gained a significant victory over the patricians with the formulation of the TWELVE TABLES (451/50 BC), regarded as the foundation of Roman civil law. The consul's judicial power passed to an urban PRAETOR (*praetor urbanus*, 367 BC), who administered the law within the city of Rome. Praetors issued an edict (EDICTUM *magistratum*) at the beginning of their term of office, which became an important source of law. The combined *edicta* of praetors and AEDILES made up the *ius honorarium* (honorary law).

In the various assemblies magistrates published proposals, which could only be voted on after a lapse of 24 days for discussion. VOTING took place by tribes or centuries, at first orally, later by secret ballot. When passed, the bill became law immediately, but enactments of the *Comitia centuriata* required the Senate's formal approval.

Plebeian power was gradually extended: finally, the *lex Hortensia* (287 BC) enacted that PLEBISCITA (resolutions of the *Concilium plebis*) should be binding on all Roman citizens, and they became the normal vehicle of legislation. The enactments of the various assemblies were called *leges*: a *lex* was a law established by the people on the proposal of a senatorial magistrate.

From 247 BC a *praetor peregrinus* was appointed to determine disputes between foreigners, or between Romans and foreigners. In *c*.177 BC the Formulary System was introduced or extended, reducing the rigid formalism of the *legis actiones*, the legal procedure confirmed by the Twelve Tables. Proceedings were conducted in two stages: (a) *in iure* (before the praetor), where the parties agreed the point at issue and embodied it in a document (the formula); (b) *in iudicio* (before the judge), where the case was argued, and the judge answered the question embodied in the formula. In 89 BC the franchise was extended to all Italians by the *lex Plautia*: Roman CITIZENSHIP was enjoyed by Italians who declared their acceptance of the civil law of Rome.

Under the Empire (27 BC–AD 476), the pre-eminent position in law was occupied by the emperor. The Senate granted Octavian (AUGUSTUS) supreme authority (IMPERIUM *maius*) and tribunician power (23 BC), and later added the powers of censor and consul. From 12 BC the emperor was also Pontifex Maximus. Augustus created a class of eminent jurists (*jurisconsulti*) empowered to expound the law, giving their opinions (*responsa prudentium*) under imperial seal. Augustus probably also introduced CONSTITUTIONES *principum* (imperial decrees), but the early emperors normally preferred to legislate through the Senate. By AD 100 most legislation was passed as SENATUS CONSULTA: the resolutions of the Senate, confirming the speech (*oratio*) of the emperor, carried the force of a *lex*. Later, *c*.AD 200, the speech itelf became binding. The Senate's formal confirmation is last recorded under PROBUS (276–82).

Under HADRIAN (117–38) the *responsa prudentium* of the official jurists were given the force of law where the jurists were unanimous. Where they differed, the judge (IUDEX) could choose whose opinion to follow. The *edicta* of urban magistrates (praetors) were codified by Salvius JULIANUS: the *edictum perpetuum* (131) became binding. The 2nd and early 3rd centuries AD were the 'classical period' of Roman law: it reached its fullest development, under the leadership of GAIUS, PAPINIAN, PAULUS, and ULPIAN. The distinction between Roman citizen and provincial largely disappeared under Caracalla, with the general extension of Roman citizenship (212).

Diocletian began the replacement of the Formulary System, finally abolished in 342: under the new system, *extraordinarium iudicium* (extraordinary procedure), most proceedings were conducted in a single stage, and there was no written formula, although the substance of the discussion was recorded. The empire was formally divided under ARCADIUS and HONORIUS (395): initially, laws continued to be passed in the names of both emperors, but Theodosius II decreed (429) that *constitutiones* could not take effect in the other half of the empire until approved by its emperor. The Law of Citations (*lex de responsis prudentium*, 426) confirmed the worth of the works of Papinian, Paulus, Gaius, Ulpian, and Modestinus. Where they were divided, the majority decision was to prevail; where equally divided, Papinian was to be followed. Only if Papinian gave no opinion could the judge follow the opinion he favoured.

The *Codex Theodosianus* (Theodosian Code), an official collection of all the imperial *constitutiones*, published in 428 in both halves of the empire, brought up to date the *Codex Hermogenianus* and *Codex Gregorianus* (which embodied imperial rescripts down to the reign of Constantine I). It was declared the sole source of law. All subsequent additions, called *novellae*, lacked the force of law in the other half of the empire until approved by its emperor. After the fall of the western empire (476), Justinian produced a further Codex (*Codex Vetus*, 529; 2nd edition, 534), as well as a *Digest* of civil law (533) and the *Institutes* (533, based upon Gaius). Together with 146 *novellae*, these were known as the *corpus iuris civile*, and remained in force until the fall of the eastern (Byzantine) empire in 1453.

See also ACTA; ADLECTIO; ADOPTIO; ADULTERY; ADVOCATUS; AMPLIATIO; CLIENS; CONTRACT; EDUCATION; INHERITANCE; INTERCESSIO; IUDICIA POPULI; IUS; JUDICIAL PROCEDURE, ROMAN; JURISPRUDENCE; MAGISTRATES, ROMAN; MAIESTAS; MANCIPATIO; MANUMISSIO; MARRIAGE, ROMAN; QUAESTIO; RELEGATIO; SACRAMENTUM; SECESSIO; SECURITY; STIPULATIO. RJB

Buckland (1963); Cracknell (1964); Jolowicz and Nicholas (1972); Nicholas (1962); Thomas (1977).

Lead Lead was mined by the Greeks at LAURIUM but was regarded as a by-product of SILVER and not much used except for WEIGHTS, clamps, and SEALS. There were also early workings in Anatolia, Sardinia, and Etruria. The Romans made much greater use of lead for water pipes and exploited sources in Spain, Gaul, Britain, and Noricum. GS

Healy (1978).

Legati Roman commanding officers. Under the Republic *legati* were senators of any seniority serving on the staff of a provincial governor (PROCONSUL). They could be delegated military commands or civil authority. Under the Principate all legions (with the exception of those in Egypt and, initially, the one in Africa) were commanded by *legati*, usually ex-PRAETORS, appointed by the emperor. In imperial provinces with only one legion the *legatus* of the legion was the governor. An imperial province with several legions was governed by a *legatus* who was an ex-CONSUL, under whom the *legati* of the legions served.

See also ARMY, ROMAN; PROVINCIA. HS

Millar (1981); Parker (1928).

Legion *see* ARMY, ROMAN.

Lelantine War the struggle between CHALCIS and ERETRIA for the fertile Lelantine plain usually dated in the later 8th century BC. According to Thucydides (1.15) this was the only war in early times in which the Greeks divided into alliances: scanty evidence makes many associations speculative, but Samos, Pharsalus, and Corinth are usually aligned with Chalcis, and Miletus and Megara with Eretria. The outcome is also uncertain, but a decisive result seems unlikely. RB

CAH III.1; Jeffery (1976).

Lemnos island in the north-east Aegean. The archaic people of Lemnos spoke a language (known from inscriptions) which may be related to ETRUSCAN. The island fell to the Persians *c.513* BC but was taken by MILTIADES *c.500*. It became an Athenian colony and *c.450* a CLERUCHY and, apart from a few brief spells, remained under Athenian control until the 2nd century AD. GS

Lenaea   Greek religious festival. The Lenaea was a festival of DIONYSUS celebrated annually at Athens and other Ionian cities in the month of Gamelion (roughly January). Very little is known of the rites except that there was a procession. But from the mid-5th century BC the festival included a dramatic competition at which, unlike the City DIONYSIA, greater emphasis was perhaps given to COMEDY than to TRAGEDY.

See also CHOREGUS; FESTIVALS, GREEK.   GS

Pickard-Cambridge (1968).

Lentulus   (d. AD 25), Roman general. Gnaeus Cornelius Lentulus, after holding the consulship in 14 BC, held a command on the Lower Danube, winning an honorary triumph against the Getae. According to TACITUS, he was 'honoured for poverty patiently endured, followed by great wealth respectably acquired and modestly employed'. He became one of the richest men, outside the imperial family, with a fortune said to amount to 400 million *sestertii*, a figure matched only by Claudius I's freedman NARCISSUS.   RJB

Grant (1971c); Wells (1984).

Leo   (d. AD 474), eastern Roman emperor, AD 457–74. Leo, a Dacian and orthodox Christian, succeeded MARCIAN. He successfully counteracted Germanic influence in the army, recruiting native Isaurian regiments (led by Zeno); but an expedition against the VANDALS in Africa, under the empress Verina's brother Basiliscus, was a failure (468). Leo was also nominal ruler of the west during interregnums, negotiating with the Vandal GAISERIC for the release of VALENTINIAN III's widow and daughters; nominating the emperor ANTHEMIUS; sending OLYBRIUS to Italy; and nominating NEPOS. Leo died in February 474, and was briefly succeeded by Leo II (474), son of his daughter Ariadne and Zeno (regent; and emperor, 474–91).

See also RICIMER.   RJB

Bury (1958); Grant (1985).

Leo I the Great   (c.AD 400–61), pope. Leo was elected bishop of Rome in 440. By confronting the problem of the relationship between church and state and promoting a close collaboration between the two, he earned the respect of his contemporaries for his diplomacy and of posterity for his contribution to the idea of papal authority. In 452 he persuaded ATTILA to leave Italy; in 455 he negotiated with the Vandal Gaiseric to spare Rome from fire; he opposed NESTORIANISM and

MANICHAEISM; and he supported Constantinople against the eastern churches. A formidable collection of his letters and sermons survives.

GS

Jalland (1941).

Leochares (4th century BC), Greek sculptor. An Athenian by birth, Leochares developed his own dramatic style of sculpture which contrasts with that of his contemporaries, LYSIPPUS, PRAXITELES, and SCOPAS. At OLYMPIA he made the gold and ivory group of the Macedonian royal family for the Philippeum. At Halicarnassus PLINY THE ELDER says he was one of several artists who worked on the MAUSOLEUM. Other works attributed to him include the Apollo Belvedere, the eagle and Ganymede, and the Demeter of Cnidus. GS

Ashmole (1972).

Leonidas king of Sparta, c.489–480 BC. Leonidas succeeded his half-brother CLEOMENES I, who had no son. As the Spartan commander, he led the Greek forces at THERMOPYLAE, including 300 Spartans (perhaps with a promise of reinforcements). Before the final stand he dismissed the other contingents, and died with his fellow citizens. His death fulfilled a Delphic oracle which prophesied that either a Spartan king must die or Sparta be sacked, and also demonstrated beyond doubt Sparta's commitment to the defence of Greece. RB

Burn (1984); Cartledge (1979).

Leonidas of Tarentum (3rd century BC), Greek epigrammatist. Leonidas led a wandering life, visiting Epirus and Cos, and a gloomy one, though his much-vaunted poverty may be poetic convention. About 100 of his EPIGRAMS are preserved in the Greek ANTHOLOGY. They are concerned with the everyday lives (rather than loves) of ordinary working people, though this taste for the mundane may reflect the contemporary affectation of the cultured élite for whom he wrote. GS

Cameron (1993); Webster (1964).

Leontini modern Lentini, city in SICILY. Founded by Chalcis in 729 BC, Leontini flourished in the 6th century. It was captured by HIPPOCRATES c.494 but after his death it was mostly under the control of SYRACUSE. It formed an alliance with Athens in 433 and in 427 its most famous citizen, the orator GORGIAS, led a delegation to request Athenian support against Syracuse. Once given, this support led ultimately to the dismal failure of the Sicilian expedition in 415. Leontini fell to the Romans in 215 BC. GS

Dunbabin (1948).

Leosthenes (d. 322 BC), Athenian general. Leosthenes supervised the return to Taenarum in the Peloponnese of Greek mercenaries disbanded by ALEXANDER THE GREAT's satraps in 324 BC. Elected Athenian general in 324/3, he contacted the anti-Macedonian HYPERIDES, deployed the mercenaries, and, after Alexander's death, led the Greek army in the revolt against ANTIPATER known as the LAMIAN WAR (323–322 BC). He was killed in the siege of Lamia. Hyperides delivered a funeral oration for him and other Athenian casualties.   EER

Bosworth (1988a); CAH VII.1; Mossé (1973).

Leotychides II king of Sparta, c.491–476 BC. Leotychides succeeded DEMARATUS, whose deposition he had abetted. He commanded the Greek naval forces in 479 and was victorious at MYCALE, but subsequently withdrew with the Spartan contingent, leaving the field to Athens. He was later caught taking bribes in Thessaly (perhaps in 476), condemned, and died in exile.   RB

Cartledge (1979).

Lepidus, Marcus Aemilius (d. 77 BC), father of the triumvir. Marcus Aemilius Lepidus, after enriching himself in the Sullan proscriptions, became consul in 78 BC on an anti-Sullan platform. Sent to deal with a revolt of dispossessed farmers in Etruria, possibly provoked by his own inflammatory rhetoric, he sided with the rebels. Then as proconsul in Cisalpine Gaul, where he had family connections, he increased his army and marched on Rome. Repelled by CATULUS at the Milvian Bridge, he was defeated by POMPEY in Etruria and died soon afterwards in Sardinia.   DP

Gruen (1974).

Lepidus, Marcus Aemilius (89–12 BC), triumvir. Marcus Aemilius Lepidus, patrician and Caesarian partisan, was consul in 46 BC, and on CAESAR's death emerged as the most powerful of his former associates after ANTONY. In 43 as governor of Gallia Narbonensis and Hispania Citerior he sided with Antony, and later joined forces with him and Octavian in the Second TRIUMVIRATE. Initially given both Spain and Gaul, he lost ground in 42 when as consul he stayed behind to keep order in Italy, while Antony and Octavian gained prestige from the defeat of Brutus and Cassius at PHILIPPI. He was subsequently deprived of Spain and Gaul on the pretext of collusion with Sextus POMPEIUS. But nothing was proved, and in 36 he successfully helped Octavian against Sextus in Sicily. When this emboldened him to challenge Octavian as an independent force, his soldiers refused to fight. Octavian stripped him of all his offices except that of Pontifex Maximus. Lepidus languished for another 24 years in banishment at Circeii.   DP

Carter (1970); Syme (1939); Weigel (1992).

Leptis Magna   city on the coast of Libya. A Punic foundation of the 6th or 5th century BC, Leptis (or Lepcis) became an ally of Rome in the 2nd century BC. It was a prosperous trading centre specializing in the export of wild animals for the GAMES. Under Trajan it became a colony and under Hadrian it acquired fine baths. But it was under Septimius SEVERUS, a native of the city, that it was given the IUS ITALICUM, a whole new quarter, and buildings of remarkable splendour. Impressive remains survive despite depredations by the Vandals.   GS

Stillwell (1976).

Lesbos   island in the north-east Aegean. Linguistically part of AEOLIS (see DIALECTS, GREEK), Lesbos was a prosperous island, deriving its wealth partly from agriculture and partly from the sea. It was an early centre of cultural activity, especially in the reign of the tyrant PITTACUS, making important contributions to the development of MUSIC, LYRIC POETRY, and ARCHITECTURE. It also played a part in the history of philosophy as the home of THEOPHRASTUS and the temporary abode of ARISTOTLE and EPICURUS.

See also MYTILENE.   GS

Letters   *see* EPISTOLOGRAPHY.

Leucas   island opposite ACARNANIA in north-west Greece. Leucas was once joined to the mainland by an isthmus of sand. The Corinthians, who colonized the island in the 7th century BC, cut through it. But by the 5th century it had built up again and ships were being hauled across it. In the 3rd century BC Leucas became the capital of the refounded Acarnanian Confederacy, but in 197 it was besieged and captured by the Romans. Probably in the 1st century BC the isthmus was cut again and a bridge was built joining the island to the mainland.   GS

Leucippus   (5th century BC), Greek philosopher. Leucippus was the originator of the atomic theory (for details *see* DEMOCRITUS), which he evolved to circumvent ELEATIC arguments denying all motion and change. Little is known about him: he has clearly been eclipsed by his disciple Democritus, who elaborated his theories. (Various unconvincing attempts have been made to differentiate the respective contributions of these two men to atomic theory.) Leucippus' birthplace is variously given as Elea, Abdera, and Miletus. Two works, entitled *The Great World System (Megas Diakosmos)* and *On the Mind*, are attributed to him by sources stemming from THEOPHRASTUS.

See also ATOMISTS; EPICURUS; PHYSICS.   JL

Bailey (1928), Kirk, Raven, and Schofield (1983).

Leuctra   10 miles south-west of THEBES, site of a battle in 371 BC in which the Boeotians, led by EPAMINONDAS, heavily defeated the Spartans and ended the latter's reputation for invincibility. Outnumbered, Epaminondas advanced (behind the cavalry which engaged the enemy cavalry) in oblique line with the Thebans in deep formation on the left opposite the Spartans. The SACRED BAND under PELOPIDAS administered the *coup de grâce*. Spartan citizen losses were devastating.   GLC

Anderson (1970); Hammond (1959).

Libanius   (AD 314–93), Greek rhetorician. Libanius was born at Antioch and educated there and at Athens before settling at Constantinople where he taught, apart from a spell at Nicomedia, until 354. Then he returned to Antioch as professor of RHETORIC where his pupils included both pagans and Christians. More than 1,600 letters survive, providing valuable evidence of the 4th-century eastern empire, and 64 speeches, including his autobiography and the funeral oration on his friend the emperor JULIAN.   GS

Liebeschuetz (1972); Wilson (1983).

Libertas   At its most basic, *libertas* was the liberty of a free man contrasted with a slave. *Libertas* also stood for citizen rights. As such, it became a political issue between POPULARES and OPTIMATES. For the Republican élite, it evoked the liberty to indulge in free competition with each other and exploit the provinces. Under the Empire it came to signify free speech and freedom from fear of death, exile, and confiscation of property.   HS

Brunt (1988); Momigliano (1975b); Wirszubski (1950).

Libius Severus   *see* RICIMER.

Libraries   It can be inferred from the jibes of Aristophanes that private individuals in the 5th century BC (such as Euripides) had collections of BOOKS, but the first institutional collection was made by ARISTOTLE for his school, the Lyceum (*see* PERIPATETIC SCHOOL). This was evidently the model for the famous library founded by PTOLEMY I SOTER at ALEXANDRIA *c*.295 BC in association with the MUSEUM. This library was made operational by Ptolemy II who wanted it to hold a complete collection of all Greek literature. It is said to have contained between 200,000 and 500,000 volumes. Its librarians (ZENODOTUS, APOLLONIUS RHODIUS, ERATOSTHENES, ARISTOPHANES OF BYZANTIUM, ARISTARCHUS) were among the leading scholars of their day and catalogues were produced under the direction of CALLIMACHUS. In the 2nd century BC a second library was founded by EUMENES II SOTER at PERGAMUM (*see* CRATES OF MALLUS). It is said to have housed 200,000 volumes, but much less is known about the activities of its librarians. Specialist libraries grew up around medical schools, synagogues, and churches.

At Rome there were large private libraries in the late Republic (e.g. those of LUCULLUS, ATTICUS, and CICERO). Caesar was the first to plan a public library and VARRO was invited to make the collection, but nothing came of it. The plan was realized in 39 BC by C. Asinius POLLIO. Two more libraries were founded by AUGUSTUS, and later emperors built more until there were said to be 26 at Rome. More were founded in the provinces and Hadrian built one in Athens. A private library became the mark of a civilized house and the remains of one have been found in HERCULANEUM.

See also SCHOLARSHIP.   GS

Fraser (1972); Pfeiffer (1968); Reynolds and Wilson (1991).

Libya To the Greeks and Romans Libya meant the continent of Africa. PHOENICIANS were the first to trade along the north coast to the west of Egypt where CARTHAGE later established colonies. The west coast was explored by Carthaginians as far as Sierra Leone and the east coast by Egyptians as far as the Horn. Other than along the Nile valley there was little penetration of the interior in antiquity.

See also ETHIOPIA.   GS

Licinius (*c.*AD 250–325), Roman emperor, AD 308–24. C. Valerius Licinianus Licinius, a Dacian, was declared Augustus in November 308, nominally replacing the western Augustus SEVERUS, although most of his territory was controlled by either CONSTANTINE I or MAXENTIUS. After GALERIUS' death (311) he came to an understanding with Constantine, married Constantine's sister Constantia (spring 313), and, after defeating MAXIMINUS (313), became Augustus of the east. An uneasy peace between Licinius and Constantine was punctuated by a war (*c.*316), and a final conflict (September 324) brought the deposition of Licinius and his son Licinius (II), Caesar 317–24. Spared on the intervention of Constantia, Licinius was put to death in 325.   RJB

Grant (1985); Parker (1958).

Licinius Stolo *see* STOLO.

Lictor Roman attendant. Lictors were the official attendants of Roman MAGISTRATES and PRIESTS. Carrying the FASCES, wearing special clothing, and walking in single file, they preceded the magistrate or priest, announcing his coming and symbolically enforcing his authority. Private citizens giving games or senators travelling abroad might also be allowed lictors, but without *fasces*. HS

Nippel (1984).

Lighthouses Since the 5th century BC the entrance to the harbour at PIRAEUS had been marked by flares that burned on columns; but the first architectural lighthouse to be constructed was the Pharos at ALEXANDRIA, built *c*.300–280 BC, possibly by Sostratus of Cnidus. One of the wonders of the ancient world, it stood for 1,250 years until it was damaged by earthquake in AD 956 and finally demolished in the 14th century. Roman coins and later imitations suggest that it rose in three tapering stages to a height of over 400 feet. At the top was a statue of Zeus Soter; below it a fire shone out to sea, its light projected by a mirror. It was the prototype for similar lighthouses that were subsequently erected throughout the ancient world. GS

Fraser (1972).

Ligures Italian people. The Ligures inhabited the coastal region to the north of Pisa and extended along the Riviera as far as the mouth of the Rhône. They were composed of a number of tribes, the most important being the Apuani and Ingauni. Their history is obscure before the 3rd century BC, and little is known of their language or material culture. The Romans campaigned successively against them from 238 BC onwards, and the conquest of the area was virtually complete by 170, although minor campaigns continued until the time of Augustus, when Liguria was incorporated into Italy as *regio* ix. HE

Potter (1987).

Lilybaeum the western tip of Sicily. An attempt by Rhodians and Cnidians to found a colony *c*.580 BC was unsuccessful. In 396 the Carthaginians founded a city there in place of Motya which had been destroyed by DIONYSIUS I. After a long siege it fell to the Romans in 241 and was incorporated into the province of SICILY. It was the seat of a quaestor in which capacity CICERO lived there in 75 BC. GS

Limes Roman frontier. *Limes*, meaning a pathway, particularly a military way used to advance into enemy territory, was applied to the

military ways, marked by forts and signal towers, that developed into
the Roman frontier system under the early Empire. Augustus was
perhaps the first to envisage permanent frontiers for the empire, but
it was not until Domitian's reign that they began to be organized (at
the price of decreased manoeuvrability and offensive capability).
Domitian built earthen forts and wooden signal towers along the newly
won German frontier (enclosing the AGRI DECUMATES), and probably also
constructed an earthen rampart with forts in the Dobrudja (Moesia).
Hadrian provided continuous barriers for parts of the northern frontier: the WALL OF HADRIAN in Britain ran north of the Stanegate, a military
road protected by intermittent forts that constituted the *limes* under
Trajan. Along a 300-mile stretch of the German and Raetian borders,
Hadrian built a wooden palisade of split oak-trunks 9 feet high,
embedded in a ditch 4 feet deep, and fastened by cross-planking. A
further Trajanic or Hadrianic *limes* has been traced in the Dobrudja,
but along most of the Danubian frontier the forts were never linked
by a wall or palisade, and the same is true of the African forts. Under
Antoninus Pius the frontiers in Britain and Germany were advanced,
but the policy of frontier wall (WALL OF ANTONINUS) or palisade was
retained. The frontier scheme was extended in the early 3rd century
with the addition of an earthen wall and ditch in Upper Germany and
a stone wall in Raetia, but the German *limes* was abandoned by
Gallienus because of the pressure of barbarian incursions. However,
Hadrian's Wall remained in use until the end of the Roman occupation of Britain, and a Syrian *limes*, reorganized by Diocletian, remained in use until the Arab invasion.   RJB

Millar (1981); Salmon (1968); Webster (1985).

Lindum   modern Lincoln, city in BRITAIN. First built as a fortress for
the Ninth Legion Hispana *c*.AD 60, and subsequently for the Second
Adiutrix, Lindum became a colony at the end of the 1st century AD.
Its strategic location at the junction of several roads ensured its continued importance and a fine walled city was built. In the 3rd century
its size was doubled but many of its buildings were dismantled in the
4th century.   GS

Wacher (1980).

Liturgy   Athenian institution obliging rich men to bear the cost of
public activities not provided by the state. Perhaps the most notable
was the *choregia*, the training and presentation of a chorus for dramatic performances (*see* CHOREGUS), but there were many others connected with FESTIVALS. In saying that there were 60 liturgies a year,
DEMOSTHENES underestimated. The cost could be as much as one talent
and in the courts men would seek to win sympathy by telling how

many liturgies they had performed. If a rich man considered he was being unfairly put upon, he could require another citizen either to undertake the duty or to exchange his property (the practice known as *antidosis*). Thus taxation of the richest was combined with patronage of the arts. The institution, which was usual in the Greek world, continued through the Hellenistic period.   GLC

Davies (1967).

Livia (57 BC–AD 29), wife of Augustus. Livia, connected to two of Rome's most powerful families, the Claudii and the Livii, married Tiberius Claudius Nero, and bore him two sons, the future emperor TIBERIUS and DRUSUS (the elder). However, while still pregnant with Drusus, she was divorced so that she could marry Octavian (AUGUSTUS), with whom she lived happily for 50 years, exercising considerable political influence during both the reign of Augustus and that of her son Tiberius.

See also CONSOLATIO AD LIVIAM.   RJB

Scullard (1982); Wells (1984).

Livilla *see* ANTONIA; DRUSUS; GAIUS; SEJANUS.

Livius Andronicus (3rd century BC), Latin poet. Lucius Livius Andronicus was a Greek-born slave from Tarentum who came to Rome as a prisoner of war. Facts about his life are hard to establish but VARRO says he was the first (in 240 BC) to produce a play at Rome. Titles of both comedies and tragedies are known, and fragments survive of a Latin 'translation' (i.e. adaptation) of Homer's *Odyssey* which was known to Horace.

See also COMEDY, ROMAN; EPIC POETRY, LATIN; TRAGEDY, ROMAN.   GS

Beare (1964); Wright (1974).

Livy (59 BC–AD 17), Roman historian. Titus Livius, Rome's greatest historian, was born and brought up in Patavium (modern Padua). Of his education we know nothing except what can be deduced from his work, namely that he had studied philosophy and rhetoric, and had an excellent command of Greek and a wide knowledge of Greek literature (some modern works wrongly imply the contrary).

Livy was not a senator and apparently played no part in public life. Equally there is no record of his ever having served in the army (though for all we know he may have done). At all events he spent most of his life in Rome, and devoted it to the composition of his monumental history 'From the Founding of the City' (*Ab Urbe Condita*), which at his death filled no fewer than 142 books.

Of these, only 35 are now preserved. These books (1–10 and 21–45) cover the period from the foundation to the battle of PYDNA (168 BC), although the period from 292 to 219 BC, narrated in books 11–20, is missing. Of these missing books, and of those after book 45, we have only a few fragments and epitomes compiled in late antiquity. These at least allow us to reconstruct the outline of the whole. Although we tend to think of Livy as a historian of early Rome, his work was in fact weighted heavily towards the late Republic and the age of the CIVIL WARS, which took up nearly half of it.

Livy was patriotic, old-fashioned, and politically conservative. Appalled by the horrors of the Civil Wars and pessimistic about the future, he found solace in the past of Rome and the example of previous generations who had withstood the Gauls, Pyrrhus, and Hannibal. His interpretation of history is essentially moralistic, and improving lessons are brought out in the presentation of leading characters, such as CAMILLUS and CATO the Censor. The speeches which Livy puts in the mouths of these men are his own free compositions, and illustrate his notion of what made them act as they did. Livy's narrative technique is superb. His finest quality is his imaginative power: his ability to recreate atmosphere and to convey the feelings of those involved in stirring events.

Livy began writing c.27 BC and continued throughout the reign of AUGUSTUS. Although he was an admirer of Augustus and shared many of his aspirations, he was in no sense an official historian, nor did he receive imperial patronage. Livy had private means and wrote of his own accord; his friendship with the emperor was the result, not the cause, of the publication of the History. He maintained a detached and independent stance on many sensitive issues; he was respectful towards Brutus and Cassius, and he was so full of praise for POMPEY that Augustus called him a 'Pompeian'.

Livy's methods have frequently been impugned and his reliability questioned. He made no claim to be an original researcher, and based his account on the works of previous historians, especially the late republican annalists, VALERIUS ANTIAS, Licinius MACER, and CLAUDIUS QUADRIGARIUS. But Livy also drew upon the earliest historians, including FABIUS PICTOR, CATO, and PISO FRUGI, and he was perhaps the first to realize the value of POLYBIUS, whom he read in Greek and used extensively in his account of the wars in the eastern Mediterranean. It is unfair to treat him as an uncritical compiler; in fact he was well aware of the limitations of his sources, and of the uncertainty of much that they reported.

See also HISTORIOGRAPHY, ROMAN.   TC

Briscoe (1973); Dorey (1971); Laistner (1947); Luce (1977); Ogilvie (1965); Walsh (1961, 1974).

Locris divided region in central Greece. The west ('Ozolian') Locrians lived on the north shore of the Gulf of Corinth; the east ('Opuntian') Locrians on the west shore of the Malean and Euboean gulfs; between them lay Doris and Phocis. The east Locrians founded the colony of Locri in south Italy and became a federal state in the 5th century BC. The west Locrians were less advanced and more loosely organized. Neither played much part in history. GS

Larsen (1968).

Logographers The logographers are defined by THUCYDIDES (1.21) as 'prose chroniclers, who are less interested in telling the truth than in catching the attention of their public, whose authorities cannot be checked, and whose subject-matter, owing to the passage of time, is mostly lost in the unreliable streams of mythology'. Lesky, rather unkindly, suggests that 'he means essentially Herodotus.' Pearson, more plausibly, thinks that he means the predecessors and contemporaries of HERODOTUS, the pioneers of HISTORIOGRAPHY. Their works have not survived, though there are quotations from them in later writers. They included mythological treatises (genealogies and attempted rationalizations), geographical works (especially travelogues), accounts of non-Greek peoples, local histories (on the foundation of cities), and attempts at chronology (tables based on lists of kings, archons, priests, etc.). Herodotus was the first to make serious use of them in order to construct coherent history. GS

Lesky (1966); Pearson (1939).

Lollius (d. c.AD 2), Roman general. Marcus Lollius held the consulship in 21 BC, and went on to serve as a legate on the Rhine, suffering defeat at the hands of invading Germanic tribes (the Sugambri, Usipetes, and Tencteri, 16 BC), who decimated his army and captured the standard of Legion V. It was a major reverse, that prompted a brief visit from Augustus, and a four-year offensive campaign headed by Augustus' step-sons TIBERIUS and DRUSUS. RJB

Drinkwater (1983).

Londinium modern London, largest city in Roman BRITAIN. Situated near the mouth of the Thames, Londinium offered facilities for trade with northern Europe and the lowest point for crossing the river. Already an important commercial centre by AD 60, it became the seat of the governor probably by the end of the 1st century. The city was destroyed by fire c.130 and, though rebuilt, was not provided with walls until the early 3rd century. They enclosed an area of about 330 acres, making it one of the largest cities in the west. After the partition under Septimius SEVERUS, Londinium became the capital of Britannia Superior and the seat of a mint from 290 to 326 and from 383 to 388. It received the title of Augusta perhaps in 306. But of 5th-century London little is known.   GS

Marsden (1980); Merrifield (1969).

Longinus (1st century AD?), Greek rhetorician. Nothing is known of this Longinus to whom the manuscript tradition ascribes authorship of a (partly) surviving treatise *On the Sublime*. Responding to Caecilius of Calacte, the writer is concerned not with his own rhetorical tradition but with the moral function of literature, with what constitutes literary greatness. Never cited in antiquity, he has been very influential among modern critics.   GS

Russell (1981).

Longus (2nd century AD?), Greek novelist. Probably from Lesbos, Longus was the author of the pastoral romance *Daphnis and Chloe*. Of compact structure, written in four books, this work breaks new ground with its depth of characterization and psychological analysis. As such it was popular with 18th- and 19th-century critics and even won the admiration of Goethe.

See also NOVEL, GREEK.   GS

Hunter (1983b); Reardon (1989).

Lucan (AD 39–65), Roman historian. Marcus Annaeus Lucanus, born at Corduba (Cordoba) in Further Spain (Baetica), was brought to Rome as an infant by his father M. Annaeus Mela, an equestrian and brother of the philosopher SENECA THE YOUNGER. There Lucan received training in philosophy and rhetoric, studying under the Stoic Annaeus Cornutus, before travelling to Athens to continue his studies. He won the favour of NERO, who recalled him to Rome and appointed him quaestor and augur. His poem in praise of Nero won a prize at the Neronian Games (AD 60), but with the publication of the first three books of his EPIC poem on the *Civil War* (62/3), he began to lose Nero's support, either through artistic jealousy or because of the poem's overtly Republican leanings. He joined the ill-fated conspiracy of Calpurnius PISO (65) against Nero: when it was discovered, Lucan was compelled to commit suicide, after allegedly seeking a pardon by revealing the names of fellow conspirators, including his own mother. Lucan's major work was the poem in 10 books (the tenth is unfinished) on the *Civil War* (*Bellum Civile*, or *Pharsalia*). The epic covers the power struggle between Pompey and Caesar: its heroes are Pompey and the Republican Stoic Cato, battling against Caesar, the enemy of freedom, culminating in Pompey's defeat at the battle of PHARSALUS (48 BC). The historical content is unreliable for, although his main source is LIVY, he dwells on certain episodes to illustrate his Republican theme, often to the exclusion of other important events, and even introduces deliberate inaccuracies for the same purpose. However, the faults of exaggeration and paradox, and frequent digression, are balanced by superb rhetoric. Although criticized by many modern authors, the epic won great fame in the Middle Ages, and its author was acclaimed by Dante as one of four Lords of Highest Song.   RJB

Ahl (1976); Dudley (1972); Grant (1979); Scullard (1982).

Lucania   region of Italy. Lucania was a mountainous area of south-west Italy, to the south of Campania and Samnium. The coastal plains were fertile and these attracted Greek colonists from c.700 BC. In the 5th century BC the colonists came into violent contact with the SABELLI, who conquered the entire region by c.390, becoming hellenized in the process. Later wars with TARENTUM led to a resounding defeat in 326 and a subsequent alliance with Rome. Lucania was not always loyal and fought against Rome during the Pyrrhic, PUNIC, and SOCIAL WARS, incurring frequent devastation, especially by Sulla.   HE

Potter (1987).

Lucian   (2nd century AD), Greek writer. Lucian was born c.AD 120 at Samosata in Commagene, so his first language was not Greek but Aramaic, but he received a Greek education. As a SOPHIST he travelled from Antioch to Italy, Gaul, Achaea, Macedonia, and Thrace. Moving to Athens c.AD 160, he gave up RHETORIC and began writing in a new form of satirical dialogue (*see* SATIRE). He was later appointed to the staff of the prefect of Egypt.

Among his surviving prose works are sophistic declamations, pamphlets, and 36 dialogues, the last owing much to MIME and Old COMEDY as well as to the Platonic form. His targets include purists and pedants, religious charlatans, philosophers, rhetoricians, historians, and the gods. Ranging over a wide variety of subjects, the dialogues sparkle with wit but are underscored by a deep reverence for the departed splendour of Greek literature. He also wrote verse, including a mock tragedy and some epigrams.

See also ATTICISM.   GS

Bowersock (1969); Branham (1989); Jones (1986); Robinson (1979); Winkler and Williams (1982).

Lucilius   (c.180–102 BC), Latin satirist. Gaius Lucilius was born at Suessa Aurunca in Campania into a noble family. He was a prominent member of the Roman literary élite and his niece was the mother of Pompey. His *Satires* (30 books), of which only fragments survive, were really a vehicle for autobiography and personal abuse of his enemies and provided the inspiration for HORACE's adaptation of the genre.

See also SATIRE.   GS

Coffey (1989); Rudd (1986).

Lucilla   *see* CLAUDIUS POMPEIANUS; COMMODUS; VERUS.

Lucius Caesar   *see* CAESAR, GAIUS.

Lucretius   (*c.*94–55 BC), Roman philosopher and poet. Titus Lucretius Carus' only work is his great didactic poem in six books *On the Nature of Things* (*De Rerum Natura*), written to eradicate superstitious fears of the intervention of the gods in human affairs and of the punishment of the soul in an AFTERLIFE. He adopted the atomic theory in order to demonstrate that the world is governed by mechanical laws of nature and that the soul too is an impermanent atomic complex that perishes with the body. Following EPICURUS, however, he rejects the strict determinism of the Greek ATOMISTS and, by attributing an element of spontaneity (a tiny swerve: *exiguum clinamen*), seeks to preserve free will for man. Although Lucretius considers himself primarily a philosopher and describes his poetry as merely the 'honey around the cup' to make the draught palatable, his true qualities as a poet have long been recognized. His contemporary, CICERO, for example, praises his 'flashes of genius' (*lumina ingenii*) and the 'artistry' (*ars*) he displays in expounding atomic physics in Latin hexameters.   JL

Dudley (1965); West (1969).

Lucullus   (*c.*117–56 BC), Roman soldier and administrator. Lucius Licinius Lucullus, politically a member of the establishment, was trained in eastern warfare under SULLA in the 80s BC, and governed Africa capably as propraetor in 77. Having secured the Mithridatic command during his consulship (74), he drove MITHRIDATES out of Bithynia and Pontus and occupied the capital of Armenia, ruled over by TIGRANES I, Mithridates' son-in-law. But he failed to capture Mithridates, his army mutinied against his strict discipline, and his fair administration of the finances of ASIA offended the *equites*, so that in 66 he was superseded by POMPEY. In 61 he opposed ratification of Pompey's eastern settlement, but soon retired to a life of private leisure, proverbial for its luxury.   DP

Gruen (1974); Keaveney (1992); Syme (1939).

Ludi   *see* GAMES, ROMAN.

Lugdunum   modern Lyon, city in GAUL. A Roman colony was founded in 43 BC where before there had been two Celtic settlements. With good communications by road and river, the colony flourished and became the capital of the province of Lugdunensis. It had an important mint (*see* COINAGE, ROMAN) and was the financial centre of the three imperial provinces known as Gallia Comata. Under its bishop IRENAEUS it had a lively Christian community in the 2nd century. Partly destroyed in the revolt of CLODIUS ALBINUS in 197, the city declined and lost its primacy to AUGUSTA TREVERORUM. It was occupied by the Burgundians *c*.470.   GS

Stillwell (1976).

Lupercalia   Roman festival. The Lupercalia, held on 15 February, began with the sacrifice of goats and a dog in the Lupercal, the cave on the PALATINE where traditionally the she-wolf had suckled ROMULUS AND REMUS. Then young men called 'Luperci', dressed only in the skins of the victims, ran around the Palatine and struck with goat thongs those whom they met, especially women wishing to conceive. The festival thus combined fertility magic with a purificatory ritual, a kind of 'beating the bounds' ceremony; if so, the Lupercalia dates back to a time when Rome was a village on the Palatine.   DP

Scullard (1981).

Lusitania   region in western SPAIN, approximately defined by modern Portugal. Its people rebelled against Rome in the 2nd century BC under VIRIATHUS and in the 1st under SERTORIUS, and were finally put down by POMPEY in 73/2. In the Augustan division of Further Spain in 27 BC Lusitania became an imperial province, while BAETICA was given to the Senate. The bridge at Alcantara is a monument to Lusitania's prosperity in the later Empire, which was due largely to the exploitation of its minerals and timber.   GS

Keay (1988).

Lyceum   *see* PERIPATETIC SCHOOL.

Lycia   territory in southern Asia Minor. Lycia is a mountainous region between CARIA and PISIDIA in south-west Asia Minor. According to Homer, Lycians fought at Troy. Conquered by the ACHAEMENIDS in 546 BC, Lycia was ruled for them by native kings. Briefly included in the Athenian Delian League (446), and under Carian control in the 4th century, Lycia fell to ALEXANDER THE GREAT. Under Ptolemaic control in the 3rd century, it was conquered by ANTIOCHUS III THE GREAT in 197. After Antiochus' defeat at MAGNESIA in 190, Rome gave Lycia to RHODES which ruled it harshly until 169 BC. The Roman province of Lycia and PAMPHYLIA was created by CLAUDIUS I in AD 43. EER

Bean (1978); Berthold (1984); Gruen (1984); Jones (1983); Magie (1975).

Lycophron tyrant of Pherae, 355–352 BC. Lycophron, son of JASON and one of the murderers of ALEXANDER OF PHERAE, became tyrant after the brief rule of Tisiphonus. He allied with Phocis and faced PHILIP II of Macedon at the disastrous battle of the Crocus Field. He was driven out of Pherae and took service under PHAYLLUS of Phocis. GLC

Westlake (1935).

Lycophron (3rd century BC), Greek poet and scholar. A native of Euboea, Lycophron moved to Alexandria c.284 BC where he was put in charge of comedy in the LIBRARY. As a dramatist he was included in the Pleiad, the élite group of seven Hellenistic tragedians; and a few lines survive of his satyr play, *Menedemus*. He was also probably the author of the surviving dramatic monologue *Alexandra* which relates the prophetic ravings of Cassandra in 1,474 lines. GS

Webster (1964).

Lycurgus (c.390–324 BC), Athenian orator and statesman. The only ATTIC ORATOR of noble blood, Lycurgus rose to power after CHAERONEA (338) and seems to have controlled the Athenian exchequer until 327. He rebuilt the theatre of Dionysus in stone, erected statues of the three great tragedians there, and had a state copy of their plays made (later lent to Alexandria and never returned); he was also responsible for strengthening the navy, building docks, and improving the harbours. As an orator he supported DEMOSTHENES' anti-Macedonian policies. His one surviving speech (*Against Leocrates*) indicates that he was more concerned with content and truth than with style. GS

Kennedy (1963).

Lycurgus Spartan lawgiver. Lycurgus was, for the Spartans, the wise lawgiver who had established all SPARTA's institutions in a coherent system, a view still reflected in Xenophon's *Lacedaemonian Constitution*. He is supposed to have been of royal blood, though not a king, and to have consulted Delphi or Crete in framing his laws. Historically, however, he is a shadowy figure. Plutarch's *Life of Lycurgus* admits at the outset: 'Concerning Lycurgus the lawgiver nothing whatsoever can be said which is not disputed'; and conflicting traditions point to a range of possible dates between about 1000 and 776 BC (all of them probably too early for the actual reforms attributed to him). In reality, his function was to guarantee the antiquity and invariability of Spartan society and to offer a rallying cry for conservative reformers.

RB

Forrest (1980); Huxley (1962).

Lydia region in western Asia Minor. Lydia spanned the two principal routes into central Anatolia, the Hermus and Cayster valleys, and was well supplied with natural resources, so it was well placed to trade with east and west. It enjoyed great prosperity under the Mermnad dynasty (*c.*675–550 BC) which began with GYGES and ended with CROESUS. In the 6th century it defeated PHRYGIA, but fell to the Persians in 550, becoming their chief satrapy in the west. It became a separate province again under Diocletian. Lydia was the first state to issue COINAGE. Its capital was at SARDES.

GS

Lydiadas (fl. 251–227 BC), tyrant of Megalopolis. Lydiadas proclaimed himself tyrant *c.*243 BC to protect a Megalopolis threatened by enemies. He abdicated in 235, joining Megalopolis to the ACHAEAN LEAGUE which he served as general in 234, 232, and 230. He opposed ARATUS OF SICYON both personally and in League policy. Lydiadas commanded the League cavalry in campaigns against the Spartan CLEOMENES III. He was killed in 227 leading a charge against the Spartans in disobedience to Aratus.

EER

CAH VII.1; Green (1990); Walbank (1933).

Lyric poetry, Greek Lyric embraces all poetry in Greek that is not epic, dramatic, or epigrammatic. It began as choral song for religious FESTIVALS, accompanied by the lyre and by dance, and is older than HOMER. Both words and MUSIC were composed by poets, and the earliest examples we have are by the 7th-century BC Spartan poet ALCMAN. The principal ingredients – honour for the gods, comments on the celebrants, moralizing myth – remained constant until the mid-5th century BC when PINDAR and BACCHYLIDES were writing. Parallel to this is the tradition of personal poetry as emotional expression which began with SAPPHO and ALCAEUS *c.*600 BC on Lesbos and continued with ANACREON. Both gave way to TRAGEDY for which the best poets began writing in the 5th century and which derives in part from lyric: both tragic and comic choruses contain examples of high-flown lyric poetry at its best. Meanwhile the dithyramb, or hymn to DIONYSUS, achieved popularity with poets such as SIMONIDES and persisted into the 4th century. The composition of hymns (not only to gods) was revived in the Hellenistic period by CALLIMACHUS, who also gave a new impetus to iambic poetry. Drinking songs (*skolia*) were always in demand.

See also CORINNA; ERINNA; EUPHORION; HERMESIANAX; HIPPONAX; IBYCUS; MIMNERMUS; SEMONIDES; STESICHORUS; TIMOTHEUS. GS

Bowra (1961); West (1974).

Lyric poetry, Latin Unlike its Greek models, Latin lyric poetry was not written to be sung to the accompaniment of a musical instrument. The genre had comparatively few exponents, perhaps because lyricism was fundamentally alien to the practical Roman temperament, and Cicero dismissed them as inconsequential.

The first Latin poet to write in Greek lyric metres was Laevius (fl. *c.*100 BC) who composed at least six books of *Erotopaegnia* of which few fragments survive. CATULLUS wrote five poems (11, 30, 34, 51, 61) in lyric metres, and many of his shorter poems in other metres deserve to be categorized as lyrics of the highest quality. HORACE is the other great practitioner of the Latin lyric in his *Odes* and *Epodes*, and his *Carmen Saeculare* actually was written to be performed by a choir. In the 1st century AD STATIUS included a few lyrics in his *Silvae* and the tragic choruses of the younger SENECA perhaps deserve to be included in the genre. Otherwise there is nothing really before AUSONIUS and the Christian hymns of AMBROSE and PRUDENTIUS. GS

Williams (1968).

Lysander (d. 395 BC), Spartan leader, honoured liberator of the Athenian empire. As nauarch (admiral of the Spartan navy), Lysander defeated the Athenians at NOTIUM (407 BC) and began his friendship with CYRUS THE YOUNGER which was to lead to victory. Replaced in a reaction against collaboration with Persia by the Panhellenist Callicratidas, who suffered serious defeat at ARGINUSAE (406), Lysander was by popular demand sent out again as *epistoleus* (second-in-command) and won the conclusive sea battle of AEGOSPOTAMI. Setting up DECARCHIES, he blockaded Athens into submission and insisted on the establishment of the THIRTY TYRANTS. His efforts to prevent the re-establishment of democracy by THRASYBULUS were blocked by PAUSANIAS. For a period he was discredited and he visited the oracle of AMMON. Having helped AGESILAUS to become king and urged war against Persia, he accompanied Agesilaus to Asia (396) seeking to reinstate the decarchies, but he was humiliated and sent home. In 395 at the start of the Corinthian War he took an army from central Greece into Boeotia. When Pausanias failed to arrive, he was killed in battle outside Haliartus. He had hoped to reform the kingship, or so his opponents alleged. GLC

Cartledge (1987); Hornblower (1983).

Lysias (*c.459–c.*380 BC), Athenian orator. Lysias was the son of a Syracusan metic who was a friend of PERICLES. He and his brothers spent some years at Thurii, returning to Athens in 412 where they prospered as shield makers. But in 404 their property was confiscated by the THIRTY TYRANTS, Lysias was arrested, and his brother Polemarchus executed. Lysias escaped to Megara where he promoted the cause of the Athenian democrats. Recalled to Athens in 403, he was briefly granted full citizen rights, but the decree was revoked. Between then and his death he is said to have composed over 200 speeches which, as a metic, he was unable to deliver himself. Of these, 35 survive, though some are incomplete and others spurious. *Against Eratosthenes* (403), delivered by Lysias to devastating effect during his brief period of citizenship, provides valuable evidence of conditions at Athens under the Thirty.   GS

Dover (1968); Kennedy (1963).

Lysimachus (*c.*360–281 BC), Macedonian general and king of Thrace. Lysimachus was a boyhood friend of ALEXANDER THE GREAT and accompanied the expedition as a 'Companion'. After Alexander's death in 323 BC, he governed Thrace for ANTIPATER and joined shifting coalitions of the DIADOCHI (against PERDICCAS, POLYPERCHON, and ANTIGONUS I MONOPHTHALMUS). He founded a capital called Lysimacheia (309), and declared himself 'king' (306). After Antigonus' death at IPSUS in 301, Lysimachus received northern and central Asia Minor. Briefly captured by barbarians north of the Danube (292), he won Macedonia and Thessaly from DEMETRIUS I POLIORCETES (*c.*288–285). After violent family intrigues, he was killed by SELEUCUS I NICATOR at the battle of Corupedium in 281.   EER

CAH VII.1; Green (1990); Hammond and Walbank (1988).

Lysippus (4th century BC), Greek sculptor. A native of Sicyon, Lysippus was one of the trio of sculptors who dominated 4th-century art, the others being PRAXITELES and SCOPAS. According to the elder PLINY he developed a new system of human proportions which made heads smaller and bodies leaner, thus making figures appear taller. He apparently worked only in bronze and made as many as 1,500 statues for patrons as far apart as south Italy and Asia Minor. Several portraits of Alexander are attributed to him; other attributions include the Apoxyomenos (youth scraping himself), the Farnese Heracles, and the Heracles Epitrapezius (seated).

See also SCULPTURE, GREEK.   GS

Johnson (1927); Pollitt (1986); Richter (1970b).

M

Macedonia The kingdom of Macedonia (or Macedon) consisted of the valleys of the Vardar and Haliacmon rivers, accessible by sea from the Thermaic Gulf and by mountainous routes from THESSALY, Illyria, and THRACE. The ancient capital was at AEGAE (modern Vergina) on the foothills of Olympus whence the Macedonians spread northwards. The Argead Dynasty, originating from ARGOS, which established itself in the mid-7th century BC, in the late 6th came under Persian suzerainty until the failure of XERXES' expedition (479). For the next 120 years Macedon was in constant danger, first from ATHENS, then from Illyrians and Boeotians (*see* ALEXANDER I; PERDICCAS II; ARCHELAUS; AMYNTAS; ALEXANDER II). Archelaus hellenized and strengthened the country militarily, but PHILIP II acceded (359) in troubled times. A Macedonian army had just suffered defeat and huge casualties from the Illyrians; Athens was seeking to restore her imperial power in the area beginning with AMPHIPOLIS. Philip reformed and trained the ARMY, consolidated the kingdom, and began extending eastwards. When ALEXANDER THE GREAT went east, ANTIPATER ruled as regent; in 323 he and his son CASSANDER secured Macedon, but uncertainty and division were not ended until the battle of IPSUS (301) (*see* ANTIGONUS I; for the 3rd century *see* DEMETRIUS I POLIORCETES; ANTIGONUS II GONATAS; DEMETRIUS II; ANTIGONUS III DOSON). PHILIP V had to confront Roman expansion. His son PERSEUS was defeated by Aemilius PAULLUS at PYDNA (168). The country was divided into four republics, and in 146 BC made into a full Roman province.   GLC

Hammond (1972); Hammond and Griffith (1979); Hammond and Walbank (1988).

Macedonian Wars three wars fought between Rome and Macedon. The First Macedonian War (215–205 bc) began when the king of

Macedon, PHILIP V, campaigned against the Illyrians and allied with HANNIBAL. Rome's response was limited, confined to attacking Philip's Greek allies, and to making an alliance with the AETOLIAN LEAGUE (212/11). The peace of Phoenice in 205 allowed Rome to concentrate on the Second PUNIC WAR.

In 200 the Senate, encouraged by Rhodes and ATTALUS I SOTER of Pergamum, decided on another war with Philip. Despite early opposition to starting the war by the *Comitia centuriata*, the consul Sulpicius Galba began hostilities by invading Macedonia. By 198 and the consulship of FLAMININUS, Philip was ready for peace. However, Flamininus prolonged the negotiations until he heard that his command had been extended for a further year and then defeated the Macedonians at CYNOSCEPHALAE (197).

In 172 BC the revival of Macedonian power under PERSEUS alarmed the Senate and led to the Third Macedonian War. At the battle of PYDNA in 168 Perseus was defeated by Aemilius PAULLUS and Macedon was broken into four republics.   LPR

Gruen (1984); Walbank (1940).

Macer (d. 66 BC), Roman historian. Gaius Licinius Macer was tribune in 73 BC, when he campaigned for the restoration of tribunician powers after SULLA's reforms, and praetor in 68. In 66 he was convicted of extortion and committed suicide. He wrote a history of Rome from the foundation, perhaps down to his own day. The work comprised at least 16 books, but only fragments survive. It was used as a source by DIONYSIUS OF HALICARNASSUS and LIVY.

See also HISTORIOGRAPHY, ROMAN.   HE

Machon (3rd century BC), Greek comic poet. A native of Corinth or Sicyon, Machon is almost the only comic dramatist known to have produced plays at Alexandria. But only two comic fragments survive and he is better known to us as the writer of iambic maxims or anecdotes concerning the utterances of well-connected prostitutes of the 5th, 4th, and 3rd centuries BC. Some 400 lines preserved by ATHENAEUS represent a lewd literary genre.   GS

Fraser (1972); Gow (1965); Webster (1964).

Macrianus (d. AD 261), Roman emperor, AD 260–1. Fulvius Julius Macrianus was the son of Titus Fulvius Macrianus, one of VALERIAN's generals in the east. The elder Macrianus rallied the Romans after Valerian's capture and, refusing the throne for himself, allowed his sons Macrianus and QUIETUS to be named emperors. Acknowledged in Syria, Asia Minor, and Egypt, and with the Persians driven back to the

Euphrates, the younger Macrianus accompanied his father into Thrace, hoping to depose GALLIENUS, but they were met by an army under Gallienus' general AUREOLUS, and killed.   RJB

Grant (1985); Parker (1958).

Macrinus (c.AD 164–218), Roman emperor, AD 217–18. Marcus Opellius Macrinus, praetorian prefect under Caracalla (AURELIUS ANTONINUS), arranged the murder of Caracalla while on campaign in Syria (April 217), and thus became the first equestrian emperor. He alienated the troops by his poor handling of an invasion of Meso- potamia by Artabanus, and was relatively easily deposed in favour of ELAGABALUS. He was put to death, as was his young son Diadumenianus, soon after a decisive battle near Antioch (June 218).   RJB

Grant (1985); Millar (1981); Parker (1958).

Macrobius (fl. ad 430), Latin writer. Ambrosius Theodosius Macrobius, though not Italian (and probably African) by birth, became praetorian prefect of Italy in ad 430. Apart from some grammatical excerpts, two of his works survive. The *Commentary on the Dream of Scipio* is a Neoplatonic discussion of the dream as recounted in Cicero's *De Re Publica*. The *Saturnalia* is a literary SYMPOSIUM, an artificial recreation of a three-day banquet given by Praetextatus at the Saturnalia of ad 384. The company of 'nobles and other learned men' includes such leading pagans as Avienus, Nicomachus Flavianus, SERVIUS, and SYMMACHUS and the conversation ranges over history, religion, philol- ogy, and especially the great pagan poet VIRGIL.   GS

Flamant (1977); Matthews (1990).

Maecenas (c.70–8 BC), Roman literary patron. Gaius Maecenas was a member of the Etruscan aristocracy and of the Roman equestrian order. He held no public office but became the trusted friend and confidant of Octavian (AUGUSTUS) on whose behalf he more than once took charge of affairs in Rome and Italy. As a literary patron (PATRONUS) he encouraged the activities of an important circle of Augustan poets, notably VIRGIL, HORACE, and PROPERTIUS. He seems to have lost the emperor's favour after 23 BC but still made him the heir to his pro- perty. Few fragments of his own writing survive.   GS

Syme (1939); Wallace-Hadrill (1989).

Maecianus (2nd century AD), Roman jurist. Lucius Volusius Maecianus was an equestrian who had a distinguished administrative and legal career. Probably a pupil of Salvius JULIANUS, he himself taught the young

Marcus AURELIUS, was an adviser to ANTONINUS PIUS, and became prefect of Egypt in AD 160–1. We know from the *Digest* that he wrote a number of lengthy legal treatises including a monograph in Greek on the law of Rhodes. A booklet on fractions survives. GS

Jolowicz and Nicholas (1972).

Maelius (d. 440/39 BC), Roman plebeian. Spurius Maelius was a rich plebeian who in 440 BC acted privately to relieve a food shortage at his own expense, by bringing corn from Etruria. He hoped to exploit the popularity this brought him to gain the consulship, or even a tyranny, but was put to death by C. Servilius Ahala, who claimed that the liberty of the Roman people was at risk. The details of the episode are only doubtfully historical. HE

Magas (fl. 300–c.250 BC), king of Cyrene. Magas was the son of BERENICE I by her first marriage, and was appointed governor of CYRENE by PTOLEMY I c.300 BC. He married a Seleucid princess, and declared himself king and independent of PTOLEMY II. The ensuing hostilities were officially halted by the engagement of their children, BERENICE (later II) and PTOLEMY (later III), and Cyrene remained at peace. Magas made alliances with Cretan cities and even had relations with the Indian king ASHOKA. EER

Bagnall (1976); CAH VII.1.

Magister militum Roman general. The *magister militum* (Master of Soldiers) was a commander in CONSTANTINE I's field army. There were two posts, *magister peditum* (Master of Foot) and *magister equitum* (Master of Horse): later, there were pairs of *magistri* at Rome and Constantinople, and subordinates in Gaul, Illyricum, and the east. Under Theodosius I there were five eastern *magistri*, but two western, of whom one, the infantry commander (e.g. STILICHO), became Master of Both Services (*magister utriusque militiae*). RJB

Bury (1958); Parker (1958).

Magister officiorum Roman bureaucrat. The *magister officiorum*, or Master of Offices (a post created by CONSTANTINE I, AD 320), was chief of the government departments and a permanent member of the imperial CONSISTORIUM. He commanded the mounted imperial bodyguard (*scholae palatinae*); acted as master of ceremonies and minister for foreign affairs; exercised judicial control over the court servants;

controlled the provision of arms and the transportation of troops; and became controller of the POSTAL SERVICE (postmaster-general, AD 396).

RJB

Bury (1958); Parker (1958).

Magistrates, Greek Magistrates represent a natural transition from monarchy, taking over the religious, judicial, and military functions of kings in the various states. As cities grew larger and more complex, magistrates would become more numerous and more specialized, finance in particular becoming important; conversely, multiplication of magistrates to form boards, and limitation of the term of office served to restrict their powers. Accountability might be further reinforced, especially in a DEMOCRACY, by a process of scrutiny before entering and on leaving office, while in an OLIGARCHY peer pressure from the permanent council would be a restraining influence. Magistrates were normally elected or chosen by lot, sometimes from an elective shortlist; voting was more normal in oligarchies, but was accepted even in democracies when the office called for expertise (e.g. generals, financial officers). At Sparta, however, EPHORS were chosen by the primitive procedure of acclamation. Within the elective framework constitutional variations were reflected in qualifications of birth, wealth, or age both for office and for the electorate, and in many cases the costs of office acted as an unofficial deterrent to all but the wealthy. In many states a magistrate gave his name to the year, like the Eponymos ARCHON at Athens.

RB

Ehrenberg (1969); Sherk (1990–93); Whibley (1913).

Magistrates, Roman Roman magistrates were annual officials elected by the people of Rome. Each magistracy was shared with a number of equal colleagues. The power of the magistrates was limited by the veto of their colleagues, senior magistrates, or the tribunes of the *plebs* (INTERCESSIO), and by the right of appeal (PROVOCATIO). Magistrates could be prosecuted for their actions after they had laid down office. By the mid-2nd century BC a hierarchy of magistracies, through some of which a politician had to progress, was established (CURSUS HONORUM). Above the minor magistrates and the TRIBUNUS MILITUM were the senior magistrates: first the QUAESTORS, then the AEDILES and the tribunes of the *plebs* (*see* TRIBUNUS PLEBIS), the latter strictly not magistrates, then the PRAETORS, and finally the CONSULS. Above the consuls were the CENSORS, elected every five years for 18 months, and the extraordinary office of DICTATOR, which was held for six months. The senior magistracies gave entrance to the SENATE.

While the magistracies had different functions, it is significant that none was a specialist post. A magistrate was expected to be able to act in administrative, financial, legal, or military spheres. Under the Empire magistrates were elected not by the people but by the Senate, increasingly at the wish of the emperor.   HS

Jolowicz and Nicholas (1972); Loewenstein (1973).

Magna Graecia 'Great Greece', the name given collectively to the Greek cities of south Italy whose inhabitants were known as Italiotes. At the instigation of CROTON, SYBARIS, and Caulonia, probably in the 5th century BC, they formed a confederacy for mutual defence against the native Italian tribes. It was broken up by DIONYSIUS I c.389 BC. By 300 most of the cities sought Roman protection. For the next two centuries they exercised a potent influence on the development of Roman culture.

See also COLONIZATION, GREEK; CUMAE; NEAPOLIS; PAESTUM; RHEGIUM; THURII.   GS

Johnston (1976); Larsen (1968); Woodhead (1962).

Magnentius (c.AD 303–53), Roman usurper, AD 350–3. Flavius Magnus Magnentius, a distinguished commander under CONSTANS, was declared emperor at Autun (January 350) and took over the western empire. He put down a rival, Nepotian, in Italy, but Illyricum was held against him. Magnentius created his brother Decentius Caesar (spring 351) to defend Gaul, and invaded Illyricum. Defeated by CONSTANTIUS II at Mursa (September 351), he lost Italy (352) and then Gaul (353), committing suicide in August 353.   RJB

Grant (1985); Salway (1981); Kent (1981).

Magnesia battle in 190 BC. After expelling the Seleucid king ANTIOCHUS III THE GREAT from Greece in 191, the Romans followed him into Asia Minor. At Magnesia, on the Maeander river, the consul Lucius Scipio and his brother, SCIPIO AFRICANUS, decisively defeated the Seleucid army. The peace terms restricted Antiochus to east of the Taurus mountains, effectively ending Seleucid influence in the eastern Mediterranean.

                                                                             LPR

Sherwin-White (1984).

Magnus Maximus *see* MAXIMUS.

Maiestas Roman treason. *Maiestas* was not easily defined: according to CICERO, treason constituted anything that detracted from the dignity, power, or greatness of the people, or from that of those given power by the people. First defined by SATURNINUS (103 BC), it was used by SULLA (*c.*82–80 BC) to prevent provincial governors from straying outside their allotted province. Caesar, in crossing the river Rubicon that separated his province of Cisalpine Gaul from Italy (49 BC), was guilty of treason, and so began the CIVIL WAR.

Under the Empire treason was defined as any insult or offence offered to the Princeps, in action, writing, or speech. The legal authority for this change derived from the Julian laws of 18 BC: the extensive series of treason trials during the reign of TIBERIUS (AD 14–37) established the revised interpretation. The use of the law of *maiestas* was accompanied by the use of public informers, the *delatores*: as there was no state prosecutor in Rome, prosecutions were brought by private citizens, who stood to gain a portion (normally a quarter) of the victim's property. The law was revived in 62 by NERO, and also used by DOMITIAN as a weapon of terror, after which it declined in importance.

See also PERDUELLIO. RJB

Grant (1979); Salmon (1968).

Majorian (d. AD 461), Roman emperor, AD 457–61. Flavius Julius Valerius Majorianus, a candidate to succeed VALENTINIAN III in 455, was passed over in favour of PETRONIUS MAXIMUS. With RICIMER he was responsible for the deposition of AVITUS (October 456), and was declared emperor in April 457. He successfully drove back the GOTHS under Theodoric II in Gaul (458–9), but an abortive expedition against the Vandals (460) led to his deposition and execution by Ricimer in August 461. RJB

Bury (1958); Grant (1985).

Malta Latin Melita, island between Sicily and Africa. Malta was a trading post of the PHOENICIANS until colonized by CARTHAGE in the 6th century BC. It was taken by the Romans in 218 BC and became part of the province of SICILY. After depredations due to VERRES, PIRACY, and the CIVIL WARS, the island slowly recovered its prosperity and became a *municipium* by the 2nd century AD. GS

Mamertines Campanian mercenaries. The Mamertines (sons of Mars) served the tyrant AGATHOCLES of Syracuse. After his death in 289 BC they seized control of MESSANA. At the river Longanus *c.*269 they were heavily defeated by HIERON II of Syracuse. Threatened with siege, they requested protection from Carthage. However, in 264 they applied to Rome for aid in expelling the Punic garrison. Rome's decision to intervene led to the First PUNIC WAR. LPR

Finley (1979).

Mancipatio   a symbolic transaction in Roman law (carried out with scales and weights and involving a formulaic oath). It is recorded in the TWELVE TABLES. *Mancipatio* usually involved the transfer of rights concerning individuals (adoption, emancipation, etc.), but was also used in transfers of slaves, land, and working animals, a survival of its agricultural origins.

See also ADOPTIO; NEXUM; SLAVERY, ROMAN.   HE

Nicholas (1962).

Manes   Roman spirits of the dead. The word was probably derived from an old Latin adjective meaning 'good'. Manes were generally mentioned on tombstones (by the formula *Dis Manibus Sacrum*) and were also worshipped at the festivals of the Feralia, Lemuria, and PARENTALIA.   HE

Ogilvie (1969).

Manichaeism   a system of belief allegedly founded by the Aramaic-speaking Christian leader Mani (AD 216–77). Manichaeism was a dualistic religion that developed from Zoroastrianism but emphasized the ethical struggle between good and evil instead of the natural one between light and darkness. Its quest for the origins of evil brought it wide popularity and it spread throughout the empire, the Near East, and as far as China. It was influenced by GNOSTICISM, Judaism, and Christianity, but it encountered strong opposition from Nestorians, Neoplatonists, Christians, and the emperor DIOCLETIAN (297). Its adherents were categorized as either Elect or Hearers according to the degree of asceticism they attained. AUGUSTINE was a Hearer for nine years.   GS

Brown (1967); Lane Fox (1986); Lieu (1985); Martin (1987).

Manilius   (fl. *c.*AD 10), Latin poet. Marcus Manilius was the author of *Astronomica*, a didactic poem on astrology. Five books (of a projected eight?) survive, the fifth incomplete, written in the second decade of the 1st century AD. The poet was learned and skilful, but nothing is known of his life. The text, both difficult and corrupt, has attracted the attention of the greatest critics.   GS

Manlius   (d. 384 BC), Roman hero. Marcus Manlius Capitolinus, according to Roman tradition, saved the CAPITOL in 390 BC from BRENNUS' attack. Manlius was woken by the sacred geese of Juno, and was able to rouse the garrison and thrust the Celts from the cliffs. In 385 he attempted to help the *plebs*, who were oppressed by debt, but a year later he was condemned for attempting to become king. He was thrown from the Tarpeian Rock, the scene of his Gallic victory.　　　LPR

Bremmer and Horsfall (1987).

Mantinea　city in south-east ARCADIA and site of two battles. Once a group of five villages, Mantinea fought at THERMOPYLAE as an ally of Sparta and later supported Sparta against the helots (*see* SERFS). But having become a democracy *c.*450 BC, it became more powerful and broke with Sparta in 420. In 418 BC the Spartans under AGIS II with some of their allies (notably the Tegeans) faced a coalition of Mantinea, Argos, and others, including Athenians, at Mantinea. THUCYDIDES' account is famous for its explanation of how advancing armies tend to veer to their right. On this occasion Agis tried to correct this at the last minute, but in vain. Spartan courage prevailed, but only just. After the peace of 387 Mantinea was forced by Sparta to demolish its walls, but after LEUCTRA (371) the city was rebuilt and joined the ARCADIAN LEAGUE. In 362 BC EPAMINONDAS at the head of the Boeotians and their Peloponnesian allies faced the Spartans, Mantineans, Athenians, and others. He concentrated his forces on the left (as at Leuctra) and won, but was himself killed. In 223 Mantinea was destroyed by ANTIGONUS III DOSON, but then refounded with the name Antigoneia.　　　GLC

Anderson (1970); Hammond (1959); Kagan (1987).

Manumissio　*see* SLAVERY, ROMAN.

Maps　The first Greek attempts to map the world were made in the 6th century BC by ANAXIMANDER and HECATAEUS OF MILETUS, but their efforts showing a circular earth surrounded by ocean were derided by HERODOTUS as naive. It was ARISTOTLE's demonstration of the sphericity of the earth that enabled a science of cartography to be established. DICAEARCHUS showed that a parallel of latitude could be drawn from Gibraltar to the Himalayas. ERATOSTHENES calculated the earth's circumference and drew both latitudes and longitudes intersecting at Rhodes which enabled him to make a new map of the world with commendable success. Further progress on the graticule was made by HIPPARCHUS and on the measurement of the earth by POSIDONIUS. The high point of ancient map making was reached in the 2nd century AD when the geographer PTOLEMY, drawing partly on the work of his predecessors and partly on the reports of travellers, produced a map which, though not as scientific as he pretended, remained a standard source until modern times. (*See* map on page 754.)

See also GEOGRAPHY.　　　GS

Dilke (1985); Neugebaur (1957).

Marathon   on the east coast of Attica, site of a battle in 490 BC in which Athens, aided by Plataeans alone, defeated a Persian sea-borne army. On the motion of MILTIADES the Athenians went out, taking up a defensive position. When it was Miltiades' turn to command, the Athenians advanced at a run, driving the Persians into a swamp and on the beach capturing seven ships. The Persian cavalry play no part in accounts of the battle. The 192 Athenian dead were buried under a mound.

See also PERSIAN WARS.   GLC

Burn (1984); CAH IV.2.

Marble   Marble was in demand for SCULPTURE in Greece from the 7th century BC and for ARCHITECTURE from the end of the 6th. It offered the greatest opportunities for embellishment, and after the mid-5th century no other material was used for large buildings at Athens. Elsewhere it was used more sparingly, often as a veneer, and few buildings were constructed solely of marble before the Hellenistic period. PAROS produced the best white marble and NAXOS the best grey. But the white marble for the Acropolis was extracted from Mt Pentelicon in Attica. In Italy the Etruscans made little use of marble and the quarries at Luna, which produced a fine white Carrara marble, were never worked very intensively. Lavish use of marble was made at Rome however, famously by AUGUSTUS, who imported different varieties from Asia Minor, Egypt, Greece, and Numidia. Coloured marbles became fashionable for interior and exterior decoration. Public buildings were constructed of marble throughout the empire.   GS

Marcellinus   *see* AMMIANUS MARCELLINUS.

Marcellus   (271–208 BC), Roman general. Marcus Claudius Marcellus was a leading general in the war against HANNIBAL. After service in the First PUNIC WAR, Marcellus as consul in 222 BC defeated the INSUBRES, winning the SPOLIA OPIMA and a TRIUMPH. In the Second Punic War he first campaigned in Italy against Hannibal (216–214), then in Sicily (214–211), capturing Syracuse, and then again in Italy (210–208), where he was killed in a skirmish near Venusia. The 'sword of Rome' to FABIUS MAXIMUS VERRUCOSUS' 'shield of Rome', Marcellus' reputation underwent much embellishment in antiquity.

See also ARCHIMEDES; PATRONUS; SCIPIO CALVUS.   HS

Lazenby (1987); Scullard (1973).

Marcellus   (42–23 BC), heir of AUGUSTUS. Marcus Claudius Marcellus was the son of Augustus' sister Octavia by her first marriage, to Gaius

Claudius Marcellus, and the husband of Augustus' only child, Julia (25 BC). Both nephew and son-in-law of Augustus, he received rapid advancement as the latter's heir. He was elected aedile without having held the quaestorship (24), and granted the right to stand for the consulship 10 years earlier than normal, but died shortly afterwards.

RJB

Salmon (1968); Wells (1984).

Marcian (c.AD 392–457), eastern Roman emperor, AD 450–7. Marcian, a distinguished soldier in his fifties, was chosen emperor in succession to THEODOSIUS II. Marcian discontinued the payment of tribute to the HUNS, who subsequently turned towards the western empire, so that his reign was relatively peaceful. The Fourth Ecumenical Council (451), at Chalcedon, established the religious supremacy of Constantinople over Alexandria. Marcian died in early 457, the last (through marriage to Theodosius' sister PULCHERIA) of the Theodosian line.

See also LEO.

RJB

Bury (1958); Grant (1985).

Marcius, Ancus king of Rome, 642–617 BC. According to tradition Ancus Marcius was the fourth king of Rome. He was of Sabine origin and was the grandson on his mother's side of NUMA POMPILIUS. Legend credits him with the construction of the first bridge over the Tiber (the Pons Sublicius), the conquest of territory between Rome and the sea along the left bank of the Tiber, and the foundation of OSTIA at the river's mouth.

HE

Scullard (1980).

Marcius Philippus (fl. 1st century BC), Roman politician. Lucius Marcius Philippus was a skilled political survivor. As consul in 91 BC Philippus, with CAEPIO, led the opposition to the tribune DRUSUS. After the death of Lucius Licinius CRASSUS, Philippus had much of Drusus' legislation revoked. He cooperated with CINNA's regime, being censor in 86, but joined SULLA in 83. Having defeated Sulla's enemies in Sardinia, Philippus became an elder statesman of the Sullan regime.

HS

van Ooteghem (1961).

Marcomanni German people. The Marcomanni, part of the SUEBI, were driven from Saxony and Thuringia (c.100 BC) to the Main valley, and from there moved to Bohemia (c.8 BC), becoming powerful under MAROBODUUS. They were saved from full-scale Roman attack by the

Pannonian–Illyrian revolt (AD 6–9), but conflict with ARMINIUS weakened Maroboduus, who was expelled (19) by Catualda. The Marcomanni effectively became Roman dependants. They fought with Rome during the reigns of Domitian and Nerva, then maintained peace until the major wars of Marcus AURELIUS' reign (c.166–72; 177–80), which finally subdued them. The Marcomanni, thereafter infrequently mentioned, remained in Bohemia until the 6th century.   RJB

Thompson (1965); Todd (1975).

Marcus Aurelius *see* AURELIUS.

Mardonius (fl. 495–479 BC), Persian noble. Mardonius was DARIUS I's nephew and son-in-law. In 492 BC he led an abortive expedition into northern Greece. In 480 he was an enthusiastic promoter of and senior commander in XERXES' expedition. Left in Greece with a picked force after Xerxes' withdrawal, he attempted unsuccessfully to win over Athens. A renewed invasion of Attica was followed by withdrawal to Boeotia, where he gave battle at PLATAEA and was killed.   RB

Burn (1984).

Marius (c.157–86 BC), Roman politician. Gaius Marius was born an equestrian and was a NOVUS HOMO. Having served under SCIPIO AEMILIANUS, he was elected a *tribunus plebis* for 119 BC, but alienated the OPTIMATES. Praetor in 115, from 109 he served with METELLUS NUMIDICUS, but attacked the handling of the war against JUGURTHA. Elected consul for 107 to command in NUMIDIA, he enrolled volunteers from the PROLETARII in the legions (the culmination of a process by which the minimum property qualification for service was removed) and, either now or later, reorganized the legions (*see* ARMY, ROMAN; STANDARDS). In 105 Marius' quaestor SULLA brought the Jugurthine war to an end.

The threat from the CIMBRI and TEUTONES secured Marius' election as consul every year from 104 to 101. Consul again in 100, he at first cooperated with the *popularis* SATURNINUS, before using his veterans to suppress him. In 88 SULPICIUS Rufus had Sulla's command against MITHRIDATES VI transferred to Marius, prompting Sulla to march on Rome. Marius fled to Africa. Returning in 87, Marius, in alliance with CINNA, took revenge on his enemies and was elected consul for 86, but died early that year.   HS

Carney (1970); van Ooteghem (1964).

Marius, Marcus Aurelius *see* VICTORINUS.

Marius Maximus (b. *c*.AD 158), Roman historian. Marius Maximus, the historian, is almost certainly Lucius Marius Maximus (consul in AD 223), a distinguished commander who, as legate of Legion I Italica under Septimius SEVERUS (193), directed the siege of PESCENNIUS NIGER in Byzantium. He wrote a sequel to SUETONIUS' *The Twelve Caesars*, not extant, but known to AMMIANUS MARCELLINUS. According to the HISTORIA AUGUSTA, which makes frequent mention of him, Maximus wrote at great length, quoting documents copiously.   RJB

Birley (1976); Parker (1958).

Mark Antony *see* ANTONY, MARK.

Maroboduus (d. *c*.AD 37), German king. Maroboduus, king of the MARCOMANNI, led his followers from the Main valley to Bohemia soon after 9 BC, and built up a strong kingdom and disciplined army, provoking a major Roman expedition under Tiberius (AD 6, diverted by the Illyrian–Pannonian revolt). He became involved in war with the CHERUSCI under ARMINIUS, and in 19 was driven into exile by Catualda, spending many years as a Roman pensioner at Ravenna.   RJB

Thompson (1965); Todd (1975).

Marriage, Greek Marriages in Greece were 'arranged': the girl had no say in the choice and was betrothed to her prospective husband by her father or nearest male relative (*kurios*) any time after the age of five. The prime concern was the continuity of the family and the *kurios* pronounced this formula to his future son-in-law: 'I give you this woman for the ploughing of legitimate children.' Betrothal (*eggue*, 'pledge') was also the moment when the size of the dowry was agreed. Marriage itself was a private contract which took effect when the bride, usually aged about 15, entered the house of her husband, usually aged about 30. There was no ceremony or state registration, but there might be a sacrifice and a banquet. A bride was introduced to the PHRATRY at the APATURIA. A wife had no independent legal status. Either party could institute divorce proceedings, but in practice it was always easier for the man.

See also ADULTERY; WOMEN, GREEK.   GS

Lacey (1968).

Marriage, Roman Early Roman practice (and law) was very similar to Greek. Betrothals were generally arranged by the parents of the future couple and took the form of a solemn and binding oath. Later this became less formal and ceased to be binding. The marriage itself involved no legal formalities but only the cohabiting of a man and a woman on a permanent basis. Formally marriage could only occur between citizens or if both parties had been granted the right to marry a member of another state (*conubium*). The latter might be withheld on grounds of class (e.g. a free person, or later one of senatorial rank, might not marry a freed person), morality (e.g. an adulteress was forbidden to remarry by Augustan law), or blood relationship. In early law the woman was transferred from the control of her father (PATRIA POTESTAS) to that of her husband (*manus*) either by symbolic purchase (*confarreatio*) or by custom (*usus*). By the end of the Republic this system had given way to one in which the wife's status and property rights were unaffected by her marriage. She then remained under *patria potestas* and in possession of her own property, though this situation was qualified by the institution of the dowry (*dos*). In early law the dowry was owned outright by the husband, but later in certain circumstances (e.g. divorce) he could be required to return all or part of it. Divorce was rare at first but had become common by the end of the Republic. Divorce by mutual consent incurred no penalty and could be instigated by either or both parties.

See also ADULTERY; CITIZENSHIP, ROMAN; WOMEN, ROMAN.   GS

Corbett (1930); Treggiari (1991).

Mars Roman god. Mars was the chief Roman god after JUPITER. He was an ancient Italian war god who was also associated with fertility. March, the first month of the primitive Roman calendar, was named after him. Almost all his festivals, for example the dances of the SALII, came in March and October at the start and end of the campaigning season. But he was also a god of agriculture; one of the prayers for farmers in CATO's book on agriculture is addressed to him. An ancient Roman legend made him an ancestor of the city as father of ROMULUS AND REMUS.   DP

Ogilvie (1969); Scullard (1981).

Marsi Italian people. The Marsi inhabited the area around the Fucine lake in the central Apennines to the east of Rome. They voluntarily made a treaty with Rome in 304 BC and supported her during the SAMNITE and PUNIC WARS. However, during the SOCIAL WAR they were among the leaders in calling for the grant of Roman citizenship. They spoke an Italic language akin to Umbrian, but under Roman influence they were quickly latinized.   HE

Potter (1987); Salmon (1982).

Martial (*c*.AD 40–104), Latin poet. Marcus Valerius Martialis was a Spaniard from Bilbilis. Moving to Rome in AD 64, he enjoyed the friendship of first his compatriots LUCAN and the younger SENECA (until their deaths in 65) and later of FRONTINUS, JUVENAL, QUINTILIAN, the younger PLINY, and SILIUS ITALICUS. But despite fashionable society and influence at court (where persistent badgering eventually won him minor reward), he consistently pleaded poverty. With Pliny's assistance he returned to Spain in 98. His first work, *Liber Spectaculorum*, celebrates the opening of the COLOSSEUM by Titus in 80. The *Xenia* and *Apophoreta* are verse mottoes to accompany gifts. But his chief work is the *Epigrams* in 12 books, mostly elegiacs, written between 86 and 101. Modelled on the EPIGRAMS of CATULLUS, they are short pieces, usually addressed to a person, concerned with some aspect of everyday life. Their range is immense; as a mirror of Roman life they are invaluable.

GS

Hutchinson (1993); Sullivan (1991).

Martianus Capella (5th century AD), Latin encyclopaedist. Martianus Minneus Felix Capella lived in Carthage where he may have taught rhetoric. He was the author of *On the Marriage of Philology and Mercury*, a handbook in prose and verse on the seven liberal arts, based partly on the work of VARRO. Its mixture of Orphic, Neopythagorean, and Chaldean theology in a fantastic mythological setting, established it as the epitome of pagan allegory in the Middle Ages.

GS

Stahl (1971–7).

Martin, St (*c*.AD 335–97), bishop of Tours. Martin was born in Pannonia and brought up in north Italy before following his father into the army. But a vision of Christ persuaded him to seek baptism and the religious life and he became a disciple of St Hilary at Poitiers. Consecrated bishop of Tours in 372, he evangelized the rural areas, promoted monasticism, and protested in vain at the execution of PRISCILLIAN. His *Life* by his friend Sulpicius Severus survives.   GS

Matthews (1990).

Marzabotto city in Italy. Marzabotto was an ETRUSCAN city in the Reno valley to the south of Bologna, probably founded in the late 6th century BC. It was at its height in the late 5th century before falling to Gaulish invaders during the 4th century. The street plan of the city is well preserved, consisting of a rectangular grid bisected by an axial road, the whole overlooked from the north by a row of temples.

HE

Scullard (1967).

Massilia modern Marseille, city at the mouth of the river Rhône, founded *c*.600 BC by Greek settlers from PHOCAEA in Ionia. It prospered as a trading centre and set up outposts of its own as far away as Spain and Corsica. Contact with Greece was maintained by means of a treasury at Delphi. In the 4th century BC adventurers from Massilia (e.g. PYTHEAS) explored north to the British Isles and Baltic and south to west Africa. Having assisted Rome in the Second PUNIC WAR, Massilia in turn appealed to Rome for help in 125 BC. Though besieged and taken by Caesar in 49 BC, the city remained more or less independent, a centre of Hellenism and an early outpost of Christianity. GS

Momigliano (1975a); Stillwell (1976).

Massinissa (*c*.237–149 BC), Numidian king. Massinissa was chief of the Massyli Numidians. He served with Carthaginian armies in Spain and campaigned against SYPHAX in NUMIDIA. When Syphax allied with Carthage (206 BC), Massinissa switched to Rome. His cavalry was a decisive factor in HANNIBAL's defeat at ZAMA in 202. After the war Carthage was forced to cede all territory which Massinissa or his ancestors had ever owned. This gave Massinissa, throughout his life, the excuse gradually to enlarge his kingdom at Carthage's expense. But he was also an advocate of Punic culture and was responsible for its survival beyond the Third Punic War. LPR

Warmington (1969a).

Mastarna king of Rome. Mastarna was an Etruscan adventurer and an associate of the VIBENNA brothers. According to Etruscan sources unearthed by the emperor CLAUDIUS, a noted Etruscologist, he eventually became king of Rome. This conflicted with the received tradition of the seven kings, a problem which Claudius solved by suggesting that Mastarna was in fact the Etruscan name of the Roman king SERVIUS TULLIUS. This identification has been rejected by some modern scholars, for whom Mastarna was an otherwise unknown eighth king.

TC

CAH VII.2; Thomsen (1980).

Mathematics Of all the sciences that engaged the attention of the Greeks, it was in mathematics – and especially in geometry – that they achieved their greatest success. The Greeks themselves find the origin of geometry in Egypt and declare that it was THALES who, after a visit to Egypt, introduced geometry into Greece. But, although the Egyptians were capable of remarkable feats of practical calculation and mensuration, they had no conception of the ideal of a rigorously deductive proof, of the method of developing a subject by a chain of theorems, based upon definitions, axioms, and postulates. These were the specific contributions of the Greeks.

The attempt by the Pythagoreans to account for the order underlying phenomena upon the basis of number led to a concentration upon arithmetic, the theory of numbers, as distinct from logistics, the art of calculating and of solving particular problems. The discovery of incommensurability, however, revealed a vital flaw in their number theory and led to a concentration upon geometry. There then ensued a period of rapid development over three centuries, culminating in the work of EUCLID, who systematized in his *Elements* earlier achievements in geometry, and of ARCHIMEDES and APOLLONIUS OF PERGE, who developed new fields of research in geometry.

Thereafter progress was rather less striking, although important advances were made by HIPPARCHUS, PTOLEMY, PAPPUS, and DIOPHANTUS, who provides the only systematic treatment of algebra during this entire period. This development of pure mathematics by the Greeks was accompanied by its application to ASTRONOMY and the various branches of PHYSICS. The later revival of Greek mathematics exercised a profound influence in the 16th and 17th centuries.

See also ARISTARCHUS OF SAMOS; EUDOXUS OF CNIDUS; HERON; HIPPIAS OF ELIS; PYTHAGORAS; SPEUSIPPUS. JL

Heath (1921).

Mauretania   land of the Moors in North Africa. The coast was opened up by PHOENICIANS who established trading stations through which timber, ebony, and purple dyes were exported. Local tribes played some part in the Jugurthine and Civil Wars. Two provinces were created by CLAUDIUS I – Mauretania Tingitana and Mauretania Caesariensis – with capitals at Tingi and Caesarea respectively; the former, the more westerly, was attached by Diocletian to the diocese of Spain. Romanization was encouraged by the foundation of *coloniae* in the 1st century AD and by the presence of the armed forces, but control of most of the country remained in the hands of local chieftains.

See also JUBA II. GS

Mausoleum   tomb of MAUSOLUS. When Mausolus, satrap of Caria, died in 353/2 BC, his monumental tomb was already well advanced. Designed by the architects Pythius and Satyrus and embellished by leading sculptors (Bryaxis, LEOCHARES, SCOPAS, and TIMOTHEUS), it was numbered among the wonders of the ancient world. Its general appearance can be reconstructed from excavation and from the elder PLINY's description: standing on a high rectangular podium were 36 Ionic columns; above them a stepped pyramid, crowned by a sculptured group of a chariot and four, rose to a height of about 134 feet. It gave its name to all subsequent 'mausolea' and was imitated in many Hellenistic and Roman buildings.   GS

Ashmole (1972); Hornblower (1982).

Mausolus satrap of Caria, 377/6–353/2 BC. The most celebrated of the Hecatomnids of Mylasa, Mausolus attained in practice considerable independence from ARTAXERXES II to whom he was formally loyal save for brief participation in the Satraps' Revolt (362 BC). His influence extended far beyond his satrapy. Possessing a fleet of 100 ships, he encouraged allies of Athens to revolt during the Greek SOCIAL WAR (357–355). He moved his capital to HALICARNASSUS which he made into a large, well-fortified city. He planned his own tomb, the extravagant and un-Greek MAUSOLEUM, which his sister, wife, and successor Artemisia completed.   GLC

Hornblower (1982).

Maxentius (c.AD 279–312), western Roman usurper, AD 306–12. Marcus Aurelius Valerius Maxentius, son of MAXIMIAN and son-in-law of GALERIUS, passed over by DIOCLETIAN in favour of SEVERUS as Caesar (305), and by Galerius in favour of CONSTANTINE I (306), was declared emperor at Rome (October 306). Maximian came out of retirement to help him, and attacks by Severus and Galerius were easily repelled (307): Maxentius then controlled Italy, Africa, and also Spain. A breach with Maxentius led Maximian to attempt to depose him (late 307), and Diocletian, Maximian, and Galerius declared Maxentius a public enemy (November 308). Maxentius was finally defeated and killed by Constantine I at the MILVIAN BRIDGE (October 312).   RJB

Grant (1985); Parker (1958).

Maximian (c.AD 240–310), Roman emperor, AD 286–305. Marcus Aurelius Valerius Maximianus, an Illyrian and fellow officer of DIOCLETIAN, was created Caesar by Diocletian (285), and promoted to Augustus (286, although subordinate to Diocletian). Based at Milan, ruling the western half of the empire, he won several victories on the Rhine frontier, but lost control of Britain to CARAUSIUS (286–93).

Britain was eventually recovered (296) by Maximian's deputy, CON-STANTIUS I CHLORUS (Caesar, 293), while Maximian himself guarded the Rhine frontier. In 297 Maximian defeated the Carpi in Pannonia, before pacifying the Quinquegetani in Africa (298). Maximian was obliged to abdicate (on the same day as Diocletian, 1 May 305) in favour of Constantius, but re-emerged (306) first in support of his son MAXENTIUS, and then in support of CONSTANTINE I against Maxentius. At a conference at Carnuntum (308), Maximian was again instructed by Diocletian to retire, but continued to scheme with and against Constantine until his death (almost certainly ordered by Constantine).

RJB

Grant (1985); Parker (1958).

Maximinus Daia (d. AD 313), eastern Roman emperor, AD 310–13. Daia (or Daza), nephew of GALERIUS, took the names Gaius Galerius Valerius Maximinus as Caesar (deputy) of the eastern Augustus, Galerius (May 305). In 310 Maximinus declared himself Augustus: after Galerius' death (May 311) he was technically senior Augustus, but accepted Constantine's seniority after MILVIAN BRIDGE (October 312). In late 312 he challenged LICINIUS, took Byzantium, but was defeated outside Heraclea (April 313). He escaped, but died at Tarsus (autumn 313).

RJB

Grant (1985); Parker (1958).

Maximinus Thrax (d. AD 238), Roman emperor, AD 235–8. Gaius Julius Verus Maximinus, a Thracian peasant promoted through the ranks because of his enormous physical strength, was chosen emperor by troops dissatisfied with SEVERUS ALEXANDER (March 235). He put down two revolts, won a victory over the Germans near Würtemburg (235), and thereafter was occupied by wars on the Danubian frontier. The hatred of the Senate for Maximinus, the first 'barbarian' emperor, led it to recognize GORDIAN I, and then to elect BALBINUS and PUPIENUS as Maximinus' rivals. Maximinus invaded Italy, but encountered stiff resistance at Aquileia, where his disheartened troops executed both him and his son Maximus (Caesar, 236–8).

RJB

Grant (1985); Parker (1958).

Maximus (d. AD 388), Roman emperor, AD 383–8. Magnus Maximus, a Spanish soldier (Macsen Wledig in Welsh literature), served with Count Theodosius in BRITAIN (c.367–9). Under THEODOSIUS I, probably as *Dux Britanniarum*, he defeated the Picts and Scots (382). Declared emperor (383), he overthrew GRATIAN in Gaul, was baptized a Christian, and ruled Britain, Gaul, and Spain. He invaded Italy (387), ousting VALENTINIAN II from Milan, but was eventually defeated and killed by Theodosius (July 388).   RJB

Grant (1985); Johnson (1980); Matthews (1990); Salway (1981); Scullard (1979).

Maximus, Petronius *see* PETRONIUS MAXIMUS.

Maximus, Pupienus *see* PUPIENUS.

Measures Measures of length were named after parts of the human body. The basic unit was the foot which varied in length from place to place, e.g. the Olympic foot measured 320mm, the Roman one 296mm. In Greece 16 fingers = 1 foot; 18 fingers = 1 short cubit; 24 fingers = 1 normal cubit; 2.5 feet = 1 pace; 6 feet = 1 fathom; 100 feet = 1 *plethron;* 600 feet = 1 stade; 30 stades = 1 parasang (a Persian measure of about 3.3 miles). At Rome 12 inches = 1 foot; 5 feet = 1 pace; 125 paces = 1 stade; 1,000 paces = 1 mile (about 95 yards short of the imperial mile).

Measures of area were related to speeds of ploughing and sowing. In Greece 1 square *plethron* = 10,000 square feet = 2/9 of an acre; 50 *plethra* = 1 *gyes* = 11 acres. At Rome 1 *iugerum* = 28,800 square Roman feet = 5/8 of an acre; 2 *iugera* = 1 *heredium;* 100 *heredia* = 1 *centuria.*

Measures of capacity in Greece were based on the *kotyle* (0.48 pint). At Athens 4 *kotylai* = 1 *choinix* (one man's corn ration for a day); 48 *choinikes* = 1 *medimnos* (11 gallons 4 pints). For liquids 12 *kotylai* = 1 *chous;* 12 *choes* = 1 *metretes* (8 gallons 5 pints). At Rome the basic unit was the *sextarius* (0.96 pint). For dry measures 16 *sextarii* = 1 *modius* (1 gallon 7 pints). For liquids 6 *sextarii* = 1 *congius;* 8 *congii* = 1 *amphora* (the volume of a cubic Roman foot by which shiploads were measured); 20 *amphorae* = 1 *culleus* (115 gallons).

See also WEIGHTS.   GS

Medes people of Asia. The Medes first appear in history as vassals of Assyria. Unified into a single kingdom during the 7th century BC, late in that century they revolted in alliance with Babylon; in 612 they captured Nineveh and effectively ended Assyrian rule. The Medes took over the northern and eastern empire, extending their power in the east and westward until they encountered the Lydians; initial conflict was followed by an alliance c.585. Hitherto PERSIA had been a Median vassal, but in 550 CYRUS, himself half-Median, led a Persian uprising, and the Persians in turn took over the Median empire, Media becoming a Persian satrapy. Elements of Median nationalism are apparent in the great revolt of 521–520, suppressed by DARIUS I; but in general the Medes enjoyed a privileged position under Persia, and Media exerted a strong cultural influence on her conqueror.   RB

CAH IV; Frye (1983); Gershevitch (1985).

Medicine It is clear from our earliest literary sources that in the heroic age of Greece attitudes towards sickness and disease were not substantially different from those of ancient Egypt and Mesopotamia, where their causes and the operation of remedies were linked with supernatural beliefs. In addition to causing death and disease, however, the gods also cured disease and healed wounds. Religious medicine thus became firmly established and priests in their temples and sanctuaries catered to an eternal human need. Patients seeking healing were able to turn for help to a wide range of gods and demi-gods (*see* INCUBATION). The most important of these was ASCLEPIUS, son of Apollo. In the last third of the 5th century, he was transformed from a minor cult hero into a major god. Originally it was assumed that his temple at COS was the cradle of Greek medicine. It was argued that HIPPOCRATES, the 'Father of Medicine', was an Asclepiad and had learned medicine at the Asclepieion at Cos, that he was the 'first to separate medicine from philosophy' and so created rational medicine. But such a view is untenable. The temple at Cos was not, in fact, built until the late 4th century BC and the affinities between Hippocratic medicine and the healing practices within the temples of Asclepius are best explained as the result of the influence of the former upon the latter.

The invention of rational medicine is one of the most impressive contributions of the ancient Greeks to Western culture. Its origins, however, must be sought, not in temple practice, but in Ionian natural philosophy. The emancipation of medicine from superstition was the outcome of the same attitude of mind which the Milesian philosophers had been the first to apply to the world about them. Their attempts to explain the world without recourse to supernatural intervention brought about a transition from mythological conjecture to rational explanation. Just as they had sought to explain in purely natural terms frightening phenomena like earthquakes, thunder, and lightning, previously regarded as manifestations of supernatural powers, so the same outlook was later applied by medical authors to explain frightening diseases like epilepsy and apoplexy.

The 60 or more treatises of the Hippocratic Corpus are virtually free from magic and supernatural intervention. Complete treatises have survived in which the causes and symptoms of disease are explained in natural terms. Without the background of Ionian rationalism, Hippocratic medicine could never have been conceived. Virtually all that sets it apart from earlier and contemporary medicine has been derived from its philosophical background, i.e. its rational attitudes, procedures, and modes of explanation; its conviction that human beings should be regarded as products of their environment, made of the same substances and subject to the same physical laws as the world at large; its belief that diseases possessed their own individual natures and ran their course within a set period of time, totally independent of supernatural interference.

A striking manifestation of this new rational attitude can be seen in the treatise on *Sacred Disease*, which seeks to demonstrate that epilepsy has a natural cause like other diseases. The same attitude is displayed in *Airs, Waters, Places*, which attempts to account for diseases generally as due to the effect of climatic and topographical factors. This rejection of belief in supernatural causation and in the efficacy of spells and incantations represents medicine's greatest and most enduring debt to philosophy. Irrational elements, however, were not completely eradicated from Greek medicine. Superstitious beliefs continued to be rife and irrational practices had become firmly entrenched as part of the folklore of ancient Greece.

During the 5th-century BC enlightenment the cult of Asclepius experienced a dramatic expansion. Although the initial influence of philosophy was so beneficial, its continued influence posed a grave threat to medicine's most advantageous development when, in the 5th century, the philosophers increasingly sought to extend their views about the world to man himself, and, as a corollary to this, began to lose their medical theories upon their philosophical postulates. The most influential philosophers in this respect were EMPEDOCLES, DIOGENES OF APPOLONIA, and the ATOMISTS. The danger inherent in this subordination of medicine to philosophy was recognized by the author of *Ancient Medicine* and a vigorous but unavailing opposition was mounted against this philosophical intrusion. Clearly conscious of the opposition between the dogmatic *a priori* methodology of the philosopher and the more empirical approach required by the physician, the author rejects attempts to resort to untestable hypotheses to explain disease. A similar attitude is displayed in *Nature of Man*, where the polemic is confined to those who hold that man is composed of a single basic substance.

Despite this vigorous opposition, the Hippocratic Corpus clearly manifests the continued influence of philosophy. Some treatises reveal the influence of a single philosopher; others are more eclectic; some even, while condemning philosophical intrusion themselves, are, nevertheless, unconsciously influenced by philosophy. *Nature of Man*, for example, so forceful in its denunciation of this practice, ironically formulates a theory which contributed more than any other to the dominance of philosophy over medicine for the next two millennia. Its author, in putting forward the theory of the four humours, which he believes to be empirically justified, subscribes in fact to a theory which developed out of the Presocratic philosophical background and is the medical analogue of the four-element theory (*see* ELEMENTS).

One irrational taboo, however, remained deeply entrenched. Religious scruples, veneration of the dead, and dread of the corpse had combined to interdict human dissection and had seriously hampered advances in the knowledge of human ANATOMY. In the 3rd century BC Greek rational medicine was transplanted to ALEXANDRIA. Here two medical *émigrés*, working in a new and stimulating environment, where they were able to dispense with the inhibitions in vogue in mainland Greece, began the systematic dissection, even vivisection, of human bodies. Striking advances were made by HEROPHILUS and ERASISTRATUS, most notably their discovery of the nervous system. Their careful dissections provided the basis and stimulus for investigations later undertaken by GALEN, whose works came ultimately to represent the supreme embodiment of Greco-Roman rational medicine.

See also ALCMAEON; BOTANY; CELSUS; DIOCLES; EDUCATION; PHILINUS; PHILISTION; PRAXAGORAS; SORANUS.   JL

Longrigg (1993); Phillips (1973); Scarborough (1969); Temkin and Temkin (1967).

Mediolanum   modern Milan, city in northern Italy. Once an important Celtic centre, Mediolanum came permanently under Roman control in 194 BC, obtaining Latin rights in 89 and Roman citizenship in 49 BC. Under the Empire it prospered and became the capital of the western empire in the 3rd century AD. The importance of its Christian community in the 4th century was demonstrated by its bishop St AMBROSE. It fell to ATTILA in 452 and ODOACER in 476.

See also CISALPINE GAUL.   GS

Matthews (1990).

Megacles   *see* ALCMAEONIDS.

Megalopolis   city in Arcadia. Megalopolis was founded after the battle of LEUCTRA (371 BC) by EPAMINONDAS as the capital of the ARCADIAN LEAGUE. Forty villages were abandoned to populate it. Regularly at odds with Sparta, it supported Macedon in the 4th century. After the abdication of LYDIADAS it joined the ACHAEAN LEAGUE in 234. Despite destruction by CLEOMENES III, it prospered again under PHILOPOEMEN but it declined in Roman times. It was the home of POLYBIUS.   GS

Megara city on the Saronic Gulf on the borders of Attica and Corinthia. It lay on the main road from central Greece to the Peloponnese and had good harbours. From the mid-8th to the mid-6th century BC it was a major colonizer, founding Megara Hyblaea in Sicily, BYZANTIUM and Chalcedon on the Bosphorus, and Heraclea Pontica in Bithynia. In the 5th century it became a bone of contention between Athens and Corinth, and PERICLES' proposal to starve it into submission by the so-called Megara Decree in 433/2 BC was one of the principal causes of the PELOPONNESIAN WAR. In the 4th century it regained some of its prosperity and was an ally of Athens against PHILIP II of Macedon. Its later history was undistinguished. GS

Legon (1981).

Megasthenes (c.350–290 BC), Seleucid envoy. Megasthenes was an Ionian Greek sent by SELEUCUS I NICATOR to the court of the Indian king SANDRACOTTUS after their treaty in 302 BC. He travelled widely in India and visited the Mauryan capital Pataliputra. His *Indica*, based on first-hand knowledge, though sometimes susceptible to fantasy, described geography, government, peoples, religion, history, archaeology, and legends. He was the most important Greek source about India, and was a source for later writers including STRABO. EER

Cary and Warmington (1929); Sedlar (1980); Woodcock (1966).

Meidias Painter (fl. 420–400 BC), Greek vase painter. Meidias was the name of an Athenian potter whose signature occurs on a hydria in London; the same style of painting has been recognized on many other vases. The painter, whose name is unknown (he may even be identified with the potter), follows the style of the ERETRIA PAINTER with his sensitively drawn figures, many of them women. GS

Burn (1987).

Mela, Pomponius (1st century AD), Latin geographer. Pomponius Mela, a Spaniard from near Gibraltar, was the first geographer to write in Latin. His *Chorographia* (3 books), composed in the 40s AD, presents a Roman view of the known world, starting from Gibraltar and working anti-clockwise round the Mediterranean to the Atlantic coast and finishing with the Middle East. Though far from original, it contains some interesting digressions. GS

Bunbury (1883).

Meleager (2nd–1st century BC), Greek epigrammatist. A Syrian from Gadara, Meleager was brought up in Tyre, and later moved to Cos where he lived to be old. His satirical works are lost, but some 130 of his erotic EPIGRAMS survive and mark him as a master of the genre. He included them in his *Garland*, the first major anthology of verse epigrams, which influenced ALEXANDRIAN POETRY at Rome and is the ultimate source of the surviving Greek ANTHOLOGY.   GS

Cameron (1993); Webster (1964).

Melian Dialogue In THUCYDIDES' account (5.84–116) of the Athenian attack on Melos in 416 BC envoys are represented seeking to persuade the Melian authorities voluntarily to submit. The argument is ruthlessly logical, leading to the conclusion that Athenian force is irresistible. Presumably something of the sort occurred, but Thucydides used the occasion to expound the nature of empire.   GLC

Gomme, Andrewes, and Dover (1970).

Melissus (fl. mid-5th century BC), Greek philosopher. Melissus was a Samian statesman and admiral who defeated an Athenian fleet which was blockading Samos in 441 BC. Whether he was actually a pupil of PARMENIDES, as DIOGENES LAËRTIUS claims (9.24), is uncertain. He does, however, like ZENO OF ELEA, accept the main tenets of Parmenides' philosophy – that reality is one, undivided, ungenerated, everlasting, homogeneous, motionless, and changeless. He produces some fresh arguments to support the latter's description of reality, but differs from him in describing it as boundless and allowing it a past and a future. Polemics may be detected in his surviving fragments levelled against contemporary philosophers, namely EMPEDOCLES, DIOGENES OF APOLLONIA, ANAXAGORAS, and, possibly, the ATOMISTS.
    See also ELEATIC 'SCHOOL'.   JL

Guthrie, vol. 2 (1965); Raven (1948).

Melos island in the Cyclades. An important source of obsidian in prehistoric times, Melos was known for its gems and jewellery in the 7th century BC. In the Peloponnesian War the island was neutral but inclined towards Sparta. In 416 BC the Athenians decided to force it to submit; but before invading they sent an embassy: its speeches are recorded by THUCYDIDES in the so-called MELIAN DIALOGUE.   GS

Memmius (d. 100 BC), Roman tribune. Gaius Memmius as *tribunus plebis* in 111 BC attacked the NOBILES who were thought to have corrupt dealings with JUGURTHA. After being praetor (*c.*104), Memmius was acquitted of extortion (*see* RES REPETUNDAE). His violent death when a candidate for the consulate prompted SCAURUS to propose the SENATUS CONSULTUM *Ultimum* which called on MARIUS to suppress SATURNINUS.

HS

Gruen (1968).

Memnon of Rhodes (fl. 353–333 BC), mercenary general. Memnon and his brother MENTOR served their brother-in-law, the Persian satrap ARTABAZUS, as mercenary commanders. Memnon fled with Artabazus into exile in Macedonia *c*.352 BC, but later succeeded Mentor as Persian general in Asia Minor. He fought against both PHILIP II's and ALEXANDER THE GREAT's invasions of Asia. Escaping from the GRANICUS RIVER, he was appointed DARIUS III's commander in 334 and began a counter-attack at sea and on the islands before dying suddenly.

EER

Bosworth (1988a); Hammond (1989); Lane Fox (1973); Parke (1933).

Menander (*c*.342–292 BC), Greek comic poet. Menander was an Athenian of good family, probably a pupil of THEOPHRASTUS and a friend of EPICURUS and DEMETRIUS OF PHALERUM. The author of over 100 plays, he was regarded as the leading exponent of New COMEDY. He is said to have died by drowning when swimming at Piraeus.

His plays were extremely popular throughout antiquity and Latin adaptations survive among the works of PLAUTUS and TERENCE. But we have no medieval manuscripts of his Greek text which, apart from sundry quotations, remained unknown until the papyrus finds of modern times. These have so far yielded one complete play (*Dyscolus*) and substantial fragments of six others as well as numerous scraps. Politics was by now too grim a subject for comedy, and Menander found domestic or private life a more suitable milieu. Though written essentially as entertainments, his plays are penetrating studies of what mattered most to the man in the Athenian agora.   GS

Goldberg (1980); Hunter (1985); Sandbach (1977); Webster (1974).

Menander (fl. 155–130 BC), king of the Indo-Greeks. Menander (the hellenized form of Milinda), the greatest king of the Indo-Greeks and probably a Buddhist, ruled a kingdom centred around Gandhara and the Punjab. He made vast forays into India as far as Pataliputra, the old Mauryan capital of SANDRACOTTUS. It is unknown whether he intended to settle this area permanently. Menander issued abundant coinage. PLUTARCH says he died in camp, but Buddhist tradition maintains that he abdicated and retired from the world.   EER

CAH VIII; Frye (1984); Narain (1957); Tarn (1984); Woodcock (1966).

Mentor of Rhodes (fl. 366–c.342/1 BC), mercenary general. Mentor was a mercenary commander under his Persian brother-in-law, the satrap ARTABAZUS. He and his brother MEMNON joined in the Satraps' Revolt (362–360 BC). Both were given territory in the Troad. When Artabazus fled to Macedon c.352, Mentor rejoined the Great King and helped reconquer Egypt (343). He arranged for Artabazus and Memnon to be recalled from exile. Mentor arrested and killed the tyrant HERMIAS (c.342/1), and died shortly afterwards. EER

Parke (1933).

Mercenaries Greece being a poor country, men always sought employment as soldiers. In the 6th century BC tyrants hired their bodyguards. In 480 Arcadians (Arcadia being the most prolific source) even offered themselves to XERXES. Later in the 5th century mercenaries are found serving Persian satraps. Even Sparta hired in 424. Such men were for the most part HOPLITES, but as the Peloponnesian War progressed, mercenary Thracian PELTASTS and light-armed from less advanced parts of Greece appeared. The Ten Thousand that CYRUS THE YOUNGER hired in 401 were famous but were merely the first of mercenary armies. The 4th century, as ISOCRATES deplored, swarmed with them, as the careers of IPHICRATES, CHARES, and CHARIDEMUS suggest. The Persians relied on them largely for the reconquest of Egypt, the Phocians in their conflict with Thebes (see Third SACRED WAR). PHILIP II of Macedon had to rely on them to a considerable extent before he had built up his ARMY. ALEXANDER THE GREAT confronted many in Persian service (see GRANICUS RIVER) and the existence of large numbers in Greece encouraged the Greeks to begin the LAMIAN WAR. Mercenary service flourished throughout Hellenistic warfare. Greek navies also depended on hired rowers and officers (see NAVY, GREEK). Roman armies were more dependent on Italian allies (SOCII) and foreign auxiliaries (AUXILIA). GLC

Griffith (1935); Parke (1933).

Mercurius Roman god. The most probable origin of Mercurius (Mercury) is that the Romans gave this name (connected with *merx* 'merchandise') to the Greek god of commerce, HERMES, whom they adopted as a god, probably in the 6th century BC. In 495 BC a temple to him was built at Rome, but outside the city boundary on the Aventine. Its dedication day, 15 May, became a festival of merchants. But Mercury also inherited other attributes from Hermes: a poem of HORACE celebrates him as trickster, messenger of the gods, inventor of the lyre, and the shepherd of the dead to the Underworld. DP

Ogilvie (1969); Scullard (1981).

Mesopotamia land between the two rivers, Tigris and EUPHRATES. Classical writers generally excluded Babylonia from their definition of Mesopotamia, confining it to the northern half of modern Iraq. The Seleucids founded many new cities and colonies in the region (*see* COLONIZATION, HELLENISTIC) but their prosperity declined under the ARSACIDS. TRAJAN campaigned there in AD 114–17, as did VERUS in 162–5 and Septimius SEVERUS in 197–9. But only Upper Mesopotamia became Roman territory in the time of Verus, and was made the province of 'Mesopotamia' by Severus.   GS

Messala Corvinus (64 BC–AD 8), Roman statesman. Marcus Valerius Messala Corvinus, who had distinguished himself during the Republican CIVIL WARS, was the colleague of Octavian (AUGUSTUS) as consul in 31 BC, and was appointed Prefect of the City by him in 26 BC. However, the latter appointment, intended to provide a deputy for Augustus during his absences from Rome, was considered unrepublican by the senatorial nobles, and Messala, himself a known Republican (who had been among BRUTUS' supporters in 42 BC), soon resigned. A wealthy senator, he became, like MAECENAS, a noted patron of the arts, surrounding himself with a literary circle that included the poet TIBULLUS.

RJB

Salmon (1968); Scullard (1982).

Messalina (*c*.AD 24–48), wife of CLAUDIUS I. Valeria Messalina, great-granddaughter of OCTAVIA, became the third wife of Claudius (*c*.AD 39) and bore him two children, Octavia and Britannicus. Claudius tolerated, or was unaware of, her many affairs, until in 48 she went through a marriage ceremony with Gaius Silius, the consul-elect, probably as part of a senatorial plot to replace Claudius with Britannicus. Claudius was persuaded by NARCISSUS to put to death both Messalina and her lover.

RJB

Salmon (1968); Scullard (1982).

Messana modern Messina, city in Sicily. At first the haunt of pirates from Cumae, a colony with the name Zancle was founded *c*.725 BC by settlers from Cumae and Chalcis. Its position on the strait and its fine natural harbour brought it a measure of prosperity. But in 490 BC it fell to ANAXILAS, tyrant of Rhegium, who introduced new settlers from Samos and Messenia and changed its name to Messene. The Doric form Messana appears on coinage from 461. In 396 it was destroyed by the Carthaginians but rebuilt by DIONYSIUS I. In 288 it was captured by the MAMERTINES whose appeal to Rome in 264 led to the First PUNIC WAR.

GS

Finley (1979).

Messapii Italian people. The Messapii were the native inhabitants of the Sallentine peninsula (the 'heel' of Italy). They retained their own language until at least 50 BC, though in other respects they were assimilated into Roman Italy. In 413 BC they supported the Athenian Sicilian expedition (*see* PELOPONNESIAN WAR) against SYRACUSE. They supported Tarentum and PYRRHUS during the Pyrrhic War, but were subjugated by Rome in 266, thereafter losing their independence.

See also BRUTTII.

HE

CAH IV; Potter (1987).

Messenia region in southern Greece. Messenia, in the south-west Peloponnese, was conquered by its neighbour SPARTA *c.*735–715 BC. A Messenian uprising two generations later failed (although there was a tradition of heroic resistance under ARISTOMENES) and the Messenians were reduced to the status of helots (*see* SERFS). Subsequent revolts, notably that following the great earthquake *c.*465, were unavailing; only after the Spartan defeat at LEUCTRA was EPAMINONDAS able to liberate Messenia and establish its capital at Messene; this stronghold was an important city in the Hellenistic and Roman periods.

RB

Cartledge (1979); Forrest (1980); Roebuck (1941).

Metals *see* BRONZE; COPPER; GOLD; IRON; LEAD; SILVER; TIN.

Metaurus battle in 207 BC. The attempt by HASDRUBAL BARCA to reinforce his brother HANNIBAL in Italy was ended at the Metaurus river in Umbria. Hasdrubal's messengers were intercepted by the Romans. The consuls Livius SALINATOR and Claudius Nero combined their armies, and caught and destroyed Hasdrubal's army before Hannibal even knew his brother had arrived in Italy.

LPR

Lazenby (1978).

Metellus Macedonicus (d. 115 BC), Roman general. Quintus Caecilius Metellus Macedonicus gained his last name from his victory, as praetor in 148 BC, over ANDRISCUS, a pretender to the throne of Macedon. As consul in 143 he put down a Celtiberian revolt in Spain. His famous speech *On the Need for Larger Families*, delivered as censor in 131, was later read by Augustus to the Senate. A staunch *nobilis*, he fiercely opposed the GRACCHI; by his death in 115, three of his sons had been consul.

DP

Astin (1967).

Metellus Numidicus (d. 91 BC), Roman general. Quintus Caecilius Metellus Numidicus was elected consul in 109 BC and appointed to the

command against JUGURTHA in Numidia. His initial success won him
the name 'Numidicus', but in 107 he was superseded by his former
officer MARIUS. His attempt when censor in 102 to remove the dema-
gogues SATURNINUS and Glaucia from the Senate was blocked by violence. In 100 he was the only senator not to swear to observe Saturninus'
agrarian law, and went into exile. Recalled by the Senate in 98, he
died in 91.   DP

Carney (1970); Gruen (1968).

Metellus Pius   (d. *c*.63 BC), Roman general. Quintus Caecilius Metellus
Pius won his surname from his efforts to recall his father METELLUS
NUMIDICUS from exile in 99 BC. During CINNA's domination he went into
exile in Africa, but in 83 joined SULLA in Italy. He was consul with
Sulla in 80, and was then sent to fight SERTORIUS in Spain. He had modest
success until POMPEY's arrival in 76 helped turn the tide. Returning in
71 he dismissed his army, triumphed, then lived in retirement until his
death.   DP

Badian (1958); Gruen (1974).

Metellus Scipio   (d. 46 BC), Roman politician. Quintus Caecilius
Metellus Scipio, a Scipio by birth and an adopted son of METELLUS PIUS,
was a leading establishment figure. When POMPEY as sole consul in 52 BC
was seeking aristocratic support against CAESAR, he found it useful to
make Metellus his consular colleague and to marry his daughter.
Metellus' obstinate resistance helped push Caesar into civil war. He
escaped from PHARSALUS, but killed himself after the Pompeians had
lost under his command at THAPSUS.   DP

Gruen (1974); Seager (1979).

Meteorology   Descriptions of the earth's surface, of its rivers, tides,
oceans, and, in particular, of phenomena above the earth (*ta meteora*),
e.g. winds, rain, comets, meteors, thunder and lightning, rainbows,
and haloes, are in evidence in early Greek literature. Initially, these
phenomena were most frequently explained as due to the supernatural
activity of anthropomorphic gods (*see* DIVINATION). Rational attitudes,
however, were brought to bear upon these matters when the Ionian
philosophers began to explain earthquakes, thunder and lightning, the
rainbow, wind, cloud, and rain as due to purely natural causes. In
Meteorologica 1–3 ARISTOTLE classifies subjects usually regarded as
belonging to meteorology in the ancient world, as (a) phenomena
above the earth, i.e. comets, meteors (which he believed to belong to
the sublunary world), rain and snow, thunder and lightning, rainbows

and haloes; and (b) matters appertaining more to physical geography, such as seas, rivers, and earthquakes. Our chief sources for ancient meteorological beliefs are ARISTOTLE, LUCRETIUS, PLINY THE ELDER, POSIDONIUS, PTOLEMY, SENECA THE YOUNGER, STRABO, and THEOPHRASTUS.

JL

Sarton (1970).

Metics resident aliens in a Greek state. Foreigners had a recognized, if inferior, status in Greek society. They were required to register and to pay a poll tax (*metoikion*) of one drachma a month. They were also liable for other taxes (EISPHORA) and civic duties (LITURGY), they must be sponsored by a citizen, but they were forbidden to own property or to marry a citizen without special permission. They had access to the law courts, they could serve in the army and navy, and a few played an important part in commerce and public life (e.g. the banker Pasion and the orators DINARCHUS, ISAEUS, and LYSIAS). Freed slaves were given the status of metics.

GS

De Ste Croix (1981); Whitehead (1977).

Meton (5th century BC), Greek astronomer. No written work has survived. Meton's date is determined by his observation of the summer solstice on 27 June 432 BC and by ARISTOPHANES' parody in the *Birds* (414). He is the first Greek we know of to have undertaken serious astronomical observations. His chief claim to fame is his introduction of a 19-year luni-solar calendar (the 'Metonic cycle') based upon the fact that 19 solar years correspond closely to 235 true synodic months. (During each 19-year cycle a thirteenth month had to be intercalated seven times.) Meton's purpose was to provide a fixed scheme for recording astronomical data. This cycle was reformed by CALLIPPUS and continued in use until the time of HIPPARCHUS.

JL

DSB IX (1974).

Micon (5th century BC), Greek painter. Micon of Athens worked as a painter and sculptor in the decades after the Persian Wars. He, together with POLYGNOTUS, was employed to paint in the great public buildings of Athens and Delphi. Their works were highly prized but have not survived. They worked together on the STOA Poikile at Athens. Micon also painted mythological scenes in the THESEUM and the Anakeion, and produced a statue of CALLIAS in Olympia.

See also PAINTING, GREEK.

GS

Miletus city in Asia Minor. In archaic times Miletus was the leading city of mainland Asia Minor, hence the favourable terms received from successive Lydian kings and CYRUS, and a major naval and commercial power (though rivalled by SAMOS). In the 7th century BC she founded numerous commercial colonies round the Black Sea, and she maintained connections with many Greek cities as well as with SYBARIS and Egypt (*see* NAUCRATIS). Despite vicious civil strife in the 6th century after the tyranny of THRASYBULUS, Miletus was at the height of her prosperity at the outbreak of the IONIAN REVOLT, precipitated by her tyrant ARISTAGORAS; as the centre of revolt, Miletus bore the brunt of Persian retaliation, and was sacked in 494. After liberation from Persia Miletus became a restive ally of Athens, from whom she finally revolted in 412. Renewed Persian influence was relieved by Alexander, and thereafter Miletus remained prosperous and locally influential.

See also ANAXIMANDER; ANAXIMENES; HECATAEUS OF MILETUS; THALES.

RB

Boardman (1980); Dunham (1915); Jeffery (1976).

Milo (d. 48 BC), Roman politician. Titus Annius Milo, as tribune in 57 BC, helped POMPEY recall CICERO by organizing gangs to counter those of CLODIUS. Gang warfare in the streets of Rome continued until Milo's men killed Clodius in January 52. In the resulting crisis Pompey was made sole consul, and Milo, who was no further use to him, was prosecuted. Pompey's soldiers surrounded the court and stopped Cicero from defending Milo, who went into exile at Massilia. In 48 Milo joined CAELIUS in a rebellion against Caesar, but was defeated and killed.

DP

Gruen (1974); Lintott (1968).

Miltiades (*c*.550–489 BC), Athenian general. Miltiades, a member of the PHILAID family, was archon in 524/3, and was subsequently sent to the Athenian colony in the CHERSONESE (founded by his uncle Miltiades) by the Peisistratidae (*see* HIPPIAS), who had assassinated his father Cimon. He joined DARIUS I's Scythian expedition as a Persian vassal, but allegedly proposed abandoning the king in Europe. He apparently took advantage of the IONIAN REVOLT to occupy Lemnos; but after the Persian victory he was forced to flee to Athens, where he was prosecuted for tyranny and acquitted. As one of the 10 generals (STRATEGOI), he was chiefly responsible for the Athenian victory at MARATHON; but a subsequent abortive expedition to Paros, in which he was injured, led to his condemnation for 'deceiving the people'. He died of his injuries soon afterwards, and the heavy fine was paid by CIMON, his son by his second marriage to a Thracian princess.

RB

Davies (1971) no. 8429; Wade-Gery (1958).

Milvian Bridge battle in AD 312. The battle of the Milvian Bridge, outside Rome, where CONSTANTINE I defeated MAXENTIUS, left Constantine as sole emperor in the west, and marks the beginning of the Christian empire. Constantine ascribed his victory to the intervention of God: EUSEBIUS' *Life of Constantine* (1.28) claims Constantine saw a vision of the Cross inscribed 'by this conquer'; according to LACTANTIUS, Constantine had the Christian monogram displayed on his soldiers' shields.

RJB

Parker (1958).

Mime, Greek A mime was a dramatic presentation of a scene from daily life. Informal mime no doubt underlies much surviving written literature. As a literary genre it has obvious links with Attic COMEDY from which it is to be distinguished by its performance (presumably a recitation), its scale, and its metre and dialect. The earliest mime writer known to us is SOPHRON who used a rhythmic Doric prose. Several of the *Idylls* of THEOCRITUS (10, 14, 15) are really mimes, as too are *Hymns* 5 and 6 of CALLIMACHUS. HERODAS claims that his mimes represent a new form – sketches from comedy put into the old Ionic of HIPPONAX.

GS

Webster (1964).

Mime, Latin Mime reached Rome from Sicily in the 3rd century BC and was given a literary form in the 1st century BC by Laberius and PUBLILIUS SYRUS. Soon it replaced ATELLANA FABULA as a tailpiece and under the Empire it monopolized the stage. It catered for a low taste: blasphemy, satire, obscenity, and explicit sex were regular fare. Yet it was patronized by Sulla and the emperors who admired its slick wit.

See also PANTOMIME.

GS

Beare (1964).

Mimnermus (7th century BC), Greek lyric poet. Mimnermus of Colophon (or perhaps Smyrna) wrote elegiac love poetry in the second half of the 7th century BC. Surviving fragments (miserably few) indicate that he produced two books: *Nanno*, a collection of short poems on a variety of themes, later admired by CALLIMACHUS; and *Smyrneis*, a part-mythological, part-historical poem about SMYRNA.

GS

West (1974).

Minerva Roman goddess. Minerva was a goddess of crafts and the arts. In Rome she was a member, with JUPITER and JUNO, of the triad worshipped in the Capitoline temple built by the kings. She was an old

Italian goddess whose cult was widespread throughout the peninsula, but at an early date she was identified with the Greek goddess ATHENA. At Rome she had a temple outside the city boundary on the Aventine, which during the Second PUNIC WAR was a centre for skilled craftsmen, and another on the Esquiline, where her cult was associated with MEDICINE. Her feast day was 19 March, the day her Aventine temple was dedicated.   DP

Ogilvie (1969); Scullard (1981).

Mining   *see* COPPER; GOLD; IRON; LEAD; SILVER; TIN.

Minturnae   city in Italy. Minturnae was a coastal town situated in southern Latium near the mouth of the river Liris. Nearby was a sacred grove and shrine to the sea-goddess Marica. It was conquered by Rome during the LATIN and SAMNITE WARS, and in 295 BC a colony was founded there. In 88 BC MARIUS took refuge from SULLA in the marshes near Minturnae.   HE

Arthur (1991); Salmon (1969).

Misenum   city in Italy, on the northern headland of the Bay of Naples. Until imperial times it was a resort town, but in 31 BC Agrippa made it a naval station. The major Roman fleet in the western Mediterranean was usually based there. The town later became a colony.

HE

Mithraism   the cult of the Indo-Persian sun god Mithras. Introduced into the Hellenistic world from the east in the 2nd century BC, Mithraism spread throughout the Roman world in the 1st century AD, particularly to the frontier provinces where it was popular with the army. Though supported by the emperors COMMODUS and DIOCLETIAN, it declined during the 4th century AD. Mithraic temples were generally subterranean, reminiscent of the cave in which Mithras slew the bull. Rituals, exclusive to men, included a form of baptism and a ceremonial meal; but parallels with Christianity are purely superficial.
See also RELIGION, ROMAN.   GS

Burkert (1987); Martin (1987); Merkelbach (1984); Ulansey (1989).

Mithridates VI   (120–63 BC), king of Pontus. Mithridates VI Eupator Dionysus ('the Great') continued the expansionist policies of his predecessors, bringing most of the Black Sea coast under his control and acquiring TIGRANES I of Armenia as a son-in-law. Attempts to control Cappadocia and Paphlagonia and to remove NICOMEDES IV from Bithynia were less successful. Raids into Mithridates' territory by Nicomedes were the immediate cause of the first of the MITHRIDATIC WARS against Rome. When finally defeated, Mithridates fled to the Crimea. There the demands on his subjects to raise new forces resulted in a revolt led by his son Pharnaces (*see* ZELA). Immune to poison, Mithridates asked one of his guards to kill him.   HS

McGing (1986).

Mithridatic Wars   The first of the Mithridatic Wars (88–66 BC) fought between Rome and MITHRIDATES VI of Pontus started when NICOMEDES IV of Bithynia raided Pontic territory. Mithridates occupied the Roman province of Asia (where he ordered the deaths of 80,000 resident Italians) and, aided by the Athenians, much of Greece. After SULLA defeated Mithridates' forces at Chaeronea and Orchomenus, peace was made in 85 and Mithridates gave up his conquests. The Second Mithridatic War in 81 was a minor affair in which Mithridates re-pelled incursions by Murena. Rome's decision in 74 to annex Bithynia caused the Third Mithridatic War. Mithridates was defeated by LUCULLUS at Cyzicus and driven from Pontus to seek refuge with his son-in-law TIGRANES I in Armenia. Lucullus defeated Mithridates and Tigranes, but mutiny in his army allowed Mithridates to recover Pontus. POMPEY, who succeeded Lucullus in 66, defeated Mithridates again and retook Pontus. Mithridates escaped to the Crimea where a revolt forced him to commit suicide.   HS

Sherwin-White (1984); Sullivan (1990).

Mnesicles   *see* PROPYLAEA.

Moesia   Roman province. Moesia included the territory of the Moesi (on the lower Danube), first defeated by M. Crassus (29 BC). Admin-istered thereafter by a prefect, and at times with its own governor, it was eventually formally organized as a province under Tiberius or even Claudius I. Moesia stretched from the river Drinus to the Black Sea, the governor also controlling the Black Sea fleet, the *Classis Moesica* (*see* NAVY, ROMAN). Under Domitian (AD 85) the province was divided into Moesia Superior and Moesia Inferior (east of the Ciabrus), and both provinces were enlarged after the conquest of DACIA (106) to the north. Moesia became a prosperous agricultural province, but was repeatedly overrun during the Gothic invasions of the mid-to-late 3rd century, although it remained part of the empire until the 6th/7th century. Many of the principal towns were colonies or *municipia* that had originally been Roman camps (e.g. Sigidunum = Belgrade), and the Latin language took firm hold.   RJB

Mócsy (1974).

Moguntiacum modern Mainz, city in Germany. A camp for two legions was established in the reign of AUGUSTUS which served as a base for operations against the Germanic tribes. The military presence was reduced to a single legion in AD 89 which from AD 92 until the 4th century was the 22nd Primigenia Pia Fidelis. A large town developed in the 1st century AD which under Domitian became the capital of GERMANIA Superior. It was destroyed by barbarians in 406 when Rome abandoned the Rhine frontier.   GS

Monarchy Although monarchy appears to have been the norm in the Mycenaean period, by the archaic period constitutional monarchy had disappeared from the Greek world, with a few exceptions on its fringes, as at CYRENE and in MACEDONIA (though 'king' often survived as the title of a magistrate). SPARTA had an unusual dual monarchy with two royal houses, which Aristotle considered a 'generalship for life'. Otherwise monarchy in Greece, lacking constitutional sanction, was regarded as TYRANNY, as were the oriental despotisms which Greeks saw as the antithesis of their own freedom; in practice, Greek states had a choice between OLIGARCHY and DEMOCRACY. The rise of Macedon and the emergence of regional strong-men such as JASON, DIONYSIUS I, and MAUSOLUS provoked renewed philosophical interest in monarchy, a development confirmed by the domination of the Hellenistic dynasties. Political philosophy now focused on the character and qualities of the monarch, actual or ideal, while oriental influences led to the development of ruler worship. Such ideas in turn influenced Roman thinking in the late Republic and early Empire, providing a constructive ideal which supplanted the hostility to kings traditional in Rome since the fall of TARQUINIUS SUPERBUS.

See also REX.   RB

Ehrenberg (1969); Price (1984); Sinclair (1967).

Money   *see* BANKING; COINAGE; FINANCE.

Monumentum Ancyranum   a simple and dignified account by AUGUSTUS of his own acts, generally known as his *Res Gestae*. It purports to be written in AD 14, the year of Augustus' death, but was probably composed earlier and updated. The document was inscribed on two bronze pillars in front of Augustus' mausoleum. These do not survive: the best-preserved copy (discovered in 1555) is on the walls of the temple of Rome and Augustus (converted into a mosque) at Ancyra (Ankara), hence the name *Monumentum Ancyranum*. Written in Latin and translated into Greek, less complete copies also survive at Apollonia (Latin and Greek) and at Antioch (Latin only). It documents Augustus' reign in the way he wished it to be portrayed: it lists the honours granted to him; his expenditure on public benefactions; his victorious military expeditions and conquests; and justifies the position of the PRINCEPS in the Roman state. RJB

Brunt and Moore (1967).

Mosaic The earliest Greek mosaics date from around 400 BC and take the form of pavements made not of cut cubes but of natural pebbles. Examples from OLYNTHUS, OLYMPIA, and Pella, mostly in black and white, show geometric and figural designs in accordance with the subject-matter favoured by the other arts. In the Hellenistic period a more varied use of colour spread from Macedonia to other parts of the Greek world, and Sicilian artists introduced a new technique of cutting and smoothing square cubes (*tesserae*) of marble, stone, and tile to make close-fitting pavements (*opus tessellatum*). The use of similar but smaller, multi-coloured, curved cubes for three-dimensional effects (*opus vermiculatum*) originated in Egypt. The subsequent invention of an effective and waterproof cement led to a proliferation of the art form throughout the Roman world and to a change from the Hellenistic preference for a single motif (*emblema*) in the centre of a room to all-over carpet designs that could be placed outside as well as in. Mural mosaic became popular in the 1st century AD and, as a medium for Christian iconography, was much favoured by the Byzantines. As with PAINTING, Roman survivals can sometimes be identified as copies of Greek originals.

See also RAVENNA. GS

Dunbabin (1978); Henig (1983).

Moschus (2nd century BC), of Syracuse, Greek poet. Moschus was a pupil of ARISTARCHUS which places him in Alexandria in the mid-2nd century BC. He wrote bucolic poetry in the tradition of THEOCRITUS but in a lighter, sweeter style. Five short hexameter poems survive as well as the epyllion *Europa*, telling how Zeus disguised as a bull abducted Europa to Crete. The story was already familiar from literature and art. GS

Fraser (1972); Webster (1964).

Mucianus (d. *c.*AD 75), Roman general and administrator. Gaius Licinius Mucianus was appointed governor of Syria by Nero in AD 67. Together with VESPASIAN, he supported OTHO's claim to the throne (69), and, after Otho's death, persuaded Vespasian to assume the purple (69). He led a large contingent of Vespasian's army to Rome, along the way repelling a Sarmatian incursion across the Danube, and, once in Rome (January 70), acted as regent until Vespasian's arrival some months later.   RJB

Salmon (1968); Scullard (1982).

Mummius Achaicus (2nd century BC), Roman commander. Lucius Mummius Achaicus became notorious for the destruction of CORINTH. As praetor in Spain in 153 BC, he won a triumph (152) over the Lusitanians. As consul in 146 he defeated the ACHAEAN LEAGUE and oversaw the sack of Corinth, whose art treasures he took to Italy. In 142 he moderated the severity of SCIPIO AEMILIANUS, his colleague as censor.   HS

Astin (1967); Gruen (1984).

Munda battle in 45 BC. At Munda in Hispania Baetica CAESAR fought the Republican army led by Titus LABIENUS and the sons of POMPEY. After an obstinate battle, a tactical move by Labienus was interpreted as flight and caused the Republican army to collapse. Labienus was killed but Sextus POMPEIUS escaped the slaughter to continue resistance.
See also BELLUM HISPANIENSE.   LPR

Municipium Italian community. *Municipia* were Italian city-states which were given Roman CITIZENSHIP but continued to exist as self-governing communities with full local autonomy. The first *municipium* was TUSCULUM, incorporated in 381 BC with full Roman citizenship. Later instances, such as CAPUA (338), Privernum (329), and CAERE (273), were given a restricted form of Roman citizenship known as 'citizenship without vote', which meant that their inhabitants assumed all the duties and obligations of Roman citizens but could not exercise political rights at Rome. It is sometimes suggested that the term *municipia* originally applied only to communities of 'citizens without vote', but this view is probably mistaken; a *municipium* can be defined as any community incorporated into the Roman state as a self-governing body of Roman citizens. When this happened it was provided with a new constitution modelled on that of Rome. Control of local affairs was placed in the hands of annually elected officials drawn from the land-owning class. These officials were known variously as aediles, praetors, or *octoviri*. After the SOCIAL WAR, when full citizenship was granted to all free inhabitants of peninsular Italy, all of Rome's former allies were organized as *municipia* with a uniform constitution under magistrates known as *quattuorviri*.

Under the Empire *municipia* began to be created outside Italy, as Roman citizenship spread to the provinces. Some of these provincial *municipia* had Latin rights, rather than full Roman citizenship, but the principle of local self-government under a standard form of constitution persisted.

See also COLONIA; IUS LATII; OPPIDUM.   HE

CAH VII.2; Humbert (1978); Sherwin-White (1973).

Museum   literally a place of the Muses, usually with an educational context (e.g. the Museum in Plato's ACADEMY). The most famous museum was the literary academy founded by PTOLEMY I SOTER in ALEXANDRIA in association with the Library. Unlike its Athenian predecessors, the academic community did not include philosophers but men of letters and scientists. Assembled by the king, they were well paid and exempt from taxation. Research took priority over teaching but not to the exclusion of the latter. After the disturbances of 146 BC it lost some of its supremacy to PERGAMUM and other rivals such as Athens, Rhodes, Antioch, and Rome, but it remained open until the end of the 4th century AD.

See also LIBRARIES; SCHOLARSHIP, GREEK.   GS

Fraser (1972); Pfeiffer (1968).

Music, Greek   Music in the Greek world was more than a major art form: it was an integral part of life and an essential feature of religion, entertainment, literature, and the rites of passage. Hymns were composed to accompany celebrations of marriage, harvest, vintage, and death; no social gathering passed without a song or some other musical performance; musical competition was just as important an ingredient as athletics in the great religious FESTIVALS; nearly all poetry – EPIC, LYRIC, and the choruses in TRAGEDY and COMEDY – was originally written to be sung (and danced); even the warrior and the athlete trained to the sound of the pipes. The philosophers stressed the value of musical EDUCATION in contributing to the attainment of good character and moral rectitude. There were professional musicians, but some musical accomplishment was the norm among citizens in classical society. At Athens the epithet *mousikos* ('muse-ish') was synonymous with having good taste.

Until the mid-5th century BC SPARTA was the musical centre of Greece and TERPANDER is said to have founded a school of music there. Two instruments were taught – the flute and the lyre – and the performer was expected to be proficient as both soloist and accompanist. The senior musical contest at the GAMES was song to the ceremonial (seven-stringed) lyre. Surviving scores are very fragmentary but suggest that rhythm was always the servant of metre. Some details of the structure of Greek music are provided by the partly surviving 4th-century BC treatise on theory by ARISTOXENUS of Tarentum.   GS

Anderson (1966); Barker (1984, 1989); Comotti (1989); Maas and Snyder (1989); Michaelides (1978); West (1992).

Music, Roman   Roman music was deeply indebted to both Etruscan and Greek influences, but music was not accorded the same esteem in either education or society at Rome as it had been in Greece. Musicians did organize themselves into GUILDS, but their status, like that of actors, was low. They were barely tolerated by, and certainly not part of, civilized society. Music, both vocal and instrumental, retained its role as an integral part of religious observances. Hymns were written for the ARVAL BROTHERS, horns and trumpets featured in the cult of the dead, and flutes accompanied prayers, sacrifices, and processions. The Roman ARMY marched to the sound of brass instruments of Etruscan origin, and music for the pipes was specially commissioned to accompany the performance of Roman COMEDY. Stringed instruments were introduced from Greece, and musical contests (for which Domitian built an ODEUM) took place occasionally. A new musical genre evolved to accompany the PANTOMIME. The emperor NERO was so proud of his voice that he never missed an opportunity to sing in public.   GS

Comotti (1989).

Mycale   headland opposite Samos where in 479 BC the Greeks defeated the Persian defensive force in Ionia. When the Persian fleet retired after SALAMIS, the Greek fleet sailed east. As the Persians refused to fight at sea with such ships as they had kept together, the Greeks landed and, helped by Greeks deserting the Persians, won a victory, the importance of which was perhaps not great.   GLC

Burn (1984); CAH IV.

Myron   (fl. mid-5th century BC), Greek sculptor. A native of Eleutherae in Attica, Myron was, with POLYCLEITUS, a pupil of Ageladas at Argos. He was held to be one of the greatest sculptors of his time and to have contributed much to the theory of symmetry and the development of the classical style. His Discobulus and Athena and Marsyas, known from Roman copies, illustrate his interest in arrested movement of the body.
   See also SCULPTURE, GREEK.   GS

Richter (1970b).

Mytilene principal city of LESBOS. Mytilene was under Persian control from 527 BC until it joined the DELIAN LEAGUE in 479. Revolts from Athens in 428 and 412 were severely punished and it remained an Athenian ally for most of the 4th century. After the death of ALEXANDER THE GREAT Mytilene was ruled in turn by Antigonus, Lysimachus, and the Ptolemies. MITHRIDATES VI EUPATOR occupied it in 88 BC and the city was stormed by the Romans in 80 but its freedom was restored by POMPEY.

GS

Stillwell (1976).

N

Nabataeans people of Arabia. The Nabataeans were nomadic traders who became settled in the territory of modern Jordan and the Negev. Their capital city was PETRA. Their wealth resulted from the overland transport of eastern perfumes, spices, and luxury goods across southern ARABIA to Mediterranean ports. These commercial contacts gave them access to Hellenistic culture, and their art and architecture display a distinctive blend of Greek and eastern styles. By the 1st century AD the sea route to India had caused overland trade to decline. Their kings remained independent of the Seleucids, but in AD 106 TRAJAN annexed their kingdom to the Roman province of Asia.   EER

Bowersock (1983); Glueck (1966, 1968, 1970); Harding (1967); Potts (1990); Sullivan (1990).

Nabis (fl. 207–192 BC), king of Sparta. Nabis became regent to the boy king Pelops of Sparta in 207 BC. Perhaps responsible for his death, Nabis seized power and reintroduced the social reforms of CLEOMENES III. He agitated against cities of the ACHAEAN LEAGUE but was subdued by PHILOPOEMEN in 200. Nabis tacitly supported PHILIP V during the Second MACEDONIAN WAR (200–197), receiving Argos in return, and was punished by FLAMININUS with the help of ATTALUS I SOTER. He retained power but was forced to relinquish Argos and Laconian ports. With Aetolian help he tried to regain his losses but was defeated by Flamininus and Philopoemen. Aetolians killed him at Sparta in 192.

EER

Cartledge and Spawforth (1989); Errington (1969); Green (1990); Gruen (1984).

Naevius (c.270–201 BC), Latin poet. Gnaeus Naevius was born in Campania and fought in the First PUNIC WAR (264–241 BC). The war was the subject of his most important work, *Bellum Punicum,* an EPIC poem written in old age in saturnian metre. His treatment of Roman history and myth inspired respectively ENNIUS and VIRGIL, but only fragments survive. He also composed original Roman tragedies (*fabulae praetextae*) as well as adapting Greek plays for the Roman stage.

GS

Wigodsky (1972); Wright (1974).

Namatianus (4th–5th century AD), Latin poet. Rutilius Claudius Namatianus was a pagan Gaul who held office at Rome under HONORIUS in AD 412–14. He described his return voyage to Gaul in 417 in a long elegiac poem, *De Reditu Suo,* of which parts of two books survive. Of considerable literary merit, it includes much anti-religious polemic and valuable commentary on contemporary events. GS

Names Most Greeks, both men and women, had only one name. A boy was often given the name of his grandfather. His father's name in the genitive (e.g. Thucydides [son] of Olorus) was sometimes added for purposes of identification. The name of a man's deme was also sometimes given but it did not become part of his name. Many names were theophoric, i.e. they incorporated the name of a god or goddess (e.g. Diogenes). Nicknames (e.g. those given to Hellenistic rulers – Soter, Auletes, etc.) were not inherited.

The Romans and other Italian peoples had at least two names – the *praenomen* or first name and the *nomen* or name of the GENS. Most also had a third name or *cognomen.* Fewer than a hundred male *praenomina* are known and only 14 are common. They are generally abbreviated: A. = Aulus; C. = Gaius; Cn. = Gnaeus; D. = Decimus; L. = Lucius; M. = Marcus; M'. = Manius; P. = Publius; Q. = Quintus; Ser. = Servius; Sex. = Sextus; Sp. = Spurius; T. = Titus; Ti. = Tiberius. Several of these had female equivalents: Gaia, Quinta. All Romans (including married women) bore the *nomen* of their father; it usually ended in -ius (m.) or -ia (f.) and was the most important name. *Cognomina,* additional personal names, often related to a personal characteristic (Naso), occupation (Pictor), or office (Censorinus). Some were handed down as subdivisions of the *gens,* e.g. Cornelius Scipio Nasica. Adopted sons took their fathers' full names, often adding their own *cognomen.* Slaves had their own names, but freedmen took their liberator's *praenomen* and *nomen,* adding their own name as a *cognomen.* GS

Kajanto (1965); Salomies (1987).

Narbo modern Narbonne, city in southern Gaul. Narbo (or Naro) was originally the capital of a tribal kingdom that grew rich on the

British TIN trade. A Roman colony was founded in 118 BC and another in 45 BC by CAESAR for veterans of his 10th legion. As the capital of Gallia Narbonensis, Narbo flourished for two centuries and acquired fine buildings. But in the 2nd century AD it declined and lost its supremacy to NEMAUSUS. The Visigoths took it in 462.   GS

Narcissus (d. AD 54), freedman of CLAUDIUS I. Narcissus rose to extraordinary power as Claudius' secretary general (*praepositus ab epistulis*), amassing a private fortune which, at over 400 million *sestertii*, matches that of LENTULUS as the largest recorded. He took the initiative in removing Claudius' unfaithful wife MESSALINA (48), but lost his preeminence after Claudius' marriage to AGRIPPINA THE YOUNGER (48), who arranged Narcissus' death soon after the accession of her son NERO (54).

RJB

Grant (1979); Wells (1984).

Nauarchos *see* NAVY, GREEK.

Naucratis Greek trading station in EGYPT. Finds show that the Greek settlement dates from the late 7th century BC. In the reign of Amasis (570–526 BC) its position was regularized as the only place in Egypt where Greek traders were allowed to live. Trading concessions were granted to a number of Greek cities and separate quarters were given to the people of Miletus, Samos, and Aegina. As the principal entrepôt between Greece and Egypt, the city flourished throughout the classical period. After Alexander's conquest much of the TRADE was moved to ALEXANDRIA, but Naucratis was the first city in Egypt with its own coinage. In the Roman period the city retained its Greek constitution but it soon fell into decline.   GS

Boardman (1980).

Naumachia mock sea battle. At Rome artificial lakes were created (the best known, on the right bank of the Tiber, was called the Naumachia) in which simulated sea battles were fought for the entertainment of the people. The first such display was given by Caesar in 46 BC. Sometimes historical engagements such as SALAMIS or ACTIUM were enacted, with criminals and prisoners of war doing the fighting. Sometimes amphitheatres (e.g. the COLOSSEUM) were flooded for the purpose.
See also GAMES, ROMAN.   GS

Naupactus city in west LOCRIS with a good harbour which commands the entrance to the Corinthian Gulf. In 456 BC it was captured by the Athenians who settled a colony of Messenian refugees there. It was an important Athenian naval base in the Peloponnesian War. After the war it was held by the Achaeans until PHILIP II of Macedon took it and presented it to Aetolia in 338. As the diplomatic centre of the AETOLIAN LEAGUE it retained its importance until 189 BC.   GS

Larsen (1968).

Navigation Both TRADE and TRAVEL in Greece were mostly sea-borne but the Greeks were not brave sailors. They had no navigational instruments, their SHIPS were small, and their sailing skills and tackle were rudimentary. The sailing season ran from March to October, though HESIOD, who voiced the general fear of the sea, recommended it should be restricted to the 50 days after the summer solstice. The construction of LIGHTHOUSES and artificial HARBOURS in the Hellenistic age and the descriptions of coasts by geographers encouraged more adventurous sailing, as did the reduction of PIRACY in the 1st century BC. The Romans were more willing to stand out to sea and to sail in the winter. The run from Puteoli to Alexandria was made direct (sometimes in only eight days), as was that from Egypt to INDIA on the monsoon winds. The average speed for a cargo vessel was 3 or 4 knots.

See also ASTRONOMY; EUDOXUS OF CYZICUS; HIPPALUS; PYTHEAS.   GS

Casson (1991); Miller (1969).

Navy, Greek The earliest naval forces consisted of SHIPS rowed by a single tier of 30 (*triakonter*) or 50 (*pentekonter*) oarsmen, and though they had extended prows, fighting was probably mainly by armed men on deck. The addition of further tiers of rowers produced the bireme and TRIREME, more powerful and manoeuvrable vessels whose main function was to disable other ships by ramming, although a contingent of hoplite marines was often retained; manoeuvrability was therefore increasingly enhanced by a lighter construction at the expense of robustness. From the mid-4th century BC on, however, this tendency was reversed by the development of heavier vessels such as quinqueremes which were simply weapons platforms, supplemented by new light types.

Naval warfare was expensive owing to the costs of ship construction and maintenance and of pay for the large crews; at Athens these were partly defrayed by the TRIERARCHY system. Lacking any space for facilities, triremes normally required beaching daily (which made effective blockading impossible) and needed regular overhauling to remain efficient. Supplies of suitable TIMBER were a major constraint on sea power, and the availability of skilled crews (often mercenaries, given the numbers required) was also important, since speed and agility could only be attained by practice.

Apart from protecting the territory and commerce of a state, naval power facilitated the transport of troops who, exceptionally, might row themselves. The close link between sea and land operations meant that naval forces were normally commanded by STRATEGOI, and the office of *nauarchos* (admiral), though found in classical Sparta, is rare before the Hellenistic period.　　　　　　　　　　　　　　　　　　　　　RB

Casson (1991); Jordan (1975); Morrison and Coates (1986); Morrison and Williams (1968); Starr (1988).

Hellenistic period: Changes in naval tactics and ship design went hand in hand in the Hellenistic period. Larger, heavier vessels which could not rely on speed and manoeuvrability for success required more manpower to propel them, and marines and war-machines to defend them. Catapults and armed men on deck warded off pursuers, who attempted to close, grapple, and board enemy ships rather than ram and disable them. Oar-power below decks was dramatically increased. SHIPS with names like '6s', '10s', '16s' (and so on up to a '40') are attested. The names apparently refer to the number of rowers in any one rowing position along the hull, assuming multiple manning of oars and banks of oars up to three. Such vessels were fashionable in the 3rd century BC but declined thereafter. '4s' and '5s' remained the standard ships of the line into the Roman period.　　　　　　　　　EER

Casson (1971, 1991); Morrison (1980); Morrison and Coates (1986).

Navy, Roman　The Roman navy was always less important than the army. This can be attributed both to a Roman antipathy towards the sea and to inherent limitations in ancient navies. Ancient oared warships were vulnerable to bad weather and normally needed to beach each night. They thus lacked strategic outreach and the ability to enforce a close blockade. Although the existence of officers called *duoviri navales* attests some earlier naval involvement, Rome first built substantial fleets during the PUNIC WARS. Despite some disasters due to poor seamanship, Roman fleets performed well against Carthage, for Rome outbuilt her opponent, and used heavy SHIPS equipped with a boarding bridge (*corvus*) as far as possible to transform naval battles into infantry engagements.

After the Punic Wars Rome allowed her fleet to decline, and for naval operations relied on ships from her Greek allies. This, with Rome's policy of keeping the fleets of other states weak, led to an epidemic of PIRACY in the Mediterranean. When the pirates threatened Rome's food supply (ANNONA), POMPEY successfully campaigned against them in 67 BC. The CIVIL WARS of the late Republic caused a revival of Roman fleets. After his father's death, Sextus POMPEIUS attempted to win power via his fleet, but was defeated by the fleets of Octavian (AUGUSTUS). The last battle of the civil wars, ACTIUM, was fought at sea.

Augustus created standing fleets, each commanded by a PRAEFECTUS, based at Misenum, Ravenna, and Alexandria. Under the Principate fleets were maintained at Boulogne, on the Rhine and Danube, and on the Black Sea. During the 3rd and 4th centuries AD Roman fleets again all but disappeared.

See also ARMY, ROMAN; WARFARE, ROMAN. HS

Casson (1991); Reddé (1986); Starr (1960); Thiel (1946).

Naxos largest island in the Cyclades. Rich deposits of high-quality MARBLE gave Naxos an important place in the development of both SCULPTURE and ARCHITECTURE in the archaic period. It played a part in the COLONIZATION of Sicily and gave its name to the city of NAXOS there. Sacked by the Persians in 490 for its part in the IONIAN REVOLT, Naxos joined the Delian League and was the first state to become subject to Athens in 470. It regained its independence but not its importance after the Peloponnesian War. GS

Stillwell (1976).

Naxos first Greek colony in Sicily. Founded by Chalcis in 735 BC, Naxos in turn colonized CATANA and LEONTINI. Its 5th-century history was unhappy. Attacked by HIPPOCRATES *c*.495, its citizens were expelled. In 415 it supported Athens against Syracuse and in 403 it was destroyed by DIONYSIUS I. The land was given to the Sicels and the population scattered. In 392 a new city was founded at nearby TAUROMENIUM. GS

Stillwell (1976).

Neanthes of Cyzicus (3rd century BC), Greek historian. Neanthes was a writer and rhetorician to whom are attributed histories of Greece and Cyzicus and colourful biographies (including one of the famous misanthrope Timon of Athens). He was criticized in antiquity for unreliability. A younger Neanthes is generally credited with authorship of a history of ATTALUS I SOTER of Pergamum, although the attribution of various of these works to one or the other writer has been disputed. EER

Brown (1958); Hansen (1971).

Neapolis modern Naples, Greek city in Italy. Little is known of its early history after its foundation by CUMAE *c*.650 BC. By the 5th century

Neapolis was the chief city of CAMPANIA and in the later 4th century it was taken by Rome. As a port it was superseded by PUTEOLI, but it remained a fashionable *municipium* and centre of Greek culture into late imperial times.   GS

Stillwell (1976).

Nearchus of Crete   (fl. 334–*c*.312 BC), admiral of ALEXANDER THE GREAT. Nearchus was a boyhood companion of Alexander. He accompanied the expedition and was appointed satrap of LYCIA and Pamphylia in 334/3 BC. He was admiral of the fleet which sailed down the Indus, explored the Persian Gulf, and reached the Tigris (326–324). His account of India and this voyage is the main source of ARRIAN's *Indica*, and was also used by STRABO. He later held office under ANTIGONUS I MONOPHTHALMUS and DEMETRIUS I POLIORCETES.   EER

Bosworth (1988a); Hammond (1989); Lane Fox (1973); Stadter (1980).

Nemausus   modern Nîmes, city in southern Gaul. Originally the capital of the local Celtic tribe, Nemausus was romanized in the 1st century BC and became a colony in 27 BC. In the 2nd century AD it succeeded NARBO as the capital of Gallia Narbonensis. Its walls date from 16 BC. A number of very impressive public buildings survive including the AMPHITHEATRE, 'Maison Carrée' (a temple dedicated to Gaius and Lucius Caesar), and nearby Pont-du-Gard AQUEDUCT.   GS

Stillwell (1976).

Nemean Games   festival held in the Argolid every second year in honour of Zeus. Originally a local festival, it became part of the panhellenic circuit in 573 BC (*see* GAMES, GREEK). In the 5th century Argos displaced Cleonae as president of the games, and in the 4th century their venue was moved from Nemea to Argos. The contests were similar to the OLYMPIC GAMES and the prize was a crown of celery.

GS

Harris (1964).

Nemesianus   (late 3rd century AD), Latin poet. Marcus Aurelius Olympius Nemesianus of Carthage was the author of four *Eclogues*, short pastoral poems in the style of CALPURNIUS SICULUS, to whom they were once attributed, and a longer didactic poem on HUNTING, *Cynegetica*, written *c*.284, of which 325 lines survive. Other poems on fishing and sailing have not survived. He is said to have contemplated an epic on the emperors Numerian and Carinus.   GS

Verdière (1974).

Neoplatonism Neoplatonism which developed at Alexandria in the 3rd century BC was a new synthesis of Platonic, Pythagorean, Aristotelian, and Stoic elements. It became the most influential philosophy of the ancient world from the mid-3rd century AD until the Neoplatonic school at Athens was closed in 529. After a lengthy period of development, Neoplatonism was given an ordered structure by PLOTINUS in the *Enneads*, published posthumously by his pupil PORPHYRY (*c*.300). In the 4th century it became more widely diffused with teaching centres established also in Syria and later at Pergamum. At this time a pupil of Porphyry, the Syrian mystic IAMBLICHUS, corrupted Plotinus' teachings by introducing alien fantasies and magical elements. Neoplatonic doctrine received its final form at the hands of PROCLUS before the closure of the Athenian school by Justinian. It survived, however, at Alexandria until the end of the 6th century.

See also NEOPYTHAGOREANISM. JL

Wallis (1972).

Neoptolemus (3rd century BC), of Parium, Greek writer. Neoptolemus was a poet and a grammarian who composed a mythological poem about Dionysus and published glossaries and works of literary criticism. His study of poetry, which is summarized by PHILODEMUS, was said by Porphyrion to be the model for HORACE's *Ars Poetica*. GS

Brink (1971).

Neopythagoreanism Although Pythagorean philosophy as such became extinct during the 4th century BC or was fused with Platonism, Pythagoreanism survived as a religious way of life. In the 2nd and 1st centuries BC, however, Pythagoreanism, combined with Platonic, Peripatetic, and Stoic elements, and accommodated to contemporary religious tendencies, was revived at Rome and Alexandria. It persisted until it was finally merged with NEOPLATONISM. These Neopythagorean writers (such as APOLLONIUS OF TYANA) reveal little trace of a common body of philosophical doctrine and were primarily interested in theological speculation, in numerical symbolism, and in the glorification of PYTHAGORAS as the founder of a religious way of life. The chief importance of Neopythagoreanism lies in its influence upon Neoplatonism and upon Jewish and Christian thought. JL

Dillon (1977).

Nepos (d. AD 480), Roman emperor, AD 474–5. Julius Nepos, related by marriage to LEO, was Leo's nominee to succeed ANTHEMIUS as Roman emperor. With eastern help Nepos deposed GLYCERIUS in June 474.

Nepos concluded a treaty with EURIC, recognizing Gothic gains in Spain and Gaul. In August 475 Nepos was deposed by his general Orestes, and replaced by ROMULUS AUGUSTULUS. Nepos lived at Salona until murdered by two retainers, still recognized as emperor by his eastern counterpart, Zeno.   RJB

Bury (1958); Grant (1985).

Nepos, Cornelius (*c*.99–24 BC), Latin biographer. Nepos was born in Cisalpine Gaul but moved to Rome where he enjoyed the society of CICERO, ATTICUS, and CATULLUS. His main work, *De Viris Illustribus*, first published in 34 BC (2nd edn. *c*.27 BC), compared Roman with foreign lives and is the earliest extant example of Latin BIOGRAPHY. The one book that survives (of the original 16) concerns foreign generals; others covered Roman generals, historians, kings, poets, orators, and scholars; lives of Atticus and the elder CATO are also preserved. Based on Greek models, the *Lives* were widely read but are of little value to historians.   GS

Dorey (1967); Geiger (1985); Momigliano (1971).

Neratius Priscus (fl. *c*.AD 100), Roman jurist. Lucius Neratius Priscus from Saepinum in Samnium rose to high office under Trajan and Hadrian. Suffect consul in AD 97 and governor of Pannonia, he was even considered a possible successor to Trajan. As a jurist he was (with CELSUS) the last head of the Proculian school. Excerpts of his *Membranae* appear in the *Digest* and PAULUS wrote a commentary *Ad Neratium*.   GS

Nero (AD 37–68), Roman emperor, AD 54–68. Lucius Domitius Ahenobarbus (Nero Claudius Drusus Germanicus Caesar after his adoption), son of Gnaeus Domitius Ahenobarbus and AGRIPPINA THE YOUNGER, was adopted by CLAUDIUS I (AD 50). He was named *princeps iuventutis* (51), and married Octavia (53), daughter of Claudius and Messalina. Nero, given preference over Claudius' own son Britannicus, succeeded in 54: Agrippina hoped to rule through her son, but Nero relied instead upon Burrus (praetorian prefect) and SENECA THE YOUNGER (his tutor). Britannicus was murdered, and Agrippina driven from court, but the years 54–8 were later seen by Trajan as a golden age of good government (the *quinquennium Neronis*): Burrus and Seneca ruled while Nero indulged in lavish entertainments. Then Nero fell in love with Poppaea Sabina, wife of OTHO, and proposed to divorce Octavia. Agrippina's disapproval precipitated her own murder (59). Next, Nero required senators and equestrians to participate in public GAMES (59), and appeared himself as musician and charioteer (60). In

62 Burrus died: one of his replacements, TIGELLINUS, encouraged Nero to further excesses. Seneca was forced into retirement, Octavia was divorced and executed (62), and treason trials on trumped-up charges began. Nero took little interest in military affairs (which included BOUDICCA's revolt and CORBULO's campaigns). However, he made generous reparations after a great fire in Rome (64), but his popularity with the people was destroyed by rumours that he had sung while Rome burned. His excesses precipitated the conspiracy of PISO (65). A kick from Nero killed the pregnant Poppaea. He now began to insist on his own divinity, and toured Greece (67), having first prizes awarded to himself everywhere. The rebellion of VINDEX was defeated (68), but Nero, declared a public enemy by the Senate (which supported GALBA), committed suicide. Nero, last of the Julio-Claudian emperors, was a memorable patron of architecture and of literature.   RJB

Grant (1985); Griffin (1984); Warmington (1969b); Wells (1984).

Nerva (*c*.AD 30–98), Roman emperor, AD 96–8. Marcus Cocceius Nerva, twice consul and distant relative of the Julio-Claudians, was chosen by the Senate to succeed DOMITIAN. He treated the Senate with great deference (the literary sources are favourable towards him as a result), and immediately paid the usual donatives to the army and the people of Rome. Measures were taken to alleviate hardship in Italy: most important was the introduction of the ALIMENTA, the Roman system of poor relief. This open-handedness was countered by setting up a five-man commission to find ways of reducing public expenditure. He garnered further support by recalling exiles banished by Domitian, and probably encouraged the blackening of Domitian's memory to his own advantage, while quietly retaining most of Domitian's legislation. However, he failed to take measures against the *delatores*, the notorious public informers. Faced with the loss of power (there was at least one abortive plot against him, led by C. Calpurnius Crassus), he mimicked GALBA by adopting a son and heir who he hoped would be popular with the troops. His choice, in October 97, of TRAJAN, governor of Upper Germany, was successful: Trajan was granted full powers and, when Nerva died three months later (January 98), Trajan succeeded peacefully.   RJB

Grant (1985); Salmon (1968); Wells (1984).

Nestorianism a theological doctrine formulated in the 5th century AD by the Syrian monk and bishop of Constantinople Nestorius (d. *c*.451). Nestorians denied the doctrine of the single nature of Christ, believing that the divine and human aspects of His nature were separate. They termed the Virgin Christotokos (mother of Christ), rejecting the term

Theotokos (mother of God). Condemned at the Council of Ephesus in 431, the Nestorians formed a separate church which flourished in Persia and parts of the Arab world until the coming of Islam. A small group known as Assyrian Christians survives to this day.   GS

Cross (1974)

New Testament the specifically Christian part of the Bible. Known in Greek as *Kaine Diatheke*, meaning the 'new covenant' between God and IIis people, it comprises the Gospels, Acts, Epistles of St PAUL, and Book of Revelation. The canon was assembled between the 2nd and 4th centuries and finally established in 367 by ST ATHANASIUS of Alexandria.   GS

Metzger (1968, 1987).

Nexum transaction in Roman law. *Nexum* was an ancient transaction, referred to in the TWELVE TABLES, by which a debtor was reduced to bondage. It involved a ritual with copper weights and a set of scales. It is unclear whether this occurred when a debtor could not pay, or when an individual voluntarily entered into bondage as part of the original contract. Debt bondage was a major social problem in early Rome, and one of the causes of the plebeian struggle. *Nexum* ceased in 326 BC when a law prohibited enslavement for private debts.

See also MANCIPATIO.   HE

CAH VII.2; Finley (1981); Nicholas (1962).

Nicaea, Council of The first 'ecumenical' (i.e. worldwide) council was convened in 325 by the emperor CONSTANTINE I at Nicaea in Bithynia to deal with the problem of ARIANISM. The principal document to emerge and survive from the council was the Nicene Creed, to which were appended four anti-Arian anathemas. Other regulations established the means of computing the date of Easter and the hierarchy among metropolitan sees which gave precedence to Rome.

See also CHRISTIANITY.   GS

Luibheid (1982).

Nicander (2nd century BC?), of Colophon, Greek poet and grammarian. The 2nd century BC was not noted for poetry. Nicander, who wrote didactic poems on scientific themes, was no scientist either. Two lengthy hexameter works are preserved, presumably for their literary perversity: *Theriaca* devotes its 958 lines to remedies against snake bite and other venomous beasts; *Alexipharmaca* (630 lines) lists cures for food poisoning. Both derive from APOLLODORUS but indiscriminately mingle recondite superstition with undigested botany and medicine. His *Metamorphoses* was used by OVID but, along with numerous other works of antiquarian prose and poetry, it is lost. GS

Gow and Scholfield (1953).

Nicanor of Stagira (*c*.360–317 BC), Macedonian general. Nicanor, a son-in-law and probably pupil of ARISTOTLE, accompanied ALEXANDER THE GREAT's expedition. He was sent back to Greece in 324 BC to deliver measures including the Exiles' Decree (ordering the repatriation of exiles throughout Greece). He commanded CASSANDER's garrison in Athens in 319, and his fleet in the Bosporus in 318 (where he defeated CLEITUS THE WHITE). A quarrel with Cassander led to his arrest and execution for treason. EER

Bosworth (1988a); Hammond and Walbank (1988).

Nicias (*c*.470–413 BC), Athenian politician and general. Nicias, a rich man loyally serving the democracy, came to prominence on the death of PERICLES (429). In the Archidamian War he proved a safe, if unspectacular, commander. He opposed the reinforcement of DEMOSTHENES at PYLOS, readily yielding the command to CLEON (425). Anxious for an end to hostilities, he was preferred to ALCIBIADES by the Spartans as agent for the peace that bears his name (421). After that the two were much opposed, notably in 418 over the alliance with Argos, and in 415 over the Sicilian expedition which Nicias tried to discredit by demanding improbably large forces. His proposal was accepted and so the city was disastrously overcommitted. Illness and caution slowed him down; fear of the people kept him in Sicily despite the advice of Demosthenes. Specially scrupulous about religion, he allowed an eclipse of the moon to delay withdrawal: disaster ensued; Nicias was captured and executed. THUCYDIDES gave him a fine epitaph. GLC

Kagan (1975, 1987).

Nicias (4th century BC), Greek painter. Nicias of Athens was a contemporary of PRAXITELES for whom he painted several statues. He was said to have been particularly successful in painting women, in distinguishing light and shade, and in making his figures stand out from the background. All his work is lost, but several wall paintings at POMPEII (Andromeda, Calypso, Io) are thought to be copies of his originals.
See also PAINTING, GREEK. GS

Robertson (1975).

Nicolaus of Damascus (b. *c.*64 BC), Greek writer. A well-educated Greek, Nicolaus enjoyed a distinguished career as adviser and court historian to HEROD THE GREAT, whom he twice accompanied to Rome. Substantial fragments survive of his biography of the young AUGUSTUS. Other writings (lost) included tragedies and comedies, philosophical and scientific works, an autobiography, and a universal history in 144 books in the style of EPHORUS from earliest times down to 4 BC.   GS

Wacholder (1962).

Nicomedes I–IV (*c.*279–75/4 BC), kings of Bithynia. Nicomedes I succeeded his father Zipoetes as king (*c.*279–*c.*255 BC) and struggled to maintain BITHYNIA's independence against the Seleucid ANTIOCHUS I SOTER. He made an alliance with Mithridates I of PONTUS, and unwisely invited the CELTS to settle in Asia Minor (*see* GALATIA). Nicomedes' hellenizing policies included founding a capital (Nicomedia) on the Propontis and striking Greek coinage. Nicomedes II, sent to Rome to argue against Bithynia's indemnity, usurped the throne of his unpopular father PRUSIAS II in 149 BC, murdering him with the help of ATTALUS II PHILADELPHUS and Rome's connivance. He remained Rome's ally, sending troops against the Macedonian pretender ARISTONICUS (133–129). Nicomedes III succeeded his father Nicomedes II *c.*127. When asked for troops by Gaius MARIUS (104), his complaint that Bithynians had been enslaved by Romans led to the Senate's order to free all enslaved freeborn allies in the provinces. His intrigues with MITHRIDATES VI of Pontus were thwarted by Rome. Nicomedes IV, succeeding Nicomedes III *c.*94, was deposed by Mithridates (*c.*92) but restored by Rome. Caught between Rome and Pontus, he owed his position to the former and was pressured to harry the latter, thus provoking the First MITHRIDATIC WAR. He bequeathed his kingdom to Rome in 75/4 BC.

EER

Gruen (1984); Jones (1983); Magie (1975); Sherwin-White (1984); Sullivan (1990).

Nicomedia   modern Ismit, city in north-west Asia Minor. Founded by NICOMEDES I *c.*265 BC, it became the capital of first the kingdom and later the province of BITHYNIA. Well placed for communications by land and sea, the city flourished and acquired fine buildings. Despite being sacked by the Goths in AD 256, it became the capital of DIOCLETIAN's eastern empire. But in the 4th century it was overshadowed by the foundation of CONSTANTINOPLE.   GS

Stillwell (1976).

Nicopolis   city in EPIRUS founded by Augustus to commemorate his victory at ACTIUM (31 BC). He peopled it with the citizens of most of the towns in the area and made it an administrative centre in place of the Acarnanian Confederacy (*see* ACARNANIA) and AETOLIAN LEAGUE. He also made it the venue of the Actian Games. Held every four years in honour of Apollo under the presidency of Sparta, they included musical and naval contests as well as athletic and equestrian events.

GS

Hammond (1967).

Nicopolis   in Pontus, site of battles in 66 and 47 BC. In 66 POMPEY succeeded LUCULLUS as commander of the war against MITHRIDATES VI. On the banks of the river Euphrates he defeated the Pontic army in a moonlit battle. Pompey later founded Nicopolis on that site. In 47 BC Pharnaces II king of Pontus defeated Gnaeus Domitius Calvinus, Caesar's subordinate, at Nicopolis.

LPR

Sherwin-White (1984).

Niger   *see* PESCENNIUS NIGER.

Nimbus   the circle of light or halo surrounding the head of a god. In Greek art Helios is often shown with a garland of solar rays. This was adopted as a symbol of divinity by the Ptolemies and from the 1st century AD by Roman emperors on their coinage. Pagan divinities are commonly represented thus in wall paintings, mosaics, and reliefs. In Christian iconography the nimbus was at first restricted to Christ; but in the 5th century it was extended to angels and in the 6th to the Virgin and other saints.

GS

Niobid Painter   (fl. 465–450 BC), Greek vase painter. The Niobid Painter is named after a vase in the Louvre that illustrates the Argonauts and the death of the Niobids. He is credited with the painting of about 90 vases, mostly large shapes. His compositions are imposing and reflect the influence of contemporary wall PAINTING, notably that of POLYGNOTUS, and SCULPTURE. His choice of subject – often epic encounters of Greeks triumphing over orientals – may have been influenced by recent events in Greek history.

GS

Arias and Hirmer (1962); Boardman (1989).

Nobiles   Roman nobility. While all PATRICIANS were *nobiles*, a man who became CONSUL, or sometimes only PRAETOR, ennobled his family. Thus, after the PLEBS were allowed to become MAGISTRATES, a plebeian nobility arose. The nobility, although consciously exclusive, was never a closed caste, as a non-noble or NOVUS HOMO could aspire to ennoble his family.

Under the Empire *nobiles* came to be thought of as only the descendants of the Republican nobility.   HS

Brunt (1982); Gelzer (1969); Hopkins (1983).

Nomothetai   Greek lawgivers. The word acquired a particular meaning in late 5th- and 4th-century BC Athens. In the 5th century what the people voted was immediately valid and a law of general import could be passed as simply as a decree about specific matters. In 403/2, when the democracy was restored, a new procedure was introduced whereby a number of *nomothetai* were appointed to consider whether the existing laws were adequate. This presented such obstacles to the passing of a law that the system was later simplified.   GLC

MacDowell (1978).

Nonnus   (5th century AD), Greek epic poet. Nonnus, from Panopolis in Egypt, was the author of *Dionysiaca*, an EPIC in 48 books. In structure and language there are close affinities between this last great poem of antiquity and the first. But its themes, the loves of Dionysus and his conquest of India, are as far from Homer as is his other remarkable work, a verse paraphrase of St John's Gospel in over 3,500 hexameters.   GS

Vian (1976–   ).

Norbanus   (d. 82 BC), Roman politician. Gaius Norbanus, one of the POPULARES, was a *tribunus plebis* in 103 BC who assisted SATURNINUS and successfully prosecuted CAEPIO. A supporter of MARIUS, he prospered under the government of CINNA, and in 83 became consul. He commanded the resistance to the forces of SULLA in 83/2 BC, but after several defeats retired to Rhodes where he committed suicide.   HS

Badian (1964).

Noricum   Roman province. Noricum was peaceably annexed by Publius Silius Nerva, governor of Illyricum, *c*.16 BC, after the Romans had imposed tributary status on the Taurisci tribe (35 BC). Sandwiched between Pannonia to the east and Raetia to the west, and bounded to the north by the Danube, Noricum was an Alpine province which provided an important northern buffer for Italy. Governed initially by a *praefectus civitatum*, it was then under an equestrian governor, based at Virunum, commanding an auxiliary force. The Marcomannic Wars (under Marcus AURELIUS) increased Noricum's military importance, and it was thereafter governed by an imperial legate, commanding the newly raised Legion II Italica, reverting to equestrian control under Gallienus. The province was split in two by Diocletian: Noricum Ripense and Noricum Mediterraneum. Noricum was overrun by repeated Germanic invasions during the 5th century, and was finally lost to the Roman empire in AD 493 when occupied by the GOTHS. RJB

Alföldy (1974); Millar (1981); Mommsen (1968).

Notitia Dignitatum a record of imperial posts, covering the eastern and western halves of the Roman empire in AD 395, providing an invaluable record of the late Roman BUREAUCRACY and the distribution of military units. It is preserved in a 15th-century copy of a manuscript now lost. The *primicerius notariorum* (head notary) maintained the list: the extant version is clearly that of the western *primicerius*, since some eastern information is abbreviated. It cannot be earlier than 395, but whereas the eastern half must be earlier than 413, the western section has been partially updated to include units raised as late as 421, and as a result shows some inconsistencies. Each half has a list of officials, from praetorian prefects to provincial governors, giving titles and ranks, brief descriptions of functions, lists of subordinates and military units. The insignia of offices and the shields of regiments were used in the preparation of diplomas of appointment. RJB

Cornell and Matthews (1982); Jones (1964); Seeck (1876).

Notium city near Ephesus where LYSANDER won a naval victory over the fleet of ALCIBIADES in 407 BC. In Alcibiades' absence Antiochus, his steersman, took 10 ships to try, by keeping eight out of sight and using two as decoys, to draw out a small number of Lysander's ships from Ephesus. The plan miscarried. In the ensuing engagement 15 Athenian ships were destroyed. The Athenians at home blamed Alcibiades. GLC

Kagan (1987).

Novel, Greek The prose romance or novel represents a late flowering of great virtuosity and originality. Ancient literary critics ignored the genre, perhaps because it lacked *gravitas*, but papyrus finds attest to its popularity and provide some guide to chronology. The Greek taste for tales of adventure which predates all written literature received added piquancy when Alexander's conquests unleashed a new current of mysteries of the Orient (and Alexander himself became the hero of a whole new romantic genre). Meanwhile the erotic element grew to dominate the literature of the Hellenistic period. Love and adventure in a Near Eastern context are the prime ingredients of the earliest novels.

The five novels that survive from the first four centuries AD were enormously influential on Byzantine and later European literature. *Chaereas and Callirhoe* by CHARITON (1st century BC or AD), in which the action swings from Syracuse to Babylon, is the earliest, but deft handling of a complicated plot indicates that the genre was already well developed. It was enriched further at the hands of XENOPHON, LONGUS, and ACHILLES TATIUS in the 2nd century, and HELIODORUS in the 3rd or 4th. Their language and erudition invite the conclusion that novels were composed as light reading for intellectuals.

See also EUHEMERUS.   GS

Bartsch (1989); Hägg (1971, 1983); Perry (1967); Reardon (1989).

Novel, Latin   Like the lyric, the novel is one of the literary genres that found little favour with Latin writers, and perhaps for the same reason: its frivolity and lack of *gravitas*. The erotic short stories or *Milesiaca* of Aristides (2nd century BC) were translated into Latin by Cornelius SISENNA (119–67 BC); and the serio-comic satires of Menippus of Gadara (3rd century BC) were adopted by Terentius VARRO (116–27 BC). The latter clearly exercised considerable influence on the satirical novel of PETRONIUS, but the *Satyricon* is really more SATIRE than novel, parodying the conventions of Greek romance. The only complete Latin novel to survive from the classical period is the *Metamorphoses* of APULEIUS (mid-2nd century AD). Based on a Milesian model, of which a version survives among works attributed to LUCIAN, it has a serious and original ending. Its affected and baroque style appealed strongly to Renaissance translators and imitators.   GS

Hägg (1983); Tatum (1979); Walsh (1970).

Novus homo   first-generation Roman politician. *Novus homo* ('new man') was the expression used to describe a politician who was the first of his family to enter the SENATE. *Novi homines* were common in the Senate, for the senatorial class needed a constant inflow of new recruits as existing families died out or lacked either the wealth or the inclination to enter the Senate. Most *novi homines* remained in the lower ranks of the Senate. A few, however, through oratory, military skill, patronage, or circumstances, rose to be PRAETOR or CONSUL and thus entered the NOBILES, although their origins could still be sneered at.

See also CATO; CICERO; MAGISTRATES; MARIUS; QUAESTOR.   HS

Hopkins (1983); Wiseman (1971).

Numa Pompilius king of Rome. Numa Pompilius was ROMULUS' successor. Of Sabine origin, he was a devout and peaceful ruler who created the major religious institutions of Rome, including the calendar of FESTIVALS and the priesthoods. There may have been a historical king Numa, but the details of his life as reported in the Roman historians are legendary. In the traditional account he is little more than a mythical stereotype, a pacific contrast to his warlike successor TULLUS HOSTILIUS.   TC

Dumézil (1970); Heurgon (1973).

Numantia city in northern SPAIN. Originally occupied by CELTS, it became the chief town of the CELTIBERIANS c.300 BC. From 195 it resisted repeated Roman assaults until it was finally captured and destroyed by SCIPIO AEMILIANUS in 133 BC. A Roman town was built over the Celtiberian one in the Augustan period. The remains of several Roman camps have been uncovered on the surrounding hills.   GS

Stillwell (1976).

Numbers The Greeks had two systems of writing numerals. The older of the two, known as the Milesian system, is alphabetic and is based on the letters of the Ionian alphabet with a few additions. The other system is acrophonic and uses the initial letters of the words of the various numerals (apart from the unit 1). The latter system was employed on all public inscriptions in Attica till the 1st century BC. It was also used in most other states from the 5th to the 3rd century when it was replaced by the former system, which is almost universal in surviving papyri.

The Roman system is based on seven signs: I = 1; V = 5; X = 10; L = 50; C = 100; D = 500; ∞ = 1,000 (M was used only as an abbreviation, not as a figure). The systems in both languages are so clumsy, especially for larger numbers, that manuscript readings are invariably corrupted and any reports of numerals in ancient literature are notoriously unreliable.   GS

Numerian (c.AD 254–84), Roman emperor, AD 283–4. Marcus Aurelius Numerianus, the younger son of CARUS, was created Caesar soon after his father's accession (282) and in the following year elevated to Augustus. He accompanied his father to Persia, and, becoming joint emperor with his elder brother CARINUS after Carus' death (late 283), led the army back towards Europe. He was murdered by his father-in-law, Arrius Aper, on the journey, and the troops elected DIOCLETIAN in his place.   RJB

Grant (1985); Parker (1958).

Numidia   part of Africa. Numidia was the name given to the area south and west of CARTHAGE inhabited by the Numidae, or nomads. By the Second PUNIC WAR these had formed into coalitions, fielding excellent cavalry, led by SYPHAX and MASSINISSA. After Syphax's death Numidia was ruled as a client kingdom of Rome by Massinissa, whose reign saw a spread of farming and urbanization. The Numidian king JUGURTHA proved a tenacious opponent of Rome in 112–106 BC. After JUBA I supported POMPEY in the CIVIL WAR, Numidia became part of the province of AFRICA. The kingdom was then briefly restored to JUBA II before being incorporated in the province of Africa Proconsularis. Romanization spread as the province's one legion was stationed in Numidia (*see* LAMBAESIS) and military colonies were founded. Septimius SEVERUS again separated Numidia from Africa, and the area was lost to the VANDALS in the 5th century AD.

See also CIRTA; PROVINCIA.   HS

Braund (1984); Garnsey (1978); Warmington (1954).

O

Octavia (64–11 BC), sister of AUGUSTUS. Octavia first married Claudius Marcellus to whom she bore a son, MARCELLUS. In 40 BC she was married to ANTONY as part of the agreement at Brundisium, and in 37 she helped to negotiate the Treaty of Tarentum. Antony repudiated her in 35 and formally divorced her just before ACTIUM, but she nevertheless brought up all his children after his death. She had two daughters by Antony, from whom were descended the future emperors GAIUS, CLAUDIUS, and NERO. Her courage and forbearance were legendary.   DP

Balsdon (1962); Carter (1970); Syme (1939).

Octavian *see* AUGUSTUS.

Odaenathus (d. AD 266/7), king of Palmyra, AD 260–6/7. Septimius Odaenathus (or Odenathus), chieftain of PALMYRA (subject to Rome), took the title of king (260) and defeated SHAPUR I of Persia. Rewarded by GALLIENUS with command of the Roman forces in the east, he disposed of QUIETUS, and became effective ruler of an extensive empire. He attacked Persia, recovering Mesopotamia and Armenia, but failed to take Ctesiphon. He was assassinated, with his elder son (*c.*266/7), and succeeded by his widow, ZENOBIA.   RJB

Parker (1958).

Odeum a small THEATRE or concert hall, used mostly for theatrical rehearsal and musical competition. The word is applied specifically to a square building in Athens, commissioned by Pericles, near the theatre of Dionysus. Its pyramidal roof, topped by a lantern, was supported by nine rows of columns, and porches were added to east and west.

Later the term was applied to a number of Roman theatres, notably that of HERODES ATTICUS on the slopes of the Athenian acropolis.   GS

Bieber (1961).

Odoacer   (d. AD 493), king of Italy, AD 476–93. Odoacer, or Odovacar, a Scirian, one of the chief officers of Orestes, deposed ROMULUS AUGUSTULUS (476) and ruled Italy as nominal deputy of the eastern emperor Zeno, a situation only formally acknowledged after NEPOS' death (480). However, he ruled increasingly openly as the first barbarian king of Italy. In 489 Theodoric II, king of the Ostrogoths, invaded: besieged in Ravenna, Odoacer was finally forced to make terms, and then killed.   RJB

Bury (1958); Grant (1985).

Oenophyta   near Tanagra, site of a battle in which the Athenians defeated the Boeotians in 457 BC. Two months after defeat by the Spartans at TANAGRA the Athenians, commanded by Myronides, marched into Boeotia and defeated the Boeotians alone. Nothing is known about the battle, but it gave Athens control of all Boeotia save THEBES until the battle of Coronea (447/6).   GLC

Ogulnius   (fl. 300–257 BC), Roman politician. Quintus Ogulnius Gallus was a tribune of the people in 300 BC when he passed the *lex Ogulnia*, against strong opposition, entitling plebeians to hold the highest priesthoods. In 292 he was part of a delegation sent to EPIDAURUS to bring the cult of ASCLEPIUS to Rome in an attempt to stop a plague. He also served on an embassy to the court of PTOLEMY II PHILADELPHUS in 272 and as consul in 269.   HE

Olbia   Greek city on the north coast of the Black Sea in modern Ukraine. Founded in the early 6th century BC by Milesian colonists, it gained early prosperity from the export of wheat and was the terminus for a major trade route into central Europe. But from the 3rd century BC it suffered barbarian attacks. It began to decline in the 2nd century and was sacked by BUREBISTAS *c.*60 BC. A Roman garrison built by HADRIAN was destroyed by the ALANI in the 3rd century AD.   GS

Oligarchy   The essence of oligarchy was the restriction of participation in government. The enfranchised group might be defined by birth, wealth, leisure, military participation, or simply by a fixed number; in all cases it was a minority of free males, usually synonymous with the wealthy. The label 'aristocracy', that is, rule based on merit, whether ability or contribution to the state, was sometimes applied to oligarchies of the well-born, who would also be wealthy and educated; but the link between birth and virtue became increasingly questionable, and aristocracy is more often used as a persuasive description of oligarchy, or by political theorists to denote the good form of a constitution, rule of the few, whose bad form is oligarchy.

Access to office was by election, often with further restrictions on eligibility, particularly a minimum age. The central institution was the council, usually small and with members serving for life. Magistrates, who tended to serve alone or in small boards, were accountable to the council; both had wide political and judicial competencies. Conversely, the assembly was usually a cipher, unless the total number enfranchised was small, when it might perform functions normally assigned to the council.

See also DEMOCRACY; MONARCHY; TYRANNY.   RB

Arnheim (1977); Donlan (1980); Sinclair (1967); Whibley (1913).

Olybrius   (4th century AD), praetorian prefect. Quintus Clodius Hermogenianus Olybrius, a Christian nobleman, married into the Anicii, a prominent aristocratic family, and became father-in-law of Petronius PROBUS. Described by AMMIANUS MARCELLINUS as humane and just, Olybrius became prefect of Rome (369–70), but fell ill: his deputy, Maximin, was, by contrast, savage and cruel. Olybrius went on to be praetorian prefect of Illyricum, then of the east, and consul in 379. He died between 384 and 395.   RJB

Hamilton and Wallace-Hadrill (1986).

Olybrius   (d. AD 472), Roman emperor, AD 472. Olybrius, from the Anicii, a distinguished senatorial family, married Placidia, daughter of VALENTINIAN III. Placidia was held captive by the Vandal GAISERIC from 455 to 461, after which Gaiseric supported Olybrius as a potential emperor. In 472 LEO, suspicious of Olybrius, sent him to Rome, but a message instructing ANTHEMIUS to execute Olybrius was intercepted by RICIMER, who declared Olybrius emperor (April). Olybrius survived both Anthemius and Ricimer, but died shortly afterwards (November).

                                                                                         RJB

Bury (1958); Grant (1985).

Olympia   in Elis, the chief sanctuary of ZEUS in Greece. The cult of Olympian Zeus was established soon after the fall of Mycenae (c.1200 BC). The shrine became a focus of pilgrimage for the whole Greek world and a depository for many of the greatest treasures of Greek art. No city was built on the site: all identifiable buildings were connected with either religion or athletics. Every four years a festival was held in honour of the god, the climax of which was the OLYMPIC GAMES, first celebrated in 776 BC. In order to guarantee pilgrims safety of travel, a sacred truce was declared and was strictly observed. The focal point of the sanctuary was the Doric temple of Zeus (built 470–456 BC), which contained the colossal gold and ivory statue of the god made by PHEIDIAS. Remains of the sculptor's workshop have been discovered nearby. The adjacent temple of HERA dates from the 7th century BC and was originally built of wood. The temples were destroyed in AD 426 by order of THEODOSIUS II.   GS

Drees (1968); Morgan (1990).

Olympias   (fl. 357–316 BC), queen of Macedon. Olympias, an Epirote princess, married PHILIP II in 357 BC and bore ALEXANDER THE GREAT in 356. Marital rift in 337 caused her departure to Epirus, but she returned after Philip's murder to support Alexander's claims to the throne. She intrigued unsuccessfully against ANTIPATER after Alexander's expedition departed, and returned again to Epirus in 331. After Alexander's death in 323, she continued to oppose Antipater and, by joining Antipater's successor POLYPERCHON in 319, thwarted Antipater's son CASSANDER. She murdered Alexander's half-brother PHILIP III ARRHIDAEUS in 317, thereby making her grandson ALEXANDER IV sole king. Cassander organized her murder in 316 by her victim's relatives.   EER

Hammond and Griffith (1979); Hammond and Walbank (1988); Macurdy (1932).

Olympic Games   the major athletic festival of the ancient world. Traditionally founded in 776 BC, the games were held every four years at OLYMPIA in honour of ZEUS for about 1,200 years until the late 4th or early 5th century AD when they were closed either by command of THEODOSIUS I in 393 or when the temple of Zeus was destroyed c.426. A list of victors from the foundation to AD 217 is preserved by EUSEBIUS.

According to PINDAR the games were founded by Heracles to commemorate the successful completion of one of his labours (the cleaning of the stables of Augeas). Another theory is that they developed out of the funeral games held to honour the local hero Pelops. A local festival may well have existed before the traditional date for the games' foundation but it is unlikely to have been organized on an international basis much before the early 8th century BC (*see* GAMES, GREEK; GEOMETRIC PERIOD).

An important and unique element of the games was the Olympic truce. This was an armistice, originally for one month, later extended to two and then three months, by which participating states were forbidden to take up arms or pursue legal disputes. Its purpose was not to stop wars but rather to ensure that wars did not stop the games and that participants and pilgrims could be guaranteed a safe passage to and from Olympia. The festival was held around the time of the second or third full moon after the summer solstice, i.e. in mid-August or mid-September when the harvest was complete (*see* FESTIVALS, GREEK).

At first there was only a single event, the stade, a foot race of about 200 yards (the length of the STADIUM). But by the mid-7th century the 'canon' of nine principal events was established: the stade, *diaulos* (double stade), *dolichos* (*c.*5,000 yards), *pentathlon* (discus, standing jump, javelin, stade, wrestling), wrestling, boxing, chariot race, horse race, and *pankration* (a violent form of all-in wrestling). Similar events for boys (from 12 to 18) and a few others for men, such as the race in heavy armour, were added later. By the 5th century BC the games lasted for five days which included various religious ceremonies, social events, and the parade of champions on the last day.

The competition was open to male citizens from all over the Greek world. Women could not compete (though they had their own games at Olympia in honour of Hera) and married women could not even watch. Participants were mostly aristocrats and full-time athletes: they were not amateurs. Training was intensive and the last month had to be spent at Elis under the eye of the 'judges of the Greeks' (Hellanodikai), as the official supervisors were known. The event itself was regarded as a paramilitary exercise and the rivalry between states for Olympic success was warfare by another name. The prize for the victor was a crown of wild olive, but the rewards in terms of prestige and even political advancement could be immense (e.g. the victory by ALCIBIADES in the chariot race of 416 BC).

The sacred truce was violated in 364 BC by the Arcadians and the decline of the games may be traced to that date. But despite the sacking of the sanctuary by SULLA and his transfer of the games to Rome in 80 BC, the festival survived and continued to be celebrated. Its increasing secularization was not sufficient to save it from the purge of pagan institutions conducted by a Christian emperor.

See also GAMES, ROMAN.   GS

Drees (1968); Easterling and Muir (1985); Finley and Pleket (1976); Harris (1964); Swaddling (1980).

Olympiodorus (fl. *c.*307–280 BC), Athenian leader. Olympiodorus was a democratic anti-Macedonian. With Aetolian help he defeated CASSANDER's attack on Athens in 306 BC, and with Phocian help pushed Cassander north of Thermopylae. He helped LACHARES against DEMETRIUS I POLIORCETES' attack, was elected archon after Athens capitulated (294–292), and led the Athenian revolt of 287. He seized Museum Hill from the Macedonian garrison, and later joined DEMOCHARES in repelling

ANTIGONUS II GONATAS from Eleusis. He may also have temporarily freed Piraeus.   EER

Ferguson (1911); Osborne (1979); Shear (1978).

Olympus, Mount   on the borders of Thessaly and Macedonia, the highest mountain in Greece (9,573 feet), by tradition the home of the gods.   GS

Olynthus   city in CHALCIDICE. Originally Thracian, Olynthus became Greek after the Persian Wars and is recorded as a member of the DELIAN LEAGUE from 454 BC. After the revolt of POTIDAEA in 432 it became the centre of the CHALCIDIAN LEAGUE and received a large influx of population from neighbouring cities. In 379 it was taken by Sparta after a long siege and the league disbanded. The city was attacked by PHILIP II of Macedon in 349 BC and, despite attempts by DEMOSTHENES to rally Athenian support, it fell the next year and was destroyed. Archaeologists have uncovered the layout of the city and the best evidence to date of what Greek HOUSES looked like.   GS

Larsen (1968); Stillwell (1976).

Omens   *see* DIVINATION.

Onesicritus   (fl. 320s BC), naval commander and historian. Onesicritus was a pupil of DIOGENES OF SINOPE the Cynic and accompanied ALEXANDER THE GREAT's expedition. He commanded Alexander's flagship on the voyage down the Indus, but quarrelled with the admiral NEARCHUS OF CRETE in the Persian Gulf. The purpose and tendency of his work on Alexander (the title of which is ambiguous) is unclear, but it contains sensational facts about India which were used by STRABO. His philosophical orientation has probably been exaggerated.   EER

Bosworth (1988a); Brown (1949); Pearson (1960).

Onesimos   (fl. 505–485 BC), Greek vase painter. Onesimos, whose name means 'profitable' and is no doubt a nickname, signed one cup made for him by EUPHRONIUS; some 10 other cups by the same potter were painted by Onesimos or his school. Most are bordered inside and out with the maeander pattern. Favourite subjects are revellers and athletes.   GS

Boardman (1975).

Onomarchus   (d. 352 BC), Phocian leader in the Third SACRED WAR. After PHILOMELUS was defeated at Neon in 354 BC, Onomarchus restored

Phocian fortunes and allied with PHERAE. In Boeotia he captured Orchomenos. In Thessaly he confronted PHILIP II (who had defeated his brother PHAYLLUS), inflicting his only defeat (353). In 352 Philip returned. Onomarchus, supporting Pherae, was defeated and killed at the Battle of the Crocus Field.   GLC

Buckler (1980).

Ophellas (fl. 326–309 BC), governor of Cyrene. Ophellas, a Macedonian officer of ALEXANDER THE GREAT, was sent by PTOLEMY (later I) in 322 BC to subdue CYRENE. He remained as a virtually independent Ptolemaic governor. His part in the revolt of 313/12, and the introduction of the Ptolemaic constitution, is unknown. He crossed the desert in 310/9 to join AGATHOCLES' attack on CARTHAGE, hoping to establish an African domain. He lost many troops and colonists and was murdered by Agathocles.   EER

Bagnall (1976); CAH VII.1; Finley (1979); Green (1990).

Opimius (2nd century BC), Roman politician. Lucius Opimius was consul in 121 BC when the SENATUS CONSULTUM *Ultimum* was passed against Gaius GRACCHUS and FULVIUS FLACCUS. Opimius had both men killed together with, it is said, 3,000 of their supporters. Hated because of this, Opimius was condemned in 109 for taking bribes while head of a commission (*c.*116) to divide NUMIDIA between JUGURTHA and Adherbal. He went into exile and was buried at Dyrrachium.   HS

Gruen (1968); Stockton (1979).

Oppian (2nd century AD), Greek epic poet. Oppian of Cilicia was the author of *Halieutica*, a didactic poem in five books on the subject of FISHING which he addressed to a Roman emperor and his son (probably Marcus Aurelius and Commodus). Another Oppian, from Apamea in Syria, dedicated a similar but inferior poem on HUNTING, *Cynegetica*, to the emperor Caracalla (AD 211–17). Inevitably, ancient tradition identified the two.   GS

Oppidum Roman town. *Oppidum* referred to the town at the centre of a MUNICIPIUM or COLONIA territory, as well as to towns which had no (judicial) territory of their own. Though common in Italy before the SOCIAL WAR, between 89 and 44 BC all Italian *oppida* were assimilated into *municipia*. Outside Italy, *oppida* were communities of citizens which soon became centres of *municipia*. They were often created on the sites of the proto-urban native communities known in Gaul and Britain as *oppida*.   HE

Optimates Roman political group. The *optimates* were not an organized party. Instead, *optimates* was the name taken by those in the SENATE who opposed the actions of the POPULARES, whom they accused of aiming at tyranny. A conservative force in Roman politics, the *optimates* sought to enhance the authority of the Senate over the people, although claiming to represent the whole people while their opponents represented only the poor.　　　　　　　　　　HS

Brunt (1988); Seager (1972a); Taylor (1949); Wirszubski (1950).

Oracles Oracles provided the gods with their principal means of communication with men (*see* DIVINATION). Conversely, they provided advice and comfort to pious mortals who wanted to know if their doings found favour with the gods. The practice of addressing questions to the resident deity of an oracular shrine seems to have had Near Eastern and Egyptian precedents. The oracle of AMMON at Siwa became known through the Greek colony at CYRENE (founded *c.*630 BC). In Greece itself the oldest oracle was said to be that of Zeus at DODONA which was known to Homer. The oracle of the dead at Ephyra, also in Epirus, possibly of similar antiquity, was consulted by PERIANDER of Corinth *c.*600 BC. The underworld could also be visited from the oracle of Trophonius at Lebadeia, as PAUSANIAS graphically describes. The god with particular responsibility for oracles was APOLLO whose shrines at DIDYMA and Claros were famous but none so famous as DELPHI. There the oracle was not founded before 750 BC but quickly attained international renown and exercised unparalleled influence over political decisions until the 4th century. The Romans were less dependent than the Greeks on oracular utterance, but lot oracles are known to have existed at Cumae and Praeneste.　　　　　GS

Easterling and Muir (1985); Parke (1967a, b).

Oratory *see* ATTIC ORATORS; RHETORIC.

Orestes *see* ROMULUS AUGUSTULUS.

Origen (*c.*AD 185–254), Greek Christian writer. The details of Origen's life are known from EUSEBIUS. Born and educated as a Christian in Alexandria, he studied in the Catechetical School of St CLEMENT. He became a teacher, and after Clement fled in the persecutions of 202 Origen succeeded him. Adopting an ascetic life-style, he made visits to Rome, Arabia, and, in 215, to Palestine where he preached. Recalled to Alexandria, he devoted himself to writing; but when on a return visit to Palestine he was ordained, he was exiled from Egypt and founded a school at Caesarea where he remained until his death.

Origen was the first Church Father to devote himself to biblical exegesis but only a fraction of his voluminous writings survives. The
apologetic *Contra Celsum* and devotional *Exhortation to Martyrdom*
survive in the original Greek, as do a short treatise on prayer, a few
homilies and letters, and parts of the commentaries on the Gospels.
The doctrinal *Principles* is preserved in Latin translation by Rufinus
together with more homilies and commentaries. Origen's influence on
subsequent scholarship was immense.

   See also CELSUS; CHRISTIANITY.   GS

Chadwick (1966); de Lange (1976).

Orosius   (5th century AD), Latin church historian. Paulus Orosius fled
from his native Spain in 414 to Africa where he was befriended by
AUGUSTINE. Augustine sent him to Jerusalem where he enlisted JEROME's
support against PELAGIANISM. On his return, Augustine persuaded him
to write a *History against the Pagans* to counter charges that Rome's
current problems were due to the victory of the Church.   GS

Momigliano (1963a).

Orpheus   *see* ORPHIC LITERATURE; ORPHISM.

Orphic literature   Greek religion had no scriptures equivalent to the
Bible or the Koran, but the followers of ORPHISM did assemble collections of writings that were said to derive from their founder, the
legendary Thracian singer. Orpheus was believed by the Greeks to be
their oldest poet, even older than Homer, and a great many poems
attributed to his authorship were in circulation. Fragments of several
Theogonies survive and indicate a debt to HESIOD. A 4th-century BC
papyrus from Derveni contains 18 lines of an Orphic poem. The extant *Hymns*, *Argonautica*, and *Lithica* are late additions to the corpus
and contribute little to our knowledge of Orphism.   GS

West (1983).

Orphism   a mystery cult associated with the Thracian poet Orpheus
which emerged during the 6th century BC. Followers of the cult believed in a divine origin for the soul and in the need for man to free
his soul from contamination by his body by means of dietary restrictions and ritual practices. A series of mortal reincarnations could
eventually liberate the soul from the cycle of rebirth and enable it to
return to its original state. To support this belief a myth was invented:
the god Dionysus, son of Zeus and Persephone, was torn to pieces and
eaten by the Titans; only his heart was saved by Athene from which
a new god was raised; the Titans were struck down by Zeus' lightning

and man was born from their ashes. Mankind thus inherited a twofold nature that included a share in the Titans' blood-guilt and a share in the divinity of Dionysus. There are evident parallels between Orphism and the religious society formed by PYTHAGORAS; Orphism also deeply impressed PLATO who incorporated elements of it in his own theory of reincarnation. In general, however, Orphism was not fashionable in the classical period. But ORPHIC LITERATURE flourished in the Hellenistic age and the cult enjoyed a revival in the 1st century BC.

See also AFTERLIFE; RELIGION, GREEK.   GS

Burkert (1987).

Oscan   ancient Italian language. Oscan was the language spoken by the native inhabitants of central southern Italy known as SABELLI, including the SAMNITES, Lucanians, and BRUTTII. An Indo-European language akin to Latin and Umbrian, it forms part of a linguistic group known as Osco-Umbrian, or simply Italic. Other Italic dialects, spoken by the SABINES, AEQUI, MARSI, PAELIGNI, etc., are similar to Oscan. Oscan is attested in several hundred surviving inscriptions and was used widely until the SOCIAL WAR, after which it was replaced by Latin. But it survived in many areas and was still spoken by some people in POMPEII in AD 79.   HE

Pulgram (1958); Salmon (1982).

Osroëne   kingdom in north-west Mesopotamia. Osroëne became a kingdom independent of Seleucid rule in 132 BC. The native Semitic kings established their capital at Edessa (modern Urfa), originally a military settlement of SELEUCUS I NICATOR. Osroëne became involved in the wars between PARTHIA and Rome. Edessa was sacked by Lucius VERUS in AD 116, and Osroëne later became a Roman province. Edessa became an important Christian centre. Frequently attacked by the SASSANIANS, Osroëne fell to the Arabs in AD 638.   EER

Drijvers (1980); Magie (1975); Segal (1970); Sullivan (1990).

Ostia   port of Rome. Ostia lay at the mouth of the TIBER and is supposed to have been founded by Ancus MARCIUS, but no trace of this early settlement has been found. Archaeology attests the foundation of a fort at the site c.400 BC. During the First PUNIC WAR in the 3rd century BC the Romans increased the size of their fleet, basing it at Ostia.

Later the Roman need for a fleet declined and Ostia became primarily a centre for Rome's maritime TRADE. This role continued as Rome grew, and the town was particularly important for trans-shipping grain imports, since many of the large transports were unable to sail up the

Tiber to Rome itself. Claudius and Trajan later improved the harbours at Ostia, acting to prevent silting and to increase protection against storms. During the 4th century AD Ostia's trading importance declined as Rome itself shrank, leading to its eventual stagnation.

Ostia is especially well known archaeologically as it was abandoned in the 9th century AD and since the 19th century it has been extensively excavated. It is therefore an important site for our knowledge of TOWN PLANNING and of humbler HOUSES. Of great interest are the pre-eminence of slaves among the population and the number of foreign cults, including CYBELE, ISIS, and Mithras (*see* MITHRAISM), probably introduced by sailors. HE

Meiggs (1960).

Ostorius Scapula (d. AD 52), governor of Britain. Publius Ostorius Scapula succeeded PLAUTIUS as governor of Britain (AD 47–52), choosing to protect Roman territory by advancing the frontiers towards the Trent. He subdued the Deceangli in north Wales, and turned against the Silures, driving CARATACUS north into the territory of the Ordovices and defeating him, possibly near Caersws. Ostorius also began the romanization of Britain, establishing the first colony at Camulodunum (Colchester, 49), before dying suddenly in 52. RJB

Salway (1981); Scullard (1979).

Ostracism Athenian banishment. The invention of ostracism is attributed to CLEISTHENES, though this has been doubted because of the delay until its first use in 487 BC. An ostracism was held once a year, if the assembly voted for it. A quorum of 6,000 was required, each voter writing on a potsherd (*ostrakon*) the name of his candidate for expulsion; the individual receiving most votes was exiled for 10 years, without loss of citizenship or property. Although the earliest victims were associates of the tyrants, ostracism seems to have been intended to defuse factional strife like that between Cleisthenes and ISAGORAS by imposing a clear choice between leaders and policies. The last recorded ostracism was that of HYPERBOLUS *c.*416 BC, though ostracism remained theoretically available in the 4th century. Some form of ostracism is also attested at Syracuse, Argos, Megara, and Miletus. RB

Meiggs and Lewis (1988) no. 21; Rhodes (1981); Thomsen (1972).

Ostrogoths *see* GOTHS.

Otho (AD 32–69), Roman emperor, AD 69. Marcus Salvius Otho, appointed governor of Lusitania (Portugal) in AD 58 by NERO (who had fallen in love with Otho's wife Poppaea Sabina, and wished to be rid of him), was the first provincial governor to declare support for GALBA against Nero (68). However, Galba adopted a successor other than Otho, so Otho had himself proclaimed emperor by the PRAETORIAN GUARD, who murdered Galba (January 69). Otho won general support from the Senate and people of Rome, and wide military support, but the Germanic legions had already proclaimed VITELLIUS. Otho was defeated near Cremona (April 69), and then committed suicide.   RJB

Grant (1985); Wellesley (1975); Wells (1984).

Ovid (43 BC–AD 17), Latin poet. Publius Ovidius Naso was born at Sulmo of an equestrian family and was destined for a public career. But after holding some minor offices he turned to poetry. His circle included GALLUS and PROPERTIUS, and by AD 8 he was Rome's leading poet when suddenly he was banished by AUGUSTUS in mysterious circumstances and spent the rest of his days at Tomis on the Black Sea. A verse autobiography (*Tristia* 4.10) survives.

The last of the Latin love elegists, Ovid was prolific and popular. *Amores* appeared first *c.*20 BC but survives in a second edition of *c.*1 BC. Many of the poems celebrate 'Corinna' who was not one of his three wives. *Ars Amatoria* (*c.*2 BC), a didactic poem on the art of love, incurred Augustus' disapproval. *Heroides* (*c.*1 BC) are rhetorical letters from mythological heroines to their former lovers. *Remedia Amoris* (*c.*AD 1), on falling out of love, is a sequel to the *Ars Amatoria*. *Fasti* (*c.*AD 4) is an aetiological calendar of the Roman year but only six books (January–June) survive. *Metamorphoses*, a mythological epic in 15 books of hexameters, was practically complete by AD 8. Ovid continued to write in exile: five books of *Tristia* and four of *Epistulae ex Ponto*, addressed to his wife and friends, beg them to work for his recall and describe his misery.   GS

Lyne (1980); Mack (1988); Syme (1978); Wilkinson (1955).

Oxyrhynchus Historian   unidentifiable author of a major history, of which fragments covering events in the Ionian War and 396–395 BC have been dug up at Oxyrhynchus in Egypt. P (as he is commonly referred to) probably dealt with the period from the end of THUCYDIDES down to the King's Peace (386). Probably contemporary with the events he describes with Thucydidean fullness and method, he is generally thought to have seriously discredited XENOPHON who now appears partial and unreliable. Evidently P was, directly or indirectly, the source of at least parts of DIODORUS SICULUS' Books 13 and 14, which are no longer to be dismissed lightly.   GLC

Bruce (1967); Cawkwell (1979).

P

Pachomius, St (*c*.AD 290–346), first abbot. Born of pagan parents in Upper Egypt, Pachomius was converted to Christianity while serving as a conscript soldier. On leaving the army he attached himself for three years to the hermit Palaemon. He then acquired his own group of disciples for whom he built a monastery *c*.320 at Tabennisi. He went on to found another 10 monasteries and to establish a pattern of communal life for them which St BASIL THE GREAT took as his model.

See also ATHANASIUS. GS

Rousseau (1985).

Pacuvius (220–*c*.130 BC), Latin tragedian. Marcus Pacuvius, nephew of ENNIUS, was born at Brindisi and moved to Rome where he practised as a painter as well as playwright. Titles and fragments of 12 tragedies survive; he also wrote satires and a historical play about Aemilius PAULLUS. Cicero regarded him as the greatest Roman tragedian.

See also TRAGEDY, ROMAN. GS

Beare (1964).

Paeligni Italian people. The Paeligni inhabited the mountainous areas of central Italy and were the eastern neighbours of the MARSI. Their capital was Corfinium. Before 300 BC they were allied to Rome and this loyalty continued until the SOCIAL WAR (91–87 BC). In 90 Corfinium became the allied capital before its conquest by the Romans. After this defeat the Paeligni received Roman citizenship and became romanized. OVID was born in the region. HE

Potter (1987); Salmon (1982).

Paeonius (fl. *c*.430–410 BC), Greek sculptor. Paeonius, a native of Mende in Thrace, is named (in an inscription on the base) as the sculptor of the surviving statue of Nike at OLYMPIA that was dedicated by the people of Messene and Naupactus from the spoils of their enemies. This refers to the Spartan defeat at PYLOS in 425 BC. The same inscription also says that Paeonius made the acroteria for the temple of Zeus at Olympia (but not the sculpture for the east pediment as PAUSANIAS wrongly states).

See also SCULPTURE, GREEK. GS

Richter (1970b).

Paestum city in Italy. Paestum lay in the coastal marshes of LUCANIA at the mouth of the river Silarus (Sele). Originally called Posidonia, it was founded *c*.600 BC by Greek colonists from SYBARIS. It fell to invading SABELLI *c*.390 who remained in control until 273 when the Romans founded the Latin colony of Paestum. Traces of the Greek city (especially three magnificent Doric temples of the 6th and 5th centuries), painted tombs of the Lucanian period, and extensive remains of the Roman colony make it a major archaeological site. HE

Pedley (1990).

Pagus an area of land (and its population), often but not always subordinate to an urban community such as an OPPIDUM or MUNICIPIUM, or a tribal group. Though Italian in origin, under the Empire *pagi* were also found in the provinces and were the smallest recognized territorial units. They were often administered by small groups of AEDILES. HE

Painting, Greek *Wall and Panel Painting*: Painting was a major art form in the Greek world and its practitioners were highly honoured. Very little survives on wall or panel – certainly nothing comparable with the remarkable frescos from the Bronze Age – but the outline of its development can be traced from other sources. These sources include south Italian tombs which were built and decorated by expatriate Greeks (presumably not of the first rank); Roman murals and mosaics from POMPEII, HÉRCULANEUM, and elsewhere which were often copied or adapted from Greek originals; accounts of painters and paintings in literature, especially by the elder PLINY and PAUSANIAS; other surviving art forms (particularly vase painting, of which more below) from which certain deductions can be made. The picture that emerges is of a gradual transition from a two-dimensional art with limited range of colour and no attempt at perspective in the ARCHAIC PERIOD to a more naturalistic style with some foreshortening in the CLASSICAL. By the end of the 5th century BC artists were mixing colours, modelling forms, and close to mastering the third dimension. The result of this evolution was HELLENISTIC realism.

POLYGNOTUS was regarded as the 'inventor' of painting and is known to have worked in Athens after the Persian Wars, sometimes with MICON. APOLLODORUS OF ATHENS seems to have been the first to mix colours and to use perspective, techniques that were further developed by his younger contemporaries ZEUXIS and PARRHASIUS. NICIAS of Athens, who worked with PRAXITELES, was a leading exponent of 4th-century realism. But the greatest artist of the Hellenistic period was, according to later writers, APELLES.

Vase Painting: Unlike other forms of painting, of which it is to some extent an index, painted POTTERY survives in profusion from all periods. As an art form in its own right its development falls into several distinct periods. In addition it provides a valuable visual reference to Greek ideas of religion and mythology and to the realities of everyday life.

In the 8th century BC the pure GEOMETRIC style that was born in Athens around 900 BC became complicated by the addition of bands of stylized animal and human figures in silhouette. From the last quarter of the 8th century the designs were less regimented and more exuberant, some figures were drawn in outline, and a number of oriental motifs were introduced, both floral (lotus, palmette) and faunal (sphinx, lion). In the second half of the 7th century the scenes became more naturalistic and the so-called black-figure style was adopted with all figures in silhouette. Corinth and Athens were the main centres, but by the mid-6th century Corinthian pottery declined with that city's fortunes, while Athens emerged as the unchallenged leader with artists such as EXECIAS and the AMASIS PAINTER. Introduction of the red-figure style, in which the figures are reserved against a black background, is attributed to the ANDOCIDES PAINTER. The two styles continued side by side to the end of the 6th century, but it was red-figure and white-ground vases that dominated the output of the 5th century, those by the NIOBID, ACHILLES, and ERETRIA painters being especially innovative and vigorous. Red-figure ware continued both in Athens and in south Italy until the end of the 4th century. In the Hellenistic period painting on pottery was largely replaced by relief decoration, but the polychrome vases of Centuripe in Sicily should be noted.

See also BERLIN PAINTER; BRYGOS PAINTER; CLEOPHRADES PAINTER; DOURIS; EPICTETUS; EUPHRANOR; EUPHRONIUS; MEIDIAS PAINTER; NIOBID PAINTER; ONESIMOS; PAN PAINTER; PENTHESILEA PAINTER. GS

Arias and Hirmer (1962); Boardman (1974, 1975, 1989); Bruno (1977); Coldstream (1968); Cook (1972); Keuls (1978); Robertson (1959); Trendall (1989).

Painting, Roman Unlike their Greek models, the work of Roman painters survives in profusion in both Italy and the provinces, with the best of it coming from Rome and Campania in the 1st centuries BC and AD. At first heavily influenced by Hellenistic originals and regularly executed by expatriate Greek artists, Roman painting gradually developed a style of its own. This can best be studied in the surviving sequence of murals at POMPEII and HERCULANEUM. The categorization into four 'Pompeian' styles, first proposed in 1882, is now applied to all Roman wall painting from 200 BC to AD 79.

Style I, dating from the early 2nd century BC, reproduces in plaster the decorative schemes that were achieved in marble in grand Hellenistic houses of the eastern Mediterranean. Style II, originating in Rome c.90 BC, reached Pompeii when it became a Roman colony in 80 BC. The imposition of an architectural screen creates an illusion of depth and provides a frame for the introduction of perspective friezes and landscape painting. Style III (c.20 BC–AD 20) replaces the realistic architecture of Style II with a more delicate and fantastic framework divided into small, brightly coloured, monochrome panels, some of which are decorated with landscapes and mythological scenes. Style IV, employed at Pompeii after the earthquake of AD 62 and also at Rome in the DOMUS AUREA, combines elements of the second and third styles in a riot of architectural fantasy and decorative detail.

Under Trajan, wall painting was largely superseded by marble veneer and MOSAIC. Later fashions were more impressionistic. Painting in the CATACOMBS set patterns for Christian iconography that were to have enduring influence. GS

Henig (1983); Ling (1991).

Palatine part of Rome. The Palatine was the chief of the seven hills of Rome, south-east of the Capitoline and dominating the Forum from the south. Roman tradition made the Palatine the site of the first settlement at Rome by ROMULUS, whose hut there was preserved in historical times, and it was here that Evander showed Aeneas the cave of the Lupercal (see LUPERCALIA). Foundations of huts and drainage channels, discovered in 1948, are evidence of Iron Age habitation on the Palatine in the 8th century BC. Since the Palatine was so close to the Forum, it became the fashionable residence of the wealthy and the politically ambitious, and house owners there included in their day HORTENSIUS HORTALUS, CICERO, CRASSUS, MILO, and ANTONY. Hortensius' house was acquired by Augustus, and became the nucleus of a complex of imperial residences. Under later emperors these quarters covered almost the whole Palatine hill, from which the word 'palace' is derived.

See also ROME, TOPOGRAPHY. DP

Platner and Ashby (1929); Richardson (1992).

Palatine Anthology *see* ANTHOLOGY, GREEK.

Palestine *see* JEWS.

Pallas (d. AD 62), freedman of ANTONIA. Pallas became the financial secretary (*a rationibus*) of CLAUDIUS I (Antonia's son), and one of the most powerful (and richest) men in his administration. He favoured Claudius' marriage to AGRIPPINA THE YOUNGER, his own mistress, an alliance that increased his own power (AD 48). However, his links with Agrippina proved his undoing: when Agrippina fell out with NERO, Pallas was dismissed (*c.*55) and eventually executed for his fortune (62).

RJB

Salmon (1968); Scullard (1982).

Palma Frontonianus (d. AD 118), Roman general. Aulus Cornelius Palma Frontonianus, consul in AD 99, was one of a group of rich and influential generals under TRAJAN. Governor of Hispania Tarraconensis (*c.*101), he was next appointed governor of Syria (*c.*105) to convert Nabataea into a province (ARABIA). His task was more one of annexation and organization than of conquest. None the less, he was rewarded by Trajan with triumphal ornaments and a second consulate (109), but was executed by HADRIAN for alleged conspiracy. RJB

CAH XI; Perowne (1960).

Palmyra modern Tadmor, city in eastern Syria. Situated half-way between DURA EUROPUS and the Mediterranean coast, the caravan city of Palmyra displays a rich and varied cultural heritage. It owed its wealth to TRADE between the Roman world and Persia, and it acted as an entrepôt where merchants from both directions would sell their goods rather than travel the whole distance across the desert. Incorporated into the Roman province of SYRIA, it expanded greatly in the 2nd century AD, acquired magnificent buildings, and became a colony *c.*212. In 260 the Palmyrene leader ODAENATHUS defeated SHAPUR I and was rewarded by Rome with independence. After his death in 266/7 his widow ZENOBIA extended Palmyra's empire over much of the Middle East before being put down by AURELIAN in 272. But the city's prosperity continued until the Arab conquest in 634. GS

Browning (1979); Colledge (1976); Michałowski (1970).

Pamphylia   region in southern Asia Minor. Essentially the coastal plain lying between LYCIA and CILICIA, Pamphylia was settled by Greeks whose dialect marks them as Arcadians. A period of Lydian domination was succeeded by 546 BC by Persian rule. Despite CIMON's victory at the EURYMEDON there is no evidence that the Persians were dislodged before the arrival of ALEXANDER THE GREAT. Part of the Seleucid empire until 189 BC when it passed to Rome, Pamphylia was incorporated into the province of Cilicia (102–44 BC). In AD 43 CLAUDIUS created the province of Lycia and Pamphylia.   GS

Bean (1979b).

Pan Painter   (fl. 480–450 BC), Greek vase painter. The Pan Painter is named after a red-figure bell-krater illustrating the death of Actaeon as its main picture and Pan in pursuit of a goatherd on the reverse. He is credited with the painting of more than 200 vases and is greatly admired for the quality of his draftsmanship despite his use of archaizing mannerisms.   GS

Arias and Hirmer (1962); Boardman (1975).

Panathenaea   Athenian religious festival. The Lesser Panathenaea was celebrated annually in the month of Hecatombaeaon (roughly July) to honour the birthday of ATHENE and the start of a new year for the city. Essential ingredients were a sacrificial procession culminating in the presentation of a new robe (*peplos*) to the goddess (illustrated in the PARTHENON frieze) and games including a chariot race. Every fourth year from 566 BC the Great Panathenaea was celebrated with enhanced pomp as a panhellenic festival.

See also CHOREGUS; FESTIVALS, GREEK.   GS

Parke (1977).

Panegyric, Latin   Panegyric is essentially a late imperial form of eulogy addressed to the emperor on a particular occasion. Deriving from the practice of the funeral oration (*see* BIOGRAPHY, LATIN), and from Ciceronian speeches such as *Pro Marcello* and *Pro Lege Manilia* in honour of the living as well as the dead, it developed in the imperial period into an act of thanks (*gratiarum actio*), formerly addressed to the Senate or people, in honour of the emperor. A collection of 12 such speeches, known as the *Panegyrici Latini*, was made in the late 4th century AD. It begins with the act of thanks that PLINY THE YOUNGER addressed to TRAJAN on his appointment to the consulship in AD 100. This is taken as the model for the subsequent speeches, all of which date from the late 3rd or 4th century and are in some way related to

Gaul. If their absurdly sycophantic content can be overlooked, they are of considerable historical interest and literary merit. Authors of panegyrics not contained in the collection include AUSONIUS in prose and pseudo-Tibullus, STATIUS, CLAUDIAN, and SIDONIUS APOLLINARIS in verse.

GS

Dorey (1975).

Pangaeus   mountain in eastern Macedonia anciently famous as a source of GOLD and SILVER as well as for its roses and an oracle of Dionysus. Gold was both mined and panned. After the reduction of THASOS in 463, control of the mines passed to Athens and in 357 to PHILIP II of Macedon. The nearby city of Philippi was refounded by Philip as a centre for the mining industry whose annual yield amounted to a thousand talents of gold.

GS

Pankration   *see* OLYMPIC GAMES.

Pannonia   Roman province. Pannonia was bounded to the north and east by the river Danube and to the south and west by Illyricum, Italy, and Noricum. Partly pacified by Octavian (AUGUSTUS) (35 BC), the southern Pannonian tribes invaded Istria (16 BC) and revolted two years later. M. AGRIPPA and M. VINICIUS commanded a successful counter-attack (13), but further campaigns under TIBERIUS were required (12 and 11 BC) before Pannonia was fully conquered. Pannonia was initially part of ILLYRICUM, but after the great Illyrian–Pannonian revolt of AD 6–9 Pannonia was organized as a separate imperial province. In *c*.106 Pannonia was subdivided into Pannonia Superior and Pannonia Inferior. Under Gallienus equestrians replaced senatorial governors, and Diocletian subdivided both provinces: Pannonia Superior was split into Pannonia Prima and Pannonia Ripariensis (north and south respectively); Pannonia Inferior into Valeria and Pannonia Secunda. Increasingly threatened by barbarian incursions in the 4th century, Pannonia was gradually abandoned after 395.

RJB

Lengyel and Radan (1980); Mócsy (1974).

Panormus   modern Palermo, city in SICILY. Founded by the PHOENICIANS in the early 7th century BC, Panormus, despite its Greek name, was never a Greek city. It became the centre of Carthaginian operations in the area and was much fought over in the First PUNIC WAR, after which it passed to Rome. Its fertile surroundings and fine harbour ensured that it remained prosperous and it became a *colonia* under AUGUSTUS.

GS

Pantheon First built by M. AGRIPPA in 27–25 BC to commemorate Augustus' victory at ACTIUM and subsequently damaged by fire in AD 80, the Pantheon was completely redesigned and rebuilt by HADRIAN between AD 118 and 128. A traditional pedimented portico with eight granite Corinthian columns leads to a domed rotunda of impressive dimensions (142 feet high and the same in diameter). The walls, of brick-faced concrete, are 18 feet thick and externally plain. The interior decoration by contrast is sumptuous, featuring variegated marbles on the floor and walls, a coffered ceiling, and at the top an oculus open to the sky. Built as a temple of all the gods and converted to a church in AD 609, the Pantheon stands primarily as a symbol of empire.

GS

MacDonald (1976); Nash (1968).

Pantomime a form of dramatic entertainment that was introduced to Rome in 22 BC. A traditional (usually mythological) theme was represented by an actor who danced silently, accompanied by instrumental music and a chorus. The single (male) actor wore masks to distinguish the various roles that he played and required considerable virtuosity to convince his audience. The performance might take place either on the stage or in a private house. Much less lewd than the MIME, it appealed to a more sophisticated taste; but it too contributed to the decline of the drama.

GS

Beare (1964).

Paphlagonia territory of northern Asia Minor. Paphlagonia lay between BITHYNIA and PONTUS on the southern shore of the Black Sea. Its coastal area was occupied by Greek settlements. The inland territory was noted for timber. Loosely under ACHAEMENID rule, after ALEXANDER THE GREAT Paphlagonia was briefly entrusted to EUMENES OF CARDIA, then divided up between Bithynia and Pontus. POMPEY joined coastal Paphlagonia to the Roman province of Bithynia and Pontus (64 BC). Inner Paphlagonia remained nominally independent under native kings subject to foreign interference. It was finally annexed by AUGUSTUS to GALATIA (6 BC), but became a province again under DIOCLETIAN.

EER

Jones (1983); Magie (1975); Sherwin-White (1984); Sullivan (1990).

Papinian (c.AD 150–212), Roman jurist. Aemilius Papinianus was born at Emesa in Syria and may have been related to JULIA DOMNA, the Syrian wife of Septimius SEVERUS. Under Severus he became praetorian prefect in 205 when both PAULUS and ULPIAN served as his assessors. He joined Severus on his British campaign of 208–11 but was murdered by

Caracalla (AURELIUS ANTONINUS) soon after the latter's accession. As a jurist he was held in high regard though his literary output was small: 37 books of *Quaestiones* and 19 of *Responsa*. His independence of judgement and sense of justice made him one of the most civilizing influences on his profession.

See also JURISPRUDENCE; LAW ROMAN. GS

Birley (1988).

Papirius Cursor (4th century BC), Roman general. Lucius Papirius Cursor was a leading general in the SAMNITE WARS, being consul repeatedly (326, 320, 319, 315, and 313 BC) and dictator, possibly twice (325 and, possibly, 309). In his dictatorship of 325 he is said to have attempted to execute FABIUS MAXIMUS RULLIANUS for fighting without orders. A Roman hero, compared with Alexander the Great, he is the subject of much romantic embellishment in the sources. HS

Salmon (1967).

Pappus (fl. AD 320), Greek mathematician. Pappus of Alexandria was the author of commentaries on EUCLID and PTOLEMY and of a work on universal geography, all of which are now lost. Parts of his great work, however, the *Collection* (*Synagogē*), a handbook of Greek MATHEMATICS, have survived (Books 3–8 and part of Book 2). This work provides invaluable historical evidence of Greek achievements in geometry, astronomy, and mechanics. JL

DSB X (1974).

Papyrus *see* BOOKS, GREEK.

Parentalia Roman festival. The Parentalia, lasting from 13 to 21 February, was a festival for private celebrations of the rites to the family dead, especially parents. As the dead were buried outside the city, during the Parentalia groups of mourners would go out to visit the family tombs and make a simple offering, described by OVID as a tile wreathed with votive garlands, a sprinkling of corn, a few grains of salt, bread soaked in wine, and some loose violets.

See also MANES. DP

Scullard (1981).

Parilia Roman festival. The Parilia was an agricultural festival for the purification of flocks, held on 21 April in honour of Pales, protector of flocks and shepherds. Beasts, stalls, and herdsmen were all purified. OVID's details include fumigating the sheep with sulphur, sweeping and decorating the stalls with branches and wreaths, and burning bonfires through which the shepherds had to jump three times. By CICERO's time it was also supposed that 21 April was the day of Rome's foundation.   DP

Scullard (1981).

Parmenides (b. *c.*515 BC), Greek philosopher. Parmenides of Elea expounded his philosophy in a single didactic poem in Greek hexameters. After an allegorical introduction, the work is divided into two parts, the *Way of Truth* and the *Way of Opinion*. In the *Way of Truth* Parmenides sets out by a series of arguments, impressive for their rigidly deductive logical exposition, to deduce all that can be said about Being. He concludes that what exists must be one, eternal, indivisible, motionless, and changeless. Then, after denying all validity to the senses and any reality to what they appear to perceive, he unexpectedly reinstates the world of appearances he has so vehemently demolished and describes a cosmogony of the familiar type. A considerable controversy has arisen regarding the import of the *Way of Opinion* and its relationship to the *Way of Truth*. It is possible that Parmenides' purpose here was dialectical and didactic, i.e. by showing how a 'modern' cosmology could be put forward upon a simple, albeit erroneous basis, Parmenides would have considerably reinforced his conclusions in the *Way of Truth*. Parmenides' rigorous, deductive reasoning, supported by the paradoxes of ZENO OF ELEA, brought the vigorous period of cosmological speculation initiated by the Milesians to a dramatic halt and, until PLATO finally exposed the fallacies inherent in his arguments, forced later philosophers to seek to evade this impasse in a variety of ways.

See also ELEATIC 'SCHOOL'; EMPEDOCLES; MELISSUS.   JL

Guthrie, vol. 2 (1965); Kirk, Raven, and Schofield (1983).

Parmenion (*c.*400–330 BC), Macedonian general. Parmenion served PHILIP II as joint commander of his Asian expedition in 336 BC. He accompanied ALEXANDER THE GREAT as second-in-command, and saw action at the battles of the GRANICUS RIVER (334), ISSUS (333), and GAUGAMELA (331). Ancient sources present him as a cautious foil to Alexander's bold tactics. This may be a literary device to compliment Alexander, but perhaps indicates Parmenion's conservative, old-fashioned military approach. Remaining behind at Ecbatana in 330 in charge of the Persian treasure, he was murdered shortly after the

execution of his son PHILOTAS. His death suggests less his own un-
trustworthiness than an attempt to whitewash the Philotas affair.

EER

Bosworth (1988a); Hammond (1989); Hammond and Griffith (1979); Hammond and Walbank (1988); Lane Fox (1973).

Paros island in the Cyclades, famous for its deposits of white MARBLE
and as the home of ARCHILOCHUS. In the 7th century BC it colonized
THASOS. In 490 it provided the Persians with a trireme, and when
MILTIADES led a retaliatory expedition the island resisted successfully.
After 480 it became subject to Athens and tried without success to
revolt in 412–410. Literary inscriptions have been recovered from the
heroön of Archilochus.

GS

Parrhasius (fl. 430–390 BC), Greek painter. A native of Ephesus where
he was the pupil of his father Euenor, Parrhasius worked mostly in
Athens and later became an Athenian. The elder PLINY describes him
as an arrogant dandy but pays tribute to the subtlety of his linework.
He is known to have done more than 20 pictures, most of them
mythological, all of them lost. His style was foppish – his Theseus was
said to be 'fed on roses' – and may be paralleled by the surviving work
of contemporary vase painters (e.g. the ERETRIA and MEIDIAS painters).
He also wrote on PAINTING.

GS

Robertson (1975).

Parthenon The Parthenon – the temple of ATHENA Parthenos – was
built on the highest point of the Athenian acropolis, on the site of an
earlier temple, between 447 and 438 BC, though the sculpture was not
finished before 432. It formed the centrepiece of PERICLES' building
programme, directed by the sculptor PHEIDIAS, and it marks the climax
of the Doric style of ARCHITECTURE. Designed by ICTINUS and constructed of Pentelic marble, the Parthenon is the architectural para-
digm of the Athenian golden age and the symbol of the city's power
and piety. The SCULPTURE, much of which is in London, illustrates
episodes in Athenian mythology and (on the frieze) a contemporary
celebration of the festival of the PANATHENAEA.

GS

Ashmole (1972); Boardman and Finn (1985); Hopper (1971); Lawrence (1984).

Parthia Occupying roughly the territory of modern Iran, Parthia was
part of the ACHAEMENID empire and was overrun by ALEXANDER THE GREAT.
It became a Seleucid satrapy (Parthyene) in the 3rd century BC, but c.247
its satrap, who had revolted from ANTIOCHUS II THEOS, was conquered

by an Arsaces who established a line of ARSACID kings ruling an independent kingdom. Parthia grew powerful and comprised extensive territories from Mesopotamia to India, divided into satrapies. Its capital was the old Median capital Ecbatana.

Parthia came to pose a serious threat to Rome's Asian provinces. Nevertheless the two powers were technically at peace when CRASSUS DIVES crossed the Euphrates in 55/4 BC and invaded Mesopotamia. Having alienated the Armenian king Artavasdes, Crassus suffered a resounding defeat at CARRHAE which greatly enhanced Parthia's prestige. Another Roman invasion, by Mark ANTONY in 36 BC, was crushed by the Parthian king PHRAATES IV. But internal divisions such as the revolt of TIRIDATES II prevented Phraates from taking full advantage of the situation and the two powers maintained an uneasy peace.

Parthian fortunes were restored by the accession of Artabanus III (AD 12–38) and the country became wealthy as a result of successful agriculture and long-distance TRADE. Parthian merchants benefited especially from the Great Silk Road which brought SILK and other luxury goods from China to Rome. Another Roman invasion, by CORBULO, was resisted by VOLOGESES I in 63 but ARMENIA was temporarily ceded to Rome. TRAJAN campaigned successfully in Parthia from 113 until illness forced his withdrawal in 117, and in 136 the ALANI invaded, but otherwise the 2nd century saw renewed prosperity for Parthia. In the revolt of PESCENNIUS NIGER (193–4) Parthia backed the loser and was punished by Septimius SEVERUS. Civil war among the Arsacids further weakened the Parthian power base culminating in the defeat of King Artabanus V c.224 by the SASSANIAN prince Ardashir.   EER

Colledge (1967); Debevoise (1938); Eddy (1961); Frye (1984); Herrmann (1977); Sherwin-White (1984); Sullivan (1990); Yarshater (1983).

Patavium   city in Italy. Patavium, modern Padua, lay in eastern CISALPINE GAUL and was probably founded by the VENETI. In 301 BC it defeated a Spartan attack. By 174 it had come under Roman control. The town lay close to the Adriatic with which it was connected by canals, and these, together with its position at a crossroads, allowed Patavium effectively to exploit its wool industry, leading to great prosperity. LIVY was born there.   HE

Paterculus   see VELLEIUS PATERCULUS.

Patria potestas   Roman family authority. The *paterfamilias* (head of household) had complete authority over all those in his power. The Roman family was agnatic – that is to say it consisted of persons related by direct descent in the male line – and any adult male citizen who had no surviving male ascendants was a *paterfamilias* (whether or not he actually had children). Conversely, a Roman remained in the power of his *paterfamilias* even though he might be a mature adult with children of his own. Such persons were not legally responsible and could own nothing. Originally only a *paterfamilias* could be a full legal person (*sui iuris*), but in time devices were found by which sons *in potestate* could be emancipated and become *sui iuris* before the death of their *paterfamilias*. In its widest sense the *familia* included inanimate property, livestock, and slaves, as well as the *pater*'s free-born descendants, and his power over them was akin to ownership (DOMINIUM). He was entitled to treat them as he wished, and had the right to sell or even to kill them. This extreme right was exercised until the end of antiquity in the practice of exposing unwanted infants, but the killing of grown-up children was tempered by custom and moral scruples, and had in practice disappeared by the time of the Empire.

See also ADOPTIO; INHERITANCE IN ROMAN LAW; MARRIAGE, ROMAN; PECULIUM; WOMEN, ROMAN.   TC

Crook (1967).

Patricians   Roman citizen class. The patricians were Roman citizens belonging to a select group of privileged clans (*see* GENS). According to tradition they were descendants of the 100 *patres* (fathers) chosen by ROMULUS to form the first SENATE. This legend oversimplifies the problem of who the patricians were, but it is true that in historical times patrician senators were called *patres*. They had certain constitutional prerogatives (*see* PATRUM AUCTORITAS), and they alone could hold the office of INTERREX. This suggests that the patriciate must have originated under the kings. The patricians also monopolized the priesthoods. Until plebeians were admitted by the law of Q. OGULNIUS (300 BC), only patricians could belong to the colleges of PONTIFICES and AUGURES, and priests such as the REX SACRORUM and the FLAMEN Dialis were always patricians. It is much less certain whether they monopolized the consulship, since some early consuls, including L. BRUTUS and Sp. CASSIUS VECELLINUS, were not patricians. The number of patricians gradually declined: around 50 patrician clans existed in the 5th century, but only 14 at the end of the Republic.   TC

CAH VII.2; Mitchell (1991); Raaflaub (1986).

Patrick, St   (*c*.AD 390–460), Christian missionary. Born in Britain to a Christian father, Patrick was captured by pirates at the age of 16 and taken as a slave to Ireland (HIBERNIA). He escaped and returned home but a vision directed him to evangelize Ireland. He devoted himself to biblical study and was ordained. Later he was sent to Ireland where he became bishop, established churches, and set about converting the people. His *Confessions* and letter to the chieftain Coroticus survive. GS

Hanson (1968).

Patrimonium Caesaris the private property of the Roman emperor. AUGUSTUS' income derived from his privately owned and inherited estates (including EGYPT), managed by imperial procurators; from the spoils of war; and from estates acquired through confiscation or bequest. Increasing confusion between the emperor's private and public income, between *patrimonium* and *fiscus* (imperial treasury), eventually led Septimius SEVERUS to establish a new private treasury, the RES PRIVATA. RJB

Salmon (1968); Scullard (1982).

Patrocles (*c*.345–*c*.275 BC), Seleucid general. Patrocles was appointed commander of Babylon by SELEUCUS (later I) in 312 BC, and later governed Seleucid lands from the Caspian Sea eastward. He wrote a work describing his circumnavigation of the Caspian Sea *c*.285, which was used by PLINY THE ELDER and STRABO. Patrocles mistakenly thought that there was a passage from the Caspian to India. His work also contained accurate information about India. ANTIOCHUS II THEOS sent Patrocles to deal with disturbances in BITHYNIA *c*.279. EER

Cary and Warmington (1929); Grainger (1990b).

Patronus responsible party in a CLIENTELA relationship. The term was used at Rome in a number of specific contexts. The former owner of a freed slave became his *patronus* and retained some jurisdiction over him (*see* SLAVERY, ROMAN). In the late Republic litigants could hire the services of a forensic *patronus* or legal assistant whose role was distinguished from that of the professional ADVOCATUS.

When a Roman general conquered another people he became their *patronus*, a relationship that he passed on to his descendants. Sicilian interests, for example, remained in the care of the Claudii Marcelli after Claudius MARCELLUS conquered the island in 211 BC. The patronage of POMPEY extended over much of the empire. That of the emperors in effect covered all of it (*see* IMPERIUM). Similarly, the interests of a MUNICIPIUM were often represented at Rome by a *patronus*, as were those of many of the GUILDS under the Empire.

Patronage of the arts, especially important in the development of poetry and drama, was a further extension of the *clientela* relationship. Many early dramatists, such as Livius Andronicus, Ennius, Plautus, and Terence, were of humble origins and would not have been heard without the assistance of a *patronus*. Later influential *patroni* included MAECENAS, PLINY THE YOUNGER, VALERIUS MESSALLA CORVINUS, and several of the emperors. GS

Saller (1982); Wallace-Hadrill (1989).

Patrum auctoritas   patrician prerogative. In early Rome decisions of the COMITIA did not become binding on the people unless they also received confirmation from the *patres*, i.e., probably, the PATRICIAN senators, rather than the whole Senate. How this so-called *patrum auctoritas* worked is not well understood, because in the later Republic it had become a meaningless formality, thanks to the *lex Publilia* of 339 BC (*see* PUBLILIUS PHILO). TC

Scullard (1980).

Paul, St   (d. *c*.AD 65), Christian apostle. Saul (later Paul) was a Jew born at Tarsus in Cilicia. After early opposition to the Church, he was converted to Christianity *c*.AD 33 and became its chief apostle to the Gentiles. He undertook missionary journeys to Cyprus, Greece, and Asia Minor, establishing churches and doing much to promote the new faith. On a visit to Jerusalem he was arrested but his trial was deferred for two years (*see* FELIX). As a Roman citizen, he appealed to Caesar and had his case transferred to Rome where he was imprisoned for another two years. After further travel he was taken back to Rome and executed. His Epistles to young churches, incorporated in the canon of the NEW TESTAMENT, exert a continuing influence on Christian doctrine. GS

Bruce (1977); Sanders (1991).

Paulinus, St   (AD 353/4–431), bishop of Nola. Pontius Meropius Anicius Paulinus, born at Bordeaux to a wealthy and noble family, studied under AUSONIUS and embarked on a public career, becoming suffect consul of Rome in 378 and governor of Campania in 381. Converted to Christianity by St AMBROSE, he was ordained in 394 and retired to Nola where he became bishop in 409. A collection of his poems and letters (to distinguished contemporaries such as AUGUSTINE and JEROME) survives. GS

Lienhard (1977).

Paullus   (228–160 BC), Roman general. Lucius Aemilius Paullus Macedonicus was a successful commander of 'philhellenic' leanings. Praetor in 191 BC, Paullus served in Spain, defeating the Lusitanians by 189. A member of the senatorial commission to Asia, he opposed the triumph of VULSO. Consul in 182, he won a triumph for his defeat of the LIGURES in 181. In 168 he was again appointed consul to end the Third MACEDONIAN WAR. He achieved this with his victory over the forces of PERSEUS at PYDNA. He carried out, allegedly against his will, a harsh settlement of Greece, which included the sack of EPIRUS. He returned to another triumph. The booty brought back was sufficient to allow the suspension of direct taxation of Roman citizens in Italy (see TRIBUTUM), although all Paullus kept for himself was Perseus' library. Censor in 164, his relative lack of wealth on his death was held to prove his probity. He was the father of SCIPIO AEMILIANUS.   HS

Gruen (1984); Reiter (1988); Scullard (1973).

Paulus, Julius   (fl. c.AD 210), Roman jurist. Few details are known of Paulus' life, but he practised as an advocate and was assessor, with ULPIAN, of PAPINIAN when he was praetorian prefect in 205. A member of the imperial council (see CONSILIUM PRINCIPIS) under both Severus and Caracalla, he was exiled by Elagabalus. Recalled by Severus Alexander, he became praetorian prefect, perhaps jointly with Ulpian. His extensive writings (320 books, including 80 on the edict, see EDICTUM) gained him a high reputation, and after Ulpian he is the most frequently excerpted author in the *Digest*.

See also JURISPRUDENCE.   GS

Pausanias   (5th century BC), Spartan regent. Pausanias was the victor of PLATAEA (479 BC) and regent for King Pleistarchus. In 478, commanding the Greek fleet round Cyprus and the Hellespont, he captured Byzantium. His high-handedness offended the allies who turned to Athens and formed the DELIAN LEAGUE. On the motion of Hetoemaridas Sparta decided to leave the war to Athens. Pausanias could not accept this and went out with some official approval, though not as regent, to Byzantium in early 476(?) to 'the war against the Hellenes'. CIMON expelled him and he dallied in the Troad, allegedly conducting treasonable exchanges with XERXES. Recalled to Sparta in late 476(?), he was tried for treason but acquitted. In 471(?) he was apparently detected communicating with Xerxes and conspiring with the helots (see SERFS) and was murdered. The whole story is highly doubtful although it comes from THUCYDIDES.   GLC

Meiggs (1972).

Pausanias   king of Sparta, 445–426 and 408/7–395 BC. During the first period of his rule Pausanias was a minor, his father Pleistoanax was in exile, and his uncle Cleomenes was regent. In 403 he persuaded a majority of the ephors to support his intervening in Athens and, characteristically of the Agiad line, made a deal with the democrats which saved Athens from the severities expected from LYSANDER. In 395 he was too late to join forces with Lysander at Haliartus and was exiled. In Tegea he wrote a tract advocating reform of the Spartan constitution. GLC

Cartledge (1987); De Ste Croix (1972).

Pausanias (2nd century AD), Greek travel writer. Possibly a native of Magnesia, Pausanias was an observant and widely read traveller who wrote a *Guide to Greece* in the 170s AD. Divided into 10 books, it concentrates on the Roman province of Achaea and was written for a readership of Roman philhellenes. Since most of the monuments were still standing at the time of writing, it is invaluable to archaeologists; but religion, myth, and local customs are also well served. GS

Habicht (1985); Levi (1971).

Peculium property held by or on behalf of someone who in Roman law was without property rights, e.g. a son, a woman, or a slave. In law the *peculium* remained the property of the father: it was a voluntary grant which he could withdraw at will. In practice, possession was nine points of the law. Under the Empire a soldier's booty was his own *peculium castrense*.
See also PATRIA POTESTAS. GS

Peisander (late 5th century BC), Athenian politician. In 415 BC Peisander was sufficiently trusted to inquire into the mutilation of the HERMAE (*see* ALCIBIADES). By 411 he was persuaded that the democracy had to be modified or abolished. He proposed the establishment of the FOUR HUNDRED and the Five Thousand, but became ever more committed to the dominance of the former. Finally he fled to the Spartans. GLC

Kagan (1987).

Peisistratids sons of PEISISTRATUS, *see* HIPPIAS.

Peisistratus (fl. *c*.560–527 BC), tyrant of Athens. Peisistratus first seized power by a ruse, probably in 561/60. His prominence was due to a regional power base as champion of the 'Hill-men' of north-east Attica and to an earlier military success against Megara. Quickly expelled by a coalition of aristocratic opponents, restored several years later with the support of the ALCMAEONID Megacles, and then, after a dispute, exiled again, he established his power definitively in 546 by military force. Despite the later Athenian hostility to tyranny, his rule was remembered as a golden age of peace and prosperity: the constitution remained unaltered, though he ensured the appointment of supporters to important offices, and rival nobles were conciliated as much as intimidated. Peisistratus was active abroad, maintaining a wide network of allies and re-establishing Athens's colonial position in the Hellespont; at home, agriculture was promoted, and lavish public works and religious and cultural programmes advanced ATHENS as a centre at the expense of regional interests. Expenditure was partly funded by a modest income tax, and Peisistratus may have struck the earliest Attic coinage. He was succeeded on his death by his sons HIPPIAS and Hipparchus.

See also LAURIUM. RB

Berve (1967); CAH III.3; Rhodes (1981).

Pelagianism a Christian doctrine introduced by the British-born monk Pelagius who came to Rome c.AD 400. Pelagius insisted that man was responsible for his own salvation without the need for divine grace and denied that each man's fate was predestined by God. He attracted the criticism of AUGUSTINE, JEROME, and OROSIUS and c.412 retired to Palestine where he found support. In 417 he was excommunicated by Pope Innocent I but the debate continued and the heresy was not finally eradicated until the late 6th century. GS

Brown (1972).

Pelopidas (c.410–364 BC), Theban general and joint architect with EPAMINONDAS of Theban hegemony. Having fled to Athens when Sparta seized the Cadmea (382 BC), he led the liberation of THEBES (379/8). Frequently Boeotarch (*see* BOEOTIAN CONFEDERACY), he was highly successful commanding the SACRED BAND at Tegea (375) and LEUCTRA (371). After invading Sparta (370/69), he concentrated on Thessaly and was taken prisoner (368). Rescued by Epaminondas, he led the embassy to ARTAXERXES II (367) and won his support for Thebes. In 364 he defeated ALEXANDER OF PHERAE at Cynoscephalae and was killed. GLC

Buckler (1980).

Peloponnese literally the island of Pelops, the Greek mainland south of the isthmus of Corinth. In a microcosm of Greece (Strabo called it 'the acropolis of all Greece') mountain ranges, rising to 7,000 feet and more, alternate with narrow fertile plains. An island but for the isthmus, it is encircled by an inhospitable coastline with deep gulfs and few harbours. Such sharp natural divisions bred a number of fiercely independent peoples, many of them untouched by political, social, and cultural movements taking place only a short distance away. The principal cities were ARGOS, CORINTH, and SPARTA. The main regions were ACHAEA, ARCADIA, ELIS, LACONIA, and MESSENIA. There were major sanctuaries at EPIDAURUS and OLYMPIA.   GS

Peloponnesian League confederation of Greek states. The Peloponnesian League was an organization consisting of SPARTA and a number of her allies; its formal constitution probably belongs shortly after 506 BC, in response to Sparta's abortive attempt to lead her allies against Athens without consultation. Thereafter, declarations of war and peace required the sanction of a League Congress, binding on all members, barring religious obligations. The allies had no mutual obligations, and might even fight one another; the formal relationship was between Sparta, the dominant partner, and individual allies. The League lasted until the decade after LEUCTRA, when allied defections caused its effective dissolution.   RB

De Ste Croix (1972).

Peloponnesian War   (431–404 BC). *Cause*: According to THUCYDIDES, the growth of Athenian power made the Spartans afraid and forced them to war. Athenian power certainly grew between 446 and 431 with the suppression of the Samian Revolt, the foundation of AMPHIPOLIS, the ever-increasing regimentation of the allies, and the accumulation of large financial reserves. Above all, ATHENS was 'the education of Hellas'. SPARTA had lost her spell over the Greek world and had to fear for her position in the Peloponnese. Sparta's particular complaints against Athens were doubtful, but in general Athens threatened the liberty of all Greeks.

The Archidamian War (431–421 BC): Sparta was confident that Athens could never dare face her army and that ravaging would force Athens to her knees within two or three years. When, reduced by the plague, Athens sought peace in 430, this confidence was confirmed. Help for the revolt of Mytilene (428) was ineffectual; and Plataea was reduced (427) merely to please the Thebans. Only when the Spartan prisoners were captured on Sphacteria (425, *see* PYLOS) did Sparta perforce commit herself to getting at the source of Athenian power, viz. the tribute-paying allies. Hence the northern campaign of BRASIDAS.

PERICLES put his trust in the navy guarding the empire and making merely retaliatory raids round the Peloponnese, confident that Sparta would see no point in continuing. The aggressive policy of DEMOSTHENES, especially the fortification of Pylos, produced a successful result – the Spartan offer of peace (425); but successful only by chance, viz. the isolation of Spartans on Sphacteria whom, demographically, Sparta could not afford to lose. At the prompting of CLEON, Sparta was rebuffed and the Spartans captured. Brasidas' success, especially at Amphipolis, induced a more sober mood. The Peace of NICIAS (421) ensued.

The peace proved unstable. Leading allies of Sparta would not accept its terms and allied with Argos. Athens allied with Argos and Sparta had to re-establish her authority, which she did at MANTINEA (418). Athens's brutal subjection of Melos (416) showed that the cause of liberating the Greeks remained urgent. When in 414 Athens raided Laconia, Sparta resumed the war and fortified Decelea.

She did so the more readily because on the proposal of ALCIBIADES Athens had involved herself in the Sicilian expedition. Its purpose is debatable: Thucydides may have exaggerated wildly. If Alcibiades had not been recalled, or if Nicias had been less cautious, Syracuse could have been reduced. By the time Demosthenes arrived with reinforcements (413), the situation was hopeless. Delayed by superstition about a lunar eclipse, the Athenians did not get away when they could. When they tried, they could not escape Syracusan vengeance. The losses of men and ships were disastrous.

The Ionian War (412–405): From Decelea the Spartans and the Boeotians systematically pillaged Attica. Huge numbers of slaves deserted and the Athenians were wholly deprived of produce. But the corn fleets still arrived and the war had to be won in Asiatic waters. Once TISSAPHERNES had negotiated a Persian–Spartan alliance (412/11), Spartan prospects greatly improved, but while that wily, wise man shilly-shallied Athens won a major naval victory at CYZICUS (410) and Sparta sought to make peace. CLEOPHON persuaded the Athenians to fight on and recover more of their disaffected allies, and in 408 CYRUS THE YOUNGER came down and took charge. In concord with LYSANDER he ensured Spartan victory. Defeat at ARGINUSAE (406), when the Spartan admiral Callicratidas was spurning Persian aid, showed that Lysander was Sparta's best hope. His victory at AEGOSPOTAMI (405) utterly finished Athenian naval power. Athens was starved into submission. GLC

De Ste Croix (1972); Hammond (1959); Hornblower (1983); Kagan (1969).

Peltasts Greek light-armed soldiers, named from their small shields (*peltae*). Peltasts, originally Thracian, first appeared in the Archidamian War, notably in DEMOSTHENES' capture of Sphacteria (*see* PYLOS). They carried a spear and a short sword and, unhindered by body armour, could move quickly. IPHICRATES made special use of them, destroying the Spartan division at Lechaeum (390). He increased the length of their spears and swords.

See also ARMS AND ARMOUR, GREEK.   GLC

Anderson (1970); Best (1969).

Penates   Roman household gods. The Penates, often linked with the LARES, were the guardian spirits of the store cupboard (*penus*) of the house. The offerings made to them by the *paterfamilias* represented the chief household cult. But there were also Penates of the state, located in the inner sanctum of VESTA's temple, though with a separate shrine on the Velia. Their origin was disputed, some identifying them with Castor and Pollux, some claiming that they had been brought by Aeneas from Troy.   DP

Scullard (1981).

Pentacosiomedimni   Athenian citizen class. The Pentacosiomedimni ('500-bushel-men') comprised the highest of SOLON's four property classes, their name reflecting their qualification, 500 measures of wet or dry produce; scholars are divided as to whether the class already existed before Solon, or was distinguished as a new top tier. They were eligible for all offices, some of which, like the treasurers of Athena, were restricted to them.

See also HIPPEIS; THETES; ZEUGITAE.   RB

Rhodes (1981).

Pentecontaetia   literally '50 years', the period between the end of the PERSIAN WARS (479 BC) and the outbreak of the PELOPONNESIAN WAR (431). Our knowledge of this period derives principally from THUCYDIDES' account, tracing the rise of Athenian power.

See also GREECE, HISTORY.   GLC

Penthesilea Painter   (fl. 465–445 BC), Greek vase painter. The Penthesilea Painter is named after a cup in Munich which illustrates Achilles and Penthesilea, a composition adapted from a wall painting. He is credited with the painting of almost 150 vases, most of them cups. His figures are noted for the intensity of their gaze.   GS

Arias and Hirmer (1962); Boardman (1989).

Perdiccas   (fl. 330–321 BC), Macedonian general. Perdiccas accompanied ALEXANDER THE GREAT's expedition as infantry, then cavalry, commander and became a member of the royal bodyguard. He succeeded HEPHAESTION as chiliarch (vizier), and after Alexander's death in 323 BC took control of the kings PHILIP III ARRHIDAEUS and ALEXANDER IV. In the ensuing struggles EUMENES OF CARDIA supported his powerful centralized control, but Perdiccas was opposed by the other jealous DIADOCHI. While attacking PTOLEMY (later I), he was assassinated by his own army.

EER

Bosworth (1988a); CAH VII.1; Green (1990); Hammond (1989); Lane Fox (1973).

Perdiccas II king of Macedon, c.450–413 BC. Perdiccas, son of ALEXANDER I, skilfully kept his throne through the Peloponnesian War by moving out of and into alliance with Athens, the real menace to his kingdom. In 432 he gave his blessing to the revolt of POTIDAEA and the formation of the CHALCIDIAN LEAGUE. In 431 he returned to alliance and in 429 warded off an invasion of Thracians under Sitalces. In 424 he helped BRASIDAS, and sometime later made peace with Athens. Thus he won a reputation for lying, but died in his bed. ARCHELAUS succeeded him.

GLC

Hammond and Griffith (1979).

Perduellio form of treason in early Roman law. Derived from a Latin word meaning 'enemy', under the early Republic it referred to any hostile activity directed against the state, with the possible exception of military offences. The terms were loosely defined in the TWELVE TABLES. The penalty was death. By the late Republic it had been subsumed under the offence of MAIESTAS.

HE

Nicholas (1962).

Peregrini non-Roman class. *Peregrini* were citizens of states other than Rome. They thus included all of Rome's Italian allies up to the SOCIAL WAR as well as all provincials with any local autonomy. *Peregrini* could not become Roman citizens unless they gave up their own status as local citizens. With the increasing extension of Roman CITIZENSHIP, this led to abuses until Augustus affirmed that all citizens were subject to local obligations (including taxes).

HE

Sherwin-White (1973).

Pergamum city in Mysia in Asia Minor. Pergamum became the capital city of the Attalid kingdom in the 3rd century BC. The Attalids began an extensive building programme funded by rich natural resources and LYSIMACHUS' treasury ('inherited' by his deputy PHILETAERUS). Situated on a lofty acropolis which dominated its surroundings, Pergamum was a model of Hellenistic TOWN PLANNING on an extensive terrace system. The upper town included palaces and fortifications, temples, a theatre, a LIBRARY which rivalled ALEXANDRIA's, and monuments celebrating military victories over the Galatians. These included the precinct of Athena and the Great Altar of Zeus, decorated with a famous sculpted frieze depicting the battle of the Gods and Giants. Lower terraces contained sanctuaries, agoras, and the largest gymnasium of the Greek world. Nearby was the healing sanctuary of ASCLEPIUS, where GALEN (a native of Pergamum) practised medicine. Pergamum ranks among the greatest Hellenistic cities in beauty, wealth, and culture. The kingdom was bequeathed to Rome in 133 BC.

See also ATTALUS I–III; EUMENES I, II.   EER

Allen (1983); CAH VII.1, VIII; Green (1990); Gruen (1984); Hansen (1971).

Periander tyrant of Corinth, *c*.625–585 BC. Periander succeeded his father CYPSELUS as tyrant of CORINTH. He fostered commerce, enlarged Corinth's naval power and her colonial empire, notably by founding POTIDAEA and gaining control of Corcyra, and established diplomatic links with THRASYBULUS of Miletus, and with Athens, Lydia, and, probably, Egypt; he himself married a daughter of Procles, tyrant of Epidaurus, whom he later deposed. Although tradition makes him a stereotype wicked tyrant, he was clearly an able ruler, reckoned in antiquity among the SEVEN SAGES. His nephew Psammetichus succeeded him, but was overthrown after three years.   RB

Andrewes (1956); Salmon (1984).

Pericles (*c*.495–429 BC), in THUCYDIDES' judgement Athens's greatest statesman. Pericles, son of XANTHIPPUS, began his long career by prosecuting CIMON (463 BC) for his conduct of the siege of Thasos and abetting EPHIALTES in his attack on the AREOPAGUS. By the late 450s he was beginning to dominate Athenian politics. General in 454(?), he proposed the recall of Cimon from ostracism, prudently accepting the inevitable, and in 451/50 he advocated restricting CITIZENSHIP to those whose parents were both Athenian. In the 440s he inaugurated his building programme (*see* ATHENS, TOPOGRAPHY; ODEUM; PARTHENON; PROPYLAEA) and dealt with the concerted Spartan invasion and Euboean revolt (446) by making the Thirty Years' Peace. He dispatched a panhellenic colony to THURII and sent CLERUCHIES round the empire. In 443 THUCYDIDES, son of Melesias, lost a trial of strength and was ostracized. Until his death from plague in 429 Pericles had such authority that Thucydides the historian spoke of 'the rule of the leading man'. Only in 430 was his counsel disregarded and he himself temporarily out of power.

Pericles' attitudes are best seen in the funeral oration Thucydides has him deliver in 431. He was the great imperialist, maintaining and extending Athenian power prudently, never contemplating a deal with Sparta that could limit empire, but also the great democrat, glorying in the freedom of individuals to do what they wished in a city offering the greatest opportunities. He firmly insisted that the Samian revolt be not tolerated and, when war was clearly coming, he refused to yield a jot to Spartan pressure and so offer hope to subject allies. He proposed the MEGARA Decree in 433/2 and occupied AEGINA, inflexible before protest. Yet he prudently kept within the peace, even as he prevented the Corcyran navy coming under Peloponnesian control, thus wrong-footing Sparta. Behind all this was the conviction that Athens was militarily unassailable. GLC

De Ste Croix (1972); Hornblower (1983); Kagan (1969).

Perioikoi Greek citizen class. Perioikoi ('dwellers about') were free men of restricted status, forming communities in an area surrounding a dominant state, as at SPARTA and Elis. Similar groups may have existed at Argos and in Thessaly and Crete, but the term might simply refer to surrounding subject communities. At Sparta Perioikoi were part of the state: they had domestic self-government, but no political rights, and served in the army as required; they were often concerned with the economic activities neglected by Spartiates. RB

Andrewes (1990); Cartledge (1979); Gschnitzer (1958).

Peripatetic School ARISTOTLE returned to Athens in 335 BC which he had left after Speusippus' appointment as head of the ACADEMY. In a grove sacred to Apollo Lyceius and the Muses, where there was a gymnasium already popular with SOPHISTS and teachers (including SOCRATES), he rented some buildings and began to teach. Among these buildings was a covered court (*peripatos*) from which the school (also known as the Lyceum) derived its name. (It is also held that it was so-called because he walked about while lecturing.) Aristotle modelled the customs of his school upon the Academy and instituted common meals and symposia. He collected manuscripts, maps, and, probably, natural objects to illustrate his lectures. Research was organized on a grand scale. (This traditional view, however, has been rejected by some who believe that the Peripatetic School as an institution was not founded until after Aristotle's death.)

After the death of ALEXANDER THE GREAT (323) anti-Macedonian feeling became rife in Athens. A charge of impiety was brought against Aristotle who left the school in THEOPHRASTUS' hands and retired to Chalcis. Under Theophrastus' leadership the school acquired buildings which were bequeathed by him to a group of scholars including STRATON, who succeeded him as head (287–269). Straton was the last great traditional head of the school. Later Peripatetics narrowed the range of scholarship and research and devoted themselves to BIOGRAPHY and literary criticism.

See also LIBRARIES.   JL

Lynch (1972).

Persecution, religious see CHRISTIANITY.

Persepolis residence and burial place of the Achaemenid kings of PERSIA. Begun by DARIUS I c.500 BC, building was continued by XERXES and only completed by ARTAXERXES I MACROCHEIR. The place was sacked and burnt by ALEXANDER THE GREAT in 331 BC, but impressive remains of palaces, halls, and fortifications survive and show a combination of Greek, Egyptian, and Mesopotamian influences.   GS

Roaf (1990).

Perseus (c.213/12–c.167 BC), king of Macedon. Perseus succeeded his father PHILIP V in 179 BC, having engineered the execution of his pro-Roman younger brother. Renewing the treaty with Rome, he continued Philip's consolidation and expansion of Macedonia. He married a Seleucid princess, married his sister to PRUSIAS II of Bithynia, and won many friends in Greece. EUMENES II SOTER of Pergamum complained to Rome about Perseus' growing power, which resulted in the Third MACEDONIAN WAR (171–168). To counter his initial military successes, Rome gave the command to L. Aemilius PAULLUS, who utterly defeated Perseus at PYDNA. He was captured, taken to Rome to march in Paullus' triumph, and died in prison.

See also ANDRISCUS.   EER

CAH VIII; Errington (1990); Green (1990); Gruen (1984); Hammond and Walbank (1988).

Persia The Persians are first attested as vassals of Assyria, and subsequently came under the control of Media. Under CYRUS they overthrew the MEDES, inheriting their empire; subsequent expansion under CAMBYSES and DARIUS I extended their domain from the Aegean to Bactria, India, and Egypt. The Persians exerted a loose control over their subjects through the system of SATRAPS, insisting on the maintenance of order and the payment of tribute, but accommodating diverse forms of subordinate political organization and tolerating religions other than their own Zoroastrianism; good communications and ample bureaucracy helped hold the empire together. The great Persian cultural achievement was the palace complexes at Susa, PERSEPOLIS, and

Pasargadae, which are a synthesis of liberal borrowings from other cultures.

Under XERXES the expansionism of earlier ACHAEMENID kings was abandoned. Although palace intrigues and revolts became more frequent, the empire remained stable, and there was no challenge to the omnipotence of the king; but Persia failed to withstand the Macedonian invasion. ALEXANDER THE GREAT maintained the satrapal system and the privileged position of the Persians. After his death Persia became part of the Seleucid empire (see SELEUCUS I NICATOR), until they in turn were displaced by the ARSACIDS.

See also SASSANIANS.   RB

CAH IV; Cook (1983); Frye (1983); Gershevitch (1985).

Persian Wars   The term 'Persian Wars' is sometimes understood as covering all Persian expansion into the Greek world from the coming of CYRUS (*c.*544 BC) to the Peace of CALLIAS (449), including the advance to, across, and round the Aegean, and the wars of the DELIAN LEAGUE, including EURYMEDON. Normally (as here) it is taken to cover the MARATHON campaign (490) and XERXES' invasion (480–479). (*See* map on page 747.)

Cause: No Persian documents exist explaining why the Persians expanded westwards. HERODOTUS' statements reflect only Greek sentiment; his claim that Persia sought to punish the Athenians for their part in the IONIAN REVOLT (499–494) is belied by the fact that both in 490 and in 480 demands for submission were sent to all Greek states. All we can say is that Persia expanded as Rome and other powers expanded, the nature of power being to expand.

Marathon: Despite a disastrous storm off Mount ATHOS, DARIUS I decided to invade by sea. Artaphernes and DATIS moved through the islands, which had sensibly submitted, and landed in Euboea, where they forced Carystus and Eretria to submit, and then at MARATHON, where they expected to be able to deploy their cavalry. The Athenians, supported by the Plataeans, took up a defensive position and waited for the Persians to start withdrawing; they then attacked and won, though how great a victory is uncertain. The Persians sailed round to Phalerum, evidently intending to land. Finding the Athenians already in position to dispute a landing, they sailed back to Asia.

Xerxes' Invasion: The Persian return to the attack was delayed by the death of Darius and problems of succession, but in the spring of 480 Xerxes set out from Sardes with an army and navy, according to the Greeks, of an immensity no modern scholar can credit. Having crossed the Hellespont on a double bridge of boats, the army, with the navy keeping roughly abreast, passed through Persian-controlled and Persian-influenced territory to THERMOPYLAE where they met a force of

Greeks under LEONIDAS, small but adequate. Xerxes had intended to outflank them by sea, but owing to losses in a storm he felt he had to try by land as well. He succeeded brilliantly at both Thermopylae and ARTEMISIUM and passed into Greece, the Greek fleet retiring to Salamis. Despite what had been agreed, the Greeks did not come out to fight in Boeotia, and the Persian army joined up with the fleet at Athens. Xerxes' motives for engaging the Greek fleet at SALAMIS have been debated. Most argue that he had to do so before passing on to attack the Peloponnesians behind a wall across the Isthmus; others that he was tricked by a seemingly traitorous message from THEMISTOCLES. When the Persian ships did enter the strait, the confined waters did not favour them and they failed. How great a failure is unclear, but some time after the battle the fleet retired to Asia and the naval war was over.

Xerxes too retired by land, leaving MARDONIUS in command of the army. In 479, having wintered in Thessaly, he again occupied Athens and then withdrew to Boeotia, waiting for the Greeks to come forth. After a surprisingly long delay PAUSANIAS led his army into Boeotia where the battle of PLATAEA was fought and won. The Persians withdrew (*see* MYCALE). Greece was free.   GLC

Burn (1984); CAH IV.

Persius (AD 34–62), Latin satirist. Aulus Persius Flaccus was a wealthy Etruscan knight from Volterra. Moving to Rome, he became a pupil of the Stoic philosopher Cornutus and a friend of LUCAN and other opponents of NERO. His six *Satires*, which owe much to HORACE and to Stoic rhetoric, are written in a vigorous, colloquial, allusive Latin. They were published posthumously by Cornutus.

See also SATIRE.   GS

Bramble (1974); Coffey (1989); Rudd (1986).

Pertinax (AD 126–93), Roman emperor, AD 193. Publius Helvius Pertinax, governor of Raetia during the Germanic invasions of 166–7, and later governor of Britain (185–7), was City Prefect and Commodus' colleague as consul (192). Offered the throne by Laetus, praetorian prefect, after Commodus' murder, and proclaimed before the praetorians, Pertinax was recognized by the Senate after an elaborate charade: he offered the throne to CLAUDIUS POMPEIANUS, who refused it, whereupon Pertinax professed reluctance to accept the post himself, but allowed the Senate to persuade him. However, his attempts to impose discipline and financial restraint cost him the support of the praetorians, and he was murdered within three months.   RJB

Grant (1985); Parker (1958); Wells (1984).

Pervigilium Veneris see ANTHOLOGY, LATIN.

Pescennius Niger (c.AD 135–94), Roman emperor, AD 193–4. Gaius Pescennius Niger Justus, from an equestrian family, held the rank of *primus pilus* and then a command in Egypt, before being admitted (by ADLECTIO) into the Senate by COMMODUS. Consul with Septimius SEVERUS (190), he was appointed governor of Syria (191), and proclaimed emperor by his legions after the murder of PERTINAX and elevation of DIDIUS JULIANUS (193). Niger enjoyed popular support in Rome, but his rival Severus' forces were superior and closer to Rome: he was prevented from advancing beyond Perinthus, and was finally defeated at Issus. He escaped, but was soon caught and executed, and his head sent to Severus.   RJB

Grant (1985); Parker (1958).

Petra Nabataean city. Petra, the capital city of the NABATAEANS in modern Jordan, lies in a hollow accessible only through a gorge. It was attacked unsuccessfully by ANTIGONUS I MONOPHTHALMUS in 312 BC. Made wealthy from the spice trade, the Nabataeans beautified Petra with buildings in Greek and eastern styles. There are extensive remains of the city (temples, gymnasia, two theatres, markets), and excellently preserved tombs and temple-tombs with architectural façades cut into the surrounding mountains.   EER

Browning (1973); Glueck (1966, 1968, 1970); Harding (1967).

Petronius (1st century AD), Latin novelist. It is likely, but not certain, that the author of the *Satyricon* is to be identified with Titus Petronius, 'arbiter of elegance' at the court of NERO. If so, he became proconsul of Bithynia and consul in AD 61 and died by his own hand in 66 after a life of notorious idleness (Tacitus, *Annals* 16.17–20). The *Satyricon* (sc. *libri*) is a work of satirical fiction (*see* SATIRE), more parody than novel; its original extent is unknown, but portions of books 14–16 survive. The centrepiece of the extant fragments is a witty description of an extravagant, vulgar, and orgiastic dinner party (*see* SYMPOSIUM) known as the *Cena Trimalchionis*. The narrative is interspersed with passages of verse in the manner of Menippus and includes bawdy anecdotes of a Milesian nature (*see* NOVEL, LATIN). The dialogue is an important witness to the colloquial language of Vulgar Latin (*see* LATIN LANGUAGE).   GS

Coffey (1989); Hägg (1983); Sullivan (1968); Walsh (1970).

Petronius Maximus (c.AD 396–455), Roman emperor, AD 455. Petronius Maximus, consul in 433 and 443, persuaded VALENTINIAN III to murder his general AETIUS (454), and then arranged Valentinian's murder (March 455). Maximus became emperor, forced Valentinian's widow Eudoxia to marry him, and gave her daughter Eudocia to his son Palladius. Eudocia was already promised to Huneric, son of the Vandal GAESERIC, who promptly invaded Italy. Maximus fled, but was killed by a stone thrown from the crowd (31 May). RJB

Bury (1958); Grant (1985).

Peucestas (c.360–c.316 BC), Macedonian general. Peucestas accompanied ALEXANDER THE GREAT'S expedition, saving Alexander's life in the attack on the Indian Malli at Multan (326/5 BC), and was appointed to the bodyguard and satrapy of Persis (325). He wore Persian dress and learned Persian, which pleased Alexander, and levied 20,000 Iranian troops in 323 for deployment with the Macedonian phalanx. After Alexander's death Peucestas initially supported but later abandoned EUMENES OF CARDIA. ANTIGONUS I MONOPHTHALMUS spared his life but his fate is unknown. EER

Billows (1990); Bosworth (1988a); Hammond (1989); Lane Fox (1973).

Phaedrus (c.15 BC–AD 50), Latin poet. Gaius Julius Phaedrus was born a Thracian slave but came to Rome and became a freedman of Augustus. Despite the unpopularity of his work and the offence that he apparently gave to SEJANUS, he succeeded in elevating the FABLE to the status of an independent genre. Five (incomplete) books of his verse fables survive, modelled on those of AESOP and written in Latin iambics. GS

Phaedrus of Sphettus (fl. c.300–270 BC), Athenian politician. Phaedrus, of the Attic deme Sphettus, was politically a 'moderate'. He held several military commands both under LACHARES (296/5 BC) and after Athens fell to DEMETRIUS I POLIORCETES in 294. He was an ambassador to PTOLEMY I. After the revolt of 287, Phaedrus and his brother CALLIAS OF SPHETTUS helped gather the harvest before the expected siege, which shows democratic sympathies although his retirement from political life afterwards perhaps indicates disagreement with the democratic government. EER

Ferguson (1911); Green (1990); Mossé (1973); Osborne (1979); Shear (1978).

Phalanx heavy infantry drawn up in battle order in Greek armies at all periods. In the HOPLITE armies of the classical age the phalanx was normally eight deep, but in the later 5th century BC new ideas came into vogue. At Delium (424) the Thebans were 25 deep. At LEUCTRA

(371) they were 50 deep. It is generally supposed that the men in a hoplite phalanx stood a shield's width apart.

See also ARMS AND ARMOUR, GREEK; ARMY, GREEK.   GLC

Pritchett (1971).

Phalaris   tyrant of Acragas, *c.*570–555 BC. Phalaris came to power about a decade after the foundation of ACRAGAS, and ruled for some 15 years. He was an able military leader, extending Acragantine influence at the expense of Greek and native neighbours and controlling Himera. Domestically, tradition makes him a stock tyrant, guilty of numerous cruelties, especially the brazen bull in which he is said to have roasted his enemies alive.

See also EPISTOLOGRAPHY, GREEK.   RB

Berve (1967); Dunbabin (1948).

Phanocles   (?3rd century BC), Greek poet. Phanocles, the gay man's HERMESIANAX, was the author of an elegiac poem entitled *Loves or Lovely Boys* which catalogued the homosexual affairs of gods and heroes. The longest of the few surviving fragments describes the murder of Orpheus.

See also HOMOSEXUALITY.   GS

Phanodemus   (4th century BC), Greek historian. Phanodemus of Athens, father of the historian Diyllus, wrote a history of Athens in at least nine books. His political activity is attested in the period 343–328 BC, though it may have been considerably longer. He seems to have concerned himself with religious matters, especially festivals. Only fragments of his history survive, the latest concerning the death of CIMON (450/49).   GLC

Jacoby (1954).

Pharnabazus   satrap of Dascylium, *c.*413–388 BC. In concert with (and also vying with) TISSAPHERNES, Pharnabazus helped Sparta win the PELOPONNESIAN WAR, proving more reliable and more accessible to Greeks than his rival. At LYSANDER's behest he had ALCIBIADES murdered when the latter was on his way to plead for Athens with the king. In the 390s, suffering from Spartan pillage, he joined with CONON in defeating the Spartan fleet at Cnidus (394) and sailed into the Corinthian Gulf (393). In 388 he was summoned to court and married ARTAXERXES' daughter. He twice failed to recover Egypt.   GLC

Dandamaev (1989).

Pharnaces I (*c*.185–*c*.159/6 BC), king of Pontus. Pharnaces attempted to expand his Black Sea kingdom *c*.183 BC by seizing the Greek city of SINOPE, and invading CAPPADOCIA, PAPHLAGONIA, and GALATIA. The Pergamene EUMENES II SOTER, ARIARATHES IV of Cappadocia, BITHYNIA, RHODES, and others who were threatened formed an alliance against him. Pharnaces refused a Roman order to desist, but was defeated by the coalition in 179. He was forced to surrender most of his conquests but kept Sinope as his capital.

See also PONTUS.   EER

CAH VIII; Gruen (1984); Jones (1983); Magie (1975).

Pharos *see* ALEXANDRIA; LIGHTHOUSES.

Pharsalus in Thessaly, battle in 48 BC. At Pharsalus, the decisive battle of the CIVIL WAR, POMPEY, with 45,000 legionaries and 7,000 cavalry, trusted in his cavalry to break through CAESAR's 21,000 legionaries and 1,000 cavalry. But Caesar's eight reserve cohorts moved up against Pompey's cavalry, using their spears as stabbing weapons, and routed them. This first defeat of Pompey's career was total, with 6,000 men killed and 29,000 captured, and gave Caesar control of the Roman world.   DP

Greenhalgh (1981).

Phayllus (d. 351 BC), Phocian general in the Third SACRED WAR. Despite defeat by PHILIP II of Macedon in 353 BC, Phayllus succeeded his brother ONOMARCHUS after his death in the Battle of the Crocus Field (352) and organized the defence of Thermopylae. He died shortly afterwards and was succeeded by Phalaecus.   GLC

Buckler (1980).

Pheidias (*c*.490–430 BC), Greek sculptor. Pheidias was an Athenian and the most celebrated sculptor of antiquity. His early commissions included a bronze group at DELPHI of Athena, Apollo, and Miltiades; the so-called Lemnian Athena; and the Athena Promachos which was erected on the acropolis *c*.456 BC. But his most famous works were the two chryselephantine statues: the first of Athena for the PARTHENON which was finished in 438 BC and is known from Roman copies, the second of Zeus for the temple of Zeus at OLYMPIA which was perhaps done around 430 BC and was one of the wonders of the ancient world. His workshop at Olympia has been identified. Pheidias was also a painter, engraver, and designer, and it may have been his artistic versatility that recommended him to PERICLES as director of all the works on the acropolis. Later he shared Pericles' unpopularity and was imprisoned on a charge of embezzling the gold supplied for his statue of Athena.

See also SCULPTURE, GREEK. GS

Richter (1970b).

Pheidippides or Philippides (fl. 490 BC), Athenian runner. Pheidippides, a professional courier, was sent to Sparta to seek assistance against the Persian expedition of 490 BC, covering some 140 miles in under two days. His vision of Pan on the way led to the promotion of the god's cult at Athens. RB

Pheidon (fl. *c.*665 BC?), king of Argos. Pheidon is described by Aristotle as a hereditary king who made himself a tyrant. He is probably to be associated with the Argive ascendancy over the Peloponnese in the second quarter of the 7th century BC, perhaps due to an early espousal of hoplite tactics, which is symbolized by victory at Hysiae and intervention by Pheidon at Olympia. Tradition associated him with the establishment of weights and measures and (erroneously) coinage.

RB

Andrewes (1956); Jeffery (1976); Tomlinson (1972).

Pherae city in THESSALY, 8 miles from the port of Pagasae. The rise of Pherae in the 4th century BC was no doubt largely due to increasing export trade in Thessalian corn. When PHILIP II of Macedon deprived it of Pagasae, it ceased to be important.

See also ALEXANDER OF PHERAE; JASON. GLC

Westlake (1935).

Pherecrates (5th century BC), Greek comic poet. Pherecrates' work is known only from fragments, but he was producing his plays at Athens between 440 and 420 BC and so was an older contemporary and rival of ARISTOPHANES. Of 19 known titles, several are named after courtesans and appear to anticipate Middle and New COMEDY in making such characters central to the action. GS

Philaids Athenian noble family. The Philaidae were one of classical Athens's leading families: under the tyranny Philaids won chariot victories and led the colony to the Chersonese, but were also viewed with suspicion by Peisistratus and his sons. MILTIADES and CIMON achieved military glory and political eminence, while another branch of the family was prominent in Athenian politics and diplomacy in the late 5th century BC; thereafter the family is less noteworthy. RB

Davies (1971) no. 8429.

Philemon (c.363–264 BC), Greek comic poet. Philemon left his native Syracuse and became an Athenian citizen in 307/6 BC; he also spent some time at the Ptolemaic court in Egypt. He contributed 97 plays to the stage of New COMEDY (of which 60 titles are known) and won at least four first prizes, but he never matched the popularity of his rival and near-contemporary MENANDER. Only fragments and adaptations by PLAUTUS survive. GS

Webster (1970).

Philetaerus (c.343–263 BC), ruler of Pergamum. Philetaerus first served ANTIGONUS I MONOPHTHALMUS, but later LYSIMACHUS put him in charge of Pergamum and a large treasury. In 282 BC he deserted to SELEUCUS I NICATOR, the growing power in Asia Minor. He consolidated his position after Lysimachus and Seleucus died in 281, but ruled under nominal Seleucid suzerainty. He defended Pergamum against Galatian attacks (278–276), and was a generous benefactor to Greek cities and sanctuaries. His adopted nephew EUMENES I succeeded him. EER

Allen (1983); CAH VII.1; Hansen (1971); McShane (1964).

Philetas (c.330–c.280 BC), of Cos, Greek poet and scholar. Philetas was the first of the Alexandrian poet-scholars, though he may never have left Cos. Among his pupils were the future PTOLEMY II (born on Cos in 308) and ZENODOTUS. As a poet he wrote epigrams and elegies and invented the pastoral genre, to be perfected by THEOCRITUS. As a scholar he composed glossaries of rare words used by earlier poets. Surviving fragments are very scanty. GS

Pfeiffer (1968); Webster (1964).

Philicus (3rd century BC), Greek poet. Though born a Corfiote, Philicus was one of the Pleiad of tragedians writing at Alexandria in the time of Ptolemy II. He was also a priest of Dionysus. No fragments or even titles of his plays survive, but we do have part of his *Hymn to Demeter* in choriambic hexameters. Addressed to his learned friends, it is of no religious significance, being aimed, like the *Hymns* of CALLIMACHUS, at a literary élite. GS

Webster (1964).

Philinus (fl. *c.*250 BC), Greek physician. Philinus of Cos was originally a pupil of Herophilus but subsequently rejected his teachings. He is said to have founded the empirical school of MEDICINE. From the few surviving fragments we learn that he rejected any diagnosis based upon the pulse and wrote about difficult words in HIPPOCRATES. JL

Von Staden (1989).

Philip I 'the Arab' (*c.*AD 204–49), Roman emperor, AD 244–9. Julius Verus Philippus, an Arabian appointed praetorian prefect by GORDIAN III, very soon seized the throne (early 244). He concluded a peace with the Persians (244), won a great victory over the Carpi on the Danube (247), and celebrated the 1,000th birthday of Rome on 21 April 248. However, DECIUS, successful commander against a Gothic invasion, was proclaimed emperor, and both Philip and his son Philip (Augustus, 246–9) were killed. RJB

Grant (1985); Parker (1958).

Philip II king of Macedon, 359–336 BC. Philip inherited from his brother a state in considerable disarray and left to his son, ALEXANDER THE GREAT, the greatest power in the world. First he formed a new ARMY. With it he proceeded to a glittering series of successes, first and most important AMPHIPOLIS, key to eastward advance. In 352, promising to settle the Third SACRED WAR, he gained the support of THESSALY (militarily powerful, as Alexander realized) and proceeded to defeat PHOCIS at the Battle of the Crocus Field (352); after this he was invulnerable in the north. When OLYNTHUS received his dissident relatives, he captured and incorporated it in his kingdom (348). In 346 he set out to finish the Sacred War. Hoping to keep him out of Greece, Athens made the Peace of PHILOCRATES; but Philip tricked the Athenians, dealt with Phocis, and, thinking he had now settled Greece, went home, perhaps already intent on war with Persia. He sought to complete the subjugation of THRACE, but Athenian hostility, led by DEMOSTHENES, drew him back to fight the devastating battle of CHAERONEA (338). He founded the League of CORINTH and retired to Macedon to prepare for the invasion of Persia. In early 336 he sent PARMENION with 10,000 troops to establish a bridgehead. By mid-summer he was murdered and buried at AEGAE.

Demosthenes would have it that Philip succeeded by trickery and bribery of traitorous Greeks. He certainly was a skilful diplomat, but his success was due above all to his strategic genius and the army he created. GLC

Cawkwell (1978); Hammond and Griffith (1979); Hatzopoulos and Loukopoulos (1980).

Philip III Arrhidaeus   (c.358–317 BC), king of Macedon. Philip, the son of PHILIP II and a secondary wife, was half-brother to ALEXANDER THE GREAT. Apparently somehow mentally defective, he was married to his half-niece Adea-Eurydice. After Alexander's death in 323 BC, he was proclaimed king at Babylon by the army, and, later, joint king with Alexander's son ALEXANDER IV. He was successively manipulated by powerful rivals (PERDICCAS, ANTIPATER, POLYPERCHON, and CASSANDER) before he and Eurydice were murdered by Alexander's mother OLYMPIAS.

EER

CAH VII.1; Errington (1990); Green (1990); Hammond and Walbank (1988).

Philip V   (238–179 BC), king of Macedon. Philip, son of DEMETRIUS II, inherited the throne upon the death of his regent ANTIGONUS III DOSON (221 BC). An educational visit to ARATUS OF SICYON led to an alliance in which Philip and the Hellenic League fought the Social War against Aetolia (220–217). Recklessly encouraged by DEMETRIUS OF PHAROS, Philip fought Rome on sea and land in Illyria, and enraged Achaea by ravaging the Peloponnese. This First MACEDONIAN WAR (215–205) ended with terms favourable to Philip. He later meddled in Egypt with ANTIOCHUS III THE GREAT (203/2), and was defeated off Chios (201) by the fleets of RHODES and ATTALUS I SOTER of Pergamum who feared him and frightened the Roman Senate into declaring war again. The Second Macedonian War against Rome (200–197) saw campaigns in Thrace, Macedonia, and Thessaly, and ended with FLAMININUS' victory over Philip at CYNOSCEPHALAE. Faced with harsh terms, Philip cooperated with Rome and concentrated on rebuilding Macedonia. Roman suspicions were correctly aroused by his aggressions in the Balkans after 185. He had a pro-Roman son executed for treason (180), thereby securing the throne for PERSEUS. He died at Amphipolis in 179. Philip was a brilliant soldier handicapped by fiery temperament and inconsistent policies. His actions led to Roman expansion and her eventual domination in Greece.

EER

CAH VII.1, VIII; Errington (1990); Green (1990); Gruen (1984); Hammond and Walbank (1988); Walbank (1940).

Philippi   in Macedonia, battle in October 42 BC. The 19 legions of BRUTUS and CASSIUS LONGINUS held Philippi against the 28 legions of ANTONY and Octavian (see AUGUSTUS). In the first battle Brutus triumphed over Octavian, but Cassius was defeated by Antony and took his own life. In the second battle, three weeks later, Octavian was ill, but Antony beat Brutus who also committed suicide. The victory in this most catastrophic of Rome's civil conflicts meant the doom of the

Republic, but gave Antony a chance to build up a power base on his prestige from it.   DP

Clarke (1981).

Philistion (fl. 4th century BC), Greek physician. According to CALLIPPUS, Philistion of Locri was the teacher of EUDOXUS. He was given the epithet 'Sicilian' because of his medical views. He adopted from EMPEDOCLES the four-element theory, but linked each ELEMENT with a single opposite: air/hot, fire/cold, earth/moist, water/dry. Like Empedocles he believed that the purpose of respiration was to cool the innate heat. Diseases were classified under three types of causes: those due to an imbalance of the elements; those due to difficulty in respiration, which took place normally throughout the whole body; and those due to external causes. The influence of 'Sicilian' medicine, so marked in the *Timaeus*, may well be due to PLATO's direct acquaintance with Philistion.   JL

Longrigg (1993).

Philistus (*c*.430–356 BC), Syracusan politician and historian. Philistus was a devoted supporter of DIONYSIUS I whom he helped to power (406/5?) but by whom he was exiled (386) to Epirus. There he began his *History of Sicily* in 13 books. Recalled by DIONYSIUS II, he commanded the tyrant's navy. When it was defeated by DION's, Philistus committed suicide. His *History* is the ultimate source of much of the Sicilian material in DIODORUS SICULUS. Cicero termed him a 'petty Thucydides'.
                                                                                             GLC

Pearson (1987).

Philo (*c*.30 BC–AD 45), Jewish scholar. Known as 'Judaeus' (the Jew), Philo was born in Alexandria where he rose to prominence in the Jewish community. He led a delegation to Rome in AD 39–40 to protest against the persecution of the JEWS by Flaccus and against the requirement that they should practise the emperor cult (*see* GAIUS). As a philosopher Philo owed much to PLATO, ARISTOTLE, and the STOICS. His own writings are mostly concerned with the elucidation of the Pentateuch and, though these had a lasting influence on early Christian literature, they cannot be said to have contributed much to the wider world of Greek philosophy.   GS

Sandmel (1979).

Philochorus (*c*.345–*c*.262 BC), Atthidographer. Philochorus of Athens was a professional seer and interpreter of sacrifices. He was also a serious scholar and the author of at least 27 works concerned with history, religion, and literature. Undoubtedly his greatest work was the ATTHIS, a history of Athens in 17 books of which 11 were devoted to his own times.   GS

Jacoby (1949).

Philocrates (4th century BC), Athenian politician, responsible for the Peace of Philocrates (346 BC). In 348 Philocrates, aiming to save OLYNTHUS, proposed to make peace with PHILIP II of Macedon. Attacked in the courts, he was successfully defended by DEMOSTHENES. In 346, for fear of Philip coming south, he made a similar proposal. He, Demosthenes (then his right-hand man), and AESCHINES went on two embassies. On the second, Demosthenes became so suspicious of Philip that he turned against his fellow ambassadors. When Philip entered Phocis to settle the Third SACRED WAR, Philocrates much to Demosthenes' fury recognized that Athens had to accept and in a famous assembly mocked Demosthenes and proposed extending the peace. In 343, when feeling was turning against maintaining the peace, Philocrates was prosecuted and, anticipating condemnation, withdrew into exile.

GLC

Cawkwell (1978).

Philodemus (c.110–c.37 BC), of Gadara, Greek philosopher and poet. Educated in Athens, Philodemus moved to Rome c.75 BC where he became a client of L. Calpurnius PISO CAESONINUS. His poetry – mostly erotic epigrams of which about 25 survive in the Greek ANTHOLOGY – was admired by Cicero and imitated by HORACE and OVID. His prose writings, of which fragments are preserved in the papyri from Piso's villa at HERCULANEUM, ranged over a wide variety of philosophical and literary subjects.

See also NEOPTOLEMUS.   GS

Brink (1971); Webster (1964).

Philomelus (d. 354 BC), Phocian leader in the Third SACRED WAR. In reaction to a decree of the DELPHIC AMPHICTYONY passed under Theban influence and requiring Phocis to pay a large fine, Philomelus occupied Delphi and, raising a mercenary army, defeated the Boeotians and Locrians. When the Amphictyony formally declared war, he began using the temple treasures to pay his mercenaries. He was defeated by the Boeotians at Neon (354 BC) and committed suicide.   GLC

Buckler (1980).

Philopoemen (*c.*253–182 BC), Achaean statesman. Philopoemen of Megalopolis opposed the Spartan CLEOMENES III, fighting him at Sellasia in 222 BC. After a decade's absence in Crete, and the death of ARATUS OF SICYON, Philopoemen was elected hipparch and then general (several times) of the ACHAEAN LEAGUE. He subdued NABIS (202–200), joining Rome in his final defeat, and incorporated Sparta and Messene into the League in 192. He dominated League policy in the face of growing Roman involvement. Captured during the revolt of Messene in 183/2, he died perhaps through poison. POLYBIUS participated in his funeral. Although considered a League hero, Philopoemen was parochial and lacked true qualities of statesmanship.

See also DEMOPHANES AND ECDELUS.   EER

Errington (1969); Green (1990); Gruen (1984).

Philotas (*c.*360–330 BC), Macedonian general. Philotas, the son of PARMENION, was the distinguished commander of ALEXANDER THE GREAT's Companion Cavalry. He and Alexander gradually became estranged for obscure reasons. Accused of suppressing evidence of a conspiracy against Alexander, he was arrested for treason in 330 BC and executed by the army. It is unknown if he was really guilty of treason, or was himself the victim of a conspiracy by jealous rivals, perhaps including the king.   EER

Bosworth (1988a); Hammond (1989); Lane Fox (1973).

Phocaea   city in Asia Minor. Phocaea pioneered Greek exploration of the western Mediterranean, reaching as far as TARTESSUS and founding a number of colonies, notably MASSILIA. Besieged by the Persians after the fall of Lydia, many inhabitants fled to their Corsican colony Alalia; driven from there by Etruscans and Carthaginians, they settled in southern Italy and founded Elea (Velia). Phocaea itself survived, reduced in power and prosperity, but still a substantial city.   RB

Boardman (1980).

Phocion (402/1–318 BC) Athenian statesman and general. Phocion was 45 times elected general. He took part in the Euboean campaign (348 BC), the expulsion of Cleitarchus from Eretria (341), the defence of Byzantium (340/39), and a defensive action in his eightieth year (322). He cautioned the Athenians against precipitate action and played the part of the moderating intermediary with the Macedonians in 338, 335, and 322. Otherwise little is known of him until the last three years of his life. However, accepting ANTIPATER's oligarchical reforms, he seemed to be a Macedonian puppet. When on the death of Antipater

CASSANDER sent Nicanor to command the garrison in Piraeus, Phocion was held responsible for his actions. POLYPERCHON sided with the democracy and Phocion was tried and condemned to death by hemlock. His character, famously steadfast and upright, and his end made comparison with SOCRATES inevitable.   GLC

Phocis   region in central Greece. Lying between BOEOTIA and western LOCRIS, Phocis occupied the fertile valleys of Crisa and the Cephissus. A federal state had emerged by the 6th century BC but it lost control of DELPHI in the First SACRED WAR and was overrun by Thessaly. Under Athenian protection in 454, it regained Delphi but switched allegiance to Sparta after the battle of Coronea (447). Persuaded to join the BOEOTIAN CONFEDERACY early in the 4th century, Phocis broke with THEBES in making another bid for Delphi in the Third SACRED WAR. Despite early successes by PHILOMELUS and ONOMARCHUS, the war weakened both sides and paved the way for PHILIP II of Macedon.   GS

Larsen (1968).

Phoenicians   By the 8th century BC the Phoenicians had long been in possession of the Lebanese ports of TYRE and SIDON and were established as traders, craftsmen, and seafarers throughout the Mediterranean. They were literate, having invented their ALPHABET (the precursor of the Greek) by 1000 BC. They traded as far as Spain and into the Red Sea, establishing small trading posts but not large-scale settlements. The exception to this was the colony at CARTHAGE, founded c.750 BC, which was a major city from the start. They also circumnavigated Africa c.600. Despite attacks on their homeland by Babylon and Assyria and the interruption of the Persian Wars in which they provided the Persians with ships, the Phoenicians continued trading until the late 4th century BC. The incorporation of their cities into the empire of ALEXANDER THE GREAT effectively put an end to their separate identity.
   See also TRADE.   GS

Grainger (1991); Moscati (1968, 1988).

Phraates IV   (d. 2 BC), king of Parthia, c.38–2 BC. Phraates IV inflicted a major defeat on Mark ANTONY's invasion of PARTHIA (36 BC). Thereafter, weakened by internal rivalries (including the pretender TIRIDATES II), he maintained peace with AUGUSTUS. He returned the standards captured from Crassus and Antony in exchange for his son, held hostage by Augustus (20 BC), and later sent his four sons to be brought up in Rome (c.10 BC). He was murdered in 2 BC.   RJB

Scott-Kilvert and Carter (1987); Wells (1984).

Phratry   Greek kinship group. A phratry ('brotherhood') consisted of one or more *gene* ('clans', *see* GENOS) whose members were theoretically kinsmen and worshipped common cults, particularly of Zeus. Phratries are attested in the political organization of many states, often as tribal divisions. In early Athens they played a significant role as subdivisions of the tribes (the details are uncertain) and in particular controlled access to citizenship. Although CLEISTHENES gave this responsibility to the DEMES, most, perhaps all, Athenians continued to belong to a phratry and to register their sons, and phratry membership could be important evidence of citizen status.   RB

Bourriot (1976); Hedrick (1991); Jones (1987); Manville (1990); Roussel (1976).

Phrygia   territory in Asia Minor. Phrygia was a kingdom of great antiquity in central Asia Minor, noted for fortified citadels and carved rock façades. Midas and Gordius (whose wagon was yoked by the 'Gordian knot') were among its legendary kings. Conquered by LYDIA by the 6th century BC, it became subject to the ACHAEMENIDS. After ALEXANDER THE GREAT's death Phrygia was controlled by successive DIADOCHI. It eventually fell to the Seleucids, and then to PERGAMUM. It was included in the Roman province of Asia after 116 BC. Eastern Phrygia, where CELTS had settled by the 2nd century BC, was incorporated into the province of GALATIA in 25 BC.   EER

Akurgal (1978); Haspels (1971); Jones (1983).

Phrynichus   (6th–5th century BC), Greek tragedian. Phrynichus was one of the earliest of the Athenian tragedians, winning first prize probably for the first time *c*.510. He wrote on many of the same subjects as his near-contemporary AESCHYLUS, including recent history. He was fined 1,000 drachmas for putting on a play about the Persian capture of MILETUS in 494, and his *Phoenissae* (476?) may have inspired Aeschylus' *Persae*.   GS

Meier (1993); Pickard-Cambridge (1962).

Phylarchus   (fl. mid-3rd century BC), Greek historian. Phylarchus wrote in Athens a history in 28 books covering the period between the deaths of PYRRHUS and CLEOMENES III (272–220 BC). His support for the social programme of the Spartan Cleomenes prejudiced his views against ARATUS OF SICYON, the ACHAEAN LEAGUE, and Macedon. His history was used by PLUTARCH for his *Lives* of Cleomenes, AGIS IV, Aratus, and Pyrrhus. The pro-Achaean POLYBIUS hated him, but his criticisms of Phylarchus' 'sensational' history are probably valid.

See also HISTORIOGRAPHY, GREEK.   EER

CAH VII.1; Walbank (1933, 1972).

Phyle Greek political division. The phyle ('tribe') was normally the principal political division in a Greek state, although their number varied, and they might be based on either geography or ancestry; the commonest patterns are the three DORIAN tribes (Hylleis, Pamphyloi, Dymanes) and the four IONIAN tribes (Geleontes, Hopletes, Argadeis, Aigikoreis), which may be supplemented by one or more tribes for those of different racial origin. Tribes in turn might contain subdivisions like the Athenian TRITTYES; but other divisions, such as the Spartan *obai*, cut across the tribal pattern. At Athens CLEISTHENES superimposed a new tribal system on the four Ionian tribes (which continued to have a limited religious and judicial significance): the new tribes were built up from DEMES on a regional basis, but the trittyes system gave them a supra-regional character as well. The tribal system then formed the basis of political and military organization, and their loyalties were reinforced by new cults, and by tribal participation in festivals. The tribes were named after native heroes, the official order being Erechtheis, Aigeis, Pandionis, Leontis, Akamantis, Oineis, Kekropis, Hippothontis, Aiantis, Antiochis. RB

Jones (1987); Roussel (1976); Whitehead (1986).

Physics the study of the natural world in all its aspects. Physics originated in 6th-century BC Ionia when the Milesian natural philosophers (THALES, ANAXIMANDER, and ANAXIMENES), convinced that there was an orderliness inherent in the multiplicity of phenomena, attempted to explain the world about them by showing how it had come to be what it is. As the basis for their evolutionary cosmogonies they sought a unifying hypothesis to account for this order and deduced natural explanations of the various phenomena from it, making no attempt to invoke, as their poetical predecessors had done, the agency of supernatural powers. They themselves called their search *historia peri physeos*, 'inquiry into nature'.

Although this period of vigorous physical speculation was brought abruptly to an end by the rigid, deductive logic of PARMENIDES, reaction to the ELEATIC impasse gave birth to two highly influential physical theories. The first, and more important of the two, the four-element theory (*see* ELEMENTS), put forward initially by EMPEDOCLES, was subsequently adopted and adapted by three of the four main schools of philosophy, the ACADEMY, the PERIPATETICS, and the STOICS. The atomic theory (*see* ATOMISTS) was formulated in answer to the self-same problems as its rival by LEUCIPPUS and DEMOCRITUS and was adopted, also with some modification, by EPICURUS. Between them these two theories dominated natural science throughout antiquity and until the 16th century. It is noteworthy that Greek physics differs from its modern counterpart in several fundamental respects: very few quantitative laws were formulated in all its branches of terrestrial physics (one can only point to PYTHAGORAS' laws of musical harmony, ARCHIMEDES' law of leverage, and some of HERON's laws of geometrical optics); comparatively little progress was made in dynamics; and systematic experimentation was only rarely employed.

See also STRATON.   JL

Longrigg (1975); Sambursky (1956).

Pilate *see* PONTIUS PILATUS.

Pindar (538–418 BC), Greek lyric poet. Pindar was born at Cynoscephalae in Boeotia and, despite education in Athens and much travel in the course of his work, he remained a Boeotian till his death at Argos at the age of 80. His poetry represents the peak of the archaic tradition of Doric choral LYRIC and his poems are called odes because they were meant to be sung.

Four books of epinician (or victory) odes survive, written to celebrate the victors at the four principal athletic FESTIVALS – the Isthmian, Nemean, Olympic, and Pythian Games. They span the period 498–446 BC and were commissioned by patrons from all over the Greek world including HIERON I of Syracuse, THERON of Acragas, and ARCESILAUS IV of Cyrene. The odes contain all the usual ingredients of hymns: moralizing, mythology, and praise of the gods. Of his other works – hymns, paeans, dithyrambs, various songs, encomia, and dirges – surviving fragments suggest similar content.   GS

Bowra (1964); Bundy (1962); Fränkel (1975); Race (1986).

Piracy Piracy was endemic throughout the Mediterranean and a constant menace to both TRAVEL and TRADE among civilized states. Among the less civilized the distinctions between war and piracy and trade were sometimes blurred. In the 5th century BC Athens championed the freedom of the seas; but when she conferred it as a favour on her allies it was unmasked as Athenian thalassocracy. As a result the Aegean was relatively free from piracy in the classical period, but the downfall of Athens made way for a resurgence of activity.

In the west there was little attempt to police the seas. Rome in the early Republic took little interest in naval concerns and even the coasts of Italy were scarcely safe. After the PUNIC WARS the fleets were allowed to decline, the naval power of RHODES was broken, and the pirates had a field day. By the start of the 1st century BC, when there was a threat to the Roman corn supply, the Senate realized that action had to be taken. The principal resorts of the pirates were in CRETE and CILICIA but the absence of a standing fleet meant that Rome's first attempts to suppress them were easily circumvented. In 67 BC POMPEY waged a successful campaign to clear the seas but the CIVIL WARS provided opportunity for a further outbreak. The creation of permanent fleets by AUGUSTUS finally ensured the safety of the seas, but only until the 3rd century AD.

See also NAVY, GREEK; NAVY, ROMAN.   GS

Ormerod (1924).

Piraeus port of ATHENS. The city of Piraeus, 4 miles south-west of Athens, occupies a rocky promontory with three natural harbours. The first fortifications were begun by HIPPIAS c.510 BC, but it was THEMISTOCLES who as archon in 493/2 realized the full potential of the site as a base for the expanding Athenian NAVY. In the 450s the city was laid out by HIPPODAMUS of Miletus and the Long Walls were built connecting it with Athens (see WALLS, LONG). These had to be destroyed after the PELOPONNESIAN WAR in 404 but they were rebuilt by Conon in 393. Piraeus was the headquarters of the Macedonian garrison which controlled Athens in the 3rd century. SULLA destroyed the city in 86 BC but it continued as a naval base into the imperial period.

Kantharos ('goblet'), the largest harbour, lay to the west of the promontory. This was divided between naval and merchant shipping and was equipped with an emporium with quays and warehouses. To the east were the smaller harbours of Zea and Munychia which were used by the fleet and provided sheds for 278 warships. Most of the population were METICS pursuing business interests and TRADE.   GS

Garland (1987); Stillwell (1976).

Pisidia mountainous region of southern Asia Minor lying to the north of PAMPHYLIA. Its principal cities, Sagalussus, Selge, and Termessus, retained their independence until the arrival of ALEXANDER THE GREAT. Under the Romans it theoretically formed part of the province of CILICIA but in practice it was governed by client kings until incorporated into the province of GALATIA by Sulpicius QUIRINIUS.   GS

Piso, Gaius Calpurnius (d. AD 65), Roman conspirator. Gaius Calpurnius Piso, member of a distinguished Republican family, was executed in AD 65 for his part in a conspiracy against NERO that included eminent senators and knights and Faenius Rufus, praetorian prefect. Most wished to replace Nero with Piso, although some favoured the younger SENECA, or a return to republicanism. The plot was betrayed, and many were executed without public trial, or committed suicide, including Piso himself, Seneca, LUCAN, and Rufus.   RJB

Salmon (1968); Scullard (1982).

Piso, Gnaeus Calpurnius   (d. AD 19), Roman politician. Gnaeus Calpurnius Piso, TIBERIUS' colleague as consul in 7 BC, was appointed governor of Syria by him (AD 17), partly as a check on GERMANICUS. Piso's independent actions led Germanicus to order him to leave Syria, shortly after which Germanicus died (AD 19), suspecting Piso of poisoning him. Tried in Rome for murder, Piso refuted the charge, but was guilty of forcibly re-entering Syria after Germanicus' death, and consequently committed suicide.   RJB

Salmon (1968); Scullard (1982).

Piso Caesoninus   (fl. 58–43 BC), Roman noble. Lucius Calpurnius Piso Caesoninus, a cultivated aristocrat of unusual integrity, became consul in 58 BC and married his daughter Calpurnia to Caesar. He failed to protect CICERO from CLODIUS, and his governorship of Macedonia was later wildly traduced by Cicero. As censor in 50 he moderated the hostility of his colleague Appius CLAUDIUS PULCHER against Caesar. He was independent enough to seek concord both in 49 and in 43, when he was a member of an embassy to ANTONY from the Senate.

See also HERCULANEUM.   DP

Syme (1939).

Piso Frugi, Lucius Calpurnius   (fl. 150–120 BC), Roman statesman and historian. As tribune in 149 BC Piso set up the first standing QUAESTIO to deal with cases of RES REPETUNDAE. He was consul in 133 and censor in 120. A staunch conservative, he was an outspoken opponent of Gaius GRACCHUS. He also wrote, probably in old age, a history of Rome from its foundation in at least seven books, of which only a few fragments survive. The arrangement was annalistic and the tone apparently moralizing; Piso used the legends of early Rome to point moral lessons, and believed that his own age was one of declining standards. Cicero placed him alongside FABIUS PICTOR and CATO the Censor as one of the founding fathers of Roman HISTORIOGRAPHY.   TC

Badian (1966b); Broughton (1951); Rawson (1991).

Piso Frugi, Lucius Calpurnius   (d. AD 32), Roman general. Lucius Calpurnius Piso Frugi, consul in 15 BC, went on to be governor of Pamphylia in Asia Minor. From there he led a force against a general uprising in Thrace, led by one Vologaesus of the Bessian tribe. It required three years of hard campaigning to subdue the area (11–9 BC), after which Piso was rewarded with triumphal honours. He was city prefect from AD 12 until his death in 32.   RJB

Scott-Kilvert and Carter (1987); Scullard (1982).

Pittacus (fl. *c.*600–580 BC), tyrant of Mytilene. Pittacus, having won fame by killing an Athenian general in single combat, was elected *aisymnetes* (an extraordinary elective dictator) by the Mytileneans about 590 BC as a solution to chronic factional strife among the aristocrats, including ALCAEUS. After 10 years of reform he resigned and returned to private life, his wisdom causing him to be numbered among the SEVEN SAGES.   RB

Andrewes (1956); Page (1955).

Placidia (*c.*AD 388–450), daughter of THEODOSIUS I (Augusta, AD 421–50). Galla Placidia, daughter of Theodosius I and Galla, and half-sister of the emperor HONORIUS, was taken hostage by ALARIC after his sack of Rome (410), and married ATHAULF (414). Returned after Athaulf's death, she was then obliged to marry CONSTANTIUS III (417), to whom she bore a son, VALENTINIAN III. After Valentinian's accession (425), Placidia ruled in her son's name for some 12 years until forced onto the sidelines by AETIUS.   RJB

Bury (1958); Matthews (1990); Oost (1968).

Plancus (fl. 45–22 BC), Roman politician. Lucius Munatius Plancus, of senatorial family from Tibur, served under CAESAR in the GALLIC and CIVIL WARS and was proconsul of Gallia Comata 44–43 BC. His polished letters to Cicero protest his Republicanism, but late in 43 he deserted BRUTUS ALBINUS and joined ANTONY and LEPIDUS, even proscribing his own brother and becoming consul with Lepidus in 42. He eventually left Antony for Octavian just before ACTIUM. He proposed the name AUGUSTUS for Octavian in 27, and was censor in 22. 'His treacheries carried him to a peaceful old age' (Syme).   DP

Carter (1970); Syme (1939).

Plataea in southern Boeotia, site of a battle in 479 BC which was the decisive engagement of the PERSIAN WARS. MARDONIUS, the Persian commander, with some difficulty drew the Greek army under PAUSANIAS into Boeotia where it took up a defensive position. The Persian mounted archers severely harassed the Greeks and cut off their supplies and water. The Greeks sought a less uncomfortable position. Mardonius attacked and the Spartans decisively fought back and routed the enemy.   GLC

Burn (1984); CAH IV.

Plato (5th–4th century BC), Greek comic poet. Plato was active at Athens from about 420 to 390, winning his first victory at the City DIONYSIA *c.*410. He seems to have been highly politicized since several of his plays were named after prominent contemporary politicians, *Hellas* was concerned with political issues in general, and *Envoys* treated an embassy to Persia.   GS

Plato (*c*.429–347 BC), Greek philosopher. Plato was born into a wealthy Athenian family. He studied initially under the Heraclitean Cratylus and is said to have entered SOCRATES' circle at an early age. He had early political ambitions, but abandoned them, alienated both by the excesses of the THIRTY TYRANTS and by the execution of Socrates (399) during the restored democracy. He withdrew from Athens and spent the next 12 years in travel. He visited Italy and Sicily in 387 where he met DIONYSIUS I, tyrant of Syracuse, and developed lifelong friendships with DION and Archytas. On his return to Athens (388) he established the ACADEMY, which he presided over for the remaining 40 years of his life. His primary object in founding the Academy was the training of potential statesmen. In 387 he travelled again to Syracuse in the hope of converting the young DIONYSIUS II to true philosophical principles of government. The attempt was a failure. Plato made a third visit in 362 when Dionysius himself promised to follow his suggestions; but he did not keep his word and Plato was kept a prisoner until the intercession of Archytas secured his release.

While Plato's philosophy reveals the influence of HERACLITUS, PARMENIDES, EMPEDOCLES, and the Pythagoreans, that of Socrates, most especially in his contribution to Plato's developed Theory of Forms and his ethical theory, is paramount. Plato provides no systematic treatise expounding his views. They have to be interpreted from his dialogues – a series of conversation-pieces of great literary and dramatic merit. We have some 30 dialogues, of which the great majority are genuine. The dialogue form presents certain difficulties. Controversy has arisen over their dates of composition. Again, in all the dialogues, except a few of the later, Socrates appears as the main interlocutor. Plato himself never appears by name. This has aroused vigorous debate as to the extent to which positive views can be ascribed to the historical Socrates. (Most scholars nowadays regard any positive doctrines to be Plato's own.) A more difficult question, however, is how the dialogues may be used to reconstruct his fundamental views, which are frequently implied rather than explicitly stated. Furthermore, since Plato himself does not appear ever to have arrived at a complete and final system, there is always an element of uncertainty in coming to conclusions about his settled views and differences of opinion inevitably arise.

See also AFTERLIFE; ARISTOTLE; ASTRONOMY; PHILISTION.   JL

Crombie (1962–3); Field (1930); Guthrie, vols. 4 and 5 (1975, 1978); Raven (1965).

Plautianus (d. AD 205), Roman politician. Gaius Fulvius Plautianus, a native of Africa, became praetorian prefect (197) under Septimius SEVERUS, who leaned heavily upon him, allowing him almost autocratic power. The marriage of Plautianus' daughter Plautilla to Caracalla (AURELIUS ANTONINUS) linked Plautianus to the imperial family (202), and he was consul (203) while still praetorian prefect. However, he incurred the enmity both of the empress JULIA DOMNA, and of Caracalla, whose allegations brought about his downfall and death.   RJB

Grant (1979); Parker (1958).

Plautius (d. after AD 57), Roman general. Aulus Plautius Silvanus commanded the Roman invasion of BRITAIN (AD 43), and became the province's first governor (43–7). With an army of four legions, plus auxiliaries, Cunobelinus' capital Camulodunum (Colchester) was quickly taken, and by the end of Plautius' governorship Rome controlled Britain up to, and beyond, the Fosse Way (roughly the Severn–Wash line), having established friendly relations with the Regni and the Iceni, and with the Brigantes further north.   RJB

Salway (1981); Scullard (1979).

Plautius Silvanus Aelianus (d. after AD 74), Roman general. Tiberius Plautius Silvanus Aelianus was a legionary legate during the conquest of Britain (AD 43), and consul in 45. As governor of Moesia under Nero, he quelled a Sarmatian revolt, raised a siege of Chersonesus (near Sebastopol) by the Scythians, settled 100,000 tribesmen south of the Danube, and sent relieving grain supplies to Rome. He was rewarded by Vespasian with triumphal ornaments and a second consulate (74), and the post of Prefect of the City.   RJB

CAH XI; ILS 986.

Plautus (c.254–184 BC), Latin comic poet. Titus Maccius Plautus was, according to tradition, born at Sarsina in Umbria; moving to Rome, he may have become a stage-hand and an actor before turning to writing comedy, but details of his life are uncertain. He was prolific and popular: his writing brought him the accolade of Roman citizenship, and in the 1st century BC he was credited with the authorship of 130 plays. VARRO identified 21 as authentic (the so-called *fabulae Varronianae*) and 21 do indeed survive, presumably the same. Two of them can be dated: *Stichus* (200 BC) and *Pseudolus* (191). Plautus certainly modelled his plays on Greek originals (especially those of MENANDER, PHILEMON, and DIPHILUS), but he also adapted them to appeal to Roman taste, he introduced a number of original Roman elements, and he disregarded Greek stage conventions.

See also COMEDY, ROMAN. GS

Beare (1964); Duckworth (1952); Hunter (1985); Segal (1987).

Plebiscitum Roman plebiscite. A plebiscite was a decision of the CONCILIUM Plebis, and at first was binding only on the PLEBS. By the *lex Hortensia* (287 BC) plebiscites gained universal validity, and became equivalent to laws (*leges*). This is also said to have been granted in 449 and 339 BC (*see* VALERIUS POTITUS; PUBLILIUS PHILO). Since important early laws (e.g. the Licinio-Sextian laws of 367 BC, *see* STOLO) were in fact plebiscites, there must be truth in this tradition; perhaps in 449 the validity of plebiscites was made conditional on further procedures, such as the PATRUM AUCTORITAS or a vote of the COMITIA, and these restrictions were partially (339) and then completely (287) removed.

See also LAW, ROMAN. TC

Scullard (1980).

Plebs Roman citizen body. In normal parlance the term *plebs* signified 'the masses', or the lower orders, of Roman society. On the other hand, a plebeian could be technically defined as any Roman citizen who was not a PATRICIAN. This situation obtained after 367 BC, but in earlier times it may not have been true that all non-patricians were plebeians. The crucial moment in the history of the *plebs* was the first SECESSIO (494 BC) when a group of poor and indebted citizens withdrew from the city and formed their own organization, with its own cults (*see* CERES), officials (AEDILES; TRIBUNUS PLEBIS), and assembly (CONCILIUM), which passed binding resolutions (PLEBISCITA). It was through this remarkable organization that the poor citizens of Rome fought for their rights: to obtain relief from debt (*see* NEXUM), fair distribution of AGER PUBLICUS, codification of the law (*see* TWELVE TABLES), and admission to the consulship and major priesthoods (*see* Q. OGULNIUS; STOLO).

TC

Brunt (1971b); CAH VII.2; Raaflaub (1986); Scullard (1980).

Pliny the Elder (AD 23/4–79), Latin scholar and writer. Gaius Plinius Secundus was born at Comum to an equestrian family. He served in the army for 12 years, mostly in Germany under his patron POMPONIUS SECUNDUS, whose biography he wrote. Returning to Italy *c*.AD 58, he withdrew from politics to his studies for the duration of Nero's reign. Under Vespasian he became procurator in Gaul, Africa, and Spain, and imperial counsellor, and commander of the fleet at Misenum. He died at Stabiae in the eruption of Vesuvius. According to his nephew PLINY THE YOUNGER, he wrote extensively on many subjects including warfare, oratory, grammar, and contemporary history (*see* AUFIDIUS BASSUS). His only surviving work is the *Natural History* (37 books), dedicated to Titus in 77. A massive, wide-ranging, and not always reliable compendium, it contains interesting digressions and provides valuable evidence of the current state of scientific knowledge.   GS

Healy (1991).

Pliny the Younger (*c.*AD 61–112), Latin writer. Gaius Plinius Caecilius Secundus was born at Comum and after his father's death was brought up by his uncle PLINY THE ELDER who adopted him. At Rome he studied rhetoric under QUINTILIAN and embarked on a long and successful public career, becoming suffect consul in AD 100 and in 110 governor of Bithynia, where he probably died. He was a friend of TACITUS, whose career followed a similar pattern. Apart from the PANEGYRIC for his consulship, his chief surviving work, and a valuable source of information on Roman high society in general and his own career in particular, is the *Letters*. In nine books (plus a tenth containing official correspondence with TRAJAN) and dating from *c.*97 to 108, they were published before his departure for Bithynia. Obviously written for publication, they represent the development of a new literary form (*see* EPISTOLOGRAPHY, LATIN), comparable with the occasional verses of MARTIAL and STATIUS.   GS

Dorey (1975); Hutchinson (1993); Sherwin-White (1966).

Plotina (d. AD 122), wife of Trajan. Pompeia Plotina was already married to TRAJAN on his accession, and remained unswervingly loyal to him. It was partly through Plotina's favour that HADRIAN eventually succeeded Trajan: she chose a wife for Hadrian, Vibia SABINA, Trajan's grand-niece (AD 100), and declared, perhaps falsely, that Trajan on his death-bed adopted Hadrian (117). Plotina was named Augusta (*c.*113), and after her death Hadrian erected a basilica in her honour at Nemausus (Nîmes).   RJB

Birley (1976); Salmon (1968).

Plotinus (AD 205–269/70), Greek Neoplatonist philosopher. Plotinus, the greatest of the NEOPLATONIST philosophers, was born at Lycopolis in Egypt. He turned to philosophy at the age of 27 and worked for 11 years under Ammonius Sacas. After joining the abortive expedition of GORDIAN III against the Persians in the hope of learning about eastern thought, he settled at Rome in 244 as a teacher of philosophy and became the leader of an influential circle there. He wrote nothing until he was 50 and then produced a series of philosophical essays intended for circulation among his pupils. These were subsequently collected by his disciple PORPHYRY and arranged by him roughly according to subject in six *Enneads* or groups of nine. Apart from the works of ARISTOTLE, the *Enneads* provide the most complete body of philosophical teaching preserved from antiquity. JL

Armstrong (1967); Wallis (1972).

Plutarch (*c.*AD 50–120), Greek prose writer. Plutarch was born and lived most of his life at Chaeronea near Thebes, but he visited Asia, Egypt, and Italy and had powerful friends at Rome. For the last 30 years of his life he was a priest at DELPHI and contributed much to the revival of the shrine. He is known to have written over 200 books of which 78 miscellaneous works (or *Moralia)* and 50 biographies survive.

The biographies are of the greatest interest and comprise 23 pairs of 'parallel lives' (a Greek compared with a Roman) and four single works. Plutarch's object was to glorify the subject and entertain the reader, not to write history. The *Lives* nevertheless contain much information that is of historical value and they were a prime source for knowledge of the ancient world in the medieval and early modern periods (*see* BIOGRAPHY, GREEK).

The *Moralia* comprise treatises on a wide variety of philosophical, rhetorical, and antiquarian subjects as well as dialogues which range over philosophical and religious issues. The aim of his later writings seems to have been to reconcile Platonist monotheism with the pagan polytheism of the established religion in which he believed devoutly. GS

C. P. Jones (1971); Russell (1973).

Polemarch *see* ARCHON.

Police, Roman Until the time of Augustus there was no formal police force in Rome, although the *triumviri capitales* or *nocturni* were responsible for quelling night-time disturbances. AUGUSTUS created three urban cohorts (*cohortes urbanae)*, later much expanded, whose task was to keep order in Rome. They were commanded by a Prefect of the City (PRAEFECTUS URBI), who also exercised judicial powers. The VIGILES (watch and fire brigade) provided an extra police force for Rome. Similar urban cohorts operated in Lyon (Lugdunum) and Carthage, but elsewhere policing was the responsibility of the governor of the province, who would use troops to enforce order.

See also VIGINTISEXVIRI.   RJB

Grant (1979); Salmon (1968).

Polis   Greek city-state. The polis was the dominant form of social and political organization in classical Greece, though certain areas such as Achaea and Aetolia were organized as *ethnoi* ('peoples'), looser federal groupings of settlements within a region. The Greek world contained many hundreds of such states, typically with a citizen population under a thousand and a correspondingly small territory; hence, large, well-documented cities such as Athens and Corinth are untypical.

A polis consisted of an urban centre (*asty*) and its surrounding territory (*chora*), which formed a political, economic, and social unity. The *chora* was normally the economic base of the state, while the *asty* provided the political centre; the formation of a polis involved a degree of centralization, and some were the product of the SYNOECISM of scattered communities. The public space of the *asty* with its AGORA and monumental buildings also formed a social focus.

Politically, the polis was equivalent to the totality of its citizens; even in a democracy they would be a minority of the population, which besides women and children might include men of subordinate status such as PERIOIKOI, METICS, SERFS, and slaves. Citizens also formed smaller groups based on locality (*see* DEME), kinship and cult (*see* PHRATRY), and political organization (*see* PHYLE). The citizens exercised power through the assembly, the council, and the courts and by electing magistrates. Within each polis inhabitants were bound together by shared religious practices; the city provided the principal focus for these, though rural cults were often important too, particularly in border regions. Law was another important unifying factor: freedom to manage its own affairs by its own laws (*autonomia*) was the ideal of every polis, defended, like its territory, by the citizen army of HOPLITES.

See also CITIZENSHIP, GREEK; GOVERNMENT; JUDICIAL PROCEDURE, GREEK.

                                                                          RB

Ehrenberg (1969); Murray and Price (1990); Osborne (1987); Rich and Wallace-Hadrill (1991); Snodgrass (1977); Starr (1986).

Pollio   (76 BC–AD 5), Roman politician and historian. Gaius Asinius Pollio, adherent of CAESAR and later of ANTONY, saved VIRGIL'S land from confiscation when serving as Antony's legate in Cisalpine Gaul in 41 BC. Consul in 40, he reconciled Antony and Octavian at the Treaty of Brundisium. After a triumph over the Parthini of Illyria in 39 and building Rome's first public LIBRARY from the booty, he switched from politics to literature. He was a friend of Virgil and HORACE, a sharp critic of other writers, but also a prolific writer himself, most famous for his history of the Civil War from 60 BC to PHILIPPI. It was praised by Horace, used by PLUTARCH and APPIAN, but has not survived.   DP

Bosworth (1972); Syme (1939).

Pollux (2nd century AD), Greek scholar and rhetorician. Julius Polydeuces (Pollux) came from Naucratis but was appointed to the chair of rhetoric at Athens some time after AD 178. His *Onomasticum*, which survives in a medieval abridgement, is a textbook of RHETORIC, intended as a guide to would-be writers of classical Attic prose. It contains a great deal of antiquarian information, e.g. on the Athenian constitution and theatrical production.   GS

Polybius (*c*.200–118 BC), Greek historian of Rome. Polybius was son of Lycortas, a wealthy aristocrat who was prominent in the politics of the ACHAEAN LEAGUE. In 180 BC he was sent as an envoy from Achaea to Egypt, and in 170/69 was Hipparch of the Achaean League. After PYDNA (168) he was one of a group of 1,000 Achaean aristocrats who were deported to Italy. Polybius was able to stay in Rome where he became a friend of SCIPIO AEMILIANUS, in whose company he visited Spain and Africa (witnessing the destruction of CARTHAGE in 146). Then he helped the Romans organize the province of Macedonia after the sack of Corinth. Later he visited Sardes and Alexandria and may have been present at Numantia when it fell to Aemilianus in 133.

Polybius wrote a panegyric on PHILOPOEMEN (whom he helped bury in 182), a work on tactics, a history of the war at Numantia, and a treatise on the equatorial region, all of which are lost. He also wrote a history in Greek, in 40 books, covering the period 264–146 BC, showing the reasons for Rome's rise to power. Books 1–5 survive intact, together with substantial fragments of the rest. The earlier parts of the history, dealing with events down to 168, were published *c*.150.

Polybius was a careful researcher, using numerous historians, private letters, public records from Achaea and Rome, and inscriptions. Most importantly, he also interviewed eyewitnesses during his time at Rome. Polybius saw history as having two purposes, to train the statesman and to teach men how to face disaster. Thus his work focuses mainly on political and military affairs and includes, in book 6, detailed discussion of the Roman army and constitution. The latter account, which presents Rome as a balanced mixture of monarchy (represented by the consuls), aristocracy (the Senate), and democracy (the *Comitia*), has been enormously influential down to the present day.

See also HISTORIOGRAPHY, GREEK.   HE

Momigliano (1975a); Walbank (1972).

Polycarp, St (*c.*AD 69–155), bishop of Smyrna. Little is known of Polycarp's long life but he was a staunch defender of orthodox Christianity and a leading figure in 2nd-century Asia Minor. Shortly after a visit to Rome he was arrested at a pagan festival and, refusing to renounce his faith, was burnt to death at the age of 86. His *Epistle to the Philippians* survives. GS

Frend (1965).

Polycleitus (fl. 450–420 BC), Greek sculptor. Polycleitus came from Argos and was, with MYRON, a pupil of the Argive sculptor Ageladas. He worked mostly in bronze, producing statues of athletes at OLYMPIA and elsewhere. Roman copies survive of his Doryphorus (spear carrier) and Diadumenus (youth binding a fillet round his head), also of an Amazon which may be his. His most celebrated work was a chryselephantine statute of Hera for the Argive Heraeum which was compared favourably by some with PHEIDIAS' statue of Olympian Zeus. The only surviving visual reference to it is on the coinage of Argos. He wrote a treatise, now lost, on the harmony of ideal human proportions.

See also SCULPTURE, GREEK. GS

Richter (1970b).

Polycles (fl. 160–120 BC), Greek sculptor. Polycles of Athens came from a long line of sculptors whose classicizing style found favour with Roman patrons in the 2nd century BC. He produced a Hercules for the temple of Ops in Rome and worked with his brother Dionysius on the cult statues for the temples of Jupiter and Juno in the Porticus Metelli. METELLUS MACEDONICUS was clearly interested in the work of living Greek artists as well as old masters.

See also SCULPTURE, GREEK. GS

Pollitt (1986).

Polycrates tyrant of Samos, *c.*546–522 BC. Polycrates presided over the peak of Samian power and prosperity; his reign is associated with great public works and the patronage of poets. The tyranny of his father Aiaces must have lapsed, since Polycrates took power by a coup, apparently against little opposition. He extended Samian sea power and influence in the Aegean, but in the 520s was obliged by Persian control of the sea to abandon his alliance with the pharaoh Amasis and support Cambyses' invasion of Egypt. He successfully resisted an assault by aristocratic dissidents backed by Sparta, but was lured to his death by Oroites, satrap of Sardes. RB

Mitchell (1975); Shipley (1987).

Polygnotus (fl. 480–450 BC), Greek painter. A native of Thasos, Polygnotus worked mostly in Athens, where he painted in the STOA Poikile (with MICON) and the THESEUM, and in DELPHI, where his Iliupersis (sack of Troy) and Nekuia (Underworld) were admired and described by PAUSANIAS in the 2nd century AD. All his works are now lost, but his success with spatial depth and emotional expression can be inferred from literary description and from contemporary vase PAINTING. ARISTOTLE described him as a skilful delineator of character. THEOPHRASTUS thought him primitive but still the first great painter.

See also PROPYLAEA.   GS

Robertson (1975).

Polyperchon (*c*.380–*c*.303 BC), Macedonian general. Polyperchon, a Macedonian on ALEXANDER THE GREAT's expedition, commanded infantry units after 333 BC. Returning to Europe with CRATERUS in 324, he so impressed ANTIPATER with his leadership during the LAMIAN WAR that he appointed Polyperchon his successor as general in Europe after 319. Although supported by EUMENES OF CARDIA and OLYMPIAS, Polyperchon was opposed by the DIADOCHI led by Antipater's son CASSANDER. His position in Greece deteriorated progressively. Polyperchon's ultimate fate is unknown.   EER

CAH VII.1; Green (1990); Hammond and Walbank (1988).

Pomerium the religious boundary of a city, beyond which the city *auspices* could not be taken. It was marked out by the founder using a plough, in accordance with an ancient and supposedly Etruscan ritual. The course of the *pomerium* was distinct from any walled circuit and from the actual limits of occupation. Proconsular authority ceased once it was crossed. The *pomerium* was marked, in Rome at least, by a series of boundary stones. In Rome we are uncertain of its precise original course, or of the various alterations made by Sulla, Caesar, Augustus, Claudius, Vespasian, and other emperors who are said to have extended it.   HE

Rykwert (1976).

Pompeianus Claudius *see* CLAUDIUS POMPEIANUS.

Pompeii city in CAMPANIA. Originally an Etruscan town, Pompeii was occupied by SAMNITES in the 5th century BC and remained Oscan-speaking until after the SOCIAL WAR when SULLA planted a colony of veterans there in 80 BC. It was then rapidly romanized and became a prosperous centre for industry and trade. Together with its neighbour

HERCULANEUM, it was engulfed by an eruption of Mt VESUVIUS in AD 79 and remained buried under a thick layer of volcanic ash and pumice. Excavations (begun in the 18th century) have revealed the remains of an astonishingly well-preserved town which have provided invaluable evidence of provincial urban life in the 1st century AD. Much of this evidence is epigraphic: trade marks and ephemeral graffiti as well as monumental inscriptions. The layout of the town follows the Greek model (see TOWN PLANNING). Public buildings are represented by an AMPHITHEATRE, THEATRE, FORUM, BASILICA, and BATHS. But even more important are the substantial remains of humbler buildings: HOUSES, shops, and workshops. Many houses were decorated with wall paintings which have been categorized into four distinct 'styles' (see PAINTING, ROMAN).

See also GARDENS. GS

Jongman (1988); Richardson (1988); Ward-Perkins and Claridge (1976).

Pompeius, Sextus (c.67–35 BC), younger son of POMPEY. Sextus Pompeius inherited his father's cause and spent his brief career fighting for the Republicans. After escapes from THAPSUS and MUNDA, he was appointed commander of the fleet by the Senate in 43 BC. Although proscribed by the Second TRIUMVIRATE, he occupied Sicily to make it a refuge for the proscribed and a base for blockading Italy, and the triumvirs were forced to include him in the Treaty of Misenum in 39. Octavian soon broke the agreement, but his attacks on Sextus were not successful until the battle of Naulochus in 36. Sextus fled to the east, but was killed by an officer of Antony. DP

Carter (1970); Hadas (1930); Syme (1939).

Pompeius Strabo (d. 87 BC), Roman general. Gnaeus Pompeius Strabo, POMPEY's father, extinguished the SOCIAL WAR in the north by his capture of Asculum as consul in 89 BC. His army had largely been recruited in Picenum where he was a locally dominant figure. He extended his influence during his consulship with a law to spread Roman citizenship in CISALPINE GAUL. For two more years he kept his army together, and marched on Rome during the civil war between CINNA and the Senate, but without making his loyalties clear. He died in mysterious circumstances in 87. DP

Badian (1964); Seager (1979).

Pompey (106–48 BC), Roman military leader. Gnaeus Pompeius Magnus, son of Gnaeus POMPEIUS STRABO, helped SULLA in 83 BC with three legions raised from his Picenum estates. After exterminating Sulla's enemies in Sicily and Africa, he used the threat of his legions to extort a triumph from Sulla. His unorthodox public career continued when the Senate gave him a special command against LEPIDUS. Then at the head of a victorious army he persuaded the Senate to send him as proconsul against SERTORIUS. He returned from Spain in 71 to another triumph and to the consulship of 70, thus flouting the rules of the CURSUS HONORUM, since he was under age, had held no previous magistracy, and was not even a member of the Senate. As consul with CRASSUS he modified Sulla's constitution, especially by restoring full rights to the tribunes.

Pompey's next opportunity came with special commands against the pirates in 67 and against MITHRIDATES VI in 66 from tribunician legislation. After spectacular military successes, which caused popular opinion to compare him to Alexander, Pompey settled the eastern provinces and doubled the treasury's revenues. His immense fame, wealth, and provincial clientele worried the *nobiles*; and, although on his return to Italy in 62 he sought cooperation with them, their opposition to his demands drove him into a coalition with CAESAR and Crassus (the First TRIUMVIRATE), for the sake of which he married Caesar's daughter, Julia. Pompey's fame was dimmed by Caesar's early victories in Gaul, and although the renewal of the triumvirate gave him another consulship in 55, the deaths of Julia and Crassus sharpened his rivalry with Caesar. The *nobiles* increasingly realized that Pompey was their best hope against the threat of Caesar. They allowed him to be sole consul in 52, and by the outbreak of CIVIL WAR in 49 had appointed him commander of the government forces against Caesar. After his defeat at PHARSALUS, he fled to Egypt where he was murdered as he landed.   DP

Greenhalgh (1980, 1981); Leach (1978); Seager (1979); Syme (1939).

Pomponius (2nd century AD), Roman jurist. Sextus Pomponius seems not to have pursued a public career but to have devoted himself to writing and teaching. He was one of the most prolific legal writers, the author of more than 300 books, half of them commissioned by HADRIAN as a commentary on the praetor's edict (*see* EDICTUM). Among several other publications, his history of Roman legal science is represented by a long extract in the *Digest*.   GS

Pomponius Mela *see* MELA, POMPONIUS.

Pomponius Secundus (d. *c*.AD 51–70), Roman soldier and poet. Publius Sabinus Pomponius Secundus, accused of MAIESTAS (treason) under Tiberius, survived seven years of imprisonment, and went on to hold the consulate (*cos. suff.* AD 44), three years after his brother Quintus (d. 42). Publius was legate of Upper Germany in 50, successfully suppressing an incursion of the CHATTI. His verses were mocked by the people under Claudius, but won praise from his friend and biographer, the elder PLINY. RJB

CAH X; Healy (1991).

Pontifex Roman priest. A *pontifex* was a member of the college of pontiffs, one of the most important Roman priestly colleges. At first exclusively patrician, the college was opened to plebeians in 300 BC by the law of Q. OGULNIUS, and the number of pontiffs increased to nine (later Sulla increased it to 15, and Caesar to 16). The pontiffs, who held office for life, were originally coopted, but after 104 were elected by a special meeting of the COMITIA *tributa* consisting of 17 tribes selected by lot. The pontifical college advised the SENATE and MAGISTRATES on all matters of state cult, and supervised the calendar of FESTIVALS. The head of the college, the Pontifex Maximus, was the most important figure in the Roman priestly hierarchy, and exercised a form of disciplinary jurisdiction over the other priests. He also kept an annual record of public business, the ANNALES *Maximi*. The post was held *ex officio* by the emperors until AD 375; since then the title has been borne by the pope. TC

Ogilvie (1969); Scullard (1981).

Pontius Pilatus (d. after AD 36), governor of Judaea. Pontius Pilatus held the post of prefect of Judaea (AD 26–36), an equestrian position combining the functions of governor and procurator. Infamous for yielding to the Jews in ordering the crucifixion of Jesus Christ (*c.*29–33), he committed a series of errors, culminating in the massacre of a group of Samaritans on Mt Gerizim, which prompted L. VITELLIUS to depose him and send him to Rome to stand trial. RJB

Scullard (1982); Williamson (1981).

Pontus territory in northern Asia Minor. Pontus lay on the southern shore of the Black Sea, east of BITHYNIA and PAPHLAGONIA and north of GALATIA and CAPPADOCIA. The fertile coastal region was good for agriculture, the mountains rich in mineral resources. Greek cities along the coast coexisted with a native population organized by tribes. Mithridates I was proclaimed king in 281 BC, but during the 3rd century Pontus remained a Seleucid ally (Mithridates II married SELEUCUS II's sister *c.*245). The kings strove to expand their territory (for example, the invasions of PHARNACES I in the 2nd century), and Pontus reached its greatest extent under MITHRIDATES VI, whose aggressive policies made him an arch-enemy of Rome and caused three MITHRIDATIC WARS (88–63 BC). POMPEY created the Roman province of Bithynia and Pontus in 64 BC, though much of Pontus remained in the hands of local dynasts until annexed with Galatia in AD 64.   EER

CAH VII.1, VIII; Eddy (1961); Gruen (1984); Jones (1983); Magie (1975); Sherwin-White (1984); Sullivan (1990).

Populares Roman political group. *Populares* were politicians who worked through, and nominally on behalf of, the people. They were not an organized party. *Populares* were typically NOBILES who used the office of *tribunus plebis* to pass measures in the *Concilium plebis* (*see* CONCILIA) to benefit the people and challenge the OPTIMATES in the SENATE. Their careers frequently ended in violence, the SENATUS CONSULTUM *Ultimum*, and death.

See also CATILINE; CINNA; CLODIUS; Gaius GRACCHUS; Tiberius GRACCHUS; MARIUS; SATURNINUS.   HS

Brunt (1988); Seager (1972a); Taylor (1949); Wirszubski (1950).

Population The nature of the evidence is such that estimates of the population of Greek city-states can only be very rough approximations. Most records relate to taxation and other civic duties which involved only the adult male citizen class. As usual Athens provides the most complete picture, but even there it is based on inadequate and unreliable information. Every 18-year-old male was registered in his DEME and deme registers were the basic qualification for attendance of the ECCLESIA. Lists were kept of those liable for military service, METICS were listed in their deme, and there may have been a poll tax on slaves. Some of this information survives and is the basis for the following figures which are rough estimates for the whole of Attica:

Date	Hoplites	Citizens	Metics	Slaves	Total
480	15,000	140,000	?	?	?
431	25,000	172,000	28,000	110,000	310,000
425	16,500	116,000	21,000	80,000	217,000
400	11,000	90,000	?	?	?
323	14,500	112,000	42,000	106,000	260,000

For some other states in the classical period only HOPLITE numbers are available: Sparta 3,000; Arcadia 6,000; Boeotia 7,000. Argos had as many citizens as Athens in 400 but fewer metics and slaves. Corinth was less than half the size of Athens. In the west Syracuse was the equal of Athens. The total population of the Greek cities of Sicily may have been 750,000.

At Rome all adult male citizens were required to register in the CENSUS. Figures surviving from the Republican period suggest the following approximations: 5th century BC 120,000; 4th century 160,000; mid-3rd century 300,000. Since returns could only be made in Rome, as the area of Roman territory grew, the scope for error increased. The figure for 125 BC of 394,736 is probably based on the registration of landholdings included in the legislation of Ti. GRACCHUS. After the extension of the CITIZENSHIP to all Italy south of the Po the figure rose to 900,000 in 70 BC. In 28 BC, when Augustus held the census with Agrippa, a more efficient procedure yielded a figure of 4,063,000, though this will have included the citizens of Cisalpine Gaul and others outside Italy. The last year for which census figures survive (AD 47) yielded about 6 million according to Tacitus.

Under the Empire figures for several provincial cities are known, though these would have included not just the urban area but also the rural environs. The free population of Alexandria, according to Diodorus, exceeded 300,000. Antioch and Carthage were similar in size and Ephesus perhaps numbered 250,000. Rome itself probably contained about 1 million free inhabitants. There are no figures for slaves, but at Pergamum Galen says there were as many slaves as there were male citizens. As for the total population of the empire, any figure is bound to be speculative, but an estimate of 54 million in AD 14 is not unreasonable. GS

Gomme (1933); Jones (1948).

Porphyry (c.AD 232–305), Greek Neoplatonist philosopher. Porphyry of Tyre studied under Longinus at Athens and in AD 262 became a devoted disciple of PLOTINUS at Rome and editor of the *Enneads*. Though lacking in originality and uncritical, he was a remarkable polymath and the author of numerous and varied works which include early philosophical and religious treatises written before his conversion to Plotinism; later works written from the Plotinian point of view; a biography of Plotinus; numerous philosophical commentaries on PLATO, ARISTOTLE, THEOPHRASTUS, and Plotinus; and several philological works.
JL

Armstrong (1967); Wallis (1972).

Porsenna, Lars (late 6th century BC), Etruscan king. Lars Porsenna was the king of Clusium who attacked Rome at the end of the 6th century BC in an attempt to restore the exiled TARQUINIUS SUPERBUS. He seized the JANICULUM, but was thwarted by Roman heroism, particularly that of Horatius, who single-handedly held the bridge over the Tiber. So far legend; the historical reality may be more complex, as a variant tradition maintained that Porsenna actually succeeded in capturing the city. HE

Alföldi (1965); Ogilvie (1976).

Portico a term in Roman ARCHITECTURE for a colonnade or range of columns, originally a development from the Greek STOA. First commonly used as an appendage to public buildings, it later acquired a domestic application to provide either exterior galleries or interior cloisters. GS

Portoria harbour dues levied in Italian harbours under the Roman Republic. Since harbours were maintained out of public funds, *portoria* were levied on goods entering and leaving a port. Under the Empire a customs duty was charged in the provinces on major trade routes at a uniform rate (usually 2.5 per cent). Until the 1st century AD collection of these levies was controlled by PUBLICANI, an office that was later transferred to imperial PROCURATORS.

See also TAXATION, ROMAN. GS

Badian (1972a).

Porus (fl. 326–317 BC), Indian king. Porus ruled considerable territory between two tributaries of the Indus, the Hydaspes (Jhelum) and Acesines (Chenab) rivers. ALEXANDER THE GREAT defeated him in battle at the Hydaspes in 326 BC (where ELEPHANTS were first deployed against Greeks). Alexander's best way of holding India was to accept Porus as an ally, increase his domain, and allow him to rule as a vassal king. Porus was murdered in 317 by a Macedonian satrap. EER

Bosworth (1988a); Hammond (1989); Lane Fox (1973).

Poseidon Greek god. The cult of Poseidon was native to Greece, long established, and universally observed. He was the god of the sea, the guardian of sailors and fishermen, and the god of earthquakes, the earth shaker, an embodiment of elemental forces. The ISTHMIAN GAMES were held in his honour, and his sanctuary at Corinth relates to that city's command of the seas; but his most famous shrines were at SUNIUM in Attica and Mycale in Ionia. In art he is bearded, carries a trident, and sometimes drives a chariot. The Romans identified him with Neptune. GS

Grimal (1986); Guthrie (1950).

Posidonius (*c.*135–51 BC), Greek prose writer. Born at Apamea in Syria and educated at Athens, Posidonius travelled widely in the western Mediterranean before settling in Rhodes. From there he led an embassy to Rome in 87 BC. His school on Rhodes was attended by CICERO, and he was twice visited by POMPEY whose fervent admirer he became. Of his writings only fragments survive, but his *Histories* related in 52 books the history of the world from where POLYBIUS left off (i.e. 146 BC) to the dictatorship of Sulla (85 BC) and included an appendix on the wars of Pompey. His vindication of Roman imperialism and his scientific observations were immensely influential.

See also MAPS; STOICS. GS

Edelstein and Kidd (1989); Kidd (1988); Reinhardt (1921).

Postal service In ancient Greece each city-state was responsible for its own mail, for which purpose it maintained ships and messengers. In Persia there was a state-run system for transporting officials as well as mail by means of a relay service along the royal roads. This public system was inherited and improved by the Seleucids, Ptolemies, and Romans in the eastern empire. First-class mail was carried by horses, second-class by runners, and parcels by camels. Messengers had to be hired for private mail. At Rome couriers were employed under the Republic. But Augustus introduced the *cursus publicus*, modelled on the system already operating in the east. Its main purpose was military for the movement of troops, but it could also be used for official transport and for mail. The service was provided and paid for by the local population. The average speed of a courier was 50 miles per day but this could be improved by a factor of three in an emergency.

See also BUREAUCRACY; ROADS, ROMAN; TRAVEL. GS

Jones (1949).

Postumius Albinus (2nd century BC), Roman historian. Aulus Postumius Albinus, consul in 151 BC, was one of a number of senators of the 2nd century BC who wrote histories of Rome in Greek. Rome's involvement with Greek communities possessing a sense of identity defined through the past created a need for Romans to construct their own history, defining Rome's place in the world and the Roman élite's place within that world. Almost nothing survives of his work, whose Hellenic pretensions were ridiculed by CATO.

See also FABIUS PICTOR; HISTORIOGRAPHY, ROMAN. HS

Badian (1966b); Scullard (1973).

Postumus (d. AD 268), Roman emperor in Gaul, AD 259–68. Marcus Cassianius Latinius Postumus, commander of the Rhine under GALLIENUS, rebelled against the central authority and established a separate Gallic empire centred on Trier (AUGUSTA TREVERORUM), comprising Gaul, Spain, and Britain. He repelled the Franks and Alamanni from Gaul, and provided a period of strong government until 268. In that year he successfully put down the rebel Laelianus at Mainz, but was assassinated after refusing to allow the plunder of the city.

See also VICTORINUS.   RJB

Parker (1958).

Potidaea   city in CHALCIDICE. Founded by Corinth *c*.600 BC to facilitate trade with Macedonia, Potidaea was minting its own coinage by the mid-6th century. It withstood a siege by the Persian ARTABAZUS in 480/79 and joined the DELIAN LEAGUE. In 432 it revolted from Athens but was subdued after a two-year siege and became a CLERUCHY until 404. In 356 it was taken by PHILIP II of Macedon but was destroyed together with OLYNTHUS in 348. In 316 a new city was built on the site named Cassandreia which remained prosperous throughout the Roman period.   GS

Alexander (1963).

Pottery, Greek   The potter's wheel had been known in Greece since the Bronze Age. The manufacture of pottery was widespread throughout the country, but CORINTH emerged as the leading producer in the mid-7th century BC, a position assumed by Athens in the mid-6th century. Both Corinthian and Attic pottery was widely exported throughout the Mediterranean world (*see* TRADE). The supremacy of Athenian potters was challenged by Boeotian and south Italian manufacturers in the mid-5th century. All three centres maintained a high standard of production until the end of the 4th century. A wide variety of shapes was produced, nearly all of them intended for some practical function. The decoration of pottery developed into a fine art (*see* PAINTING, GREEK), though the painted ornament of the ARCHAIC and CLASSICAL PERIODS largely gave way to moulded and appliqué relief in HELLENISTIC times. Potter and painter seem to have been equally respected professions and many vases are signed with the names of both.

See also AMASIS; DOURIS; EPICTETUS; EUPHRONIUS; EXECIAS; INDUSTRY; LAMPS.
                                                                        GS

Noble (1988); Sparkes (1991); Webster (1972).

Pottery, Roman   Early Roman pottery was deeply influenced by centres of production in Etruria and Magna Graecia. Painted decoration was in decline by the start of the 3rd century BC, to be replaced by black gloss finishes and moulded relief. Arretine ware (originally from Arezzo in Etruria), usually red in colour and decorated in relief, was made in the 1st century BC and the 1st AD and was followed by similar red-gloss ware from the provinces of Gaul (*see* SAMIAN WARE, TERRA SIGILLATA), Germany, and Africa. Painted decoration enjoyed a revival in the later Empire, but it was a humdrum affair compared with the work of earlier Greek artists. By the 3rd century AD GLASS had largely replaced pottery as the medium for everyday tableware.   GS

Charleston (1955); Hayes (1972, 1980); Henig (1983); Peacock (1982).

Praefectura Roman assize town. Under the Republic magistrates (*praefecti*) were sent to a new MUNICIPIUM to assist the introduction of new citizen rights. These occasional visits later became annual, supplementing but not replacing local magistrates. The system lasted until the end of the SOCIAL WAR (89 BC), but after this *praefecturae* became assimilated to MUNICIPIA.   HE

Sherwin-White (1973).

Praefectus Roman army officer. Under the Republic units of Italian allies (SOCII) were commanded by *praefecti*. After the SOCIAL WAR *praefecti* were commanders of cavalry units. Under the Principate a regular EQUESTRIAN military career became established: first *praefectus* of an auxiliary infantry unit (*cohortis*), then TRIBUNUS MILITUM, and then *praefectus* of a cavalry unit (*equitum* or *alae*). Higher equestrian *praefecti* commanded the PRAETORIAN GUARD, the VIGILES, the legions in Egypt, and the fleets of the NAVY. The PRAEFECTUS URBI was a senator and commanded the urban cohorts. In the 3rd century AD *praefecti* were appointed to further military commands.

See also ANNONA.   HS

Keppie (1983); Webster (1985).

Praefectus praetorio praetorian commander. The *praefectus praetorio*, or praetorian prefect, commanded the PRAETORIAN GUARD. The commanders, usually two in number, were normally equestrians. After SEJANUS, prefects normally accompanied the emperor, acting as his military, and increasingly also his judicial, deputies. The great era of the prefecture was the early 3rd century (post-holders included the lawyers PAPINIAN and ULPIAN), and in the later 3rd century some prefects reached the imperial throne (e.g. MACRINUS, PHILIP I 'THE ARAB'). Under DIOCLETIAN there were four praetorian prefects, one attached to each ruler; under Constantine, shorn of their military functions, these became immensely powerful civil administrators, each responsible for a geographical area.

See also PLAUTIANUS; TIGELLINUS; TURBO. RJB

Bury (1958); Millar (1977); Parker (1958).

Praefectus urbi Roman city prefect. A magistracy for Rome instituted by AUGUSTUS, urban prefects were drawn from the Senate and were often of consular status. The office was held for a number of years, though not with a fixed term. The prefect's prime responsibility was maintaining law and order in the city of Rome (see POLICE) and he was thus placed in charge of the urban cohorts. He also had a separate court of justice which by the 3rd century AD had superseded those of other magistrates. After its refoundation in AD 330, Constantinople also acquired an urban prefect. HE

Praeneste city in Italy. Praeneste, modern Palestrina, lay in the western Apennines of central Italy, to the east of Rome. Its strategic position led to frequent conflict with Rome during the 4th century BC, before it was finally defeated in the LATIN WAR. In 82 BC SULLA sacked it because of its support for the son of MARIUS, after which it was refounded as a colony. Praeneste was famous for its cult of FORTUNA, to whom a huge temple complex in Hellenistic style was built at the end of the 2nd century BC. HE

Lewis (1971).

Praetextatus (AD 320–84), praetorian prefect. Vettius Agorius Praetextatus, a pagan aristocrat of ability and learning, was a friend of SYMMACHUS and an informant of AMMIANUS MARCELLINUS. He was appointed governor of Achaea by Julian (362), and later, as Prefect to the City, he quieted Christian rioting at Rome (367–8). He was a member of an embassy to VALENTINIAN I (370–1) that won an end to the torture of senators, and was later Prefect of Italy. RJB

Hamilton and Wallace-Hadrill (1986); Jones, Martindale, and Morris (1971).

Praetor Roman magistrate. The praetorship was an annual magistracy essential for the CURSUS HONORUM ranking above the quaestorship but below the consulate. While the most important MAGISTRATES, who came to be called CONSULS during the 4th century BC, were originally called praetors, the first praetor in the later sense, the *praetor urbanus*, was created in 367 BC to take over from the consuls aspects of civil jurisdiction. In *c.*242 a second praetor, the *praetor peregrinus*, was created to superintend cases involving foreigners. Further praetors were created to govern various provinces acquired by Rome. SULLA raised the number of praetors to eight (probably from six) and fixed a minimum age of 39. Henceforth praetors were intended to remain in Rome for their year in office, the *praetor urbanus* and *praetor peregrinus* continuing their functions while the other six acted as presidents of the standing criminal courts (*see* QUAESTIO), before going out to govern provinces the following year.

Under the Principate the praetorship, held at about the age of 30, remained an important post which qualified a man for the lesser provincial governorships. The praetors' numbers rose to 18 in the mid-2nd century AD; their most important functions remained judicial, and they gained the right to give games in Rome. HS

Jolowicz and Nicholas (1972); Millar (1977).

Praetorian guard The praetorian guard was the Roman emperor's bodyguard, organized by AUGUSTUS (27 BC). There were nine cohorts of veterans, each 500 strong. They were paid at three times the legionary rate, received frequent donatives, and served for 16 years. From 2 BC they were commanded by two equestrian prefects, and each cohort by a tribune. SEJANUS brought the cohorts together in a single camp just outside Rome (AD 23), giving them great political power both to install rulers (e.g. GAIUS, CLAUDIUS I) and to depose them (e.g. NERO, GALBA). Gaius increased the number of cohorts to 12, while Vitellius replaced the guard with 16 cohorts from the German legions loyal to him. Vespasian reverted to nine cohorts, and a tenth was later added, perhaps by Domitian. Septimius Severus replaced the guard with Illyrians loyal to himself, and, in addition, doubled the size of each cohort. The guard was eventually disbanded by Constantine I.

See also PRAEFECTUS PRAETORIO. RJB

Millar (1977); Parker (1958); Scullard (1982).

Praetorian prefect *see* PRAEFECTUS PRAETORIO.

Praxagoras (fl. *c.*340 BC), Greek physician. Praxagoras of Cos was considerably influenced by 'Sicilian' MEDICINE (*see* PHILISTION) and held that the heart was the seat of the intellect and that digestion was a form of putrefaction. He differed from Sicilian opinion, however, in believing that respiration served to provide nourishment for the psychic humour rather than cool the innate heat. He differentiated between veins and arteries, holding that blood flows through the former and air (*pneuma*) through the latter, a misconception which dominated Greek medicine for over four and a half centuries. He stressed the diagnostic importance of the arterial pulse and took an important step towards the discovery of the nervous system made by his pupil HEROPHILUS by conjecturing that attenuated arteries (*neura*) served as channels for the *pneuma* which transmitted motions from the heart to the extremities. Praxagoras is thus a transitory figure standing between the old medicine and the new medicine soon to arise in Alexandria. Only fragments of his work survive. JL

DSB XI (1975); Longrigg (1993).

Praxiteles (fl. 370–330 BC), Greek sculptor. Praxiteles of Athens was the son of the sculptor Cephisodotus. Together with LYSIPPUS and SCOPAS he dominated art in the 4th century BC and deeply influenced subsequent generations. In the course of a long career he is said to have made well over 75 statues, most of them in mainland Greece. He worked in both marble and bronze, but preferred the former, and liked his marbles to be painted by NICIAS. Most of his subjects were religious, the most celebrated being the Aphrodite of Cnidus which was much admired in antiquity but is now known only from Roman copies. Other lost works included the Apollo Sauroctonus (the lizard slayer), the Eros of Thespiae, the Eros of Parium, the Phryne of Delphi, the Aphrodite of Arles, the Artemis of Gabii, and the leaning satyr. The Hermes with the infant Dionysus at Olympia, which PAUSANIAS attributed to Praxiteles, is probably an original work, though some doubt its authenticity.

See also PAINTING, GREEK; SCULPTURE, GREEK. GS

Richter (1970b); Robertson (1975).

Priene city in western Asia Minor and a member of the Ionian League (*see* IONIANS). The original site is not known. It was refounded on its present site in the 4th century BC where it flourished briefly until the sea receded and deprived it of trade. Remains of a well-laid-out Hellenistic city survive (*see* HIPPODAMUS of Miletus). Its diminishing prosperity meant that unlike other Greek cities in Ionia it was not overlaid with subsequent Roman building. GS

Bean (1979a); Wycherley (1967).

Priests, Greek In Greek society there was no such thing as training and ordination to the priesthood. Priests and priestesses were appointed to the service of a god or goddess without any special authority or knowledge. They must simply be of good character, full citizens, and free from pollution (but not necessarily celibate). The leading role at an act of public worship would normally be taken by someone of high standing (at Athens the ARCHON Basileus; at SPARTA one of the kings;

elsewhere a magistrate elected for a specific period or for life). Similarly in the domestic context sacrifice would be conducted by the head of the house. But a sanctuary was the property of a god and was cared for by a priest (or priests) dedicated to that god's service. Such priesthoods were often inherited (e.g. the ELEUSINIAN MYSTERIES were administered by the Eumolpidae), brought great prestige, and could carry a stipend. GS

Burkert (1985); Parker (1983).

Priests, Roman The modern term 'priest' is an imprecise and somewhat misleading translation of the Latin *sacerdos*. In general, Roman priests were not professional holy men with a special calling, and not necessarily even particularly religious. Most Roman priests were aristocrats drawn from the political class, and combined their priesthoods with tenure of political and military office (the REX SACRORUM and FLAMEN Dialis were exceptions). They were also enrolled in colleges, and gave advice on religious matters rather than directly participating in cult.

See also ARVAL BROTHERS; AUGURES; AUGUSTALES; EPULONES; FETIALES; GUILDS; HARUSPICES; PONTIFEX; RELIGION, ROMAN; SALII; SODALES; VESTALS.

TC

Beard and North (1990); Ogilvie (1969); Scullard (1981); Szemler (1972).

Primus (b. *c*.AD 20), Roman soldier. Marcus Antonius Primus, commander of a Danubian legion in AD 69, supported VESPASIAN against VITELLIUS. Without waiting for MUCIANUS, Vespasian's principal general, Primus attacked Italy, overwhelming Vitellius' poorly led army at the second battle of Bedriacum (Cremona), before going on to take Rome itself. Primus held Rome for a few weeks after which his personal ambitions, if any, were ended by the arrival of Mucianus to serve as regent for Vespasian. RJB

Grant (1979); Wellesley (1975).

Princeps Roman imperial title. *Princeps* was the unofficial title by which the early Roman emperors preferred to be known. *Princeps*, the leading man, was a title with good Republican antecedents, chosen for that reason by AUGUSTUS, who was anxious to avoid titles like *Rex* (king) or *Dictator*. His use of *Princeps* was an extension of his claim to have restored the Roman Republic, that he was the leading citizen of a free city, but the significance was soon lost with the increasingly obvious autocracy under later emperors. *Princeps* was not an abbreviation of *Princeps Senatus*, denoting the senior man in the Senate, although Augustus undoubtedly also held that position, enrolling himself at the head of the list of senators in the census of 28 BC. The title *princeps iuventutis*, denoting the leader of the equestrian order, was sometimes given to princes of the imperial house (e.g. TITUS and DOMITIAN) indicating their status as heirs apparent.   RJB

Salmon (1968); Wells (1984).

Priscillian   (d. AD 385), Christian heretic. A native of Avila, Priscillian was a layman who preached a form of GNOSTICISM which attracted many adherents in Spain and Gaul. Despite opposition he was consecrated bishop of Avila in 380. Rebuffed by the pope and AMBROSE, Priscillian and his followers were condemned by a council at Bordeaux in 384. Priscillian appealed to the emperor at Trier but despite protests from MARTIN he was executed. In Spain, where he was considered a martyr, the heresy gained a mass following and continued into the 6th century.

GS

Chadwick (1976).

Probus   (AD 232–82), Roman emperor, AD 276–82. Marcus Aurelius Probus was born at Sirmium in August 232. An experienced general and colleague of AURELIAN, he was proclaimed emperor by the army of the east to succeed TACITUS, successfully rivalling FLORIANUS (276). He repelled Germanic incursions into Gaul, before constructing a series of forts along the further bank of the Rhine. He defeated an invasion of Illyricum by the Vandals (278), and then moved east (279). Rebellions in the west forced his return: Proculus, in Lyon, and Bonosus were put down (281), but the elevation of CARUS by the army in Raetia led to Probus' murder at Sirmium.   RJB

Crees (1965); Grant (1985); Parker (1958).

Probus   (c.AD 328–c.388), praetorian prefect. Sextus Claudius Petronius Probus, according to AMMIANUS MARCELLINUS, was known throughout the Roman world for his high birth, powerful influence, and vast riches. He was praetorian prefect of Illyricum (364), of Gaul (366), and of Italy (368–75, and 383). Painted as an unscrupulous character by Ammianus, he organized the defence of Sirmium against the QUADI and SARMATIANS (373), but was lucky to escape punishment by Valentinian I for financial extortion (375).   RJB

Hamilton and Wallace-Hadrill (1986); Jones, Martindale, and Morris (1971).

Proclus   (c.AD 410–85), Greek Neoplatonist philosopher, mathematician, and astronomer. Born in Constantinople, Proclus was the last important member of the Neoplatonist movement. After early education at Xanthus and Alexandria, he joined the ACADEMY and rose to be its head after studying under Plutarch and Syrianus. He was vastly learned and a prolific author. He employed his talents systematizing and perfecting NEOPLATONISM. As the last great systematizer of Greek philosophical thought, his indirect influence upon medieval thought via the writings of Dionysius the Areopagite was considerable. In the Renaissance Proclus' Platonism was much in vogue. His extant works include philosophical treatises, several commentaries on PLATO's dialogues, and scientific and literary works.   JL

Armstrong (1967); Wallis (1972).

Proconsul   Roman magistrate. A proconsul held the authority (IMPERIUM) of a CONSUL, while not holding the office, to command an army or govern a PROVINCIA. First recorded in 326 BC when PUBLILIUS PHILO had his consular authority prolonged (*prorogatio imperii*), *prorogatio* became a normal practice to overcome the shortage of MAGISTRATES with *imperium* to govern the empire. After SULLA, the consuls and PRAETORS were to remain in Rome while the provinces were to be governed by ex-magistrates as proconsuls. AUGUSTUS commanded his provinces as proconsul, his governors being LEGATI ranked as propraetors, while the 'senatorial' provinces were governed by ex-consuls or ex-praetors as proconsuls.   HS

Jashemski (1950); Richardson (1976).

Procopius   *see* VALENS; VALENTINIAN I.

Procurator   Roman agent. A procurator, in Republican times, was the agent of a wealthy individual or corporation, and, under the Empire, a personal agent of the emperor. Procurators were essentially financial agents, normally equestrians, but sometimes freedmen, and with the widening of their powers, gradually became public servants. By the 2nd century there was a well-established career structure. They could serve as procurators (finance officers) of provinces, or as governors of minor provinces; they controlled the mint, the mines, the gladiatorial schools, and the various administrative departments, ruled by the secretary-general, financial secretary, and judicial secretary. Senior equestrian procurators qualified for the prefectures, the most important being, in rising order, the fleet, the fire brigade (VIGILES), the grain supply (ANNONA), Egypt, and the PRAETORIAN GUARD. During the 3rd century procurators were frequently used as substitutes for senatorial governors (*see* VICARIUS), while in the 4th century procurators retained their financial function, but were called *rationales*.

See also BUREAUCRACY, ROMAN; FINANCE, ROMAN.   RJB

Parker (1958); Salmon (1968).

Proletarii the lowest class of Roman citizens. *Proletarii* owned little or no property and were excluded from the system of CENSUS classes. They voted in a single century, giving them little political power. They were exempted from military service until the mid-2nd century BC, but then increasingly began to be recruited as the minimum property qualification was reduced, and eventually disregarded, especially after MARIUS' levy in 107. In the 1st century BC most Roman soldiers were drawn from the *proletarii*.

See also ARMY, ROMAN.   HE

Brunt (1988); Gabba (1976); Nicolet (1980).

Propertius (*c*.50–2 BC), Latin poet. Sextus Propertius came from an equestrian family in Umbria whose estates suffered in the confiscations of 41–40 BC. He received an education in rhetoric but chose poetry in preference to a public career. He settled in Rome and published four books of elegies between 29 and 16 BC. The first brought him into contact with the literary circle of MAECENAS and he expressed admiration for VIRGIL, but as a pacifist he was out of sympathy with many of the ideals of the Augustan age. He was acquainted with OVID and he acknowledged his debt to the Alexandrian poets. Many of the earlier poems are focused on his mistress Cynthia, identified with a married woman called Hostia. Later poems are less concerned with love: in book 3 Propertius proclaims himself the Roman Callimachus; book 4, which includes the lament for Cornelia, is a forceful Roman miscellany.   GS

Griffin (1985); Hubbard (1974); Lyne (1980).

Propylaea a term in Greek ARCHITECTURE for a monumental gateway. The best-known example provides the only entrance to the Athenian acropolis. Designed by Mnesicles and built between 437 and 432 BC of Pentelic marble, it was an elaborate building with five doorways, the central one measuring some 14 feet in width by 24 feet in height. Doric porticoes face both outwards and inwards, flanked by loggias on both sides which contain a mixture of Doric and Ionic columns. One of the wings (to the north) was designed as a picture gallery and housed paintings by POLYGNOTUS and other artists. No expense was spared in the building's decoration.   GS

Bundgaard (1957); Hopper (1971).

Proscription a published list of Roman citizens who were declared outlaws with a price on their heads and whose property was confiscated. This device was first used by SULLA in 82 BC. The proscribed were hunted down and killed, and their descendants barred from public office. Sulla's ruthlessness was deeply etched in Roman memories, but a second proscription list was published by Antony, Lepidus, and Octavian during the CIVIL WAR of 43–42 BC.   DP

Scullard (1982).

Prostitution   In Athens prostitution was legalized and widely available. Prostitutes were usually of foreign birth, as were most concubines and courtesans of the classical period (e.g. ASPASIA, the Milesian mistress of Pericles). They ranged from the cheap tarts of Piraeus to the sophisticated entertainers at the SYMPOSIUM. Slaves were employed in sacred prostitution at temples (*see* HIERODOULOI), as in the cult of Aphrodite at Corinth. At Rome male and female prostitution was officially practised. MESSALINA, wife of Claudius, is satirized by Juvenal as the Roman whore *par excellence*.   GS

Protagoras   (*c.*490–420 BC), Greek sophist. Protagoras of Abdera, one of the most famous of the SOPHISTS, visited Athens on several occasions and became a friend of PERICLES. He professed to teach 'virtue' (*aretē*), i.e. efficiency in the conduct of life. He was widely respected and was appointed to draw up the laws for the new colony at THURII in 444/3 BC. He wrote at least two main treatises: the *Truth* (or the *Throwers*) and *On the Gods*. The former work opens with his well-known dictum 'man is the measure of all things' which is generally understood in antiquity to imply relativity of knowledge and to entail scepticism about any scientific claim to universal validity. In the latter, he expresses an agnostic attitude towards belief in the gods. He evidently did not extend his scepticism to moral issues, however, since he apparently adhered to a conventional morality and urged men to respect the moral code of their own communities.   JL

Guthrie, vol. 3 (1969); Kennedy (1963); Kerferd (1981).

Provincia   Roman overseas possession. (*See* map on page 752.) The primary meaning of the term *provincia* was the sphere of operations of a Roman MAGISTRATE. While this meaning was never lost, a *provincia* came to be understood as an area of territory outside Italy directly ruled by Rome. SICILY became Rome's first major overseas province in 211 BC. Roman possessions in SPAIN were organized into two provinces in 197, AFRICA and MACEDONIA–ACHAEA were organized in 146, ASIA after 133, and GAUL around 100 (*see also* CISALPINE GAUL). The slow annexation of territories was not caused by reluctance to possess an empire. The empire was not considered co-extensive with the provinces. In most senses client kings and peoples were part of the empire. Although imperialism did not necessarily require annexation, in the last century of the Republic many new provinces were organized (*see* CYRENAICA; SYRIA).

Under the Republic the provinces were governed by senators, at first usually magistrates, later normally ex-magistrates, who often looked to corruption to fund political careers and élite status (*see* RES REPETUNDAE).

Under AUGUSTUS the provinces were divided into 'imperial' (ruled by the emperor via LEGATI) and 'senatorial' (ruled by ex-magistrates chosen, in theory, by the SENATE). It is, however, clear that the emperor could always interfere in senatorial provinces.

While new provinces (BRITAIN; DACIA) were created under the Empire, the system remained basically the same until the 3rd century AD, when provinces were subdivided into smaller units (*see* DIOCLETIAN).

See also IMPERIUM; VICARIUS.   HS

Lintott (1981); North (1981); Richardson (1986).

Provocatio   Roman right of appeal. The right of appeal to the people against a magistrate's judicial verdict was supposedly granted to Roman citizens by P. VALERIUS PUBLICOLA in 509 BC, reiterated in 449 by the Valerio-Horatian laws (*see* VALERIUS POTITUS) and again in 300 by another *lex Valeria* (*see* VALERIUS CORVUS). Some historians accept only the law of 300 as historical, rejecting the earlier ones as fiction; but there is no good reason in principle why they should not all be authentic, and a clause in the TWELVE TABLES guaranteeing the people's sovereignty in capital cases seems to presuppose the existence of a right of appeal.   TC

Lintott (1972); Scullard (1980).

Proxenos   Greek political representative. A *proxenos* was a resident citizen of one state who looked after the interests of another state and its citizens in his own, receiving the title of *proxenos* and other privileges and, where possible, protection. He combined some of the functions of a diplomatic mission and an intelligence service. A state might have several *proxenoi* in one place, and the position was often hereditary.   RB

Adcock and Mosley (1975); Meiggs (1972); Walbank (1978); Wallace (1970).

Prudentius   (AD 348–*c*.410), Christian Latin poet. Aurelius Prudentius Clemens was born in Spain and educated in rhetoric. He enjoyed a successful public career culminating in two provincial governorships and a position in the imperial court at Rome before devoting himself to Christian poetry. He wrote hymns and a celebration of the Christian martyrs as well as didactic poems on the doctrine of the Trinity, the origin of sin, the battle of sins and vices, and a verse polemic against SYMMACHUS.   GS

Binns (1974); Palmer (1989); Peebles (1951).

Prusias I (*c*.230–*c*.182 BC), king of Bithynia. Prusias, son of Ziaelas and grandson of NICOMEDES I, attempted to expand his kingdom by warring with Byzantium (220–219 BC) and the Galatians (217). He was PHILIP V's ally in the First MACEDONIAN WAR (214–205), attacking Rome's ally ATTALUS I SOTER of Pergamum. Philip rewarded him with cities on the Propontis (Cius and Myrleia). BITHYNIA wisely remained neutral in Rome's war with ANTIOCHUS III THE GREAT, but the settlement after MAGNESIA (190) gave Bithynian territory to EUMENES II SOTER and caused hostilities between them. Although supported by Philip V and the Gauls, and aided by the advice of the refugee Carthaginian general HANNIBAL, Prusias was forced to renounce the disputed territories.
                                                                              EER

CAH VIII; Gruen (1984); Hammond and Walbank (1988).

Prusias II (*c*.182–149 BC), king of Bithynia. Prusias succeeded his father PRUSIAS I, and joined fellow Asian dynasts in the alliance against PHARNACES I of Pontus (*c*.183–179 BC). As a brother-in-law of PERSEUS of Macedon, Prusias sought to avoid Roman hostility after Perseus' defeat. Continuing his father's enmity to Pergamum, Prusias declared war on ATTALUS II SOTER (156–154) and launched an invasion despite Rome's orders. He was forced to seek terms and pay an indemnity. His growing unpopularity at home and with Rome led to his murder by supporters of his son NICOMEDES (II), who was aided by Attalus and encouraged by Rome.
    See also BITHYNIA.   EER

CAH VIII; Gruen (1984); Sherwin-White (1984).

Prytanis Athenian official. Each tribal contingent of 50 councillors served in turn as an executive committee of the BOULE; they were called Prytaneis, and their term of office a 'prytany'. They met every day in their state building, the Prytaneion, and a third of them at a time were required to be there continuously during their prytany. Their chairman, the *epistates*, was chosen daily by lot (no one served twice) and effectively functioned as head of state for the day; in the 5th century BC he presided over the council and assembly, and in the 4th selected the board of presidents (*proedroi*) by lot.   RB

Hansen (1991); Rhodes (1972).

Ptolemy I Soter (*c*.367/6–283/2 BC), king of Egypt. Ptolemy, a Macedonian boyhood friend of ALEXANDER THE GREAT, served as Companion, bodyguard, and general during the expedition. After Alexander's death in 323 BC, he became satrap of Egypt and executed CLEOMENES OF NAUCRATIS. Ptolemy kidnapped Alexander's body, *en route* to Macedonia, diverting it to ALEXANDRIA (where the tomb later became the focus of the Ptolemaic ruler cult). He joined the DIADOCHI who opposed PERDICCAS (the latter was killed trying to invade Egypt in 321/20), and joined CASSANDER, LYSIMACHUS, and SELEUCUS (later I) in 315 against ANTIGONUS I MONOPHTHALMUS. He thwarted an invasion of Egypt by Antigonus' son DEMETRIUS I POLIORCETES at the battle of Gaza in 312, but lost a naval battle off Cypriot Salamis in 306. At some time he renounced his queen (a daughter of ANTIPATER) and married BERENICE I. He took the titles 'king' in 305 and 'saviour' later. After Antigonus' death at IPSUS in 301, Ptolemy reoccupied Palestine and Syria; five 'Syrian Wars' against the Seleucids ensued during the next century. He consolidated control over Cyprus and parts of the Cyclades and Asia Minor. Ptolemy organized the economic, administrative, and military structure of his empire, and instituted the MUSEUM and LIBRARY at Alexandria. He wrote a history of Alexander which was used as a main source by ARRIAN. EER

Bosworth (1980, 1988a, b); CAH VII.1; Fraser (1972); Green (1990).

Ptolemy II Philadelphus (308–246 BC), king of Egypt. Ptolemy II, son of PTOLEMY I and BERENICE I, was joint king from 285 BC and succeeded in 283 (instead of his elder half-brother PTOLEMY CERAUNUS). In the First Syrian War (274–271) Ptolemy invaded Syria and was victorious over ANTIOCHUS II THEOS. He was helped in affairs by his queen ARSINOË II, his full sister whom he married *c*.274 after the renunciation of ARSINOË I. He deified himself and Arsinoë in 272/1 and later adopted her cult title 'brother/sister-loving'. Ptolemy supported Athens in the War of CHREMONIDES (*c*.266–261), and fought the Second Syrian War (*c*.260–253). Its outcome was indecisive, but Ptolemy married his daughter BERENICE SYRA to Antiochus. His long, prosperous reign left ALEXANDRIA the capital of the Mediterranean. EER

CAH VII.1; Fraser (1972); Green (1990).

Ptolemy III Euergetes (*c*.288–222/1 BC), king of Egypt. Ptolemy III 'the benefactor' was the son of PTOLEMY II and ARSINOË I. His marriage to BERENICE II upon his accession in 246 BC united Egypt and Cyrene. In the Third Syrian War (246–241) Ptolemy invaded Syria to support his sister BERENICE SYRA's son as heir to the Seleucid throne. To avenge their murders, he fought the Seleucid successor SELEUCUS II CALLINICUS but was forced to make peace. Ptolemy intervened in Greece to counter Macedonian influence. He was first allied with ARATUS OF SICYON (and elected general of the ACHAEAN LEAGUE in 243); but when Aratus turned towards Macedon, Ptolemy supported the Spartan CLEOMENES III, whom he received in exile in 222.   EER

CAH VII.1; Fraser (1972); Green (1990).

Ptolemy IV Philopator (c.244–204), king of Egypt. 'Father-loving' Ptolemy IV, the son of PTOLEMY III and BERENICE III, acceded to the throne in 221 BC and married his full sister ARSINOË III. More interested in self-indulgence and leisure than kingship, Ptolemy was controlled by devious ministers. The Fourth Syrian War (221–217) saw invasions of Palestine by ANTIOCHUS III THE GREAT, but Ptolemy defeated him at RAPHIA in 217 only with the help of native Egyptian troops. Serious internal revolts and the secession of Upper Egypt (207) followed. Ptolemy continued to prefer pseudo-intellectual pursuits to public affairs, and tolerated the removal of his queen from court. His sudden death was concealed for a time by his ministers.   EER

CAH VII.1; Fraser (1972); Green (1990); Gruen (1984).

Ptolemy V Epiphanes (210–180 BC), king of Egypt. Ptolemy V, '[god] made manifest', was the son of PTOLEMY IV and ARSINOË III. The accession c.204 BC of a young child controlled by his father's unscrupulous ministers meant trouble for Egypt. The Macedonian PHILIP V and the Seleucid ANTIOCHUS III THE GREAT plotted to divide Egypt; in the Fifth Syrian War (202–195) Antiochus invaded Syria despite Roman disapproval. Ptolemy concluded peace in 195 and married Antiochus' daughter two years later. Although his reign saw the loss of territory in Asia Minor, the Aegean, and Palestine (200), Upper and Lower Egypt were reunited and native revolts quelled. The Rosetta Stone commemorates Ptolemy's majority and coronation as pharaoh at Memphis in 197.   EER

CAH VIII; Fraser (1972); Green (1990); Gruen (1984).

Ptolemy VI–XV kings of Egypt. Ptolemy VI Philometor (r. 180–145 BC) succeeded as a minor and ruled jointly with his mother until her death in 176. He married his full sister CLEOPATRA II. After the Sixth Syrian War against ANTIOCHUS IV EPIPHANES (170–168), they ruled jointly but uneasily with their mutual brother Ptolemy VIII Euergetes, finally dividing the kingdom in 164/3. Intervening in dynastic struggles over the Seleucid ALEXANDER BALAS, Ptolemy VI was killed in 145. His young son Ptolemy VII was murdered by his uncle Ptolemy VIII when the latter returned to Alexandria. Ptolemy VIII married his widowed sister CLEOPATRA II, and, later, their daughter CLEOPATRA III. Cleopatra II revolted in 132 by offering the throne to the Seleucid DEMETRIUS II, but Ptolemy VIII helped to unseat him. He ruled peacefully with both queens from 124 to 116. Ptolemy IX Lathyrus and Ptolemy X, sons of Ptolemy VIII and Cleopatra III, bitterly contested the throne while meddling in Seleucid dynastic struggles between ANTIOCHUS VIII GRYPUS and ANTIOCHUS IX CYZICENUS (both Seleucids had married sisters of the Ptolemaic princes). In 107 Ptolemy IX became an independent king in Cyprus, but returned to Alexandria in 88; he defeated his brother and ruled until his death in 81. Ptolemy IX's heir, a daughter, was murdered by Ptolemy X's son, Ptolemy XI. His murder by the Alexandrians in 80 extinguished the legitimate Ptolemaic line. Ptolemy XII Auletes ('the fluteplayer') (r. 80–51 BC) succeeded as an illegitimate son of Ptolemy IX. His pro-Roman feelings made him unpopular among the Alexandrians, but Rome secured his throne. In 51 his daughter CLEOPATRA VII acceded jointly with her younger brother and husband Ptolemy XIII. When he died fighting CAESAR in 47, Cleopatra married her other brother Ptolemy XIV but had him killed in 44. Ptolemy XV, the son of Cleopatra VII and (allegedly) Caesar, was known as Caesarion.   EER

Fraser (1972); Green (1990); Gruen (1984); Sherwin-White (1984); Sullivan (1990).

Ptolemy Ceraunus   (fl. 287–279 BC), king of Macedon. Ptolemy 'the thunderbolt' was the eldest son of PTOLEMY I but the throne passed to his half-brother PTOLEMY II. After meddling in the court of LYSIMACHUS, he fled to SELEUCUS I NICATOR but murdered him after Lysimachus' death in 281 BC. Proclaimed king by the Macedonian army, Ptolemy defeated the navy of ANTIGONUS II GONATAS (his rival for the Macedonian throne), and married Lysimachus' widow, his own half-sister ARSINOË (later II). He was killed attacking the Galatians in 279.   EER

CAH VII.1; Errington (1990); Green (1990); Hammond and Walbank (1988).

Ptolemy of Alexandria   (c.AD 100–70), Egyptian astronomer, geographer, and mathematician. Claudius Ptolemaeus, from Ptolemais in Upper Egypt, lived in Alexandria where he superintended the MUSEUM. His principal astronomical work, known by its Arabic title as the *Almagest* (13 books), is based on HIPPARCHUS' geocentric conception of the universe and observations made by Ptolemy himself between AD 127 and 147. It superseded all previous work in the field and remained the standard textbook for more than a thousand years. Equally important was Ptolemy's *Geography* (eight books plus an atlas of MAPS) which aimed 'to reform the map of the world'. (*See* map on page 754.) Though erroneous in many respects (e.g. a serious underestimate of the earth's circumference), it was the most accurate of the ancient geographies and the basis of all medieval work on the subject. Ptolemy wrote numerous other works on ASTRONOMY, astrology, music, and optics, some of which survive in Latin or Arabic translation.   GS

Miller (1969); Toomer (1984).

Publicani   Roman tax collectors. *Publicani* performed the two kinds of services which the Roman state needed and which it could not do itself. The first was provision of supplies for the army and of goods and services for civic projects like public buildings. The second was the collection of money to pay for these essential services, the money coming both from revenues inside Italy such as harbour dues (PORTORIA) and the leasing of public land and from provincial TAXATION. Both provision of materials and collection of revenue were put out to contract by a form of public auction. Tax contracts were sold to the highest bidder, who then recouped at a profit. The buyers were members of the EQUESTRIAN ORDER, often formed into companies made necessary by the large capital sums involved, and gaining great wealth from such contracts as that to collect the tithe from the province of Asia. Their power, considerable under the Republic, diminished under the Principate when direct taxes were collected by government-appointed officials.   DP

Badian (1972a).

Publilius Philo   (fl. 340–315 BC), Roman statesman. Quintus Publilius Philo was the leading political figure of his generation. He held four consulships (339, 327, 320, 315 BC), was the first plebeian praetor (336), and the first PROCONSUL (326). In 339 he sponsored the *leges Publiliae*, which enacted that PLEBISCITA should have the force of law, that one of the censors must be a plebeian, and that the PATRUM AUCTORITAS should be given before rather than after the vote of the COMITIA. In 326 Philo negotiated a treaty with Naples, the first between Rome and a Greek city.   TC

Broughton (1951); CAH VII.2.

Publilius Syrus   (1st century BC), Latin writer. Publilius was a slave from Antioch who came to Rome in the time of Julius Caesar. A witty actor, he won his freedom and achieved popularity throughout Italy as a composer of MIME. The moralizing maxims of mimographers achieved proverbial status in the 1st century AD and a large collection survives that is attributed to Publilius.   GS

Pulcheria   (AD 399–453), sister of THEODOSIUS II (Augusta, AD 414–53). Pulcheria, the daughter of Arcadius and Eudoxia, and a pious orthodox Christian, acted as regent for her younger brother Theodosius II from 414, and continued to exercise power after his majority (416). Eventually discord with Theodosius' empress EUDOCIA, fomented by the eunuch Chrysaphius, caused her retirement (c.443) to the palace of Hebdomon. On Crysaphius' fall, shortly before Theodosius' death, she regained her influence, and married Theodosius' chosen successor MARCIAN.   RJB

Bury (1958); Grant (1985); Holum (1983).

Punic Wars   three wars fought between Rome and Carthage. After centuries of friendship, Rome's decision to intervene in Sicily and aid the MAMERTINES against Carthage led to the *First Punic War* (264–241 BC). Rome challenged Carthaginian naval supremacy by building 100 ships, modelled on a captured Punic warship, in 260. In 256 REGULUS, the consul, defeated a Punic fleet at Ecnomus and then invaded Africa. This expedition ended in disaster when the Spartan mercenary Xanthippus retrained the Carthaginian army and defeated Regulus in 255 BC. The war continued in Sicily, but exhaustion and apathy on both sides led to stagnation. The appointment of HAMILCAR BARCA and his notable successes with limited resources galvanized the Romans to build a new fleet (243) of 200 quinqueremes. In 241 a decisive naval victory off the Aegates islands brought the war to an end.

Carthage turned her attention to building an empire in Spain and, under the leadership of Hamilcar and later HASDRUBAL, exploited its mineral wealth and manpower. However, when in 219 HANNIBAL besieged SAGUNTUM, a Roman ally within Carthage's sphere of influence, it led to the *Second Punic War* (218–201 BC). (*See* map on page 750.) This war was dominated by the generalship of Hannibal who crossed the Alps in winter to arrive in Italy in 218 with 20,000 men and 6,000 cavalry. Despite great victories at TICINUS, TREBBIA, Lake TRASIMENE, and CANNAE, Hannibal was unable to break Roman resolve; and although he maintained himself undefeated in Italy for 16 years, he failed to damage the core of the Roman alliance: the Latins, Umbrians, and Picentines. Because of Roman naval superiority he suffered from a lack of reinforcements, having to employ the Celtic tribes of Cisalpine Gaul. The Romans were able to exploit the Italian fear of the Gauls and to present themselves as the protectors of Italy. In 207 Hannibal's brother HASDRUBAL BARCA attempted to join him in Italy but was defeated and killed at the river METAURUS. Roman manpower was great enough to enable the Romans to fight Hannibal in Italy while conducting campaigns in other theatres. In 212 MARCELLUS captured Syracuse, and in 209 SCIPIO AFRICANUS captured New Carthage (Cartagena) and by 206 had expelled the Carthaginians from Spain. Success in Spain proved to be the key to victory because its capture denied Carthage vital men and resources and freed troops for a Roman invasion of North Africa. Hannibal was recalled to fight Scipio Africanus but was defeated at ZAMA in 202. Carthage was reduced to being an African client of Rome but was continually forced to cede land to Rome's main ally in the region, MASSINISSA.

The Third Punic War (149–146 BC) began when Massinissa finally provoked the Carthaginians into attacking him. At the urgings of CATO, who had visited Carthage, the Romans issued an ultimatum containing demands that could not reasonably be met, and forced Carthage into war. Carthage succumbed in 146 after a three-year siege in which only a tenth of the population survived to be sold into slavery. The consul SCIPIO AEMILIANUS demolished the city and ploughed salt into its ashes. LPR

Caven (1980); Toynbee (1965); Warmington (1969a).

Pupienus (d. AD 238), Roman emperor, AD 238. Marcus Clodius Pupienus Maximus was a member of the board of 20 selected by the Senate to organize the defence of Italy against MAXIMINUS THRAX in 238, and, after GORDIAN I's death, was chosen joint emperor with BALBINUS. Pupienus became army commander, Balbinus civil commander. Resentment of Pupienus' German bodyguard was the direct cause of the assassination of both emperors by the praetorian guard, and the elevation of GORDIAN III. RJB

Grant (1985); Parker (1958).

Puteoli modern Pozzuoli, city in CAMPANIA. The site was colonized by Greeks from CUMAE c.520 BC and known as Dicaearchia. In the 4th century it passed to Roman control as Puteoli and resisted HANNIBAL in 215. In 194 it received a Roman colony and from the 2nd century on it flourished as a commercial port. It handled most of Rome's TRADE with the east, including corn, and seems not to have been diminished by the growth of OSTIA. Most of the population were engaged in commerce, but it was also a fashionable resort where wealthy Romans such as SULLA and CICERO built villas. GS

Stillwell (1976).

Pydna　battle in 168 BC. At Pydna, in Macedonia, Aemilius PAULLUS defeated King PERSEUS of Macedon. The Macedonian phalanx lost its order on broken ground and the maniples (*see* ARMY, ROMAN) acting individually, were able to infiltrate its ranks and cut the pikemen to pieces. Perseus fled but was later captured, and Macedon was divided into four republics.　　　　　　　　　　　　　　　　　　　　LPR

Connolly (1975); Gruen (1984).

Pylos　headland on the north side of the Bay of Navarino in the south-west Peloponnese. DEMOSTHENES fortified it in 425 BC as a base for expatriate Messenians to operate in Messenia and shake Spartan control. BRASIDAS failed to recapture it by sea. When the Spartans occupied the adjacent island of Sphacteria, the besiegers became the besieged. Demosthenes captured them and Athens used them as hostages to prevent invasion and enforce a peace.

See also PELOPONNESIAN WAR.　　　　　　　　　　　　　　　　　GLC

Kagan (1975).

Pyrgi　city in Italy. Pyrgi, modern Santa Severa, was an Etruscan port and sanctuary in the territory of CAERE on the west coast of Italy, about 30 miles north-west of OSTIA. Although its culture was Etruscan, excavations at the site have revealed extensive outside influences, which imply the presence of communities of foreign traders. The most important find was a bilingual inscription in Etruscan and Phoenician recording a dedication to the Phoenician goddess Astarte by the local ruler of Caere. The text dates from the early 5th century and proves among other things the existence at that period of links between CARTHAGE and central Italy.　　　　　　　　　　　　　　　　　　　HE

Coarelli (1974); Pallottino (1975).

Pyrrhon　(*c*.365–275 BC), Greek philosopher. Pyrrhon of Elis was the founder of Greek scepticism (*see* SCEPTICS). He is said to have been taught by Bryson, the Megarian philosopher, and then by the Democritean Anaxarchus whom he accompanied on Alexander's expedition to India. He left no writings and it is consequently difficult to determine how much later sceptics derived directly from him. His pupil TIMON of Phlius, however, defended Pyrrhon's position. From his works and other sceptical sources it may be inferred that due to the deceptions inherent in sense perception Pyrrhon concluded that positive knowledge was impossible, that judgement should be withheld about all things, and that appearances followed without commitment to any definite attitude towards them. Thus the sceptic is led to a state of imperturbability, his ultimate goal in life. JL

Long (1974).

Pyrrhus (319–272 BC), king of Epirus. Pyrrhus, a cousin of ALEXANDER THE GREAT, faced dynastic quarrels and exile in his early reign. In 302 BC Pyrrhus fled to his brother-in-law DEMETRIUS I POLIORCETES who, after IPSUS, sent him as hostage to PTOLEMY I. With Ptolemaic support he returned as king to EPIRUS after CASSANDER's death in 297. He unsuccessfully intrigued against Demetrius over the Macedonian succession, and joined the DIADOCHI's coalition against him after 292. Greatly expanding his Epirote kingdom, he expelled Demetrius in 288 and was proclaimed king of Macedon, although LYSIMACHUS later drove him back to Epirus. From 280 to 275 Pyrrhus fought campaigns for Greeks in Italy and Sicily against Rome and Carthage (winning a costly 'pyrrhic victory' at Heraclea). Ever an adventuring opportunist, he returned and opposed ANTIGONUS II GONATAS in Macedon and Greece. Allied with the Spartan CLEONYMUS, Pyrrhus invaded the Peloponnese in 272, attacked Sparta, and was driven back by Gonatas and AREUS I. He was killed in a street battle at Argos. EER

CAH VII.1, VIII; Errington (1990); Green (1990); Gruen (1984); Hammond (1967); Hammond and Walbank (1988).

Pythagoras (fl. *c*.530 BC), Greek philosopher. Pythagoras left Samos in 532/1 BC to escape the tyranny of POLYCRATES and settled at CROTON in south Italy, where he founded a religious community. The members of the brotherhood, which was open to both men and women, were bound by vows of secrecy and practised strict rules of abstinence. To show their respect they attributed their own discoveries to Pythagoras himself. No work of his has survived, although many were fathered upon him. Even by Aristotle's time he had become a figure of legend with the result that it is difficult to distinguish myth from reality. Eventually the Crotoniates rose in revolt and Pythagoras had to flee to Metapontum where he died.

Pythagoras evidently believed that the soul was immortal, confined within the body as a tomb and condemned to a cycle of reincarnation as a man, an animal, or even a plant. It was possible, however, to win release by purification. By contemplating the order inherent in the world about him and by assimilating himself to it, man became progressively purified until he eventually escaped the cycle of birth and achieved immortality. It seems likely that Pythagoras himself had discovered the numerical ratios determining the principal intervals of the musical scale and was led in consequence to his unifying hypothesis that 'all things are number', the belief that the world and everything in it was expressible in terms of number (or proportion). Starting from this first principle, Pythagoras and his followers devoted themselves first to arithmetic, using a notation consisting of patterns of dots (whence, incidentally, is derived our notion of 'square numbers'). The most important of these figures is the 'tetraktys of the decad' (attributed to Pythagoras himself) which represents the number 10 as the sum of the first four integers. Later, discovery of the incommensurability of side and diagonal of a right-angled triangle led to a greater concentration upon geometry. (It is unclear whether Pythagoras himself or a later follower was the discoverer of the theorem which bears his name.) Pythagoras' preoccupation with MATHEMATICS also led to advances in ASTRONOMY, most especially in the attempt to represent the motions of the heavenly bodies upon a geometrical basis.

See also NEOPYTHAGOREANISM.   JL

Guthrie, vol. 1 (1962); Kirk, Raven, and Schofield (1983).

Pytheas (late 4th century BC), Greek explorer. Pytheas was a native of MASSILIA and a member of its seafaring community. He explored the waters of northern Europe and wrote an account of his voyage. The account is lost but parts of it are briefly described by STRABO and PLINY THE ELDER. It seems that he sailed through the Straits of Gibraltar and up the Atlantic coast to Britain which he circumnavigated. From Britain he visited the island of 'Thule' (Iceland?) and the Baltic before returning via the English Channel to the Mediterranean. His observations contributed to the development of cartography.

See also NAVIGATION.   GS

Hawkes (1977).

Pythian Games festival held at DELPHI in honour of APOLLO. From earliest times the centrepiece was a musical competition for a hymn to the god. Originally held every eight years, the festival was reorganized in 582 BC and became four-yearly like the OLYMPIC GAMES, to which it ranked second in importance. Athletic and equestrian events were included, but music still took pride of place. The prize was a wreath of bay.

See also FESTIVALS, GREEK; GAMES, GREEK.   GS

Harris (1964).

Q

Quadi German tribe. The Quadi (part of the SUEBI) were forced from the Main (*c.*7 BC), and settled in Moravia, some being allowed by the Romans to move to Pannonia (*c.*AD 50). Domitian's war secured peace until the Marcomannic Wars (166–80). The Quadi (with the MARCOMANNI and SARMATIANS) remained a permanent threat to the empire, and in the 5th century some of the Quadi joined the VANDALS and ALANI, finally settling in Spain.   RJB

Thompson (1965); Todd (1975).

Quaestio Roman criminal court. A crime against the state too serious to be tried by a MAGISTRATE, or an appeal against such a trial (*see* PROVOCATIO), would be tried by a *quaestio*, at first an *ad hoc* court under a magistrate appointed by the SENATE or people, from which there was no appeal. In 149 BC PISO FRUGI set up the first permanent *quaestio* (*perpetua*) to try extortion cases (*see* RES REPETUNDAE). In the following years other standing courts were established to try various crimes.

The power of the *quaestiones* made the composition of the juries a political issue. Gaius GRACCHUS enacted that the juries should be drawn from the EQUESTRIAN ORDER. Conflict over the juries continued. SULLA gave them back to the Senate and formalized the *quaestiones*, each under a PRAETOR. From 70 BC senators, equestrians, and men of the TRIBUNUS AERARIUS class each composed one-third of the juries. CAESAR removed the *tribuni aerarii*. AUGUSTUS reorganized the *quaestiones*, and they continued into the 3rd century AD.

See also LAW, ROMAN.   HS

Brunt (1988); Jones (1972).

Quaestor Roman magistrate. The quaestorship was the lowest regular magistracy, usually held after that of TRIBUNUS MILITUM. Although the kings are said to have appointed quaestors to try capital crimes, in the historical period quaestors were primarily financial officials, two being in charge of the AERARIUM, others holding posts throughout Italy and the provinces. The number of quaestors rose from the original two until SULLA fixed it at 20, making the quaestorship compulsory for the CURSUS HONORUM, with a minimum age requirement of 30, and giving automatic elevation to the SENATE. CAESAR doubled the number of quaestors, but AUGUSTUS returned it to 20 and lowered the minimum age to 25. Under the Principate the *aerarium* was removed from the quaestors, and imperial officials gradually took over their duties in Italy. Quaestors continued to serve as financial officials of provincial governors, and two were quaestors of the emperor who read out his communications to the Senate.

The officials in charge of the finances of a colony or MUNICIPIUM were also called quaestors.

See also MAGISTRATES, ROMAN.   HS

Harris (1976); Jolowicz and Nicholas (1972); Millar (1977).

Quietus (d. AD 261), Roman emperor, AD 260–1. Fulvius Julius Quietus, younger son of the elder Macrianus, was created emperor in AD 260, together with his elder brother, the younger MACRIANUS. Left in Syria with the praetorian prefect Ballista, while his father and brother invaded Europe, Quietus was besieged in Emesa and killed by ODAENATHUS of Palmyra.   RJB

Grant (1985); Parker (1958).

Quinquereme *see* SHIPS.

Quintilian (*c.*AD 33–100), Latin writer. Marcus Fabius Quintilianus, a native of Calgurris in Spain, was educated in Rome under the orator Domitius Afer. After his return to Spain he was recalled by Galba and in 88 became Rome's first professional salaried teacher of RHETORIC. His pupils included PLINY THE YOUNGER and the heirs of Domitian. His only surviving work is the *Institutio Oratoria* in 12 books, published probably in 96. This wide-ranging study covers every aspect of the young orator's EDUCATION from infancy to his emergence as a qualified speaker. It includes an illuminating critique of Greek and Latin authors from the orator's standpoint. For Quintilian the aim of education was to produce not a pedant but a civilized man of high principles (*vir bonus*). He admired CICERO and adapted Ciceronian precepts to the needs of his time. His work exercised profound influence over

subsequent ancient and Renaissance writers. Two collections of declamations attributed to him are almost certainly spurious.   GS

Bonner (1977); Dorey (1975); Kennedy (1969).

Quintillus   (d. AD 270), Roman emperor, AD 270. Marcus Aurelius
Claudius Quintillus was the younger, and less able, brother of CLAUDIUS
II. Left by Claudius in command of an army concentrated around
Aquileia, he was proclaimed emperor by these troops after Claudius'
death in early 270, and recognized by the Senate. He was opposed,
however, by AURELIAN, and after Aurelian's proclamation at Sirmium,
Quintillus was deserted by his forces and committed suicide, having
reigned for only a few months.   RJB

Grant (1985); Parker (1958).

Quintus   (4th century AD), of Smyrna, Greek epic poet. Quintus was
the author of the extant *Posthomerica* (14 books), an EPIC in Homeric
hexameters which continues the story of the *Iliad* from the death of
Hector to the fall of Troy. It was perhaps intended to fill the gap
between the two epics of Homer and to supersede the account of the
EPIC CYCLE.   GS

Vian (1959).

Quirinal   part of Rome. The Quirinal was the most northerly of the
Roman hills, lying to the west of the Viminal and north of the FORUM
ROMANUM. It was traditionally connected with the SABINES, and there are
indications that it may have been the site of an early settlement parallel to that on the PALATINE, but this has not yet been confirmed by
archaeology. During the Republic several temples were built there
(including those to QUIRINUS, Fortuna, Salus, and Semo Sancus), while
under the early Empire it was the site of many luxurious houses and
formed Augustus' *regio* vi. Diocletian and Constantine built large bath
complexes there. It was included in the WALL OF SERVIUS.   HE

Momigliano (1963b); Platner and Ashby (1929); Richardson (1992); Robinson
(1992).

Quirinius   (d. AD 21), Roman general. Publius Sulpicius Quirinius,
consul in 12 BC, was one of the most able and loyal of Augustus'
generals. His successes included dealing with the Marmaridae, a tribe
to the south of the province of Cyrene (before 12 BC), and later, as
governor of Galatia and Pamphylia, subduing the Homanades tribe
(*c*.AD 1) in Asia Minor. His most famous act, however, was as the
governor of Syria: St Luke's gospel (2:2) records the census (tax

assessment) of Judaea conducted by Cyrenius (Quirinius, AD 6), a census made necessary by the deposition of Archelaus and the conversion of Judaea into a Roman province.   RJB

Millar (1981); Scullard (1982).

Quirinus   Roman god. Quirinus was an obscure god, possibly of Sabine origin, connected with the QUIRINAL hill, where a temple was built to him in 293 BC, and with Quirites, an alternative name for the Roman people. Quirinus was also a member of an ancient trinity of gods, perhaps representing fertility, along with JUPITER (sovereignty) and MARS (war). At some point, perhaps relatively late, he was identified with ROMULUS. His festival was celebrated on 17 February.   HE

Dumézil (1970); Scullard (1981).

Qumran   *see* DEAD SEA SCROLLS.

R

Raetia Roman province. Raetia was an Alpine province, which (with NORICUM to the east) provided an important northern buffer for Italy. The territory included parts of Bavaria and Switzerland, and the Tyrol. The Camunni and the Vennones were defeated by P. Silius Nerva (16 BC), and DRUSUS and TIBERIUS defeated the Raeti and Vindelici. At first under the governor of Gaul, Raetia later had its own governor, based in Augusta Vindelicorum, commanding an auxiliary force. With the region's increased military importance during Marcus AURELIUS' Marcomannic Wars, an imperial legate commanding Legion III Italica governed Raetia. Under Gallienus Raetia reverted to equestrian control, and Diocletian's administrative reorganization split Raetia in two, although the military command remained unified under a *dux Raetiarum*. Germanic tribes exerted increasing pressure, and some territory was abandoned to the ALAMANNI after 389. From *c.*450 most of the plain was reoccupied by Germanic tribes and by *c.*482 Rome retained only the Alpine regions.   RJB

Millar (1981); Mommsen (1968).

Raphia battle in 217 BC. Raphia, in south-west Palestine near Gaza, was the site of a battle during the Fourth Syrian War between PTOLEMY IV and ANTIOCHUS III, who had invaded Ptolemaic Syria and Palestine *en route* to Egypt. Here the Ptolemies first deployed African ELEPHANTS against the Seleucids' Indian elephants. Although the Indian animals proved superior, Antiochus was defeated with the help of Ptolemy's native Egyptian troops. Hereafter Antiochus turned his attention eastward to his Asian empire.   EER

Bar-Kochva (1976); CAH VII.1; Scullard (1974).

Ravenna city in northern Italy. Perhaps an Etruscan foundation, Ravenna was an Umbrian city before it came under Roman control c.190 BC. It gained citizenship in 89 and was used by CAESAR as a base before he crossed the Rubicon in 49. AUGUSTUS made it the base for his Adriatic fleet which brought it enduring commercial prosperity and a cosmopolitan population. In AD 402 it became the capital of the western emperor HONORIUS and subsequently of the barbarian kings ODOACER and Theodoric II. From the 5th century date some of the city's finest surviving buildings, notably the Orthodox Baptistery (originally baths) and the tomb of Galla PLACIDIA (celebrated for its magnificent interior mosaic decoration). The monuments of Ravenna illustrate better than those of any other Italian city the fashions of art and architecture in late antiquity.   GS

Krautheimer (1975); Matthews (1990).

Recuperator Roman juryman. *Recuperatores* were used in certain cases to replace a IUDEX. Initially their use was restricted to cases involving PEREGRINI, though this was later extended to include cases between citizens. Cases tried before *recuperatores* were resolved faster than those coming before a *iudex* because of restrictions on both the length of the trial and the number of witnesses. It is not known why certain citizen trials came before *recuperatores*.   HE

Nicholas (1962).

Red-figure *see* PAINTING, GREEK.

Regia religious building in Rome. The Regia was a trapezoidal building in the Forum, between the Sacred Way and the House of the Vestals. In the late Republic it was the place where the PONTIFEX Maximus carried out his sacred duties, but its name indicates that it had formerly belonged to the king – either the REX or the REX SACRORUM (or both). Recent excavations have shown that, although rebuilt several times, the Regia had existed since the late 7th century BC.   TC

CAH VII.2; Platner and Ashby (1929); Richardson (1992).

Regillus, Lake battle c.496 BC. At Lake Regillus, near TUSCULUM in Latium, the dictator Aulus POSTUMIUS defeated the LATIN LEAGUE and its ally TARQUINIUS SUPERBUS. The resulting treaty, signed by Sp. CASSIUS VECELLINUS c.493, helped the Latins and the Romans to resist the attacks of the VOLSCI and the AEQUI. Livy's battle account is focused on the 'epic' deeds of individual aristocrats. After the victory, a temple to Castor was founded in Rome.   LPR

CAH VII.2.

Regio the term for a quarter of the city of ROME. Under the Republic there were four *regiones;* but AUGUSTUS increased their number to 14 and reorganized their administration under AEDILES, PRAETORS, and TRIBUNI PLEBIS. The *regiones* were subdivided into 265 parishes (*vici*), each of which was in the care of four elected VICOMAGISTRI. The same word was also used for the 11 *regiones* into which Augustus divided ITALY. (*See* map on page 756.)   GS

Regulus (3rd century BC), Roman general. Marcus Atilius Regulus captured BRUNDISIUM during his first consulate (267 BC). During his second (256), in the First PUNIC WAR, he led an expedition against Carthage. After winning a naval battle at Ecnomus he landed in Africa and captured Tunis. He failed to come to terms with the Carthaginians, however, and in 255 was defeated and captured. He was later sent to Rome to negotiate, unsuccessfully, and voluntarily returned to Carthage where he was put to death by torture.   HE

Regulus (fl. later 1st century AD), Roman informer. Marcus Aquilius Regulus was a notorious informer during the reign of NERO (AD 54–68), and became prominent again, for the same reason, during the last years of DOMITIAN (*c*.89–96). Informers such as Regulus were encouraged to act as *agents provocateurs*, and could be handsomely rewarded for bringing the often trivial charges that, after the formality of a trial, led to the condemnation of, in particular, a number of prominent senators.   RJB

Salmon (1968).

Relegatio a form of Roman punishment that entailed expulsion from Roman territory. It was applied with different levels of severity, from temporary banishment without loss of citizenship or property to the extreme form known as *deportatio*, by which the victim was sent to a specific place, usually an island, for life. In the early Principate it was used by emperors to get rid of high-placed persons, including relatives, who had become a threat or an embarrassment (*see* e.g. JULIA MAJOR).   TC

Religion, Greek Public religion centred on worship of the gods of Olympus who were ruled by ZEUS. Our knowledge of it derives partly from literature and partly from archaeology. Many of its beliefs and practices were absorbed into Roman religion; almost none survived the fall of paganism. Private religion focused on the cult of the dead and the various mystery cults. Some of its manifestations survived in the folk religion of the Christian era. In the archaic and early classical periods piety was the order of the day; in the 4th and subsequent centuries BC a degree of scepticism was fostered by contemporary poets and philosophers (*see* SOPHISTS; STOICS).

Public Religion: The most conspicuous surviving evidence of Greek religion is architectural. A temple (*see* ARCHITECTURE, GREEK) was dedicated to one particular god or goddess whose cult provided the focus of public religion for the neighbourhood. It was the god's dwelling place, and it contained his image. It did not house his worshippers, who congregated at the altar outside the building. Rituals such as offerings, libations, sacrifices, and prayers were performed at the altar by PRIESTS who were the servants of the god. The shrine itself was not always a building: it might take the form of a cave, or tree, or mountain top. Similarly, the object of the cult was not necessarily a god: it might equally be a hero (*see* HERO CULT).

FESTIVALS were celebrated at regular intervals and provided an opportunity for the local community to enjoy a feast and to honour the god. Processions with dancing and hymns were a common feature; sometimes athletic, musical, or dramatic competition formed a part of the programme.

Since the gods were thought to intervene directly in human affairs, it was necessary to placate them by means of offerings and sacrifices. It was also advisable to consult them before taking any important decision, for which purpose ORACLES existed to serve both public and private interests.

Above all, public religion in Greece was inextricably bound up in the organization of the POLIS. It was part and parcel of the social and political identity of the community. As such it was inescapable. In the Hellenistic period it developed a further dimension in the shape of the RULER CULT.

Private Religion: Below the level of public religion was a whole series of religious subcultures which may have played a far more important role in the lives of ordinary people but about which we know far less. Most important of these were the mystery cults (*see* ELEUSINIAN MYSTERIES; ORPHISM) which were secret and involved some sort of initiation procedure. Because they required a degree of personal commitment that went beyond the obligations attaching to membership of the polis, they are likely to have inspired a greater sense of responsibility and devotion in their initiates than the public cults.

Another expression of private religion and of family identity is seen in the cult of the dead (*see* BURIAL PRACTICES, GREEK). The traditions associated with it presuppose an unquestioned belief in the AFTERLIFE around which so many private rituals revolved.

If oracles provided the public means for gods to guide men's behaviour, signs and their interpretation by seers were their private counterpart (*see* DIVINATION). Because the Greeks had no revealed scriptures, signs formed the principal regular channel of communication with the supernatural and were ignored at men's peril.

See also HERMETICA; ISIS. GS

Burkert (1983, 1985, 1987); Dodds (1951); Easterling and Muir (1985); Festugière (1954); Lawson (1910); Martin (1987); Parker (1983).

Religion, Roman Roman religion was founded on the sense of spirits everywhere. Instead of examining empirically such crucial processes as harvest, pregnancy, and trade, the Romans preferred to assume that everything was the result of divine agency. Their view was polytheistic: different gods controlled the different parts of life. Such gods could be highly particularized. Each Roman household had its own shrine with its own individual protecting gods (the LARES and PENATES). A list of gods that a farmer could invoke included First Plougher, Second Plougher, Harrower, Sower, Top Dresser, Hoer, Raker, etc. Each copse, lake, river, and spring was thought to have its own immanent spirit. Different trade GUILDS pinned their hopes not on statistical analysis but on their own particular gods. Towns had their patron deities.

From this crowd of spirits certain gods emerged as leading powers. Under Etruscan influence the trio of JUPITER, JUNO, and MINERVA in their temple on the Capitoline Hill became dominant, with Jupiter, Best and Greatest, as the special Roman champion. As Rome came into contact with the Greek world, her principal gods were identified with their appropriate Greek counterparts (such as MARS with ARES and Vulcan with HEPHAESTUS) and adopted their iconography and mythology (*see* RELIGION, GREEK).

Romans spent much time trying to ensure that the appropriate gods were on their side. The three main means, common to both public and private religion, were (a) prayer, by which a request could be brought to the notice of the gods; (b) SACRIFICE, which could induce a god to grant the request; (c) DIVINATION, by which the will of the gods could be made known to men. All three methods involved intricate procedures, based on traditional rituals. Provided that the rites were properly carried out, there was a good chance that the god concerned would show favour. A worshipper was not expected to love his god or to behave morally because of his religion. But the details had to be punctiliously observed: the squeaking of a rat could invalidate a ceremony. This business-like, contractual nature of Roman religion is seen clearly in the common practice of vows, public and private. A public vow might be a promise made by a magistrate on behalf of the state to build a new temple, if a certain battle was won. A private individual might fix on a temple wall a tablet containing his promise of a sacrifice, if his son came safe home from war.

There was no priestly class at Rome. In the home the *paterfamilias* carried out the necessary ritual. State religion was looked after by PRIESTS who were drawn from the political élite and pronounced on religious matters under the supervision of the Senate. Official calendars gave Romans the timetable for their annual FESTIVALS. Many will have been of only antiquarian interest, but festivals like the LUPERCALIA and the PARENTALIA still made an impact.

In practice Roman religion was more diverse than this picture. Stoicism and Epicureanism influenced the upper classes, and Oriental cults like MITHRAISM and the BACCHANALIA swept through Italy sporadically. Under the Principate the RULER CULT was firmly established but in the 4th century AD CHRISTIANITY became the religion of the empire.

See also ISIS. DP

Beard and North (1990); CAH VII.2; Dumézil (1970); Liebeschuetz (1979); Ogilvie (1969); Scullard (1981).

Remus *see* ROMULUS AND REMUS.

Res Gestae *see* MONUMENTUM ANCYRANUM.

Res privata imperial finance department. The *res privata principis* was a new private treasury created by Septimius SEVERUS (AD 193–211). As the bulk of the emperor's private income (PATRIMONIUM) went into the imperial treasury (*fiscus*), Severus instituted the *res privata* to receive the confiscated property of Pescennius Niger and Clodius Albinus, and all future imperial acquisitions. It rapidly surpassed the *patrimonium*, and was administered by an official equal in rank to the controller of the *fiscus*.

See also CONSISTORIUM; FINANCE, ROMAN. RJB

Parker (1958).

Res repetundae extortion. Trials for *res repetundae*, the abuse of power by Roman MAGISTRATES or pro-magistrates in the provinces (*see* PROVINCIA), usually extortion of money from provincials, were, from 149 BC, heard in the first standing court (QUAESTIO *perpetua*) established at Rome by PISO FRUGI. The court and its procedures were thoroughly reformed by Gaius GRACCHUS, after whom the composition of the jury became a bone of contention. Members of the SENATE were eager to control the courts and reluctant to condemn governors who were members of their own order. Members of the EQUESTRIAN ORDER, from which the PUBLICANI were drawn, were keen to condemn governors who interfered with the exploitation of provinces by *publicani* (*see* RUTILIUS RUFUS).

See also LAW, ROMAN; PROCONSUL.   HS

Jones (1972).

Rex Roman king. Traditionally Rome was ruled by seven kings: ROMULUS, NUMA POMPILIUS, TULLUS HOSTILIUS, Ancus MARCIUS, TARQUINIUS PRISCUS, SERVIUS TULLIUS, and TARQUINIUS SUPERBUS. With the exception of Romulus, all seem to have been historical figures. The monarchy disappeared at the end of the 6th century BC, though it is uncertain whether it developed into the Republic, as some modern scholars believe, or was overthrown by a revolution, as the Roman tradition maintained. Little is known for certain about the nature of Roman kingship, although it seems that succession was elective, not hereditary (*see* INTERREX). Some features of royal power, such as the FASCES, were supposedly inherited by the republican magistrates, and the king's priestly role was reflected in the institution of the REX SACRORUM. In the late Republic the term *rex* was disliked in political circles, and was rejected by CAESAR and the emperors.   HE

CAH VII.2; Heurgon (1973); Weinstock (1971).

Rex Sacrorum Roman priest. The Rex Sacrorum was a priest who under the Republic performed the religious functions of the former REX. According to tradition, the founders of the Republic enacted that the priest-king should be a patrician, a lifelong member of the pontifical college subordinate to the PONTIFEX Maximus, and wholly excluded from political office and membership of the Senate. In the late Republic the Rex Sacrorum was an obscure figure, who nevertheless still had a role in the religious calendar, performing sacrifices at the beginning of each month and on certain other days.   TC

CAH VII.2; Scullard (1981).

Rhegium modern Reggio di Calabria, city on the toe of Italy opposite MESSANA. Founded from Zancle (Messana) by Chalcidians and Messenians *c.*720 BC, Rhegium occupied a strategic position controlling the straits. Under ANAXILAS its power grew but in 387 it was destroyed by Syracuse under DIONYSIUS I. It later resisted the assaults of the BRUTTII, PYRRHUS, and HANNIBAL and as a loyal ally of Rome became a *municipium* after 90 BC. It was the home of the Greek poet IBYCUS and remained Greek-speaking throughout antiquity.   GS

Dunbabin (1948).

Rhetoric, Greek If oratory was the child of DEMOCRACY, then rhetoric, which is the study of the theory of oratory, was its grandchild. The establishment of democracies in many parts of the Greek world from the 6th century BC on meant that the prime management skill required by the politician anxious to succeed was the power to persuade. PERICLES was by all accounts an impressive performer. Although oratory as a literary genre did not take root before the last quarter of the 5th century BC, the theory of it had already been propounded by the SOPHISTS in the preceding decades, and once literary oratory emerged as a primarily Athenian genre, rhetoric followed it as the Athenian discipline *par excellence*. Schools of rhetoric, such as that established by ISOCRATES, provided an EDUCATION that was far more relevant to the needs of the day than anything offered by the philosophical institutes such as Plato's ACADEMY. DEMOSTHENES was its most celebrated practitioner, ARISTOTLE its most influential theoretician. His *Rhetoric* considered the theory of rhetorical debate, its effect on the audience, and its style, and it propounded the tripartite distinction between judicial, deliberative, and epideictic oratory.

With the demise of the city-state, political oratory lost its purpose, but rhetoric survived to become the mainstay of higher education and the principal vehicle for the universal spread of Greek culture. Theories were developed and handbooks written; but for our knowledge of rhetoric in the Hellenistic period we are dependent on Latin sources. CICERO's *De Inventione* follows a Hellenistic division of the subject into five categories: content, arrangement, style, memory, delivery. However artificial the theory, it was always closely linked with forensic practice and major political issues were discussed in the schools. Greek rhetoric enjoyed a new lease of life in the more peaceful conditions of the later Empire with the notable achievements of HERMOGENES OF TARSUS in the 3rd century and LIBANIUS in the 4th.

See also ATTICISM. GS

Kennedy (1963, 1972); Vickers (1988).

Rhetoric, Latin Rhetorical theory, based on Greek models, was introduced to Rome in the last quarter of the 2nd century BC. The earliest textbook to survive is the anonymous *Rhetorica ad Herennium* (*c*.85 BC) which divides the subject into the five Hellenistic categories (invention, arrangement, delivery, memory, and style) but subjects it to an original Latin analysis. Closely related to this is the *De Inventione* of CICERO which is not a complete handbook but provides further evidence of Rome's debt to and adaptation of Greek techniques. Cicero later refined his own attitude to rhetorical EDUCATION in his *De Oratore* (55 BC), commending the orator who could speak well on any topic, and in his *Orator* (46 BC) in which he contrasted DEMOSTHENES (and by implication himself) as the model orator with the narrow-minded fanaticism of the so-called Atticists.

Under the Principate oratory moved its focus from politics to the law court; and the practice of declamation (*declamatio*), which had always formed a part of rhetorical training, acquired a new status as an independent genre. Despite criticism from many quarters for its bad taste (SENECA THE ELDER) and artificiality (TACITUS), the influence of *declamatio* on education and on literature was profound and enduring. Rhetorical studies flourished none the less, as is clear from the *Institutio* of QUINTILIAN, and the impact of a rhetorical education on the style of Latin poetry and drama is evident in the work of such writers as HORACE, JUVENAL, LUCAN, OVID, SENECA THE YOUNGER, and VIRGIL. But there is no denying that oratory was on the decline (*see* the *Dialogus* of Tacitus), and with the revival of Greek letters in the later Empire the baton of rhetoric was passed back to its original holders.

See RHETORIC, GREEK.   GS

Bonner (1977); Kennedy (1972); Vickers (1988).

Rhianus (b. *c.*275 BC), Greek epic poet and scholar. Rhianus was a Cretan and may not have belonged to the Alexandrian circle, though he clearly operated in its tradition. His poetry included a mythological epic on Heracles (four books) and a historical treatment of the Second Messenian War (*c.*660 BC; *see* ARISTOMENES), as well as topographical poems and epigrams. His scholarly edition of Homer is represented by more than 40 readings in the Homeric scholia.   GS

Pfeiffer (1968); Wade-Grey (1966); Webster (1964).

Rhine (Latin Rhenus), river in northern Europe. From the time of CAESAR the Rhine traditionally formed the northern frontier of the empire, despite the temporary occupation of the AGRI DECUMATES. A fleet (*classis Germanica*) was stationed by AUGUSTUS at COLONIA AGRIPPINENSIS in 12 BC and eight legions were deployed along the length of the frontier, between which the river provided a vital means of communication. It was also an important artery for TRADE with northern Europe. It was finally abandoned in 406 in the face of a massive barbarian invasion of ALANI, SUEBI, and VANDALS.   GS

Millar (1981).

Rhodes Greek island. Rhodes's three city-states (Lindus, Ialysus, and Camirus) synoecized into a single state, with a capital also called Rhodes, in 408/7 BC. The 4th century saw the establishment of a stable democracy, domination by CARIA (355–333), and the imposition of a garrison by ALEXANDER THE GREAT *c.*332. During the DIADOCHI's struggles Rhodes refused to help ANTIGONUS I MONOPHTHALMUS against PTOLEMY I, and was unsuccessfully besieged for a year (305/4) by DEMETRIUS I

POLIORCETES (*see* CHARES OF LINDUS). Remaining a staunch Ptolemaically, Rhodes attained considerable prosperity through her commercially favourable geographical position, and, after *c*.250, took over from Egypt policing the seas against PIRACY. She cooperated with Rome against PHILIP V and ANTIOCHUS III, receiving vast territory in Asia Minor as a reward. Her ambivalent attitude towards PERSEUS led to Roman punishment, and an unequal alliance in 168. Though remaining independent and prosperous, Rhodes ceased to be a power. She resisted MITHRIDATES VI in 88 and was sacked by CASSIUS in 43 BC.   EER

Berthold (1984); Green (1990); Gruen (1984); Sherwin-White (1984).

Ricimer   (d. AD 472), Roman politician. Flavius Ricimer, grandson of the Visigothic king Wallia, was 'kingmaker' of the western Roman empire and effective ruler of Italy from 456 to 472. As Master of Soldiers (MAGISTER MILITUM), he won a naval victory over the Vandals off Corsica (456), and deposed AVITUS (October 456), replacing him with MAJORIAN (April 457). Majorian's failure against the Vandals led Ricimer to remove him (August 461) and appoint Libius Severus (November 461–August 465), a mere figurehead; then for 20 months Ricimer ruled alone. He accepted LEO's nominee ANTHEMIUS (April 467), and married Anthemius' daughter, but eventually replaced Anthemius with OLYBRIUS (472), shortly before his own death (August).   RJB

Bury (1958); Grant (1985).

Roads, Roman   As Rome's power extended, so did the network of her roads, first in Italy and then throughout the Mediterranean basin, until there were 53,000 miles of major roads. They often connected Rome with fortified outposts (colonies) in hostile territory. Troops and supplies could move swiftly along them. Later followed TRADE and fraternization with the natives. Roads of earlier powers such as the Etruscans tended to be well made only in limited areas, but Roman roads were thoroughly constructed over long stretches. The secret of their permanence was their foundation of large stones overlaid by smaller stones, sometimes bound by cement. The surface could be of gravel, cobbles, or paving stones. The roads were given a camber and side ditches for drainage. Often the foundations were laid on top of a high mound or *agger*. Wherever practicable the roads were straight; surveyors took sightings from one high point to the next or in flat country used smoke from fires. Milestones gave the distance from some centre and often the name of the builder of the road and the date. Under the Republic the CENSORS were responsible for roads and let out contracts for their construction and repair.

Today, centuries after the completion of their task of controlling and romanizing the provinces, Roman roads often provide the basis of modern transport systems.

See also AEMILIA, VIA; APPIA, VIA; EGNATIA, VIA; FLAMINIA, VIA; POSTAL SERVICE. DP

Chevallier (1976); Potter (1987); Wiseman (1987).

Roman confederacy *see* SOCII.

Rome, history *To 31 BC:* The beginnings of Rome are lost in legend. According to the story, the city took its name from ROMULUS, who founded it in 753 BC and became its first king. Traditionally Rome had seven kings (*see* REX), the last of whom, TARQUINIUS SUPERBUS, was expelled in 509 BC and replaced by a republic.

It is difficult to know how much truth there is in these legends. Archaeologists have established that one or more villages existed on the site from the end of the Bronze Age (*c*.1000 BC) and that by 600 BC the settlement had developed into a substantial city-state. At the time of the overthrow of Tarquin, which is probably an authentic historical event, Rome possessed an extensive territory, a strong army, and a wide network of commercial and diplomatic contacts.

Under the Republic power was exercised by two annual CONSULS, who commanded the army and ruled the city. They were advised by a council of elders (the SENATE), and in the course of time were joined by other MAGISTRATES (*see* PRAETOR; QUAESTOR, etc.) who, like the consuls, were annually elected.

At first all political and religious offices were dominated by the PATRICIANS; but during the 4th century other wealthy citizens, representing the plebeians, also obtained access to magistracies and priesthoods (*see* OGULNIUS; STOLO). This was a victory for the PLEBS, who in 494 BC had formed their own assembly and elected TRIBUNES to represent them. The tribunes agitated for the codification of the law, which was realized in 450 BC with the publication of the TWELVE TABLES, and managed to secure better economic conditions for their followers. In 287 BC the plebeians obtained the right to pass legally binding enactments in their assemblies (*see* PLEBISCITUM), and at this point the struggle between the patricians and plebeians was finally ended.

In the 4th century, after a temporary setback in 390 when the city was sacked by the Gauls (*see* BRENNUS), the Romans gradually expanded their power. Part of the land they conquered was used to found colonies (*see* COLONIZATION, ROMAN); the rest was left to its original owners who were obliged to become allies (SOCII) and to fight for Rome in subsequent wars. This arrangement increased Rome's manpower resources and pushed her into further conquests. By 272 BC she had conquered all of peninsular Italy; its peoples were now allies, and over 25 colonies had been founded.

Shortly afterwards the Romans became involved in a major overseas war, when they challenged the Carthaginians for the control of SICILY. In spite of immense losses, the Romans finally emerged as victors in the First PUNIC WAR (264–241BC), and Sicily became the first province. The Second Punic War began in 218 when HANNIBAL sought revenge by invading Italy. In spite of spectacular victories, Hannibal failed to win over Rome's Italian allies and was gradually worn down; he withdrew from Italy in 204 and was finally defeated at ZAMA.

As a result the Romans obtained further provinces from the former Carthaginian possessions in Spain, and were drawn into imperialistic ventures in the eastern Mediterranean. In the following decades they decisively defeated the major Hellenistic kingdoms in Greece and Asia Minor (see MACEDONIAN WARS). By 167 BC Rome dominated the whole Mediterranean. After a third Punic War (149–146) Carthage was destroyed and AFRICA became a Roman province. GREECE was made a province at the same time; ASIA followed in 133, and then southern GAUL in 121, CILICIA in 101, and CYRENAICA in 96.

These overseas conquests had a dramatic effect on all aspects of life at home. In the first place they consolidated the power of the NOBILES, who dominated the Senate and senior magistracies. The growth of empire also increased the wealth of the upper classes, who hastened to invest it in land. This led to the growth of large estates (LATIFUNDIA), worked by war captives imported as slaves (see SLAVERY, ROMAN). Slave labour replaced the small peasant proprietors, who formed the backbone of the Roman ARMY but found that prolonged military service in distant theatres made it increasingly difficult to maintain their farms. Roman and Italian peasants were thus the victims of their own success, and were driven off the land to a life of penury. Peasant displacement led not only to discontent, but also to growing military problems, since the law laid down a property qualification for service in the army.

As the rich grew richer, they began to adopt luxurious and increasingly sophisticated habits. The influence of Greek culture became pervasive; architecture, literature, and the visual arts flourished, as the Romans imitated all the trappings of Greek civilization, to the dismay of traditionalists like CATO the Censor.

The widening gulf between rich and poor eventually gave rise to violent conflict. In 133 BC Tiberius GRACCHUS attempted to reclaim AGER PUBLICUS from the rich and redistribute it to the poor. There was furious opposition, and Gracchus himself was murdered. Ten years later his brother Gaius suffered the same fate when he attempted to bring in a series of radical reforms.

In the following generation Rome faced hostile military threats in every part of the empire, leading to wars against JUGURTHA, the CIMBRI, and the Italian *socii* (*see* SOCIAL WAR). These crises showed the ruling oligarchy to be corrupt and incompetent, and they were only resolved by elevating able and ambitious individuals to positions of power, and by creating a professional army from the proletariat.

These measures solved the military problems, but had fatal political consequences, because they provided the poor with a means to redress their grievances, and ambitious nobles with the chance to gain personal power by means of armed force. The first CIVIL WAR was between MARIUS and SULLA (88–86 BC). Both men marched against the city and massacred their political opponents; in 81 Sulla set himself up as dictator. His attempts at reform were ineffectual, however, and the same lethal trends continued. A fresh series of military crises in the 70s enabled POMPEY to gain a temporary pre-eminence; but he could not prevent other leaders from imitating him. In 49 BC his rival, Julius CAESAR, the victor of the GALLIC WARS, invaded Italy and once again plunged the empire into civil war. After defeating Pompey at PHARSALUS Caesar became consul and dictator for life.

Caesar embarked on a series of grandiose reforms, but his monarchical tendencies aroused opposition. On 15 March 44 BC he fell victim to the conspiracy of BRUTUS and CASSIUS LONGINUS. They were unable to restore the Republic, however, because Caesar's chief aides, ANTONY and LEPIDUS, had the support of his armies; in 43 they joined Caesar's heir, the 19-year-old OCTAVIAN, in a ruling TRIUMVIRATE. Lepidus was soon squeezed out, and the empire was uneasily divided between Octavian and Antony until 31 BC, when the issue was decided in Octavian's favour at ACTIUM. Mark Antony and his mistress CLEOPATRA committed suicide, leaving Octavian in complete control of the empire.

TC

Boardman, Griffin, and Murray (1986); Brunt (1971b, 1988); CAH VII.2, VIII; Crawford (1978); Grant (1979); Hopkins (1978); Mommsen (1861); Nicolet (1980); Scullard (1980, 1982).

31 BC–AD 476: The history of Rome from 31 BC is dominated by the emperors. The first emperor, AUGUSTUS (31 BC–AD 14), evolved a position as a constitutional monarch that placed emphasis upon powers with respectable Republican precedents, rather than upon his real power base, the legions. All the emperors up to MACRINUS (AD 217–18) were senators, and although the emperors became increasingly openly autocratic from the Flavian period (AD 69–96), most tried to work with the SENATE: the emperor CARUS (AD 282–3) was the first to omit to obtain the sanction of the Senate for his elevation.

The emperor's position was technically that of PRINCEPS (leading man), wielding powers that were of Republican nature and exceptional only in their extent and their concentration in the hands of an individual. The emperor depended upon the powers of IMPERIUM *maius* and *tribunicia potestas*, with certain consular powers. He was chief priest (PONTIFEX Maximus) and, as his position became more obvious, the need, felt by earlier emperors, to avoid the consulship and censorship became less acute: the Flavians held the consulship in most years (frequently VESPASIAN and TITUS together), and DOMITIAN was censor throughout his reign (AD 81–96).

The constitutional ambiguities were most acutely felt in the naming of successors. Augustus marked out his successors by adopting them, establishing the 'dynastic' principle: when the emperor had a son, he intended him to succeed (e.g. Vespasian was succeeded by Titus); where he had no son, he adopted one. The candidate nominally had to be acceptable to the Senate: in practice, the approval of the PRAETORIAN GUARD and of the legions was more important.

The Senate and people of Rome, effectively deprived of their constitutional rights in elections and legislation, instead gained relative peace and economic prosperity. Imperial control gradually extended to most aspects of life, including the price of food, the corn supply, the maintenance of public buildings and aqueducts. Frequent donatives were distributed on behalf of the emperor, games and shows kept the people entertained, and large amounts of the profit from the empire were used to adorn the city. The Roman emperors built extensively: most of the buildings, e.g. the COLOSSEUM, begun by Vespasian (AD 69–79) and completed by his son Titus (79–81), were in Rome, although other areas benefited as well, e.g. Achaea under NERO (AD 54–68) and HADRIAN (AD 117–38); Africa, particularly LEPTIS MAGNA, under Septimius SEVERUS (AD 193–211).

The reign of Augustus was the last great age of Roman expansion, after which the essential shape of the empire was established, circling the Mediterranean and extending north to the Danube and the Rhine (and beyond). Further territory was incorporated by CLAUDIUS I, who began the conquest of Britain (AD 43); and by TRAJAN who established the provinces of Dacia (AD 106) and Arabia (106) as well as the short-lived provinces of Armenia, Mesopotamia, and Cappodocia (abandoned 117). The empire reached its greatest extent following the Parthian campaigns under Marcus AURELIUS (AD 162–6) and Septimius Severus (AD 198), with the annexation of Mesopotamia, which extended Roman power eastwards to the Tigris.

The early imperial period saw a gradual transition from the expansionist policy of the Republican period to a more defensive, fixed-frontier policy. The land between the upper Rhine and upper Danube (the AGRI DECUMATES) was occupied by the Flavians (AD 69–96), shortening the northern frontier, and informal frontiers were gradually replaced by more permanent structures (*see* LIMES; WALL OF HADRIAN). This defensive outlook became more deeply ingrained as population pressure from migrating Germanic tribes (GERMANI) to the north of the empire, as well as internal pressures, and the military threat posed by the Sassanian empire in Persia, forced the Romans onto the defensive in the 3rd and 4th centuries AD.

The provinces of the empire gained greatly from the relative peace provided by the *pax Romana*, enjoying considerable local independence and a general increase in prosperity up to the mid-3rd century AD. Most provinces became substantially romanized, with the spread of Roman-style urban society and amenities, and the growth of an empire-wide trading network in commodities such as corn, wine, oils, metals, pottery, and glass. A substantial road network, built largely for military purposes, also aided communications and commerce, as did a single currency. In the west, Latin culture predominated, although in the east Greek culture (Hellenism) remained pre-eminent, and Greek remained the language of the educated classes. The pagan Roman empire successfully assimilated many foreign religions by equating newly encountered gods with members of its own pantheon (e.g. Jupiter Dolichenus). Adherents of monotheistic religions such as Christianity were occasionally persecuted for political reasons until, under CONSTANTINE I (AD 307–37), Christianity became the official religion of the empire.

From *c*.AD 238 many provinces suffered the effects of increasingly frequent and severe barbarian incursions, which forced the abandonment of Roman territory north of the Rhine and Danube (Agri Decumates, *c*.259/60; Dacia, *c*.270). Beset by internal and external threats, GALLIENUS (AD 253–68) was forced to tolerate the breakaway Gallic and Palmyrene empires. AURELIAN (AD 270–75) succeeded in reuniting the empire, and, to counter the problems of the empire, DIOCLETIAN (AD 284–305) established a tetrarchic system of two Augusti and two subordinate Caesars. During the 3rd and 4th centuries AD the centre of gravity of the empire gradually shifted eastwards, and Constantine established a new capital at CONSTANTINOPLE (Byzantium, modern Istanbul), dedicated in AD 330.

THEODOSIUS I (AD 379–95) formally split the empire between his two sons ARCADIUS (eastern emperor, AD 395–408) and HONORIUS (western emperor, AD 395–423). In the 5th century the western empire depended increasingly upon barbarian generals to stem the tide of barbarian invasions. The threat of invasion prompted Honorius to move the capital of the western empire from Rome to RAVENNA (AD 404): Rome itself was sacked by the Goths under ALARIC (AD 410), and again by the VANDALS under Gaiseric (AD 455). Finally, it became part of the kingdom of ODOACER (first barbarian king of Italy, AD 476–93), who deposed

ROMULUS AUGUSTULUS (AD 475–6). The eastern empire, however, survived, and as the Byzantine empire remained unconquered until the Turkish invasion of 1453. RJB

Grant (1979); Millar (1981); Wells (1984).

Rome, topography   Archaeology has confirmed the tradition that the earliest (8th-century BC) Roman settlement was on the PALATINE while the ESQUILINE provided the main cemetery. It was the three peaks of the Palatine and four of the Esquiline that together made up the seven hills upon which Rome was traditionally built. The first city was a collection of hilltop villages. Between the Palatine, the Esquiline, and the CAPITOL (soon to become a citadel) was a marshy valley. Once drained by the CLOACA MAXIMA, this valley became at the end of the 7th century the FORUM ROMANUM, the city's principal market-place. Further urbanization occurred on the Palatine, a cult centre was built on the AVENTINE, and a CIRCUS in the valley between them. The first bridge over the Tiber, the Pons Sublicius, is credited to Ancus MARCIUS. In time, a city of four *regiones* (*see* REGIO) emerged – Palatine, Esquiline, CAELIUS MONS, QUIRINAL – which was enclosed by the so-called WALL OF SERVIUS (now dated to the 4th century BC). Later in the Republic AQUEDUCTS were built, the first in 312 BC; the Tiber was provided with new bridges and quays; Sulla built a new TABULARIUM (record office), Pompey a fine THEATRE, and Caesar another forum. Such was the city of bricks inherited by AUGUSTUS.

Augustan additions, not all in marble, included a new forum, a palace on the Palatine, three aqueducts, and the PANTHEON, ARA PACIS, and mausoleum in the CAMPUS MARTIUS; many older monuments were rebuilt, notably in the Forum Romanum, and the city was divided into 14 new *regiones*. (*See* map on page 756.) After the fire of AD 64 Nero added a palace (DOMUS AUREA) and boulevard (Via Sacra) in the Hellenistic style as well as BATHS and a GYMNASIUM. Then followed the COLOSSEUM, more baths, fora, temples, and aqueducts, Hadrian's mausoleum and the rebuilt Pantheon, and a number of imperial statements such as TRIUMPHAL ARCHES and the columns of Trajan and Marcus Aurelius. In the later 3rd century the enlarged city was encircled by the WALL OF AURELIAN. In the 4th century Rome emerged as a Christian city with the great churches of St Peter, St John Lateran, St Paul-outside-the-Walls, Sta Maria in Trastevere, and many others. (*See* map on page 757.) GS

Nash (1968); Platner and Ashby (1929); Richardson (1992); Robinson (1992); Stillwell (1976); Todd (1978).

Romulus and Remus   founders of Rome. According to the best-known version of the legend, Romulus and Remus were the twin sons of the god MARS and Rea Silvia, a princess of ALBA LONGA. Her uncle, the cruel king Amulius, ordered the babies to be drowned in the Tiber; but they were rescued by a she-wolf and brought up by shepherds. When they grew up the boys resolved to found a new city, but they quarrelled and in the ensuing fight Remus was killed. Romulus then founded his city on the PALATINE; he obtained citizens by offering asylum to refugees and vagabonds, and provided them with wives by arranging the rape of the SABINE women. As king of Rome Romulus created institutions such as the three TRIBUS, the CURIAE, and the SENATE. After his death he was worshipped as the god QUIRINUS. The story of the twins is very ancient (a famous bronze statue of the she-wolf dates from the 6th century BC). It has many mythical parallels and folk-tale elements, and is certainly pure legend. But it nevertheless expresses some profound historical truths. For instance, the story of the asylum reflects the Roman practice of granting CITIZENSHIP to outsiders.　　　　TC

Bremmer and Horsfall (1987); Grant (1971b).

Romulus Augustulus　last Roman emperor, AD 475–6. Romulus Augustus, known as Augustulus, was the son of Julius NEPOS' general Orestes. Elevated by his father in August 475 in place of Nepos, he was in fact a usurper, but has become known as the last Roman emperor in the west. Orestes ruled for exactly a year until killed by ODOACER, who spared the young Augustulus, gave him a pension, and sent him to live with relatives in Campania.　　　　RJB

Bury (1958); Grant (1985).

Rosalia　Roman festival. Rosalia, a rose festival, was never a fixed public festival except locally. Such festivals are recorded as occurring in different places on various days of May, June, and July. The Romans were so fond of roses, using them extravagantly at public and private banquets, that the prime purpose of a Rosalia was probably to honour the rose, though members of a family could also use the day to meet at the grave of their dead and deck it with roses.　　　　DP

Roscius Gallus　(d. 62 BC), Roman actor. Quintus Roscius Gallus, a native of Latium, was the most famous comic actor of his day, though he also played tragic parts. His earnings were enormous, and Sulla made him an *eques*. He was a friend of CICERO, to whom he gave his first important brief and who later defended him in a private suit. Though handsome, he had a squint, and to hide it is said to have introduced the wearing of masks while acting.　　　　DP

Rostra　Roman speaker's platform. The Rostra was the long, straight-fronted stone platform in the Forum from which the speakers addressed the people. It was on the south side of the open assembly space called the COMITIUM. It took its name from the bronze prows (*rostra*) of the Latin ships with which it was decorated after Rome's capture of them at Antium in 338 BC during the Latin War. Julius Caesar built new *rostra* at the west end of the Forum.   DP

Nash (1968); Platner and Ashby (1929); Richardson (1992).

Roxane (fl. 327–311 BC), wife of Alexander the Great. Roxane, daughter of a Bactrian nobleman, married ALEXANDER THE GREAT in 327 BC. Ancient sources attest his love for her, but the match was politically useful for pacifying the north-eastern satrapies and for dynastic considerations. Roxane bore him a posthumous son in 323, ALEXANDER IV. ANTIPATER took them to Macedonia in 320; after his death they fled to OLYMPIAS in Epirus. Olympias' murder left them the pawns of CASSANDER, who murdered them both.   EER

Errington (1990); Green (1990); Hammond and Walbank (1988).

Roxolani   *see* SARMATIANS.

Rubicon, river   *see* CAESAR, JULIUS; CIVIL WARS.

Rufinus   (d. AD 395), praetorian prefect. Flavius Rufinus, a native of Aquitaine, became effective ruler of the eastern Roman empire after THEODOSIUS I's death (January 395). He held the post of Master of Offices (MAGISTER OFFICIORUM) (in Constantinople) from 388, was consul in 392, and then became praetorian prefect of the east in succession to TATIANUS. As praetorian prefect he dominated the young ARCADIUS, but was murdered, almost certainly at the instigation of STILICHO, on 27 November 395.   RJB

Bury (1958); Grant (1985).

Rufus   (d. after AD 69), Roman politician. Lucius Verginius Rufus, son of an equestrian, became a senator and eventually consul (AD 63). As governor of Upper Germany, he put down the revolt of VINDEX (68). A genuine Republican, Rufus refused to bid for the throne, placed himself at the disposal of the Senate, and accepted its recognition of GALBA (68). He was immediately recalled by Galba from his command, but Galba's successor, OTHO, prudently appointed Rufus consul (69).

                                                                RJB

Salmon (1968); Scullard (1982).

Ruler cult, Greek   It was not unprecedented in the Greek world for honours similar to those paid to a god to be heaped on a ruler or commander (such as LYSANDER) who had saved his people from the brink of destruction; but deification as such did not occur before the Macedonian period. PHILIP II had already planned a *heroön*, a temple of godlike kings, for himself at Olympia at the time of his death. It was completed by ALEXANDER THE GREAT whose phenomenal achievements brought him voluntary formal recognition as a god. The cult of Alexander and his successors arose for largely political reasons in the wake of the acquisition of a vast territorial empire which needed to find a means to express its loyalty. Its characteristic features were: dedications to the ruler; worship of the ruler as a god by the cities that he founded; statues of the ruler erected in existing temples; inclusion of the ruler and his cult in the official list of divinities of the polis; establishment of a dynastic cult in each of the successor kingdoms.

GS

Lane Fox (1973).

Ruler cult, Roman As Roman power spread, various manifestations of that power were awarded religious cult. Not only were the goddess Roma and other non-individual aspects of Rome given cult, but, from the end of the 3rd century BC, so were individual Romans, such as MARCELLUS, SCIPIO AFRICANUS, and FLAMININUS. CAESAR was given divine honours in Rome in his lifetime and deified after death. Henceforth emperors popular with the Senate underwent apotheosis after death. From AUGUSTUS, reigning Roman emperors were offered cult in both the Greek east, which had a tradition of ruler cult, and the west. Although emperors exercised some control over these cults, they should not be interpreted with a Christian bias as merely *political* arrangements of no *religious* significance. Enacting the cult of the emperor gave provincials a method of defining via ritual their place within the empire and their relationship with the power that ruled over them.

See also RELIGION, ROMAN; RULER CULT, GREEK. HS

Fishwick (1987–); Hopkins (1978); Price (1984).

Rutilius Rufus (fl. 115–90 BC), Roman politican and historian. Publius Rutilius Rufus was defeated by SCAURUS for the consulate of 115 BC. One of the LEGATI of METELLUS NUMIDICUS against JUGURTHA, he became consul in 105. Rutilius offended the PUBLICANI while governing ASIA on behalf of SCAEVOLA and was prosecuted for extortion (*see* RES REPETUNDAE) in 92. The injustice of this prompted DRUSUS to attempt reform of the courts (*see* QUAESTIO). Rutilius went into exile at Smyrna where he composed a bitter and influential history of his times. HS

Badian (1964).

S

Sabelli Italian people. The Sabelli expanded from central Italy and imposed their language on the indigenous populations of the south in the 5th century BC. They conquered CAMPANIA (*c.*450–420), LUCANIA (*c.*420–390), and the BRUTTII (*c.*356). 'Sabelli' was later used as a Roman term for speakers of OSCAN, i.e. the Apuli, Bruttii, Campani, Lucani, and Samnites, but probably also including the Aequi, Marsi, Paeligni, and Vestini. The term seems to have had cultural significance, but no political importance.

See also VOLSCI.   HE

Potter (1987); Salmon (1967).

Sabina (AD 88–137), wife of Hadrian. Vibia Sabina, great-niece of TRAJAN, was chosen by PLOTINA, Trajan's wife, as a suitable wife for HADRIAN (AD 100). Hadrian found Sabina moody and difficult, and might have divorced her had he been a private citizen. However, she displayed no open opposition, and Hadrian insisted that she be accorded due respect: both Septicius Clarus, the praetorian prefect, and SUETONIUS were dismissed from court for behaving too informally towards her.   RJB

Birley (1976); Perowne (1960).

Sabines Italian people. The Sabines inhabited the Apennines immediately to the north-east of Rome, including the towns of Amiternum, Nursia, and Reate, as well as the fertile Ager Sabinus. They were famous for their bravery and their austerity. According to the legend of the rape of the Sabine women, the population of early Rome was partly Sabine (*see* QUIRINAL; ROMULUS), and at least two of the kings,

NUMA POMPILIUS and Ancus MARCIUS, were of Sabine origin. The Sabines fought the Romans sporadically until 449 BC, when they were badly defeated. Nothing is heard of them again until 290, when they were conquered by Manius Curius DENTATUS who confiscated some territory, sold some into slavery, and made the rest 'citizens without vote' (*see* MUNICIPIUM). After becoming full Roman citizens in 268, they were rapidly romanized. This was probably made easier as a result of gradual infiltration during earlier periods. Sabine influence has been detected in Roman religious practices and in the Latin language, though they themselves probably spoke a form of OSCAN.   HE

Heurgon (1973); Poucet (1985); Salmon (1982).

Sabinus   (1st century AD), Roman jurist. Masurius Sabinus was of humble origins and attained equestrian rank only in his fiftieth year. He was the author of a standard work on private law. One of the two schools of law to which most jurists belonged down to the 2nd century was named after him, the other being named after its leader Proculus. Nothing is known of their organization or their doctrinal differences. Prominent heads of the Sabinians included JAVOLENUS PRISCUS and JULIANUS.

See also JURISPRUDENCE.   GS

Sacramentum   In early Roman law (*see* TWELVE TABLES) *sacramentum* referred to a fixed sum of money deposited by both parties in a case. The loser of the case forfeited this sum, which was handed over to the state. The *sacramentum* was also the military oath of allegiance sworn by a Roman recruit. The terms of the oath were to serve his commander, not desert him until formally released, and act on behalf of the Republic. The personal element in the oath was important in the late Republic, when armies might follow their commanders against the state. Under the Principate the oath to the emperor was renewed annually.

See also ARMY, ROMAN; STIPENDIUM.   HS

Nicholas (1962); Watson (1969).

Sacred Band   élite unit of 300 formed at THEBES by Gorgidas after the liberation (379/8 BC). It was used by PELOPIDAS at Tegyra (375) and at LEUCTRA (371) to devastating effect. At CHAERONEA (338) it was annihilated. It consisted of pairs of lovers who in fighting for each other fought fiercely for Thebes.   GLC

Buckler (1980).

Sacred Wars   wars fought at the instigation of the DELPHIC AMPHICTYONY. The *First Sacred War* (c.595–586 BC) was allegedly waged by a coalition of forces from Thessaly, Sicyon, and Athens to wrest control of the Delphic sanctuary from Crisa. After the war the priesthood was re-formed and the reorganized Amphictyony transferred its centre from Anthela to DELPHI.

In the *Second Sacred War* (*c.*449 BC) Sparta liberated Delphi from domination by Phocis and, shortly afterwards, in a separate expedi-tion, Athens restored Phocian control, though Delphi recovered her independence soon afterwards.

The *Third Sacred War* (356–346 BC) was a conflict between THEBES and PHOCIS ostensibly for control of Delphi. Thebes, dominating the DELPHIC AMPHICTYONY, had Phocis heavily fined for a trivial offence. PHILOMELUS occupied Delphi, using the temple treasures to pay his mercenary army, but was defeated at Neon. ONOMARCHUS was success-ful against Boeotia, but PHILIP II of Macedon defeated the Phocians and the Pheraeans at the Battle of the Crocus Field (352). Onomarchus committed suicide. PHAYLLUS kept Philip out of Thermopylae. Phalaecus took over, but the fatal alliance of Philip and Thebes was formed. By 347 the temple treasures were running out, both sides were exhausted, and Philip made it known that he would end the war in 346. Despite Athenian efforts to keep him out by the Peace of Philocrates, he came unopposed: Phalaecus must have done a secret deal. Philip settled the Sacred War and, in reality, the future of Greece.   RB/GLC

Buckler (1980); Parke and Wormell (1956).

Sacrifice   Literally the performance of a sacred ritual, sacrifice, espe-cially animal sacrifice, formed the principal element of ancient reli-gious practice and the commonest medium for making offering to the gods. Distinction may be made between sacrifice for praise, for thanksgiving, for expiation, and for intercession; between offerings to the gods, the heroes, and the dead; and between public and private ritual (*see* RELIGION, GREEK *and* ROMAN). Bloodless offerings were typi-cally the first fruits, beans, cakes, grain, and cheese, but libations of milk and wine also featured. Much commoner was the sacrifice of a domestic animal (usually goat, sheep, or ox) at the altar or graveside. The victim was festooned before being ritually slaughtered, flayed, butchered, and roasted. The worshippers then shared the flesh with the god in a sort of communion feast. Local variations in the details of the ancient rites are as numerous as modern interpretations of their significance. Animal sacrifice often accompanied formal oath-taking ceremonies. There is no evidence for human sacrifice in the Greco-Roman world.

See also BURIAL PRACTICES; FESTIVALS.   GS

Burkert (1983); Easterling and Muir (1985); Parker (1983).

Saguntum city in Spain besieged in 219 BC. The town of Saguntum was the short-term cause of the Second PUNIC WAR. It was an ally of Rome in a recognized Carthaginian sphere of influence. Hannibal attacked it in 219 BC in defiance of Roman warnings and, after a difficult and costly siege lasting eight months, captured the town. The Romans made no effort to relieve it, but used it as a pretext for making war on Carthage. LPR

Lazenby (1978).

Salamis battle in 480 BC in which XERXES' fleet was defeated in the strait between Attica and the island of Salamis. The Greek fleet, about 310 strong, refused battle on the open sea. The Persian fleet, perhaps roughly equal, sailed into the strait and could not exploit the superior seamanship of the PHOENICIANS. Losses on both sides are uncertain, but Xerxes decided not to try again.

See also PERSIAN WARS. GLC

Burn (1984); CAH IV.

Salamis city on the east coast of CYPRUS. The first Cypriot coinage was issued by Salamis in the mid-6th century BC. At a battle near Salamis in 498 the Cypriots were beaten by the Persians for their part in the IONIAN REVOLT. Under King EVAGORAS (411–374/3) Salamis became a haven for Greek philosophers and artists. Despite defeat in a naval battle off Salamis in 306 by DEMETRIUS I POLIORCETES, PTOLEMY I gained control of the island, but the capital was moved from Salamis to Paphos *c.*200 BC. GS

Stillwell (1976).

Salii Roman ritual dancers. The Salii were 24 priests of MARS who each March and October, at the start and the end of the campaigning season, engaged in ritual song and war dance throughout the city. The most striking feature of their old Italian war dress was the 'figure-of-eight' shield on their left arms. These shields were copies of the original shield which was said to have fallen from heaven as a gift from JUPITER to King NUMA POMPILIUS. During the processions they beat their shields with their swords and halted at certain places to perform elaborate dances to the tune of a flute. Afterwards they enjoyed feasts which became proverbial for their opulence. DP

Beard and North (1990); Scullard (1981).

Salinator (b. 254 BC), Roman general. Marcus Livius Salinator as consul in 219 BC won a triumph over the Illyrians. He was, however, tried for misappropriation of booty and retired from Rome until 210. As consul in 207, Salinator, after being reconciled with his colleague C. Claudius Nero, an ex-subordinate who had testified against him, defeated HASDRUBAL BARCA at the METAURUS, for which he won a second triumph.

See also PUNIC WARS.   HS

Lazenby (1978); Scullard (1973).

Sallust (86–34 BC), Roman historian. Gaius Sallustius Crispus, a senator of Sabine origin, as tribune in 52 BC attacked CLODIUS and CICERO after MILO's death, but was himself removed from the Senate in 50 by the censor, Appius CLAUDIUS PULCHER. He joined CAESAR, commanded a legion for him in 49, and after being praetor was appointed in 47 the first governor of Africa Nova. On his return to Rome he was acquitted of extortion (probably through Caesar's influence), retired from politics, and settled down in his magnificent gardens to a more successful career as a historian. He composed two monographs, *The War with Catiline* and *The Jugurthine War*, followed by his longest work, the *Histories*, dealing in five books with the period from 78 to 67 BC. The two monographs survive completely, but only four speeches, two letters, and some snippets from the *Histories*.

He wrote about CATILINE because of 'the novelty of his crime and the danger to which the state was exposed', and his main aim may have been to produce a vivid account of this crisis. But the conspiracy is also shown as exemplifying Rome's political and moral decline after 146 BC caused by the vices of the *nobiles*, with CATO and Caesar rising above the general degradation. Caesar, however, despite Sallust's connections with him, is not favoured more than Cato.

The war with JUGURTHA was chosen for similar reasons, for the long-lasting, bloody, fluctuating nature of the struggle, and because it marked the beginning of successful opposition to the *nobiles*. Sallust, however, can see merit in individual *nobiles* such as METELLUS NUMIDICUS.

Sallust's geography and chronology can be inaccurate, his philosophical prologues are merely neat expressions of commonplaces, and he is not free of political bias. But his narrative is taut, swift, and compelling with characters vividly drawn and speeches of genuine dramatic power. His new style, modelled in its brevity and rhetoric and archaisms on Thucydides and the elder Cato, greatly influenced TACITUS.

See also HISTORIOGRAPHY, ROMAN.   DP

Earl (1961); Paul (1984); Syme (1964).

Salvius Julianus *see* JULIANUS.

Samian ware the name commonly given to the red-coloured POTTERY from GAUL more properly known as TERRA SIGILLATA. Originally founded by Italian immigrants at the start of the 1st century AD, the industry developed away from Arretine styles but retained classical motifs for decoration. Production throughout Gaul and the Rhineland was on a massive scale and swamped the market for two centuries, not only in the western provinces but also in Italy and Greece. GS

Samnites Italian people. The Samnites were an OSCAN-speaking confederation of tribes who occupied the southern central Apennines. They were a mainly pastoral people with few urban centres and no coinage; nevertheless Samnium was densely populated. There are many hillforts throughout the region which testify to the raiding and warfare of the Samnites. They had a formidable army whose arms and formations were adopted by Rome during the SAMNITE WARS. A distinct national awareness gave the Samnite League a strong sense of unity. Its chief magistrate, the *meddix*, seems to have had political, military, and religious duties. LPR

CAH VII.2; Salmon (1967).

Samnite Wars three wars fought between Rome and the SAMNITES. The *First Samnite War* (343–341 BC) was fought for control of Campania when CAPUA appealed to Rome for aid against the Samnites. After a number of victories the Romans gained control of the region. The *Second Samnite War* (326–304 BC) was an important phase in Rome's conquest of Italy. Despite humiliation at the CAUDINE FORKS in 321, the Romans pursued an offensive strategy which wore down Samnite resolve. In the *Third Samnite War* (298–290 BC) the Samnites formed coalitions with Etruscans, Gauls, and Umbrians, but Roman victories at Sentinum in 295 and Aquilonia in 293 broke Samnite power. LPR

CAH VII.2; Salmon (1967).

Samos Greek island. In the archaic age Samos was a major east Aegean power, reaching her zenith under POLYCRATES. Following a period of Persian domination, she emerged as a leading ally of Athens, remaining loyal, despite political upheavals, until the end of the PELOPONNESIAN WAR. The DECARCHIES established by LYSANDER quickly fell, but after a brief independence Samos again came under Persian control. Both Persians and Samians were ejected in 365 BC and replaced by an Athenian CLERUCHY; the Samians were not restored until 322. Thereafter, in the Hellenistic and Roman periods, Samos enjoyed prosperity, but had little independence or power. RB

Shipley (1987).

Samothrace island in the north Aegean. Thracian inhabitants were joined by Aeolic Greek colonists c.700 BC. In the 6th century the island minted a silver coinage and founded colonies on the mainland. In the 5th century its power declined but it retained its importance as the centre of a mystery cult of the Great Gods, who included the non-Greek deities known as Cabiri. The sanctuary was endowed with fine buildings in the Hellenistic period and the cult continued to operate till the 4th century AD.   GS

Stillwell (1976).

Sandracottus (323/2–297 BC), Indian king. Sandracottus (Greek form of the native name Chandragupta) founded the Mauryan dynasty of northern India after defeating in 323/2 BC the last Nanda king. He was powerful enough to resist the invasion of SELEUCUS I NICATOR in 303, who ceded him several satrapies in return for 500 war ELEPHANTS. His capital at Pataliputra (modern Patna) was visited by MEGASTHENES, the Seleucid ambassador to his court. Sandracottus was the grandfather of ASHOKA.   EER

Sedlar (1980); Smith (1981); Thapar (1966, 1973); Woodcock (1966).

Sappho (born c.630 BC), Greek lyric poet. Sappho was a slightly older contemporary of ALCAEUS and came from the same aristocratic background on LESBOS. She lived mostly in Mytilene, but was exiled to Sicily sometime between 604 and 596 BC. On her return she seems to have become involved with other young women in the cult of Aphrodite; but she also married and had a daughter. Her poetry, nine books of lyrics of which numerous fragments survive, is personal and passionate, addressed mostly to her girls. CATULLUS imitated her in two of his poems.   GS

Kirkwood (1974); Page (1955).

Sarapis Egyptian god. The cult of Sarapis was a creation of Ptolemaic ALEXANDRIA. Its origins seem to lie with the cult of the sacred bull Apis at Memphis who in death was identified with the god of the underworld, Osiris. The most likely reason for the creation of a new deity is that PTOLEMY I SOTER wished to provide the Greek population of Egypt with a patron god. Egyptian elements were therefore combined with Greek and the new god was identified with both Dionysus and Hades. His cult, together with that of his wife ISIS, was spread by commercial contacts throughout the Hellenistic world. In the Roman period the cult of Sarapis was somewhat eclipsed by the mysteries of Isis.   GS

Fraser (1972).

Sarcophagi   A sarcophagus is a coffin, generally made of stone or clay, though some wooden ones from Hellenistic times have survived in southern Russia and in Egypt. Plain sarcophagi were used by the Greeks of all periods; painted clay sarcophagi first appeared in eastern Greece in the late 6th century BC; sculptured sarcophagi were made by Greek craftsmen for the kings of Sidon in the 5th and 4th centuries BC, of which the most famous example is the so-called Alexander sarcophagus. Sculptured sarcophagi of stone and clay were used by the ETRUSCANS from the 6th century BC, most commonly in the form of a casket surmounted by either a gabled lid or an effigy of the deceased. Richly carved marble sarcophagi were produced throughout the Roman world with effect from the 2nd century AD when cremation was largely superseded by inhumation.

See also BURIAL PRACTICES.   GS

Strong (1976).

Sardes   city in western Asia Minor and the capital of LYDIA. After a century of economic prosperity and artistic achievement, Sardes fell to CYRUS in 546 BC who made it the western capital of the Persian empire. Liberated by ALEXANDER THE GREAT in 334 BC, it changed hands several times in the Hellenistic period before being passed to Rome in the will of ATTALUS III PHILOMETOR of Pergamum. Under the Romans it remained prosperous as an administrative centre and was adorned with fine buildings.   GS

Stillwell (1976).

Sardinia   island in the western Mediterranean. Greek colonists showed little interest in Sardinia, and after the defeat of a Greek fleet off CORSICA in 535 BC it was annexed by CARTHAGE. Seized by Rome in 238 BC, it became a joint province with Corsica in 227. Under the Empire it became a separate province but it never really prospered despite being an important source of grain and metals. Outside the main cities of Caralis and Turris the island was only slightly romanized and the organization of the interior remained tribal.

See also ANNONA.   GS

Guido (1963); Rickman (1980).

Sarmatians   nomadic people. The Sarmatians originated east of the river Tanais, but moved westwards from *c.*250 BC, displacing the Scythians. Both major groupings accepted client status with Rome: the Roxolani, settling by the Danube estuary, were defeated by Augustus and Nero; the Iazyges settled between the middle Danube and the river Theiss, forming a buffer between Roman Pannonia and the Dacian tribes. Population pressures forced further tribal movements in the 2nd/3rd centuries AD, the Iazyges joining the MARCOMANNI against Aurelius (168–79), and the Roxolani invading Moesia with the GOTHS. The Sarmatian problem largely evaporated after Constantine I settled large numbers of them within the empire.

See also ALANI.   RJB

Wilkes (1983).

Sassanians Persian people. The Sassanians inherited the territory of Achaemenid PERSIA and Arsacid PARTHIA. The Sassanian empire (AD 224–636) at its zenith stretched from Syria to India, from Georgia to the Persian Gulf, and was in frequent conflict on its western borders with the Romans, disputing possession of Asia Minor (Assyria, Armenia, and Mesopotamia) and Syria. The emperor VALERIAN was captured by SHAPUR I (259), GALERIUS defeated Narses in Armenia, forcing territorial concessions (298), and SHAPUR II campaigned against the Romans from the 330s to the 370s. The empire survived until 636 when the Arabs overran Mesopotamia, and the Sassanians withdrew eastwards into Iran.   RJB

Grant (1979); Herrmann (1977); Millar (1981).

Satire '*Satura*', wrote QUINTILIAN (*Inst.* 10.1.93), 'is our [sc. Rome's] supreme achievement.' The word means a miscellany of different things, so inevitably its definition varied from one writer to the next. Essentially it was a piece of verse, or prose mixed with verse, that was intended to entertain the reader and denigrate contemporary society. As such it owes a clear debt to Athenian Old COMEDY and, according to Livy (7.2), some of the earliest *saturae* assumed a simple dramatic form. ENNIUS was the first to write verse satire and so was described by HORACE as the 'originator' (*auctor*) of the genre; the term 'founder' (*inventor*) he reserved for LUCILIUS who gave it its modern satirical connotation. Horace himself followed Lucilius in composing hexameter satires which are conversational without being too malicious and contain a significant philosophical element. PERSIUS also admired Lucilius, though his satires are more like homilies. But the greatest exponent of the genre was undoubtedly JUVENAL who abandoned all inhibition in his personal assaults while at the same time raising satire to the highest of literary forms. Such was the corruption of his age that he claimed to find it 'difficult not to write satire' (1.30).

The satires of Menippus (3rd century BC) and the dialogues of LUCIAN provided VARRO with a model for his *Menippean Satires* which combined prose with passages of verse in several metres. The same form was used by the younger SENECA in his malicious lampoon on the emperor Claudius, *Apocolocyntosis*, and by PETRONIUS in his satirical novel, *Satyricon*. GS

Braund (1989); Coffey (1989); Rudd (1986); Sullivan (1962).

Satrap Persian governor. A satrap was the governor of a satrapy, one of the provinces of the Persian empire, a system properly organized, though not invented, by DARIUS I. Normally Persian, and often of royal blood, satraps had wide powers, being answerable only to the king, and were responsible for collecting tribute, maintaining order, administering justice, and providing troops for royal armies as necessary.
See also PERSIA. RB

CAH IV; Cook (1983); Tuplin (1987).

Saturnalia Roman festival. The Saturnalia, celebrated at the winter solstice from 17 to 23 December, was the merriest festival of the year. It opened with a great sacrifice at the temple of Saturn in the Forum, followed by a banquet, which apparently anyone could attend. During the festival shops, schools, and courts were closed, war was interrupted, and gambling was allowed in public. In the home masters waited on their slaves; presents of little pottery dolls were given to children and wax candles to friends. A mock king was chosen as Master of Revels, and ruled for a week, in which the Golden Age of Saturn was recalled. Western tradition preserves many features of the Saturnalia in the Christmas festival. DP

Scullard (1981).

Saturninus (d. 100 BC), Roman tribune. Lucius Appuleius Saturninus was a turbulent tribune in the mould of the POPULARES. As *tribunus plebis* in 103 and 100 BC Saturninus cooperated with MARIUS to get land voted for Marius' veterans. Saturninus also established a court (*see* QUAESTIO) for treason (*see* MAIESTAS), instituted subsidized corn distributions for the people (*see* ANNONA), and proposed more sweeping land distribution than the measures for the veterans. After the violent death of MEMMIUS, a candidate for the consulate, the SENATE passed the SENATUS CONSULTUM *Ultimum* at the urging of SCAURUS. Marius then turned against Saturninus and used force to suppress him. HS

Gruen (1968); Lintott (1968).

Satyr play In the 5th century BC the performance of three tragedies was always followed by a lighter piece or satyr play by the same author. Described by DEMETRIUS (*On Style* 169) as 'tragedy at play', the satyr play was essentially mythological burlesque. Its chorus was composed of satyrs, led by their father Silenus; the tone was humorous and spirited but not satirical. One complete play (EURIPIDES' *Cyclops*) survives, together with half of SOPHOCLES' *Ichneutae* and numerous Aeschylean fragments.

See also DIONYSIA.   GS

Sutton (1980).

Saxons German people. The Saxons settled in the Cimbric Chersonese (Holstein) in the 2nd century AD, replaced the CHAUCI on the lower Elbe by *c.*AD 200, and expanded into Frisia and the lower Rhine valley. From the 4th century they clashed with the FRANKS, and expanded east and south. They were infamous pirates, raiding and settling along the northern coasts of Gaul, and increasingly began to establish themselves in Britain during the 5th century.   RJB

Johnson (1980); Salway (1981); Todd (1975).

Scaevola (d. 82 BC), Roman advocate. Quintus Mucius Scaevola was the leading lawyer of his time (*see* ADVOCATUS). As consul in 95 BC, with Lucius Licinius CRASSUS, he passed the *lex Licinia Mucia* establishing a QUAESTIO for aliens illegally claiming CITIZENSHIP. With RUTILIUS RUFUS, he reorganized the province of ASIA. Scaevola stayed in Rome under CINNA's regime, but was killed in 82. He wrote the first systematic treatise on civil law.

See also JURISPRUDENCE.   HS

Badian (1964).

Scaurus (d. 89 BC), Roman politician. Marcus Aemilius Scaurus was a poor patrician who rose to a position of great influence. Consul in 115 BC, he won a triumph over the LIGURES. Hostile to JUGURTHA, he became censor in 109. As an OPTIMATE, he proposed the SENATUS CONSULTUM *Ultimum* of 100 which led to MARIUS using force to suppress SATURNINUS and his followers.   HS

Badian (1964); Gruen (1968).

Sceptics Scepticism proper begins with PYRRHON (*c.*365–275 BC) and his school, although it has its roots in earlier thought of the SOPHISTS. The Sceptics inferred from the contradictions inherent in sense perception that knowledge is impossible and therefore judgement must be suspended. Pyrrhon's scepticism was essentially practical and aimed to produce imperturbability of mind. Pyrrhon himself left no writings, but Sextus Empiricus (*c.*AD 200) provides us with full details of Sceptic doctrine. Scepticism was introduced into the ACADEMY by ARCESILAUS and formed the basis of Academic teaching until the headship of Antiochus (78 BC). JL

Long (1974).

Scerdilaidas (fl. 230–205 BC), Illyrian chieftain. Scerdilaidas, probably of royal birth, led Illyrian forces against EPIRUS in 230 BC, and joined DEMETRIUS OF PHAROS in attacking Greece, thereby breaking an Illyrian treaty with Rome. In 220/19 he made an alliance with the Macedonian PHILIP V, further angering Rome, but broke it off in 217 and invaded Macedonia. Philip drove him back by 213/12. Scerdilaidas signed the Aetolian treaty with Rome in 212/11, and harried Philip during the First MACEDONIAN WAR. EER

CAH VIII; Gruen (1984); Hammond (1967); Hammond and Walbank (1988).

Scholarship, Greek Pfeiffer defines scholarship as 'the art of understanding, explaining, and restoring the literary tradition'. It was initiated by the poets of the Hellenistic age who wished to preserve and interpret the work of their predecessors. BOOKS had been in circulation since the 5th century BC, but it was only with the foundation of a LIBRARY at Alexandria by Ptolemy I that the raw material for scholarship became available. The collection grew from 200,000 papyrus rolls in 285 BC to 700,000 in the 1st century BC and was administered and catalogued by a succession of scholar librarians.

The old order was gone, in literature as in politics, but the newcomers were determined to select and preserve the best of the old. They were poets themselves and they worked primarily on poetic texts, beginning with Homer. PHILETAS of Cos was the first with his glossaries of rare words, though the first 'edition' of Homer had been prepared by ANTIMACHUS of Colophon at the end of the 5th century BC. The first librarian was ZENODOTUS of Ephesus who made critical editions of Homer, Hesiod, and Pindar. His successors, notably ARISTOPHANES OF BYZANTIUM and ARISTARCHUS OF SAMOTHRACE, developed more sophisticated editorial techniques, decided which writers and which of their works deserved to survive, and thus established the canon of classical literature.

Finally came the work of interpretation. Commentaries were written on all the major texts (*see* SCHOLIA), and studies made of metre, grammar, and language. Nor was Alexandria the only centre of scholarly activity: there was also a large library at PERGAMUM where there was more emphasis on prose texts.

See also APOLLODORUS; CRATES OF MALLUS; DIONYSIUS THRAX; ERATOSTHENES; HARPOCRATION; HEPHAESTION. GS

Pfeiffer (1968); Reynolds and Wilson (1991); Wilson (1983).

Scholarship, Latin The study of grammar and poetry was introduced to Rome by the visiting Greek scholar CRATES OF MALLUS in 168 BC. QUINTILIAN mentions some early grammarians and there is evidence of an interest in literary matters in the poetry of ACCIUS and LUCILIUS; but the first Roman deserving the title of scholar is L. Aelius Stilo (*c.*154– 74 BC) who probably absorbed the rudiments of Alexandrian scholarship when exiled to Rhodes in 100 BC. Among his concerns was the authenticity of the plays of PLAUTUS. His most influential pupil was the polymath M. Terentius VARRO (116–27 BC) whose researches in literary history, drama, and linguistics provided a model for subsequent generations of critics and scholars.

Scholarly activity under the Empire was further stimulated by the foundation of the Palatine Library under its first director HYGINUS. Early in the 1st century AD Verrius FLACCUS composed the first Latin lexicon, *De Significatu Verborum*, which partly survives in an abridged version. Grammatical studies were pursued by Quintilian, and contributions to literary criticism were made by the elder SENECA, PETRONIUS, and PERSIUS. Towards the end of the 1st century M. Valerius Probus is said to have produced critical editions of a number of poetic texts but there is no firm evidence of his work in the manuscript traditions. The decline of creative writing in the 2nd century was complemented by increased antiquarian interest in earlier writers evident in the works of FRONTO, GELLIUS, and APULEIUS. The 3rd and 4th centuries saw the publication of several major commentaries, notably those of Acron and Porphyrion on Horace, DONATUS on Terence and Virgil, and SERVIUS also on Virgil. GS

Reynolds and Wilson (1991).

Scholia explanatory notes to a text, preserved in the margins of medieval manuscript copies. Extant scholia to Greek texts such as Homer, Hesiod, Pindar, and the dramatists are likely to owe much to the work of Alexandrian scholars such as ZENODOTUS, ARISTOPHANES OF BYZANTIUM, and ARISTARCHUS OF SAMOTHRACE and more to the exegetical outpourings of DIDYMUS; but theirs were all independent commentaries, and many other hands added to them before they emerged as marginal scholia at the end of antiquity. Similar sets of marginal annotations were appended to manuscripts of Latin texts with effect from the 3rd century AD. GS

Reynolds and Wilson (1991); Wilson (1983).

Schools *see* EDUCATION.

Science *see* ANATOMY; ASTRONOMY; BOTANY; ENGINEERING; MATHEMATICS; METEOROLOGY; PHYSICS; ZOOLOGY.

Scipio (d. 211 BC), Roman general. Publius Cornelius Scipio, the younger brother of SCIPIO CALVUS and father of SCIPIO AFRICANUS, as consul in 218 BC was sent to Spain to prevent HANNIBAL reaching Italy. Having missed Hannibal in France, he returned to Italy to be defeated at TICINUS and TREBBIA. In Spain as proconsul from 217, he campaigned successfully with his brother, defeating HASDRUBAL BARCA in 215, until 211 when they were defeated and killed in separate battles.

See also PUNIC WARS.   HS

Lazenby (1978).

Scipio Aemilianus (c.185–129 BC), Roman general and politician. Publius Cornelius Scipio Aemilianus was the son of Aemilius PAULLUS, under whom he served at PYDNA (168 BC), but was adopted by the elder son of SCIPIO AFRICANUS. He volunteered for service in Spain in 151 and distinguished himself as a *tribunus militum* in 149/8. Although too young and not of sufficient rank, he was elected consul for 147, and destroyed CARTHAGE in 146, bringing the PUNIC WARS to an end.

As censor in 142 his desire for a moral purge of the state was thwarted by his colleague MUMMIUS ACHAICUS. In 134 he was consul for the second time and entrusted with the war in SPAIN, which he brought to a close with the capture of NUMANTIA in 133. On his return to Rome he opposed the Gracchan land commission and as a result lost much popularity. When found dead in unexplained circumstances, he was thought to have been murdered; high among the suspects was his wife, the sister of the Gracchi.

Aemilianus was paradoxically fond of traditional Roman ways and Greek culture. His association with intellectuals such as POLYBIUS encouraged CICERO to make him a central character in several dialogues.

See also Tiberius GRACCHUS; LAELIUS; TERENCE.   HS

Astin (1967).

Scipio Africanus (236–183 BC), Roman general. Publius Cornelius Scipio Africanus, the son of Publius Cornelius SCIPIO and brother of SCIPIO ASIAGENUS, was one of Rome's most successful generals and was compared to Alexander the Great. Said to have saved his father's life at the battle of TICINUS and rallied the survivors of CANNAE, in 210 BC he was given a proconsular command in Spain, thus becoming the first private citizen to hold such a command. A string of victories, including the defeat of HASDRUBAL BARCA at Baecula, and diplomacy based on his father's work among the Spaniards drove the Carthaginians out of Spain by 206.

As consul in 205 Scipio's plan of invading Africa while HANNIBAL was still in Italy was opposed by FABIUS MAXIMUS VERRUCOSUS, but Scipio won the issue and, after training his troops in Sicily, crossed to Africa in 204. Successes in Africa brought Hannibal back from Italy in 203, and in 202, with the aid of the cavalry of MASSINISSA, Scipio defeated Hannibal at ZAMA, thus ending the Second PUNIC WAR.

Scipio was censor in 199 and consul for the second time in 194, when he argued against FLAMININUS' policy of evacuating Greece. In 190 Scipio went to Asia, nominally as his brother's legate, to command in the war against ANTIOCHUS III THE GREAT, but through illness did not command at MAGNESIA. In the 180s the Scipios were politically attacked by CATO; and Africanus, after defending his brother in 187, retired into private life at Liternum, where he died in 183.   HS

Scullard (1970, 1973); Walbank (1967).

Scipio Asiagenus   (fl. 207–187 BC), Roman general. Lucius Cornelius Scipio Asiagenus (or Asiaticus), son of Publius Cornelius SCIPIO, was much overshadowed by his brother SCIPIO AFRICANUS, whose legate he was from 207 to 202 BC in Spain, Sicily, and Africa. As consul in 190 Asiagenus was sent against ANTIOCHUS III THE GREAT, but on the understanding that his brother, nominally his legate, was to command. Victory at MAGNESIA under his authority won him the name Asiagenus and a triumph in 188.

Charged with peculation in 187, he was defended by his brother and saved from imprisonment by Tiberius GRACCHUS. But in 184 CATO as censor removed Asiagenus from equestrian status.   HS

Scullard (1973).

Scipio Calvus   (d. 211 BC), Roman general. Gnaeus Cornelius Scipio Calvus, the brother of Publius Cornelius SCIPIO and uncle of SCIPIO AFRICANUS, as consul in 222 BC with his colleague MARCELLUS defeated the INSUBRES of Cisalpine Gaul. From 218 he campaigned successfully in Spain together with his brother, who arrived in 217. They defeated HASDRUBAL BARCA at Iberia in 215, but were defeated and killed in separate engagements in 211.

See also PUNIC WARS.   HS

Lazenby (1978).

Scopas   (fl. 370–330 BC), Greek sculptor. Scopas of Paros was a contemporary of PRAXITELES and LYSIPPUS and one of the dominant figures in 4th-century art. Like Praxiteles, he preferred to work in marble and most of his subjects are religious. Roman copies survive of his Pothos (Desire) and Meleager; other works, such as the Apollo Smintheus and Aphrodite Pandemus, are known only from representations on coins. Unlike Praxiteles, he also had architectural associations: he is recorded as the architect of the temple of Athena Alea at Tegea (some fragments of its sculpture survive), as one of the sculptors employed on the MAUSOLEUM, and as having carved one of the columns for the temple of Artemis at Ephesus.

See also SCULPTURE, GREEK.   GS

Ashmole (1972); Richter (1970b); Stewart (1977).

Sculpture, Greek Our knowledge of Greek sculpture derives from original works (which survive in appreciable quantities), from Roman copies (see SCULPTURE, ROMAN), from descriptions in literature (notably the elder PLINY and PAUSANIAS), and from inscriptions (especially statue bases and dedications). Most was either religious or commemorative in inspiration. Cult statues were required for cellas and sanctuaries, and religious and mythological scenes in relief for temple decoration; athletic and military victories had to be celebrated; the dead were commemorated; and from the 5th century BC portraits of public figures were commissioned. The materials most commonly used were stone (MARBLE or limestone), BRONZE, wood, TERRACOTTA, and for chryselephantine statues a combination of gold and ivory. Stone sculpture was generally painted, and often accessories (such as eyes, jewellery, weapons, reins) were added in a different material.

Archaic Period: The production of monumental stone sculpture in Greece seems to have begun around 650 BC. Greek contact with the east increased after Egypt's conquest of Assyria in 672 BC and Egyptian influence is evident in the statuary of the ARCHAIC PERIOD. A favourite subject was the *kouros* or free-standing nude youth, life-size or bigger, in a standard pose with fists clenched and the left foot slightly forward. The female equivalent (*kore*) was clothed in close-fitting drapery. Seated and striding figures were also represented, both strikingly similar to Egyptian prototypes. But the trend towards realism in the portrayal of human anatomy gradually became more pronounced so that by the 5th century BC sculpture had lost most of its oriental flavour.

Architectural sculpture followed a similar progression and offered scope for more ambitious composition. Episodes from mythology such as the story of the Argonauts, the judgement of Paris, and battles between gods and giants were favoured subjects for a narrative frieze that might stretch all round a building. Acroteria generally took the form of fabulous beasts – sphinxes, griffins, or gorgons. Graves were marked by a carved stone shaft surmounted by a sphinx, though a simple palmette later replaced the sphinx.

Classical Period: By the start of the CLASSICAL PERIOD the standing male figure had matured into the more realistic pose of such works as the bronze charioteer at Delphi and the striding bronze Poseidon (or Zeus)

in Athens. The climax of this development towards anatomical harmony is represented by the work of POLYCLEITUS who, like MYRON, favoured various athletic stances. But the most famous sculptor of the 5th century (perhaps of antiquity) was PHEIDIAS who was charged by PERICLES with the supervision of all the works on the Athenian acropolis. His chryselephantine statues of Athena for the PARTHENON and Zeus for OLYMPIA are lost, but the surviving sculptures from the Parthenon bear witness to his genius. Work of similar quality was done throughout Greece by pupils and successors of Pheidias such as AGORACRITUS, ALCAMENES, and PAEONIUS.

Sculpture in the 4th century BC was dominated by the work of three artists – PRAXITELES, SCOPAS, and LYSIPPUS. The first is represented by a major surviving work – the Hermes at Olympia – which is testimony to the achievement of the age, though some doubt its authenticity. The relaxed majesty of the 5th century had been succeeded by a more personalized humanity and intensity of expression which may also be observed in 4th-century Attic gravestones.

Hellenistic Period: An even greater realism, sometimes verging on the melodramatic, characterizes the sculpture of the HELLENISTIC PERIOD. Swirling drapery, writhing bodies, and expressions of anguish on the 2nd-century reliefs from PERGAMUM contrast with the restraint of earlier times. At the same time the classicizing tendencies of artists such as EUBULIDES and POLYCLES kept 5th-century traditions alive and were much admired by Roman patrons.

See also ANTENOR; ANTIGONUS OF CARYSTUS; CHARES OF LINDUS; CRESILAS; DAMOPHON; ENDOIOS; EUPHRANOR; LEOCHARES; SILANION; TIMOTHEUS.   GS

Bieber (1954); Boardman (1978, 1985); Richter (1970a, b); Ridgway (1970, 1978, 1981); Smith (1991); Stewart (1979, 1990).

Sculpture, Roman   The first sculptors employed at Rome were ETRUSCANS. Their liking for working in bronze, for clothing their statues, and for setting up statues of public figures was shared by the Romans. But from the 2nd century BC Greek artists flocked to Rome and were commissioned to copy Greek originals by wealthy patrons who were obsessed with a desire to exhibit the outward trappings of Hellenic culture. As a result Greek religious iconography was adopted wholesale at Rome, and sculpture in the round never really progressed beyond the adaptation of Greek models.

Architectural sculpture, however, took over the Greek form of commemorative relief and developed it in a purely Roman fashion. Roman sculptors replaced the mythological subject-matter of their Greek predecessors with representations of historical events. Appearing first on the base of the statue of Aemilius PAULLUS at Delphi on which episodes from the battle of PYDNA were shown, the theme was continued throughout Roman history and may be observed on such monuments as the ARA PACIS, the columns of TRAJAN and Marcus AURELIUS, and every TRIUMPHAL ARCH in the capital and throughout the empire.

The other form in which Roman sculptors, or rather Greek sculptors working under Roman patronage, achieved distinction was individual portraiture. Its most distinctive characteristic was extreme realism combined with a curious emphasis of the subject's less attractive features. Under AUGUSTUS there was a return to more idealized portraiture, but the realism reappeared under the Flavians and again in the 3rd century AD.   GS

Bieber (1977); Lawrence (1972); Strong (1961).

Scythians   nomadic tribe from Central Asia. In the late 8th century BC they moved into southern Russia and the Ukraine from where they expelled the CIMMERIANS and where they established their own kingdom of Royal Scythia. They traded with the Greek cities of the Black Sea coast, buying pottery and jewellery in exchange for foodstuffs (especially wheat) and furs. They were expert horsemen and were among the first to put mounted archers in the field, defeating a Macedonian force c.325 BC. They were also skilled metalworkers and much fine goldwork has been recovered from their tombs.   GS

Talbot Rice (1958).

Seals   Seals were in use in Greece from earliest times primarily to provide documents and other items with a 'signature' or means of identification. Cut from stone or precious metal, or sometimes from ivory or glass, they were usually worn as signet rings; occasionally they were strung round the neck or kept in a case. The scarab form, adopted from Egypt, was especially popular in the 5th century BC. The impression was made in wax or LEAD on documents and in clay on larger items. The device was normally a representation of a god or hero or animal, or later a person. The engraving of sealstones remained a fine art throughout antiquity.

See also GEMS.   GS

Boardman (1970); Richter (1968, 1971).

Secessio   the term used in Latin sources to describe the withdrawal of the PLEBS to a hill outside the city. It was an extreme form of civil disobedience, particularly because it implied draft evasion. The first secession traditionally occurred in 494 BC and resulted in the formation of the plebeian organization (*see* TRIBUNUS PLEBIS). At least four further secessions are recorded, the last of them in 287 BC (*see* PLEBISCITUM), but in 121 BC Gaius GRACCHUS attempted to revive the

tradition of secession when he and his followers withdrew to the
AVENTINE.   TC

Scullard (1980).

Security   In Roman law security could be received either in the form
of an oral contract (STIPULATIO) or by rights over the property of a
debtor. This security could be realized through either DOMINIUM (to be
received back if the debt was settled) or MANCIPATIO. *Stipulatio* could
be given on the same property to different creditors, with the earlier
claim taking priority if needing to be realized.

See also NEXUM.   HE

Nicholas (1962).

Segesta   city in north-west SICILY. Segesta was the chief city of the
Elymi who with the PHOENICIANS retained possession of western Sicily
until the island passed under Roman control in the mid-3rd century
BC. By the 5th century the city was partly hellenized: its temples were
Doric and its alphabet Greek. To further its traditional quarrel with
SELINUS it sought the help of first Athens, encouraging the disastrous
Sicilian expedition of 415 BC, and then CARTHAGE, provoking war be-
tween Greeks and Carthaginians in 409. It deserted Carthage at the
start of the First PUNIC WAR and was made a free city by Rome. Some
fine buildings survive.   GS

Finley (1979).

Seisachtheia   *see* SOLON.

Sejanus   (d. AD 31), praetorian prefect. Lucius Aelius Sejanus, son of
Seius Strabo, a wealthy equestrian, became his father's colleague as
praetorian prefect (AD 14), and sole prefect in 17. Efficient and
hardworking, he became TIBERIUS' intimate adviser, but was extremely
ambitious and almost universally hated. The suspicion that he seduced
GERMANICUS' sister, Livilla, and induced her to poison her husband,
DRUSUS (23), may well be justified. He concentrated the PRAETORIAN GUARD
in a single camp outside Rome (23), and after Tiberius' retirement
from Rome (26) wielded immense power until Tiberius, warned of
Sejanus' ambitions by the younger ANTONIA, sent Macro to Rome to
denounce and execute him.   RJB

Salmon (1968); Wells (1984).

Seleuceia on Tigris   city in Babylonia. Seleuceia was founded by
SELEUCUS (later I) to replace BABYLON as his capital when his rule in

Babylonia was confirmed in 312 BC. It became an important commercial centre, since trade from the Persian Gulf could reach it up the Tigris and Euphrates (to which the city was connected by canal). Seleuceia had a large mixed population of Greeks, natives, and Jews, and it was the major Greek city in Babylonia, retaining its importance even after the foundation of Syrian ANTIOCH. It passed into Parthian control in 141 BC, was burnt by TRAJAN, and finally destroyed by AVIDIUS CASSIUS in AD 164.   EER

Hopkins (1972); Stillwell (1976).

Seleucus I Nicator   (c.358–281 BC), Seleucid king. Seleucus 'the conqueror' accompanied ALEXANDER THE GREAT's expedition as one of the Macedonian 'Companions'. He commanded the Bodyguard in India and was appointed chiliarch (vizier) after Alexander's death. He became satrap of Babylonia in 321 BC, but the increasingly powerful ANTIGONUS I MONOPHTHALMUS caused his flight to PTOLEMY I in 315. The defeat of Antigonus' son DEMETRIUS I POLIORCETES at Gaza in 312 allowed Seleucus' return to Babylon (when the 'Seleucid era' officially began). He founded a capital city at SELEUCEIA ON TIGRIS. Seleucus regained much of Alexander's eastern empire and proclaimed himself king in 305/4. Antigonus' defeat at IPSUS in 301 gave the Seleucid empire a Mediterranean orientation, as the foundation of ANTIOCH in Syria in 300 shows. Seleucus won all of Asia Minor by finally capturing Demetrius (bent on recovering his father's territory) in 286, and by defeating LYSIMACHUS at Corupedium in 281. While invading Europe to annex Thrace he was murdered by PTOLEMY CERAUNUS.   EER

CAH VII.1; Grainger (1990b); Green (1990).

Seleucus II Callinicus   (c.265–225 BC), Seleucid king. Seleucus 'the triumphant' was the eldest son of ANTIOCHUS II and LAODICE I, claiming the throne over BERENICE SYRA's infant son (who was murdered). He fought the Third Syrian War against Berenice's brother PTOLEMY III (246–241 BC), only succeeding after sharing the throne with his brother ANTIOCHUS HIERAX. Antiochus later rebelled and the empire was divided. Seleucus regained sole control only after Antiochus' defeat by ATTALUS I SOTER, though much of Seleucid Asia Minor was lost to Pergamum.
   See also ARIARATHES III.   EER

CAH VII.1; Green (1990).

Selinus   city on the south coast of SICILY. Founded from Megara Hyblaea in 651 BC, Selinus occupies a strategic position and is the most westerly of the Greek cities of the island. Despite a long-standing quarrel with SEGESTA, it prospered and erected magnificent temples, the remains of which survive. It enjoyed good relations with Carthage until Segesta provoked a war in 409 which culminated in the destruction of Selinus, Acragas, Gela, and Himera. A second Carthaginian destruction in the First PUNIC WAR was final. GS

Finley (1979).

Semonides (7th century BC), Greek lyric poet. Semonides was born on Samos but led a Samian colony to Amorgos. He is said to have written two books of iambics and two of elegiacs, the latter on the history of Samos. But apart from two passages preserved by Stobaeus, the longer of which runs to 118 lines and mocks women in terms of the animals they resemble (the lazy sow, the barking bitch, etc.), little of his work survives. GS

Lloyd-Jones (1975).

Senate *To 31 BC:* The Roman Senate was in origin the council of the kings (*see* REX). Its members were chosen by the kings. After the abolition of the monarchy, members were theoretically enrolled by first the CONSULS, later the CENSORS. However, by the historical period membership had become a prerogative of those who had been MAGISTRATES. SULLA formalized this by giving QUAESTORS automatic entry. Censors could still remove men. There was no property qualification until AUGUSTUS, although we can assume possession of the EQUESTRIAN qualification. Senators were debarred from trade, and were thus a landed class. Senators liked to see their order as hereditary, but in fact new men (*see* NOVUS HOMO) always formed a significant percentage. The Senate thus formed a means of integration for the citizen élite. Although ROMULUS traditionally instituted a Senate of 100, the first historically recorded membership was 300. Sulla increased this to 600, and CAESAR to 900, before Augustus returned it to 600.

Although the Senate was strictly only an advisory body (*see* SENATUS CONSULTUM), it was usually seen as being in legitimate control of the Republic. This was only partly due to its institutionalized political functions. Magistrates were expected to consult the Senate. It negotiated with foreign embassies, assigned provinces to magistrates, prolonged commands, and voted funds. It was, however, also the focus of communication between the gods and man, being the final arbiter in religious crises. The Senate also formed the only expression of continuity in political institutions. It was the symbol of consensus among the élite and the historical validation of their status. When in the late Republic general élite consensus gave way to intense conflict, attacks on the authority of the Senate, and its eventual overthrow, destroyed the Republic and brought a return to monarchy.

See also CURIA; CURSUS HONORUM; LAW, ROMAN; NOBILES; PATRICIANS; SENATE, IMPERIAL.   HS

Beard and Crawford (1985); Brunt (1982); Gelzer (1969); Hopkins (1983); Wiseman (1971).

31 BC–476 AD: The Senate was retained by AUGUSTUS as a vital part of the fiction of the restoration of the Republic, and throughout the Empire the emperor's powers were in theory granted by the Senate. Augustus reduced the Senate to its former size of 600 and allowed it to govern Italy and other provinces without large armies. However, the emperor soon came to control both the AERARIUM (the state treasury) and the whole senatorial administration. Senatorial elections were reduced in importance by the emperor's powers of *nominatio* and *commendatio*, and the emperor could directly control the Senate's composition by the power of ADLECTIO, or through the censorship. In addition, Augustus imposed a property qualification of one million *sestertii*. The title *princeps senatus* (leading senator) passed to the emperor.

The Senate lost many functions, but developed important judicial ones. SENATUS CONSULTA, initially the Senate's advice to the magistrates, achieved the status of laws by the late 2nd century AD, but the Senate's power was restricted by the emperor's right to convene, preside over, and bring business before it. None the less, although attendance declined, the Senate retained a reputation for competence. 'Good' emperors allowed it to try its own members, while 'bad' ones could receive *damnatio memoriae*. Its Roman composition altered to include provincials, primarily Italian, southern Gaullish, or Spanish in the 1st century, and, in the 2nd/3rd centuries, included many Africans and Orientals. Gallienus reduced the role of senators in military command and provincial government, while under Constantine the distinction between senator and equestrian almost disappeared. A senate in CONSTANTINOPLE (from 330) achieved equal status with that of Rome (359), and by *c.*384 each senate had *c.*2,000 members. In the 5th century the Senate declined in power still further, but remained the formal representative of the Roman people (upper class), and continued its legislative functions. It is last heard of in 603.   RJB

Millar (1977); Talbert (1984).

Senatus Consultum   senatorial decision. Under the Republic a decision of the SENATE was in theory only advice to MAGISTRATES and lacked the force of law, although in practice it would seldom be ignored. Most controversial was the *Senatus Consultum Ultimum*, which called on the CONSULS to employ all means to save the state (*see* INTERCESSIO; PROVOCATIO). As this was used by OPTIMATES to suppress the POPULARES, it is unsurprising that its legality was defended by the former and attacked by the latter.

Under the Principate, *senatus consulta* came to have the force of law, but by the 3rd century AD were subsumed into imperial law-making.

See also LAW, ROMAN; PLEBISCITUM.   HS

Jolowicz and Nicholas (1972); Lintott (1968); Wirszubski (1950).

Seneca the Elder   (*c.*55 BC–AD 40), Latin rhetorician. Lucius Annaeus Seneca was born at Corduba in Spain and educated at Rome where he taught rhetoric. Little is known of his life, but he had three sons – Novatus Gallio, governor of Achaea, SENECA THE YOUNGER, and Mela, father of LUCAN – for whom in old age he compiled his anthology of oratorical quotations and exercises, *Oratorum Sententiae Divisiones Colores*: five (of an original 10) books of *Controversiae* and one book (of an original two) of *Suasoriae* survive and provide valuable evidence of the training in RHETORIC known as *declamatio*.   GS

Bonner (1977); Fairweather (1981); Sussman (1978).

Seneca the Younger   (*c.*4 BC–AD 65), Roman politician, philosopher, and dramatist. Lucius Annaeus Seneca was born at Corduba in Spain, the second son of SENECA THE ELDER. At Rome he studied rhetoric and philosophy before embarking on a public career. His brilliance as an orator incurred the jealousy of the emperor GAIUS and in AD 41 he was exiled to Corsica for alleged adultery with the emperor's sister. Recalled in 49, he became tutor to the young NERO and praetor. As chief adviser to Nero after his accession in 54, he enjoyed a position of influence and power, from which, as the emperor's conduct degenerated, he retired in 62 to pursue his literary interests. In 65 he was implicated in the conspiracy of PISO and forced to take his own life.

Of his voluminous writings the following works survive: 12 books of STOIC *Dialogi*, exercises in RHETORIC and philosophy; the moral tracts *De Beneficiis* (seven books) and *De Clementia* (incomplete); seven books of *Naturales Quaestiones* concerned with meteorology and other natural phenomena; 20 books of *Epistulae Morales ad Lucilium*, an artificial correspondence (*see* EPISTOLOGRAPHY, LATIN); nine tragedies, for recitation, not performance (*see* TRAGEDY, ROMAN); 77 epigrams; *Apocolocyntosis*, a SATIRE on the deification of the emperor Claudius.

GS

Costa (1974); Dudley (1972); Griffin (1976); Hutchinson (1993); Pratt (1983).

Senones   Gallic people. The Senones migrated into CISALPINE GAUL in the 5th century BC and settled between Ravenna and Ancona. Led by

BRENNUS, they captured Rome in 390 BC. Allied with the ETRUSCANS and SAMNITES, they were defeated at Sentinum in 295 but continued to fight the Romans. In 283 Dolabella destroyed their army and established a Roman colony at Sena Gallica (Senigallia).   LPR

Beresford Ellis (1990).

Sententia in Latin literature, and specifically in the language of the rhetorical schools, a terse and moralizing expression that functions like an aphorism. Such expressions are especially common in the works of Juvenal, Lucan, Martial, Seneca, and Tacitus.   GS

Sepeia near Tiryns, scene of a battle c.494 BC. CLEOMENES I invaded ARGOS, Sparta's Peloponnesian rival, by sea, giving battle at Sepeia. Having won by a stratagem, he pursued the Argives into a sacred wood; here, he lured out individuals by trickery and killed them until discovered, then burnt the rest to death. On his return home he was prosecuted for failure to assault the city of Argos, but acquitted. RB

Burn (1984); Tomlinson (1972).

Septuagint the Greek version of the Old Testament. The name (from *septuaginta*, late Latin for 70) derives from an apocryphal story that when PTOLEMY II PHILADELPHUS asked for a translation of the Jewish Law he was sent 70 (or 72) scholars from Jerusalem who executed the work on the island of Pharos. In fact the translation was done over a period of time by several hands and was mostly complete before the start of the Christian era. It was used principally by Jewish migrants into Egypt who had become Greek speakers and by Christians who adopted it as their Bible. Variations between its text and that of the DEAD SEA SCROLLS are the subject of current research.   GS

Fraser (1972).

Serfs In various areas of Greece the indigenous population had been reduced to subjection as agricultural serfs (but *see* Athenaeus 263 for a voluntary relationship). They were not chattels, but retained their social organization and occupied their original homes and land, in a status between freedom and servitude. The best-attested are the Messenian and Laconian helots, who constituted the labour force of SPARTA, paying a proportion of their produce to their masters; their racial and social coherence encouraged revolts, hence Sparta's repressive treatment of them. Similar groups existed at Syracuse, Sicyon, and Argos and in Thessaly and Crete.

See also SLAVERY, GREEK.   RB

Cartledge (1979); Finley (1981).

Sertorius (d. 72 BC), Roman soldier and administrator. Quintus Sertorius, a Sabine *eques*, after early military experience under Marius against the Germans and under Didius in Spain, helped CINNA capture Rome for the Marians in 87 BC, though opposing Marius' bloodbath. After his praetorship in 83, he went to Spain as a governor. Driven out after Sulla's victory, he returned in 80 to organize a revolt with strong support from discontented Iberian tribes among whom he won a reputation for humanity and generosity. He also provided a base for Marian refugees from Sulla's regime and survivors of LEPIDUS' rebellion, creating a counter-Senate from among them and always claiming to represent the legitimate Roman government. By his charismatic leadership and his skill at guerrilla warfare, he retained his control of most of the peninsula until Pompey and Metellus began to wear him down in 75–74. Failure made him more cruel towards the natives. In 72 he was murdered by his jealous lieutenant Perperna.   DP

Curchin (1991); Gabba (1976).

Servianus (*c*.AD 47–136), Roman politician. Lucius Julius Ursus Servianus married HADRIAN's sister, Domitia Paulina. Though 31 years older than Hadrian, he was jealous of the favour shown him by the future emperor TRAJAN. He was consul in 90 (or 93), and governor of Upper Germany in 97, and consul twice more (102 and 134). In 136 he was accused of plotting with his 18-year-old grandson, Pedanius Fuscus, Hadrian's nearest male relative, and put to death.   RJB

Perowne (1960).

Servilius Vatia Isauricus (134–44 BC), Roman soldier and politician. Publius Servilius Vatia Isauricus fought for SULLA in the CIVIL WAR, and was one of the leaders of the Senate during a long political career. After his consulship in 79 BC he held a five-year command against the pirates in Cilicia. He got his surname from his victories over the Isaurians, and triumphed on his return to Rome. He failed to become Pontifex Maximus in 63 against competition from Julius Caesar, but was censor in 55.   DP

Gruen (1974); Magie (1975).

Servius (late 4th–early 5th century AD), Latin grammarian. Servius appears as a character in MACROBIUS' *Saturnalia* but nothing is known of his life. He was the author of a detailed commentary on the works of VIRGIL which survives in two versions, of which the longer incorporates material by other scholars including DONATUS. Designed for use in schools, it concentrates on matters of grammar and style but also contains much of antiquarian interest.   GS

Kaster (1988).

Servius Tullius (6th century BC), king of Rome. Servius Tullius, the sixth and best-loved of the Roman kings, reigned traditionally from 578 to 535 BC. There are differing traditions about his origins (see MASTARNA): according to the standard Roman legend he was born a slave in the house of TARQUINIUS PRISCUS, but grew up to become his trusted lieutenant and eventual successor. He was celebrated as a reformer, who held the first CENSUS, reorganized the tribes and the COMITIA, extended the POMERIUM, and surrounded the city with a wall. Many of these developments can, in fact, be dated to the 6th century BC. Servius was eventually murdered by his successor, TARQUINIUS SUPERBUS.

See also COINAGE, ROMAN; DIANA; LATIN LEAGUE; TRIBUS; WALL OF SERVIUS.

TC

CAH VII.2; Ogilvie (1976); Thomsen (1980).

Sestos city of the Thracian CHERSONESE. Its strategic location overlooking the Dardanelles and its fine harbour ensured that it played a major part in both PERSIAN and PELOPONNESIAN WARS. In 480 BC it received Xerxes' bridge of boats, and in 479/8 it was the first city to be freed by the Athenian fleet. In 411–404 it was the Athenian base for naval operations against Sparta. Under the Romans it became a free city but its importance declined.

GS

Seven Sages name given in ancient tradition to seven men of practical wisdom of the period c.620–550 BC. The lists vary according to authority but four names are invariably included: THALES of Miletus, Bias of Priene, PITTACUS of Mytilene, and SOLON of Athens. Plato (*Protagoras* 343be) added CHILON of Sparta, Cleobulus of Lindus, and Myson of Chen. The Seven Sages were held to represent ancient wisdom and their teachings were handed down as popular aphorisms.

JL

Severus, Flavius Valerius (d. AD 307), Roman emperor, AD 306–7. Flavius Valerius Severus, an Illyrian soldier, became western Caesar after MAXIMIAN's forced retirement and CONSTANTIUS I's elevation to Augustus (May 305). Severus' portion was Italy, Pannonia, and Africa. After Constantius' death (July 306) Severus became Augustus, with CONSTANTINE I technically his subordinate. GALERIUS, now senior Augustus, ordered Severus to attack the usurper MAXENTIUS, but Severus' troops (loyal to Maximian, Maxentius' father) mutinied. Severus was imprisoned by Maximian and put to death by Maxentius.

RJB

Grant (1985); Parker (1958).

Severus, Lucius Septimius (AD 145/6–211), Roman emperor, AD 193–211. Lucius Septimius Severus, from Leptis Magna, owed his advancement to a fellow African, Aemilius Laetus, last of Commodus' praetorian prefects. Severus, governor of Upper Pannonia, claimed the throne (April 193), posing as the avenger of PERTINAX to gain support against DIDIUS JULIANUS. He won the backing of the Rhine and Danube legions, and bought off CLODIUS ALBINUS with the title of Caesar, before invading Italy. Julianus' support evaporated, and Severus was declared emperor. Severus disbanded the PRAETORIAN GUARD, replacing it with men from his own legions. He then confronted PESCENNIUS NIGER, who was defeated and killed (spring 194). After an invasion of Parthia (195) the province of Osroene was established. Severus next turned against Albinus, elevating his elder son Bassianus (CARACALLA, by his second wife JULIA DOMNA) to Caesar (June 196). After Albinus' defeat (19 February 197) at Lyon, and subsequent suicide, Severus soon began a second Parthian campaign. Ctesiphon fell to the Romans (March 198), and Severus took the title Parthicus Maximus, promoting Caracalla to Augustus, and his second son, GETA, to Caesar. MESOPOTAMIA was subsequently annexed as a Roman province.

Severus' administrative reforms included a reorganization of imperial finances, and an increased role for equestrians, to whom new legions and provinces were assigned (*see* BUREAUCRACY). The PRAETORIAN PREFECT lost many of his military functions, but became a powerful judicial and administrative figure, the post being held by the eminent jurist Papinian, after the execution of Severus' favourite PLAUTIANUS. A building programme, both in Rome (e.g. the Arch of Severus) and Africa (particularly LEPTIS MAGNA), belongs to this period. The last years of Severus (208–11) were occupied with war in Britain, partly to secure the loyalty of the army to his warring sons, partly to counter barbarian incursions in 207. Roman armies penetrated southern Scotland and much reconstruction was undertaken on Hadrian's Wall, before Severus' death at York (4 February 211).   RJB

Birley (1988); Grant (1985); Parker (1958); Wells (1984).

Severus Alexander   (AD 208–35), Roman emperor, AD 222–35. (Marcus Julius) Gessius Alexianus Bassianus, son of Julia Mammaea, was the second grandson of Julia Maesa to become emperor. Adopted in July 221 as the heir of his cousin ELAGABALUS, he took the name Marcus Aurelius Severus Alexander and became emperor after the murder of Elagabalus. Alexander discarded the religious fanaticism of Elagabalus, and his restraint and courtesy assured his popularity with Senate and people. Real power was held initially by Julia Maesa, and, after her death, by Julia Mammaea and her praetorian prefect, Ulpian. An invasion of Mesopotamia (230) by the Persians under Ardashir was repulsed (232–3) and Alexander celebrated a triumph, although his own part had been undistinguished. German invasions across the Rhine and Danube proved Alexander's undoing: he attempted to negotiate a settlement rather than offer battle, and so lost the support of his troops. Alexander and Mammaea were murdered, and replaced by MAXIMINUS THRAX (March 235). RJB

Grant (1985); Parker (1958); Wells (1984).

Shapur I (d. AD 272), king of Persia, c.AD 241–72. Shapur (or Sapor) succeeded his father Ardashir (Artaxerxes) as king of SASSANIAN Persia, taking the title 'King of Kings of Iran and Non-Iran'. He launched three major invasions against Rome (242–4, c.256–7, and 259–60), during which he overran Mesopotamia and Armenia, temporarily held Antioch (c.256), and captured the emperor VALERIAN (260) near Edessa, before ODAENATHUS of Palmyra forced his retreat. A rock-cut sculpture at Naqsh-i-Rustam shows Valerian kneeling before Shapur. RJB

Grant (1979); Millar (1981); Parker (1958).

Shapur II (d. AD 379), king of Persia, AD 309–79. Shapur (or Sapor) became king of SASSANIAN Persia in 309/10, while very young. In 334 he invaded Armenia, but was expelled by Constantine's nephew Hannibalian (336). During the early years of CONSTANTIUS II's reign he three times besieged Nisibis in Mesopotamia (338, 346, 350), was diverted by barbarian incursions along his northern and eastern frontiers, but returned to the attack (359), fighting further campaigns against Constantius II, JULIAN, and Valens. RJB

Hamilton and Wallace-Hadrill (1986); Parker (1958).

Ships Underwater archaeology and the reconstruction of ancient vessels have made important contributions to the understanding of ships and shipbuilding in antiquity. Both warships and cargo ships were equipped with oars and sails, but when a TRIREME made ready for battle she abandoned her tackle, and rowers took up space which on a merchant ship was more profitably used for cargo. Warships were built for speed and manoeuvrability since apart from ramming opponents their offensive capability was limited. The first Greek warships (see NAVY, GREEK) were propelled by a single bank of oarsmen. In order to maintain her naval supremacy Athens developed the trireme, a high-performance vessel with a total of 170 rowers arranged in three banks on each side. In the Hellenistic period the number of banks was increased to four (quadrireme) and five (quinquereme) and more. The Romans (see NAVY, ROMAN) used the quinquereme with some success against the Carthaginians, but their preference was to use heavier ships as boarding platforms. Merchant ships were designed to sail more slowly on longer voyages in worse weather and with heavier cargo. They relied on sail and were therefore subject to wind conditions, but in normal circumstances they could make 3–4 knots. In Hellenistic times ships of 150 tons were common and up to 500 tons not rare. Roman freighters often had two or three masts.

See also NAVIGATION; TIMBER.

GS

Casson (1991); Morrison and Coates (1986); White (1984).

Sicilian expedition *see* PELOPONNESIAN WAR.

Sicily *To 350 BC*: The first wave of Greek COLONIZATION in Sicily began with NAXOS and SYRACUSE, and included CATANA, LEONTINI, GELA, MESSANA (or Zancle), and Megara Hyblaea; these in turn planted colonies such as SELINUS, ACRAGAS, and Himera. The western part of the island was controlled by the Phoenicians, but the indigenous Sicans and Sicels were gradually displaced, although Elymian SEGESTA remained independent. Archaic Sicily came to be dominated by the empire of Gela (*see* HIPPOCRATES) and Syracuse (*see* GELON, HIERON I) whose aggressive expansion led to an abortive Carthaginian intervention in support of their opponents at HIMERA.

The 460s saw an unsuccessful Sicel nationalist movement led by DUCETIUS. Continued fear of Syracuse enabled Athens, who had been building up her diplomatic contacts in Sicily, to intervene during the PELOPONNESIAN WAR on an increasing scale until her final defeat in 413; thereafter, her former allies looked to CARTHAGE for support. Carthaginian successes led to the rise of DIONYSIUS I, who held Carthage at bay during his tyranny, and raised Syracusan power to new heights, being courted by both Athens and Sparta; but on his death Syracuse became embroiled in civil war (*see* DION, DIONYSIUS II) and Carthaginian influence revived.

See also ANAXILAS; PHALARIS; THERON.

RB

CAH V; Dunbabin (1948); Finley (1979); Freeman (1891–4).

350–211 BC: In response to the appeal of Syracusan aristocrats to their mother city Corinth for help against Dionysius II, Corinth sent TIMOLEON in 345. He eventually liberated Syracuse and defeated Carthage, but his social and political reforms throughout Sicily did not outlive him, and civil war returned to Syracuse (*c.334*). AGATHOCLES established a populist tyranny there from 317 to 289, despite repressive measures. After PYRRHUS' expedition, HIERON II established control, defeated the MAMERTINES (*c.269*), and ruled a prosperous and peaceful Syracuse. After his death (215), Syracuse supported Carthage in the Second PUNIC WAR, leading to her capture by Rome in 211 and the unification of Sicily into a Roman province.

EER

CAH VII.2, VIII; Finley (1979); Green (1990).

Roman province: After the capture of Syracuse in 211 BC Sicily became Rome's first major overseas PROVINCIA. The province was governed by a praetor, later by a proconsul or propraetor, assisted by two quaestors. Sicily's agricultural productivity made the province important for the Roman corn supply (ANNONA) and led to the creation of large estates (LATIFUNDIA). The slaves who worked the estates underpinned the great slave revolts of 135–132 and 104–100 BC. Sicily was notoriously ill-governed by VERRES in 73–71 BC. In the era of the Second TRIUMVIRATE Sicily was held by Sextus POMPEIUS, until he was ejected by AUGUSTUS in 36 BC. Under the Empire Sicily remained an undisturbed Roman province until the barbarian invasions of the 5th century AD.   HS

Bradley (1989); Finley (1979).

Sicyon   city in southern Greece. Sicyon emerged from subjection to Argos under a tyranny founded by Orthagoras *c.*660 BC. The tyrant CLEISTHENES initiated a period of prosperity and cultural activity in the 6th century. The tyranny was ended by Sparta in the 550s and Sicyon joined the Peloponnesian League. In 303 BC DEMETRIUS I POLIORCETES moved the city from the plain to a superior inland site. In the 3rd century Sicyon was united with the ACHAEAN LEAGUE by ARATUS OF SICYON, but its prosperity was later eclipsed by Corinth.   GS

Andrewes (1956); Griffin (1982); Walbank (1933).

Sidon   city and port of the PHOENICIANS. Hellenized in the 5th century, Sidon was captured in the 4th century first by EVAGORAS of Cyprus and then by ALEXANDER THE GREAT, but continued to be ruled by a native dynasty until the 3rd century when it became a republic. Conquered by the Seleucids in 200 BC, it was granted freedom in 111 and became a Roman colony under Elagabalus. Always prosperous, Sidon was the centre of purple-dyeing and (from the 1st century BC) GLASS-blowing industries.   GS

Sidonius Apollinaris   (*c.*AD 431–86), Latin poet and letter writer. Gaius Sollius Apollinaris Sidonius was born at Lugdunum of a distinguished Gallo-Roman family. As the son-in-law of the emperor AVITUS he moved to Rome upon his accession and delivered a verse PANEGYRIC in his honour on 1 January 456, for which he was honoured with a statue in the Forum of Trajan. Two years later he delivered a second panegyric for MAJORIAN, and in 468 a third for ANTHEMIUS which earned him the prefecture of Rome. Returning to Gaul in 469, he became bishop of Clermont. In addition to the panegyrics and various other poems, nine books of letters survive, addressed to family and friends.
     GS

Stevens (1933).

Siegecraft, Greek Greek cities were traditionally captured by block-ades. Simple siege devices like mounds, tunnels, battering rams, and fire are attested in the PELOPONNESIAN WAR, but simple FORTIFICATIONS could withstand them. DIONYSIUS I of Syracuse revolutionized siegecraft by inventing artillery (bolt-shooting catapults like crossbows) and mobile storeyed towers (brought up on specially constructed moles) which protected catapults, rams, and boarding bridges. PHILIP II of Macedon used similar tactics, and ALEXANDER THE GREAT fully appreciated the art of siegecraft. He also used stone-throwing torsion catapults (using sinews or hair), and mounted his machines on ships. Defending cities vastly improved their fortifications and also used artillery. DEMETRIUS I POLIORCETES (the 'besieger') employed the ultimate Hellenistic siege tactics. In his siege of RHODES (305/4 BC) towers containing catapults were mounted on ships guarded by floating booms. His 'City-Taker' was a nine-storeyed tower with catapults on each level. He also de-ployed covered galleries to protect men and machines, and boring and battering rams mounted on rollers operated by windlasses and pulleys.

See also ARCHIMEDES; SIEGECRAFT, ROMAN.   EER

Connolly (1981); Lawrence (1979); Marsden (1969); Tarn (1930).

Siegecraft, Roman The standard Roman system of siegecraft from the 3rd century BC onwards was bicircumvallation, a development of the technique used by the Greeks to starve defenders into submission. A first line of booby traps, trenches, and ramparts, joining the army's camps, fenced the defenders in, while a second line faced outwards against a possible relieving force. In offensive siegecraft the Romans fell far short of the Greeks, and real sieges were largely confined to the east, where there was a tradition of siegecraft. They used some of the Greeks' tools – iron-headed rams, siege towers, mechanically operated grappling hooks – but made no innovations, and preferred undermin-ing and ramp-building. Torsion catapults were widely used, both bolt-firing and stone-firing (*catapultae* and *ballistae*; the names were later reversed). As an alternative to approaching the walls in hide-covered frames, the infantry attacked in tortoise formation (*testudo*), in a rectangular block, with shields locked together both around and above them.   RJB

Connolly (1981); Hackett (1989).

Silanion (fl. 360–330 BC), Greek sculptor. Silanion of Athens is known to have produced three sculptures of mythological subjects – Achilles, Theseus, and Dying Jocasta – and a number of portraits: Sappho, Corinna, Plato, the sculptor Apollodorus, and at least one boxer at Olympia. Copies survive of the Corinna and Plato, and an original bronze head of a boxer from Olympia may be his. He also wrote a treatise on proportion. GS

Richter (1970b).

Silius Italicus (*c.*AD 26–101), Latin poet and lawyer. Tiberius Catius Asconius Silius Italicus was a wealthy and successful advocate who became consul in AD 68 and governor of Asia *c.*77. Retiring to Rome, he enjoyed the cultured society of men such as MARTIAL and the younger PLINY and took to writing poetry. An admirer of Cicero (whose house he bought) and Virgil (whose tomb he restored), he composed *Punica*, an EPIC poem in 17 books on the Second PUNIC WAR. The narrative owes most to LIVY and the poetry to VIRGIL, but the style is rhetorical and verbose. GS

von Albrecht (1964).

Silk Production of real silk was confined to China until the 6th century AD but by the 5th century BC it was being imported into western Asia in the form of cloth or yarn. During the Hellenistic period it spread into the Greek world and by the early Empire it had reached Rome via PARTHIA and the Phoenician cities of TYRE and SIDON. At Rome it was so expensive that it was said to be worth its weight in gold, and its use was attacked by moralists. An inferior raw silk was produced on the island of Cos from the 4th century BC and was for a long time the only available material for home-made silk garments.

See also TRADE. GS

Miller (1969).

Silver Silver was less popular than GOLD for jewellery, though it was for long the rarer and more valuable metal. But it was used for COINAGE; to make vases and statuettes; and later by the Romans for domestic furniture and especially for tableware. Its introduction was said to be due to the PHOENICIANS. In the classical Greek period it was found in Attica (where the mines of LAURIUM produced large quantities until 413 BC), Macedonia (on Mt PANGAEUS), Lydia, and Colchis. Sources in Spain, Sardinia, Gaul, Dacia, and Britain were exploited by the Romans. The metal was hammered into sheets which were riveted or soldered together. Decoration was then added by chasing, stamping, engraving, or repoussé working. Further effects could be produced by gilding or niello inlay. GS

Healy (1978); Strong (1966).

Simonides (*c.*556–468 BC), Greek lyric poet. Simonides was born on Ceos but like his younger contemporary Pindar he travelled widely as a professional poet. He was brought to Athens by HIPPARCHUS and then invited to Thessaly. By the 490s he was back in Athens where he defeated AESCHYLUS in the competition for an epitaph on the dead at Marathon. Finally he moved to Syracuse c.476 to the court of HIERON I whom he reconciled to THERON of Acragas. As a poet he was original, influential, and versatile, composing hymns, paeans, dithyrambs, epinician odes, dirges, elegies, and epigrams. He was uncle to BACCHYLIDES. GS

Bowra (1961).

Sinope city on the southern shore of the Black Sea. Founded by Miletus probably c.630 BC, Sinope occupies a defensive position on a peninsula with two good harbours. It was an important trading station exporting timber and minerals and standing at the end of a caravan route from the Euphrates. It received Athenian settlers c.437 but remained mostly free until the 2nd century BC. In 183 it was taken by PHARNACES I and made the capital of PONTUS. After harsh treatment in the Third MITHRIDATIC WAR it was captured by LUCULLUS in 70 BC and given its freedom. Caesar made it a Roman colony in 47 BC and in the 3rd century it received IUS ITALICUM. GS

Sisenna (119–67 BC), Roman historian. Lucius Cornelius Sisenna was praetor in 78 BC, defended VERRES in 70, and was a legate of Pompey in 67, dying in Crete. He wrote a history in at least 12 books, covering the SOCIAL WAR and Sullan CIVIL WAR, possibly continuing Sempronius ASELLIO. He was noted for his brilliant style, and was criticized for pro-Sullan bias. The work survives only in fragments. HE

Badian (1964); Rawson (1991).

Slavery, Greek The use of unfree labour was widespread in ancient Greece. In some cases this consisted of SERFS, working the land they occupied for their conquerors, with a social organization and some minimal rights. Chattel slaves were different, first in coming predominantly from outside the Greek world, and secondly in being the property either of a state or (usually) of individual owners. Numbers are hard to establish, but for Athens estimates of 60,000–100,000 seem reasonable; that would be between a quarter and a third of the POPULATION, and nowhere are they likely to have outnumbered free men. The richest individuals might own 1,000 or more slaves as an asset, to be hired out as labourers, for example in the Athenian silver mines at LAURIUM; but moderate groups of a few to a few dozen seem to have been more normal: such slaves were mostly agricultural or industrial workers or domestic servants. Prices varied according to ability, but the average slave might have cost 150–200 drachmas, and required feeding and clothing, so slave ownership, though widespread, was far from universal.

The treatment of slaves varied enormously: at one extreme, slaves in the Athenian silver mines were simply a labour force, working in appalling conditions, while at the other the slaves of craftsmen could be craftsmen themselves, working beside their masters, or even independently, with the possibility of manumission. Slaves could earn money, but slave marriages and children do not seem to have been common. Although often moderately treated, slaves were generally regarded as inferior, even by the philosophers, although some SOPHISTS dissented, and their only legal protection lay in their owners' property rights. Nevertheless, revolts did not occur, because slaves were racially and culturally heterogeneous and relatively dispersed, but they might run away where possible. RB

Cartledge (1985); De Ste Croix (1981); Finley (1960); Garlan (1982); Vogt (1974); Wiedemann (1981).

Slavery, Roman Roman slaves, though persons, were the property of their owners, to whom they owed absolute obedience. They had virtually no rights, being regarded as pieces of equipment which happened to be alive. The acquisition of an empire and years of unchecked piracy flooded Italy with cheap slaves. Hundreds of thousands of prisoners were enslaved in the great wars of conquest, such as Caesar's GALLIC WAR. By the end of the Republic slaves, at two million plus, formed more than 20 per cent of the population of Italy. Numbers ranged from the one or two slaves of an ordinary family to the thousands owned by great nobles like DOMITIUS AHENOBARBUS or CRASSUS.

Slaves were employed in all spheres of human activity, other than military and political. No job was peculiar to slaves, but the two basic types were the workers and the thinkers. 'Working' slaves were used especially in the mines and on the vast estates of the rich. 'Thinking' slaves might be doctors, teachers, accountants, bailiffs, overseers, secretaries, etc.: they held such jobs because of the Roman reluctance to work for someone else and their recognition that people reared in the culture of the Greek east had the necessary skills.

Although a few owners like Cicero (see TIRO) treated their slaves humanely, the general attitude was probably more cruel. In court slaves were only examined under torture. At GLADIATOR shows they were publicly killed for the amusement of the free. There were three great slave revolts in Sicily and Italy between 139 and 71 BC (see SPARTACUS).

Manumission, however, was common, if only because sometimes an owner could see that he would get more work out of a new slave. Freed slaves had some citizen rights, and the sons of freedmen were full members of the citizen body.

See also CITIZENSHIP, ROMAN.   DP

Bradley (1987); Finley (1980, 1990); Hopkins (1978); Wiedemann (1981).

Smyrna modern Izmir, city on the west coast of Asia Minor. Settled by Aeolic Greeks *c.*1000 BC, Smyrna was fortified in the 9th century when it came under the control of Ionians from Colophon. After a period of prosperity the city was destroyed by Alyattes of Lydia *c.*600 BC and again by the Persians *c.*545. Refounded on its present site by ALEXANDER THE GREAT, Smyrna flourished and remained throughout antiquity one of the principal cities of Asia. Smyrnaean poets included BION, HOMER (?), MIMNERMUS, and QUINTUS.   GS

Stillwell (1976).

Social institutions   *see* CITIZENSHIP; INHERITANCE; MARRIAGE; WOMEN.

Social War, Greek   (357–355 BC), a war fought by Athens against dissident members of the Second Athenian Confederacy, Rhodes, Chios, Cos, and Byzantium. Athens's endeavours to recover AMPHIPOLIS and the Thracian Chersonese, the menacing conduct of CHARES, and the promise of protection by MAUSOLUS excited revolt. Militarily, Athens was barely adequate. When Chares lent help to ARTABAZUS, ARTAXERXES III threatened reprisals if Athens did not end the war. Thus the allies gained their freedom.   GLC

Sealey (1976).

Social War, Roman   (91–87 BC), a war between Rome and her Italian allies (SOCII). Rome's manpower problems in the 2nd century BC put an increased military burden on the allies. Although abroad the Greeks thought of the allies as Romans, at home the allies were denied access to decision-making and the benefits of empire. After some reverses, Rome won the war largely by conceding Roman CITIZENSHIP to all of Italy south of the river Po. The war created dangerous precedents. Roman magnates acquired 'private' armies, and Italians became accustomed to fighting Italians.

See also ARMY, ROMAN.   HS

Brunt (1988); Gabba (1976).

Socii Rome's Italian allies. The Roman conquest of Italy resulted in a system of military alliances by which defeated communities remained theoretically independent but were in practice reduced to subjects. This relationship was enshrined in treaties of alliance (*foedera*: hence 'federal', 'confederate', etc.) which the Italian peoples made with Rome, on terms that were more or less favourable, depending on whether they submitted voluntarily or were defeated in war. The model was the treaty of 493 BC between Rome and the LATIN LEAGUE. By the time of the Punic Wars more than 150 separate treaties had been concluded, and all the peoples of non-Roman Italy had become *socii*. The treaties stipulated military partnership, but in practice the allies were obliged to assist the Romans by sending contingents of troops to fight alongside the legions. In the middle Republic Roman armies always contained a large proportion, varying between half and two-thirds, of allied troops. By the time of the Gracchi the system had become exploitative, and in 91 BC allied discontent gave rise to the SOCIAL WAR, as a result of which the allies were given Roman CITIZENSHIP and incorporated in the Roman state.   TC

CAH VIII; Gabba (1976).

Socrates   (469–399 BC), Greek philosopher. Socrates was a native Athenian, the son of a sculptor and a midwife. Apart from military service at Potidaea, Amphipolis, and Delium, he rarely left the city. Initially he was interested in natural philosophy and is said to have been a pupil of Archelaus. He subsequently abandoned these interests – later parodied by ARISTOPHANES in the *Clouds* – and devoted himself to ethical enquiry which he pursued by relentlessly cross-questioning those who had pretensions to wisdom with a view to convincing them that their assumptions were ill-founded. His striking and charming personality, unusual appearance, great intellectual ability, and moral courage attracted to him a diverse circle of devoted friends, including young men of good family looking for an intellectual training which would equip them for a public career. Socrates pretended to know nothing himself and believed that he had a divine mission to serve as an intellectual midwife bringing to birth other men's ideas. He wrote nothing himself and it is mainly through PLATO's early dialogues and XENOPHON's *Memorabilia* that we know about his teaching and personality.

Being free from ambition, Socrates avoided politics, but was twice placed in situations where he displayed great moral courage. After ARGINUSAE, as president of the Assembly, he refused to put to the vote an illegal motion for the trial of the generals *en bloc*. He also defied the order of the THIRTY TYRANTS to arrest a man whom they had condemned. Under the restored democracy, however, he was tried and sentenced to death for 'introducing new gods and corrupting the young'. The real weight of the charge doubtless lay in the accusation that he was a subversive influence upon the minds of young men. Refusing escape on the ground that it was illegal, he drank the hemlock.

Socrates' defence and final days are described by Plato in the *Apology* and *Phaedo*.   JL

Guthrie, vol. 3 (1969).

Sodales   members of a Roman association. The Latin term *sodales* means something like 'companions', and was applied to men grouped together for some common end. Warrior bands of *sodales* played a part in the history of archaic Italy; for instance MASTARNA was one of the *sodales* of Caeles VIBENNA (*see also* VALERIUS PUBLICOLA). Members of religious colleges were also sometimes called *sodales*, for example the ARVAL BROTHERS, FETIALES, SALII, and the otherwise unknown *Sodales Titii*.
                                                                          TC

Stibbe, Colonna, De Simone, and Versnel (1980).

Solon   (fl. *c*.594 BC), Athenian lawgiver. Solon was elected archon for 594/3 BC with full powers to resolve the dangerous conflicts between rich and poor in Athenian society and forestall a tyranny. The nature of the *Seisachtheia* ('Shaking off of burdens'), his social and economic reforms, is uncertain, but it seems that Solon abolished loans on the security of the person, and hence debt slavery, and dissolved a quasifeudal relationship between peasant and aristocrat (*hektemorage*). His political reforms are clearer: distinctions of birth were superseded by the establishment of four economically defined classes, PENTACOSIOMEDIMNI, HIPPEIS, ZEUGITAE, and THETES, with political rights assigned accordingly. The minimum privileges, participation in the assembly and courts, may have existed previously, but their value was increased: an elective council of 400 was created alongside the AREOPAGUS to prepare business for the ECCLESIA, and Solon established the right of appeal from a magistrate to the people (HELIAEA) and opened the right to prosecute to any citizen for most offences. Solon's law code, which retained only the homicide law from DRACO's code, covered every area of life, and became the basis of classical Athenian LAW. His surviving poetry shows that Solon, though himself a EUPATRID, sought to achieve a compromise between the two sides but pleased neither: discontent and political strife continued, to be exploited by PEISISTRATUS. But though he failed to achieve his immediate objective, the substance of his reforms survived, and he was revered as one of the founders of Athenian democracy.   RB

Forrest (1966); Murray (1993); Rhodes (1981).

Sophists   The term *sophistes* originally meant a wise man or expert in some art or craft. It was applied, for example, to members of the SEVEN SAGES. In the 5th century BC, however, it came to be especially applied to itinerant teachers, who travelled from city to city giving instruction for a fee. Although the subjects they taught were diverse, they were invariably aimed at achieving success in life. PROTAGORAS, for example, professed to teach *aretē* (virtue or efficiency in the conduct of life) while GORGIAS specialized in RHETORIC, which was one of the chief means to attain success in a democracy. Less scrupulous sophists, however, claimed to be able to teach easy ways to success and to impart the ability to argue for any point of view without regard for morality and truth. In consequence, there developed a wide scepticism about the possibility of attaining truth through reason and the validity of any code of conduct. The cynical disbelief of such men in all moral restraints together with their pursuit of selfish, personal desires resulted in the terms 'sophist' and 'sophistic' becoming invested with pejorative connotations.   JL

Bowerstock (1969); Guthrie, vol. 3 (1969); Kerferd (1981).

Sophocles   (*c.*496–406 BC), Greek tragedian. Sophocles was born into a wealthy family at Colonus near Athens. As a boy he led the victory song after Salamis in 480 BC. He had a public career, serving as imperial treasurer in 443 and as a general, first with PERICLES in 441 and later with NICIAS. He was a priest of a healing cult, and after his death he was acknowledged as a hero in recognition of his services to Asclepius.

As a tragedian he was immensely prolific, with 123 plays credited to his name, and highly successful: he won 24 victories (the first in 468 when AESCHYLUS was competing) and never came lower than second. Seven complete plays survive: *Ajax, Antigone, Electra, Oedipus Coloneus, Oedipus Tyrannus, Philoctetes, Trachiniae*; and about half of the satyr play *Ichneutae. Oedipus Coloneus* was produced posthumously in 401. *Oedipus Tyrannus* was considered the model TRAGEDY by ARISTOTLE.   GS

Knox (1964); Winnington-Ingram (1980).

Sophron   (5th century BC), writer of Greek mime. Sophron of Syracuse was perhaps the first to give literary form to the popular genre of prose comedy centred on everyday life and known as MIME. Little of his work survives, but he was admired by PLATO and exerted considerable influence on his fellow Sicilian THEOCRITUS.   GS

Soranus   (2nd century AD), Greek physician. Soranus of Ephesus studied in Alexandria and practised at Rome during the reigns of Trajan and Hadrian. Two of his works have survived in Greek, a treatise on fractures and another on gynaecology in four books. Only fragments of *On Acute and Chronic Diseases* have survived but we possess a complete Latin translation by Caelius Aurelianus.   JL

Temkin (1956).

Sortes   *see* DIVINATION.

Sosius Senecio   (d. after AD 107), Roman general. Quintus Sosius Senecio, consul in AD 99, was a prominent figure during the reign of TRAJAN. An extremely able general, he was, in addition, a friend of PLUTARCH, a correspondent of the younger PLINY, and a friend to the young HADRIAN. He was valued greatly by Trajan, and honoured by him with a second consulship (107, as the colleague of SURA, consul for the third time) and a statue, privileges granted only rarely.   RJB

Birley (1976).

Spain   as a Roman province. After the Second PUNIC WAR at the end of the 3rd century BC Rome controlled an eastern coastal strip of Spain (Hispania Citerior, 'nearer Spain') and the south-eastern coastal district with the Guadalquivir valley (Hispania Ulterior, 'further Spain'). To rule these areas two new praetors were created in 197 BC. During the 2nd century BC frequent warfare, most notably against VIRIATHUS and the Lusitanians of modern Portugal and the CELTIBERIANS of north central Spain, brought a gradual extension of Roman control.

After the defeat of the Celtiberians at NUMANTIA in 133, SCIPIO AEMILIANUS and a senatorial commission drew up a *lex* (defining law) for each PROVINCIA. At this time Rome only controlled just over half of the Iberian peninsula. Although Spain saw Roman military activity in the 1st century BC, most notably the war against SERTORIUS which was ended by POMPEY, and CAESAR's campaign against Pompeian forces during the CIVIL WARS, the remainder of the peninsula was not conquered until the reign of AUGUSTUS. A new province of LUSITANIA was created, while Citerior (renamed Tarraconensis) was greatly enlarged. Ulterior was now renamed BAETICA.

Caesar and Augustus founded numerous colonies in Spain (*see* COLONIZATION, ROMAN). Although proceeding at vastly different rates in different areas, with Baetica far ahead of Tarraconensis and Lusitania, the romanization of Spain was profound. VESPASIAN reduced the garrison to just one legion and granted Latin rights to the whole peninsula. Senators were recruited from the 1st century BC, a process which culminated in the accession of the emperor TRAJAN, a native of Baetica. Some of the most important Latin writers of the 1st century AD came from Spain: the elder and younger SENECA, LUCAN, the agricultural writer COLUMELLA, the orator QUINTILIAN, and the poet MARTIAL.

Spain suffered barbarian incursions in the 3rd century AD, and was reorganized into six provinces by DIOCLETIAN. The peninsula was lost to the VISIGOTHS (*see* GOTHS) in the 5th century AD.   HS

Curchin (1991); Keay (1988); Richardson (1986); Sutherland (1939).

Sparta   Sparta began in the 9th century BC as a confederation of villages in the Eurotas valley. Having taken control of LACONIA, Sparta made the crucial decision *c.*735 to invade MESSENIA, annexing her land and reducing the Messenians to serfdom as helots (*see* SERFS). Two generations later the Messenians revolted, probably encouraged by Argos's victory over Sparta at Hysiae in 669, and were only reduced after prolonged hard fighting. Thereafter, Sparta was locked into an unbreakable circle: Messenian land and helot labour left Spartiates free to be professional soldiers, whose principal function was to guard against helot revolts.

During the 7th century Sparta underwent internal reforms. The date and details are controversial: Spartan tradition ascribed the complete developed form of their society to the legislation of LYCURGUS, but it probably developed gradually and piecemeal. In 706 political disorder had necessitated the dispatch of Sparta's only colony in the west, TARENTUM. Some time later a constitutional settlement ('the Great *Rhetra*') defined in writing the relationship of APELLA, GEROUSIA, and kings, recognizing limited rights for all citizens. Sparta fascinated ancient political theorists, who attributed her famed stability to a blend of monarchy (unusually double), aristocracy (the Gerousia), and democracy (the EPHORS and Apella); but in reality Sparta was an oligarchy, a model for and supporter of similar regimes.

In the same period the army underwent reorganization to accommodate HOPLITE weapons and tactics. Meanwhile the assignment of an equal allotment of land to each citizen established a theoretical economic equality, paralleled by a notoriously rigorous state-organized system of EDUCATION, the *agoge*, which turned Spartan boys into soldiers. Hence Spartan citizens called themselves *homoioi*, 'equals' (or 'alike'). Despite this uniformity, and the dominance of the state, Sparta's celebrated austerity developed slowly: the poetry of ALCMAN and artistic remains, especially pottery and bronzework, attest a lively archaic culture.

Having secured Messenia, Sparta attempted to annex Arcadia likewise. Failure precipitated a change of policy under ANAXANDRIDAS and CHILON: a combination of diplomacy and warfare extended Spartan influence throughout the Peloponnese, and it grew further under CLEOMENES I; it is no surprise that Sparta should have led Greece in the PERSIAN WARS, arguably her finest hour. Her subsequent cautious avoidance of overseas commitments, however, allowed the growth of

Athenian power, and once a rival began to encroach on Sparta's allies, the PELOPONNESIAN WAR was inevitable.

Sparta's victory in 404 again left her the dominant power in Greece, but at the expense of an accommodation with Persia and a peace which alienated her allies. There were also internal problems: the career of LYSANDER exemplified Sparta's difficulties with ambitious individuals, while the conspiracy of Cinadon revealed increasing tension between non-citizens and Spartiates; the citizen population, already declining in the 5th century, was now perilously low. Victory under AGESILAUS in the Corinthian War restored Sparta's position in mainland Greece; but she was unable to prevent the formation of a new Athenian empire or to check the rise of THEBES, who finally defeated her decisively at LEUCTRA. The ensuing liberation of Messenia effectively destroyed Spartan power; thereafter her influence was confined to the Peloponnese.

See also CARNIA; CRYPTEIA; DORIANS; PELOPONNESIAN LEAGUE; PERIOIKOI.

RB

Cartledge (1979); Cartledge and Spawforth (1989); Forrest (1980); Huxley (1962); Murray (1993); Oliva (1971); Rawson (1969).

Spartacus   (d. 71 BC), Roman slave. Spartacus, a Thracian gladiator, escaped from Capua and in 73 BC led a slave revolt which spread through southern Italy and ultimately attracted 90,000 slaves. These huge forces overran southern Italy for three years, defeating a succession of Roman commanders sent against them including the consuls of 72, and would have invaded Sicily, if their pirate transports had not failed them. Spartacus was finally defeated and killed in Lucania in 71 by CRASSUS, who subsequently crucified any rebels he captured. Pompey, returning from Spain, exterminated the few rebels that escaped. His courage and abilities made Spartacus a legend in his lifetime.   DP

Bradley (1989); Rubinsohn (1987).

Spartocids   ruling dynasty at Panticapaeum in the Crimea (*see* CHERSONESE, TAURIAN). The Spartocids, whose name derives from their founder Spartocus, began their rule in 438/7 BC. Athens courted their favour because she depended on them for the corn she needed to import. They, perhaps content to have a secure market, accorded Athens privileged access.   GLC

Rostovtzeff (1941).

Speusippus   (*c*.407–339 BC), Greek philosopher. Speusippus of Athens succeeded his uncle, PLATO, as head of the ACADEMY and held office from

347 until his death. Only fragments remain of his voluminous writings. He wrote on Pythagorean MATHEMATICS and endorsed the search for the elements of numbers, taken over by Plato from the Pythagoreans, but refused to equate numbers with Platonic Ideas, which he rejected. Speusippus further developed the method of classification begun by Plato with his dialectical illustrations, and in ethics held that pleasure is neither good nor evil in itself and that goodness is to be found only in the last stages of development.   JL

Guthrie, vol. 5 (1978).

Sphacteria battle in 425 BC, *see* PYLOS.

Spolia opima spoils of victory. *Spolia opima* were spoils offered to Jupiter Feretrius by a Roman general who had killed an enemy leader in single combat. Roman tradition knew of three such occasions: Romulus' legendary victory over the king of Caenina, the defeat of Lars Tolumnius of Veii by A. Cornelius Cossus (*c.*428 BC), and the victory of M. Claudius MARCELLUS over Viridomarus (222 BC). Octavian rejected the claim of Marcus Licinius CRASSUS to the *spolia opima* in 28 BC.   DP

Versnel (1970).

Sport *see* EDUCATION; GAMES; OLYMPIC GAMES.

Stadium The first stadium, or running track, in Greece was built at OLYMPIA in the mid-6th century BC. It was a stade (600 Greek feet, *c.*200 yards) in length, whence its name, which was also the name of the sprinting race. Like THEATRES, stadia were usually placed against the side of a hill with a natural embankment to provide seating. Stone seating was rare and introduced late, if at all. The stadium at Athens, first built in the 4th century BC, was reconstructed in marble in the 2nd century AD by HERODES ATTICUS and again in 1896 for the first Olympic Games of modern times.
See also GAMES.   GS

Drees (1968).

Standards Roman military symbol. The early legion had five standards. MARIUS gave each legion an eagle (*aquila*) as its standard. Subunits of a legion carried standards called *signa*. Under the Principate a legion also used symbols specific to itself, and *imagines*, portraits of reigning and deified emperors. Standards were given quasi-divine honours. In the late Empire the *draco*, of barbarian origin, and the *labarum*, a Christian symbol, were introduced.

See also ARMS AND ARMOUR, ROMAN; ARMY, ROMAN.   HS

Keppie (1984); Parker (1928); Webster (1985).

Statilius Taurus   (d. *c*.15 BC), Roman general. Titus Statilius Taurus, a NOVUS HOMO and consul in 37 BC, became the greatest of AUGUSTUS' generals after AGRIPPA. Besides fighting in Sicily, Illyricum, and Spain, he commanded the land army at ACTIUM, and for his services in Africa in 34 he was given a triumph, commemorated by an amphitheatre built in the Campus Martius. He gained a second consulship in 25, and in 16 BC was put in charge of Rome during Augustus' absence in Gaul. His descendants included several consuls and Nero's third wife, Messalina.   DP

Carter (1970); Syme (1939).

Statius   (*c*.AD 45–96), Latin poet. Publius Papinius Statius was born at Naples, the son of a schoolmaster. Moving to Rome, he enjoyed popularity as a poet and imperial patronage under DOMITIAN. His epic on the emperor's German wars is lost, but three other works survive. The *Thebaid* is an EPIC in 12 books, owing much to VIRGIL, on the quarrel between Eteocles and Polynices, written between AD 80 and 91. The *Achilleis*, another epic, was left unfinished. The *Silvae* is a collection of 32 occasional poems in various metres which Statius published between 92 and his death.   GS

Dudley (1972); Hardie (1983); Vessey (1973).

Stesichorus   (*c*.632–553 BC), Greek lyric poet. Stesichorus was born in south Italy at either Mataurus or Locri but lived mostly at Himera in Sicily. A younger contemporary of ALCMAN, he was one of the earliest poet musicians of choral LYRIC and the first literary representative of Greek culture in the west. His subject-matter is closely linked to epic: the wooden horse of Troy, the Calydonian boar hunt, the funeral games of Pelias. Of the 26 books of his collected poems only fragments survive, but enough to show that his episodic treatment of myth represents an important stage in the transition from EPIC to TRAGEDY.

GS

Bowra (1961).

Stilicho   (d. AD 408), Roman regent. Stilicho, of Vandal birth, was appointed Master of Both Services (*see* MAGISTER MILITUM) in Italy by THEODOSIUS I (394), and became regent for HONORIUS and effective ruler of the western empire from 395. He marched against ALARIC in Thessaly, but turned back on the order of Arcadius, and then put down the rebellion of GILDO (397–8). He twice defeated Alaric in Italy (402,

403), but allowed his escape, hoping for aid in annexing eastern Illyricum. He defeated a Gothic invasion of Italy, led by Radagaisus (405–6), but failed to stop further Germanic invasions of Gaul (406–8). His unpopularity finally led to his execution. RJB

Bury (1958); Grant (1985); Matthews (1990).

Stipendium Roman military service. In the Republic the maximum service required in the legions was 16 years. The norm was probably six years. The length of service ruined many of the Italian peasants who served, and this led to manpower problems. The reforms of MARIUS and the enfranchisement of the Italian allies (SOCII) eased the problem. AUGUSTUS twice regularized the terms of service; 16 years, plus four as veterans, with the legions, and 12 for praetorians in 13 BC; and 20 years, plus five as veterans, with the legions, 16 for praetorians, and 25 for auxiliaries in AD 5.

See also ARMY, ROMAN; SACRAMENTUM; SOCIAL WAR, ROMAN. HS

Brunt (1971a); Gabba (1976); Smith (1958).

Stipulatio Roman legal contract. A *stipulatio* was a verbal contract whereby a person gave an undertaking to another in the form of an answer to a question. Thus: 'Do you promise to do so-and-so?' 'I promise.' There were certain essential formalities. Both parties had to be present; the response had to fit the question precisely (i.e. to use the same verb); no conditions or qualifications could be added; and there were to be no interruptions during the exchange. Witnesses were not necessary. The procedure was as old as the TWELVE TABLES, and was central to the Roman law of obligations. It was used extensively in civil litigation; for example, a magistrate could order a *stipulatio* in order to reinforce a judgement. In the course of time written stipulations were admitted, and were normal in Cicero's time; by the age of Justinian they had replaced the oral form altogether.

See also SECURITY. TC

Watson (1965).

Stoa a term in Greek ARCHITECTURE applied to a long open colonnade. Stoas were commonly built in sanctuaries or market-places to provide shelter from sun, wind, and rain. They served a variety of functions including those of market, classroom, lawcourt, council chamber, and informal meeting place. The Stoa Poikilē at Athens, where ZENO OF CITTIUM taught his pupils (*see* STOICS), was renowned for its paintings by POLYGNOTUS. The Stoa of Attalus (2nd century BC) has been reconstructed as a museum for the Agora. GS

Coulton (1976).

Stoics The Stoic school was founded at Athens by ZENO OF CITIUM *c.*300 BC and was named after the STOA Poikilē (Painted Colonnade) in which he taught. The history of the school is usually divided into three distinct periods: Early Stoa (foundation to the first half of the 2nd century BC); Middle Stoa (2nd and 1st centuries BC); and Late Stoa (Roman Empire). Zeno was the author of the fundamental doctrines which were adopted by Cleanthes, his successor as head of the school. CHRYSIPPUS, however, the third head, elaborated the system and his views became established as orthodox.

During the Middle Stoa, Panaetius, under the influence of Platonic and Aristotelian ideas, revised the whole system and rejected the doctrine of world conflagration. He adapted Stoic ethics to suit the needs of the Roman nobility, and it is largely due to him that Stoicism became so influential within these circles at Rome. A further revision was undertaken by his pupil POSIDONIUS, and through him Stoicism influenced scientists like Geminus and STRABO. During the final period, Stoicism became predominantly preoccupied with ethical concerns. Its most important exponents during the 1st century AD were SENECA THE YOUNGER and EPICTETUS. At this time, too, Stoicism provided a philosophic basis for opposition to the principle of one-man imperial rule, especially during the reigns of Nero and Domitian. Its most important representative, however, in the 2nd century was the emperor Marcus AURELIUS. Although Stoicism exercised an important influence upon NEOPLATONISM, the school itself gradually declined in the 3rd century.

See also DIO CHRYSOSTOM. JL

Long (1974); Sandbach (1975).

Stolo (4th century BC), Roman lawgiver. The plebeian tribune Gaius Licinius Stolo, together with his colleague L. Sextius Lateranus, proposed a series of measures which were passed in 367 BC and subsequently became known as the Licinio-Sextian Laws. They included action to relieve debt (*see* NEXUM), imposed a limit of 500 *iugera* on individual holdings of AGER PUBLICUS, and gave plebeians the right to hold the consulship; as a result L. Sextius became the first plebeian consul in 366 BC. Stolo was himself consul a few years later. According to a nice story which may or may not be true, he was convicted and fined for occupying more *ager publicus* than was permitted under his own law. TC

CAH VII.2.

Strabo (64 BC–*c.*AD 24), Greek geographer. A Pontic Greek from Amasea, Strabo spent much of his early life studying in Rome before setting off on his travels in the course of which he visited Egypt,

Ethiopia, and Arabia Felix. In 7 BC he returned to Amasea where he died. His *Historical Sketches* in 47 books are lost, but his *Geography* (17 books) survives. As GEOGRAPHY it is entirely derivative, but it preserves all that we know of ERATOSTHENES' Homeric geography and as a source of historical information and contemporary detail it is a treasure house.   GS

Strategos Greek magistrate and general. In most Greek states the generals (*strategoi*) were also magistrates, usually elected, and allowed repeated terms of office in recognition of the need for expertise. As state officials, they were frequently supervised by their cities, and liable to prosecution in cases of failure or insufficient success. At Athens 10 *strategoi*, one for and (normally) from each tribe, replaced the POLEMARCH as commanders in the field; they were also responsible for the call-up and for the conduct of judicial proceedings in the military sphere. Normally they exercised strategic command independently or in groups in different theatres rather than as a board (the tribal contingents being under subordinate officers), and from the mid-4th century BC some generals began to be annually assigned to particular regular duties.

Because it was an elective position allowing iteration, the generalship offered 5th-century Athenian politicians a continuing position of authority (though not all politicians were *strategoi*, and vice versa). The 4th century saw the emergence of the specialist general, often commanding mercenaries, and employed by his own state either irregularly (since unpopularity might necessitate a period of service abroad) or not at all (*see* CHABRIAS; CHARES; IPHICRATES).   RB

Hansen (1991); MacDowell (1978); Pritchett, part II (1974).

Stratocles (*c*.350–293/2 BC), Athenian politician. Stratocles attacked DEMOSTHENES in the HARPALUS trial in 324 BC, but is best known for espousing the cause of ANTIGONUS I MONOPHTHALMUS and DEMETRIUS I POLIORCETES in Athens after 307, being responsible for the lavish honours granted to them. His pro-Macedonian policies lasted until Antigonus' defeat at IPSUS in 301, despite opposition from CASSANDER's supporters. He lost political power after Ipsus, but regained some influence when Demetrius again won control of Athens in 294.   EER

Ferguson (1911); Mossé (1973); Shear (1978).

Straton (d. *c*.268 BC), Greek philosopher. After a period of study at the Lyceum (*see* PERIPATETIC SCHOOL) under THEOPHRASTUS, Straton left Athens to take up an appointment at Alexandria as tutor to the future PTOLEMY II PHILADELPHUS. There he seems to have taken part in the establishment of the MUSEUM. He returned to Athens at the death of Theophrastus (287 BC) to succeed him as head of the Lyceum where he remained until his death. A partially preserved list of his writing includes works on logic, ethics, cosmology, zoology, psychology, physiology, and physics. Only fragments remain of his works. His main interest lay in PHYSICS and his preoccupation with the natural world earned him the sobriquet 'the physicist'.   JL

DSB XIII (1976).

Suebi   German people. The Suebi were a major grouping of Germanic peoples, including the Hermunduri, MARCOMANNI, Naristi, Nemetes, QUADI, Semnones, Triboci, and Vangiones. They expanded south-west-wards, reaching the Rhine *c.*100 BC. DRUSUS (7 BC) forced the Quadi and Marcomanni eastwards, into Moravia and Bohemia: pressure on these tribes from the GOTHS precipitated the Marcomannic Wars (AD 168–79) against Rome. The Semnones, like the ALAMANNI, clashed with the Romans from the 3rd century onwards.   RJB

Thompson (1965); Todd (1975).

Suetonius   (*c.*AD 69–*c.*140), Roman biographer. Gaius Suetonius Tranquillus, son of a Roman equestrian, was a close friend of the younger PLINY, who tells us that Suetonius practised briefly at the bar, but avoided political life before becoming chief secretary to HADRIAN (who later dismissed him for over-familiarity towards the empress SABINA). Suetonius wrote on a number of subjects: *Royal Biographies*; *Roman Manners and Customs*; *The Roman Year*; *Offices of State*; *Cicero's Republic*; *The Physical Defects of Mankind*; *An Essay on Nature*; *Greek Objurgations*; *Grammatical Problems*; *Critical Signs Used in Books*; *Methods of Reckoning Time*; *Roman Festivals*; *Roman Dress*; *Greek Games*; and *Lives of Famous Whores*. Fragments of his *Illustrious Writers* survive, while his most famous work, *The Twelve Caesars* (a series of biographies of Julius Caesar and the emperors Augustus to Domitian), survives intact. Suetonius took care to check his facts and quote conflicting evidence, but frequently concentrates on scandalous incidents in the Caesars' domestic lives.

See also BIOGRAPHY, LATIN; HISTORIA AUGUSTA.   RJB

Graves (1957); Wallace-Hadrill (1983).

Suetonius Paulinus   (d. after AD 69), Roman general. Gaius Suetonius Paulinus, governor of Britain (AD 58–61), continued the Roman advance begun by PLAUTIUS and OSTORIUS SCAPULA. He pacified the Silures in south Wales (58/9), and, after overrunning the Deceangli in north Wales, attacked Mona (Anglesey, 60). Thus occupied, Paulinus was unable to prevent BOUDICCA's sacking of Colchester, London, and Verulamium (St Albans). His savage reprisals after defeating the rebellion led to his replacement by a more conciliatory governor.   RJB

Salway (1981); Scullard (1979).

Sulla   (*c*.138–78 BC), Roman dictator. Lucius Cornelius Sulla Felix came from an obscure patrician family. After early military successes he became consul for 88 BC and was allotted the command against MITHRIDATES. When SULPICIUS RUFUS transferred this command to MARIUS, Sulla took the unprecedented step of persuading his army of six legions to march on Rome. He took control by violence before departing to fight Mithridates. When CINNA's regime sent out another army with a new commander to replace him, Sulla made peace with Mithridates, won over the other Roman army, and settled the affairs of Greece and Asia on his own authority. Returning to Italy in 83, he once again led his army against the established government in Rome. A brutal CIVIL WAR ensued, from which Sulla emerged victorious in 82. He then embarked on a massacre of his opponents by means of PROSCRIPTION lists, and was installed as dictator to revise the constitution. His solution was to increase the powers of the Senate, which he doubled in size, to reduce the tribunes to impotence, and to impose checks on senior magistrates. The resulting regime soon showed itself unworthy of Sulla's ruthless efforts on its behalf, and few of his measures survived the reaction after his death, while his violent methods set an example to later ambitious dynasts seeking to overthrow the traditional regime.   DP

Badian (1970a); Gruen (1974); Keaveney (1982).

Sulpicius   (d. 88 BC), Roman politician. Publius Sulpicius Rufus was a member of Lucius CRASSUS' circle and a friend of DRUSUS. In 95 BC he prosecuted NORBANUS. In 88 as tribune he devoted himself to securing full political rights for the newly enfranchised Italians, in the teeth of opposition from the OPTIMATES. He also passed a law transferring the Mithridatic command from SULLA to MARIUS, who was one of his chief supporters. When Sulla marched on Rome, he was captured and executed and his laws annulled.   HE

Sundials   *see* ANAXIMANDER; TIME, MEASUREMENT OF.

Sunium   The temple of POSEIDON at Sunium on the southernmost tip of Attica was built *c*.444 BC on the foundations of an earlier temple which had been destroyed by the Persians. Probably by the same architect as the THESEUM in Athens, it had a Doric peristyle but a continuous frieze with Ionic mouldings. The site – a rocky headland 200 feet above the sea – overlooks one of the busiest shipping lanes in Greece and became a favourite resort of pirates.   GS

Lawrence (1984); Stillwell (1976).

Sura   (d. soon after AD 110), Roman general. Lucius Linicius Sura was a prominent general, and a close friend of (and speech-writer for) the emperor TRAJAN. He was consul three times (in AD 97, 102, and 107, the last as the colleague of SOSIUS SENECIO). He became extremely wealthy, and built a gymnasium for the people of Rome. When Sura died, he was accorded a public funeral and a statue, and Trajan built baths in his honour.   RJB

Birley (1976).

Sybaris   city in Calabria. Sybaris was founded c.720 BC as an Achaean colony in the rich farmland of southern Italy. The city prospered from agriculture and trade, especially with Miletus and Etruria (since it commanded the land route across the toe of Italy) and enjoyed a famously luxurious life-style. Sybaris was destroyed by its neighbour and rival CROTON in 510, but was later replaced by the foundation of THURII nearby.   RB

Dunbabin (1948).

Sybota   near the southern tip of Corcyra where a sea battle was fought in 433 BC by Corinthians against Corcyrans. A small force of Athenian ships stood by to help the Corcyrans if necessary, in accordance with the recently negotiated defensive alliance. Corinth therefore held back and both sides claimed victory. The old-fashioned tactics demonstrated how Athenian ships, expert in ramming, were in advance of the Greeks generally.

See also NAVY, GREEK.   GLC

Kagan (1969).

Symmachia   literally 'fighting side by side', so the Greek word for 'alliance'. It is distinguished from *epimachia* which was the word for a purely defensive alliance ('if anyone attacks you, I will defend you'). The PERSIAN WARS demonstrated that the full form ('to think the same persons friends and enemies') was necessary.

There were simple alliances of one state with another; but leagues described themselves in terms of alliances (e.g. the DELIAN LEAGUE was 'the Athenians and the allies'); and in the 4th century BC a league, e.g. the Second Athenian Confederacy, was an alliance between a single state on the one hand and Athens and her allies on the other, i.e. an alliance with an alliance. Various common peaces of the 4th century were described as 'peace and alliance', 'alliance' referring to joint action against breaches of the peace. GLC

Ehrenberg (1969).

Symmachus (*c*.AD 340–402), Roman orator. Quintus Aurelius Symmachus was a member of the Roman senatorial class, received a training in rhetoric, and was highly regarded as an orator. He became governor of Bruttium in AD 365 and of Africa in 373, prefect of Rome in 384, and consul in 391. Typically of his class, he was a pagan, more devoted to estate management than to political activity. Fragments of eight speeches, including three PANEGYRICS, are preserved. But he is best remembered for his letters (over 900 survive), collected in 10 books, of which nine are private and one his official correspondence as prefect. GS

Binns (1974); Matthews (1990).

Symmoria group of Athenian citizens liable for tax in the 4th century BC. When the arrangements for paying EISPHORA (capital levy to underwrite a war) were reformed in 378/7, taxpayers were grouped into 'symmories'. In 358/7, when the law of PERIANDER divorced payment of the costs of a trireme from service as a commander, the same method was adopted. GLC

Sympoliteia term used to designate a single state formed out of two or more states. By the 4th century BC various forms of unification were in vogue. *Sympoliteia* was the most complete, involving the establishment of a single set of laws for two or more previously separate cities, e.g. the Chalcidians of Thrace. The term was also used for the unification of peoples, e.g. the Achaeans who all shared one constitution where originally there had been 12 cities.

See also ACHAEAN LEAGUE; AETOLIAN LEAGUE. GLC

Ehrenberg (1969).

Symposium Greek drinking party. The symposium was a social ritual taking the form of an after-dinner entertainment for Greek men. Musical interludes might be provided by servant girls, but the principal ingredients were wine and conversation. Gatherings of intellectuals centring on the circle of Socrates are described by PLATO and XENOPHON. Less intellectual occasions would include the playing of games and singing of drinking songs. A caricature of the degeneracy of the Roman symposium is provided by PETRONIUS. GS

Lissarrague (1990); Murray (1990).

Synesius (*c*.AD 370–413), Greek Christian writer. Born and brought up a pagan at Cyrene, Synesius studied under the Neoplatonist philosopher Hypatia at Alexandria. He led a successful mission to Constantinople in 399 and married a Christian in 403 but had to abandon his marriage on his election to the bishopric of Ptolemais in 410. His writings include letters, hymns, and pamphlets as well as a treatise on dreams and an attack on excessive monastic asceticism.   GS

Liebeschuetz (1990); Momigliano (1963a).

Synoecism unification into one state. The Greeks used the term *synoecismus* to denote the grouping of two or more communities into a single state; it implies the establishment of a political union and centre (whether pre-existing or specially founded), though not necessarily the gathering of population into a single settlement. The synoecism of ATTICA was attributed to Theseus in the mythical period, and celebrated in an annual festival, the Synoecia.
See also POLIS.   RB

Ehrenberg (1969); Moggi (1976).

Syphax (d. 201 BC), Numidian chief. Syphax, chief of the Masaesyli Numidians, revolted from Carthage and in 213 BC allied with Rome. He was opposed by MASSINISSA, king of the Massyli, who campaigned against him. In 206 Syphax transferred his allegiance to Carthage and expelled Massinissa from his kingdom. In 203 he was captured after a Carthaginian defeat on the Great Plains, and died in chains in Rome in 201.   LPR

Warmington (1969a).

Syracuse city in Sicily. Syracuse, founded from Corinth (trad. 733 BC), was the leading city in Sicily. Her rise to eminence began under the tyranny of GELON and HIERON I who by conquest and population transfers built Syracuse into a major military power, which won victories over Carthage at HIMERA and the Etruscans at Cumae (474). After Hieron the tyranny was replaced by a democracy which defeated DUCETIUS and during the PELOPONNESIAN WAR thwarted Athens's first intervention (427–424) and defeated a full-scale assault (415–413); but victory was followed by renewed Carthaginian activity and political upheaval (*see* HERMOCRATES), culminating in the tyranny of DIONYSIUS I. Dionysius drove back the Carthaginians, and raised Syracusan power and prosperity to new heights, but fresh internal conflict under DIONYSIUS II and DION again weakened the city. Matters were restored by TIMOLEON, but his constitution was overthrown by the tyranny of AGATHOCLES. On his death the Carthaginians benefited from another period of instability, and Syracuse only regained her position under HIERON II. However, his conflict with the MAMERTINES drew the Romans into Sicily; although Hieron was treated as an ally, his son's support for HANNIBAL led to the sack of Syracuse, which subsequently became the governmental centre of the Roman province of Sicily.   RB

CAH V; Dunbabin (1948); Finley (1979); Loicq-Berger (1967); Woodhead (1962).

Syria   Roman province. After the defeat of the Armenian king TIGRANES I in the Third MITHRIDATIC WAR, Pompey created the province of Syria (64–63 BC). The province consisted of the cities of the region (ANTIOCH, Beirut, Damascus, Laodicea, SIDON) and contained the client kingdoms of COMMAGENE, ARABIA, Nabataea, and Judaea, the ITURAEAN tetrarchy, and other minor principalities. Commagene was annexed to the province in AD 72; Ituraea partly in 24 BC, partly in AD 93. Judaea (*see* JEWS) became a separate province in AD 70, Nabataea (*see* NABATAEANS) in AD 105. Under Septimius Severus the province was divided between north (Syria Coele) and south (Syria Phoenice).

Syria was a rural province, though Antioch was always one of the great cities of the empire. The Aramaic language continued to be used and the impact of hellenization was minimal. Syria was famous for wine, wool and linen, and purple dyes. It was also an important recruiting ground for the Roman army. And the province benefited from trade between the Mediterranean and MESOPOTAMIA (*see* PALMYRA).

Syria was an important military frontier, guarding Rome against PARTHIA and the SASSANIANS. Under the Principate its consular governor commanded four legions, and under the late Empire the eastern field army was based at Antioch.   HE

Magie (1975); Sherwin-White (1984).

T

Tabularium record office in Rome. The Tabularium contained the major ARCHIVES of the Roman Republic. Originally it held financial documents, but later also laws promulgated by the Senate. Under the Empire it held imperial constitutions. It was attached to the treasury in the temple of Saturn and was administered by the urban QUAESTORS. In 78 BC the records were moved to a new building on the CAPITOL, facing the Forum Romanum.   HE

Tacitus (c.AD 56–c.120), Roman historian. Cornelius Tacitus is perhaps the most famous of Roman historians, but we know relatively little of his life. His name was Publius or Gaius Cornelius Tacitus, and he was born in AD 56 or 57, probably in a provincial town in Gallia Narbonensis (southern France) or Cisalpine Gaul (northern Italy). The son of a Roman equestrian, he studied at Rome with the leading orators of the day. He rose to senatorial rank, and passed through a normal senatorial career, surviving the reign of Domitian (81–96) to become consul under Nerva (97), and, eventually, governor of Asia (112–13). He died sometime after 115: it is probable that he lived and worked up to the end of Trajan's reign and even for some years into that of Hadrian (117–38). He married the daughter of AGRICOLA in 77, and was an intimate friend of the younger PLINY, who addressed a number of his letters to him.

Tacitus became one of the best-known orators of his day, and in one of his written works, the *Dialogue on Orators* (of uncertain date, but dedicated to a consul of 102, and probably by Tacitus), four historical characters discuss the rival merits of oratory and literature, and the reasons for the decline in oratory under the early Empire. Tacitus' earliest works are the *Agricola* and the *Germania*, short monographs published *c*.98. The *Agricola* is partly a biography, almost a eulogy, of his father-in-law, but also includes useful historical and geographical material on Britain from the conquest onwards. The *Germania* is a study of the character, customs, and geography of central Europe and the German tribes.

Tacitus' principal works are the *Histories* and the *Annals* of imperial Rome. The *Histories*, covering AD 68–96 (from the death of Nero to Domitian), is the earlier work, perhaps published in instalments between 105 and 108. Only about a third survives, covering the year of the four emperors (AD 69) and the first nine months of the following year. The *Annals*, Tacitus' last and greatest work, spanned the reigns of Tiberius, Gaius, Claudius, and Nero (AD 14–68): 40 years out of 54 survive.

Tacitus, more dependable than SUETONIUS or DIO CASSIUS, is our best literary source for the years of the early Principate. He was meticulous in his attempts to verify his facts, although, perhaps inevitably, he displayed an anti-imperial, pro-senatorial bias, as he was a member of the Senate that felt the full impact of imperial oppression under Domitian. Tacitus' style varied: the *Dialogue on Orators* shows the influence of CICERO, while the later works, particularly the *Annals*, exhibit the great variety and epigrammatic terseness for which he is famous. He preferred short sentences, perhaps because his works were designed to be declaimed in the first instance. By his own claim, his sources included the official archives (ACTA SENATUS), and he undoubtedly consulted the works of many authors of the 1st century AD. Some of them he names, including Cluvius Rufus and Fabius Rusticus (who wrote on the period from Augustus to Nero), and the elder PLINY.

See also HISTORIOGRAPHY, ROMAN; RHETORIC, LATIN.   RJB

Goodyear (1970); Grant (1971c); Mattingly and Handford (1970); Syme (1958); Wellesley (1975).

Tacitus (*c*.AD 200–76), Roman emperor, AD 275–6. Marcus Claudius Tacitus, a Roman and a senator, who claimed descent from the historian Tacitus, was chosen by the Senate as a stop-gap emperor (autumn 275) after the assassination of AURELIAN. Allegedly already 75 years old, Tacitus accepted the nomination out of a sense of duty, and, aided by his praetorian prefect FLORIANUS, acted vigorously to repel a Gothic invasion of Asia Minor. He died at Tyana, perhaps murdered, in the spring of 276.   RJB

Grant (1985); Parker (1958).

Tagus title of the chief magistrate in THESSALY. The office was curious in that a *tagus* was only appointed in an emergency, but once appointed he retained it for life. It is found in literature only in XENOPHON's account of JASON of Pherae and his successor ALEXANDER (who appears to have usurped it); but presumably prominent Thessalians of earlier periods were so titled. After Jason it was replaced by the archonship (held by PHILIP II of Macedon from 352 BC onwards).   GLC

Westlake (1935).

Tanagra   city in Boeotia, site of a major (though thinly attested) battle in 457 BC between 1,500 Spartans with 10,000 allied troops and 14,000 Athenians and allies. The Spartan force, cut off in Boeotia, had to fight their way out. That they did march home by way of Megara proves that they were, as THUCYDIDES reported, victorious.   GLC

Kagan (1969).

Tarentum   Greek Taras, modern Taranto, city in south Italy. Traditionally founded in 706 BC by Spartans (specifically Parthenians, the illegitimate offspring of Spartan women and helots), Tarentum stands on a peninsula commanding the best port in south Italy. Aristocratic rule was replaced by democracy c.475 BC. By the mid-5th century the decline of CROTON brought Tarentum increased wealth and power which peaked in the 4th century under Archytas. Later the city needed help to fend off the Italian tribes and turned first to Sparta and then to mercenary leaders including PYRRHUS of Epirus. He was finally defeated in 275 leaving Tarentum to surrender to the Romans. In 213 it fell to HANNIBAL but was retaken in 209 and plundered by the Romans. Thereafter it declined and lost much of its prestige to BRUNDISIUM. It was the home of the Latin poet LIVIUS ANDRONICUS.   GS

Brauer (1986); Dunbabin (1948); Stillwell (1976).

Tarpeian Rock   a cliff within the city of Rome from which traitors and murderers were thrown. Its precise location is unknown, but it seems to have been on the south-west corner of the CAPITOL, overlooking the Forum Romanum. It was named after Tarpeia, who betrayed Rome to the Sabines during their war against Romulus.   HE

Platner and Ashby (1929); Richardson (1992); Robinson (1992).

Tarquinii   city in Italy. Tarquinii, modern Tarquinia, lies close to the coast, about 50 miles north-west of Rome. It began as a VILLANOVAN settlement, and became a major Etruscan city in the 7th and 6th centuries BC. It fought a series of major wars against Rome in the 4th century, but made a treaty in 351. It is most famous today for its cemetery which has been extensively excavated, revealing painted chamber tombs dating from the 6th to the 1st century BC. HE

Coarelli (1974); Scullard (1967).

Tarquinius Priscus king of Rome, 616–579 BC. Lucius Tarquinius Priscus was the fifth king of Rome according to tradition. He was son of Demaratus, a Corinthian aristocrat who had left Corinth to escape the tyranny of CYPSELUS and fled to TARQUINII. His son, Lucumo, migrated to Rome because of its reputation for admitting foreigners, and eventually became king with the name Lucius Tarquinius. He enlarged the Senate, won victories against the Latins, Sabines, and Etruscans, and began construction of the temple of Capitoline Jupiter. HE

Ogilvie (1976).

Tarquinius Superbus king of Rome, 534–510 BC. Tarquinius Superbus was the son or grandson of TARQUINIUS PRISCUS and traditionally the seventh and last king of Rome. He seized the throne after murdering SERVIUS TULLIUS, and ruled as a tyrant. He was expelled by a group of aristocrats after the rape of Lucretia by his son Sextus. His attempt to return with the help of Lars PORSENNA was a failure, and he died in exile at Cumae in 4925 BC.

See also TUSCULUM. HE

Ogilvie (1976).

Tarraco modern Tarragona, city in north-east SPAIN. Known as Cissa in the pre-Roman period, the city was destroyed by P. and Cn. SCIPIO in 218 BC. Refortified, it became the Roman base for action against the Carthaginians and Iberians. Under Caesar it became a Roman colony and under Augustus the chief city of Hispania Tarraconensis. Sacked by the Franks in AD 257, it revived sufficiently to be lauded by AUSONIUS in 370, but fell to the Visigoths in 476. GS

Stillwell (1976).

Tarsus city in CILICIA. There was a Greek colony at Tarsus by the 8th century BC. The city was autonomous under Persian rule and was issuing Greek coinage by the 5th century. After the conquests of ALEXANDER THE GREAT it was disputed between the Seleucids and the Ptolemies and was temporarily renamed Antioch on the Cydnus. Occupied by POMPEY in 66 BC, it was granted freedom by Mark ANTONY, and from AD 72 became the capital of the province of Cilicia. It was the birthplace of St PAUL. GS

Stillwell (1976).

Tartessus   region of Spain. The mineral wealth of Tartessus, an indigenous culture situated around the lower Guadalquivir river, attracted the attention of both Greeks and PHOENICIANS. Merchants from PHOCAEA, the principal Greek visitors, established friendly relations and traded lucratively in tin, copper, and silver from the late 7th century BC. But by c.500 they had been excluded by the Phoenicians, whose contacts were earlier and based on substantial settlements in the region.   RB

Aubert Semmler (1988).

Tatianus   (d. after AD 394), praetorian prefect. Tatianus was praetorian prefect of the east under the emperor THEODOSIUS I from AD 389 to 393 and consul in 391, while his son Proclus held the post of prefect of the city (of Constantinople) from 389 to 392. Both fell foul of the ambitious RUFINUS, Tatianus' successor as praetorian prefect, who engineered their arrest and condemnation, probably in 394. Tatianus was exiled to Lycia and his son was executed.   RJB

Bury (1958).

Tauromenium   modern Taormina, city in eastern SICILY. Tauromenium was founded in 392 BC by DIONYSIUS I soon after the destruction of nearby NAXOS. Andromachus, father of the historian TIMAEUS, became tyrant in 358. But c.316 it passed to Syracusan control, first under AGATHOCLES and later HIERON II. On the death of the latter (215 BC) Tauromenium accepted Roman rule. After the foundation of a colony by Augustus in 30 BC it flourished.   GS

Finley (1979).

Taxation, Greek   Little is known of early Greek practices. The Athenian tyrants are said by THUCYDIDES to have exacted a 5 per cent tax on agricultural produce and we hear of similar taxation by tyrants elsewhere. In the Athenian democracy (as always the source of most of our evidence) there was no general regular direct taxation, although the LITURGY system was a way of taxing the very rich. In times of crisis money was raised by the war tax (EISPHORA), a form of capital levy. But there were many indirect taxes, most notably perhaps the 2 per cent surcharge on imports and exports. Thus taxation fell on citizens and non-citizens alike. Right of collection was sold to the highest bidder. In the Hellenistic period rulers taxed both directly and indirectly; commonly there was a 10 per cent tax on agricultural produce. Taxes in Ptolemaic Egypt were particularly severe.

See also METICS.   GLC

Ehrenberg (1969); Michell (1957).

Taxation, Roman Roman taxation varied according to time and place. Direct taxation (TRIBUTUM; property and poll taxes) was levied in the provinces, but not (from 167 BC) in Italy, in colonies, or in communities granted immunity (IMMUNITAS). Most taxes were indirect (*see* VECTIGAL), the most important being customs duties (PORTORIA), levied on both internal and external trade. An inheritance tax was levied on Roman citizens only, and there was also a tax on the manumission of slaves.

The early emperors curtailed the inefficient and corrupt Republican system under which the censors and provincial governors farmed out tax collection to syndicates, whose agents (PUBLICANI) did the actual collection, particularly of the DECUMANA, a tithe (one-tenth) of the grain harvest on public land (AGER PUBLICUS) in Italy and Sicily. *Publicani* became less important as imperial officials (PROCURATORS) took over their functions. Provincial cities were responsible for collection of their own taxes. Regular censuses were conducted for tax purposes, and newly incorporated provinces underwent an immediate CENSUS.

From the 3rd century, because of the devaluation of the COINAGE, taxes were largely levied in kind (the ANNONA). Constant military expenditure demanded very high levels of taxation. Diocletian increased taxation still further, but also made collection increasingly efficient.

See also FINANCE, ROMAN.   RJB

Grant (1979); Salmon (1968); Wells (1984).

Taxiles (later 3rd century BC), Indian king. Taxiles, the royal name of King Omphis, ruled the territory between the Indus and Hydaspes (Jhelum) rivers. He welcomed ALEXANDER THE GREAT, who made his base at the capital Taxila, and fought with him against his rival, the Indian king PORUS, at the battle of the Hydaspes in 326 BC. First placed under a Macedonian satrap, he later became co-governor and finally independent. By 312 his domain was absorbed by SANDRACOTTUS.   EER

Bosworth (1988a); Hammond (1989).

Technology *see* ENGINEERING.

Tegea city in southern Greece. After a war with Sparta Tegea joined the Peloponnesian League *c.*550 BC and supported Sparta for two centuries apart from a brief revolt in 470–465. But at MANTINEA (362) Tegea fought with the Thebans. In 316 it withstood a siege by CASSANDER but in 222 it fell to ANTIGONUS III DOSON. Its buildings were restored in the Hellenistic period but it failed to regain its earlier importance. The temple of Athena Alea, destroyed in 395 BC, was rebuilt in the mid-4th century by SCOPAS.   GS

Stillwell (1976).

Temenos the precinct or enclosed area surrounding an altar and usually including a temple. GS

Temples *see* ARCHITECTURE.

Temple officials *see* PRIESTS.

Terence (*c.*185–159 BC), Latin comic poet. Publius Terentius Afer was born in Carthage and brought to Rome as a slave of the senator Terentius Lucanus, whose name he took on gaining his freedom. Supported by his friends SCIPIO AEMILIANUS and LAELIUS, he produced his first play, *Andria*, in 166 BC. Five others followed before his untimely death: *Hecyra* in 165, *Heauton Timorumenos* in 163, *Eunuchus* and *Phormio* in 161, *Adelphi* in 160. Of these, *Hecyra* and *Phormio* were adapted from Apollodorus of Carystus and the rest from MENANDER. Terence was more faithful to his Greek originals than his predecessor PLAUTUS had been. He substituted portraiture for caricature, realism for farce, artistry in plot and language for bawdy humour. Thus his plays appealed less to the masses, and more to discriminating aristocrats and connoisseurs. They retained their popularity and influence throughout antiquity and received the accolade of a commentary by the 4th-century grammarian DONATUS.

See also COMEDY, ROMAN. GS

Beare (1964); Duckworth (1952); Goldberg (1986); Hunter (1985); Sandbach (1977).

Terpander (7th century BC), Greek musician and poet. Born at Antissa on Lesbos, Terpander lived at Sparta where he won a victory at the CARNEA in 676 BC and where he is said to have founded a school of MUSIC. He is credited with the introduction of the seven-stringed lyre and with setting the works of Homer to music. The few surviving fragments of his own poetry are of doubtful authenticity. GS

West (1992).

Terracotta Terracotta – fired clay – was used for a variety of purposes in addition to POTTERY. Architectural uses included roof tiles, bricks, SARCOPHAGI, and decorative features such as metopes and acroteria. Everyday items such as toys, LAMPS, and tokens were made of clay, as were theatrical masks. It was also commonly used for a number of sculptural purposes including statues, figurines, and small reliefs. As such, it developed along the same lines as larger-scale SCULPTURE and was always brightly painted.

Terracotta statuettes were chiefly used for votive purposes and therefore represented the deity of the sanctuary concerned. Gods such as Demeter, Persephone, and Dionysus, who offered protection in the underworld, were especially popular. They were produced in large quantities throughout the Greco-Roman world. Notable centres of production developed in Boeotia, Cyprus, and Crete in the archaic period, Melos, Locri, and Tarentum in the 5th century BC, Athens and Tanagra in the 4th century, Asia Minor and Egypt in the Hellenistic period, and Gaul and Germany in the first two centuries AD.   GS

Henig (1983); Higgins (1968, 1987).

Terra sigillata a mass-produced form of POTTERY which occurred throughout the Roman world in the imperial period. Whether moulded or wheel-made, it was distinguished by its red-coloured glaze which was sometimes embellished with relief or stamped decoration. The principal areas of manufacture were: Italy, where it originated in the 1st century BC as Arretine ware, from which a number of plain wares developed; Greece and Asia Minor in the 1st century AD; Gaul, where it became known as SAMIAN WARE; Spain, which was an extension of the Gaulish industry; North Africa in the late Roman and Byzantine periods.   GS

Tertullian (c.AD 160–220), Latin Christian writer. Quintus Septimius Florens Tertullianus was born a pagan at Carthage and trained as a lawyer. Converted to Christianity c.195, he devoted himself to writing in defence of the Church against popular charges of atheism and magic and about various ethical and moral issues. Having attacked a number of heresies including GNOSTICISM, he later became associated with the Montanists who stressed the virtues of asceticism and martyrdom and the exclusion of idolatry. He nevertheless remained dogmatically orthodox, and as the first Latin theologian (author of 31 surviving works) he occupies a special place in the history of political and religious thought.   GS

Chadwick (1986b).

Tessera Roman token, ticket, or tag. *Tesserae* in the form of discs, usually made of metal, clay, or bone, were used for many purposes. Attached to bags of coins, they indicated that the contents had been tested for genuineness. Often bearing a stamped type or legend, they identified the recipients of imperial largesse. They also served as admission tickets to the games and public shows.   GS

Testimonium evidence in Roman law. *Testimonium* was evidence given by a witness (*testis*). Witnesses were required for legal transactions such as transfers of property, certain types of marriage, and especially wills (*testamenta*). Only adult male citizens could witness such transactions. Children, slaves, foreigners, lunatics, criminals, and disreputable persons such as actors were excluded, as were women, with the exception of the VESTAL Virgins. A rather different kind of *testimonium* was that given by witnesses who testified to facts in civil and criminal cases. Here the evidence of women, foreigners, and slaves was admitted under certain conditions (e.g. slaves had to be tortured), and in criminal proceedings witnesses could be forced to testify. Witnesses gave their evidence in person and under oath; false witness was severely punished.   TC

Jolowicz and Nicholas (1972).

Testudo   *see* SIEGECRAFT, ROMAN.

Tetrarchy   *see* DIOCLETIAN.

Tetrarchy   one of the four divisions of THESSALY. The four were Thessaliotis, Hestiaeotis, Pelasgiotis, and Phthiotis, each under a tetrarch. When and how the system was instituted and how long it lasted is unknown. PHILIP II of Macedon revived it in 344 or 342 BC. The system was copied in the Hellenistic period. GALATIA was so divided.
  See also DIOCLETIAN.   GLC

Westlake (1935).

Tetricus   (d. after AD 274), Roman emperor in Gaul, AD 270–3. Gaius Pius Esuvius Tetricus, governor of Aquitania under VICTORINUS, was the last ruler of POSTUMUS' breakaway Gallic empire, appointing his own son, Tetricus, Caesar. Barely able to contain Germanic invasions of Gaul, and brought to battle near Châlons by AURELIAN, Tetricus deserted his army and surrendered. Although paraded alongside ZENOBIA during Aurelian's subsequent triumph (274), Tetricus was restored to his senatorial rank and property and given the post of *corrector Lucaniae.*   RJB

Parker (1958).

Teutones   German people. The Teutones and CIMBRI between 113 and 102 BC wandered through the Celtic lands from Noricum to Spain, periodically posing a threat to Rome and causing panic in Italy and the provinces of Cisalpine and Transalpine Gaul. After defeating a number of Roman armies, the Teutones were annihilated by MARIUS at Aquae Sextiae (Aix) in 102.   LPR

Chadwick (1970).

Thales (*c*.625–547 BC), Greek natural philosopher. In the century after his death Thales of Miletus became an epitome of practical ingenuity and is invariably listed as one of the SEVEN SAGES. ARISTOTLE describes him as the founder of natural philosophy and believes that he held WATER to be the material cause. It seems more likely, however, that Thales put forward as his unifying hypothesis the view that things came from water and thus conceived it as a 'remote ancestor' rather than a persistent material substrate. From this hypothesis Thales, apparently, deduced natural explanations for phenomena such as earthquakes, and supplanted supernatural explanations previously in vogue. It is in the light of this innovation that Thales' importance should be assessed rather than basing it upon dubious reports of his prediction of the solar eclipse of 585 BC or of his founding theoretical MATHEMATICS in Greece.

See also ANAXIMANDER; PHYSICS.   JL

DSB XIII (1976); Kirk, Raven, and Schofield (1983).

Thamugadi modern Timgad, city in NUMIDIA. Founded as a colony for veterans by TRAJAN in AD 100, the city was planned like a fortified camp but was equipped with fine public buildings. It flourished for four centuries, becoming in the 4th century a centre of the schismatic church of the DONATISTS. Impressive remains of its buildings and mosaics survive.   GS

Stillwell (1976).

Thapsus about 100 miles south of Carthage, site of a battle in 46 BC. By the winter of 47/6 BC the Pompeians had gathered in the area an army of 14 legions and 15,000 cavalry, commanded by Q. METELLUS SCIPIO and King JUBA II. To deal with such a force, Caesar risked shipping across his eight legions in winter. While he was besieging Thapsus, he lured Scipio into a battle and decisively defeated him. Plutarch reports 50,000 killed on Scipio's side and 50 on Caesar's.   DP

Thargelia Greek religious festival. The Thargelia was a pre-harvest festival, celebrated at Athens and in Ionia in the month of Thargelion (May–June) in honour of Apollo. First fruits of the corn were carried in procession and a purification ritual was enacted in which a scapegoat (*pharmakos*), who symbolized evil, was flogged or stoned to ensure a good harvest.

See also CHOREGUS; FESTIVALS, GREEK.   GS

Thasos island in the north Aegean. Thasos was colonized *c*.680 BC by Ionian Greeks from PAROS led by Telesicles, father of the poet

ARCHILOCHUS. It prospered in the 6th century, largely on the strength of its GOLD mines and those of Mt PANGAEUS which it also controlled. After the Persian Wars, in which it offered no resistance, it allied with Athens apart from attempted revolts in 465 and 411. In 340 it fell to PHILIP II of Macedon and in 196 to Rome. But it remained prosperous and when production in the mines slackened in the 3rd century BC it found a new source of income in the export of WINE. Thasos was the birthplace of the painter POLYGNOTUS.   GS

Theatre, Greek The architectural form of the Greek theatre derives from the circular dancing area (*orchestra*) where choruses (which were the antecedents of TRAGEDY and COMEDY) were sung and danced. The theatre, like the STADIUM, was normally sited at the foot of a hill so that the embankment behind provided a natural auditorium. At first, therefore, there was no need for any building except an altar to DIONYSUS in whose honour the drama was performed. Action took place in and just behind the *orchestra* where a wooden platform made a low stage. A backdrop was provided by a simple tent or hut (*skene*); chorus and actors made their entrances and exits by means of ramps on either side.

As theatrical entertainment grew more popular and as the dramatists introduced changes in technique, so the form of the theatre evolved. Stone seating, rising in wedge-shaped tiers, replaced earlier wooden benches; and more elaborate seats at the front were provided for priests and officials. The *skene* acquired architectural shape in the 4th century BC with a colonnade (*proskenion*) in front supporting a platform which later came to be used as a raised stage. The theatre of Dionysus in Athens, where the plays of AESCHYLUS, SOPHOCLES, EURIPIDES, and ARISTOPHANES were produced, dates from the 5th century BC and is the oldest surviving theatre, though its visible remains are later. Other theatres are preserved throughout the Greek world, notably at EPIDAURUS (*c.*350 BC) where ancient plays are still regularly performed.   GS

Berve and Gruben (1963); Bieber (1961).

Theatre, Roman The first Roman theatre was not built until the 1st century BC. Before that the plays of PLAUTUS and TERENCE were performed on makeshift stages in the FORUM before circles of wooden seats. As the role of the chorus diminished, so the *orchestra* contracted to a mere semi-circle. Meanwhile, the stage building (or *scenae frons*) rose in height to the top of the auditorium (*cavea*) and acquired an elaborate façade as well as a roof. The availability of concrete meant that free-standing theatres could now be built on top of arched vaults without the natural support of a hillside. External treatment was similar to that of the AMPHITHEATRE, as was the provision of underground passages and stairways. Fine examples survive at POMPEII, Orange, Aspendos, Sabratha, and TAUROMENIUM.

See also ODEUM. GS

Bieber (1961).

Thebes leading city of BOEOTIA. In the 6th century BC Thebes began subjecting the rest of Boeotia, but in the PERSIAN WARS, having voluntarily sided with XERXES, she was disgraced. After OENOPHYTA (457) Athens controlled Boeotia until the Battle of Coronea (447) when the BOEOTIAN CONFEDERACY was established in the form it kept until the King's Peace (387/6). During the PELOPONNESIAN WAR Theban cavalry supported Spartan invasions of Attica, and the attempt of DEMOSTHENES to prevent it ended in disaster at Delium (424). After 421 Thebes showed herself increasingly independent. After 404 strained relations turned to open antipathy, ISMENIAS funding THRASYBULUS and the Thebans refusing to accompany AGESILAUS to Asia. The Corinthian War ensued. When recalled, Agesilaus conceived bitter hatred for Thebes and used the King's Peace to dissolve the Confederacy. In 382 supporters of Sparta persuaded Phoebidas to occupy the Cadmea. After liberation (379/8) Thebes grew increasingly ambitious until in 371 she could stand alone and fight. LEUCTRA made Spartan ruin and Theban hegemony inevitable. EPAMINONDAS and PELOPIDAS dominated the 360s. Distracted and exhausted by the Third SACRED WAR, the Thebans were forced to ally with PHILIP II of Macedon. In 339 they seized Thermopylae and fought heroically at CHAERONEA (338). In 335 the city rebelled against the Macedonian garrison and was razed. Resurrected by CASSANDER, Thebes never recovered her importance. GLC

Buckler (1980); Cloché (1952); Larsen (1968).

Thebes city in Upper Egypt. Thebes, in ancient times, and briefly in the 7th century BC, capital of Egypt, was already known to Homer as a hundred-gated city of proverbial wealth. Archaeological evidence indicates that it was visited by Greeks in the archaic period (*see* EGYPT), and it remained an important town into the Hellenistic period, gradually declining thereafter.

See also AMMON. RB

Boardman (1980); Burkert (1976).

Themistocles (*c.*524–459 BC), Athenian statesman. Themistocles began his public career as archon in 493/2, when he started the fortification of PIRAEUS. In 483/2 he persuaded the Athenians to devote the greatly increased revenues from the LAURIUM silver mines to enlarging their navy, against opposition from ARISTIDES, who was ostracized. In

480 he organized Athenian resistance to Xerxes, leading the Athenian contingent to Thessaly and commanding the Athenian navy at ARTEMISIUM and SALAMIS, where his stratagem lured the Persian fleet into the narrows; during the succeeding winter he led reprisals against medizing islanders. After the Persian withdrawal Themistocles arranged the reconstruction of Athens's walls by subterfuge against Spartan opposition. But subsequently his opposition to Sparta found little favour, his popularity declined, and he was ostracized (perhaps in 471) and migrated to Argos. Denounced by Sparta, he was condemned *in absentia* at Athens for treason and fled via Corcyra and northern Greece to Persia. Here he won the favour of Artaxerxes I and was rewarded with the gift of several cities including Magnesia, where he lived until his death; the tradition that he committed suicide is dubious.

RB

Frost (1980); Lenardon (1978); Podlecki (1975).

Theocritus (*c.*300–*c.*260 BC), Greek poet. Theocritus was a native of Syracuse and addressed one poem to HIERON II, probably in 275. But he lived mostly in Cos and Alexandria, and *c.*272 he was writing a panegyric for PTOLEMY II. Little else is known of his life but it may be assumed that the bucolic poems are early and that it was for them that he earned his reputation. His botanical observations are precise and suggest an east Aegean location, even for those *Idylls* set in Magna Graecia. Other surviving poems include minor epics, aetiology, epigrams, and MIMES. His handling of certain episodes in the legend of the Argonauts has led some to believe that he sided with CALLIMACHUS in his feud with APOLLONIUS RHODIUS. But feud or no feud, there is every reason to suppose that he would have been acquainted with Callimachus. His mimes find a parallel in those of HERODAS.   GS

Griffiths (1979); Hutchinson (1988); Webster (1964).

Theodora   *see* CONSTANTIUS I CHLORUS.

Theodoric (d. AD 451), king of the Visigoths, AD 418–51. Theodoric I, grandson of ALARIC, made repeated efforts (largely frustrated by AETIUS) to enlarge the new federate Gothic kingdom within the Roman empire. An alliance with the VANDALS turned to hatred when Theodoric's daughter, wife of the Vandal heir, Huneric, was repudiated and mutilated to allow a Roman–Vandal alliance. Theodoric was persuaded by AVITUS to help the Romans repel an invasion by ATTILA, but was killed during a drawn battle.

See also GOTHS.   RJB

Bury (1958); Todd (1972).

Theodorus (6th century BC), Greek artist. Theodorus of Samos was a versatile artist, architect, and inventor. He is recorded as a metal-worker in bronze (a self-portrait) and silver (a bowl for CROESUS), as a gem engraver (POLYCRATES' ring), painter, sculptor (the Pythian Apollo at Samos), architect (the 'Scias' at Sparta), and writer (of a book on the Heraeum at Samos). He is said to have introduced the lathe, lever, and line, the rules of proportion, and the arts of clay modelling and bronze casting.   GS

Theodosian Code *see* LAW, ROMAN; THEODOSIUS II.

Theodosius the Elder *see* BRITAIN.

Theodosius I (*c*.AD 346–95), Roman emperor, AD 379–95. Flavius Theodosius, son of Valentinian's general Theodosius, was appointed emperor in the east by GRATIAN after the death of VALENS, with the primary task of dealing with the GOTHS. His solution was the rapid extension of 'federate' status, whereby whole tribes were settled within the empire. He owes his title 'the Great' to his rigid adherence to the Nicene Christian creed: he deposed Arian bishops, punished heretics severely, and, influenced by AMBROSE, banned all pagan worship (391) (*see* CHRISTIANITY). Theodosius came to dominate the entire empire, intervening to defeat MAXIMUS (388), and restore VALENTINIAN II, whose sister, Galla, was his second wife (387). Theodosius' deputy in Gaul, Arbogastes, replaced Valentinian with his protégé Eugenius (392), causing Theodosius to return to put down Eugenius (394). Thereafter Theodosius ruled alone, though with the succession clearly marked out by the appointment as junior Augusti of his sons by Aelia Flacilla, ARCADIUS (383) and HONORIUS (393).   RJB

Grant (1985); Matthews (1990).

Theodosius II (AD 401–50), eastern Roman emperor, AD 408–50. Theodosius II, son of Arcadius and Eudoxia, was dominated succes-sively by the regent Anthemius, praetorian prefect of the east, by his sister PULCHERIA (*c*.414–43), and then by the eunuch Chrysaphius. At Pulcheria's bidding he married EUDOCIA (421), and in 425 intervened in the west to install his cousin as VALENTINIAN III. He was responsible for the fortification of CONSTANTINOPLE, for the founding of a university there, and for the compilation of the legal code known as the Theodosian Code (438). He mounted an abortive expedition against the Vandals (441), and held off the HUNS by the payment of subsidies.
See also LAW, ROMAN.   RJB

Bury (1958); Grant (1985).

Theognis (6th century BC), Greek elegiac poet. Theognis of Megara is credited with the authorship of about 700 elegiac couplets which survive in the manuscript tradition. Most are short drinking songs, written for aristocratic male society and especially for the SYMPOSIUM; some are moralizing maxims, others deal with the love of boys. No doubt an original core was written by a poet called Theognis; but problems of chronology and differences in tone and content indicate the participation of other poets (MIMNERMUS and TYRTAEUS among them); and almost certainly the collection represents an Alexandrian anthology. GS

Fränkel (1975); West (1974).

Theophrastus (c.371–287 BC), Greek philosopher. Theophrastus of Eresus was a pupil and colleague of ARISTOTLE. He later succeeded him as head of the PERIPATETIC SCHOOL (322 BC). Only a fraction of his works has survived: two books on BOTANY, *History of Plants* and *Causes of Plants*; *Characters*, a collection of descriptive character sketches; a short treatise on *Metaphysics*; and fragments of two other works, *The Doctrines of the Natural Philosophers* and the *Laws*. All of these works reveal strong Aristotelian influence. However, although Theophrastus worked mainly within the framework of Aristotelian philosophy, he was clearly not prepared to accept that system in its entirety and frequently challenges, rejects, or corrects particular aspects of it.

See also DIOCLES; DOXOGRAPHERS; STRATON. JL

DSB XIII (1976); Kennedy (1963).

Theopompus (4th century BC), Greek historian. Theopompus of Chios accompanied his father into exile for pro-Spartan sympathies no later than 371 BC and was restored in the 330s by ALEXANDER THE GREAT. Like EPHORUS a pupil of ISOCRATES, he turned to writing history: first a *History of Greece* in 12 books covering the period from the end of THUCYDIDES to the Battle of Cnidus (394); then, impressed by the rise of PHILIP II of Macedon, a *History of Philip* in 58 books (of which large portions were not directly concerned with Philip). Only fragments remain. His style was colourful, his manner highly censorious. His values and beliefs remain obscure.

See also HISTORIOGRAPHY, GREEK. GLC

Boardman and Vaphopoulou-Richardson (1986); Connor (1968).

Theorika Athenian state subsidy for theatre seats. Poorer citizens who were so registered were encouraged to attend the theatre and were entitled to a subsidy of two obols each at each performance. The subsidy was administered by magistrates who wielded considerable financial influence. According to a law passed in the 4th century BC by EUBULUS any peacetime surplus cash had to be placed in the Theoric Fund which subsidized a programme of public works.

See also FINANCE, GREEK; TRAGEDY, GREEK.   GS

Theoroi   Greek religious envoys. *Theoroi* (literally observers) were the delegates sent to represent their own city at another city's festival. Every state sent *theoroi* to the panhellenic festivals. The word was also used of envoys sent out to announce a forthcoming festival, to consult an oracle, or to offer sacrifice at a distant shrine. It was thus applied generally to religious envoys, and in some cities *theoroi* were elected magistrates.   GS

Theoxenia   Greek religious festival. The Theoxenia was a festival at which the gods were entertained as guests at a banquet. At Delphi it was a major event, held in the month of Theoxenios (March–April), inevitably dominated by Apollo, and celebrated by PINDAR in *Paean* 6. Elsewhere, notably at Athens and Sparta, the Dioscuri (Castor and Polydeuces) were the guests of honour and places were laid for two in a closed room. The meal was later shared by the worshippers.

See also FESTIVALS, GREEK.   GS

Thera   modern Santorini, Greek island. After the destruction of its Minoan civilization by volcanic eruption, Thera was resettled by Spartan colonists. Though bare, the island was famous for its wine, and it also lay conveniently between Crete and the Cyclades. Its most significant achievement was the foundation of CYRENE *c.*630 BC in response to a crisis caused by severe drought; islanders had the right subsequently to claim Cyrenean citizenship.   RB

Craik (1980); Jeffery (1976).

Theramenes   (d. 404/3 BC), Athenian statesman. Theramenes took a principal part in the FOUR HUNDRED (411 BC). Turning against the extremists, he led the movement to establish the Five Thousand, a moderate oligarchy or modified democracy. As trierarch at ARGINUSAE (406), he was accused of failing to rescue drowning sailors, but turned the accusation on the generals. In 404 he negotiated the peace with Sparta which spared Athens the loss of her walls, and he was a popular member of the THIRTY TYRANTS. He opposed CRITIAS, the extreme oligarch, on ideological grounds and was executed.   GLC

Hignett (1952); Kagan (1987); Ostwald (1986).

Thermopylae   narrow pass between the mountains and the sea providing the only practical route from the north into central Greece. In

480 BC LEONIDAS with 4,000 Greeks failed to hold the pass against XERXES. When frontal assault proved ineffective, Xerxes sent an out-flanking force on the mountain path which was unknown to Leonidas and most of the Greeks. When he realized what was happening, Leonidas dismissed most of his force. Of 300 Spartans only one sur-vived.

The same route was found by the Gauls who invaded Greece in 279 BC under BRENNUS. A combined Greek army confronted him at Thermopylae, but he drew off the Aetolian contingent, turned the pass and reached Delphi. In 192 BC the Aetolians invited ANTIOCHUS III THE GREAT to invade Greece. The Romans under Glabrio stopped his ad-vance from Euboea to Aetolia at Thermopylae in 191, and he departed for Asia.   EER

Bar-Kochva (1976); Burn (1984); CAH VIII; Rankin (1987).

Theron tyrant of Acragas, c.488–472 BC. Theron, descended from a noble family prominent in the overthrow of PHALARIS, ruled Acragas from 488 to his death in 472 BC; he was an ally of GELON, with whom he had ties of marriage. His seizure of Himera in 483 provoked a Carthaginian invasion, defeated by Gelon and Theron at the battle of HIMERA. His son Thrasydaeus inherited the tyranny, but was soon overthrown.   RB

Berve (1967); Dunbabin (1948).

Theseum The temple of HEPHAESTUS at Athens, popularly known as the Theseum, was built between 449 and 444 BC and is the best-preserved Doric temple in Greece. Probably by the same architect as the temple of Poseidon at SUNIUM, it is constructed of Pentelic marble and overlooks the Agora. The metopes illustrate the exploits of Theseus and Heracles.   GS

Lawrence (1984).

Thesmophoria Greek religious festival. The Thesmophoria was a women's festival celebrated throughout Greece in the autumn to hon-our DEMETER, goddess of agriculture. Occurring just before the sowing of the corn, its purpose was to ensure a fertile crop. The central feature was the sacrifice of a pig. The exclusion of men was presumably successful: ARISTOPHANES gives few details in his play *Thesmophoriazusae*.

See also FESTIVALS, GREEK; WOMEN, GREEK.   GS

Thesmothetai *see* ARCHON.

Thespiae city in central Greece. Thespians fought with distinction at THERMOPYLAE (480 BC) and their city was destroyed by Xerxes. Rebuilt by Athens, it incurred the enmity of THEBES. A member of the BOEOTIAN CONFEDERACY after 446 BC, it provided Sparta with a base for operations against Thebes after 382. It remained prosperous throughout the Hellenistic and Roman periods, organizing a panhellenic festival of the Muses, the Mouseia, every four years on the slopes of nearby Mt Helicon.   GS

Thespis (6th century BC), Greek tragedian. Thespis of Icaria near Athens was regarded by the ancients as the inventor of TRAGEDY. It seems that he was the first to present tragedy at the City DIONYSIA when that festival was being reorganized by PEISISTRATUS *c*.534: his prize was a goat. He may have introduced the speaking actor and improved the mask. Many legends are associated with his name and a few fragments of doubtful authenticity.   GS

Pickard-Cambridge (1962).

Thessalonica city in Macedonia. Founded by CASSANDER *c*.316 BC and named after his wife, Thessalonica stood at the head of routes north into Central Europe, west over the Pindus to the Adriatic, and east to Byzantium (*see* EGNATIA, VIA). It therefore acquired both commercial and strategic significance and soon became the chief port of Macedonia. After 146 BC it was the capital of the Roman province of Macedonia and enjoyed increasing prosperity in the imperial period. It became a Roman colony *c*.AD 250 but its greatest period began with the division of the empire. As the residence of the emperor GALERIUS it acquired a palace complex and hippodrome. In 379–80 THEODOSIUS I fortified the city and used it as the base of his operations against the Goths. In the mid-5th century it became the seat of the prefects of Illyricum, and there was renewed building activity including a new circuit of walls and many churches.   GS

Thessaly region of northern Greece. The great plain of Thessaly, surrounded by mountains, with access to the sea only by the Peneus gorge and the Gulf of Pagasae to the south-east, was well suited to the rearing of horses. Landed aristocracy naturally held sway, large families such as the ALEUADAE of Larisa, the Echecratids of Pharsalus, and the Scopads of Crannon. (For early organization *see* TETRARCHY.) The Aleuadae submitted to Persia in the 480s BC; but on a number of occasions in the 6th and 5th centuries Athens received the help of Thessalian cavalry, though never to great advantage. In the 4th century PHERAE, well placed to exploit the export of corn, became a powerful rival to Larisa and Pharsalus. In the 370s JASON was appointed TAGUS and built up considerable power. His successor ALEXANDER OF PHERAE was in the 360s a powerful irritant and provoked Theban expansion into Thessaly under PELOPIDAS. In the Third SACRED WAR the Thessalians took the opportunity to pursue their age-old enmity with Phocis, save for Pherae. PHILIP II of Macedon, summoned as ally, became archon and destroyed Pheraean and Phocian power at the Battle of the Crocus Field (352). Thessaly with its considerable military potential remained in thrall to Macedon, and Thessalian cavalry played an important part in ALEXANDER THE GREAT's campaigns. In the LAMIAN WAR (323/2) Thessaly broke free temporarily. Liberation from Macedonian rule came in 196 when a new Thessalian Confederacy was established. In 148 BC it was incorporated in the Roman province of MACEDONIA.   GLC

CAH III.3; Hornblower (1983); Westlake (1935).

Thetes   Athenian working class. The Thetes were the lowest of SOLON's four property classes with an annual income of less than 200 measures of produce. Solon admitted them to the ECCLESIA and the HELIAEA but not to the BOULE or the magistracies. In war they could not serve as HOPLITES, but they fought as light-armed troops and archers and provided crew and officers for the Athenian NAVY.

See also HIPPEIS; PENTACOSIOMEDIMNI; ZEUGITAE.   GS

Rhodes (1981).

Thirty Tyrants   leaders of the oligarchic revolution at Athens in 404 BC. Claiming that the terms of the peace with Sparta had not been fulfilled, LYSANDER intervened. Thirty Constitutional Commissioners (*syngrapheis*) were appointed, led by the extremists CRITIAS and Charicles and the moderate THERAMENES. Under the protection of a Spartan garrison they proceeded to institute a murderous regime. This was opposed by Theramenes, who was executed. SOCRATES refused to have any part in their bloody deeds. THRASYBULUS, who had with other democrats fled to Thebes, occupied Phyle and, when the Thirty failed to remove him, he advanced to Piraeus. There he resisted 'the men of the city' and Critias was killed in battle. The Thirty were forced to withdraw to Eleusis where they were all later put to death.   GLC

Hornblower (1983); Ostwald (1986).

Thirty Tyrants   Roman usurpers. The Thirty Tyrants (a deliberate and unwarranted comparison with the classical Athenian THIRTY TYRANTS) is the collective title given by the HISTORIA AUGUSTA ('Pollio') to a series of mid-3rd-century AD usurpers (many challenging GALLIENUS). These were individual usurpers, and the number was made up only by including figures such as VICTORINUS' mother (Victoria) and son

(Victorinus Junior). The *Historia*'s list comprises: in the Gallic provinces, POSTUMUS, Postumus Junior, Lollianus (LAELIANUS), MARIUS, Victorinus, Victoria, Victorinus Junior, Tetricus, Tetricus Junior; in Syria, Cyriades, Balista, Macrianus, MACRIANUS Junior, QUIETUS; in Palmyra, ODAENATHUS, ZENOBIA, Herodes, Herennius, Timolaus, Maeonius; in Egypt, AEMILIANUS; in Isauria, Trebellianus; in the east, Saturninus; at Carthage, Celsus; in Illyricum, Ingenuus, Regalianus, Valens, AUREOLUS; in Thessaly, Piso; in Achaea, (another) Valens. Titus (usurper under Maximinus Thrax) and Censorinus (under Claudius II) complete the 30 if the women are omitted: the number can be augmented by e.g. Faustinus (alleged rebel against Tetricus).   RJB

Syme (1968).

Thrace   region north of the Aegean and west of the Black Sea, inhabited by a people of Indo-European but not Greek descent. The Aegean coast was colonized by Greeks from the 8th century BC, that of the Propontis from the 7th, and that of the Black Sea from the 6th (*see* COLONIZATION, GREEK). But the colonists did not penetrate the interior and the Thracians were untouched by hellenization. Thrace fell to the Persians *c*.516 BC. Soon after the Persian Wars a native Odrysian dynasty emerged and ruled until the mid-4th century when Thrace fell to PHILIP II of Macedon. After PYDNA (168 BC) western Thrace was incorporated into the Roman province of Macedonia, while the rest of the region was ruled by a native dynasty until AD 48 when it became the Roman province of Thrace. It remained a land of few cities, though colonies were founded at Aprus and Deultum.

See also CHERSONESE, THRACIAN.   GS

Danov (1976); A. H. M. Jones (1971).

Thrasybulus of Athens   (d. 389 BC), Athenian statesman. As trierarch in Samos in 411 BC Thrasybulus sought to restore democracy there and had ALCIBIADES recalled. Although general at CYZICUS (410), he was merely trierarch at ARGINUSAE (406) and survived the same charge as THERAMENES. In 404 he withdrew to Thebes whence, helped by ISMENIAS, he occupied the border post of Phyle. When the THIRTY TYRANTS failed to dislodge him, he took Piraeus, defeated 'the men of the city', and expelled the Thirty, becoming with ANYTUS a leader of the restored democracy. In 395, disdaining Persian overtures, he involved Athens in the Corinthian War, commanding at Nemea but retiring during CONON's return. After the failure to make peace (392) he set out with a fleet and regained a number of Athens's former subject allies. He was killed at Aspendus.

GLC

Kagan (1987); Ostwald (1986); Strauss (1986).

Thrasybulus of Miletus (fl. *c*.590 BC), tyrant of Miletus. Thrasybulus successfully resisted a series of annual Lydian assaults, and eventually made a treaty of friendship and alliance with King Alyattes of Lydia; this was partly due to a shared friendship with PERIANDER of Corinth, whom Thrasybulus supported in turn (Herodotus 5.92).   RB

Berve (1967); Jeffery (1976).

Thucydides (mid-5th century BC), Athenian politician and opponent of PERICLES. Thucydides, son of Melesias, was a relative of CIMON and shared the same values. He opposed Pericles' use of the accumulated tribute of the DELIAN LEAGUE for his building programme. In 443 BC in a trial of strength he was ostracized. After his return little more is heard of him.   GLC

Kagan (1969); Ostwald (1986).

Thucydides (*c*.455–400 BC), Greek historian of the PELOPONNESIAN WAR. Thucydides, son of Olorus, relative of CIMON, was an Athenian aristocrat and intellectual colossus who 'went over' to PERICLES, the champion of empire and democracy. He caught the plague in 430/29 BC but survived. Blamed for losing AMPHIPOLIS as general in 424, he was exiled and did not return until the end of the war (404). He began collecting material for his *History* at its outbreak (431). Exile enabled him to visit the Peloponnese. The work remains unfinished: Book 8 breaks off in mid-sentence in 411.

How and when he composed his history has absorbed many. He might be expected to have published the Archidamian War (431–421) separately and perhaps covered the Sicilian expedition (415–413) in another work. But all parts bear traces of revision and in a sense the *History* is a unified whole. In a world without proper maps and full reports, collecting material must have been most exacting; autopsy was not always possible and cross-questioning participants laborious. The speeches probably reflect actual speeches, but it is debated how much they report what was said or what Thucydides thought or what he thought his speakers thought.

His purpose, he professed, was to provide posterity with a warning of how men are likely to behave as long as men are men. War is the vehicle, but essentially he is concerned with men's desire for power over others and their ruthless pursuit of it. Empire in the broad sense is inevitable, not a matter for praise or censure, but one empire could be more admirable than another. The admirer of Pericles who chose to include his funeral oration must rate as the admirer of Athenian empire. But his attitude to DEMOCRACY, fostered by Pericles as a necessary concomitant of naval empire, is more debated. Many have seen

Thucydides as a sympathizer with the moderate oligarchy established by THERAMENES in 411. Perhaps his attitude had changed.

Some development is to be presumed. In the earlier books individuals are much less prominent than in the later. Some have supposed that he changed his mind about the cause of the war, or about ALCIBIADES' value to the state, or about the practicability of the Sicilian expedition; others that the MELIAN DIALOGUE and the funeral oration do represent 'developments' in his thought. Perhaps he should have developed more. His omission of Athenian relations with Persia is astounding. After CYRUS THE YOUNGER took charge (408) Persia was decisive, and what Thucydides had written must have seemed insufficient.

His accuracy is extraordinary. Rarely can he be seriously faulted (though his account of PAUSANIAS is disquietingly incredible). He is generally thought unjust to CLEON, perhaps to Alcibiades also. He is certainly too ready to attribute motives where he must have lacked evidence.

One idea dominates: in interstate relations expediency alone rules. The vision is bleak, perhaps true.

See also HISTORIOGRAPHY, GREEK.   GLC

Connor (1984); Hornblower (1987); Westlake (1968).

Thugga   modern Dougga, city in North Africa about 60 miles southwest of CARTHAGE. The original population was part Punic and part Libyan: an inscription in both languages survives on a mausoleum of the 3rd century BC. Annexed by Rome in 46 BC, Thugga became part of the province of AFRICA. At first the native and Roman communities coexisted separately, but economic development brought them together and the city was equipped with fine public buildings. It became a *municipium* in AD 205 and a colony in 261.   GS

Stillwell (1976).

Thurii   city in south Italy. Founded in 443 BC by Athens as a panhellenic colony to replace the destroyed city of SYBARIS, Thurii flourished as a port. But constant problems with local tribes in the 4th century drove it to accept Roman protection and as such it opposed PYRRHUS and HANNIBAL. Despite the planting of a Latin colony in 193 BC, the city declined and was eventually abandoned.   GS

Dunbabin (1948).

Tiber   river in Italy. The Tiber rises in the Apennines near Arretium and flows generally southwards for 250 miles before issuing into the sea at Ostia, 16 miles south-west of Rome. Its tawny colour is caused by the silt it carries down with it. It formed the eastern border of

Etruria and the northern border of Latium. At Rome its division into two around the Tiber island made this the first crossing point from the river mouth. DP

Platner and Ashby (1929); Richardson (1992).

Tiberius (42 BC–AD 37), Roman emperor, AD 14–37. Tiberius Julius Caesar, son of Tiberius Claudius Nero and LIVIA, became Octavian's step-son (38 BC). He received the lost standards from the PARTHIANS (20), served with distinction on the northern frontier (16–12), and was consul in 13 and 7. After AGRIPPA's death (12 BC), Tiberius was compelled to divorce his wife Vipsania Agrippina (daughter of Agrippa and mother of the younger DRUSUS) to marry Augustus' daughter JULIA (11 BC). In 6 BC Tiberius retired to Rhodes: he returned to Rome in AD 2, and in 4 AUGUSTUS adopted him. He was granted tribunician power for 10 years and proconsular *imperium* on the northern frontier, but was required to adopt his nephew GERMANICUS and grant him precedence over Drusus. Tiberius crushed revolts in Pannonia and Illyricum, and retrieved the situation after VARUS' German disaster. He celebrated a triumph (12), and in 13 became virtual co-emperor with the extension of his tribunician power and the grant of *imperium proconsulare maius*.

He succeeded Augustus in AD 14: although popular with the army, he was ageing, reserved, and embittered. His civil government was excellent in the early years. In general, he followed the policies of Augustus (although not slavishly so): his foreign policy was one of consolidation and non-aggression. An increase in treason trials was partly due to the necessity to establish precedents in law, and many early cases, brought by informers (*delatores*), were dismissed by Tiberius. Tiberius' retirement to Capri (26) left the praetorian prefect, SEJANUS, as virtual regent in Rome until replaced in 31. Tiberius made Germanicus' son GAIUS and his own grandson Gemellus joint heirs (35), probably hoping to live until Gemellus' majority. The generally harsh verdict on Tiberius' reign is somewhat unjust: the provinces enjoyed peace and increasing prosperity, his administration and foreign policy were good, and he provided a period of stability by continuing Augustus' policies. RJB

Grant (1985); Levick (1976); Scullard (1982); Seager (1972b).

Tibullus (c.55–19 BC), Latin poet. Albius Tibullus seems to have come from an equestrian family in rural Latium. He associated himself with M. Valerius MESSALLA CORVINUS with whom he may have campaigned in Gaul. But he abandoned military and political ambitions in favour of poetry, becoming a friend of HORACE and acquaintance of OVID. His *oeuvre* is slight but accessible: three books of elegies are attributed to him, of which the third is spurious. Book 1 celebrates his love for Delia and Marathus; Book 2 is a miscellany including poems for another mistress (Nemesis) and for Messalla. GS

Cairns (1979); Lyne (1980).

Tibur city in Italy. Tibur, modern Tivoli, lies 17 miles north-east of Rome. It was an important centre of early Latium. Excavations have revealed an Iron Age cemetery of the 9th century BC. It frequently fought Rome in the 4th century BC and remained an independent town until it acquired Roman citizenship *c.*90 BC. Located 800 feet above sea level, it became a fashionable resort: CATULLUS and AUGUSTUS had villas there, and impressive remains of a villa of HADRIAN are still visible (*see* AR-CHITECTURE, ROMAN). The most important monument in the town is the temple of Hercules Victor, part of a major complex in Greek style, dating from the late 2nd century BC. DP

Stillwell (1976).

Ticinus battle in 218 BC. The first battle fought by HANNIBAL in Italy was at the river Ticinus, near Pavia. He proved his cavalry's superiority by soundly defeating the Roman and allied cavalry led by Publius Cornelius SCIPIO, forcing him to withdraw his consular army to Placentia (Piacenza). LPR

Lazenby (1978).

Tigellinus (d. AD 69), praetorian prefect. Ofonius Tigellinus, a vicious Sicilian who became prefect of the VIGILES, was one of two men appointed by NERO to replace Burrus as praetorian prefect (AD 62). Tigellinus encouraged Nero in his excesses, and, after the conspiracy of PISO (65), conducted a purge of Nero's opponents. He abandoned Nero when the latter was challenged by GALBA (68), was left unpunished by Galba, but was forced to suicide by OTHO (69). RJB

Salmon (1968); Scullard (1982); Wellesley (1975).

Tigranes I (fl. 100–*c.*56 BC), king of Armenia. Tigranes, a former Parthian hostage, was given the throne of ARMENIA by Parthia. He expanded his kingdom to the south at Parthia's expense. In 83 BC he invaded Cilicia, Syria, and Phoenicia, and was offered the Seleucid throne by the inhabitants of ANTIOCH, tired of warring Seleucid princes. He founded a new capital, TIGRANOCERTA, which he populated from conquered cities. An alliance in 69 with his father-in-law MITHRIDATES VI involved him in war with Rome. Tigranocerta was captured by

LUCULLUS in 69, and in 66 POMPEY forced his surrender. He retreated to his original territory and remained a Roman vassal.   EER

Der Nersessian (1969); Magie (1975); Sullivan (1990).

Tigranocerta city in Armenia. Tigranocerta was founded in the 1st century BC by TIGRANES I as his southern capital. He synoecized cities of conquered territory to add to its population, which included Greeks. It was captured in 69 BC by LUCULLUS, who sent home its forced inhabitants, and again by CORBULO in AD 59. The SASSANIANS destroyed Tigranocerta in the 4th century AD. It was renamed Martyropolis in the 5th century, after its famous Christian Church of the Martyrs.

                                                                     EER

Der Nersessian (1969); Magie (1975); Sherwin-White (1984); Sullivan (1990).

Timaeus (c.356–260 BC), Greek historian. Timaeus was the son of Andromachus, the ruler of Tauromenium in Sicily. He fled to Athens (c.317 BC) in order to escape the regime of AGATHOCLES. He probably remained in Athens for 50 years, where he worked on his *History* in learned isolation.

The *History*, in at least 38 books, dealt with events in Italy, Sicily, and Libya, and thus included the rise of Rome, whose importance Timaeus was the first to appreciate. Numerous fragments of the *History* survive, and its influence was widespread. Keen on research, Timaeus was, however, criticized by POLYBIUS for being an 'armchair historian', out of touch with the real world.   HS

Brown (1958); Momigliano (1977); Pearson (1987).

Timber Good-quality timber was always in demand for architectural projects and for shipbuilding. Timber in quantity was also required for house-building, for making tools and furniture, and for fuel. Western Greece is well enough watered to produce a fair supply; eastern Greece is drier and was seriously deforested by the classical period. Many states therefore looked to their colonies: Macedonia, Thrace, Sicily, and south Italy were the best sources. In the Hellenistic period reserves in Syria, Cilicia, and Cyprus became available. The Romans had plentiful supplies near to hand in Italy and the western Mediterranean.

See also ARBORICULTURE.   GS

Meiggs (1982).

Time, measurement of In Greek and Roman times the day ran from sunrise to sunset and, whatever its length, was divided into 12 equal 'hours'. The time was told either by a sundial, invented by ANAXIMANDER from a Babylonian model, or a water clock (*clepsydra*), which allowed water to trickle into a cistern in which was a float that operated a pointer. Neither method was particularly accurate.

The Athenian year began with the first new moon after the summer solstice. It was divided into 12 lunar months, each of 29 or 30 days, whose names (and approximate modern equivalents), all associated with FESTIVALS, were: Hekatombaion (July), Metageitnion (August), Boedromion (September), Pyanopsion (October), Maimakterion (November), Poseideon (December), Gamelion (January), Anthesterion (February), Elaphebolion (March), Mounichion (April), Thargelion (May), Skirophorion (June). At irregular intervals, usually every two or three years, an additional month was intercalated to bring this lunar calendar into line with the solar year. Months were not divided into weeks but into decads of 10 days each: the first 10 'waxing', the last 10 'waning', the middle 10 unspecified. For dating purposes the year at Athens was named after the chief ARCHON, at Sparta after the first EPHOR. Sittings of the BOULE were governed by a 'prytany' calendar which divided the year into 10 'months' of 36 or 37 days each. This corresponded more or less exactly with the solar year and was the system generally followed in inscriptions until the end of the 5th century BC. Thereafter the two calendars began on the same day.

The Roman year originally consisted of only 10 months and omitted the 'dead' months of January and February. These were added by Numa Pompilius, but March remained the beginning of the year until 163 BC. March, May, July, and October each had 31 days, February 28, the rest 29 each, giving a total of 355 days. An additional 'month' of 22 or 23 days was intercalated between 23 and 24 February, but this resulted in such confusion that in 46 BC Julius CAESAR set about reform. He adapted the Egyptian solar calendar, introduced the months that are still in use today, and repeated 23 February in leap years. The Julian calendar remained in use until 1582 when it was modified by Pope Gregory XIII. Certain days in the calendar were marked with an F (= *dies fasti*), others with an N (= *dies nefasti*), indicating that public business might or might not be transacted. Days of the month were calculated in relation to the Kalends (1st), Nones (9th), or Ides (13th), except that in March, May, July, and October Nones fell on the 7th and Ides on the 15th. The nearest thing to a week was the eight-day interval between market days (*nundinae*), but this bore no relation to the month. Years were designated by the names of the consuls in office together with (under the Empire) the regnal year of the emperor. The point of departure for the dating of events was the foundation of the city (*ab urbe condita* = AUC), which by the end of the Republican period was identified with the year 753 BC.

See also ASTRONOMY; CALLIPPUS; ERATOSTHENES; METON.   GS

Gibbs (1976); Michels (1967); Mikalson (1976); Pritchett (1963).

Timoleon (c.365–c.334 BC), liberator of Sicily. Timoleon, a confirmed anti-tyrant from Corinth, was sent by his city in 345 BC to rescue Syracuse from the tyrant DIONYSIUS II. He liberated Syracuse, despite Sicilian opposition supported by Carthage, and instituted constitutional reforms. Timoleon removed tyrants from other Sicilian cities, defeated Carthage at the battle of the Crimisus river c.339, and encouraged widespread immigration from Greece to SICILY. Despite occasional setbacks, his programmes were successful, pacified Greek Sicily (albeit temporarily), and stimulated prosperity. He retired to Syracuse with extensive civic honours. The historian TIMAEUS' lavish praise of Timoleon is perhaps over-generous to an autocratic leader who was himself voted dictatorial powers.   EER

Finley (1979); Talbert (1974).

Timon (c.320–230 BC), Greek philosopher. After studying in Megara with Stilpo, Timon of Phlius went to Elis and became a follower of the sceptical philosopher PYRRHON. Pyrrhon himself wrote nothing and his views are known to us primarily through Timon's works, fragments of which have been preserved in later writers. Timon defended his master's position in verse and prose. Many of the fragments preserved are derived from his *Silloi* ('Squints' or lampoons) in which he attacked the views of other philosophers.   JL

Long (1974).

Timotheus (c.450–c.360 BC), Greek lyric poet. A native of Miletus, Timotheus wrote choral poetry at Athens which was not popular. A large papyrus fragment preserves over 200 lines of his lyric nome entitled *The Persians*, for which EURIPIDES composed the prologue. The verse, written as prose (i.e. without line breaks), is turgid; but the manuscript, dating from the 4th century BC, is one of the earliest extant Greek BOOKS.   GS

Timotheus (c.415–354 BC), Athenian general. Son of Conon and a pupil of ISOCRATES, Timotheus played an important part in extending the Second Athenian Confederacy in the 370s BC by diplomacy rather than force. In 375 his resounding naval victory over Sparta at Alyzeia gained Athens a share in the hegemony under the renewed peace and himself great glory. In 373, accused (unsuccessfully) of delaying the resumption of war, he went to serve Persia against Egypt. After the fall of CALLISTRATUS (366) Timotheus, as general again, won Samos and operated successfully in the north. In the SOCIAL WAR he was heavily fined for not cooperating with CHARES.   GLC

Timotheus (fl. 380–340 BC), Greek sculptor. Timotheus is known to have worked on the architectural sculpture of both the temple of Asclepius at Epidaurus (c.370 BC) and the MAUSOLEUM (c.350 BC). The elder PLINY mentions him as working with Bryaxis, LEOCHARES, and SCOPAS at Halicarnassus. But his work cannot be distinguished from that of his colleagues, so no other sculpture can be ascribed to him with any degree of certainty.   GS

Robertson (1975).

Tin As an ingredient of BRONZE, tin was in demand from an early period. The main source was Britain, but tin was also found in the Erzegebirge in Central Europe and in Spain and Brittany. Trade routes from Britain led either overland across France and on into Etruria or by sea round the coast of Spain, where other valuable metals such as SILVER were to be found. MASSILIA was the chief entrepôt for the overland trade, though the Greeks had earlier used their colonies at Cumae and Pithecoussae. The maritime route was preferred by the PHOENICIANS who sought to preserve it by the foundation of CARTHAGE and other settlements in the western Mediterranean.

See also CASSITERIDES; NARBO.   GS

Healy (1978).

Tiridates II (d. after c.23 BC), Parthian pretender. Tiridates, probably a general of the Parthian king PHRAATES IV, rebelled c.30 BC, and may have succeeded in expelling Phraates briefly. However, he was soon defeated and fled to Syria. Augustus allowed him to stay there, but gave him no aid, and removed Phraates' son to Rome as a hostage. According to DIO CASSIUS, Tiridates went to Rome himself (c.23 BC) and successfully persuaded Augustus to refuse Phraates' request for his extradition.   RJB

Scott-Kilvert and Carter (1987).

Tiro (103–4 BC), secretary to CICERO. Marcus Tullius Tiro was, in turn, the slave, freedman, and biographer of Cicero. Having invented his own system of shorthand, he was able to take down his master's correspondence at speed. Together with ATTICUS he is to be credited with the posthumous collection, editing, and publication of the letters and some of the speeches.

See also BOOKS, LATIN.   GS

Tissaphernes (d. 395 BC), Persian commander. Tissaphernes was largely responsible for the conduct of Persian policy towards the Greeks from c.413 to 395 BC. When Athens transgressed the peace, Tissaphernes negotiated an alliance with Sparta (412/11). Whether he needed ALCIBIADES so to advise him or not, he was more concerned to prolong the war than to end it. Superseded by CYRUS THE YOUNGER (408), he retired to his Carian estate and forewarned ARTAXERXES II of his brother's preparations. At CUNAXA (401) he saved the day and was restored to the satrapy of Ionia. His rule provoked the Asiatic Greeks to appeal to Sparta. Heavily defeated by AGESILAUS in 395, he was executed at Artaxerxes' command. GLC

Dandamaev (1989); Kagan (1987).

Titus (AD 39–81), Roman emperor, AD 79–81. Titus Caesar Vespasianus, elder son of VESPASIAN and Flavia Domitilla, served in Germany and Britain, and completed the suppression of the Jewish revolt (AD 70). Under Vespasian he was consul six times, and was granted the powers of *imperium proconsulare* and *tribunicia potestas* from 71. He bowed to Roman prejudices, putting aside his mistress, the Jewess BERENICE, and demonstrated considerable administrative ability. He succeeded peacefully (79), and was one of the most popular Roman emperors, largely because of his open-handed behaviour and constant shows and games. His private life, however, was frugal, and he continued most of Vespasian's policies. The Flavian amphitheatre (COLOSSEUM) was completed by Titus, and he constructed elaborate public baths nearby. He took vigorous measures to alleviate the hardship resulting from three major disasters: the eruption of VESUVIUS on 24 August 79, which buried Pompeii and Herculaneum; a great fire in Rome; and an outbreak of plague.

See also DOMITIAN. RJB

Grant (1985); Jones (1984); Salmon (1968); Wells (1984).

Toga white woollen garment worn by Roman citizens. The *toga praetexta* had a purple border and was worn by boys and by some priests and magistrates. On reaching manhood males assumed the *toga virilis* which was *de rigueur* on formal occasions. Women too had earlier worn the toga; but most later changed to the *stola*, leaving the toga for prostitutes.

See also DRESS, ROMAN. GS

Tombs *see* BURIAL PRACTICES.

Torquatus (4th century BC), Roman dictator. Titus Manlius Imperiosus earned the name Torquatus in 361 BC, when he defeated a huge Gaul in single combat and despoiled him of his torque. He became dictator in 353 and was consul three times (347, 344, and 340). While campaigning against the Latins in 340, he executed his son for disobeying a command and engaging in single combat. Such a severe degree of discipline became known as 'Manlian'.   LPR

Oakley (1985).

Town planning Early Greek cities were often centred on an ACROPOLIS or a natural harbour. From the 6th century BC many cities were provided with FORTIFICATIONS. Inside the walls the streets were narrow, meandering, mostly unpaved, and lined with small HOUSES. A marketplace or AGORA provided the commercial, social, religious, and political centre of the city. A THEATRE usually occupied a convenient slope. The STADIUM and burial grounds were generally outside the walls. In time a rectangular grid plan with wider streets was developed, attributed to HIPPODAMUS of Miletus. In the Hellenistic period long colonnaded streets were built and the Hippodamian plan was universally imposed. The Hellenistic city was the model for most Roman city planners, though they were also influenced by traditions of military ARCHITECTURE and surveying (*see* GROMATICI). The FORUM took the place of the agora, drainage improved, and housing tended more towards high-rise blocks (*insulae*). As in the Greek world new foundations could be laid out according to a premeditated plan while older cities 'just growed'. GS

Ward-Perkins (1974); Wycherley (1967).

Trade The first people to exploit Mediterranean trade on a large scale were the PHOENICIANS. They established trading stations throughout the region from Spain to the Red Sea. Most Greek states were more or less self-sufficient until the archaic age when they became unable to sustain a growing population. At the same time local INDUSTRY began to develop and also a need to barter its products with goods from overseas. The desire for trade and hunger for land constituted the two principal motives for the first waves of COLONIZATION by the Greeks from the 8th to the 6th century BC. Many colonies were chosen for the quality of their harbours and their access to marketable items such as corn, timber, and minerals.

The growth of trade coincided with the invention of COINAGE around the end of the 7th century BC. Despite problems caused by different weight standards between cities, coinage facilitated small-scale commercial dealings, and the distribution of coins provides valuable evidence of trading patterns. Transportation was mostly by sea. It was therefore slow and seasonal. Cargo SHIPS, built to carry maximum loads with minimum crew, were dependent on sail and wind.

Much of Athens's trade was in the hands of METICS (resident aliens), many of whom lived in PIRAEUS. The chief exports were oil, wine, silver, pottery, arms, and marble. Imports included grain, slaves, timber for shipbuilding, iron, copper, flax, and luxury goods. Dealings were regulated by market commissioners. Both imports and exports carried a 2 per cent tax. Special measures were taken to protect the corn supply, most of which came from the Black Sea. Merchants often formed GUILDS, but primarily for social rather than economic reasons.

The conquests of Alexander the Great opened up new markets in the east, and the trade in luxury items, silks, perfumes, and spices expanded rapidly bringing great wealth to certain areas. DELOS in particular flourished on the trade in slaves. Other commercial centres included Rhodes, Ephesus, Miletus, Thessalonica, Olbia, Antioch on the Orontes, Tyre, Sidon, Seleuceia on Tigris, and Alexandria.

The Romans inherited the trading empire of the Greek east and expanded it west as far as the Atlantic and north to the Baltic. Rome was the commercial centre and its principal ports were PUTEOLI and OSTIA. PIRACY which had long inhibited maritime trade was greatly reduced by the campaigns of POMPEY in 67 BC. Meanwhile overland trade within the empire was made faster and safer by the network of ROADS. There was free trade under the Republic, though harbour dues (PORTORIA) were levied on goods entering and leaving Italian harbours, and under the Empire a low customs duty was charged in the provinces. Goods from outside the empire, however, were taxed heavily (25 per cent on luxuries from the east, for example). The trade in cheap products, which had begun to fall off as local industries expanded, received a further blow in the 3rd century AD with the collapse of the coinage and the new system of TAXATION introduced by DIOCLETIAN. Meanwhile the trade in luxury goods such as silk became a state monopoly and all overseas trade was strictly controlled by the state.

See also BANKING; FINANCE; FOOD AND DRINK; SLAVERY; *and entries for individual commodities and cities.*   GS

Boardman (1980); D'Arms (1981); Garnsey, Hopkins, and Whittaker (1983); Hopper (1979); Miller (1969); Rostovtzeff (1941, 1957).

Tragedy, Greek Tragedy was an Athenian phenomenon of the 5th century BC. By 500 BC the presentation of drama was institutionalized as part of the City DIONYSIA, a festival celebrated every March in honour of DIONYSUS (*see* THESPIS). COMEDY was included for the first time in 486. A second festival known as the LENAEA, held every January, also for Dionysus, established by the mid-5th century, also included plays. By the 4th century plays were produced at festivals elsewhere in Attica and the fashion quickly spread throughout the Greek world. But by then the period of creativity was over and the canon of great tragedians was fixed for all time with the works of AESCHYLUS, SOPHOCLES, and EURIPIDES.

Presentation took the form of a competition similar to the great athletic contests. Each competitor produced, directed, choreographed, wrote the music for, and at first even acted in four of his own plays – three tragedies (which might be linked as a trilogy such as Aeschylus' *Oresteia*) and a SATYR PLAY. The performance took place in the THEATRE of Dionysus on the slopes of the Acropolis before an audience that could number 14,000 (women and children may have been excluded) in the open air and in the daytime. State subsidies (THEORIKA) enabled the poor to attend.

Production was highly stylized and included interludes of singing and dancing performed by the chorus. Both actors and chorus (all male) wore masks. The subject-matter was usually (but not invariably) mythological, with variation in interpretation, motivation, and characterization to suit the dramatist's purpose. That purpose, which may have included social, political, and moral concerns, was above all else dramatic: to create suspense, to challenge the audience both emotionally and intellectually, and to win the prize.

See also AGATHON; ION; LYCOPHRON; PHRYNICHUS.   GS

Herington (1985); Meier (1993); Pickard-Cambridge (1968); Taplin (1978); Vickers (1973); Walcot (1976).

Tragedy, Roman Despite the meagreness of surviving fragments, tragedy in the Republican period was at least as popular at Rome as COMEDY and most of the early dramatists (LIVIUS ANDRONICUS, NAEVIUS, ENNIUS) wrote both. Tragedies, like comedies, were generally modelled on Greek exemplars, but with the musical component transferred from the chorus to the principal characters; some, however, were based on themes from Roman history and mythology, and there was a new element of patriotism that would not have found a place on the Athenian stage. PACUVIUS was the first dramatist at Rome to write only tragedies, and his younger contemporary ACCIUS was most admired as a tragedian; but his death (*c*.85 BC) signalled the end of tragedy as a dramatic form. OVID wrote a play called *Medea* but it was no more intended for the stage than were the tragedies of the younger SENECA, nine of which survive.   GS

Beare (1964); Hutchinson (1993); Pratt (1983).

Trajan (AD 53–117), Roman emperor, AD 98–117. Marcus Ulpius Traianus was a Spaniard, son of the distinguished ex-consul Ulpius Traianus. Popular with the troops as governor of Upper Germany, he was chosen by NERVA as his successor, and immediately made co-emperor (October 97). Three months later he succeeded Nerva peacefully, but did not come to Rome until over a year later. Trajan treated the Senate with respect, avoiding numerous consulships, and, in contrast to the reign of Domitian, his reign was seen as something of a golden age. His modest behaviour, and that of his wife Plotina and sister Marciana, won him the title *optimus princeps*, best of leaders. He was an energetic and able administrator, paying great attention to Italy and the provinces, and undertook a substantial building programme in Rome, the most spectacular building being his FORUM, dedicated in 112. However, it is for his military leadership that he is best remembered: the first of two tough campaigns (101–2) against DECEBALUS in DACIA reduced Dacia to client status and is commemorated on Trajan's Column in Rome; after the second (105–6), Dacia was incorporated into the empire. The enormous booty from the war, and the revenue from the Dacian gold mines, financed Trajan's public works and donatives and the extension of the system of ALIMENTA (poor relief). Further expansion of the empire took place in the east: the governor of Syria incorporated the Nabataean kingdom as the province of ARABIA, and Trajan fought a major Parthian War (113 onwards), reducing Armenia (a client kingdom) to provincial status and creating two new provinces, Assyria and Mesopotamia, out of Parthian territory, before renewed Parthian invasions forced Trajan to return much territory to client kings. Trajan died on 9 August 117, *en route* for Rome: it is unclear whether, on his deathbed, he adopted his relative HADRIAN as his successor.   RJB

Grant (1985); Salmon (1968); Wells (1984).

Trajan Decius   *see* DECIUS.

Transportation   *see* POSTAL SERVICE; ROADS, ROMAN; SHIPS; TRAVEL.

Trasimene, Lake   battle in 217 BC. At Lake Trasimene, near Perusia, HANNIBAL ambushed the consular army of FLAMINIUS. Flaminius had hoped to catch the Carthaginians between his legions and those of the consul Servilius Geminus, but he was attacked on the march and his men were trapped along the edge of the lake. Those who did not drown were captured and a similar fate befell Servilius' 4,000 cavalry. After these disasters FABIUS MAXIMUS VERRUCOSUS was appointed dictator.   LPR

Lazenby (1978).

Travel   In the Greek world travel was slow, strenuous, and dangerous. The absence of satisfactory roads restricted overland journeys to short distances. Travel by sea was seasonal, and even in the open season was still vulnerable to storms and PIRACY. Voyages were rarely undertaken for pleasure: generally they were motivated by some serious purpose such as COLONIZATION, TRADE, or WARFARE. But clearly some people were prepared to travel long distances, e.g. in order to attend a panhellenic festival or consult an oracle.

The Persian system of royal roads, equipped with staging posts, was inherited by the Hellenistic world; and an even more impressive network of ROADS was developed by the Romans, first in Italy, and later throughout the empire. Meanwhile at sea the scourge of piracy was temporarily removed by the campaign of POMPEY in 67 BC. As a result travel in the Roman world became safer and faster; and, though it could never be described as comfortable, travelling for pleasure was a realistic possibility in peacetime.

See also FESTIVALS; HERMES; NAVIGATION; ORACLES; POSTAL SERVICE.   GS

Casson (1974).

Treasury   Athens had many treasuries and a treasurer (*tamias*) for each, but the evolution of a single finance officer was slow. The Theoric Commissioner of the 350s BC was in effect such. In the 330s LYCURGUS was certainly in control of the financial administration and probably had a special title. Where the money was kept is obscure. 'Receivers' (*apodektai*) received the sums due to the state and promptly paid them over to the treasurers of the separate funds. It is unclear when a central treasury was instituted.

See also FINANCE, GREEK.   GLC

Ehrenberg (1969); Rhodes (1972).

Trebbia   battle in 218 BC. At the river Trebbia, in Cisalpine Gaul, HANNIBAL defeated the consuls Sempronius Longus and Publius Cornelius SCIPIO. The Romans were tricked into attacking across the river, swollen by the spring thaw and still icy cold. They were quickly fatigued by the cold and, when attacked in the rear by a previously hidden Punic force, their resistance collapsed. Only 10,000 Romans, a quarter of the army, managed to escape.   LPR

Lazenby (1978).

Trebonianus Gallus   (*c.*AD 206–53), Roman emperor, AD 251–3. Gaius Vibius Trebonianus Gallus, commander in Moesia under DECIUS, was proclaimed emperor by the army after Decius' death. He bought off the Goths, but proved ineffective against a Persian invasion of Mesopotamia and against further Gothic incursions, and the army in Moesia chose its commander Aemilianus to replace him. During a battle at Interamna, north of Rome, Gallus and his son Volusianus (Gallus' colleague as Augustus, 251–3) were both murdered.   RJB

Grant (1985); Parker (1958).

Trebonius (d. 43 BC), Roman soldier and administrator. Gaius Trebonius, son of an *eques*, was tribune in 55 BC, when he carried a law conferring five-year commands on POMPEY and CRASSUS. He served CAESAR well as an officer in Gaul from 55 to 50, and in 49 laid siege to Massilia. He was appointed *consul suffectus* by Caesar in 45 although a NOVUS HOMO, but in 44 he took part in his assassination. Appointed proconsul of Asia in 43, he was murdered by DOLABELLA.

DP

Trees *see* ARBORICULTURE; TIMBER.

Treveri Gallic people. The Treveri, a Gallic tribe settled in the Moselle basin, were conquered by Caesar, but rebelled in 29 BC, AD 21, and again in 70. Thereafter they remained loyal to Rome, becoming highly romanized, although their territory was several times devastated by barbarian incursions in the mid-3rd century. In the late 3rd century an imperial court was established at Trier (AUGUSTA TREVERORUM), capital of the Treveri, which remained an imperial stronghold until taken by the barbarians, *c.*430.

RJB

Drinkwater (1983); King (1990); Matthews (1990); Wightman (1970).

Tribunus aerarius Roman class. The *tribuni aerarii* were responsible for the collection of the TRIBUTUM and its payment to the troops. The abolition of *tributum* in 167 BC ended this function, but the *tribuni aerarii* continued to exist as a citizen class, just below the EQUESTRIAN ORDER in wealth. From 70 BC *tribuni aerarii* composed one-third of the jury of a QUAESTIO, until Caesar removed them in 46 BC.

HS

Nicolet (1980).

Tribunus militum Roman army officer. In a legion under the Republic there were six military tribunes, all of EQUESTRIAN standing. The increased use of LEGATI made these officers less important. Under the Principate there were two types of military tribune, one of senatorial birth (*laticlavius*) and five of equestrian birth (*angusticlavii*), in each legion. The *laticlavius* was a young man usually hoping to go on to be QUAESTOR. The office of *tribunus angusticlavius* became normal in an equestrian career (*see* PRAEFECTUS). In the late Empire *tribunus* became a more general title for a military commander.

See also ARMY, ROMAN.

HS

Keppie (1983); Webster (1985).

Tribunus plebis The tribunes of the Roman PLEBS were traditionally created at the first SECESSIO (494 BC). There were probably only two tribunes at first, but their number was later increased to 10 per year, elected by the CONCILIUM *plebis*. The tribunes acted as champions of the *plebs*, and derived their power and standing from a *lex sacrata*, a solemn oath of the *plebs*, who swore to defend their tribunes and invoked curses on anyone who caused them harm. They thus became sacrosanct, and this inviolability enabled the tribunes to exercise the right of INTERCESSIO (veto). The tribunes convened the plebeian assembly, and proposed measures which if approved became PLEBISCITA. After plebeians were admitted to the consulship in 367 BC (*see* STOLO), the tribunate became a stepping stone in the career of ambitious plebeian NOBILES, and the tribunes' powers were used as weapons in political struggles between noble factions. But it was still possible for radical tribunes to promote popular reforms. In the late Republic tribunes like the GRACCHI, SATURNINUS, and P. SULPICIUS Rufus fought to improve the conditions of the poor and to call the ruling oligarchy to account. In 81 BC SULLA severely restricted the tribunes' powers; but they were restored by POMPEY in 70, and tribunes continued to play a leading part in Roman politics to the end of the Republic. Under the Principate tribunes ceased to have any practical function; but the emperors themselves, starting with Augustus in 23 BC, held the 'tribunician power', which symbolized their role as champions of the people.   TC

Brunt (1971b); Finley (1983).

Tribus   division of the Roman people. In early times the Roman people were supposedly divided into three tribes (the word *tribus* may be connected with Latin *tres* = three) called Ramnes, Tities, and Luceres. In historical times these original tribes had been replaced by a system of local tribes, to which Roman citizens belonged by virtue of residence. Tradition ascribes the local tribes to SERVIUS TULLIUS, who divided the city into four tribes, and the countryside into a number of 'rustic' tribes. By 495 BC there were 17 rustic tribes. As Rome expanded during the 4th and 3rd centuries, further tribes were created to incorporate newly won territory; by 241 BC the number of tribes had reached 35 (4 urban, 31 rustic). After that it was decided not to create any further tribes, but to include all additional territory in the existing 35. The tribes were used as the basis of army recruitment, and as constituent voting units in the CONCILIUM *plebis* and COMITIA *tributa*.
          TC

Taylor (1960).

Tributum   Roman tax. *Tributum* was an emergency property tax levied on Roman citizens, theoretically refundable after the crisis had been resolved. It was first imposed in 406 BC during the siege of Veii. The collection of *tributum* from Roman citizens was suspended in 167 BC (*see* TRIBUNUS AERARIUS), after which the Roman treasury depended on income from provincial TAXATION. In the course of time *tributum* became a general term for direct taxes raised in the provinces.   RJB

Crawford (1985); Jones (1974); Nicolet (1980).

Triclinium   Roman dining room. At dinner the Romans reclined on three-seater couches on three sides of a square table. This arrangement, and by transference the room in which it took place, was known as the *triclinium*. Places were assigned according to strict social etiquette: the host's family took the left-hand couch with the host himself at the inside end; guests took the other two, the guest of honour being placed next to the host.   GS

Trierarchy   command of a trireme. At Athens trierarchy was a form of military service which members of the property class of HIPPEIS were obliged to perform. Essentially the trierarch's function was to pay, while the steersman possessed the real nautical experience. Service could be frequent and, as Athenians became poorer in the Peloponnesian War, a shared trierarchy was introduced requiring service for only half a year. Since equipment drawn from the Commissioners of the Docks was unreliable, trierarchs preferred to keep their own. The navy lists of the 4th century BC record and carry over debts for decades. In 358/7 service and payment were separated. All the reforms proposed in the Demosthenic period were concerned solely with securing a more equitable system of paying.

See also NAVY, GREEK.   GLC

Jordan (1972).

Trireme   Greek warship. The trireme was the backbone of the Greek NAVY in the classical period. Manned by 170 oarsmen in three banks on each side, it was a long slender ship (the shipsheds at PIRAEUS measured *c.*120 feet by 12) capable of relatively high speed (a recorded journey of 130 miles in a day suggests an average of 8.6 knots). Light and easily manoeuvrable, it was equipped with a ram which was its only weapon in battle.

See also NAVIGATION; SHIPS; TRIERARCHY.   GS

Morrison and Coates (1986).

Trittyes   Athenian political division. Originally Athens had four tribes, divided into 12 trittyes ('thirds'). Under the reforms of CLEISTHENES each of the 10 new tribes was formed from three new trittyes, one from each of the three zones, City, Coast, and Inland, into which

Attica was divided; the trittyes in turn formed groups of demes, not always adjacent ones. Trittyes had officers, cults, and property and, apparently, some military functions.

See also DEME; PHYLE.   RB

Jones (1987); Traill (1975).

Triumph Roman celebration of victory. A triumph at Rome was the ritual procession by a victorious general from the Campus Martius to the temple of Jupiter Capitolinus. The conditions for a triumph were defeat of a foreign enemy, with at least 5,000 of them killed, by a magistrate with *imperium*, who had to bring home his army to show that the war was won. Because *imperium* lapsed inside Rome itself, the general had to wait outside until the Senate had given him permission to retain his command inside the city for the day of the triumph only. The victorious general, richly dressed and wreathed in bay, stood on a four-horse chariot, preceded by his lictors and followed by his troops. The procession was joined by the magistrates and senators, captives, slaves bearing spoils, and sacrificial animals. There were some 100 triumphs between 220 and 70 BC. They conferred great prestige and were keenly sought by magistrates, who were thus encouraged in belligerence and brutality.   DP

Harris (1979); Versnel (1970).

Triumphal arch one of the most solid and most characteristic of all Roman architectural monuments. Generally set up to commemorate a military victory or TRIUMPH, the arch offered scope for visual propaganda to enhance the reputation and prestige of the victor. The first examples are recorded at Rome at the start of the 2nd century BC, but the majority date from the imperial period when their use was restricted to the emperors themselves. An Augustan arch took the form of a simple archway between pairs of engaged columns or pilasters and was usually surmounted by a bronze group of the emperor with a chariot and four. Later, side arches were added and the sculptural decoration became more elaborate.

See also SCULPTURE, ROMAN.   GS

Triumvirate The 'First Triumvirate' is the name misleadingly applied to the wholly unofficial agreement between CAESAR, POMPEY, and CRASSUS in 60 BC to work for their mutual political advantage. 'Conspiracy' or 'tyranny' were the names used by their enemies. Relying on armed force, they broke the monopoly of the power of the *nobiles*, and paved the way for one-man rule. Crassus died in 55, but Caesar and Pompey did not formally separate until the Civil War of 49.

The 'Second Triumvirate', an agreement between ANTONY, LEPIDUS, and Octavian (AUGUSTUS) to rule the Roman world together for five years, was made legal on 23 November 43 BC. Their powers were practically absolute. In 42 they carried out a wholesale proscription and defeated the Republicans at PHILIPPI. The Triumvirate was later renewed for another five years, but Lepidus was soon deposed, and the union between Antony and Octavian finally broken at ACTIUM in 31.

DP

Carter (1970), Gruen (1974); Weigel (1992).

Trogus (fl. late 1st century BC), Roman historian. Pompeius Trogus, a historian of the Augustan period, wrote a *Universal History*, in Latin, in 44 books. Trogus' history dealt with the peoples outside Italy, thus forming a useful complement to the work of other authors, and in particular LIVY, on the history of Rome itself. Unfortunately, Trogus' work survives only in an epitome produced by Justin, and in fragmentary quotations by such as the elder PLINY.

RJB

Salmon (1968); Scullard (1982).

Trophy It was common practice for a victorious Greek army to set up a suit of armour belonging to the enemy as a 'trophy' to mark the site of victory on the battlefield. A trophy might also be dedicated in the sanctuary of the god held responsible for the victory. From the 4th century BC trophies assumed a more permanent monumental form such as a tower surmounted by a sculptured trophy. This practice was continued by Roman emperors, e.g. TRAJAN's trophy near Adamclisi to celebrate his Dacian victories.

GS

Tullus Hostilius king of Rome, 673–642 BC. Tullus Hostilius was traditionally the third king of Rome. Legend portrays him as a ferocious and warlike figure. He captured and destroyed ALBA LONGA and built the first Senate House, the Curia Hostilia.

HE

Scullard (1980).

Turbo (d. AD 120s/130s), praetorian prefect. Quintus Marcius Turbo, an experienced soldier and administrator, was a trusted general of the emperors TRAJAN and HADRIAN. He quelled the unrest in Africa and Egypt (AD 116–17), and was recalled by Hadrian to take up an extraordinary command of both Pannonia and Dacia, to oversee the consolidation of Dacia as part of the empire. Praetorian prefect in Rome from 119, he served with great dedication until eventually dismissed by Hadrian.

RJB

Perowne (1960); Salmon (1968).

Tusculum city in Italy. The Latin city of Tusculum lay in the Alban Hills about 15 miles south-east of Rome. It was an important city in the 6th century BC, and its leading citizen, Octavus Mamilius, married a daughter of TARQUINIUS SUPERBUS. After the overthrow of Tarquin Tusculum led the Latins against Rome, a revolt which ended in defeat at Lake REGILLUS (496). In 381 Tusculum was annexed by Rome and became the first MUNICIPIUM. It later joined the Latin revolt of 340 but was reduced in 338 (*see* LATIN WAR). In later times Tusculum became a fashionable country retreat where well-to-do Romans, including CICERO, had villas. HE

CAH VII.2.

Twelve Tables Roman law code. The Twelve Tables were produced in 451–450 BC by the DECEMVIRI, a board of lawgivers specially appointed for the purpose. The Tables were subsequently regarded as the foundation of Roman LAW. The full text does not survive, but a sample of the contents is preserved in quotations. These take the form of terse injunctions and prohibitions in archaic language. For example: 'If he summons him to court, let him go. If he does not go, summon a witness. Then he shall seize him.' 'If he has maimed another's limb, unless he settles with him, let there be retaliation.' The Twelve Tables were not a systematic code in the modern sense, and the Decemvirs evidently made no attempt to set out the whole of the law on any subject. Rather, they seem to have dealt specifically with perceived difficulties and matters of current dispute. The chief topics covered in the surviving texts are: the family, marriage, and divorce; inheritance, ownership, and transfer of property; torts and delicts; debt, slavery, and NEXUM. Public law – the constitutional rules governing the political system – seems not to have been included. TC

CAH VII.2; Watson (1975).

Tyranny Greeks used the term *tyrannos* to denote a monarch whose position was unconstitutional. Originally tyrants seized power through popular support; the term only gradually became pejorative, and their unrestricted power occasioned envy as well as hatred, though for the philosophers (particularly PLATO) the tyrant is generally a villain. Although tyrannies occurred in later periods of Greek history (e.g. DIONYSIUS I, GELON, JASON), they are particularly prevalent *c*.650–500 BC, as a stage in political evolution between aristocracy and, usually, OLIGARCHY. Though often of the aristocracy (e.g. PEISISTRATUS), or just outside it (e.g. CYPSELUS), the usurpers exploited discontent with aristocratic exclusiveness and misbehaviour. A general increase in prosperity undermined the claims of birth, while the emergence of the

HOPLITE army meant that aristocrats were no longer the city's only defenders. Several tyrants are said to have been successful military leaders, and the acquiescence of the new army may be assumed in most cases. Others appealed to an ethnic minority (*see* CLEISTHENES OF SICYON), or pursued populist policies, including public works, which also promoted a new urban centre at the expense of local nobles. Tyrants intermarried and lent each other material and moral support; but, as discontent lessened, their popularity tended to diminish, and their sons, lacking legitimacy, found power hard to retain without repression; few tyrannies extended to the third generation.

See also DIONYSIUS II; HIERON I; HIPPIAS; PERIANDER; PITTACUS; POLYCRATES; THRASYBULUS.   RB

Andrewes (1956); Berve (1967).

Tyre city of the PHOENICIANS. Like its neighbour SIDON, Tyre was established as a major city with trading links throughout the Mediterranean before the 8th century BC. In 332 BC it was besieged by ALEXANDER THE GREAT and destroyed. It recovered and after Ptolemaic and Seleucid rule was declared free in 126 BC. Incorporated into the Roman province of Syria by Pompey, it became a Roman colony and was given IUS ITALICUM in the 2nd century AD.   GS

Stillwell (1976).

Tyrtaeus (7th century BC), Greek elegiac poet. Tyrtaeus was a Spartan general in the Second Messenian War (mid-7th century BC) and took part in the capture of Messene (*see* MESSENIA). His poems, which were collected into five books by the Alexandrians, included war songs, elegiac exhortations (of which four survive), and a *Constitution* for the Spartans. They are said to have filled his countrymen with a new fighting spirit.   GS

West (1974).

U

Ulpian (d. AD 228), Roman jurist. Domitius Ulpianus was born at Tyre and was the pupil and successor of another Syrian, PAPINIAN. He was prominent as a jurist in the reign of Caracalla (AD 211–17). Like PAULUS, he was banished by Elagabalus, recalled by Severus Alexander, and became praetorian prefect. The last, and perhaps the greatest, of the Roman jurists before the codification of Justinian, he was murdered in 228 in a mutiny of the Praetorian Guard. His literary output was considerable and wide-ranging: his textbooks, monographs, and commentaries synthesized the work of his predecessors and make up nearly a third of the *Digest*.

See also JURISPRUDENCE.   GS

Birley (1988); Honoré (1982).

Umbrians   Italian people. The Umbrians inhabited north central Italy, stretching from the Apennines to the Adriatic coast, bordering Cisalpine Gaul to the north and Picenum to the east. They spoke an Italic language related to OSCAN which is known from inscriptions, the most famous being the IGUVIUM TABLES. The Roman conquest of Umbria began in 310 BC (*see* FABIUS MAXIMUS RULLIANUS) and was completed by 266.

                                                                            HE

Harris (1971); Salmon (1982).

Urbanization   *see* MUNICIPIUM; POLIS.

Utica   city in Africa. Utica was one of the earliest trading stations of the PHOENICIANS. After the destruction of CARTHAGE in 146 BC it became capital of the new Roman province of AFRICA. Settled by influential Roman citizens, Utica supported POMPEY in the CIVIL WAR that ended the Republic and was the scene of CATO's suicide. Under the Empire it was eclipsed by a resurgent Carthage and its port became silted up; but it rescued its fortunes by adopting an agricultural economy.   GS

Stillwell (1976).

V

Vaballathus *see* ZENOBIA.

Valens (d. *c.*AD 69), Roman general. Fabius Valens, previously a supporter of GALBA, supported VITELLIUS against OTHO in his bid to become emperor (AD 69). Together with CAECINA ALIENUS, he led the Germanic legions into Italy, defeating Otho's forces outside Cremona. Rewarded with the consulship for 69, he was at first too ill to lead Vitellius' forces against VESPASIAN. He took command after Caecina's defection to Vespasian's cause, but was soon captured by the Flavian forces.

RJB

Salmon (1968); Wellesley (1975).

Valens (*c.*AD 328–78), eastern Roman emperor, AD 364–78. Flavius Valens, named Augustus by his brother VALENTINIAN I (March 364), ruled the eastern third of the empire from Constantinople. The less able of the brothers, Valens was a strict Arian, and showed less religious tolerance than Valentinian. The usurper Procopius (365–6) failed to depose him, but his later years were dominated by the GOTHS, who crossed the Danube and were allowed to settle. Maltreated by Valens' officials, the Visigoths ravaged the Balkans and other tribes crossed the Danube (376). Valens, not waiting for GRATIAN's aid, was completely defeated and killed by the Visigoths at Hadrianople (Adrianople, Thrace; 9 August 378).

RJB

Grant (1985); Hamilton and Wallace-Hadrill (1986).

Valentinian I (AD 321–75), Roman emperor, AD 364–75. Flavius Valentinianus, a Danubian officer, was chosen emperor at Nicaea by the army after the death of JOVIAN (February 364), and was the last really able western emperor. Ruling from Milan, he held the west and centre of the empire, including Illyricum, and named his younger brother VALENS as Augustus in the east (March 364). After a serious illness (367), he named his young son GRATIAN Augustus, to ensure the succession. AMMIANUS MARCELLINUS criticizes Valentinian's cruelty, jealousy, greed, and timidity, but praises many qualities, including his religious tolerance and his skill in warfare. Much of the reign was occupied with campaigning: leaving Valens to deal with the usurper Procopius, Valentinian won a number of victories against the Germanic tribes, and established a new line of defences along the northern frontiers. He sent Count Theodosius (father of Theodosius I) to save BRITAIN from barbarian incursions; and repelled further Germanic invasions in 374–5.

RJB

Grant (1985); Matthews (1990); Salway (1981).

Valentinian II (AD 371–92), Roman emperor, AD 375–92. Flavius Valentinianus, son of VALENTINIAN I, was declared emperor, aged four, by the army at Aquincum (Belgrade) and given the central portion of the empire (Italy, Illyricum, and Africa) by GRATIAN and VALENS. Initially dominated by Gratian (d. 383), he became nominal ruler of the whole of the western empire after MAXIMUS' defeat by THEODOSIUS I (388). Dominated, however, by Theodosius, he was sent to Gaul, and died (probably murdered) at Vienne.

RJB

Grant (1985), Matthews (1990).

Valentinian III (AD 419–55), Roman emperor, AD 425–55. Flavius Placidus Valentinianus, son of PLACIDIA and CONSTANTIUS III, was installed as western emperor by THEODOSIUS II, in place of the usurper John (423–5). Last of the male line of the house of Valentinian, he was dominated first by Placidia and, increasingly, by AETIUS. Convinced by the eunuch Heraclius and PETRONIUS MAXIMUS of Aetius' treason, he killed the latter with his own hand (454), and was himself killed by Aetius' retainers.

RJB

Bury (1958); Grant (1985).

Valerian (*c*.AD 190–260), Roman emperor, AD 253–60. Publius Licinius Valerianus, Trajan DECIUS' regent in Rome, was summoned to assist Decius' successor TREBONIANUS GALLUS against Aemilianus, governor of Moesia. Too late to prevent the murder of Gallus, Valerian took possession of the empire himself, after Aemilianus had been killed by his own troops (253). Valerian moved to counter Persian incursions

(256/7), leaving his son, GALLIENUS, to rule the west: he repelled an invasion of Syria by SHAPUR I (257), but was unable to deal with a combination of Gothic invasions, plague, and a further advance by Shapur. Foolishly agreeing to meet Shapur, he was captured, and died in Persia (260).   RJB

Grant (1985); Parker (1958).

Valerius Antias (early 1st century BC), Roman annalist. Valerius Antias wrote a history of Rome in at least 75 books, running from the foundation down to his own times, the age of Sulla. The work survives only in meagre fragments, which do not allow us properly to judge its quality. But he was used as a source by LIVY who was aware of Antias' shortcomings and reproached him for exaggeration and inaccuracy. Antias was a contemporary of CLAUDIUS QUADRIGARIUS and MACER.

See also HISTORIOGRAPHY, ROMAN.   HE

Badian (1966b); Cornell (1986); Wiseman (1979).

Valerius Corvus (4th century BC), Roman hero. Marcus Valerius Maximus earned the name Corvus ('crow') in 349 BC when he was aided by a crow in a single combat with a Gaul. The crow represented death and battle to the Celts and this story resembles a similar event in the Irish epic *Tain-Bo-Cuailnge*. Valerius was an influential senator and a successful general, holding six consulships (348, 346, 343, 335, 300, and 299) and winning four triumphs. In 300 he passed a law granting the right of appeal (PROVOCATIO).   LPR

Hubert (1987); Oakley (1985).

Valerius Flaccus (*c.*AD 40–92), Latin poet. Gaius Valerius Flaccus was clearly a public figure since he held one of the religious offices reserved for magistrates, but nothing else is known of his life. His only known work is the EPIC poem *Argonautica* in eight books, left unfinished at his death. It owes much to APOLLONIUS RHODIUS and to VIRGIL and is less rhetorical than most contemporary poetry.   GS

Valerius Maximus (early 1st century AD), Roman historian. Valerius Maximus accompanied Sextus Pompeius to Asia in AD 27 and on his return composed a handbook of historical examples for use by rhetoricians, dedicated to the emperor Tiberius. The work comprises nine books and groups the examples under headings, according to the moral or philosophical points they illustrate. Each section is subdivided into stories concerning Romans and foreigners. His main sources were CICERO and LIVY.   HE

Dorey (1975).

Valerius Messalla Corvinus (64 BC–AD 8), Roman soldier and man of letters. Marcus Valerius Messalla Corvinus, a patrician, fought for the Republicans at PHILIPPI in 42 BC, transferred to Antony, but later joined Octavian. He fought for him against Sextus POMPEIUS and at ACTIUM. Augustus used him in the abortive attempt to set up an urban prefect in 25 BC, and in 11 BC as *curator aquarum*. As a patron of literature, Messalla included TIBULLUS and OVID in his circle. He was also famous for his oratory, public works, and knowledge of grammar.   DP

Syme (1939).

Valerius Potitus (5th century BC), Roman statesman. Lucius Valerius Potitus was one of the leaders of the revolt against the DECEMVIRI and after their downfall was elected consul (449 BC) with M. Horatius Barbatus. The two consuls triumphed over the AEQUI and the SABINES (respectively), and issued the so-called Valerio-Horatian Laws. These recognized the sacrosanctity of the TRIBUNES, made PLEBISCITA binding on the people, and guaranteed the citizens' right of appeal (PROVOCATIO). The traditional account is full of high-minded romance, but the central elements are probably historical.   TC

Scullard (1980).

Valerius Publicola (fl. 510–500 BC), Roman lawgiver. Publius Valerius Publicola was renowned, with L. BRUTUS, as one of the founding fathers of the Republic. As consul in 509 BC he gave the people the right of appeal (PROVOCATIO). He held three further consulships (508, 507, 504 BC) and won notable victories over the ETRUSCANS and SABINES. Although once widely regarded as legendary, he is now taken more seriously by historians after the discovery at Satricum of an archaic inscription, dating from *c*.500 BC, which records a dedication to Mars by 'the SODALES [i.e. the armed retinue] of Publius Valerius'.   TC

Stibbe, Colonna, De Simone, and Versnel (1980).

Vandals The Vandals, originally from Jutland, moved to Hungary *c*.AD 170, where their mailed cavalry posed an increasing threat to Roman RAETIA. In the 5th century they joined with the SUEBI and the ALANI, invading first Gaul (406) and then Spain (409). The Romans were obliged to grant them federate status, and the Asding Vandals settled in Galicia, the Siling Vandals in Baetica. The VISIGOTHS destroyed the Silings and broke up the Alani: the remnants joined the Asdings, under Guntheric (thereafter king of the Vandals and Alani). The Vandals became the most feared power in the Mediterranean, and under GAISERIC they invaded Mauretania (429) and seized Carthage (439), which Gaiseric ruled, nominally as a Roman vassal, but essentially as an independent king. The Vandals mounted attacks from Carthage on Sicily, Sardinia, and Corsica and, in 455, they sacked Rome. The Vandal threat continued after Gaiseric's death (477) until crushed by Belisarius (533). RJB

Todd (1972).

Varro, Gaius Terentius (fl. 218–200 BC), Roman soldier and administrator. Gaius Terentius Varro was a NOVUS HOMO who became consul in 216 BC. Defeated by HANNIBAL at CANNAE, Varro extricated a small force and was thanked by the Senate for not despairing of the Republic. He went on to serve in Picenum and Etruria. Hostile aristocratic sources depicted Varro, probably unfairly, as a low-class rabble-rouser, comparable to FLAMINIUS, and made him a scapegoat for Cannae.
See also PUNIC WARS. HS

Lazenby (1978); Scullard (1973).

Varro, Marcus Terentius (116–27 BC), Latin writer and scholar. Marcus Terentius Varro came probably from the Sabine town of Reate and was educated at Rome under L. Aelius Stilo and at Athens under Antiochus of Ascalon. He held the offices of quaestor, tribune of the *plebs*, and praetor and fought for POMPEY in Spain. Later, reconciled to Caesar, he was commissioned to assemble a LIBRARY. After Caesar's death he was outlawed and his library plundered; but he lived on to pursue his studies and was dubbed by QUINTILIAN 'the most learned of Romans'.

Of his numerous works (he is credited with over 600 volumes) only two survive; *De Lingua Latina* (five books of an original 25) on etymology and linguistics; *De Re Rustica* (six books out of 25) on AGRICULTURE. Lost works included 110 *Menippean Satires* (*see* SATIRE), 41 books of *Antiquitates* (both 'human' and 'divine'), 76 dialogues, 15 books of biographical sketches, and an encyclopaedia of the liberal arts (later used by MARTIANUS CAPELLA). His learning was unrivalled for both its breadth and depth.
See also SCHOLARSHIP, LATIN. GS

Skydsgaard (1967).

Varus (d. AD 9), Roman general. Publius Quinctilius Varus, related to AUGUSTUS through his wife Claudia Pulchra (grand-daughter of Octavia), was a competent governor, successful in Syria, but owed his appointment as commander on the Rhine (AD 9) to imperial favour. Through unpopular taxation and rulings, he provoked a rebellion amongst

Germanic tribes between the Rhine and the Elbe, and was ambushed by ARMINIUS in the Teutoburg forest: Varus' three legions were annihilated and he committed suicide.   RJB

Salmon (1968); Scullard (1982).

Vase painting *see* PAINTING, GREEK.

Vectigal the Roman term for an indirect tax, applied to rents from state property such as public land, mines, and salt-works, and to various other taxes, the most important being the PORTORIA (harbour dues). Under the Empire, the inhabitants of Italy were exempt from TRIBUTUM, direct TAXATION, so they paid only *vectigalia*. *Vectigalia* provided a considerable proportion of the state revenue, and their yield was increased by the extension of citizenship. Collection of *vectigalia* was initially farmed out to companies of PUBLICANI, but they were replaced, in the 2nd century AD, by single *conductores*, and, later still, by state officials.   RJB

Grant (1979); Salmon (1968); Scullard (1982).

Veii city in Italy. The ETRUSCAN city of Veii was a VILLANOVAN foundation, lying about nine miles north of Rome. The two cities were ancient rivals and fought a series of wars in the 5th century BC, before Veii finally fell to Rome in 396 and its territory was annexed. Veii suffered from its proximity to Rome and stagnated, despite becoming a MUNICIPIUM under Augustus.   HE

CAH VII.2; Potter (1979).

Velleius Paterculus (fl. AD 7–30), Roman historian. Gaius Velleius Paterculus, a Campanian, became quaestor in AD 7, served under Tiberius in Germany for eight years, and in AD 15 reached the praetorship. His one literary work, a compendium of Roman history in two books, was dedicated in AD 30 to Marcus Vinicius, consul of that year. The first book sketches very briefly Rome's history down to the fall of Carthage in 146 BC, but with a gap between ROMULUS and PYDNA (168). The second book, six times as long, is complete and takes the story down to AD 30. Overall the work shows Roman history building up to the perfect climax of the rule of the fulsomely praised TIBERIUS. Velleius admits his brief summary was written hurriedly: some of his sentences are labyrinthine, and his epigrams lack the bite and point of those of TACITUS. But his frequent character sketches are readable and often illuminating, e.g. those of Pompey and Caesar, and he does offer a connected account of the period from the Gracchi to Tiberius.

See also HISTORIOGRAPHY, ROMAN. DP

Dorey (1975).

Veneti Gallic people. The Gallic Veneti occupied the coast of Brittany. In 56 BC CAESAR was forced to build a fleet to overcome their naval power before he could subdue them. LPR

Chadwick (1970).

Veneti Italian people. The Italian Veneti lived on the Adriatic coast around the mouth of the river Po, and gave their name to Venice. They were more ancient than the Gallic tribes of Cisalpine Gaul and spoke an Italic dialect similar to Latin. They were often anti-Gallic and sided with Rome on several occasions. In 302 BC they repulsed a landing by a Greek fleet under CLEONYMUS. LPR

Chilver (1941).

Ventidius (*c.*94–38 BC), Roman general. Publius Ventidius, an Italian, was captured in infancy at Asculum (89 BC). But he rose to be an army contractor, although vilified by his enemies as a 'muleteer', and attached himself to CAESAR, through whom he entered the Senate. Praetor in 43, he raised three legions which reinforced ANTONY after Mutina, and became *consul suffectus* later in the year. In 39 and 38 he was sent by Antony to drive the Parthians out of Syria and Asia. His brilliant victories were honoured with a triumph, and his death, which soon followed, with a public funeral. DP

Syme (1939).

Venus *see* APHRODITE.

Ver sacrum Italian ceremony. In mythical accounts of early Italy the *ver sacrum* ('sacred spring') was an offering to the gods of the whole product of one spring season. In the allotted period all livestock born were sacrificed. Children from this spring, on reaching maturity, were sent away to find new land under a leader who followed a sacred animal. LPR

CAH VII.2; Scullard (1981).

Vercingetorix (1st century BC), Gallic chief. Vercingetorix, a young noble of the ARVERNI, in 52 BC led the general revolt against CAESAR. Using extreme discipline to mould the tribes into a unified army, he avoided battle and employed scorched-earth tactics. He was trapped with 80,000 men in the hillfort of Alesia which Caesar surrounded with siege works. He surrendered to save the army from starvation and was executed after Caesar's triumph in 44.   LPR

Connolly (1975); Hubert (1987).

Verres   (d. 43 BC), governor of Sicily. Gaius Verres, as praetor in 74 BC, openly took bribes, and as proconsul in Sicily from 73 to 71 BC plundered the island for his own enrichment. He probably expected to be acquitted on an extortion charge with the help of bribery, powerful friends, and HORTENSIUS HORTALUS to defend him, but was overcome by the legal skills of CICERO. He retired to Massilia, where he was proscribed and killed by Antony in 43 BC.   DP

Seager (1979).

Verulamium   modern St Albans, city in BRITAIN. Already the tribal capital of the Catuvellauni, Verulamium was first occupied by the Romans in AD 43–4 and laid out as a city c.50. Destroyed in the rebellion of BOUDICCA (AD 60–1), the city was rebuilt by 79 when a new forum was dedicated to the emperor Vespasian. It was later fortified and enlarged and building activity continued until the end of the 5th century.   GS

Wheeler and Wheeler (1936).

Verus   (AD 130–69), Roman emperor, AD 161–9. Lucius Aurelius Commodus Verus, son of HADRIAN's intended successor L. Aelius Verus (d. 1 January 138), was adopted by ANTONINUS PIUS, together with Marcus AURELIUS, at Hadrian's insistence. Verus later married Lucilla (b. AD 146), daughter of Aurelius and FAUSTINA THE YOUNGER. When Aurelius became emperor (161), he took Verus as his colleague. Verus was appointed commander of the Roman counter-attack against a Parthian invasion, which was a complete success due only to the skill of the subordinate commanders. Verus' indolence and love of luxury made him an unsuitable emperor and his death removed a block on the effective rule of Aurelius.   RJB

Grant (1985); Parker (1958); Salmon (1968).

Vespasian   (AD 9–79), Roman emperor, AD 69–79. Titus Flavius Vespasianus, born at Raete (central Italy), distinguished himself as a soldier in Thrace, Germany, and Britain. Governor of Judaea in AD 68, he supported OTHO after NERO's assassination, and then VITELLIUS after

Otho's death. However, persuaded by MUCIANUS, governor of Syria, and TITUS, his own son, he allowed himself to be proclaimed emperor by the Egyptian legions (1 July 69). The Danubian legions, led by Antonius PRIMUS and Arrius Varus, invaded Italy and defeated Vitellius (69), and Vespasian reached Rome in mid-70.

The revolt of CIVILIS was put down by Petilius Cerialis, and Vespasian then reorganized the AUXILIA so that they no longer served in their native country or under native officers. Commagene and Armenia Minor were annexed (72), and a general policy of consolidation of the frontiers was maintained. Vespasian founded numerous *coloniae* and *municipia*, particularly in Spain. He assumed the office of censor, filling the gaps in the Senate with a new aristocracy (which included TRAJAN, AGRICOLA, and M. Annius Verus, ancestor of Marcus AURELIUS). Although remaining courteous towards the Senate, he saw no reason to avoid the consulship, holding it in every year except 73 and 78, on six occasions with Titus as his colleague. He restricted unnecessary expenditure and increased revenues by raising taxes and revoking exemptions, and was thus able to spend freely on buildings (e.g. the COLOSSEUM; the temple of Peace), roads, art, and education. Vespasian was succeeded by his son, the first emperor to be so.   RJB

Grant (1985); Nicols (1978); Salmon (1968); Wells (1984).

Vesta Roman goddess. Vesta, the goddess of the hearth, was worshipped both at family hearths and at the state hearth in a round temple in the Forum. This contained no image of Vesta, but a fire which was permanently kept alight by the VESTALS. If it went out, a public calamity was presaged. Aeneas was said to have brought the fire from Troy together with the PENATES and a statue of Pallas Athene which assured the safety of Rome. The statue and Penates were kept in an inner sanctum of the temple.   DP

Platner and Ashby (1929); Richardson (1992); Scullard (1981).

Vestals Roman priestesses. The six Vestals were virgins who guarded the fire of the state hearth. Chosen between the ages of 6 and 10, they served for 30 years, living next door to the temple of VESTA in the Forum. If the fire ever went out, they relit it by rubbing sticks together. They has great privileges, but a Vestal guilty of unchastity was entombed alive.   DP

Beard (1980); Beard and North (1990).

Vesuvius volcano on the Bay of Naples. Vesuvius had not erupted since well before historical times and was widely regarded as extinct.

Its slopes were planted with vines and crowded with villas. A serious earthquake in AD 62 passed unheeded. The volcano's eruption on 24 August AD 79 was therefore a total surprise. It buried the cities of HERCULANEUM and POMPEII. An eye-witness account survives in the letters of PLINY THE YOUNGER.　　　　　　　　　　　　　　　　　　GS

Ward-Perkins and Claridge (1976).

Vibenna　name of two Etruscan adventurers. Aulus and Caelius (or Caeles) Vibenna were figures of Etruscan legend who, with their friend MASTARNA, played an obscure but significant part in the history of early Rome. Antiquarians of the 1st century BC linked them with the Tarquins, a connection borne out by an Etruscan painting (from the 4th-century BC François Tomb at Vulci) which shows a battle involving the Vibenna brothers, Mastarna, and other figures including a Gnaeus Tarquinius from Rome.

See also CAELIUS MONS.　　　　　　　　　　　　　　　　　　TC

Alföldi (1965); CAH VII.2.

Vicarius　(literally, substitute) a title given to an equestrian acting as governor of a Roman province. During the early Empire a *vicarius* only functioned when the governor was absent, or died in office, but during the 3rd century provinces were frequently entrusted to a *vicarius*, a PROCURATOR of equestrian rank, instead of to a senatorial governor. Diocletian (AD 284–305) grouped the provinces into 12 dioceses, each controlled by a *vicarius*.　　　　　　　　　　　　　　　　　　RJB

Millar (1981); Parker (1958).

Vicomagister　local Roman magistrate. A *vicomagister* was elected by one of the 265 parishes, or *vici*, of the city of Rome. The positions, revived by Augustus in 7 BC, carried various local responsibilities, including supervision of worship of the *Lares compitales* (guardian spirits, between which stood the *genius Augusti*, guardian spirit of Augustus' family) at shrines at crossroads. Such local posts gave an outlet for the potentially disruptive energies of freedmen, who could not join the army.

See also REGIO.　　　　　　　　　　　　　　　　　　RJB

Salmon (1968); Scullard (1982).

Victor　*see* AURELIUS VICTOR.

Victorinus　(d. AD 270), Roman emperor in Gaul, AD 268–70. Marcus Piavonius Victorinus, a tribune of the guards at Trier under POSTUMUS, inherited the latter's Gallic empire after a brief reign by Marcus Aurelius Marius. It is likely that Spain returned to its Roman allegiance at this time, and that Victorinus' empire thus comprised Britain and Gaul. A rebellion at Autun was defeated after a siege of seven months, but Victorinus was killed soon afterwards at Cologne and succeeded by TETRICUS. RJB

Parker (1958).

Vigiles   The *vigiles*, or watch, were a force established by Augustus, to provide both night-watchmen and a public fire brigade service for Rome. In 21 BC the aedile M. Egnatius Rufus formed a private fire brigade: faced with a potential private army, Augustus executed Rufus and set up the public service, initially of 600 slaves, but later expanded to a corps of 7,000 freedmen (AD 6), divided into seven 1,000-strong cohorts each responsible for two of the 14 districts of Rome. It was a semi-military force, commanded by an equestrian prefect. The strength of the *vigiles* was later trebled by Septimius SEVERUS.

   See also POLICE, ROMAN. RJB

Grant (1979); Millar (1981); Salmon (1968).

Vigintisexviri   Roman magistrates. The Republican *vigintisexviri* (26 men) were junior magistrates, reduced to 20 men, *vigintiviri*, by the time of Augustus: the *iiiviri monetales* (mint officials); the *iiiviri capitales* (dealing with cases carrying the death penalty); the *ivviri viarum curandarum* (in charge of the streets of Rome); the *xviri stlitibus iudicandis* (judging cases concerning the freedom of citizens). Members of the senatorial order normally held one of these posts before progressing to the QUAESTORship. RJB

Scott-Kilvert and Carter (1987); Scullard (1982).

Villa   *see* ARCHITECTURE, ROMAN.

Villanovan culture   the early Iron Age culture prevalent in western areas of Italy, especially Campania, south Etruria, and Tuscany, and also in Emilia-Romagna along the northern edge of the Apennines. The culture in fact takes its name from a site near Bologna which was discovered in 1853. The most characteristic feature of the Villanovan culture is the practice of cremation and the disposal of the ashes in distinctive biconical urns. These were placed in pits, and grouped to form 'urnfields', similar to those of Bronze Age central Europe, whence the practice was probably derived. In the 8th century BC cremation died out, and gave way to inhumation, and many of the larger Villanovan sites developed into city-states. The major ETRUSCAN cities all had Villanovan antecedents.

See also BONONIA; LATIAL CULTURE.   TC

CAH IV; Hencken (1968); Ridgway and Ridgway (1979).

Vindex (d. AD 68), Roman rebel. Gaius Julius Vindex, governor of Gallia Lugdunensis (central Gaul), rebelled against NERO in March AD 68. A romanized Gaul, he was perhaps attempting to win a degree of autonomy for Gaul but, although he raised a large force, not all the tribes joined him, and Lyon remained loyal to Rome. After only a few months he was defeated by the three legions of Verginius RUFUS at Vesontio (Besançon) and committed suicide.   RJB

Grant (1979); Salmon (1968).

Vindobona modern Vienna, city on the river Danube. First fortified by the Romans early in the 1st century AD, Vindobona became a legionary camp *c*.AD 100 (first for the 13th, then the 14th, and after 115 for the 10th). Destroyed in the wars against the MARCOMANNI, it was rebuilt and became a *municipium* and a naval base for the Danube fleet. Marcus AURELIUS died there. It was abandoned by the Romans early in the 5th century.   GS

Vinicius (d. after AD 1), Roman general. Marcus Vinicius was a prominent subordinate commander under AUGUSTUS. He helped to secure the passes between northern Italy and Transalpine Gaul by defeating tribes in the Vallis Poenina (Valais) (*c*.25 BC). He was briefly entrusted with command of the war in Pannonia (13 BC) until relieved by M. AGRIPPA, and, with L. DOMITIUS AHENOBARBUS, was again in charge of the Danubian frontier during TIBERIUS' retirement to Rhodes (6 BC onwards).   RJB

Salmon (1968); Scullard (1982).

Virgil (70–19 BC), Latin poet. Publius Vergilius Maro came from a village near Mantua. Of humble origins (his father was a potter), he received a good education at Cremona, Milan, and Rome and seems to have been destined for a senatorial career. But after a single appearance in the courts, he forsook public life and, having been introduced to the circle of CATULLUS by his friend POLLIO, he turned instead to poetry and philosophy. After the publication of his first book (*Eclogues*) he was patronized by MAECENAS who introduced him to Octavian (AUGUSTUS). He also enjoyed the society of HORACE and Varius. Returning from a visit to Greece, he died at Brundisium and was buried at Naples. He was unmarried.

Apart from a number of spurious juvenilia (*see* APPENDIX VIRGILIANA), three works survive. The *Eclogues* (more properly *Bucolics*) are modelled on the *Idylls* of THEOCRITUS and were written between 45 and 37 BC. The 10 hexameter poems of pastoral romance interweave traditional Greek elements with contemporary Roman themes. The four books of *Georgics*, modelled on the didactic poems of NICANDER but described by their author as Hesiodic, were composed between 36 and 29 BC. In celebration of Italian country life and values they treat, in turn, of crops, trees, cattle, and bees. The *Aeneid*, an EPIC poem in 12 books, recounts the adventures of the hero Aeneas from the sack of Troy to the foundation of ALBA LONGA. Both truly Homeric in concept and truly Roman in treatment, it is Virgil's, and Rome's, supreme poetic achievement.

See also ALEXANDRIAN POETRY, LATIN.   GS

Cairns (1989); Camps (1969); Griffin (1986); Hardie (1986); Otis (1963); Wilkinson (1969).

Viriathus (2nd century BC), Lusitanian chief. Viriathus, a shepherd and bandit, led the Lusitani (in modern Portugal, where he is still a national hero) from 147 to 139 BC. He fought Rome with great success and encouraged the CELTIBERIANS to revolt in 144. In 140 he forced the surrender of 20,000 Romans under terms which the Senate chose to ignore. In 139 Caepio arranged the assassination of Viriathus by his own servants.   LPR

Knapp (1977).

Visigoths *see* GOTHS.

Vitellius (AD 15–69), Roman emperor, AD 69. Aulus Vitellius, son of Lucius VITELLIUS, served as proconsul of Africa under CLAUDIUS I, and was appointed governor of Lower Germany by GALBA (AD 68). He was almost immediately proclaimed emperor by his troops (69). His generals VALENS and CAECINA ALIENUS invaded Italy, defeating Galba's successor, OTHO (April 69): Otho committed suicide and the Senate recognized Vitellius as emperor. The praetorian cohorts, which had supported Otho, were replaced by troops from the Germanic legions; but Vitellius had no money to pay the promised bonus, and alienated the Danubian legions (which had also supported Otho), putting to death their centurions. The historical sources highlight Vitellius' cruelty and gluttony, but this is the biased verdict of his victorious enemies. VESPASIAN was proclaimed emperor (July 69), and the Danubian legions under PRIMUS invaded Italy, defeating the Vitellians. Vitellius held out until Rome itself was captured and he himself was killed (December 69). RJB

Grant (1985); Salmon (1968); Wellesley (1975); Wells (1984).

Vitellius (d. after AD 51), Roman administrator. Lucius Vitellius, father of the emperor VITELLIUS, was the close friend and chief adviser of the emperor CLAUDIUS I. He was legate of Syria under Tiberius (35–7), negotiating successfully with the Parthian king, Artabanus III, for the retention of a Roman nominee, Mithridates, on the Armenian throne. He removed from office PONTIUS PILATUS, governor of Judaea (36), and conciliated the Jews, requiring Roman troops to avoid bringing their standards onto Jewish soil. RJB

Scullard (1982).

Viticulture The vine was one of the mainstays of Mediterranean AGRICULTURE. It was a long-term crop, requiring several years between first planting and producing; it was capital-intensive, in that the farmer needed not only land and vines but also stakes and props and a fence or wall to protect the plantation; and it was labour-intensive, needing about three times as many workers as corn. CATO describes an Italian vineyard of some 66 acres which was worked by two oxen, three asses, an overseer, his wife, and 16 slaves. Vines were planted in long rows, often interspersed with fruit trees and vegetables. The crop was so important that some states took legal measures to protect it. THASOS forbad the import of foreign wine; Ptolemaic Egypt taxed it heavily; and Rome protected its local trade by restricting viticulture in certain areas outside Italy.

See also WINE. GS

Rostovtzeff (1941, 1957); White (1967).

Vitruvius (1st century BC), Roman architect. Vitruvius Pollio worked for both Julius CAESAR and AUGUSTUS as an architect, but the only building that he mentions as his own was a basilica at Fanum. He seems to have had no connection with any of the great projects of the time and his fame derives entirely from his treatise *On Architecture* which survives in 10 books. The work is both objective and comprehensive and touches on every aspect of the architect's training and the range of skills required for professional practice. It was enormously influential in the Renaissance. GS

Plommer (1973).

Vologeses I king of Parthia, *c*.AD 51–80. Vologeses I established himself as king of Parthia around AD 51, and built a new capital,

Vologesokerta, on the Tigris. He established his brother Tiridates I in Armenia, but, distracted by a revolt probably led by his own son Vardanes, was unable to prevent CORBULO from deposing Tiridates. Vologeses later tied down Corbulo in Syria, compelled the surrender in Armenia of Paetus (62, Corbulo's replacement in Cappadocia), and restored Tiridates. RJB

Millar (1981); Scullard (1982).

Volsci Italian people. At the beginning of the 5th century BC the Volscians overran southern Latium and penetrated as far as the southern edge of the Alban Hills. They were probably a tribe of the SABELLI, people from the central Apennines, speaking an OSCAN-type dialect. Their main centres in Latium were ANTIUM, Circeii, and Anxur, but another group of Volscians was established inland in the middle Liris valley, around Sora, Arpinum, and Atina. Together with the AEQUI they were enemies of the Latins, and the legend of CORIOLANUS may recall a time when they threatened Rome itself. They were finally defeated in the LATIN WAR. TC

CAH VII.2; Salmon (1982).

Volusianus *see* TREBONIANUS GALLUS.

Voting at Rome. Voting in the COMITIA *curiata* soon became a formality. In the *Comitia centuriata* it proceeded via the 193 centuries, a majority in each century producing one vote. The richest centuries voted first, and voting ceased when a majority was reached. The procedure was basically similar in the *Comitia tributa* and *Concilium plebis* (*see* CONCILIA) which were organized into 35 tribes (TRIBUS). Before 139 BC each vote was given singly and out loud. Between 139 and 107 BC secret ballots were introduced for the assemblies' three functions: elections, legislation, and jurisdiction. Voting in the assemblies was phased out under the Principate. HS

Nicolet (1980); Staveley (1972); Taylor (1966).

Vulcan *see* HEPHAESTUS.

Vulgate the Latin version of the Bible. The term is used specifically to refer to the revision of the biblical text undertaken by JEROME *c.*AD 382 at the request of Pope Damasus. He tackled the NEW TESTAMENT first, for which he collated some ancient Greek manuscripts but changed the Latin text only where necessary. For the Old Testament his first versions of the Psalms were based on the Greek text of the SEPTUAGINT.

But his move to Bethlehem in 387 enabled him to study the Hebrew text and to undertake a new translation of the whole of the Old Testament from Hebrew into Latin, completed c.404. It survives in more than 8,000 manuscripts. GS

Kelly (1975).

Vulso (fl. 197–187 BC), Roman general. Gnaeus Manlius Vulso succeeded SCIPIO ASIAGENUS in the east as consul in 189 BC. He gained much booty from his defeat of the Galatians of Asia Minor. Returning to Rome via Thrace, he lost many men and some of his booty. His request for a triumph, although opposed by Aemilius PAULLUS, was granted. He was held responsible for the introduction to Rome of eastern luxury and its bad moral effects. HS

Scullard (1973); Toynbee (1965).

W

Wall of Antoninus The Antonine Wall, begun c.AD 142 under ANTONINUS PIUS, advanced the Roman frontier in Britain from the WALL OF HADRIAN to the Forth–Clyde line. It was 37 miles long, built of turf on a stone foundation about 14 feet wide, and 10 or perhaps 12 feet high. A ditch ran to the north, and a military way to the south; 16 forts are known, three more are assumed; a few fortlets are known, but no turrets (beacon platforms were probably used instead). Most plausibly, a withdrawal (c.158) was reversed by Pius, and the wall abandoned by the mid-160s (though a date up to c.180 remains possible).

See also LIMES.   RJB

Breeze and Dobson (1987); Robertson (1990).

Wall of Aurelian Prompted by barbarian invasions of Italy, AURELIAN began a new wall to enclose Rome, which had long since outgrown the WALL OF SERVIUS. Begun in AD 271 and finished during the reign of PROBUS, the wall was 12 miles long and enclosed, as far as was practical, all 14 city wards (REGIONES). It had a standard width of 12 feet and was 20 feet high, with rectangular interval towers topped by artillery platforms. It was a defensive structure, but not designed to withstand a prolonged siege, containing 18 gateways flanked by projecting towers (four of them double-arched) as well as numerous posterns.   RJB

Richmond (1971); Todd (1978).

Wall of Hadrian Hadrian's Wall spanned the Tyne–Solway gap. Begun after HADRIAN's visit to Britain (AD 122), it was stone-built from

Newcastle upon Tyne to the Irthing, and turf-built from there to Bowness-on-Solway. It was between 6 and 10 feet wide, and probably about 15 feet high. Just over 70 miles (76 Roman miles) long, there were milecastles throughout and two turrets between each. A ditch ran to the north, and a frontier zone to the south was delineated by the *vallum*, a ditch flanked by raised banks. A series of forts several miles behind the wall (e.g. Vindolanda) was soon moved up to the wall (e.g. Housesteads). Later modifications extended the wall east to Wallsend, and replaced the turf wall in stone. Hadrian's Wall, briefly replaced by the WALL OF ANTONINUS, was repaired in the 160s, and a military way added behind it. The wall, substantially rebuilt under Septimius SEVERUS (*c*.205–7) and restored by Count Theodosius (*c*.369/70), probably remained occupied up to (and beyond) 410.

See also LIMES.   RJB

Breeze and Dobson (1987); Collingwood Bruce (1978); Graham (1979).

Wall of Servius   This wall surrounding Rome was built in 378 BC and enclosed the hills, though in a somewhat irregular fashion. It was of stone construction (possibly built with the assistance of Greek work-men), 15 feet thick, at least 28 feet high, though 2nd-century BC modifications increased the height to about 52 feet. The wall was pierced by numerous gates on roads leading out of the city. By the time of Augustus it had fallen into neglect and its fabric was often incorporated into private architecture. The wall was traditionally at-tributed to King SERVIUS TULLIUS, though he seems to have been re-sponsible for only an earlier rampart on the eastern side of the city.

                                                                        HE

Todd (1978).

Wall of Severus   *see* WALL OF HADRIAN.

Walls, Long   (of Athens). In the 450s BC walls were built connecting Athens and PIRAEUS (which had been walled by THEMISTOCLES in the 480s) and Athens and the eastern end of the Bay of Phalerum. On PERICLES' proposal a third wall was built parallel to the former giving a passage about 180 yards wide and 4 miles long. These 'Long Walls' had to be demolished under the terms of peace in 404. The Phalerum wall was not rebuilt when CONON helped rebuild the others in 393/2.   GLC

Wycherley (1978).

Warfare, Greek   Much Greek warfare was a small-scale, local affair, intended to resolve political or territorial disputes. The invaders' threat to devastate the defenders' crops drew them out to give battle: a HOPLITE encounter determined the outcome, after which the victors returned their opponents' dead for burial, set up a TROPHY, and made an appropriate settlement. Casualties were usually moderate, perhaps 5 per cent for the victors and 15 per cent for the losers. Such warfare was necessarily seasonal, since the agricultural year dictated the effectiveness of the threat and the availability of men. States did not normally seek to destroy opponents, and their rudimentary siegecraft would have made this difficult.

The PELOPONNESIAN WAR altered matters: Athens's economic and naval power negated the normal tactics, while the opposed leagues proved resilient and capable of absorbing reverses; their extent made the war more complex, and the need to maintain them engendered an escalating ruthlessness and brutality. Likewise, the wars of PHILIP II and ALEXANDER THE GREAT laid more stress on pursuit, to inflict casualties and confusion, and on successful sieges to extend territorial control.

See also ARMY, GREEK; SIEGECRAFT, GREEK.   RB

Anderson (1970); Garlan (1975); Grundy (1911); Hanson (1983); Pritchett, part IV (1985).

Warfare, Roman   Rome was always primarily a land power. From the earliest times Rome's ARMY was based on heavy infantry. The early phalanx was replaced in the 4th century BC by the more flexible legion. Although continuing to evolve, the legion existed into the late Empire.

The legions were skilled in SIEGECRAFT, their skills being daily practised entrenching a camp. The camp made them strategically slower, but it increased their tactical security. The legions were at their best in high-intensity warfare of pitched battle and siege. Lighter units of auxiliaries were availabe for lower-intensity operations and supporting roles in high-intensity operations. Under the Principate, to preserve the lives of Roman citizens, attempts were made to replace legions with auxiliaries in pitched battle. From the 3rd century AD heavy cavalry began to replace heavy infantry as the main strike force in Roman warfare.

See also ARMS AND ARMOUR, ROMAN; NAVY, ROMAN.   HS

Adcock (1940); Hackett (1989); Luttwak (1976); Parker (1928).

Water   Water was significant in three areas. The first was the purely practical business of drinking, washing, and bathing. The Greeks relied on public fountains for most purposes. The Romans developed the AQUEDUCT to provide cities with a more regular supply, while the institution of BATHS became a central feature of society. Secondly, philosophers such as THALES produced cosmological theories that placed both the origins and the ultimate destiny of the world in water (*see* ELEMENTS). Thirdly, in religion it had certain symbolic values: rites of passage were purified by water as were oracular consultations; nature was fertilized by it; and it was offered to the souls of the dead who thirsted.   GS

Bruun (1991); Hodge (1992).

Weaving   Everyday clothing was generally woven in the home. Fancier goods were made by craftsmen and were often imported from the east. Few have survived, but illustrations in art and literature attest to their high quality. The upright loom was used with the warp held taut by weights and the weft thrown across, starting at the top and working downwards, by means of a pointed shuttle. The weft, which was much finer than the warp, was then pressed upwards by a comb. The alternative style of starting at the bottom, which enabled the weaver to sit, was introduced to Rome from Egypt in the 1st century BC.

See also INDUSTRY.   GS

Hoffmann (1964).

Weights   Greek weights were usually square and made of LEAD, inscribed with the name of the city, the denomination, and a type to symbolize the weight: the standard Attic series used the astragalus (= 1 stater), dolphin (= 1 mna), amphora (= ¹/₃ stater), and tortoise (= ¹/₄ stater). Many other types and several weight standards were in use elsewhere. The weights adopted by SOLON for the COINAGE at Athens were roughly as follows: 1 obol (12 measures of barley) = 0.72gm; 1 drachma (6 obols) = 4.31gm; 1 mina (100 drachmae) = 431gm; 1 talent (60 minae) = 25.86kg.

Roman weights were less varied than Greek and were generally in the form of a spherical piece of metal or stone, flattened on top and bottom, with the denomination inscribed on the top. The system was based on the pound (= 327gm) which was divided into 12 ounces.

See also MEASURES.   GS

Wine   Wine, diluted with water, was drunk at all levels of society throughout the ancient world. Its production was therefore universal, but certain regions acquired particular fame for the quality of their vintages, notably CHIOS, Cos, Lemnos, and THASOS in Greece and Alba Longa and Campania in Italy. The grapes were first trodden before being pressed, the juice from the trodden grapes being used to improve the flavour of poor wine. The juice extracted by pressing was transferred to storage vats for fermentation and bottled after about six months. The wine was usually drunk after three to four years, though some Italian wines took longer to mature.

See also FOOD AND DRINK; SYMPOSIUM; VITICULTURE.   GS

Lissarrague (1990); White (1984).

Women, Greek   Greek women led lives which by modern standards were isolated and underprivileged. Legally and politically, the wives and daughters of citizens had no more rights than slaves and they were expected to spend most of their time in the home where they had their own quarters. Here, however, in a wealthy context they ruled a world of their own and were responsible for the management of the domestic finances, slaves, and crafts such as baking, spinning, and weaving. In poorer homes they would work alongside their husbands and fathers and perform tasks otherwise left to slaves. Women took major roles in religion, notably in processions and as priestesses, and they had their own festivals such as the THESMOPHORIA. They also occupied the traditional position of 'influence behind the throne'. That they were aware of, and occasionally frustrated by, their unscripted role in the functioning of society is demonstrated by the comedies of ARISTOPHANES. Non-citizen women led more liberated lives, sometimes working as entertainers at the SYMPOSIUM, as courtesans, or as prostitutes. ASPASIA rose from such a background to become the wife of PERICLES.

See also ADULTERY; MARRIAGE, GREEK; PROSTITUTION; SLAVERY, GREEK.

GS

Just (1989); Lacey (1968); Pomeroy (1975, 1990); Sealey (1990).

Women, Roman   Under the early Republic authority in the Roman family (PATRIA POTESTAS) was wielded exclusively by the head of the household (*paterfamilias*) who had absolute power over his wife and children. Women could not own property or transact business in their own right. In the home, however, they were powerful and influential and they were no longer confined to women's quarters, as Greek women had been. From the 2nd century BC the patriarchal system began to break down and the position of women became more emancipated. EDUCATION was available for girls as well as boys. Some women acquired wealth, others (e.g. CLODIA and FULVIA) sought political power. Divorce became easier and so common that under the Empire measures had to be taken to promote MARRIAGE. No woman ruled Rome in her own right, though AGRIPPINA THE YOUNGER came close to it and many others held positions of great influence. A remark by CATO illustrates the change in the position of women: 'All men rule over women; we Romans rule over all men; and our wives rule over us.'

See also ADULTERY; MARRIAGE, ROMAN; PROSTITUTION; SLAVERY, ROMAN.

GS

Balsdon (1962); Dixon (1988); Gardner (1986); Pomeroy (1975).

Wrestling   *see* GAMES, GREEK.

X

Xanthippus (*c*.520–475 BC), Athenian politician. Xanthippus was the father of PERICLES by the ALCMAEONID Agariste. He led the prosecution of MILTIADES in 489, and was ostracized in 484. After his recall he commanded the Athenian forces at MYCALE and the siege of SESTOS, and was archon in 479/8.   RB

Davies (1971) no. 11811.I.

Xanthus (5th century BC), of Lydia, Greek historian. Xanthus, son of Candaules, was an older contemporary of HERODOTUS. He wrote a history of Lydia in four books, which was certainly used by NICOLAUS OF DAMASCUS. Whether Herodotus drew on him, as EPHORUS asserted, is more doubtful.

   See also HISTORIOGRAPHY, GREEK.   GLC

Pearson (1939).

Xenocrates (*c*.395–314 BC), Greek philosopher. Xenocrates of Chalcedon, a student of PLATO, became the third head of the ACADEMY, after SPEUSIPPUS. Like Speusippus, he reveals the influence of Pythagorean mathematical philosophy. However, whereas Plato had separated ideal from mathematical numbers and Speusippus recognized mathematical numbers only, Xenocrates identified the two. Although a prolific author, only scanty information regarding his views has survived. According to Sextus Empiricus he was responsible for the formal division of philosophy into three parts – physics, ethics, and logic – which became standard in Hellenistic times.   JL

Guthrie, vol. 5 (1978).

Xenophanes (*c.570–c.*478 BC), Greek poet and philosopher. Xenophanes left his native Colophon *c.*545 BC when Ionia fell to the Persians and lived the rest of his life in exile, mostly in Sicily. A philosophical poet, he attacked HOMER and HESIOD for their treatment of the gods, and his theological ideas had far-reaching influence. He also wrote epics on the foundation of Colophon and Elea and was regarded by Plato as the founder of the ELEATIC SCHOOL. GS

Kirk, Raven, and Schofield (1983).

Xenophon (*c.*428–354 BC), Greek writer. Xenophon was born a member of the wealthy Athenian class of HIPPEIS. As such he was peripherally involved in the oligarchic revolution of 404 BC and gladly accepted the opportunity offered by CYRUS THE YOUNGER's mercenary army, in which he fought at CUNAXA. After the arrest of the generals Xenophon was one of those who took command of the Ten Thousand and led them back to Asiatic Greece. He preferred not to go home and, despite being regarded by the Spartans with suspicion, increased his experience of war by serving under the Spartan generals Thibron and Dercyllidas. When AGESILAUS arrived (396), close friendship ensued and he marched back to Greece with him (394), serving at Coronea. Athens had exiled him, so Agesilaus found him an estate near Olympia where he lived the life of the Peloponnesian landed gentleman for 20 years. In the disturbances after LEUCTRA he had to remove to Corinth where he spent the rest of his life.

Xenophon's literary activity is diverse, its chronology obscure. He had attended SOCRATES in youth and he perhaps began with a Socratic *Apology*, affecting to be Socrates' defence at his trial, followed by the *Memorabilia*, in which the element of personal reminiscence is debated. In the late 370s or early 360s he turned to his account of the Ten Thousand, the *Anabasis* or 'March Up-country', and to continuing THUCYDIDES down to the end of the Peloponnesian War (*Hellenica* 1–2.3.10). Where the *Cyropaedeia* ('Education of Cyrus') fits in is a puzzle; perhaps it came before the *Anabasis*. In 359 on the death of Agesilaus he wrote his encomium (*Agesilaus*) and in the 350s continued the history of Greece (*Hellenica*) down to MANTINEA (362). The *Poroi* ('Revenues') was his advice to Athens (perhaps taken by EUBULUS) on how to get over the near-bankruptcy to which imperialist policies had reduced her. Other works of uncertain date are the *Oeconomicus* ('On Estate Management'), *Symposium*, *Hipparchicus* ('Cavalry Commander'), *Cynegeticus* ('On Hunting'), and *On Horsemanship*.

Xenophon wrote with great charm and a deceptive freshness. His *Anabasis*, written long after the events it describes, is perhaps not the straightforward record it seems but, in large degree, a personal apologia, tinged with panhellenism, the creed he shared with Agesilaus. His philosophy was second-rate but the record of Socrates is a valuable corrective to PLATO who transformed Socrates' ideas. The *Cyropaedeia*, to Romans a most engrossing tale, is to us wearisome. It is the *Hellenica* that most attracts and distracts modern scholarship.

The *Hellenica* is essentially Xenophon's memoirs, not history. It reflects his prejudices and the restriction of his interests. Its omissions astonish but it is a splendid illumination of the 'best men' of the Peloponnese who looked to Sparta as the ideal society and the inspiration of the good life. For literary reasons it has outlived other, probably superior, histories of Greece. But through all his work Xenophon, poker-faced and oblique, shows himself the *kaloskagathos*, the gentleman.

See also HISTORIOGRAPHY, GREEK; HORSES. GLC

Anderson (1974); Cawkwell (1972b, 1979).

Xenophon of Ephesus (2nd century AD), Greek novelist. Xenophon was the author of a romance entitled *Ephesiaca* or *Anthea and Habrocomes* which survives in a five-book abridgement of the original 10 books. It contains all the traditional elements of the genre (*see* NOVEL, GREEK) but the characterization is poor and the work finds little favour with modern critics. GS

Perry (1967); Reardon (1989); Schmeling (1980).

Xerxes king of Persia, 486–465 BC. Xerxes inherited the expedition against Greece from his father DARIUS I, but extensive preparations, compounded by revolts in Egypt and Babylon, delayed its departure. Xerxes led the expedition in person, as Darius had intended to, but withdrew after defeat at SALAMIS, delegating command to MARDONIUS. Despite defeat and a Greek counter-offensive, his power was unshaken, though he abandoned further attempts at expansion. He built extensively at PERSEPOLIS, and was eventually assassinated in a palace intrigue and succeeded by his youngest son, ARTAXERXES I.

See also PERSIAN WARS. RB

Burn (1984); CAH IV; Cook (1983).

Z

Zaleucus (fl. *c.*660 BC), lawgiver of Locri. Zaleucus was admired for the law code which he gave to Italian Locri, reputedly the earliest written laws. Among attested measures, he is said to have fixed the penalty for each offence, though he also maintained the principle of an eye for an eye, and to have restricted the alienability of land. Protected by sanctions, his laws survived almost unchanged for 200 years. RB

Dunbabin (1948); Gagarin (1986).

Zama battle in 202 BC. At Zama, in Numidia, HANNIBAL was defeated by SCIPIO AFRICANUS. Scipio exploited the cavalry advantage which his ally MASSINISSA gave him by sweeping the Carthaginian cavalry from the battlefield. Outnumbered and with many of his troops of inferior quality, Hannibal nevertheless gave the Romans a hard struggle until the Roman cavalry returned and fell upon the Punic rear. The battle ended the Second PUNIC WAR. LPR

Lazenby (1978).

Zancle *see* MESSANA.

Zela battle in 47 BC. At Zela, in Asia Minor, CAESAR fought the Pontic king Pharnaces II. After a swift campaign, Caesar occupied high ground opposite the Pontic camp. He was amused to observe the phalanx of Pharnaces advancing across very rough terrain, and surprised to see it attempting to attack his position on the hill. Caesar's easy victory was reported in the famous dispatch '*veni, vidi, vici*' ('I came, I saw, I conquered').

See also BELLUM ALEXANDRINUM. LPR

Zeno of Citium (*c*.333–262 BC), Greek Stoic philosopher. Zeno came to Athens (*c*.311) and attended the lectures of Polemon, head of the ACADEMY, and of Diodorus Cronus, the Megarian philosopher, but he was subsequently converted to cynicism by CRATES OF THEBES. He developed his own philosophy through studying the works of ANTISTHENES. He taught in the STOA Poikilē (from which his school derived its name) a comprehensive tripartite system comprising logic and theory of knowledge (*Logicon*), physics (*Physicon*), and ethics (*Ethicon*). In physics he was strongly influenced by PERIPATETIC philosophy to which he accommodated aspects of HERACLITUS' philosophy. His logic and theory of knowledge reveal the influence of Antisthenes and Diodorus. In ethics he taught that the only true good is virtue, the only real evil, moral weakness.

See also CHRYSIPPUS; STOICS. JL

Long (1974).

Zeno of Elea (*c*.490–454 BC), Greek philosopher. Zeno's book was written in his youth to defend PARMENIDES' arguments and to reduce his opponents' hypotheses to absurdity by deducing contradictory consequences from them. Hence Aristotle (fr. 65) calls him the 'inventor of dialectic'. Belief in plurality and motion is vigorously attacked in this way. Zeno's paradoxes were not conceived to attack a special physical or metaphysical theory (e.g. Pythagoreanism), as some scholars have claimed, but rather to be of general validity against popular beliefs and thereby indirectly support the deductions of Parmenides.

See also ELEATIC 'SCHOOL'. JL

Kirk, Raven, and Schofield (1983); Lee (1936).

Zenobia (d. after AD 272), queen of Palmyra, AD 266/7–72. Septimia Zenobia, widow of ODAENATHUS of PALMYRA, ruled Syria in the name of her young son, Vaballathus. She added Egypt (269) and Cappadocia and Galatia (269–70) to her empire, but failed to take Bithynia and thus reach Chalcedon. Zenobia discarded her technical subordination to Rome (271), so AURELIAN marched against her, finally capturing Palmyra (272). Zenobia walked in golden chains at Aurelian's subsequent triumph (274), but was then granted a pension. RJB

Grant (1979); Parker (1958).

Zenodotus (b. *c*.325 BC), Greek scholar. Zenodotus of Ephesus was a pupil of PHILETAS of Cos before being summoned to Alexandria *c*.284 by PTOLEMY II and appointed tutor to the royal family and the first librarian. He undertook the formidable task of collecting and classifying texts for the LIBRARY, he compiled a Homeric glossary, and he made the first critical editions of the works of Homer, Hesiod, and Pindar.

GS

Pfeiffer (1968).

Zeugitae Athenian citizen class. The Zeugitae ('yoke-men') were the third of SOLON's four property classes, and the lowest with a financial qualification, namely 200 measures of produce; they are generally supposed to have been equivalent to the hoplites in the pre-Solonian division of classes. They were initially confined to the ordinary magistracies, but became eligible for the archonship from 457/6 BC.

See also HIPPEIS; PENTACOSIOMEDIMNI; THETES.   RB

Rhodes (1981).

Zeus father of the Greek gods. Zeus was first, and universally, the sky god. By extension he was the weather god in charge of all natural phenomena such as storms, thunder, and lightning. As the cloud gatherer he lived on the mountain tops, and specifically on the highest of them all, Olympus, where he ruled over his extended family of gods and goddesses. Zeus was the father of men as well as gods and was honoured as the guardian of political liberty, of law and order, oaths, and moral behaviour. The justice that he dispensed was impartial, supreme, and inexorable. In art he was bearded and regal. His most famous image was the chryselephantine statue by PHEIDIAS at Olympia.

See also DIVINATION; HERA; OLYMPIA.   GS

Guthrie (1950); Lloyd-Jones (1971).

Zeuxis (fl. 430–390 BC), Greek painter. Zeuxis was born at Heraclea in south Italy and moved to Athens as a young man *c*.430 BC. His painting of Eros in the temple of Aphrodite is mentioned by ARISTOPHANES in the *Acharnians* (425 BC). Other works included a Helen, a Penelope, and a Centaur family. He spent the last decade of the century at the court of ARCHELAUS in Macedon where he decorated the royal palace. QUINTILIAN said that he discovered the principles of light and shade, and the elder PLINY that he 'entered the door that was opened by APOLLODORUS and stole his art'.

See also PAINTING, GREEK.   GS

Robertson (1975).

Zoology The origin of life, and of man in particular, engaged the interest of the Greeks from the earliest times. The belief that man and other animals came into being from the earth is frequently encountered in Greek mythology. The development of Ionian natural philosophy, however, introduced rational attitudes into accounts of the origin of life at an early date when ANAXIMANDER put forward the theory that the first living creatures, enclosed in prickly membranes, arose from primeval moisture evaporated by the sun. In the doxographical evidence recording Anaximander's beliefs scholars have found foreshadowings of the theories of adaptation to environment, the survival of the fittest, and the evolution of species. But, although his insight that the first living creatures must have had initially some protection to take the place of that normally afforded by the parent is impressively imaginative, there is no justification for the claim that his theories anticipate modern evolutionary doctrine.

Similar anticipations have been found in EMPEDOCLES' thought, but although one may justifiably find expressed here a theory of the survival of the fittest, any evolutionary thought is the mechanical outcome of his general physical system. There is no direct line of genetic evolution of more specialized organisms from primitive prototypes through the mechanism of heredity. A more reliable anticipation of Darwin may be seen in the Hippocratic treatise *De Genitura/De Natura Pueri/De Morbis* 4 which, doubtless under the influence of DEMOCRITUS, sets forth a theory of pangenesis remarkably like his *Variations of Animals and Plants under Domestication*. It may be said with some justification that with the exception of this work ancient zoology begins and ends with ARISTOTLE. The most important of his zoological treatises are the *History of Animals* (nine books), *On the Generation of Animals* (five books), *On the Parts of Animals* (four books), *On the Motion of Animals* (one book), and *On the Progression of Animals* (one book). These works, which present a great wealth of observation (more than 500 species of animals are mentioned), exactness of description, careful ordering, and classification, laid the foundations of systematic zoology for the next two thousand years.   JL

Sarton (1970).

Zosimus (d. after AD 498), historian of Rome. Zosimus, a Greek historian, perhaps the sophist Zosimus of Gaza or the sophist Zosimus of Ascalon, wrote a history (*Historia Nova*) of the Roman Empire from Augustus to 410, completed after 498. It began with a brief survey of the years to 270, and was fuller thereafter, drawing upon EUNAPIUS and Olympiodorus (whose history ran from AD 407 to 425). He was a pagan: his writing is anti-Christian, and favourable to JULIAN.   RJB

Buchanan and Davis (1967); Bury (1958); Ridley (1982).

Bibliography

Ackrill, J.L. (1981). *Aristotle the Philosopher*. Oxford: Oxford University Press.

Adams, W.Y. (1977). *Nubia. Corridor to Africa*. London: Allen Lane.

Adcock, F.E. (1940). *The Roman Art of War*. Cambridge, Mass.: Harvard University Press.

—— (1957). *The Greek and Macedonian Art of War*. Berkeley and Los Angeles: University of California Press.

—— (1966). *Marcus Crassus, Millionaire*. Cambridge: Heffer.

Adcock, F.E., and Mosley, D.J. (1975). *Diplomacy in Ancient Greece*. London: Thames & Hudson.

Ahl, F.M. (1976). *Lucan: An Introduction*. Ithaca, NY: Cornell University Press.

Akurgal, E. (1978). *Ancient Civilizations and Ruins of Turkey from Prehistoric Times until the End of the Roman Empire*. 4th edn. Istanbul: Haset Kitabevi.

Alexander, J.A. (1963). *Potidaea, its History and Remains*. Athens, Ga.: University of Georgia Press.

Alföldi, A. (1965). *Early Rome and the Latins*. Ann Arbor: University of Michigan Press.

Alföldy, G. (1974). *Noricum*. London: Routledge & Kegan Paul.

Allen, R.E. (1983). *The Attalid Kingdom: A Constitutional History*. Oxford: Clarendon Press.

Allen, W.S. (1978). *Vox Latina*. 2nd edn. Cambridge: Cambridge University Press.

—— (1987). *Vox Graeca: The Pronunciation of Classical Greek*. 3rd edn. Cambridge: Cambridge University Press.

Alty, J.H.M. (1982). 'Dorians and Ionians', *Journal of Hellenic Studies*, 102. 1–14.

Ameling, W. (1983). *Herodes Atticus.* Hildesheim, Zürich, New York: Georg Olms.

Amit, M. (1973). *Great and Small Poleis.* Brussels: Latomus.

Anderson, J.K. (1961). *Ancient Greek Horsemanship.* Berkeley and Los Angeles: University of California Press.

—— (1970). *Military Theory and Practice in the Age of Xenophon.* Berkeley and Los Angeles: University of California Press.

—— (1974). *Xenophon.* London: Duckworth.

Anderson, W.D. (1966). *Ethos and Education in Greek Music: The Evidence of Poetry and Philosophy.* Cambridge, Mass.: Harvard University Press.

Andrewes, A. (1956). *The Greek Tyrants.* London: Hutchinson.

—— (1966). 'The Government of Classical Sparta' in Badian (1966a).

—— (1990). 'Argive *Perioikoi*' in Craik (1990).

Andronikos, M. (1974). *Vergina: The Royal Tombs and the Ancient City.* Athens: Ekdotike Athenon.

Arias, P.E., and Hirmer, M. (1962). *A History of Greek Vase Painting.* London: Thames & Hudson.

Armstrong, A.H. (ed.) (1967). *The Cambridge History of Later Greek and Early Medieval Philosophy.* Cambridge: Cambridge University Press.

Arnheim, M.T.W. (1977). *Aristocracy in Greek Society.* London: Thames & Hudson.

Arthur, P. (1991). *Romans in Northern Campania.* London: British School at Rome.

Ashby, T. (1935). *The Aqueducts of Ancient Rome.* Oxford: Clarendon Press.

Ashmole, B. (1972). *Architect and Sculptor in Classical Greece.* London: Phaidon.

Astin, A.E. (1958). *The Lex Annalis before Sulla.* Brussels: Collection Latomus 32.

—— (1967). *Scipio Aemilianus.* Oxford: Clarendon Press.

—— (1978). *Cato the Censor.* Oxford: Clarendon Press.

Atkinson, J.A. (1980). *A Commentary on Q. Curtius Rufus'* Historiae Alexandri Magni. Amsterdam: J.C. Gieben.

Aubert Semmler, M.E. (1988). 'Spain' in Moscati (1988).

Auguet, R. (1972). *Cruelty and Civilization: The Roman Games.* London: Allen & Unwin.

Aujac, G. (1975). *La Géographie dans le monde antique.* Paris: Presses Universitaires de France.

Austin, M.M. (1970). *Greece and Egypt in the Archaic Age.* Cambridge: Cambridge Philological Society.

Avi-Yonah, M. (1984). *The Jews under Roman and Byzantine Rule.*

A Political History of Palestine from the Bar Kokhba War to the Arab Conquest. Jerusalem: Magnes Press, Hebrew University.

Badian, E. (1958). *Foreign Clientelae, 264–70 BC*. Oxford: Clarendon Press.

—— (1961). 'Harpalus', *Journal of Hellenic Studies*, 81. 16–43.

—— (1964). *Studies in Greek and Roman History*. Oxford: Blackwell.

—— (ed.) (1966a). *Ancient Society and Institutions: Studies Presented to Victor Ehrenberg on his 75th Birthday*. Oxford: Blackwell.

—— (1966b). 'The Early Historians' in Dorey (1966).

—— (1970a). *Lucius Sulla, the Deadly Reformer*. Sydney: Sydney University Press.

—— (1970b). *Titus Quinctius Flamininus: Philhellenism and Realpolitik*. Cincinnati: Cincinnati University Press.

—— (1972a). *Publicans and Sinners*. Oxford: Blackwell.

—— (1972b). 'Tiberius Gracchus and the Beginning of the Roman Revolution', *Aufsteig und Niedergang der Römischen Welt*, 1.i.668–731.

Bagnall, R.S. (1976). *The Administration of the Ptolemaic Possessions outside Egypt*. Leiden: E.J. Brill.

Bailey, C. (1928). *The Greek Atomists and Epicurus*. Oxford: Clarendon Press.

Balsdon, J.P.V.D. (1962). *Roman Women*. London: Bodley Head.

Barber, G.L. (1935). *The Historian Ephorus*. Cambridge: Cambridge University Press.

Barker, A. (1984). *Greek Musical Writings*, I: *The Musician and his Art*. Cambridge: Cambridge University Press.

—— (1989). *Greek Musical Writings*, II: *Harmonic and Acoustic Theory*. Cambridge: Cambridge University Press.

Barker, P. (1981). *The Armies and Enemies of Imperial Rome*. 4th edn. Worthing: Wargames Research Group.

Bar-Kochva, B. (1976). *The Seleucid Army. Organization and Tactics in the Great Campaigns*. Cambridge: Cambridge University Press.

Barnes, T.D. (1982). *Constantine and Eusebius*. Cambridge, Mass.: Harvard University Press.

Barrett, A.A. (1989). *Caligula, the Corruption of Power*. London: Batsford.

Bartsch, S. (1989). *Decoding the Ancient Novel: The Reader and the Role of Description in Heliodorus and Achilles Tatius*. Princeton, NJ: Princeton University Press.

Bean, G.E. (1978). *Lycian Turkey*. London: Benn.

—— (1979a). *Aegean Turkey*. 2nd edn. London: Benn.

—— (1979b). *Turkey's Southern Shore*. 2nd edn. London: Benn.

—— (1980). *Turkey beyond the Maeander*. 2nd edn. London: Benn.

Beard, M. (1980). 'The Sexual Status of the Vestal Virgins', *Journal of Roman Studies*, 70. 12–27.

Beard, M., and Crawford, M. (1985). *Rome in the Late Republic.* London: Duckworth.

Beard, M., and North, J.A. (eds.) (1990). *Pagan Priests.* London: Duckworth.

Beare, W. (1964). *The Roman Stage.* 3rd edn. London: Methuen.

Bennett, H. (1923). *Cinna and his Times.* Chicago: Chicago University Press.

Beresford Ellis, P. (1990). *The Celtic Empire.* London: Guild.

Bernstein, A.E. (1978). *Tiberius Sempronius Gracchus: Tradition and Apostasy.* Ithaca, NY: Cornell University Press.

Berthold, R.M. (1984). *Rhodes in the Hellenistic Age.* Ithaca, NY: Cornell University Press.

Berve, H. (1956). *Dion.* Mainz: Abhandlungen der Mainzer Akademie, 10.

—— (1967). *Die Tyrannis bei den Griechen.* 2 vols. Munich: C.A. Beck.

Berve, H., and Gruben, G. (1963). *Greek Temples, Theatres and Shrines.* London: Thames & Hudson.

Best, J.G.P. (1969). *Thracian Peltasts and their Influence on Greek Warfare.* Groningen: Wolters-Noordhoff.

Bickerman, E. (1988). *The Jews in the Greek Age.* Cambridge, Mass.: Harvard University Press.

Bieber, M. (1954). *The Sculpture of the Hellenistic Age.* New York: Columbia University Press.

—— (1961). *History of the Greek and Roman Theater.* 2nd edn. Princeton, NJ: Princeton University Press.

—— (1977). *Ancient Copies. Contributions to the History of Greek and Roman Art.* New York: New York University Press.

Billows, R.A. (1990). *Antigonus the One-Eyed and the Creation of the Hellenistic State.* Berkeley and Los Angeles: University of California Press.

Binns, J.W. (ed.) (1974). *Latin Literature of the Fourth Century.* London: Routledge & Kegan Paul.

Birley, A.R. (1976). *Lives of the Later Caesars.* Harmondsworth: Penguin.

—— (1977). *The Roman Emperor Hadrian.* Northumberland: Barcombe Publications.

—— (1987). *Marcus Aurelius.* New edn. London: Eyre & Spottiswoode.

—— (1988). *Septimius Severus. The African Emperor.* New edn. London: Eyre & Spottiswoode.

Bishop, M.C., and Coulston, J.C.N. (1993). *Roman Military Equipment.* London: Batsford.

Blank, D.L. (1982). *Ancient Philosophy and Grammar: The Syntax of Apollonius Dyscolus.* Chico, CA: Scholars Press.

Blockley, R.C. (1983). *The Fragmentary Classicising Historians of the Later Roman Empire.* Vol. 2. Liverpool: Francis Cairns.

Boardman, J. (1970). *Greek Gems and Finger Rings*. London: Thames & Hudson.

—— (1974). *Athenian Black Figure Vases*. London: Thames & Hudson.

—— (1975). *Athenian Red Figure Vases: The Archaic Period*. London: Thames & Hudson.

—— (1978). *Greek Sculpture: The Archaic Period*. London: Thames & Hudson.

—— (1980). *The Greeks Overseas*. 3rd edn. London: Thames & Hudson.

—— (1985). *Greek Sculpture: The Classical Period*. London: Thames & Hudson.

—— (1989). *Athenian Red Figure Vases: The Classical Period*. London: Thames & Hudson.

Boardman, J., and Finn, D. (1985). *The Parthenon and its Sculptures*. London: Thames & Hudson.

Boardman, J., Griffin, J., and Murray, O. (eds.) (1986). *The Oxford History of the Roman World*. Oxford: Oxford University Press.

Boardman, J., and Vaphopoulou-Richardson, C.E. (eds.) (1986). *Chios: A Conference at the Homereion in Chios 1984*. Oxford: Clarendon Press.

Boëthius, A. (1960). *The Golden House of Nero*. Ann Arbor: University of Michigan Press.

—— (1978). *Etruscan and Early Roman Architecture*. 2nd edn. Harmondsworth: Penguin.

Bolton, J.D.P. (1962). *Aristeas of Proconnesus*. Oxford: Clarendon Press.

Bonfante, G., and Bonfante, L. (1983). *The Etruscan Language: An Introduction*. Manchester: Manchester University Press.

Bonfante, L. (ed.) (1986). *Etruscan Life and Afterlife: A Handbook of Etruscan Studies*. Warminster: Aris & Phillips.

—— (1990). *Etruscan*. London: British Museum.

Bonner, R.J., and Smith, G. (1930–8). *The Administration of Justice from Homer to Aristotle*. 2 vols. Chicago: University of Chicago Press.

Bonner, S.F. (1977). *Education in Ancient Rome: From the Elder Cato to the Younger Pliny*. London: Methuen.

Bosworth, A.B. (1972). 'Asinius Pollio and Augustus', *Historia*, 21. 441–73.

—— (1980). *A Historical Commentary on Arrian's* History of Alexander. Vol. 1. Oxford: Clarendon Press.

—— (1988a). *Conquest and Empire. The Reign of Alexander the Great*. Cambridge: Cambridge University Press.

—— (1988b). *From Arrian to Alexander. Studies in Historical Interpretation*. Oxford: Clarendon Press.

Bourriot, F. (1976). *Recherches sur la nature du génos: étude d'histoire sociale Athénienne – périodes archaïque et classique.* Lille: Université Lille III.

Bowersock, G.W. (1969). *Greek Sophists in the Roman Empire.* Oxford: Clarendon Press.

—— (1978). *Julian the Apostate.* London: Duckworth.

—— (1983). *Roman Arabia.* Cambridge, Mass.: Harvard University Press.

Bowman, A.K. (1986). *Egypt after the Pharaohs, 332 BC–AD 642.* London: British Museum.

Bowra, C.M. (1945). *From Virgil to Milton.* London: Macmillan.

—— (1961). *Greek Lyric Poetry from Alcman to Simonides.* 2nd edn. Oxford: Clarendon Press.

—— (1964). *Pindar.* Oxford: Clarendon Press.

Bradley, K.R. (1987). *Slaves and Masters in the Roman Empire: A Study in Social Control.* New York, Oxford: Oxford University Press.

—— (1989). *Slavery and Rebellion in the Roman World, 140–70 BC.* London: Batsford.

Bramble, J. (1974). *Persius and the Programmatic Satire.* Cambridge: Cambridge University Press.

Branham, B.B. (1989). *Unruly Excellence: Lucian and the Comedy of Traditions.* Cambridge, Mass.: Harvard University Press.

Brauer, G.C. (1986). *Taras. Its History and Coinage.* New Rochelle, NY: A.D. Caratzas.

Braund, D. (1984). *Rome and the Friendly King. The Character of Client Kingship.* London: Croom Helm.

Braund, S.H. (ed.) (1989). *Satire and Society in Ancient Rome.* Exeter: University of Exeter.

Breeze, D.J., and Dobson, B. (1987). *Hadrian's Wall.* 3rd edn. Harmondsworth: Penguin.

Bremmer, J.N., and Horsfall, N.M. (1987). *Roman Myth and Mythography.* London: Institute of Classical Studies.

Brink, C.O. (1971). *Horace on Poetry: The 'Ars Poetica'.* Cambridge: Cambridge University Press.

Briscoe, J. (1973). *A Commentary on Livy, Books XXXI–XXXIII.* Oxford: Clarendon Press.

Brock, M.D. (1911). *Studies in Fronto and his Age.* Cambridge: Cambridge University Press.

Broughton, T.R.S. (1951–2). *The Magistrates of the Roman Republic.* 2 vols. New York: American Philological Association.

Brown, P.R.L. (1967). *Augustine of Hippo.* London: Faber & Faber.

—— (1972). *Religion and Society in the Age of St Augustine.* London: Faber & Faber.

Brown, T.S. (1949). *Onesicritus. A Study in Hellenistic Historiography.* Berkeley and Los Angeles: University of California Press.

—— (1958). *Timaeus of Tauromenium*. Berkeley and Los Angeles: University of California Press.

Browning, I. (1973). *Petra*. London: Chatto & Windus.

—— (1979). *Palmyra*. London: Chatto & Windus.

Browning, R. (1975). *The Emperor Julian*. London: Weidenfeld & Nicolson.

—— (1983). *Medieval and Modern Greek*. 2nd edn. Cambridge: Cambridge University Press.

Bruce, F.F. (1977). *Paul: Apostle of the Free Spirit*. Exeter: Paternoster.

Bruce, I.A.F. (1967). *An Historical Commentary on the* Hellenica Oxyrhynchia. Cambridge: Cambridge University Press.

Brun, P. (1983). *Eisphora – Syntaxis – Stratiotika*. Paris: Les Belles Lettres.

Bruno, V.J. (1977). *Form and Colour in Greek Painting*. London: Thames & Hudson.

Brunt, P.A. (1966). 'Athenian Settlements Abroad in the Fifth Century BC' in Badian (1966a).

—— (1971a). *Italian Manpower, 225 BC–AD 14*. Oxford: Clarendon Press.

—— (1971b). *Social Conflicts in the Roman Republic*. London: Chatto & Windus.

—— (1982). '*Nobilitas* and *Novitas*', *Journal of Roman Studies*, 72. 1–17.

—— (1988). *The Fall of the Roman Republic and Related Essays*. Oxford: Clarendon Press.

Brunt, P.A., and Moore, J.M. (eds.) (1967). *Res Gestae Divi Augusti: The Achievements of the Divine Augustus*. Oxford: Clarendon Press.

Bruun, C. (1991). *The Water Supply of Ancient Rome: A Study of Roman Imperial Administration*. Helsinki: Societas Scientiarum Fennica.

Buchanan, J.J., and Davis, H.T. (1967). *Zosimus, Historia Nova, The Decline of Rome*. San Antonio, Tex.: Trinity University Press.

Buck, C.D. (1955). *Greek Dialects*. Chicago: University of Chicago Press.

Buck, R.J. (1979). *A History of Boeotia*. Edmonton: University of Alberta Press.

Buckland, W.W. (1963). *A Textbook of Roman Law from Augustus to Justinian*. 3rd edn. Rev. P. Stein. Cambridge: Cambridge University Press.

Buckler, J. (1980). *The Theban Hegemony 371–362 BC*. Cambridge, Mass.: Harvard University Press.

Bugh, G.R. (1988). *The Horsemen of Athens*. Princeton, NJ: Princeton University Press.

Bunbury, E.H. (1883). *A History of Ancient Geography*. 2nd edn. London: John Murray.

Bundgaard, J.A. (1957). *Mnesicles*. Copenhagen: Gyldendal.

Bundy, E.L. (1962). *Studia Pindarica*. Berkeley and Los Angeles: University of California Press.

Burck, E. (ed.) (1979). *Das römische Epos, Grundriss der Literaturgeschichte nach Gattungen*. Darmstadt: Wissenschaftliche Buchgesellschaft.

Burkert, W. (1976). 'Das hunderttorige Theben und die Datierung der Ilias', *Wiener Studien*, n.s. 10, 5–21.

—— (1983). *Homo Necans. The Anthropology of Ancient Greek Sacrificial Ritual and Myth*. Berkeley and Los Angeles: University of California Press.

—— (1985). *Greek Religion: Archaic and Classical*. Oxford: Blackwell.

—— (1987). *Ancient Mystery Cults*. Cambridge, Mass.: Harvard University Press.

Burn, A.R. (1960). *The Lyric Age of Greece*. London: Edward Arnold.

—— (1984). *Persia and the Greeks. The Defence of the West c.546–478 BC*. 2nd edn. London: Duckworth.

Burn, L. (1987). *The Meidias Painter*. Oxford: Clarendon Press.

Burnett, A. (1987). *Coinage in the Roman World*. London: Seaby.

Burney, C., and Lang, D.M. (1971). *The Peoples of the Hills. Ancient Ararat and Caucasus*. London: Weidenfeld & Nicolson.

Bury, J.B. (1958). *History of the Later Roman Empire from the Death of Theodosius I to the Death of Justinian*. 2 vols. New edn. New York: Dover Publications.

Bury, J.B., and Meiggs, R. (1975). *A History of Greece*. 4th edn. London: Macmillan.

CAH = *Cambridge Ancient History*. 2nd edn. Ed. F.W. Walbank, A.E. Astin, M.W. Frederiksen, R.M. Ogilvie. Vols. III.1 (1982), III.2 (1991), III.3, IV (1988), V (1992), VII.1 (1984), VII.2 (1989), VIII (1989). 1st edn. Ed. S.A. Cook, F.E. Adcock, M.P. Charlesworth. Vols. X (1934), XI (1936). Cambridge: Cambridge University Press.

Cairns, F. (1979). *Tibullus: A Hellenistic Poet at Rome*. Cambridge: Cambridge University Press.

—— (1989). *Virgil's Augustan Epic*. Cambridge: Cambridge University Press.

Calder, W.M., and Stern, J. (eds.) (1970). *Pindaros und Bakchylides*. Darmstadt: Wissenschaftliche Buchgesellschaft.

Cameron, Alan (1970). *Claudian. Poetry and Propaganda at the Court of Honorius*. Oxford: Clarendon Press.

—— (1976). *Circus Factions. Blues and Greens at Rome and Byzantium*. Oxford: Clarendon Press.

—— (1993). *The Greek Anthology from Meleager to Planudes*. Oxford: Clarendon Press.

Camps, W.A. (1969). *An Introduction to Virgil's* Aeneid. Oxford: Oxford University Press.

Capuis, L. (1968). *Alkamenes*. Florence: Olschki.

Carney, T.F. (1970). *A Biography of Gaius Marius*. 2nd edn. Chicago: Argonaut.

Carson, R.A.G. (1990). *Coins of the Roman Empire*. London, New York: Routledge.

Carter, J.M. (1970). *The Battle of Actium: The Rise and Triumph of Augustus Caesar*. London: Hamish Hamilton.

Cartledge, P.A. (1979). *Sparta and Lakonia*. London: Routledge & Kegan Paul.

—— (1985). 'Rebels and *Sambos* in Classical Greece: A Comparative View' in Cartledge and Harvey (1985).

—— (1987). *Agesilaus*. London: Duckworth.

—— (1990). *Aristophanes and his Theatre of the Absurd*. Bristol: Bristol Classical Press.

Cartledge, P.A., and Harvey, F.D. (eds.) (1985). *Crux: Essays in Greek History Presented to G.E.M. De Ste Croix on his 75th Birthday*. London: Duckworth.

Cartledge, P.A., Millett, P., and Todd, S. (eds.) (1990). *Nomos: Essays in Athenian Law, Politics and Society*. Cambridge: Cambridge University Press.

Cartledge, P.A., and Spawforth, A. (1989). *Hellenistic and Roman Sparta: A Tale of Two Cities*. London: Routledge.

Cary, M. (1949). *The Geographic Background of Greek and Roman History*. Oxford: Clarendon Press.

Cary, M., and Warmington, E.H. (1929). *The Ancient Explorers*. London: Methuen.

Casson, L. (1971). *Ships and Seamanship in the Ancient World*. Princeton, NJ: Princeton University Press.

—— (1974). *Travel in the Ancient World*. London: Allen & Unwin.

—— (1991). *The Ancient Mariners: Seafarers and Seafighters of the Mediterranean in Ancient Times*. 2nd edn. Princeton, NJ: Princeton University Press.

Casson, S. (1937). *Ancient Cyprus*. London: Methuen.

Caven, B. (1980). *The Punic Wars*. London: Weidenfeld & Nicolson.

—— (1990). *Dionysius I, War-Lord of Sicily*. New Haven, Conn.: Yale University Press.

Cawkwell, G.L. (1963). 'Eubulus', *Journal of Hellenic Studies*, 83. 47–67.

—— (1972a). 'Epaminondas and Thebes', *Classical Quarterly*, 22. 254–78.

—— (1972b). Introduction to *Xenophon: The Persian Expedition*. Harmondsworth: Penguin.

—— (1978). *Philip of Macedon.* London: Faber & Faber.

—— (1979). Introduction to *Xenophon: A History of My Time.* Harmondsworth: Penguin.

—— (1981). 'Philip and the Amphictyonic League' in Hatzopoulos and Louthopoulos (1981).

Chadwick, H. (1966). *Early Christian Thought and the Classical Tradition.* Oxford: Clarendon Press.

—— (1976). *Priscillian of Avila.* Oxford: Clarendon Press.

—— (1986a). *Augustine.* Oxford: Oxford University Press.

—— (1986b). *The Early Church.* 2nd edn. Harmondsworth: Penguin.

Chadwick, N. (1970). *The Celts.* Harmondsworth: Penguin.

Chamoux, F. (1953). *Cyrène sous la monarchie des Battiades.* Paris: de Boccard.

Charbonneaux, J. (1958). *Les Bronzes grecs.* Paris: Presses Universitaires de France.

Charbonneaux, J., Martin, R., and Villard, F. (1971). *Archaic Greek Art.* London: Thames & Hudson.

—— (1973). *Classical Greek Art: 480–330 BC.* London: Thames & Hudson.

Charles-Picard, G., and Charles-Picard, C. (1961). *Daily Life in Carthage in the Time of Hannibal.* London: Allen & Unwin.

Charleston, R.J. (1955). *Roman Pottery.* London: Faber & Faber.

Chevallier, R. (1976). *Roman Roads.* London: Batsford.

Chilver, G.E.F. (1941). *Cisalpine Gaul.* Oxford: Clarendon Press.

Clarke, M.L. (1971). *Higher Education in the Ancient World.* London: Routledge & Kegan Paul.

—— (1981). *The Noblest Roman: Marcus Brutus and his Reputation.* London: Thames & Hudson.

Clay, J.S. (1989). *The Politics of Olympus. Form and Meaning in the Major Homeric Hymns.* Princeton, NJ: Princeton University Press.

Cloché, P. (1952). *Thèbes de Béotie.* Namur: Bibliothèque de la Faculté de Philosophie et Lettres de Namur, Fasc. 13.

Coarelli, F. (ed.) (1974). *Etruscan Cities.* London: Cassell.

Coffey, M. (1989). *Roman Satire.* 2nd edn. Bristol: Bristol Classical Press.

Cohen, E.E. (1973). *Ancient Athenian Maritime Courts.* Princeton, NJ: Princeton University Press.

Cohen, G.M. (1978). *The Seleucid Colonies. Studies in Founding, Administration and Organization.* Wiesbaden: Franz Steiner.

Coldstream, J.N. (1968). *Greek Geometric Pottery: A Survey of Ten Local Styles and their Chronology.* London: Methuen.

—— (1977). *Geometric Greece.* London: Ernest Benn.

Colledge, M.A.R. (1967). *The Parthians.* London: Thames & Hudson.

—— (1976). *The Art of Palmyra.* London: Thames & Hudson.

Collingwood, R.G., and Myres, J.N.L. (1937). *Roman Britain and the English Settlements*. 2nd edn. Oxford: Clarendon Press.

Collingwood Bruce, J. (1978). *Handbook to the Roman Wall*. New edn. Rev. C. Daniels. Newcastle: Harold Hill & Son.

Comotti, G. (1989). *Music in Greek and Roman Culture*. Baltimore and London: Johns Hopkins University Press.

Conacher, D.J. (1968). *Euripidean Drama: Myth, Theme, and Structure*. Toronto: Toronto University Press.

Connolly, P. (1975). *The Roman Army*. London: Macdonald.

—— (1981). *Greece and Rome at War*. London: Macdonald.

Connor, W.R. (1968). *Theopompus and Fifth Century Athens*. Washington, DC: Center for Hellenic Studies.

—— (1984). *Thucydides*. Princeton, NJ: Princeton University Press.

Cook, J.M. (1983). *The Persian Empire*. London: Dent.

Cook, R.M. (1972). *Greek Painted Pottery*. 2nd edn. London: Methuen.

Corbett, P.E. (1930). *The Roman Law of Marriage*. Oxford: Clarendon Press.

Cornell, T.J. (1986). 'The Formation of the Historical Tradition of Early Rome' in Moxon, Smart, and Woodman (1986).

Cornell, T.J., and Matthews, J.F. (1982). *Atlas of the Roman World*. Oxford: Phaidon.

Costa, C.D.N. (ed.) (1974). *Seneca*. London: Routledge & Kegan Paul.

Cottrell, L. (1960). *Enemy of Rome*. London: Evans Brothers.

Coulton, J.J. (1976). *The Architectural Development of the Greek Stoa*. Oxford: Clarendon Press.

—— (1977). *Greek Architects at Work*. London: Elek.

Cracknell, D.G. (1964). *Law Students' Companion, no.4: Roman Law*. London: Butterworth.

Craik, E.M. (1980). *The Dorian Aegean*. London: Routledge.

—— (ed.) (1990). *'Owls to Athens': Essays on Classical Subjects for Sir Kenneth Dover*. Oxford: Clarendon Press.

Crawford, M.H. (1978). *The Roman Republic*. London: Fontana.

—— (ed.) (1983). *Sources for Ancient History*. Cambridge: Cambridge University Press.

—— (1985). *Coinage and Money under the Roman Republic*. London: Methuen.

Crees, J.H.E. (1965). *The Reign of the Emperor Probus*. Rome: Studia Historica 13.

Crombie, I.M. (1962–3). *An Examination of Plato's Doctrines*. 2 vols. London: Routledge & Kegan Paul.

Crook, J.A. (1955). *Concilium Principis, Imperial Councils and Councillors from Augustus to Diocletian*. Cambridge: Cambridge University Press.

—— (1967). *Life and Law of Rome*. London: Thames & Hudson.

Cross, F.L. (ed.) (1974). *Oxford Dictionary of the Christian Church*. 2nd edn. London: Oxford University Press.

Cunliffe, B. (1971). *Fishbourne: A Roman Palace and its Garden*. London: Thames & Hudson.

—— (1988). *Greeks, Romans and Barbarians. Spheres of Interaction*. London: Batsford.

Curchin, L.A. (1991). *Roman Spain: Conquest and Assimilation*. London, New York: Routledge.

Dandamaev, M.A. (1989). *A Political History of the Achaemenid Empire*. Leiden: E.J. Brill.

Danov, C.M. (1976). *Altthrakien*. Berlin: de Gruyter.

D'Arms, J.H. (1970). *Romans on the Bay of Naples. A Social and Cultural Study of the Villas and their Owners from 150 BC to AD 400*. Cambridge, Mass.: Harvard University Press.

—— (1981). *Commerce and Social Standing in Ancient Rome*. Cambridge, Mass.: Harvard University Press.

Davies, J.K. (1967). 'Demosthenes on Liturgies: A Note', *Journal of Hellenic Studies*, 87. 33–40.

—— (1971). *Athenian Propertied Families 600–300 BC*. Oxford: Clarendon Press.

Davies, M. (1989). *The Epic Cycle*. Bristol: Bristol Classical Press.

Davies, W.D., and Finkelstein, L. (eds.) (1989). *Cambridge History of Judaism*. Vol. 2: *The Hellenistic Age*. Cambridge: Cambridge University Press.

Debevoise, N.C. (1938). *A Political History of Parthia*. Chicago: University of Chicago Press.

de Blois, L. (1976). *The Policy of the Emperor Gallienus*. Leiden: E.J. Brill.

de Lange, N.R.M. (1976). *Origen and the Jews: Studies in Jewish–Christian Relations in Third-century Palestine*. Cambridge: Cambridge University Press.

Delano-Smith, C. (1979). *Western Mediterranean Geography*. London: Academic Press.

den Boer, W. (1972). *Some Minor Roman Historians*. Leiden: E.J. Brill.

Der Nersessian, S. (1969). *The Armenians*. London: Thames & Hudson.

Dessau, H. (1889). 'Über Zeit und Persönlichkeit der Scriptores Historiae Augustae', *Hermes*, 24. 337–92.

De Ste Croix, G.E.M. (1953). 'Demosthenes' *TIMHMA* and the Athenian Eisphora in the Fourth Century BC', *Classica et Mediaevalia*, 14. 30–70.

—— (1972). *The Origins of the Peloponnesian War*. London: Duckworth.

—— (1981). *The Class Struggle in the Ancient Greek World*. London: Duckworth.

Develin, R. (1989). *Athenian Officials 684–321 BC*. Cambridge: Cambridge University Press.

Dewald, C., and Marincola, J. (1987). *Herodotus and the Invention of History*. Buffalo: S.U.N.Y. [*Arethusa*, vol. 20.]

Dicks, D.R. (1970). *Early Greek Astronomy to Aristotle*. London: Thames & Hudson.

Dilke, O.A.W. (1962). 'The Roman Surveyors', *Greece and Rome*, 9. 170ff.

—— (1985). *Greek and Roman Maps*. London: Thames & Hudson.

Dillon, J. (1977). *The Middle Platonists*. London: Duckworth.

Dixon, S. (1988). *The Roman Mother*. London: Croom Helm.

Dodds, E.R. (1951). *The Greeks and the Irrational*. Berkeley and Los Angeles: University of California Press.

Donlan, W. (1980). *The Aristocratic Ideal in Ancient Greece*. Lawrence, Kans.: Coronado Press.

Dorey, T.A. (ed.) (1965). *Cicero*. London: Routledge & Kegan Paul.

—— (ed.) (1966). *Latin Historians*. London: Routledge & Kegan Paul.

—— (ed.) (1967). *Latin Biography*. London: Routledge & Kegan Paul.

—— (ed.) (1971). *Livy*. London: Routledge & Kegan Paul.

—— (ed.) (1975). *Empire and Aftermath. Silver Latin*, II. London: Routledge & Kegan Paul.

Douglas, A.E. (1968). *Cicero*. Oxford: Greece and Rome New Survey 2.

Dover, K.J. (1968). *Lysias and the Corpus Lysiacum*. Berkeley and Los Angeles: University of California Press.

—— (1972). *Aristophanic Comedy*. London: Batsford.

—— (1978). *Greek Homosexuality*. London: Duckworth.

Downey, G. (1961). *A History of Antioch in Syria from Seleucid Times to the Arab Conquest*. Princeton, NJ: Princeton University Press.

—— (1963). *Ancient Antioch*. Princeton, NJ: Princeton University Press.

Drees, L. (1968). *Olympia: Gods, Artists and Athletes*. London: Pall Mall.

Drijvers, H.J.W. (1980). *Cults and Beliefs at Edessa*. Leiden: E.J. Brill.

Drinkwater, J.F. (1983). *Roman Gaul: The Three Provinces, 58 BC–AD 260*. London: Croom Helm.

DSB = *Dictionary of Scientific Biography*. Ed. C.C. Gillispie. 15 vols. New York: Scribner, 1970–8.

Duckworth, G.E. (1952). *The Nature of Roman Comedy*. Princeton, NJ: Princeton University Press.

Dudley, D.R. (1937). *A History of Cynicism*. Cambridge: Cambridge University Press.

—— (ed.) (1965). *Lucretius*. London: Routledge & Kegan Paul.

—— (ed.) (1972). *Neronians and Flavians: Silver Latin*. Vol. 1. London: Routledge & Kegan Paul.

Due, B. (1980). *Antiphon: A Study in Argumentation*. Copenhagen: Museum Tusculanum.

Dumézil, G. (1970). *Archaic Roman Religion*. 2 vols. Chicago: University of Chicago Press.

Dunbabin, K.M.D. (1978). *The Mosaics of Roman North Africa. Studies in Iconography and Patronage*. Oxford: Clarendon Press.

Dunbabin, T.J. (1948). *The Western Greeks*. Oxford: Clarendon Press.

Dunham, A.G. (1915). *A History of Miletus*. London: University of London Press.

Earl, D.C. (1961). *The Political Thought of Sallust*. Cambridge: Cambridge University Press.

—— (1963). *Tiberius Gracchus: A Study in Politics*. Brussels: Collection Latomus 66.

Easterling, P.E., and Muir, J.V. (eds.) (1985). *Greek Religion and Society*. Cambridge: Cambridge University Press.

Eddy, S.K. (1961). *The King is Dead: Studies in the Near Eastern Resistance to Hellenism 334–31 BC*. Lincoln, Nebraska: University of Nebraska Press.

Edelstein, L., and Kidd, I.G. (eds.) (1989). *Posidonius*. Vol. 1: *The Fragments*. 2nd edn. Cambridge: Cambridge University Press.

Edwards, J. (ed.) (1988). *The Roman Cookery of Apicius*. London: Century.

Edwards, M.W. (1987). *Homer, Poet of the* Iliad. Baltimore, MD: Johns Hopkins University Press.

Ehrenberg, V. (1969). *The Greek State*. 2nd edn. London: Methuen.

Ellis, J.R., and Milns, R.D. (1970). *The Spectre of Philip*. Sydney: Sydney University Press.

Ellis, W.M. (1989). *Alcibiades*. London: Routledge.

Emery, Walter B. (1965). *Egypt in Nubia*. London: Hutchinson.

Emlyn-Jones, C.J. (1980). *The Ionians and Hellenism*. London: Routledge.

Erim, K.T. (1986). *Aphrodisias*. London: Muller, Blond & White.

Errington, R.M. (1969). *Philopoemen*. Oxford: Clarendon Press.

—— (1990). *A History of Macedonia*. Berkeley and Los Angeles: University of California Press.

Exler, F.X.J. (1923). *The Form of the Ancient Greek Letter*. Washington, DC: Catholic University of America.

Fairweather, J. (1981). *Seneca the Elder*. Cambridge: Cambridge University Press.

Farnell, L.R. (1921). *Greek Hero Cults and Ideas of Immortality*. Oxford: Clarendon Press.

Ferguson, W.S. (1911). *Hellenistic Athens. An Historical Essay*. London: Macmillan.

Festugière, A.-J. (1954). *Personal Religion among the Greeks*. Berkeley and Los Angeles: University of California Press.

Field, G.C. (1930). *Plato and his Contemporaries*. London: Methuen.

Figuera, T. (1981). *Aegina*. New York: Arno Press.

—— (1991). *Athens and Aegina in the Age of Imperial Colonization*. Baltimore, Md.: Johns Hopkins University Press.

Filoramo, G. (1990). *A History of Gnosticism*. Oxford: Blackwell.

Finegan, J. (1969). *The Archaeology of the New Testament. The Life of Jesus and the Beginning of the Early Church*. Princeton, NJ: Princeton University Press.

Finley, M.I. (ed.) (1960). *Slavery in Classical Antiquity*. Cambridge: Heffer.

—— (1965). 'Technical Innovation and Economic Progress in the Ancient World', *Economic History Review*, 18. 29–45.

—— (1977). *The World of Odysseus*. 2nd edn. London: Chatto & Windus.

—— (1979). *Ancient Sicily*. 2nd edn. London: Chatto & Windus.

—— (1980). *Ancient Slavery and Modern Ideology*. London: Chatto & Windus.

—— (1981). *Economy and Society in Ancient Greece*. London: Chatto & Windus.

—— (1983). *Politics in the Ancient World*. Cambridge: Cambridge University Press.

—— (1985). *Democracy Ancient and Modern*. 2nd edn. London: Hogarth Press.

—— (ed.) (1990). *Classical Slavery*. London: Chatto & Windus.

Finley, M.I., and Pleket, H.W. (1976). *The Olympic Games: The First Thousand Years*. London: Chatto & Windus.

Fishwick, D. (1987–). *The Imperial Cult in the Latin West: Studies in the Ruler Cult of the Western Provinces of the Roman Empire*. Vol. 1.i–ii 1987; Vol. 2.i 1991; Vol. 2.ii 1992. Leiden: E.J. Brill.

Flamant, J. (1977). *Macrobe et le Néo-Platonisme latin à la fin du IVe siècle*. Leiden: E.J. Brill.

Fontenrose, J. (1978). *The Delphic Oracle*. Berkeley and Los Angeles: University of California Press.

Fornara, C.W. (1968). 'The "Tradition" about the Murder of Hipparchus', *Historia*, 17. 400–24.

—— (1970). 'The Cult of Harmodius and Aristogeiton', *Philologus*, 114. 155–80.

—— (1983). *The Nature of History in Ancient Greece and Rome*. Berkeley and Los Angeles: University of California Press.

Forrest, W.G. (1957). 'Colonisation and the Rise of Delphi', *Historia*, 6. 160–75.

—— (1966). *The Emergence of Greek Democracy*. London: Weidenfeld & Nicolson.

—— (1980). *A History of Sparta 950–192 BC*. 2nd edn. London: Duckworth.

Fowden, G. (1986). *The Egyptian Hermes. A Historical Approach to the Late Pagan Mind*. Cambridge: Cambridge University Press.

Fraenkel, E. (1957). *Horace*. Oxford: Clarendon Press.

Fränkel, H. (1975). *Early Greek Poetry and Philosophy*. Oxford: Blackwell.

Fraser, P.M. (1972). *Ptolemaic Alexandria*. 3 vols. Oxford: Clarendon Press.

Frederiksen, M. (1984). *Campania*. London: British School at Rome.

Freeman, E.A. (1891–4). *The History of Sicily*. 4 vols. Oxford: Clarendon Press.

Frend, W.H.C. (1965). *Martyrdom and Persecution in the Early Church*. Oxford: Blackwell.

—— (1985). *The Donatist Church. A Movement of Protest in Roman North Africa*. 3rd edn. Oxford: Clarendon Press.

Friedrich, P. (1979). *The Meaning of Aphrodite*. Chicago and London: University of Chicago Press.

Frier, B.W. (1979). *Libri Annales Pontificum Maximorum: The Origins of the Annalistic Tradition*. Rome: American Academy in Rome.

—— (1985). *The Rise of the Roman Jurists: Studies in Cicero's pro Caecina*. Princeton, NJ: Princeton University Press.

Frost, F.J. (1980). *Plutarch's Themistocles: A Historical Commentary*. Princeton, NJ: Princeton University Press.

Frye, R.N. (1984). *The History of Ancient Iran*. Munich: Beck.

Fuhrmann, M. (1992). *Cicero and the Roman Republic*. Oxford: Blackwell.

Gabba, E. (1956). *Appiano e la storia delle guerre civili*. Florence: La Nuova Italia.

—— (1976). *Republican Rome: The Army and the Allies*. Oxford: Blackwell.

—— (1991). *Dionysius and the History of Archaic Rome*. Berkeley and Los Angeles: University of California Press.

Gagarin, M. (1981). *Drakon and Early Athenian Homicide Law*. New Haven, Conn.: Yale University Press.

—— (1986). *Early Greek Law*. Berkeley and Los Angeles: University of California Press.

Gardner, J.F. (1986). *Women in Roman Law and Society*. London: Croom Helm.

Garlan, Y. (1975). *War in the Ancient World*. Trans. J. Lloyd. London: Chatto & Windus.

—— (1982). *Les Esclaves en Grèce ancienne*. Paris: Maspero.

Garland, R. (1985). *The Greek Way of Death*. London: Duckworth.

—— (1987). *The Piraeus: From the Fifth to the First Century BC*. London: Duckworth.

Garnsey, P.D.A. (1978). 'Rome's African Empire under the Principate', in Garnsey and Whittaker, C.R. (eds.), *Imperialism in the Ancient World*. Cambridge: Cambridge University Press.

Garnsey, P.D.A., Hopkins, K., and Whittaker, C.R. (eds.) (1983). *Trade in the Ancient Economy*. London: Chatto & Windus.

Garnsey, P.D.A., and Saller, R. (1987). *The Roman Empire. Economy, Society and Culture*. London: Duckworth.

Geiger, J. (1985). *Cornelius Nepos and Ancient Political Biography*. Stuttgart: Franz Steiner.

Gelzer, M. (1969). *The Roman Nobility*. Oxford: Blackwell.

Gershevitch, I. (ed.) (1985). *Cambridge History of Iran*. Vol. 2: *The Median and Achaemenid Periods*. Cambridge: Cambridge University Press.

Gibbs, S.L. (1976). *Greek and Roman Sundials*. New Haven and London: Yale University Press.

Glueck, N. (1966). *Deities and Dolphins: The Story of the Nabataeans*. London: Cassell.

—— (1968). *Rivers in the Desert: A History of the Negev*. 2nd edn. New York: Norton.

—— (1970). *The Other Side of the Jordan*. 2nd edn. Cambridge, Mass.: American School of Oriental Research.

Goell, T. (1952). 'Nimrud Dagh: The Tomb of Antiochus I, King of Commagene', *Archaeology*, 5. 136–44.

Goldberg, S.M. (1980). *The Making of Menander's Comedy*. London: Athlone Press.

—— (1986). *Understanding Terence*. Princeton, NJ: Princeton University Press.

Gomme, A.W. (1933). *Population of Athens*. Oxford: Blackwell.

Gomme, A.W., Andrewes, A., and Dover, K.J. (1970). *A Historical Commentary on Thucydides*. Vol. 4. Oxford: Clarendon Press.

Goodman, M. (1987). *The Ruling Class of Judaea. The Origins of the Jewish Revolt against Rome AD 66–70*. Cambridge: Cambridge University Press.

Goodyear, F.R.D. (1970). *Tacitus*. Oxford: Clarendon Press.

Gordon, A.E. (1983). *Illustrated Introduction to Latin Epigraphy*. Berkeley and Los Angeles: University of California Press.

Gould, J. (1989). *Herodotus*. London: Weidenfeld & Nicolson.

Gow, A.S.F. (ed.) (1965). *Machon, The Fragments*. Cambridge: Cambridge University Press.

Gow, A.S.F., and Scholfield, A.F. (eds.) (1953). *Nicander: The Poems and Poetical Fragments*. Cambridge: Cambridge University Press.

Graham, A.J. (1964). *Colony and Mother City in Ancient Greece*. Manchester: Manchester University Press.

Graham, F. (1979). *The Roman Wall, Comprehensive History and Guide*. Newcastle upon Tyne: Frank Graham.

Grainger, J.D. (1990a). *Cities of Seleukid Syria*. Oxford: Clarendon Press.

—— (1990b). *Seleukos Nikator: Constructing a Hellenistic Kingdom*. London: Routledge.

—— (1991). *Hellenistic Phoenicia*. Oxford: Clarendon Press.

Grant, M. (1970a). *The Ancient Historians*. London: Weidenfeld & Nicolson.

—— (1970b). *The Roman Forum*. London: Weidenfeld & Nicolson.

—— (1971a). *Gladiators*. 2nd edn. Harmondsworth: Penguin.

—— (1971b). *Roman Myths*. London: Weidenfeld & Nicolson.

—— (1971c). *Tacitus: The Annals of Imperial Rome*. Rev. edn. Harmondsworth: Penguin.

—— (1974). *Julius Caesar*. London: Weidenfeld & Nicolson.

—— (1979). *History of Rome*. 2nd edn. London: Weidenfeld & Nicolson.

—— (1980). *The Etruscans*. London: Weidenfeld & Nicolson.

—— (1985). *The Roman Emperors. A Biographical Guide to the Rulers of Imperial Rome 31 BC–AD 476*. London: Weidenfeld & Nicolson.

Grant, R.M. (1980). *Eusebius as Church Historian*. Oxford: Oxford University Press.

Graves, R. (1957). *Gaius Suetonius Tranquillus: The Twelve Caesars*. Harmondsworth: Penguin.

Green, P. (1990). *Alexander to Actium. The Historical Evolution of the Hellenistic Age*. Berkeley and Los Angeles: University of California Press.

Greenhalgh, P.A.L. (1973). *Early Greek Warfare*. Cambridge: Cambridge University Press.

—— (1980). *Pompey: The Roman Alexander*. London: Weidenfeld & Nicolson.

—— (1981). *Pompey: The Republican Prince*. London: Weidenfeld & Nicolson.

Griffin, A. (1982). *Sicyon*. Oxford: Clarendon Press.

Griffin, J. (1980). *Homer*. Oxford: Oxford University Press.

—— (1985). *Latin Poets and Roman Life*. London: Duckworth.

—— (1986). *Virgil*. Oxford: Oxford University Press.

Griffin, M.T. (1976). *Seneca: A Philosopher in Politics*. Oxford: Clarendon Press.

—— (1984). *Nero. The End of a Dynasty*. London: Batsford.

Griffith, G.T. (1935). *The Mercenaries of the Hellenistic World*. Cambridge: Cambridge University Press.

Griffith, M. (1977). *The Authenticity of 'Prometheus Bound'*. Cambridge: Cambridge University Press.

Griffiths, F.T. (1979). *Theocritus at Court*. Mnemosyne supplement LV. Leiden: E.J. Brill.

Grimal, P. (1986). *Dictionary of Classical Mythology*. Oxford: Blackwell.

Gruen, E.S. (1968). *Roman Politics and the Roman Criminal Courts, 149–78 BC*. Cambridge, Mass.: Harvard University Press.

—— (1974). *The Last Generation of the Roman Republic*. Berkeley and Los Angeles: University of California Press.

—— (1984). *The Hellenistic World and the Coming of Rome*. Berkeley and Los Angeles: University of California Press.

Grundy, G.B. (1911). *Thucydides and the History of his Age*. London: John Murray.

Gschnitzer, F. (1958). *Abhängige Orte im griechischen Altertum*. Munich: Beck. [*Zetemata* 17.]

Guido, M. (1963). *Sardinia*. London: Thames & Hudson.

Guthrie, W.K.C. (1950). *The Greeks and their Gods*. London: Methuen.

—— (1962–81). *History of Greek Philosophy*. 6 vols. Cambridge: Cambridge University Press.

Habicht, C. (1985). *Pausanias' Guide to Ancient Greece*. Berkeley and Los Angeles: University of California Press.

—— (1990). *Cicero the Politician*. Baltimore and London: Johns Hopkins University Press.

Hackett, J. (1989). *Warfare in the Ancient World*. London: Sidgwick & Jackson.

Hadas, M. (1930). *Sextus Pompey*. New York: Columbia University Press.

Hägg, T. (1971). *Narrative Technique in Ancient Greek Romances*. Stockholm: Almqvist & Wiksell.

—— (1983). *The Novel in Antiquity*. Oxford: Blackwell.

Halliday, W.R. (1913). *Greek Divination*. London: Macmillan.

Hamilton, M. (1906). *Incubation, or the Cure of Disease in Pagan Temples and Christian Churches*. St Andrews: Henderson.

Hamilton, W., and Wallace-Hadrill, A. (1986). *Ammianus Marcellinus: The Later Roman Empire AD 354–378*. Harmondsworth: Penguin.

Hammond, N.G.L. (1959). *A History of Greece to 322 BC*. Oxford: Clarendon Press.

—— (1967). *Epirus*. Oxford: Clarendon Press.

—— (1972). *A History of Macedonia*. Vol. 1. Oxford: Clarendon Press.

—— (1989). *Alexander the Great: King, Commander, and Statesman*. 2nd edn. Bristol: Bristol Classical Press.

Hammond, N.G.L., and Griffith, G.T. (1979). *A History of Macedonia*. Vol. 2: *550–336 BC*. Oxford: Clarendon Press.

Hammond, N.G.L., and Walbank, F.W. (1988). *A History of Macedonia*. Vol. 3: *336–167 BC*. Oxford: Clarendon Press.

Hands, A.R. (1968). *Charities and Social Aid in Greece and Rome*. London: Thames & Hudson.

Hansen, E.V. (1971). *The Attalids of Pergamon.* Ithaca, NY: Cornell University Press.

Hansen, M.H. (1975). *Eisangelia.* Odense: Odense University Press.

—— (1983). *The Athenian Ecclesia I.* Copenhagen: Museum Tusculanum.

—— (1987). *The Athenian Assembly in the Age of Demosthenes.* Oxford: Blackwell.

—— (1989). *The Athenian Ecclesia II.* Copenhagen: Museum Tusculanum.

—— (1991). *The Athenian Democracy in the Age of Demosthenes.* Oxford: Blackwell.

Hanson, R.P.C. (1968). *St Patrick: His Origins and Career.* Oxford: Clarendon Press.

Hanson, V.D. (1983). *Warfare and Agriculture in Classical Greece.* Pisa: Giardini.

—— (1989). *The Western Way of War.* London: Hodder & Stoughton.

—— (ed.) (1991). *Hoplites.* London: Routledge.

Hanson, W.S. (1987). *Agricola and the Conquest of the North.* London: Batsford.

Harden, D.B. (1987). *Glass of the Caesars.* Milan: Olivetti.

Hardie, A. (1983). *Statius and the* Silvae. *Poets, Patrons and Epideixis in the Graeco-Roman World.* Liverpool: Francis Cairns.

Hardie, P.R. (1986). *Virgil's* Aeneid: *Cosmos and Imperium.* Oxford: Clarendon Press.

Harding, G.L. (1967). *The Antiquities of Jordan.* 2nd edn. London: Lutterworth Press.

Harris, H.A. (1964). *Greek Athletes and Athletics.* London: Hutchinson.

Harris, W.V. (1971). *Rome in Etruria and Umbria.* Oxford: Clarendon Press.

—— (1976). 'The Development of the Quaestorship', *Classical Quarterly,* 26. 92–106.

—— (1979). *War and Imperialism in Republican Rome, 327–70* BC. Oxford: Clarendon Press.

Harrison, A.R.W. (1968–71). *The Law of Athens.* 2 vols. Oxford: Clarendon Press.

Hartley, B.R. (1988). *The Brigantes.* Gloucester: Alan Sutton.

Hartley, B.R., and Wacher, J. (eds.) (1983). *Rome and her Northern Provinces.* Gloucester: Alan Sutton.

Hasluck, F.W. (1910). *Cyzicus.* Cambridge: Cambridge University Press.

Haspels, C.H.E. (1971). *The Highlands of Phrygia. Sites and Monuments.* 2 vols. Princeton, NJ: Princeton University Press.

Hatzopoulos, M.B., and Loukopoulos, L.D. (eds.) (1981). *Philip of Macedon.* London: Heinemann.

Hawkes, C.F.C. (1977). *Pytheas: Europe and the Greek Explorers.* Oxford: Blackwell.

Hayes, J.W. (1972). *Late Roman Pottery*. London: British School at Rome.

—— (1980). *Supplement to Late Roman Pottery*. London: British School at Rome.

Head, B.V. (1911). *Historia Nummorum*. 2nd edn. Oxford: Clarendon Press.

Healy, J.F. (1978). *Mining and Metallurgy in the Greek and Roman World*. London: Thames & Hudson.

—— (1991). *Pliny the Elder, Natural History, a Selection*. Harmondsworth: Penguin.

Hearsey, J.E.N. (1963). *City of Constantine*. London: John Murray.

Heath, T.L. (1913). *Aristarchus of Samos*. Oxford: Clarendon Press.

—— (1921). *A History of Greek Mathematics*. 2 vols. Oxford: Clarendon Press.

Heather, P.J. (1991). *Goths and Romans*. Oxford: Clarendon Press.

Heckel, W. (1984). Introduction and notes to Quintus Curtius Rufus, *The History of Alexander*. Trans. J. Yardley. Harmondsworth: Penguin.

Hedrick, C.W. (1991). *The Decrees of Demotionidai*. Atlanta, Ga.: American Philological Association.

Heichelheim, F.M. (1964). *An Ancient Economic History*. Vol. 2. Leiden: Sijthoff.

Hencken, H. (1968). *Tarquinia, Villanovans and Early Etruscans*. Cambridge, Mass.: American School of Prehistoric Research, Peabody Museum.

Henig, M. (ed.) (1983). *A Handbook of Roman Art*. Oxford: Phaidon.

Herington, J. (1985). *Poetry into Drama. Early Tragedy and the Greek Poetic Tradition*. Berkeley and Los Angeles: University of California Press.

Herrington, C.J. (1955). *Athena Parthenos and Athena Polias*. Manchester: Manchester University Press.

Herrmann, G. (1977). *The Iranian Revival*. Oxford: Elsevier–Phaidon.

Hertling, L., and Kirschbaum, E. (1960). *The Roman Catacombs and their Martyrs*. London: Darton, Longman & Todd.

Heurgon, J. (1973). *The Rise of Rome to 264 BC*. London: Batsford.

Higgins, R. (1968). *Greek Terracottas*. London: Methuen.

—— (1980). *Greek and Roman Jewellery*. 2nd edn. London: Methuen.

—— (1987). *Tanagra and the Figurines*. London: Trefoil Books.

Highet, G. (1954). *Juvenal the Satirist*. Oxford: Clarendon Press.

Hignett, C. (1952). *A History of the Athenian Constitution to the End of the Fifth Century BC*. Oxford: Clarendon Press.

Hodge, A.T. (1992). *Roman Aqueducts and Water Supply*. London: Duckworth.

Hodges, H. (1977). *Technology in the Ancient World*. New York: Knopf.

Hoffman, M. (1964). *The Warp-Weighted Loom*. Oslo: Universitetsforlaget.

Holford-Strevens, L.A. (1988). *Aulus Gellius*. London: Duckworth.

Holland Smith, J. (1971). *Constantine the Great*. New York: Scribner.

Holt, F.L. (1988). *Alexander the Great and Bactria*. Leiden: E.J. Brill.

Holtz, L. (1981). *Donat et la tradition de l'enseignement grammatical*. Paris: CNRS.

Holum, K.G. (1983). *Theodosian Empresses. Women and Imperial Dominion in Late Antiquity*. Berkeley and Los Angeles: University of California Press.

Honoré, A.M. (1962). *Gaius: A Biography*. Oxford: Clarendon Press.

—— (1982). *Ulpian*. Oxford: Clarendon Press.

Hopkins, C. (ed.) (1972). *Topography and Architecture of Seleucia on the Tigris*. Ann Arbor: University of Michigan Press.

—— (1979), ed. B. Goldman. *The Discovery of Dura-Europos*. New Haven, Conn.: Yale University Press.

Hopkins, K. (1978). *Conquerors and Slaves: Sociological Studies in Roman History*, vol.1. Cambridge: Cambridge University Press.

—— (1983). *Death and Renewal. Sociological Studies in Roman History*, vol.2. Cambridge: Cambridge University Press.

Hopper, R.J. (1971). *The Acropolis*. London: Weidenfeld & Nicolson.

—— (1979). *Trade and Industry in Classical Greece*. London: Thames & Hudson.

Hornblower, J. (1981). *Hieronymus of Cardia*. Oxford: Clarendon Press.

Hornblower, S. (1982). *Mausolus*. Oxford: Clarendon Press.

—— (1983). *The Greek World 479–323 BC*. London: Methuen.

—— (1987). *Thucydides*. London: Duckworth.

Hornblower, S., and Greenstock, M.C. (1986). *The Athenian Empire*. 3rd edn. London: London Association of Classical Teachers.

Hubbard, M.E. (1974). *Propertius*. London: Duckworth.

Hubert, H. (1987). *The Greatness and Decline of the Celts*. London: Constable.

Hull, D.B. (1964). *Hounds and Hunting in Ancient Greece*. Chicago: University of Chicago Press.

Humbert, M. (1978). *Municipium et civitas sine suffragio: l'organisation de la conquête jusqu'à la guerre sociale*. Rome: École Française de Rome.

Humphrey, J.H. (1986). *Roman Circuses: Arenas for Chariot Racing*. London: Batsford.

—— (ed.) (1991). *Literacy in the Roman World*. Ann Arbor: Journal of Roman Archaeology, suppl. vol. 3.

Hunt, E.D. (1982). *Holy Land Pilgrimage in the Later Roman Empire* AD *312–460*. Oxford: Clarendon Press.

Hunter, R.L. (ed.) (1983a). *Eubulus. The Fragments*. Cambridge: Cambridge University Press.

—— (1983b). *A Study of 'Daphnis and Chloe'*. Cambridge: Cambridge University Press.

—— (1985). *The New Comedy of Greece and Rome*. Cambridge: Cambridge University Press.

Hurwit, J.M. (1985). *The Art and Culture of Early Greece, 1100–480* BC. Ithaca, NY: Cornell University Press.

Hutchinson, G.O. (1988). *Hellenistic Poetry*. Oxford: Clarendon Press.

—— (1993). *Latin Literature from Seneca to Juvenal: A Critical Study*. Oxford: Clarendon Press.

Huxley, G.L. (1962). *Early Sparta*. London: Faber & Faber.

—— (1966). *The Early Ionians*. London: Faber & Faber.

—— (1969). *Greek Epic Poetry from Eumelos to Panyassis*. London: Faber & Faber.

Huzar, E.G. (1978). *Mark Antony*. Minneapolis: Minnesota University Press.

Hyland, A. (1990). *Equus: The Horse in the Roman World*. London: Batsford.

ILS = *Inscriptiones Latinae Selectae*. Ed. H. Dessau. Berlin: 1892–1916; repr. Chicago: Ares, 1979.

Jacobsthal, P. (1956). *Greek Pins and their Connexions with Europe and Asia*. Oxford: Clarendon Press.

Jacoby, F. (1923–58). *Die Fragmente der griechischen Historiker*. Leiden: E.J. Brill.

—— (1949). *Atthis: The Local Chronicles of Ancient Athens*. Oxford: Clarendon Press.

Jaeger, W.W. (1940). 'Diocles of Carystus: A New Pupil of Aristotle', *Philosophical Review*, 49. 393–414.

—— (1948). *Aristotle: Fundamentals of the History of his Development*. Trans. R. Robinson. Oxford: Clarendon Press.

Jalland, T. (1941). *The Life and Times of St Leo the Great*. London: SPCK.

James, E. (1980). *Visigothic Spain*. Oxford: Clarendon Press.

—— (1988). *The Franks*. Oxford: Blackwell.

Janko, R.C.M. (1982). *Homer, Hesiod and the Hymns*. Cambridge: Cambridge University Press.

Jashemski, W.F. (1950). *Origin and History of Proconsular and Propraetorian Imperium to 27* BC. Chicago: Chicago University Press.

Jeffery, L.H. (1976). *Archaic Greece: The City-States c.700–500* BC. London: Ernest Benn.

—— (1990). *The Local Scripts of Archaic Greece*. 2nd edn. Rev. A.W. Johnston. Oxford: Clarendon Press.

Jenkins, G.K. (1990). *Ancient Greek Coins*. 2nd edn. London: Seaby.

Johnson, F.P. (1927). *Lysippus*. Durham, NC: Duke University Press.

Johnson, S. (1980). *Later Roman Britain*. London: Routledge & Kegan Paul.

Johnston, A. (1976). *The Emergence of Greece*. Oxford: Elsevier–Phaidon.

Jolowicz, H.F., and Nicholas, B. (1972). *Historical Introduction to the Study of Roman Law*. 3rd edn. Cambridge: Cambridge University Press.

Jones, A.H.M. (1948). *Ancient Economic History*. London: H.K. Lewis.

—— (1949). *The Greek City from Alexander to Justinian*. Oxford: Clarendon Press.

—— (1964). *The Later Roman Empire 284–602*. 2 vols. Oxford: Blackwell.

—— (1967). *Sparta*. Oxford: Clarendon Press.

—— (1970). *Augustus*. London: Chatto & Windus.

—— (1971). *The Cities of the Eastern Roman Provinces*. 2nd edn. Oxford: Clarendon Press.

—— (1972). *The Criminal Courts of the Roman Republic and Principate*. Oxford: Blackwell.

—— (1974). *The Roman Economy: Studies in Ancient Economic and Administrative History*. Oxford: Blackwell.

—— (1983). *The Cities of the Eastern Roman Provinces*. 2nd edn. Amsterdam: Hakkert.

Jones, A.H.M., Martindale, J.R., and Morris, J. (1971). *The Prosopography of the Later Roman Empire*. Vol. 1: AD 260–395. Cambridge: Cambridge University Press.

Jones, B.W. (1979). *Domitian and the Senatorial Order*. Philadelphia: American Philosophical Society, Memoirs no. 132.

—— (1984). *The Emperor Titus*. London: Croom Helm.

Jones, C.P. (1971). *Plutarch and Rome*. Oxford: Clarendon Press.

—— (1986). *Culture and Society in Lucian*. Cambridge, Mass.: Harvard University Press.

Jones, J.W. (1956). *The Law and Legal Theory of the Greeks*. Oxford: Clarendon Press.

Jones, N.F. (1987). *Public Organization in Ancient Greece: A Documentary Study*. Philadelphia, Pa.: American Philosophical Society.

Jongman, W. (1988). *The Economy and Society of Pompeii*. Amsterdam: J.C. Gieben.

Jordan, B. (1975). *The Athenian Navy in the Classical Period*. Berkeley and Los Angeles: University of California Press.

Just, R. (1989). *Women in Athenian Law and Life*. London: Routledge.

Kagan, D. (1969). *The Outbreak of the Peloponnesian War*. Ithaca and London: Cornell University Press.

—— (1975). *The Archidamian War*. Ithaca and London: Cornell University Press.

—— (1987). *The Fall of the Athenian Empire*. Ithaca and London: Cornell University Press.

Kahn, C.H. (1960). *Anaximander and the Origins of Greek Cosmology*. New York: Columbia University Press.

Kajanto, I. (1965). *The Latin Cognomina*. Helsinki: Societas Scientiarum Fennica.

Karouzou, S. (1956). *The Amasis Painter*. Oxford: Clarendon Press.

Kaster, R.A. (1988). *Guardians of Language: The Grammarian and Society in Late Antiquity*. Berkeley and Los Angeles: University of California Press.

Kazhdan, A.P. (ed.) (1991). *Oxford Dictionary of Byzantium*. 3 vols. New York: Oxford University Press.

Kearns, E. (1985). 'Change and Continuity in Religious Structures after Cleisthenes' in Cartledge and Harvey (1985).

Keaveney, A. (1982). *Sulla: The Last Republican*. London: Croom Helm.

—— (1992). *Lucullus: A Life*. London: Routledge.

Keay, S.J. (1988). *Roman Spain*. London: British Museum.

Kebric, R.B. (1977). *In the Shadow of Macedon. Duris of Samos*. Wiesbaden: Franz Steiner.

Kelly, J.M. (1975). *Studies in the Civil Judicature of the Roman Republic*. Oxford: Clarendon Press.

Kelly, J.N.D. (1975). *Jerome: His Life, Writings, and Controversies*. London: Duckworth.

—— (1977). *Early Christian Doctrines*. 5th edn. London: Black.

Kennedy, G.A. (1958). 'The Oratory of Andocides', *American Journal of Philology*, 79. 32–43.

—— (1963). *The Art of Persuasion in Greece*. Princeton, NJ: Princeton University Press.

—— (1969). *Quintilian*. New York: Twayne.

—— (1972). *The Art of Rhetoric in the Roman World*. Princeton, NJ: Princeton University Press.

Kenney, E.J., and Clausen, W.V. (eds.) (1982). *The Cambridge History of Classical Literature*. Vol. 2: *Latin Literature*. Cambridge: Cambridge University Press.

Kent, J.P.C. (1978). *Roman Coins*. London: Thames & Hudson.

—— (1981). *The Roman Imperial Coinage*. Ed. C.H.V. Sutherland and R.G. Carson. Vol. 8: *The Family of Constantine I* AD 337–364. London: Spink.

Keppie, L. (1983). *Colonization and Veteran Settlement in Italy 47–14 BC*. London: British School at Rome.

—— (1984). *The Making of the Roman Army from Republic to Empire.* London: Batsford.

—— (1991). *Understanding Roman Inscriptions.* London: Batsford.

Kerferd, G.B. (1981). *The Sophistic Movement.* Cambridge: Cambridge University Press.

Keuls, E.C. (1978). *Plato and Greek Painting.* Leiden: E.J. Brill.

Kidd, I.G. (1988). *Posidonius.* Vol. 2: *The Commentary.* Cambridge: Cambridge University Press.

Kindstrand, J.F. (1976). *Bion of Borysthenes: A Collection of the Fragments with Introduction and Commentary.* Stockholm: Almqvist & Wiksell.

King, A. (1990). *Roman Gaul and Germany.* London: British Museum.

Kirk, G.S. (1965). *Homer and the Epic.* Cambridge: Cambridge University Press.

—— (1976). *Homer and the Oral Tradition.* Cambridge: Cambridge University Press.

Kirk, G.S., Raven, J.E., and Schofield, M. (1983). *The Presocratic Philosophers.* 2nd edn. Cambridge: Cambridge University Press.

Kirkwood, G.M. (1974). *Early Greek Monody.* Ithaca, NY: Cornell University Press.

Knapp, R.C. (1977). *Aspects of the Roman Experience in Iberia, 206–100 BC.* Valladolid: Anejos de Hispania antiqua 9.

Knox, B.M.W. (1964). *The Heroic Temper.* Berkeley and Los Angeles: University of California Press.

Kokkinos, N. (1992). *Antonia Augusta: Portrait of a Great Roman Lady.* London: Routledge.

Kraay, C.M. (1976). *Archaic and Classical Greek Coins.* London: Methuen.

Krautheimer, R. (1975). *Early Christian and Byzantine Architecture.* Harmondsworth: Penguin.

Kurtz, D.C. (1975). *Athenian White Lekythoi: Patterns and Painters.* Oxford: Clarendon Press.

—— (1983). *The Berlin Painter.* Oxford: Clarendon Press.

Kurtz, D.C., and Boardman, J. (1971). *Greek Burial Customs.* London: Thames & Hudson.

Lacey, W.K. (1968). *The Family in Classical Greece.* London: Thames & Hudson.

Laistner, M.L.W. (1947). *The Greater Roman Historians.* Berkeley and Los Angeles: University of California Press.

Lamberton, R. (1988). *Hesiod.* New Haven, Conn.: Yale University Press.

Landels, J.G. (1978). *Engineering in the Ancient World.* Berkeley and Los Angeles: University of California Press.

Lane Fox, R. (1973). *Alexander the Great*. London: Allen Lane.
—— (1985). 'Aspects of Inheritance in the Greek World' in Cartledge and Harvey (1985).
—— (1986). *Pagans and Christians*. Harmondsworth: Penguin.
Larsen, J.A.O. (1968). *Greek Federal States. Their Institutions and History*. Oxford: Clarendon Press.
Lateiner, D. (1989). *The Historical Method of Herodotus*. Toronto: University of Toronto Press.
Lausberg, M. (1982). *Das Einzeldistichon: Studien zum antiken Epigramm*. Munich: Wilhelm Fink.
Lawrence, A.W. (1972). *Greek and Roman Sculpture*. London: Cape.
—— (1979). *Greek Aims in Fortification*. Oxford: Clarendon Press.
—— (1984). *Greek Architecture*. 4th edn. Rev. R.A. Tomlinson. Harmondsworth: Penguin.
Lawson, J.C. (1910). *Modern Greek Folklore and Ancient Greek Religion*. Cambridge: Cambridge University Press.
Lazenby, J.F. (1978). *Hannibal's War*. Warminster: Aris & Phillips.
—— (1985). *The Spartan Army*. Warminster: Aris & Phillips.
Leach, J. (1978). *Pompey the Great*. London: Croom Helm.
Lee, H.D.P. (1936). *Zeno of Elea*. Cambridge: Cambridge University Press.
Legon, R.P. (1981). *Megara. The Political History of a Greek City-State to 336 BC*. Ithaca, NY: Cornell University Press.
Lenardon, R.J. (1978). *The Saga of Themistocles*. London: Thames & Hudson.
Lengyel, A., and Radan, G.T.B. (eds.) (1980). *The Archaeology of Roman Pannonia*. Budapest: Akademiai Kiado and University Press of Kentucky.
Lesky, A. (1966). *A History of Greek Literature*. London: Methuen.
Lévêque, P. (1955). *Agathon*. Lyon: Université, Faculté des Lettres.
Levi, P. (1971). *Pausanias: Guide to Greece*. 2 vols. Harmondsworth: Penguin.
—— (1980). *Atlas of the Greek World*. Oxford: Phaidon.
Levick, B. (1976). *Tiberius the Politician*. London: Thames & Hudson.
—— (1990). *Claudius*. New Haven, Conn.: Yale University Press.
Lewis, N. (1974). *Papyrus in Classical Antiquity*. Oxford: Clarendon Press.
—— (1983). *Life in Egypt under Roman Rule*. Oxford: Clarendon Press.
—— (1986). *The Greeks in Ptolemaic Egypt: Case Studies in the Social History of the Hellenistic World*. Oxford: Clarendon Press.
Lewis, R.G. (1971). 'A Problem in the Siege of Praeneste, 82 BC', *Proceedings of the British School at Rome*, 39. 32–9.
Lezzi-Hafter, A. (1988). *Der Eretria-Maler: Werke und Weggefährten*. 2 vols. Mainz: Von Zabern.

Liebeschuetz, J.H.W.G. (1972). *Antioch. City and Imperial Administration in the Later Roman Empire.* Oxford: Clarendon Press.

—— (1979). *Continuity and Change in Roman Religion.* Oxford: Clarendon Press.

—— (1990). *Barbarians and Bishops. Army, Church, and State in the Age of Arcadius and Chrysostom.* Oxford: Clarendon Press.

Lienhard, J.T. (1977). *Paulinus of Nola and Early Western Monasticism.* Cologne and Bonn: Peter Hanstein.

Lieu, S.N.C. (1985), *Manicheism in the Later Roman Empire and Medieval China.* Manchester: Manchester University Press.

—— (ed.) (1986). *The Emperor Julian, Panegyric and Polemic.* Liverpool: Liverpool University Press.

Lilla, S.R.C. (1971). *Clement of Alexandria.* Oxford: Oxford University Press.

Linderski, J. (1986). 'The Augural Law' in Temporini (1986).

Lindsay, J. (1963). *Daily Life in Roman Egypt.* London: Frederick Muller.

Ling, R. (1989). *Classical Greece.* Oxford: Phaidon.

—— (1991). *Roman Painting.* Cambridge: Cambridge University Press.

Lintott, A.W. (1968). *Violence in Republican Rome.* Oxford: Clarendon Press.

—— (1972). 'Provocatio: From the Struggle of the Orders to the Principate' in Temporini (1972).

—— (1981). 'What was the Imperium Romanum?', *Greece and Rome,* 28. 53–67.

—— (1982). *Violence, Civil Strife and Revolution in the Classical City.* London: Croom Helm.

—— (1990). 'Electoral Bribery in the Roman Republic', *Journal of Roman Studies,* 80. 1–16.

Lissarrague, F. (1990). *The Aesthetics of the Greek Banquet: Images of Wine and Ritual.* Princeton, NJ: Princeton University Press.

Lloyd, G.E.R. (1968). *Aristotle: The Growth and Structure of his Thought.* Cambridge: Cambridge University Press.

—— (1978). *Hippocratic Writings.* Harmondsworth: Penguin.

Lloyd-Jones, P.H.J. (1971). *The Justice of Zeus.* Berkeley and Los Angeles: University of California Press.

—— (1975). *Females of the Species.* London: Duckworth.

Loewenstein, K. (1973). *The Governance of Rome.* The Hague: M. Nijhoff.

Loicq-Berger, M.-P. (1967). *Syracuse: Histoire culturelle d'une cité grecque.* Brussels: Latomus.

Long, A.A. (1974). *Hellenistic Philosophy.* London: Duckworth.

Longrigg, J. (1975). 'Elementary Physics in the Lyceum and Stoa', *Isis,* 66. 211–29.

—— (1976). 'The "Roots" of All Things', *Isis*, 67. 420–38.

—— (1993). *Greek Rational Medicine*. London: Routledge.

Lord, A.B. (1960). *The Singer of Tales*. Cambridge, Mass.: Harvard University Press.

Luce, T.J. (1977). *Livy: The Composition of his History*. Princeton, NJ: Princeton University Press.

—— (ed.) (1982). *Ancient Writers*. New York: Scribner.

Luibheid, C. (1982). *The Council of Nicaea*. Galway: Galway University Press.

Luttwak, E.N. (1976). *The Grand Strategy of the Roman Empire from the First Century* AD *to the Third*. Baltimore, MD: Johns Hopkins University Press.

Lynch, J.P. (1972). *Aristotle's School: A Study of a Greek Educational Institution*. Berkeley and Los Angeles: University of California Press.

Lyne, R.O.A.M. (1980). *The Latin Love Poets: From Catullus to Horace*. Oxford: Clarendon Press.

Maas, M., and Snyder, J.McI. (1989). *Stringed Instruments of Ancient Greece*. New Haven and London: Yale University Press.

MacBain, B. (1982). *Prodigy and Expiation: A Study on Religion and Politics in Republican Rome*. Brussels: Latomus.

MacDonald, W.L. (1976). *The Pantheon. Design, Meaning, and Progeny*. London: Allen Lane.

—— (1982). *The Architecture of the Roman Empire*, I: *An Introductory Study*. 2nd edn. New Haven and London: Yale University Press.

—— (1986). *The Architecture of the Roman Empire*, II: *An Urban Appraisal*. New Haven and London: Yale University Press.

MacDowell, D.M. (1963). *Athenian Homicide Law in the Age of the Orators*. Manchester: Manchester University Press.

—— (1978). *The Law in Classical Athens*. London: Thames & Hudson.

—— (1986). *Spartan Law*. Edinburgh: Scottish Academic Press.

McGing, B.C. (1986). *The Foreign Policy of Mithridates VI Eupator, King of Pontus*. Leiden: E.J. Brill.

Mack, S. (1988). *Ovid*. New Haven, Conn.: Yale University Press.

McKay, A.G. (1975). *Houses, Villas and Palaces in the Roman World*. London: Thames & Hudson.

Maclagan, M. (1968). *The City of Constantinople*. London: Thames & Hudson.

Macleod, C.W. (1982). 'Politics and the *Oresteia*', *Journal of Hellenic Studies*, 102. 124–44.

MacMullen, R. (1969). *Constantine*. London: Weidenfeld & Nicolson.

McShane, R.B. (1964). *The Foreign Policy of the Attalids of Pergamum*. Urbana: University of Illinois Press.

Macurdy, G.H. (1932). *Hellenistic Queens*. Baltimore, Md.: Johns Hopkins University Press.

Maenchen-Helfen, D.J. (1973). *The World of the Huns*. Berkeley and Los Angeles: University of California Press.

Magie, D. (1975). *Roman Rule in Asia Minor to the End of the Third Century after Christ*. 2 vols. New York: Arno Press.

Manville, P.B. (1990). *The Origins of Citizenship in Ancient Athens*. Princeton, NJ: Princeton University Press.

Marrou, H.I. (1956) *A History of Education in Antiquity*. London: Sheed & Ward.

Marsden, E.W. (1964). *The Campaign of Gaugamela*. Liverpool: Liverpool University Press.

—— (1969). *Greek and Roman Artillery. Historical Development*. Oxford: Clarendon Press.

Marsden, P. (1980). *Roman London*. London: Thames & Hudson.

Marshall, B.A. (1976). *Crassus: A Political Biography*. Amsterdam: A.M. Hakkert.

Martin, L. (1987). *Hellenistic Religions. An Introduction*. New York: Oxford University Press.

Matthews, J. (1989). *The Roman Empire of Ammianus*. London: Duckworth.

—— (1990). *Western Aristocracies and Imperial Court AD 364–425*. New edn. Oxford: Clarendon Press.

Mattingly, H., and Handford, S.A. (1970). *Tacitus: The Agricola and the Germania*. Harmondsworth: Penguin.

Meier, C. (1993). *The Political Art of Greek Tragedy*. Cambridge: Polity Press.

Meiggs, R. (1960). *Roman Ostia*. Oxford: Clarendon Press.

—— (1972). *The Athenian Empire*. Oxford: Clarendon Press.

—— (1982). *Trees and Timber in the Ancient Mediterranean World*. Oxford: Clarendon Press.

Meiggs, R., and Lewis, D.M. (1988). *A Selection of Greek Historical Inscriptions to the End of the Fifth Century BC*. 2nd edn. Oxford: Clarendon Press.

Merkelbach, R. (1984). *Mithras*. Königstein: Anton Hain.

Merrifield, R. (1969). *Roman London*. London: Cassell.

Metzger, B.M. (1968). *The Text of the New Testament: Its Transmission, Corruption, and Restoration*. 2nd edn. Oxford: Clarendon Press.

—— (1987). *The Canon of the New Testament: Its Origin, Development, and Significance*. Oxford: Clarendon Press.

Michaelides, S. (1978). *The Music of Ancient Greece – An Encyclopaedia*. London: Faber & Faber.

Michałowski, K. (1970). *Palmyra*. London: Pall Mall.

Michell, H. (1957). *Economics of Ancient Greece.* Cambridge: Heffer.
—— (1964). *Sparta.* Cambridge: Cambridge University Press.
Michels, A.K. (1967). *The Calendar of the Roman Republic.* Princeton, NJ: Princeton University Press.
Mikalson, J.D. (1976). *The Sacred and Civil Calendar of the Athenian Year.* Princeton, NJ: Princeton University Press.
Millar, F.G.B. (1964). *A Study of Cassius Dio.* Oxford: Clarendon Press.
—— (1977). *The Emperor in the Roman World (31 BC–AD 337).* London: Duckworth.
—— (1981). *The Roman Empire and its Neighbours.* 2nd edn. London: Duckworth.
—— (1983). 'Epigraphy' in Crawford (1983).
Miller, J.I. (1969). *The Spice Trade of the Roman Empire 29 BC–AD 641.* Oxford: Clarendon Press.
Mitchell, B.M. (1966). 'Cyrene and Persia', *Journal of Hellenic Studies,* 86. 99–113.
—— (1975). 'Herodotus and Samos', *Journal of Hellenic Studies,* 95. 75–91.
Mitchell, R.E. (1991). *Patricians and Plebeians.* Ithaca, NY: Cornell University Press.
Mócsy, A. (1974). *Pannonia and Upper Moesia: A History of the Middle Danubian Provinces of the Roman Empire.* London: Routledge & Kegan Paul.
Moggi, M. (1976). *I synecismi interstatali greci I: dalle origini al 338.* Pisa: Marlin.
Momigliano, A.D. (ed.) (1963a). *The Conflict between Paganism and Christianity in the Fourth Century.* Oxford: Clarendon Press.
—— (1963b). 'An Interim Report on the Origins of Rome', *Journal of Roman Studies,* 53. 95–121.
—— (1971). *The Development of Greek Biography.* Cambridge, Mass.: Harvard University Press.
—— (1975a). *Alien Wisdom. The Limits of Hellenization.* Cambridge: Cambridge University Press.
—— (1975b). 'Dio of Prusa, the Rhodian "libertas" and the Philosophers', in Momigliano (ed.), *Quinto contributo alla storia degli studi classici e del mondo antico.* Rome: Ed. di Storia e Letteratura.
—— (1977). *Essays in Ancient and Modern Historiography.* Oxford: Blackwell.
—— (1990). *The Classical Foundations of Modern Historiography.* Berkeley and Los Angeles: University of California Press.
Mommsen, T. (1861). *History of Rome.* London: Richard Bentley.
—— (1968). *The Provinces of the Roman Empire. The European Provinces.* Ed. T.R.S. Broughton. Chicago: University of Chicago Press.

Moretti, G. (1948). *Ara Pacis Augustae*. Rome: Institutio Poligrafico dello Stato.

Morgan, C. (1990). *Athletes and Oracles: The Transformation of Olympia and Delphi in the Eighth Century* BC. Cambridge: Cambridge University Press.

Morkholm, O. (1966). *Antiochus IV of Syria*. Copenhagen: Gyldendal.

Morrison, J.S. (1980). *Long Ships and Round Ships: Warfare and Trade in the Mediterranean, 3000 BC–500 AD*. London: HMSO.

Morrison, J.S., and Coates, J.F. (1986). *The Athenian Trireme. The History and Reconstruction of an Ancient Greek Warship*. Cambridge: Cambridge University Press.

Morrison, J.S., and Williams, R.T. (1968). *Greek Oared Ships 900–322 BC*. Cambridge: Cambridge University Press.

Moscati, S. (1968). *The World of the Phoenicians*. London: Weidenfeld & Nicolson.

—— (ed.) (1988). *The Phoenicians*. Milan: Bompiani.

Mossé, C. (1973). *Athens in Decline, 404–86 BC*. Trans. J. Stewart. London: Routledge & Kegan Paul.

Moxon, I.S., Smart, J.D., and Woodman, A.J. (eds.) (1986). *Past Perspectives*. Cambridge: Cambridge University Press.

Murray, G. (1934). *The Rise of the Greek Epic*. 4th edn. London: Oxford University Press.

Murray, O. (1972). 'Herodotus and Hellenistic Culture', *Classical Quarterly*, n.s. 22. 200–13.

—— (ed.) (1990). *Sympotica: A Symposium on the Symposion*. Oxford: Clarendon Press.

—— (1993). *Early Greece*. 2nd edn. London: Fontana.

Murray, O., and Price, S.R.F. (eds.) (1990). *The Greek City from Homer to Alexander*. Oxford: Clarendon Press.

Musurillo, H.A. (ed.) (1954). *The Acts of the Pagan Martyrs*. Oxford: Clarendon Press.

Mylonas, G.E. (1961). *Eleusis and the Eleusinian Mysteries*. Princeton, NJ: Princeton University Press.

Narain, A.K. (1957). *The Indo-Greeks*. Oxford: Clarendon Press.

Nash, E. (1968). *A Pictorial Dictionary of Ancient Rome*. 2 vols. 2nd edn. London: Thames & Hudson.

Neugebaur, O. (1957). *The Exact Sciences in Antiquity*. 2nd edn. Providence, RI: Brown University Press.

Nicholas, B. (1962). *An Introduction to Roman Law*. Oxford: Clarendon Press.

Nicolet, C. (1980). *The World of the Citizen in Republican Rome*. London: Batsford.

Nicols, J. (1978). *Vespasian and the Partes Flavianae*. Wiesbaden: Steiner.

Nippel, W. (1984). 'Policing Rome', *Journal of Roman Studies*, 74. 20–9.

Noble, J.V. (1988). *The Techniques of Painted Attic Pottery*. 2nd edn. London: Thames & Hudson.

North, J.A. (1979). 'Religious Toleration in Republican Rome', *Proceedings of the Cambridge Philological Society*, 25. 85–103.

—— (1981). 'The Development of Roman Imperialism', *Journal of Roman Studies*, 71. 1–9.

Oakley, S.P. (1985). 'Single Combat in the Roman Republic', *Classical Quarterly*, 35. 392–410.

Ogilvie, R.M. (1965). *A Historical Commentary on Livy I–V*. Oxford: Clarendon Press.

—— (1969). *The Romans and their Gods in the Age of Augustus*. London: Chatto & Windus.

—— (1976). *Early Rome and the Etruscans*. London: Fontana.

—— (1978). *The Library of Lactantius*. Oxford: Clarendon Press.

Oliva, P. (1971). *Sparta and her Social Problems*. Prague: Academia; Amsterdam: Hakkert.

Oost, S.I. (1968). *Galla Placidia Augusta*. Chicago: University of Chicago Press.

Ormerod, H.A. (1924). *Piracy in the Ancient World. An Essay in Mediterranean History*. Liverpool: Liverpool University Press.

Osborne, M.J. (1979). 'Kallias, Phaidros, and the Revolt of Athens in 287 BC', *Zeitschrift für Papyrologie und Epigraphie*, 35. 181–94.

—— (1981–3). *Naturalisation in Athens*. 4 vols. Brussels: Academie.

Osborne, R. (1985). *Demos: The Discovery of Classical Attika*. Cambridge: Cambridge University Press.

—— (1987). *Classical Landscape with Figures*. London: George Philip.

—— (1990). 'The *Demos* and its Divisions in Classical Athens' in Murray and Price (1990).

Ostwald, M. (1969). *Nomos and the Beginnings of the Athenian Democracy*. Oxford: Clarendon Press.

—— (1986). *From Popular Sovereignty to the Sovereignty of Law. Society and Politics in Fifth Century Athens*. Berkeley and Los Angeles: University of California Press.

Otis, B. (1963). *Virgil: A Study in Civilized Poetry*. Oxford: Clarendon Press.

Page, D.L. (1951). *Alcman, the Partheneion*. Oxford: Clarendon Press.

—— (1955). *Sappho and Alcaeus*. Oxford: Clarendon Press.

Pagels, E.H. (1979). *The Gnostic Gospels*. New York: Random House.

Palagia, O. (1980). *Euphranor*. Leiden: E.J. Brill.

Pallottino, M. (1975). *The Etruscans*. 2nd edn. London: Allen Lane.

—— (1991). *A History of Earliest Italy*. London: Routledge.

Palmer, A.-M. (1989). *Prudentius on the Martyrs*. Oxford: Clarendon Press.

Palmer, L.R. (1954). *The Latin Language*. London: Faber & Faber.

—— (1980). *The Greek Language*. London: Faber & Faber.

Palmer, R.E.A. (1970). *The Archaic Community of the Romans*. Cambridge: Cambridge University Press.

Parke, H.W. (1933). *Greek Mercenary Soldiers*. Oxford: Clarendon Press.

—— (1967a). *Greek Oracles*. London: Hutchinson.

—— (1967b). *The Oracles of Zeus*. Oxford: Blackwell.

—— (1977). *Festivals of the Athenians*. London: Thames & Hudson.

Parke, H.W., and Wormell, D.E.W. (1956). *The Delphic Oracle*. 2 vols. Oxford: Blackwell.

Parker, H.M.D. (1928). *The Roman Legions*. Cambridge: Heffer.

—— (1958). *A History of the Roman World from* AD *138 to 337*. 2nd edn. Rev. B.H. Warmington. London: Methuen.

Parker, R. (1983). *Miasma. Pollution and Purification in Early Greek Religion*. Oxford: Oxford University Press.

Parry, A. (ed.) (1971). *The Making of Homeric Verse*. Oxford: Clarendon Press.

Paul, G.M. (1984). *A Historical Commentary on Sallust's* Bellum Jugurthinum. Liverpool: Francis Cairns.

Peacock, D.P.S. (1982). *Pottery in the Roman World: An Ethnoarchaeological Approach*. London and New York: Longman.

Pearson, L. (1939). *The Early Ionian Historians*. Oxford: Clarendon Press.

—— (1960). *The Lost Histories of Alexander the Great*. New York: American Philological Association.

—— (1962). 'The Pseudo-History of Messenia and its Authors', *Historia*, 11. 397–426.

—— (1976). *The Art of Demosthenes*. Meisenheim am Glan: Anton Hain.

—— (1987). *The Greek Historians of the West: Timaeus and his Predecessors*. Atlanta, GA: American Philological Association.

Pédech, P. (1976). *La Géographie des grecs*. Paris: Presses Universitaires de France.

Pedley, J.G. (1990). *Paestum: Greeks and Romans in Southern Italy*. London: Thames & Hudson.

Peebles, B. (1951). *The Poet Prudentius*. New York: McMullen.

Percival, J. (1976). *The Roman Villa: An Historical Introduction*. London: Batsford.

Perkins, A. (1973). *The Art of Dura-Europus*. Oxford: Clarendon Press.

Perowne, S. (1960). *Hadrian*. London: Hodder & Stoughton.

Perry, B.E. (1952). *Aesopica*. Vol. 1. Urbana, Ill.: University of Illinois Press.

—— (1967). *The Ancient Romances. A Literary–Historical Account of their Origins.* Berkeley and Los Angeles: University of California Press.

Pfeiffer, R. (1968). *History of Classical Scholarship: From the Beginnings to the End of the Hellenistic Age.* Oxford: Clarendon Press.

Phillips, E.D. (1973). *Greek Medicine.* London: Thames & Hudson.

Pichlmayr, F. (ed.) (1911). *Aurelius Victor.* Leipzig: Teubner.

Pickard-Cambridge, A. (1914). *Demosthenes and the Last Days of Greek Freedom.* New York and London: Knickerbocker Press.

—— (1962). *Dithyramb, Tragedy and Comedy.* 2nd edn. Oxford: Clarendon Press.

—— (1968). *The Dramatic Festivals of Athens.* 2nd edn. Rev. J. Gould and D.M. Lewis. Oxford: Clarendon Press.

Platner, S.B., and Ashby, T. (1929). *Topographical Dictionary of Ancient Rome.* Oxford: Clarendon Press.

Plommer, H. (1973). *Vitruvius and Later Roman Building Manuals.* Cambridge: Cambridge University Press.

Podlecki, A.J. (1966). *The Political Background of Aeschylean Tragedy.* Ann Arbor: University of Michigan Press.

—— (1975). *The Life of Themistocles.* Montreal: McGill and Queen's University Press.

Poliakoff, M.B. (1987). *Combat Sports in the Ancient World: Competition, Violence, and Culture.* New Haven and London: Yale University Press.

Pollitt, J.J. (1986). *Art in the Hellenistic Age.* Cambridge: Cambridge University Press.

Pomeroy, S. (1975). *Goddesses, Whores, Wives and Slaves: Women in Classical Antiquity.* New York: Schocken Books.

—— (1990). *Women in Hellenistic Egypt. From Alexander to Cleopatra.* 2nd edn. Detroit: Wayne State University Press.

Posner, E. (1972). *Archives in the Ancient World.* Cambridge, Mass.: Harvard University Press.

Potter, T.W. (1979). *The Changing Landscape of South Etruria.* London: Elek.

—— (1987). *Roman Italy.* London: British Museum.

Potts, D.T. (1990). *The Arabian Gulf in Antiquity.* Vol. II: *From Alexander the Great to the Coming of Islam.* Oxford: Clarendon Press.

Poucet, J. (1985). *Les Origines de Rome. Tradition et histoire.* Brussels: Facultés Universitaires Saint Louis.

Poultney, J.W. (1959). *The Bronze Tables of Iguvium.* New York: American Philological Association.

Powell, B.B. (1991). *Homer and the Origin of the Greek Alphabet.* Cambridge: Cambridge University Press.

Powell, T.G.E. (1960). *The Celts*. 2nd edn. London: Thames & Hudson.

Pratt, N. (1983). *Seneca's Drama*. Chapel Hill: University of North Carolina Press.

Price, S.R.F. (1984). *Rituals and Power: The Roman Imperial Cult in Asia Minor*. Cambridge: Cambridge University Press.

Pritchett, W.K. (1963). *Ancient Athenian Calendars on Stone*. Berkeley and Los Angeles: University of California Press.

—— (1965–91). *The Greek State at War*. 5 vols. Berkeley and Los Angeles: University of California Press.

—— (1971). *Ancient Greek Military Practices*. Part 1. Berkeley and Los Angeles: University of California Press.

Pulgram, E. (1958). *The Tongues of Italy*. Cambridge, Mass.: Harvard University Press.

Quinn, K. (1972). *Catullus: An Interpretation*. London: Batsford.

—— (1979). *Texts and Contexts: The Roman Writers and their Audience*. London: Routledge & Kegan Paul.

Raaflaub, K.A. (ed.) (1986). *Social Struggles in Archaic Rome: New Perspectives on the Conflict of the Orders*. Berkeley and Los Angeles: University of California Press.

—— (1989). 'Contemporary Perceptions of Democracy in Fifth-century Athens', *Classica et Mediaevalia*, 40. 33–70.

Race, W.H. (1986). *Pindar*. Boston, Mass.: Twayne.

Rajak, T. (1983). *Josephus, the Historian and his Society*. London: Duckworth.

Rankin, H.D. (1987). *Celts and the Classical World*. London: Croom Helm.

Raven, J.E. (1948). *Pythagoreans and Eleatics*. Cambridge: Cambridge University Press.

—— (1965). *Plato's Thought in the Making*. Cambridge: Cambridge University Press.

Rawson, B. (ed.) (1986). *The Family in Ancient Rome: New Perspectives*. London: Croom Helm.

Rawson, E.D. (1969). *The Spartan Tradition in European Thought*. Oxford: Clarendon Press.

—— (1973). 'Scipio, Laelius, Furius and the Ancestral Religion', *Journal of Roman Studies*, 63. 161–74.

—— (1975). *Cicero, a Portrait*. London: Allen Lane.

—— (1985). *Intellectual Life in the Late Roman Republic*. London: Duckworth.

—— (1991). *Roman Culture and Society: Collected Papers*. Oxford: Clarendon Press.

Reardon, B.P. (ed.) (1989). *Collected Ancient Greek Novels*. Berkeley and Los Angeles: University of California Press.

Reddé, M. (1986). *Mare Nostrum: les infrastructures, le dispositif et l'histoire de la marine militaire sous l'empire romain*. Rome: École Française.

Reinhardt, K. (1921). *Poseidonios*. Munich: Oskar Beck.

Reiter, W. (1988). *Aemilius Paullus. Conqueror of Greece*. London: Croom Helm.

Reynolds, L.D., and Wilson, N.G. (1991). *Scribes and Scholars: A Guide to the Transmission of Greek and Latin Literature*. 3rd edn. Oxford: Clarendon Press.

Rhodes, P.J. (1972). *The Athenian Boule*. Oxford: Clarendon Press.

—— (1981). *A Commentary on the Aristotelian* Athenaion Politeia. Oxford: Clarendon Press.

Rich, J., and Wallace-Hadrill, A. (eds.) (1991). *City and Country in the Ancient World*. London: Routledge.

Richardson, J.S. (1976). *Roman Provincial Administration 222 BC– AD 117*. Basingstoke: Macmillan.

—— (1986). *Hispaniae: Spain and the Development of Roman Imperialism 218–82 BC*. Cambridge: Cambridge University Press.

Richardson, L. (1988). *Pompeii: An Architectural History*. Baltimore, Md.: Johns Hopkins University Press.

—— (1992). *A New Topographical Dictionary of Rome*. Baltimore, Md.: Johns Hopkins University Press.

Richmond, I.A. (1971). *The City Wall of Imperial Rome*. Maryland: McGrath.

Richter, G.M.A. (1968–71). *Engraved Gems of the Greeks, Etruscans and Romans*. 2 vols. London: Phaidon.

—— (1970a). *Kouroi: Archaic Greek Youths*. 3rd edn. London: Phaidon.

—— (1970b). *The Sculpture and Sculptors of the Greeks*. 4th edn. New Haven, Conn.: Yale University Press.

Rickman, G.E. (1980). *The Corn Supply of Ancient Rome*. Oxford: Clarendon Press.

Ridgway, B.S. (1970). *The Severe Style in Greek Sculpture*. Princeton, NJ: Princeton University Press.

—— (1978). *The Archaic Style in Greek Sculpture*. Princeton, NJ: Princeton University Press.

—— (1981). *Fifth Century Styles in Greek Sculpture*. Princeton, NJ: Princeton University Press.

Ridgway, D., and Ridgway, F.R. (eds.) (1979). *Italy before the Romans*. London: Academic Press.

Ridley, R.T. (1982). *Zosimus, New History*. Sydney: University of Sydney.

Rivet, A.L.F. (1988). *Gallia Narbonensis: Southern Gaul in Roman Times*. London: Batsford.

Rizzo, F.P. (1970). *La repubblica di Siracusa nel momento di Ducezio.* Palermo: U. Manfredi.

Roaf, M. (1990). *Cultural Atlas of Mesopotamia and the Ancient Near East.* Oxford and New York: Facts on File.

Roberts, C.H., and Skeat, T.C. (1983). *The Birth of the Codex.* London: British Academy.

Robertson, A.S. (1990). *The Antonine Wall. A Handbook to the Surviving Remains.* 4th edn. Glasgow: Glasgow Archaeological Society.

Robertson, M. (1959). *Greek Painting.* Geneva: Weber.

—— (1975). *A History of Greek Art.* 2 vols. Cambridge: Cambridge University Press.

Robinson, C. (1979). *Lucian and his Influence in Europe.* London: Duckworth.

Robinson, H.R. (1975). *The Armour of Imperial Rome.* London: Arms & Armour Press.

Robinson, O.F. (1992). *Ancient Rome.* London: Routledge.

Roebuck, C.A. (1941). *A History of Messenia from 369 to 146 BC.* Chicago: University of Chicago Libraries.

Romm, J.S. (1992). *The Edges of the Earth in Ancient Thought.* Princeton, NJ: Princeton University Press.

Ross, D.D. (1969). *Style and Tradition in Catullus.* London: Oxford University Press.

—— (1975). *Backgrounds to Augustan Poetry: Gallus, Elegy and Rome.* Cambridge: Cambridge University Press.

Rossi, L. (1971). *Trajan's Column and the Dacian Wars.* London: Thames & Hudson.

Rostovtzeff, M.I. (1941). *The Social and Economic History of the Hellenistic World.* 3 vols. Oxford: Clarendon Press.

—— (1957). *The Social and Economic History of the Roman Empire.* 2nd edn. Oxford: Clarendon Press.

Rousseau, P. (1985). *Pachomius: The Making of a Community in Fourth-century Egypt.* Berkeley and Los Angeles: University of California Press.

Roussel, D. (1976). *Tribu et cité.* Paris: Les Belles Lettres.

Rubinsohn, W.Z. (1987). *Spartacus' Uprising and Soviet Historical Writing.* Oxford: Oxbow.

Rudd, N. (1966). *The Satires of Horace.* Cambridge: Cambridge University Press.

—— (1986). *Themes in Roman Satire.* London: Duckworth.

Rudolph, K. (1983). *Gnosis.* Edinburgh: T. and C. Clark.

Ruehl, F. (1887). *Eutropius, Breviarium ab urbe condita.* Repr. Stuttgart: Teubner, 1975.

Ruether, R. (1969). *Gregory of Nazianzus: Rhetor and Philosopher.* Oxford: Clarendon Press.

Russell, D.A. (1973). *Plutarch*. London: Duckworth.

—— (1981). *Criticism in Antiquity*. London: Duckworth.

Rykwert, J. (1976). *The Idea of a Town*. London: Faber & Faber.

Sacks, K.S. (1990). *Diodorus Siculus and the First Century*. Princeton, NJ: Princeton University Press.

Saller, R.P. (1982). *Personal Patronage under the Early Empire*. Cambridge: Cambridge University Press.

Salmon, E.T. (1967). *Samnium and the Samnites*. Cambridge: Cambridge University Press.

—— (1968). *A History of the Roman World from 30 BC to AD 138*. 6th edn. London: Methuen.

—— (1969). *Roman Colonization under the Republic*. London: Thames & Hudson.

—— (1982). *The Making of Roman Italy*. London: Thames & Hudson.

Salmon, J.B. (1984). *Wealthy Corinth*. Oxford: Clarendon Press.

Salomies, O. (1987). *Die römischen Vornamen. Studien zur römischen Namengebung*. Helsinki: Societas Scientiarum Fennica.

Salway, P. (1981). *Roman Britain*. Oxford: Clarendon Press.

Sambursky, S. (1956). *The Physical World of the Greeks*. London: Routledge & Kegan Paul.

Sandbach, F.H. (1975). *The Stoics*. London: Chatto & Windus.

—— (1977). *The Comic Theatre of Greece and Rome*. London: Chatto & Windus.

Sanders, E.P. (1991). *Paul*. Oxford: Oxford University Press.

Sanders, L.J. (1987). *Dionysius I of Syracuse and Greek Tyranny*. London: Croom Helm.

Sandmel, S. (1979). *Philo of Alexandria: An Introduction*. Oxford: Oxford University Press.

Sandy, G.N. (1982). *Heliodorus*. Boston, Mass.: Twayne.

Sansone, D. (1989). *Plutarch: The Lives of Aristeides and Cato*. Warminster: Aris & Phillips.

Sarton, G. (1970). *A History of Science*. Vol. 1: *Ancient Science through the Golden Age of Greece*. New York: Norton.

Scarborough, J. (1969). *Roman Medicine*. Ithaca, NY: Cornell University Press.

Schmeling, G.L. (1980). *Xenophon of Ephesus*. Boston, Mass.: Twayne.

Schulz, F. (1946). *History of Roman Legal Science*. Oxford: Clarendon Press.

Schürer, E. (1973–87), ed. G. Vermes, F. Millar, and M. Black. *The History of the Jewish People*. 3 vols. Edinburgh: T. and C. Clark.

Scott-Kilvert, I., and Carter, J. (1987). *Cassius Dio: The Roman History, The Reign of Augustus*. Harmondsworth: Penguin.

Scullard, H.H. (1967). *The Etruscan Cities and Rome*. London: Thames & Hudson.

—— (1970). *Scipio Africanus: Soldier and Politician*. London: Thames & Hudson.

—— (1973). *Roman Politics, 220–150 BC*. 2nd edn. Oxford: Clarendon Press.

—— (1974). *The Elephant in the Greek and Roman World*. London: Thames & Hudson.

—— (1979). *Roman Britain, Outpost of the Empire*. London: Thames & Hudson.

—— (1980). *A History of the Roman World, 753–146 BC*. 4th edn. London: Methuen.

—— (1981). *Festivals and Ceremonies of the Roman Republic*. London: Thames & Hudson.

—— (1982). *From the Gracchi to Nero. A History of Rome from 133 BC to AD 68*. 5th edn. London: Methuen.

Seager, R. (1972a). 'Cicero and the Word *Popularis*', *Classical Quarterly*, 22. 328–38.

—— (1972b). *Tiberius*. London: Eyre Methuen.

—— (1979). *Pompey: A Political Biography*. Oxford: Blackwell.

Sealey, B.R.I. (1976). *A History of the Greek City States*. Berkeley and Los Angeles: University of California Press.

Sealey, R. (1990). *Women and Law in Classical Greece*. Chapel Hill, NC: University of North Carolina Press.

—— (1993). *Demosthenes and his Time. A Study in Defeat*. Oxford: Oxford University Press.

Sedlar, J.W. (1980). *India and the Greek World. A Study in the Transmission of Culture*. Totowa, NJ: Rowman & Littlefield.

Seeck, O. (1876). *Notitia Dignitatum*. Repr. Frankfurt: Minerva, 1962.

Segal, E. (1987). *Roman Laughter*. 2nd edn. Oxford: Oxford University Press.

Segal, J.B. (1970). *Edessa. 'The Blessed City'*. Oxford: Clarendon Press.

Sestieri, A.-M. (1992). *The Iron-Age Community of Osteria dell'Osa*. Cambridge: Cambridge University Press.

Shackleton Bailey, D.R. (ed.) (1965–70). *Cicero's Letters to Atticus*. 7 vols. Cambridge: Cambridge University Press.

Shear, T.L. (1978). *Kallias of Sphettos and the Revolt of Athens in 286 BC*. Princeton, NJ: American School of Classical Studies.

Sherk, R. (1990–93). 'The Eponymous Officials of Greek Cities', *Zeitschrift für Papyrologie und Epigraphik*, 83. 249–88; 84. 231–95; 88. 225–60; 93. 223–72; 96. 267–95.

Sherwin-White, A.N. (1966). *The Letters of Pliny. A Social and Historical Commentary*. Oxford: Clarendon Press.

—— (1973). *The Roman Citizenship*. 2nd edn. Oxford: Clarendon Press.

—— (1977). 'Roman Involvement in Anatolia, 167–88 BC', *Journal of Roman Studies*, 67. 62–75.

—— (1982). 'The Lex Repetundarum and the Political Ideas of Gaius Gracchus', *Journal of Roman Studies*, 72. 18–31.

—— (1984). *Roman Foreign Policy in the East 168 BC–AD 1*. London: Duckworth.

Sherwin-White, S.M. (1978). *Ancient Cos. An Historical Study from the Dorian Settlement to the Imperial Period*. Göttingen: Vandenhoeck & Ruprecht.

—— (1985). 'Ancient Archives: The Edict of Alexander to Priene, a Reappraisal', *Journal of Hellenic Studies*, 105. 69–89.

Shinnie, P.L. (1967). *Meroë: A Civilization of the Sudan*. London: Thames & Hudson.

Shipley, G. (1987). *A History of Samos 800–188 BC*. Oxford: Clarendon Press.

Sinclair, T.A. (1967). *A History of Greek Political Thought*. London: Routledge.

Skutsch, O. (1985). *The Annals of Quintus Ennius*. Oxford: Clarendon Press.

Skydsgaard, J.E. (1967). *Varro the Scholar*. Copenhagen: Munksgaard.

Smith, R.E. (1958). *Service in the Post-Marian Roman Army*. Manchester: Manchester University Press.

Smith, R.R.R. (1988). *Hellenistic Ruler Portraits*. Oxford: Clarendon Press.

—— (1991). *Hellenistic Sculpture*. London: Thames & Hudson.

Smith, V.A. (1981) *Oxford History of India*. 4th edn. Ed. P Spear. Delhi: Oxford University Press.

Smith, W.D. (1979). *The Hippocratic Tradition*. Ithaca, NY: Cornell University Press.

Snodgrass, A.M. (1967). *Arms and Armour of the Greeks*. London: Thames & Hudson.

—— (1977). *Archaeology and the Rise of the Greek State*. Cambridge: Cambridge University Press.

Snowden, F.M. (1970). *Blacks in Antiquity: Ethiopians in the Greco-Roman Experience*. Cambridge, Mass.: Harvard University Press.

Solmsen, F. (1979). *Isis among the Greeks and Romans*. Cambridge, Mass.: Harvard University Press.

Soulahti, J. (1963). *The Roman Censors. A Study on Social Structure*. Helsinki: Academia Scientiarum Fennica.

Sparkes, B.A. (1991). *Greek Pottery: An Introduction*. Manchester: Manchester University Press.

Spiller, G. (ed.) (1991). *The Mediterranean Diets in Health and Disease*. New York: Van Nostrand Reinhold.

Stadter, P.A. (1980). *Arrian of Nicomedia*. Chapel Hill: University of North Carolina Press.

Stahl, W.H. (1971–7). *Martianus Capella and the Seven Liberal Arts*. 2 vols. London and New York: Columbia University Press.

Staniforth, M. (1964). *Marcus Aurelius: Meditations*. Harmondsworth: Penguin.

Starr, C.G. (1960). *The Roman Imperial Navy 31 BC–AD 324*. 2nd edn. Cambridge: Heffer.

—— (1986). *Individual and Community: The Rise of the Polis 800–500 BC*. Oxford: Clarendon Press.

—— (1988). *The Influence of Sea Power on Ancient History*. Oxford: Clarendon Press.

—— (1990). *The Birth of Athenian Democracy*. Oxford: Clarendon Press.

Staveley, E.S. (1972). *Greek and Roman Voting and Elections*. London: Thames & Hudson.

Stern, M. (ed.) (1974–84). *Greek and Latin Authors on Jews and Judaism*. 3 vols. Jerusalem: Israel Academy of Sciences and Humanities.

Stevens, C.E. (1933). *Sidonius Apollinaris and his Age*. Oxford: Clarendon Press.

Stewart, A.F. (1977). *Skopas of Paros*. Park Ridge, NJ: Noyes Press.

—— (1979). *Attika. Studies in Athenian Sculpture of the Hellenistic Age*. London: Society for the Promotion of Hellenic Studies.

—— (1990). *Greek Sculpture: An Exploration*. 2 vols. New Haven and London: Yale University Press.

Stibbe, C.M., Colonna, G., De Simone, C., and Versnel, H.S. (1980). *Lapis Satricanus*. The Hague: Nederlands Institut te Rome.

Stillwell, R. (ed.) (1976). *The Princeton Encyclopedia of Classical Sites*. Princeton, NJ: Princeton University Press.

Stipcevic, A. (1977). *The Illyrians*. New York: Noyes Press.

Stockton, D. (1971). *Cicero: A Political Biography*. Oxford: Clarendon Press.

—— (1979). *The Gracchi*. Oxford: Clarendon Press.

Strauss, B.S. (1986). *Athens after the Peloponnesian War*. London: Croom Helm.

Stronach, D.M. (1978). *Pasargadae*. Oxford: Clarendon Press.

Strong, D.E. (1961). *Roman Imperial Sculpture*. London: Tiranti.

—— (1966). *Greek and Roman Gold and Silver Plate*. London: Methuen.

—— (1976). *Roman Art*. Harmondsworth: Penguin.

Stroud, R.S. (1968). *Drakon's Law on Homicide*. Berkeley and Los Angeles: University of California Press.

Stylianou, P.J. (1989). *The Age of the Kingdoms. A Political History of Cyprus in the Archaic and Classical Periods*. Leukosia: Archbishop Makarios Foundation.

Sullivan, J.P. (ed.) (1962). *Critical Essays on Roman Literature: Satire*. London: Routledge & Kegan Paul.

—— (1968). *The Satyricon of Petronius*. London: Faber & Faber.

—— (1991). *Martial: The Unexpected Classic: A Literary and Historical Study*. Cambridge: Cambridge University Press.

Sullivan, R.D. (1990). *Near Eastern Royalty and Rome, 100–30 BC*. Toronto: University of Toronto Press.

Susini, G. (1973). *The Roman Stonecutter: An Introduction to Latin Epigraphy*. Oxford: Blackwell.

Sussman, L.A. (1978). *The Elder Seneca*. Leiden: E.J. Brill.

Sutherland, C.H.V. (1939). *The Romans in Spain 217 BC–AD 117*. London: Methuen.

—— (1974). *Roman Coins*. London: Barrie & Jenkins.

Sutton, D.F. (1980). *The Greek Satyr Play*. Meisenheim am Glan: Anton Hain.

Swaddling, J. (1980). *The Ancient Olympic Games*. London: British Museum.

Syme, R. (1939). *The Roman Revolution*. Oxford: Clarendon Press.

—— (1958). *Tacitus*. Oxford: Clarendon Press.

—— (1964). *Sallust*. Berkeley and Los Angeles: University of California Press.

—— (1968). *Ammianus and the Historia Augusta*. Oxford: Clarendon Press.

—— (1971). *Emperors and Biography. Studies in the Historia Augusta*. Oxford: Clarendon Press.

—— (1978). *History in Ovid*. Oxford: Clarendon Press.

—— (1980). *Some Arval Brethren*. Oxford: Clarendon Press.

Symons, D.J. (1987a). *Costume of Ancient Greece*. London: Batsford.

—— (1987b). *Costume of Ancient Rome*. London: Batsford.

Szemler, G.J. (1972). *The Priests of the Roman Republic*. Brussels: Latomus.

Talbert, R.J.A. (1974). *Timoleon and the Revival of Greek Sicily*. Cambridge: Cambridge University Press.

—— (1984). *The Senate of Imperial Rome*. Princeton, NJ: Princeton University Press.

Talbot Rice, T. (1958). *The Scythians*. London: Thames & Hudson.

Taplin, O. (1978). *Greek Tragedy in Action*. London: Methuen.

Tarn, W.W. (1913). *Antigonos Gonatas*. Oxford: Oxford University Press.

—— (1930). *Hellenistic Military and Naval Developments*. Cambridge: Cambridge University Press.

—— (1984).*The Greeks in Bactria and India*. 3rd edn. Rev. F.L. Holt. Chicago: Ares.

Tarn, W.W., and Griffith, G.T. (1952). *Hellenistic Civilization*. 3rd edn. London: Edward Arnold.

Tatton-Brown, V. (1987). *Ancient Cyprus*. London: British Museum.

Tatum, J. (1979). *Apuleius and the* Golden Ass. Ithaca, NY: Cornell University Press.

Taylor, L.R. (1931). *The Divinity of the Roman Emperor*. Middletown, Conn.: American Philological Association.

—— (1949). *Party Politics in the Age of Caesar*. Berkeley and Los Angeles: University of California Press.

—— (1960). *The Voting Districts of the Roman Republic*. Rome: American Academy in Rome.

—— (1962). 'Forerunners of the Gracchi', *Journal of Roman Studies*, 52. 19–27.

—— (1966). *Roman Voting Assemblies from the Hannibalic War to the Dictatorship of Caesar*. Ann Arbor: University of Michigan Press.

Taylor, M.W. (1981). *The Tyrant Slayers*. New York: Arno Press.

Temkin, O. (1956). *Soranus' Gynecology*. Baltimore, Md.: Johns Hopkins University Press.

Temkin, O. and Temkin, C.L. (eds.) (1967). *Ancient Medicine*. Baltimore, Md.: Johns Hopkins University Press.

Temporini, H. (ed.) (1972). *Aufstieg und Niedergang der römischen Welt*, vol.I.1. Berlin: De Gruyter.

—— (ed.) (1986). *Aufstieg und Niedergang der römischen Welt*, vol.II.16.3. Berlin: De Gruyter.

Thapar, R. (1966). *A History of India*. Vol. I. Harmondsworth: Penguin.

—— (1973). *Asoka and the Decline of the Mauryas*. 2nd edn. Delhi: Oxford University Press.

Thee, F.C.R. (1984). *Julius Africanus and the Early Christian View of Magic*. Tübingen: J.C.B. Mohr.

Thiel, J.H. (1946). *Studies on the History of Roman Sea-power in Republican Times*. Amsterdam: North Holland.

—— (1954). *A History of Roman Sea-power before the Second Punic War*. Amsterdam: North Holland.

—— (1966). *Eudoxus of Cyzicus*. Groningen: J.B. Wolters.

Thomas, J.A.C. (1977). *Textbook of Roman Law*. Amsterdam: North Holland.

Thomas, R. (1989). *Oral Tradition and Written Record in Classical Athens*. Cambridge: Cambridge University Press.

Thompson, D.J. (1988). *Memphis under the Ptolemies*. Princeton, NJ: Princeton University Press.

Thompson, E.A. (1965). *The Early Germans*. Oxford: Oxford University Press.

—— (1975). *A History of Attila and the Huns*. New edn. Westport, Conn.: Greenwood Press.

Thompson, H.A., and Wycherley, R.E. (1972). *The Agora of Athens: The History, Shape and Uses of an Ancient City Center*. Princeton, NJ: American School of Classical Studies at Athens.

Thomsen, R. (1964). *Eisphora*. Copenhagen: Gyldendal.

—— (1972). *The Origin of Ostracism: A Synthesis*. Copenhagen: Gyldendal.

—— (1980). *King Servius Tullius: A Historical Synthesis*. Copenhagen: Gyldendal.

Tillyard, H.J.W. (1908). *Agathocles*. Cambridge: Cambridge University Press.

Tod, M.N. (1948). *A Selection of Greek Historical Inscriptions*. Vol. 2: *From 403 to 323 BC*. Oxford: Clarendon Press.

Todd, M. (1972). *Everyday Life of the Barbarians: Goths, Franks and Vandals*. London: Batsford.

—— (1975). *The Northern Barbarians 100 BC–AD 300*. London: Hutchinson.

—— (1978). *The Walls of Rome*. London: Elek.

—— (1981). *Roman Britain 55 BC–AD 400*. London: Fontana.

Tomlinson, R.A. (1972). *Argos and the Argolid*. London: Routledge.

—— (1983). *Epidauros*. London: Granada.

—— (1989). *Greek Architecture*. Bristol: Bristol Classical Press.

Toomer, G.J. (1984). *Ptolemy's Almagest*. London: Duckworth.

Toynbee, A.J. (1965). *Hannibal's Legacy: The Hannibalic War's Effects on Roman Life*. 2 vols. London: Oxford University Press.

Toynbee, J.M.C. (1971). *Death and Burial in the Roman World*. London: Thames & Hudson.

Tozzi, P. (1978). *La rivolta ionica*. Pisa: Giardini.

Traill, J.S. (1975). *The Political Organization of Attica*. Princeton, NJ: American School of Classical Studies at Athens.

Travlos, J. (1971). *Pictorial Dictionary of Ancient Athens*. London: Thames & Hudson.

Treggiari, S. (1991). *Roman Marriage: Iusti Coniuges from the Time of Cicero to the Time of Ulpian*. Oxford: Clarendon Press.

Trendall, A.D. (1989). *Red Figure Vases of South Italy and Sicily: A Handbook*. London: Thames & Hudson.

Trump, D.H. (1966). *Central and Southern Italy before Rome*. London: Thames & Hudson.

Tuplin, C. (1987). 'The Administration of the Achaemenid Empire' in *Coinage and Administration in the Athenian and Persian Empires*. Ed. I. Carradice. Oxford: B.A.R. International Series 343.

Ulansey, D. (1989). *The Origins of the Mithraic Mysteries: Cosmology and Salvation in the Ancient World*. Oxford: Oxford University Press.

van Groningen, B.A. (1977). *Euphorion*. Amsterdam: Hakkert.

van Ooteghem, J. (1961). *Lucius Marcius Philippus et sa famille*. Brussels: Académie Royale de Belgique.

—— (1964). *Caius Marius*. Brussels: Académie Royale de Belgique.

Verdière, R. (1974). *Prolégomènes à Nemesianus*. Leiden: E.J. Brill.

Vermes, G. (1987). *The Dead Sea Scrolls in English*. 3rd edn. Harmondsworth: Penguin.

Vermes, G., and Vermes, P. (1977). *The Dead Sea Scrolls: Qumran in Perspective*. London: Collins.

Versnel, H.S. (1970). *Triumphus: An Inquiry into the Origin, Development and Meaning of the Roman Triumph*. Leiden: E.J. Brill.

Vessey, D. (1973). *Statius and the* Thebaid. Cambridge: Cambridge University Press.

Vian, F. (1959). *Recherches sur les Posthomerica de Quintus de Smyrne*. Paris: C. Klincksieck.

—— (ed.) (1976–). Nonnos de Panopolis: *Les Dionysiaques*. Paris: Les Belles Lettres.

Vickers, B. (1973). *Towards Greek Tragedy*. London: Longman.

—— (1988). *In Defence of Rhetoric*. Oxford: Clarendon Press.

Vogt, J. (1974). *Ancient Slavery and the Ideal of Man*. Trans. T. Wiedemann. Oxford: Blackwell.

Volkmann, H. (1958). *Cleopatra: A Study in Politics and Propaganda*. Trans. T.J. Cadoux. London: Elek.

von Albrecht, M. (1964). *Silius Italicus, Freiheit und Gebundenheit römischer Epik*. Amsterdam: Schippers.

von Staden, H. (1989). *Herophilus: The Art of Medicine in Early Alexandria*. Cambridge: Cambridge University Press.

Wacher, J. (1980). *Roman Britain*. London: Dent.

Wacholder, B.Z. (1962). *Nicolaus of Damascus*. Berkeley and Los Angeles: University of California Press.

Wade-Gery, H.T. (1958). *Essays in Greek History*. Oxford: Blackwell.

—— (1966). 'The Rhianos-Hypothesis' in Badian (1966a).

Walbank, F.W. (1933). *Aratos of Sicyon*. Cambridge: Cambridge University Press.

—— (1940). *Philip V of Macedon*. Cambridge: Cambridge University Press.

—— (1967). 'The Scipionic Legend', *Proceedings of the Cambridge Philological Society*, 13. 54–69.

—— (1972). *Polybius*. Berkeley and Los Angeles: University of California Press.

—— (1981). *The Hellenistic World*. Brighton: Harvester.

Walbank, M.B. (1978). *Athenian Proxenies of the Fifth Century* BC. Toronto: Stevens.

Walcot, P. (1976). *Greek Drama in its Theatrical and Social Context*. Cardiff: University of Wales Press.

Walker, D.S. (1967). *A Geography of Italy*. London: Methuen.

Wallace, M.B. (1970). 'Early Greek Proxenies', *Phoenix*, 24. 189–208.

Wallace, R.W. (1989). *The Areopagus Council to 307* BC. Baltimore, Md.: Johns Hopkins University Press.

Wallace-Hadrill, A. (1983). *Suetonius. The Scholar and his Caesars.* London: Duckworth.

—— (ed.) (1989). *Patronage in Ancient Society.* London: Routledge.

Wallis, R.T. (1972). *Neoplatonism.* London: Duckworth.

Walsh, P.G. (1961). *Livy: His Historical Aims and Methods.* Cambridge: Cambridge University Press.

—— (1970). *The Roman Novel: The 'Satyricon' of Petronius and the 'Metamorphoses' of Apuleius.* Cambridge: Cambridge University Press.

—— (1974). *Livy.* Oxford: Clarendon Press.

Ward, A.M. (1977). *Marcus Crassus and the Late Roman Republic.* Columbia: University of Missouri Press.

Warde Fowler, W. (1899). *The Roman Festivals.* London: Macmillan.

Ward-Perkins, J.B. (1974). *Cities of Ancient Greece and Italy: Planning in Classical Antiquity.* New York: George Braziller.

—— (1977). *Roman Architecture.* New York: Abrams.

Ward-Perkins, J.B., and Claridge, A. (1976). *Pompeii* AD *79.* Bristol: Imperial Tobacco Ltd.

Warmington, B.H. (1954). *The North African Provinces from Diocletian to the Vandal Conquest.* Cambridge: Cambridge University Press.

—— (1969a). *Carthage.* 2nd edn. Harmondsworth: Penguin.

—— (1969b). *Nero, Reality and Legend.* London: Chatto & Windus.

Warmington, E.H. (1934). *Ancient Geography.* London and Toronto: Dent.

Watson, A. (1965). *The Law of Obligations in the Later Roman Republic.* Oxford: Clarendon Press.

—— (1971). *The Law of Succession in the Later Roman Republic.* Oxford: Clarendon Press.

—— (1975). *Rome of the Twelve Tables.* Princeton, NJ: Princeton University Press.

Watson, G.R. (1969). *The Roman Soldier.* London: Thames & Hudson.

Webb, P.H. (1933). *The Roman Imperial Coinage.* Ed. H. Mattingly, and E.A. Sydenham. Vol. 5, pt. 2. London: Spink.

Webster, G. (1978). *Boudicca. The British Revolt against Rome,* AD *60.* London: Batsford.

—— (1985). *The Roman Imperial Army of the First and Second Centuries* AD. 3rd edn. London: A. & C. Black.

Webster, T.B.L. (1964). *Hellenistic Poetry and Art.* London: Methuen.

—— (1970). *Studies in Later Greek Comedy.* 2nd edn. Manchester: Manchester University Press.

—— (1972). *Potter and Patron in Classical Athens.* London: Methuen.

—— (1974). *An Introduction to Menander.* Manchester: Manchester University Press.

Wegner, M. (1979). *Euthymides und Euphronios*. Münster: Aschendorff.

Weigel, R.D. (1992). *Lepidus: The Tarnished Triumvir*. London: Routledge.

Weinstock, S. (1971). *Divus Julius*. Oxford: Clarendon Press.

Weitzmann, K., and Kessler, H.L. (1990). *The Frescoes of the Dura Synagogue and Christian Art*. Washington, DC: Dumbarton Oaks Research Library and Collection.

Wellesley, K. (1975). *The Long Year, AD 69*. London: Elek.

Wells, C.M. (1984). *The Roman Empire*. London: Fontana.

West, A.B. (1918). *The History of the Chalcidic League*. Madison, Wis.: Bulletin of the University of Wisconsin no. 969.

West, D. (1969). *The Imagery and Poetry of Lucretius*. Edinburgh: Edinburgh University Press.

West, M.L. (1974). *Studies in Greek Elegy and Iambus*. Berlin and New York: De Gruyter.

—— (1983). *The Orphic Poems*. Oxford: Clarendon Press.

—— (1992). *Ancient Greek Music*. Oxford: Clarendon Press.

Westermann, W.L. (1955). *The Slave Systems of Greek and Roman Antiquity*. Philadelphia, Pa.: American Philosophical Society.

Westlake, H.D. (1935). *Thessaly in the Fourth Century BC*. London: Methuen.

—— (1968). *Individuals in Thucydides*. Cambridge: Cambridge University Press.

—— (1969). *Essays on the Greek Historians and Greek History*. Manchester: Manchester University Press.

Wheeler, R.E.M. (1968). *Early India and Pakistan to Ashoka*. London: Thames & Hudson.

Wheeler, R.E.M., and Wheeler, T.V. (1936). *Verulamium, a Belgic and Two Roman Cities*. Oxford: Oxford University Press for the Society of Antiquaries.

Whibley, L. (1913). *Greek Oligarchies, their Character and Organisation*. Cambridge: Cambridge University Press.

White, K.D. (1967). *Agricultural Implements of the Roman World*. Cambridge: Cambridge University Press.

—— (1970). *Roman Farming*. London: Thames & Hudson.

—— (1975). *Farm Equipment of the Roman World*. Cambridge: Cambridge University Press.

—— (1984). *Greek and Roman Technology*. London: Thames & Hudson.

Whitehead, D. (1977). *The Ideology of the Athenian Metic*. Cambridge: Cambridge Philological Society.

—— (1986). *The Demes of Attica, 508/7–c.250 BC*. Princeton, NJ: Princeton University Press.

—— (1990). *Aineias the Tactician: How to Survive under Siege*. Oxford: Clarendon Press.

Whitman, C.H. (1974). *Euripides and the Full Circle of Myth*. Cambridge, Mass.: Harvard University Press.

Wiedemann, T.E.J. (1981). *Greek and Roman Slavery*. London: Croom Helm.

—— (1992). *Emperors and Gladiators*. London: Routledge.

Wightman, E.M. (1970). *Roman Trier and the Treveri*. London: Hart-Davis.

Wigodsky, M. (1972). *Vergil and Early Latin Poetry*. Wiesbaden: Frank Steiner.

Wilamowitz-Moellendorff, U. von (1881). *Antigonos von Karystos. Philologische Untersuchungen*, 4.

Wilkes, J.J. (1969). *Dalmatia*. London: Routledge & Kegan Paul.

—— (1983). 'Romans, Dacians and Sarmatians, 255–289' in Hartley and Wacher (1983).

—— (1992). *The Illyrians*. Oxford: Blackwell.

Wilkinson, J. (1981). *Egeria's Travels*. 2nd edn. Warminster: Aris & Phillips.

Wilkinson, L.P. (1955). *Ovid Recalled*. Cambridge: Cambridge University Press.

—— (1969). *The Georgics – A Critical Survey*. Cambridge: Cambridge University Press.

Will, E. (1956). *Doriens et ioniens*. Paris: Publications de la Faculté de l'Université de Strasbourg no. 132.

Willets, R.F. (1965). *Ancient Crete, a Social History*. London: Routledge.

—— (1967). *The Law Code of Gortyn*. Berlin: De Gruyter.

Williams, G. (1968). *Tradition and Originality in Roman Poetry*. Oxford: Clarendon Press.

Williams, S. (1985). *Diocletian and the Roman Recovery*. London: Batsford.

Williamson, G.A. (1981). *Josephus: The Jewish War*. New edn. Rev. E.M. Smallwood. Harmondsworth: Penguin.

Wilson, N.G. (1983). *Scholars of Byzantium*. London: Duckworth.

Winkler, J.J. (1985). *Auctor and Actor: A Narratological Reading of Apuleius's* The Golden Ass. Berkeley and Los Angeles: University of California Press.

Winkler, J.J., and Williams, G. (1982). *Later Greek Literature*. Cambridge: Cambridge University Press.

Winnington-Ingram, R.P. (1980). *Sophocles: An Interpretation*. Cambridge: Cambridge University Press.

Winter, F.E. (1971). *Greek Fortifications*. London: Routledge & Kegan Paul.

Wirszubski, C. (1950). *Libertas as a Political Idea at Rome during the Late Republic and Early Principate.* Cambridge: Cambridge University Press.

Wiseman, T.P. (1971). *New Men in the Roman Senate, 139 BC–AD 14.* Oxford: Clarendon Press.

—— (1979). *Clio's Cosmetics.* Leicester: Leicester University Press.

—— (1985). *Catullus and his World: A Reappraisal.* Cambridge: Cambridge University Press.

—— (1987). *Roman Studies, Literary and Historical.* Liverpool: Francis Cairns.

Witt, R.E. (1971). *Isis in the Graeco-Roman World.* London: Thames & Hudson.

Wlosok, A. (1960). *Laktanz und die philosophische Gnosis.* Heidelberg: Carl Winter.

Wolfram, H. (1988). *History of the Goths.* Berkeley and Los Angeles: University of California Press.

Woodcock, G. (1966). *The Greeks in India.* London: Faber & Faber.

Woodhead, A.G. (1962). *The Greeks in the West.* London: Thames & Hudson.

—— (1981). *The Study of Greek Inscriptions.* 2nd edn. Cambridge: Cambridge University Press.

Wormell, D.E.W. (1935). 'The Literary Tradition Concerning Hermias of Atarneus', *Yale Classical Studies,* 5. 55–92.

Wright, F.A. (1937). *Marcus Agrippa, Organizer of Victory.* London: Routledge.

Wright, J. (1974). *Dancing in Chains: The Stylistic Unity of the Comoedia Palliata.* Rome: American Academy.

Wright, W.C. (1922). *Philostratus and Eunapius: The Lives of the Sophists.* Cambridge, Mass.: Harvard University Press.

Wycherley, R.E. (1967). *How the Greeks Built Cities.* 2nd edn. London: Macmillan.

—— (1978). *The Stones of Athens.* Princeton, NJ: Princeton University Press.

Yarshater, E. (ed.) (1983). *Cambridge History of Iran.* Vol. 3: *The Seleucid, Parthian, and Sassanian Periods.* Cambridge: Cambridge University Press.

Yavetz, Z. (1983). *Julius Caesar and his Public Image.* London: Thames & Hudson.

Zanker, P. (1988). *The Power of Images in the Age of Augustus.* Ann Arbor: Michigan University Press.

Zeller, E. (1883). *A History of Eclecticism in Greek Philosophy.* Trans. S.F. Alleyne. London: Longman.

Zuntz, G. (1955). *The Political Plays of Euripides.* Manchester: Manchester University Press.

Appendixes

AGIADS   Aristodemus   EURYPONTIDS

Eurysthenes

Agis I

Echestratus

Leobotas

Doryssus

Agesilaus I

Archelaus
(c.785–760)

Teleclus
(c.760–740)

Alcamenes
(c.740–700)

Polydorus
(c.700–665)

Eurycrates
(c.665–640)

Anaxander
(c.640–615)

Eurycratidas
(c.615–590)

Leon
(c.590–560)

Procles

Eurypon

Prytanis

Polydectes

Eunomus

Charilaus
(c.775–750)

Nicander
(c.750–720)

Theopompus
(c.720–675)

Anaxandridas I
(c.675–660)

Archidamus I
(c.660–645)

Anaxilaus
(c.645–625)

Leotychidas I
(c.625–600)

Hippocratidas
(c.600–575)

=(1) -------- **Anaxàndridas II** -------- =(2)
(c.560–525)

Agasicles
(c.575–550)

Agesilaus

Dorieus **Leonidas** = Gorgo Cleombrotus **Cleomenes I**
(c.489–480)   (c.520–489)

Ariston
(c.550–515)

Menares

Gorgo

Pleistarchus
(c.480–458)

Pausanias
(Regent 480–c.471)

Demaratus **Leotychidas II**
(c.515–491)   (c.491–476)

Pleistoanax
(458–408)

Zeuxidamus

Agesipolis I
(395–380)

Pausanias
(445–426 and 408–395)

Archidamus II = Lampito
(c.469–427)

Cleombrotus I
(380–371)

Agesipolis II
(371–370)

Acrotatus

Cleomenes II
(370–309)

Agis II **Agesilaus II**
(427–c.401) (c.401–360)

Cleonymus

Areus I
(309–265)

Agis III **Archidamus III**
(338–330)   (c.360–338)

Leonidas II
(c.254–235)

Eudamidas I
(330–305)

Acrotatus
(265–c.262)

Cleomenes III **Eucleidas**
(235–222)   (227–222)

Chilonis = **Cleombrotus II**
        (243–241)

Archidamus IV
(c.305–275)

Eudamidas II
(c.275–244)

Areus II
(c.262–254)

Agesipolis

Agis IV **Archidamus V**
(c.244–241) (228–227)

Eudamidas III
(241–228)

Agesipolis III
(219–215)

The two royal houses of Sparta

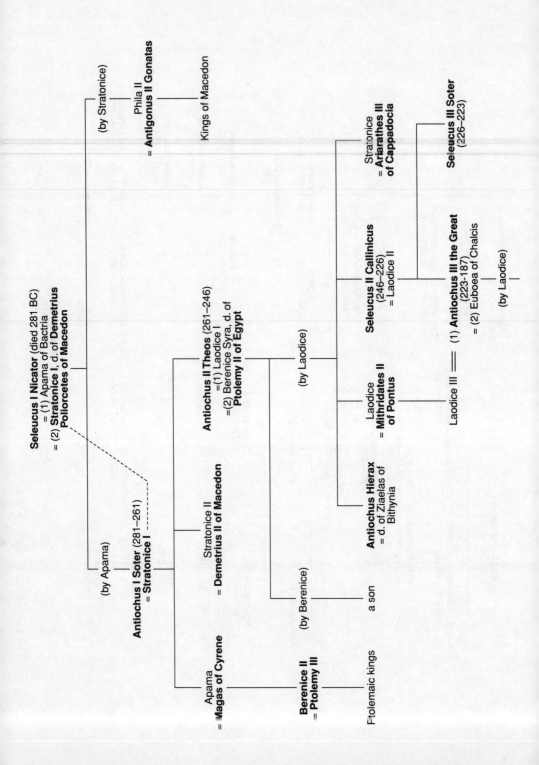

Seleucus I Nicator (died 281 BC)
= (1) Apama of Bactria
= (2) **Stratonice** I, d. of **Demetrius Poliorcetes of Macedon**

(by Apama)

(by Stratonice)

Phila II
= **Antigonus II Gonatas**

Kings of Macedon

Antiochus I Soter (281–261)
= **Stratonice** I

Stratonice II
= **Demetrius II of Macedon**

Antiochus II Theos (261–246)
= (1) Laodice I
= (2) Berenice Syra, d. of **Ptolemy II of Egypt**

Apama
= **Magas of Cyrene**

Berenice II
= **Ptolemy III**

(by Berenice)

a son

Ptolemaic kings

(by Laodice)

Antiochus Hierax
= d. of Ziaelas of Bithynia

Laodice
= **Mithridates II of Pontus**

Seleucus II Callinicus (246–226)
= Laodice II

Stratonice
= **Ariarathes III of Cappadocia**

Laodice III = (1) **Antiochus III the Great** (223–187)
= (2) Euboea of Chalcis

Seleucus III Soter (226–223)

(by Laodice)

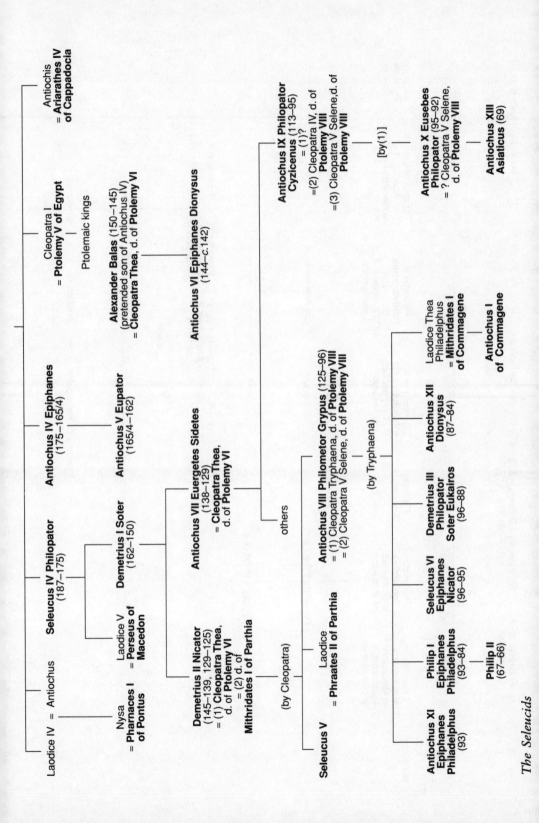

The Seleucids

Laodice IV = Antiochus

Nysa
= Pharnaces I
of Pontus

Seleucus IV Philopator
(187–175)

Laodice V
= Perseus of Macedon

Demetrius I Soter
(162–150)

Antiochus IV Epiphanes
(175–165/4)

Antiochus V Eupator
(165/4–162)

Cleopatra I
= Ptolemy V of Egypt

Ptolemaic kings

Antiochis
= Ariarathes IV
of Cappadocia

Demetrius II Nicator
(145–139, 129–125)
= (1) Cleopatra Thea,
d. of Ptolemy VI
= (2) d. of
Mithridates I of Parthia

Antiochus VII Euergetes Sidetes
(138–129)
= Cleopatra Thea,
d. of Ptolemy VI

Alexander Balas (150–145)
(pretended son of Antiochus IV)
= Cleopatra Thea, d. of Ptolemy VI

Antiochus VI Epiphanes Dionysus
(144–c.142)

others

(by Cleopatra)

Laodice
= Phraates II of Parthia

Seleucus V

Antiochus VIII Philometor Grypus (125–96)
= (1) Cleopatra Tryphaena, d. of Ptolemy VIII
= (2) Cleopatra V Selene, d. of Ptolemy VIII

Antiochus IX Philopator
Cyzicenus (113–95)
= (1)?
=(2) Cleopatra IV, d. of
Ptolemy VIII
=(3) Cleopatra V Selene,d. of
Ptolemy VIII

(by Tryphaena)

[by(1)]

Antiochus XI
Epiphanes
Philadelphus
(93)

Philip I
Epiphanes
Philadelphus
(93–84)

Philip II
(67–66)

Seleucus VI
Epiphanes
Nicator
(96–95)

Demetrius III
Philopator
Soter Eukairos
(96–88)

Antiochus XII
Dionysus
(87–84)

Laodice Thea
Philadelphus
= Mithridates I
of Commagene

Antiochus I
of Commagene

Antiochus X Eusebes
Philopator (95–92)
= ? Cleopatra V Selene,
d. of Ptolemy VIII

Antiochus XIII
Asiaticus (69)

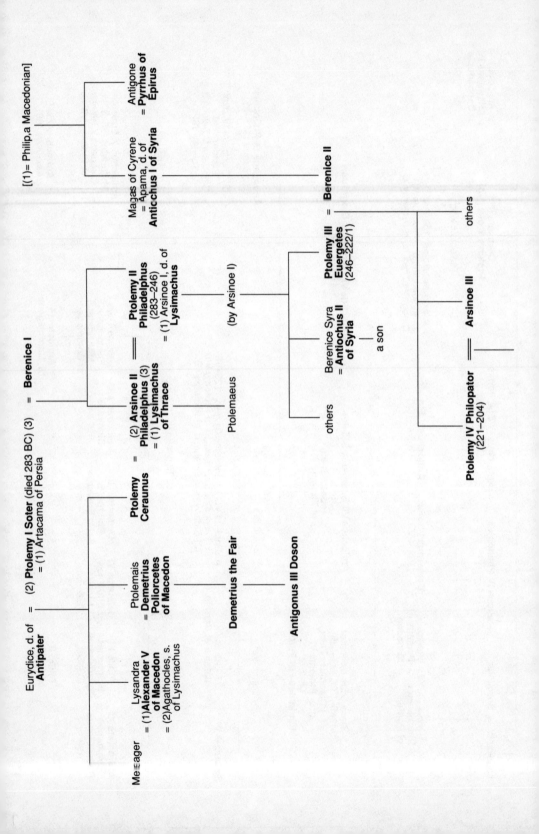

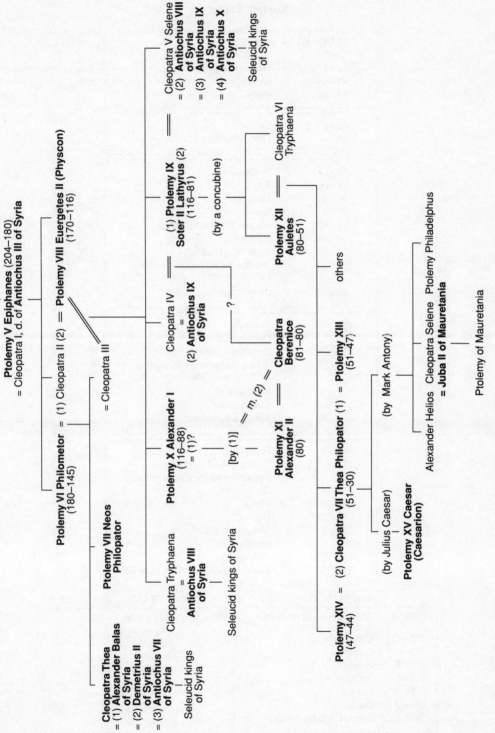

The Ptolemies

Roman Emperors

31 BC–AD 14	Augustus	**JULIO-CLAUDIANS**
14–37	Tiberius	
37–41	Gaius (Caligula)	
41–54	Claudius I	
54–68	Nero	

68–9	Galba	
69	Otho, Vitellius	

69–79	Vespasian	**FLAVIANS AND ANTONINES**
79–81	Titus	
81–96	Domitian	
96–8	Nerva	
98–117	Trajan (97–8 with Nerva)	
117–38	Hadrian	
138–61	Antoninus Pius	
161–80	Marcus Aurelius (161–9 with Lucius Verus)	
180–92	Commodus	

193	Pertinax	**SEVERANS**
193	Didius Julianus	
193–211	Septimius Severus	
211–17	Aurelius Antoninus (Caracalla) (211–12 with Geta)	
217–18	Macrinus	
218–22	Elagabalus	
222–35	Severus Alexander	

235–8	Maximinus
238	Gordian I and II (in Africa)
238	Balbinus and Pupienus (in Italy)
238–44	Gordian III
244–9	Philip
249–51	Decius
251–3	Trebonianus Gallus
253	Aemilianus
253–60	Valerian
253–68	Gallienus (253–60 with Valerian)

WEST		EAST	
259–74	Gallic empire of Postumus, Victorinus, Tetricus	260–72	Palmyrene empire of Odaenathus, Zenobia, Vaballath
268–70	Claudius II		
270	Quintillus		
270–5	Aurelian		
275–6	Tacitus		
276–82	Probus		
282–3	Carus		
283–4	Carinus and Numerian		

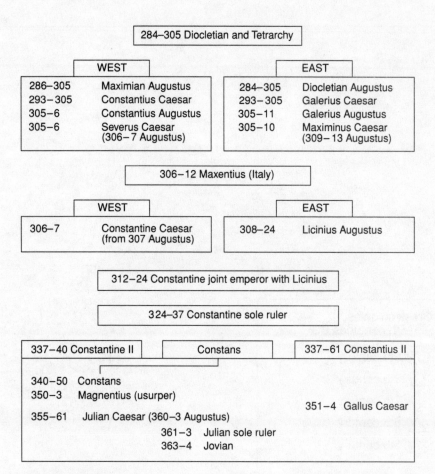

284–305 Diocletian and Tetrarchy

WEST		EAST	
286–305	Maximian Augustus	284–305	Diocletian Augustus
293–305	Constantius Caesar	293–305	Galerius Caesar
305–6	Constantius Augustus	305–11	Galerius Augustus
305–6	Severus Caesar (306–7 Augustus)	305–10	Maximinus Caesar (309–13 Augustus)

306–12 Maxentius (Italy)

WEST		EAST	
306–7	Constantine Caesar (from 307 Augustus)	308–24	Licinius Augustus

312–24 Constantine joint emperor with Licinius

324–37 Constantine sole ruler

337–40 Constantine II	Constans	337–61 Constantius II

340–50	Constans	
350–3	Magnentius (usurper)	
		351–4 Gallus Caesar
355–61	Julian Caesar (360–3 Augustus)	
	361–3 Julian sole ruler	
	363–4 Jovian	

364–75	Valentinian	364–78	Valens
375–83	Gratian	379–95	Theodosius I
	375–92 Valentinian II (Italy, Illyricum)		
383–8	Maximus (usurper)		
392–4	Eugenius (usurper)		
395–423	Honorius (395–408 Stilicho as regent)	395–408	Arcadius
421	Constantius III		
423–5	John (usurper)	408–50	Theodosius II
425–55	Valentinian III	450–7	Marcian
455	Petronius Maximus	457–74	Leo
455–6	Avitus	474–91	Zeno
457–61	Majorian	(475–6	Basiliscus)
461–5	Libius Severus		
467–72	Anthemius		
472	Olybrius		
473–4	Glycerius		
474–5	Nepos		
475–6	Romulus Augustulus		

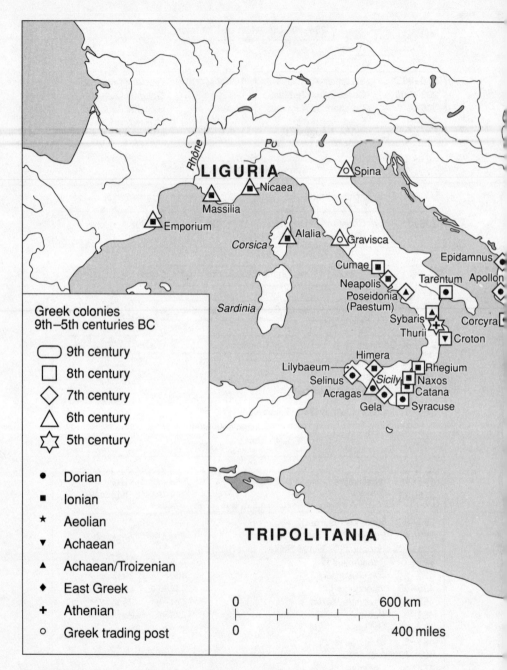

Greek colonization, 9th–5th centuries BC. *(After Levi.)*

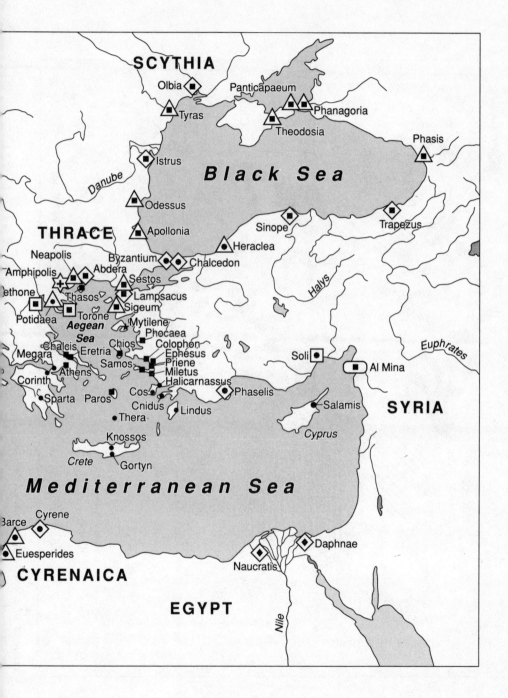

SCYTHIA

Olbia

Panticapaeum

Tyras

Phanagoria

Theodosia

Phasis

Istrus

Black Sea

Danube

Odessus

THRACE

Apollonia

Sinope

Trapezus

Heraclea

Neapolis

Byzantium

Chalcedon

Amphipolis

Abdera

Halys

ethone

Sestos

Thasos

Lampsacus

Euphrates

Potidaea

Torone

Sigeum

*Aegean
Sea*

Mytilene

Phocaea

Chalcis

Chios

Colophon

Soli

Megara

Eretria

Ephesus

Al Mina

Athens

Samos

Priene

Miletus

SYRIA

Corinth

Halicarnassus

Sparta

Paros

Cos

Phaselis

Cnidus

Lindus

Salamis

Thera

Cyprus

Knossos

Crete

Gortyn

M e d i t e r r a n e a n   S e a

Barce

Cyrene

Daphnae

Euesperides

Naucratis

CYRENAICA

EGYPT

Nile

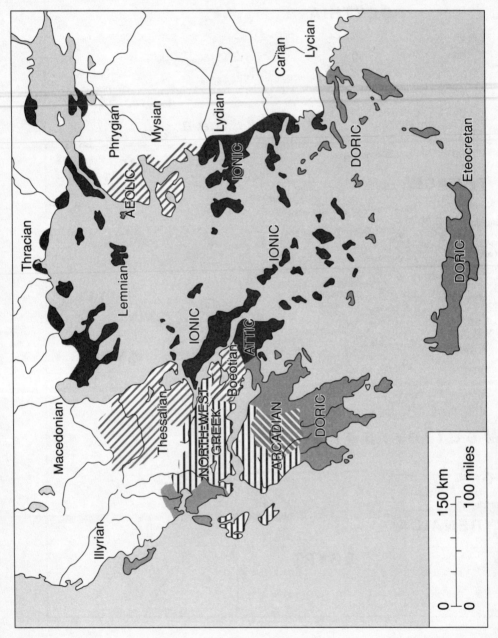

Dialects of the Greek world. (After Levi.)

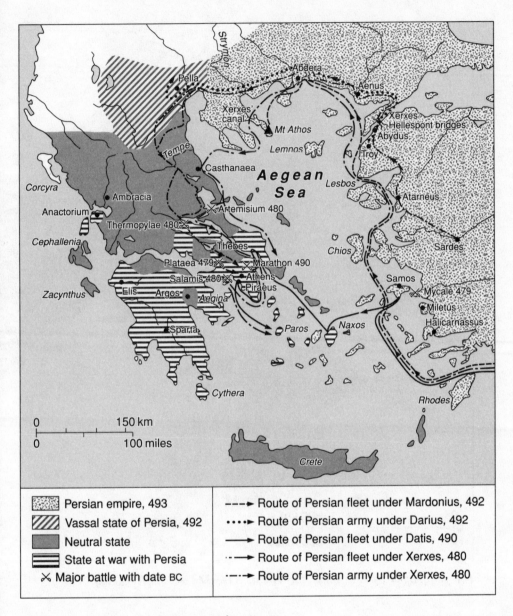

The Persian Wars, 492–479 BC. (After Levi.)

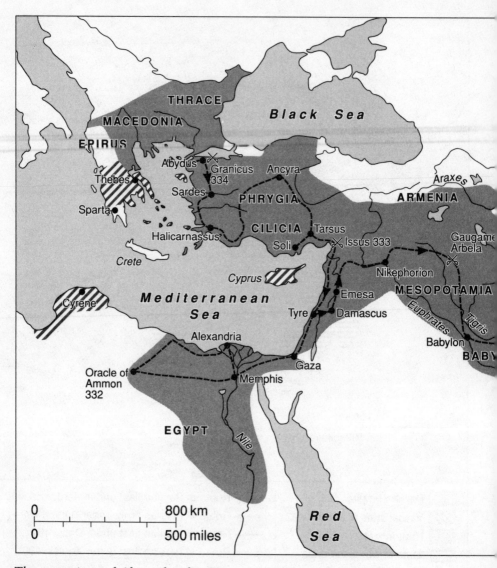

The campaigns of Alexander the Great, 334–323 BC. *(After Levi.)*

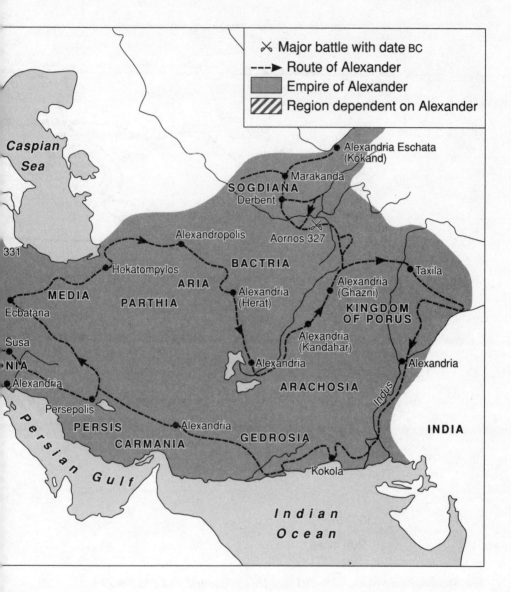

× Major battle with date BC
---→ Route of Alexander
▓ Empire of Alexander
▨ Region dependent on Alexander

**Caspian
Sea**

Alexandria Eschata
(Kokand)

Marakanda

SOGDIANA

Derbent

Alexandropolis

Aornos 327

331

BACTRIA

Hekatompylos

Taxila

ARIA

MEDIA   **PARTHIA**

Ecbatana

Alexandria
(Herat)

Alexandria
(Ghazni)

**KINGDOM
OF PORUS**

Susa

NIA

Alexandria
(Kandahar)

Alexandria

Alexandria

Persepolis

ARACHOSIA

Alexandria

Indus

PERSIS   Alexandria

CARMANIA   **GEDROSIA**   **INDIA**

P e r s i a n   G u l f

Kokola

*I n d i a n
O c e a n*

The Second Punic War, 218–201 BC. (After Cornell and Matthews.)

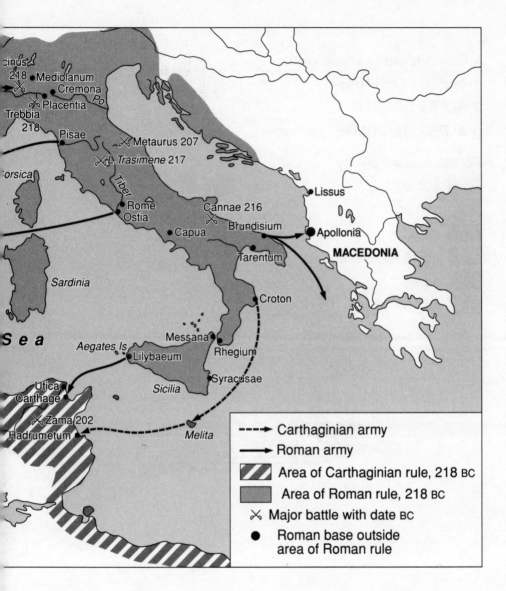

cinus
218
Mediolanum
Cremona
Placentia
Po
Trebbia
218
Pisae
Corsica
Metaurus 207
L. Trasimene 217
Tiber
Rome
Ostia
Capua
Cannae 216
Brundisium
Tarentum
Lissus
Apollonia
MACEDONIA
Sardinia
Croton
Sea
Aegates Is
Messana
Lilybaeum
Rhegium
Sicilia
Syracusae
Utica
Carthage
Zama 202
Hadrumetum
Melita

-----▶ Carthaginian army

——▶ Roman army

Area of Carthaginian rule, 218 BC

Area of Roman rule, 218 BC

✕ Major battle with date BC

● Roman base outside
area of Roman rule

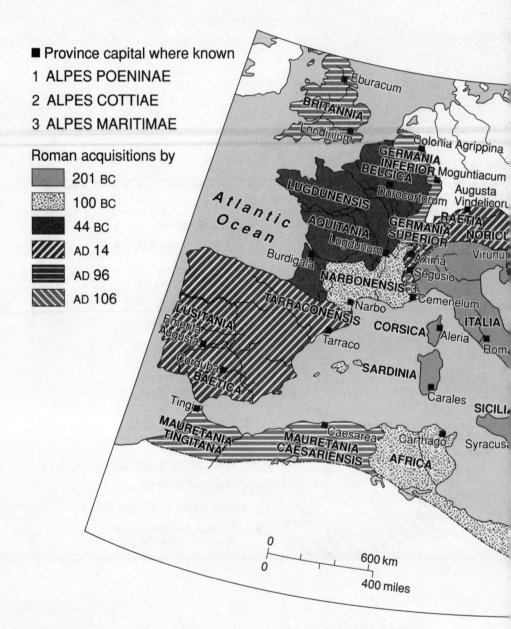

- ■ Province capital where known
- 1 ALPES POENINAE
- 2 ALPES COTTIAE
- 3 ALPES MARITIMAE

Roman acquisitions by

	201 BC
	100 BC
	44 BC
	AD 14
	AD 96
	AD 106

Growth of the Roman empire to AD *106. (After Cornell and Matthews.)*

Carnuntum
Aquincum
NNONIA
ALMATIA
Sarmizegetusa
DACIA
Viminacium
MOESIA
MOESIA
alonae SUPERIOR INFERIOR
THRACIA
MACEDONIA
Thessalonica
Perinthus

Black Sea

Amastris
BITHYNIA AND
PONTUS
Nicomedia
Ancyra
CAPPADOCIA
Caesarea

EPIRUS
ACHAEA
Corinthus

ASIA
Ephesus
GALATIA
Tarsus
LYCIA
AND
CILICIA
PAMPHYLIA
Antiochia
SYRIA

Gortyn
CRETA
Paphos
CYPRUS
Bostra

Mediterranean Sea
Caesarea
JUDAEA

Cyrene
Alexandria
ARABIA

CYRENAICA
AEGYPTUS

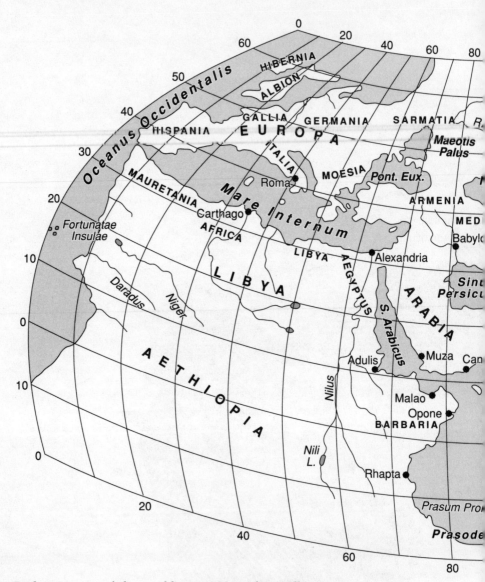

Ptolemy's map of the world c.AD 150. (After Miller.)

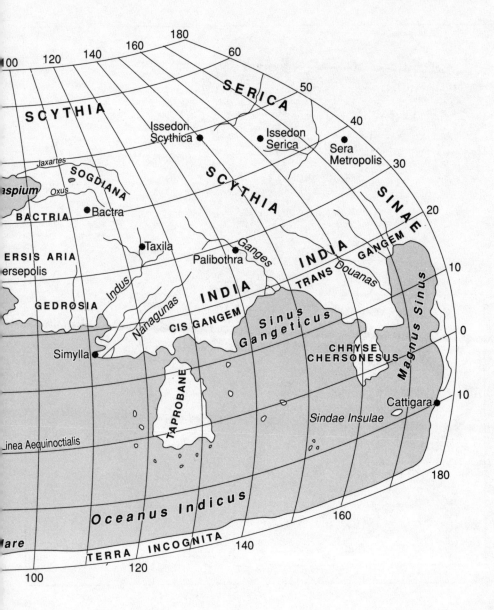

TRANSPADANA
XI

VENETIA
X

Po

LIGURIA
IX

AEMILIA
VIII

Arno

UMBRIA
VI

ETRURIA
VII

Tiber

PICENUM
V

SAMNIUM
IV

Rome

LATIUM

I

CAMPANIA

APULIA
II

LUCANIA

III

BRUTTIUM

VII

XIV

Wall of Servius

VII

VI

IX

Wall of Aurelian

IV

V

VIII

III

V

XIV

X

I

Tiber

XI

II

XIII

XII

I

ROME

0   150 m

0   300 km

0   200 miles

Key

I	Porta Capena	VI	Alta Semita	XI	Circus Maximus
II	Caelimontium	VII	Via Lata	XII	Piscina Publica
III	Isis et Serapis	VIII	Forum Romanum	XIII	Aventinus
IV	Templum Pacis	IX	Circus Flaminius	XIV	Trans Tiberim
V	Esquiliae	X	Palatium		

The regiones of Augustan Italy and Augustan Rome. (After Cornell and Matthews.)

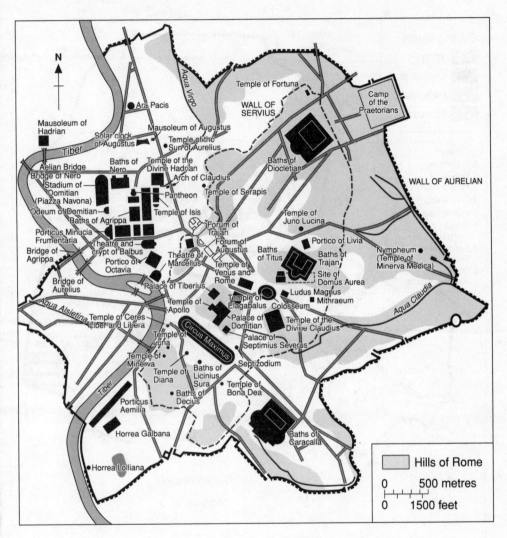

The city of Rome in the 3rd century AD. *(After Cornell and Matthews.)*

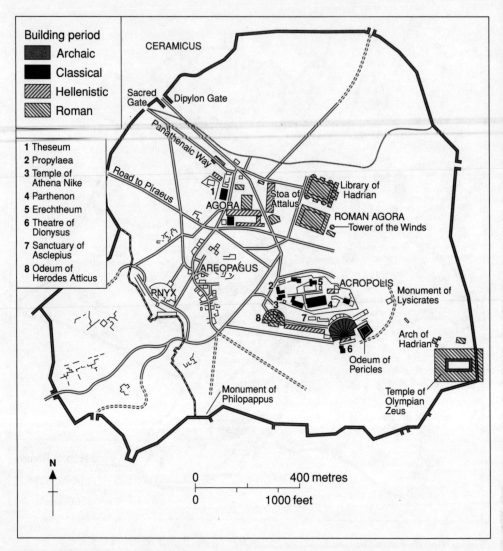

The city of Athens. (After Levi.)